ROGET'S II
The New Thesaurus

Expanded Edition

ROGET'S II
The New Thesaurus

Expanded Edition

By the editors of
The American Heritage Dictionary

Houghton Mifflin Company • Boston

Library of Congress Cataloging-in-Publication Data

Roget's II.

    1. English language—Synonyms and antonyms.
PE1591.R715   1988   423'.1   88-8842
ISBN 0-395-48317-4
ISBN 0-395-48318-2

Manufactured in the United States of America

EDITORIAL STAFF

PREFACE

Roget's II: The New Thesaurus, an entirely new work, represents a significant change from traditional thesaurus making. The lexicographic staff of Houghton Mifflin Company, publishers of *The American Heritage Dictionary, Second College Edition*, has recognized the problems encountered by thesaurus users. Complex index referencing systems have burdened the user's search, and word groupings by vague meanings have confounded selection of suitable words. Consequently, *Roget's II* has been carefully prepared to provide rapid access to synonyms, which are grouped by precise meanings, facilitating the choice of appropriate words to express thoughts. Thousands of near-synonyms, near-antonyms, and antonyms have been added at appropriate entries as an additional feature felt to be helpful to writers searching for just the right word.

For ease of use and clarity in word selection *Roget's II* is organized in an innovative format. In the left-hand column of each page all entries are arranged in alphabetical order and are classified by part of speech. Every word is accurately defined, as is each sense of a word for which more than one meaning has been included. Sentences and phrases using the entry words in context provide guidance in usage. In the right-hand column synonyms, idioms, near-synonyms, near-antonyms, and antonyms are listed alphabetically within groups and are presented adjacent to each defined meaning of each discrete sense.

Secondary entries are included in the single alphabetical listing and are also precisely defined. They are directionally cross-referred to main entries with full synonym presentation. This efficient system eliminates the need for complicated indexes and redundant listings.

Since *Roget's II* defines all entry words and their corresponding synonyms, the work is self-contained. Therefore the user does not need to verify a meaning by consulting a dictionary. Controversial synonyms are labeled, providing usage guidance.

It is intended that *Roget's II* be a source of appropriate words to express thoughts or ideas, guiding the user away from the common pitfall of selecting an unsuitable word. Consequently, only synonyms are *exhaustively* listed.

New computerized editing and typesetting technology have supplemented the traditional methods of lexicography in preparing *Roget's II*. The manuscript typesetting, alphabetizing, final cross-referencing, and accuracy-verification functions were accomplished by computer programs.

Research and investigation for this thesaurus began thirteen years ago. On the basis of experience gained during the preparation of the American Heritage Dictionaries, it was believed that a new thesaurus could provide the user with the kind of clear guidance found in these dictionaries. The editors worked with consultant Robert Masters to explore new ideas for organization and presentation of synonyms. Houghton Mifflin's dictionary staff was also aided by the work of independent lexicographers in the development of this work.

An abiding objective of our word-reference publishing is to provide authoritative information about our language and guidance in its effective use. We believe *Roget's II: The New Thesaurus* will serve the user well in selecting the right words to express thoughts precisely and to add colorful variety to expression.

INTRODUCTION

Roget's II: The New Thesaurus is a book devoted entirely to meaning. In contrast to the old-fashioned thesaurus, which groups undifferentiated words together with an undefined entry word, this book provides an analysis—a definition—of the meaning or meanings of each entry word in the book. Synonyms are grouped according to meaning. What, then, *is* meaning?

Meaning

The meaning of even a single word is rather more complex than one might imagine. The most obvious aspect of meaning is *denotation*, that is, the thing meant, the concept or object referred to. The denotation of the word *chair*, for example, is that it is a piece of furniture, that it has a seat, legs, a back, and often arms, and that one person can sit on it. So long as it has these features, a person can identify a chair as a chair irrespective of the fact that it may be big or small, made of chrome or wood, upholstered or caned— in short, no matter what other features it may have. Furthermore, a chair is distinct from all other pieces of furniture upon which one can sit. It is different from a stool because a stool is backless and armless. It is different from a couch, on which one or more may recline, and different from a chaise longue, which has a seat long enough to support the outstretched legs of the sitter. Thus the denotation of a word includes those features that are criterial and so serve to define and distinguish.

In addition to its denotation, a word may have a *connotation*, that is, the configuration of suggestive or associative implications constituting the general sense of an expression beyond its literal sense. Differences of style, expressiveness, and other characteristics such that a given term conveys a given denotation more—or less—formally, colorfully, humorously, and the like, constitute the connotations of the word. For example, both *mouth* and *trap* denote the opening in the body through which food is ingested. *Mouth*, however, is what might be called a neutral term; it conveys information but has no connotations. *Trap*, on the other hand, is a slang word and is often considered to be somewhat vulgar. An *alcoholic* drinks habitually and to excess, and the word is neutral; *lush*, however, is a slang term with pejorative overtones.

Words expressive of emotion frequently have connotations, but many that are not emotive also have them. Many sets of words of identical denotation participate in a spectrum of greater to lesser formality. For example, of the cluster *transpire, happen, occur, befall, betide, hap*, and *bechance*, all meaning "to take place, come to pass," *transpire* is the most formal; *happen* and *occur* are neutral—nonconnotative; *befall* and *betide* have a somewhat archaic flavor; *hap* is archaic; and *bechance* is rare. All of these facts beyond the bare denotation of the terms constitute the connotations of these words. In *Roget's II* labels, such as *Informal, Regional,* and *Slang,* identify restrictions with respect to level or style of usage.

Two or more words may have the same denotation and connotation and yet differ in their *range of applicability*; that is, they cannot be used interchangeably in the same context. *Cancel* and *vacate*, both having the same denotation ("to annul or invalidate") and both being nonconnotative, can nevertheless not be used interchangeably, because *vacate* is a legal term. One might *cancel* a magazine subscription, but one would hardly *vacate* it. *Extension* and *production* both refer to the act of making something longer, but *production* is used only in geometry, whereas *extension* applies generally. *Slowly* and *adagio* have the same denotation, but *adagio* is a technical term in music. Terms of restricted range of applicability are identified in *Roget's II* by such labels as *Architecture*, *Mythology*, or *Journalism*.

Synonymy and Synonyms

Given the complexity of meaning, a person searching for an alternative word must be sure that the synonym chosen is accurate and precise. Because of its emphasis on the meaning or meanings of a word *Roget's II* is specifically designed to offer the user a choice of synonyms that lie within the denotative range of the word or sense of the word with which they correspond.

A *synonym* is a word that differs in form from but has a meaning identical or very similar to that of another word. It is often said that there is no such thing as an absolute synonym for any word, that is, a form that is identical in every aspect of meaning so that the two can be applied interchangeably. According to this extreme view the only true synonyms are terms having precisely the same denotation, connotation, and range of applicability. As it turns out, these so-called true synonyms are frequently technical terms and almost always concrete words coming from linguistically disparate sources. Good examples of such pairs are *celiac* (from Greek)/*abdominal* (from Latin) and *car* (from Latin)/*automobile* (from French). These meet the criteria for true synonymy: they have precisely the same denotations, connotations, and range of applicability, and they are used in identical contexts.

This view of synonymy is far too restrictive, however. In *Roget's II* synonymous terms are those having nearly identical denotations. English, because of its linguistic history and its large wordstock, is rich in such words. Speakers very often have a choice from among a set of words of differing origin but the same denotation. A man may be *bearded* (from Old English), *barbate* (from Latin), *bewhiskered* (from Scandinavian), or *whiskered* (from Scandinavian). One may go to the *shore* (from Middle Low German), the *coast* (from Latin), or the *littoral* (from Latin). One can refer to the sense of *hearing* (from Old English) or to the *acoustic* (from Greek), *auditory* (from Latin), *aural* (from Latin), or *auricular* (from Latin) sense. One can make clothing from *cloth* (from Germanic), *fabric* (from Latin), *material* (from Latin), or *textiles* (from Latin). The reason for choosing one of these words over another is frequently stylistic: one may prefer a simpler or a more complex word; one may prefer a more formal or a less formal term. But the fact that they share a denotation makes them synonymous and available as substitutes for words one has in mind so that one can be more precise, express oneself more colorfully, or avoid repetition. All of the terms included in the synonymies in *Roget's II* share the same denotation.

HOW TO USE THIS BOOK

The Entries

Roget's II: The New Thesaurus contains five kinds of entries introduced by boldface head words: main entries having synonym lists (and sometimes near-synonyms, near-antonyms, and antonyms), indented subentries in smaller type representing very close historical relatives and derivatives of the main entries, secondary entries referring you to the main-entry synonym lists, and directional cross-reference entries guiding you from secondary to primary variant spellings and from secondary entries to synonymized subentries.

fall *verb*
  1. To move downward in response to gravity: *Apples fell from the tree.*
....

fall down *verb*
Informal. To be unsuccessful.
fall off *verb*
  1. To slope downward.
....

fallacy *noun*
  1. An erroneous or false idea: *an educational philosophy grounded on fallacy.*
....

fall down *verb*
....

falsity *noun*
  1. An erroneous or false idea
  2. Betrayal, esp. of a moral obligation.
  3. An untrue declaration.

  1. ***Syns:*** descend, drop.
....

FAIL.

  1. DROP.
....

  1. ***Syns:*** erroneousness, error, fallaciousness, falsehood, falseness, falsity, untruth.
....

SEE **fall.**

  1. FALLACY.
  2. FAITHLESSNESS.
  3. LIE^2 *noun*

Entry Order

Main entries, secondary entries, and directional cross-references are listed alphabetically. For instance, the first entry in this book is **aback**. It is followed in turn by the separate entries **abandon, abandoned, abandonment, abase,** and **abash.**

Subentry order is as follows: two-word verbs derived from single-word verb head words usually appear as indented subentries directly under the base verbs. Two-word verb subentries are also alphabetized:

fall *verb*
  fall down *verb*
....
  fall off *verb*
....
  fall on (or **upon**) *verb*
....

fall through *verb*

. . . .

fall *noun*

. . . .

Each of the two-word verb subentries shown above is also entered in directional cross-reference form at its own alphabetical place elsewhere in the book (see "Directional Cross-References").

Components of Main Entries

These are the components of a typical main entry:

destroy *verb*

1. To cause the complete ruin or wreckage of: *paintings destroyed by fire; drugs that destroyed her health; news that destroyed his hopes.*

1. *Syns:* demolish, destruct, dynamite, finish, ruin, ruinate (*Regional*), shatter, sink, smash, total, torpedo, undo, wrack, wreck. —*Idiom* put the kibosh on.

The head word **(destroy)** is followed on the same line by an italic part-of-speech label (*verb*). A boldface sense number (in this case **1.**) appears in all multisense entries in the left-hand column beneath the head word, followed by a basic meaning element—a concise denotation of the sense shared by the head word and its synonyms. In this example the basic meaning element shared by **destroy** and its fourteen synonyms is "to cause the complete ruin or wreckage of." The basic meaning element is supplemented by at least one illustrative example showing a typical usage context for the head word and its synonyms. Definition 1 of the main entry **destroy** contains three italic examples: *paintings destroyed by fire, drugs that destroyed her health,* and *news that destroyed his hopes.* These examples show both concrete and figurative uses of **destroy**. The synonyms are all substitutable for the head word in the example.

In the right-hand column the appropriate sense number (**1.**) is followed by the italic boldface abbreviation *Syns*, which introduces the list of words synonymous with **destroy**: demolish, destruct, dynamite, finish, ruin, ruinate (*Regional*), shatter, sink, smash, total, torpedo, undo, wrack, and wreck.

When appropriate, idioms equivalent to the synonyms are shown at the ends of synonym lists. These idioms are phrases with a meaning identical to the basic meaning element shared by all the synonyms. In the entry shown here, "put the kibosh on" is an idiom that is equivalent to **destroy** and its fourteen synonyms.

Scattered throughout the text are thousands of carefully chosen near-synonyms, near-antonyms, and antonyms. Near-synonyms, introduced by the boldface italic head *Near-syns*, appear after the synonym lists to which they are related:

adventurous *adjective*

1. Taking or willing to take risks: *Adventurous pioneers settled the American West.*

1. *Syns:* adventuresome, audacious, enterprising, venturesome, venturous.
Near-syns: bold, brash, daredevil, daring, foolhardy, harebrained, impetuous, imprudent, madcap, rash, reckless.
Near-ants: cautious, reserved.
Ant: unadventurous.

2. Involving possible risk, loss, or injury.

2. DANGEROUS.

Near-synonyms are words that are closely related to the head words at which they appear; yet, they do not share with those head words irreducible elements of denotation, or meaning.

Antonyms, or words directly opposite in meaning to the head words at which they appear, are to be found, when applicable, at the ends of some entries or senses. Near-antonyms, words closely related to true antonyms, and having meanings nearly opposite those of the synonyms, appear, when applicable, throughout the text:

acknowledge *verb*

1. To recognize, often reluctantly, the reality or truth of: *He acknowledged his mistake.*

    1. ***Syns:*** admit, allow, avow, concede, confess, fess up (*Slang*), grant, own (up).
    Near-ants: disallow, disavow, disown, nix (*Slang*), reject; contradict, impugn, negate.
    Ant: deny.

2. To express recognition of: *acknowledged his duty toward his family.*

    2. ***Syns:*** admit, recognize.

The editors have made a special effort to include *only* those near-synonyms, near-antonyms, and antonyms most commonly sought by you, the readers. Inclusion of these new features in this revision is a response to requests from those of you who use our thesaurus.

Components of the Secondary Entries

Secondary entries contain head words, parts of speech, a definition or definitions, and small-capital cross-references to main entries:

ghoul *noun*
A perversely bad, cruel, or wicked person.   FIEND.

reprove *verb*

1. To castigate for the purpose of improving.
2. To criticize for a fault or offense.

    1. CORRECT *verb*.
    2. CALL DOWN at **call**.

Secondary entries enable you to locate the main entries where full synonym lists are entered. If you have the word *ghoul* in mind, for instance, but seek a different, better, or more colorful word, you look up **ghoul**. You see that it is cross-referred to the main entry **fiend**. When you turn to **fiend**, you find seven synonyms and one idiom from which to choose:

fiend *noun*

1. A perversely bad, cruel, or wicked person: *a fiend who tormented and killed his prisoners.*

    1. ***Syns:*** archfiend, beast, ghoul, monster, ogre, tiger, vampire. —*Idiom* devil incarnate.

If, on the other hand, you start with the word *reprove* in the sense meaning "to criticize another for a fault or offense," you will find the appropriate cross-reference entry at definition 2 of **reprove**, directing you to the subentry **call down** at the main entry **call**. And at **call down** there are sixteen synonyms and four idioms from which to choose:

call *verb*

. . . .

    call down *verb*
    Informal. To criticize for a fault or offense: *got called down for failing to meet the deadline.*

    Syns: admonish, bawl out (*Informal*), castigate, chastise, chew out (*Slang*), chide, dress down, lambaste (*Slang*), rap[1] (*Informal*), rebuke, reprimand, reproach, reprove, scold, tax, upbraid. —*Idioms* bring (*or* call *or* take) to task, haul (*or* rake) over the coals, let someone have it, rap on (*or* over) the knuckles.

Every synonym is entered at its own alphabetical place with a cross-reference to the appropriate main entry. Near-synonyms, near-antonyms, and antonyms—freestanding elements within entries—are not cross-referenced because it was felt that inclusion of such cross-references would needlessly clutter the text and possibly confuse the busy user.

Subentries

Only the closest historical relatives of head words are indented subentries. For instance, **abandon** *noun* is a subentry of the verb **abandon**, but **abandonment** is a separate entry. Two-word verbs derived from single-word verbs are shown as subentries of the single-word verbs (as in the case of **call down** at **call**) unless the two-word verbs have themselves generated noun or adjective derivatives. In this case the two-word verb is the head word, and the derivative is its subentry. For example, **fade out** *verb* is a main entry followed by the subentry **fade-out** *noun*.

Directional Cross-References

Directional cross-references help you locate subentries of main entries and variant spellings that differ markedly from the spellings of primary variants. For example, **call down**, as noted above, is a subentry at **call**; hence **call down** is also entered in directional cross-reference form at its own alphabetical place in the overall C sequence:

call down *verb*　　　　　　　　　　　　　　　SEE **call**.

By the same token the variant spelling **aeon** is shown at its own alphabetical place in the A sequence as:

aeon *noun*　　　　　　　　　　　　　　　SEE **eon**.

Variants

Equal and secondary variants are tagged as such in the synonym lists. An equal variant is a spelling of a word that is just as acceptable as the primary spelling. Equal variants of synonyms and idioms in synonym lists are signaled by use of the italic connective *or:*

down-at-heel *or* down-at-the-heel

A secondary variant is a spelling that is less common than the primary form but nevertheless acceptable. Secondary variants are signaled in synonym lists by parentheses plus the italic connective *also:*

lese majesty (*also* lèse majesté)
dialogue (*also* dialog)

Some words have more than one variant. These, too, are shown:

naive (*also* naïve, naif, naïf)

All such variants are given at main- and secondary-entry head words in synonym lists.

When a single idiom can be worded in a variety of ways, the variant wordings are given parenthetically. For instance, the idiom in the synonym list at definition 4 of **fall** *verb* is: take a fall (*or* header *or* plunge *or* spill *or* tumble).

Homographs

A homograph is a word that is spelled the same as another word but that differs in meaning and origin and may differ in pronunciation or syllabication. Homographs are signaled by superscript numerals following the words to which they refer. Homograph numbers are used in head words, cross-references, and synonym lists:

fell[1] *verb*
1. To bring down, as with a saw or ax.　　　1. CUT *verb*.

fell[2] *adjective*
Showing or suggesting a disposition to be violently　FIERCE.
destructive without scruple or restraint.

fell[3] *noun*
The skin of an animal.　　　　　　　HIDE[2] *noun*.

In the synonym lists at **cut, fierce,** and **hide²** the synonyms are styled as fell¹, fell², and fell³, respectively. Notice also that the cross-reference to HIDE² contains the proper homograph number for that main entry.

Labels

You don't need to consult a dictionary when you use *Roget's II* because all words requiring labels have been clearly tagged in synonym lists and in main and secondary entries. The kinds of labels used in this book are temporal labels (*Archaic, Obs.*), usage labels (*Informal, Slang,* and *Poetic*), dialect labels (such as *Regional* and *Chiefly Regional*), language labels (such as *French, Brit.,* and *Chiefly Brit.*), field labels (such as *Law* and *Motion Pic. & T.V.*), and status labels (such as *Rare*).

Archaic labels are used with words once common but now characteristic of a style no longer prevalent in spoken and written English. For example, *affright,* meaning "to fill with fear," is an archaic synonym of *frighten* and is labeled as such. *Obs.,* for "obsolete," indicates that a term is used only in quotation or intentional archaism. For instance, the obsolete term *affectionated,* meaning "feeling and expressing affection," is labeled (*Obs.*). *Roget's II* contains very few archaic and obsolete terms.

Usage labels such as *Informal, Slang,* and *Poetic* indicate various levels of usage and styles of expression that may or may not be appropriate in all contexts or situations. *Informal* generally applies to those words that are commonly used in the spoken language and in ordinary writing but that might not be considered appropriate in very formal or official context or circumstances. The word *chummy,* for example, carries an *Informal* label in the synonym list at **friendly,** and *dizzy,* meaning "given to lighthearted silliness," carries the same label when it appears in the synonym list at sense of 1 of **giddy.** Slang, on the other hand, is a style of language characteristic of very casual speech. Slang comprises words and special senses of words denoting things in an exceptionally vivid, humorous, irreverent, or sarcastic manner. For example, in the synonym list at **die** the following terms bear *Slang* labels: check out, croak, kick in, and kick off. The label *Poetic* applies to words most often used in verse. An example of a term labeled *Poetic* is *aurora* when it is used to mean "dawn."

Dialect labels such as *Regional* and *Chiefly Regional* indicate that a term is indigenous to a particular geographic area. For example, the word *piece,* a synonym of **distance,** is used by speakers only in a limited part of the United States. Hence it carries the label *Regional.* The word *unluck,* meaning "misfortune," is labeled *Chiefly Regional* because it is used chiefly but not exclusively in the southern part of this country.

Language labels such as *Brit.* distinguish between British English and American English. Examples of British Commonwealth labels include: bluebottle (*Brit.*), a synonym at **policeman;** bonny (*Scot.*), a synonym at **beautiful;** *funk²* (*Chiefly Brit.*), a synonym at **cowardice;** and bail³ (*Austral.*), a synonym at **rob.** In a few instances idioms are labeled if they are clearly British; at definition 1 of **escape** *verb* the idiom "do a bunk" carries a *Brit.* label. In some cases *Slang* and *Regional* labels are combined with *Brit.* labels to show special usage levels and styles. For example, the adjective *chuffy,* meaning "glum," is labeled *Brit. Regional* because it occurs in certain provincial British dialects. And the verb *dip,* meaning "to pawn," is not only a Briticism; it is also considered a slang term in British English. Hence it is labeled *Brit. Slang.*

Some synonyms are labeled according to the fields of knowledge with which they are primarily associated. For instance, the word *dissolve* has a special meaning, "to make a film image disappear gradually." This sense is therefore labeled *Motion Pic. & T.V.* in the synonym list at sense 1 of **fade out** *verb,* a main entry also carrying this label. Another example is the sense of **competence** meaning "conferred power"—a sense carrying the label *Law.*

The status label *Rare* means that a term is seldom if ever used. The verb *discuss,* meaning "to eat," is an example of a synonym so labeled.

The eight parts of speech are labeled in italics and appear in all boldface entries and subentries.

Abbreviations Used in This Book

An alphabetical list of the abbreviations used in *Roget's II* along with their expansions is given below.

Anat.	Anatomy	*Med.*	Medicine
Archit.	Architecture	*Mil.*	Military
Austral.	Australian	*Motion Pic. & T.V.*	Motion Pictures & Television
Biol.	Biology	*Mus.*	Music
Bot.	Botany	*Myth.*	Mythology
Brit.	British	*Naut.*	Nautical
Can.	Canadian	*New Zeal.*	New Zealand
Chem.	Chemistry	*Obs.*	Obsolete
Eccles.	Ecclesiastical	*Path.*	Pathology
Econ.	Economics	*Phon.*	Phonetics
Ed.	Education	*Physiol.*	Physiology
Eng.	English	*Print.*	Printing
esp.	especially	*Psychoanal.*	Psychoanalysis
Geol.	Geology	*Psychol.*	Psychology
Geom.	Geometry	*Rhet.*	Rhetoric
Gk.	Greek	*Rom.*	Roman
Hist.	History	*Scot.*	Scottish
Ir.	Irish	*usu.*	usually
Jour.	Journalism	*Vet. Med.*	Veterinary Medicine
Ling.	Linguistics	*Zool.*	Zoology

A

aback *adverb*
Without adequate preparation.

UNAWARES.

abandon *verb*
1. To give up without intending to return or claim again: *abandoned his wife and children.*

1. **Syns:** desert[3], forsake, leave[1], quit, throw over, walk out on.
   Near-syns: cast (off *or* aside), drop, renounce, reject, repudiate; chuck[1] (*Informal*), discard, junk, scrap[1].
   Ant: reclaim.

2. To let (something) go.
3. To give up a possession, claim, or right.
4. To cease trying to accomplish or continue: *abandoned her studies for lack of funds.*

2. RELINQUISH.
3. ABDICATE.
4. **Syns:** desist, discontinue, forswear (*also* foreswear), give up, lay off (*Slang*), quit, renounce, stop, swear off (*Informal*). —*Idioms* call it a day, call it quits, hang up the fiddle, have done with, throw in the towel.

5. To yield (oneself) unrestrainedly, as to a particular impulse.

5. GIVE OVER at **give**.

abandon *noun*
1. A complete surrender of inhibitions: *playing the flute with abandon.*
2. A careless, often reckless disregard for consequences: *rides his motorcycle with abandon.*

1. **Syns:** abandonment, incontinence, unrestraint, wantonness, wildness.
2. **Syns:** heedlessness, thoughtlessness.

abandoned *adjective*
1. Having been given up and left alone: *an abandoned house.*
2. Lacking in moral restraint: *an abandoned brute.*

1. **Syns:** derelict, deserted, destitute (*Obs.*), forlorn, forsaken, lorn (*Poetic*).
2. **Syns:** dissolute, incontinent, licentious, profligate, unbridled, unconstrained, uncontrolled, ungoverned, uninhibited, unrestrained, wanton, wild.

abandonment *noun*
1. The act of forsaking: *his abandonment of his family.*
2. A giving up of a possession, claim, or right.
3. A complete surrender of inhibitions.

1. **Syn:** desertion.
2. ABDICATION.
3. ABANDON *noun*.

abase *verb*
To deprive of esteem, self-worth, or effectiveness.

HUMBLE *verb*.

abash *verb*
To cause (a person) to be self-consciously distressed.

EMBARRASS.

abashed *adjective*
Distressed and ill at ease.

EMBARRASSED.

abashment *noun*
Self-conscious distress.

EMBARRASSMENT.

abate *verb*
1. To grow or cause to grow gradually less.
2. To become less active or intense.

1. DECREASE *verb*.
2. SUBSIDE.

abatement *noun*
1. The act or process of decreasing.
2. An amount deducted.
3. The act or process of becoming less active or intense.

1. DECREASE *noun*.
2. DEDUCTION.
3. WANE *noun*.

abbreviate *verb*
1. To make short or shorter.

1. SHORTEN.

  2. To make short or shorter by or as if by cutting.   2. TRUNCATE.

abdicate *verb*

To give up a possession, claim, or right: *The queen abdicated the throne in 1948.*

Syns: abandon, cede, demit, hand over, quitclaim, relinquish, render (up), renounce, resign, surrender, waive, yield.

abdication *noun*

A giving up of a possession, claim, or right: *her abdication of her responsibilities.*

Syns: abandonment, demission, quitclaim, renunciation, resignation, surrender, waiver.

abduct *verb*

To seize and detain (a person) unlawfully.   KIDNAP.

abecedarian also **abecedary** *noun*

One lacking professional skill and ease in a particular pursuit.   AMATEUR.

abecedary *noun*   SEE **abecedarian.**

aberrance or **aberrancy** *noun*

The condition of being abnormal.   ABNORMALITY.

aberrancy *noun*   SEE **abberance.**

aberrant *adjective*

  1. Departing from the normal.   1. ABNORMAL.

  2. Straying from a proper course or standard.   2. ERRANT.

aberration *noun*

  1. The condition of being abnormal.   1. ABNORMALITY.

  2. Serious mental illness or disorder impairing a person's capacity to function normally and safely.   2. INSANITY.

abet *verb*

To give support or assistance.   HELP *verb.*

abeyance also **abeyancy** *noun*

The condition of being temporarily inactive: *hold a decision in abeyance; cancer kept in abeyance with chemotherapy.*

Syns: dormancy, intermission, latency, quiescence (*also* quiescency), remission, suspension.

abeyancy *noun*   SEE **abeyance.**

abeyant *adjective*

Existing in a temporarily inactive and hidden form.   LATENT.

abhor *verb*

To regard with utter contempt and disdain.   DESPISE.

abhorrence *noun*

  1. Extreme hostility and dislike.   1. HATE *noun.*

  2. A feeling of fear and repugnance.   2. HORROR.

abhorrent *adjective*

So objectionable as to elicit despisal.   FILTHY.

abide *verb*

  1. To put up with.   1. ENDURE.

  2. To remain in existence or in a certain state for an indefinitely long time.   2. ENDURE.

  3. To stop temporarily and remain, as if reluctant to leave.   3. PAUSE *verb.*

  4. To have as one's domicile, usu. for an extended period.   4. LIVE[1].

  5. To continue to be in a place.   5. REMAIN.

  abide by *verb*

To act in conformity with.   FOLLOW.

abide by *verb*   SEE **abide.**

abiding *adjective*

Existing or remaining in the same state for an indefinitely long time.   CONTINUING.

ability *noun*

  1. Physical, mental, financial, or legal power to perform: *had the ability to learn physics.*

  1. *Syns:* ableness, capability, capacity, competence (*also* competency), faculty, might.

2. Natural or acquired facility in a specific activity: *has fine technical ability.*

2. *Syns:* adeptness, command, craft, expertise, expertism, expertness, knack, know-how (*Informal*), mastery, proficiency, skill.
Near-syns: adroitness, deftness, handiness; ingenuity, resourcefulness.

abjuration *noun*
A formal statement of disavowal.

RETRACTION.

abjure *verb*
To disavow (something previously written or said) irrevocably and usu. formally.

RETRACT.

ablaze *adjective*
On fire.

BLAZING.

able *adjective*
Having the ability to perform well: *an able attorney.*

Syns: adept, au fait (*French*), capable, competent, good, proficient, qualified, skilled, skillful.
Near-syns: alert, clever, keen, proper, sharp; effective, effectual.
Ants: inept; unable.

able-bodied *adjective*
Physically strong and healthy: *able-bodied young men helping to move the furniture.*

Syns: strapping, sturdy.

ableness *noun*
Physical, mental, financial, or legal power to perform.

ABILITY.

abnormal *adjective*
Departing from the normal: *an abnormal interest in bats.*

Syns: aberrant, anomalistic, anomalous, atypical (*also* atypic), deviant, deviate, deviating, deviative, divergent, preternatural, unnatural.
Near-syns: irregular, uncustomary, unrepresentative, unusual, untypical.
Ant: normal.

abnormality *noun*
The condition of being abnormal: *an abnormality in his vision.*

Syns: aberrance *or* aberrancy, aberration, anomalism, anomaly, deviance, deviancy, deviation, preternaturalness.

abode *noun*
A building or shelter where one lives.

HOME.

abolish *verb*
1. To put an end to formally and with authority: *The Thirteenth Amendment abolished slavery.*

1. *Syns:* abrogate, annihilate, annul, cancel, invalidate, negate, nullify, repeal, rescind, set aside, vitiate, void.
2. To destroy all traces of.
2. ANNIHILATE.

abolishment *noun*
An often formal act of putting an end to.

ABOLITION.

abolition *noun*
An often formal act of putting an end to: *the abolition of slavery.*

Syns: abolishment, abrogation, annihilation, annulment, defeasance, extinguishment, invalidation, negation, nullification, repeal, rescindment, rescission.

abominable *adjective*
1. Eliciting or deserving hate.
2. Too awful to be described.

1. HATEFUL.
2. UNSPEAKABLE.

abominate *verb*
To regard with extreme dislike and hostility.

HATE *verb.*

abomination *noun*
1. Extreme hostility and dislike.
2. An object of extreme dislike.

1. HATE *noun.*
2. HATE *noun.*

aboriginal *adjective*
Belonging to one because of the place or circumstances of one's birth.

NATIVE *adjective.*

abort *verb*
To bring forth a nonviable fetus prematurely.

MISCARRY.

abound *verb*
To overflow with.

TEEM[1].

abounding *adjective*
Full of animation and activity.

ALIVE.

about *adverb*
1. In or toward a former location or condition.
2. Toward the back.
3. Near to in quantity or amount.

1. BACK *adverb.*
2. BACKWARD *adverb.*
3. APPROXIMATELY.

about-face *verb*
To turn sharply around.

DOUBLE *verb.*

abracadabra *noun*
1. Wordy, unclear jargon.
2. Esoteric, formulaic, and often incomprehensible speech relating to the occult.

1. GIBBERISH.
2. GIBBERISH.

abrade *verb*
To make (the skin) raw by or as if by friction.

CHAFE.

abridge *verb*
To make short or shorter by or as if by cutting.

TRUNCATE.

abridgment *noun*
A short summary prepared by cutting down a larger work.

SYNOPSIS.

abrogate *verb*
To put an end to formally and with authority.

ABOLISH.

abrogation *noun*
An often formal act of putting an end to.

ABOLITION.

abrupt *adjective*
1. Happening quickly and without warning: *his abrupt departure for New York.*
2. Rudely unceremonious: *gave an abrupt, barely civil answer.*

1. **Syns:** hasty, hurried, precipitant, precipitate, sudden.
2. **Syns:** blunt, brief, brusque, crusty, curt, gruff, short, short-spoken, snippety, snippy.
   Near-syns: bluff, brisk, crisp, terse, sharp; impetuous, quick.

3. So sharply inclined as to be almost perpendicular.

3. STEEP[1].

abscond *verb*
To break loose and leave suddenly, as from confinement or from a difficult or threatening situation.

ESCAPE *verb.*

absence *noun*
1. Failure to be present: *his constant absence from meetings.*
2. The condition of lacking a usual or needed amount: *an absence of reliable information.*

1. **Syns:** absentation, nonappearance, nonattendance.
2. **Syns:** dearth, default (*Obs.*), defect, deficiency, lack, miss (*Regional*), want.

absent *adjective*
1. Not present: *absent from her office.*
2. Deficient in a usual or needed amount: *junk foods in which nutrition is absent.*
3. So lost in thought as to be unaware of one's surroundings.

1. **Syns:** away, gone, missing, wanting.
2. **Syns:** lacking, wanting.

3. ABSENT-MINDED.

absentation *noun*
Failure to be present.

ABSENCE.

absent-minded *adjective*
So lost in thought as to be unaware of one's surroundings: *an absent-minded professor.*

Syns: absent, abstracted, bemused, distrait, faraway, inattentive, inconscient, preoccupied. —*Idioms* a million miles away, off in the clouds.

absolute *adjective*
1. Having and exercising complete political power and control: *an absolute ruler*.

1. ***Syns:*** absolutist (*also* absolutistic), arbitrary, autarchic (*also* autarchical), autocratic, despotic, dictatorial, monocratic, totalitarian, tyrannical (*also* tyrannic), tyrannous.
Near-ants: circumscribed, limited, restrained, restricted.

2. Supremely excellent in quality or nature.
3. Free from extraneous elements.
4. Completely such, without qualification or exception.
5. Without limitations or mitigating conditions.

2. PERFECT.
3. PURE *adjective*.
4. UTTER².
5. UNCONDITIONAL.

absolutely *adverb*
1. Without question: *absolutely the finest painting in the gallery*.
2. In truth.
3. It is so; as you say or ask.

1. ***Syns:*** certainly, doubtless, positively.

2. REALLY.
3. YES *adverb*.

absolution *noun*
The act or an instance of forgiving.

FORGIVENESS.

absolutism *noun*
1. A government in which a single leader or party exercises absolute control over all citizens and every aspect of their lives: *Absolutism prevailed before the coup d'état*.
2. A political doctrine advocating the principle of absolute rule: *a strong belief in absolutism held by reactionaries*.

1. ***Syns:*** autarchy, autocracy, dictatorship, monocracy.

2. ***Syns:*** authoritarianism, autocracy, despotism, dictatorship, totalitarianism.

absolutist also **absolutistic** *adjective*
Having and exercising complete political power and control.

ABSOLUTE.

absolutistic *adjective*

SEE **absolutist.**

absolve *verb*
1. To free from a charge or imputation of guilt.
2. To free from an obligation or duty.

1. CLEAR *verb*.
2. EXCUSE *verb*.

absorb *verb*
1. To take in and incorporate, esp. mentally: *quickly absorbed new ideas*.
2. To occupy the full attention of: *His medical practice absorbed him*.

1. ***Syns:*** assimilate, digest, imbibe, insorb, soak up.
2. ***Syns:*** consume, engross, immerse, monopolize, preoccupy.

absorbed *adjective*
Having one's thoughts fully occupied: *absorbed in painting*.

Syns: consumed, deep, engrossed, immersed, intent, preoccupied, rapt, wrapped up.
Near-ants: apathetic, disinterested, indifferent, unconcerned, uninterested.
Ant: distracted.

absorbent *adjective*
Having a capacity or tendency to absorb or soak up: *an absorbent fabric*.

Syns: absorptive, assimilating, assimilative, bibulous.

absorbing *adjective*
Catching and holding the full attention: *an absorbing book*.

Syns: consuming, engrossing, enthralling, gripping.

absorption *noun*
1. The process of absorbing and incorporating, esp. mentally: *her absorption of her mentor's opinions*.
2. Total occupation of the attention or of the mind: *complete absorption in the work at hand*.

1. ***Syns:*** assimilation, digestion.

2. ***Syns:*** engrossment, enthrallment, preoccupation.

absorptive *adjective*
Having a capacity or tendency to absorb or soak up.

ABSORBENT.

absquatulate *verb*
Slang. To break loose and leave suddenly, as from confinement or from a difficult or threatening situation.

ESCAPE *verb*.

abstain *verb*
To hold oneself back.

REFRAIN.

abstemious *adjective*
Exercising moderation and self-restraint in appetites and behavior.

TEMPERATE.

abstentious *adjective*
Exercising moderation and self-restraint in appetites and behavior.

TEMPERATE.

abstinence *noun*
The practice of refraining from use of alcoholic beverages.

TEMPERANCE.

abstinent *adjective*
Exercising moderation and self-restraint in appetites and behavior.

TEMPERATE.

abstract *adjective*
1. Existing only in concept and not in reality.
2. Concerned with or restricted to a theory or theories.

1. THEORETICAL.
2. THEORETICAL.

abstract *noun*
A short summary prepared by cutting down a larger work.

SYNOPSIS.

abstract *verb*
1. To remove from association with.
2. To recapitulate the salient facts of.

1. DETACH.
2. REVIEW *verb*.

abstracted *adjective*
So lost in thought as to be unaware of one's surroundings.

ABSENT-MINDED.

abstraction *noun*
The condition of being so lost in solitary thought as to be unaware of one's surroundings.

TRANCE.

abstruse *adjective*
Beyond the understanding of an average mind.

DEEP *adjective*.

absurd *adjective*
So senseless as to be laughable.

FOOLISH.

absurdity *noun*
Foolish behavior.

FOOLISHNESS.

abundance *noun*
Prosperity and a sufficiency of life's necessities.

PLENTY *noun*.

abundant *adjective*
1. Characterized by abundance.
2. Large in number or yield.

1. GENEROUS.
2. HEAVY *adjective*.

abuse *verb*
1. To hurt or injure by maltreatment: *abused their lungs by smoking heavily.*
2. To use wrongly and improperly: *Some employees abused their privileges and arrived at noon.*

1. *Syns:* ill-use, maltreat, mishandle, mistreat, misuse.
2. *Syns:* misapply, misappropriate, misemploy, mishandle, misuse, pervert. *Near-syns:* exploit; corrupt, debase, profane, prostitute; mar, spoil.

3. To take advantage of unfairly: *abused her hospitality by staying too long.*
4. To attack with harsh, often insulting language.

3. *Syns:* exploit, impose (on *or* upon), presume (on *or* upon), use (*Informal*).
4. REVILE.

abuse *noun*
1. Wrong, often corrupt use: *the abuse of power.*

1. *Syns:* abusion (*Obs.*), misapplication, misappropriation, misemployment, mishandling, misuse, perversion.

2. Physically harmful treatment: *Child abuse is a crime.*
3. Harsh, often insulting language.

2. *Syns:* maltreatment, mistreatment, misusage.
3. VITUPERATION.

abusion *noun*
Obs. Wrong, often corrupt use.   ABUSE *noun.*

abusive *adjective*
Of, relating to, or characterized by verbal abuse: *Syns:* contumelious, invective, obloquious,
abusive remarks.   opprobrious, reviling, scurrilous,
     vituperative.

abut *verb*
To be contiguous or next to.   ADJOIN.

abutting *adjective*
Sharing a common boundary.   ADJOINING.

abysmal *adjective*
1. Extending far downward or inward from a surface.   1. DEEP *adjective.*
2. Open wide.   2. YAWNING.

abyssal *adjective*
Open wide.   YAWNING.

academic *adjective*
1. Characterized by a narrow concern for book learning   1. PEDANTIC.
   and formal rules, without knowledge or experience
   of practical matters.
2. Concerned with or restricted to a theory or theories.   2. THEORETICAL.

accede *verb*
To respond affirmatively; receive with agreement or   ASSENT *verb.*
compliance.

accelerate *verb*
To increase the speed of.   SPEED UP at **speed.**

accent *noun*
1. Special weight placed upon something considered   1. EMPHASIS.
   important.
2. A particular vocal quality that indicates some   2. TONE.
   emotion or feeling.
accent *verb*
To accord emphasis to.   EMPHASIZE.

accented *adjective*
Expressed or performed with emphasis.   EMPHATIC.

accentuate *verb*
To accord emphasis to.   EMPHASIZE.

accentuated *adjective*
Expressed or performed with emphasis.   EMPHATIC.

accentuation *noun*
Special weight placed upon something considered   EMPHASIS.
important.

accept *verb*
1. To receive (something given or offered) willingly and   1. *Syns:* embrace, take up, welcome.
   gladly: *going to Sweden to accept the award.*
2. To admit to one's possession, presence, or awareness.   2. RECEIVE.
3. To allow admittance, as to a group: *was accepted for*   3. *Syns:* admit, receive, take in.
   membership in the country club.
4. To be favorably disposed toward.   4. APPROVE.
5. To regard (something) as true or real.   5. BELIEVE.
6. To put up with.   6. ENDURE.
7. To respond affirmatively; receive with agreement or   7. ASSENT.
   compliance.
8. To perceive and recognize the meaning of.   8. UNDERSTAND.

acceptable *adjective*
1. Capable of being accepted: *an acceptable applicant;*   1. *Syns:* admissible, unobjectionable.
   an acceptable gift.
2. Of moderately good quality but less than excellent: 2. *Syns:* adequate, average, common,
   an acceptable dissertation by a capable student.   decent, fair, fairish, goodish,
     indifferent, O.K. (*Informal*), passable,
     respectable, satisfactory, sufficient, tidy
     (*Informal*), tolerable.

Near-syns: all right, good, ordinary, mediocre, middling (*Informal*), unexceptional; bearable.
Ant: unacceptable.

acceptance *noun*
1. The act or process of accepting: *his acceptance of the suggestion.*
2. Favorable regard: *The theory slowly gained acceptance.*

1. **Syns:** acquiescence, agreement, assent, consent, nod, yes.
2. **Syns:** approbation, approval, favor.

acceptant *adjective*
Ready and willing to receive favorably, as new ideas.

RECEPTIVE.

acceptation *noun*
That which is signified by a word or expression.

MEANING.

accepted *adjective*
Generally approved or agreed upon: *accepted behavior.*

Syns: conventional, orthodox, received, sanctioned.

acception *noun*
That which is signified by a word or expression.

MEANING.

acceptive *adjective*
Ready and willing to receive favorably, as new ideas.

RECEPTIVE.

access *noun*
1. The right to enter or make use of.
2. A sudden, violent expression, as of emotion.
3. A sudden and often acute manifestation of a disease.

1. ADMISSION.
2. OUTBURST.
3. SEIZURE.

accessible *adjective*
1. Easily approached.
2. Available for use.

1. APPROACHABLE.
2. OPEN *adjective.*

accession *noun*
Something tending to augment something else.

ADDITION.

accessory *noun*
Something that attaches as a supplementary part.

ATTACHMENT.

accessory *adjective*
Giving or able to give help or support.

AUXILIARY *adjective.*

accident *noun*
1. An unexpected and usu. undesirable event: *a traffic accident.*

2. An unexpected random event.

1. **Syns:** casualty, contretemps, misadventure, mischance, misfortune, mishap.
2. CHANCE *noun.*

accidental *adjective*
1. Occurring unexpectedly: *an accidental meeting.*

2. Not part of the real or essential nature of a thing: *The secondary plot was accidental to the novel.*

1. **Syns:** casual, chance, contingent, fluky, fortuitous, inadvertent, odd.
2. **Syns:** adscititious (*also* adcititious), adventitious, incident (*Archaic*), incidental, supervenient.

acclaim *verb*
To express warm approval of.

PRAISE *verb.*

acclaim *noun*
An expression of warm approval.

PRAISE *noun.*

acclimate *verb*
1. To make or become suitable to a particular situation or use.
2. To make resistant to hardship, esp. through continued exposure.

1. ADAPT.

2. HARDEN.

acclimation *noun*
Adjustment to a changing environment.

ADAPTATION.

acclimatization *noun*
Adjustment to a changing environment.

ADAPTATION.

acclimatize *verb*
1. To make or become suitable to a particular situation or use.

1. ADAPT.

2. To make resistant to hardship, esp. through continued exposure.

2. HARDEN.

acclivity   *noun*
An upward slope.

ASCENT.

accolade   *noun*
Recognition of achievement or superiority or a sign of this.

DISTINCTION.

accommodate   *verb*
   1. To have the room or capacity for: *a room that can accommodate a large crowd.*
   2. To make or become suitable to a particular situation or use.
   3. To bring into accord.
   4. To provide with often temporary lodging.
   5. To perform a service or a courteous act.

1. *Syns:* contain, hold.

2. ADAPT.

3. HARMONIZE.
4. HARBOR *verb*.
5. OBLIGE.

accommodating   *adjective*
Ready to do favors for another.

OBLIGING.

accommodation   *noun*
The condition of being made suitable to an end.

ADAPTATION.

accompaniment   *noun*
   1. One that accompanies another: *Unemployment is an accompaniment of recessions.*
   2. Something added to another for embellishment or completion: *Croutons are a good accompaniment to soup.*

1. *Syns:* associate, attendant, companion, concomitant.
2. *Syns:* augmentation, complement, enhancement, enrichment.

accompany   *verb*
To be with or go with (another): *Thunder accompanies lightning. Jack accompanied his niece to the première.*

Syns: attend, companion, company (*Rare*), consort (*Obs.*), escort. —*Idiom* go hand in hand with.

accompanying   *adjective*
Occurring in company with: *war and its accompanying horrors.*

Syns: attendant, attending, coincident, concomitant, concurrent.

accomplish   *verb*
To succeed in doing: *accomplished her objective and won the race.*

Syns: achieve, attain, gain, reach, realize, score.
Near-syns: complete, consummate, fulfill, perfect; succeed, win.

accomplished   *adjective*
Very proficient as a result of practice and study: *an accomplished musician.*

Syns: finished, practiced, skilled.

accomplishment   *noun*
   1. Something completed successfully: *Winning the race was a real accomplishment.*
   2. Something done.

1. *Syns:* achievement, acquirement, acquisition, attainment, effort, feat.
2. ACT *noun*.

accord   *verb*
   1. To come to an understanding or to terms.
   2. To be compatible or in correspondence.
   3. To give formally or officially.
   4. To let have as a favor or privilege.

1. AGREE.
2. AGREE.
3. CONFER.
4. GRANT *verb*.

accord   *noun*
   1. Harmonious mutual understanding.
   2. The quality or condition of being in complete mutual agreement.
   3. An act or state of agreeing between parties regarding a course of action.
   4. A formal, usu. written settlement between nations.
   5. Pleasing agreement, as of musical sounds.

1. AGREEMENT.
2. UNANIMITY.

3. AGREEMENT.

4. TREATY.
5. HARMONY.

accordance   *noun*
   1. The act or state of agreeing or conforming.
   2. The act of conferring, as of an honor.

1. AGREEMENT.
2. CONFERMENT.

accordant *adjective*
1. In keeping with one's needs or expectations.
2. Having components pleasingly combined.

1. AGREEABLE.
2. SYMMETRICAL.

accost *verb*
To approach for the purpose of speech: *was accosted by petitioners outside the door of the chamber.*

Syns: greet, hail, salute.

accouchement *noun*
French. The act or process of bringing forth young.

BIRTH *noun.*

account *noun*
1. A recounting of past events.
2. A statement of causes or motives: *She was asked to give an account for her tardiness.*

1. STORY.
2. *Syns:* explanation, justification, rationale, rationalization, reason. —*Idiom* why and wherefore.

3. A precise list of fees or charges: *My account has been paid in full.*
4. A measure of those qualities that determine merit, desirability, usefulness, or importance.
5. A feeling of deference, approval, and liking.
6. The quality of being suitable or adaptable to an end.
7. A harbored grievance demanding satisfaction.

3. *Syns:* bill[1], invoice, reckoning, statement, tab.
4. WORTH.

5. ESTEEM *noun.*
6. USE *noun.*
7. SCORE *noun.*

account *verb*
To look upon in a particular way.

REGARD *verb.*

account for *verb*
To offer reasons for or a cause of: *He had grown up in several different countries, which accounted for his unplaceable foreign accent.*

Syns: explain, justify, rationalize.

accountable *adjective*
1. Legally obligated.
2. Capable of being accounted for.

1. LIABLE.
2. EXPLAINABLE.

account for *verb*

SEE **account.**

accouter *verb*
To supply what is needed for some activity or purpose.

FURNISH.

accouterments *noun*
Things needed for a task, journey, or other purpose.

OUTFIT *noun.*

accredit *verb*
1. To regard as belonging to or resulting from another.
2. To give authority to.

1. ATTRIBUTE *verb.*
2. AUTHORIZE.

accretion *noun*
The result or product of building up.

BUILD-UP at **build up.**

accrue *verb*
To bring together so as to increase in mass or number.

ACCUMULATE.

acculturate *verb*
To fit for companionship with others, esp. in attitude or manners.

SOCIALIZE.

accumulate *verb*
To bring together so as to increase in mass or number: *accumulated a great deal of money in a short time. Snow began to accumulate on the pavement.*

Syns: accrue, agglomerate, aggregate, amass, collect[1], cumulate, garner, gather, hive, pile up, roll up.
Near-syns: assemble, lay (up *or* by), heap, mass, stock, stockpile, store; hoard, treasure.
Ant: dissipate.

accumulation *noun*
1. A quantity accumulated: *an accumulation of junk in the attic.*

1. *Syns:* acervation, agglomeration, aggregation, amassment, assemblage, collection, congeries, cumulation, cumulus, garner, mass.

2. The result or product of building up.

2. BUILD-UP at **build up.**

accumulative *adjective*
Increasing, as in force, by successive additions: *the accumulative unhealthy effect of smoking.*

Syns: additive, additory, cumulative.

accuracy *noun*
1. Freedom from error: *checked the results for accuracy.*

    1. **Syns:** accurateness, correctness, exactitude, exactness, preciseness, precision, rightness.

2. Correspondence with fact or truth.

    2. VERACITY.

accurate *adjective*
1. Having no errors: *an accurate calculation of expenses.*

    1. **Syns:** correct, errorless.

2. Conforming to fact: *an accurate description of the house.*

    2. **Syns:** correct, exact, faithful, precise, proper, right, rigorous, true, veracious, veridical.

accurateness *noun*
Freedom from error.

    ACCURACY.

accurse *verb*
Rare. To invoke evil or injury upon.

    CURSE *verb.*

accursed *adjective*
So annoying or detestable as to deserve condemnation.

    DAMNED.

accusal *noun*
A charging of someone with a misdeed.

    ACCUSATION.

accusant *noun*
1. One that accuses.
2. One that makes a formal complaint, esp. in court.

    1. ACCUSER.
    2. COMPLAINANT.

accusation *noun*
A charging of someone with a misdeed: *an accusation that she had committed murder.*

    Syns: accusal, accuse (*Obs.*), charge, denouncement, denunciation, imputation, incrimination, indictment (*Law*).

accusative *adjective*
Containing, relating to, or involving an accusation.

    ACCUSATORIAL.

accusatorial *also* **accusatory** *adjective*
Containing, relating to, or involving an accusation: *pointing an accusatorial finger at the defendant.*

    Syns: accusative, accusive, denunciative, denunciatory, incriminating, incriminative.

accusatory *adjective*

    SEE **accusatorial.**

accuse *verb*
To make an accusation against: *accused the senator of accepting a bribe.*

    Syns: arraign, charge (with), denounce, denunciate, incriminate, inculpate, indict, tax.

accuse *noun*
Obs. A charging of someone with a misdeed.

    ACCUSATION.

accused *noun*
Law. A person against whom an action is brought: *The accused pleaded innocent.*

    Syns: defendant (*Law*), respondent (*Law*).

accuser *noun*
One that accuses: *confronted his accuser in open court.*

    Syns: accusant, denouncer, denunciator, incriminator, indictor (*also* indicter).

accusive *adjective*
Containing, relating to, or involving an accusation.

    ACCUSATORIAL.

accustom *verb*
To make familiar through constant practice or use: *She accustomed her eyes to the bright sunlight.*

    Syns: acquaint (*Obs.*), condition, familiarize (*Archaic*), habituate, inure, wont.

accustomable *adjective*
Obs. Commonly practiced or used.

    CUSTOMARY.

accustomary *adjective*
Archaic. Commonly practiced or used.

    CUSTOMARY.

accustomed *adjective*
1. Familiar through repetition: *crickets making their accustomed noises.*

    1. **Syns:** chronic, habitual, routine.

2. Commonly practiced or used.

    2. CUSTOMARY.

    accustomed to *adjective*

In the habit of: *He was a bachelor and accustomed to doing things his own way.*

Syns: used to, wont to.

accustomed to *adjective*
SEE **accustomed.**

ace¹ *noun*
The least bit.
DAMN *noun.*

ace² *noun*
1. *Informal.* A person with a high degree of knowledge or skill.
2. Something, esp. something held in reserve, that gives one a decisive advantage.

1. EXPERT *noun.*
2. TRUMP *noun.*

acerb *adjective*
1. So sharp as to cause mental pain.
2. Having a noticeably sharp, pungent taste or smell.
3. Having a taste characteristic of that produced by acids.
4. Given to or expressing sarcasm.

1. BITING.
2. BITTER *adjective.*
3. SOUR *adjective.*
4. SARCASTIC.

acerbic *adjective*
1. So sharp as to cause mental pain.
2. Having a noticeably sharp, pungent taste or smell.
3. Having a taste characteristic of that produced by acids.
4. Given to or expressing sarcasm.

1. BITING.
2. BITTER *adjective.*
3. SOUR *adjective.*
4. SARCASTIC.

acerbity *noun*
Ironic, bitter humor designed to wound.
SARCASM.

acervation *noun*
A quantity accumulated.
ACCUMULATION.

acetose *adjective*
SEE **acetous.**

acetous also **acetose** *adjective*
Having a taste characteristic of that produced by acids.
SOUR *adjective.*

ache *verb*
1. To have or cause a feeling of physical pain or discomfort.
2. To have a strong longing for.
3. To experience or express compassion.

1. HURT *verb.*
2. DESIRE *verb.*
3. FEEL *verb.*

ache *noun*
A sensation of physical discomfort occurring as the result of disease or injury.
PAIN *noun.*

Acheronian *adjective*
Dark and depressing.
GLOOMY.

Acherontic *adjective*
Dark and depressing.
GLOOMY.

achieve *verb*
To succeed in doing.
ACCOMPLISH.

achievement *noun*
1. Something completed successfully.
2. A great or heroic deed.

1. ACCOMPLISHMENT.
2. FEAT.

aching *adjective*
Marked by, causing, or experiencing physical pain.
PAINFUL.

acicular *adjective*
Having an end tapering to a point.
POINTED.

aciculate *adjective*
Having an end tapering to a point.
POINTED.

acid *adjective*
1. So sharp as to cause mental pain.
2. Having a taste characteristic of that produced by acids.

1. BITING.
2. SOUR *adjective.*

acidic *adjective*
So sharp as to cause mental pain.
BITING.

acidulous *adjective*
Having a taste characteristic of that produced by acids.
SOUR *adjective.*

acknowledge *verb*
1. To recognize, often reluctantly, the reality or truth of: *He acknowledged his mistake.*

2. To express recognition of: *acknowledged his duty toward his family.*

acknowledgement *noun*

acknowledgment also **acknowledgement** *noun*
1. The act of admitting to something: *her acknowledgment of her error.*
2. Favorable notice, as of an achievement.

acme *noun*
The highest point or state.

acquaint *verb*
1. To make known socially: *The couple got acquainted at a party.*
2. To cause to know about or be aware of.
3. *Obs.* To make familiar through constant practice or use.

acquaintance *noun*
1. Personal knowledge derived from participation or observation: *has a more than passing acquaintance with baroque music.*
2. A person whom one knows casually: *met several acquaintances on the street.*

acquaintant *noun*
Obs. A person whom one knows casually.

acquainted *adjective*
Having good knowledge of.

acquiesce *verb*
To respond affirmatively; receive with agreement or compliance.

acquiescence *noun*
1. The act or process of accepting.
2. The quality or state of willingly carrying out the wishes of others.

acquiescent *adjective*
1. Disposed to accept or agree.
2. Submitting without objection or resistance.

acquire *verb*
To come into possession of.

acquirement *noun*
Something completed successfully.

acquisition *noun*
Something completed successfully.

acquisitive *adjective*
Having a strong urge to obtain or possess something, esp. material wealth, in quantity.

acquisitiveness *noun*
Excessive desire for more than one needs or deserves.

acquit *verb*
1. To conduct oneself in a specified way.
2. To free from a charge or imputation of guilt.

acres *noun*
Law. Usu. extensive real estate.

acrid *adjective*
1. So sharp as to cause mental pain.

---

1. *Syns:* admit, allow, avow, concede, confess, fess up (*Slang*), grant, own (up).
   Near-ants: disallow, disavow, disown, nix (*Slang*), reject; contradict, impugn, negate.
   Ant: deny.
2. *Syns:* admit, recognize.

SEE **acknowledgment.**

1. *Syns:* admission, avowal, confession.

2. RECOGNITION.

CLIMAX *noun.*

1. *Syns:* introduce, present[2], quaint[2] (*Archaic*).
2. INFORM.
3. ACCUSTOM.

1. *Syns:* experience, familiarity.

2. *Syns:* acquaintant (*Obs.*), friend.

ACQUAINTANCE.

FAMILIAR *adjective.*

ASSENT *verb.*

1. ACCEPTANCE.
2. OBEDIENCE.

1. WILLING.
2. PASSIVE.

GET.

ACCOMPLISHMENT.

ACCOMPLISHMENT.

GREEDY.

GREED.

1. ACT *verb.*
2. CLEAR *verb.*

LAND *noun.*

1. BITING.

2. Having a noticeably sharp, pungent taste or smell.

acridity *noun*
The quality or state of feeling bitter.

acrimonious *adjective*
Bitingly hostile.

acrimony *noun*
The quality or state of feeling bitter.

act *noun*
1. The process of doing: *the act of thinking.*
2. Something done: *an act of bravery.*

3. The formal product of a legislative or judicial body.
4. *Informal.* A display of insincere behavior: *Her concern is just an act.*

5. A short theatrical piece within a larger production.

act *verb*
1. To play the part of: *acted Juliet in summer stock.*

2. To produce on the stage.
3. To conduct oneself in a specified way: *always acts like a lady.*

4. To behave affectedly or insincerely: *is usually just acting when he shows interest.*

5. To react in a specified way.

act for *verb*
To perform the duties of another: *In his brother's absence he acted for him.*

act up *verb*
1. *Informal.* To behave in a rowdy or unruly fashion.
2. *Informal.* To work improperly due to mechanical difficulties.

act for *verb*

actify *verb*
To arouse to action.

acting *adjective*
Temporarily assuming the duties of another.

acting *noun*
1. The art and occupation of an actor: *went into acting as a profession.*
2. A display of insincere behavior.

action *noun*
1. The process of doing.
2. Something done.
3. *Law.* A legal proceeding to demand justice or enforce a right.
4. A hostile encounter between opposing military forces.

action *verb*
Law. To institute or subject to legal proceedings.

actions *noun*
The manner in which one behaves.

activate *verb*
To arouse to action: *trying to activate his wish to learn.*

active *adjective*
1. In action or full operation: *an active volcano; an active imagination; an active savings account.*

---

2. BITTER *adjective.*

RESENTMENT.

RESENTFUL.

RESENTMENT.

1. **Syn:** action.
2. **Syns:** accomplishment, action, actus, deed, doing, thing.
3. LAW.
4. **Syns:** acting, dissemblance, masquerade, play-acting, pose, pretense, sham, show, simulation.
5. SKETCH *noun.*

1. **Syns:** do, enact, impersonate, perform, play-act, portray, represent.
2. STAGE *verb.*
3. **Syns:** acquit, bear, behave, carry, comport, demean[1], deport, disport, do, quit.
4. **Syns:** affect, assume, counterfeit, dissemble, fake, feign, play-act, pose, pretend, put on, sham, simulate.
5. FUNCTION.

Syns: function, officiate, serve.

1. MISBEHAVE.
2. MALFUNCTION.

SEE **act.**

ACTIVATE.

TEMPORARY.

1. **Syns:** dramatics, play-acting, playing, stage.
2. ACT *noun.*

1. ACT *noun.*
2. ACT *noun.*
3. LAWSUIT.

4. COMBAT *noun.*

SUE.

BEHAVIOR.

Syns: actify, activize, actuate, dynamize, energize, galvanize, stimulate.

1. **Syns:** alive, functioning, going, live[2], operative, running, working.
   Near-syns: dynamic, energetic,

2. Moving or performing quickly, lightly, and easily.
3. Disposed to action.

activity *noun*
Energetic physical action: *growing fat from too much food and too little activity.*

activize *verb*
To arouse to action.

actor *noun*
1. A theatrical performer: *an actor on Broadway.*
2. One who participates.

actual *adjective*
1. Occurring or existing in act or fact: *The actual world as opposed to the ideal.*
2. In agreement or correspondence with fact: *made an actual contribution to the investigation.*
3. Based on fact: *an actual account of what happened.*

actuality *noun*
1. The state or fact of having reality: *ideas true in possibility but not in actuality.*
2. Something that exists: *turned my dream into an actuality.*
3. The quality of being factual: *The story was in actuality not true.*

actualization *noun*
The condition of being in full force or operation.

actualize *verb*
To make real or actual.

actually *adverb*
1. In point of fact: *She said she was working when actually she was reading a novel.*
2. At this moment.
3. In truth.

actuate *verb*
1. To arouse to action.
2. To set or keep going.
3. To put into action or use.

act up *verb*

actus *noun*
Something done.

acumen *noun*
Skill in perceiving, discriminating, or judging.

acuminate *verb*
To give a sharp edge to.

   acuminate *adjective*
   Biol. Having an end tapering to a point.

acumination *noun*
Biol. A sharp or tapered end.

acuminous *adjective*
Biol. Having an end tapering to a point.

acute *adjective*
1. Possessing or displaying perceptions of great accuracy and sensitivity: *an acute observer of the passing scene.*

2. Having an end tapering to a point.
3. Having or suggesting keen, discerning intellect.
4. *Mus.* Elevated in pitch.

---

vigorous; busy, diligent, industrious; alert, vigilant, wide-awake.
Ant: inactive.
2. NIMBLE.
3. VIGOROUS.

Syns: exercise, exercising, exertion.

ACTIVATE.

1. ***Syns:*** player, thespian.
2. PARTICIPANT.

1. ***Syns:*** existent, existing, extant.

2. ***Syns:*** indisputable, real, true, undeniable.
3. ***Syns:*** factual, hard, sure-enough.

1. ***Syns:*** being, existence.

2. ***Syns:*** materiality, reality.

3. ***Syns:*** fact, factuality, factualness, reality.

EFFECT *noun.*

REALIZE.

1. ***Syns:*** genuinely, indeed, really.

2. NOW.
3. REALLY.

1. ACTIVATE.
2. DRIVE *verb.*
3. USE *verb.*
SEE **act.**

ACT *noun.*

DISCERNMENT.

SHARPEN.

POINTED.

POINT *noun.*

POINTED.

1. ***Syns:*** keen[1], perceptive, sensitive, sharp.
Near-syns: accurate, meticulous, precise; observant.
Ants: dull; obtuse.
2. POINTED.
3. INCISIVE.
4. HIGH.

5. Marked by severity or intensity.

5. SHARP.

6. So serious as to be at the point of crisis.

6. CRITICAL.

adage *noun*
A usu. pithy and familiar statement expressing an observation or principle generally accepted as wise or true.

PROVERB.

adamant *adjective*
Firmly, often unreasonably immovable in purpose or will.

STUBBORN.

adamantine *adjective*
Firmly, often unreasonably immovable in purpose or will.

STUBBORN.

adapt *verb*
To make or become suitable to a particular situation or use: *The family quickly adapted to country life.*

Syns: acclimate, acclimatize, accommodate, adjust, conform, fashion, fit, reconcile (to *or* with), square, suit, tailor, tailor-make.

adaptable *adjective*
Capable of adapting or being adapted: *An adaptable person can live happily almost anywhere.*

Syns: adaptative, adaptive, adjustable, elastic, flexible, plastic, pliable, pliant, supple.

adaptation also **adaption** *noun*
1. The condition of being made suitable to an end: *the adaptation of the novel as a film.*
2. Adjustment to a changing environment: *made a quick adaptation to the new job.*

1. *Syns:* accommodation, adjustment, conformation.
2. *Syns:* acclimation, acclimatization.

adaptative *adjective*
Capable of adapting or being adapted.

ADAPTABLE.

adaption *noun*

SEE **adaptation.**

adaptive *adjective*
Capable of adapting or being adapted.

ADAPTABLE.

adcititious *adjective*

SEE **adscititious.**

add *verb*
1. To join so as to form a larger or more comprehensive entity: *added a new wing to the library.*
2. To combine (figures) to form a sum: *adding the debit column in the ledger.*

1. *Syns:* annex, append, plus.
2. *Syns:* cast, figure, foot (up), sum (up), summate, tally, tot[2] (up), total, totalize, tote[2] (up).

add up to *verb*
1. To have or convey a particular idea.
2. To come to in number or quantity.

1. MEAN[1].
2. AMOUNT *verb.*

added *adjective*
Being an addition.

ADDITIONAL.

addition *noun*
1. The act or process of adding: *the waiter's addition of the price of the dinner and the tax.*
2. Something tending to augment something else: *The young lawyer proved a real addition to the staff.*

1. *Syns:* summation, totalization.
2. *Syns:* accession, augmentation.

additional *adjective*
1. Being an addition: *What additional information do you need?*
2. Going beyond what currently exists.

1. *Syns:* added, extra, fresh, further, more, new, other.
2. FURTHER *adjective.*

additionally *adverb*
In addition: *Additionally he pleased us by the excellence of his work.*

Syns: also, besides, further, furthermore, item, more, still. —*Idioms* as well, to boot.

additive *adjective*
1. Involving addition: *additive, not subtractive.*
2. Increasing, as in force, by successive additions.

1. *Syns:* additory, plus.
2. ACCUMULATIVE.

additory *adjective*
1. Involving addition.
2. Increasing, as in force, by successive additions.

1. ADDITIVE.
2. ACCUMULATIVE.

addle   *verb*
To cause to be unclear in mind or intent.   CONFUSE.

addled   *adjective*
Mentally uncertain.   CONFUSED.

address   *verb*
1. To direct speech to: *addressed her softly.*
2. To talk to (an audience) formally: *addressed the meeting.*
3. To bring an appeal or request to the attention of: *addressed the mayor for a solution to the problem.*
4. To mark (a written communication) with its destination: *addressed the envelope.*
5. To devote (oneself or one's efforts).
6. To cause (something) to be conveyed to a destination.
7. To attempt to gain the affection of.

1. *Syns:* speak (to), talk (to).
2. *Syns:* bespeak (*Archaic*), lecture, prelect (*also* praelect), speak (to).
3. *Syns:* appeal (to), apply (to), approach, petition, sue.
4. *Syns:* direct, superscribe.

5. APPLY.
6. SEND.

7. COURT *verb.*

address   *noun*
1. A usu. formal oral communication to an audience.
2. A written inscription on a deliverable item giving its destination: *put the wrong address on the package.*
3. Behavior through which one reveals one's personality.
4. The ability to say and do the right thing at the right time.
5. Skillfulness in the use of the hands or body.

1. SPEECH.
2. *Syns:* direction (*Archaic*), superscription.

3. BEARING.

4. TACT.

5. DEXTERITY.

addresses   *noun*
Romantic attentions.   COURTSHIP.

adduce   *verb*
To bring forward and quote for formal consideration.   PRESENT[2] *verb.*

add up to   *verb*   SEE **add.**

adept   *adjective*
Having or demonstrating a high degree of knowledge or skill.   EXPERT *adjective.*

adept   *noun*
A person with a high degree of knowledge or skill in a particular field.   EXPERT *noun.*

adeptness   *noun*
Natural or acquired facility in a specific activity.   ABILITY.

adequacy   *noun*
An adequate quantity.   ENOUGH *noun.*

adequate   *adjective*
1. Of moderately good quality but less than excellent.
2. Being what is needed without being in excess.

1. ACCEPTABLE.
2. SUFFICIENT *adjective.*

adhere   *verb*
To hold fast to.   BOND *verb.*

adherence   *noun*
The close physical union of two objects.   BOND *noun.*

adherent   *noun*
One who supports and adheres to another.   FOLLOWER.

adhesion   *noun*
The close physical union of two objects.   BOND *noun.*

adhesive   *adjective*
Having the property of adhering.   STICKY.

adieu   *noun*
A separation of two or more people.   PARTING *noun.*

ad interim   *adjective*
Latin. Temporarily assuming the duties of another.   TEMPORARY.

adjacent   *adjective*
Sharing a common boundary.   ADJOINING.

adjoin *verb*

To be contiguous or next to: *a lot that adjoins ours.*

Syns: abut (on, upon, *or* against), border (on *or* upon), bound[2], butt[2] (on), join (*Informal*), juxtapose, meet[1], neighbor, touch, verge (on *or* upon).

adjoining *adjective*

Sharing a common boundary: *took adjoining rooms in the hotel.*

Syns: abutting, adjacent, approximal, bordering, conterminous, contiguous, joined (*Informal*), juxtaposed, meeting, neighboring, next, touching.

Near-syns: attached, close, closest, connected, hitched, linked, near, nearby, nearest.

Ant: detached.

adjourn *verb*

To put off until a later time.

DEFER[1].

adjournment *noun*

The act of putting off or the condition of being put off.

DELAY *noun.*

adjudge *verb*

To make a decision about (a controversy, dispute, etc.) after deliberation, as in a court of law.

JUDGE *verb.*

adjudicate *verb*

To make a decision about (a controversy, dispute, etc.) after deliberation, as in a court of law.

JUDGE *verb.*

adjunct *noun*

Something that attaches as a supplementary part.

ATTACHMENT.

adjust *verb*

1. To alter (parts of a device) for proper functioning: *adjust the valves.*
2. To make or become suitable to a particular situation or use.

1. **Syns:** attune, fix, regulate, set[1], tune (up).
2. ADAPT.

adjustable *adjective*

Capable of adapting or being adapted.

ADAPTABLE.

adjustment *noun*

The condition of being made suitable to an end.

ADAPTATION.

adjutant *noun*

A person who holds a position auxiliary to another and assumes some of his responsibilities.

ASSISTANT.

adjuvant *adjective*

Giving or able to give help or support.

AUXILIARY *adjective.*

ad-lib *adjective*

Informal. Spoken, performed, or composed with little or no preparation or forethought.

EXTEMPORANEOUS.

ad-lib *verb*

Informal. To compose or recite without preparation.

IMPROVISE.

ad-lib *noun*

Informal. Something improvised.

IMPROVISATION.

admeasure *verb*

To set aside or distribute as a share.

ALLOT.

administer *verb*

1. To have charge of (the affairs of others): *administer a colony.*
2. To oversee the provision or execution of: *administer justice.*
3. To provide as a remedy: *administer a sedative.*
4. To mete out by means of some action.

1. **Syns:** administrate, direct, govern, head, manage, run, superintend.
2. **Syns:** administrate, carry out, execute.
3. **Syns:** dispense, give (out).
4. GIVE *verb.*

administerial *adjective*

Of, for, or relating to administration or administrators.

ADMINISTRATIVE.

administrable *adjective*

Capable of being governed.

GOVERNABLE.

administrant *noun*
A person having administrative or managerial authority in an organization.

EXECUTIVE *noun*.

administrate *verb*
1. To have charge of (the affairs of others).
2. To oversee the provision or execution of.

1. ADMINISTER.
2. ADMINISTER.

administration *noun*
1. Authoritative control over the affairs of others: *was responsible for the administration of the province.*
2. The giving of a medication, esp. by prescribed dosage: *the administration of an antibiotic.*

1. *Syns:* direction, government, management, superintendence.
2. *Syns:* application, dispensation, dispensing.

administrational *adjective*
Of, for, or relating to administration or administrators.

ADMINISTRATIVE.

administrative *adjective*
Of, for, or relating to administration or administrators: *an administrative secretary.*

Syns: administerial, administrational, executive, managerial, ministerial.

administrator *noun*
A person having administrative or managerial authority in an organization.

EXECUTIVE *noun*.

admirable *adjective*
Deserving admiration: *She has some really admirable qualities.*

Syns: commendable, estimable, laudable, meritorious, meritorious, praiseworthy, worthy.
Near-syns: invaluable, precious, priceless; desirable, pleasant, satisfying; deserving.
Ants: despicable; worthless.

admiration *noun*
1. A feeling of deference, approval, and liking.
2. *Archaic.* The emotion aroused by something awe-inspiring or astounding.

1. ESTEEM *noun*.
2. WONDER *noun*.

admire *verb*
1. To regard with great pleasure or approval: *admired the view.*
2. To have a high opinion of: *admired him for his honesty.*

1. *Syns:* appreciate, enjoy, relish.

2. *Syns:* consider, esteem, honor, regard, respect, value. —*Idiom* look up to.

admirer *noun*
1. One who ardently admires: *an admirer of Shakespeare's plays.*
2. A man who courts a woman.

1. *Syns:* devotee, fan² (*Informal*), fancier, lover.
2. BEAU.

admissible *adjective*
1. Capable of being accepted.
2. Capable of being allowed.

1. ACCEPTABLE.
2. PERMISSIBLE.

admission *noun*
1. The state of being allowed entry: *her admission to college.*

2. The right to enter or make use of: *It was months before he was allowed admission into the club.*
3. The act of admitting to something.

1. *Syns:* admittance, entrance¹, immission (*Archaic*), ingress (*also* ingression), introduction, intromission.
2. *Syns:* access, admittance, entrance¹, entrée, entry, ingress (*also* ingression).
3. ACKNOWLEDGMENT.

admit *verb*
1. To serve as a means of entrance for: *This ticket admits one adult.*
2. To allow admittance, as to a group.
3. To afford an opportunity for.
4. To recognize, often reluctantly, the reality or truth of.
5. To express recognition of.

1. *Syns:* immit (*Archaic*), intromit, let in.

2. ACCEPT.
3. PERMIT *verb*.
4. ACKNOWLEDGE.

5. ACKNOWLEDGE.

admittance *noun*
1. The state of being allowed entry.
2. The right to enter or make use of.

1. ADMISSION.
2. ADMISSION.

admix *verb*
To put together into one mass so that the constituent parts are more or less homogeneous.

MIX *verb*.

admixture *noun*
Something produced by mixing.

MIXTURE.

admonish *verb*
To criticize for a fault or offense.

CALL DOWN at **call**.

admonishing *adjective*
Giving warning.

CAUTIONARY.

admonishment *noun*
1. Advice to beware, as of a person or thing.
2. Words expressive of strong disapproval.

1. WARNING *noun*.
2. REBUKE *noun*.

admonition *noun*
1. Advice to beware, as of a person or thing.
2. Words expressive of strong disapproval.

1. WARNING *noun*.
2. REBUKE *noun*.

admonitory *adjective*
Giving warning.

CAUTIONARY.

ado *noun*
Busy and useless activity.

FUSS *noun*.

adopt *verb*
1. To take, as another's idea, and make one's own: *adopted a competitor's sales techniques.*
2. To accept officially.

1. *Syns:* embrace, espouse, take on (*or* up).
2. PASS *verb*.

adopted *adjective*
Being fictitious and not real.

ASSUMED.

adoption *noun*
A ready taking up of something: *their adoption of sophisticated clothing.*

Syns: embracement, embracing, espousal.

adorable *adjective*
Easy to love: *an adorable baby.*

Syns: lovable, sweet.

adorant *adjective*
Feeling or showing reverence.

REVERENT.

adoration *noun*
1. The act of adoring, esp. reverently: *prayed with solemn adoration.*
2. Deep and ardent affection: *his adoration of his young wife.*

1. *Syns:* idolization, reverence, veneration, worship.
2. *Syns:* devotion, fancy (*Obs.*), love.

adore *verb*
1. To regard with great awe and devotion: *a saint adored for his kindness.*
2. To feel deep, devoted love for: *adored her husband.*

3. *Informal.* To like or enjoy enthusiastically, often excessively: *She adores skiing.*

1. *Syns:* idolize, revere, reverence, venerate, worship.
2. *Syns:* affect^2 (*Archaic*), affection^1, love, worship.
3. *Syns:* delight in, dote on (*or* upon), eat up (*Slang*), groove on (*Slang*), love.

adoring *adjective*
Feeling or showing reverence.

REVERENT.

adorn *verb*
1. To furnish with decorations: *a gown adorned with lace.*

2. To endow with beauty and elegance by way of a notable addition.

1. *Syns:* bedeck, deck (out), decorate, dress (up), embellish, garnish, ornament, trim.
2. GRACE *verb*.

adornment *noun*
Something that adorns: *jewels and other adornments.*

Syns: decoration, embellishment, garnishment, garniture, ornament, ornamentation, trim, trimming.

adroit *adjective*
1. Exhibiting or possessing skill and ease in performance.
2. Showing art or skill in performing or doing.
3. Well done or executed.

1. DEXTEROUS.

2. ARTFUL.
3. NEAT.

adroitness *noun*
Skillfulness in the use of the hands or body.   DEXTERITY.

adscititious also **adcititious** *adjective*
Not part of the real or essential nature of a thing.   ACCIDENTAL *adjective*.

adulate *verb*
To compliment excessively and ingratiatingly.   FLATTER.

adulation *noun*
Excessive, ingratiating praise.   FLATTERY.

adulator *noun*
One who flatters another excessively.   SYCOPHANT.

adult *adjective*
Having reached full growth and development.   MATURE *adjective*.

adulterant *noun*
One that contaminates.   CONTAMINANT.

adulterate *verb*
To make impure or inferior by deceptively adding   ***Syns:*** debase, doctor (up), dope, load,
foreign substances: *adulterated coffee.*   sophisticate.

adulterated *adjective*
Mixed with other substances.   IMPURE.

adulteration *noun*
The state of being contaminated.   CONTAMINATION.

adulterator *noun*
One that contaminates.   CONTAMINANT.

adumbrate *verb*
1. To give an indication of something in advance: **1.** ***Syns:*** foreshadow, prefigure, presage.
   events that adumbrated later developments.
2. To tell about or make known (future events) in   **2.** PREDICT.
   advance, esp. by means of special knowledge or
   inference.
3. To draw up a preliminary plan or version of.   **3.** DRAFT *verb*.
4. To make dark or darker.   **4.** SHADE *verb*.
5. To make dim or indistinct.   **5.** OBSCURE *verb*.

adumbration *noun*
Comparative darkness that results from the blocking of   SHADE *noun*.
light rays.

advance *verb*
1. To cause to move forward or upward, as toward a   **1.** ***Syns:*** forward, foster, further, promote.
   goal: *advance a worthy cause.*
2. To go forward, esp. toward a conclusion.   **2.** COME.
3. To bring forward and quote for formal consideration. **3.** PRESENT^2.
4. To raise in rank.   **4.** PROMOTE.
5. To attain a higher status, rank, or condition.   **5.** RISE.
6. To supply (money), esp. on credit.   **6.** LEND.

advance *noun*
1. Forward movement: *recent advances in science; the*   **1.** ***Syns:*** advancement, furtherance,
   advance of technology.   headway, march^1, ongoing, progress,
                                                                   progression.
2. The amount by which something is increased.   **2.** INCREASE *noun*.

advance *adjective*
Going before: *got advance warning of the storm's*   ***Syns:*** antecedent, anterior, precedent,
approach.   preceding, prior.

advanced *adjective*
1. Ahead of current trends or customs: *advanced ideas.* **1.** ***Syns:*** forward, precocious, progressive.
2. Far along in life or time.   **2.** OLD.

advancement *noun*
1. A progression upward in rank: *a quick advancement*   **1.** ***Syns:*** elevation, jump, promotion,
   in her career.   upgrading.
2. Forward movement.   **2.** ADVANCE *noun*.

advances *noun*
Preliminary actions intended to elicit a favorable   ***Syns:*** approach(es), overture(s).
response: *rejected her advances out of hand.*

advantage *noun*
1. A factor conducive to superiority and success: *Give the slow starters a 30-second advantage.*
2. A dominating position, as in a conflict: *had the advantage in the argument.*

3. Something beneficial: *gave the children many advantages.*
4. Something that contributes to or increases one's well-being.
5. A state of health, happiness, and prospering.
6. The quality of being suitable or adaptable to an end.

advantage *verb*
To derive advantage.

advantageous *adjective*
1. Affording profit.
2. Affording benefit.

advent *noun*
1. The act or fact of coming near.
2. The act of arriving.

adventitious *adjective*
Not part of the real or essential nature of a thing.

adventure *noun*
An exciting, often hazardous undertaking: *a mountain-climbing adventure.*

adventure *verb*
1. To expose to possible loss or damage.
2. To run the risk of.

adventurer *noun*
1. One who engages in exciting, risky pursuits: *explorers and other adventurers.*
2. A free-lance fighter.
3. One who speculates for quick profits.

adventuresome *adjective*
Taking or willing to take risks.

adventurous *adjective*
1. Taking or willing to take risks: *Adventurous pioneers settled the American West.*

2. Involving possible risk, loss, or injury.

adventurousness *noun*
Willingness to take risks.

adversary *noun*
One that opposes another in a battle, contest, controversy, or debate.

adverse *adjective*
1. Acting against or in opposition.
2. Tending to discourage, retard, or make more difficult.

adversity *noun*
Bad fortune.

advert *verb*
To call or direct attention to (an occurrence, situation, etc.).

---

1. **Syns:** allowance, handicap, head start, odds, start, vantage.
2. **Syns:** better[1], bulge (*Slang*), draw, drop, edge, forehand, jump, superiority, vantage. —*Idioms* inside track, upper hand.
3. **Syns:** benefit, blessing, boon[1], favor, gain, profit.
4. INTEREST *noun.*

5. WELFARE.
6. USE *noun.*

BENEFIT.

1. PROFITABLE.
2. BENEFICIAL.

1. APPROACH *noun.*
2. ARRIVAL.

ACCIDENTAL *adjective.*

Syns: emprise (*also* emprize), enterprise, venture.

1. RISK *verb.*
2. HAZARD *verb.*

1. **Syns:** daredevil, venturer.

2. MERCENARY *noun.*
3. SPECULATOR.

ADVENTUROUS.

1. **Syns:** adventuresome, audacious, enterprising, venturesome, venturous. **Near-syns:** bold, brash, daredevil, daring, foolhardy, harebrained, impetuous, imprudent, madcap, rash, reckless. **Near-ants:** cautious, reserved. **Ant:** unadventurous.
2. DANGEROUS.

DARING *noun.*

OPPONENT.

1. OPPOSING.
2. UNFAVORABLE.

MISFORTUNE.

REFER.

advertent *adjective*
Concentrating the mental powers on something.

ATTENTIVE.

advertise also **advertize** *verb*
1. To make known vigorously the positive features of (a product): *advertise a new camera.*

1. *Syns:* ballyhoo (*Informal*), build up, cry (up), plug (*Informal*), promote, publicize, push (*Slang*), talk up.

2. To bring to public notice.
3. To make (information) generally known: *The girl advertised her engagement by wearing a diamond ring.*

2. ANNOUNCE.
3. *Syns:* blaze² (around), blazon, broadcast, bruit (about), disseminate, noise (about *or* abroad), promulgate. —*Idioms* spread far and wide, spread the word.

advertising *noun*
The act or profession of promoting something, as a product: *Advertising can be a lucrative occupation.*

Syns: promotion, publicity.

advertize *verb*

SEE **advertise.**

advice *noun*
An opinion as to a decision or course of action: *hopes to get sound advice before purchasing the house.*

Syns: advisement, counsel, recommendation.

advice(s) *noun*
New information, esp. about recent events and happenings.

NEWS.

advisable *adjective*
Worth doing, esp. for practical reasons: *Checking the data is advisable.*

Syns: counselable (*also* counsellable), expedient, recommendable, well².

advise *verb*
1. To give recommendations to (someone) about a decision or course of action: *My attorney advised me to sue.*

1. *Syns:* counsel, recommend.

2. To cause to know about or be aware of.
3. To meet and exchange views to reach a decision.

2. INFORM.
3. CONFER.

advised *adjective*
1. Resulting from deliberation and careful thought: *a badly advised decision.*

1. *Syns:* calculated, considered, deliberated, studied, studious (*Rare*), thought-out, weighed.

2. Provided with information; made aware.

2. INFORMED.

advisement *noun*
1. A careful considering of a matter: *The judge took the case under advisement.*

1. *Syns:* calculation, consideration, deliberation, lucubration (*Archaic*), study.

2. An opinion as to a decision or course of action.

2. ADVICE.

adviser also **advisor** *noun*
One who advises another, esp. officially or professionally: *a financial adviser.*

Syns: consultant, counsel, counselor (*also* counsellor), mentor.

advisor *noun*

SEE **adviser.**

advisory *adjective*
Giving advice: *the college advisory board.*

Syns: consultative, consultatory, consulting.

advocate *verb*
To aid the cause of by approving or favoring.

SUPPORT *verb.*

aegis *noun*
Aid or support given by a patron.

PATRONAGE.

aeon *noun*

SEE **eon.**

aerate *verb*
To expose to circulating air.

AIR *verb.*

aerial *adjective*
1. Of or relating to air.
2. So light and insubstantial as to resemble air or a thin film.
3. Imposingly high.

1. AIRY.
2. FILMY.

3. LOFTY.

aerosphere *noun*
The gaseous mixture enveloping the earth.

AIR *noun*.

aery *adjective*
So light and insubstantial as to resemble air or a thin film.

FILMY.

aesthetic or **esthetic** *adjective*
Showing good taste.

TASTEFUL.

afeard also **afeared** *adjective*
Regional. Filled with fear or terror.

AFRAID.

afeared *adjective*

SEE **afeard**.

affability *noun*
The quality of being pleasant and friendly.

AMIABILITY.

affable *adjective*
1. Characterized by kindness and warm, unaffected courtesy.
2. Pleasant and friendly.

1. GRACIOUS.

2. AMIABLE.

affair *noun*
1. Something that concerns or involves one personally.
2. A large or important social gathering.
3. An intimate sexual relationship between two people.
4. Something to be done, considered, or dealt with.

1. BUSINESS.
2. PARTY *noun*.
3. LOVE *noun*.
4. MATTER *noun*.

affect[1] *verb*
To evoke a usu. strong mental or emotional response from: *a play that deeply affects its audience*.

Syns: get (to) (*Informal*), impact, impress, influence, move, strike, sway, touch.

affect[2] *verb*
1. To take on or give a false appearance of.
2. *Archaic*. To feel deep, devoted love for.

1. ASSUME.
2. ADORE.

affectation *noun*
Artificial behavior adopted to impress others: *That accent is mere affectation*.

Syns: affectedness, airs, lug(s), mannerism, pretense.

affected[1] *adjective*
Emotionally aroused: *affected by a powerful novel*.

Syns: impressed, inspired, moved, stirred, struck, swayed, touched.

affected[2] *adjective*
1. Artificially genteel: *put on an affected British accent*.

2. Having concern.
3. Not genuine or sincere.

1. *Syns:* artificial, la-di-da (*also* la-de-da) (*Informal*), lardy-dardy (*Slang*), mannered, precious, pretentious.
2. CONCERNED.
3. ARTIFICIAL.

affectedness *noun*
Artificial behavior adopted to impress others.

AFFECTATION.

affecting *adjective*
Exciting a deep, usu. somber response: *an affecting climax to the story*.

Syns: impressive, moving, poignant, stirring, touching.

affection[1] *noun*
1. The condition of being closely tied to another by affection or faith.
2. A complex and usu. strong subjective response, as of love, hate, etc.

1. ATTACHMENT.

2. EMOTION.

affection *verb*
To feel deep, devoted love for.

ADORE.

affection[2] *noun*
1. A pathological condition of mind or body.
2. A distinctive element.

1. DISEASE.
2. QUALITY.

affectionate *adjective*
Feeling and expressing affection: *an affectionate parent*.

Syns: affectionated (*Obs*.), affectuous (*Obs*.), doting, fond, loving.

affectionated *adjective*
Obs. Feeling and expressing affection.

AFFECTIONATE.

affective *adjective*
Relating to, arising from, or appealing to the emotions.

EMOTIONAL.

affectivity *noun*
A complex and usu. strong subjective response, as love, hate, etc.   EMOTION.

affectuous *adjective*
Obs. Feeling and expressing affection.   AFFECTIONATE.

afferent *adjective*
Transmitting impulses from sense organs to nerve centers.   SENSORY.

affianced *adjective*
Pledged to marry.   ENGAGED.

affianced *noun*
A person to whom one is engaged to be married.   INTENDED *noun*.

affiliate *verb*
To unite or be united in a relationship.   ASSOCIATE *verb*.

affiliate *noun*
1. One who is united in a relationship with another.   1. ASSOCIATE *noun*.
2. A local unit of a business or an auxiliary controlled by such a business.   2. SUBSIDIARY.

affiliation *noun*
The state of being associated.   ASSOCIATION.

affinity *noun*
The quality or state of being alike.   LIKENESS.

affirm *verb*
1. To make valid and binding by a formal legal act.   1. CONFIRM.
2. To put into words positively and with conviction.   2. ASSERT.

affirmation *noun*
1. An act of confirming officially.   1. CONFIRMATION.
2. The act of asserting positively.   2. ASSERTION.

affirmative *adjective*
1. Giving assent.   1. FAVORABLE.
2. Of a constructive nature.   2. POSITIVE.

affirmatory *adjective*
Giving assent.   FAVORABLE.

affix *verb*
1. To join one thing to another.   1. ATTACH.
2. To ascribe (a misdeed, error, etc.) to.   2. FIX *verb*.

afflation *noun*
1. Divine guidance and motivation imparted directly.   1. INSPIRATION.
2. The act of breathing in.   2. INSPIRATION.

afflatus *noun*
Divine guidance and motivation imparted directly.   INSPIRATION.

afflict *verb*
To bring great harm or suffering to: *afflicted with painful chronic ailments.*

Syns: agonize, curse, excruciate, plague, rack, scourge, smite, strike, torment, torture.
Near-syns: annoy, bother, harass, harrow, irk, pester, vex, worry.
Ant: comfort.

afflicted *adjective*
Having a painful ailment.   MISERABLE.

affliction *noun*
1. Something hard to bear physically or emotionally.   1. BURDEN *noun*.
2. A state of physical or mental suffering.   2. DISTRESS *noun*.
3. A cause of suffering or harm.   3. CURSE *noun*.

afflictive *adjective*
1. Marked by, causing, or experiencing physical pain.   1. PAINFUL.
2. Difficult to accept.   2. BITTER *adjective*.

affluent *adjective*
Possessing a large amount of money, land, or other material possessions.   RICH.

afford *verb*
To make (something) readily available.   OFFER *verb*.

affray *noun*
A quarrel or fight marked by very noisy, disorderly,   BRAWL *noun*.
and often violent behavior.

affright *verb*
Archaic. To fill with fear.   FRIGHTEN.

affright *noun*
Archaic. Great agitation and anxiety caused by the   FEAR *noun*.
expectation or the realization of danger.

affront *verb*
To cause resentment or hurt by callous, rude behavior.   INSULT *verb*.

affront *noun*
An act that offends a person's sense of pride or dignity.   INDIGNITY.

afield *adverb*
Not in the right way or on the proper course.   WRONG *adverb*.

afire *adjective*
On fire.   BLAZING.

aflame *adjective*
On fire.   BLAZING.

à fond *adverb*
1. *French*. To the fullest extent.   1. COMPLETELY.
2. *French*. In a complete manner.   2. COMPLETELY.

aforehand *adverb*
Chiefly Regional. Before the expected time.   EARLY *adverb*.

aforetime *adverb*
Archaic. At a time in the past.   EARLIER.

afraid *adjective*
Filled with fear or terror: *was afraid of snakes*.   *Syns:* afeard (*also* afeared) (*Regional*),
                                                              aghast, apprehensive, ascared (*Chiefly
                                                              Regional*), fearful, fearsome, frightened,
                                                              petrified, scared.
                                                              Near-ants: brave, dauntless, fearless,
                                                              intrepid; assured, calm, collected,
                                                              confident, poised, self-assured, self-
                                                              possessed.
                                                              Ant: unafraid.

afresh *adverb*
Once more.   NEW *adverb*.

after *adjective*
1. Located in the rear.   1. BACK *adjective*.
2. Following something else in time.   2. LATER *adjective*.

after *adverb*
At a subsequent time.   LATER *adverb*.

afterlife *noun*
Endless life after death.   IMMORTALITY.

aftermath *noun*
Something brought about by a cause.   EFFECT *noun*.

afterward also **afterwards** *adverb*
At a subsequent time.   LATER *adverb*.

afterwards *adverb*   SEE **afterward.**

afterwhile *adverb*
At a subsequent time.   LATER *adverb*.

again *adverb*
Once more.   NEW *adverb*.

age *noun*
1. A particular time notable for its distinctive   1. *Syns:* day(s), epoch, era, period, time(s).
characteristics: *the Edwardian Age*.

2. *Informal.* A long time: *haven't seen you for ages.*

2. **Syns:** eon (*also* aeon), eternity, long[1].
—*Idioms* blue moon, dog's age, donkey's years, forever and a day, forever and ever, month of Sundays.

3. Old age: *the weakness and frailty of age.*

3. **Syns:** agedness, caducity, elderliness, senectitude, senescence, years.

age *verb*
1. To grow old: *He is aging fast.*
2. To bring or come to full development.

1. **Syns:** get along (*or* on), olden, senesce.
2. MATURE *verb.*

aged *adjective*
1. Brought to full flavor and richness by aging: *aged cheese.*
2. Far along in life or time.
3. Belonging to, existing, or occurring in times long past.

1. **Syns:** matured, mellow, ripe, ripened.

2. OLD.
3. OLD.

agedness *noun*
Old age.

AGE *noun.*

ageless *adjective*
Existing unchanged forever: *the ageless themes of love and hate.*

Syns: dateless, eternal, eterne (*Archaic*), timeless.
Near-syns: lasting, permanent, perpetual; immutable, inalterable, intemporal, unalterable, unchanging, unvarying.
Ant: transient.

agency *noun*
That by which something is accomplished or some end achieved.

MEANS.

agenda *noun*
An organized list of procedures, activities, events, etc.

PROGRAM.

agent *noun*
That by which something is accomplished or some end achieved.

MEANS.

age-old *adjective*
Belonging to, existing, or occurring in times long past.

OLD.

agglomerate *verb*
To bring together so as to increase in mass or number.

ACCUMULATE.

agglomeration *noun*
A quantity accumulated.

ACCUMULATION.

aggrandize *verb*
1. To make or become greater or larger.
2. To raise to a high position or status.

1. INCREASE *verb.*
2. EXALT.

aggrandizement *noun*
The act of raising to a high position or status or the condition of being so raised.

EXALTATION.

aggravate *verb*
1. To increase in intensity or severity.
2. *Informal.* To trouble the nerves or peace of mind of, esp. by repeated vexations.

1. INTENSIFY.
2. ANNOY.

aggravating *adjective*
Informal. Troubling the nerves or peace of mind, as by repeated vexations.

VEXATIOUS.

aggravation *noun*
1. *Informal.* Something that annoys.
2. *Informal.* The feeling of being annoyed.
3. *Informal.* Needless trouble.

1. ANNOYANCE.
2. ANNOYANCE.
3. BOTHER *noun.*

aggregate *verb*
1. To bring together so as to increase in mass or number.
2. To come to in number or quantity.

ACCUMULATE.

2. AMOUNT *verb.*

aggregate *noun*

1. A number or quantity obtained as a result of addition.
2. An amount or quantity from which nothing is left out or held back.

aggregation *noun*
A quantity accumulated.

aggress *verb*
To set upon with violent force.

aggression *noun*
1. *Psychoanal.* Hostile behavior: *could not control his aggression.*

2. The act of attacking.

aggressive *adjective*
1. Inclined to act in a hostile way: *an aggressive person, always ready to argue.*

2. Marked by boldness and assertiveness: *an aggressive executive.*

aggressiveness also **aggressivity** *noun*
Hostile behavior.

aggressivity *noun*

aggressor *noun*
One who starts a hostile action: *fought the foreign aggressors.*

aggrieve *verb*
1. To cause suffering or painful sorrow to.
2. To do a wrong to; treat unjustly.

aggroup *verb*
To come or bring into a group or groups.

aghast *adjective*
1. Filled with fear or terror.
2. Overcome with intense feeling, as of amazement, horror, or dismay.

agile *adjective*
Moving or performing quickly, lightly, and easily.

agileness *noun*

agility also **agileness** *noun*
The quality or state of being agile: *fielded all questions with agility.*

agitate *verb*
1. To cause to move to and fro violently: *land and sea agitated by tremors.*

2. To impair or destroy the composure of: *a mind agitated by grief.*

3. To alter the settled state or position of.

agitation *noun*
1. The condition of being physically agitated: *a ship tossed by the agitation of the sea.*
2. A state of discomposure: *almost incoherent from his agitation.*

1. TOTAL *noun.*

2. WHOLE *noun.*

ACCUMULATION.

ATTACK *verb.*

1. **Syns:** aggressiveness (*also* aggressivity), belligerence, belligerency, combativeness, contentiousness, hostility.
2. ATTACK *noun.*

1. **Syns:** belligerent, combative, contentious, militant, offensive, pushy (*Informal*).
2. **Syns:** assertive, assertory, go-getting, hard-hitting.
   Near-syns: militant, pushing, pushy, self-assertive; domineering, imperious, tough.
   Ants: laid-back (*Informal*); different.

AGGRESSION.
SEE **aggressiveness**.

Syns: assailant, assailer, attacker.

1. DISTRESS *verb.*
2. WRONG *verb.*

GROUP *verb.*

1. AFRAID.
2. SHOCKED.

NIMBLE.
SEE **agility**.

Syns: dexterity, dexterousness, nimbleness, quickness.

1. **Syns:** churn, convulse, rock^2, shake.
   Near-syns: bounce, jar, jog, joggle, jolt, jostle, jounce, rattle, roil, ruffle, stir.
2. **Syns:** bother, discombobulate (*Slang*), discompose, disquiet, disturb, flurry, fluster, perturb, rock^2, ruffle, shake (up), toss, unsettle, upset.
3. DISTURB.

1. **Syns:** commotion, convulsion, turbulence, upset.
2. **Syns:** disquiet, dither, flap (*Slang*), flurry, fluster, flutter, lather (*Slang*), perturbation, stew (*Informal*), tumult, turmoil, upset.

agitator *noun*
One who agitates, esp. politically: *The British considered Samuel Adams an agitator.*

Syns: fomenter, instigator.

agnate *adjective*
Connected by or as if by kinship or common origin.

RELATED.

agog *adjective*
Intensely desirous or interested.

EAGER.

agonize *verb*
1. To bring great harm or suffering to.
2. To twist and turn, as in pain, struggle, or embarrassment.

1. AFFLICT.
2. WRITHE.

agonizing *adjective*
Extraordinarily painful or distressing.

TORMENTING.

agony *noun*
A state of physical or mental suffering.

DISTRESS *noun.*

agree *verb*
1. To come to an understanding or to terms: *agreed on all major points.*
2. To be compatible or in correspondence: *The copy agrees with the original.*

1. *Syns:* accord, coincide, concord, concur, get together, harmonize.
2. *Syns:* accord, check out, comport, conform (to), consist, correspond, fit, gee (*Informal*), harmonize, jibe (*Informal*), match, quadrate, rhyme (*also* rime), square, tally.

3. To respond affirmatively; receive with agreement or compliance.

3. ASSENT *verb.*

agreeability *noun*
The quality of being pleasant and friendly.

AMIABILITY.

agreeable *adjective*
1. To one's liking: *an agreeable change in your attitude.*

1. *Syns:* favorable, good, gratifying, nice, pleasant, pleasing, pleasurable, welcome.

2. Pleasant and friendly.
3. In keeping with one's needs or expectations: *a theory that was agreeable to current ideas.*

2. AMIABLE.
3. *Syns:* accordant (with), compatible, conformable (to), congenial, congruous, consistent, consonant (with *or* to), correspondent, corresponding.

4. Disposed to accept or agree.

4. WILLING.

agreeableness *noun*
The quality of being pleasant and friendly.

AMIABILITY.

agreed *adverb*
It is so; as you say or ask.

YES *adverb.*

agreement *noun*
1. The act or state of agreeing or conforming: *agreement between forecasts and sales.*

1. *Syns:* accordance, conformance, conformation, conformity, correspondence, tallying.

2. The act or process of accepting.
3. Harmonious mutual understanding: *We are in agreement on the issue.*

2. ACCEPTANCE.
3. *Syns:* accord, chime, concord, concordance, concurrence, consonance, harmony, rapport, tune.

4. An act or state of agreeing between parties regarding a course of action: *an agreement with the union on overtime.*
5. A legally binding arrangement between parties: *an author-publisher agreement.*

4. *Syns:* accord, arrangement, bargain, deal (*Informal*), pact, understanding.
5. *Syns:* bond, compact², contract, convention, covenant, pact.
Near-syns: bargain, deal, transaction; peace, treaty.

6. A formal, usu. written settlement between nations.

6. TREATY.

agrestal also **agrestial** *adjective*
In a primitive state; not domesticated or cultivated.

WILD *adjective.*

agrestial *adjective*

SEE **agrestal.**

agrestic also **agrestical** *adjective*
Of or pertaining to the countryside. COUNTRY *adjective.*

ahead *adverb*
Before the expected time. EARLY *adverb.*

aid *verb*
To give support or assistance. HELP *verb.*

aid *noun*
1. The act or an instance of helping. 1. HELP *noun.*
2. A person who helps. 2. HELPER.

aidant *adjective*
Affording support or assistance. HELPFUL.

aide *noun*
A person who holds a position auxiliary to another and assumes some of his responsibilities. ASSISTANT.

aidful *adjective*
Archaic. Affording benefit. BENEFICIAL.

aiding *adjective*
1. Giving or able to give help or support. 1. AUXILIARY *adjective.*
2. Affording support or assistance. 2. HELPFUL.

aidless *adjective*
Devoid of help or protection. HELPLESS.

ail *verb*
To cause anxious uneasiness in. WORRY *verb.*

ailing *adjective*
Affected or tending to be affected with minor health problems. SICKLY.

ailment *noun*
1. A pathological condition of mind or body. 1. DISEASE.
2. A minor illness, esp. one of a temporary nature. 2. INDISPOSITION.

aim *verb*
1. To move (a weapon, blow, etc.) in the direction of someone or something: *aimed the gun at the bird.* 1. *Syns:* cast, direct, head, lay[1] (*Mil.*), level, point, present[2], set[1], train, turn, zero in.
2. To have in mind as a goal or purpose. 2. INTEND.
3. To strive toward a goal: *aimed at a better education.* 3. *Syns:* aspire, seek. —*Idiom* set one's sights on.

aim *noun*
1. What one intends to do or achieve. 1. INTENTION.
2. Something strongly desired. 2. AMBITION.
3. The thread or current of thought uniting or occurring in all the elements of a text or discourse. 3. THRUST *noun.*

aimless *adjective*
Without aim, purpose, or intent: *an aimless conversation.* *Syns:* desultory, objectless, purposeless. *Near-ants:* deliberate, methodical, systematic; arranged, ordered, organized, planned. *Ant:* purposeful.

air *noun*
1. The gaseous mixture enveloping the earth: *air polluted with smoke.* 1. *Syns:* aerosphere, atmosphere.
2. A natural movement or current of air. 2. WIND[1] *noun.*
3. The celestial regions as seen from the earth: *Clouds filled the air.* 3. *Syns:* firmament, heaven(s), sky, welkin (*Archaic*).
4. A general impression produced by a predominant quality or characteristic: *exhibited an air of unease.* 4. *Syns:* ambiance (*also* ambience), atmosphere, aura, feel, feeling, mood, smell, tone.
5. Behavior through which one reveals one's personality. 5. BEARING.
6. A pleasing succession of musical tones forming a usu. brief aesthetic unit. 6. MELODY.

air *verb*

1. To expose to circulating air: *air a room.*
2. To utter publicly: *air my opinions.*

airless *adjective*
1. Oppressive due to a lack of fresh air: *a hot, airless closet.*
2. Marked by an absence of circulating air: *couldn't run on airless days.*

airs *noun*
Artificial behavior adopted to impress others.

airy *adjective*
1. Of or relating to air: *airy white clouds.*
2. Imposingly high.
3. Exposed to or characterized by the presence of freely circulating air or wind: *an airy hillside.*
4. So light and insubstantial as to resemble air or a thin film.
5. Displaying light-hearted nonchalance: *had an airy disregard for all rules.*

akin *adjective*
Connected by or as if by kinship or common origin.

alabaster also **alabastrine** *adjective*
Of a moderately white color.

alabastrine *adjective*

à la mode *adjective*
Being or in accordance with the current fashion.

alarm *noun*
1. A signal that warns of imminent danger: *The troops responded to the alarm.*
2. Great agitation and anxiety caused by the expectation or the realization of danger.

alarm *verb*
1. To fill with fear.
2. To notify (someone) of imminent danger or risk.

alarming *adjective*
Causing or able to cause fear.

alarmist *noun*
One who needlessly alarms others: *alarmists predicting global war.*

alarum *noun*
Archaic. A signal that warns of imminent danger.

albescent *adjective*
Of a moderately white color.

alcoholic *adjective*
Containing alcohol.

alert *adjective*
1. Vigilantly attentive: *alert to danger.*

2. Mentally quick and original.

alert *noun*
A signal that warns of imminent danger.

alert *verb*
To notify (someone) of imminent danger or risk.

alertness *noun*
The condition of being aware.

alibi *noun*
Informal. An explanation offered to justify an action.

---

1. **Syns:** aerate, ventilate, wind[1].
2. **Syns:** blow off (*Slang*), come out with, express, put, state, vent, ventilate.

1. **Syns:** breathless, close[1], stifling, stuffy.

2. **Syns:** breathless, breezeless, still, windless.

AFFECTATION.

1. **Syns:** aerial, atmospheric, pneumatic.
2. LOFTY.
3. **Syns:** blowy, breezy, gusty, windy.

4. FILMY.

5. **Syns:** breezy, buoyant, corky (*Informal*), debonair (*also* debonaire), jaunty. —*Idiom* free and easy.

RELATED.

FAIR *adjective.*
SEE **alabaster.**

FASHIONABLE.

1. **Syns:** alarum (*Archaic*), alert, tocsin, warning.
2. FEAR *noun.*

1. FRIGHTEN.
2. WARN.

FEARFUL.

Syns: scaremonger, terrorist. —*Idiom* sheep in wolf's clothing.

ALARM *noun.*

FAIR *adjective.*

HARD *adjective.*

1. **Syns:** observant, open-eyed, vigilant, wakeful, wary, watchful, wide-awake. **Near-syns:** attentive, aware, cautious, heedful, mindful; careful, unsleeping.
2. CLEVER.

ALARM *noun.*

WARN.

AWARENESS.

EXCUSE *noun.*

alien *adjective*
1. Of, from, or characteristic of another place or part of the world.   1. FOREIGN.
2. Not part of the essential nature of a thing.   2. FOREIGN.

alien *noun*
A person coming from another country.   FOREIGNER.

alien *verb*
To change the ownership of (property) by means of a legal document.   TRANSFER.

alienate *verb*
1. To make distant, hostile, or unsympathetic.   1. ESTRANGE.
2. *Law.* To change the ownership of (property) by means of a legal document.   2. TRANSFER.

alienation *noun*
1. The act of estranging or the condition of being estranged.   1. ESTRANGEMENT.
2. Serious mental illness or disorder impairing a person's capacity to function normally and safely.   2. INSANITY.

alight[1] *verb*
To come to rest on the ground.   LAND *verb*.

alight on (or **upon**)   *verb*
Archaic. To find or meet by chance.   COME ACROSS at **come**.

alight[2] *adjective*
On fire.   BLAZING.

alight on (or **upon**)   *verb*   SEE **alight**[1].

align *verb*
1. To be formally associated, as by treaty.   1. ALLY *verb*.
2. To place in or form a line or lines.   2. LINE *verb*.

aligned *adjective*
Closely connected by or as if by a treaty.   ALLIED.

alike *adjective*
Possessing the same or almost the same characteristics.   LIKE[2].

alikeness *noun*
The quality or state of being alike.   LIKENESS.

aliment *noun*
That which sustains the mind or spirit.   FOOD.

alimentary *adjective*
Of or relating to food or nutrition.   NUTRITIVE.

alimentation *noun*
The means needed to support life.   LIVING *noun*.

alimony *noun*
The means needed to support life.   LIVING *noun*.

alive *adjective*
1. Marked by or exhibiting life: *The patient is still alive.*   1. *Syns:* animate, animated, live[2], living, vital.
2. In action or full operation.   2. ACTIVE.
3. Having existence or life: *the best chess player alive.*   3. *Syns:* around (*Informal*), existent, existing, extant, living.
4. Full of animation and activity: *a street alive with pedestrians.*   4. *Syns:* abounding, overflowing, replete, rife, teeming.
5. Marked by comprehension, cognizance, and perception.   5. AWARE.

all *adjective*
Including every constituent or individual.   WHOLE *adjective*.

all *noun*
An amount or quantity from which nothing is left out or held back.   WHOLE *noun*.

all *adverb*
Without exception; in its entirety.   PURELY.

all-around *adjective*   SEE **all-round**.

allay *verb*
1. To make or become calm.
2. To make less severe or more bearable.

1. CALM *verb*.
2. RELIEVE.

allayment *noun*
Freedom, esp. from pain.

RELIEF.

allegation *noun*
A statement of something as fact.

CLAIM *noun*.

allege *verb*
1. To state to be true.
2. *Archaic.* To bring forward and quote for formal consideration.

1. CLAIM *verb*.
2. PRESENT[2] *verb*.

allegiance *noun*
Faithfulness or devotion to a person, a cause, obligations, or duties.

FIDELITY.

allegiant *adjective*
Adhering firmly and devotedly, as to a person, a cause, or a duty.

FAITHFUL.

alleviate *verb*
To make less severe or more bearable.

RELIEVE.

alleviation *noun*
Freedom, esp. from pain.

RELIEF.

alliance *noun*
1. An association, esp. of nations for a common cause: *a Western alliance against the Warsaw Pact countries.*
2. The state of being associated.

1. **Syns:** Anschluss (*German*), coalition, confederacy, confederation, federation, league, union.
2. ASSOCIATION.

allied *adjective*
1. Closely connected by or as if by a treaty: *Libya and its allied countries.*
2. Connected by or as if by kinship or common origin.

1. **Syns:** aligned, confederated, federated, unified.
2. RELATED.

all in *adjective*
Informal. Extremely tired.

EXHAUSTED.

all-inclusive *adjective*
Covering a wide scope.

GENERAL.

allness *noun*
The state of being entirely whole.

COMPLETENESS.

allocate *verb*
1. To set aside or distribute as a share.
2. To set aside for a specified purpose.

1. ALLOT.
2. APPROPRIATE *verb*.

allocation *noun*
That which is allotted.

ALLOTMENT.

allocution *noun*
A usu. formal oral communication to an audience.

SPEECH.

allot *verb*
• To set aside or distribute as a share: *Each sailor was allotted four ounces of grog.*

Syns: admeasure, allocate, allow, apportion, assign, give, lot, mete (out), portion.

allotment *noun*
That which is allotted: *a gas allotment of 50 gallons a month.*

Syns: allocation, allowance, cut (*Informal*), divvy (*Slang*), lot, measure, part, portion, quantum, quota, ration, share.

all-out *adjective*
1. Covering all aspects with painstaking accuracy.
2. Completely such, without qualification or exception.

1. THOROUGH.
2. UTTER[2].

all-overs *noun*
Chiefly Regional. A state of nervous restlessness or agitation.

JITTERS.

allow *verb*
1. To recognize, often reluctantly, the reality or truth of.

1. ACKNOWLEDGE.

2. To set aside or distribute as a share.   2. ALLOT.
3. To afford an opportunity for.   3. PERMIT *verb*.
4. To give one's consent to.   4. PERMIT *verb*.
5. To neither forbid nor prevent.   5. PERMIT *verb*.

allowable *adjective*
Capable of being allowed.   PERMISSIBLE.

allowance *noun*
1. Approval for an action, esp. as granted by one in authority.   1. PERMISSION.
2. That which is allotted.   2. ALLOTMENT.
3. A factor conducive to superiority and success.   3. ADVANTAGE *noun*.
4. An accommodation made in the light of special or extenuating circumstances.   4. CONCESSION.

alloyed *adjective*
Mixed with other substances.   IMPURE.

all right *adverb*
It is so; as you say or ask.   YES *adverb*.

all-round also **all-around** *adjective*
1. Covering a wide scope.   1. GENERAL.
2. Having many aspects, uses, or abilities.   2. VERSATILE.

allude *verb*
To call or direct attention to (an occurrence, situation, etc.).   REFER.

allure *verb*
1. To direct or impel to oneself by some quality or action.   1. ATTRACT.
2. To beguile or draw into a wrong or foolish course of action.   2. TEMPT.

allure *noun*
The power or quality of attracting.   ATTRACTION.

allurement *noun*
1. The power or quality of attracting.   1. ATTRACTION.
2. Something that attracts, esp. with the promise of pleasure or reward.   2. LURE *noun*.

alluring *adjective*
1. Pleasing to the eye or mind.   1. ATTRACTIVE.
2. Tending to seduce.   2. SEDUCTIVE.

allusive *adjective*
Tending to bring something, as a memory, mood, or image, subtly or indirectly to mind.   SUGGESTIVE.

alluvion *noun*
An abundant, usu. overwhelming flow.   FLOOD *noun*.

ally *verb*
1. To be formally associated, as by treaty: *That nation has allied itself with the Arabs.*   1. *Syns:* align, confederate, federate, league.
2. To unite or be united in a relationship.   2. ASSOCIATE *verb*.

ally *noun*
1. One nation associated with another in a common cause: *England and America were allies against the Nazis.*   1. *Syns:* coalitionist, confederate, leaguer.
2. One who is united in a relationship with another.   2. ASSOCIATE *noun*.

almost *adverb*
Near to in quantity or amount.   APPROXIMATELY.

alms *noun*
Something given to a charity or cause.   DONATION.

almsman *noun*
One who begs habitually or for a living.   BEGGAR *noun*.

almswoman *noun*
One who begs habitually or for a living.   BEGGAR *noun*.

alone *adjective*
1. Lacking the company of others: *was alone after her husband's death.*

2. Set away from all others.
3. Without equal or rival.

alone *adverb*
1. Without the presence or aid of another: *I'll finish the job alone.*

2. To the exclusion of anyone or anything else.

aloneness *noun*
The quality or state of being alone: *Aloneness often engenders depression.*

aloof *adjective*
1. Lacking interest in one's surroundings or worldly affairs.
2. Not friendly, sociable, or warm in manner.

aloofness *noun*
Dissociation from one's surroundings or worldly affairs.

already *adverb*
1. At a time in the past.
2. At the very time.

also *adverb*
In addition.

alter *verb*
To make or become different.

alterable *adjective*
Capable of or liable to change.

alterant *noun*
An agent that stimulates or precipitates a reaction, development, or change.

alteration *noun*
1. The process or result of making or becoming different.
2. A usu. physical change of one thing into another.

altercation *noun*
A discussion, often heated, in which a difference of opinion is expressed.

alterity *noun*
The condition of being unlike or dissimilar.

alternate *verb*
To do, use, or occur in successive turns.

alternate *noun*
One that takes the place of another.

alternation *noun*
Occurrence in successive turns.

alternative *noun*
The power or right of choosing.

altitude *noun*
The distance of something from a given level.

altitudinous *adjective*
Having a rather great upward projection.

alto *adjective*
Mus. Being a sound produced by a relatively small frequency of vibrations.

altogether *adverb*
1. To the fullest extent.
2. Without exception.

---

1. **Syns:** companionless, lonely, lonesome, solitary, unaccompanied.
   Near-ants: attended, chaperoned, companioned, escorted.
   Ant: accompanied.
2. SOLITARY.
3. UNIQUE.

1. **Syns:** single-handedly, solely, solo.
   —*Idioms* all by oneself, all by one's lonesome.
2. SOLELY.

Syns: isolation, lonelihood, loneliness, loneness, solitude.

1. DETACHED.

2. COOL *adjective.*

DETACHMENT.

1. EARLIER.
2. EVEN[1] *adverb.*

ADDITIONALLY.

CHANGE *verb.*

CHANGEABLE.

CATALYST.

1. CHANGE *noun.*

2. CONVERSION.

ARGUMENT.

DIFFERENCE.

ROTATE.

SUBSTITUTE *noun.*

ROTATION.

CHOICE *noun.*

ELEVATION.

HIGH.

LOW *adjective.*

1. COMPLETELY.
2. PURELY.

altruism *noun*
Kindly, charitable interest in others. BENEVOLENCE.
altruistic *adjective*
Of or concerned with charity. BENEVOLENT.
amalgam *noun*
Something produced by mixing. MIXTURE.
amalgamate *verb*
To put together into one mass so that the constituent MIX *verb.*
parts are more or less homogeneous.
amalgamation *noun*
Something produced by mixing. MIXTURE.
amaranthine *adjective*
Enduring for all time. ENDLESS.
amaroidal *adjective*
Having a noticeably sharp, pungent taste or smell. BITTER *adjective.*
amass *verb*
To bring together so as to increase in mass or number. ACCUMULATE.
amassment *noun*
1. A quantity accumulated. 1. ACCUMULATION.
2. The result or product of building up. 2. BUILD-UP at **build up.**
amateur *noun*
One lacking professional skill and ease in a particular ***Syns:*** abecedarian (*also* abecedary),
pursuit: *a foreign policy jeopardized by the mistakes of* dabbler, dilettante, nonprofessional,
amateurs. smatterer, tyro, uninitiate.
 Near-syns: apprentice, beginner,
 greenhorn, neophyte, novice; putterer,
 tinkerer.
 Ants: expert, master, pro (*Informal*),
 professional.

amateurish *adjective*
Lacking the required professional skill: *an amateurish* ***Syns:*** dilettante, dilettantish, dilettantist,
attempt to negotiate. jackleg (*Informal*), unskilled, unskillful.
amative *adjective*
Of, concerning, or promoting sexual love or desire. EROTIC.
amatory *adjective*
Of, concerning, or promoting sexual love or desire. EROTIC.
amaze *verb*
To impress strongly by what is unexpected or unusual. SURPRISE *verb.*
amaze *noun*
Archaic. The emotion aroused by something awe- WONDER *noun.*
inspiring or astounding.
amazement *noun*
The emotion aroused by something awe-inspiring or WONDER *noun.*
astounding.
amazing *adjective*
So remarkable as to elicit disbelief. FABULOUS.
ambiance also **ambience** *noun*
1. The totality of surrounding conditions and 1. ENVIRONMENT.
   circumstances affecting growth or development.
2. A general impression produced by a predominant 2. AIR *noun.*
   quality or characteristic.
ambidextrous *adjective*
1. Having many aspects, uses, or abilities. 1. VERSATILE.
2. Not being what one purports to be. 2. INSINCERE.
ambience *noun* SEE **ambiance.**
ambiguity *noun*
1. An expression or term liable to more than one 1. ***Syns:*** amphibology, double entendre,
   interpretation: *a political speech filled with* equivocality, equivocation, equivoque
   ambiguities. (*also* equivoke), tergiversation.
2. The quality or state of being ambiguous. 2. VAGUENESS.
3. The use or an instance of equivocal language. 3. EQUIVOCATION.

ambiguous *adjective*
1. Liable to more than one interpretation: *an ambiguous remark by the governor.*

2. Not affording certainty: *an ambiguous position.*

1. **Syns:** amphibological, cloudy, equivocal, nebulous, obscure, sibylline, uncertain, unclear, unexplicit, unintelligible, vague.
   Near-ants: clear, intelligible, lucid, perspicuous; certain, categorical, express, specific, unequivocal.
   Ant: explicit.
2. **Syns:** borderline, chancy, clouded, doubtable, doubtful, dubious, dubitable, equivocal, iffy (*Informal*), indecisive, indeterminate, open, problematical (*also* problematic), questionable, uncertain, unclear, undecided, unsettled, unsure. —*Idioms* at issue, in doubt, in question, up in the air.

ambiguousness *noun*
The quality or state of being ambiguous.

VAGUENESS.

ambit *noun*
1. A line around a closed figure or area.
2. An area within which something or someone exists, acts, or has influence or power.

1. CIRCUMFERENCE.
2. RANGE *noun.*

ambition *noun*
1. A strong desire to achieve something: *had an ambition to be a lawyer.*
2. Something strongly desired: *achieved his one ambition.*
3. The wish, power, and ability to begin and follow through with a plan or task: *a woman of great energy and ambition.*

1. **Syns:** ambitiousness, aspiration.

2. **Syns:** aim, goal, mark, object[1], objective.
3. **Syns:** drive, enterprise, gumption (*Informal*), initiative, push (*Informal*).

ambitious *adjective*
Full of ambition: *an ambitious young artist.*

Syns: aspiring, emulous.

ambitiousness *noun*
A strong desire to achieve something.

AMBITION.

amble *verb*
To walk at a leisurely pace.

STROLL *verb.*

amble *noun*
An act of walking, esp. for pleasure.

WALK *noun.*

ambrosial *adjective*
Highly pleasing, esp. to the sense of taste.

DELICIOUS.

ambulate *verb*
To go on foot.

WALK *verb.*

ambuscade *verb*
1. To wait concealed in order to attack (someone).
2. To attack suddenly and without warning.

1. LAY FOR at **lay**[1].
2. AMBUSH.

ambush *verb*
1. To attack suddenly and without warning: *highwaymen who hid behind thickets and ambushed passing travelers.*
2. To wait concealed in order to attack (someone).

1. **Syns:** ambuscade, bushwhack, surprise, waylay.

2. LAY FOR at **lay**[1].

ameliorate *verb*
To advance to a more desirable state.

IMPROVE.

amelioration *noun*
1. Something that improves.
2. Steady improvement, as of an individual or a society.

1. IMPROVEMENT.
2. PROGRESS *noun.*

amenable *adjective*
1. Willing to carry out the wishes of others.
2. Ready and willing to receive favorably, as new ideas.

1. OBEDIENT.
2. RECEPTIVE.

amend *verb*
1. To make right what is wrong.
2. To prepare a new version of.
3. To advance to a more desirable state.

1. CORRECT *verb*.
2. REVISE.
3. IMPROVE.

amendment *noun*
1. The act or process of revising.
2. Something that improves.

1. REVISION.
2. IMPROVEMENT.

amends *noun*
Something to make up for loss or damage.

COMPENSATION.

amenities *noun*
Courteous acts that contribute to smoothness and ease in dealings and social relationships: *Even when he was angry, he observed the amenities.*

Syns: civilities, courtesies, pleasantries, proprieties.

amenity *noun*
1. Anything that increases physical comfort: *a sunny apartment with all the amenities.*
2. The quality of being pleasant and friendly.

1. *Syns:* comfort, convenience, facility.
2. AMIABILITY.

ament *noun*
A mentally deficient person.

FOOL *noun*.

amerce *verb*
To impose a fine on.

FINE² *verb*.

amercement *noun*
A sum of money levied as punishment for an offense.

FINE² *noun*.

amiability *noun*
The quality of being pleasant and friendly: *negotiations carried on in amiability; a woman of surprising amiability.*

Syns: affability, agreeability, agreeableness, amenity, amiableness, cordiality, friendliness, geniality, pleasantness.

amiable *adjective*
1. Pleasant and friendly: *met on the street and had an amiable conversation; found her to be an amiable enough companion.*

1. *Syns:* affable, agreeable, complaisant, cordial, easy, easygoing, genial, good-natured, good-tempered.
Near-syns: attentive, courteous, mannerly; good-humored, lenient, mild, obliging; kind, kindly; responsive, warm, warmhearted.
Ant: sullen.

2. Of or befitting a friend or friends.

2. FRIENDLY.

amiableness *noun*
The quality of being pleasant and friendly.

AMIABILITY.

amicable *adjective*
1. Of or befitting a friend or friends.
2. Exhibiting accord in feeling or action.

1. FRIENDLY.
2. HARMONIOUS.

amical *adjective*
Exhibiting accord in feeling or action.

HARMONIOUS.

amigo *noun*
Span. A person whom one knows well, likes, and trusts.

FRIEND.

amiss *adjective*
Not in accordance with what is usual or expected: *We knew something was amiss when he failed to keep the appointment.*

Syns: awry, wrong.

amiss *adverb*
Not in the right way or on the proper course.

WRONG *adverb*.

amnesiac *adjective*
Unable to remember.

FORGETFUL.

amnesty *noun*
The act or an instance of forgiving.

FORGIVENESS.

amok *adjective*

SEE **amuk.**

amorist *noun*
A man amorously attentive to women.

GALLANT *noun*.

amorous *adjective*
1. Feeling or devoted to sexual love or desire.
2. Of, concerning, or promoting sexual love or desire.

1. EROTIC.
2. EROTIC.

amorousness *noun*
The passionate affection and desire felt by lovers for each other.

LOVE *noun*.

amorphous *adjective*
Having no distinct shape.

SHAPELESS.

amount *noun*
1. A number or quantity obtained as a result of addition.
2. The general sense or significance, as of an action, statement, etc.
3. A measurable whole.

1. TOTAL *noun*.
2. IMPORT *noun*.
3. QUANTITY.

amount *verb*
1. To come to in number or quantity: *The total purchase amounts to ten dollars.*
2. To be equivalent or tantamount: *criticism that amounted to rejection.*

1. *Syns:* add up to, aggregate, number, reach, run, total.
2. *Syns:* constitute, correspond, equal.
   —*Idiom* have all the earmarks.

amour *noun*
1. The passionate affection and desire felt by lovers for each other.
2. An intimate sexual relationship between two people.

1. LOVE *noun*.
2. LOVE *noun*.

amour-propre *noun*
1. A regarding of oneself with undue favor.
2. A sense of one's own dignity or worth.

1. EGOTISM.
2. PRIDE *noun*.

amphibological *adjective*
Liable to more than one interpretation.

AMBIGUOUS.

amphibology *noun*
An expression or term liable to more than one interpretation.

AMBIGUITY.

ample *adjective*
1. Of full measure; not narrow or restricted.
2. Characterized by abundance.
3. Large in expanse.
4. Having plenty of room.

1. FULL.
2. GENEROUS.
3. BROAD.
4. ROOMY.

amplification *noun*
The act of increasing in dimensions, scope, or inclusiveness.

EXPANSION.

amplify *verb*
1. To make or become greater or larger.
2. To increase markedly in level or intensity, esp. of sound.
3. To express at greater length or in greater detail.

1. INCREASE *verb*.
2. ELEVATE.
3. ELABORATE *verb*.

amplitude *noun*
1. The quality or state of being large in amount, extent, or importance.
2. Great extent, amount, or dimension.
3. The amount of space occupied by something.

1. SIZE.
2. BULK.
3. SIZE.

amuck also **amok** *adjective*
Out of control.

RUNAWAY *adjective* at **run away**.

amulet *noun*
A small object worn or kept for its supposed magical power.

CHARM *noun*.

amuse *verb*
To occupy in an agreeable or pleasing way: *I amused myself with a game of solitaire.*

Syns: distract, divert, entertain, recreate.

amusement *noun*
1. The condition of being amused: *They perform music for their own amusement.*

1. *Syns:* distraction, diversion, entertainment, recreation.

2. Something, esp. a performance or show, designed to entertain: *A puppeteer provided amusement for the party.*

amusing *adjective*
  1. Entertaining or pleasing: *an amusing game of bridge.*
  2. Arousing laughter: *a very amusing joke.*

analogize *verb*
  To represent as similar.

analogon *noun*
  Something closely resembling or analogous to something else.

analogous *adjective*
  Possessing the same or almost the same characteristics.

analogue *noun*
  Something closely resembling or analogous to something else.

analogy *noun*
  The quality or state of being alike.

analysis *noun*
  1. The separation of a whole into its parts for study: *a harmonic analysis of a Bach fugue.*
  2. A close or systematic study: *made an analysis of the election to determine why the victor had won.*

analytic also **analytical** *adjective*
  Able to reason validly.

analyze *verb*
  1. To separate into parts for study: *analyzed the ore and found it contained iron.*
  2. To study closely or systematically: *analyzing Shakespeare's plays to find recurring motifs.*

Ananias *noun*
  One who tells lies.

anarchy *noun*
  A lack of civil order or peace.

anathema *noun*
  1. An object of extreme dislike.
  2. A denunciation invoking a wish or threat of evil or injury.

anathematize *verb*
  To invoke evil or injury upon.

anatomize *verb*
  To separate into parts for study.

ancestor *noun*
  1. A person from whom one is descended: *My ancestors were farmers.*
  2. A forerunner: *The harpsichord is the ancestor of the modern piano.*

ancestral *adjective*
  Of or from one's ancestors: *lived in the ancestral home.*

ancestry *noun*
  One's ancestors or their character: *a young man of Italian-German ancestry.*

anchor *verb*
  To make secure.

ancient *adjective*
  1. Of, existing, or occurring in a distant period.
  2. Long past.

---

2. *Syns:* distraction, diversion, entertainment, recreation.

1. *Syns:* distracting, diverting.

2. *Syns:* comic, comical, droll, funny, humorous, killing (*Slang*), laughable, risible, zany.

LIKEN.

PARALLEL *noun.*

LIKE².

PARALLEL *noun.*

LIKENESS.

1. *Syns:* breakdown, dissection, resolution.

2. *Syns:* examination, inspection, investigation, review, survey.

LOGICAL.

1. *Syns:* anatomize, break down, dissect, resolve.
2. *Syns:* examine, inspect, investigate.

LIAR.

DISORDER *noun.*

1. HATE *noun.*
2. CURSE *noun.*

CURSE *verb.*

ANALYZE.

1. *Syns:* antecedent, ascendant, father, forebear, forefather, progenitor.
2. *Syns:* antecedent, precursor, predecessor, prototype.

Syns: hereditary, inherited, patrimonial.

Syns: birth, blood, bloodline, descent, extraction, family, genealogy, line, lineage, origin, parentage, pedigree, seed.

FASTEN.

1. EARLY *adjective.*
2. HIGH.

3. Belonging to, existing, or occurring in times long past.

3. OLD.

ancient *noun*
An elderly person.

SENIOR *noun.*

ancillary *adjective*
Giving or able to give help or support.

AUXILIARY *adjective.*

anecdote *noun*
An entertaining and often oral account of a real or fictitious occurrence.

YARN.

anemic *adjective*
1. Being weak in quality or substance.
2. Of or associated with sickness.

1. PALE *adjective.*
2. SICKLY.

anesthetic *adjective*
Lacking passion and emotion.

INSENSITIVE.

anew *adverb*
Once more.

NEW *adverb.*

anfractuous *adjective*
1. Not taking a direct or straight line or course.
2. Repeatedly curving in alternate directions.

1. INDIRECT.
2. WINDING.

angel *noun*
1. A pure, uncorrupted person.
2. *Informal.* A person who supports or champions an activity, institution, etc.
3. One who assumes financial responsibility for another.

1. INNOCENT *noun.*
2. PATRON.

3. SPONSOR.

angelic also **angelical** *adjective*
Free from evil and corruption.

INNOCENT *adjective.*

anger *noun*
A strong feeling of displeasure or hostility: *Strong criticism often evokes anger.*

Syns: indignation, irateness, ire.

anger *verb*
1. To cause to feel or show anger: *His condescending attitude angered her.*

1. *Syns:* burn up (*Informal*), enrage, incense[1], infuriate, ire, madden, provoke, steam up (*Informal*). —*Idioms* make one hot under the collar, make one's blood boil, put one's back up, put one's dander up.

2. To be or become angry: *She angered at the slightest hint of criticism.*

2. *Syns:* blow up (*Informal*), boil (over) (*Slang*), bristle, burn (up), explode, flare up, fume, rage, seethe. —*Idioms* blow a fuse, blow one's stack (*or* top), breathe fire, fly off the handle, get hot under the collar, get one's dander up, hit the ceiling, lose one's temper, see red.

angle *verb*
1. To cause to move, esp. at an angle.
2. To direct (material) to the interests of a particular group.
3. To try to obtain, usu. by subtleness and cunning.

1. BEND *verb.*
2. BIAS *verb.*

3. HINT *verb.*

angle *noun*
1. A way of considering a matter.
2. The position from which something is observed or considered.
3. *Slang.* A clever, unexpected new trick or method.

1. LIGHT[1] *noun.*
2. POINT OF VIEW.

3. WRINKLE[2].

angry *adjective*
Feeling or showing anger: *an angry customer; an angry expression on his face.*

Syns: choleric, enraged, furious, incensed, indignant, irate, ireful, mad, maddened, seething, sore (*Informal*), wrathful. —*Idioms* fit to be tied, foaming at the

mouth, hot under the collar, in a rage (*or* temper).
Near-ants: calm, placid, tolerant, tranquil; content, pleased, relaxed, satisfied.

angst *noun*
Anxious concern. — ANXIETY.

anguish *noun*
A state of physical or mental suffering. — DISTRESS *noun*.

anguish *verb*
To cause suffering or painful sorrow to. — DISTRESS *verb*.

angular *adjective*
Having little flesh or fat on the body. — THIN *adjective*.

anhydrous *adjective*
Having little or no liquid or moisture. — DRY *adjective*.

anima *noun*
The vital principle or animating force within living beings. — SPIRIT.

animal *adjective*
Relating to the desires and appetites of the body. — PHYSICAL.

animalism *noun*
A preoccupation with the body and satisfaction of its desires. — PHYSICALITY.

animality *noun*
A preoccupation with the body and satisfaction of its desires. — PHYSICALITY.

animalize *verb*
To ruin utterly in character or quality. — CORRUPT *verb*.

animate *verb*
1. To make alive. — 1. QUICKEN.
2. To make lively or animated. — 2. LIGHT[1] *verb*.
3. To arouse the emotions of; make ardent. — 3. FIRE *verb*.
4. To raise the spirits of. — 4. ELATE.
5. To impart courage, inspiration, and resolution to. — 5. ENCOURAGE.

animate *adjective*
1. Marked by or exhibiting life. — 1. ALIVE.
2. Very brisk, alert, and high-spirited. — 2. LIVELY.

animated *adjective*
1. Marked by or exhibiting life. — 1. ALIVE.
2. Very brisk, alert, and high-spirited. — 2. LIVELY.

animating *adjective*
Serving to enliven. — STIMULATING.

animation *noun*
1. A lively, emphatic, eager quality or manner. — 1. SPIRIT.
2. Capacity or power for work or vigorous activity. — 2. ENERGY.
3. High spirits. — 3. ELATION.

animosity *noun*
Deep-seated hatred, as between longtime opponents or rivals. — ENMITY.

animus *noun*
1. The vital principle or animating force within living beings. — 1. SPIRIT.
2. Deep-seated hatred, as between longtime opponents or rivals. — 2. ENMITY.

annals *noun*
A chronological record of past events. — HISTORY.

annex *verb*
To join so as to form a larger or more comprehensive entity. — ADD.

annihilate *verb*
1. To destroy all traces of: *a cholera epidemic that annihilated most of the population; an administration committed to annihilating poverty.*

2. To put an end to formally and with authority.
3. *Informal.* To render totally ineffective by decisive defeat.
4. To kill savagely and indiscriminately: *The night raiders annihilated the settlers.*
5. To remove or destroy completely.

annihilation *noun*
1. Utter destruction: *the Nazis' attempted annihilation of the Jewish people.*

2. An often formal act of putting an end to.

annotation *noun*
Critical explanation or analysis.

announce *verb*
1. To bring to public notice: *The management announced that Horowitz would play a concert.*

2. To make known the presence or arrival of.

announcement *noun*
1. The act of announcing: *The press listened attentively during the President's announcement.*

2. A public statement: *an announcement of a cease-fire.*

annoy *verb*
1. To trouble the nerves or peace of mind of, esp. by repeated vexations: *The constant requests for a donation finally began to annoy her.*

2. To disturb by repeated attacks: *small children annoying the cat by pulling its tail.*

annoyance *noun*
1. Something that annoys: *Headaches are a relatively minor annoyance.*

2. The act of annoying: *used tactics of annoyance to force the tenants to move.*
3. The feeling of being annoyed: *He won, much to his rival's annoyance.*

annoying *adjective*
Troubling the nerves or peace of mind, as by repeated vexations.

annul *verb*
1. To put an end to formally and with authority.
2. To remove or invalidate by or as if by running a line through or wiping clean.

1. **Syns:** abolish, blot out, clear, eradicate, erase, exterminate, extinguish, extirpate, liquidate, obliterate, remove, root out, rub out, snuff out, stamp out, uproot, wipe out. —*Idioms* do away with, put an end to.
2. ABOLISH.
3. OVERWHELM.

4. **Syns:** butcher, decimate, massacre, slaughter.
5. ABOLISH.

1. **Syns:** eradication, extermination, extinction, extinguishment, extirpation, liquidation, obliteration.
2. ABOLITION.

COMMENTARY.

1. **Syns:** advertise (*also* advertize), annunciate, broadcast, declare, proclaim, promulgate, publish.
2. USHER IN at **usher.**

1. **Syns:** annunciation, broadcast, declaration, proclamation, promulgation, pronouncement, publication.
2. **Syns:** declaration, edict, manifesto, notice, proclamation, pronouncement.

1. **Syns:** aggravate (*Informal*), bother, bug (*Slang*), chafe, disturb, exasperate, fret, gall[2], get, irk, irritate, nettle, peeve, provoke, ruffle, thorn, vex. —*Idioms* get in one's hair, get on one's nerves, get under one's skin. **Near-ants:** comfort, console, solace; gratify, please, relax, satisfy. **Ant:** soothe.
2. **Syns:** bedevil, beleaguer, beset, harass, harry, pester, plague, tease, worry.

1. **Syns:** aggravation (*Informal*), besetment, bother, botheration, botherment, irritant, irritation, nuisance, peeve, plague.
2. **Syns:** bothering, harassment, pestering, provocation, vexation.
3. **Syns:** aggravation (*Informal*), bother, botheration, exasperation, irritation, vexation.

VEXATIOUS.

1. ABOLISH.
2. CANCEL.

annular *adjective*
Having the shape of a curve everywhere equidistant   ROUND.
from a fixed point.

annulment *noun*
An often formal act of putting an end to.   ABOLITION.

annunciate *verb*
To bring to public notice.   ANNOUNCE.

annunciation *noun*
The act of announcing.   ANNOUNCEMENT.

anomalism *noun*
The condition of being abnormal.   ABNORMALITY.

anomalous *adjective*
Departing from the normal.   ABNORMAL.

anomaly *noun*
The condition of being abnormal.   ABNORMALITY.

anonymity *noun*
The quality or state of being obscure.   OBSCURITY.

anonymous *adjective*
Having an unknown name or author: *a panel of*   **Syns:** nameless, unnamed, unsigned.
medical experts and anonymous young addicts; received
an anonymous letter.

anschauung *noun*
German. The power to discern the true nature of a   INSTINCT.
person or situation.

Anschluss *noun*
German. An association, esp. of nations for a common   ALLIANCE.
cause.

answer *noun*
1. Something spoken or written as a return to a   1. **Syns:** comeback (*Slang*), rejoinder,
    question, demand, etc.: *gave him a nasty answer.*   reply, response, retort.
2. Something worked out to explain, resolve, or provide   2. **Syns:** result, solution.
    a method for dealing with and settling a problem:
    found the answer to the crossword puzzle.

answer *verb*
1. To speak or act in response to: *answering a question;*   1. **Syns:** rejoin, reply, respond, retort,
    answered his letter. Answer when you're spoken to!   return.
2. To supply fully or completely.   2. SATISFY.
3. To meet a need or requirement.   3. SERVE.

answerable *adjective*
Legally obligated.   LIABLE.

Antaean *adjective*
Of extraordinary size and power.   GIANT *adjective.*

antagonism *noun*
1. A state of mind brought on by something that is   1. ANTIPATHY.
    antipathetic.
2. Deep-seated hatred, as between longtime opponents   2. ENMITY.
    or rivals.
3. The condition of being in conflict.   3. OPPOSITION.

antagonist *noun*
One that opposes another in a battle, contest,   OPPONENT.
controversy, or debate.

antagonistic *adjective*
Acting against or in opposition.   OPPOSING.

ante *noun*
Slang. Something valuable risked on an uncertain   BET *noun.*
outcome.

antecede *verb*
To come, exist, or occur prior to in time.   PRECEDE.

antecedence *noun*
The act, condition, or right of preceding.   PRECEDENCE.

antecedent *noun*
1. That which produces an effect.
2. A person from whom one is descended.
3. A forerunner.
4. A closely similar case in existence or in the past.

antecedent *adjective*
1. Going before.
2. Just gone by or elapsed.

antedate *verb*
To come, exist, or occur prior to in time.

antediluvial *adjective*

antediluvian also **antediluvial** *adjective*
1. Of, existing, or occurring in a distant period.
2. Belonging to, existing, or occurring in times long past.

antediluvian *noun*
An old-fashioned person who is reluctant to change or innovate.

anterior *adjective*
1. Going before.
2. Just gone by or elapsed.

anthropoid *adjective*
Resembling a man or human being.

anthropomorphic *adjective*
Resembling a man or human being.

anthropomorphous *adjective*
Resembling a man or human being.

antic *noun*
A mischievous act.

antic *adjective*
Conceived or done with no reference to reality or common sense.

anticipant *adjective*
Having or marked by expectation.

anticipate *verb*
1. To anticipate confidently.
2. To know in advance.

anticipated *adjective*
Known to be about to arrive.

anticipation *noun*
1. The condition of looking forward to something, esp. with eagerness: *a look of happy anticipation on the children's faces.*
2. Something expected.

anticipative *adjective*
Having or marked by expectation.

anticipatory *adjective*
Having or marked by expectation.

antidote *noun*
Something that corrects or counteracts.

antipathetic *adjective*
1. Arousing deep-seated dislike: *an authoritarian person, in every way antipathetic.*
2. Characterized by a natural or innate opposition.
3. Acting against or in opposition.

antipathy *noun*
1. A state of mind brought on by something that is antipathetic: *felt a real antipathy toward violent behavior.*
2. Deep-seated hatred, as between longtime opponents or rivals.

1. CAUSE *noun.*
2. ANCESTOR.
3. ANCESTOR.
4. PRECEDENT.

1. ADVANCE *adjective.*
2. PAST *adjective.*

PRECEDE.

SEE **antediluvian.**

1. EARLY *adjective.*
2. OLD.

SQUARE *noun.*

1. ADVANCE *adjective.*
2. PAST *adjective.*

MANLIKE.

MANLIKE.

MANLIKE.

PRANK.

FANTASTIC.

EXPECTANT.

1. EXPECT.
2. FORESEE.

DUE *adjective.*

1. *Syns:* expectancy (*also* expectance), expectation.
2. EXPECTATION.

EXPECTANT.

EXPECTANT.

REMEDY *noun.*

1. *Syns:* aversive, hateful, repellent, uncongenial, unsympathetic.
2. CONTRARY *adjective.*
3. OPPOSING.

1. *Syns:* antagonism, aversion, hostility, repellence (*also* repellency).
2. ENMITY.

antipodal *adjective*
Diametrically opposed.   OPPOSITE *adjective.*

antipode *noun*
That which is diametrically opposed to another.   OPPOSITE *noun.*

antipodean *adjective*
Diametrically opposed.   OPPOSITE *adjective.*

antipole *noun*
That which is diametrically opposed to another.   OPPOSITE *noun.*

antiquated *adjective*
Of a style or method formerly in vogue.   OLD-FASHIONED.

antique *adjective*
1. Belonging to, existing, or occurring in times long   1. OLD.
   past.
2. Of a style or method formerly in vogue.   2. OLD-FASHIONED.

antiseptic *adjective*
Free from dirt, stain, or impurities.   CLEAN *adjective.*

antithesis *noun*
1. The condition of being in conflict.   1. OPPOSITION.
2. That which is diametrically opposed to another.   2. OPPOSITE *noun.*

antithetical also **antithetic** *adjective*
1. Characterized by a natural or innate opposition.   1. CONTRARY *adjective.*
2. Diametrically opposed.   2. OPPOSITE *adjective.*

antonymous *adjective*
Characterized by a natural or innate opposition.   CONTRARY *adjective.*

anxiety *noun*
Anxious concern: *feeling anxiety about the outcome of*   *Syns:* angst, anxiousness, care, disquiet,
the trial.   disquietude, distress, perturbation,
                                                         unease, uneasiness, worry.

anxious *adjective*
1. In a state of uneasiness: *anxious about her high*   1. *Syns:* concerned, disquieted, distressed,
   fever and pain.   disturbed, nervous, troubled, uneasy,
                                                            unsettled, worried.
2. Intensely desirous or interested.   2. EAGER.

anxiousness *noun*
Anxious concern.   ANXIETY.

A-one *adjective*
Informal. Exceptionally good of its kind.   EXCELLENT.

apace *adverb*
In a rapid way.   FAST *adverb.*

apanage *noun*   SEE **appanage.**

apart *adjective*
1. Set away from all others.   1. SOLITARY.
2. Without equal or rival.   2. UNIQUE.

apart *adverb*
As a separate unit.   SEPARATELY.

apartheid *noun*
The policy or practice of excluding a minority group   SEGREGATION.
from full freedom or participation in a society.

apathetic *adjective*
Without emotion or interest: *renters apathetic about*   *Syns:* disinterested, impassive, indifferent,
rising property taxes.   insensible, lethargic, listless, phlegmatic,
                                                        stolid, unconcerned, uninterested,
                                                        unresponsive.
                                                        Near-syns: dull, inert, sluggish; torpid;
                                                        dry, limp, spiritless.
                                                        Near-ants: involved, interested; alert.

apathy *noun*
Lack of emotion or interest: *looked at the turmoil*   *Syns:* disinterest, disregard, impassivity,
around him with complete apathy.   indifference, insensibility, lassitude,
                                                        lethargy, listlessness, phlegm, stolidity,
                                                        unconcern, unresponsiveness.

ape *verb*
To copy (the manner or expression of another), esp. in
an exaggerated or mocking way.   IMITATE.
ape *noun*
Slang. A person who treats others violently and   THUG.
roughly, esp. for hire.
aperture *noun*
An open space allowing passage.   HOLE *noun.*
apery *noun*
The act, practice, or art of copying the manner or   MIMICRY.
expression of another.
apex *noun*
1. The highest point or state.   1. CLIMAX *noun.*
2. The highest point.   2. HEIGHT.
3. A sharp or tapered end.   3. POINT *noun.*
aphonic *adjective*
Lacking the power or faculty of speech.   DUMB.
aphorism *noun*
A usu. pithy and familiar statement expressing an   PROVERB.
observation or principle generally accepted as wise or
true.
aphoristic *adjective*
Precisely meaningful and tersely cogent.   PITHY.
aphrodisia *noun*
Sexual hunger.   DESIRE *noun.*
aphrodisiac *adjective*
Of, concerning, or promoting sexual love or desire.   EROTIC.
aping *noun*
The act, practice, or art of copying the manner or   MIMICRY.
expression of another.
apish *adjective*
Copying another in an inferior or obsequious way.   IMITATIVE.
aplomb *noun*
1. A stable, calm state of the emotions.   1. BALANCE *noun.*
2. A firm belief in one's own powers.   2. CONFIDENCE.
apocalypse *noun*
Something disclosed, esp. something not previously   REVELATION.
known or realized.
apocalyptic also **apocalyptical** *adjective*
Portending future disaster.   FATEFUL.
apogee *noun*
The highest point or state.   CLIMAX *noun.*
apologetic *adjective*
Expressing or inclined to express an apology: *an*   ***Syns:*** contrite, penitent, regretful,
apologetic smile; an apologetic letter.   repentant, sorry.
apologetic *noun*
A statement that justifies or defends past actions,   APOLOGY.
policies, etc.
apologia *noun*
A statement that justifies or defends past actions,   APOLOGY.
policies, etc.
apology *noun*
1. A statement of acknowledgment expressing regret or   1. ***Syns:*** excuse, regrets. —*Idiom* mea
asking pardon: *made an apology for being late.*   culpa.
2. A statement that justifies or defends past actions, 2. ***Syns:*** apologetic, apologia, defense,
policies, etc.: *The report was nothing more than an* justification.
apology for capital punishment.
apostasy *noun*
An instance of defecting from or abandoning a cause.   DEFECTION.
apostate *noun*
A person who has defected.   DEFECTOR.

apostatize *verb*
To abandon one's cause or party usu. to join another.   DEFECT *verb*.

apostle *noun*
A person doing religious or charitable work in a foreign   MISSIONARY *noun*.
country.

apostolic *adjective*
Of missionaries or their work.   MISSIONARY *adjective*.

apotheosis *noun*
The act of raising to a high position or status or the   EXALTATION.
condition of being so raised.

apotheosize *verb*
To raise to a high position or status.   EXALT.

appall *verb*
To deprive of courage or the power to act as a result of   DISMAY *verb*.
fear, anxiety, or disgust.

appalled *adjective*
Overcome with intense feeling, as of amazement,   SHOCKED.
horror, or dismay.

appalling *adjective*
1. Very bad.   1. TERRIBLE.
2. Causing or able to cause fear.   2. FEARFUL.

appanage also **apanage** *noun*
A privilege granted a person by virtue of birth.   BIRTHRIGHT.

apparatus *noun*
1. Something, as a machine, devised for a particular   1. DEVICE.
function.
2. Things needed for a task, journey, or other purpose.   2. OUTFIT *noun*.

apparel *noun*
Articles worn to cover the body.   DRESS *noun*.

apparel *verb*
To put clothes on.   DRESS *verb*.

apparent *adjective*
1. Readily seen, perceived, or understood: *exploded in*   1. **Syns:** clear, clear-cut, crystal-clear,
anger for no apparent reason; a danger that was   distinct, evident, manifest, noticeable,
apparent at once; antagonism that was apparent to   obvious, patent, plain, visible. —*Idioms*
everyone.   in plain sight, in view.
2. Appearing as such but not necessarily so: *His*   2. **Syns:** ostensible, outward, seeming,
apparent gruffness hid a deep kindness.   semblant, superficial.
    Near-syns: deceptive, delusive,
    delusory, illusive, illusory, misleading;
    factitious, fake, false, pseudo, sham.
    Ants: actual, genuine, real.

apparently *adverb*
On the surface: *apparently calm but inwardly seething*   **Syns:** evidently, seemingly. —*Idioms* on
with rage.   the face of it, to all outward appearances.

apparition *noun*
A supernatural being.   GHOST *noun*.

appeal *noun*
1. An earnest or urgent request: *made a frantic appeal*   1. **Syns:** beseechment, entreaty,
for help.   imploration, plea, prayer, suit,
    supplication.
2. An application to a higher authority, as for sanction   2. **Syns:** petition, suit.
or a decision: *about to make an appeal to the*
supreme court to review the case.
3. The power or quality of attracting.   3. ATTRACTION.

appeal *verb*
1. To make an earnest or urgent request: *appealed to*   1. **Syns:** beg, beseech, conjure, entreat,
passers-by to chase the mugger; appealed for help.   implore, plead with, pray, supplicate.
2. To make application to a higher authority: *appealing*   2. **Syns:** apply, petition, sue.
to the grievance committee to settle the problem.

3. To direct or impel to oneself by some quality or action.

3. ATTRACT.

4. To bring an appeal or request to the attention of.

4. ADDRESS *verb*.

appealer *noun*
One that asks a higher authority for something, as a favor or redress: *the latest appealer of that court decision.*

Syns: appellant, petitioner, suitor.

appealing *adjective*
Pleasing to the eye or mind.

ATTRACTIVE.

appear *verb*
1. To come into view: *A ship appeared on the horizon.*

1. *Syns:* emerge, issue, loom, materialize, show, show up (*Informal*). —*Idioms* make (*or* put in) an appearance, meet (*or* strike) the eye.

2. To have the appearance of: *He appeared to be sleeping, but he was wide awake.*

2. *Syns:* look, seem, sound[1]. —*Idiom* strike one as (being).

3. To begin to appear or develop.

3. DAWN *verb*.

appearance *noun*
1. The act of coming into view: *the surprise appearance of an unexpected witness.*

1. *Syns:* emergence, materialization.

2. The act of arriving.

2. ARRIVAL.

3. The way something or someone looks: *Her elegant appearance showed good taste.*

3. *Syns:* aspect, look(s), mien.

4. The character projected by someone to the public.

4. IMAGE *noun*.

appease *verb*
1. To ease the anger or agitation of.

1. PACIFY.

2. To grant or have what is demanded by (a need or desire).

2. SATISFY.

appellant *noun*
One that asks a higher authority for something, as a favor or redress.

APPEALER.

appellation *noun*
The word or words by which one is called and identified.

NAME *noun*.

appellative *noun*
The word or words by which one is called and identified.

NAME *noun*.

append *verb*
To join so as to form a larger or more comprehensive entity.

ADD.

appendage *noun*
Something resembling or structurally analogous to a tree branch.

BRANCH *noun*.

appertain *verb*
1. To be the property of a person or thing.

1. BELONG.

2. To be pertinent.

2. APPLY.

appetence also **appetency** *noun*
1. A desire for food or drink.

1. APPETITE.

2. A strong wish for what promises enjoyment or pleasure.

2. DESIRE *noun*.

appetency *noun*

SEE **appetence**.

appetent *adjective*
Intensely desirous or interested.

EAGER.

appetite *noun*
1. A desire for food or drink: *Though he has a healthy appetite, he is no glutton.*

1. *Syns:* appetence (*also* appetency), hunger, stomach, taste, thirst.

2. A strong wish for what promises enjoyment or pleasure.

2. DESIRE *noun*.

3. A liking or personal preference for something.

3. TASTE *noun*.

appetition *noun*
A strong wish for what promises enjoyment or pleasure.

DESIRE *noun*.

applaud *verb*
1. To express approval, esp. by clapping: *The audience applauded the cast.*
2. To express warm approval of.

    1. *Syns:* cheer, clap (for), root[2]. —*Idiom* give someone a hand.
    2. PRAISE.

applause *noun*
1. Approval expressed by clapping: *a round of applause at the end of the concert.*
2. An expression of warm approval.

    1. *Syns:* hand (*Informal*), ovation, plaudit.
    2. PRAISE *noun.*

apple-polish *verb*
Informal. To support slavishly every opinion or suggestion of a superior.

    FAWN.

apple-polisher *noun*
Informal. One who flatters another excessively.

    SYCOPHANT.

applesauce *noun*
Slang. Something that does not have or make sense.

    NONSENSE.

appliance *noun*
Something, as a machine, devised for a particular function.

    DEVICE.

applicable *adjective*
Related to the matter at hand.

    RELEVANT.

applicant *noun*
A person who applies for or seeks a job or position: *a job applicant; an applicant for admission to college.*

    Syns: aspirant, candidate, hopeful, petitioner, seeker.

application *noun*
1. A specific use: *Geometry has many practical applications.*
2. The fact of being related to the matter at hand.
3. Steady attention and effort, as to one's work.
4. A document used in applying, as for a job: *You'll have to fill out an application.*
5. The giving of a medication, esp. by prescribed dosage.
6. The act of putting into play.
7. The condition of being put to use.

    1. *Syns:* employment, implementation, operation, utilization.
    2. RELEVANCE.
    3. DILIGENCE.
    4. *Syn:* form.
    5. ADMINISTRATION.
    6. EXERCISE *noun.*
    7. DUTY.

apply *verb*
1. To devote (oneself or one's efforts): *Fred applied himself to his studies.*

2. To put into action or use.
3. To be pertinent: *This rule does not apply to you.*

4. To ask for employment, acceptance, or admission: *applying for a job; applied to college.*
5. To bring an appeal or request to the attention of.
6. To make application to a higher authority.
7. To have recourse to when in need.

    1. *Syns:* address, bend, buckle, concentrate, dedicate, devote, direct, focus (on), give, turn.
    2. USE *verb.*
    3. *Syns:* appertain, bear on (*or upon*), concern, involve, pertain, refer, relate. —*Idioms* have a bearing on, have to do with.
    4. *Syns:* petition, put in (*Informal*), sign up.
    5. ADDRESS *verb.*
    6. APPEAL *verb.*
    7. RESORT TO at **resort.**

appoint *verb*
1. To select for an office or position: *The board of directors appointed Martin president. Jane appointed herself my conscience.*
2. To supply what is needed for some activity or purpose.

    1. *Syns:* designate, make, name, nominate, tap[1] (*Slang*).

    2. FURNISH.

appointee *noun*
A person who is appointed to an office or position: *a new consular appointee.*

    Syns: designee, nominee.

appointment *noun*
1. The act of appointing to an office or position: *The appointment of a Chief Justice is an important decision.*

    1. *Syns:* designation, naming, nomination.

2. A post of employment.

3. A commitment to appear at a certain time and place.

4. A piece of equipment for comfort or convenience.

apportion *verb*
To set aside or distribute as a share.

apportionment *noun*
The act of distributing or the condition of being distributed.

apposite *adjective*
Related to the matter at hand.

appraisal *noun*
The act or result of judging the worth or value of something or someone.

appraise *verb*
To make a judgment as to the worth or value of.

appraisement *noun*
The act or result of judging the worth or value of something or someone.

appreciable *adjective*
Capable of being noticed or apprehended mentally.

appreciate *verb*
1. To recognize the worth, quality, importance, etc., of: *Many art lovers appreciate Renoir.*

2. To regard with great pleasure or approval.

appreciation *noun*
1. Recognition of worth, quality, importance, etc.: *a great appreciation of music and sculpture.*

2. A being grateful: *expressed their appreciation with a small present.*

3. A feeling of deference, approval, and liking.

appreciative *adjective*
Showing or feeling gratitude.

apprehend *verb*
1. To take into custody as a prisoner.

2. To perceive and recognize the meaning of.

3. To perceive directly with the intellect.

4. *Obs.* To be intuitively aware of.

5. To be afraid of.

apprehension *noun*
1. A seizing and holding by law.

2. Intellectual hold.

apprehensive *adjective*
Filled with fear or terror.

apprise also **apprize** *verb*
To cause to know about or be aware of.

apprize *verb*

approach *verb*
1. To come near in space or time: *approached the house; approaching three o'clock.*

2. To come near in quality, amount, etc.

3. To make overtures to, esp. for the purpose of achieving a desired result: *approached the boss about a raise.*

---

2. POSITION.

3. ENGAGEMENT.

4. FURNISHING.

ALLOT.

DISTRIBUTION.

RELEVANT.

ESTIMATE *noun.*

ESTIMATE *verb.*

ESTIMATE *noun.*

PERCEPTIBLE.

1. *Syns:* cherish, enjoy, esteem, go for (*Informal*), prize, relish, respect, savor, treasure, value.
Near-ants: contemn, disapprove, disdain, rebuke, scorn; decry, denigrate, depreciate, devalue, disparage.
Ant: despise.

2. ADMIRE.

1. *Syns:* admiration, awareness, comprehension, enjoyment, liking, receptivity, responsiveness, taste.

2. *Syns:* gratefulness, gratitude, thankfulness, thanks.

3. ESTEEM *noun.*

GRATEFUL.

1. ARREST *verb.*
2. UNDERSTAND.
3. KNOW.
4. PERCEIVE.
5. FEAR *verb.*

1. ARREST *noun.*
2. GRASP *noun.*

AFRAID.

INFORM.

SEE **apprise.**

1. *Syn:* near. —*Idioms* come close to, draw near to.
2. RIVAL *verb.*
3. *Syns:* address, sound[1].

4. To go about the initial step in doing (something).
5. To bring an appeal or request to the attention of.

4. START *verb*.
5. ADDRESS *verb*.

approach *noun*
1. The act or fact of coming near: *The dog's barking announced the approach of the guests. Cold winds mark the approach of winter.*
2. A method used in dealing with something: *a new approach to solving the fuel shortage.*

1. Syns: advent, coming, convergence, imminence, nearness.
2. Syns: attack, course, line, modus operandi (*Latin*), plan, procedure, tack, technique.

approachable *adjective*
Easily approached: *Despite his fame, he remained approachable and sympathetic.*

Syns: accessible, friendly, responsive, warm, welcoming.

approach(es) *noun*
Preliminary actions intended to elicit a favorable response.

ADVANCES.

approaching *adjective*
In the relatively near future.

COMING.

approbate *verb*
To be favorably disposed toward.

APPROVE.

approbation *noun*
Favorable regard.

ACCEPTANCE.

approbatory *adjective*
Serving to compliment.

COMPLIMENTARY.

appropriate *adjective*
1. Suitable for a particular person, condition, occasion, or place: *wore appropriate clothes to the wedding; music appropriate for that drama; an appropriate choice of words.*

1. Syns: apt, befitting, correct, felicitous, fit, fitting, happy, meet[2], proper, right, suited.
Near-syns: applicable, germane, just, pertinent, relevant, suitable; opportune, pat, timely.
Ant: inappropriate.

2. Suited to one's end or purpose.
3. Consistent with prevailing or accepted standards or circumstances.

2. CONVENIENT.
3. JUST *adjective*.

appropriate *verb*
1. To set aside for a specified purpose: *Congress appropriated money for public education.*
2. To lay claim to for oneself or as one's right.

1. Syns: allocate, designate, earmark.
2. ASSUME.

appropriation *noun*
1. The act of taking something for oneself.
2. Something, as a gift, granted for a definite purpose.

1. USURPATION.
2. GRANT *noun*.

approval *noun*
1. Official acceptance or permission: *receiving approval for the formation of a fact-finding committee.*

1. Syns: authorization, concurrence, consent, endorsement, O.K. (*Informal*), sanction.

2. Favorable regard.
3. An act of confirming officially.

2. ACCEPTANCE.
3. CONFIRMATION.

approve *verb*
1. To be favorably disposed toward: *do not approve of gambling.*

1. Syns: accept, approbate, countenance, favor, go for, hold with, subscribe to.
—*Idioms* take kindly to, think well (or highly) of.

2. To accept officially.
3. To make valid and binding by a formal legal act.

2. PASS *verb*.
3. CONFIRM.

approximal *adjective*
Sharing a common boundary.

ADJOINING.

approximate *verb*
1. To calculate approximately.
2. To come near in quality, amount, etc.

1. ESTIMATE *verb*.
2. RIVAL *verb*.

approximately *adverb*
Near to in quantity or amount: *Approximately 40 people came to the meeting.*

Syns: about, almost, nearly, roughly.

approximation *noun*
A rough or tentative calculation.

ESTIMATE *noun.*

appulse *noun*
Violent, forcible contact between two or more things.

COLLISION.

apropos *adjective*
Related to the matter at hand.

RELEVANT.

apt *adjective*
1. Suitable for a particular person, condition, occasion, or place.
2. Having or showing a tendency or likelihood.

1. APPROPRIATE *adjective.*

2. INCLINED.

aptitude *noun*
An innate capability.

TALENT.

aptness *noun*
An innate capability.

TALENT.

aquake *adjective*
Marked by or affected with tremors.

TREMULOUS.

aquiver *adjective*
Marked by or affected with tremors.

TREMULOUS.

arbiter *noun*
A person, usu. appointed, who decides the issues or results, or supervises the conduct, of a competition or conflict.

JUDGE *noun.*

arbitrary *adjective*
1. Determined or marked by whim or caprice rather than reason: *The use of the color red to mean "stop" is arbitrary.*
2. Based on individual judgment or discretion: *made an arbitrary choice because there was no basis for choosing logically.*
3. Having and exercising complete political power and control.

1. *Syns:* capricious, chance, random, whimsical, willful.

2. *Syns:* discretionary, judgmental, personal, subjective.

3. ABSOLUTE.

arbitrate *verb*
To make a decision about (a controversy, dispute, etc.) after deliberation, as in a court of law.

JUDGE *verb.*

arbitrator *noun*
A person, usu. appointed, who decides the issues or results, or supervises the conduct, of a competition or conflict.

JUDGE *noun.*

Arcadian *adjective*
Of or pertaining to the countryside.

COUNTRY *adjective.*

arcane *adjective*
Difficult to explain or understand.

MYSTERIOUS.

arced *adjective*
Deviating from a straight line.

BENT *adjective.*

archaic *adjective*
Of a style or method formerly in vogue.

OLD-FASHIONED.

arched *adjective*
Deviating from a straight line.

BENT *adjective.*

archetypal *adjective*
Having the nature of, constituting, or serving as a type.

TYPICAL.

archetype *noun*
A first form from which varieties arise or imitations are made.

ORIGINAL *noun.*

archetypic also **archetypical** *adjective*
Having the nature of, constituting, or serving as a type.

TYPICAL.

archfiend *noun*
A perversely bad, cruel, or wicked person. FIEND.

architect *noun*
One that creates, founds, or originates. ORIGINATOR.

arciform *adjective*
Deviating from a straight line. BENT *adjective*.

arctic *adjective*
Very cold. FRIGID.

ardent *adjective*
1. Showing or having enthusiasm.   1. ENTHUSIASTIC.
2. Intensely desirous or interested.   2. EAGER.
3. Fired with intense feeling.   3. PASSIONATE.
4. Marked by much heat.   4. HOT *adjective*.

ardor *noun*
1. Passionate devotion to or interest in a cause,   1. ENTHUSIASM.
   subject, etc.
2. Powerful, intense emotion.   2. PASSION.

ardorless *adjective*
Deficient in or lacking sexual desire. FRIGID.

arduous *adjective*
1. Imposing a severe test of bodily or spiritual   1. BURDENSOME.
   strength.
2. So sharply inclined as to be almost perpendicular.   2. STEEP[1].

arduously *adverb*
With effort. HARD *adverb*.

area *noun*
1. A part of the earth's surface: *an agricultural area;*   1. **Syns:** belt, locality, neighborhood,
   an urban area.   quarter, region, tract. —*Idiom* neck of
        the woods.
2. A surrounding site.   2. LOCALITY.
3. A rather small part of a geographic unit considered   3. NEIGHBORHOOD.
   in regard to its inhabitants or distinctive
   characteristics.
4. A sphere of activity, study, or interest: *Comparative*   4. **Syns:** arena, bag (*Slang*), department,
   literature is his area.   domain, field, orbit, province, realm,
        scene (*Slang*), subject, terrain,
        territory, world.

arena *noun*
A sphere of activity, study, or interest. AREA.

argot *noun*
An often regional form of a language not considered DIALECT.
standard.

arguable *adjective*
In doubt or dispute. DEBATABLE.

argue *verb*
1. To put forth reasons for or against, often excitedly: 1. **Syns:** contend, debate, dispute, moot.
   The senator argued in favor of the amendment. We
   argued the pros and cons of gas rationing.
2. To engage in a quarrel: *constantly argues with his*   2. **Syns:** bicker, contend, dispute, fight,
   wife.   hassle, quarrel, quibble, squabble, tiff,
        wrangle. —*Idioms* bandy (*or* have)
        words, cross swords, have it out, join
        (*or* take) issue, lock horns.
3. To give grounds for believing in the existence or   3. INDICATE.
   presence of.

argue into *verb*
To succeed in causing (a person) to act in a certain way. PERSUADE.

argue into *verb* SEE **argue.**

argument *noun*
1. A discussion, often heated, in which a difference of opinion is expressed: *regularly had arguments about money.*

2. A course of reasoning: *The argument is that conservation will prevent shortages.*
3. A fact or circumstance that gives logical support to an assertion, claim, or proposal.
4. What a speech, piece of writing, or artistic work is about.

argumentation *noun*
The presentation of an argument: *an attorney skilled in argumentation.*

argumentative *adjective*
Given to arguing: *an argumentative old curmudgeon.*

argute *adjective*
Elevated in pitch.

aria *noun*
A pleasing succession of musical tones forming a usu. brief aesthetic unit.

arid *adjective*
1. Having little or no liquid or moisture.
2. Having little or no precipitation.
3. Arousing no interest or curiosity.

ariose *adjective*
Having or producing a pleasing melody.

arise *verb*
1. To come into being.
2. To begin to develop.
3. To have as a source.
4. To leave one's bed.
5. To move from a lower to a higher position.

aristarch *noun*
A person who finds fault, often severely and willfully.

aristocracy *noun*
People of the highest social level.

aristocratic *adjective*
Of high birth or social position.

aristoi *noun*
People of the highest social level.

arithmetic *noun*
Arithmetic calculations.

arm *noun*
1. Something resembling or structurally analogous to a tree branch.
2. A component of government that performs a given function.

arm *verb*
To put (explosive material) into a weapon.

armistice *noun*
A temporary cessation of hostilities by mutual consent of the contending parties.

---

1. *Syns:* altercation, clash, contention, controversy, debate, disagreement, dispute, fight, hassle, polemic, quarrel, rhubarb (*Slang*), row^2, run-in, spat, squabble, tangle (*Informal*), tiff, unpleasantness, words, wrangle.
2. *Syns:* case, point, reason.

3. REASON *noun.*

4. SUBJECT *noun.*

Syns: debate, disputation, forensics.

Syns: combative, contentious, disputatious, eristic, litigious, polemical, quarrelsome, scrappy.
Near-syns: controversial, fiery, hotheaded, impetuous; belligerent, bellicose.

HIGH.

MELODY.

1. DRY *adjective.*
2. DRY *adjective.*
3. BORING.

MELODIOUS.

1. BEGIN.
2. DAWN *verb.*
3. STEM *verb.*
4. GET UP at **get**.
5. RISE *verb.*

CRITIC.

SOCIETY.

NOBLE.

SOCIETY.

FIGURES.

1. BRANCH *noun.*
2. BRANCH *noun.*

LOAD *verb.*

TRUCE.

army *noun*
A very large number of things grouped together. CROWD *noun*.

aroma *noun*
1. The quality of something that may be perceived by the olfactory sense. 1. SMELL *noun*.
2. A sweet or pleasant odor. 2. FRAGRANCE.
3. A distinctive yet intangible quality deemed typical of a given thing. 3. FLAVOR *noun*.

aromatic *adjective*
Having a pleasant odor. FRAGRANT.

aromatize *verb*
To fill with a pleasant odor. SCENT *verb*.

around *adverb*
1. From one end to the other. 1. THROUGH *adverb*.
2. Toward the back. 2. BACKWARD *adverb*.
3. In or toward a former location or condition. 3. BACK *adverb*.

around *adjective*
Informal. Having existence or life. ALIVE.

around-the-clock *adjective* SEE **round-the-clock**.

arouse *verb*
1. To induce or elicit (a reaction or emotion): *Her magic tricks aroused wonder in the children.* 1. *Syns:* awaken, foment, kindle, raise, rouse, stir[1] (up), waken.
2. To elicit a strong emotional response from. 2. INSPIRE.
3. To stir to action or feeling. 3. PROVOKE.
4. To cease sleeping. 4. WAKE *verb*.

arraign *verb*
To make an accusation against. ACCUSE *verb*.

arrange *verb*
1. To put into a deliberate order: *arranging figures in sequential order.* 1. *Syns:* array, assort, classify, dispose, distribute, group, marshal, order, organize, range, rank[1], sort, systematize.
2. To plan the details or arrangements of: *arranging a formal dinner for 12.* 2. *Syns:* lay out, prepare, schedule, work out.
3. To come to an agreement about: *eventually arranged the terms of the cease-fire.* 3. *Syns:* conclude, fix, negotiate, set[1], settle.
4. To put into correct or conclusive form. 4. SETTLE.
5. To combine and adapt in order to attain a particular effect. 5. HARMONIZE.

arrangement *noun*
1. A way or condition of being arranged: *Every year we change the arrangement of the furniture.* 1. *Syns:* disposal, disposition, distribution, formation, grouping, layout, line-up (*also* lineup), order, ordering, sequence.
2. An act or state of agreeing between parties regarding a course of action. 2. AGREEMENT.

arrangements *noun*
Plans made in preparation for some undertaking: *We're making arrangements for our trip to Nassau.* *Syns:* preparations, provisions.

arrant *adjective*
1. Conspicuously bad or offensive. 1. FLAGRANT.
2. Characterized by or done without shame. 2. SHAMELESS.
3. Completely such, without qualification or exception. 3. UTTER[2].

array *verb*
1. To put clothes on. 1. DRESS *verb*.
2. To put into a deliberate order. 2. ARRANGE.

array *noun*
1. An impressive or ostentatious exhibition. 1. DISPLAY *noun*.
2. A number of individuals making up or considered a unit. 2. GROUP *noun*.

arrear or **arrears** *noun*
Something, such as money, owed by one person to
another.   DEBT.

arrearage *noun*
1. A condition of owing something to another.   1. DEBT.
2. Something, such as money, owed by one person to   2. DEBT.
another.

arrears *noun*   SEE **arrear.**

arrest *verb*
1. To take into custody as a prisoner: *got arrested for*   1. *Syns:* apprehend, bag (*Slang*), bust
automobile theft.   (*Slang*), collar (*Slang*), detain, nab
                                                                                     (*Slang*), pick up, pinch (*Slang*), run
                                                                                     in, seize.
2. To prevent the occurrence or continuation of a   2. STOP *verb.*
movement, action, or operation.
3. To compel the attention, interest, imagination, etc., 3. GRIP *verb.*
of.

arrest *noun*
1. The act of stopping.   1. STOP *noun.*
2. A seizing and holding by law: *made five arrests*   2. *Syns:* apprehension, bust (*Slang*),
yesterday; resisted arrest violently.   detention, nab (*Slang*), pickup, pinch,
                                                                                     seizure.

arresting *adjective*
Readily attracting notice.   NOTICEABLE.

arrestive *adjective*
Readily attracting notice.   NOTICEABLE.

arrival *noun*
1. The act of arriving: *the mayor's arrival at city hall.* 1. *Syns:* advent, appearance, coming.
2. One that arrives: *a late arrival at the party.*   2. *Syns:* comer, incomer, visitor.
3. The achievement of something desired, planned, or   3. SUCCESS.
attempted.

arrive *verb*
1. To come to a particular place: *arrived at the office at* 1. *Syns:* blow in (*Slang*), check in
nine sharp.   (*Informal*), get in, pull in, reach, show
                                                                                     up, turn up.
2. To gain wealth or fame.   2. SUCCEED.

arrive at *verb*
To reach a goal or objective: *Management and the union*   *Syns:* attain, gain, get to, hit on (*or*
arrived at an understanding.   upon).

arrive at *verb*   SEE **arrive.**

arrogance *noun*
The quality of being arrogant: *Even his walk showed*   *Syns:* disdain, haughtiness, hauteur,
his arrogance.   insolence (*also* insolency), loftiness,
                                                                                lordliness, overbearingness, presumption,
                                                                                pride, superciliousness, superiority.

arrogant *adjective*
Overly convinced of one's own superiority and   *Syns:* disdainful, haughty, high-and-
importance: *An arrogant man treats others with*   mighty, hoity-toity (*also* highty-tighty),
condescension.   insolent, lofty, lordly, overbearing,
                                                                                overweening, presumptuous, proud,
                                                                                supercilious, superior. —*Idiom* on one's
                                                                                high horse.
                                                                                Near-ants: abject, fawning, obsequious,
                                                                                submissive, subservient, truckling;
                                                                                humble, mild.
                                                                                Ant: meek.

arrogate *verb*
To lay claim to for oneself or as one's right.   ASSUME.

arrogation *noun*
The act of taking something for oneself.   USURPATION.

arrondi *adjective*
French. Deviating from a straight line.

BENT *adjective.*

art *noun*
1. A skill in doing or performing that is attained by study, practice, or observation: *"The art of saying things well is useless to a man who has nothing to say."* Macaulay.

1. **Syns:** craft, expertise, knack, know-how (*Informal*), technique.

2. Deceitful cleverness: *used all the art at his disposal to manipulate his colleagues.*

2. **Syns:** artfulness, artifice, craft, craftiness, cunning, foxiness, guile, wiliness.

artful *adjective*
1. Showing art or skill in performing or doing: *an artful rendition of a Chopin mazurka.*

1. **Syns:** adroit, deft, dexterous, masterful, masterly, skillful.

2. Deceitfully clever: *used artful means to get exactly what she wanted.*

2. **Syns:** crafty, cunning, foxy, guileful, scheming, sly, tricky, wily.

artfulness *noun*
Deceitful cleverness.

ART.

article *noun*
1. An individually considered portion of a whole.

1. ELEMENT.

2. Something having material existence.

2. OBJECT[1].

articulate *adjective*
1. Produced by the voice.

1. VOCAL.

2. Fluently persuasive and forceful.

2. ELOQUENT.

articulate *verb*
1. To produce or make (speech sounds).

1. PRONOUNCE.

2. To put into words.

2. SAY *verb.*

3. To make into a whole by joining a system of parts.

3. INTEGRATE *verb.*

articulation *noun*
1. The use of the speech organs to produce sounds.

1. VOICING.

2. The act or an instance of expressing in words.

2. EXPRESSION.

artifice *noun*
1. Deceitful cleverness.

1. ART.

2. An indirect, usu. cunning means of gaining an end.

2. TRICK *noun.*

artificial *adjective*
1. Made by human beings, not nature: *an artificial lake.*

1. **Syns:** manmade, manufactured, synthetic.

2. Made to imitate something else: *artificial pearls; artificial flowers.*

2. **Syns:** imitation, manmade, mock, pretend (*Informal*), sham, synthetic.
Near-syns: dummy, ersatz, fake, false, papier-mâché, phony, pretend (*Informal*); simulated, substitute.
Ant: genuine, real.

3. Not genuine or sincere: *an artificial display of affection.*

3. **Syns:** affected, feigned, insincere, phony (*also* phoney) (*Informal*), pretended, spurious.

4. Artificially genteel.

4. AFFECTED[2].

5. Marked by unnaturalness, pretension, and often a slavish love of fads.

5. PLASTIC.

artistic *adjective*
Showing good taste.

TASTEFUL.

artless *adjective*
1. Free from guile, cunning, or deceit: *the artless bewilderment of a child.*

1. **Syns:** guileless, ingenuous, innocent, naive (*also* naïve, naif, naïf), natural, simple, unaffected, unsophisticated, unstudied.

2. Of a plain and unsophisticated nature.

2. RUSTIC *adjective.*

artsy *adjective*
Pretentiously artistic.

ARTY.

artsy-craftsy or **arty-crafty** *adjective*
Pretentiously artistic.

ARTY.

arty   *adjective*
Pretentiously artistic: *arty movies.*

Syns: artsy, artsy-craftsy (*or* arty-crafty), contrived, precious, pretentious.

arty-crafty   *adjective*
SEE **artsy-craftsy.**

aruspex   *noun*
SEE **haruspex.**

ascared   *adjective*
Chiefly Regional. Filled with fear or terror.
AFRAID.

ascend   *verb*
1. To move upward on or along: *ascending a mountain.*
2. To move from a lower to a higher position.
3. To attain a higher status, rank, or condition.

1. *Syns:* climb, go up, mount, scale^2.
2. RISE *verb.*
3. RISE *verb.*

ascendancy   *noun*
The condition or fact of being dominant.
DOMINANCE.

ascendant   *adjective*
Having pre-eminent significance.
RULING *adjective.*

ascendant   *noun*
A person from whom one is descended.
ANCESTOR.

ascension   *noun*
1. The act of rising or moving upward.
2. The act of moving upward on or along.

1. RISE *noun.*
2. ASCENT.

ascent   *noun*
1. The act of moving upward on or along: *the mountaineer's ascent of the Matterhorn.*
2. The act of rising or moving upward.
3. An upward slope: *climbed the steep ascent to the top of the hill.*

1. *Syns:* ascension, climb, climbing, mounting, scaling.
2. RISE *noun.*
3. *Syns:* acclivity, grade, gradient, rise, slope.

ascertain   *verb*
To obtain knowledge or awareness of something not known before, as through observation, study, etc.
DISCOVER.

ascribe   *verb*
To regard as belonging to or resulting from another.
ATTRIBUTE *verb.*

ascription   *noun*
The act of attributing.
ATTRIBUTION.

aseptic   *adjective*
Arousing no interest or curiosity.
BORING.

ashake   *adjective*
Marked by or affected with tremors.
TREMULOUS.

ashen   *adjective*
Lacking color.
PALE *adjective.*

ashiver   *adjective*
Marked by or affected with tremors.
TREMULOUS.

ashy   *adjective*
Lacking color.
PALE *adjective.*

aside   *noun*
1. The act of digressing.
2. An instance of digressing.

1. DIGRESSION.
2. DIGRESSION.

ask   *verb*
1. To put a question to (someone): *He asked her what was wrong.*
2. To seek an answer to (a question): *have to ask the right questions if you're going to learn.*
3. To have as a need or prerequisite.
4. To request that someone take part in or be present at a particular occasion.
5. To endeavor to obtain (something) by expressing one's needs or desires.

1. *Syns:* examine, inquire (*also* enquire) (of), interrogate, query, question, quiz.
2. *Syns:* pose, put, raise.
3. DEMAND *verb.*
4. INVITE.
5. REQUEST *verb.*

askance   *adverb*
With skepticism.
SKEPTICALLY.

asleep   *adjective*
1. In a state of sleep.
2. No longer alive.

1. SLEEPING.
2. DEAD *adjective.*

3. Lacking physical feeling or sensitivity.   **3.** DEAD *adjective*.

asomatous *adjective*
Having no body, form, or substance.   IMMATERIAL.

aspect *noun*
  1. A disposition of the facial features that conveys meaning, feeling, or mood.   **1.** EXPRESSION.
  2. An outward appearance.   **2.** FACE *noun*.
  3. The way something or someone looks.   **3.** APPEARANCE.
  4. A way of considering a matter.   **4.** LIGHT[1] *noun*.
  5. The particular angle from which something is considered.   **5.** PHASE.

asperity *noun*
Something that obstructs progress and requires great effort to overcome.   DIFFICULTY.

asperous *adjective*
Having a coarse, irregular surface.   ROUGH.

asperse *verb*
To make defamatory statements about.   LIBEL *verb*.

aspersion *noun*
The expression of injurious, malicious statements about someone.   LIBEL *noun*.

asphyxiate *verb*
To stop the breathing of.   CHOKE.

aspirant *noun*
  1. One who aspires: *aspirants for the presidency.*   **1.** *Syns:* aspirer, hopeful, yearner.
  2. A person who applies for or seeks a job or position.   **2.** APPLICANT.

aspiration *noun*
  1. A strong desire to achieve something.   **1.** AMBITION.
  2. A fervent hope, wish, or goal.   **2.** DREAM *noun*.

aspire *verb*
  1. To have a fervent hope or aspiration: *aspiring to great knowledge; aspires to become an actress.*   **1.** *Syns:* dream, hope. —*Idioms* reach for the stars, set one's heart (*or* sights) on.
  2. To strive toward a goal.   **2.** AIM *verb*.

aspirer *noun*
One who aspires.   ASPIRANT.

aspiring *adjective*
Full of ambition.   AMBITIOUS.

ass *noun*
One deficient in judgment and good sense.   FOOL *noun*.

assail *verb*
  1. To attack with harsh, often insulting language.   **1.** REVILE *verb*.
  2. To set upon with violent force.   **2.** ATTACK *verb*.

assailable *adjective*
Open to attack and capture because of a lack of protection.   VULNERABLE.

assailant *noun*
One who starts a hostile action.   AGGRESSOR.

assailer *noun*
One who starts a hostile action.   AGGRESSOR.

assailment *noun*
The act of attacking.   ATTACK *noun*.

assault *verb*
  1. To set upon with violent force.   **1.** ATTACK *verb*.
  2. To compel (another) to participate in or submit to a sexual act.   **2.** RAPE.

assault *noun*
The act of attacking.   ATTACK *noun*.

assay *verb*
  1. To make an attempt to do or make.   **1.** ATTEMPT *verb*.
  2. To make a judgment as to the worth or value of.   **2.** ESTIMATE *verb*.

3. To subject to a procedure that ascertains effectiveness, value, proper function, or other quality.

assay *noun*
1. An effort to do or make something.
2. A procedure that ascertains effectiveness, value, proper function, or other quality.

assemblage *noun*
1. A quantity accumulated.
2. A number of persons who have come or been gathered together.

assemble *verb*
1. To bring together: *assembling the staff for the meeting.*

2. To come together: *A crowd quickly assembled to watch the motorcade.*

3. To create by forming, combining, or altering materials.

assembly *noun*
1. A number of persons who have come or been gathered together: *an assembly of jurors waiting to be called.*

2. A formal assemblage of the members of a group.

assent *verb*
To respond affirmatively; receive with agreement or compliance: *assented to the board's decision.*

assent *noun*
The act or process of accepting.

assenting *adjective*
Giving assent.

assert *verb*
1. To put into words positively and with conviction: *Some critics assert that he is the world's greatest pianist.*
2. To defend, maintain, or insist on the recognition of (one's rights, for example): *She asserted her independence and went back to work.*
3. To state to be true.

assertion *noun*
1. The act of asserting positively: *bold assertions of cultural superiority.*
2. A statement of something as fact.

assertive *adjective*
1. Marked by boldness and assertiveness.
2. Bold and definite in character.

assertory *adjective*
Marked by boldness and assertiveness.

assess *verb*
1. To make a judgment as to the worth or value of.
2. To establish and apply as compulsory.

assessment *noun*
1. The act or result of judging the worth or value of something or someone.
2. A compulsory contribution, usu. of money, that is required of persons or groups of persons for the support of a government.

---

3. TEST *verb*.

1. ATTEMPT *noun*.
2. TEST *noun*.

1. ACCUMULATION.
2. ASSEMBLY.

1. *Syns:* call, collect[1], convene, convoke, gather, get together, marshal, muster, round up, summon.
2. *Syns:* aggroup, cluster, collect[1], congregate, convene, forgather (*also* foregather), gather, get together, muster.
3. MAKE *verb*.

1. *Syns:* assemblage, body, company, conclave, congregation, congress, convocation, crowd, gathering, group, meeting, muster, troop.
2. CONVENTION.

Syns: accede (to), accept, acquiesce (in), agree, consent.

ACCEPTANCE.

FAVORABLE.

1. *Syns:* affirm, asseverate, aver, avouch, avow, declare, hold, maintain, state. —*Idiom* have it.
2. *Syns:* claim, vindicate.

3. CLAIM *verb*.

1. *Syns:* affirmation, averment, avowal, declaration, statement.
2. CLAIM *noun*.

1. AGGRESSIVE.
2. EMPHATIC.

AGGRESSIVE.

1. ESTIMATE *verb*.
2. IMPOSE.

1. ESTIMATE *noun*.

2. TAX *noun*.

assets *noun*
All property or goods having economic value.   RESOURCES.

asseverate *verb*
To put into words positively and with conviction.   ASSERT.

assiduity *noun*
Steady attention and effort, as to one's occupation.   DILIGENCE.

assiduous *adjective*
Characterized by steady attention and effort.   DILIGENT.

assiduousness *noun*
Steady attention and effort, as to one's occupation.   DILIGENCE.

assign *verb*
1. To set aside or distribute as a share.   1. ALLOT.
2. To ascribe (a misdeed, error, etc.) to.   2. FIX *verb*.
3. To regard as belonging to or resulting from another.   3. ATTRIBUTE *verb*.
4. To appoint and send to a particular place.   4. STATION *verb*.
5. *Law.* To change the ownership of (property) by   5. TRANSFER.
   means of a legal document.

assignation *noun*
A commitment to appear at a certain time and place.   ENGAGEMENT.

assignment *noun*
The act of attributing.   ATTRIBUTION.

assimilate *verb*
1. To take in and incorporate, esp. mentally.   1. ABSORB.
2. To represent as similar.   2. LIKEN.

assimilating *adjective*
Having a capacity or tendency to absorb or soak up.   ABSORBENT.

assimilation *noun*
The process of absorbing and incorporating, esp.   ABSORPTION.
mentally.

assimilative *adjective*
Having a capacity or tendendy to absorb or soak up.   ABSORBENT.

assist *verb*
To give support or assistance.   HELP *verb*.

assist *noun*
The act or an instance of helping.   HELP *noun*.

assistance *noun*
The act or an instance of helping.   HELP *noun*.

assistant *noun*
1. A person who holds a position auxiliary to another   1. **Syns:** adjutant, aide, auxiliary,
   and assumes some of his responsibilities: *an*   coadjutant, coadjutor, lieutenant,
   editorial assistant; the colonel's office assistant.   second[2].
2. A person who helps.   2. HELPER.

assisting *adjective*
Giving or able to give help or support.   AUXILIARY *adjective*.

assistive *adjective*
Affording support or assistance.   HELPFUL.

assize *noun*
Eng. Hist. The formal product of a legislative or   LAW *noun*.
judicial body.

associate *verb*
1. To unite or be united in a relationship: *Mr. Elkins*   1. **Syns:** affiliate, ally, bind, combine,
   was associated with the firm of Harper and Brothers.   conjoin, connect, join, link, relate.
2. To come or bring together in one's mind or   2. **Syns:** bracket, connect, correlate,
   imagination: *I always associate lilacs with spring.*   couple, identify, link.
3. To keep company: *I told you not to associate with*   3. **Syns:** consort, fraternize, hang out
   him; he's bad news.   (*Slang*), hobnob, run around
                                                                      (*Informal*), troop (with). —*Idiom* rub
                                                                      elbows.

associate *noun*
1. One who is united in a relationship with another: 1. **Syns:** affiliate, ally, cohort (*Informal*),

The politician's associates suffered the consequences when the scandal was exposed.
2. One who keeps company with another: *One of his closest associates is a member of Congress.*

3. One that accompanies another.

association *noun*
1. The state of being associated: *The architect and the builder work in close association.*

2. A group of people united in a relationship and having some interest, activity, or purpose in common.
3. A feeling, thought, idea, etc., associated in one's mind or imagination with someone or something specific.
4. A group of athletic teams that play each other.

assort *verb*
1. To distribute into groups according to kinds: *assorted plates by size.*
2. To put into a deliberate order.

assorted *adjective*
Consisting of a number of different kinds.

assortment *noun*
A collection of various things: *Under the Christmas tree was piled a large assortment of packages.*

assuage *verb*
1. To ease the anger or agitation of.
2. To make less severe or more bearable.

assuagement *noun*
Freedom, esp. from pain.

assume *verb*
1. To take upon oneself: *He assumed responsibility for his widowed aunt.*
2. To take for granted without proof.
3. To lay claim to for oneself or as one's right: *assumed the authority to close the office early.*

4. To take on or give a false appearance of: *assuming a sober, dignified expression.*

5. To behave affectedly or insincerely.
6. To put (an article of clothing) on one's person.

assumed *adjective*
1. Being fictitious and not real: *an assumed name.*

2. Based on inference, not fact.

assuming *adjective*
Having or exhibiting excessive and arrogant self-confidence.

assumption *noun*
1. Something taken to be true without proof: *acted on the assumption that both countries were interested in world peace.*

colleague, confederate, copartner, fellow, partner.
2. **Syns:** buddy (*Informal*), chum, companion, comrade, crony, mate, pal (*Informal*).
Near-syns: acquaintance, friend, confidant, familiar, intimate; brother-in-arms, comrade-in-arms, sidekick (*Slang*).
3. ACCOMPANIMENT.

1. **Syns:** affiliation, alliance, combination, conjunction, connection, cooperation, partnership.
2. UNION.

3. SUGGESTION.

4. CONFERENCE.

1. **Syns:** categorize, class, classify, group, pigeonhole, separate, sort, sort out.
2. ARRANGE.

VARIOUS.

Syns: conglomeration, diversity, gallimaufry, hodgepodge, jumble, medley, mélange (*also* melange), miscellany, mishmash, olio, patchwork, salmagundi, variety. —*Idioms* grab bag, mixed bag.

1. PACIFY.
2. RELIEVE.

RELIEF.

1. **Syns:** incur, shoulder, tackle, take on, take over, take up, undertake.
2. SUPPOSE.
3. **Syns:** appropriate, arrogate, commandeer, pre-empt (*also* preempt, preëmpt), seize, take, usurp.
4. **Syns:** affect[2], counterfeit, fake, feign, pretend, put on, simulate. —*Idiom* make believe.
5. ACT *verb*.
6. DON.

1. **Syns:** adopted, made-up, pseudonymic, pseudonymous.
2. PRESUMPTIVE.

PRESUMPTUOUS.

1. **Syns:** postulate, postulation, premise, presumption, presupposition, supposition, surmise, theory, thesis.

2. The act of taking something for oneself.   **2.** USURPATION.

3. Excessive and arrogant self-confidence.   **3.** PRESUMPTION.

assumptive *adjective*

  1. Having or exhibiting excessive and arrogant self-confidence.   **1.** PRESUMPTUOUS.

  2. Based on probability or presumption.   **2.** PRESUMPTIVE.

assurance *noun*

  1. A firm belief in one's own powers.   **1.** CONFIDENCE.

  2. The quality or state of being safe.   **2.** SAFETY.

  3. A statement that expresses a commitment on the part of its maker as to its truthfulness or to the fulfillment of its conditions.   **3.** WORD *noun*.

assure *verb*

  1. To cause (another) to believe something.   **1.** CONVINCE.

  2. To render certain.   **2.** GUARANTEE *verb*.

assured *adjective*

  1. Having no doubt.   **1.** SURE.

  2. Having a firm belief in one's own powers.   **2.** CONFIDENT.

astonish *verb*

To impress strongly by what is unexpected or unusual.   SURPRISE.

astonishing *adjective*

  1. So remarkable as to elicit disbelief.   **1.** FABULOUS.

  2. Causing momentary shock.   **2.** STARTLING.

astound *verb*

To impress strongly by what is unexpected or unusual.   SURPRISE.

astounding *adjective*

  1. So remarkable as to elicit disbelief.   **1.** FABULOUS.

  2. Causing momentary shock.   **2.** STARTLING.

astral *adjective*

  1. Very broad and noble in character, scope, or grasp.   **1.** GRAND.

  2. Pre-eminent in rank or position.   **2.** HIGHEST.

astrict *verb*

To check the freedom and spontaneity of.   CONSTRAIN.

astringent *adjective*

Having a noticeably sharp, pungent taste or smell.   BITTER *adjective*.

astute *adjective*

Having or showing a clever awareness and resourcefulness in practical matters.   SHREWD.

astuteness *noun*

Skill in perceiving, discriminating, or judging.   DISCERNMENT.

asylum *noun*

  1. Something that physically protects, esp. from danger.   **1.** COVER *noun*.

  2. An institution that provides care and shelter.   **2.** HOME.

  3. The state of being protected or safeguarded, as from danger or hardship.   **3.** REFUGE.

asymmetric also **asymmetrical** *adjective*

Not straight, uniform, or symmetrical.   IRREGULAR.

asymmetry *noun*

Lack of smoothness or regularity.   IRREGULARITY.

athirst *adjective*

  1. Needing or desiring drink.   **1.** THIRSTY.

  2. Intensely desirous or interested.   **2.** EAGER.

atingle *adjective*

Feeling a very strong emotion.   THRILLED.

atman *noun*

Hinduism. The vital principle or animating force within living beings.   SPIRIT.

atmosphere *noun*

  1. The gaseous mixture enveloping the earth.   **1.** AIR *noun*.

2. A general impression produced by a predominant quality or characteristic.

3. A distinctive yet intangible quality deemed typical of a given thing.

4. The totality of surrounding conditions and circumstances affecting growth or development.

atmospheric *adjective*
Of or relating to air.

atramentous *adjective*
Of the darkest achromatic visual value.

atrium *noun*
An area partially or entirely enclosed by walls or buildings.

atrocious *adjective*
1. Disgracefully and grossly offensive.
2. Extremely unpleasant to the senses or feelings.

atrociousness *noun*
1. The quality of passing all moral bounds.
2. The quality or state of being flagrant.

atrocity *noun*
1. The quality or state of being flagrant.
2. The quality of passing all moral bounds.
3. A monstrous offense or evil.

atrophy *noun*
Descent to a lower level or condition.

attach *verb*
To join one thing to another: *the hinges to which the door is attached.*

attachment *noun*
1. Something that attaches as a supplementary part: *bought an attachment for the vacuum cleaner.*
2. The condition of being closely tied to another by affection or faith: *felt a strong attachment for her friend.*

attack *verb*
1. To set upon with violent force: *Germany attacked the Soviet Union in 1941.*

2. To start work on vigorously: *City Hall is attacking the problem of substandard housing.*

attack *noun*
1. The act of attacking: *a sneak attack that left the city in ruins.*

2. A sudden and often acute manifestation of a disease.
3. A method used in dealing with something.

attackable *adjective*
Open to attack and capture because of a lack of protection.

attacker *noun*
One who starts a hostile action.

attain *verb*
1. To succeed in doing.
2. To reach a goal or objective.

attainable *adjective*
Capable of being obtained or used.

attainment *noun*
Something completed successfully.

attaint *noun*
Archaic. A mark of discredit or disgrace.

---

2. AIR *noun.*

3. FLAVOR *noun.*

4. ENVIRONMENT.

AIRY.

BLACK *adjective.*

COURT *noun.*

1. OUTRAGEOUS.
2. OFFENSIVE *adjective.*

1. ENORMITY.
2. FLAGRANCY.

1. FLAGRANCY.
2. ENORMITY.
3. OUTRAGE *noun.*

DETERIORATION.

Syns: affix, clip^2, connect, couple, fasten, fix, moor, secure.

1. **Syns:** accessory, adjunct, supplement.

2. **Syns:** affection^1, bond, devotion, fondness, love, loyalty, tie.

1. **Syns:** aggress, assail, assault, beset, fall on (*or* upon), go at, have at, hit, pitch into (*Informal*), sail in (*or* into), storm, strike.

2. **Syns:** go at, sail in (*or* into), tackle, wade in (*or* into).

1. **Syns:** aggression, assailment, assault, offense, offensive, onrush, onset, onslaught, strike.

2. SEIZURE.
3. APPROACH *noun.*

VULNERABLE.

AGGRESSOR.

1. ACCOMPLISH.
2. ARRIVE AT at **arrive.**

AVAILABLE.

ACCOMPLISHMENT.

STAIN *noun.*

attempt *verb*

To make an attempt to do or make: *Let me attempt to explain. She left without attempting a retort.*

Syns: assay, endeavor, essay, offer, seek, strive, try, undertake. —*Idioms* have a go at, have (*or* make *or* take) a shot at, make a stab at, take a crack (*or* whack) at.

attempt *noun*

1. An effort to do or make something: *the child's first awkward attempt to walk.*
2. An earnest try.

1. **Syns:** assay, endeavor, essay, offer, take (*Slang*), trial, try, undertaking.
2. EFFORT.

attend *verb*

1. To be with or go with (another).
2. To work and care for.
3. To have the care and supervision of.
4. To perceive by ear, usu. attentively.
5. To occur as a consequence.

1. ACCOMPANY.
2. SERVE.
3. TEND[2].
4. HEAR.
5. FOLLOW.

attend to *verb*

To put into correct or conclusive form.

SETTLE.

attendant *noun*

1. A person who helps.
2. One that accompanies another.

1. HELPER.
2. ACCOMPANIMENT.

attendant *adjective*

Occurring in company with.

ACCOMPANYING.

attending *adjective*

Occurring in company with.

ACCOMPANYING.

attend to *verb*

SEE **attend.**

attention *noun*

1. Concentration of the mental powers on something: *The speaker held my full attention.*
2. The act of noting, observing, or taking into account.

1. **Syns:** attentiveness, concentration, consideration, heedfulness.
2. NOTICE *noun.*

attentive *adjective*

1. Concentrating the mental powers on something: *an attentive audience.*

1. **Syns:** advertent, heedful, intent, observant. —*Idioms* all ears (*or* eyes), on the ball.
   Near-syns: alert, aware, mindful, regardful, watchful; concerned, eager, interested, keen; concentrating.
   Ants: inattentive, distracted.

2. Full of polite concern for the well-being of others: *very attentive to her guests.*

2. **Syns:** considerate, courteous, gallant, polite, solicitous, thoughtful.

attentiveness *noun*

Concentration of the mental powers on something.

ATTENTION.

attenuate *verb*

1. To lessen the strength of by or as if by admixture.
2. To become diffuse.
3. To lessen or deplete the nerve, energy, or strength of.

1. DILUTE *verb.*
2. THIN *verb.*
3. ENERVATE.

attenuate *adjective*

Having little flesh or fat on the body.

THIN *adjective.*

attest *verb*

1. To assure the certainty or validity of.
2. To confirm formally as true, accurate, or genuine.
3. To give grounds for believing in the existence or presence of.
4. To give evidence or testimony under oath.

1. CONFIRM.
2. CERTIFY.
3. INDICATE.

4. TESTIFY.

attestant *noun*

One who testifies, esp. in court.

WITNESS *noun.*

attestation *noun*

That which confirms.

CONFIRMATION.

attire *noun*

Articles worn to cover the body.

DRESS *noun.*

attire *verb*
To put clothes on.

DRESS *verb*.

attitude *noun*
1. A frame of mind affecting one's thoughts or behavior.
2. A general cast of mind with regard to something.
3. The way in which a person holds or carries his body.
4. The way in which one is placed or arranged.

1. POSTURE *noun*.
2. SENTIMENT.
3. POSTURE *noun*.
4. POSITION *noun*.

attitudinize *verb*
1. To represent oneself in a given character or as other than what one is.
2. To assume an exaggerated or unnatural attitude or pose.

1. POSE *verb*.
2. POSTURE *verb*.

attract *verb*
1. To direct or impel to oneself by some quality or action: *A new celebrity attracted the crowd's attention. A handsome man attracts all eyes.*
2. To arouse the interest and attention of.

1. *Syns:* allure, appeal, draw, lure, magnetize, pull, take.
2. INTEREST *verb*.

attracting *adjective*
Pleasing to the eye or mind.

ATTRACTIVE.

attraction *noun*
The power or quality of attracting: *the attraction of living in a big city. City life holds no attraction for the farm family. She is a woman of great attraction to men.*

Syns: allure, allurement, appeal, attractiveness, call, charisma, charm, draw, enchantment, fascination, glamour (*also* glamor), lure, magnetism, pull, witchery.

attractive *adjective*
1. Pleasing to the eye or mind: *an attractive woman; an attractive offer.*

1. *Syns:* alluring, appealing, attracting, bewitching, captivating, charming, come-hither, enchanting, engaging, enticing, entrancing, fascinating, fetching, glamorous (*also* glamourous), lovely, magnetic, prepossessing, pretty, sweet, taking, tempting, winning, winsome.
Near-ants: abhorrent, disgusting, distasteful, loathsome, obnoxious, repugnant, revolting, sickening, vile.
Ants: repellent, repulsive.

2. Having qualities that delight the eye.
3. Pleasingly suited to the wearer.

2. BEAUTIFUL.
3. BECOMING.

attractiveness *noun*
The power or quality of attracting.

ATTRACTION.

attribute *verb*
To regard as belonging to or resulting from another: *a painting attributed to da Vinci.*

Syns: accredit, ascribe, assign, charge, credit, impute, lay[1], refer.

attribute *noun*
1. A distinctive element.
2. An object associated with and serving to identify something else.

1. QUALITY *noun*.
2. SYMBOL *noun*.

attribution *noun*
The act of attributing: *the attribution of a previously unknown symphony to Mozart.*

Syns: ascription, assignment, credit, imputation.

attrition *noun*
A feeling of regret for one's sins or misdeeds.

PENITENCE.

attune *verb*
1. To alter (parts of a device) for proper functioning.
2. To bring (oneself) into harmony with one's environment.
3. To bring into accord.

1. ADJUST.
2. ADJUST.
3. HARMONIZE.

atypical also **atypic** *adjective*
1. Departing from the normal.
2. Not usual or ordinary.

1. ABNORMAL.
2. UNUSUAL.

au courant *adjective*
French. Modern.

CONTEMPORARY *adjective.*

audacious *adjective*
1. Rude and disrespectful.
2. Having or showing courage.
3. Taking or willing to take risks.

1. IMPUDENT.
2. BRAVE *adjective.*
3. DARING *adjective.*

audacity *noun*
1. The state or quality of being impudent.
2. Willingness to take risks.

1. IMPUDENCE.
2. DARING *noun.*

audience *noun*
1. The body of persons who admire a public personality, esp. an entertainer.
2. A chance to be heard.

1. PUBLIC *noun.*
2. HEARING.

audition *noun*
1. The sense by which sound is perceived.
2. A chance to be heard.

1. HEARING.
2. HEARING.

au fait *adjective*
1. *French.* Having the ability to perform well.
2. *French.* Conforming to accepted standards.

1. ABLE.
2. CORRECT *adjective.*

aught *noun*
Archaic. No thing; not anything.

NOTHING *noun.*

augment *verb*
To make or become greater or larger.

INCREASE *verb.*

augmentation *noun*
1. Something tending to augment something else.
2. Something added to another for embellishment or completion.
3. The act of increasing or rising.

1. ADDITION.
2. ACCOMPANIMENT.
3. INCREASE *noun.*

augur *verb*
To tell about or make known (future events) by or as if by supernatural means.

PROPHESY.

augur *noun*
A person who foretells future events by or as if by supernatural means.

PROPHET.

augury *noun*
A phenomenon that serves as a sign or warning of some future good or evil.

OMEN.

august *adjective*
1. Raised to or occupying a high position or rank.
2. Large and impressive in size, scope, or extent.

1. EXALTED.
2. GRAND.

au naturel *adjective*
Not wearing any clothes.

NUDE.

aura *noun*
A general impression produced by a predominant quality or characteristic.

AIR *noun.*

aureate *adjective*
Characterized by language that is elevated and sometimes pompous in style.

SONOROUS.

auricular *adjective*
Known about by very few.

CONFIDENTIAL.

auriflamme *noun*

SEE **oriflamme.**

aurora *noun*
Poetic. The first appearance of daylight in the morning.

DAWN *noun.*

auspex *noun*
A person who foretells future events by or as if by supernatural means.

PROPHET.

auspices *noun*
Aid or support given by a patron.   PATRONAGE.

auspicious *adjective*
1. Indicative of future success.   1. FAVORABLE.
2. Occurring at a fitting or advantageous time.   2. OPPORTUNE.

austere *adjective*
1. Cold and forbidding.   1. BLEAK.
2. *Archaic.* Having a noticeably sharp, pungent taste   2. BITTER *adjective.*
   or smell.

austerity *noun*
The fact or condition of being rigorous and unsparing.   SEVERITY.

autarchic also **autarchical** *adjective*
Having and exercising complete political power and   ABSOLUTE.
control.

autarchy *noun*
A government in which a single leader or party   ABSOLUTISM.
exercises absolute control over all citizens and every
aspect of their lives.

authentic *adjective*
1. Not counterfeit or copied: *an authentic painting by*   1. *Syns:* bona fide, genuine, good,
   Rembrandt.   indubitable, original, real, true,
                                                                      undoubted, unquestionable.
                                                                      Near-ants: artificial, deceptive,
                                                                      delusive, delusory, fake, false,
                                                                      misleading.
                                                                      Ants: unauthentic, spurious.
2. Worthy of belief because of precision, faithfulness to   2. *Syns:* authoritative, convincing,
   an original, etc.: *an authentic re-creation of a*   credible, faithful, true, trustworthy,
   Revolutionary War battle.   valid.

authenticate *verb*
1. To establish as true or genuine.   1. PROVE.
2. To assure the certainty or validity of.   2. CONFIRM.

authentication *noun*
That which confirms.   CONFIRMATION.

authenticity *noun*
The quality of being authentic: *recognized the*   *Syns:* genuineness, legitimacy, realness,
authenticity of the painting.   truthfulness, validity.

author *noun*
One that creates, founds, or originates.   ORIGINATOR.

author *verb*
To be the author of (a published work or works).   PUBLISH.

authoritarian *adjective*
1. Characterized by or favoring absolute obedience to   1. *Syns:* autocratic, despotic, dictatorial,
   authority: *Nazi Germany was an authoritarian*   doctrinaire, totalitarian, tyrannical
   society.   (*also* tyrannic).
2. Tending to dictate.   2. DICTATORIAL.

authoritarian *noun*
One who imposes or favors absolute obedience to   *Syns:* autocrat, despot, dictator, martinet,
authority: *always felt his parents were authoritarians.*   tyrant.

authoritarianism *noun*
A political doctrine advocating the principle of absolute   ABSOLUTISM.
rule.

authoritative *adjective*
1. Exercising authority: *an authoritative young*   1. *Syns:* commanding, dominant, lordly,
   executive.   masterful, mighty, powerful, weighty.
2. Having or arising from authority: *an authoritative*   2. *Syns:* conclusive, official, sanctioned,
   interpretation of Mozart; an authoritative order.   standard.
3. Worthy of belief because of precision, faithfulness to   3. AUTHENTIC.
   an original, etc.

authority *noun*
1. The right and power to command, decide, rule, or judge: *The mayor has the authority to convene the school committee.*

2. A person or group having the right and power to command, decide, rule, or judge: *governmental authorities; school authorities.*
3. A person with a high degree of knowledge or skill in a particular field.
4. Conferred power.

authorization *noun*
Approval for an action, esp. as granted by one in authority.

authorize *verb*
1. To give authority to: *I authorized my partner to negotiate in my behalf.*
2. To give one's consent to.

autochthonal *adjective*
autochthonic *adjective*
autochthonous also **autochthonal, autochthonic** *adjective*
Belonging to one because of the place or circumstances of one's birth.

autocracy *noun*
1. A government in which a single leader or party exercises absolute control over all citizens and every aspect of their lives.
2. A political doctrine advocating the principle of absolute rule.

autocrat *noun*
One who imposes or favors absolute obedience to authority.

autocratic *adjective*
1. Having and exercising complete political power and control.
2. Characterized by or favoring absolute obedience to authority.

autograph *verb*
To affix one's signature to.

automatic *adjective*
1. Acting or happening without apparent forethought, prompting, or planning.
2. Performed or performing automatically and impersonally.

autonomous *adjective*
Having political independence.

autonomy *noun*
The condition of being politically free.

auxiliary *adjective*
1. Giving or able to give help or support: *an auxiliary division of the fire department.*

2. Used or held in reserve: *an auxiliary supply of oil; an auxiliary engine.*

auxiliary *noun*
A person who holds a position auxiliary to another and assumes some of his responsibilities.

avail *verb*
To be an advantage to.

1. *Syns:* clout (*Informal*), command, control, domination, dominion, jurisdiction, mastery, might, power, prerogative, say-so (*Informal*), sway.
2. *Syns:* higher-up (*Informal*), official. —*Idiom* the powers that be.

3. EXPERT *noun*.

4. FACULTY.

PERMISSION.

1. *Syns:* accredit, commission, empower, enable, entitle, license, qualify.
2. PERMIT *verb*.
SEE **autochthonous**.
SEE **autochthonous**.

NATIVE *adjective*.

1. ABSOLUTISM.

2. ABSOLUTISM.

AUTHORITARIAN *noun*.

1. ABSOLUTE.

2. AUTHORITARIAN *adjective*.

SIGN *verb*.

1. SPONTANEOUS.

2. PERFUNCTORY.

FREE *adjective*.

FREEDOM.

1. *Syns:* accessory, adjuvant, aiding, ancillary, assisting, collateral, contributory, helping, subsidiary.
2. *Syns:* back-up, emergency, reserve, secondary, standby, supplemental, supplementary.

ASSISTANT.

PROFIT *verb*.

avail *noun*
The quality of being suitable or adaptable to an end.   USE *noun*.

available *adjective*
Capable of being obtained or used: *All the available*   **Syns:** attainable, disponible, gettable,
information indicated that war was imminent.   obtainable, procurable. —*Idiom* to be had.

avarice *noun*
Excessive desire for more than one needs or deserves.   GREED.

avaricious *adjective*
Having a strong urge to obtain or possess something,   GREEDY.
esp. material wealth, in quantity.

avenge *verb*
To exact revenge for: *avenged his sister's death by*   **Syns:** fix (*Informal*), pay back, pay off,
killing her murderer.   redress, repay, requite, vindicate.
                                                              —*Idioms* even the score, get even with,
                                                              pay back in full measure (*or* in kind *or* in
                                                              one's own coin), settle (*or* square)
                                                              accounts, take an eye for an eye, wreak
                                                              vengeance on.

avengement *noun*
The act of retaliating.   RETALIATION.

avenging *noun*
The act of retaliating.   RETALIATION.

avenue *noun*
A course affording passage from one place to another.   WAY.

aver *verb*
To put into words positively and with conviction.   ASSERT.

average *noun*
Something, as a type, number, quantity, or degree, that   **Syns:** mean^3, median, medium, norm, par.
represents a midpoint between extremes on a scale of
valuation: *much more intelligent than the average.*

average *adjective*
1. Of moderately good quality but less than excellent.   1. ACCEPTABLE.
2. Being of no special quality or type.   2. ORDINARY *adjective*.
3. To be expected.   3. COMMON *adjective*.

averment *noun*
The act of asserting positively.   ASSERTION.

averse *adjective*
Not inclined or willing to do or undertake.   INDISPOSED.

averseness *noun*
The state of not being disposed or inclined.   INDISPOSITION.

aversion *noun*
1. A state of mind brought on by something that is   1. ANTIPATHY.
   antipathetic.
2. Extreme repugnance excited by something offensive.   2. DISGUST *noun*.
3. A feeling of fear and repugnance.   3. HORROR.

aversive *adjective*
Arousing deep-seated dislike.   ANTIPATHETIC.

avert *verb*
1. To change the direction or course of.   1. TURN *verb*.
2. To prohibit from occurring by advance planning or   2. PREVENT.
   action.

avid *adjective*
1. Intensely desirous or interested.   1. EAGER.
2. Having a strong urge to obtain or possess   2. GREEDY.
   something, esp. material wealth, in quantity.
3. Having an insatiable appetite for an activity or   3. VORACIOUS.
   pursuit.

avidity *noun*
Excessive desire for more than one needs or deserves.   GREED.

avidness *noun*
The quality or condition of being voracious.   VORACITY.

avoid *verb*

To keep away from: *They drove through the countryside, avoiding cities. Referees must avoid taking sides.*

Syns: bypass, dodge, duck, elude, escape, eschew, evade, get around, shun. —*Idioms* fight shy of, give a wide berth to, have no truck with, keep (*or* stay *or* steer) clear of.

avoidance *noun*

The act, an instance, or a means of avoiding.

avoirdupois *noun*

Informal. The state or quality of being physically heavy.

ESCAPE *noun.*

HEAVINESS.

avouch *verb*

To put into words positively and with conviction.

ASSERT.

avow *verb*

1. To recognize, often reluctantly, the reality or truth of.

2. To put into words positively and with conviction.

1. ACKNOWLEDGE.

2. ASSERT.

avowal *noun*

1. The act of admitting to something.

2. The act of asserting positively.

1. ACKNOWLEDGMENT.

2. ASSERTION.

await *verb*

To anticipate confidently.

EXPECT.

awake *adjective*

1. Not in a state of sleep.

2. Marked by comprehension, cognizance, and perception.

1. WAKEFUL.

2. AWARE.

awake *verb*

To cease sleeping.

WAKE *verb.*

awaken *verb*

1. To cease sleeping.

2. To induce or elicit (a reaction or emotion).

1. WAKE *verb.*

2. AROUSE.

award *noun*

1. Something given in return for a service or accomplishment.

2. A memento received as a symbol of excellence or victory.

1. REWARD *noun.*

2. TROPHY.

award *verb*

1. To give formally or officially.

2. To let have as a favor or privilege.

1. CONFER.

2. GRANT *verb.*

aware *adjective*

Marked by comprehension, cognizance, and perception: *I am aware of my own shortcomings.*

Syns: alive (to), awake (to), cognizant, conversant (with), hip (to) (*Slang*), knowing, mindful, sensible, sentient, wise[1] (to). —*Idiom* on to.

awareness *noun*

1. The condition of being aware: *His awareness of danger made him cautious.*

2. Recognition of worth, quality, importance, etc.

1. **Syns:** alertness, cognizance, consciousness, perception, sense.

2. APPRECIATION.

awash *adjective*

Full to the point of flowing over.

BIG *adjective.*

away *adjective*

Not present.

ABSENT.

awe *noun*

The emotion aroused by something awe-inspiring or astounding.

WONDER *noun.*

awful *adjective*

1. Causing or able to cause fear.

2. Very bad.

1. FEARFUL.

2. TERRIBLE.

awfully *adverb*

Informal. To a high degree.

VERY *adverb.*

awkward *adjective*
1. Lacking dexterity and grace in physical movement: *an awkward girl with huge hands and feet; an awkward dancer.*

2. Clumsily lacking in the ability to do or perform.
3. Difficult to handle or manage: *an awkward bundle to carry.*

4. Characterized by embarrassment and discomfort: *an awkward silence.*
5. Causing self-conscious distress.
6. Characterized by inappropriateness and gracelessness, esp. in expression.

awry *adjective*
Not in accordance with what is usual or expected.

axiom *noun*
A broad and basic rule or truth.

ay *noun & adverb*

aye also **ay** *noun*
An affirmative vote or voter.

aye also **ay** *adverb*
It is so; as you say or ask.

1. *Syns:* clumsy, gawky, graceless, inept, klutzy (*Slang*), lumbering, lumpish, ungainly, ungraceful. —*Idiom* all thumbs.
2. UNSKILLFUL.
3. *Syns:* bulky, clumsy, cumbersome, cumbrous, inconvenient, unhandy, unmanageable, unwieldy.
4. *Syns:* constrained, uncomfortable, uneasy.
5. EMBARRASSING.
6. UNFORTUNATE *adjective*.

AMISS *adjective*.

LAW *noun*.

SEE **aye**.

YES *noun*.

YES *adverb*.

B

babble *verb*
1. To talk rapidly, incoherently, or indistinctly: *babies babbling in their cribs.*

2. To talk volubly, persistently, and usu. inconsequentially.

babble *noun*
1. Unintelligible or foolish talk: *a babble of voices in the airport; a speech that was just so much babble.*

2. Incessant and usu. inconsequential talk.

babbling *adjective*
Emitting a murmuring sound felt to resemble a laugh.

babe *noun*
1. A very young child.
2. *Slang.* A guileless, unsophisticated person.

babel *noun*
Sounds or a sound, esp. when loud, confused, or disagreeable.

baby *noun*
1. A very young child: *a tiny baby in its mother's arms.*

1. *Syns:* blather, chatter, gabble, gibber, jabber, prate, prattle.
Near-syns: clack, drivel, drool, jaw (*Slang*), rattle, yak (*Slang*), yammer, yap (*Slang*).
2. CHATTER *verb*.

1. *Syns:* blather, blatherskite, double-talk, gabble, gibberish, jabber, jabberwocky (*also* jabberwock), nonsense, prate, prattle, twaddle.
2. CHATTER *noun*.

LAUGHING.

1. BABY *noun*.
2. INNOCENT *noun*.

NOISE *noun*.

1. *Syns:* babe, bambino, infant, neonate, newborn, nursling. —*Idiom* bundle of joy.

2. A person who behaves in a childish, weak, or spoiled way: *a real baby who is afraid to assert herself.*

2. *Syns:* milksop, milquetoast, mollycoddle, weakling. —*Idiom* mama's boy (*or* girl).

baby *verb*
To treat with indulgence and often overtender care: *annoys her son by hovering over him and babying him.*

Syns: cater to, coddle, cosset, indulge, mollycoddle, overindulge, pamper, spoil.

babyish *adjective*
1. Of or like a baby: *a lovely babyish face.*
2. Of or characteristic of a child, esp. in immaturity.

1. *Syns:* cherubic, childlike, infantile.
2. CHILDISH.

back *noun*
The part or area farthest from the front: *the back of the house.*

Syns: posterior, rear[1], rearward.

back *verb*
1. To move in a reverse direction: *As she talked she kept backing slowly toward the door.*

1. *Syns:* backtrack, fall back, retreat, retrocede, retrograde, retrogress. —*Idiom* retrace one's steps.

2. To aid the cause of by approving or favoring.
3. To present evidence in support of: *backed his claim by showing the receipts.*
4. To supply capital to or for.
5. To assure the certainty or validity of.

2. SUPPORT *verb.*
3. *Syns:* buttress, corroborate, justify, substantiate.
4. FINANCE *verb.*
5. CONFIRM.

back down (or **out**) *verb*
To abandon a former position or commitment: *She accepted the invitation but backed down at the last minute.*

Syns: fink out (*Slang*), retreat.

back *adjective*
1. Located in the rear: *the back porch.*

1. *Syns:* after, hind, hindmost (*also* hindermost), posterior, postern, rear[1].
2. *Syn:* outlying.

2. Distant from a center of activity: *back roads.*

back *adverb*
1. In or toward a former location or condition: *going back to their home town.*
2. Toward the back.

1. *Syns:* about, around, backward (*also* backwards), rearward, round.
2. BACKWARD *adverb.*

backbiting *adjective*
Damaging to the reputation.

LIBELOUS.

backbreaking *adjective*
Imposing a severe test of bodily or spiritual strength.

BURDENSOME.

back down (or **out**) *verb*

SEE **back.**

backer *noun*
A person who supports or champions an activity, institution, etc.

PATRON.

backfire *verb*
To produce an unexpected and undesired result: *His elaborate plan to bypass his boss backfired.*

Syns: boomerang, bounce back, rebound.

background *noun*
Past events surrounding a person or thing.

HISTORY.

backing *noun*
Aid or support given by a patron.

PATRONAGE.

backland *noun*
An uninhabited region left in its natural state.

WILD *noun.*

backlog *noun*
A supply stored or hidden for future use.

HOARD *noun.*

backside *noun*
The part of one's back on which one rests in sitting.

BOTTOM *noun.*

backslide *verb*
To slip from a higher or better condition to a former, usu. lower or poorer one.

RELAPSE *verb.*

backslide *noun*
A slipping from a higher or better condition to a lower or poorer one.

LAPSE *noun.*

backsliding *noun*
A slipping from a higher or better condition to a lower or poorer one.

LAPSE *noun*.

backtrack *verb*
To move in a reverse direction.

BACK *verb*.

back-up *adjective*
Used or held in reserve.

AUXILIARY *adjective*.

backward *adjective*
1. Directed or facing toward the back or rear: *a backward glance.*
2. Not progressing and developing as fast as others, as in economic and social aspects: *backward peoples; backward countries.*
3. Economically and socially below standard.
4. Clinging to obsolete ideas.
5. Reticent or reserved in manner.
6. Having only a limited ability to learn and understand: *a backward child.*

7. Exhibiting lack of education or knowledge.

1. *Syns:* retrograde, retrogressive.
2. *Syns:* behindhand, lagging, underdeveloped, undeveloped.
3. DEPRESSED.
4. UNPROGRESSIVE.
5. MODEST.
6. *Syns:* dull, retarded, simple, simple-minded, slow, slow-witted, weak-minded.
   Near-syns: feebleminded, half-witted, imbecilic, limited, moronic.
7. IGNORANT.

backward also **backwards** *adverb*
1. In or toward a former location or condition.
2. Toward the back: *jumped backward to avoid the oncoming taxi.*

1. BACK *adverb*.
2. *Syns:* about, around, back, rearward, round.

backwards *adverb*

SEE **backward**.

bad *adjective*
1. Below a standard of quality: *a really bad book.*

2. Morally objectionable.
3. Misbehaving, often in a troublesome way.
4. Not pleasant or agreeable.
5. Bringing, predicting, or characterized by misfortune: *a run of bad luck; bad times.*
6. Impaired because of decay: *a bad apple.*

1. *Syns:* bum (*Informal*), deficient, unsatisfactory. —*Idioms* below par, not up to scratch (*or* snuff).
2. EVIL *adjective*.
3. NAUGHTY.
4. UNPLEASANT.
5. *Syns:* evil, ill, inauspicious, unfavorable.
6. *Syns:* decayed, decomposed, putrid, rotten, spoiled.
   Near-syns: moldy, musty, rancid, worm-eaten; putrefied; turned; stale.
   Ant: good.

7. Causing harm or injury.

7. HARMFUL.

bad *noun*
Whatever is destructive or harmful.

EVIL *noun*.

bad *adverb*
Informal. In such a way as to inflict hardship or difficulty.

HARD *adverb*.

badge *noun*
An emblem of honor worn on one's clothing.

DECORATION.

badger *verb*
1. To torment with persistent insult or ridicule.
2. To trouble persistently from or as if from all sides.

1. BAIT *verb*.
2. BESIEGE.

badland *noun*
A tract of unproductive land.

BARREN *noun*.

badly *adverb*
1. In such a way as to inflict hardship or difficulty.
2. Not in the right way or on the proper course.

1. HARD *adverb*.
2. WRONG *adverb*.

bad-mannered *adjective*
Lacking good manners.

RUDE.

badness *noun*
Whatever is destructive or harmful.

EVIL *noun*.

bad-tempered *adjective*
Having or showing a bad temper.   ILL-TEMPERED.

baffle *verb*
To prevent from accomplishing a purpose.   FRUSTRATE.

bag *verb*
1. To curve outward past the normal or usual limit.   1. BULGE *verb*.
2. *Slang.* To gain possession of, esp. after a struggle or   2. TAKE *verb*.
   chase.
3. *Slang.* To take into custody as a prisoner.   3. ARREST *verb*.

bag *noun*
1. *Slang.* Something at which a person excels.   1. FORTE.
2. *Slang.* A sphere of activity, study, or interest. 2. AREA.
3. *Slang.* An ugly, frightening old woman.   3. WITCH *noun*.

baggage *noun*
A vulgar, promiscuous woman who flouts propriety.   SLUT.

bail¹ *noun*
1. *Law.* Money supplied for the temporary release of an   1. BOND *noun*.
   arrested person that guarantees his appearance for
   trial.
2. One who posts bond.   2. BONDSMAN.

bail² *verb*
To take a substance, as liquid, from a container by   DIP *verb*.
plunging the hand or a utensil into it.

bail out *verb*
To catapult oneself from a disabled aircraft.   EJECT.

bail³ *verb*
Austral. To take property or possessions from (a person,   ROB.
company, etc.) unlawfully and usu. forcibly.

bail out *verb*   SEE **bail²**.

bailsman *noun*
One who posts bond.   BONDSMAN.

bairn *noun*
Scot. A young person between birth and puberty. CHILD.

bait *verb*
1. To torment with persistent insult or ridicule: 1. *Syns:* badger, bullyrag, heckle, hector,
   Neighborhood toughs baited minority groups with   hound, needle (*Informal*), ride
   racist remarks.   (*Informal*), taunt. —*Idiom* wave the
                                                          red flag in front of the bull.
2. To excite (another) by exposing something desirable   2. TANTALIZE.
   while keeping it out of reach.

bait *noun*
Something that leads one into a place or situation from   LURE *noun*.
which escape is difficult.

bake *verb*
To feel or look hot.   BURN *verb*.

baking *adjective*
Marked by much heat.   HOT *adjective*.

balance *noun*
1. A stable state characterized by the cancellation of   1. *Syns:* counterpoise, equilibrium,
   all forces by equal opposing forces: *Man has upset*   equipoise, stasis.
   the balance of nature by destroying certain species.
2. A stable, calm state of the emotions: *regained his*   2. *Syns:* aplomb, composure, cool (*Slang*),
   balance slowly after the divorce.   coolness, equanimity, poise, self-
                                                          possession.
3. Satisfying arrangement marked by even distribution   3. PROPORTION.
   of elements, as in a design.
4. What remains after a part has been used or   4. *Syns:* leavings, remainder, remains,
   subtracted: *a balance due of $50.*   remnant, residue, rest².

balance *verb*
1. To put in balance: *balancing the weights on both*   1. *Syns:* counterbalance, equalize,
   sides of the scale.   stabilize, steady.

   2. To act as an equalizing weight or force to: *Her basic kindness balances her quick temper.*

   3. To place or be placed on a narrow or insecure surface: *balancing a glass on the edge of the table.*
   4. To examine so as to note the similarities and differences of.
   5. To make up for the defects of.

balanced *adjective*
   1. Neither favorable nor unfavorable.
   2. Having components pleasingly combined.
   3. Characterized by or displaying symmetry, esp. correspondence in scale or measure.
   4. Possessing, proceeding from, or exhibiting good judgment and prudence.

bald *adjective*
   1. Without the usual covering.
   2. Without addition, decoration, or qualification.

balderdash *noun*
Something that does not have or make sense.

bald-faced *adjective*
Characterized by or done without shame.

baleful *adjective*
   1. Portending future disaster.
   2. Strongly suggestive of great harm, menace, or evil.

balk *verb*
To prevent from accomplishing a purpose.

   balk *noun*
A large, oblong piece of wood or other material, used esp. for construction.

balky *adjective*
Given to acting in opposition to others.

ball *noun*
A party or gathering for dancing.

balloon *verb*
To curve outward past the normal or usual limit.

ballot *verb*
To select by vote for an office.

balloter *noun*
One who votes.

ballup *noun*

ball up *verb*
   1. *Slang.* To harm irreparably through inept handling; make a mess of.
   2. *Slang.* To put into total disorder.

   ballup *noun*
Slang. A lack of order or regular arrangement.

ballyhoo *verb*
   1. *Informal.* To make known vigorously the positive features of (a product).
   2. *Informal.* To increase or seek to increase the importance or reputation of by favorable publicity.

   ballyhoo *noun*
Informal. A systematic effort to increase the importance or reputation of by favorable publicity.

balm *verb*
To make or become calm.

balmy *adjective*
   1. Free from severity or violence, as in movement.
   2. *Slang.* So senseless as to be laughable.

---

   2. *Syns:* compensate (for), counteract, counterbalance, counterpoise, countervail, make up (for), offset, set off.
   3. *Syns:* perch, poise.

   4. COMPARE.

   5. COMPENSATE.

   1. FAIR *adjective.*
   2. SYMMETRICAL.
   3. SYMMETRICAL.

   4. SANE.

   1. BARE *adjective.*
   2. BARE *adjective.*

NONSENSE.

SHAMELESS.

   1. FATEFUL.
   2. MALIGN *adjective.*

FRUSTRATE.

BEAM *noun.*

CONTRARY *adjective.*

DANCE *noun.*

BULGE *verb.*

ELECT *verb.*

ELECTOR.

SEE **ball up.**

   1. BOTCH *verb.*

   2. CONFUSE.

DISORDER *noun.*

   1. ADVERTISE.

   2. PROMOTE.

PROMOTION.

CALM *verb.*

   1. GENTLE *adjective.*
   2. FOOLISH.

baloney also **boloney** *noun*
Slang. Something that does not have or make sense. NONSENSE.

bambino *noun*
A very young child. BABY *noun.*

bamboozle *verb*
Informal. To cause to accept what is false, esp. by trickery or misrepresentation. DECEIVE.

ban *verb*
1. To refuse to allow. 1. FORBID.
2. To keep from being published or transmitted. 2. CENSOR.

ban *noun*
A refusal to allow. FORBIDDANCE.

banal *adjective*
1. Without freshness or appeal due to overuse. 1. TRITE.
2. Lacking the qualities requisite for spiritedness and originality. 2. INSIPID.

banality *noun*
1. A trite expression or idea. 1. CLICHÉ *noun.*
2. The state or quality of being insipid. 2. INSIPIDITY.

band¹ *noun*
A thin strip of material or color: *wore a red band on her head.* **Syns:** bandeau, fillet, strip², stripe.

band *verb*
To encircle with or as if with a band: *The equator bands the earth. The waist on this dress is banded in velvet.* **Syns:** begird, belt, cincture, compass, encompass, engird, engirdle, gird, girdle, girt, ring.

band² *noun*
1. A group of performers: *a band of actors touring the country.* 1. **Syns:** company, corps, party, troop, troupe.
2. An organized group of criminals, hoodlums, or wrongdoers. 2. GANG.
3. A usu. small number of individuals. 3. GROUP *noun.*

band *verb*
To assemble or join in a group: *The parents of the handicapped banded together to pressure the legislature.* **Syns:** combine, gang up (*Informal*), league, unite.

bandage *verb*
To apply therapeutic materials to (a wound). DRESS *verb.*

bandeau *noun*
A thin strip of material or color. BAND¹ *noun.*

banderol *noun* SEE **banderole.**

banderole also **banderol, bannerol** *noun*
Fabric used esp. as a symbol. FLAG¹ *noun.*

bandy *verb*
To give and receive. EXCHANGE.

bane *noun*
1. Anything that is injurious, destructive, or fatal. 1. POISON *noun.*
2. A cause of suffering or harm. 2. CURSE *noun.*
3. Something that causes total loss or severe impairment of one's health, fortune, honor, hopes, etc. 3. RUIN *noun.*

baneful *adjective*
1. Extremely destructive or harmful. 1. VIRULENT.
2. Portending future disaster. 2. FATEFUL.

bang *noun*
1. A forceful movement causing a loud noise. 1. SLAM *noun.*
2. A sudden sharp, explosive noise. 2. REPORT *noun.*
3. An earsplitting, explosive noise. 3. BLAST *noun.*
4. A sudden sharp, powerful stroke. 4. BLOW².
5. *Slang.* A strong, pleasant feeling of excitement or stimulation. 5. THRILL *noun.*
6. A dazzling, often sudden instance of success. 6. HIT *noun.*

bang *verb*
1. To strike, set down, or close in such a way as to make a loud noise: *banged the door behind him.*
2. To make an earsplitting, explosive noise.

1. *Syns:* clap, crash, slam, whack.

2. BLAST *verb.*

bang *adverb*
Informal. Without the slightest deviation in any respect.

PRECISELY.

banish *verb*
1. To force to leave a country or place by official decree: *was banished for fomenting a rebellion.*
2. To rid one's mind of.

1. *Syns:* deport, exile, expatriate, expel, ostracize, transport.

2. DISMISS.

banishment *noun*
Enforced removal from one s native country by official decree.

EXILE *noun.*

bank¹ *verb*
To place (money) in a bank: *banks her savings rather than keeping the money at home.*

Syns: deposit, lay away, salt away (*Informal*), sock away (*Informal*).

bank on (or **upon**) *verb*
Informal. To place trust or confidence in.

DEPEND ON at **depend.**

bank² *noun*
A group of things gathered haphazardly.

HEAP *noun.*

bank *verb*
To put into a disordered pile.

HEAP *verb.*

bank on (or **upon**) *verb*

SEE **bank¹.**

bankroll *verb*
Slang. To supply capital to or for.

FINANCE.

bankrupt *verb*
To reduce to financial insolvency.

RUIN *verb.*

bankruptcy *noun*
The condition of being financially insolvent.

FAILURE.

banned *adjective*
Not allowed.

FORBIDDEN.

banner *noun*
Fabric used esp. as a symbol.

FLAG¹ *noun.*

banner *adjective*
Exceptionally good of its kind.

EXCELLENT.

bannerol *noun*

SEE **banderole.**

banquet *noun*
A large meal elaborately prepared or served.

FEAST.

bantam *adjective*
Notably below average in amount, size, or scope.

LITTLE.

banter *verb*
To tease or mock good-humoredly.

JOKE *verb.*

baptize *verb*
To give a name or title to.

NAME *verb.*

bar *noun*
1. Anything that impedes or prevents entry or passage: *His extreme conservatism is a bar to his acceptance by the workers.*

1. *Syns:* barricade, barrier, block, hamper, hindrance, hurdle, impediment, obstacle, obstruction, snag, stop, traverse, wall.

2. A relatively long, straight, rigid piece of metal or other solid material.

2. STICK *noun.*

3. A judicial assembly.

3. COURT *noun.*

bar *verb*
1. To shut in with or as if with bars: *In a rage, she barred herself in her room.*

1. *Syns:* confine, lock, wall.

2. To keep from being admitted, included, or considered.

2. EXCLUDE.

3. To stop or prevent passage of.

3. OBSTRUCT.

barbarian *noun*
An unrefined, rude person.

BOOR.

barbarian *adjective*
1. Lacking in delicacy or refinement.
2. Not civilized.

1. COARSE.
2. UNCIVILIZED.

barbaric *adjective*
1. Not civilized.
2. Lacking in delicacy or refinement.

1. UNCIVILIZED.
2. COARSE.

barbarism *noun*
A term whose form offends against established usage standards.

CORRUPTION.

barbarity *noun*
A cruel act or an instance of cruel behavior.

CRUELTY.

barbarous *adjective*
1. Not civilized.
2. Showing or suggesting a disposition to be violently destructive without scruple or restraint.

1. UNCIVILIZED.
2. FIERCE.

bard *noun*
Someone who writes verse.

POET.

bare *adjective*
1. Without the usual covering: *a bare hillside.*

1. *Syns:* bald, denuded, exposed, naked, nude.
Near-syns: arid, bleak, desert, desolate; stripped, uncovered.
Ant: covered.

2. Not wearing any clothes.
3. Containing nothing.
4. Without addition, decoration, or qualification: *just the bare facts, please.*
5. Just sufficient: *won the election by a bare majority.*
6. Being what is specified and nothing more.

2. NUDE.
3. EMPTY *adjective.*
4. *Syns:* bald, dry, plain, simple, unadorned, unvarnished.
5. *Syns:* mere, scant.
6. MERE.

bare *verb*
1. To make bare: *bared his head to the sun.*

1. *Syns:* denude, disrobe, divest, expose, strip[1], uncover.

2. To make visible; bring to view.

2. REVEAL.

barefaced *adjective*
Characterized by or done without shame.

SHAMELESS.

barely *adverb*
By a very little; almost not: *could barely hear the music through the static.*

Syns: just, hardly, scarce.
Near-syns: almost, approximately, nearly.

bareness *noun*
The state of being without clothes.

NUDITY.

bargain *noun*
1. An agreement, esp. one involving a sale or exchange: *kept his part of the bargain and mowed the lawn.*

1. *Syns:* compact[2], contract, covenant, deal (*Informal*), transaction.

2. An act or state of agreeing between parties regarding a course of action.

2. AGREEMENT.

3. Something offered or bought at a low price: *a book that is a real bargain.*

3. *Syns:* buy, giveaway (*Informal*), steal (*Slang*).

bargain *verb*
1. To argue about the terms, as of a sale.
2. To enter into a formal agreement.

1. HAGGLE.
2. CONTRACT *verb.*

bargain on (or **for**) *verb*
To anticipate confidently.

EXPECT.

bargain on (or **for**) *verb*

SEE **bargain.**

bark *verb*
1. To make a sudden sharp, explosive noise.
2. To speak abruptly and sharply.

1. CRACK *verb.*
2. SNAP *verb.*

bark *noun*
A sudden sharp, explosive noise.

REPORT *noun.*

barnacle *noun*
One who depends on another for support without reciprocating.

PARASITE.

barnyard *adjective*
Offensive to accepted standards of decency.

OBSCENE.

baronial *adjective*
Large and impressive in size, scope, or extent.

GRAND.

baroque *adjective*
Elaborately and heavily ornamented.

ORNATE.

barrage *noun*
A concentrated outpouring, as of missiles, words, or blows: *was hit with a barrage of insults.*

Syns: bombardment, burst, cannonade, fusillade, hail¹, salvo, shower, storm, volley.

barrage *verb*
To direct a barrage at: *barraging the speaker with questions.*

Syns: bombard, cannonade, pepper, shower.

barrel *noun*
Informal. A great deal.

HEAP *noun.*

barrel *verb*
Slang. To move swiftly.

RUSH *verb.*

barren *adjective*
1. Unable to produce offspring: *a barren couple who plan to adopt.*
2. Lacking or unable to produce growing plants or crops: *a barren desert; barren soil.*

1. *Syns:* childless, infecund, infertile, sterile.
2. *Syns:* infertile, unproductive.
   Near-syns: arid, desert, dry, parched; bleak, depleted, impoverished, poor, worn-out; fallow; hardscrabble.
   Ant: fertile.

3. Having no useful result.
4. Lacking a desirable element.

3. FUTILE.
4. EMPTY *adjective.*

barren *noun*
A tract of unproductive land: *the pine barrens of New Jersey.*

Syns: badland, desert¹, waste, wasteland, wilderness.

barrenness *noun*
1. Total lack of ideas, meaning, or substance.
2. Empty, unfilled space.
3. The state or condition of being unable to reproduce sexually.

1. EMPTINESS.
2. NOTHINGNESS.
3. STERILITY.

barricade *noun*
Anything that impedes or prevents entry or passage.

BAR *noun.*

barrier *noun*
1. Anything that impedes or prevents entry or passage.
2. A solid structure that encloses an area or separates one area from another.

1. BAR *noun.*
2. WALL *noun.*

bar sinister *noun*
A mark of discredit or disgrace.

STAIN *noun.*

basal *adjective*
1. Of or treating the simplest aspects.
2. Arising from or going to the root or source.

1. ELEMENTARY.
2. RADICAL *adjective.*

base¹ *noun*
1. The lowest or supporting part or structure: *built on a base of solid rock.*

1. *Syns:* basis, bed, bottom, foot, footing, foundation, fundament, ground, groundwork, seat, substratum, underpinning.

2. Anything on which something immaterial, such as an argument or charge, rests.
3. A fundamental principle or underlying concept.
4. A center of organization, supply, or activity: *the biggest army base in the East.*
5. *Ling.* The main part of a word to which affixes are attached.

2. BASIS.

3. BASIS.
4. *Syns:* complex, headquarters, installation, station.
5. THEME.

base *verb*
To take or serve as the basis for: *bases her opinions on facts; opinions based on facts.*

Syns: build, establish, found, ground, predicate, rest¹, root in, seat.

base² *adjective*
1. Having or proceeding from low moral standards.
2. Lacking high station or birth.
3. Of decidedly inferior quality.

1. SORDID.
2. LOWLY.
3. SHODDY.

baseborn *adjective*
1. Lacking high station or birth.
2. Born out of wedlock.

1. LOWLY.
2. ILLEGITIMATE.

baseless *adjective*
Having no basis or foundation in fact: *a baseless accusation.*

Syns: bottomless, groundless, idle, unfounded, unwarranted.
Near-syns: indefensible, unjustifiable, unsupported, untenable; empty, vain; foundationless, uncalled-for, ungrounded.

bash *noun*
1. *Informal.* A sudden sharp, powerful stroke.
2. *Slang.* A big, exuberant party.
3. *Slang.* A large or important social gathering.

1. BLOW².
2. BLAST *noun.*
3. PARTY.

bash *verb*
Informal. To deliver (a powerful blow) suddenly and sharply.

HIT *verb.*

bashful *adjective*
Reticent or reserved in manner.

MODEST.

basic *adjective*
1. Of or being an irreducible element.
2. Arising from or going to the root or source.
3. Constituting or forming part of the essence of something.
4. Of or treating the simplest aspects.

1. ELEMENTAL.
2. RADICAL *adjective.*
3. ESSENTIAL *adjective.*
4. ELEMENTARY.

basic *noun*
A fundamental, irreducible constituent of a whole.

ELEMENT.

basically *adverb*
In regard to the essence of a matter.

ESSENTIALLY.

basin *noun*
1. The region drained by a river system: *Much of the country lies within the Mississippi-Missouri basin.*
2. An area sunk below its surroundings.

1. *Syn:* watershed.
2. DEPRESSION.

basis *noun*
1. Anything on which something immaterial, such as an argument or charge, rests: *making decisions on the basis of expediency.*
2. The lowest or supporting part or structure.
3. A fundamental principle or underlying concept: *Freedom of speech is a basis of democracy.*
4. A justifying fact or consideration: *made an accusation totally without basis.*
5. An established position from which to operate or deal with others: *We're on a friendly enough basis.*

1. *Syns:* base¹, footing, foundation, ground, groundwork.
2. BASE¹ *noun.*
3. *Syns:* base¹, cornerstone, foundation, fundamental, root¹, rudiment.
4. *Syns:* foundation, justification, reason, warrant.
5. *Syns:* footing, status, terms.

bask *verb*
To take extravagant pleasure.

LUXURIATE.

bass *adjective*
Being a sound produced by a relatively small frequency of vibrations.

LOW *adjective.*

bastard *adjective*
Born out of wedlock.

ILLEGITIMATE.

bastardize *verb*
To ruin utterly in character or quality.

CORRUPT *verb.*

bastardy *noun*
The condition of being of illegitimate birth.

ILLEGITIMACY.

baste *verb*
To hit heavily and repeatedly.

BEAT *verb*.

bat¹ *noun*
Slang. A drinking bout.

BENDER.

bat² *noun*
Slang. An ugly, frightening old woman.

WITCH *noun*.

bat³ *verb*
To open and close the eyes rapidly.

BLINK *verb*.

batch *noun*
A number of individuals making up or considered a unit.

GROUP *noun*.

bate *verb*
To become less active or intense.

SUBSIDE.

bathe *verb*
1. To make moist.
2. To flow against or along.

1. WASH.
2. WASH.

bathetic *adjective*
1. Affectedly or extravagantly emotional.
2. Without freshness or appeal due to overuse.

1. SENTIMENTAL.
2. TRITE.

bathos *noun*
The quality or condition of being affectedly or overly emotional.

SENTIMENTALITY.

batten *verb*
To make a large profit.

CLEAN UP at **clean.**

batter *verb*
1. To injure or damage, as by abuse or heavy wear: *a house that was battered by the hurricane.*

1. *Syns:* knock about, knock around, mangle, maul, rough up.
Near-syns: bruise, contuse; shatter, wreck; disable, disfigure, scar.

2. To hit heavily and repeatedly with violent blows.

2. BEAT *verb*.

battle *noun*
1. An intense competition: *a political battle; a battle of wits.*
2. A hostile encounter between opposing military forces.

1. *Syns:* struggle, vying.

2. COMBAT *noun*.

battle *verb*
To strive in opposition to.

CONTEND.

battle-ax or **battle-axe** *noun*
A person, esp. a woman, who habitually uses loud, abusive language.

SCOLD *noun*.

battle-axe *noun*

SEE **battle-ax.**

batty *adjective*
Slang. Afflicted with or exhibiting irrationality and mental unsoundness.

INSANE.

bauble *noun*
A small, showy article.

NOVELTY.

bawd *noun*
A woman who engages in sexual intercourse for payment.

PROSTITUTE.

bawl *verb*
1. To cry loudly, as a healthy child does from pain or distress: *The unhappy infant kicked and bawled.*
2. To make inarticulate sounds of grief or pain, usu. accompanied by tears.
3. To speak or say very loudly.
4. To say (something) with a shout.

1. *Syns:* howl, wail, yowl.

2. CRY *verb*.

3. ROAR *verb*.

4. SHOUT *verb*.

bawl out *verb*
1. *Informal.* To reprimand loudly or harshly: *got bawled out for insubordination.*

1. *Syns:* berate, rate² , tell off (*Informal*), tongue-lash, wig (*Brit.*). —*Idioms* call on the carpet, give hell to.

2. *Informal.* To criticize for a fault or offense.

2. CALL DOWN at **call.**

bawl *noun*
A loud, deep, prolonged sound.   ROAR *noun.*
bawling *noun*
Λ fit of crying.   CRY *noun.*
bawl out *verb*   SEE **bawl.**
bay[1] *noun*
A body of water partly enclosed by land but having a   *Syns:* bight, cove.
wide outlet to the sea: *sailboats bobbing in the blue*
water of the bay.
bay[2] *verb*
To utter or emit a long, mournful, plaintive sound.   HOWL *verb.*
bazoo *noun*
Any derisive sound of disapproval.   HISS *noun.*
be *verb*
  1. To have reality or life: *I think, therefore I am.*   1. *Syns:* breathe, exist, live[1], subsist.
  2. To have being or actuality.   2. EXIST.
beak *noun*
  1. The horny projection forming a bird's jaws.   1. BILL[2].
  2. *Informal.* The structure on the human face that   2. NOSE *noun.*
     contains the nostrils and organs of smell and forms
     the beginning of the respiratory tract.
beam *noun*
  1. A large, oblong piece of wood or other material, used   1. *Syns:* balk, timber.
     esp. for construction: *a dining-room ceiling featuring*
     exposed beams.
  2. A series of particles or waves traveling close   2. *Syns:* ray, shaft.
     together in parallel paths: *A beam of light peeped*
     through the curtains.
  beam *verb*
  1. To emit a bright light: *A hot sun beamed in the sky.*   1. *Syns:* blaze[1], burn, gleam, glow,
                                                       incandesce, radiate, shine.
  2. To curve the lips upward in expressing amusement,   2. SMILE *verb.*
     pleasure, or happiness.
beaming *adjective*
Giving off or reflecting light readily or in large   BRIGHT.
amounts.
bean *noun*
Slang. The uppermost part of the body.   HEAD *noun.*
bear *verb*
  1. To hold up: *men bearing the burden of leadership*   1. *Syns:* carry, support, sustain.
     in wartime.
  2. To hold on one's person.   2. CARRY *verb.*
  3. To move while supporting.   3. CARRY *verb.*
  4. To hold and turn over in the mind: *often bore*   4. *Syns:* harbor, nurse.
     grudges.
  5. To be endowed with as a visible characteristic or   5. *Syns:* carry, display, exhibit, have,
     form: *sisters bearing a strong resemblance to their*   possess.
     mother.
  6. To conduct oneself in a specified way.   6. ACT *verb.*
  7. To put up with.   7. ENDURE.
  8. To give birth to: *a woman who has borne three*   8. *Syns:* birth (*Chiefly Regional*), bring
     children.   forth, deliver, have. —*Idiom* be
                                                       brought abed (*or* to bed) of.
  9. To bring forth (a product): *fruit trees that bear well.*   9. *Syns:* produce, yield.
  10. To exert pressure: *an old man bearing heavily on*   10. *Syns:* press, push.
      his cane.
  11. To proceed in a specified direction: *Bear right at the*   11. *Syns:* go, head, make, set out, strike
      next intersection.   out.
  12. To cause to come along with oneself.   12. BRING.
  bear on (or **upon**) *verb*
  To be pertinent.   APPLY.

bear out   *verb*
1. To assure the certainty or validity of.
2. To establish as true or genuine.

1. CONFIRM.
2. PROVE.

bear up   *verb*
To withstand stress or difficulty: *bore up well during his mother's long illness.*

Syns: endure, hold up, stand up.

bearable   *adjective*
Capable of being tolerated: *It's more discomfort than pain—quite bearable.*

Syns: endurable, sufferable, tolerable.
Near-syns: acceptable, allowable, livable, satisfactory, supportable, sustainable.
Ant: unbearable.

beard   *verb*
To confront boldly and courageously.

DEFY.

bearer   *noun*
A person who carries messages or is sent on errands: *gave the bearer a receipt for the package.*

Syns: carrier, courier, messenger, runner.

bearing   *noun*
1. Behavior through which one reveals one's personality: *a person of dignified bearing.*

1. *Syns:* address, air, demeanor, gest (*also* geste) (*Archaic*), manner, mien, port (*Archaic*), presence, style.
Near-syns: attitude, carriage, pose, posture, stand; poise; aspect, comportment, deportment.

2. One's place and direction relative to one's surroundings: *can't find my bearing in this strange city.*
3. The fact of being related to the matter at hand.
4. A connecting relation.
5. The compass direction in which a ship or aircraft moves.

2. *Syns:* bearings, location, orientation, position, situation.
3. RELEVANCE.
4. CONCERN.
5. HEADING.

bearings   *noun*
One's place and direction relative to one's surroundings.

BEARING.

bear on (or **upon**)   *verb*

SEE **bear.**

bear out   *verb*

SEE **bear.**

bear up   *verb*

SEE **bear.**

beast   *noun*
A perversely bad, cruel, or wicked person.

FIEND.

beat   *verb*
1. To hit heavily and repeatedly with violent blows: *mugged and beaten black and blue.*

1. *Syns:* baste, batter, belabor, buffet, drub, hammer, lambaste (*Slang*), pound, pummel, thrash, thresh (*Rare*). —*Idiom* rain blows on.

2. To punish with blows or lashes: *beat the boy for smoking.*

2. *Syns:* flog, hide^2, lay into, lick (*Slang*), thrash, trim (*Informal*), whip.

3. To shape, break, or flatten with repeated blows: *beat copper into bowls.*

3. *Syns:* forge^1, hammer, pound.

4. To mix rapidly to a frothy consistency: *beat egg whites for a meringue.*

4. *Syns:* whip, whisk.

5. To move (wings, arms, etc.) up and down.

5. FLAP *verb.*

6. To indicate (time or rhythm), as with repeated gestures or sounds: *a conductor beating the meter with his baton.*

6. *Syns:* count, mark.

7. To make rhythmic contractions, sounds, or movements: *His heart beat with excitement.*

7. *Syns:* palpitate, pulsate, pulse, throb.

8. To win a victory over, as in battle or a competition.
9. *Informal.* To be greater or better than.
10. *Slang.* To make incapable of finding something to think, do, or say.
11. To be projected with blinding intensity.

8. DEFEAT *verb.*
9. SURPASS.
10. NONPLUS.

11. GLARE *verb.*

beat off   *verb*

To turn or drive away.   PARRY.

beat *noun*

1. A repeated stroke or blow, esp. one that produces a   1. **Syns:** clunk, pounding, thump.
   sound: *the beat of galloping hoofs.*
2. A periodic contraction or sound of something   2. **Syns:** palpitation, pulsation, pulse,
   coursing: *the beat of a heart.*   throb.
3. An area regularly covered, as by a policeman or   3. **Syns:** circuit, province, round, route.
   reporter: *The Upper West Side is my beat.*
4. The regular recurrence of strong and weak elements,   4. RHYTHM.
   such as stressed and unstressed notes in music.

beat *adjective*

Informal. Extremely tired.   EXHAUSTED.

beating *noun*

1. A punishment dealt with blows or lashes: *gave him   1. **Syns:** flogging, hiding, licking (*Slang*),
   a beating for lying.*   thrashing, whipping.
2. The act of defeating or the condition of being   2. DEFEAT *noun.*
   defeated.

beatitude *noun*

A condition of supreme well-being and good spirits.   HAPPINESS.

beat off *verb*   SEE **beat.**

beau *noun*

A man who courts a woman: *a flirt surrounded by*   **Syns:** admirer, courter, suitor, swain.
beaus.

beau geste *noun*

An act requiring special generosity.   COURTESY.

beau ideal *noun*

One that is worthy of imitation or duplication.   MODEL *noun.*

beauteous *adjective*

Having qualities that delight the eye.   BEAUTIFUL.

beautiful *adjective*

Having qualities that delight the eye: *the most*   **Syns:** attractive, beauteous, bonny (*Scot.*),
beautiful face I ever saw.   comely, fair, good-looking, gorgeous,
                                                          handsome, lovely, pretty, pulchritudinous,
                                                          ravishing, sightly. —*Idiom* easy on the
                                                          eyes.
                                                          Near-syns: choice, elegant, exquisite,
                                                          stunning; splendid, sublime; eye-
                                                          appealing, eye-filling, well-favored.
                                                          Ants: ugly, unbeautiful.

beautify *verb*

To endow with beauty and elegance by way of a notable   GRACE *verb.*
addition.

beauty *noun*

1. A woman regarded as beautiful: *was a real beauty in   1. **Syns:** belle, doll (*Slang*), knockout
   her day.*   (*Slang*), looker (*Slang*), lovely,
                                                              stunner. —*Idiom* sight for sore eyes.
2. A special feature or quality that confers superiority. 2. VIRTUE.

becalm *verb*

To make or become calm.   CALM *verb.*

beckon *verb*

To solicit (danger) playfully and provocatively, often   COURT *verb.*
unwittingly.

becloud *verb*

To make dim or indistinct.   OBSCURE *verb.*

beclouded *adjective*

Covered by or as if by a thin coating or film.   FILMY.

become *verb*

1. To come to be: *As time went on she became more and   1. **Syns:** come, get, grow, turn (out), wax.
   more like her mother. New York became my home.*
2. To be appropriate or suitable to.   2. SUIT *verb.*
3. To look good on or with.   3. FLATTER.

4. To be in keeping with.   **4.** FIT *verb.*

becoming   *adjective*
   1. Pleasingly suited to the wearer: *wore a becoming*   **1.** *Syns:* attractive, flattering.
      hat.   *Near-ants:* unattractive, unflattering;
                                    distasteful, inappropriate, unsuitable.
                                    Ant: unbecoming.
   2. Conforming to accepted standards.   **2.** CORRECT *adjective.*
becrush   *verb*
   To press forcefully so as to break up into a pulpy mass.   CRUSH *verb.*
bed   *noun*
   The lowest or supporting part or structure.   BASE[1] *noun.*
   bed   *verb*
   1. To provide with often temporary lodging.   **1.** HARBOR *verb.*
   2. To go to bed.   **2.** RETIRE.
   3. To engage in sexual relations with.   **3.** TAKE *verb.*
bedamn   *verb*
   To use profane or obscene language.   SWEAR *verb.*
bedaub   *verb*
   To spread with a greasy, sticky, or dirty substance.   SMEAR *verb.*
bedaze   *verb*
   To stun the senses, as with a heavy blow, a shock, or   DAZE *verb.*
   fatigue.
bedazzle   *verb*
   To confuse with bright light.   DAZE *verb.*
bedeck   *verb*
   To furnish with decorations.   ADORN.
bedevil   *verb*
   1. To trouble persistently from or as if from all sides.   **1.** BESIEGE.
   2. To disturb by repeated attacks.   **2.** ANNOY.
bedim   *verb*
   To make dim or indistinct.   OBSCURE *verb.*
bedlamite   *adjective*
   Afflicted with or exhibiting irrationality and mental   INSANE.
   unsoundness.
bedog   *verb*
   To keep (another) under surveillance by moving along   FOLLOW.
   behind.
bedraggled   *adjective*
   Showing signs of wear and tear or neglect.   SHABBY.
bee   *noun*
   An impulsive, often illogical turn of mind.   FANCY *noun.*
beef   *noun*
   1. *Informal.* A circumstance regarded as a cause for   **1.** GRIEVANCE.
      protest or complaint.
   2. *Slang.* An expression of dissatisfaction.   **2.** COMPLAINT.
   beef   *verb*
   Slang. To express negative feelings, esp. of   COMPLAIN.
   dissatisfaction or resentment.
   beef up   *verb*
   Slang. To make or become greater or larger.   INCREASE *verb.*
beef up   *verb*   SEE **beef.**
beetle   *verb*
   To incline downward or over.   HANG *verb.*
befall   *verb*
   1. To take place.   **1.** COME.
   2. To take place by chance.   **2.** CHANCE *verb.*
   3. To happen to one.   **3.** COME.
befit   *verb*
   1. To be appropriate or suitable to.   **1.** SUIT *verb.*
   2. To be in keeping with.   **2.** FIT *verb.*

befitting *adjective*
1. Conforming to accepted standards.
2. Suited to one's end or purpose.
3. Suitable for a particular person, condition, occasion, or place.

1. CORRECT *adjective*.
2. CONVENIENT.
3. APPROPRIATE *adjective*.

befog *verb*
To make dim or indistinct.

OBSCURE *verb*.

before *adverb*
1. At a time in the past.
2. Until then.

1. EARLIER.
2. EARLIER.

beforehand *adverb*
1. Until then.
2. Before the expected time.

1. EARLIER.
2. EARLY *adverb*.

beforetime *adverb*
Rare. At a time in the past.

EARLIER.

befoul *verb*
1. To make dirty.
2. To make physically impure.
3. To cast aspersions on.

1. DIRTY *verb*.
2. CONTAMINATE.
3. BLACKEN.

befuddle *verb*
To cause to be unclear in mind or intent.

CONFUSE.

befuddled *adjective*
Mentally uncertain.

CONFUSED.

befuddlement *noun*
A stunned or bewildered condition.

DAZE *noun*.

beg *verb*
1. To ask or ask for as charity: *begging for quarters on street corners.*
2. To make an earnest or urgent request.

1. **Syns:** bum (*Slang*), cadge (*Informal*), mooch (*Slang*), panhandle (*Slang*).
2. APPEAL *verb*.

begats *noun*
1. *Slang.* A group consisting of those descended directly from the same parents or ancestors.
2. *Slang.* A written record of ancestry.

1. PROGENY.
2. GENEALOGY.

beget *verb*
To be the biological father of.

FATHER *verb*.

beggar *noun*
1. One who begs habitually or for a living: *beggars and derelicts annoying passers-by.*

2. An impoverished person.
3. One who humbly entreats.

1. **Syns:** almsman, almswoman, bummer[1] (*Slang*), cadger (*Informal*), mendicant, moocher (*Slang*), panhandler (*Slang*).
2. PAUPER *noun*.
3. SUPPLICANT.

beggary *noun*
1. The condition of being a beggar: *forced into beggary after years of unemployment.*
2. The condition of being extremely poor.

1. **Syns:** mendicancy, mendicity.
2. POVERTY.

begin *verb*
1. To come into being: *Charity begins at home.*
2. To go about the initial step in doing (something).

1. **Syns:** arise, commence, originate, start.
2. START *verb*.

beginner *noun*
One who is just starting to learn or do something: *As a beginner I played scales.*

Syns: fledgling, freshman, initiate, innocent, neophyte, novice, novitiate (*also* noviciate), rookie (*Slang*), tenderfoot, tyro.

beginning *noun*
1. The act or process of bringing or being brought into existence: *assumed responsibility for the beginning of the strike.*

2. The initial stage of a developmental process.
beginning *adjective*

1. **Syns:** commencement, genesis, inauguration, inception, initiation, kickoff (*Informal*), launching, leadoff, opening, start.
2. BIRTH *noun*.

1. Indicating the start of something: *the beginning stages of the negotiations.*
2. At or near the start of a period, development, or series.
3. Of or treating the simplest aspects.

begird *verb*
1. To encircle with or as if with a band.
2. To shut in on all sides.

begrime *verb*
To make dirty.

begrudge *verb*
To feel envy for.

beguile *verb*
To cause to accept what is false, esp. by trickery or misrepresentation.

beguiled *adjective*
Affected with intense romantic attraction.

béguin *noun*
French. An extravagant, short-lived romantic attachment.

behave *verb*
1. To conduct oneself in a specified way.
2. To react in a specified way.

behavior *noun*
1. The manner in which one behaves: *always on his best behavior when his in-laws are there.*

2. The way in which a machine or other thing performs or functions: *studying the behavior of matter at extremely low temperatures.*

behemoth *noun*
One that is extraordinarily large and powerful.

behemothic *adjective*
Of extraordinary size and power.

behest *noun*
An authoritative indication to be obeyed.

behind *noun*
The part of one's back on which one rests in sitting.
behind *adverb*
1. Not on time.
2. So as to fall behind schedule.

behindhand *adjective*
1. Not progressing and developing as fast as others, as in economic and social aspects.
2. Not being on time.
behindhand *adverb*
1. Not on time.
2. So as to fall behind schedule.

behold *verb*
To apprehend (images) by use of the eyes.

beholden *adjective*
Owing something, as gratitude or appreciation, to another.

beholder *noun*
Someone who observes.

behoove *verb*
To be appropriate or suitable to.

being *noun*
1. The fact or state of existing.
2. The state or fact of having reality.
3. The condition of being in full force or operation.

---

1. **Syns:** inceptive, initial, introductory.

2. EARLY *adjective.*

3. ELEMENTARY.

1. BAND[1] *verb.*
2. SURROUND.

DIRTY *verb.*

ENVY *verb.*

DECEIVE.

INFATUATED.

INFATUATION.

1. ACT *verb.*
2. ACT *verb.*

1. **Syns:** actions, comportment, conduct, demeanor, deportment, havings (*Scot.*), havior (*Regional*), way.
2. **Syns:** functioning, operation, performance, reaction, working.

GIANT *noun.*

GIANT *adjective.*

COMMAND *noun.*

BOTTOM *noun.*

1. LATE *adverb.*
2. SLOW *adverb.*

1. BACKWARD *adjective.*

2. LATE *adjective.*

1. LATE *adverb.*
2. SLOW *adverb.*

SEE.

OBLIGED.

WATCHER.

SUIT *verb.*

1. EXISTENCE.
2. ACTUALITY.
3. EFFECT *noun.*

4. A member of the human race.

5. One that exists independently.

6. A basic trait or set of traits that define and establish the character of something.

belabor *verb*
To hit heavily and repeatedly.

belated *adjective*
Not being on time.

belatedness *noun*
The quality or condition of not being on time.

belay *verb*
1. *Naut.* To prevent the occurrence or continuation of a movement, action, or operation.

2. *Rare.* To come to a cessation.

belch *verb*
To send forth (confined matter) violently.

beldam also **beldame** *noun*
An ugly, frightening old woman.

beldame *noun*

beleaguer *verb*
1. To surround with hostile troops.

2. To trouble persistently from or as if from all sides.

3. To disturb by repeated attacks.

belie *verb*
1. To give an inaccurate view of by representing falsely or misleadingly.

2. To prove or show to be false.

belief *noun*
1. Mental acceptance of the truth or actuality of something: *What she tells you is not worthy of belief.*

2. Something believed or accepted as true by a person: *It is her belief that the end justifies the means.*

3. Absolute certainty in the trustworthiness of another.

believable *adjective*
Worthy of being believed: *a completely believable account of the biggest hurricane in years.*

believe *verb*
1. To regard (something) as true or real: *I don't believe a word he says.*

2. To have confidence in the truthfulness of: *Do you believe her?*

3. To have an opinion: *He believes that jogging is good for the health.*

4. To view in a certain way.

belittle *verb*
To think, represent, or speak of as small or unimportant: *belittled the accomplishments of his major political opponent.*

---

4. HUMAN BEING.

5. THING.

6. ESSENCE.

BEAT *verb.*

LATE *adjective.*

LATENESS.

1. STOP *verb.*

2. STOP *verb.*

ERUPT.

WITCH *noun.*

SEE **beldam.**

1. BESIEGE.

2. BESIEGE.

3. ANNOY.

1. DISTORT.

2. REFUTE.

1. *Syns:* credence, credit, faith.

2. *Syns:* conviction, feeling, idea, mind, notion, opinion, persuasion, position, sentiment, view.

3. CONFIDENCE.

Syns: colorable, credible, creditable, plausible.

1. *Syns:* accept, buy (*Slang*), go for (*Slang*), swallow (*Slang*).
Near-ants: distrust, doubt, mistrust, suspect; challenge, question; reject, turn down.
Ants: disbelieve, misbelieve.

2. *Syns:* credit, trust. —*Idiom* take at one's word.

3. *Syns:* consider, deem, figure (*Informal*), hold, opine, think. —*Idiom* be of the opinion.

4. FEEL *verb.*

Syns: decry, depreciate, derogate, detract (from), discount, disparage, downgrade, knock (*Slang*), minimize, run down (*Informal*), talk down. —*Idiom* make light (*or* little) of.
Near-syns: criticize, discredit, dispraise; underestimate, underrate.
Ants: magnify, praise.

belittlement *noun*
The act or an instance of belittling: *a belittlement of his sister's accomplishments.*

Syns: depreciation, derogation, detraction, disparagement.

belittling *adjective*
Tending or intending to belittle.

DISPARAGING.

belle *noun*
A woman regarded as beautiful.

BEAUTY.

bellicose *adjective*
1. Having or showing an eagerness to fight.
2. Of, pertaining to, or inclined toward war.

1. BELLIGERENT.
2. MILITARY.

bellicosity *noun*
1. Warlike or hostile attitude or nature.
2. The power or will to fight.

1. BELLIGERENCE.
2. FIGHT *noun.*

belligerence *noun*
1. Warlike or hostile attitude or nature: *greeted my suggestion with real belligerence.*

1. *Syns:* bellicosity, belligerency, combativeness, contentiousness, hostility, pugnacity, truculence (*also* truculency).

2. Hostile behavior.
3. The power or will to fight.

2. AGGRESSION.
3. FIGHT *noun.*

belligerency *noun*
1. Warlike or hostile attitude or nature.
2. Hostile behavior.
3. The power or will to fight.
4. A state of open, prolonged fighting.

1. BELLIGERENCE.
2. AGGRESSION.
3. FIGHT *noun.*
4. CONFLICT *noun.*

belligerent *adjective*
1. Having or showing an eagerness to fight: *a belligerent, loose-tongued drunkard.*

1. *Syns:* bellicose, combative, contentious, hostile, pugnacious, quarrelsome, scrappy (*Informal*), truculent, warlike.
Near-syns: aggressive, antagonistic, fierce, hot-tempered; battling, fighting; militant.
Ant: friendly.

2. Inclined to act in a hostile way.
3. Of or engaged in warfare: *a belligerent nation.*

2. AGGRESSIVE.
3. *Syns:* combatant, fighting, warring.
—*Idiom* at war.

bellow *verb*
1. To speak or say very loudly.
2. To say (something) with a shout.

1. ROAR *verb.*
2. SHOUT *verb.*

bellow *noun*
A loud, deep, prolonged sound.

ROAR *noun.*

belly *verb*
To curve outward past the normal or usual limit.

BULGE *verb.*

bellyache *verb*
Slang. To express negative feelings, esp. of dissatisfaction or resentment.

COMPLAIN.

bellyacher *noun*
Slang. A person who habitually complains or grumbles.

GROUCH *noun.*

belong *verb*
1. To be the property of a person or thing: *The necklace once belonged to her grandmother.*
2. To have a proper or suitable place: *The clean shirts belong in the bureau.*

1. *Syns:* appertain, pertain.

2. *Syns:* fit, go.

belongings *noun*
1. Those articles that belong to someone: *lost all her personal belongings in the fire.*

1. *Syns:* effects, goods, possessions, stuff (*Informal*), things.
Near-syns: fixtures, furnishings, furniture; accessories, baggage, equipment, paraphernalia, trappings; chattels, movables.

2. One's portable property.

beloved *noun*
A person who is much loved.

beloved *adjective*
1. Regarded with much love and tenderness.
2. Given special, usu. doting treatment.

belt *noun*
1. A part of the earth's surface.
2. *Slang.* A sudden sharp, powerful stroke.
3. *Slang.* An act of drinking or the amount swallowed.

belt *verb*
1. To encircle with or as if with a band.
2. *Slang.* To deliver (a powerful blow) suddenly and sharply.

bemask *verb*
To change or modify so as to prevent recognition of the true identity or character of.

bemean *verb*
To deprive of esteem, self-worth, or effectiveness.

bemire *verb*
To soil with mud.

bemired *adjective*
Covered or soiled with mud.

bemud *verb*
Archaic. To soil with mud.

bemuse *verb*
To stun the senses, as with a heavy blow, a shock, or fatigue.

bemused *adjective*
So lost in thought as to be unaware of one's surroundings.

benchmark *noun*
A means by which individuals are compared and judged.

bend *verb*
1. To swerve from a straight line: *a highway that bends to the left.*
2. To cause to move, esp. at an angle: *The prism bent the emerging light rays.*
3. To influence or be influenced in a certain direction.
4. To devote (oneself or one's efforts).
5. To be unable to hold up: *a bridge that bent under the weight of the train.*

6. To incline the body.
7. To make willing or receptive.

bend *noun*
Something bent: *the car rounding the bend.*

bender *noun*
Slang. A drinking bout: *went on a week's bender.*

bending *adjective*
Having bends, curves, or angles.

benediction *noun*
A short prayer said at meals.

benefact *verb*
To give support or assistance.

benefaction *noun*
1. A charitable deed.

---

2. EFFECTS.

DARLING *noun.*

1. DARLING *adjective.*
2. FAVORITE *adjective.*

1. AREA.
2. BLOW[2].
3. DRINK *noun.*

1. BAND[1] *verb.*
2. HIT *verb.*

DISGUISE *verb.*

HUMBLE *verb.*

MUDDY *verb.*

MUDDY *adjective.*

MUDDY *verb.*

DAZE *verb.*

ABSENT-MINDED.

STANDARD *noun.*

1. *Syns:* bow, crook, curve, round.

2. *Syns:* angle, deflect, refract, turn.

3. DISPOSE.
4. APPLY.
5. *Syns:* break, cave in (*Informal*), collapse, crumple, fold (*Informal*), give, go. —*Idiom* give way.
6. STOOP.
7. DISPOSE.

Syns: bow, crook, curvation, curvature, curve, round, turn.

Syns: bat[1] (*Slang*), binge (*Slang*), booze, brannigan (*Slang*), carousal, carouse, compotation, drunk, tear[1] (*Slang*).

CROOKED.

GRACE *noun.*

HELP *verb.*

1. BENEVOLENCE.

2. Something given to a charity or cause.

benefactor *noun*
1. A person who gives to a charity or cause.
2. A person who supports or champions an activity, institution, etc.

benefic *adjective*
Affording benefit.

beneficence *noun*
1. Kindly, charitable interest in others.
2. A charitable deed.
3. Something given to a charity or cause.

beneficent *adjective*
Affording benefit.

beneficial *adjective*
Affording benefit: *a beneficial climate.*

benefit *verb*
1. To derive advantage: *benefited from the stock split.*
2. To be an advantage to.

benefit *noun*
1. A state of health, happiness, and prospering.
2. The quality of being suitable or adaptable to an end.
3. Something beneficial.
4. Something that contributes to or increases one's well-being.
5. *Archaic.* A kindly act.

benevolence *noun*
1. Kindly, charitable interest in others: *ruled his subjects with benevolence.*

2. A charitable deed: *was grateful for their financial benevolence.*

benevolent *adjective*
1. Characterized by kindness and concern for others: *a benevolent ruler.*

2. Of or concerned with charity: *a benevolent fund.*

benevolentness *noun*
Kindly, charitable interest in others.

benighted *adjective*
1. Clinging to obsolete ideas.
2. Exhibiting lack of education or knowledge.

---

2. DONATION.

1. DONOR.
2. PATRON.

BENEFICIAL.

1. BENEVOLENCE.
2. BENEVOLENCE.
3. DONATION.

BENEFICIAL.

Syns: advantageous, aidful (*Archaic*), benefic, beneficent, benignant, favorable, good, helpful, propitious, salutary, toward (*Rare*), useful.
Near-ants: baneful, deleterious, noxious, pernicious.
Ants: detrimental, harmful.

1. ***Syns:*** advantage, capitalize (on), profit.
2. PROFIT *verb.*

1. WELFARE.
2. USE *noun.*
3. ADVANTAGE *noun.*
4. INTEREST *noun.*

5. FAVOR *noun.*

1. ***Syns:*** altruism, beneficence, benevolentness, benignancy, charitableness, charity, good will, grace, kindliness, kindness.
Near-syns: amity, favor, friendliness, friendship, generosity, helpfulness, rapport, tolerance.
Ants: animosity, hatred, ill-will.
2. ***Syns:*** benefaction, beneficence, benignity (*Archaic*), favor, kindness, oblation, office(s), philanthropy.

1. ***Syns:*** benign, benignant, big, chivalrous, good, humane, humanitarian, kind, kindhearted, kindly.
2. ***Syns:*** altruistic, charitable, eleemosynary, philanthropic (*also* philanthropical).
Near-syns: bighearted, generous, good, humane, humanitarian, liberal, openhanded.
Ant: uncharitable.

BENEVOLENCE.

1. UNPROGRESSIVE.
2. IGNORANT.

benightedness *noun*
The condition of being ignorant; lack of knowledge or learning. — IGNORANCE.

benign *adjective*
1. Characterized by kindness and concern for others.
2. Having or showing a tender, considerate, and helping nature.
3. Indicative of future success.

1. BENEVOLENT.
2. KIND[1].

3. FAVORABLE.

benignancy *noun*
Kindly, charitable interest in others. — BENEVOLENCE.

benignant *adjective*
1. Affording benefit.
2. Characterized by kindness and concern for others.
3. Having or showing a tender, considerate, and helping nature.

1. BENEFICIAL.
2. BENEVOLENT.
3. KIND[1].

benignity *noun*
Archaic. A charitable deed. — BENEVOLENCE.

bent *adjective*
1. Deviating from a straight line: *a bent tree limb.*

1. *Syns:* arced, arched, arciform, arrondi (*French*), bowed, curved, curvilinear, rounded.

2. On an unwavering course of action.

2. SET[1] *adjective.*

bent *noun*
1. An inclination to something: *a strong bent toward conservatism.*

1. *Syns:* bias, disposition, leaning, partiality, penchant, predilection, predisposition, proclivity, proneness, propensity, squint, tendency, turn.

2. An innate capability.

2. TALENT.

benumb *verb*
1. To render less sensitive.
2. To stun the senses, as with a heavy blow, a shock, or fatigue.
3. To render helpless, as by emotion.

1. DEADEN.
2. DAZE *verb.*

3. PARALYZE.

benumbed *adjective*
1. Lacking physical feeling or sensitivity.
2. Lacking responsiveness or alertness.

1. DEAD *adjective.*
2. DULL *adjective.*

bequeath *verb*
1. To convey (something) from one generation to the next.
2. *Law.* To give (property) to another person after one's death.

1. HAND DOWN at **hand.**

2. LEAVE[1].

berate *verb*
To reprimand loudly or harshly. — BAWL OUT at **bawl.**

bereave *verb*
To take or keep something away from. — DEPRIVE.

berth *noun*
1. A particular position in a designated order of importance.
2. Steady or regular employment.
3. A post of employment.

1. PLACE *noun.*

2. JOB.
3. POSITION *noun.*

berth *verb*
To provide with often temporary lodging. — HARBOR *verb.*

beseech *verb*
To make an earnest or urgent request. — APPEAL *verb.*

beseechment *noun*
An earnest or urgent request. — APPEAL *noun.*

beseem *verb*
Archaic. To be appropriate or suitable to. — SUIT *verb.*

beset *verb*
1. To shut in on all sides.
2. To surround with hostile troops.

1. SURROUND.
2. BESIEGE.

3. To set upon with violent force.
4. To trouble persistently from or as if from all sides.
5. To disturb by repeated attacks.

3. ATTACK *verb*.
4. BESIEGE.
5. ANNOY.

besetment *noun*
Something that annoys.

ANNOYANCE.

besides *adverb*
In addition.

ADDITIONALLY.

besiege *verb*
1. To surround with hostile troops: *besiege a fortress.*

2. To shut in on all sides.
3. To trouble persistently from or as if from all sides: *was besieged with complaints.*

1. *Syns:* beleaguer, beset, blockade, invest (*Mil.*), siege.
2. SURROUND.
3. *Syns:* badger, bedevil, beleaguer, beset, harass, harry, hound, importune, pester, plague.

besiegement *noun*
A prolonged surrounding of an objective by hostile troops.

SIEGE *noun*.

besmear *verb*
1. To spread with a greasy, sticky, or dirty substance.
2. To cast aspersions on.

1. SMEAR *verb*.
2. BLACKEN.

besmirch *verb*
To cast aspersions on.

BLACKEN.

besoil *verb*
To make dirty.

DIRTY *verb*.

besotted *adjective*
Intoxicated with alcoholic liquor.

DRUNK *adjective*.

bespatter *verb*
1. To hurl or scatter liquid upon.
2. To mark or soil with spots.
3. To cast aspersions on.

1. SPLASH.
2. SPOT *verb*.
3. BLACKEN.

bespeak *verb*
1. To give grounds for believing in the existence or presence of.
2. To claim in advance.
3. *Archaic.* To talk to (an audience) formally.

1. INDICATE.
2. BOOK *verb*.
3. ADDRESS *verb*.

bespeckle *verb*
To mark with many small spots.

SPECKLE.

besprinkle *verb*
To scatter or release in drops or small particles.

SPRINKLE.

best *adjective*
1. Surpassing all others in quality: *the best diamonds available.*

2. Much more than half: *The best part of the week is gone.*

best *noun*
That which is superlative: *chose only the best among many paintings.*

1. *Syns:* bettermost (*Chiefly Regional*), optimal, optimum, superb, superlative, unsurpassed.
2. *Syns:* better[1], bettermost (*Chiefly Regional*), greater, larger, largest.

Syns: choice, cream, crème de la crème (*French*), elite (*also* élite), flower, pick, prize, top. —*Idioms* cream of the crop, flower of the flock, pick of the bunch, top cream.

best *verb*
1. To get the better of.
2. To win a victory over, as in battle or a competition.
3. To be greater or better than.

1. TRIUMPH *verb*.
2. DEFEAT *verb*.
3. SURPASS.

bestain *verb*
To soil with foreign matter.

STAIN *verb*.

bestial *adjective*
Showing or suggesting a disposition to be violently destructive without scruple or restraint.

FIERCE.

bestialize *verb*
To ruin utterly in character or quality.

CORRUPT *verb.*

bestow *verb*
1. To give formally or officially.
2. To make a gift of.
3. To present as a gift to a charity or cause.
4. *Archaic.* To provide with often temporary lodging.

1. CONFER.
2. GIVE *verb.*
3. DONATE.
4. HARBOR *verb.*

bestowal *noun*
The act of conferring, as of an honor.

CONFERMENT.

bestride *verb*
To sit with a leg on each side of.

STRIDE.

bet *verb*
1. To make a bet on: *We bet on the winner.*

1. *Syns:* gamble, game, lay¹, lay down, play, post, put, stake, wager. —*Idiom* take a flyer.
Near-syns: chance, hazard, risk, speculate, venture.

2. To put up as a stake in a game or speculation.

2. GAMBLE *verb.*

bet *noun*
1. Something valuable risked on an uncertain outcome: *My bet on the race is $50.*
2. A venture depending on chance.

1. *Syns:* ante (*Slang*), pot (*Card Games*), stake, wager.
2. GAMBLE *noun.*

bête noire *noun*
French. An object of extreme dislike.

HATE *noun.*

bethink *verb*
To renew (an image or thought) in the mind.

REMEMBER.

betide *verb*
1. To take place.
2. To happen to one.

1. COME.
2. COME.

betimes *adverb*
1. Before the expected time.
2. At times.

1. EARLY *adverb.*
2. NOW *adverb.*

betoken *verb*
1. To give grounds for believing in the existence or presence of.
2. To give reason for expecting.

1. INDICATE.

2. PROMISE *verb.*

betray *verb*
1. To be treacherous to: *betrayed his comrades.*

2. To disclose in a breach of confidence: *betrayed my secret.*

1. *Syns:* cross (up), double-cross (*Slang*), rat (on) (*Slang*), sell out (*Slang*).
2. *Syns:* blab, discover (*Archaic*), divulge, expose, give away, let out, reveal, spill (*Informal*), tell, uncover, unveil. —*Idioms* let slip, let the cat out of the bag, spill the beans, tell all.

3. To victimize (someone) by underhandedness.
4. To cause to accept what is false, esp. by trickery or misrepresentation.

3. DECEIVE.
4. DECEIVE.

betrayal *noun*
An act of betraying: *suffered betrayal to the Gestapo.*

Syns: betrayment, double-cross (*Slang*), sellout (*Slang*), treachery. —*Idiom* Judas kiss.

betrayer *noun*
One who betrays: *a treacherous betrayer hanged by his comrades.*

Syns: double-crosser (*Slang*), Judas, rat (*Slang*), traitor.

betrayment *noun*
An act of betraying.

BETRAYAL.

betrothal *noun*
The act or condition of being pledged to marry.

ENGAGEMENT.

betrothed *adjective*
Pledged to marry.

ENGAGED.

betrothed *noun*

A person to whom one is engaged to be married.

betrothment *noun*
The act or condition of being pledged to marry.

better¹ *adjective*
1. Of greater excellence than another: *This book is better than that one.*
2. Much more than half.

better *verb*
1. To advance to a more desirable state.
2. To be greater or better than.

better *noun*
1. A dominating position, as in a conflict.
2. One who stands above another in rank.

better *adverb*
To a greater extent: *were better suited for the job than the others.*

better² *noun*

betterment *noun*
1. Something that improves.
2. Steady improvement, as of an individual or a society.

bettermost *adjective*
1. *Chiefly Regional.* Surpassing all others in quality.
2. *Chiefly Regional.* Much more than half.

bettor also **better** *noun*
One who bets: *throngs of bettors at the race.*

bevel *adjective*
Angled at a slant.

beveled *adjective*
Angled at a slant.

bever *noun*
Chiefly Regional. A light meal.

beverage *noun*
Any liquid that is fit for drinking.

bevy *noun*
A usu. small number of individuals.

beware *verb*
To be careful.

bewilder *verb*
To cause to be unclear in mind or intent.

bewildered *adjective*
Mentally uncertain.

bewitch *verb*
1. To act upon with or as if with magic.
2. To please greatly or irresistibly.

bewitched *adjective*
Affected with intense romantic attraction.

bewitching *adjective*
1. Pleasing to the eye or mind.
2. Tending to seduce.
3. Pertaining to magic.

bias *noun*
1. An inclination for or against that inhibits impartial judgment: *a decision influenced by personal bias.*

2. An inclination to something.

bias *verb*
1. To cause to have a prejudiced view: *His past experiences have biased his outlook.*
2. To influence or be influenced in a certain direction.

INTENDED *noun.*

ENGAGEMENT.

1. **Syns:** preferable, superior.

2. BEST *adjective.*

1. IMPROVE.
2. SURPASS.

1. ADVANTAGE *noun.*
2. SUPERIOR *noun.*

Syn: more.

SEE **bettor.**

1. IMPROVEMENT.
2. PROGRESS *noun.*

1. BEST *adjective.*
2. BEST *adjective.*

Syns: gambler, gamester, player, speculator.

BIAS *adjective.*

BIAS *adjective.*

BITE *noun.*

DRINK *noun.*

GROUP *noun.*

LOOK OUT.

CONFUSE.

CONFUSED.

1. CHARM *verb.*
2. CHARM *verb.*

INFATUATED.

1. ATTRACTIVE.
2. SEDUCTIVE.
3. WITCHING *adjective.*

1. **Syns:** one-sidedness, partiality, prejudice, prepossession, tendentiousness.
2. BENT *noun.*

1. **Syns:** color, jaundice, prejudice, prepossess, warp.
2. DISPOSE.

3. To direct (material) to the interests of a particular group: *a magazine biased toward conservatives.*
4. To have an effect or impact upon.
bias *adjective*
Angled at a slant: *a bias fold.*

biased also **biassed** *adjective*
1. Exhibiting bias: *a biased remark in favor of the tax.*

3. *Syns:* angle, skew, slant.

4. INFLUENCE *verb.*

Syns: bevel, beveled, biased (*also* biassed), diagonal, oblique, slanted, slanting.

1. *Syns:* colored, one-sided, partial, partisan, prejudiced, prejudicial, prepossessed, tendentious.
Near-ants: detached, dispassionate, impartial, open-minded; fair, honest, just, right.
Ants: neutral, objective, unbiased.

2. Angled at a slant.
biassed *adjective*
bibelot *noun*
A small, showy article.
bibulous *adjective*
Having a capacity or tendency to absorb or soak up.
bicker *verb*
To engage in a quarrel.
bid *verb*
1. To request that someone take part in or be present at a particular occasion.
2. To make an offer of.
3. To give orders to.
bid *noun*
1. A spoken or written request for someone to take part or be present.
2. Something offered.
biddable *adjective*
Willing to carry out the wishes of others.
biddie *noun*
bidding *noun*
An authoritative indication to be obeyed.
biddy also **biddie** *noun*
Slang. An ugly, frightening old woman.
bide *verb*
1. To continue to be in a place.
2. To have as one's domicile, usu. for an extended period.
3. To stop temporarily and remain, as if reluctant to leave.
biff *noun*
Slang. A sudden sharp, powerful stroke.
biff *verb*
Slang. To deliver (a powerful blow) suddenly and sharply.
biform *adjective*
Composed of two parts or things.
bifurcate *verb*
To separate into branches or branchlike parts.
big *adjective*
1. Notably above average in amount, size, or scope: *a big inheritance.*

2. BIAS *adjective.*
SEE **biased.**

NOVELTY.

ABSORBENT.

ARGUE.

1. INVITE.

2. GO *verb.*
3. COMMAND *verb.*

1. INVITATION.

2. OFFER *noun.*

OBEDIENT.
SEE **biddy.**

COMMAND *noun.*

WITCH *noun.*

1. REMAIN.
2. LIVE[1].

3. PAUSE *verb.*

BLOW[2].

HIT *verb.*

DOUBLE *adjective.*

BRANCH *verb.*

1. *Syns:* considerable, extensive, good, great, healthy, large, large-scale, sizable (*also* sizeable), tidy (*Informal*).
Near-syns: hulking, whopping; ample, biggish, roomy, spacious, voluminous; major.
Ant: little.

2. Having reached full growth and development.
3. Having great significance.
4. Characterized by kindness and concern for others.
5. Willing to give of oneself and one's possessions.
6. Full to the point of flowing over: *eyes big with tears.*

2. MATURE *adjective.*
3. IMPORTANT.
4. BENEVOLENT.
5. GENEROUS.
6. **Syns:** awash, brimful, brimming, overflowing.

big   *noun*
An important, influential person.

DIGNITARY.

Big Brother   *noun*
An absolute ruler, esp. one who is harsh and oppressive.

DICTATOR.

biggish   *adjective*
Somewhat big.

SIZABLE.

bighead   *noun*
Informal. An exaggerated belief in one's own importance.

EGOTISM.

bigheadedness   *noun*
Informal. An exaggerated belief in one's own importance.

EGOTISM.

big-hearted   *adjective*
Willing to give of oneself and one's possessions.

GENEROUS.

big-heartedness   *noun*
The quality or state of being generous.

GENEROSITY.

bight   *noun*
A body of water partly enclosed by land but having a wide outlet to the sea.

BAY¹.

big-league   *adjective*
Being among the leaders of a particular class: *a big-league publisher.*

Syns: big-time (*Slang*), blue-chip, heavyweight (*Informal*), major, major-league.

bigness   *noun*
The quality or state of being large in amount, extent, or importance.

SIZE.

bigoted   *adjective*
Not tolerant of the beliefs, opinions, etc., of others.

INTOLERANT.

bigotry   *noun*
Irrational suspicion or hatred of a particular group, race, or religion.

PREJUDICE *noun.*

big shot   *noun*
Slang. An important, influential person.

DIGNITARY.

big-time   *adjective*
Slang. Being among the leaders of a particular class.

BIG-LEAGUE.

big-timer   *noun*
Slang. An important, influential person.

DIGNITARY.

big wheel   *noun*
Slang. An important, influential person.

DIGNITARY.

bigwig   *noun*
Informal. An important, influential person.

DIGNITARY.

bilge   *noun*
Something that does not have or make sense.

NONSENSE.

bilk   *verb*
Slang. To get money or something else from by deceitful trickery.

CHEAT *verb.*

bill¹   *verb*
To present a statement of fees or charges to: *Bill me next month.*

Syn: invoice.

bill   *noun*
1. A precise list of fees or charges.
2. A printed list of the order of events and other pertinent information for a public performance.

1. ACCOUNT *noun.*
2. PROGRAM.

bill² *noun*
1. The horny projection forming a bird's jaws: *The pelican has a large bill.*
2. The projecting rim on the front of a cap: *The bill shades my eyes.*

1. **Syn:** beak.
2. **Syns:** brim, peak, visor.

billet *verb*
To provide with often temporary lodging.

HARBOR *verb.*

billet *noun*
1. A particular position in a designated order of importance.
2. A post of employment.

1. PLACE *noun.*
2. POSITION *noun.*

billingsgate *noun*
Harsh, often insulting language.

VITUPERATION.

binary *adjective*
Composed of two parts or things.

DOUBLE *adjective.*

bind *verb*
1. To be morally bound to do.
2. To apply therapeutic materials to (a wound).
3. To unite or be united in a relationship.
4. To make fast or firmly fixed by means of a cord, rope, etc.

1. COMMIT.
2. DRESS *verb.*
3. ASSOCIATE *verb.*
4. TIE *verb.*

bind *noun*
Informal. A difficult, embarrassing situation.

PREDICAMENT.

bine *noun*
A young stemlike growth arising from a plant.

SHOOT *noun.*

binge *noun*
1. A period of uncontrolled self-indulgence: *a shopping binge.*
2. *Slang.* A drinking bout.

1. **Syns:** blowoff (*Informal*), fling, jag (*Slang*), orgy, rampage, spree.
2. BENDER.

bird *noun*
Slang. Any derisive sound of disapproval.

HISS *noun.*

birdbrained *adjective*
Slang. Given to lighthearted silliness.

GIDDY.

bird-dog *verb*
To keep (another) under surveillance by moving along behind.

FOLLOW.

birth *noun*
1. The act or process of bringing forth young: *witnessed the birth of my son.*

2. The initial stage of a developmental process: *the birth of Christianity.*

3. One's ancestors or their character.

1. **Syns:** accouchement (*French*), birthing (*Chiefly Regional*), childbearing, childbirth, delivery, labor, lying-in, parturition, travail.
2. **Syns:** beginning, commencement, dawn, dawning, genesis, inception, nascence (*also* nascency), onset, opening, origin, outset, spring, start.
3. ANCESTRY.

birth *verb*
Chiefly Regional. To give birth to.

BEAR.

birthing *noun*
Chiefly Regional. The act or process of bringing forth young.

BIRTH *noun.*

birthright *noun*
1. A privilege granted a person by virtue of birth: *Free speech is the birthright of Americans.*
2. Any special privilege accorded a firstborn: *The estate was the eldest son's birthright.*

1. **Syns:** appanage (*also* apanage), droit, perquisite, prerogative, right.
2. **Syns:** heritage, inheritance, legacy, patrimony.

bistered *adjective*
Of a complexion tending toward brown or black.

DARK *adjective.*

bit¹ *noun*
1. A tiny amount: *doesn't make a bit of difference.*

1. **Syns:** crumb, dab, dash, doit, dram, drop, fragment, grain, hoot, iota, jot,

minim, mite, modicum, molecule, ort,
ounce, particle, scrap[1], scruple, shred,
smidgen (*Informal*), smitch (*Informal*),
snap, speck, spot (*Chiefly Brit.
Informal*), tittle, whit.

2. A small portion of food: *a bit of cheese*.

2. **Syns:** bite, crumb, morsel, mouthful,
piece.

3. A rather short period: *waited for a bit*.

3. **Syns:** space, spell[3], stretch, time, while.

4. *Informal*. A particular kind of activity: *did the
intellectual bit*.

4. **Syn:** routine. —*Idiom* song and dance.

bit[2] *verb*
To control, restrict, or arrest.

RESTRAIN.

bitch *verb*
Slang. To express negative feelings, esp. of
dissatisfaction or resentment.

COMPLAIN.

bitchy *adjective*
Slang. Characterized by intense ill will or spite.

MALEVOLENT.

bite *verb*
1. To seize, as food, with the teeth: *The dog bit into the
meat*.

1. **Syns:** champ (*also* chomp), gnash,
gnaw.

2. To consume gradually, as by chemical reaction,
friction, etc.: *acid biting into the silver*.

2. **Syns:** corrode, eat, erode, gnaw, wear,
wear away.

3. To feel or cause to feel a sensation of heat or
discomfort.

3. STING *verb*.

bite *noun*
1. A small portion of food.

1. BIT[1].

2. *Informal*. A light meal: *has a bite before bed every
night*.

2. **Syns:** bever (*Chiefly Regional*), morsel,
snack, snap (*Chiefly Brit. Regional*).

3. A cutting quality.

3. EDGE *noun*.

biting *adjective*
1. So sharp as to cause mental pain: *biting criticism*.

1. **Syns:** acerb, acerbic, acid, acidic, acrid,
caustic, cutting, incisive, mordacious,
mordant, penetrating, pungent,
scathing, slashing, stinging, truculent,
vitriolic, vituperative.

2. Having or suggesting keen, discerning intellect.

2. INCISIVE.

bitter *adjective*
1. Having a noticeably sharp, pungent taste or smell: *a
bitter wine*.

1. **Syns:** acerb, acerbic, acrid, amaroidal,
astringent, austere (*Archaic*), harsh,
sour.

2. Causing sharp, often prolonged discomfort: *the bitter
climate of the Sahara*.

2. **Syns:** brutal, hard, harsh, rough,
rugged, severe.

3. Very cold.

3. FRIGID.

4. Difficult to accept: *the bitter truth*.

4. **Syns:** afflictive, distasteful, grievous,
indigestible, painful, unpalatable.
Near-syns: bad, disagreeable,
displeasing, disturbing, offensive,
unpleasant; galling, vexatious; woeful.

5. Bitingly hostile.

5. RESENTFUL.

bitter *verb*
To make or become bitter.

EMBITTER.

bitterness *noun*
The quality or state of feeling bitter.

RESENTMENT.

bizarre *adjective*
1. Deviating from the customary.

1. ECCENTRIC *adjective*.

2. Conceived or done with no reference to reality or
common sense.

2. FANTASTIC.

3. Resembling a freak.

3. FREAKISH.

blab *verb*
1. To disclose in a breach of confidence.

1. BETRAY.

2. To engage in or spread gossip.

2. GOSSIP *verb*.

blab *noun*
Incessant and usu. inconsequential talk.   CHATTER *noun*.

blabber *verb*
To talk volubly, persistently, and usu.   CHATTER *verb*.
inconsequentially.

blabber *noun*
Incessant and usu. inconsequential talk.   CHATTER *noun*.

blabby *adjective*
Inclined to gossip.   GOSSIPY.

black *adjective*
1. Of the darkest achromatic visual value: *a black hat*.   1. **Syns:** atramentous, ebon (*Poetic*),
                                                               ebony, inky, jet[1], jet-black, jetty, onyx,
                                                               pitch-black, pitchy, sable, sooty.
2. Having no light: *a black cave*.   2. **Syns:** caliginous (*Rare*), dark, inky,
                                                               pitch-dark.
3. Covered or stained with or as if with dirt or other   3. DIRTY *adjective*.
   impurities.
4. Characterized by intense ill will or spite.   4. MALEVOLENT.
5. Dark and depressing.   5. GLOOMY.
6. Morally objectionable.   6. EVIL *adjective*.

black *verb*
1. To make dirty.   1. DIRTY *verb*.
2. To make or receive a bruise or bruises on.   2. BRUISE *verb*.

black-a-vised *adjective*
Of a complexion tending toward brown or black.   DARK *adjective*.

blackball *verb*
1. To exclude from normal social or professional   1. **Syns:** blacklist, boycott, ostracize, shut
   activities: *suspected troublemakers blackballed from*   out.
   jobs.
2. To prevent or forbid authoritatively.   2. VETO *verb*.

blacken *verb*
1. To make dirty.   1. DIRTY *verb*.
2. To cast aspersions on: *blackened the good name of a*   2. **Syns:** befoul, besmear, besmirch,
   great statesman.   bespatter, denigrate, dirty, smear,
                                                               smudge, smut, soil, stain, sully, taint,
                                                               tarnish. —*Idioms* give a black eye to,
                                                               throw mud on.

black eye *noun*
1. A bruise surrounding the eye: *got a black eye in the*   1. **Syns:** mouse (*Slang*), shiner (*Slang*).
   fight.   —*Idiom* eye in mourning.
2. A mark of discredit or disgrace.   2. STAIN *noun*.

black-hearted *adjective*
Characterized by intense ill will or spite.   MALEVOLENT.

blackish *adjective*
Somewhat black: *blackish clouds*.   **Syns:** dark, dusky.

blackjack *verb*
To compel by pressure or threats.   COERCE.

blacklist *verb*
To exclude from normal social or professional activities. BLACKBALL.

blackout *noun*   SEE **black out**.

black out *verb*
1. To suffer temporary loss of consciousness: *blacked*   1. **Syns:** faint, keel over, pass out
   out from lack of oxygen.   (*Informal*), swoon.
2. To keep from being published or transmitted.   2. CENSOR.

blackout *noun*
A temporary loss of consciousness: *suffered blackouts at* **Syns:** faint, swoon, syncope (*Path.*).
high altitudes.   —*Idiom* dead faint.

blade *noun*
The cutting part of a sharp instrument.   EDGE *noun*.

blamable also **blameable** *adjective*
Deserving blame.   BLAMEWORTHY.

blame *verb*
1. To find fault with: *no one to blame but myself.*

    1. **Syns:** censure, condemn, criticize, cut up (*Informal*), denounce, denunciate, fault, pan (*Informal*), rap[1] (*Slang*), reprehend, reprobate.
    Near-syns: accuse, charge, knock, impute.

2. To ascribe (a misdeed, error, etc.) to.

    2. FIX *verb.*

blame *noun*
1. Responsibility for an error or crime: *The blame for the cover-up is mine.*

    1. **Syns:** culpability, fault, guilt, onus.

2. A finding fault: *said nothing to them in the way of blame.*

    2. **Syns:** censure, condemnation, criticism, denunciation, reprehension, reprobation.

blameable *adjective*

    SEE **blamable.**

blamed *adjective*
So annoying or detestable as to deserve condemnation.

    DAMNED.

blameful *adjective*
Deserving blame.

    BLAMEWORTHY.

blameless *adjective*
1. Free from guilt or blame.
2. Beyond reproach.

    1. INNOCENT *adjective.*
    2. EXEMPLARY.

blameworthy *adjective*
Deserving blame: *behavior that was blameworthy if not criminal.*

    Syns: blamable (*also* blameable), blameful, censurable, culpable, guilty, reprehensible. —*Idiom* at fault.

blanch also **blench** *verb*
To lose normal coloration; turn pale.

    PALE *verb.*

blanched *adjective*
Lacking color.

    PALE *adjective.*

bland *adjective*
1. Free from severity or violence, as in movement.
2. Lacking the qualities requisite for spiritedness and originality.
3. Without definite or distinctive characteristics.
4. Effortlessly gracious and tactful in social manner.

    1. GENTLE *adjective.*
    2. INSIPID.
    3. NEUTRAL.
    4. SUAVE.

blandish *verb*
1. To persuade or try to persuade by gentle, persistent urging or flattery.
2. To compliment excessively and ingratiatingly.

    1. COAX.
    2. FLATTER.

blandishment *noun*
Excessive, ingratiating praise.

    FLATTERY.

blandness *noun*
The state or quality of being insipid.

    INSIPIDITY.

blank *adjective*
Lacking expression.

    EXPRESSIONLESS.

blanket *verb*
To extend over the surface of.

    COVER *verb.*

blankety-blank *adjective*
Informal. So annoying or detestable as to deserve condemnation.

    DAMNED.

blankness *noun*
1. Total lack of ideas, meaning, or substance.
2. A desolate sense of loss.

    1. EMPTINESS.
    2. EMPTINESS.

blare *verb*
1. To be projected with blinding intensity.
2. To have or produce a blatantly startling effect.

    1. GLARE *verb.*
    2. SCREAM *verb.*

blare *noun*
An intense, blinding light.

    GLARE *noun.*

blaring *adjective*
Marked by extremely high volume and intensity of sound.

LOUD *adjective*.

blarney *noun*
Excessive, ingratiating praise.

FLATTERY.

blaspheme *verb*
To use profane or obscene language.

SWEAR *verb*.

blasphemous *adjective*
Showing irreverence and contempt for something sacred.

SACRILEGIOUS.

blasphemy *noun*
1. A profane or obscene term.
2. An act of disrespect or impiety toward something regarded as sacred.

1. SWEAR *noun*.
2. SACRILEGE.

blast *noun*
1. A violent release of confined energy, usu. accompanied by a loud sound and shock waves: *a bomb blast.*
2. An earsplitting, explosive noise: *the blast of jet afterburners.*
3. *Informal.* A big, exuberant party: *a pregraduation blast.*

1. *Syns:* blowout, blowup, burst, detonation, explosion, fulmination.
2. *Syns:* bang, boom, burst, roar, thunder.
3. *Syns:* bash (*Slang*), blowout (*Slang*), celebration, shindig (*Slang*).

blast *verb*
1. To release or cause to release energy suddenly and violently, esp. with a loud noise.
2. To make an earsplitting, explosive noise: *Jet fighters blasted off the runway.*
3. To spoil or destroy: *Our hopes have been blasted.*
4. *Slang.* To render totally ineffective by decisive defeat.

1. EXPLODE.
2. *Syns:* bang, boom, roar, thunder.
3. *Syns:* blight, dash, nip, wreck.
4. OVERWHELM.

blasted *adjective*
Slang. So annoying or detestable as to deserve condemnation.

DAMNED.

blatant *adjective*
1. Characterized by or done without shame.
2. Offensively loud and insistent.

1. SHAMELESS.
2. VOCIFEROUS.

blather *verb*
To talk rapidly, incoherently, or indistinctly.

BABBLE *verb*.

blather *noun*
1. Unintelligible or foolish talk.
2. Something that does not have or make sense.

1. BABBLE *noun*.
2. NONSENSE.

blatherskite *noun*
Unintelligible or foolish talk.

BABBLE *noun*.

blaze¹ *verb*
1. To undergo combustion.
2. To emit a bright light.
3. To be projected with blinding intensity.
4. To have or produce a blatantly startling effect.

1. BURN *verb*.
2. BEAM *verb*.
3. GLARE *verb*.
4. SCREAM *verb*.

blaze *noun*
1. The visible signs of combustion.
2. An intense, blinding light.

1. FIRE *noun*.
2. GLARE *noun*.

blaze² *verb*
To make (information) generally known.

ADVERTISE.

blazing *adjective*
1. On fire: *The forest is blazing.*

1. *Syns:* ablaze, afire, aflame, alight², burning, comburent, conflagrant, fiery, flaming, flaring, ignited. —*Idioms* in a blaze, in flames.

2. Extremely bright: *blazing sunlight.*
3. Fired with intense feeling.

2. *Syns:* brilliant, dazzling, glaring, glary.
3. PASSIONATE.

blazon *verb*
To make (information) generally known.

ADVERTISE.

bleach *verb*
To lose normal coloration; turn pale.

PALE *verb*.

bleak *adjective*
1. Cold and forbidding: *a bleak, silent man.*

1. **Syns:** austere, dour, grim, hard, harsh, severe.
Near-ants: calm, mild, peaceful, soft, warm; attractive.
Ant: pleasant.

2. Dark and depressing.

2. GLOOMY.

blear *verb*
To make dim or indistinct.

OBSCURE *verb*.

blear *adjective*
Not clearly perceived or perceptible.

UNCLEAR.

bleary *adjective*
1. Not clearly perceived or perceptible.
2. Extremely tired.

1. UNCLEAR.
2. EXHAUSTED.

bleed *verb*
To flow or leak out slowly.

OOZE *verb*.

blemish *noun*
1. Something that mars the appearance or causes inadequacy or failure.
2. A mark of discredit or disgrace.

1. DEFECT *noun*.

2. STAIN *noun*.

blemish *verb*
To spoil the soundness or perfection of.

INJURE.

blench[1] *verb*
To draw away involuntarily, usu. due to fear or disgust.

FLINCH.

blench[2] *verb*

SEE **blanch.**

blend *verb*
1. To put together into one mass so that the constituent parts are more or less homogeneous.
2. To combine and adapt in order to attain a particular effect.

1. MIX *verb*.

2. HARMONIZE.

blend *noun*
Something produced by mixing.

MIXTURE.

bless *verb*
1. To make sacred by a religious rite.
2. To feel and express gratitude to.

1. SANCTIFY.
2. THANK.

blessed *adjective*
1. Regarded with particular reverence or respect.
2. So annoying or detestable as to deserve condemnation.

1. HOLY.
2. DAMNED.

blessedness *noun*
1. The quality of being holy or sacred.
2. A condition of supreme well-being and good spirits.

1. HOLINESS.
2. HAPPINESS.

blessing *noun*
1. Something beneficial.
2. A short prayer said at meals.

1. ADVANTAGE *noun*.
2. GRACE *noun*.

blight *verb*
To spoil or destroy.

BLAST *verb*.

blind *adjective*
1. Without the sense of sight: *was blind from birth.*

1. **Syns:** dark (*Regional*), eyeless, sightless, unseeing.

2. Unwilling or unable to perceive: *was blind to the danger.*
3. *Slang.* Intoxicated with alcoholic liquor.
4. Screened from the view of oncoming drivers: *a blind intersection.*

2. **Syns:** dull, purblind, uncomprehending, unperceptive.
3. DRUNK *adjective*.
4. **Syns:** concealed, hidden.

blind *verb*
To confuse with bright light.

DAZE *verb*.

blind *noun*
A shelter for concealing hunters: *a duck blind.*

Syns: hide[1] (*Brit.*), stand.

blind alley *noun*
Informal. A course leading nowhere: *reached a blind alley in the negotiations.*

Syn: cul-de-sac. —*Idiom* dead-end street.

blindness *noun*
The condition of not being able to see: *suffered blindness after the accident.*

Syn: sightlessness.

blink *verb*
1. To open and close the eyes rapidly: *blinked in the glare.*
2. To shine with intermittent gleams: *The ship's signal blinked in the night.*

1. *Syns:* bat[3], nictitate (*also* nictate), twinkle (*Archaic*), wink.
2. *Syns:* coruscate, flash, flicker, glimmer, twinkle, wink.

blink at *verb*
To pretend not to see: *The senator merely blinked at the corruption.*

Syns: connive at, dissemble (*Obs.*), ignore, pass over, wink at. —*Idioms* be blind to, close (*or* shut) one's eyes to, look the other way, turn a blind eye to.

blink *noun*
1. A brief closing of the eyes: *One blink and the bird was gone.*
2. A quick look.
3. A sudden quick light: *saw a blink from the signal in the dark.*

1. *Syns:* nictitation (*also* nictation), wink.
2. GLANCE[1] *noun.*
3. *Syns:* coruscation, flash, flicker, glance[1], gleam, glimmer, glint, spark, twinkle, wink.

blink at *verb*

SEE **blink.**

blinker *noun*
Slang. An organ of vision.

EYE *noun.*

blip *verb*
To hit with a quick, sharp blow of the hand.

SLAP *verb.*

blister *verb*
To criticize harshly and devastatingly.

SLAM *verb.*

blistering *adjective*
Marked by much heat.

HOT *adjective.*

blithe *adjective*
1. Characterized by joyful exuberance.
2. Free from care or worry.

1. GAY *adjective.*
2. LIGHT[2].

blithesome *adjective*
Characterized by joyful exuberance.

GAY *adjective.*

bloated *adjective*
Characterized by an exaggerated show of dignity or self-importance.

POMPOUS.

bloc *noun*
A group of individuals united in a common cause.

COMBINE *noun.*

block *verb*
1. To stop or prevent passage of.
2. To plug up something, as a hole, space, or container.

1. OBSTRUCT.
2. FILL.

block out *verb*
1. To draw up a preliminary plan or version of.
2. To cut off from sight: *The trees block out the view.*

1. DRAFT *verb.*
2. *Syns:* close[1], hide[1], obscure, obstruct, screen, shroud, shut out.

block *noun*
1. Anything that impedes or prevents entry or passage.
2. *Slang.* The uppermost part of the body.

1. BAR *noun.*
2. HEAD *noun.*

blockade *verb*
To surround with hostile troops.

BESIEGE.

blockhead *noun*
Slang. A mentally dull person.

DULLARD.

blockheaded *adjective*
Lacking in intelligence.

STUPID.

block out *verb*

SEE **block.**

blocky *adjective*
Short, heavy, and solidly built.   STOCKY.

blond also **blonde** *adjective*
Having light hair.   FAIR *adjective*.

blonde *adjective*   SEE **blond**.

blood *noun*
1. The fluid circulated by the heart through the   1. **Syns:** claret (*Slang*), gore.
   vascular system: *lost a lot of blood during the
   operation.*
2. The crime of murdering someone.   2. MURDER *noun*.
3. One's ancestors or their character.   3. ANCESTRY.

blood bath *noun*
The savage killing of many victims.   MASSACRE *noun*.

bloodcurdling *adjective*
Causing great horror.   HORRIBLE.

bloodhound *verb*
To follow closely or persistently.   DOG *verb*.

bloodless *adjective*
1. Lacking color.   1. PALE *adjective*.
2. Being weak in quality or substance.   2. PALE *adjective*.
3. Lacking passion and emotion.   3. INSENSITIVE.

bloodletting *noun*
The savage killing of many victims.   MASSACRE *noun*.

bloodline *noun*
One's ancestors or their character.   ANCESTRY.

bloodshed *noun*
The savage killing of many victims.   MASSACRE *noun*.

bloodstained *adjective*
Of or covered with blood.   BLOODY *adjective*.

bloodsucker *noun*
One who depends on another for support without   PARASITE.
reciprocating.

bloodsucking *adjective*
Of or characteristic of a parasite.   PARASITIC.

bloodthirsty *adjective*
Eager for bloodshed.   MURDEROUS.

bloody *adjective*
1. Of or covered with blood: *a bloody knife.*   1. **Syns:** bloodstained, ensanguined, gory,
                                                             imbrued (*also* embrued).
2. Attended by or causing bloodshed: *a bloody battle.* 2. **Syns:** sanguinary, sanguineous.
3. Eager for bloodshed.   3. MURDEROUS.

bloody *verb*
To cover with blood: *bloodied my hands while cleaning   **Syns:** ensanguine, imbrue (*also* embrue).
the fish.*

bloom *noun*
1. The showy reproductive structure of a plant: *rose   1. **Syns:** blossom, floret, flower.
   blooms.*
2. A condition or time of vigor and freshness: *the   2. **Syns:** blossom, efflorescence,
   bloom of Greek civilization.*   florescence, flower, flush, prime.
3. A fresh, rosy complexion: *was pale and had lost her 3. **Syns:** blossom, blush, flush, glow.
   bloom.*

bloom *verb*
1. To bear flowers: *roses blooming on the fence.*   1. **Syns:** blossom, blow³, burgeon,
                                                             effloresce, flower.
2. To grow rapidly and luxuriantly.   2. FLOURISH.

bloomer *noun*
Slang. A stupid, clumsy mistake.   BLUNDER *noun*.

blooming *adjective*
1. Bright and clear; not dull or faded.   1. FRESH.
2. Of a healthy, reddish color.   2. RUDDY.

3. *Slang.* Completely such, without qualification or exception.

3. UTTER[2].

4. *Slang.* So annoying or detestable as to deserve condemnation.

4. DAMNED.

blooper *noun*
Informal. A stupid, clumsy mistake.

BLUNDER *noun.*

blossom *noun*
1. The showy reproductive structure of a plant.
2. A condition or time of vigor and freshness.
3. A fresh, rosy complexion.

1. BLOOM *noun.*
2. BLOOM *noun.*
3. BLOOM *noun.*

blossom *verb*
1. To bear flowers.
2. To grow rapidly and luxuriantly.

1. BLOOM *verb.*
2. FLOURISH.

blot *noun*
A mark of discredit or disgrace.

STAIN *noun.*

blot out *verb*
1. To remove or invalidate by or as if by running a line through or wiping clean.
2. To destroy all traces of.

1. CANCEL.

2. ANNIHILATE.

blot out *verb*

SEE **blot**.

bloviate *verb*
To speak in a loud, pompous, or prolonged manner.

RANT.

blow[1] *verb*
1. To be in a state of motion, as air: *The wind is blowing.*
2. To breathe hard.
3. *Slang.* To talk with excessive pride.
4. To release or cause to release energy suddenly and violently, esp. with a loud noise.
5. *Slang.* To spend (money) excessively and usu. foolishly.
6. *Slang.* To harm irreparably through inept handling; make a mess of.
7. *Slang.* To move or proceed away from a place.
8. *Slang.* To pay for the food, drink, or entertainment of another.

1. *Syns:* puff, winnow.

2. PANT.
3. BOAST *verb.*
4. EXPLODE.

5. WASTE *verb.*

6. BOTCH *verb.*

7. GO *verb.*
8. TREAT *verb.*

blow in *verb*
Slang. To come to a particular place.

ARRIVE.

blow *noun*
1. A natural movement or current of air.
2. *Slang.* An act of boasting.

1. WIND[1].
2. BOAST *noun.*

blow[2] *noun*
1. A sudden sharp, powerful stroke: *a blow on the head.*

1. *Syns:* bang, bash (*Informal*), belt (*Slang*), biff (*Slang*), bop (*Informal*), clout, conk, crack, hit, lick, paste (*Slang*), pound, smack[1], smacker, sock (*Slang*), swat, thwack, wallop (*Informal*), welt (*Informal*), whack, whop.

2. Something that jars the mind or emotions.

2. SHOCK *noun.*

blow[3] *verb*
To bear flowers.

BLOOM *verb.*

blow-by-blow *adjective*
Characterized by attention to detail.

DETAILED.

blower *noun*
Slang. One given to boasting.

BRAGGART *noun.*

blowhard *noun*
Slang. One given to boasting.

BRAGGART *noun.*

blow in *verb*

SEE **blow[1]**.

blowoff *noun*

SEE **blow off**.

blow off *verb*
Slang. To utter publicly.   AIR *verb*.
blowoff *noun*
Informal. A period of uncontrolled self-indulgence.   BINGE.
blowout *noun*   SEE **blow out.**
blow out *verb*
To come open or fly apart suddenly and violently, as   BURST *verb*.
from internal pressure.
blowout *noun*
1. A violent release of confined energy, usu.   **1.** BLAST *noun*.
   accompanied by a loud sound and shock waves.
2. *Slang*. A big, exuberant party.   **2.** BLAST *noun*.
blowup *noun*   SEE **blow up.**
blow up *verb*
1. To release or cause to release energy suddenly and   **1.** EXPLODE.
   violently, esp. with a loud noise.
2. To come open or fly apart suddenly and violently, as **2.** BURST *verb*.
   from internal pressure.
3. To be or become angry.   **3.** ANGER *verb*.
blowup *noun*
1. A violent release of confined energy, usu.   **1.** BLAST *noun*.
   accompanied by a loud sound and shock waves.
2. A sudden, violent expression, as of emotion.   **2.** OUTBURST.
blowy *adjective*
Exposed to or characterized by the presence of freely   AIRY.
circulating air or wind.
blub *verb*
To make inarticulate sounds of grief or pain, usu.   CRY *verb*.
accompanied by tears.
blubber *verb*
To make inarticulate sounds of grief or pain, usu.   CRY *verb*.
accompanied by tears.
blubbering *noun*
A fit of crying.   CRY *noun*.
bludgeon *verb*
To domineer or drive into compliance by the use of   INTIMIDATE.
threats, force, etc.
blue *adjective*
1. *Informal*. In low spirits.   **1.** DEPRESSED.
2. Bordering on indelicacy or impropriety.   **2.** RACY.
blue *verb*
Brit. Slang. To spend (money) excessively and usu.   WASTE *verb*.
foolishly.
blue blood *noun*
People of the highest social level.   SOCIETY.
blue-blooded *adjective*
Of high birth or social position.   NOBLE.
bluebottle *noun*
Brit. A member of a law-enforcement agency.   POLICEMAN.
blue-chip *adjective*
Being among the leaders of a particular class.   BIG-LEAGUE.
bluecoat *noun*
A member of a law-enforcement agency.   POLICEMAN.
blue-eyed *adjective*
Given special, usu. doting treatment.   FAVORITE *adjective*.
bluenose *noun*
A person who is too much concerned with being proper,   PRUDE.
modest, or righteous.
bluenosed *adjective*
Marked by excessive concern for propriety and good   GENTEEL.
form.

blueprint   *noun*
A method for making, doing, or accomplishing   DESIGN *noun*.
something.

blueprint   *verb*
1. To work out and arrange the parts or details of.   1. DESIGN *verb*.
2. To form a strategy for.   2. DESIGN *verb*.

blue-ribbon   *adjective*
Exceptionally good of its kind.   EXCELLENT.

blues   *noun*
Informal. A feeling or spell of dismally low spirits.   GLOOM.

bluff   *verb*
To cause to accept what is false, esp. by trickery or   DECEIVE.
misrepresentation.

blunder   *noun*
A stupid, clumsy mistake: *a million-dollar*   *Syns:* bloomer (*Slang*), blooper (*Informal*),
manufacturing blunder.   boner (*Slang*), bull, bungle, foozle,
fumble, goof (*Slang*), miscue, rock[1], screw-
up (*Slang*), stumble, trip.
Near-syns: fault, lapse, misdoing, mistake,
slip; boo-boo (*Informal*), muff;
impropriety, indecorum; error; faux pas.

blunder   *verb*
1. To move awkwardly or clumsily: *blundered around*   1. *Syns:* bumble[1], lurch, stumble, wallow.
    in the dark and fell.
2. To harm irreparably through inept handling; make a   2. BOTCH *verb*.
    mess of.

blunderer   *noun*
A stupid, clumsy person: *a store mismanaged by*   *Syns:* blunderhead, botcher, bungler,
blunderers.   foozler, fumbler. —*Idiom* bull in a china
shop.

blunderhead   *noun*
A stupid, clumsy person.   BLUNDERER.

blunt   *verb*
1. To make or become less sharp-edged.   1. DULL *verb*.
2. To render less sensitive.   2. DEADEN.

blunt   *adjective*
1. Not physically sharp or keen.   1. DULL *adjective*.
2. Rudely unceremonious.   2. ABRUPT.

blur   *verb*
To make dim or indistinct.   OBSCURE *verb*.

blurred   *adjective*
Covered by or as if by a thin coating or film.   FILMY.

blurt   *verb*
To speak suddenly or sharply, as from surprise or   EXCLAIM.
emotion.

blurt   *noun*
A sudden, sharp utterance.   EXCLAMATION.

blush   *verb*
To become red in the face: *blushed with embarrassment.*   *Syns:* color, crimson, flush, glow, mantle,
redden.

blush   *noun*
A fresh, rosy complexion.   BLOOM *noun*.

bluster   *verb*
To speak or say very loudly.   ROAR *verb*.

board   *verb*
1. To provide with often temporary lodging.   1. HARBOR *verb*.
2. To go aboard (a means of transport).   2. TAKE *verb*.

boards   *noun*
The raised platform on which theatrical performances   STAGE *noun*.
are given.

boast *verb*
1. To talk with excessive pride: *boasted about their wealth.*

2. To be possessed of.
boast *noun*
An act of boasting: *big boasts about his strength.*

boaster *noun*
One given to boasting.
boastful *adjective*
Characterized by or given to boasting: *boastful remarks about his ability.*

bob *verb*
Obs. To make a noise by striking.
bob *noun*
Obs. An audible blow.
bobby *noun*
Brit. Slang. A member of a law-enforcement agency.
bodement *noun*
A phenomenon that serves as a sign or warning of some future good or evil.
bodiless *adjective*
Having no body, form, or substance.
bodily *adjective*
Of or pertaining to the human body: *bodily organs; bodily cleanliness.*
body *noun*
1. The physical frame of a dead person or animal: *lowered the body into the coffin.*
2. The main part: *The body of the paper discusses nuclear energy.*
3. *Informal.* A member of the human race.
4. A separate and distinct portion of matter: *celestial bodies.*
5. A measurable whole.
6. A group of people organized for a particular purpose.
7. A number of individuals making up or considered a unit.
8. A number of persons who have come or been gathered together.
body *verb*
To serve as the image of.
boff *noun*
A dazzling, often sudden instance of success.
bog *verb*
To interfere with the progress of.
bogey *noun*
boggle *verb*
1. To harm irreparably through inept handling; make a mess of.
2. To overwhelm with surprise, wonder, or bewilderment.
bogie *noun*
bogle *noun*
A supernatural being.

1. **Syns:** blow[1] (*Slang*), brag, crow, gasconade, rodomontade (*also* rhodomontade), vaunt.
2. COMMAND *verb.*

Syns: blow[1] (*Slang*), brag, braggadocio, fanfaronade, gasconade, rodomontade (*also* rhodomontade).

BRAGGART *noun.*

Syns: braggadocian, braggart, braggy, rodomontade (*also* rhodomontade).
Near-syns: arrogant, pretentious, cocksure, bigheaded, conceited, swellheaded, vainglorious, vaunting.
Ant: modest.

TAP[1] *verb.*

TAP[1] *noun.*

POLICEMAN.

OMEN.

IMMATERIAL.

Syns: corporal, corporeal, fleshly, personal, physical, somatic.

1. **Syns:** cadaver, carcass, corpse, corpus, mort (*Rare*), remains, stiff (*Slang*).
2. **Syns:** bulk, corpus, substance.

3. HUMAN BEING.
4. **Syns:** mass, object[1].

5. QUANTITY.
6. FORCE *noun.*
7. GROUP *noun.*

8. ASSEMBLY.

REPRESENT.

HIT *noun.*

HINDER.
SEE **bogy.**

1. BOTCH.

2. STAGGER.

SEE **bogy.**

GHOST *noun.*

bogus *adjective*
Fraudulently or deceptively imitative.

COUNTERFEIT *adjective*.

bogy also **bogey, bogie** *noun*
A supernatural being.

GHOST *noun*.

bohunk *noun*
Slang. A large, ungainly, and dull-witted person.

LUMP[1] *noun*.

boil *verb*
1. To cook (food) in liquid heated to the point of steaming: *boiled the potatoes.*
2. To be in a state of emotional or mental turmoil: *was silently boiling over the delay.*
3. *Slang.* To be or become angry.
4. To move swiftly.

1. *Syns:* parboil, seethe (*Archaic*), simmer, stew.
2. *Syns:* bubble, burn, churn, ferment, moil, seethe, simmer, smolder.
3. ANGER *verb*.
4. RUSH *verb*.

boil away *verb*
To pass off as vapor, esp. due to being heated.

EVAPORATE.

boil down *verb*
To reduce in complexity or scope: *My complaints can be boiled down to this.*

Syn: simplify.

boil away *verb*

SEE **boil**.

boil down *verb*

SEE **boil**.

boiling *adjective*
Marked by much heat.

HOT.

boisterous *adjective*
Offensively loud and insistent.

VOCIFEROUS.

bold *adjective*
1. Rude and disrespectful.
2. Having or showing courage.
3. Taking or willing to take risks.
4. Standing out prominently: *a bold handwriting.*

5. So sharply inclined as to be almost perpendicular.

1. IMPUDENT.
2. BRAVE *adjective*.
3. DARING *adjective*.
4. *Syns:* conspicuous, prominent, pronounced.
5. STEEP[1].

boldacious *adjective*
Brit. Regional. Rude and disrespectful.

IMPUDENT.

boldfaced *adjective*
Rude and disrespectful.

IMPUDENT.

boldness *noun*
1. The state or quality of being impudent.
2. Willingness to take risks.

1. IMPUDENCE.
2. DARING *noun*.

bollix up *verb*
Slang. To harm irreparably through inept handling; make a mess of.

BOTCH.

boloney *noun*

SEE **baloney**.

bolster *verb*
To keep from yielding or failing during stress or difficulty.

SUSTAIN.

bolt *noun*
A sudden and involuntary movement.

JUMP *noun*.

bolt *verb*
1. To move suddenly and involuntarily.
2. To leave hastily.
3. To move swiftly.
4. To swallow (food or drink) greedily or rapidly in large amounts.

1. JUMP *verb*.
2. RUN *verb*.
3. RUSH *verb*.
4. GULP *verb*.

bomb *noun*
Slang. One that fails completely.

FAILURE.

bombard *verb*
To direct a barrage at.

BARRAGE *verb*.

bombardment *noun*
A concentrated outpouring, as of missiles, words, or blows.

BARRAGE *noun*.

bombastic *adjective*
Characterized by language that is elevated and sometimes pompous in style.

SONOROUS.

bombed *adjective*
Slang. Intoxicated with alcoholic liquor.

DRUNK *adjective.*

bombinate *verb*
To make a continuous low-pitched droning sound.

HUM *verb.*

bombination *noun*
A continuous low-pitched droning sound.

HUM *noun.*

bona fide *adjective*
Not counterfeit or copied.

AUTHENTIC.

bond *noun*
1. That which unites or binds: *the bond of matrimony.*

2. A legally binding arrangement between parties.
3. The close physical union of two objects: *a tight bond between wall and wallpaper.*
4. The condition of being closely tied to another by affection or faith.
5. *Law.* Money supplied for the temporary release of an arrested person that guarantees his appearance for trial: *Bond was set at $100,000.*

1. *Syns:* knot, ligament, ligature, link, linkage, nexus, tie, vinculum, yoke.
2. AGREEMENT.
3. *Syns:* adherence, adhesion, cohesion.

4. ATTACHMENT.

5. *Syn:* bail[1].

bond *verb*
To hold fast to: *plastics bonded with cement.*

Syns: adhere (to), clag (*Brit. Regional*), cleave, cling, cohere, stick.

bonds *noun*
Something that physically confines the legs or arms: *prisoners in bonds.*

Syns: chains, fetters, gyves (*Archaic*), irons, manacles, restraints, shackles.

bondsman *noun*
One who posts bond: *The bondsman and the attorney conferred.*

Syns: bail[1], bailsman.

bone-dry *adjective*
Having little or no liquid or moisture.

DRY *adjective.*

boner *noun*
Slang. A stupid, clumsy mistake.

BLUNDER *noun.*

bone up *verb*
To study hard, esp. when pressed for time: *had to bone up for the examination.*

Syns: cram (*Informal*), grind, mug up.
—*Idiom* burn the midnight oil.

bong *verb*
To give forth or cause to give forth a clear, resonant sound.

RING[2].

bonkers *adjective*
Slang. Afflicted with or exhibiting irrationality and mental unsoundness.

INSANE.

bonny *adjective*
1. *Scot.* Having qualities that delight the eye.
2. *Scot.* Having pleasant, desirable qualities.

1. BEAUTIFUL.
2. GOOD *adjective.*

bonus *noun*
A sum of money offered for a special service, as the apprehension of a criminal.

REWARD *noun.*

bony *adjective*
Having little flesh or fat on the body.

THIN *adjective.*

boo *noun*
Any derisive sound of disapproval.

HISS *noun.*

booby trap *noun*
A source of danger or difficulty not easily foreseen and avoided.

PITFALL.

boodle *noun*
1. *Slang.* Money, property, or a favor given, offered, or promised to a person in a position of trust as an inducement to dishonest behavior.

1. BRIBE *noun.*

2. *Slang.* A large sum of money.   **2.** FORTUNE.

3. *Slang.* Goods or property seized unlawfully, esp. by a victor in wartime.   **3.** PLUNDER *noun.*

boohoo *verb*
To make inarticulate sounds of grief or pain, usu. accompanied by tears.   CRY *verb.*

boohoos *noun*
A fit of crying.   CRY *noun.*

book *noun*
A printed and bound work: *a book on birds.*   **Syns:** tome, volume.

book *verb*
1. To register in or as if in a book.   **1.** LIST¹ *verb.*
2. To claim in advance: *booked a room.*   **2.** **Syns:** bespeak, engage, reserve.

bookish *adjective*
1. Devoted to study or reading.   **1.** STUDIOUS.
2. Characterized by a narrow concern for book learning and formal rules, without knowledge or experience of practical matters.   **2.** PEDANTIC.

booky *adjective*
Characterized by a narrow concern for book learning and formal rules, without knowledge or experience of practical matters.   PEDANTIC.

boom *verb*
1. To make an earsplitting, explosive noise.   **1.** BLAST *verb.*
2. To make a continuous deep, reverberating sound.   **2.** RUMBLE.
3. To fare well.   **3.** PROSPER.

boom *noun*
An earsplitting, explosive noise.   BLAST *noun.*

boomerang *verb*
To produce an unexpected and undesired result.   BACKFIRE.

booming *adjective*
Improving, growing, or succeeding steadily.   FLOURISHING.

boon¹ *noun*
Something beneficial.   ADVANTAGE *noun.*

boon² *adjective*
Characterized by joyful exuberance.   GAY *adjective.*

boor *noun*
An unrefined, rude person: *a boor who interrupted constantly.*   **Syns:** barbarian, bosthoon (*Ir.*), bounder (*Chiefly Brit.*), chuff, churl, grobian, mucker, Philistine (*also* philistine), vulgarian, yahoo.
Near-syns: boob (*Slang*), buffoon, oaf, hick, clown; loon, rustic.

boorish *adjective*
Lacking in delicacy or refinement.   COARSE.

boost *verb*
1. To move (something) to a higher position.   **1.** ELEVATE.
2. To increase in amount.   **2.** RAISE *verb.*
3. To increase or seek to increase the importance or reputation of by favorable publicity.   **3.** PROMOTE.

boost *noun*
1. An instance of lifting or being lifted.   **1.** LIFT *noun.*
2. The act of increasing or rising.   **2.** INCREASE *noun.*
3. The amount by which something is increased.   **3.** INCREASE *noun.*

boot¹ *verb*
1. *Slang.* To end the employment of.   **1.** DISMISS.
2. *Slang.* To put out by force.   **2.** EJECT.

boot *noun*
A strong, pleasant feeling of excitement or stimulation.   THRILL *noun.*

boot² *verb*
Archaic. To be an advantage to.   PROFIT *verb.*

bootleg *verb*
To import or export secretly and illegally.   SMUGGLE.

bootlegger *noun*
A person who engages in smuggling.   SMUGGLER.

bootless *adjective*
Having no useful result.   FUTILE.

bootlick *verb*
To support slavishly every opinion or suggestion of a   FAWN.
superior.

booty *noun*
Goods or property seized unlawfully, esp. by a victor in   PLUNDER *noun*.
wartime.

booze *noun*
Slang. A drinking bout.   BENDER.

booze *verb*
Slang. To take alcoholic liquor, esp. excessively or   DRINK *verb*.
habitually.

boozed *adjective*
Slang. Intoxicated with alcoholic liquor.   DRUNK *adjective*.

boozehound *noun*
Slang. A person who is habitually drunk.   DRUNKARD.

boozer *noun*
Slang. A person who is habitually drunk.   DRUNKARD.

boozy *adjective*
Slang. Intoxicated with alcoholic liquor.   DRUNK *adjective*.

bop *verb*
Informal. To deliver (a powerful blow) suddenly and   HIT *verb*.
sharply.

bop *noun*
Informal. A sudden sharp, powerful stroke.   BLOW².

border *noun*
1. A fairly narrow line or space forming a boundary: *a flower border around the sundial; the border of the property.*

    1. **Syns:** borderline (*also* border line), brim, brink, edge, edging, fringe, margin, perimeter (*Mil.*), periphery, rim, terminus (*Rare*), verge.

2. The line or area separating geopolitical units: *crossed the Canadian border.*

    2. **Syns:** borderland, boundary, march², marchland.

border *verb*
1. To put or form a border on: *Pansies border the flower beds.*
2. To be contiguous or next to.
3. To come near in quality, amount, etc.

    1. **Syns:** bound², edge, fringe, margin, rim, skirt, verge.
    2. ADJOIN.
    3. RIVAL *verb*.

bordering *adjective*
Sharing a common boundary.   ADJOINING.

borderland *noun*
The line or area separating geopolitical units.   BORDER *noun*.

borderline *also* **border line** *noun*
1. A fairly narrow line or space forming a boundary.
2. A transitional interval beyond which some new action or different state of affairs is likely to begin or occur.

    1. BORDER *noun*.
    2. VERGE *noun*.

borderline *adjective*
Not affording certainty.   AMBIGUOUS.

bore *verb*
To fatigue with dullness or tedium: *Your stories bore me.*

    Syns: ennui, pall, tire, weary.

bore *noun*
An unpleasant, tiresome person.   DRIP *noun*.

boreal *adjective*
Very cold.   FRIGID.

boredom *noun*
The condition of being bored: *nearly died of boredom at the party.*

boresome *adjective*
Arousing no interest or curiosity.

boring *adjective*
Arousing no interest or curiosity: *a boring play.*

bosky *adjective*
Full of shade.

bosom *noun*
The seat of a person's innermost emotions and feelings.

bosom *verb*
Archaic. To put one's arms around affectionately.

boss *noun*
1. Someone who directs and supervises workers: *The construction boss told the carpenters to build shelves in each office.*
2. One who is highest in rank or authority.
3. A professional politician who controls a party or political machine: *the boss of Tammany Hall.*

boss *verb*
1. To direct and watch over the work and performance of others.
2. To command in an arrogant manner: *wouldn't let him boss her children.*

boss *adjective*
1. Having or exercising authority.
2. *Slang.* Exceptionally good of its kind.

bossy *adjective*
Tending to dictate.

bosthoon *noun*
Ir. An unrefined, rude person.

botch *verb*
To harm irreparably through inept handling; make a mess of: *The mechanic botched the repair, and the car wouldn't run.*

botch *noun*
A ruinous state of disorder: *He really made a botch of his marriage.*

botcher *noun*
A stupid, clumsy person.

botchery *noun*
A ruinous state of disorder.

bother *verb*
1. To trouble the nerves or peace of mind of, esp. by repeated vexations.
2. To impair or destroy the composure of.

Syns: ennui, tedium, yawn (*Informal*).

BORING.

Syns: arid, aseptic, boresome, dreary (*also drear*), dry, dull, humdrum, irksome, monotonous, sterile, stuffy, tedious, tiresome, tiring, uninteresting, weariful, wearisome, weary.
Near-ants: exciting, inspiring, provocative, stimulating, stirring.
Ants: absorbing, engrossing, interesting.

SHADY.

HEART.

EMBRACE *verb.*

1. **Syns:** director, foreman, head, manager, overseer, superintendent, supervisor, taskmaster. —*Idiom* straw boss.
2. CHIEF *noun.*
3. **Syns:** chief, chieftain (*Slang*), leader, ringleader.

1. SUPERVISE *verb.*

2. **Syns:** dictate to, dominate, domineer, order (around), rule, tyrannize.

1. PRINCIPAL.
2. EXCELLENT.

DICTATORIAL.

BOOR.

Syns: ball up (*Slang*), blow[1] (*Slang*), blunder, boggle, bollix up (*Slang*), bungle, foul up (*Slang*), fumble, goof up (*Slang*), gum up (*Slang*), louse up (*Slang*), mess up, mishandle, mismanage, muck up, muddle, muff, screw up (*Slang*), snafu (*Slang*), spoil. —*Idiom* make a muck of.
Near-syns: butcher, mangle, murder; mar, ruin, wreck.

Syns: botchery, hash, mess, mess-up, muddle, mull[1], muss, shambles, snafu (*Slang*).

BLUNDERER.

BOTCH *noun.*

1. ANNOY.

2. AGITATE.

bother *noun*
1. Something that annoys.
2. The feeling of being annoyed.
3. Needless trouble: *went through a lot of bother for nothing.*

1. ANNOYANCE.
2. ANNOYANCE.
3. *Syns:* aggravation (*Informal*), botheration, bustle, fuss, pother, vexation.

botheration *noun*
1. Something that annoys.
2. The feeling of being annoyed.
3. Needless trouble.

1. ANNOYANCE.
2. ANNOYANCE.
3. BOTHER *noun.*

bothering *noun*
The act of annoying.

ANNOYANCE.

botherment *noun*
Something that annoys.

ANNOYANCE.

bothersome *adjective*
Troubling the nerves or peace of mind, as by repeated vexations.

VEXATIOUS.

bottom *noun*
1. The lowest or supporting part or structure.
2. A side or surface that is below or under: *put a sticker on the bottom of the drawer.*
3. A point of origin from which ideas, influences, etc., emanate.
4. *Informal.* The part of one's back on which one rests in sitting: *gave him a playful swat on the bottom.*

5. A very low level, position, or degree.

1. BASE[1] *noun.*
2. *Syns:* underneath, underside.

3. CENTER *noun.*

4. *Syns:* backside, behind, buttocks, derrière, fanny (*Slang*), posterior, rear[1] (*Informal*), rump, seat.
5. LOW *noun.*

bottom *adjective*
1. Opposite to or farthest from the top: *the bottom drawer of the bureau.*
2. Arising from or going to the root or source.

1. *Syns:* lowermost, lowest, nethermost, undermost.
2. RADICAL *adjective.*

bottomless *adjective*
Having no basis or foundation in fact.

BASELESS.

boulevard *noun*
A course affording passage from one place to another.

WAY.

bounce *verb*
1. To spring back after colliding with something: *The ball bounced up and down.*
2. To move in a lively way: *bounced out of bed bright and early.*
3. *Slang.* To put out by force.
4. *Slang.* To end the employment of.

1. *Syn:* rebound.

2. *Syns:* bound[1], jump, leap, spring.

3. EJECT.
4. DISMISS.

bounce back *verb*
To produce an unexpected and undesired result.

BACKFIRE.

bounce *noun*
1. An act of bouncing or a bouncing movement: *a bounce of the ball.*
2. A sudden lively movement: *a quick bounce of her head.*
3. Capacity to bounce: *a ball with plenty of bounce.*

4. The ability to recover quickly from depression or discouragement.
5. A lively, emphatic, eager quality or manner.

1. *Syns:* bound[1], rebound.

2. *Syns:* bound[1], jump, leap, spring.

3. *Syns:* resilience (*also* resiliency), spring, springiness.
4. RESILIENCE.

5. SPIRIT.

bounce back *verb*

SEE **bounce.**

bouncy *adjective*
Very brisk, alert, and high-spirited.

LIVELY.

bound[1] *verb*
To move in a lively way.

BOUNCE *verb.*

bound *noun*
1. An act of bouncing or a bouncing movement.

1. BOUNCE *noun.*

2. A sudden lively movement.   **2.** BOUNCE *noun.*

bound² *verb*
1. To fix the limits of.   **1.** DETERMINE.
2. To be contiguous or next to.   **2.** ADJOIN.
3. To put or form a border on.   **3.** BORDER *verb.*

bound³ *adjective*
Owing something, as gratitude or appreciation, to another.   OBLIGED.

boundary *noun*
The line or area separating geopolitical units.   BORDER *noun.*

bounded *adjective*
Having distinct limits.   DEFINITE.

bounden *adjective*
Owing something, as gratitude or appreciation, to another.   OBLIGED.

bounder *noun*
Chiefly Brit. An unrefined, rude person.   BOOR.

boundless *adjective*
Having no ends or limits.   ENDLESSNESS.

boundlessness *noun*
The state or quality of being infinite.   INFINITY.

bound(s) *noun*
1. A demarcation point or boundary beyond which something does not extend or occur.   **1.** END *noun.*
2. The boundary surrounding a certain area.   **2.** LIMIT *noun.*

bounteous *adjective*
Characterized by abundance.   GENEROUS.

bountiful *adjective*
Characterized by abundance.   GENEROUS.

bountifulness *noun*
Prosperity and a sufficiency of life's necessities.   PLENTY *noun.*

bounty *noun*
A sum of money offered for a special service, as the apprehension of a criminal.   REWARD *noun.*

bouquet *noun*
1. Cut flowers that have been arranged in a usu. small bunch: *a bouquet of roses on the table.*   **1.** *Syns:* nosegay, posy.
2. An expression of admiration or congratulation.   **2.** COMPLIMENT *noun.*
3. A sweet or pleasant odor.   **3.** FRAGRANCE.

bout *noun*
1. A limited, often assigned period of activity, duty, or opportunity.   **1.** TURN *noun.*
2. An often prolonged period, as of illness.   **2.** SIEGE *noun.*

boutade *noun*
An impulsive, often illogical turn of mind.   FANCY *noun.*

bow *verb*
1. To incline the body.   **1.** STOOP.
2. To swerve from a straight line.   **2.** BEND *verb.*
3. To give in from or as if from a gradual loss of strength.   **3.** SUCCUMB.
4. To conform to the will or judgment of another, esp. out of respect or courtesy.   **4.** DEFER².
5. To make one's formal entry, as into society.   **5.** COME OUT at **come.**

bow *noun*
1. An inclination of the head or body, as in greeting, consent, courtesy, submission, or worship: *gave a bow of acknowledgment.*   **1.** *Syns:* curtsy, genuflection, kowtow, nod, obeisance.
2. Something bent.   **2.** BEND *noun.*

bowdlerize *verb*
To examine (material) and remove parts considered harmful or improper for publication or transmission.   CENSOR.

bowed *adjective*
Deviating from a straight line. BENT *adjective*.

bowl over *verb*
To overwhelm with surprise, wonder, or bewilderment. STAGGER.

box[1] *noun*
A difficult, embarrassing situation. PREDICAMENT.

box[2] *noun*
A quick, sharp blow, esp. with the hand. SLAP *noun*.

box *verb*
To hit with a quick, sharp blow of the hand. SLAP *verb*.

boy *noun*
Informal. A grown man, referred to familiarly, jokingly, **Syns:** chap, fellow.
or as a member of one's set or group: *had a night on*
the town with the boys.

boycott *verb*
To exclude from normal social or professional activities. BLACKBALL.

boyfriend also **boy friend** *noun*
Informal. A man who is the favored companion of a **Syns:** beau, fellow (*Informal*).
woman: *went to dinner with her boyfriend.*

brace[1] *noun*
Two items of the same kind together. COUPLE *noun*.

brace[2] *verb*
To prepare (oneself) for action. GIRD.

brace *noun*
A means or device that keeps something erect, stable, SUPPORT *noun*.
or secure.

bracer *noun*
A medicine that restores or increases vigor. TONIC *noun*.

bracing *adjective*
Producing or stimulating physical, mental, or emotional TONIC *adjective*.
vigor.

bracket *noun*
A division of persons or things by quality, rank, or CLASS *noun*.
grade.

bracket *verb*
To come or bring together in one's mind or imagination. ASSOCIATE *verb*.

brag *verb*
To talk with excessive pride. BOAST *verb*.

brag *noun*
1. An act of boasting. 1. BOAST *noun*.
2. One given to boasting. 2. BRAGGART *noun*.

brag *adjective*
Exceptionally good of its kind. EXCELLENT.

braggadocian *adjective*
Characterized by or given to boasting. BOASTFUL.

braggadocio *noun*
1. An act of boasting. 1. BOAST *noun*.
2. One given to boasting. 2. BRAGGART *noun*.

braggart *noun*
One given to boasting: *just another self-important* **Syns:** blower (*Slang*), blowhard (*Slang*),
braggart. boaster, brag, braggadocio, bragger,
fanfaron (*Obs.*). —*Idiom* hot-air artist.
Near-syns: bluffer, blusterer, loudmouth
(*Slang*), windbag.

braggart *adjective*
Characterized by or given to boasting. BOASTFUL.

bragger *noun*
One given to boasting. BRAGGART *noun*.

braggy *adjective*
Characterized by or given to boasting. BOASTFUL.

brain *noun*
1. The seat of the faculty of intelligence and reason.
2. *Slang.* A person of great mental ability.
3. A person considered with respect to intelligence.

1. HEAD *noun.*
2. MIND *noun.*
3. MIND *noun.*

brain child *noun*
Informal. Something invented.

INVENTION.

brainless *adjective*
Displaying a complete lack of forethought and good sense.

MINDLESS.

brain(s) *noun*
Informal. The faculty of thinking, reasoning, and acquiring and applying knowledge.

INTELLIGENCE.

brainsick *adjective*
Afflicted with or exhibiting irrationality and mental unsoundness.

INSANE.

brainsickness *noun*
Serious mental illness or disorder impairing a person's capacity to function normally and safely.

INSANITY.

brainstorm *noun*
A sudden, exciting thought.

INSPIRATION.

brainwash *verb*
To teach to accept a system of thought uncritically.

INDOCTRINATE.

brain wave *noun*
A sudden, exciting thought.

INSPIRATION.

brainwork *noun*
The act or process of thinking.

THOUGHT.

brainy *adjective*
Informal. Having or showing intelligence, often of a high order.

INTELLIGENT.

brake *verb*
To control, restrict, or arrest.

RESTRAIN.

branch *noun*
1. Something resembling or structurally analogous to a tree branch: *The eastern branch of the road led to the city.*
2. An area of academic study that is part of a larger body of learning: *Biology is a branch of science.*
3. A local unit of a business or an auxiliary controlled by such a business.
4. A part of a family, tribe, or other group, or of such a group's language, that is believed to stem from a common ancestor: *Germanic is a branch of Indo-European.*
5. A component of government that performs a given function: *the executive branch.*
6. A small stream.

1. *Syns:* appendage, arm, fork, offshoot.
2. *Syns:* discipline, specialty.
3. SUBSIDIARY.
4. *Syns:* division, offshoot, subdivision.
5. *Syns:* arm, division, organ, wing.
6. *Syns:* brook[1], creek, run.

branch *verb*
To separate into branches or branchlike parts: *The highway branches here.*

Syns: bifurcate, diverge, divide, fork, ramify, subdivide.

brand *noun*
A name or other device placed on merchandise to signify its ownership or manufacture.

MARK *noun.*

brand *verb*
1. To set off by or as if by a mark indicating ownership or manufacture.
2. To mark with disgrace or infamy.

1. MARK *verb.*
2. STIGMATIZE.

brandish *verb*
1. To wield boldly and dramatically.
2. To make a public and usu. ostentatious show of.

1. FLOURISH.
2. DISPLAY *verb.*

brand-new *adjective*
Not previously known or used.

FRESH.

brannigan *noun*
Slang. A drinking bout.   BENDER.

brash *adjective*
1. Characterized by unthinking boldness and haste.   1. RASH[1].
2. Having or exhibiting excessive and arrogant self-   2. PRESUMPTUOUS.
   confidence.
3. Lacking sensitivity and skill in dealing with others.   3. TACTLESS.

brashness *noun*
1. Excessive and arrogant self-confidence.   1. PRESUMPTION.
2. Foolhardy boldness or disregard of danger.   2. TEMERITY.

brass *noun*
1. *Informal.* Excessive and arrogant self-confidence.   1. PRESUMPTION.
2. *Brit. Slang.* Something, as coins, printed bills, etc.,   2. MONEY.
   used as a medium of exchange.

brassbound *adjective*
Firmly, often unreasonably immovable in purpose or   STUBBORN.
will.

brass-tacks *adjective*
Precisely meaningful and tersely cogent.   PITHY.

brassy *adjective*
1. *Informal.* Having or exhibiting excessive and   1. PRESUMPTUOUS.
   arrogant self-confidence.
2. *Informal.* Characterized by or done without shame.   2. SHAMELESS.

brattle *verb*
Chiefly Scot. To make or cause to make a succession of   RATTLE *verb.*
short, sharp sounds.

brave *adjective*
Having or showing courage: *a brave effort to rescue the*   **Syns:** audacious, bold, courageous,
drowning child.   dauntless, doughty, fearless, fortitudinous,
                                                         gallant, game, gutsy (*Informal*), gutty,
                                                         heroic, intrepid, mettlesome, plucky, stout,
                                                         stouthearted, unafraid, undaunted,
                                                         valiant, valorous.
                                                         Near-syns: boldhearted, bravehearted,
                                                         lionhearted, manful, manly, spunky,
                                                         stalwart; gritty, steadfast, venturesome.
                                                         Ant: cowardly.

brave *verb*
To confront boldly and courageously.   DEFY.

brave *noun*
Obs. One who is habitually cruel to smaller or weaker   BULLY *noun.*
people.

braveness *noun*
The quality of mind enabling one to face danger or   COURAGE.
hardship resolutely.

bravery *noun*
The quality of mind enabling one to face danger or   COURAGE.
hardship resolutely.

braw *adjective*
Scot. Having pleasant, desirable qualities.   GOOD *adjective.*

brawl *noun*
A quarrel or fight marked by very noisy, disorderly,   **Syns:** affray, broil, donnybrook, fracas,
and often violent behavior: *The party ended in a*   fray, free-for-all, melee (*also* mêlée), riot,
shameful brawl.   row[2], ruckus (*Informal*), ruction, tumult,
                                                         uproar.
                                                         Near-syns: dogfight, fight, maul, rough-
                                                         and-tumble, scrap, scuffle, set-to; fistfight,
                                                         slugfest; rumpus.

brawl *verb*
To quarrel noisily: *often call the police because the*   **Syns:** broil, caterwaul, riot, squabble,
neighbors constantly brawl.   wrangle.

brawn *noun*
The state or quality of being physically strong.   STRENGTH.
brawny *adjective*
1. Characterized by marked muscular development; powerfully built.   1. MUSCULAR.
2. Having great physical strength.   2. STRONG.
bray *verb*
To break up into tiny particles.   CRUSH *verb*.
brazen *adjective*
1. Rude and disrespectful.   1. IMPUDENT.
2. Having or exhibiting excessive and arrogant self-confidence.   2. PRESUMPTUOUS.
3. Characterized by or done without shame.   3. SHAMELESS.
brazenfaced *adjective*
Characterized by or done without shame.   SHAMELESS.
brazenness *noun*
1. The state or quality of being impudent.   1. IMPUDENCE.
2. Excessive and arrogant self-confidence.   2. PRESUMPTION.
breach *noun*
1. An act or instance of breaking a law or regulation or of nonfulfillment of an obligation, promise, etc.: *was reproached for breach of good faith.*   1. *Syns:* contravention, infraction, infringement, transgression, trespass, violation.
2. An opening, esp. in a solid structure: *Water poured through the breach in the dike.*   2. *Syns:* break, cleft, gap, hole, perforation, rent², rupture.
3. An interruption in friendly relations: *a policy dispute that could create a breach between our two countries.*   3. *Syns:* break, disaffection, estrangement, fissure, rent², rift, rupture, schism.
4. An interval during which continuity is suspended.   4. GAP.
breach *verb*
1. To fail to fulfill (a promise) or conform to (a regulation).   1. VIOLATE.
2. To make a hole or other opening in: *breached the walls during the attack.*   2. *Syns:* break through, hole, perforate, pierce, puncture, rupture.
bread *noun*
1. Something fit to be eaten.   1. FOOD.
2. The means needed to support life.   2. LIVING.
3. *Slang.* Something, as coins, printed bills, etc., used as a medium of exchange.   3. MONEY.
breadth *noun*
A wide and open area, as of land, sky, or water.   EXPANSE.
breadthen *verb*
To make or become broad or broader.   BROADEN.
break *verb*
1. To crack or split into two or more fragments by means of or as a result of force, a blow, or strain: *He's afraid he'll break his glasses. The mirror broke into hundreds of pieces.*   1. *Syns:* cleave, disjoin, disjoint, fracture, rive, shatter, shiver, smash, splinter, sunder.
2. To become separated from: *At a certain speed space vehicles break free of the earth's gravity.*   2. *Syns:* disengage, dissociate.
3. To become or cause to become apart one from another.   3. DIVIDE.
4. To make or become unusable or inoperative: *broke my watch; a typewriter that broke.*   4. *Syns:* bust (*Slang*), fail, ruin.
5. To give way mentally and emotionally.   5. BREAK DOWN.
6. To impair severely the spirit, health, effectiveness, etc., of: *broke the enemy's resistance.*   6. *Syns:* crush, destroy, overwhelm, ruin, subdue.
7. To make (an animal) docile.   7. GENTLE *verb*.
8. To pass into or through by overcoming resistance.   8. PENETRATE.
9. To cut short; discontinue: *determined to break her smoking habit.*   9. *Syns:* cut out (*Slang*), give up, kick (*Slang*), leave off, stop.
10. To refuse or fail to obey.   10. DISOBEY.

11. To reduce to financial insolvency.
12. To lower in rank or grade.
13. To make known.
14. To be made public.
15. To find the key to: *broke the Japanese military code and hastened the war's end.*
16. To interrupt regular activity for a short period: *We'll break for lunch at one.*
17. To be unable to hold up.
18. To spade or dig (soil) to bring the undersoil to the surface.
19. To fail to fulfill (a promise) or conform to (a regulation).

11. RUIN *verb*.
12. DEMOTE.
13. COMMUNICATE.
14. COME OUT at **come**.
15. *Syns:* crack, decipher, puzzle out.
16. *Syn:* recess. —*Idioms* take a break, take a breather, take five.
17. BEND *verb*.
18. TURN *verb*.
19. VIOLATE.

break in *verb*
1. To enter forcibly and illegally: *Thieves broke in and stole the stereo.*
2. To interject remarks or questions into another's discourse.

1. *Syns:* burglarize, housebreak, trespass.
2. INTERRUPT.

break off *verb*
1. To stop suddenly, as a conversation, activity, relationship, etc.
2. To terminate a relationship or association by or as if by leaving one another.

1. SUSPEND.
2. SEPARATE *verb*.

break through *verb*
To make a hole or other opening in.

BREACH *verb*.

break up *verb*
1. To bring or come to a forced end: *The police may have to break up this fight. Their marriage broke up.*
2. To reduce or become reduced to pieces or components: *Over the centuries rock breaks up into particles from erosion.*
3. *Slang.* To express great amusement or mirth: *The audience broke up at the comedienne's act.*
4. To make a division into parts, sections, or branches.
5. To terminate a relationship or association by or as if by leaving one another.

1. *Syns:* halt[1], stop.
2. *Syns:* crumble, decompose, disintegrate, dissolve, fragment, fragmentize.
3. *Syns:* guffaw, howl (*Slang*), roar.
4. DIVIDE.
5. SEPARATE *verb*.

break *noun*
1. A usu. narrow partial opening caused by splitting and rupture.
2. An opening, esp. in a solid structure.
3. A cessation of continuity or regularity: *a break in the conversation.*
4. An interval during which continuity is suspended.
5. A pause or interval, as from work or duty: *going to take a coffee break.*

6. *Informal.* A favorable or advantageous combination of circumstances.
7. An interruption in friendly relations.
8. The act or an instance of escaping, as from confinement or difficulty.

1. CRACK *noun*.
2. BREACH *noun*.
3. *Syns:* discontinuity, disruption, interruption, pause, suspension.
4. GAP.
5. *Syns:* breather (*Informal*), intermission, recess, respite, rest[1], time-out.
6. OPPORTUNITY.
7. BREACH *noun*.
8. ESCAPE *noun*.

breakable *adjective*
Easily broken or damaged.

FRAGILE.

breakage *noun*
An act, instance, or consequence of breaking: *wholesale breakage of china during the move.*

Syns: damage, destruction, impairment, wreckage.

breakdown *noun*

SEE **break down**.

break down *verb*
1. To collapse or shatter by or as if by breaking: *The firemen broke down the door.*
2. To cease functioning properly.

1. *Syns:* destroy, smash, tear down.
2. FAIL.

3. To separate into parts for study.
4. To give way mentally and emotionally: *She broke down from the pressure.*
5. To become or cause to become rotten or unsound.
6. To suddenly lose all health or strength.
7. To fall in.

breakdown   *noun*
1. A sudden sharp decline in mental, emotional, or physical health: *Stress caused a complete breakdown.*
2. An abrupt, disastrous failure.
3. The separation of a whole into its parts for study.
4. The condition of being decayed.
5. A cessation of proper mechanical functions.

break in   *verb*

breakneck   *adjective*
Characterized by great celerity.

break off   *verb*

breakout   *noun*

break out   *verb*
1. To become manifest suddenly and in full force: *In 1967 a war broke out in the Middle East.*
2. To break loose and leave suddenly, as from confinement or from a difficult or threatening situation.

    breakout   *noun*
    The act or an instance of escaping, as from confinement or difficulty.

break through   *verb*

break up   *verb*

breast   *noun*
The seat of a person's innermost emotions and feelings.

breath   *noun*
1. The act or process of breathing: *the runner's labored breath.*
2. Air breathed out, evidenced by vapor, odor, or heat: *could see my breath in the frosty air.*
3. Air breathed in: *took an audible breath.*
4. A barely perceivable indication of something.

breathe   *verb*
1. To draw air into the lungs in the process of respiration: *breathing rapidly from exertion.*
2. To expel air in the process of respiration: *breathed out loudly.*
3. To breathe in and out: *breathing deeply.*
4. To have reality or life.
5. To tell in confidence.

breather   *noun*
Informal. A pause or interval, as from work or duty.

breathless   *adjective*
1. Marked by an absence of circulating air.
2. Oppressive due to a lack of fresh air.

breed   *verb*
1. To produce sexually or asexually others of one's kind.
2. To be the biological father of.
3. To bring into existence and foster the development of.
4. To give rise to.

    breed   *noun*
    A class that is defined by the common attribute or attributes possessed by all its members.

---

3. ANALYZE.
4. *Syns:* break, cave in, collapse, crack (up), fold (*Informal*), snap.
5. DECAY *verb.*
6. COLLAPSE *verb.*
7. CAVE IN at **cave.**

1. *Syns:* collapse, crackup (*Informal*).
2. COLLAPSE *noun.*
3. ANALYSIS.
4. DECAY *noun.*
5. FAILURE.

SEE **break.**

FAST *adjective.*

SEE **break.**

SEE **break out.**

1. *Syns:* burst forth, erupt, explode, flare (up).
2. ESCAPE *verb.*

ESCAPE *noun.*

SEE **break.**

SEE **break.**

HEART.

1. *Syn:* respiration.
2. *Syn:* exhalation.
3. *Syn:* inhalation.
4. TRACE *noun.*

1. *Syns:* inhale, inspire.
2. *Syns:* exhale, expire.
3. *Syn:* respire.
4. BE.
5. CONFIDE.

BREAK *noun.*

1. AIRLESS.
2. AIRLESS.

1. REPRODUCE.
2. FATHER *verb.*
3. GROW.
4. GENERATE.

KIND[2].

breeding *noun*
The process by which an organism produces others of its kind.

REPRODUCTION.

breeze *noun*
1. A natural movement or current of air.
2. A gentle wind: *We went sailing, but there was no breeze.*
3. *Informal.* An easily accomplished task: *Chopping onions is a breeze with a food processor.*

1. WIND[1].
2. *Syn:* zephyr.
3. *Syns:* cinch (*Informal*), pushover (*Informal*), snap (*Informal*), walkaway (*Informal*), walkover (*Informal*). —*Idioms* child's play, duck soup.

breeze *verb*
Informal. To move swiftly and effortlessly: *two young girls breezing down the street.*

Syns: waltz, zip.

breezeless *adjective*
Marked by an absence of circulating air.

AIRLESS.

breezy *adjective*
1. Displaying light-hearted nonchalance.
2. Exposed to or characterized by the presence of freely circulating air or wind.

1. AIRY.
2. AIRY.

briary *adjective*

SEE **briery.**

bribe *noun*
Money, property, or a favor given, offered, or promised to a person in a position of trust as an inducement to dishonest behavior: *offered the judge a bribe to find in his favor.*

Syns: boodle (*Slang*), fix, graft, payoff (*Informal*), payola (*Slang*).

bribe *verb*
To give, offer, or promise a bribe to: *tried to bribe the senator to vote in favor of the tax law.*

Syns: buy, buy off, fix, pay off (*Informal*). —*Idioms* grease someone's palm (*or* hand), tickle someone's palm (*or* hand).

bridal *noun*
The act or ceremony by which two people become husband and wife.

WEDDING.

bridle *verb*
To control, restrict, or arrest.

RESTRAIN.

brief *adjective*
1. Not long in time or duration: *Spring is all too brief.*
2. Marked by or consisting of few words: *a brief explanation.*

1. *Syn:* short.
2. *Syns:* compendious, concise, condensed, laconic, lean[2], short, succinct, summary, terse. —*Idiom* to the point. *Near-ants:* diffuse, long-winded, prolix, rambling, verbose, voluble. *Ant:* wordy.

3. Rudely unceremonious.
4. Accomplished in very little time.

3. ABRUPT.
4. QUICK *adjective.*

brief *noun*
A short summary prepared by cutting down a larger work.

SYNOPSIS.

brief *verb*
To make short or shorter by or as if by cutting.

TRUNCATE.

briery also **briary** *adjective*
Full of sharp, needlelike protuberances.

THORNY.

brig *noun*
A place for the confinement of persons in lawful detention.

JAIL *noun.*

bright *adjective*
1. Giving off or reflecting light readily or in large amounts: *a bright brass doorknob; bright, sparkling diamonds.*

1. *Syns:* beaming, brilliant, effulgent, incandescent, irradiant, lambent, lucent, luminous, lustrous, radiant, refulgent, shining. *Near-ants:* dark, dusky, gloomy,

murky; colorless, drab, dreary, lackluster, somber; cloudy, gray overcast.
Ants: dim, dull.

2. Full of color.
    2. COLORFUL.
3. Indicative of future success.
    3. FAVORABLE.
4. Being in or showing good spirits.
    4. CHEERFUL.
5. Mentally quick and original.
    5. CLEVER.

brighten *verb*
1. To become brighter or fairer.   1. CLEAR *verb.*
2. To make lively or animated.   2. LIGHT¹ *verb.*

brilliance also **brilliancy** *noun*
1. Exceptional brightness and clarity, as of a cut and polished stone.   1. FIRE *noun.*
2. Brilliant, showy splendor.   2. GLITTER *noun.*

brilliancy *noun*   SEE **brilliance.**

brilliant *adjective*
1. Giving off or reflecting light readily or in large amounts.   1. BRIGHT.
2. Having or showing intelligence, often of a high order.   2. INTELLIGENT.
3. Indicative of future success.   3. FAVORABLE.

brim *noun*
A fairly narrow line or space forming a boundary.   BORDER *noun.*

brimful *adjective*
1. Full to the point of flowing over.   1. BIG *adjective.*
2. Completely filled.   2. FULL.

brimming *adjective*
1. Full to the point of flowing over.   1. BIG *adjective.*
2. Completely filled.   2. FULL.

bring *verb*
1. To cause to come along with oneself: *Soldiers brought the prisoner back for questioning.*   1. *Syns:* bear, carry, convey, fetch, take.
2. To succeed in causing (a person) to act in a certain way.   2. PERSUADE.
3. To be the cause of.   3. CAUSE *verb.*
4. To achieve a certain price: *His stamp collection should bring $1,000.*   4. *Syns:* bring in, fetch (*Informal*), realize, sell for.

bring about *verb*
To be the cause of.   CAUSE *verb.*

bring around *verb*
1. To succeed in causing (a person) to act in a certain way.   1. PERSUADE.
2. To cause to come back to life or consciousness.   2. REVIVE.

bring down *verb*
1. To cause to fall, as from a shot or blow: *brought his opponent down with a left hook to the jaw.*   1. DROP *verb.*
2. To bring about the downfall of.   2. OVERTHROW.

bring forth *verb*
To give birth to.   BEAR.

bring in *verb*
1. To make as income or profit.   1. RETURN *verb.*
2. To achieve a certain price.   2. BRING.

bring off *verb*
To carry to a successful conclusion.   EFFECT *verb.*

bring on *verb*
To cause to happen suddenly or unexpectedly.   PRECIPITATE *verb.*

bring out *verb*
To present for circulation, exhibit, or sale.   PUBLISH.

bring up *verb*

1. To take care of and educate (a child): *was brought up by conservative parents.*
2. To put forward a topic for discussion.
3. To call or direct attention to (an occurrence, situation, etc.).

bring about *verb*
bring around *verb*
bring down *verb*
bring forth *verb*
bring in *verb*
bring off *verb*
bring on *verb*
bring out *verb*
bring up *verb*

brink *noun*
1. A fairly narrow line or space forming a boundary.
2. A transitional interval beyond which some new action or different state of affairs is likely to begin or occur.

brio *noun*
A lively, emphatic, eager quality or manner.

brisk *adjective*
1. Moving or performing quickly, lightly, and easily.
2. Disposed to action.

brisky *adjective*
Disposed to action.

bristle *verb*
1. To overflow with.
2. To be or become angry.

brittle *adjective*
Easily broken or damaged.

broach *verb*
To put forward a topic for discussion: *did not know how to broach the subject tactfully.*

broad *adjective*
1. Extending over a large area from side to side: *broad shoulders; a broad smile.*
2. Large in expanse: *a broad, velvety lawn.*

3. Covering a wide scope.
4. Not narrow or conservative in thought, expression, or conduct: *a woman of broad views on social reform.*
5. Easily seen through due to a lack of subtlety.
6. Bordering on indelicacy or impropriety.

broadcast *verb*
1. To make (information) generally known.
2. To bring to public notice.

broadcast *noun*
The act of announcing.

broaden *verb*
1. To make or become broad or broader: *The turnpike broadens at the tollgate.*
2. To make or become more comprehensive or inclusive.

broad-minded *adjective*
Not narrow or conservative in thought, expression, or conduct.

broadness *noun*
The extent of something from side to side.

---

1. **Syns:** raise, rear[2].
2. BROACH.
3. REFER.

SEE **bring.**
SEE **bring.**
SEE **bring.**
SEE **bring.**
SEE **bring.**
SEE **bring.**
SEE **bring.**
SEE **bring.**
SEE **bring.**

1. BORDER *noun.*
2. VERGE *noun.*

SPIRIT.

1. NIMBLE.
2. VIGOROUS.

VIGOROUS.

1. TEEM[1].
2. ANGER *verb.*

FRAGILE.

Syns: bring up, introduce, moot, put forth, raise.

1. **Syn:** wide.

2. **Syns:** ample, expansive, extended, extensive, spacious.
   Near-syns: big, considerable, large, major, sizable.

3. GENERAL.
4. **Syns:** broad-minded, liberal, open-minded, progressive, tolerant.
5. UNSUBTLE.
6. RACY.

1. ADVERTISE.
2. ANNOUNCE.

ANNOUNCEMENT.

1. **Syns:** breadthen, widen.

2. EXTEND.

BROAD *adjective.*

WIDTH.

broad-spectrum *adjective*
Covering a wide scope. GENERAL.

Brobdingnagian *adjective*
Of extraordinary size and power. GIANT *adjective*.

broil *noun*
A quarrel or fight marked by very noisy, disorderly, BRAWL *noun*.
and often violent behavior.

broil *verb*
1. To feel or look hot. 1. BURN *verb*.
2. To quarrel noisily. 2. BRAWL *verb*.

broiling *adjective*
Marked by much heat. HOT *adjective*.

broke *adjective*
Informal. Having little or no money or wealth. POOR.

broken-down *adjective*
Showing signs of wear and tear or neglect. SHABBY.

broker *noun*
Someone who acts as an intermediate agent in a GO-BETWEEN.
transaction.

bromide *noun*
A trite expression or idea. CLICHÉ *noun*.

bromidic *adjective*
Without freshness or appeal due to overuse. TRITE.

Bronx cheer *noun*
Slang. Any derisive sound of disapproval. HISS *noun*.

brood *noun*
1. A group consisting of those descended directly from 1. PROGENY.
the same parents or ancestors.
2. The offspring, as of an animal, bird, etc., that are 2. YOUNG *noun*.
the result of one breeding season.

brood *verb*
To turn over in the mind, moodily and at length: *He's* **Syns:** despond, dwell on (*or* upon), fret,
brooding about his decline in popularity and worrying mope, stew (*over or* about) (*Informal*),
about the upcoming election. worry. —*Idiom* be in a brown study.

brook¹ *noun*
A small stream. BRANCH *noun*.

brook² *verb*
To put up with. ENDURE.

brotherhood *noun*
The condition of being friends. FRIENDSHIP.

brouhaha *noun*
A condition of intense public interest or excitement. SENSATION.

browbeat *verb*
To domineer or drive into compliance by the use of INTIMIDATE.
threats, force, etc.

browbeater *noun*
One who is habitually cruel to smaller or weaker BULLY *noun*.
people.

brown-nose *verb*
Slang. To support slavishly every opinion or suggestion FAWN.
of a superior.

browse *verb*
1. To look through reading matter casually: *browsed* 1. **Syns:** dip into, flip (through), glance at
through the magazine looking at advertisements. (*or* over *or* through), leaf through, riffle
through, run through, scan, skim,
thumb through.
2. To go through a place, viewing or inspecting in a 2. **Syns:** roam, stroll, wander.
leisurely way: *browsing around in the department*
store.

bruise   *verb*
To make or receive a bruise or bruises on: *bruised his shoulder when he fell off the horse; skin that bruises easily.*

Syns: black, contuse.

bruit   *verb*
1. To make (information) generally known.
2. To spread as news.

1. ADVERTISE.
2. NOISE *verb.*

brume   *noun*
A thick, heavy atmospheric condition offering reduced visibility due to the presence of suspended particles.

HAZE *noun.*

brummagem   *noun*
An inferior substitute imitating an original.

COPY *noun.*

brunet also **brunette**   *adjective*
Of a complexion tending toward brown or black.

DARK *adjective.*

brunette   *adjective*

SEE **brunet.**

brush   *noun*
1. Light and momentary contact with another person or thing: *a brush of her fingers on the piano keys.*
2. A brief, hostile exposure to or contact with something, as danger, opposition, etc.: *has frequent brushes with the law.*

1. *Syns:* flick, glance[1], graze, skim.

2. *Syns:* clash, encounter, run-in, skirmish.

brush   *verb*
To make light and momentary contact with, as in passing: *His arm brushed mine in the elevator.*

Syns: flick, glance[1], graze, kiss, shave, skim.

brusque   *adjective*
Rudely unceremonious.

ABRUPT.

brutal   *adjective*
Causing sharp, often prolonged discomfort.

BITTER *adjective.*

brutality   *noun*
A cruel act or an instance of cruel behavior.

CRUELTY.

brutalize   *verb*
To ruin utterly in character or quality.

CORRUPT *verb.*

bubble   *noun*
A fantastic, impracticable plan or desire.

ILLUSION.

bubble   *verb*
1. To form or cause to form foam.
2. To be in a state of emotional or mental turmoil.

1. FOAM *verb.*
2. BOIL *verb.*

buck[1]   *verb*
To take a stand against.

CONTEST *verb.*

buck up   *verb*
Informal. To impart strength and confidence to.

ENCOURAGE.

buck[2]   *verb*
To break up into tiny particles.

CRUSH *verb.*

bucket   *verb*
To move swiftly.

RUSH *verb.*

buckle   *verb*
1. To devote (oneself or one's efforts).
2. To fall in.

1. APPLY.
2. CAVE IN at **cave.**

buckram   *adjective*
So rigidly constrained, formal, or awkward as to lack all grace and spontaneity.

STIFF *adjective.*

bucks   *noun*
Slang. Something, as coins, printed bills, etc., used as a medium of exchange.

MONEY.

buck up   *verb*

SEE **buck**[1].

bucolic   *adjective*
Of or pertaining to the countryside.

COUNTRY *adjective.*

bud   *noun*
1. A source of further growth and development.
2. A young person between birth and puberty.

1. GERM.
2. CHILD.

buddy   *noun*
Informal. One who keeps company with another.   ASSOCIATE *noun*.

budge   *verb*
To make a slight movement.   STIR[1] *verb*.

budget   *noun*
A measurable whole.   QUANTITY.

buff   *verb*
To give a gleaming luster to, usu. through friction.   GLOSS *verb*.

buffet   *noun*
A quick, sharp blow, esp. with the hand.   SLAP *noun*.

   buffet   *verb*
1. To hit with a quick, sharp blow of the hand.   **1.** SLAP *verb*.
2. To hit heavily and repeatedly.   **2.** BEAT *verb*.

bug   *noun*
1. *Informal.* A minute organism usu. producing   **1.** GERM.
   disease.
2. *Slang.* Something that mars the appearance or   **2.** DEFECT *noun*.
   causes inadequacy or failure.
3. *Slang.* A person who is ardently devoted to a   **3.** ENTHUSIAST.
   particular subject or activity.

   bug   *verb*
1. *Slang.* To trouble the nerves or peace of mind of,   **1.** ANNOY.
   esp. by repeated vexations.
2. To monitor (telephone calls) with a concealed   **2.** TAP[2] *verb*.
   listening device connected to the circuit.

bugbear   *noun*
1. *Archaic.* A supernatural being.   **1.** GHOST *noun*.
2. An object of extreme dislike.   **2.** HATE *noun*.

buggy   *adjective*
Slang. Afflicted with or exhibiting irrationality and   INSANE.
mental unsoundness.

bughouse   *adjective*
Slang. Afflicted with or exhibiting irrationality and   INSANE.
mental unsoundness.

bugs   *adjective*
Slang. Afflicted with or exhibiting irrationality and   INSANE.
mental unsoundness.

build   *verb*
1. To make or form (a structure): *built a skyscraper;*   **1.** *Syns:* construct, erect, put up, raise,
   built a sand castle for the children.   rear[2].
                                                             Near-ants: demolish, destroy,
                                                             dismantle, level, raze, wreck.
2. To create by forming, combining, or altering   **2.** MAKE.
   materials.
3. To take or serve as the basis for.   **3.** BASE[1] *verb*.
4. To become greater in number, amount, or intensity.   **4.** RISE *verb*.

   build in   *verb*
To construct or include as an integral or permanent   *Syns:* incorporate, integrate.
part: *Be sure to build in the sum allowed for cost*
overruns.

   build   *noun*
Bodily type.   CONSTITUTION.

builder   *noun*
1. A person or business that makes or builds   **1.** *Syns:* constructor, erector, maker,
   something: *the builder of a house; an automobile*   manufacturer.
   builder.
2. A person instrumental in the growth of something,   **2.** *Syns:* contributor, creator, developer,
   esp. in its early stages: *one of the builders of the*   pioneer.
   space age.

build in   *verb*   SEE **build**.

building   *noun*
A usu. permanent construction, as a house, store, etc.:
put up a 25-story building on the site.

Syns: edifice, pile, structure.

build-up also **buildup**   *noun*

SEE **build up.**

build up   *verb*
1. To increase or seek to increase the importance or
   reputation of by favorable publicity.
2. To make or become greater or larger.
3. To achieve an increment of gradually.
4. To make known vigorously the positive features of
   (a product).

1. PROMOTE.
2. INCREASE *verb.*
3. GAIN *verb.*
4. ADVERTISE.

build-up also **buildup**   *noun*
1. The result or product of building up: *the build-up of
   ashes in the fireplace; the build-up of tensions during
   the strike.*

2. *Informal.* A systematic effort to increase the
   importance or reputation of by favorable publicity.

1. *Syns:* accretion, accumulation,
   amassment, development, enlargement,
   increase, increment, multiplication,
   proliferation.
2. PROMOTION.

built   *adjective*
Informal. Having a full, voluptuous figure.

SHAPELY.

built-in   *adjective*
1. Constructed as a nondetachable part of a larger
   unit: *a built-in bookcase.*
2. Forming an essential element: *a built-in sense of
   danger.*

1. *Syns:* component, constituent,
   incorporated.
2. *Syns:* congenital, constitutional, inborn,
   inbred, inherent, innate, intrinsic,
   natural.

bulge   *noun*
1. A part that protrudes or extends outward: *a bulge
   under his jacket indicating a pistol.*
2. *Slang.* A dominating position, as in a conflict.

1. *Syns:* jut, knob, knot, projection,
   protrusion, protuberance.
2. ADVANTAGE *noun.*

bulge   *verb*
To curve outward past the normal or usual limit:
Money and cosmetics are making her purse bulge.

Syns: bag, balloon, belly, jut, overhang,
pouch, project, protrude, protuberate,
stand out, stick out.

bulk   *noun*
1. Great extent, amount, or dimension: *Whales have
   monstrous bulk.*
2. A measurable whole.
3. The main part.
4. The greatest part or portion.

1. *Syns:* amplitude, magnitude, mass,
   size, volume.
2. QUANTITY.
3. BODY *noun.*
4. WEIGHT *noun.*

bulky   *adjective*
1. Extremely large; having great mass: *a bulky volume
   of poetry.*
2. Having a large body, esp. in girth: *a bulky man
   having trouble climbing the stairs.*
3. Difficult to handle or manage.

1. *Syns:* massive, oversize (*also
   oversized*).
2. *Syns:* hulking, hulky, stout.

3. AWKWARD.

bull   *noun*
1. A stupid, clumsy mistake.
2. *Slang.* Something that does not have or make sense.
3. *Slang.* A member of a law-enforcement agency.

1. BLUNDER *noun.*
2. NONSENSE.
3. POLICEMAN.

bulldogged   *adjective*
Tenaciously unwilling to yield.

OBSTINATE.

bulldoggish   *adjective*
Tenaciously unwilling to yield.

OBSTINATE.

bulldoggy   *adjective*
Tenaciously unwilling to yield.

OBSTINATE.

bulldoze   *verb*
1. To domineer or drive into compliance by the use of
   threats, force, etc.
2. *Slang.* To do or achieve by forcing obstacles out of
   one's way.

1. INTIMIDATE.
2. PUSH *verb.*

bulldozer *noun*
One who is habitually cruel to smaller or weaker people. BULLY *noun*.

bullet *verb*
To move swiftly. RUSH *verb*.

bullheaded *adjective*
Tenaciously unwilling to yield. OBSTINATE.

bullheadedness *noun*
The quality or state of being stubbornly unyielding. OBSTINACY.

bullwork *noun*
Physical exertion that is usu. difficult and exhausting. LABOR *noun*.

bully *noun*
One who is habitually cruel to smaller or weaker people: *A swaggering bully is often a real coward.*

Syns: brave (*Obs.*), browbeater, bulldozer, hector, intimidator.
Near-syns: antagonizer, heckler, persecutor, pest, tease, tormenter, tough.

bully *verb*
To domineer or drive into compliance by the use of threats, force, etc. INTIMIDATE.

bully *adjective*
Informal. Exceptionally good of its kind. EXCELLENT.

bullyrag *verb*
1. To domineer or drive into compliance by the use of threats, force, etc. 1. INTIMIDATE.
2. To torment with persistent insult or ridicule. 2. BAIT *verb*.

bum *verb*
1. *Slang.* To ask or ask for as charity. 1. BEG.
2. *Informal.* To pass time without working or in avoiding work. 2. IDLE *verb*.

bum *noun*
A self-indulgent person who spends time avoiding work or other useful activity. WASTREL.

bum *adjective*
Informal. Below a standard of quality. BAD.

bumble¹ *verb*
To move awkwardly or clumsily. BLUNDER *verb*.

bumble² *verb*
To make a continuous low-pitched droning sound. HUM *verb*.

bumble *noun*
A continuous low-pitched droning sound. HUM *noun*.

bumbling *adjective*
Clumsily lacking in the ability to do or perform. UNSKILLFUL.

bummer¹ *noun*
Slang. One who begs habitually or for a living. BEGGAR.

bummer² *noun*
Slang. A great disappointment or regrettable fact. SHAME *noun*.

bump *verb*
1. To proceed with sudden, abrupt movements: *an old car bumping down the road.* 1. **Syns:** jerk, jolt.
2. To come together or come up against with force. 2. COLLIDE.
3. *Informal.* To lower in rank or grade. 3. DEMOTE.
4. To put out by force. 4. EJECT.

bump into *verb*
Informal. To find or meet by chance. COME ACROSS at **come**.

bump *noun*
1. Violent, forcible contact between two or more things. 1. COLLISION.
2. A small raised area of skin resulting from a light blow, an insect sting, etc.: *Wasp bites cause bumps.* 2. **Syns:** bunch, knob, knot, lump¹, swelling.
3. An unevenness or elevation on a surface: *a bump in the road.* 3. **Syns:** hump, knob, lump¹, nub, protuberance.

bump into *verb* SEE **bump**.

bump-off *noun*   SEE **bump off.**

bump off *verb*
Slang. To take the life of (a person or persons)   MURDER *verb.*
unlawfully.

  bump-off *noun*
  Slang. The crime of murdering someone.   MURDER *noun.*

bunch *noun*
1. *Informal.* A number of individuals making up or   1. GROUP *noun.*
   considered a unit.
2. *Informal.* A usu. small number of individuals.   2. GROUP *noun.*
3. *Informal.* A particular social group.   3. CROWD *noun.*
4. A small raised area of skin resulting from a light   4. BUMP *noun.*
   blow, an insect sting, etc.

buncombe *noun*   SEE **bunkum[1].**

bundle *noun*
1. A number of individuals making up or considered a   1. GROUP *noun.*
   unit.
2. *Slang.* A large sum of money.   2. FORTUNE.

bungle *verb*
To harm irreparably through inept handling; make a   BOTCH *verb.*
mess of.

  bungle *noun*
  A stupid, clumsy mistake.   BLUNDER *noun.*

bungler *noun*
A stupid, clumsy person.   BLUNDERER.

bunk[1] *verb*
To provide with often temporary lodging.   HARBOR *verb.*

bunk[2] *noun*
Slang. Something that does not have or make sense.   NONSENSE.

bunk[3] *verb*
Brit. To break loose and leave suddenly, as from   ESCAPE *verb.*
confinement or from a difficult or threatening situation.

bunkum[1] also **buncombe** *noun*
Something that does not have or make sense.   NONSENSE.

bunkum[2] *adjective*
Regional. Having good health.   HEALTHY.

Bunyanesque *adjective*
Of extraordinary size and power.   GIANT *adjective.*

buoy *verb*
To raise the spirits of.   ELATE *verb.*

  buoy up *verb*
  To keep from yielding or failing during stress or   SUSTAIN.
  difficulty.

buoyancy *noun*
The ability to recover quickly from depression or   RESILIENCE.
discouragement.

buoyant *adjective*
Displaying light-hearted nonchalance.   AIRY.

buoy up *verb*   SEE **buoy.**

bur *verb & noun*   SEE **burr.**

burble *verb*
To flow or move with a low, slapping sound.   WASH.

burbling *adjective*
Emitting a murmuring sound felt to resemble a laugh.   LAUGHING.

burden *noun*
1. Something carried physically: *the camel's burden of*   1. *Syns:* cargo, freight, haul, impost, load.
   spices.
2. Something hard to bear physically or emotionally: 2. *Syns:* affliction, cross, trial.
   the burden of a guilty conscience.

3. A duty or responsibility that is a source of anxiety, worry, or hardship: *the burden of supporting dependent relatives.*

3. *Syns:* millstone, onus, tax, weight.

4. The general sense or significance, as of an action, statement, etc.

4. IMPORT *noun.*

burden *verb*
To place a burden or heavy load on.

CHARGE *verb.*

burdensome *adjective*
Imposing a severe test of bodily or spiritual strength: *burdensome farm chores.*

Syns: arduous, backbreaking, demanding, difficult, effortful, exacting, exigent, formidable, hard, heavy, laborious, onerous, oppressive, rigorous, rough, severe, taxing, tough, trying, weighty. *Near-ants:* easy, effortless; facile, light, simple, unexacting, untaxing, untrying.

burg *noun*
Informal. A large and important town.

CITY *noun.*

burgeon *verb*
1. To bear flowers.

1. BLOOM *verb.*

2. To become greater in number, amount, or intensity.

2. RISE *verb.*

burglarize *verb*
To enter forcibly and illegally.

BREAK IN at **break.**

burial *noun*
An act of placing a body in a grave or tomb: *Burial immediately followed the funeral.*

Syns: entombment, inhumation, interment.

buried *adjective*
Lying beyond what is obvious or avowed.

ULTERIOR.

burke *verb*
To evade, as a topic, esp. by circumlocution.

SKIRT *verb.*

burlesque *noun*
A false, derisive, or impudent imitation of something.

MOCKERY.

burlesque *verb*
To copy (the manner or expression of another), esp. in an exaggerated or mocking way.

IMITATE.

burly *adjective*
Characterized by marked muscular development; powerfully built.

MUSCULAR.

burn *verb*
1. To undergo combustion: *Wood shavings burn readily.*

1. *Syns:* blaze[1], combust, conflagrate, flame (up), flare.

2. To undergo or cause to undergo damage by or as if by fire: *burned the rug with a cigarette.*

2. *Syns:* char, scorch, sear, singe.

3. To emit a bright light.

3. BEAM *verb.*

4. To feel or look hot: *He's burning with fever.*

4. *Syns:* bake, broil, roast, scorch, swelter.

5. To be in a state of emotional or mental turmoil.

5. BOIL.

6. To feel or cause to feel a sensation of heat or discomfort.

6. STING *verb.*

7. To cause to become sore or inflamed.

7. IRRITATE.

8. To be or become angry.

8. ANGER *verb.*

burn out *verb*
To lose so much strength and power as to become ineffective or motionless.

RUN DOWN.

burn up *verb*
Informal. To cause to feel or show anger.

ANGER *verb.*

burn *noun*
Damage that results from burning: *a burn in the tablecloth.*

Syns: char, scorch, sear, singe.

burning *adjective*
1. On fire.

1. BLAZING.

2. Marked by much heat.

2. HOT *adjective.*

3. Fired with intense feeling.

3. PASSIONATE.

4. Of immediate import: *a burning issue; burning needs.*

4. *Syns:* crying, exigent, imperative, importunate, instant, pressing, urgent.

burnish *verb*
To give a gleaming luster to, usu. through friction.

GLOSS *verb.*

burn out *verb*

SEE **burn.**

burn up *verb*

SEE **burn.**

burr also **bur** *verb*
To make a continuous low-pitched droning sound.

HUM *verb.*

burr also **bur** *noun*
A continuous low-pitched droning sound.

HUM *noun.*

burrow *noun*
A hollow place used as an animal's dwelling.

HOLE *noun.*

burst *verb*
1. To come open or fly apart suddenly and violently, as from internal pressure: *The balloon burst.*
2. To release or cause to release energy suddenly and violently, esp. with a loud noise.

1. *Syns:* blow out, blow up, bust (*Informal*), explode, pop.
2. EXPLODE.

burst forth *verb*
To become manifest suddenly and in full force.

BREAK OUT.

burst *noun*
1. A violent release of confined energy, usu. accompanied by a loud sound and shock waves.
2. An earsplitting, explosive noise.
3. A sudden, violent expression, as of emotion.
4. A concentrated outpouring, as of missiles, words, or blows.

1. BLAST *noun.*
2. BLAST *noun.*
3. OUTBURST.
4. BARRAGE *noun.*

burst forth *verb*

SEE **burst.**

bursting *adjective*
1. Completely filled.
2. Intensely desirous or interested.

1. FULL.
2. EAGER.

bury *verb*
1. To place (a corpse) in or as if in a grave: *bury the dead.*
2. To put or keep out of sight.
3. *Slang.* To win a victory over, as in battle or a competition.

1. *Syns:* entomb, inhume, inter, lay away (*Informal*). —*Idiom* lay to rest.
2. HIDE[1] *verb.*
3. DEFEAT *verb.*

bush *noun*
An uninhabited region left in its natural state.

WILD *noun.*

bush *verb*
Slang. To make extremely tired.

EXHAUST.

bush up *verb*
Chiefly Regional. To put or keep out of sight.

HIDE[1] *verb.*

bushed *adjective*
Slang. Extremely tired.

EXHAUSTED.

bushel *noun*
Informal. An indeterminately great amount or number.

HEAP *noun.*

bush up *verb*

SEE **bush.**

bushwhack *verb*
To attack suddenly and without warning.

AMBUSH.

business *noun*
1. Activity pursued as a livelihood: *Her business is advertising.*

1. *Syns:* calling, employ (*Archaic*), employment, job, line, occupation, pursuit, racket (*Slang*), trade, vocation, work.

2. Commercial, industrial, or professional activity in general: *laws regulating business; when business is slow.*

2. *Syns:* commerce, industry, trade, trading, traffic.

3. The commercial transactions of customers with a supplier.

3. PATRONAGE.

4. A commercial organization.

4. COMPANY.

5. Something that concerns or involves one personally: *Do you think that's any of your business?*

5. **Syns:** affair, concern, lookout.
Near-syns: care, matter, responsibility, thing.

businesslike *adjective*
1. Showing characteristics advantageous to or of use in business: *businesslike procedures.*
2. Marked by sober sincerity.

1. **Syns:** efficient, methodical, systematic (*also* systematical).
2. SERIOUS.

businessperson *noun*
A person engaged in buying and selling.

DEALER.

buss *noun*
The act or an instance of kissing.

KISS *noun.*

buss *verb*
To touch or caress with the lips, esp. as a sign of passion or affection.

KISS *verb.*

bust *verb*
1. *Informal.* To come open or fly apart suddenly and violently, as from internal pressure.
2. *Slang.* To make or become unusable or inoperative.
3. *Slang.* To reduce to financial insolvency.
4. *Slang.* To lower in rank or grade.
5. *Slang.* To make (an animal) docile.
6. *Slang.* To take into custody as a prisoner.
7. To hit with a quick, sharp blow of the hand.

1. BURST *verb.*
2. BREAK *verb.*
3. RUIN *verb.*
4. DEMOTE.
5. GENTLE *verb.*
6. ARREST *verb.*
7. SLAP *verb.*

bust *noun*
1. *Slang.* One that fails completely.
2. *Slang.* The condition of being financially insolvent.
3. *Slang.* A seizing and holding by law.
4. *Slang.* A quick, sharp blow, esp. with the hand.

1. FAILURE.
2. FAILURE.
3. ARREST *noun.*
4. SLAP *noun.*

busted *adjective*
Slang. Having little or no money or wealth.

POOR.

bustle *noun*
1. Needless trouble.
2. Agitated, excited movement and activity.

1. BOTHER *noun.*
2. STIR[1] *noun.*

bustle *verb*
1. To be nervously or uselessly active.
2. To move swiftly.

1. FUSS *verb.*
2. RUSH *verb.*

busy *adjective*
1. Involved in activity or work: *Call when you're not so busy.*
2. Excessively filled with detail: *a busy advertising layout.*

1. **Syns:** employed, engaged, occupied.
2. **Syns:** cluttered, crowded, fussy.

busy *verb*
To make busy: *busying myself with legal matters.*

Syns: engage, engross, occupy.

busybody *noun*
1. A person given to intruding in other people's affairs.
2. A person who snoops.

1. MEDDLER.
2. SNOOP *noun.*

but *adverb*
To the exclusion of anyone or anything else.

SOLELY.

butcher *verb*
To kill savagely and indiscriminately.

ANNIHILATE.

butcher *noun*
One who murders another.

MURDERER.

butchery *noun*
The savage killing of many victims.

MASSACRE *noun.*

butt[1] *noun*
An act or instance of using force so as to propel ahead.

PUSH *noun.*

butt[2] *verb*
To be contiguous or next to.

ADJOIN.

butt[3] *noun*
1. A person who is easily deceived or victimized.
2. An object of amusement or laughter.

1. DUPE *noun.*
2. JOKE *noun.*

butt[4] *noun*
Residual matter.   END *noun*.
butter *verb*
To spread with a greasy, sticky, or dirty substance.   SMEAR *verb*.
  butter up *verb*
  Informal. To compliment excessively and ingratiatingly.   FLATTER.
butter up *verb*   SEE **butter**.
butt in *verb*
  1. To force or come in as an improper or unwanted   1. INTRUDE.
     element.
  2. *Slang.* To intervene officiously or indiscreetly in the   2. MEDDLE.
     affairs of others.
buttinsky *noun*
Slang. A person given to intruding in other people's   MEDDLER.
affairs.
buttocks *noun*
The part of one's back on which one rests in sitting.   BOTTOM *noun*.
button-down *adjective*
Informal. Conforming to established practice or   CONVENTIONAL.
standards.
buttress *noun*
A means or device that keeps something erect, stable,   SUPPORT *noun*.
or secure.
  buttress *verb*
  To present evidence in support of.   BACK *verb*.
buy *verb*
  1. To acquire in exchange for money or something of   1. *Syn:* purchase.
     equal value: *bought a house.*
  2. To give, offer, or promise a bribe to.   2. BRIBE *verb*.
  3. *Slang.* To regard (something) as true or real.   3. BELIEVE.
  buy off *verb*
  To give, offer, or promise a bribe to.   BRIBE *verb*.
  buy *noun*
  1. Something bought or capable of being bought: *a*   1. *Syn:* purchase.
     major buy in cotton futures.
  2. Something offered or bought at a low price.   2. BARGAIN *noun*.
buyable *adjective*
Capable of being bribed.   CORRUPTIBLE.
buyer *noun*
One who buys goods or services.   PATRON.
buy off *verb*   SEE **buy**.
buzz *verb*
  1. To make a continuous low-pitched droning sound.   1. HUM *verb*.
  2. To engage in or spread gossip.   2. GOSSIP *verb*.
  3. *Informal.* To communicate with (someone) by   3. TELEPHONE.
     telephone.
  buzz *noun*
  1. A continuous low-pitched droning sound.   1. HUM *noun*.
  2. Idle, often sensational and groundless talk about   2. GOSSIP *noun*.
     others.
  3. *Informal.* A telephone communication.   3. CALL *noun*.
by-and-by *noun*
Time that is yet to be.   FUTURE *noun*.
bygone *adjective*
Of a style or method formerly in vogue.   OLD-FASHIONED.
bypass *verb*
  1. To keep away from.   1. AVOID.
  2. To evade, as a topic, esp. by circumlocution.   2. SKIRT *verb*.
  3. To pass around but not through.   3. SKIRT *verb*.
by-product *noun*
Something derived from another.   DERIVATIVE *noun*.

by-sitter *noun*
Someone who observes.   WATCHER.

bystander *noun*
Someone who observes.   WATCHER.

byword *noun*
A usu. pithy and familiar statement expressing an   PROVERB.
observation or principle generally accepted as wise or
true.

Byzantine *adjective*
Difficult to understand due to intricacy.   COMPLEX *adjective*.

C

cabal *noun*
A secret plan to achieve an evil or illegal end.   PLOT *noun*.

cabalistic *adjective*
Difficult to explain or understand.   MYSTERIOUS.

cabbage *noun*
Slang. Something, as coins, printed bills, etc., used as a MONEY.
medium of exchange.

cache *verb*
To put or keep out of sight.   HIDE¹ *verb*.

cachinnate *verb*
To express amusement, mirth, or scorn by smiling and   LAUGH *verb*.
emitting loud, inarticulate sounds.

cachinnation *noun*
An act of laughing.   LAUGH *noun*.

cackle *verb*
To express amusement, mirth, or scorn by smiling and   LAUGH *verb*.
emitting loud, inarticulate sounds.

  cackle *noun*
  An act of laughing.   LAUGH *noun*.

cacophonic also **cacophonical** *adjective*   SEE **cacophonous**.

cacophonous also **cacophonic, cacophonical**
adjective
Characterized by unpleasant discordance of sound.   INHARMONIOUS.

cadaver *noun*
The physical frame of a dead person or animal.   BODY *noun*.

cadaverous *adjective*
1. Gruesomely suggestive of ghosts or death.   **1.** GHASTLY.
2. Lacking color.   **2.** PALE *adjective*.
3. Physically haggard.   **3.** WASTED.

cadence also **cadency** *noun*
The regular recurrence of strong and weak elements,   RHYTHM.
such as stressed and unstressed notes in music.

cadenced *adjective*
Marked by a regular rhythm.   RHYTHMICAL.

cadency *noun*   SEE **cadence**.

cadge *verb*
Informal. To ask or ask for as charity.   BEG.

cadger *noun*
Informal. One who begs habitually or for a living.   BEGGAR *noun*.

caducity *noun*
Old age.   AGE *noun*.

cage *verb*
To confine within a limited area.   ENCLOSE.

cagey also **cagy** *adjective*
Having or showing a clever awareness and   SHREWD.
resourcefulness in practical matters.

cagy *adjective*   SEE **cagey.**

Cain *noun*
One who murders another.   MURDERER.

cajole *verb*
To persuade or try to persuade by gentle, persistent   COAX.
urging or flattery.

cake *verb*
To make or become physically hard.   HARDEN.

calaboose *noun*
Slang. A place for the confinement of persons in lawful   JAIL *noun*.
detention.

calamitous *adjective*
Causing ruin or destruction.   FATAL.

calamity *noun*
An occurrence inflicting widespread destruction and   DISASTER.
distress.

calculate *verb*
1. To ascertain by mathematics: *astronomers*   1. *Syns:* cast, cipher, compute, figure
   calculating the positions of the planets.   (out), reckon.
2. To make a judgment as to the worth or value of.   2. ESTIMATE *verb*.
3. To note (items) one by one so as to get a total.   3. COUNT *verb*.

calculated *adjective*
1. Planned, weighed, or estimated in advance: *took a*   1. *Syns:* considered, deliberate,
   calculated risk.   intentional, premeditated.
2. Resulting from deliberation and careful thought.   2. ADVISED.

calculating *adjective*
Coldly planning to achieve selfish aims: *a calculating*   *Syns:* designing, scheming.
and shrewd businessman.

calculation *noun*
1. The act, process, or result of calculating: *made a*   1. *Syns:* computation, figuring, reckoning.
   quick calculation of the cost.
2. Careful forethought to avoid harm or risk.   2. CAUTION *noun*.
3. A careful considering of a matter.   3. ADVISEMENT.

calendar *noun*
An organized list of procedures, activities, events, etc.   PROGRAM.

caliber *noun*
1. A division of persons or things by quality, rank, or   1. CLASS *noun*.
   grade.
2. Degree of excellence.   2. QUALITY.
3. A level of superiority that is usu. high.   3. MERIT *noun*.

caliginous *adjective*
Rare. Having no light.   BLACK.

call *verb*
1. To demand to appear, come, or assemble: *calling the*   1. *Syns:* convene, convoke, muster, send
   doctor; called a meeting.   for, summon.
2. To speak or say very loudly.   2. ROAR *verb*.
3. To communicate with (someone) by telephone.   3. TELEPHONE.
4. To give a name or title to.   4. NAME *verb*.
5. To describe with a word or term: *called me a liar.*   5. *Syns:* characterize, designate, label,
                                                                        style, tag, term.
6. To go to or seek out the company of in order to   6. VISIT *verb*.
   socialize.

7. To bring together.
8. To calculate approximately.
9. To tell about or make known (future events) in advance, esp. by means of special knowledge or inference.

call down *verb*
Informal. To criticize for a fault or offense: *got called down for failing to meet the deadline.*

call for *verb*
1. To be a proper or sufficient occasion for: *This calls for champagne.*
2. To have as a need or prerequisite.
3. To ask for urgently or insistently.

call off *verb*
To decide not to go ahead with (something previously arranged).

call *noun*
1. A loud cry.
2. The power or quality of attracting.
3. That which provides a reason or justification.
4. A telephone communication: *Give him a call when you arrive.*
5. An act or an instance of going or coming to see another.
6. The act of demanding.

call down *verb*
called-for *adjective*
Imposed on one by authority, command, or convention.

call for *verb*

call girl *noun*
A woman who engages in sexual intercourse for payment.

calligraphic *adjective*
Of or pertaining to representation by means of writing.

calling *noun*
1. An inner urge to pursue an activity or perform a service.
2. Activity pursued as a livelihood.

call off *verb*
callous *adjective*
Totally lacking in compassion.

calm *adjective*
1. Not excited or emotionally agitated: *spoke in a calm voice.*

2. Motionless and undisturbed.
3. Not easily excited, even under pressure.

calm *noun*
1. An absence of motion or disturbance.
2. Lack of emotional agitation: *kept his calm during the emergency.*

---

7. ASSEMBLE.
8. ESTIMATE *verb*.
9. PREDICT.

Syns: admonish, bawl out (*Informal*), castigate, chastise, chew out (*Slang*), chide, dress down, lambaste (*Slang*), rap¹ (*Informal*), rebuke, reprimand, reproach, reprove, scold, tax, upbraid. —*Idioms* bring (*or* call *or* take) to task, haul (*or* rake) over the coals, let someone have it, rap on (*or* over) the knuckles.

1. *Syns:* justify, occasion, warrant.
2. DEMAND *verb*.
3. DEMAND *verb*.

CANCEL.

1. SHOUT *noun*.
2. ATTRACTION.
3. CAUSE *noun*.
4. *Syns:* buzz (*Informal*), ring¹ (*Informal*).
5. VISIT *noun*.
6. DEMAND *noun*.
SEE **call**.

REQUIRED.
SEE **call**.

PROSTITUTE.

GRAPHIC.

1. VOCATION.
2. BUSINESS.
SEE **call**.

COLD-BLOODED.

1. *Syns:* composed, placid, serene, tranquil, unruffled.
Near-syns: collected, cool, easy, easygoing; imperturbable, nonchalant, unflappable.
Ant: agitated.
2. STILL *adjective*.
3. COOL *adjective*.

1. STILLNESS.
2. *Syns:* calmness, composure, cool (*Slang*), equanimity, head, sang-froid, serenity, tranquillity *or* tranquility.

calm *verb*
1. To make or become calm: *calmed her fears.*

2. To ease the anger or agitation of.
calm down *verb*
To ease the anger or agitation of.
calm down *verb*
calmness *noun*
Lack of emotional agitation.
calumniate *verb*
To make defamatory statements about.
calumnious *adjective*
Damaging to the reputation.
calumny *noun*
The expression of injurious, malicious statements about someone.
camouflage *verb*
To change or modify so as to prevent recognition of the true identity or character of.
campaign *noun*
An organized effort to accomplish a purpose.
campestral *adjective*
Of or pertaining to the countryside.
camp follower *noun*
A woman who engages in sexual intercourse for payment.
can *verb*
1. To prepare (food) for storage and future use.
2. *Slang.* To end the employment of.
can *noun*
Slang. A place for the confinement of persons in lawful detention.
canard *noun*
An untrue declaration.
cancel *verb*
1. To remove or invalidate by or as if by running a line through or wiping clean: *canceled checks; going to cancel his magazine subscription; an order canceled by the President.*
2. To decide not to go ahead with (something previously arranged): *canceled the concert because of illness.*
3. To make ineffective by applying an opposite force or amount: *Two opposing votes cancel each other.*
4. To put an end to formally and with authority.
cancellation *noun*
The act of erasing or the condition of being erased.
candid *adjective*
Speaking or spoken freely and sincerely.
candidate *noun*
A person who applies for or seeks a job or position.
candy *verb*
To make superficially more acceptable or appealing.
candyman *noun*
Slang. A person who sells narcotics illegally.

1. **Syns:** allay, balm, becalm, compose, lull, quiet, settle, soothe, still, tranquilize (*also* tranquillize).
Near-ants: bother, discompose, disquiet, disturb, perturb.
Ants: agitate; arouse, upset.
2. PACIFY.

PACIFY.

SEE **calm.**

CALM *noun.*

LIBEL *verb.*

LIBELOUS.

LIBEL *noun.*

DISGUISE *verb.*

DRIVE *noun.*

COUNTRY *adjective.*

PROSTITUTE.

1. CONSERVE *verb.*
2. DISMISS.

JAIL *noun.*

LIE[2] *noun.*

1. **Syns:** annul, blot out, cross out, erase, expunge, rub out, scratch out, strike out, undo, vacate (*Law*), wipe out, x out.
2. **Syns:** call off, drop, kill (*Slang*), scratch (*Informal*), scrub (*Informal*).
3. **Syns:** counteract, neutralize.
4. ABOLISH

ERASURE.

FRANK.

APPLICANT.

SWEETEN.

PUSHER.

cane *noun*
A fairly long, straight piece of solid material used esp. as a support in walking.   STICK *noun*.

canker *verb*
1. To ruin utterly in character or quality.   1. CORRUPT *verb*.
2. To have a destructive effect on.   2. POISON *verb*.

cannonade *noun*
A concentrated outpouring, as of missiles, words, or blows.   BARRAGE *noun*.

cannonade *verb*
To direct a barrage at.   BARRAGE *verb*.

canny *adjective*
1. Astute but lacking in ethics or principles.   1. SHARP *adjective*.
2. Careful in the use of material resources.   2. ECONOMICAL.

canon *noun*
A principle governing the affairs of man within or among political units.   LAW *noun*.

canonical *adjective*
Adhering to beliefs or practices approved by authority or tradition.   ORTHODOX.

cant¹ *verb*
1. To depart or cause to depart from true vertical or horizontal.   1. INCLINE *verb*.
2. To lean suddenly, unsteadily, and erratically from the vertical axis.   2. LURCH *verb*.

cant *noun*
Deviation from a particular direction.   INCLINATION.

cant² *noun*
1. Specialized expressions indigenous to a particular field, subject, trade, or subculture.   1. LANGUAGE.
2. An often regional form of a language not considered standard.   2. DIALECT.

cantankerous *adjective*
Having or showing a bad temper.   ILL-TEMPERED.

canted *adjective*
Departing from true vertical or horizontal.   INCLINED.

cap *verb*
1. To reach or bring to a climax.   1. CLIMAX *verb*.
2. To extend over the surface of.   2. COVER *verb*.
3. To put a topping on.   3. TOP *verb*.

capability *noun*
Physical, mental, financial, or legal power to perform.   ABILITY.

capable *adjective*
Having the ability to perform well.   ABLE.

capacious *adjective*
1. Of full measure; not narrow or restricted.   1. FULL.
2. Having plenty of room.   2. ROOMY.

capacity *noun*
1. Physical, mental, financial, or legal power to perform.   1. ABILITY.
2. The ability or power to seize or attain.   2. GRASP *noun*.

caper *verb*
To leap and skip about playfully.   GAMBOL.

caper *noun*
A mischievous act.   PRANK.

capital *adjective*
1. Most important, influential, or significant.   1. PRIMARY.
2. Exceptionally good of its kind.   2. EXCELLENT.
3. Conspicuously bad or offensive.   3. FLAGRANT.

capital *noun*
1. All property or goods having economic value.   1. RESOURCES.

2. The monetary resources of a government, organization, or individual.

2. FUNDS.

capitalist *noun*
One who is occupied with or expert in large-scale financial affairs.

FINANCIER.

capitalize *verb*
1. To supply capital to or for.
2. To derive advantage.

1. FINANCE.
2. BENEFIT *verb*.

capitulate *verb*
To give in from or as if from a gradual loss of strength.

SUCCUMB.

capitulation *noun*
The act of submitting or surrendering to the power of another.

SURRENDER *noun*.

caprice *noun*
An impulsive, often illogical turn of mind.

FANCY *noun*.

capricious *adjective*
1. Following no predictable pattern: *a capricious flirt; a capricious storm; capricious stock-market fluctuations.*

1. *Syns:* changeable, erratic, fantastic (*also* fantastical), fickle, freakish, inconsistent, inconstant, lubricious, mercurial, temperamental, ticklish, uncertain, unpredictable, unstable, unsteady, variable, volatile, whimsical.

2. Determined or marked by whim or caprice rather than reason.

2. ARBITRARY.

captain *verb*
To have authoritative charge of.

LEAD *verb*.

captious *adjective*
Inclined to judge too severely.

CRITICAL.

captivate *verb*
To please greatly or irresistibly.

CHARM *verb*.

captivated *adjective*
Affected with intense romantic attraction.

INFATUATED.

captivating *adjective*
Pleasing to the eye or mind.

ATTRACTIVE.

capture *verb*
1. To obtain possession or control of: *The Dodgers captured the pennant.*
2. To obtain possession of, esp. after a struggle or chase.

1. *Syns:* cop (*Slang*), gain, get, take, win.
2. TAKE *verb*.

carcass *noun*
The physical frame of a dead person or animal.

BODY *noun*.

card *noun*
Informal. A person whose words or actions provoke or are intended to provoke amusement or laughter.

JOKER.

cardboard *adjective*
So rigidly constrained, formal, or awkward as to lack all grace and spontaneity.

STIFF *adjective*.

cardinal *adjective*
1. Dominant in importance or influence.
2. Most important, influential, or significant.

1. PIVOTAL.
2. PRIMARY.

care *noun*
1. A cause of worry: *Her main care is how to support the family.*
2. Anxious concern.
3. Cautious attentiveness: *handled the glass with care.*

1. *Syns:* concern, trouble. —*Idiom* thorn in one's side.
2. ANXIETY.
3. *Syns:* carefulness, caution, gingerliness, heed, heedfulness, regard.
Near-ants: carelessness, disregard, heedlessness, unconcern; boredom, ennui.

4. Attentiveness to detail.

5. The function of watching, guarding, or overseeing: *left the keys to the house in his care.*

6. The systematic application of remedies to effect a cure.

care *verb*
To have an objection: *I don't care if you go.*

care for *verb*
To have the care and supervision of.

care for *verb*

carefree *adjective*
Free from care or worry.

careful *adjective*
   1. Cautiously attentive: *gave the will a careful reading.*

   2. Trying attentively to avoid danger, risk, or error.
   3. Showing or marked by attentiveness to all aspects or details: *a careful worker; fine, careful work.*

carefulness *noun*
   1. Careful forethought to avoid harm or risk.
   2. Cautious attentiveness.

careless *adjective*
   1. Lacking or marked by a lack of care: *hurt her by a careless remark.*

   2. Indifferent to correctness, accuracy, or neatness: *a careless writer.*

caress *verb*
To touch or stroke affectionately: *patted and caressed the little boy.*

careworn *adjective*
Pale and exhausted because of worry, sleeplessness, etc.

cargo *noun*
Something carried physically.

caricature *noun*
A false, derisive, or impudent imitation of something.

caritas *noun*
Kind, forgiving, or compassionate treatment of or disposition toward others.

cark *verb*
   1. To be troubled.
   2. To cause anxious uneasiness in.

carnage *noun*
The savage killing of many victims.

carnal *adjective*
Relating to the desires and appetites of the body.

carnality *noun*
A preoccupation with the body and satisfaction of its desires.

carol *verb*
To utter words or sounds in musical tones.

carom also **carrom** *verb*
To strike a surface at such an angle as to be deflected.

carousal *noun*
A drinking bout.

carouse *verb*
To behave riotously.

---

4. THOROUGHNESS.

5. *Syns:* charge, custody, guardianship, keeping, superintendence, supervision, trust.

6. TREATMENT.

Syns: mind, object[2].

TEND[2].

SEE **care.**

LIGHT[2].

1. *Syns:* heedful, mindful, observant, watchful.

2. WARY.
3. *Syns:* meticulous, painstaking, scrupulous.

1. CAUTION *noun.*
2. CARE *noun.*

1. *Syns:* feckless, heedless, inattentive, thoughtless, unconcerned, unmindful. *Near-syns:* forgetful; incautious, lax, neglectful, negligent, rash, slack; uncaring, uninterested, unthinking. *Ant:* careful.
2. *Syns:* messy, slapdash, slipshod, sloppy, slovenly, untidy.

Syns: cuddle, fondle, pet[1].

HAGGARD.

BURDEN *noun.*

MOCKERY.

GRACE *noun.*

1. WORRY *verb.*
2. WORRY *verb.*

MASSACRE *noun.*

PHYSICAL.

PHYSICALITY.

SING.

GLANCE[1] *verb.*

BENDER.

REVEL *verb.*

carouse *noun*
A drinking bout.   BENDER.

carp *verb*
To raise unnecessary or trivial objections.   QUIBBLE.

carp at *verb*
To scold or find fault constantly.   NAG.

carp at *verb*   SEE **carp**.

carper *noun*
A person who finds fault, often severely and willfully.   CRITIC.

carping *adjective*
Inclined to judge too severely.   CRITICAL.

carriage *noun*
1. The way in which a person holds or carries his body.   1. POSTURE *noun*.
2. The moving of persons or goods from one place to   2. TRANSPORTATION.
   another.

carrier *noun*
A person who carries messages or is sent on errands.   BEARER.

carrom *verb*   SEE **carom**.

carry *verb*
1. To move while supporting: *carried the groceries into*   1. **Syns:** bear, convey, lug, schlep
   the house.   (*Slang*), tote[1] (*Informal*), transport.
2. To serve as a conduit.   2. CONDUCT *verb*.
3. To hold on one's person: *I never carry much money.*   3. **Syns:** bear, have, pack (*Informal*),
                                                                 possess.
4. To sustain the weight of.   4. SUPPORT *verb*.
5. To conduct oneself in a specified way.   5. ACT *verb*.
6. To be accepted or approved.   6. PASS *verb*.
7. To have as an accompaniment, condition, or   7. **Syns:** entail, involve.
   consequence: *a crime that carries a heavy penalty.*
8. To have for sale: *All drugstores carry aspirin.*   8. **Syns:** keep, stock.
9. To make known.   9. COMMUNICATE.
10. To cause (a disease) to pass to another or others.   10. COMMUNICATE.
11. To cause to come along with oneself.   11. BRING.
12. To hold up.   12. BEAR.
13. To be endowed with as a visible characteristic or   13. BEAR.
    form.
14. To proceed on a certain course or for a certain   14. EXTEND.
    distance.

carry away *verb*
To move or excite greatly: *completely carried away by*   **Syns:** enrapture, send (*Slang*), thrill,
the music.   transport.

carry off *verb*
1. To cause the death of.   1. KILL.
2. To seize and detain (a person) unlawfully.   2. KIDNAP.

carry on *verb*
1. To control the course of (an activity).   1. CONDUCT *verb*.
2. To involve oneself in (an activity).   2. PARTICIPATE.
3. To engage in (a war or campaign).   3. WAGE *verb*.
4. To continue without halting despite difficulties or   4. **Syns:** go on, hang on, keep going, keep
   setbacks: *carried on with her work as if he hadn't*   on, persevere, persist.
   said a word.
5. To behave in a rowdy or unruly fashion.   5. MISBEHAVE.
6. To show enthusiasm.   6. ENTHUSE.

carry out *verb*
1. To oversee the provision or execution of.   1. ADMINISTER.
2. To compel observance of.   2. ENFORCE.
3. To carry to a successful conclusion.   3. EFFECT *verb*.
4. To engage in (a war or campaign).   4. WAGE *verb*.

carry through *verb*
To carry to a successful conclusion.   EFFECT *verb*.

carry away *verb*   SEE **carry**.

carry off *verb*   SEE **carry.**
carry on *verb*   SEE **carry.**
carry out *verb*   SEE **carry.**
carry through *verb*   SEE **carry.**
cartel *noun*
   1. A group of individuals united in a common cause.   1. COMBINE *noun.*
   2. A combination of businesses closely interconnected   2. COMBINE *noun.*
     for common profit.
carve *verb*
   To separate into parts with or as if with a sharp-edged   CUT *verb.*
   instrument.
Casanova *noun*
   1. A man amorously attentive to women.   1. GALLANT *noun.*
   2. A man who philanders.   2. PHILANDERER.
case *noun*
   1. One that is representative of a group or class.   1. EXAMPLE.
   2. A course of reasoning.   2. ARGUMENT.
   3. *Law.* A legal proceeding to demand justice or enforce   3. LAWSUIT.
     a right.
   case *verb*
   Slang. To look at carefully or critically.   EXAMINE.
caseharden *verb*
   To make resistant to hardship, esp. through continued   HARDEN.
   exposure.
casehardened *adjective*
   Physically toughened so as to have great endurance.   HARD *adjective.*
cash *noun*
   Something, as coins, printed bills, etc., used as a   MONEY.
   medium of exchange.
cashier *verb*
   To end the employment of.   DISMISS.
Cassandra *noun*
   A prophet of misfortune or disaster.   PESSIMIST.
cast *verb*
   1. To move (a weapon, blow, etc.) in the direction of   1. AIM *verb.*
     someone or something.
   2. To combine (figures) to form a sum.   2. ADD.
   3. To ascertain by mathematics.   3. CALCULATE.
   4. To form a strategy for.   4. DESIGN *verb.*
   5. To send through the air with a motion of the hand   5. THROW *verb.*
     or arm.
   6. To send out heat, light, or energy.   6. SHED *verb.*
   7. *Brit. & Vet. Med.* To bring forth a nonviable fetus   7. MISCARRY.
     prematurely.
   cast about *verb*
   To try to find.   SEEK.
   cast away *verb*
   To damage, disable, or destroy (a seacraft).   WRECK *verb.*
   cast down *verb*
   1. To make sad or gloomy.   1. DEPRESS.
   2. To cause unhappiness by failing to satisfy the hopes,   2. DISAPPOINT.
     desires, or expectations of.
   cast out *verb*
   To rid one's mind of.   DISMISS.
   cast *noun*
   1. A disposition of the facial features that conveys   1. EXPRESSION.
     meaning, feeling, or mood.
   2. The external outline of a thing.   2. FORM *noun.*
   3. A shade of a color, esp. a pale or delicate variation.   3. TINT *noun.*
   4. A model for making a mold.   4. FORM *noun.*

5. A class that is defined by the common attribute or attributes possessed by all its members.

6. An act of throwing.

7. Something that is foretold by or as if by supernatural means.

cast about *verb*

cast away *verb*

cast down *verb*

castigate *verb*
To criticize for a fault or offense.

cast out *verb*

castrate *verb*
To render incapable of reproducing sexually.

castration *noun*
The act or an instance of making one incapable of reproducing sexually.

casual *adjective*
1. Unconstrained by rigid standards.
2. Occurring unexpectedly.

casualness *noun*
Lack or avoidance of formality.

casualty *noun*
1. An unexpected and usu. undesirable event.
2. A termination of life, usu. as the result of an accident or a disaster.
3. One that is made to suffer injury, loss, or death.

casuistry *noun*
Plausible but invalid reasoning.

cataclysm *noun*
1. An occurrence inflicting widespread destruction and distress.
2. An abundant, usu. overwhelming flow.
3. A momentous or sweeping change.

cataclysmal *adjective*

cataclysmic also **cataclysmal** *adjective*
Causing ruin or destruction.

catacomb *noun*
A burial place or receptacle for human remains.

catalog *verb & noun*

catalogue also **catalog** *verb*
To register in or as if in a book.

catalogue also **catalog** *noun*
A series of names, words, etc., printed or written down.

catalyst *noun*
An agent that stimulates or precipitates a reaction, development, or change: *a biochemical catalyst used in testing; was a catalyst for good.*

cataract *noun*
An abundant, usu. overwhelming flow.

catastrophe *noun*
An occurrence inflicting widespread destruction and distress.

catastrophic *adjective*
Causing ruin or destruction.

catcall *noun*
Any derisive sound of disapproval.

catch *verb*
1. To get hold of (something moving): *The outfielder caught the fly ball.*
2. To gain possession of, esp. after a struggle or chase.

---

5. KIND².

6. THROW *noun*.

7. PROPHECY.

SEE **cast**.

SEE **cast**.

SEE **cast**.

CALL DOWN at **call**.

SEE **cast**.

STERILIZE.

STERILIZATION.

1. EASYGOING.
2. ACCIDENTAL *adjective*.

INFORMALITY.

1. ACCIDENT.
2. FATALITY.

3. VICTIM.

FALLACY.

1. DISASTER.

2. FLOOD *noun*.
3. REVOLUTION.

SEE **cataclysmic**.

FATAL.

GRAVE¹.

SEE **catalogue**.

LIST¹ *verb*.

LIST¹ *noun*.

Syns: alterant, ferment, leaven, leavening, yeast.

FLOOD *noun*.

DISASTER.

FATAL.

HISS *noun*.

1. *Syns:* clutch, grab, nab, seize, snatch.
   —*Idiom* lay hands on.
2. TAKE *verb*.

3. To grasp at (something) eagerly, forcibly, and abruptly with the jaws.

4. To gain control of or an advantage over by or as if by trapping: *hoping to catch her in her own lies.*

5. To have a sudden, overwhelming effect on.
6. To become or cause to become stuck or lodged: *The bone caught in his throat.*
7. To make secure.
8. To come upon, esp. suddenly or unexpectedly.
9. To deliver (a powerful blow) suddenly and sharply.
10. To become affected with a disease.
11. To perceive, esp. barely or fleetingly: *caught a glimpse of the President's motorcade.*
12. To perceive and recognize the meaning of.
13. To go aboard (a means of transport).

catch on *verb*
Informal. To perceive and recognize the meaning of.

catch up *verb*
1. To come up even with (another): *running hard to catch up with the other joggers.*
2. To draw in in such a way that extrication is difficult.
3. To compel the attention, interest, imagination, etc., of.

catch *noun*
1. The act of catching, esp. a sudden taking and holding: *retrieved the flyaway hat with a leaping catch.*
2. A device for fastening or for checking motion: *The catch of my necklace broke.*
3. *Informal.* A tricky or unsuspected condition: *an offer so generous that I'm sure there's a catch to it.*
4. *Informal.* A person or thing worth catching: *was considered quite a catch in his day.*

catching *adjective*
Capable of transmission by infection.

catch on *verb*

catch up *verb*

catechism *noun*
A set of questions or exercises designed to determine knowledge or skill.

catechization *noun*
A set of questions or exercises designed to determine knowledge or skill.

categorical *adjective*
Clearly, fully, and sometimes emphatically expressed.

categorize *verb*
1. To assign to a class or classes.
2. To distribute into groups according to kinds.

category *noun*
A subdivision of a larger group.

cater to *verb*
1. To comply with the wishes or ideas of (another).
2. To treat with indulgence and often overtender care.

caterwaul *verb*
To quarrel noisily.

catharsis *noun*
A freeing from sin, guilt, or defilement.

cathartic *adjective*
Of, relating to, or tending to eliminate.

---

3. SNAP *verb.*

4. *Syns:* enmesh, ensnare, entangle, entrap, snare, tangle, trammel, trap, web.

5. SEIZE.
6. *Syns:* fix, lodge, stick.

7. FASTEN.
8. TAKE *verb.*
9. HIT *verb.*
10. CONTRACT *verb.*
11. *Syns:* descry, detect, discern, espy, get (*Informal*), spot, spy.

12. UNDERSTAND.
13. TAKE *verb.*

UNDERSTAND.

1. *Syn:* overtake.

2. INVOLVE.
3. GRIP *verb.*

1. *Syns:* clutch, grab, seizure, snatch.

2. *Syns:* clasp, fastener, hook.

3. *Syns:* rub, snag.

4. *Syns:* plum, prize.

COMMUNICABLE.

SEE **catch.**

SEE **catch.**

TEST *noun.*

TEST *noun.*

DEFINITE.

1. CLASS *verb.*
2. ASSORT.

CLASS *noun.*

1. HUMOR *verb.*
2. BABY *verb.*

BRAWL *verb.*

PURIFICATION.

ELIMINATIVE.

catholic *adjective*
So pervasive and all-inclusive as to exist in or affect the whole world.

UNIVERSAL *adjective*.

catholicon *noun*
Something believed to cure all human disorders.

PANACEA.

catlike *adjective*
So slow, deliberate, and secret as to escape observation.

STEALTHY.

catnap *noun*
A brief sleep.

NAP *noun*.

catnap *verb*
To sleep for a brief period.

NAP *verb*.

cat's-paw also **cats-paw** *noun*
A person used or controlled by others.

PAWN².

cause *noun*
1. That which produces an effect: *Scientists are seeking the cause of cancer.*
2. A basis for an action or decision: *gave his wife cause to be angry.*
3. That which provides a reason or justification: *no cause for alarm.*
4. A goal or set of interests served with dedication: *working in the cause of peace.*
5. *Law.* A legal proceeding to demand justice or enforce a right.

1. *Syns:* antecedent, reason.
2. *Syns:* ground, motivation, motive, reason, spring.
3. *Syns:* call, justification, necessity, occasion.
4. *Syn:* crusade.
5. LAWSUIT.

cause *verb*
To be the cause of: *a loss that caused pain. Drunken drivers often cause accidents.*

Syns: bring about, effect, effectuate, engender, generate, induce, ingenerate, lead to, make, occasion, produce, result in, secure. —*Idioms* bring to pass (*or* effect), give rise to.

caustic *adjective*
1. So sharp as to cause mental pain.
2. Given to or expressing sarcasm.

1. BITING.
2. SARCASTIC.

causticity *noun*
Ironic, bitter humor designed to wound.

SARCASM.

caution *noun*
1. Careful forethought to avoid harm or risk: *climbed the icy steps with caution.*

1. *Syns:* calculation, carefulness, circumspection, gingerliness, precaution, wariness.
   Near-syns: acumen, astuteness, canniness, discretion, foresight, forethought; insight, sagacity, wisdom.

2. Advice to beware, as of a person or thing.
3. Cautious attentiveness.
4. The exercise of good judgment or common sense in practical matters.
5. An instance that warns or discourages prospective imitators.

2. WARNING *noun*.
3. CARE *noun*.
4. PRUDENCE.
5. EXAMPLE.

caution *verb*
To notify (someone) of imminent danger or risk.

WARN.

cautionary *adjective*
Giving warning: *sent him a cautionary letter before he filed suit.*

Syns: admonishing, admonitory, monitory, warning.

cautious *adjective*
Trying attentively to avoid danger, risk, or error.

WARY.

cave *noun*
A hollow beneath the earth's surface: *Water trickled out of the cave.*

Syns: cavern, grotto.

cave in *verb*
1. To fall in: *The roof caved in from the heavy snow.*

1. *Syns:* break down, buckle, collapse, give, go.

2. *Informal.* To be unable to hold up.

2. BEND *verb.*

3. To suddenly lose all health or strength.

3. COLLAPSE *verb.*

4. To give way mentally and emotionally.

4. BREAK DOWN.

caveat *noun*
Advice to beware, as of a person or thing.

WARNING *noun.*

cave in *verb*

SEE **cave.**

cavern *noun*
A hollow beneath the earth's surface.

CAVE.

cavernous *adjective*
1. Open wide.

1. YAWNING.

2. Curving inward.

2. HOLLOW *adjective.*

cavil *verb*
To raise unnecessary or trivial objections.

QUIBBLE.

caviler *noun*
A person who finds fault, often severely and willfully.

CRITIC.

caviling *adjective*
Inclined to judge too severely.

CRITICAL.

cavity *noun*
A space in an otherwise solid mass.

HOLE *noun.*

cavort *verb*
To leap and skip about playfully.

GAMBOL.

cease *verb*
1. To bring or come to a natural or proper end.

1. CLOSE[1] *verb.*

2. To stop suddenly, as a conversation, activity, relationship, etc.

2. SUSPEND.

3. To come to a cessation.

3. STOP *verb.*

4. To prevent the occurrence or continuation of a movement, action, or operation.

4. STOP *verb.*

cease *noun*
A concluding or terminating.

END *noun.*

cease-fire *noun*
A temporary cessation of hostilities by mutual consent of the contending parties.

TRUCE.

ceaseless *adjective*
Existing or occurring without interruption or end.

CONTINUAL.

cede *verb*
1. To give up a possession, claim, or right.

1. ABDICATE.

2. To change the ownership of (property) by means of a legal document.

2. TRANSFER.

ceiling *noun*
1. The greatest amount or number allowed.

1. LIMIT *noun.*

2. The greatest quantity or highest degree attainable.

2. MAXIMUM *noun.*

celebrate *verb*
1. To mark (a day or event) with ceremonies of respect, festivity, or rejoicing: *We always celebrate Christmas with prayers and carols.*

1. *Syns:* commemorate, keep, observe, solemnize.

2. To show happy satisfaction in an event, esp. by merrymaking: *celebrated by giving a party.*

2. *Syns:* rejoice, revel. —*Idioms* kill the fatted calf, make merry.

3. To pay tribute or homage to.

3. HONOR *verb.*

celebrated *adjective*
Widely known and esteemed.

EMINENT.

celebration *noun*
1. The act of observing a day or event with ceremonies: *the celebration of Passover.*

1. *Syns:* commemoration, observance.

2. The act of showing happy satisfaction in an event: *During the graduation celebration speeches were made.*

2. *Syns:* festivity, merrymaking, rejoicing, revelry, revels.

3. A big, exuberant party.

3. BLAST *noun.*

celebrity *noun*
1. Wide recognition for one's deeds.

1. FAME.

2. A famous person: *All the celebrities arrived for the première of the play.*

celeritous *adjective*
Characterized by great celerity.

celerity *noun*
1. Rapidness of movement or activity.
2. Rate of motion or performance.

celestial *adjective*
1. Of or relating to the heavens.
2. Of or relating to heaven.

censor *verb*
1. To examine (material) and remove parts considered harmful or improper for publication or transmission: *censoring the prisoner's mail.*
2. To keep from being published or transmitted: *censored the news story.*

censorious *adjective*
Inclined to judge too severely.

censurable *adjective*
Deserving blame.

censure *verb*
1. To find fault with.
2. To feel or express strong disapproval of.

censure *noun*
A finding fault.

center *noun*
1. A point or area equidistant from all sides of something: *put the flowers in the center of the table.*
2. A point of origin from which ideas, influences, etc., emanate: *tried to get to the center of the problem.*
3. A place of concentrated activity, influence, or importance: *New York is a great urban center.*

center *verb*
To direct toward a common center.

center *adjective*
At, in, near, or being the center.

central *adjective*
1. At, in, near, or being the center: *the central part of the state.*
2. Dominant in importance or influence.
3. Not extreme.

cerebral *adjective*
1. Relating to or performed by the mind.
2. Appealing to or engaging the intellect.

cerebrate *verb*
1. To use the powers of the mind, as in conceiving ideas, drawing inferences, and making judgments.
2. To consider carefully and at length.

cerebration *noun*
The act or process of thinking.

ceremonial *adjective*
Of or characterized by ceremony.

ceremonial *noun*
A formal act or set of acts prescribed by ritual.

ceremonious *adjective*
Fond of or given to ceremony: *The Japanese are a ceremonious people.*

---

2. *Syns:* hero, luminary, name, notable, personage. —*Idioms* big name, person of note.
   Near-syns: idol, star, superstar; big-name, somebody; worthy.

FAST *adjective.*

1. HASTE *noun.*
2. SPEED *noun.*

1. HEAVENLY.
2. HEAVENLY.

1. *Syns:* bowdlerize, expurgate, screen.
   Near-syns: excise, exscind; blue-pencil, delete, edit, red-pencil; purify.
2. *Syns:* ban, black out, hush up, stifle, suppress. —*Idiom* put the lid on.

CRITICAL.

BLAMEWORTHY.

1. BLAME *verb.*
2. DEPLORE.

BLAME *noun.*

1. *Syns:* middle, midpoint, midst.

2. *Syns:* bottom, core, focus, heart, hub, quick, root[1].

3. *Syns:* focus, headquarters, heart, hub, seat.

CONCENTRATE *verb.*

CENTRAL.

1. *Syns:* center, medial, median, mid, middle.
2. PIVOTAL.
3. MIDDLE *adjective.*

1. MENTAL.
2. INTELLECTUAL *adjective.*

1. THINK.

2. PONDER.

THOUGHT.

RITUAL *adjective.*

CEREMONY.

Syns: conventional, courtly, formal, polite, punctilious.

ceremoniousness *noun*
Strict observance of social conventions.

CEREMONY.

ceremony *noun*
1. A formal act or set of acts prescribed by ritual: *performed the wedding ceremony.*

1. **Syns:** ceremonial, liturgy, observance, office (*Eccles.*), rite, ritual, service.

2. A conventional social gesture or act without intrinsic purpose.

2. RITUAL *noun.*

3. Strict observance of social conventions: *welcomed the pope with great ceremony.*

3. **Syns:** ceremoniousness, formality, protocol.

certain *adjective*
1. Sure to happen: *certain death.*

1. **Syns:** inescapable, inevitable, unavoidable.

2. In a definite and final form; not likely to change.

2. FIRM[1].

3. Established beyond a doubt: *It is absolutely certain that chaos will result.*

3. **Syns:** inarguable, incontestable, incontrovertible, indisputable, indubitable, irrefutable, positive, sure, undeniable, undisputable, unquestionable.

4. Such as could not possibly fail or disappoint.
5. Having no doubt.
6. Known positively.

4. SURE.
5. SURE.
6. DEFINITE.

certainly *adverb*
1. Without question.
2. It is so; as you say or ask.

1. ABSOLUTELY.
2. YES *adverb.*

certainty *noun*
1. The fact or condition of being without doubt.
2. A clearly established fact: *It is by no means a certainty that a virus causes cancer.*

1. SURENESS.
2. **Syn:** cinch (*Slang*). —*Idiom* sure thing.

certify *verb*
1. To confirm formally as true, accurate, or genuine: *This letter certifies that the bearer was employed by us.*

1. **Syns:** attest, testify, vouch for, witness. —*Idiom* bear witness to.
   Near-syns: assert, aver, avouch, avow, guarantee, profess, warrant.

2. To assume responsibility for the quality, worth, or durability of.

2. GUARANTEE *verb.*

certitude *noun*
The fact or condition of being without doubt.

SURENESS.

cessation *noun*
1. A concluding or terminating.
2. The condition of being stopped.
3. The act of stopping.

1. END *noun.*
2. STOP *noun.*
3. STOP *noun.*

cesspit *noun*
A place known for its great filth or corruption.

PIT *noun.*

cesspool *noun*
A place known for its great filth or corruption.

PIT *noun.*

chafe *verb*
1. To make (the skin) raw by or as if by friction: *chafed her knee when she fell on the concrete.*

1. **Syns:** abrade, excoriate, fret, gall[1].
   Near-syns: graze, scrape, scratch, skin; damage, hurt, impair, injure; inflame, irritate.

2. To worry over trifles.
3. To trouble the nerves or peace of mind of, esp. by repeated vexations.

2. FUSS *verb.*
3. ANNOY.

chaff *verb*
To tease or mock good-humoredly.

JOKE *verb.*

chafing *adjective*
Being unable to endure irritation or opposition.

IMPATIENT.

chagrin *noun*
Self-conscious distress.

EMBARRASSMENT.

chagrin *verb*
To cause (a person) to be self-consciously distressed.

EMBARRASS.

chagrined *adjective*
Distressed and ill at ease.

EMBARRASSED.

chain *noun*
1. A number of things placed or occurring one after the other.
2. An unbroken sequence of events.

1. SERIES.

2. RUN *noun*.

chains *noun*
Something that physically confines the legs or arms.

BONDS.

challenge *verb*
1. To take a stand against.
2. To confront boldly and courageously.
3. To call on another to do something requiring boldness.
4. To come near in quality, amount, etc.

1. CONTEST *verb*.
2. DEFY.
3. DARE *verb*.

4. RIVAL *verb*.

challenge *noun*
1. An act of taunting another to do something bold or rash.
2. Behavior or an act that is intentionally provocative.
3. The act of expressing strong or reasoned opposition.

1. DARE *noun*.

2. DEFIANCE.

3. OBJECTION.

champ also **chomp** *verb*
1. To seize, as food, with the teeth.
2. To bite and grind with the teeth.

1. BITE *verb*.
2. CHEW.

champion *adjective*
Exceptionally good of its kind.

EXCELLENT.

champion *verb*
To aid the cause of by approving or favoring.

SUPPORT *verb*.

chance *noun*
1. The quality shared by random, unintended, or unpredictable events or this quality regarded as the cause of such events: *left the result up to chance.*
2. The likelihood of a given event occurring: *There's very little chance that he'll win the election.*
3. A favorable or advantageous combination of circumstances.
4. A possibility of danger or harm.
5. An unexpected random event: *We met quite by chance.*

1. *Syns:* fortuitousness, fortuity, fortune, hap[1] (*Archaic*), hazard, luck.
   Near-syns: break, fluke; fate, lot.
2. *Syns:* likeliness, odds, outlook, probability, prospect.

3. OPPORTUNITY.

4. RISK *noun*.
5. *Syns:* accident, fluke, fortuity, hap[1] (*Archaic*), happenstance (*also* happenchance).

chance *verb*
1. To take place by chance: *It chanced that she was there too.*
2. To run the risk of.

1. *Syns:* befall, hap[1] (*Archaic*), happen.

2. HAZARD *verb*.

chance on (or **upon**) *verb*
To find or meet by chance.

COME ACROSS at **come**.

chance *adjective*
1. Occurring unexpectedly.
2. Determined or marked by whim or caprice rather than reason.

1. ACCIDENTAL *adjective*.
2. ARBITRARY.

chance on (or **upon**) *verb*

SEE **chance**.

chancy *adjective*
1. Not affording certainty.
2. Involving possible risk, loss, or injury.

1. AMBIGUOUS.
2. DANGEROUS.

change *verb*
1. To make or become different: *a series of events that will change the world.*
2. To give up in return for something else: *"Would you change places with me?" I asked.*

3. To leave or discard for another: *changed planes in Chicago; changed the subject.*
4. To render incapable of reproducing sexually.

1. *Syns:* alter, modify, mutate, turn, vary.

2. *Syns:* commute, exchange, interchange, substitute, swap (*also* swop) (*Informal*), switch, trade.
3. *Syns:* shift, switch.

4. STERILIZE.

change *noun*
1. The process or result of making or becoming different: *The change in her personality was amazing.*
2. The process or result of giving a different form or appearance: *cultural changes resulting from occupation by foreign troops.*
3. The act of exchanging or substituting: *a change of clothes.*

1. *Syns:* alteration, modification, mutation, permutation, variation.
2. *Syns:* conversion, metamorphosis, transfiguration, transformation, translation, transmutation.
3. *Syns:* commutation, exchange, interchange, shift, substitution, swap (*also* swop) (*Informal*), switch, trade, transposition (*also* transposal).

changeable *adjective*
1. Capable of or liable to change: *changeable fall weather.*

1. *Syns:* alterable, fluid, mutable, uncertain, unsettled, unstable, unsteady, variable, variant, various (*Archaic*).
Near-ants: constant, invariable, permanent; certain, fixed, immutable; abiding, enduring, persistent.
Ants: unchangeable, unchanging.

2. Changing easily, as in expression.
3. Following no predictable pattern.

2. MOBILE.
3. CAPRICIOUS.

changeover *noun*
1. The process or an instance of passing from one form, state, or stage to another.
2. A usu. physical change of one thing into another.

1. TRANSITION.
2. CONVERSION.

channel *verb*
To serve as a conduit.

CONDUCT *verb.*

chant *verb*
To utter words or sounds in musical tones.

SING.

chaos *noun*
A lack of order or regular arrangement.

DISORDER *noun.*

chaotic *adjective*
Characterized by physical confusion.

CONFUSED.

char *verb*
To undergo or cause to undergo damage by or as if by fire.

BURN *verb.*

char *noun*
Damage that results from burning.

BURN *noun.*

character *noun*
1. The combination of emotional, intellectual, and moral qualities that distinguishes an individual: *Goodness is the foundation of a great man's character.*
2. A distinctive element.
3. Moral or ethical strength: *a person of real character.*

1. *Syns:* complexion, disposition, make-up (*also* makeup), nature.
2. QUALITY.
3. *Syns:* fiber, honesty, integrity, principles, probity, rectitude.

4. *Archaic.* A statement attesting to personal qualifications, character, and dependability.
5. Public estimation of someone.
6. A person portrayed in fiction or drama: *the cast of characters.*
7. An important, influential person.
8. *Informal.* A person who is appealingly odd or curious: *an old character talking to the pigeons.*
9. A conventional mark used in a writing system: *Chinese characters are used in Japanese texts.*

4. REFERENCE.
5. REPUTATION.
6. *Syns:* persona, personage.
7. DIGNITARY.
8. *Syns:* card (*Slang*), oddball (*Slang*), oddity, original, quiz.
9. *Syns:* sign, symbol.

characteristic *adjective*
Serving to identify or set apart an individual or group.

DISTINCTIVE.

characteristic *noun*
1. A distinctive element.

1. QUALITY.

2. An activity done without thinking.

characterize *verb*
1. To describe with a word or term.
2. To make noticeable or different.

charade *noun*
The presentation of something false as true.

charge *verb*
1. To place a burden or heavy load on: *The ship's hold was charged with coal.*

2. To be morally bound to do.
3. To place a trust upon.
4. To give orders to.
5. To regard as belonging to or resulting from another.
6. To make or become full; put into as much as can be held.
7. To put (explosive material) into a weapon.
8. To cause to be filled with a particular mood or tone: *an atmosphere charged with excitement.*
9. To make an accusation against.

charge *noun*
1. The function of watching, guarding, or overseeing.
2. A person who relies on another for support.
3. An authoritative indication to be obeyed.
4. A charging of someone with a misdeed.
5. An amount paid or to be paid for a purchase.
6. A fixed amount of money charged for a privilege or service.
7. A swift advance or attack: *a cavalry charge.*
8. An act or course of action that is demanded of one, as by position, custom, law, or religion.
9. A quantity of explosives put into a weapon.

charisma *noun*
The power or quality of attracting.

charitable *adjective*
1. Not strict or severe.
2. Concerned with human welfare and the alleviation of suffering.

charitableness *noun*
1. Kindly, charitable interest in others.
2. Forbearing or lenient treatment.

charity *noun*
1. Kindly, charitable interest in others.
2. Kind, forgiving, or compassionate treatment of or disposition toward others.
3. Forbearing or lenient treatment.
4. Something given to a charity or cause.

charlatan *noun*
One who is not what he claims to be.

charm *verb*
1. To act upon with or as if with magic: *charms the authorities into waiving the regulations.*

2. To please greatly or irresistibly: *charmed the audience with the pas de deux.*

charm *noun*
1. The power or quality of attracting.
2. A small object worn or kept for its supposed magical power: *wore a good-luck charm.*

charmer *noun*
One that seduces.

2. HABIT.

1. CALL *verb.*
2. DISTINGUISH.

PRETENSE.

1. **Syns:** burden, cumber, encumber, freight, lade, load, saddle, tax, weigh, weight.
2. COMMIT.
3. ENTRUST.
4. COMMAND *verb.*
5. ATTRIBUTE *verb.*
6. FILL *verb.*

7. LOAD *verb.*
8. **Syns:** freight, impregnate, permeate, pervade, saturate, suffuse, transfuse.
9. ACCUSE *verb.*

1. CARE *noun.*
2. DEPENDENT *noun.*
3. COMMAND *noun.*
4. ACCUSATION.
5. COST *noun.*
6. TOLL[1].

7. **Syns:** race, rush.
8. DUTY.

9. LOAD *noun.*

ATTRACTION.

1. TOLERANT.
2. HUMANITARIAN.

1. BENEVOLENCE.
2. TOLERANCE.

1. BENEVOLENCE.
2. GRACE *noun.*

3. TOLERANCE.
4. DONATION.

FAKE *noun.*

1. **Syns:** bewitch, enchant, ensorcel, enthrall, entrance[2], spell[2], spellbind, witch.
2. **Syns:** beguile, bewitch, captivate, enchant, entrance[2], fascinate.

1. ATTRACTION.
2. **Syns:** amulet, fetish, juju, periapt, phylactery (*Archaic*), talisman.

SEDUCER.

charming *adjective*
1. Pleasing to the eye or mind.
2. Giving great pleasure or delight.

1. ATTRACTIVE.
2. DELIGHTFUL.

chart *noun*
An orderly, columnar display of data.

TABLE *noun.*

chart *verb*
1. To form a strategy for.
2. To show graphically the direction or location of, as by using coordinates.

1. DESIGN *verb.*
2. PLOT *verb.*

charter *verb*
To engage the temporary use of (something) for a fee.

HIRE *verb.*

chary *adjective*
1. Trying attentively to avoid danger, risk, or error.
2. Careful in the use of material resources.

1. WARY.
2. ECONOMICAL.

chase *verb*
To follow (another) with the intent of overtaking and capturing.

PURSUE.

chase *noun*
The following of another in an attempt to overtake and capture.

PURSUIT.

chaste *adjective*
Morally beyond reproach, esp. in sexual conduct: *a chaste nun.*

Syns: decent, modest, nice, pure, virtuous. **Near-ants:** lascivious, lecherous, licentious, lustful; coarse, ribald, vulgar; obscene. **Ant:** unchaste.

chasten *verb*
To castigate for the purpose of improving.

CORRECT *verb.*

chastise *verb*
To criticize for a fault or offense.

CALL DOWN at **call.**

chastity *noun*
The condition of being chaste: *Victorian ideas of chastity.*

Syns: decency, modesty, purity, virtue, virtuousness.

chat *noun*
1. Spoken exchange.
2. Incessant and usu. inconsequential talk.

1. CONVERSATION.
2. CHATTER *noun.*

chat *verb*
To engage in spoken exchange.

CONVERSE[1] *verb.*

chattel *noun*
A piece of equipment for comfort or convenience.

FURNISHING.

chattels *noun*
One's portable property.

EFFECTS.

chatter *verb*
1. To talk volubly, persistently, and usu. inconsequentially: *chattered for hours about his operation.*

1. **Syns:** babble, blabber, clack, gab (*Informal*), gas (*Slang*), go on (*Informal*), jabber, jaw (*Slang*), palaver, prate, prattle, rattle on, run on, spiel (*Slang*), yak (*Slang*). —*Idioms* run off at the mouth, shoot the breeze (*or* the bull).

2. To talk rapidly, incoherently, or indistinctly.
3. To make or cause to make a succession of short, sharp sounds.

2. BABBLE *verb.*
3. RATTLE.

chatter *noun*
Incessant and usu. inconsequential talk: *I don't have time for chatter, so I'll get right to the point.*

Syns: babble, blab, blabber, chat, chitchat, gab (*Informal*), jabber, palaver, prate, prattle, yak (*Slang*). —*Idiom* small talk.

chatty *adjective*
1. Given to conversation.
2. In the style of conversation.

1. TALKATIVE.
2. CONVERSATIONAL.

chaw *verb*
  Regional. To bite and grind with the teeth.   CHEW.

cheap *adjective*
  1. Low in price: *Tomatoes are cheap in August.*
      1. **Syns:** inexpensive, low, low-cost, low-priced.
      Near-ants: costly, dear, high, high-priced, pricey.
      Ant: expensive.

  2. Of decidedly inferior quality.   **2.** SHODDY.
  3. Ungenerously or pettily reluctant to spend money.   **3.** STINGY.

cheapen *verb*
  1. To become or make less in price or value.   **1.** DEPRECIATE.
  2. To lower in character or quality.   **2.** DEBASE.

cheapskate also **cheap skate** *noun*
  Slang. A stingy person.   MISER.

cheat *verb*
  1. To get money or something else from by deceitful trickery: *cheated the American Indians out of their land.*
      1. **Syns:** bilk (*Slang*), chisel (*Slang*), cozen, defraud, diddle (*Slang*), do (*Slang*), flimflam (*Slang*), gull, gyp (*also* gip) (*Informal*), mulct, rook (*Slang*), stick (*Slang*), sting (*Slang*), swindle, take, trim (*Informal*), victimize.
      Near-syns: befool, dupe, extort, fleece, fool, con (*Slang*); beguile, deceive, delude, double-cross, mislead.

  2. To be sexually unfaithful to another.   **2.** PHILANDER *verb.*

cheat *noun*
  1. An act of cheating: *He pulled off a big cheat when he sold us that car.*
      1. **Syns:** flimflam (*Slang*), fraud, gyp (*Informal*), swindle.
  2. A person who cheats: *is a sneak and a cheat.*
      2. **Syns:** cheater, chiseler (*Slang*), crook (*Informal*), diddler (*Slang*), flimflammer (*Slang*), gyp (*Informal*), gypper (*Informal*), sharper, swindler, trickster.

cheater *noun*
  A person who cheats.   CHEAT *noun.*

check *noun*
  1. The act of examining carefully.   **1.** EXAMINATION.
  2. The act of stopping.   **2.** STOP *noun.*

check *verb*
  1. To look at carefully or critically.   **1.** EXAMINE.
  2. To subject to a test of knowledge or skill.   **2.** TEST *verb.*
  3. To subject to a procedure that ascertains effectiveness, value, proper function, or other quality.
      3. TEST *verb.*
  4. To prevent from accomplishing a purpose.   **4.** FRUSTRATE.
  5. To control, restrict, or arrest.   **5.** RESTRAIN.
  6. To prevent the occurrence or continuation of a movement, action, or operation.
      6. STOP *verb.*

check in *verb*
  Informal. To come to a particular place.   ARRIVE.

check out *verb*
  1. To be compatible or in correspondence.   **1.** AGREE.
  2. *Slang.* To cease living.   **2.** DIE.

check in *verb*   SEE **check.**

checkmate *verb*
  To prevent from accomplishing a purpose.   FRUSTRATE.

check out *verb*   SEE **check.**

checkup *noun*
  1. A medical inquiry into a patient's state of health.   **1.** EXAMINATION.

2. The act of examining carefully.   2. EXAMINATION.

cheek *noun*
1. The state or quality of being impudent. 1. IMPUDENCE.
2. Excessive and arrogant self-confidence. 2. PRESUMPTION.

cheekiness *noun*
Excessive and arrogant self-confidence.   PRESUMPTION.

cheeky *adjective*
1. Rude and disrespectful.   1. IMPUDENT.
2. Having or exhibiting excessive and arrogant self-   2. PRESUMPTUOUS.
   confidence.

cheer *noun*
A condition of supreme well-being and good spirits.   HAPPINESS.

cheer *verb*
1. To give great or keen pleasure to.   1. DELIGHT *verb*.
2. To express approval, esp. by clapping.   2. APPLAUD.

cheer (on) *verb*
To impart courage, inspiration, and resolution to.   ENCOURAGE.

cheer (up) *verb*
To impart strength and confidence to.   ENCOURAGE.

cheerful *adjective*
1. Being in or showing good spirits: *gave a cheerful   1. **Syns:** bright, cheery, chipper
   wave of the hand to the onlookers.*   (*Informal*), happy, lighthearted, sunny.
                                               Near-ants: blue (*Informal*), depressed,
                                               doleful, melancholy; joyless, mournful,
                                               woeful; dour, morose, sullen; austere,
                                               grim.
                                               Ants: gloomy, glum.
2. Providing joy and pleasure.   2. GLAD.

cheerfulness *noun*
A condition of supreme well-being and good spirits.   HAPPINESS.

cheering *adjective*
Inspiring confidence or hope.   ENCOURAGING.

cheerless *adjective*
Dark and depressing.   GLOOMY.

cheery *adjective*
1. Being in or showing good spirits.   1. CHEERFUL.
2. Providing joy and pleasure.   2. GLAD.

cheesy *adjective*
Slang. Of decidedly inferior quality.   SHODDY.

chef *noun*
A person who prepares food for eating.   COOK *noun*.

chef d'oeuvre *noun*
French. An outstanding and ingenious work.   MASTERPIECE.

cherish *verb*
1. To have the highest regard for: *cherished their   1. **Syns:** prize, treasure. —*Idiom* hold
   friendship.*   dear.
2. To recognize the worth, quality, importance, etc., of.   2. APPRECIATE.

cherubic *adjective*
Of or like a baby.   BABYISH.

chew *verb*
To bite and grind with the teeth: *Many athletes chew   **Syns:** champ (*also* chomp), chaw
tobacco.*   (*Regional*), chump[2], crump, crunch,
                                               masticate, munch.

chew out *verb*
Slang. To criticize for a fault or offense.   CALL DOWN at **call.**

chew over *verb*
To consider carefully and at length.   PONDER.

chew out *verb*   SEE **chew.**
chew over *verb*   SEE **chew.**

chic *adjective*
Being or in accordance with the current fashion.   FASHIONABLE.

chicanery *noun*
Lack of straightforwardness and honesty in action.   INDIRECTION.

chicken *noun*
Slang. An ignoble, uncourageous person.   COWARD.

chicken *adjective*
Slang. Ignobly lacking in courage.   COWARDLY.

chicken feed *noun*
Slang. A small or trifling amount of money.   PEANUTS.

chickenhearted *adjective*
Ignobly lacking in courage.   COWARDLY.

chide *verb*
To criticize for a fault or offense.   CALL DOWN at **call.**

chiding *noun*
Words expressive of strong disapproval.   REBUKE *noun.*

chief *adjective*
1. Most important, influential, or significant.   1. PRIMARY.
2. Having or exercising authority.   2. PRINCIPAL.

chief *noun*
1. One who is highest in rank or authority: *makes out*   1. **Syns:** boss, chieftain, director, head,
   a weekly report for his chief.   headman, hierarch, honcho (*Informal*),
                                                              leader, master. —*Idioms* cock of the
                                                              walk, first fiddle.
2. A professional politician who controls a party or   2. BOSS *noun.*
   political machine.

chieftain *noun*
1. One who is highest in rank or authority.   1. CHIEF *noun.*
2. *Slang.* A professional politician who controls a party 2. BOSS *noun.*
   or political machine.

child *noun*
1. A young person between birth and puberty: *a group*   1. **Syns:** bairn (*Scot.*), bud, innocent,
   of children with their teacher.   juvenile, kid (*Informal*), moppet, tot[1],
                                                              youngster.
2. One descended directly from the same parents or   2. DESCENDANT *noun.*
   ancestors.
3. A guileless, unsophisticated person.   3. INNOCENT *noun.*
4. One who is not yet legally of age.   4. MINOR *noun.*

childbearing *noun*
The act or process of bringing forth young.   BIRTH *noun.*

childbirth *noun*
The act or process of bringing forth young.   BIRTH *noun.*

childish *adjective*
Of or characteristic of a child, esp. in immaturity: **Syns:** babyish, immature, infantile,
childish, sulking behavior.   juvenile, puerile.
                                                         Near-syns: fatuous, foolish, silly, simple;
                                                         naive, unsophisticated; backward,
                                                         retarded, slow.
                                                         Ants: adult, mature.

childless *adjective*
Unable to produce offspring.   BARREN *adjective.*

childlike *adjective*
Of or like a baby.   BABYISH.

children *noun*
Those descended from another.   DESCENDANTS.

chill *adjective*
1. Marked by a low temperature.   1. COLD *adjective.*
2. Lacking all friendliness and warmth.   2. COLD *adjective.*

chill *noun*
Relative lack of warmth.   COLD *noun.*

chilliness *noun*
Relative lack of warmth.   COLD *noun.*

chilly *adjective*
1. Marked by a low temperature.
2. Not friendly, sociable, or warm in manner.

1. COLD *adjective*.
2. COOL *adjective*.

chime *noun*
Harmonious mutual understanding.

AGREEMENT.

chime *verb*
To give forth or cause to give forth a clear, resonant sound.

RING².

chime in *verb*
To interject remarks or questions into another's discourse.

INTERRUPT.

chime in *verb*

SEE **chime.**

chimera *noun*
A fantastic, impracticable plan or desire.

ILLUSION.

chimerical also **chimeric** *adjective*
1. Of, pertaining to, or in the nature of an illusion; lacking reality.
2. Existing only in the imagination.

1. ILLUSIVE.
2. IMAGINARY.

chink *noun*
A usu. narrow partial opening caused by splitting and rupture.

CRACK *noun*.

chintzy *adjective*
Tastelessly showy.

GAUDY.

chip in *verb*
1. *Informal.* To give in common with others.
2. To interject remarks or questions into another's discourse.

1. CONTRIBUTE.
2. INTERRUPT.

chipper *adjective*
1. *Informal.* Being in or showing good spirits.
2. Very brisk, alert, and high-spirited.

1. CHEERFUL.
2. LIVELY.

chisel *verb*
Slang. To get money or something else from by deceitful trickery.

CHEAT *verb*.

chiseler *noun*
Slang. A person who cheats.

CHEAT *noun*.

chitchat *noun*
Incessant and usu. inconsequential talk.

CHATTER *noun*.

chivalric *adjective*
Respectfully attentive, esp. to women.

GALLANT *adjective*.

chivalrous *adjective*
1. Characterized by kindness and concern for others.
2. Characterized by elaborate but usu. formal courtesy.
3. Respectfully attentive, esp. to women.

1. BENEVOLENT.
2. GRACIOUS.
3. GALLANT *adjective*.

chivalrousness *noun*
Respectful attention, esp. toward women.

GALLANTRY.

chivalry *noun*
Respectful attention, esp. toward women.

GALLANTRY.

choate *adjective*
Lacking nothing essential or normal.

COMPLETE *adjective*.

chockablock *adjective*
Completely filled.

FULL.

chock-full also **chuck-full, choke-full** *adjective*
Completely filled.

FULL.

choice *noun*
1. The act of choosing: *Did price influence your choice?*
2. The power or right of choosing: *I had no choice but to accept his decision.*
3. Unrestricted freedom to choose.
4. One that is selected.
5. That which is superlative.

1. *Syns:* election, option, preference, selection.
2. *Syns:* alternative, option.
3. WILL¹ *noun*.
4. ELECT *noun*.
5. BEST *noun*.

choice *adjective*
1. Singled out in preference.
2. Of fine quality: *had a choice glass of wine.*

3. Appealing to refined taste.

choke *verb*
1. To interfere with or stop the normal breathing of, esp. by constricting the windpipe: *choked the victim to death.*
2. To stop the breathing of: *a tight collar that almost chokes him.*
3. To hold (something requiring an outlet) in check.
4. To plug up something, as a hole, space, or container.

choke-full *adjective*

choking *noun*
The act of restraining forcefully.

choler *noun*
1. A tendency to become angry or irritable.
2. Violent or unrestrained anger.

choleric *adjective*
1. Easily annoyed.
2. Feeling or showing anger.

chomp *verb*

choose *verb*
1. To make a choice from a number of alternatives: *You'll have to choose which cities you most want to visit.*

2. To have the desire or inclination to: *I can do exactly as I choose.*

choosy *adjective*
Very difficult to please.

chop¹ *verb*
1. To bring down, as with a saw or ax.
2. To decrease, as in length or amount, by or as if by severing or excising.

chop *noun*
A quick, sharp blow, esp. with the hand.

chop² *verb*
Naut. To turn aside sharply from a straight course.

chore *noun*
1. A piece of work that has been assigned.
2. A difficult or tedious undertaking.

chortle *verb*
To laugh quietly.

chosen *adjective*
Singled out in preference.

chow *noun*
Slang. Something fit to be eaten.

chow *verb*
Slang. To take (food) into the body as nourishment.

christen *verb*
To give a name or title to.

chronic *adjective*
1. Of long duration: *suffering from chronic feelings of doubt.*
2. Subject to a disease or habit for a long time: *a chronic alcoholic; a chronic liar.*
3. Familiar through repetition.

---

1. SELECT *adjective.*
2. *Syns:* fine, first-class, prime, select, superior, top-quality.
3. DELICATE.

1. *Syns:* strangle, throttle.

2. *Syns:* asphyxiate, smother, stifle, suffocate.
3. REPRESS.
4. FILL.
SEE **chock-full.**

REPRESSION.

1. TEMPER *noun.*
2. FURY.

1. TESTY.
2. ANGRY.
SEE **champ.**

1. *Syns:* cull, elect, opt for, pick (out), select, single out.
Near-ants: decline, refuse, repudiate, spurn; abnegate, eschew, forgo.
Ant: reject.
2. *Syns:* desire, like¹, please, want, will¹, wish. —*Idioms* have a mind, see fit.

NICE.

1. CUT *verb.*
2. CUT BACK.

SLAP *noun.*

SWERVE.

1. TASK *noun.*
2. TASK *noun.*

CHUCKLE.

SELECT *adjective.*

FOOD.

EAT.

NAME *verb.*

1. *Syns:* continuing, lingering, persistent, prolonged, protracted.
2. *Syns:* confirmed, habitual, habituated, inveterate.
3. ACCUSTOMED.

chronicle *noun*
   1. A recounting of past events.   **1.** STORY.
   2. A chronological record of past events.   **2.** HISTORY.
chubby *adjective*
   Well-rounded and usu. short in physique.   PLUMP[1].
chuck[1] *verb*
   1. *Informal.* To let go or get rid of as being no longer   **1.** DISCARD.
      of use, value, etc.
   2. *Informal.* To put out by force.   **2.** EJECT.
chuck[2] *noun*
   Regional. Something fit to be eaten.   FOOD.
chuck[3] *verb*
   Obs. To laugh quietly.   CHUCKLE.
chuck-full *adjective*   SEE **chock-full.**
chuckle *verb*
   To laugh quietly: *The baby chuckled while playing with*   *Syns:* chortle, chuck[3] (*Obs.*).
   his toys.   *Near-syns:* giggle, snicker; guffaw, laugh.
chuff *noun*
   1. An unrefined, rude person.   **1.** BOOR.
   2. A stingy person.   **2.** MISER.
   chuff *adjective*
   Regional. Broodingly and sullenly unhappy.   GLUM.
chuffy *adjective*
   Brit. Regional. Broodingly and sullenly unhappy.   GLUM.
chum *noun*
   One who keeps company with another.   ASSOCIATE *noun.*
chummy *adjective*
   1. *Informal.* Very closely associated.   **1.** FAMILIAR *adjective.*
   2. *Informal.* Of or befitting a friend or friends.   **2.** FRIENDLY.
chump[1] *noun*
   Slang. A person who is easily deceived or victimized.   DUPE *noun.*
chump[2] *verb*
   To bite and grind with the teeth.   CHEW.
chunk *noun*
   An irregularly shaped mass of indefinite size.   LUMP[1] *noun.*
chunky *adjective*
   Short, heavy, and solidly built.   STOCKY.
church *noun*
   Those who accept and practice a particular religious   FAITH.
   belief.
   church *adjective*
   Of or relating to a church or to an established religion.   SPIRITUAL.
churchly *adjective*
   Of or relating to a church or to an established religion.   SPIRITUAL.
churchman *noun*
   A person ordained for service in a Christian church.   PREACHER.
churl *noun*
   An unrefined, rude person.   BOOR.
churlish *adjective*
   Lacking in delicacy or refinement.   COARSE.
churn *verb*
   1. To cause to move to and fro violently.   **1.** AGITATE.
   2. To be in a state of emotional or mental turmoil.   **2.** BOIL.
chutzpah *noun*
   Slang. Foolhardy boldness or disregard of danger.   TEMERITY.
cinch *noun*
   1. *Informal.* An easily accomplished task.   **1.** BREEZE *noun.*
   2. *Slang.* A clearly established fact.   **2.** CERTAINTY.
   cinch *verb*
   Slang. To render certain.   GUARANTEE *verb.*

cincture   *verb*
To encircle with or as if with a band.   BAND[1] *verb.*

cinerarium   *noun*
A burial place or receptacle for human remains.   GRAVE[1].

cipher   *verb*
To ascertain by mathematics.   CALCULATE.

cipher   *noun*
A totally insignificant person.   NONENTITY.

circle   *noun*
1. A closed plane curve everywhere equidistant from a   1. **Syns:** circuit, gyre, orb (*Archaic*), ring[1],
   fixed point or something shaped like this: *a bracelet*   wheel.
   that looks like a circle of diamonds.
2. A course, process, or journey that ends where it   2. **Syns:** circuit, cycle, orbit, round, tour,
   began or repeats itself: *drove full circle—Boston to*   turn.
   New York and back.
3. A group of people sharing an interest, activity, or   3. **Syns:** crowd, group, set[2].
   achievement: *popular in musical circles.*   **Near-syns:** clan, clique, ring; friends,
                                                             intimates; associates, companions,
                                                             comrades; cronies.
4. A particular social group.   4. CROWD *noun.*

circle   *verb*
1. To move or cause to move in circles or around an   1. TURN *verb.*
   axis or center.
2. To shut in on all sides.   2. SURROUND.

circuit   *noun*
1. A course, process, or journey that ends where it   1. CIRCLE *noun.*
   began or repeats itself.
2. A closed plane curve everywhere equidistant from a   2. CIRCLE *noun.*
   fixed point or something shaped like this.
3. A line around a closed figure or area.   3. CIRCUMFERENCE.
4. Circular movement around a point or about an axis.   4. REVOLUTION.
5. An area regularly covered, as by a policeman or   5. BEAT *noun.*
   reporter.
6. A group of athletic teams that play each other.   6. CONFERENCE.

circuitous   *adjective*
Not taking a direct or straight line or course.   INDIRECT.

circular   *adjective*
1. Not taking a direct or straight line or course.   1. INDIRECT.
2. Having the shape of a curve everywhere equidistant   2. ROUND.
   from a fixed point.

circulate   *verb*
1. To pass (something) out.   1. DISTRIBUTE.
2. To move freely as a liquid.   2. FLOW *verb.*
3. To become known far and wide.   3. GET ABOUT.

circulation   *noun*
Circular movement around a point or about an axis.   REVOLUTION.

circumference   *noun*
A line around a closed figure or area: *walked around*   **Syns:** ambit, circuit, compass, perimeter,
the circumference of the property.   periphery.

circumlocutional   *adjective*
Characterized by excessive and obfuscatory wordiness.   TAUTOLOGICAL.

circumlocutionary   *adjective*
Characterized by excessive and obfuscatory wordiness.   TAUTOLOGICAL.

circumlocutious   *adjective*
Characterized by excessive and obfuscatory wordiness.   TAUTOLOGICAL.

circumlocutory   *adjective*
Characterized by excessive and obfuscatory wordiness.   TAUTOLOGICAL.

circumnavigate   *verb*
To pass around but not through.   SKIRT *verb.*

circumscribe   *verb*
To place a limit on.   LIMIT *verb.*

circumscribed *adjective*
Kept within certain limits. RESTRICTED.

circumscription *noun*
1. Something that limits or restricts. 1. RESTRICTION.
2. The act of limiting or condition of being limited. 2. RESTRICTION.

circumspect *adjective*
Trying attentively to avoid danger, risk, or error. WARY.

circumspection *noun*
1. Careful forethought to avoid harm or risk. 1. CAUTION *noun*.
2. The exercise of good judgment or common sense in 2. PRUDENCE.
practical matters.

circumstance *noun*
1. One of the conditions or facts attending an event 1. *Syns:* detail, fact, factor, particular.
and having some bearing on it: *Tell me the*
circumstances under which you left.
2. Something that happens: *a victim of circumstance.* 2. *Syns:* event, happening, incident,
occurrence.
3. Something significant that happens. 3. EVENT.

circumstances *noun*
Existing surroundings that affect an activity. CONDITIONS.

circumstantial *adjective*
Characterized by attention to detail. DETAILED.

circumvent *verb*
1. To pass around but not through. 1. SKIRT *verb*.
2. To evade, as a topic, esp. by circumlocution. 2. SKIRT *verb*.

circumvolution *noun*
Circular movement around a point or about an axis. REVOLUTION.

cite *verb*
1. To refer to by name. 1. NAME *verb*.
2. To bring forward and quote for formal consideration. 2. PRESENT[2] *verb*.

citify *verb*
To imbue with city ways, manners, and customs: *After* *Syns:* metropolitanize, urbanize.
living in New York for six months she became
thoroughly citified.

citizen *noun*
A person owing loyalty to and entitled to the protection *Syns:* national, subject.
of a given state: *an American citizen arrested on*
suspicion of spying.

city *noun*
A large and important town: *The city of Budapest* *Syns:* burg (*Informal*), metropolis,
straddles the Danube. municipality.

city *adjective*
Of, in, or belonging to a city: *city government; city life.* *Syns:* metropolitan, municipal, urban.

civic *adjective*
Of, concerning, or affecting the community or the PUBLIC *adjective*.
people.

civil *adjective*
1. Characterized by good manners. 1. COURTEOUS.
2. Of, concerning, or affecting the community or the 2. PUBLIC *adjective*.
people.

civilities *noun*
Courteous acts that contribute to smoothness and ease AMENITIES.
in dealings and social relationships.

civility *noun*
1. Well-mannered behavior toward others. 1. COURTESY.
2. A courteous act. 2. COURTESY.

civilization *noun*
The total product of human creativity and intellect at a CULTURE.
particular time.

civilize *verb*
To fit for companionship with others, esp. in attitude or manners. SOCIALIZE.

civilized *adjective*
Characterized by discriminating taste and broad knowledge as a result of development or education. CULTURED.

civilizing *adjective*
Promoting culture. CULTURAL.

clack *noun*
A light, sharp noise. SNAP *noun*.

clack *verb*
1. To make a light, sharp noise. 1. SNAP *verb*.
2. To make or cause to make a succession of short, sharp sounds. 2. RATTLE.
3. To talk volubly, persistently, and usu. inconsequentially. 3. CHATTER *verb*.

clacket *verb*
Regional. To make a light, sharp noise. SNAP *verb*.

clad *verb*
1. To put clothes on. 1. DRESS *verb*.
2. To furnish with a covering of a different material. 2. FACE *verb*.

clag *verb*
Brit. Regional. To hold fast to. BOND *verb*.

claggy *adjective*
Regional. Having the property of adhering. STICKY.

claim *verb*
1. To assert one's right to: *claimed his share of the profits.* 1. **Syn:** demand. —*Idiom* lay claim to.
2. To defend, maintain, or insist on the recognition of (one's rights, for example). 2. ASSERT.
3. To state to be true: *claims she can write poetry and novels with equal ease.* 3. **Syns:** allege, assert, contend, declare, maintain, say.
Near-ants: contradict, deny, gainsay; challenge, question; query.

claim *noun*
1. A legitimate or supposed right to demand something as one's rightful due: *the Arabs' claim to lands conquered by Israel; keyboard virtuosity as her claim to fame.* 1. **Syns:** dibs (*Slang*), pretense, pretension, title.
2. A statement of something as fact: *an advertisement that makes false claims.* 2. **Syns:** allegation, assertion, contention, declaration.
3. A right or legal share in something. 3. INTEREST *noun*.

claimant *noun*
1. One who sets forth a claim to a royal title: *The Comte de Paris is the claimant to the throne of France.* 1. **Syns:** claimer, pretender.
2. One that makes a formal complaint, esp. in court. 2. COMPLAINANT.

claimer *noun*
One who sets forth a claim to a royal title. CLAIMANT.

clamber *verb*
To move or climb hurriedly, esp. on all fours. SCRAMBLE.

clamor *verb*
To speak or say very loudly. ROAR *verb*.

clamor *noun*
1. Sounds or a sound, esp. when loud, confused, or disagreeable. 1. NOISE *noun*.
2. A loud, deep, prolonged sound. 2. ROAR *noun*.
3. Offensively loud and insistent utterances, esp. of disapproval. 3. VOCIFERATION.

clamorous *adjective*
Offensively loud and insistent. VOCIFEROUS.

clampdown *noun*
Informal. Sudden punitive action. — SUPPRESSION.

clan *noun*
A group of people sharing common ancestry. — FAMILY.

clandestine *adjective*
Existing or operating in a way so as to ensure complete concealment and confidentiality. — SECRET *adjective*.

clandestinely *adverb*
In a secret way. — SECRETLY.

clap *verb*
1. To strike, set down, or close in such a way as to make a loud noise. — 1. BANG *verb*.
2. To express approval, esp. by clapping. — 2. APPLAUD.
3. To make a sudden sharp, explosive noise. — 3. CRACK *verb*.

claptrap *noun*
Something that does not have or make sense. — NONSENSE.

claret *noun*
Slang. The fluid circulated by the heart through the vascular system. — BLOOD *noun*.

clarification *noun*
1. Something that serves to explain or clarify. — 1. EXPLANATION.
2. The act or process of removing physical impurities. — 2. PURIFICATION.

clarified *adjective*
Made pure, esp. by a commercial refining process. — REFINED.

clarify *verb*
1. To make clear or clearer: *tried to clarify the point of law for his client*. — 1. *Syns:* clear, clear up, elucidate, illuminate. —*Idiom* shed (*or* throw) light on (*or* upon).
   Near-ants: befog, cloud, obfuscate, obscure; confuse, muddle.
2. To make or become clear by the removal of impurities. — 2. REFINE.

clarity *noun*
1. The quality of being clear and easy to perceive or understand: *a photograph remarkable for its clarity; an actor renowned for the clarity of his speech*. — 1. *Syns:* clearness, distinctness, limpidity, lucidity, perspicuity, plainness.
2. The condition of being clean and free of contaminants. — 2. PURITY.

clash *verb*
1. To strike together with a loud, harsh noise: *cymbals clashing*. — 1. *Syns:* crash, smash.
2. To fail to be in accord. — 2. CONFLICT *verb*.

clash *noun*
1. A brief, hostile exposure to or contact with something, as danger, opposition, etc. — 1. BRUSH *noun*.
2. A loud striking together: *a clash of cymbals*. — 2. *Syns:* crash, smash.
3. A state of disagreement and disharmony. — 3. CONFLICT *noun*.
4. A discussion, often heated, in which a difference of opinion is expressed. — 4. ARGUMENT.

clashing *adjective*
In sharp opposition. — CONFLICTING.

clasp *noun*
1. A device for fastening or for checking motion. — 1. CATCH *noun*.
2. An act or means of holding something. — 2. HOLD *noun*.
3. The act of embracing. — 3. EMBRACE *noun*.

clasp *verb*
1. To take firmly with the hand and maintain a hold on. — 1. GRASP *verb*.
2. To put one's arms around affectionately. — 2. EMBRACE *verb*.

class *noun*

1. A subdivision of a larger group: *the class of concertgoers who enjoy chamber music.*
2. A division of persons or things by quality, rank, or grade: *a painter of the highest class.*
3. Degree of excellence.
4. *Slang.* High style in quality, manner, or dress: *a new restaurant with real class.*

1. *Syns:* category, classification, order, set[2].
2. *Syns:* bracket, caliber, grade, league (*Informal*), order, rank[1], tier.
3. QUALITY.
4. *Syns:* quality, refinement.

class *verb*

1. To assign to a class or classes: *classed farmers separately from those whose work entails only service.*

1. *Syns:* categorize, classify, grade, group, pigeonhole, place, rank[1], rate[1].
   Near-syns: appraise, gauge, judge; consider, hold, regard; mark, score.

2. To distribute into groups according to kinds.

2. ASSORT.

classic *adjective*

1. Having the nature of, constituting, or serving as a type.
2. Characterized by enduring excellence, appeal, and importance.

1. TYPICAL.

2. VINTAGE *adjective*.

classical *adjective*

1. Having the nature of, constituting, or serving as a type.
2. Characterized by enduring excellence, appeal, and importance.

1. TYPICAL.

2. VINTAGE *adjective*.

classification *noun*

A subdivision of a larger group.

CLASS *noun*.

classified *adjective*

Of or being information available only to authorized persons.

CONFIDENTIAL.

classify *verb*

1. To assign to a class or classes.
2. To distribute into groups according to kinds.
3. To put into a deliberate order.

1. CLASS *verb*.
2. ASSORT.
3. ARRANGE.

classy *adjective*

Slang. Being or in accordance with the current fashion.

FASHIONABLE.

clatter *verb*

To make or cause to make a succession of short, sharp sounds.

RATTLE.

clean *adjective*

1. Free from dirt, stain, or impurities: *clean clothing; clean water.*

1. *Syns:* antiseptic, cleanly, immaculate, spotless, stainless, unsoiled, unsullied.
   Near-ants: dingy, grimy, grubby, messy, slovenly; fetid, filthy, foul, rank, unwholesome.
   Ants: dirty, unclean.

2. Without imperfections or blemishes: *the clean lines of a fine antique.*
3. According to the rules.
4. Free from evil and corruption.
5. Not lewd or obscene: *a clean joke.*
6. *Slang.* Free from guilt or blame.

2. *Syns:* perfect, regular.
3. SPORTSMANLIKE.
4. INNOCENT *adjective*.
5. *Syns:* decent, modest, wholesome.
6. INNOCENT *adjective*.

clean *verb*

1. To make or become clear by the removal of impurities.

1. REFINE.

2. To make or keep (an area) clean and orderly.

2. TIDY *verb*.

clean out *verb*

1. To remove the contents of.
2. *Informal.* To reduce to financial insolvency.

1. EMPTY *verb*.
2. RUIN *verb*.

clean up *verb*

Informal. To make a large profit: *cleaned up on the stock market.*

Syns: batten, profit. —*Idiom* make a killing.

clean *adverb*
Informal. To the fullest extent.   COMPLETELY.

cleaner *noun*
Something that purifies.   PURIFIER.

cleaning *noun*
The act or process of removing physical impurities.   PURIFICATION.

cleanliness *noun*
The condition of being clean and free of contaminants.   PURITY.

cleanly *adjective*
Free from dirt, stain, or impurities.   CLEAN *adjective*.

    cleanly *adverb*
In a fair, sporting manner.   FAIR *adverb*.

cleanness *noun*
The condition of being clean and free of contaminants.   PURITY.

clean out *verb*   SEE **clean.**

cleanse *verb*
1. To make or become clear by the removal of impurities.   1. REFINE.
2. To free from sin, guilt, or defilement.   2. PURIFY.

cleanser *noun*
Something that purifies.   PURIFIER.

cleansing *noun*
1. The act or process of removing physical impurities.   1. PURIFICATION.
2. A freeing from sin, guilt, or defilement.   2. PURIFICATION.

clean up *verb*   SEE **clean.**

clear *adjective*
1. Free from what obscures or dims: *a glass of clear, sediment-free claret.*   1. *Syns:* limpid, lucid, pellucid, transparent.
2. Free from clouds, mist, etc.: *a clear day.*   2. *Syns:* cloudless, fair, fine[1], sunny, unclouded.
3. Admitting light so that objects beyond can be seen.   3. TRANSPARENT.
4. Readily seen, perceived, or understood.   4. APPARENT.
5. Easily seen through due to a lack of subtlety.   5. UNSUBTLE.
6. Clearly defined; not ambiguous.   6. SHARP *adjective*.
7. Without any doubt.   7. DECIDED.
8. Free from flaws or blemishes: *a clear, radiant complexion.*   8. *Syns:* flawless, unblemished, unbroken, unmarked.
9. Free from obstructions: *The road ahead is clear.*   9. *Syns:* open, unimpeded, unobstructed.
10. Freed from contact or connection: *The rope is clear of the scaffolding.*   10. *Syns:* disengaged, free, unfastened.
11. Containing nothing.   11. EMPTY *adjective*.

    clear *verb*
1. To make clear or clearer.   1. CLARIFY.
2. To make or keep (an area) clean and orderly.   2. TIDY *verb*.
3. To become brighter or fairer: *If the weather clears, we can enjoy the picnic.*   3. *Syns:* brighten, clear up.
4. To free from something objectionable or undesirable.   4. RID.
5. To free from an entanglement: *cleared himself from the unsatisfactory relationship.*   5. *Syns:* disengage, disentangle, extricate, untangle.
6. To destroy all traces of.   6. ANNIHILATE.
7. To rid of obstructions: *cleared the streets for the motorcade.*   7. *Syn:* open.
8. To remove the contents of.   8. EMPTY *verb*.
9. To free from a charge or imputation of guilt: *The jury cleared the defendant of the murder charge.*   9. *Syns:* absolve, acquit, disculpate, exculpate, exonerate, purge (*Law*), vindicate.
10. To be accepted or approved.   10. PASS *verb*.
11. To pass by or over safely or successfully: *Our car barely cleared the snowdrift.*   11. *Syns:* hurdle, negotiate.
12. To set right by giving what is due.   12. SETTLE.

13. To make as income or profit.

clear out *verb*
Informal. To leave hastily.

clear up
1. To become brighter or fairer.
2. To make clear or clearer.
3. To find a solution for.

clear *adverb*
Informal. All the way: *From here you can see clear to the park.*

clearance *noun*
The act or process of eliminating.

clear-cut *adjective*
1. Without any doubt.
2. Clearly, fully, and sometimes emphatically expressed.
3. Readily seen, perceived, or understood.
4. Having or suggesting keen, discerning intellect.

clearness *noun*
The quality of being clear and easy to perceive or understand.

clear out *verb*

clear-sightedness *noun*
Skill in perceiving, discriminating, or judging.

clear up *verb*

cleave *verb*
1. To crack or split into two or more fragments by means of or as a result of force, a blow, or strain.
2. To separate into parts with or as if with a sharp-edged instrument.
3. To separate or pull apart by force.

cleft *noun*
1. An opening, esp. in a solid structure.
2. A usu. narrow partial opening caused by splitting and rupture.

clemency *noun*
Kind, forgiving, or compassionate treatment of or disposition toward others.

clement *adjective*
Not strict or severe.

clench *verb*
To take firmly with the hand and maintain a hold on.

clench *noun*
An act or means of holding something.

clergyman *noun*
A person ordained for service in a Christian church.

cleric *noun*
A person ordained for service in a Christian church.

clerical *noun*
A person ordained for service in a Christian church.

clerk *noun*
Archaic. A person ordained for service in a Christian church.

clever *adjective*
1. Mentally quick and original: *The child is clever but not brilliant.*

---

13. RETURN *verb*.

RUN *verb*.

1. CLEAR *verb*.
2. CLARIFY.
3. RESOLVE *verb*.

Syns: completely, entirely, fully.

ELIMINATION.

1. DECIDED.
2. DEFINITE.

3. APPARENT.
4. INCISIVE.

CLARITY.

SEE **clear**.

DISCERNMENT.
SEE **clear**.

1. BREAK *verb*.

2. CUT *verb*.

3. TEAR[1].

1. BREACH *noun*.

2. CRACK *noun*.

GRACE *noun*.

TOLERANT.

GRASP *verb*.

HOLD *noun*.

PREACHER.

PREACHER.

PREACHER.

PREACHER.

1. *Syns:* alert, bright, intelligent, keen[1], quick-witted, sharp, sharp-witted, smart. —*Idiom* smart as a tack (*or* whip).
Near-ants: asinine, fatuous, foolish, simple, simple-minded.
Ant: dull.

2. Amusing or pleasing because of wit or originality: *made the audience laugh with a few clever, offbeat comparisons.*
3. Exhibiting or possessing skill and ease in performance.
4. Astute but lacking in ethics or principles.

clew *noun*

cliché *noun*
A trite expression or idea: *a short story marred by clichés.*

cliché *adjective*
Without freshness or appeal due to overuse.

click *noun*
A light, sharp noise.

click *verb*
1. To make a light, sharp noise.
2. *Slang.* To turn out well.
3. *Informal.* To interact with another or others in a meaningful fashion.

client *noun*
One who buys goods or services.

clientele *noun*
Customers or patrons collectively.

climacteric *adjective*
So serious as to be at the point of crisis.

climactic *adjective*
Of or constituting a climax: *The climactic moment of the event was the presentation of the award.*

climate *noun*
1. The totality of surrounding conditions and circumstances affecting growth or development.
2. A prevailing quality, as of thought, behavior, or attitude, of a given period.

climatize *verb*
To make resistant to hardship, esp. through continued exposure.

climax *noun*
1. The highest point or state: *a public figure at the climax of his popularity.*

2. The greatest quantity or highest degree attainable.

climax *verb*
To reach or bring to a climax: *The movie climaxes with realistic scenes of an invasion.*

climb *verb*
1. To move upward on or along.
2. To attain a higher status, rank, or condition.

climb *noun*
The act of moving upward on or along.

climbing *noun*
The act of moving upward on or along.

clinch *verb*
1. To take firmly with the hand and maintain a hold on.
2. *Slang.* To put one's arms around affectionately.

clinch *noun*
Slang. The act of embracing.

2. *Syns:* scintillating, smart, sparkling, sprightly, witty.

3. DEXTEROUS.

4. SHARP *adjective.*
SEE **clue.**

Syns: banality, bromide, commonplace, platitude, stereotype, truism.

TRITE.

SNAP *noun.*

1. SNAP *verb.*
2. SUCCEED.
3. RELATE.

PATRON.

PATRONAGE.

CRITICAL.

Syns: crowning, culminating, peak.

1. ENVIRONMENT.

2. TEMPER *noun.*

HARDEN.

1. *Syns:* acme, apex, apogee, crest, crown, culmination, height, meridian, payoff (*Informal*), peak, pinnacle, summit, zenith.
2. MAXIMUM *noun.*

Syns: cap, crown, culminate, peak, top off.
Near-syns: conclude, end, finish, terminate.

1. ASCEND.
2. RISE *verb.*

ASCENT.

ASCENT.

1. GRASP *verb.*

2. EMBRACE *verb.*

EMBRACE *noun.*

clincher *noun*
Informal. Something, esp. something held in reserve, that gives one a decisive advantage.

TRUMP *noun.*

cling *verb*
To hold fast to.

BOND *verb.*

clink *noun*
Slang. A place for the confinement of persons in lawful detention.

JAIL *noun.*

clip¹ *verb*
1. To decrease, as in length or amount, by or as if by severing or excising.
2. *Informal.* To deliver (a powerful blow) suddenly and sharply.
3. *Slang.* To exploit (another) by charging too much for something.

1. CUT BACK.
2. HIT *verb.*
3. SKIN *verb.*

clip *noun*
1. *Informal.* A quick, sharp blow, esp. with the hand.
2. *Informal.* Rate of motion or performance.

1. SLAP *noun.*
2. SPEED *noun.*

clip² *verb*
1. To join one thing to another.
2. *Brit. Regional.* To put one's arms around affectionately.

1. ATTACH.
2. EMBRACE *verb.*

clitter *verb*
To make or cause to make a succession of short, sharp sounds.

RATTLE.

cloak *verb*
1. To surround and cover completely so as to obscure.
2. To cover as if with clothes.
3. To change or modify so as to prevent recognition of the true identity or character of.
4. To prevent (something) from being known.

1. WRAP *verb.*
2. CLOTHE.
3. DISGUISE *verb.*
4. COVER *verb.*

cloak *noun*
1. A garment wrapped about a person.
2. A deceptive outward appearance.

1. WRAP *noun.*
2. FAÇADE.

cloak-and-dagger *adjective*
Existing or operating in a way so as to ensure complete concealment and confidentiality.

SECRET *adjective.*

clobber *verb*
1. *Slang.* To win a victory over, as in battle or a competition.
2. *Slang.* To deliver (a powerful blow) suddenly and sharply.
3. *Slang.* To render totally ineffective by decisive defeat.

1. DEFEAT *verb.*
2. HIT *verb.*
3. OVERWHELM.

clobbering *noun*
Slang. The act of defeating or the condition of being defeated.

DEFEAT *noun.*

clock *verb*
To record the speed or duration of.

TIME *verb.*

clod *noun*
1. An irregularly shaped mass of indefinite size.
2. A large, ungainly, and dull-witted person.
3. An unpleasant, tiresome person.

1. LUMP¹ *noun.*
2. LUMP¹ *noun.*
3. DRIP *noun.*

clog *verb*
To plug up something, as a hole, space, or container.

FILL.

cloggy *adjective*
Having the property of adhering.

STICKY.

cloister *verb*
To put into solitude.

SECLUDE.

cloistered *adjective*
Solitary and shut off from society.

SECLUDED.

clomp *verb*
  To make a dull sound by or as if by striking a surface
  with a heavy object.

THUD *verb*.

close¹ *adjective*
  1. Not far from another in space, time, or relation: *an airport that is close to town; a birthday close to my own.*

  1. **Syns:** immediate, near, near-at-hand, nearby, nigh, proximate. — *Idioms* at hand, under one's nose, within a stone's throw, within hailing distance. **Near-syns:** abutting, adjacent, adjoining, contiguous; handy, next-door; nearest, next. **Ant:** remote.

  2. Having all parts near to each other.
  3. Affording little room for movement.
  4. Nearly equivalent or even: *a close race; a close election.*
  5. Stretched tightly.
  6. Not deviating from correctness, accuracy, or completeness: *keeping a close watch on the prisoner.*
  7. Very closely associated.
  8. Not speaking freely or openly.
  9. Ungenerously or pettily reluctant to spend money.
  10. Oppressive due to a lack of fresh air.

  2. THICK.
  3. TIGHT *adjective*.
  4. **Syns:** neck-and-neck (*Informal*), tight.

  5. TAUT.
  6. **Syns:** exact, faithful, full, rigorous, strict.
  7. FAMILIAR *adjective*.
  8. TACITURN.
  9. STINGY.
  10. AIRLESS.

close *verb*
  1. To move an appropriate barrier into (an opening): *Close the door behind you.*
  2. To plug up something, as a hole, space, or container.
  3. To cut off from sight.
  4. To bring or come to a natural or proper end: *She closes letters with greetings. The play closed after ten performances.*

  1. **Syns:** put to, shut.
  2. FILL.
  3. BLOCK OUT at **block**.
  4. **Syns:** cease, complete, conclude, consummate, end, finish, terminate, ultimate, wind up (*Informal*), wrap up. —*Idiom* put (*or* set) a period to.

  5. To come together: *His arms closed around her in a tight embrace.*

  5. **Syns:** converge, meet¹.

close in *verb*
  To surround and advance upon: *The skyscrapers seemed to close in on us.*

  Syns: enclose, envelop, fence, hedge, hem.

close off *verb*
  To set apart from a group.

  ISOLATE.

close out *verb*
  To get rid of completely by selling, esp. in quantity or at a discount.

  SELL OFF at **sell**.

close *noun*
  1. A concluding or terminating.
  2. The last part.

  1. END *noun*.
  2. END *noun*.

close *adverb*
  To a point near in time, space, or relation: *stuck close together; standing close by.*

  Syns: hard, near, nearby, nigh.

close² *noun*
  An area partially or entirely enclosed by walls or buildings.

  COURT *noun*.

close-at-hand *adjective*
  Being within easy reach.

  CONVENIENT.

close-by *adjective*
  Being within easy reach.

  CONVENIENT.

close-fisted *adjective*
  Ungenerously or pettily reluctant to spend money.

  STINGY.

close in *verb*

  SEE **close¹**.

close-minded *adjective*
  1. Not tolerant of the beliefs, opinions, etc., of others.
  2. Tenaciously unwilling to yield.

  1. INTOLERANT.
  2. OBSTINATE.

close-mouthed *adjective*
Not speaking freely or openly. TACITURN.

close off *verb* SEE **close¹**.

close out *verb* SEE **close¹**.

closet *verb*
To enclose so as to hinder or prohibit escape. IMPRISON.

closing *adjective*
Coming after all others. LAST¹ *adjective*.

closing *noun*
A concluding or terminating. END *noun*.

closure *noun*
A concluding or terminating. END *noun*.

clot *verb*
To change or be changed from a liquid into a soft, semisolid, or solid mass. COAGULATE.

clothe *verb*
1. To cover as if with clothes: *trees clothed in leafy splendor.*

    1. **Syns:** cloak, drape, mantle, robe.
    Near-syns: array, clad, dress, enclothe, garb, swathe.
    Ant: unclothe.

2. To put clothes on. 2. DRESS *verb*.
3. To surround and cover completely so as to obscure. 3. WRAP *verb*.

clothes *noun*
Articles worn to cover the body. DRESS *noun*.

clothing *noun*
Articles worn to cover the body. DRESS *noun*.

cloud *verb*
To make dim or indistinct. OBSCURE *verb*.

cloud *noun*
A very large number of things grouped together. CROWD *noun*.

clouded *adjective*
Not affording certainty. AMBIGUOUS.

cloudiness *noun*
The quality or state of being ambiguous. VAGUENESS.

cloudless *adjective*
Free from clouds, mist, etc. CLEAR *adjective*.

cloudy *adjective*
1. Not clearly perceived or perceptible. 1. UNCLEAR.
2. Liable to more than one interpretation. 2. AMBIGUOUS.

clout *noun*
1. A sudden sharp, powerful stroke. 1. BLOW².
2. *Informal.* The right and power to command, decide, rule, or judge. 2. AUTHORITY.
3. *Informal.* The power to produce an effect by indirect means. 3. INFLUENCE *noun*.
4. *Informal.* Effective means of influencing, compelling, or punishing. 4. MUSCLE *noun*.

clout *verb*
To deliver (a powerful blow) suddenly and sharply. HIT *verb*.

clown *noun*
A person whose words or actions provoke or are intended to provoke amusement or laughter. JOKER.

clown *verb*
Informal. To make jokes; behave playfully. JOKE *verb*.

cloy *verb*
To satisfy to the full or to excess. SATIATE.

club *noun*
A group of people united in a relationship and having some interest, activity, or purpose in common. UNION.

clue also **clew** *noun*
1. A piece of information useful in a search. 1. LEAD *noun*.

2. A subtle pointing out.   **2.** HINT *noun.*

clump *noun*
  1. An irregularly shaped mass of indefinite size.   **1.** LUMP¹ *noun.*
  2. A number of individuals making up or considered a   **2.** GROUP *noun.*
    unit.

  clump *verb*
  1. To move heavily.   **1.** LUMP¹ *verb.*
  2. To make a dull sound by or as if by striking a   **2.** THUD *verb.*
    surface with a heavy object.

clumsy *adjective*
  1. Lacking dexterity and grace in physical movement.   **1.** AWKWARD.
  2. Clumsily lacking in the ability to do or perform.   **2.** UNSKILLFUL.
  3. Lacking sensitivity and skill in dealing with others. **3.** TACTLESS.
  4. Difficult to handle or manage.   **4.** AWKWARD.

clunk *noun*
  A repeated stroke or blow, esp. one that produces a   BEAT *noun.*
  sound.

  clunk *verb*
  To make a dull sound by or as if by striking a surface   THUD *verb.*
  with a heavy object.

cluster *noun*
  A number of individuals making up or considered a   GROUP *noun.*
  unit.

  cluster *verb*
  To come together.   ASSEMBLE *verb.*

clutch *noun*
  1. The act of catching, esp. a sudden taking and   **1.** CATCH *noun.*
    holding.
  2. An act or means of holding something.   **2.** HOLD *noun.*
  3. A number of individuals making up or considered a   **3.** GROUP *noun.*
    unit.

  clutch *verb*
  1. To get hold of (something moving).   **1.** CATCH *verb.*
  2. To take firmly with the hand and maintain a hold   **2.** GRASP *verb.*
    on.

clutching *adjective*
  Fearful of the loss of position or affection.   JEALOUS.

clutter *noun*
  A lack of order or regular arrangement.   DISORDER *noun.*

cluttered *adjective*
  Excessively filled with detail.   BUSY *adjective.*

coadjutant *noun*
  A person who holds a position auxiliary to another and   ASSISTANT.
  assumes some of his responsibilities.

coadjute *verb*
  To work together toward a common end.   COOPERATE.

coadjutor *noun*
  A person who holds a position auxiliary to another and   ASSISTANT.
  assumes some of his responsibilities.

coadjuvancy *noun*
  Joint work toward a common end.   COOPERATION.

coagency *noun*
  Joint work toward a common end.   COOPERATION.

coagulate *verb*
  To change or be changed from a liquid into a soft,   ***Syns:*** clot, congeal, gelatinize, jell, set¹.
  semisolid, or solid mass: *Egg white coagulates when
  heated.*

coalesce *verb*
  To bring or come together into a united whole.   COMBINE *verb.*

coalition *noun*
  1. An association, esp. of nations for a common cause.   **1.** ALLIANCE.

2. A group of individuals united in a common cause.

3. A bringing together into a whole.

coalitionist *noun*

One nation associated with another in a common cause.

coarse *adjective*

1. Lacking in delicacy or refinement: *coarse language; coarse manners; a coarse person who offended others.*

2. Displaying a lack of knowledge or skill.

3. Offensive to accepted standards of decency.

4. Consisting of or covered with large particles: *coarse sand.*

5. Having a coarse, irregular surface.

coast *verb*

To pass smoothly, quietly, and undisturbed on or as if on a slippery surface.

coax *verb*

To persuade or try to persuade by gentle, persistent urging or flattery: *She succeeded in coaxing her parents to buy her a car.*

cockcrow *noun*

The first appearance of daylight in the morning.

cock-eyed *adjective*

1. *Slang.* So senseless as to be laughable.

2. *Slang.* Intoxicated with alcoholic liquor.

coddle *verb*

To treat with indulgence and often overtender care.

coefficient *adjective*

Working together toward a common end.

coequal *noun*

One that is very similar to another in rank or position.

coerce *verb*

1. To compel by pressure or threats: *coerced them into the car at gunpoint.*

2. To cause (a person or thing) to act or move in spite of resistance.

coerced *adjective*

Done under force.

coercion *noun*

Power used to overcome resistance.

coercive *adjective*

Accomplished by force.

coetaneous *adjective*

Belonging to the same period of time as another.

coeval *adjective*

Belonging to the same period of time as another.

coeval *noun*

One of the same time or age as another.

coexistent *adjective*

Belonging to the same period of time as another.

coextensive *adjective*

Lying in the same plane and not intersecting.

cogent *adjective*

1. Serving to convince.

---

2. COMBINE *noun*.

3. UNIFICATION.

ALLY *noun*.

1. **Syns:** barbarian, barbaric, boorish, churlish, crass, crude, earthy, gross, ill-bred, Philistine (*also* philistine), raw, rough, rude, tasteless, uncivilized, uncouth, uncultivated, unpolished, unrefined, vulgar.
   Near-ants: considerate, courtly, gracious; charming, cultivated, polished, refined.

2. CRUDE.

3. OBSCENE.

4. **Syns:** grainy, granular, gritty, rough.

5. ROUGH.

SLIDE *verb*.

Syns: blandish, cajole, soft-soap (*Informal*), sweet-talk (*Informal*), wheedle.

DAWN *noun*.

1. FOOLISH.

2. DRUNK *adjective*.

BABY *verb*.

COOPERATIVE.

PEER[2].

1. **Syns:** blackjack, dragoon, force, hijack (*also* highjack) (*Informal*), shotgun (*Informal*), strong-arm (*Informal*).

2. FORCE *verb*.

FORCED.

FORCE *noun*.

FORCIBLE.

CONTEMPORARY *adjective*.

CONTEMPORARY *adjective*.

CONTEMPORARY *noun*.

CONTEMPORARY *adjective*.

PARALLEL *adjective*.

1. CONVINCING.

2. Based on good judgment, reasoning, or evidence.   2. SOUND².

cogitate *verb*
1. To use the faculty of reason.   1. REASON *verb*.
2. To think about seriously.   2. CONSIDER.
3. To consider carefully and at length.   3. PONDER.
4. To use the powers of the mind, as in conceiving ideas, drawing inferences, and making judgments.   4. THINK.

cogitation *noun*
The act or process of thinking.   THOUGHT.

cogitative *adjective*
Of, characterized by, or disposed to thought.   THOUGHTFUL.

cognate *adjective*
Connected by or as if by kinship or common origin.   RELATED.

cognizance *noun*
1. The condition of being aware.   1. AWARENESS.
2. The act of noting, observing, or taking into account.   2. NOTICE *noun*.

cognizant *adjective*
Marked by comprehension, cognizance, and perception.   AWARE.

cognomen *noun*
The word or words by which one is called and identified.   NAME *noun*.

cohere *verb*
To hold fast to.   BOND *verb*.

coherence *noun*
Logical agreement among things or parts.   CONSISTENCY.

cohesion *noun*
The close physical union of two objects.   BOND *noun*.

cohort *noun*
1. One who supports and adheres to another.   1. FOLLOWER.
2. *Informal.* One who is united in a relationship with another.   2. ASSOCIATE *noun*.

coil *verb*
To move or proceed on a repeatedly curving course.   WIND².

coincide *verb*
1. To occur at the same time: *The two incidents coincided.*   1. *Syn:* concur.
2. To come to an understanding or to terms.   2. AGREE.

coincident *adjective*
1. Occurring in company with.   1. ACCOMPANYING.
2. Existing or occurring at the same moment.   2. SIMULTANEOUS.

coinstantaneous *adjective*
Existing or occurring at the same moment.   SIMULTANEOUS.

cold *adjective*
1. Marked by a low temperature: *a cold night.*   1. *Syns:* chill, chilly, cool, nippy, shivery.
2. *Informal.* Lacking consciousness.   2. UNCONSCIOUS.
3. Not affected by or showing emotion: *a cold person unable to respond.*   3. *Syns:* cold-blooded, emotionless, unaffected, unemotional.
    Near-ants: cordial, friendly, genial, hearty, warm.
4. Dark and depressing.   4. GLOOMY.
5. Lacking all friendliness and warmth: *a cold farewell.*   5. *Syns:* chill, emotionless, frigid, glacial, icy.
6. Deficient in or lacking sexual desire.   6. FRIGID.

cold *noun*
Relative lack of warmth: *the winter cold.*   *Syns:* chill, chilliness, coldness, coolness, coolth.

cold-blooded *adjective*
1. Totally lacking in compassion: *a cold-blooded killer.*   1. *Syns:* callous, cold-hearted, compassionless, hard-boiled (*Informal*), hardened, hardhearted, heartless,

obdurate, stonyhearted, unfeeling.
—*Idiom* cold of heart.
Near-syns: brutal, cruel, merciless, ruthless, tough; unemotional, unsympathetic; cantankerous, peevish.

2. Not affected by or showing emotion.

2. COLD *adjective.*

cold-hearted *adjective*
Totally lacking in compassion.

COLD-BLOODED.

coldness *noun*
Relative lack of warmth.

COLD *noun.*

cold-shoulder *verb*

SEE **cold shoulder.**

cold shoulder *noun*
Informal. A deliberate slight.

SNUB *noun.*

  cold-shoulder *verb*
  Informal. To slight (someone) deliberately.

SNUB *verb.*

collaborate *verb*
To work together toward a common end.

COOPERATE.

collaboration *noun*
Joint work toward a common end.

COOPERATION.

collaborative *adjective*
Working together toward a common end.

COOPERATIVE.

collapse *verb*
1. To suddenly lose all health or strength: *collapsed from exhaustion.*

2. To give way mentally and emotionally.
3. To be unable to hold up.
4. To fall in.
5. To cease to function, as a mechanical device.
6. To undergo capture, defeat, or ruin.
7. To undergo sudden financial failure: *The stock market collapsed.*

1. ***Syns:*** break down, cave in, conk out (*Slang*), crack, crack up (*Informal*), drop, give out, give way, succumb.
2. BREAK DOWN.
3. BEND *verb.*
4. CAVE IN at **cave.**
5. BREAK DOWN.
6. SURRENDER *verb.*
7. ***Syns:*** break, bust, crash, fail, fold (*Informal*), go under. —*Idioms* go bust, go on the rocks, go to the wall.

collapse *noun*
1. An abrupt, disastrous failure: *the 1929 stock-market collapse.*
2. A sudden sharp decline in mental, emotional, or physical health.
3. A disastrous, overwhelming defeat or ruin.

1. ***Syns:*** breakdown, crash, debacle, smash, smashup, wreck.
2. BREAKDOWN at **break down.**

3. FALL *noun.*

collar *verb*
Slang. To take into custody as a prisoner.

ARREST *verb.*

collate *verb*
To examine so as to note the similarities and differences of.

COMPARE.

collateral *adjective*
1. In a position of subordination.
2. Giving or able to give help or support.
3. Lying in the same plane and not intersecting.

1. SUBORDINATE *adjective.*
2. AUXILIARY *adjective.*
3. PARALLEL *adjective.*

colleague *noun*
1. One who is united in a relationship with another.
2. One that is very similar to another in rank or position.

1. ASSOCIATE *noun.*
2. PEER².

collect¹ *verb*
1. To bring together so as to increase in mass or number.
2. To bring together.
3. To come together.
4. To bring one's emotions under control.

1. ACCUMULATE.

2. ASSEMBLE.
3. ASSEMBLE.
4. COMPOSE.

collect² *noun*
A formula of words used in praying.

PRAYER.

collected *adjective*
Not easily excited, even under pressure.

COOL *adjective.*

collection *noun*
1. A quantity accumulated.
2. A number of individuals making up or considered a unit.

1. ACCUMULATION.
2. GROUP *noun.*

collide *verb*
To come together or come up against with force: *The two cars collided.*

Syns: bump, crash.

collision *noun*
Violent, forcible contact between two or more things: *the collision of the two spacecraft with Earth.*

Syns: appulse, bump, concussion, crash, impact, jar, jolt, percussion, shock, smash, wallop.

colloquial *adjective*
In the style of conversation.

CONVERSATIONAL.

colloquialist *noun*
One given to conversation.

CONVERSATIONALIST.

colloquist *noun*
One given to conversation.

CONVERSATIONALIST.

colloquium *noun*
A meeting for the exchange of views.

CONFERENCE.

colloquy *noun*
Spoken exchange.

CONVERSATION.

collude *verb*
To work out a secret plan to achieve an evil or illegal end.

PLOT *verb.*

collusion *noun*
A secret plan to achieve an evil or illegal end.

PLOT *noun.*

colony *noun*
An area subject to rule by an outside power.

POSSESSION.

colophon *noun*
A name or other device placed on merchandise to signify its ownership or manufacture.

MARK *noun.*

color *noun*
1. The property by which the sense of vision can distinguish between objects, as a red apple and a green apple, that are very similar or identical in form and size: *Red, yellow, and blue are primary colors.*
2. Something that imparts color: *painted the room using a new washable color.*
3. Skin tone, esp. of the face.
4. A deceptive outward appearance.
5. Appearance of truth or authenticity.

1. *Syns:* hue, shade, tone.

2. *Syns:* colorant, coloring, dye, dyestuff, pigment, stain, tincture.
3. COMPLEXION.
4. FAÇADE.
5. VERISIMILITUDE.

color *verb*
1. To impart color to: *colored the shingles brown.*
2. To immerse in a coloring solution.
3. To give an inaccurate view of by representing falsely or misleadingly.
4. To cause to have a prejudiced view.
5. To give a deceptively attractive appearance to: *color a lie.*

1. *Syns:* dye, stain, tint.
2. DIP *verb.*
3. DISTORT.

4. BIAS *verb.*
5. *Syns:* gild, gloss (over), gloze (over), palliate, sugarcoat, varnish, veneer, whitewash. —*Idioms* lend a good color to, paper over the cracks, put a gloss on, put a good face on.

6. To become red in the face.

6. BLUSH *verb.*

colorable *adjective*
Worthy of being believed.

BELIEVABLE.

colorant *noun*
Something that imparts color.

COLOR *noun.*

coloration *noun*
Skin tone, esp. of the face.   COMPLEXION.

colored *adjective*
Exhibiting bias.   BIASED.

colorful *adjective*
1. Full of color: *a colorful bed of pansies.*   1. **Syns:** bright, gay, showy, vivid.
                                                         Near-syns: florid, garish, gaudy, loud;
                                                         flashy, splashy.
                                                         Ant: colorless.

2. Evoking strong mental images through   2. **Syns:** picturesque, vivid.
   distinctiveness: *colorful writing; a colorful character.*

coloring *noun*
1. Something that imparts color.   1. COLOR *noun.*
2. Skin tone, esp. of the face.   2. COMPLEXION.
3. A deceptive outward appearance.   3. FAÇADE.

colorless *adjective*
1. Lacking color.   1. PALE *adjective.*
2. Lacking liveliness, charm, or surprise.   2. DULL *adjective.*
3. Without definite or distinctive characteristics. 3. NEUTRAL.

colorlessness *noun*
The state or quality of being insipid.   INSIPIDITY.

colors *noun*
Fabric used esp. as a symbol.   FLAG[1] *noun.*

colossal *adjective*
Of extraordinary size and power.   GIANT *adjective.*

column *noun*
A group of people or things arranged in a row.   LINE *noun.*

comb *verb*
To make a thorough search of.   SCOUR.

combat *noun*
A hostile encounter between opposing military forces: **Syns:** action, battle, engagement.
sent the infantry into combat.

combat *verb*
1. To strive in opposition to.   1. CONTEND.
2. To take a stand against.   2. CONTEST *verb.*
3. To oppose actively and with force.   3. RESIST.

combatant *noun*
One who engages in a combat or struggle.   FIGHTER.

combatant *adjective*
Of or engaged in warfare.   BELLIGERENT.

combative *adjective*
1. Inclined to act in a hostile way.   1. AGGRESSIVE.
2. Having or showing an eagerness to fight.   2. BELLIGERENT.
3. Given to arguing.   3. ARGUMENTATIVE.

combativeness *noun*
1. Hostile behavior.   1. AGGRESSION.
2. Warlike or hostile attitude or nature.   2. BELLIGERENCE.
3. The power or will to fight.   3. FIGHT *noun.*

combinate *verb*
To bring or come together into a united whole.   COMBINE *verb.*

combination *noun*
1. The result of combining: *Water is a combination of* 1. **Syns:** conjugation, melding, unification,
   hydrogen and oxygen.   union.
2. The state of being associated.   2. ASSOCIATION.
3. A group of individuals united in a common cause. 3. COMBINE *noun.*

combinational *adjective*
Of, relating to, or tending to produce combination: *the* **Syns:** combinative, combinatorial,
combinational tendencies of these substances.   combinatory, conjugational, conjugative.

combinative *adjective*
Of, relating to, or tending to produce combination. COMBINATIONAL.

combinatorial *adjective*
Of, relating to, or tending to produce combination. COMBINATIONAL.

combinatory *adjective*
Of, relating to, or tending to produce combination. COMBINATIONAL.

combine *verb*
1. To bring or come together into a united whole: *combine oxygen with hydrogen; artistic expression combined with technique.*
    1. *Syns:* coalesce, combinate, compound, concrete, conjoin, conjugate, connect, couple, join, link, marry, meld, unite, wed, yoke.
2. To make a part of a united whole.
    2. EMBODY.
3. To unite or be united in a relationship.
    3. ASSOCIATE *verb.*
4. To assemble or join in a group.
    4. BAND[2] *verb.*
5. To put together into one mass so that the constituent parts are more or less homogeneous.
    5. MIX *verb.*

combine *noun*
1. A group of individuals united in a common cause: *a combine of citizens demanding tax relief.*
    1. *Syns:* bloc, cartel, coalition, combination, faction, party, ring[1].
2. A combination of businesses closely interconnected for common profit: *a large oil combine.*
    2. *Syns:* cartel, pool, syndicate, trust.

combined *adjective*
Joined together into a whole: *the combined influences of poverty and inflation.*
Syns: conjoint, fused, melded.

comburent *adjective*
On fire. BLAZING.

combust *verb*
To undergo combustion. BURN *verb.*

come *verb*
1. To take place: *Will war come?*
    1. *Syns:* befall, betide, come about, come off, develop, hap[1] (*Archaic*), happen, occur, pass, transpire.
2. To take place at a set time: *Christmas comes on December 25.*
    2. *Syns:* fall, occur.
3. To happen to one: *Depression came to her quickly.*
    3. *Syns:* befall, betide.
4. To go forward, esp. toward a conclusion: *This project is coming just fine.*
    4. *Syns:* advance, come along, get along, march[1], move (along), proceed, progress.
5. To have as a source.
    5. STEM *verb.*
6. To have as one's home or place of origin: *I come from Virginia.*
    6. *Syns:* hail[2], originate.
7. To come to be.
    7. BECOME.

come about *verb*
To take place. COME.

come across *verb*
1. To find or meet by chance: *come across the lost sock; come across an old friend.*
    1. *Syns:* alight on (*or* upon) (*Archaic*), bump into (*Informal*), chance on (*or* upon), come on (*or* upon), find, happen on (*or* upon), light on (*or* upon), run across, run into, stumble on (*or* upon), tumble (on). —*Idiom* meet up with.
2. *Slang.* To give in common with others.
    2. CONTRIBUTE.

come along *verb*
To go forward, esp. toward a conclusion. COME.

come around (or **round**) *verb*
To regain one's health. RECOVER.

come by *verb*
1. To come into possession of.
    1. GET.
2. To go to or seek out the company of in order to socialize.
    2. VISIT *verb.*

come in *verb*
1. To come or go into (a place).
    1. ENTER.

2. To complete a race or competition in a specified position.

2. RUN *verb.*

come into *verb*
To receive (property) from one who has died.

INHERIT.

come off *verb*
1. To take place.
2. To turn out well.

1. COME.
2. SUCCEED.

come out *verb*
1. To be made public: *didn't want the whole story to come out.*
2. To make one's formal entry, as into society: *came out at the debutante ball.*

1. *Syns:* break, get out, leak (out), out, transpire. —*Idiom* come to light.
2. *Syns:* bow, debut (*also* début).

come out with *verb*
To utter publicly.

AIR *verb.*

come over *verb*
Informal. To go to or seek out the company of in order to socialize.

VISIT *verb.*

come through *verb*
1. To turn out well.
2. To exist in spite of adversity.
3. *Informal.* To give in common with others.

1. SUCCEED.
2. SURVIVE.
3. CONTRIBUTE.

come about *verb*

SEE **come.**

come across *verb*

SEE **come.**

come along *verb*

SEE **come.**

come around (or **round**) *verb*

SEE **come.**

comeback *noun*

SEE **come back.**

come back *verb*
To go again to a former place.

RETURN *verb.*

comeback *noun*
1. A return to former prosperity or status: *made a political comeback.*
2. *Slang.* A spirited, incisive reply.
3. *Slang.* Something spoken or written as a return to a question, demand, etc.

1. *Syn:* recovery.
2. RETORT *noun.*
3. ANSWER *noun.*

come by *verb*

SEE **come.**

comedian *noun*
A person whose words or actions provoke or are intended to provoke amusement or laughter.

JOKER.

comedown *noun*
A sudden drop to a lower condition or status.

DESCENT.

comedy *noun*
The quality of being laughable or comical.

HUMOR *noun.*

come-hither *adjective*
Pleasing to the eye or mind.

ATTRACTIVE.

come in *verb*

SEE **come.**

come into *verb*

SEE **come.**

comely *adjective*
1. Having qualities that delight the eye.
2. Conforming to accepted standards.

1. BEAUTIFUL.
2. CORRECT *adjective.*

come off *verb*

SEE **come.**

come-on *noun*

SEE **come on.**

come on (or **upon**) *verb*
To find or meet by chance.

COME ACROSS at **come.**

come-on *noun*
Something that attracts, esp. with the promise of pleasure or reward.

LURE *noun.*

come out *verb*

SEE **come.**

come out with *verb*

SEE **come.**

come over *verb*

SEE **come.**

comer *noun*
1. *Informal.* One showing much promise: *The young executive is a real comer.*
2. One that arrives.

1. **Syn:** up-and-comer. —*Idioms* man (*or* woman) on the way up, rising star.
2. ARRIVAL.

comestible *adjective*
Fit to be eaten.

EDIBLE.

comestible *noun*
Something fit to be eaten.

FOOD.

come through *verb*

SEE **come.**

comeupance *noun*

SEE **comeuppance.**

comeuppance also **comeupance** *noun*
Informal. Something justly deserved.

DUE *noun.*

comfort *verb*
1. To give hope to in time of grief or pain: *comforted the widow.*
2. To make less severe or more bearable.

1. **Syns:** consolate (*Obs.*), console, solace, soothe.
2. RELIEVE.

comfort *noun*
1. Steady good fortune or financial security.
2. A consoling in time of grief or pain: *gave comfort to the bereaved.*
3. Anything that increases physical comfort.

1. PROSPERITY.
2. **Syns:** consolation, solace.

3. AMENITY.

comfortable *adjective*
1. Affording pleasurable ease: *a comfortable new house.*

1. **Syns:** comfy (*Informal*), cozy (*also* cosy), easeful, easy, snug, soft (*Informal*).
   Near-ants: annoying, bothersome, irking, vexatious; troubling.
   Ant: uncomfortable.

2. Enjoying steady good fortune or financial security.
3. *Informal.* Being what is needed without being in excess.

2. PROSPEROUS.
3. SUFFICIENT.

comfortless *adjective*
Causing discomfort.

UNCOMFORTABLE.

comfy *adjective*
Informal. Affording pleasurable ease.

COMFORTABLE.

comic *noun*
A person whose words or actions provoke or are intended to provoke amusement or laughter.

JOKER.

comic *adjective*
1. Arousing laughter.
2. Deserving laughter.

1. AMUSING.
2. LAUGHABLE.

comical *adjective*
1. Arousing laughter.
2. Deserving laughter.

1. AMUSING.
2. LAUGHABLE.

comicality also **comicalness** *noun*
The quality of being laughable or comical.

HUMOR *noun.*

comicalness *noun*

SEE **comicality.**

coming *adjective*
1. In the relatively near future: *the coming years.*

1. **Syns:** approaching, forthcoming, upcoming.

2. Occurring right after another.
3. Being or occurring in the time ahead.
4. *Informal.* Showing great promise: *Roller discos are the coming thing.*
5. *Informal.* Improving, growing, or succeeding steadily.

2. FOLLOWING *adjective.*
3. FUTURE *adjective.*
4. **Syns:** promising, up-and-coming.

5. FLOURISHING.

coming *noun*
1. The act of arriving.
2. The act or fact of coming near.

1. ARRIVAL.
2. APPROACH *noun.*

coming-out *noun*
Informal. The instance or occasion of being presented for the first time to society.

PRESENTATION.

command *verb*
1. To give orders to: *commanded the brigade to attack.*

1. **Syns:** bid, charge, direct, enjoin, instruct, order, require, tell.

2. To have authoritative charge of.
2. LEAD *verb.*
3. To be possessed of: *commands great prestige; commands five languages.*
3. **Syns:** boast, enjoy, have, hold, possess.
4. To rise above, esp. so as to afford a view of.
4. DOMINATE.

command *noun*
1. An authoritative indication to be obeyed: *gave the command to fire.*

1. **Syns:** behest, bidding, charge, commandment, dictate, direction, directive, injunction, instruction, mandate, order, word.

2. The capacity to lead others.
2. LEAD *noun.*
3. The right and power to command, decide, rule, or judge.
3. AUTHORITY.
4. The act of exercising controlling power or the condition of being so controlled.
4. DOMINATION.
5. Natural or acquired facility in a specific activity.
5. ABILITY.
6. The degree of skill exhibited in any performance.
6. TECHNIQUE.

commandeer *verb*
1. To lay claim to for oneself or as one's right.
1. ASSUME.
2. To take quick and forcible possession of.
2. SEIZE.

commandeering *noun*
The act of taking quick and forcible possession of.

SEIZURE.

commanding *adjective*
1. Exercising controlling power or influence.
1. DOMINANT.
2. Exercising authority.
2. AUTHORITATIVE.

commandment *noun*
An authoritative indication to be obeyed.

COMMAND *noun.*

comme il faut *adjective*
French. Conforming to accepted standards.

CORRECT *adjective.*

commemorate *verb*
1. To mark (a day or event) with ceremonies of respect, festivity, or rejoicing.
1. CELEBRATE *verb.*
2. To honor or keep alive the memory of.
2. MEMORIALIZE.

commemoration *noun*
1. The act of observing a day or event with ceremonies.
1. CELEBRATION.
2. Something, as a structure or custom, serving to honor or keep alive a memory.
2. MEMORIAL *noun.*

commemorative *adjective*
Serving to honor or keep alive a memory.

MEMORIAL *adjective.*

commence *verb*
1. To go about the initial step in doing (something).
1. START *verb.*
2. To come into being.
2. BEGIN.
3. To begin to appear or develop.
3. DAWN *verb.*

commencement *noun*
1. The act or process of bringing or being brought into existence.
1. BEGINNING *noun.*
2. The initial stage of a developmental process.
2. BIRTH *noun.*

commend *verb*
1. To pay a compliment to.
1. COMPLIMENT *verb.*
2. To express warm approval of.
2. PRAISE *verb.*
3. To give over to another for care, use, or performance.
3. ENTRUST.

commendable *adjective*
Deserving admiration.

ADMIRABLE.

commendation *noun*
1. An expression of admiration or congratulation.
1. COMPLIMENT *noun.*

2. An expression of warm approval.   2. PRAISE *noun*.

commendatory *adjective*
Serving to compliment.   COMPLIMENTARY.

commensurable *adjective*
1. Properly or correspondingly related in size, amount,   1. PROPORTIONAL.
   or scale.
2. Characterized by or displaying symmetry, esp.   2. SYMMETRICAL.
   correspondence in scale or measure.

commensurate *adjective*
1. Properly or correspondingly related in size, amount,   1. PROPORTIONAL.
   or scale.
2. Characterized by or displaying symmetry, esp.   2. SYMMETRICAL.
   correspondence in scale or measure.

comment *noun*
1. An expression of fact or opinion: *made a positive*   1. *Syns:* note, obiter dictum, observation,
   comment about the party.   remark.
2. Evaluative and critical discourse.   2. REVIEW *noun*.
3. Critical explanation or analysis.   3. COMMENTARY.
4. Something said.   4. WORD *noun*.

comment *verb*
To make observations: *commented on the artist's*   *Syns:* note, observe, remark.
technique.

commentary *noun*
1. Critical explanation or analysis: *commentaries on*   1. *Syns:* annotation, comment, exegesis,
   the Old Testament.   interpretation, note.
2. A narrative of experiences undergone by the writer: 2. *Syns:* memoir, reminiscence.
   Caesar's Commentaries on the Gallic War.
3. Evaluative and critical discourse.   3. REVIEW *noun*.

commentator *noun*
A person who evaluates and reports on the worth of   CRITIC.
something.

commerce *noun*
Commercial, industrial, or professional activity in   BUSINESS.
general.

commingle *verb*
To put together into one mass so that the constituent   MIX *verb*.
parts are more or less homogeneous.

commiserable *adjective*
Arousing or deserving pity.   PITIFUL.

commiserate *verb*
To experience or express compassion.   FEEL *verb*.

commiseration *noun*
Sympathetic, sad concern for someone in misfortune.   PITY.

commiserative *adjective*
Feeling or expressing sorrow.   SYMPATHETIC.

commission *verb*
To give authority to.   AUTHORIZE.

commission *noun*
An assignment one is sent to carry out.   MISSION.

commit *verb*
1. To be responsible for or guilty of (an error or crime):   1. *Syns:* perpetrate, pull off (*Informal*).
   committed murder.
2. To give over to another for care, use, or   2. ENTRUST.
   performance.
3. To place officially in confinement: *commit a criminal*   3. *Syns:* consign, institutionalize, send up
   to prison.   (*Informal*).
4. To be morally bound to do: *was committed to defend*   4. *Syns:* bind, charge, obligate, pledge.
   his country.

commitment *noun*
An act or course of action that is demanded of one, as   DUTY.
by position, custom, law, or religion.

committal *noun*
An act or course of action that is demanded of one, as by position, custom, law, or religion.

DUTY.

commix *verb*
To put together into one mass so that the constituent parts are more or less homogeneous.

MIX *verb*.

commodious *adjective*
Having plenty of room.

ROOMY.

commodities *noun*
Products bought and sold in commerce.

GOODS.

common *adjective*
1. Belonging to, shared by, or applicable to all alike: *National security is a common concern for Americans.*
2. Belonging or pertaining to the whole.
3. Occurring quite often: *Traffic accidents are common phenomena.*

1. **Syns:** communal, conjoint, general, intermutual, joint, mutual, public.

2. GENERAL.
3. **Syns:** everyday, familiar, frequent, ordinary, regular, routine, widespread.
   Near-ants: infrequent, occasional, unfrequent; casual, chance, incidental.
   Ants: rare, uncommon.

4. Being of no special quality or type.
5. To be expected: *the common problems of city life.*

4. ORDINARY *adjective*.
5. **Syns:** average, commonplace, general, matter-of-course, normal, ordinary, typical (*also* typic), usual.

6. Known widely and unfavorably.
7. Of moderately good quality but less than excellent.
8. Of mediocre quality.
9. Of decidedly inferior quality.
10. Lacking high station or birth.
11. *Chiefly Regional.* Unconstrained by rigid standards.

6. NOTORIOUS.
7. ACCEPTABLE.
8. INFERIOR.
9. SHODDY.
10. LOWLY.
11. EASYGOING.

common *noun*
A tract of cultivated land belonging to and used by a community: *picnics on the town common.*

Syn: green.

commonage *noun*
The common people.

COMMONALTY.

commonality *noun*

SEE **commonalty.**

commonalty also **commonality** *noun*
The common people: *laws protecting both the nobility and the commonalty.*

Syns: commonage, commoners, commons, crowd, masses, mob, plebeians, plebs, populace, public, ruck[1]. —*Idiom* third estate.

commoners *noun*
The common people.

COMMONALTY.

commonly *adverb*
For the most part.

USUALLY.

commonplace *adjective*
1. Being of no special quality or type.
2. To be expected.
3. Without freshness or appeal due to overuse.
4. Of or suitable for ordinary days or routine occasions.

1. ORDINARY *adjective*.
2. COMMON *adjective*.
3. TRITE.
4. EVERYDAY.

commonplace *noun*
1. A regular or customary matter, condition, or course of events.
2. A trite expression or idea.

1. USUAL *noun*.
2. CLICHÉ.

commons *noun*
The common people.

COMMONALTY.

common sense *noun*
The ability to make sensible decisions: *had enough common sense to study hard.*

Syns: gumption, judgment, sense, wisdom. —*Idiom* horse sense.

Near-syns: discretion, prudence; brains, intelligence, smarts (*Slang*), wit.

commonsensible *adjective*
Possessing, proceeding from, or exhibiting good judgment and prudence.

SANE.

commonsensical *adjective*
Possessing, proceeding from, or exhibiting good judgment and prudence.

SANE.

commotion *noun*
1. The condition of being physically agitated.
2. An interruption of regular procedure or of public peace.

1. AGITATION.
2. DISTURBANCE.

communal *adjective*
Belonging to, shared by, or applicable to all alike.

COMMON *adjective*.

communalize *verb*
To place under government or group ownership or control.

SOCIALIZE.

communicable *adjective*
1. Capable of transmission by infection: *measles and other communicable diseases.*
2. Disposed to be open, sociable, and talkative.

1. *Syns:* catching, contagious, infectious, taking.
2. OUTGOING.

communicate *verb*
1. To make known: *communicate information.*

1. *Syns:* break, carry, convey, disclose, get across, impart, pass, report, tell, transmit.

2. To put into words.
3. To give expression to, as by gestures, facial aspects, or bodily posture.
4. *Informal.* To interact with another or others in a meaningful fashion.
5. To cause (a disease) to pass to another or others: *typhus communicated from one to another.*

2. SAY *verb*.
3. EXPRESS *verb*.

4. RELATE.

5. *Syns:* carry, convey, give, pass, spread, transmit.

communication *noun*
1. The exchange of ideas by writing, speech, or signals: *Good communication is essential to a successful business.*
2. Something communicated, as information: *I have read your latest communication.*
3. A situation allowing exchange of ideas or messages.

1. *Syns:* communion, converse[1] (*Rare*), intercommunication, intercourse.

2. *Syns:* message, word.

3. TOUCH *noun*.

communicative *adjective*
Disposed to be open, sociable, and talkative.

OUTGOING.

communion *noun*
1. Those who accept and practice a particular religious belief.
2. The exchange of ideas by writing, speech, or signals.

1. FAITH.

2. COMMUNICATION.

community *noun*
Persons as an organized body.

PUBLIC *noun*.

commutation *noun*
The act of exchanging or substituting.

CHANGE *noun*.

commute *verb*
1. To give up in return for something else.
2. To change into a different form, substance, or state.

1. CHANGE *verb*.
2. CONVERT.

comp *noun*
Informal. A free ticket entitling one to transportation or admission.

PASS *noun*.

compact[1] *adjective*
1. Having all parts near to each other.
2. Precisely meaningful and tersely cogent.
3. Characterized by an economy of artistic expression.

1. THICK.
2. PITHY.
3. TIGHT *adjective*.

compact[2] *noun*
1. A legally binding arrangement between parties.

1. AGREEMENT.

2. An agreement, esp. one involving a sale or exchange.

compactness *noun*
The quality, condition, or degree of being thick.

companion *noun*
1. One of a matched pair of things.
2. One who keeps company with another.
3. One that accompanies another.
companion *verb*
To be with or go with (another).
companionable *adjective*
Liking company: *a companionable person.*

companionless *adjective*
Lacking the company of others.
companionship *noun*
A pleasant association among people.
company *noun*
1. A commercial organization: *a new computer company.*

2. A number of persons who have come or been gathered together.
3. A person or persons visiting one: *had company for dinner.*
4. A pleasant association among people: *enjoyed their company.*
5. A group of performers.
company *verb*
Rare. To be with or go with (another).
comparable *adjective*
Possessing the same or almost the same characteristics.
comparative *adjective*
Being such by comparison with some standard: *comparative affluence.*
compare *verb*
1. To examine so as to note the similarities and differences of: *compare prices; compare one poet's verse with that of another.*
2. To be equal or alike: *These concerts compare well with last season's.*

3. To represent as similar.
comparison *noun*
The quality or state of being alike.
compass *noun*
1. A line around a closed figure or area.
2. An area within which something or someone exists, acts, or has influence or power.
3. The ability or power to seize or attain.
compass *verb*
1. To shut in on all sides.
2. To perceive and recognize the meaning of.
compassion *noun*
Sympathetic, sad concern for someone in misfortune.
compassionate *adjective*
1. Concerned with human welfare and the alleviation of suffering.
2. Feeling or expressing pity.
3. Feeling or expressing sorrow.

2. BARGAIN *noun.*

THICKNESS.

1. MATE *noun.*
2. ASSOCIATE *noun.*
3. ACCOMPANIMENT.

ACCOMPANY.

Syns: convivial, sociable, social.
Near-syns: amiable, complacent, good-natured, sympathetic.

ALONE *adjective.*

COMPANY *noun.*

1. Syns: business, concern, corporation, enterprise, establishment, firm², house, outfit.
2. ASSEMBLY.
3. Syns: guest, visitant, visitor.

4. Syns: companionship, fellowship, society.
5. BAND² *noun.*

ACCOMPANY.

LIKE².

Syn: relative.

1. Syns: balance, collate.

2. Syns: correspond (to), equal, match, measure up (to), parallel, stack up (*Informal*), touch.
3. LIKEN.

LIKENESS.

1. CIRCUMFERENCE.
2. RANGE *noun.*

3. GRASP *noun.*

1. SURROUND.
2. UNDERSTAND.

PITY.

1. HUMANITARIAN.

2. PITYING.
3. SYMPATHETIC.

compassionate *verb*
To experience or express compassion.

FEEL *verb*.

compassionless *adjective*
Totally lacking in compassion.

COLD-BLOODED.

compatible *adjective*
In keeping with one's needs or expectations.

AGREEABLE.

compatriot *noun*
A person who is from one's own country.

COUNTRYMAN.

compeer *noun*
One that is very similar to another in rank or position.

PEER[2].

compel *verb*
To cause (a person or thing) to act or move in spite of resistance.

FORCE *verb*.

compendious *adjective*
Marked by or consisting of few words.

BRIEF.

compensate *verb*
1. To make up for the defects of: *His lack of height was compensated by agility.*
2. To act as an equalizing weight or force to.
3. To give compensation to: *They were compensated for their travel expenses.*
4. To give payment to in return for goods or services rendered.

1. *Syns:* balance, counterbalance, counterpoise, countervail, neutralize, offset, outweigh, redeem, set off.
2. BALANCE *verb*.
3. *Syns:* indemnify, pay, recompense, redress, reimburse, remunerate, repay, requite.
4. PAY *verb*.

compensation *noun*
1. Something to make up for loss or damage: *compensation for work-related injuries.*

2. Something given in exchange for goods or services rendered.

1. *Syns:* amends, indemnification, indemnity, offset, quittance, recompense, redress, remuneration, reparation, requital, restitution, satisfaction, setoff.
2. PAYMENT.

compensative *adjective*
Affording compensation.

COMPENSATORY.

compensatory *adjective*
Affording compensation: *was awarded compensatory damages.*

Syns: compensative, indemnificatory, remunerative.

compete *verb*
To strive against (others) for victory: *competed against the best athletes in the Olympics.*

Syns: contend, contest, rival, vie.

competence also **competency** *noun*
1. Physical, mental, financial, or legal power to perform.
2. *Law.* Conferred power.

1. ABILITY.
2. FACULTY.

competency *noun*

SEE **competence**.

competent *adjective*
1. Having the necessary strength or ability.
2. Having the ability to perform well.
3. Being what is needed without being in excess.

1. EQUAL *adjective*.
2. ABLE.
3. SUFFICIENT.

competition *noun*
1. A struggle with others for victory or supremacy: *competition between political parties; cutthroat competition between auto dealers.*
2. A trial of skill or ability: *an archery competition.*
3. One that competes.

1. *Syns:* contest, corrivalry, race, rivality, rivalry, strife, striving, war, warfare. —*Idiom* tug of war.
2. *Syns:* contest, meet[1].
3. COMPETITOR.

competitive *adjective*
Given to competition: *a competitive business.*

Syns: competitory, emulous, vying.

competitor *noun*
One that competes: *competitors for that market.*

Syns: competition, contender, contestant, corrival, opponent, rival.

competitory *adjective*
Given to competition.

COMPETITIVE.

complain *verb*
To express negative feelings, esp. of dissatisfaction or resentment: *complained about the inadequate service.*

Syns: beef (*Slang*), bellyache (*Slang*), bitch (*Slang*), gripe (*Informal*), grouch, grouse (*Informal*), grumble, kick (*Informal*), murmur, whine, yawp (*also* yaup).
Near-syns: fret, fuss, mutter, nag, pester, repine, wail; squawk.

complainant *noun*
One that makes a formal complaint, esp. in court: *The complainant has filed suit.*

Syns: accusant, claimant, plaintiff (*Law*).

complainer *noun*
A person who habitually complains or grumbles.

GROUCH *noun.*

complaint *noun*
1. An expression of dissatisfaction: *received many complaints about the car.*
2. A pathological condition of mind or body.
3. A minor illness, esp. one of a temporary nature.

1. *Syns:* beef (*Slang*), grievance, gripe (*Informal*), grumble.
2. DISEASE.
3. INDISPOSITION.

complaisant *adjective*
1. Pleasant and friendly.
2. Ready to do favors for another.

1. AMIABLE.
2. OBLIGING.

complement *noun*
1. Something that completes another: *An attractively set table is a complement to fine food.*
2. Something added to another for embellishment or completion.

1. *Syns:* completion, expletive (*Rare*), supplement.
2. ACCOMPANIMENT.

complement *verb*
To fill in what is lacking and make perfect: *A good wine complements any meal.*

Syns: complete, fill out, round off, round out, supplement.

complemental *adjective*
Forming or serving as a complement.

COMPLEMENTARY.

complementary *adjective*
Forming or serving as a complement: *wall colors complementary to the decor.*

Syns: complemental, completing, supplemental.

complete *adjective*
1. Lacking nothing essential or normal: *developed a complete strategy.*
2. Not shortened by omissions: *a complete anthology.*

3. Not more or less.
4. Covering all aspects with painstaking accuracy.
5. Including every constituent or individual.
6. Having reached completion: *The novel is at last complete.*

1. *Syns:* choate, entire, full, intact, integral, perfect, whole.
2. *Syns:* unabridged, uncut, unexpurgated.
3. ROUND.
4. THOROUGH.
5. WHOLE *adjective.*
6. *Syns:* completed, concluded, done, ended, finished, terminated, through.
   —*Idiom* all wrapped up.
   Near-syns: accomplished, achieved, executed, realized; attained, encompassed.
   Ant: incomplete.

7. Completely such, without qualification or exception.

7. UTTER[2].

complete *verb*
1. To fill in what is lacking and make perfect.
2. To bring or come to a natural or proper end.

1. COMPLEMENT *verb.*
2. CLOSE[1] *verb.*

completed *adjective*
Having reached completion.

COMPLETE *adjective.*

completely *adverb*
1. To the fullest extent: *completely wrong.*

   1. **Syns:** à fond (*French*), altogether, clean (*Informal*), dead, entirely, flat, fully, quite, thoroughly, well[2], wholly. —*Idiom* through and through.

2. In a complete manner: *completely investigated the crash.*

   2. **Syns:** à fond (*French*), exhaustively, intensively, thoroughly. —*Idioms* in and out, inside out, up and down.

3. All the way.

   3. CLEAR *adverb.*

completeness *noun*
The state of being entirely whole: *maintained the completeness of his empire.*

   Syns: allness, entireness, entirety, integrity, oneness, totality, wholeness.

completing *adjective*
Forming or serving as a complement.

   COMPLEMENTARY.

completion *noun*
1. A concluding or terminating.
2. Something that completes another.

   1. END *noun.*
   2. COMPLEMENT *noun.*

complex *adjective*
1. Consisting of two or more interconnected parts: *complex flower structures.*
2. Difficult to understand due to intricacy: *Inflation is a complex problem.*

   1. **Syns:** composite, compound.
   2. **Syns:** Byzantine, complicated, convoluted, daedal, daedalian, elaborate, gordian, intricate, involute, involved, knotty, labyrinthine, perplexing, tangled.
   Near-ants: comprehensible, defined, distinct, plain; clear, explicable, uncomplicated, uninvolved.
   Ant: simple.

complex *verb*
To make complex, intricate, or perplexing.

   COMPLICATE.

complex *noun*
1. A usu. large entity composed of interconnected parts: *the military-industrial complex.*
2. A center of organization, supply, or activity.
3. *Informal.* An exaggerated concern: *had a complex about flying.*

   1. **Syns:** complexus, system.
   2. BASE[1] *noun.*
   3. **Syns:** hangup (*Informal*), preoccupation, prepossession.

complexion *noun*
1. Skin tone, esp. of the face: *a dark complexion.*
2. The combination of emotional, intellectual, and moral qualities that distinguishes an individual.
3. A person's customary manner of emotional response.

   1. **Syns:** color, coloration, coloring.
   2. CHARACTER.
   3. DISPOSITION.

complexity *noun*
Something complex: *the complexities of nuclear physics.*

   Syns: complication, intricacy.

complexus *noun*
A usu. large entity composed of interconnected parts.

   COMPLEX *noun.*

compliance also **compliancy** *noun*
The quality or state of willingly carrying out the wishes of others.

   OBEDIENCE.

compliancy *noun*

   SEE **compliance.**

compliant *adjective*
Willing to carry out the wishes of others.

   OBEDIENT.

complicate *verb*
To make complex, intricate, or perplexing: *a crisis complicated by a lack of communication.*

   Syns: complex, embarrass, entangle, mix up, perplex, ravel, snarl[1], tangle.
   Near-syns: entangle, muddle; disarrange, disorder, jumble, upset.
   Ant: simplify.

complicated *adjective*
1. Difficult to understand due to intricacy.
2. Complexly detailed.

   1. COMPLEX *adjective.*
   2. ELABORATE *adjective.*

complication *noun*
Something complex.

COMPLEXITY.

compliment *verb*
1. To pay a compliment to: *complimented the pianist on his performance.*
2. To express warm approval of.
3. To look good on or with.

1. **Syns:** commend, praise, recommend.
   —*Idiom* take off one's hat to.
2. PRAISE *verb*.
3. FLATTER.

compliment *noun*
An expression of admiration or congratulation: *deserved compliments on her scholarly work.*

Syns: bouquet, commendation, orchid(s), praise, tribute.

complimentary *adjective*
1. Serving to compliment: *complimentary remarks.*
2. Costing nothing.

1. **Syns:** approbatory, commendatory.
2. FREE *adjective*.

compliment(s) *noun*
1. An act requiring special generosity.
2. An expression of warm approval.

1. COURTESY.
2. PRAISE *noun*.

comply *verb*
To act in conformity with.

FOLLOW.

complying *adjective*
Willing to carry out the wishes of others.

OBEDIENT.

component *noun*
One of the individual entities contributing to a whole.

ELEMENT.

component *adjective*
Constructed as a nondetachable part of a larger unit.

BUILT-IN.

comport *verb*
1. To conduct oneself in a specified way.
2. To be compatible or in correspondence.

1. ACT *verb*.
2. AGREE.

comportment *noun*
The manner in which one behaves.

BEHAVIOR.

compose *verb*
1. To form by artistic effort: *composed a piano sonata.*
2. To bring one's emotions under control: *composed herself in spite of the danger.*
3. To be the constituent parts of.
4. To make or become calm.

1. **Syns:** create, indite, produce, write.
2. **Syns:** collect[1], contain, control, cool (down), restrain, simmer down.
3. CONSTITUTE.
4. CALM *verb*.

composed *adjective*
1. Not excited or emotionally agitated.
2. Not easily excited, even under pressure.

1. CALM *adjective*.
2. COOL *adjective*.

composite *adjective*
Consisting of two or more interconnected parts.

COMPLEX *adjective*.

composition *noun*
1. Something that is the result of creative effort: *a composition for flute and oboe; a composition in black and red.*
2. A relatively brief discourse written esp. as an exercise: *a composition for English class.*
3. A settlement of differences through mutual concession.

1. **Syns:** opus, piece, production, work.

2. **Syns:** essay, paper, theme.

3. COMPROMISE *noun*.

compos mentis *adjective*
Latin. Of sound mind; mentally healthy.

SANE.

composure *noun*
1. Lack of emotional agitation.
2. A stable, calm state of the emotions.

1. CALM *noun*.
2. BALANCE *noun*.

compotation *noun*
A drinking bout.

BENDER.

compound *adjective*
Consisting of two or more interconnected parts.

COMPLEX *adjective*.

compound *verb*
1. To bring or come together into a united whole.
2. To put together into one mass so that the constituent parts are more or less homogeneous.

1. COMBINE *verb*.
2. MIX *verb*.

compound *noun*
Something produced by mixing.   MIXTURE.

comprehend *verb*
1. To perceive and recognize the meaning of.   1. UNDERSTAND.
2. To perceive directly with the intellect.   2. KNOW.
3. To have as an integral part.   3. CONTAIN.

comprehensible *adjective*
Capable of being readily understood.   UNDERSTANDABLE.

comprehension *noun*
1. Intellectual hold.   1. GRASP *noun*.
2. Recognition of worth, quality, importance, etc.   2. APPRECIATION.

comprehensive *adjective*
Covering a wide scope.   GENERAL.

compress *verb*
1. To act on with a steady pushing force.   1. CROWD *verb*.
2. To subject to compression.   2. SQUEEZE *verb*.
3. To reduce in size by or as if by drawing together. 3. CONTRACT *verb*.

compression *noun*
A compressing of something.   CONSTRICTION.

comprise *verb*
1. To be the constituent parts of.   1. CONSTITUTE.
2. To have as an integral part.   2. CONTAIN.

compromise *noun*
A settlement of differences through mutual concession: **Syns:** composition, give-and-take, medium,
a union-management compromise.   mid-course.
                                                          Near-syns: compact, contract, deal, pact,
                                                          peace; agreement, arrangement, bargain,
                                                          understanding.

compromise *verb*
1. To make a concession: *were unable to compromise on* 1. **Syn:** concede. —*Idioms* give and take,
   the wording of the treaty.   go fifty-fifty, meet halfway.
2. To expose to possible loss or damage.   2. RISK *verb*.

compulsory *adjective*
1. Imposed on one by authority, command, or   1. REQUIRED.
   convention.
2. Done under force.   2. FORCED.

compunction *noun*
1. A feeling of uncertainty about the fitness or   1. QUALM.
   correctness of an action.
2. A feeling of regret for one's sins or misdeeds.   2. PENITENCE.

compunctious *adjective*
Feeling or expressing regret for one's sins or misdeeds. REMORSEFUL.

computation *noun*
1. The act, process, or result of calculating.   1. CALCULATION.
2. Arithmetic calculations.   2. FIGURES.

compute *verb*
1. To ascertain by mathematics.   1. CALCULATE.
2. To note (items) one by one so as to get a total.   2. COUNT *verb*.

comrade *noun*
One who keeps company with another.   ASSOCIATE *noun*.

comradeship *noun*
The condition of being friends.   FRIENDSHIP.

con *verb*
1. To look at carefully or critically.   1. EXAMINE.
2. To commit to memory.   2. MEMORIZE.
3. To apply one's mind to the acquisition of knowledge. 3. STUDY *verb*.

concatenate *verb*
To make into a whole by joining a system of parts.   INTEGRATE *verb*.

concave *adjective*
Curving inward.   HOLLOW *adjective*.

concavity *noun*
An area sunk below its surroundings. DEPRESSION.

conceal *verb*
1. To put or keep out of sight. 1. HIDE[1] *verb*.
2. To prevent (something) from being known. 2. COVER *verb*.

concealed *adjective*
1. Lying beyond what is obvious or avowed. 1. ULTERIOR.
2. Screened from the view of oncoming drivers. 2. BLIND *adjective*.

concealment *noun*
The habit, practice, or policy of keeping secrets. SECRECY.

concede *verb*
1. To recognize, often reluctantly, the reality or truth of. 1. ACKNOWLEDGE.
2. To cease opposition. 2. GIVE IN at **give**.
3. To make a concession. 3. COMPROMISE *verb*.
4. To let have as a favor or privilege. 4. GRANT *verb*.

conceit *noun*
1. A regarding of oneself with undue favor. 1. EGOTISM.
2. An impulsive, often illogical turn of mind. 2. FANCY *noun*.

conceit *verb*
Rare. To find agreeable. LIKE[1].

conceited *adjective*
1. Thinking too highly of oneself. 1. EGOTISTICAL.
2. Unduly preoccupied with one's own appearance. 2. VAIN.

conceivable *adjective*
1. Capable of being anticipated, considered, or imagined. 1. EARTHLY.
2. Likely to happen or to be true. 2. PROBABLE.

conceive *verb*
1. To form mental images of. 1. IMAGINE.
2. To perceive and recognize the meaning of. 2. UNDERSTAND.

concentrate *verb*
1. To direct toward a common center: *The enemy concentrated its firepower on the inner city.* 1. *Syns:* center, converge, focalize, focus.
2. To devote (oneself or one's efforts). 2. APPLY.

concentrated *adjective*
1. Not diffused or dispersed: *Concentrated effort is required.* 1. *Syns:* exclusive, fixed, intensive, undivided, unswerving, whole.
2. Having a high concentration of the distinguishing ingredient. 2. STRONG.
3. Intensely sustained, esp. in activity. 3. HEAVY *adjective*.

concentration *noun*
1. A converging at a common center: *heavy troop concentrations on the border.* 1. *Syns:* confluence, conflux, convergence.
2. Concentration of the mental powers on something. 2. ATTENTION.

concept *noun*
That which exists in the mind as the product of careful mental activity. IDEA.

conception *noun*
That which exists in the mind as the product of careful mental activity. IDEA.

conceptual *adjective*
Existing only in the imagination. IMAGINARY.

concern *noun*
1. A being personally interested in: *You are the object of our concern.* 1. *Syns:* concernment, interest, interestedness, regard.
2. Something that concerns or involves one personally. 2. BUSINESS.
3. Thoughtful attention. 3. CONSIDERATION.
4. A connecting relation: *a matter of no concern to our plans.* 4. *Syns:* bearing, concernment, pertinence (*also* pertinency), relevance (*also* relevancy).

5. The quality or state of being important.

6. A cause of worry.

7. A commercial organization.

8. *Informal.* A small, specialized mechanical device.

concern *verb*

1. To be pertinent.

2. To cause anxious uneasiness in.

concerned *adjective*

1. Having concern: *All those concerned attended the meeting.*

2. In a state of uneasiness.

concernment *noun*

1. A connecting relation.

2. The quality or state of being important.

3. A being personally interested in.

concert *noun*

Pleasing agreement, as of musical sounds.

concession *noun*

An accommodation made in the light of special or extenuating circumstances: *made a concession due to her inexperience.*

conciliate *verb*

1. To ease the anger or agitation of.

2. To re-establish friendship between.

conciliation *noun*

A re-establishment of friendship or harmony.

concise *adjective*

Marked by or consisting of few words.

conclave *noun*

A number of persons who have come or been gathered together.

conclude *verb*

1. To bring or come to a natural or proper end.

2. To make up or cause to make up one's mind.

3. To put into correct or conclusive form.

4. To come to an agreement about.

5. To draw a conclusion from evidence or reasoning.

concluded *adjective*

Having reached completion.

concluding *adjective*

Coming after all others.

conclusion *noun*

1. A concluding or terminating.

2. The last part.

3. A position reached after consideration.

4. A position arrived at by reasoning from premises or general principles.

conclusive *adjective*

1. Determining or having the power to determine an outcome.

2. Having or arising from authority.

3. Serving the function of deciding or settling with finality.

conclusively *adverb*

In conclusion.

concoct *verb*

To use ingenuity in making, developing, or achieving.

concomitant *adjective*

Occurring in company with.

---

5. IMPORTANCE.

6. CARE *noun.*

7. COMPANY *noun.*

8. GADGET.

1. APPLY.

2. WORRY *verb.*

1. *Syns:* affected[2], interested, involved.
Near-ants: aloof, incurious, indifferent; apathetic, bored.
Ants: unconcerned, uninterested.

2. ANXIOUS.

1. CONCERN *noun.*

2. IMPORTANCE.

3. CONCERN *noun.*

HARMONY.

Syn: allowance.

1. PACIFY.

2. RECONCILE.

RECONCILIATION.

BRIEF.

ASSEMBLY.

1. CLOSE[1] *verb.*

2. DECIDE.

3. SETTLE.

4. ARRANGE.

5. INFER.

COMPLETE *adjective.*

LAST[1] *adjective.*

1. END *noun.*

2. END *noun.*

3. DECISION.

4. DEDUCTION.

1. DECISIVE.

2. AUTHORITATIVE.

3. DEFINITIVE.

LAST[1] *adverb.*

INVENT.

ACCOMPANYING.

concomitant *noun*
One that accompanies another.   ACCOMPANIMENT.

concord *verb*
To come to an understanding or to terms.   AGREE.

   concord *noun*
   1. Harmonious mutual understanding.   1. AGREEMENT.
   2. A formal, usu. written settlement between nations.   2. TREATY.
   3. The state of individuals who are in utter agreement.   3. HARMONY.
   4. Pleasing agreement, as of musical sounds.   4. HARMONY.

concordance *noun*
Harmonious mutual understanding.   AGREEMENT.

concordant *adjective*
Having components pleasingly combined.   SYMMETRICAL.

concourse *noun*
The act or fact of coming together.   JUNCTION.

concrete *adjective*
1. Having actual reality.   1. REAL.
2. Composed of or relating to things that occupy space   2. PHYSICAL.
   and can be perceived by the senses.

   concrete *verb*
   1. To bring or come together into a united whole.   1. COMBINE *verb*.
   2. To make or become physically hard.   2. HARDEN.

concupiscence *noun*
Sexual hunger.   DESIRE *noun*.

concupiscent *adjective*
Feeling or devoted to sexual love or desire.   EROTIC.

concupiscible *adjective*
Archaic. Arousing erotic desire.   DESIRABLE.

concur *verb*
1. To occur at the same time.   1. COINCIDE.
2. To come to an understanding or to terms.   2. AGREE.

concurrence *noun*
Harmonious mutual understanding.   AGREEMENT.

concurrent *adjective*
1. Occurring in company with.   1. ACCOMPANYING.
2. Belonging to the same period of time as another. 2. CONTEMPORARY *adjective*.
3. Lying in the same plane and not intersecting.   3. PARALLEL *adjective*.
4. Being in or characterized by complete agreement. 4. UNANIMOUS.

concursion *noun*
The act or fact of coming together.   JUNCTION.

concussion *noun*
Violent, forcible contact between two or more things. COLLISION.

condemn *verb*
1. To pronounce judgment against: *condemned the*   1. ***Syns:*** damn, doom, sentence.
   dissidents to hard labor.
2. To find fault with.   2. BLAME *verb*.
3. To feel or express strong disapproval of.   3. DEPLORE.

condemnation *noun*
A finding fault.   BLAME *noun*.

condemnatory *adjective*
Containing or imposing a condemnation: *a*   ***Syn:*** condemning.
condemnatory decree.

condemned *adjective*
Sentenced to terrible, irrevocable punishment: *a*   ***Syns:*** doomed, fated, foredoomed, lost.
condemned man on death row.   ***Near-ants:*** delivered, redeemed.
                                                     Ant: saved.

condemning *adjective*
Containing or imposing a condemnation.   CONDEMNATORY.

condensation *noun*
A short summary prepared by cutting down a larger   SYNOPSIS.
work.

condense *verb*
To make thick or thicker, esp. through evaporation or condensation.
THICKEN.

condensed *adjective*
Marked by or consisting of few words.
BRIEF.

condescend *verb*
1. To descend to a level considered inappropriate to one's dignity: *condescended to empty the garbage.*
1. *Syns:* deign, stoop, vouchsafe.
2. To treat in a superciliously indulgent manner: *a snob who condescended to all the neighbors.*
2. *Syns:* patronize, talk down (to).

condescendence *noun*
Superciliously indulgent treatment, esp. of those considered inferior.
CONDESCENSION.

condescending *adjective*
Exhibiting condescension: *a condescending snob.*
Syn: patronizing.

condescension *noun*
Superciliously indulgent treatment, esp. of those considered inferior: *His overt condescension toward us is repellent.*
Syns: condescendence, patronization, patronizing.

condiment *noun*
A substance that imparts taste.
FLAVORING.

condition *noun*
1. Manner of being or form of existence: *a patient in a weakened condition; a house restored to its former condition.*
1. *Syns:* mode, posture, situation, state, status.
2. Something indispensable: *Eating is a condition to survival.*
2. *Syns:* essential, must, necessity, precondition, prerequisite, requirement, requisite, sine qua non.
3. A restricting or modifying element.
3. PROVISION.
4. A state of sound readiness.
4. TRIM *noun.*

condition *verb*
To make familiar through constant practice or use.
ACCUSTOM.

conditional *adjective*
1. Depending on or containing a condition or conditions: *a conditional surrender.*
1. *Syns:* provisional, provisionary, provisory, qualified, tentative.
   Near-syns: limited, modified, restricted; iffy (*Informal*), uncertain.
   Ant: unconditional.
2. Determined or to be determined by someone or something else.
2. DEPENDENT *adjective.*

conditioned *adjective*
Determined or to be determined by someone or something else.
DEPENDENT *adjective.*

conditions *noun*
Existing surroundings that affect an activity: *poor working conditions.*
Syns: circumstances, environment.

condonable *adjective*
Admitting of forgiveness or pardon.
PARDONABLE.

condonation *noun*
The act or an instance of forgiving.
FORGIVENESS.

condone *verb*
To grant forgiveness for a fault, offense, or injury.
FORGIVE.

conduce *verb*
To have a share in (an act, result, etc.); have a hand in.
CONTRIBUTE.

conducive *adjective*
Tending to contribute to a result.
CONTRIBUTIVE.

conduct *verb*
1. To control the course of (an activity): *conduct the affairs of state; conduct an experiment.*
1. *Syns:* carry on, direct, manage, operate, steer, supervise.
2. To show the way to.
2. GUIDE *verb.*

3. To serve as a conduit: *Most metals conduct electricity.*

3. *Syns:* carry, channel, convey, transmit.

4. To engage in (a war or campaign).

4. WAGE *verb.*

conduct *noun*
The manner in which one behaves.

BEHAVIOR.

conductor *noun*
Something or someone that shows the way.

GUIDE *noun.*

confab *noun*
Informal. An exchanging of views.

CONFERENCE.

confab *verb*
Informal. To meet and exchange views to reach a decision.

CONFER.

confabulate *verb*
1. To engage in spoken exchange.
2. To meet and exchange views to reach a decision.

1. CONVERSE[1] *verb.*
2. CONFER.

confabulation *noun*
1. Spoken exchange.
2. An exchanging of views.
3. An exchange of views in an attempt to reach a decision.

1. CONVERSATION.
2. CONFERENCE.
3. DELIBERATION.

confabulator *noun*
One given to conversation.

CONVERSATIONALIST.

confabulatory *adjective*
In the style of conversation.

CONVERSATIONAL.

confederacy *noun*
An association, esp. of nations for a common cause.

ALLIANCE.

confederate *verb*
To be formally associated, as by treaty.

ALLY *verb.*

confederate *noun*
1. One nation associated with another in a common cause.
2. One who is united in a relationship with another.

1. ALLY *noun.*
2. ASSOCIATE *noun.*

confederated *adjective*
Closely connected by or as if by a treaty.

ALLIED.

confederation *noun*
1. An association, esp. of nations for a common cause.
2. A group of people united in a relationship and having some interest, activity, or purpose in common.

1. ALLIANCE.
2. UNION.

confer *verb*
1. To meet and exchange views to reach a decision: *confer with one's associates.*

1. *Syns:* advise (with), confab (*Informal*), confabulate, consult, parley, powwow, talk.

2. To give formally or officially: *conferred honors on them.*

2. *Syns:* accord, award, bestow, grant, present[2].

conferee also **conferree** *noun*
One who participates in a conference: *nine conferees on the panel.*

Syns: deliberant, discussant, discussor.

conference *noun*
1. A meeting for the exchange of views: *a teachers' conference.*

1. *Syns:* colloquium, discussion, powwow, seminar. —*Idiom* rap session.

2. An exchanging of views: *needed several hours of conference with each student.*

2. *Syns:* confab (*Informal*), confabulation, discussion, rap[1] (*Slang*), ventilation.

3. An exchange of views in an attempt to reach a decision.

3. DELIBERATION.

4. A group of athletic teams that play each other: *Southern Conference football clubs.*

4. *Syns:* association, circuit, league.

5. A formal assemblage of the members of a group.

5. CONVENTION.

6. The act of conferring, as of an honor.

6. CONFERMENT.

conferment *noun*
The act of conferring, as of an honor: *conferment of an honorary doctorate.*

conferral *noun*
The act of conferring, as of an honor.

conferree *noun*

confess *verb*
To recognize, often reluctantly, the reality or truth of.

confession *noun*
The act of admitting to something.

confessor *noun*
One in whom secrets are confided.

confidant also **confidante** *noun*
One in whom secrets are confided: *her closest friend and confidant.*

confidante *noun*

confide *verb*
1. To tell in confidence: *reluctantly confided my secret in her.*
2. To give over to another for care, use, or performance.

confidence *noun*
1. Absolute certainty in the trustworthiness of another: *had confidence in the President.*
2. The fact or condition of being without doubt.
3. A firm belief in one's own powers: *had a lot of confidence.*

confident *adjective*
1. Having a firm belief in one's own powers: *a confident man.*

2. Having no doubt.

confidential *adjective*
1. Known about by very few: *a confidential executive decision.*

2. Indicating intimacy and mutual trust: *drew me aside in a confidential way.*
3. Of or being information available only to authorized persons: *confidential government documents.*

configuration *noun*
The external outline of a thing.

confine *verb*
1. To shut in with or as if with bars.
2. To enclose so as to hinder or prohibit escape.
3. To put in jail.
4. To place a limit on.

confinement *noun*
The act of limiting or condition of being limited.

confine(s) *adjective*
1. A demarcation point or boundary beyond which something does not extend or occur.
2. The boundary surrounding a certain area.

confining *adjective*
Affording little room for movement.

Syns: accordance, bestowal, conference, conferral, presentation.

CONFERMENT.

SEE **conferee.**

ACKNOWLEDGE.

ACKNOWLEDGMENT.

CONFIDANT.

Syns: confessor, repository.

SEE **confidant.**

1. **Syns:** breathe, whisper.

2. ENTRUST.

1. **Syns:** belief, faith, reliance, trust.

2. SURENESS.
3. **Syns:** aplomb, assurance, self-assurance, self-confidence, self-possession.

1. **Syns:** assured, secure, self-assured, self-confident, self-possessed.
Near-ants: afraid, doubtful, dubious, fearful, jittery, nervous.
Ant: apprehensive.

2. SURE.

1. **Syns:** auricular, hush-hush (*Informal*), inside (*Slang*), private, privy (*Archaic*).
2. **Syns:** familiar, intimate[1], privy (*Obs.*).

3. **Syns:** classified, privileged (*Law*), restricted.

FORM *noun.*

1. BAR *verb.*
2. IMPRISON.
3. JAIL *verb.*
4. LIMIT *verb.*

RESTRICTION.

1. END *noun.*

2. LIMIT *noun.*

TIGHT *adjective.*

confirm *verb*
1. To assure the certainty or validity of: *a suspicion confirmed by evidence.*

   1. ***Syns:*** attest, authenticate, back (up), bear out, corroborate, justify, substantiate, testify (to), validate, verify, warrant.
   Near-ants: confute, controvert, disprove, refute, traverse; impugn, negate.
   Ant: deny.

2. To establish as true or genuine.
   2. PROVE.
3. To make valid and binding by a formal legal act: *Congress must confirm the treaty.*
   3. ***Syns:*** affirm, approve, ratify.
4. To make firmer in a particular conviction or habit: *scandals that confirmed their distrust of politicians.*
   4. ***Syns:*** fortify, harden, strengthen.

confirmation *noun*
1. An act of confirming officially: *Senate confirmation of the treaty.*
   1. ***Syns:*** affirmation, approval, ratification.
2. That which confirms: *found in the ledger confirmation of fraud.*
   2. ***Syns:*** attestation, authentication, corroboration, evidence, proof, substantiation, testament, testimonial, testimony, validation, verification.

confirmed *adjective*
1. Firmly established by long standing: *confirmed habits difficult to break.*
   1. ***Syns:*** entrenched, hard-shell (*also* hard-shelled), ingrained, inveterate, irradicable, set[1], settled.
2. Subject to a disease or habit for a long time.
   2. CHRONIC.

confiscate *verb*
To take quick and forcible possession of.
   SEIZE.

confiscation *noun*
The act of taking quick and forcible possession of.
   SEIZURE.

conflagrant *adjective*
On fire.
   BLAZING.

conflagrate *verb*
To undergo combustion.
   BURN *verb.*

conflagration *noun*
The visible signs of combustion.
   FIRE *noun.*

conflict *noun*
1. A state of open, prolonged fighting: *the conflict in Vietnam.*
   1. ***Syns:*** belligerency, hostilities, strife, war, warfare.
2. A state of disagreement and disharmony: *family conflicts.*
   2. ***Syns:*** clash, contention, difficulty, disaccord, discord, dissension, dissent, dissentience, dissidence, dissonance, friction, inharmony, strife, variance.
   crosscurrents

conflict *verb*
To fail to be in accord: *Your story conflicts with hers.*
   Syns: clash, contradict, disaccord, discord, jar (with). —*Idiom* go (*or* run) counter to.

conflicting *adjective*
In sharp opposition: *conflicting statements.*
   Syns: clashing, disconsonant, discrepant, incongruent, incongruous, inconsistent.

confluence *noun*
1. A converging at a common center.
   1. CONCENTRATION.
2. The act or fact of coming together.
   2. JUNCTION.

conflux *noun*
A converging at a common center.
   CONCENTRATION.

conform *verb*
1. To make or become suitable to a particular situation or use.
   1. ADAPT.
2. To make conventional.
   2. CONVENTIONALIZE.
3. To be compatible or in correspondence.
   3. AGREE.
4. To act in conformity with.
   4. FOLLOW.

5. To bring into accord.   **5.** HARMONIZE.

conform to   *verb*
To be in keeping with.   FIT *verb.*

conformable   *adjective*
1. Willing to carry out the wishes of others.   **1.** OBEDIENT.
2. In keeping with one's needs or expectations.   **2.** AGREEABLE.

conformance   *noun*
1. The act or state of agreeing or conforming.   **1.** AGREEMENT.
2. An act of willingly carrying out the wishes of others.   **2.** OBEDIENCE.

conformation   *noun*
1. The condition of being made suitable to an end.   **1.** ADAPTATION.
2. The act or state of agreeing or conforming.   **2.** AGREEMENT.

conformist   *adjective*
Conforming to established practice or standards.   CONVENTIONAL.

conformity   *noun*
1. The act or state of agreeing or conforming.   **1.** AGREEMENT.
2. Logical agreement among things or parts.   **2.** CONSISTENCY.
3. An act of willingly carrying out the wishes of others.   **3.** OBEDIENCE.

conform to   *verb*   SEE **conform.**

confound   *verb*
1. To cause to be unclear in mind or intent.   **1.** CONFUSE.
2. To take (one thing) mistakenly for another.   **2.** CONFUSE.
3. To cause (a person) to be self-consciously distressed.   **3.** EMBARRASS.
4. To make incapable of finding something to think, do, or say.   **4.** NONPLUS.

confounded   *adjective*
1. So annoying or detestable as to deserve condemnation.   **1.** DAMNED.
2. Distressed and ill at ease.   **2.** EMBARRASSED.
3. Overcome with intense feeling, as of amazement, horror, or dismay.   **3.** SHOCKED.

confront   *verb*
1. To meet face-to-face, esp. defiantly: *enemy troops confronting each other.*   **1.** *Syns:* accost, encounter, face, front.
2. To come up against.   **2.** ENCOUNTER *verb.*

confrontation   *noun*
A face-to-face, usu. hostile meeting: *a confrontation between union and management.*   *Syns:* encounter, face-off.

confuse   *verb*
1. To cause to be unclear in mind or intent: *The purpose of camouflage is to confuse the enemy. I was totally confused by the complex memorandum. The heavy traffic confused the novice driver.*   **1.** *Syns:* addle, befuddle, bewilder, confound, discombobulate (*Slang*), dizzy, fuddle, mix up, perplex, throw. —*Idiom* make one's head reel (*or* swim *or* whirl).
     Near-syns: distract, muddle; misguide, mislead, perturb, upset; bother, disquiet.

2. To put into total disorder: *had hopelessly confused his finances.*   **2.** *Syns:* ball up (*Slang*), disorder, jumble, mess up, muddle, scramble, snafu (*Slang*), snarl[1].

3. To take (one thing) mistakenly for another: *confused aggressiveness with ruthlessness.*   **3.** *Syns:* confound, misdeem, mistake, mix up.
4. To cause (a person) to be self-consciously distressed.   **4.** EMBARRASS.

confused   *adjective*
1. Characterized by physical confusion: *a confused sea of faces; a confused pile of clothes.*   **1.** *Syns:* chaotic, confusional, disordered, helter-skelter, higgledy-piggledy, jumbled, mixed-up, muddled, topsy-turvy, upside-down.

2. Mentally uncertain: *I am totally confused by this problem.*

2. Syns: addled, befuddled, bewildered, discombobulated (*Slang*). —*Idiom* turned around.

confusedness *noun*
A lack of order or regular arrangement.

DISORDER *noun*.

confusion *noun*
1. A lack of order or regular arrangement.
2. Self-conscious distress.

1. DISORDER *noun*.
2. EMBARRASSMENT.

confusional *adjective*
Characterized by physical confusion.

CONFUSED.

confute *verb*
To prove or show to be false.

REFUTE.

congeal *verb*
1. To change or be changed from a liquid into a soft, semisolid, or solid mass.
2. To make or become physically hard.

1. COAGULATE
2. HARDEN.

congener *noun*
Something closely resembling or analogous to something else.

PARALLEL *noun*.

congenial *adjective*
1. Characterized by kindness and warm, unaffected courtesy.
2. Of or befitting a friend or friends.
3. Affording pleasure or comfort.
4. In keeping with one's needs or expectations.
5. Exhibiting accord in feeling or action.

1. GRACIOUS.
2. FRIENDLY.
3. GRATEFUL.
4. AGREEABLE.
5. HARMONIOUS.

congenital *adjective*
1. Possessed at birth.
2. Of or arising from the most basic structure of an individual.
3. Forming an essential element.

1. INNATE.
2. CONSTITUTIONAL *adjective*.
3. BUILT-IN.

congeries *noun*
A quantity accumulated.

ACCUMULATION.

congest *verb*
To plug up something, as a hole, space, or container.

FILL.

conglomeration *noun*
A collection of various things.

ASSORTMENT.

congratulate *verb*
To be proud of (oneself) because of some accomplishment, achievement, etc.

PRIDE *verb*.

congregate *verb*
To come together.

ASSEMBLE.

congregation *noun*
A number of persons who have come or been gathered together.

ASSEMBLY.

congress *noun*
1. A number of persons who have come or been gathered together.
2. A group of people united in a relationship and having some interest, activity, or purpose in common.
3. A formal assemblage of the members of a group.

1. ASSEMBLY.
2. UNION.
3. CONVENTION.

congruity *noun*
Logical agreement among things or parts.

CONSISTENCY.

congruous *adjective*
1. In keeping with one's needs or expectations.
2. Having components pleasingly combined.

1. AGREEABLE.
2. SYMMETRICAL.

conjectural *adjective*
Presumed to be true, real, or genuine, esp. on inconclusive grounds.

SUPPOSED.

conjecture *verb*
To draw an inference on the basis of inconclusive
evidence or insufficient information.　　　　GUESS *verb*.

　conjecture *noun*
　1. A judgment, estimate, or opinion arrived at by　　1. GUESS *noun*.
　　guessing.
　2. Abstract reasoning.　　　　　　　　　　　　2. THEORY.

conjectured *adjective*
Based on inference, not fact.　　　　　　　　PRESUMPTIVE.

conjoin *verb*
　1. To bring or come together into a united whole.　1. COMBINE *verb*.
　2. To unite or be united in a relationship.　　　2. ASSOCIATE *verb*.

conjoint *adjective*
　1. Joined together into a whole.　　　　　　　1. COMBINED.
　2. Belonging to, shared by, or applicable to all alike.　2. COMMON *adjective*.

conjugal *adjective*
Of, relating to, or typical of marriage.　　　　MARITAL.

conjugality *noun*
The state of being united as husband and wife.　MARRIAGE.

conjugate *verb*
To bring or come together into a united whole.　COMBINE *verb*.

conjugation *noun*
The result of combining.　　　　　　　　　　COMBINATION.

conjugational *adjective*
Of, relating to, or tending to produce combination.　COMBINATIONAL.

conjugative *adjective*
Of, relating to, or tending to produce combination.　COMBINATIONAL.

conjunction *noun*
The state of being associated.　　　　　　　　ASSOCIATION.

conjuration *noun*
　1. The use of skillful tricks and deceptions to produce　1. MAGIC *noun*.
　　entertainingly baffling effects.
　2. The use of supernatural powers to influence or　2. MAGIC *noun*.
　　predict events.

conjure *verb*
To make an earnest or urgent request.　　　　APPEAL.

conjury *noun*
　1. The use of skillful tricks and deceptions to produce　1. MAGIC *noun*.
　　entertainingly baffling effects.
　2. The use of supernatural powers to influence or　2. MAGIC *noun*.
　　predict events.

conk *noun*
　1. A sudden sharp, powerful stroke.　　　　　1. BLOW^2.
　2. *Slang*. The uppermost part of the body.　　2. HEAD *noun*.

　conk out *verb*
　1. To cease functioning properly.　　　　　　1. FAIL.
　2. *Slang*. To suddenly lose all health or strength.　2. COLLAPSE *verb*.

conk out *verb*　　　　　　　　　　　　SEE **conk.**

connate *adjective*
Connected by or as if by kinship or common origin.　RELATED.

connatural *adjective*
　1. Connected by or as if by kinship or common origin.　1. RELATED.
　2. Of or arising from the most basic structure of an　2. CONSTITUTIONAL *adjective*.
　　individual.

connect *verb*
　1. To bring or come together into a united whole.　1. COMBINE *verb*.
　2. To join one thing to another.　　　　　　　2. ATTACH.
　3. To unite or be united in a relationship.　　　3. ASSOCIATE *verb*.
　4. To come or bring together in one's mind or　4. ASSOCIATE *verb*.
　　imagination.

5. *Informal.* To interact with another or others in a meaningful fashion.

5. RELATE.

connection *noun*
1. A point or position at which two or more things are joined.
2. The state of being associated.
3. A feeling, thought, idea, etc., associated in one's mind or imagination with someone or something specific.
4. A logical or natural association between two or more things.
5. *Slang.* An acquaintance who is in a position to help.

1. JOINT *noun.*

2. ASSOCIATION.
3. SUGGESTION.

4. RELATION.

5. CONTACT *noun.*

conniption *noun*
Informal. An angry outburst.

TEMPER *noun.*

connivance also **connivence** *noun*
A secret plan to achieve an evil or illegal end.

PLOT *noun.*

connive *verb*
To work out a secret plan to achieve an evil or illegal end.

PLOT *verb.*

connive at *verb*
To pretend not to see.

BLINK AT at **blink.**

connive at *verb*

SEE **connive.**

connivence *noun*

SEE **connivance.**

connotation *noun*
A feeling, thought, idea, etc., associated in one's mind or imagination with someone or something specific.

SUGGESTION.

connote *verb*
To have or convey a particular idea.

MEAN[1].

connubial *adjective*
Of, relating to, or typical of marriage.

MARITAL.

connubiality *noun*
The state of being united as husband and wife.

MARRIAGE.

conquer *verb*
1. To win a victory over, as in battle or a competition.
2. To get the better of.

1. DEFEAT *verb.*
2. TRIUMPH *verb.*

conquering *adjective*
Pertaining to, having the nature of, or experiencing triumph.

VICTORIOUS.

conqueror *noun*
One that conquers: *the conqueror of Wales.*

Syns: conquistador, master, victor, winner.

conquest *noun*
The act of conquering: *the Norman Conquest.*

Syns: triumph, victory, win.

conquistador *noun*
One that conquers.

CONQUEROR.

consanguine *adjective*

SEE **consanguineous.**

consanguineous also **consanguine** *adjective*
Connected by or as if by kinship or common origin.

RELATED.

conscienceless *adjective*
Lacking scruples or principles.

UNSCRUPULOUS.

conscious *adjective*
Tending toward awareness and appreciation.

MINDFUL.

consciousness *noun*
The condition of being aware.

AWARENESS.

conscript *verb*
To enroll compulsorily in military service.

DRAFT *verb.*

conscription *noun*
Compulsory enrollment in military service.

DRAFT *noun.*

consecrate *verb*
1. To make sacred by a religious rite.
2. To give over by or as if by vow to a higher purpose.

1. SANCTIFY.
2. DEVOTE.

consecrated *adjective*
Given over exclusively to a single use or purpose.

SACRED.

consecution *noun*
1. A way in which things follow each other in space or time.
2. A number of things placed or occurring one after the other.

1. ORDER *noun*.

2. SERIES.

consecutive *adjective*
Following one after another in an orderly pattern: *It was cloudy for six consecutive days.*

Syns: sequent, sequential, serial, subsequent, subsequential, succedent, succeeding, successional, successive.
Near-syns: after, ensuing, following, later, next.

consensus *noun*
The quality or condition of being in complete mutual agreement.

UNANIMITY.

consent *noun*
1. The act or process of accepting.
2. Approval for an action, esp. as granted by one in authority.

1. ACCEPTANCE.
2. PERMISSION.

consent *verb*
1. To respond affirmatively.
2. To give one's consent to.

1. ASSENT *verb*.
2. PERMIT *verb*.

consequence *noun*
1. Something brought about by a cause.
2. The quality or state of being important.

1. EFFECT *noun*.
2. IMPORTANCE.

consequent *adjective*
Consistent with reason and intellect.

LOGICAL.

consequential *adjective*
1. Having great significance.
2. Having or exercising influence.

1. IMPORTANT.
2. INFLUENTIAL.

conservancy *noun*
The careful guarding of an asset.

CONSERVATION.

conservation *noun*
The careful guarding of an asset: *wildlife conservation.*

Syns: conservancy, husbandry, management, preserval, preservation.

conservative *adjective*
1. Strongly favoring retention of the existing order: *a conservative politician.*

1. **Syns:** orthodox, right, rightist, right-wing, Tory, traditionalist (*also* traditionalistic).

2. Kept within sensible limits: *a conservative estimate; conservative attire.*

2. **Syns:** discreet, moderate, reasonable, restrained, temperate.
Near-syns: cautious, chary, controlled, wary; circumspect, proper, prudent, vigilant.

3. Able to preserve.

3. PRESERVATIVE.

conservative *noun*
One who strongly favors retention of the existing order: *a political conservative.*

Syns: fundamentalist, praetorian, rightist, right-winger, Tory.

conservator *noun*
Law. A person who is legally responsible for the person or property of another considered by law to be incompetent to manage his affairs.

GUARDIAN.

conservatory *adjective*
Able to preserve.

PRESERVATIVE.

conserve *verb*
1. To protect (an asset) from loss or destruction: *conserve energy.*
2. To prepare (food) for storage and future use: *conserve strawberries.*

1. **Syns:** husband, preserve, save.

2. **Syns:** can, preserve, put up.

consider *verb*
1. To think about seriously: *considered all the options first.*

2. To look upon in a particular way.
3. To have an opinion.
4. To have a high opinion of.
5. To be occupied or concerned.
6. To direct the eyes on an object.

considerable *adjective*
1. Notably above average in amount, size, or scope.
2. Having great significance.

considerably *adverb*
To a considerable extent: *sales considerably higher than forecast.*

considerate *adjective*
Full of polite concern for the well-being of others.

considerately *adverb*
In a considerate manner: *Treat your parents considerately.*

consideration *noun*
1. Thoughtful attention: *consideration for the feelings of others.*
2. A careful considering of a matter.
3. Concentration of the mental powers on something.
4. Something given in exchange for goods or services rendered.
5. A feeling of deference, approval, and liking.

considered *adjective*
1. Resulting from deliberation and careful thought.
2. Planned, weighed, or estimated in advance.

consign *verb*
1. To give over to another for care, use, or performance.
2. To cause (something) to be conveyed to a destination.
3. To place officially in confinement.

consist *verb*
1. To have as an inherent basis: *The beauty of the style consists in its simplicity.*
2. To be compatible or in correspondence.

consist of *verb*
To be the constituent parts of.

consistence *noun*

consistency also **consistence** *noun*
Logical agreement among things or parts: *The statements lack consistency.*

consistent *adjective*
1. Remaining continually unchanged: *a consistent advocate of reform.*

2. In keeping with one's needs or expectations.

consistently *adverb*
In an expected or customary manner.

consist of *verb*

consolate *verb*
Obs. To give hope to in time of grief or pain.

---

1. *Syns:* cogitate, entertain, excogitate, study, think over.
   Near-syns: contemplate, meditate, mind, muse, reason, reflect, speculate; examine, inspect, scrutinize.
2. REGARD *verb.*
3. BELIEVE.
4. ADMIRE.
5. DEAL *verb.*
6. LOOK *verb.*

1. BIG.
2. IMPORTANT.

Syns: far, quite, well[2]. —*Idioms* by a long shot (*or* way), by a wide margin, by far.

ATTENTIVE.

Syns: solicitously, well[2].

1. *Syns:* concern, regard, solicitude, thoughtfulness.
2. ADVISEMENT.
3. ATTENTION.
4. PAYMENT.

5. ESTEEM *noun.*

1. ADVISED.
2. CALCULATED.

1. ENTRUST.

2. SEND.

3. COMMIT.

1. *Syns:* dwell, exist, inhere, lie[1], repose, reside, rest[1].
2. AGREE.

CONSTITUTE.
SEE **consistency.**

Syns: coherence, conformity, congruity, correspondence.

1. *Syns:* constant, invariable, same, unchanging, unfailing.
   Near-ants: changeable, fluctuant, inconstant, irregular, variable, varying.
   Ant: inconsistent.
2. AGREEABLE.

USUALLY.
SEE **consist.**

COMFORT *verb.*

consolation *noun*
A consoling in time of grief or pain.   COMFORT *noun*.

console *verb*
To give hope to in time of grief or pain.   COMFORT *verb*.

consolidation *noun*
A bringing together into a whole.   UNIFICATION.

consonance *noun*
1. Harmonious mutual understanding.   1. AGREEMENT.
2. *Mus.* Pleasing agreement, as of musical sounds.   2. HARMONY.

consonant *adjective*
1. Characterized by harmony of sound.   1. HARMONIOUS.
2. In keeping with one's needs or expectations.   2. AGREEABLE.

consort *verb*
1. To keep company.   1. ASSOCIATE *verb*.
2. *Obs.* To be with or go with (another).   2. ACCOMPANY.

consort *noun*
A husband or wife.   SPOUSE.

conspicuous *adjective*
1. Readily attracting notice.   1. NOTICEABLE.
2. Standing out prominently.   2. BOLD.

conspiracy *noun*
A secret plan to achieve an evil or illegal end.   PLOT *noun*.

conspire *verb*
To work out a secret plan to achieve an evil or illegal PLOT *verb*.
end.

constable *noun*
Brit. A member of a law-enforcement agency.   POLICEMAN.

constancy *noun*
Faithfulness or devotion to a person, a cause,   FIDELITY.
obligations, or duties.

constant *adjective*
1. Remaining continually unchanged.   1. CONSISTENT.
2. Having no variations.   2. EVEN[1] *adjective*.
3. Existing or occurring without interruption or end.   3. CONTINUAL.
4. Adhering firmly and devotedly, as to a person, a   4. FAITHFUL.
   cause, or a duty.

consternate *verb*
To deprive of courage or the power to act as a result of DISMAY *verb*.
fear, anxiety, or disgust.

consternation *noun*
1. A sudden or complete loss of courage in the face of 1. DISMAY *noun*.
   trouble or danger.
2. Great agitation and anxiety caused by the   2. FEAR *noun*.
   expectation or the realization of danger.

constituent *adjective*
Constructed as a nondetachable part of a larger unit.   BUILT-IN.

constituent *noun*
One of the individual entities contributing to a whole. ELEMENT.

constitute *verb*
1. To be the constituent parts of: *Ten members*   1. *Syns:* compose, comprise, consist of,
   constitute a quorum.   form, make, make up.
2. To cause to be by official action.   2. ENACT.
3. To bring into existence formally.   3. FOUND.
4. To put in force by legal authority.   4. ESTABLISH.
5. To be equivalent.   5. AMOUNT *verb*.

constitution *noun*
Bodily type: *a strong constitution.*   *Syns:* build, habit (*Rare*), habitus,
                                                        physique.

constitutional *adjective*
1. Of or arising from the most basic structure of an individual: *constitutional weaknesses*.

2. Constituting or forming part of the essence of something.

constitutional *noun*
A usu. brief and regular journey on foot, esp. for exercise: *a morning constitutional through the park*.

constitutive *adjective*
Constituting or forming part of the essence of something.

constrain *verb*
1. To check the freedom and spontaneity of: *a friendship now constrained by tension*.
2. To subject to compression.
3. To act on with a steady pushing force.
4. To control, restrict, or arrest.
5. To cause (a person or thing) to act or move in spite of resistance.

constrained *adjective*
1. Characterized by embarrassment and discomfort.
2. Tending to keep one's thoughts and emotions to oneself.
3. Done under force.

constrainment *noun*
The act of limiting or condition of being limited.

constraint *noun*
1. Power used to overcome resistance.
2. Something that limits or restricts.
3. The act of limiting or condition of being limited.

constrict *verb*
1. To render narrow or narrower: *constricted blood vessels*.
2. To subject to compression.
3. To reduce in size by or as if by drawing together.
4. To check the freedom and spontaneity of.

constriction *noun*
1. A becoming narrow or narrower: *a constriction of the small bowel*.
2. A compressing of something: *The tight collar produced a painful constriction of my neck*.

constringe *verb*
1. To subject to compression.
2. To render narrow or narrower.

construct *verb*
1. To create by forming, combining, or altering materials.
2. To make or form (a structure).

construction *noun*
Something that serves to explain or clarify.

constructor *noun*
A person or business that makes or builds something.

construe *verb*
1. To make understandable.
2. To understand in a particular way.
3. To express in another language, while systematically retaining the original sense.

consuetude *noun*
An accepted way of doing something.

1. *Syns:* congenital, connatural, elemental, inborn, inbred, indigenous, indwelling, ingenerate, ingrained, inherent, innate, intrinsic.
2. ESSENTIAL *adjective*.

Syns: hike, turn, walk.

ESSENTIAL *adjective*.

1. *Syns:* astrict, constrict, cramp, inhibit.

2. SQUEEZE *verb*.
3. CROWD *verb*.
4. RESTRAIN.
5. FORCE *verb*.

1. AWKWARD.
2. RESERVED.

3. FORCED.

RESTRICTION.

1. FORCE *noun*.
2. RESTRICTION.
3. RESTRICTION.

1. *Syns:* constringe, narrow.

2. SQUEEZE *verb*.
3. CONTRACT *verb*.
4. CONSTRAIN.

1. *Syn:* stricture (*Path.*).

2. *Syns:* compression, squeeze, squeezing.

1. SQUEEZE *verb*.
2. CONSTRICT.

1. MAKE.

2. BUILD *verb*.

EXPLANATION.

BUILDER.

1. EXPLAIN.
2. INTERPRET.
3. TRANSLATE.

CONVENTION.

consult *verb*
To meet and exchange views to reach a decision. CONFER.

consultant *noun*
One who advises another, esp. officially or professionally. ADVISER.

consultation *noun*
An exchange of views in an attempt to reach a decision. DELIBERATION.

consultative *adjective*
Giving advice. ADVISORY.

consultatory *adjective*
Giving advice. ADVISORY.

consulting *adjective*
Giving advice. ADVISORY.

consume *verb*
1. To eat completely or entirely: *consumed eight pancakes in a flash.*
2. To take (food) into the body as nourishment.
3. To do away with completely and destructively: *a body consumed with cancer; a building consumed by flames.*
4. To use all of.
5. To be depleted.
6. To spend (money) excessively and usu. foolishly.
7. To occupy the full attention of.
8. To use up foolishly or needlessly.

1. **Syns:** devour, dispatch, eat up, polish off (*Informal*), punish (*Informal*), put away, shift.
2. EAT.
3. **Syns:** devour, eat, eat up, swallow (up), waste.
4. EXHAUST.
5. GO *verb.*
6. WASTE *verb.*
7. ABSORB.
8. WASTE *verb.*

consumed *adjective*
Having one's thoughts fully occupied. ABSORBED.

consumer *noun*
One who consumes goods and services: *gas consumers.* **Syns:** customer, user.

consuming *adjective*
Catching and holding the full attention. ABSORBING.

consummate *verb*
To bring or come to a natural or proper end. CLOSE[1] *verb.*

consummate *adjective*
1. Supremely excellent in quality or nature.
2. Completely such, without qualification or exception.

1. PERFECT *adjective.*
2. UTTER[2].

consummation *noun*
1. A concluding or terminating.
2. The condition of being fulfilled.

1. END *noun.*
2. FULFILLMENT.

consumption *noun*
1. A quantity consumed: *Gas consumption has markedly increased.*
2. A contagious disease producing lesions esp. of the lungs.

1. **Syns:** usage, use.
2. TUBERCULOSIS.

consumptive *adjective*
1. Tending to consume and destroy: *tasks consumptive of my time; a consumptive fire.*
2. *Path.* Pertaining to or afflicted with tuberculosis.

1. **Syns:** desolating, ravaging, wasting.
2. TUBERCULAR.

contact *noun*
1. A coming together so as to be touching: *body contact.*
2. A situation allowing exchange of ideas or messages.
3. An acquaintance who is in a position to help: *received the information from a government contact.*

1. **Syns:** contingence, touch.
2. TOUCH *noun.*
3. **Syns:** connection (*Slang*), source.

contact *verb*
1. To bring into or make contact with: *a burn where the acid contacted his body.*
2. *Informal.* To succeed in communicating with.

1. **Syn:** touch.
2. REACH.

contagion *noun*
Anything that is injurious, destructive, or fatal. POISON *noun.*

contagious *adjective*
Capable of transmission by infection.

COMMUNICABLE.

contain *verb*
1. To have within: *Orange juice contains vitamin C.*
2. To have as an integral part: *The estate contains a manor house and grounds.*

3. To have the room or capacity for.
4. To bring one's emotions under control.

1. **Syns:** have, hold.
2. **Syns:** comprehend, comprise, embody, embrace, encompass, have, include, involve, subsume, take in.
3. ACCOMMODATE.
4. COMPOSE.

contaminant *noun*
One that contaminates: *sewage and other contaminants.*

Syns: adulterant, adulterator, contamination, contaminator, impurity, poison, pollutant.

contaminate *verb*
1. To make physically impure: *water contaminated with radioactive wastes.*

2. To make morally impure.

1. **Syns:** befoul, foul, poison, pollute.
   Near-syns: dirty, ruin, soil, spoil.
   Ant: purify.
2. TAINT *verb.*

contaminated *adjective*
Ceremonially or religiously unfit.

IMPURE.

contaminating *adjective*
Morally detrimental.

UNWHOLESOME.

contamination *noun*
1. The state of being contaminated: *radioactive contamination.*
2. One that contaminates.

1. **Syns:** adulteration, pollution.

2. CONTAMINANT.

contaminative *adjective*
Morally detrimental.

UNWHOLESOME.

contaminator *noun*
One that contaminates.

CONTAMINANT.

contemn *verb*
To regard with utter contempt and disdain.

DESPISE.

contemplate *verb*
1. To have in mind as a goal or purpose.
2. To direct the eyes on an object.
3. To consider carefully and at length.

1. INTEND.
2. LOOK *verb.*
3. PONDER.

contemplative *adjective*
Of, characterized by, or disposed to thought.

THOUGHTFUL.

contemporanean *noun*
1. A person of the present age.
2. One of the same time or age as another.

1. CONTEMPORARY *noun.*
2. CONTEMPORARY *noun.*

contemporanean *adjective*
Belonging to the same period of time as another.

CONTEMPORARY *adjective.*

contemporaneous *adjective*
Belonging to the same period of time as another.

CONTEMPORARY *adjective.*

contemporary *adjective*
1. Belonging to the same period of time as another: *a fact documented by two contemporary sources.*

1. **Syns:** coetaneous, coeval, coexistent, concurrent, contemporanean, contemporaneous, synchronic (*also* synchronical), synchronous.
   Near-syns: coincident, concomitant; current, existing, present; connected, related, simultaneous.

2. In existence now.
3. Modern: *was very contemporary in his thinking.*

2. PRESENT[1] *adjective.*
3. **Syns:** au courant (*French*), mod (*Informal*), up-to-date, up-to-the-minute.

4. Existing or occurring at the same moment.

4. SIMULTANEOUS.

contemporary *noun*
1. One of the same time or age as another: *a contemporary of Tolstoy.*

1. **Syns:** coeval, contemporanean.

2. A person of the present age: *Shostakovich and other contemporaries.*

2. Syns: contemporanean, modern.

contemporize *verb*
To make contemporary.

MODERNIZE.

contempt *noun*
1. The disposition boldly to defy or resist authority or an opposing force.
2. The feeling of despising.

1. DEFIANCE.
2. DESPISAL.

contempt *verb*
Archaic. To regard with utter contempt and disdain.

DESPISE.

contemptible *adjective*
1. Having or proceeding from low moral standards.
2. So objectionable as to elicit despisal.

1. SORDID.
2. FILTHY.

contemptuous *adjective*
Marked by defiance.

DEFIANT.

contend *verb*
1. To strive in opposition to: *contended with heavy traffic; two nations contending for nuclear superiority.*

1. Syns: battle, combat, fight, oppugn, struggle, tilt, vie, war, wrestle.
Near-syns: contest, oppose, resist, withstand.

2. To state to be true.
3. To strive against (others) for victory.
4. To put forth reasons for or against.
5. To engage in a quarrel.

2. CLAIM *verb.*
3. COMPETE.
4. ARGUE.
5. ARGUE.

contender *noun*
One that competes.

COMPETITOR.

content *adjective*
Having achieved satisfaction, as of one's goal.

FULFILLED.

contention *noun*
1. A state of disagreement and disharmony.
2. A discussion, often heated, in which a difference of opinion is expressed.
3. A statement of something as fact.
4. A hypothetical, controversial proposition.

1. CONFLICT *noun.*
2. ARGUMENT.
3. CLAIM *noun.*
4. THESIS.

contentious *adjective*
1. Inclined to act in a hostile way.
2. Having or showing an eagerness to fight.
3. Given to arguing.

1. AGGRESSIVE.
2. BELLIGERENT.
3. ARGUMENTATIVE.

contentiousness *noun*
1. Hostile behavior.
2. Warlike or hostile attitude or nature.
3. The power or will to fight.

1. AGGRESSION.
2. BELLIGERENCE.
3. FIGHT *noun.*

conterminous *adjective*
Sharing a common boundary.

ADJOINING.

contest *verb*
1. To take a stand against: *contested the court ruling.*

1. Syns: buck[1], challenge, combat, dispute, fight, oppose, recalcitrate, resist, traverse.
Near-syns: duel, repel, withstand; assail, assault, attack; frustrate, thwart.
Ant: capitulate.

2. To strive against (others) for victory.

2. COMPETE.

contest *noun*
1. A struggle with others for victory or supremacy.
2. A trial of skill or ability.

1. COMPETITION.
2. COMPETITION.

contestant *noun*
One that competes.

COMPETITOR.

contestation *noun*
A hypothetical, controversial proposition.

THESIS.

contested *adjective*
In doubt or dispute.   DEBATABLE.

contexture *noun*
A distinctive, complex underlying pattern or structure.   TEXTURE.

contiguous *adjective*
Sharing a common boundary.   ADJOINING.

continent *adjective*
Exercising moderation and self-restraint in appetites   TEMPERATE.
and behavior.

contingence *noun*
A coming together so as to be touching.   CONTACT *noun*.

contingency *noun*
Something that may occur or be done.   POSSIBILITY.

contingent *adjective*
1. Determined or to be determined by someone or   1. DEPENDENT *adjective*.
   something else.
2. Occurring unexpectedly.   2. ACCIDENTAL *adjective*.

continual *adjective*
Existing or occurring without interruption or end: *were*   ***Syns:*** ceaseless, constant, continuous,
irritated by their continual complaints.   endless, eternal, everlasting, incessant,
                                                    interminable, nonstop, perpetual,
                                                    relentless, round-the-clock (*also* around-
                                                    the-clock), timeless, unceasing, unending,
                                                    uninterrupted, unremitting.
                                                    Near-ants: ephemeral, evanescent, short-
                                                    lived, temporary, transient.

continuance *noun*
An uninterrupted course: *were concerned about the*   ***Syns:*** continuation, persistence (*also*
continuance of the symptoms.   persistency), run.

continuation *noun*
1. Uninterrupted existence or succession: *a*   1. ***Syns:*** continuity, continuum, duration,
   continuation of the hostilities.   endurance, persistence (*also*
                                                        persistency).
2. An uninterrupted course.   2. CONTINUANCE.

continue *verb*
1. To go on after an interruption: *I continued working*   1. ***Syns:*** pick up, recommence, renew,
   after lunch.   reopen, restart, resume, take up.
                                                        Near-ants: cease, discontinue, end,
                                                        halt, postpone, quit, stop.
2. To remain in existence or in a certain state for an   2. ENDURE.
   indefinitely long time.

continuing *adjective*
1. Existing or remaining in the same state for an   1. ***Syns:*** abiding, enduring, inveterate,
   indefinitely long time: *enjoyed a continuing*   lasting, long-lasting, long-lived, long-
   friendship with them.   standing, old, perdurable, perennial.
2. Of long duration.   2. CHRONIC.

continuity *noun*
Uninterrupted existence or succession.   CONTINUATION.

continuous *adjective*
Existing or occurring without interruption or end. CONTINUAL.

continuum *noun*
Uninterrupted existence or succession.   CONTINUATION.

contort *verb*
To alter and spoil the natural form or appearance of.   DEFORM.

contour *noun*
A line marking and shaping the outer form of an   OUTLINE *noun*.
object.

contra *noun*
That which is diametrically opposed to another.   OPPOSITE *noun*.

contraband *verb*
To import or export secretly and illegally.   SMUGGLE.

contrabandist *noun*
A person who engages in smuggling.   SMUGGLER.

contract *verb*
1. To enter into a formal agreement: *contracted with*   1. **Syns:** bargain, covenant.
   local workers to harvest the cucumbers.
2. To become affected with a disease: *contracted*   2. **Syns:** catch, develop, get, sicken, take.
   diphtheria.   —*Idiom* come down with.
3. To reduce in size by or as if by drawing together: 3. **Syns:** compress, constrict, shrink.
   contract an arm muscle.
4. To assume an obligation.   4. PLEDGE *verb*.

contract *noun*
1. A legally binding arrangement between parties.   1. AGREEMENT.
2. An agreement, esp. one involving a sale or   2. BARGAIN *noun*
   exchange.

contradict *verb*
1. To fail to be in accord.   1. CONFLICT *verb*.
2. To refuse to admit the truth, reality, value, or worth 2. DENY.
   of.

contradiction *noun*
A refusal to grant the truth of a statement or charge.   DENIAL.

contradictory *adjective*
Diametrically opposed.   OPPOSITE *adjective*.

contradictory *noun*
That which is diametrically opposed to another.   OPPOSITE *noun*.

contradistinction *noun*
1. The condition of being in conflict.   1. OPPOSITION.
2. Striking difference between compared individuals.   2. CONTRAST *noun*.

contradistinguish *verb*
To compare so as to reveal differences.   CONTRAST *verb*.

contraposition *noun*
1. The condition of being in conflict.   1. OPPOSITION.
2. That which is diametrically opposed to another.   2. OPPOSITE *noun*.

contraption *noun*
1. Something, as a machine, devised for a particular   1. DEVICE.
   function.
2. A small, specialized mechanical device.   2. GADGET.

contrariety *noun*
The condition of being in conflict.   OPPOSITION.

contrarious *adjective*
Rare. Given to acting in opposition to others.   CONTRARY *adjective*

contrary *adjective*
1. Characterized by a natural or innate opposition: *a*   1. **Syns:** antipathetic, antithetical (*also*
   policy contrary to ethical principles.   antithetic), antonymous, opposite,
                                                             repugnant (*Logic*).
2. Given to acting in opposition to others: *a contrary* 2. **Syns:** balky, contrarious (*Rare*),
   person who refused to conform.   difficult, froward, impossible, ornery,
                                                             perverse, wayward.
3. Diametrically opposed.   3. OPPOSITE *adjective*.

contrary *noun*
1. The condition of being in conflict.   1. OPPOSITION.
2. That which is diametrically opposed to another.   2. OPPOSITE *noun*.

contrast *verb*
To compare so as to reveal differences: *a poem*   **Syns:** contradistinguish, set off (against).
contrasting good and evil.

contrast *noun*
Striking difference between compared individuals: *the*   **Syns:** contradistinction, counterpoint.
contrast between father and son.

contravene *verb*
1. To fail to fulfill (a promise) or conform to (a   1. VIOLATE.
   regulation).

2. To refuse to admit the truth, reality, value, or worth
of.

contravention *noun*
An act or instance of breaking a law or regulation or of
nonfulfillment of an obligation, promise, etc.

contretemps *noun*
An unexpected and usu. undesirable event.

contribute *verb*
1. To give in common with others: *All employees
contributed to the retirement fund.*

2. To have a share in (an act, result, etc.), have a hand
in: *All of us contributed to the cost over: un.*
3. To present as a gift to a charity or cause.

contribution *noun*
Something given to a charity or cause.

contributive *adjective*
Tending to contribute to a result: *factors contributive to
international tension.*

contributor *noun*
1. A person who gives to a charity or cause.
2. A person instrumental in the growth of something,
esp. in its early stages.
3. A person who supports or champions an activity,
institution, etc.

contributory *adjective*
Giving or able to give help or support.

contrite *adjective*
1. Expressing or inclined to express an apology.
2. Feeling or expressing regret for one's sins or
misdeeds.

contriteness *noun*
A feeling of regret for one's sins or misdeeds.

contrition *noun*
A feeling of regret for one's sins or misdeeds.

contrivance *noun*
1. Something invented.
2. A small, specialized mechanical device.
3. Something, as a machine, devised for a particular
function.

contrive *verb*
1. To use ingenuity in making, developing, or
achieving.
2. To form a strategy for.

contrived *adjective*
Pretentiously artistic.

control *verb*
1. To exercise authority or influence over: *The Romans
controlled a huge empire.*

2. To bring one's emotions under control.
3. To keep the mechanical operation of (a device)
within proper parameters.

control *noun*
1. The right and power to command, decide, rule, or
judge.
2. The act of exercising controlling power or the
condition of being so controlled.
3. The continuous exercise of authority over a political
unit.

---

2. DENY.

BREACH *noun*.

ACCIDENT.

1. *Syns:* chip in (*Informal*), come across
(*Slang*), come through (*Informal*),
donate, kick in (*Slang*), subscribe.
2. *Syns:* conduce (to *or* toward), partake
(in), share (in).
3. DONATE.

DONATION.

Syn: conducive.

1. DONOR.
2. BUILDER.

3. PATRON.

AUXILIARY *adjective*.

1. APOLOGETIC *adjective*.
2. REMORSEFUL.

PENITENCE.

PENITENCE.

1. INVENTION.
2. GADGET.
3. DEVICE.

1. INVENT.

2. DESIGN *verb*.

ARTY.

1. *Syns:* direct, dominate, govern, rule.
—*Idioms* be at the helm, be in the
driver's seat, hold sway over, hold the
reins.
2. COMPOSE.
3. GOVERN.

1. AUTHORITY.

2. DOMINATION.

3. GOVERNMENT.

4. The keeping of one's thoughts and emotions to oneself.

4. RESERVE *noun*.

controllable *adjective*
Capable of being governed.

GOVERNABLE.

controlled *adjective*
Tending to keep one's thoughts and emotions to oneself.

RESERVED.

controlling *adjective*
Exercising controlling power or influence.

DOMINANT.

controversy *noun*
A discussion, often heated, in which a difference of opinion is expressed.

ARGUMENT.

controvert *verb*
To refuse to admit the truth, reality, value, or worth of.

DENY.

contumacious *adjective*
Marked by defiance.

DEFIANT.

contumacy *noun*
The disposition boldly to defy or resist authority or an opposing force.

DEFIANCE.

contumelious *adjective*
1. Of, relating to, or characterized by verbal abuse.
2. Rude and disrespectful.

1. ABUSIVE.
2. IMPUDENT.

contumely *noun*
1. Harsh, often insulting language.
2. An act that offends a person's sense of pride or dignity.

1. VITUPERATION.
2. INDIGNITY.

contuse *verb*
To make or receive a bruise or bruises on.

BRUISE *verb*.

conundrum *noun*
Anything that arouses curiosity or perplexes because it is unexplained, inexplicable, or secret.

MYSTERY.

convalesce *verb*
To regain one's health.

RECOVER.

convene *verb*
1. To demand to appear, come, or assemble.
2. To bring together.
3. To come together.

1. CALL *verb*.
2. ASSEMBLE.
3. ASSEMBLE.

convenience *noun*
Anything that increases physical comfort.

AMENITY.

convenience *verb*
To perform a service or a courteous act.

OBLIGE.

convenient *adjective*
1. Suited to one's end or purpose: *found a convenient excuse not to go.*

2. Being within easy reach: *found a convenient location for the shelves.*

1. **Syns:** appropriate, befitting, expedient, fit, good, meet[2] (*Archaic*), proper, suitable, tailor-made, useful.
2. **Syns:** close-at-hand, close-by, handy, near-at-hand, nearby.
Near-syns: close, near, nigh; immediate, neighboring, next.
Ant: inconvenient.

convention *noun*
1. A formal assemblage of the members of a group: *a medical convention.*
2. A legally binding arrangement between parties.
3. A formal, usu. written settlement between nations.
4. An accepted way of doing something: *social conventions.*

1. **Syns:** assembly, conference, congress, convocation, meeting.
2. AGREEMENT.
3. TREATY.
4. **Syns:** consuetude, form, usage.

conventional *adjective*
1. Conforming to established practice or standards: *conventional attire; a conventional view of society.*

1. **Syns:** button-down (*Informal*), conformist, establishmentarian, orthodox, square (*Slang*), straight (*Slang*), traditional.

Near-syns: conservative; temperate; constrained, restrained.
Ant: unconventional.

2. Generally approved or agreed upon.
3. Fond of or given to ceremony.

2. ACCEPTED.
3. CEREMONIOUS.

conventionalize *verb*
To make conventional: *conventionalized decorating schemes.*

Syns: conform, stylize.

converge *verb*
1. To come together.
2. To direct toward a common center.

1. CLOSE[1] *verb.*
2. CONCENTRATE.

convergence *noun*
1. A converging at a common center.
2. The act or fact of coming near.
3. The act or fact of coming together.

1. CONCENTRATION.
2. APPROACH *noun.*
3. JUNCTION.

conversant *adjective*
1. Having good knowledge of.
2. Marked by comprehension, cognizance, and perception.

1. FAMILIAR *adjective.*
2. AWARE.

conversation *noun*
Spoken exchange: *a telephone conversation with a friend.*

Syns: chat, colloquy, confabulation, converse[1], coze, dialogue (*also* dialog), parley, talk.

conversational *adjective*
1. In the style of conversation: *a conversational narrative.*
2. Given to conversation.

1. **Syns:** chatty, colloquial, confabulatory, informal.
2. TALKATIVE.

conversationalist *also* **conversationist** *noun*
One given to conversation: *an excellent conversationalist at parties.*

Syns: colloquialist, colloquist, confabulator, discourser, talker.
SEE **conversationalist.**

conversationist *noun*

converse[1] *verb*
To engage in spoken exchange: *conversed softly in the corner.*

Syns: chat, confabulate, coze, discourse, speak, talk, visit (*Informal*).

converse *noun*
1. Spoken exchange.
2. *Rare.* The exchange of ideas by writing, speech, or signals.

1. CONVERSATION.
2. COMMUNICATION.

converse[2] *adjective*
Diametrically opposed.

OPPOSITE *adjective.*

converse *noun*
That which is diametrically opposed to another.

OPPOSITE *noun.*

conversion *noun*
1. A usu. physical change of one thing into another: *the company's conversion from domestic to military production.*

1. **Syns:** alteration, changeover, shift, transformation.
Near-syns: change, modification, qualification; innovation, novelty.

2. The process or result of giving a different form or appearance.

2. CHANGE *noun.*

3. A fundamental change in one's beliefs: *conversion from the Methodist to the Catholic faith.*

3. **Syns:** metanoia, rebirth, regeneration.

convert *verb*
1. To change into a different form, substance, or state: *convert water into ice; convert a country from democracy to police state.*

1. **Syns:** commute, metamorphize, metamorphose, mutate, transfer, transfigure, transform, translate, transmogrify, transmute, transpose, transubstantiate.

2. To convince (another) to adopt a particular faith or belief: *Missionaries converted the islanders to Christianity.*

2. **Syns:** lead, persuade.

convey *verb*
1. To cause to come along with oneself.
2. To move while supporting.
3. To cause to be transferred from one to another.
4. To serve as a conduit.
5. To make known.
6. To put into words.
7. To give expression to, as by gestures, facial aspects, or bodily posture.
8. To cause (a disease) to pass to another or others.
9. *Law.* To change the ownership of (property) by means of a legal document.

1. BRING.
2. CARRY *verb.*
3. PASS *verb.*
4. CONDUCT *verb.*
5. COMMUNICATE.
6. SAY *verb.*
7. EXPRESS *verb.*
8. COMMUNICATE.
9. TRANSFER.

conveyance *noun*
1. The moving of persons or goods from one place to another.
2. *Law.* A making over of legal ownership or title.
3. *Archaic.* The crime of taking someone else's property without consent.

1. TRANSPORTATION.
2. GRANT *noun.*
3. LARCENY.

conviction *noun*
1. Something believed or accepted as true by a person.
2. The fact or condition of being without doubt.

1. BELIEF.
2. SURENESS.

convince *verb*
1. To cause (another) to believe something: *Convince me that I'm wrong!*
2. To succeed in causing (a person) to act in a certain way.

1. *Syns:* assure, persuade, satisfy, win over.
2. PERSUADE.

convincing *adjective*
1. Serving to convince: *a convincing argument.*

1. *Syns:* cogent, persuasive, satisfactory, satisfying, solid, sound[2], telling. *Near-syns:* conclusive, decisive, definitive, demonstrated, established, validated, verified. *Ant:* unconvincing.

2. Worthy of belief because of precision, faithfulness to an original, etc.

2. AUTHENTIC.

convivial *adjective*
1. Liking company.
2. Spent, marked by, or enjoyed in the company of others.
3. Of or befitting a friend or friends.

1. COMPANIONABLE.
2. SOCIAL.
3. FRIENDLY.

convocation *noun*
1. A formal assemblage of the members of a group.
2. A number of persons who have come or been gathered together.

1. CONVENTION.
2. ASSEMBLY.

convoke *verb*
1. To demand to appear, come, or assemble.
2. To bring together.

1. CALL *verb.*
2. ASSEMBLE.

convoluted *adjective*
Difficult to understand due to intricacy.

COMPLEX *adjective.*

convulse *verb*
To cause to move to and fro violently.

AGITATE.

convulsion *noun*
1. The condition of being physically agitated.
2. A condition of anguished struggle and disorder.
3. A momentous or sweeping change.

1. AGITATION.
2. THROE.
3. REVOLUTION.

cook *verb*
To prepare (food) for eating by the use of heat: *cooked his steak rare.*

Syn: do.

cook up *verb*
Informal. To use ingenuity in making, developing, or achieving.

INVENT.

cook *noun*
A person who prepares food for eating: *an excellent cook.*

Syns: chef, cuisinier.

cook up *verb*

SEE **cook.**

cool *adjective*
1. Not easily excited, even under pressure: *a cool and controlled person.*

1. *Syns:* calm, collected, composed, cool-headed, detached, disimpassioned, even[1], even-tempered, imperturbable, nonchalant, unflappable (*Slang*), unruffled.
Near-ants: fervent, fervid, impassioned, passionate; perturbed, upset.
Ant: agitated.

2. Not friendly, sociable, or warm in manner: *a shy, cool person.*

2. *Syns:* aloof, chilly, distant, frosty, offish, remote, reserved, reticent, solitary, standoffish, unapproachable, uncommunicative, undemonstrative, withdrawn.

3. Marked by a low temperature.
4. *Slang.* Particularly excellent.

3. COLD *adjective.*
4. MARVELOUS.

cool *verb*
To bring one's emotions under control.

COMPOSE.

cool *noun*
1. *Slang.* A stable, calm state of the emotions.
2. *Slang.* The state or quality of being nonchalant.
3. *Slang.* Lack of emotional agitation.

1. BALANCE *noun.*
2. NONCHALANCE.
3. CALM *noun.*

cooler *noun*
Slang. A place for the confinement of persons in lawful detention.

JAIL *noun.*

cool-headed *adjective*
Not easily excited, even under pressure.

COOL *adjective.*

coolie also **cooly** *noun*
One who labors.

LABORER.

coolness *noun*
1. Relative lack of warmth.
2. A stable, calm state of the emotions.

1. COLD *noun.*
2. BALANCE *noun.*

coolth *noun*
Relative lack of warmth.

COLD *noun.*

cooly *noun*

SEE **coolie.**

coop *verb*
To confine within a limited area.

ENCLOSE.

coop *noun*
Slang. A place for the confinement of persons in lawful detention.

JAIL *noun.*

cooperant *adjective*
Working together toward a common end.

COOPERATIVE.

cooperate *verb*
To work together toward a common end: *The two agencies cooperated on the energy policy.*

Syns: coadjute, collaborate.

cooperation *noun*
1. Joint work toward a common end: *mutual cooperation among the allies to achieve peace.*
2. The state of being associated.

1. *Syns:* coadjuvancy, coagency, collaboration, synergy, teamwork.
2. ASSOCIATION.

cooperative *adjective*
Working together toward a common end: *a cooperative effort.*

Syns: coefficient, collaborative, cooperant, synergetic.
Near-ants: competitive; antagonistic, conflicting.
Ant: uncooperative.

coordinate also **co-ordinate** *verb*
1. To bring into accord.

1. HARMONIZE.

2. To combine and adapt in order to attain a particular effect.　**2.** HARMONIZE.

cop *noun*
Informal. A member of a law-enforcement agency.　POLICEMAN.
　cop *verb*
　1. *Slang.* To obtain possession or control of.　**1.** CAPTURE.
　2. *Slang.* To take (another's property) without permission.　**2.** STEAL *verb.*

copartner *noun*
One who is united in a relationship with another.　ASSOCIATE *noun.*

copious *adjective*
　1. Characterized by abundance.　**1.** GENEROUS.
　2. Large in number or yield.　**2.** HEAVY *adjective.*

copper *noun*
Slang. A member of a law-enforcement agency.　POLICEMAN.

copulate *verb*
To engage in sexual relations with.　TAKE *verb.*

copy *noun*
　1. An inferior substitute imitating an original: *an inexpensive copy of the tiara.*　**1.** *Syns:* brummagem, ersatz, imitation, pinchbeck, simulacrum (*also* simulacre), simulation.
　2. Something closely resembling another: *copies of Louis XV furniture.*　**2.** *Syns:* duplicate, facsimile, reduplication, replica, replication, reproduction. —*Idiom* carbon copy.
　3. A representation of a person or thing.　**3.** LIKENESS.
　copy *verb*
　1. To make a copy of: *copied an original design.*　**1.** *Syns:* duplicate, image, imitate, reduplicate, replicate, reproduce. *Near-syns:* counterfeit, fake, sham, simulate; burlesque, mock, parody. *Ant:* originate.
　2. To take as a model.　**2.** FOLLOW.

coquet *verb*
To make amorous advances without serious intentions.　FLIRT *verb.*

coquetry *noun*
The practice of flirting.　FLIRTATION.

coquette *noun*
A woman who leads men on.　FLIRT *noun.*

coquettish *adjective*
Given to flirting.　FLIRTATIOUS.

cordial *adjective*
　1. Characterized by kindness and warm, unaffected courtesy.　**1.** GRACIOUS.
　2. Pleasant and friendly.　**2.** AMIABLE.

cordiality *noun*
The quality of being pleasant and friendly.　AMIABILITY.

core *noun*
　1. The most central and material part.　**1.** HEART.
　2. A point of origin from which ideas, influences, etc., emanate.　**2.** CENTER *noun.*

corkscrew *verb*
To move or proceed on a repeatedly curving course.　WIND^2.

corky *adjective*
Informal. Displaying light-hearted nonchalance.　AIRY.

corner *noun*
　1. A difficult, embarrassing situation.　**1.** PREDICAMENT.
　2. Exclusive control or possession.　**2.** MONOPOLY.

cornerstone *noun*
A fundamental principle or underlying concept.　BASIS.

corny *adjective*
Slang. Without freshness or appeal due to overuse.　TRITE.

corollary *noun*
Something brought about by a cause.   EFFECT *noun*.
corporal *adjective*
Of or pertaining to the human body.   BODILY.
corporation *noun*
A commercial organization.   COMPANY *noun*.
corporeal *adjective*
1. Of or pertaining to the human body.   1. BODILY.
2. Composed of or relating to things that occupy space   2. PHYSICAL.
   and can be perceived by the senses.
corps *noun*
1. A group of people organized for a particular purpose.   1. FORCE *noun*.
2. A group of performers.   2. BAND² *noun*.
corpse *noun*
The physical frame of a dead person or animal.   BODY *noun*.
corpselike *adjective*
Gruesomely suggestive of ghosts or death.   GHASTLY.
corpulent *adjective*
Having too much flesh.   FAT *adjective*.
corpus *noun*
1. The physical frame of a dead person or animal.   1. BODY *noun*.
2. The main part.   2. BODY *noun*.
3. A measurable whole.   3. QUANTITY.
correct *verb*
1. To make right what is wrong: *correct an error*.   1. ***Syns:*** amend, emend, mend, rectify,
                                                              remedy, right.
                                                              Near-ants: damage, harm, hurt, impair,
                                                              injure, mar, spoil, wreck.
2. To castigate for the purpose of improving: *correct a* 2. ***Syns:*** chasten, chastise, rebuke,
   child for being rude.   reprove.
3. To subject (one) to a penalty for a wrong.   3. PUNISH.
correct *adjective*
1. Having no errors.   1. ACCURATE.
2. Conforming to fact.   2. ACCURATE.
3. Conforming to accepted standards: *correct social*   3. ***Syns:*** au fait (*French*), becoming,
   behavior.   befitting, comely, comme il faut
                                                              (*French*), decent, decorous, de rigueur
                                                              (*French*), nice, proper, respectable,
                                                              right, seemly.
4. Suitable for a particular person, condition, occasion, 4. APPROPRIATE *adjective*
   or place.
correction *noun*
A penalty imposed for wrongdoing.   PUNISHMENT.
corrective *adjective*
Tending to correct: *took corrective measures to ease the* ***Syns:*** emendatory, reformatory, remedial.
tension.
  corrective *noun*
  Something that corrects or counteracts.   REMEDY *noun*.
correctly *adverb*
In a fair, sporting manner.   FAIR *adverb*.
correctness *noun*
1. Freedom from error.   1. ACCURACY.
2. Correspondence with fact or truth.   2. VERACITY.
3. Conformity to recognized standards, as of conduct or   3. DECENCY.
   appearance.
correlate *verb*
To come or bring together in one's mind or imagination.   ASSOCIATE *verb*.
  correlate *noun*
  Something closely resembling or analogous to   PARALLEL *noun*.
  something else.

correlation *noun*
A logical or natural association between two or more things.

RELATION.

correspond *verb*
1. To be compatible or in correspondence.
2. To be equal or alike.
3. To be equivalent.

1. AGREE.
2. COMPARE.
3. AMOUNT *verb*.

correspond to *verb*
To be in keeping with.

FIT *verb*.

correspondence *noun*
1. The act or state of agreeing or conforming.
2. Logical agreement among things or parts.

1. AGREEMENT.
2. CONSISTENCY.

correspondent *noun*
Something closely resembling or analogous to something else.

PARALLEL *noun*.

correspondent *adjective*
In keeping with one's needs or expectations.

AGREEABLE.

corresponding *adjective*
1. In keeping with one's needs or expectations.
2. Possessing the same or almost the same characteristics.

1. AGREEABLE.
2. LIKE².

correspond to *verb*

SEE **correspond.**

corrival *noun*
One that competes.

COMPETITOR.

corrivalry *noun*
A struggle with others for victory or supremacy.

COMPETITION.

corroborate *verb*
1. To present evidence in support of.
2. To assure the certainty or validity of.
3. To establish as true or genuine.

1. BACK *verb*.
2. CONFIRM.
3. PROVE.

corroboration *noun*
That which confirms.

CONFIRMATION.

corrode *verb*
To consume gradually, as by chemical reaction, friction, etc.

BITE *verb*.

corrosive *adjective*
1. Given to or expressing sarcasm.
2. Serving to corrupt.

1. SARCASTIC.
2. CORRUPTIVE.

corrosiveness *noun*
Ironic, bitter humor designed to wound.

SARCASM.

corrupt *adjective*
1. Utterly reprehensible in nature or behavior: *a corrupt parent who debased the child.*

1. *Syns:* degenerate, depraved, flagitious, miscreant, nefarious, perverse, rotten, unhealthy, villainous.
Near-syns: crooked, devious, shadowy; baneful, deleterious, detrimental, noxious, pernicious; infamous, vile.
Ants: honest, pure.

2. Marked by dishonesty, esp. in matters of public trust: *corrupt police officers who accepted bribes.*

2. *Syns:* crooked, dishonest, venal.

3. Ruthlessly seeking personal advantage: *corrupt politicians who line their pockets at taxpayers' expense.*

3. *Syns:* mercenary, praetorian, unethical, unprincipled, unscrupulous, venal.

corrupt *verb*
1. To ruin utterly in character or quality: *public taste corrupted by pornography.*

1. *Syns:* animalize, bastardize, bestialize, brutalize, canker, debase, debauch, demoralize, deprave, pervert, stain, vitiate, warp.

2. To make morally impure.

2. TAINT *verb*.

3. To subject (someone having the public's trust) to improper influence: *The mob corrupted the city council.*

corrupted *adjective*
Lowered in character or quality: *a man corrupted by his lust for power.*

corruptible *adjective*
Capable of being bribed: *a corruptible congressman— easy pickings for the mob.*

corrupting *adjective*
Morally detrimental.

corruption *noun*
1. Immoral, degrading acts or habits: *condemned the luxury and corruption of the ruling classes.*
2. Departure from what is legally, ethically, and morally correct: *impeached for corruption in high office.*
3. A term whose form offends against established usage standards: *Many writers consider "finalize" a corruption of good English.*

corruptive *adjective*
Serving to corrupt: *The presence of drugs was a corruptive factor.*

corruptness *noun*
Departure from what is legally, ethically, and morally correct.

coruscate *verb*
1. To shine with intermittent gleams.
2. To emit light suddenly in rays or sparks.

coruscation *noun*
A sudden quick light.

cosmic *adjective*
So pervasive and all-inclusive as to exist in or affect the whole world.

cosmopolitan *adjective*
1. Experienced in the ways of the world; lacking natural simplicity.
2. So pervasive and all-inclusive as to exist in or affect the whole world.

cosmos *noun*
The totality of all existing things.

cosset *verb*
To treat with indulgence and often overtender care.

cost *noun*
1. An amount paid or to be paid for a purchase: *The cost of the dress is $60.*
2. Something expended to obtain a benefit or desired result: *Production costs offset sales.*
3. A loss sustained in the accomplishment of or as the result of something: *a revolution brought about at the cost of many lives.*

cost *verb*
To require a specified price: *The painting costs $10,000.*

cost-free *adjective*
Costing nothing.

costive *adjective*
Ungenerously or pettily reluctant to spend money.

costly *adjective*
1. Bringing a high price: *costly paintings.*

---

3. *Syns:* buy, purchase.

Syns: debased, debauched, depraved, perverted, vitiated. —*Idiom* gone to the dogs.

Syns: buyable, purchasable, venal.

UNWHOLESOME.

1. *Syns:* depravity, immorality, turpitude, vice, wickedness.
2. *Syns:* corruptness, crookedness, dishonesty, improbity.

3. *Syns:* barbarism, solecism, vulgarism.

Syns: corrosive, injurious.

CORRUPTION.

1. BLINK *verb.*
2. FLASH *verb.*

BLINK *noun.*

UNIVERSAL *adjective.*

1. SOPHISTICATED.

2. UNIVERSAL *adjective.*

UNIVERSE.

BABY *verb.*

1. *Syns:* charge, price, tab.

2. *Syns:* disbursement, expense, expenditure, outlay.
3. *Syns:* expense, price, sacrifice, toll[1].

Syns: go for, sell for.

FREE *adjective.*

STINGY.

1. *Syns:* dear, expensive, high, high-priced. —*Idiom* high as smoke.

2. Of great value.　　2. VALUABLE.

costume *noun*
Clothes or other personal effects, such as make-up, worn to conceal one's identity.　　DISGUISE *noun*.

cosy *adjective*　　SEE **cozy.**

cotton *verb*
1. To support slavishly every opinion or suggestion of a superior.　　1. FAWN.
2. *Informal.* To live or act together in harmony.　　2. GET ALONG at **get.**

couch *verb*
To convey in language or words of a particular form.　　PHRASE *verb*.

counsel *verb*
To give recommendations to (someone) about a decision or course of action.　　ADVISE.

counsel *noun*
1. An opinion as to a decision or course of action.　　1. ADVICE.
2. An exchange of views in an attempt to reach a decision.　　2. DELIBERATION.
3. One who advises another, esp. officially or professionally.　　3. ADVISER.

counselable also **counsellable** *adjective*
Worth doing, esp. for practical reasons.　　ADVISABLE.

counsellable *adjective*　　SEE **counselable.**

counsellor *noun*　　SEE **counselor.**

counselor or **counsellor** *noun*
One who advises another, esp. officially or professionally.　　ADVISER.

count *verb*
1. To note (items) one by one so as to get a total: *Count your change.*　　1. *Syns:* calculate, compute, enumerate, number, numerate, reckon, tale, tally, tell off.
2. To be of significance or importance: *an opinion that counts for naught; felt that honesty counted too.*　　2. *Syns:* import, matter, signify, weigh.
3. To indicate (time or rhythm), as with repeated gestures or sounds.　　3. BEAT *verb*.

count on *verb*
1. *Informal.* To anticipate confidently.　　1. EXPECT.
2. To place trust or confidence in.　　2. DEPEND ON at **depend.**

count out *verb*
To keep from being admitted, included, or considered.　　EXCLUDE.

count *noun*
A noting of items one by one: *kept an accurate count of the words.*　　*Syns:* numeration, reckoning, tab, tally.

countenance *noun*
1. A disposition of the facial features that conveys meaning, feeling, or mood.　　1. EXPRESSION.
2. The front surface of the head.　　2. FACE *noun*.
3. An outward appearance.　　3. FACE *noun*.

countenance *verb*
1. To be favorably disposed toward.　　1. APPROVE.
2. To lend supportive approval to.　　2. ENCOURAGE.

counter *noun*
1. That which is diametrically opposed to another.　　1. OPPOSITE *noun*.
2. A spirited, incisive reply.　　2. RETORT *noun*.

counter *verb*
1. To place in opposition or be in opposition to.　　1. OPPOSE.
2. To return like for like, esp. to return an unfriendly or hostile action with a similar one.　　2. RETALIATE.

counter *adjective*
Diametrically opposed.　　OPPOSITE *adjective*.

counteract *verb*
1. To act as an equalizing weight or force to.
2. To make ineffective by applying an opposite force or amount.

1. BALANCE *verb*.
2. CANCEL.

counteraction *noun*
The act of retaliating.

RETALIATION.

counteragent *noun*
Something that corrects or counteracts.

REMEDY *noun*.

counterattack *noun*
The act of retaliating.

RETALIATION.

counterbalance *verb*
1. To put in balance.
2. To act as an equalizing weight or force to.
3. To make up for the defects of.

1. BALANCE *verb*.
2. BALANCE *verb*.
3. COMPENSATE.

counterblow *noun*
The act of retaliating.

RETALIATION.

counterfactual *adjective*
Devoid of truth.

FALSE.

counterfeit *adjective*
Fraudulently or deceptively imitative: *counterfeit bills; counterfeit love.*

Syns: bogus, ersatz, fake, false, fraudulent, phony (*also* phoney) (*Informal*), pseudo, sham, spurious, supposititious, supposititious.

counterfeit *verb*
1. To make a fraudulent copy of: *counterfeited the signature on the check.*
2. To behave affectedly or insincerely.
3. To take on or give a false appearance of.

1. ***Syns:*** fake, falsify, forge[1].
2. ACT *verb*.
3. ASSUME.

counterfeit *noun*
A fraudulent imitation: *The painting is a clever counterfeit of an old master.*

Syns: fake, forgery, phony (*also* phoney) (*Informal*), sham.

countermeasure *noun*
Something that corrects or counteracts.

REMEDY *noun*.

counterpart *noun*
1. One holding a position corresponding to that of one in another organization or hierarchy: *Each foreign diplomat was seated next to his American counterpart at the banquet.*
2. Something closely resembling or analogous to something else.

1. ***Syn:*** vis-à-vis. —*Idiom* opposite number.
2. PARALLEL *noun*.

counterpoint *noun*
Striking difference between compared individuals.

CONTRAST *noun*.

counterpoise *noun*
A stable state characterized by the cancellation of all forces by equal opposing forces.

BALANCE *noun*.

counterpoise *verb*
1. To act as an equalizing weight or force to.
2. To make up for the defects of.

1. BALANCE *verb*.
2. COMPENSATE.

counterstroke *noun*
The act of retaliating.

RETALIATION.

countertype *noun*
Something closely resembling or analogous to something else.

PARALLEL *noun*.

countervail *verb*
1. To act as an equalizing weight or force to.
2. To make up for the defects of.

1. BALANCE *verb*.
2. COMPENSATE.

countless *adjective*
Too great to be calculated.

INCALCULABLE.

count on *verb*

SEE **count**.

count out *verb*

SEE **count**.

country *noun*
1. A rural area: *a farm in the country.*

2. An organized geopolitical unit.
3. *Informal.* A particular area used for or associated with a specific individual or activity.

country *adjective*
Of or pertaining to the countryside: *a quiet country scene.*

countryman *noun*
A person who is from one's own country: *The President addressed his countrymen.*

countryside *noun*
A rural area.

couple *noun*
1. Two items of the same kind together: *a couple of pistols; sang a couple of songs.*
2. Two persons united, as by marriage.

couple *verb*
1. To bring or come together into a united whole.
2. To join one thing to another.
3. To come or bring together in one's mind or imagination.

couple with *verb*
To engage in sexual relations with.

couple with *verb*

coupling *noun*
A point or position at which two or more things are joined.

courage *noun*
The quality of mind enabling one to face danger or hardship resolutely: *a soldier decorated for courage in battle.*

courageous *adjective*
Having or showing courage.

courageousness *noun*
The quality of mind enabling one to face danger or hardship resolutely.

courier *noun*
A person who carries messages or is sent on errands.

course *verb*
1. To move freely as a liquid.
2. To come forth or emit in abundance.

course *noun*
1. A method used in dealing with something.
2. The compass direction in which a ship or aircraft moves.
3. A number of things placed or occurring one after the other.

court *verb*
1. To attempt to gain the affection of: *court a girl.*

---

1. **Syn:** countryside. —*Idiom* God's country.
2. STATE *noun.*
3. TERRITORY.

Syns: agrestic (*also* agrestical), Arcadian, bucolic, campestral, hick (*Informal*), pastoral, provincial, rural, rustic.

Syn: compatriot. —*Idiom* fellow citizen.

COUNTRY *noun.*

1. **Syns:** brace[1], doublet, pair.

2. PAIR.

1. COMBINE *verb.*
2. ATTACH.
3. ASSOCIATE *verb.*

TAKE *verb.*

SEE **couple.**

JOINT *noun.*

Syns: braveness, bravery, courageousness, dauntlessness, fearlessness, fortitude, gallantry, guts (*Slang*), heart, intrepidity, mettle, moxie (*Slang*), nerve, pluck, resolution, spirit, spunk (*Informal*), valiancy (*also* valiance), valor.
Near-syns: audacity, boldness, heroism.
Ant: cowardice.

BRAVE *adjective.*

COURAGE.

BEARER.

1. FLOW *verb.*
2. FLOW *verb.*

1. APPROACH *noun.*
2. HEADING.

3. SERIES.

1. **Syns:** address, pursue, romance (*Informal*), rush, spark, sue (*Archaic*), woo.

2. To solicit (danger) playfully and provocatively, often unwittingly: *courted economic disaster; a stunt pilot who courted death.*

court *noun*
1. An area partially or entirely enclosed by walls or buildings: *My window opens onto a court.*

2. A judicial assembly: *called the court to order.*

courteous *adjective*
1. Characterized by good manners: *a courteous person who took my coat.*
2. Full of polite concern for the well-being of others.

courteousness *noun*
Well-mannered behavior toward others.

courter *noun*
A man who courts a woman.

courtesan *noun*
A woman who engages in sexual intercourse for payment.

courtesies *noun*
Courteous acts that contribute to smoothness and ease in dealings and social relationships.

courtesy *noun*
1. Well-mannered behavior toward others: *common courtesy.*
2. A courteous act: *Little courtesies like thank-you notes are important.*
3. An act requiring special generosity: *received free drinks by courtesy of the airline.*

courtier *noun*
One who flatters another excessively.

courting *noun*
Romantic attentions.

courtliness *noun*
Respectful attention, esp. toward women.

courtly *adjective*
1. Characterized by elaborate but usu. formal courtesy.
2. Respectfully attentive, esp. to women.
3. Fond of or given to ceremony.

courtship *noun*
Romantic attentions: *a long courtship before marriage.*

courtyard *noun*
An area partially or entirely enclosed by walls or buildings.

cove *noun*
A body of water partly enclosed by land but having a wide outlet to the sea.

covenant *noun*
1. A declaration that one will or will not do a certain thing.
2. A legally binding arrangement between parties.

covenant *verb*
1. To guarantee by a solemn promise.
2. To enter into a formal agreement.

cover *verb*
1. To extend over the surface of: *Snow covered the ground.*

---

2. **Syns:** beckon, invite, provoke, tempt, toy (with).

1. **Syns:** atrium, close², courtyard, curtilage, enclosure, quad, quadrangle, yard.
2. **Syns:** bar, lawcourt, tribunal.

1. **Syns:** civil, genteel, mannerly, polite, well-bred, well-mannered.
2. ATTENTIVE.

COURTESY.

BEAU.

PROSTITUTE.

AMENITIES.

1. **Syns:** civility, courteousness, politeness.
2. **Syn:** civility.
3. **Syns:** beau geste, compliment(s), favor, indulgence.

SYCOPHANT.

COURTSHIP.

GALLANTRY.

1. GRACIOUS.
2. GALLANT *adjective.*
3. CEREMONIOUS.

Syns: addresses, courting, suit.

COURT *noun.*

BAY¹.

1. PROMISE *noun.*

2. AGREEMENT.

1. PLEDGE *verb.*
2. CONTRACT *verb.*

1. **Syns:** blanket, cap, overcast, overlay, spread over.
Near-syns: conceal, hide, screen, shield; enclose, envelop, shroud, wrap.
Ants: bare, uncover.

2. To journey over (a specified distance).

3. *Jour.* To observe, analyze, and relate the details of (an event): *covered the elections.*

4. To prevent (something) from being known: *tried to cover up the scandal.*

cover up *verb*
To change or modify so as to prevent recognition of the true identity or character of.

cover *noun*
1. Something that physically protects, esp. from danger: *sought cover in the house from the attackers.*

2. A deceptive outward appearance.

3. A professed rather than a real reason.

coverage *noun*
Jour. The extent to which an event is reported: *election coverage.*

covert *adjective*
1. Existing or operating in a way so as to ensure complete concealment and confidentiality.

2. Lying beyond what is obvious or avowed.

covert *noun*
1. Something that physically protects, esp. from danger.

2. A hiding place.

cover up *verb*

covet *verb*
1. To have a strong longing for.
2. To feel envy for.

covetous *adjective*
1. Resentfully or painfully desirous of another's advantages.

2. Having a strong urge to obtain or possess something, esp. material wealth, in quantity.

covetousness *noun*
1. Resentful or painful desire for another's advantages.

2. Excessive desire for more than one needs or deserves.

cow *verb*
To domineer or drive into compliance by the use of threats, force, etc.

coward *noun*
An ignoble, uncourageous person: *a coward who deserted his comrades under fire.*

cowardice *noun*
Ignoble lack of courage: *desertion and other acts of cowardice.*

cowardliness *noun*
Ignoble lack of courage.

cowardly *adjective*
Ignobly lacking in courage: *cowardly turncoats.*

2. TRAVERSE *verb.*

3. *Syn:* report.

4. *Syns:* cloak, conceal, enshroud, hide[1], hush (up), mask, shroud, veil. —*Idioms* keep under cover, keep under wraps, veil in secrecy.

DISGUISE *verb.*

1. *Syns:* asylum, covert, harbor, harborage, haven, protection, refuge, retreat, sanctuary, shelter.

2. FAÇADE.

3. PRETENSE.

Syn: reportage.

1. SECRET *adjective.*

2. ULTERIOR.

1. COVER *noun.*

2. HIDE-OUT.

SEE **cover.**

1. DESIRE *verb.*
2. ENVY *verb.*

1. ENVIOUS.

2. GREEDY.

1. ENVY *noun.*
2. GREED.

INTIMIDATE.

Syns: chicken (*Slang*), craven, dastard, funk[2] (*Chiefly Brit.*), poltroon (*Archaic*), yellow-belly (*Slang*). —*Idiom* gutless wonder.

Syns: cowardliness, cravenness, dastardliness, faint-heartedness, funk[2] (*Chiefly Brit.*), gutlessness, poltroonery, pusillanimity, unmanliness, yellowness (*Slang*). —*Idioms* white feather, yellow streak.

COWARDICE.

Syns: chicken (*Slang*), chickenhearted, craven, dastardly, faint-hearted, gutless, lily-livered, pusillanimous, unmanly, yellow (*Slang*), yellow-bellied (*Slang*).

coy *adjective*
1. Given to flirting.
2. Reticent or reserved in manner.

1. FLIRTATIOUS.
2. MODEST.

coze *verb*
To engage in spoken exchange.

CONVERSE[1] *verb*.

coze *noun*
Spoken exchange.

CONVERSATION.

cozen *verb*
1. To get money or something else from by deceitful trickery.
2. To cause to accept what is false, esp. by trickery or misrepresentation.

1. CHEAT *verb*.

2. DECEIVE.

cozy also **cosy** *adjective*
Affording pleasurable ease.

COMFORTABLE.

crab *noun*
Informal. A person who habitually complains or grumbles.

GROUCH *noun*.

crabbed *adjective*
Having or showing a bad temper.

ILL-TEMPERED.

crabby *adjective*
Having or showing a bad temper.

ILL-TEMPERED.

crack *noun*
1. A usu. narrow partial opening caused by splitting and rupture: *a crack in the ice.*
2. A sudden sharp, powerful stroke.
3. A sudden sharp, explosive noise.
4. *Slang.* A brief trial.
5. A very brief time.
6. *Informal.* A flippant or sarcastic remark: *made a crack about women drivers.*

1. *Syns:* break, chink, cleft, fissure, rift, split.
2. BLOW[2].
3. REPORT *noun*.
4. TRY *noun*.
5. FLASH *noun*.
6. *Syns:* cut (*Informal*), dig, jab, quip, wisecrack.

crack *verb*
1. To make a sudden sharp, explosive noise: *The rifle cracked in the silent woods.*
2. To undergo partial breaking: *The ice cracked under my weight.*
3. To give way mentally and emotionally.
4. To suddenly lose all health or strength.
5. To find the key to.

1. *Syns:* bark, clap, pop, snap.

2. *Syns:* fissure, rupture, snap, split.

3. BREAK DOWN.
4. COLLAPSE *verb*.
5. BREAK *verb*.

crack *adjective*
Having or demonstrating a high degree of knowledge or skill.

EXPERT *adjective*.

crackajack *adjective & noun*

SEE **crackerjack.**

crackdown *noun*
Sudden punitive action.

SUPPRESSION.

cracked *adjective*
Afflicted with or exhibiting irrationality and mental unsoundness.

INSANE.

crackerjack also **crackajack** *adjective*
Slang. Having or demonstrating a high degree of knowledge or skill.

EXPERT *adjective*.

crackerjack also **crackajack** *noun*
Slang. A person with a high degree of knowledge or skill in a particular field.

EXPERT *noun*.

crackers *adjective*
Chiefly Brit. Slang. Afflicted with or exhibiting irrationality and mental unsoundness.

INSANE.

crackle *verb*
To make a series of short, sharp noises: *The fire crackled as it consumed the dry branches.*

Syns: crepitate, splutter, sputter.

crackpot *noun*
An insanely foolish or strange person: *a crackpot who wrote incoherent letters to the President.*

Syns: crank, cuckoo, ding-a-ling (*Informal*), dingbat (*Informal*), eccentric, harebrain, kook (*Slang*), loon, loony (*also* luny), lunatic, nut (*Slang*), screwball, weirdie (*also* weirdy, weirdo) (*Slang*).
SEE **crack up.**

crackup *noun*
crack up *verb*
 1. *Informal.* To undergo wrecking.
 2. *Informal.* To suddenly lose all health or strength.
 crackup *noun*
 1. A wrecking of a vehicle.
 2. *Informal.* A sudden sharp decline in mental, emotional, or physical health.

 1. CRASH *verb.*
 2. COLLAPSE *verb.*

 1. CRASH *noun.*
 2. BREAKDOWN at **break down.**

cracky *adjective*
Chiefly Brit. Regional. Afflicted with or exhibiting irrationality and mental unsoundness.

INSANE.

craft *noun*
 1. Natural or acquired facility in a specific activity.
 2. A skill in doing or performing that is attained by study, practice, or observation.
 3. Deceitful cleverness.
 4. Lack of straightforwardness and honesty in action.

 1. ABILITY.
 2. ART.

 3. ART.
 4. INDIRECTION.

craftiness *noun*
 1. Deceitful cleverness.
 2. Lack of straightforwardness and honesty in action.

 1. ART.
 2. INDIRECTION.

craftsmanship *noun*
The technique, style, and quality of working.

WORK *noun.*

crafty *adjective*
Deceitfully clever.

ARTFUL.

cragged *adjective*
Having a coarse, irregular surface.

ROUGH.

craggy *adjective*
Having a coarse, irregular surface.

ROUGH.

cram *verb*
 1. To fill to excess by compressing or squeezing tightly.
 2. To congregate closely around or against.
 3. *Informal.* To study hard, esp. when pressed for time.

 1. CROWD *verb.*
 2. CROWD *verb.*
 3. BONE UP.

crammed *adjective*
Completely filled.

FULL.

cramp *verb*
To check the freedom and spontaneity of.

CONSTRAIN.

 cramp *noun*
 Something that limits or restricts.

RESTRICTION.

cramped *adjective*
Affording little room for movement.

TIGHT *adjective.*

crank *noun*
 1. *Informal.* A person who habitually complains or grumbles.
 2. An insanely foolish or strange person.

 1. GROUCH *noun.*

 2. CRACKPOT.

cranky *adjective*
Having or showing a bad temper.

ILL-TEMPERED.

crap *noun*
Slang. Something that does not have or make sense.

NONSENSE.

crappy *adjective*
Slang. Of decidedly inferior quality.

SHODDY.

crapulence *noun*
The condition of being intoxicated with alcoholic liquor.

DRUNKENNESS.

crapulent *adjective*
Intoxicated with alcoholic liquor.

DRUNK *adjective.*

crapulous *adjective*
Intoxicated with alcoholic liquor.

DRUNK *adjective*.

crash *noun*
1. A wrecking of a vehicle: *a plane crash.*

1. *Syns:* crackup, pileup, smash, smashup, wreck.

2. Violent, forcible contact between two or more things.
2. COLLISION.
3. A loud striking together.
3. CLASH *noun*.
4. A forceful movement causing a loud noise.
4. SLAM *noun*.
5. An abrupt, disastrous failure.
5. COLLAPSE *noun*.

crash *verb*
1. To undergo wrecking: *The plane crashed.*

1. *Syns:* crack up (*Informal*), pile up, smash, smash up.

2. To come together or come up against with force.
2. COLLIDE.
3. To strike, set down, or close in such a way as to make a loud noise.
3. BANG *verb*.
4. To strike together with a loud, harsh noise.
4. CLASH *verb*.
5. To undergo sudden financial failure.
5. COLLAPSE *verb*.
6. *Slang*. To go to bed.
6. RETIRE.

crash *adjective*
Informal. Designed to meet emergency needs as quickly as possible: *a crash program to save energy; a hospital crash tray.*

Syns: hurry-up, rush.

crashing *adjective*
Completely such, without qualification or exception.

UTTER².

crass *adjective*
Lacking in delicacy or refinement.

COARSE.

crave *verb*
1. To have a strong longing for.
1. DESIRE *verb*.
2. To have a greedy, obsessive desire.
2. LUST *verb*.

craven *adjective*
Ignobly lacking in courage.

COWARDLY.

craven *noun*
An ignoble, uncourageous person.

COWARD.

cravenness *noun*
Ignoble lack of courage.

COWARDICE.

craving *noun*
A strong wish for what promises enjoyment or pleasure.

DESIRE *noun*.

crawl *verb*
1. To move along in a crouching or prone position: *soldiers crawling through barbed-wire obstacles.*

1. *Syns:* creep, slide, snake, worm.

2. To advance slowly: *Time crawls.*
2. *Syns:* creep, drag, inch.
3. To overflow with.
3. TEEM¹.
4. To experience a repugnant tingling sensation: *a person who made my skin crawl.*

4. *Syns:* creep, formicate. —*Idiom* have the creeps.

crawl *noun*
A very slow rate of speed: *Time passed at a crawl.*

Syn: creep. —*Idiom* snail's pace.

crawly *adjective*
Experiencing a repugnant tingling sensation: *My skin felt crawly after the horror movie.*

Syns: creepy (*Informal*), goose-pimply.

craze *verb*
To make insane.

DERANGE.

craze *noun*
1. A subject or activity that inspires lively interest.
1. ENTHUSIASM.
2. The current custom.
2. FASHION *noun*.

crazed *adjective*
Afflicted with or exhibiting irrationality and mental unsoundness.

INSANE.

craziness *noun*
1. Serious mental illness or disorder impairing a person's capacity to function normally and safely.

1. INSANITY.

2. Foolish behavior.
2. FOOLISHNESS.

crazy *adjective*
1. Afflicted with or exhibiting irrationality and mental unsoundness.
2. So senseless as to be laughable.
3. *Informal.* Showing or having enthusiasm.

1. INSANE.

2. FOOLISH.
3. ENTHUSIASTIC.

cream *noun*
That which is superlative.

BEST *noun.*

cream *verb*
1. To form or cause to form foam.
2. *Slang.* To render totally ineffective by decisive defeat.

1. FOAM *verb.*
2. OVERWHELM.

creamy *adjective*
Bright and clear; not dull or faded.

FRESH.

crease *noun*
1. A line made by the doubling of one part over another.
2. An indentation or seam on the skin, esp. on the face.

1. FOLD *noun.*

2. LINE *noun.*

create *verb*
1. To form by artistic effort.
2. To cause to come into existence.
3. To bring into existence formally.

1. COMPOSE.
2. PRODUCE.
3. FOUND.

creation *noun*
1. The act of founding or establishing.
2. Any fictitious idea accepted as part of an ideology by an uncritical group; a received idea.
3. The totality of all existing things.

1. FOUNDATION.
2. MYTH.

3. UNIVERSE.

creative *adjective*
Characterized by or productive of new things or new ideas.

INVENTIVE.

creativity *noun*
The power or ability to invent.

INVENTION.

creator *noun*
1. A person instrumental in the growth of something, esp. in its early stages.
2. One that creates, founds, or originates.

1. BUILDER.

2. ORIGINATOR.

creature *noun*
A member of the human race.

HUMAN BEING.

credence *noun*
Mental acceptance of the truth or actuality of something.

BELIEF.

credible *adjective*
1. Worthy of being believed.
2. Worthy of belief because of precision, faithfulness to an original, etc.

1. BELIEVABLE.
2. AUTHENTIC.

credit *verb*
1. To have confidence in the truthfulness of.
2. To regard as belonging to or resulting from another.

1. BELIEVE.
2. ATTRIBUTE *verb.*

credit *noun*
1. Mental acceptance of the truth or actuality of something.
2. The act of attributing.
3. Favorable notice, as of an achievement.

1. BELIEF.

2. ATTRIBUTION.
3. RECOGNITION.

creditable *adjective*
1. Worthy of being believed.
2. Deserving honor or respect.

1. BELIEVABLE.
2. HONORABLE.

creed *noun*
1. A system of religious belief.
2. Those who accept and practice a particular religious belief.

1. RELIGION.
2. FAITH.

creek *noun*
A small stream.

BRANCH *noun.*

creep *verb*
1. To move along in a crouching or prone position.
2. To move silently and furtively.
3. To advance slowly.
4. To experience a repugnant tingling sensation.

1. CRAWL *verb.*
2. SNEAK *verb.*
3. CRAWL *verb.*
4. CRAWL *verb.*

creep *noun*
A very slow rate of speed.

CRAWL *noun.*

creepy *adjective*
Informal. Experiencing a repugnant tingling sensation.

CRAWLY.

crème de la crème *noun*
1. *French.* That which is superlative.
2. *French.* People of the highest social level.

1. BEST *noun.*
2. SOCIETY.

crepehanger *noun*
A prophet of misfortune or disaster.

PESSIMIST.

crepitate *verb*
To make a series of short, sharp noises.

CRACKLE.

crest *noun*
1. The highest point.
2. The greatest quantity or highest degree attainable.
3. The highest point or state.

1. HEIGHT.
2. MAXIMUM *noun.*
3. CLIMAX *noun.*

cretin *noun*
A mentally deficient person.

FOOL *noun.*

crew *noun*
A group of people organized for a particular purpose.

FORCE *noun.*

crib *verb*
Informal. To reproduce (the artistic work of another) illicitly.

PIRATE *verb.*

cribber *noun*
Informal. One who illicitly reproduces the artistic work of another.

PIRATE *noun.*

crime *noun*
1. A serious breaking of the public law: *Car theft and armed robbery are crimes.*

1. **Syns:** felony (*Law*), illegality, misdeed, offense, trespass, violation.
Near-syns: breach, break, infringement.

2. A wicked act: *white-collar crimes such as stealing supplies.*

2. **Syns:** diablerie (*also* diablery), evil, evildoing, iniquity, misdeed, offense, sin, tort, transgression, wrong, wrongdoing.

3. Something that offends one's sense of propriety, fairness, or justice: *It is a crime to waste food.*

3. **Syns:** outrage, sin.

4. *Informal.* A great disappointment or regrettable fact.

4. SHAME *noun.*

criminal *adjective*
Of, involving, or being a crime: *criminal activities such as extortion and blackmail.*

Syns: illegal, illegitimate, illicit, lawless, unlawful, wrongful.

criminal *noun*
One who commits a crime: *killers and other criminals.*

Syns: felon (*Law*), lawbreaker, malefactor, offender.
Near-syns: crook, gangster, hood, mobster, racketeer, thug; fugitive, outlaw; con (*Slang*), convict, jailbird; trespasser, wrongdoer.

crimp *verb*
To make irregular folds in, esp. by pressing or twisting.

WRINKLE[1] *verb.*

crimple *verb*
To make irregular folds in, esp. by pressing or twisting.

WRINKLE[1] *verb.*

crimson *verb*
To become red in the face.

BLUSH *verb.*

crinkle *noun*
1. A line made by the doubling of one part over another.
2. An indentation or seam on the skin, esp. on the face.

1. FOLD *noun*.
2. LINE *noun*.

crinkle *verb*
To make irregular folds in, esp. by pressing or twisting.

WRINKLE[1] *verb*.

cripple *verb*
1. To deprive of, or of the use of, a limb or bodily member: *was badly crippled in the crash*.
2. To render powerless or motionless by inflicting severe injury.

1. **Syns:** dismember, maim, mutilate.
2. DISABLE.

crisis *noun*
1. A highly volatile, dangerous situation requiring immediate remedial action: *The Middle East situation has reached the point of crisis.*
2. A decisive point: *decided to adopt a new lifestyle as the result of a midlife crisis.*

1. **Syns:** emergency, extremity. —*Idiom* flash point.
2. **Syns:** crossroad(s), exigency (*also* exigence), head, juncture, pass. —*Idioms* turning point, zero hour.

crisscross *verb*
To pass through or over.

CROSS *verb*.

criterion *noun*
A means by which individuals are compared and judged.

STANDARD *noun*.

critic *noun*
1. A person who evaluates and reports on the worth of something: *an art critic*.
2. A person who finds fault, often severely and willfully: *a chronic critic of everyone*.

1. **Syns:** commentator, judge, reviewer.
2. **Syns:** aristarch, carper, caviler, criticizer, faultfinder, hypercritic, knocker (*Slang*), momus. **Near-ants:** backer, supporter; advocate, champion.

critical *adjective*
1. Inclined to judge too severely: *an unnecessarily critical attitude*.
2. Characterized by careful and exact evaluation: *a critical appraisal of the athlete's abilities*.
3. So serious as to be at the point of crisis: *a critical shortage of fuel*.

1. **Syns:** captious, carping, caviling, censorious, faultfinding, hypercritical, overcritical.
2. **Syns:** discerning, discriminating, penetrating.
3. **Syns:** acute, climacteric, crucial, desperate, dire, exigent. **Near-syns:** consequential, decisive, important, momentous, significant, weighty. **Ant:** trivial.

criticism *noun*
1. A finding fault.
2. Evaluative and critical discourse.

1. BLAME *noun*.
2. REVIEW *noun*.

criticize *verb*
1. To find fault with.
2. To write a critical report on.

1. BLAME *verb*.
2. REVIEW *verb*.

criticizer *noun*
A person who finds fault, often severely and willfully.

CRITIC.

critique *noun*
Evaluative and critical discourse.

REVIEW *noun*.

critique *verb*
To write a critical report on.

REVIEW *verb*.

croak *verb*
Slang. To cease living.

DIE.

crocked *adjective*
Slang. Intoxicated with alcoholic liquor.

DRUNK *adjective*.

crone *noun*
An ugly, frightening old woman.   WITCH *noun.*

crony *noun*
One who keeps company with another.   ASSOCIATE *noun.*

crook *verb*
To swerve from a straight line.   BEND *verb.*

crook *noun*
1. Something bent.   1. BEND *noun.*
2. *Informal.* A person who cheats.   2. CHEAT *noun.*

crooked *adjective*
1. Having bends, curves, or angles: *a crooked tree limb;*   1. ***Syns:*** bending, curved, curving,
   a crooked country lane.   devious, twisting.
                                                             Near-syns: meandering, rambling,
                                                             serpentine, tortuous, winding; indirect,
                                                             roundabout.
                                                             Ant: straight.
2. Not straight, uniform, or symmetrical.   2. IRREGULAR.
3. Marked by dishonesty, esp. in matters of public   3. CORRUPT *adjective.*
   trust.

crookedness *noun*
1. Lack of smoothness or regularity.   1. IRREGULARITY.
2. Departure from what is legally, ethically, and   2. CORRUPTION.
   morally correct.

crop *verb*
1. *Brit. Regional.* To gather (grain) left by reapers. 1. GLEAN.
2. To decrease, as in length or amount, by or as if by   2. CUT BACK.
   severing or excising.
3. To make short or shorter by or as if by cutting.   3. TRUNCATE.

crop *noun*
The produce gathered from the land.   HARVEST *noun.*

cropping *noun*
The act or process of bringing in a crop.   HARVEST *noun.*

cross *verb*
1. To go across: *crossed the ocean.*   1. ***Syns:*** transit, transverse, traverse.
2. To pass through or over: *at the corner where Elm*   2. ***Syns:*** crisscross, crosscut, cut across,
   crosses Main Street.   decussate, intercross, intersect.
3. To be treacherous to.   3. BETRAY.

cross out *verb*
To remove or invalidate by or as if by running a line   CANCEL.   *Crosscurrents*
through or wiping clean.

cross *noun*
Something hard to bear physically or emotionally.   BURDEN *noun.*

cross *adjective*
Having or showing a bad temper.   ILL-TEMPERED.

crosscut *verb*
To pass through or over.   CROSS *verb.*

cross-examine *verb*
To question thoroughly and relentlessly to verify facts. INTERROGATE.

cross-eye *noun*
The condition of not having the visual axes parallel.   SQUINT *noun.*

cross-eyed *adjective*
Marked by or affected with a squint.   SQUINTY.

crossing *adjective*
Situated or lying across.   TRANSVERSE.

cross-interrogate *verb*
To question thoroughly and relentlessly to verify facts. INTERROGATE.

cross out *verb*   SEE **cross.**

cross-question *verb*
To question thoroughly and relentlessly to verify facts. INTERROGATE.

crossroad(s) *noun*
A decisive point.   CRISIS.

crosswise *adjective*
Situated or lying across.

TRANSVERSE.

crouch *verb*
To stoop low with the limbs pulled in close to the body: *crouched behind the tree and listened.*

Syns: huddle, hunch, hunker, squab (*Brit. Regional*), squat.

crow *verb*
1. To talk with excessive pride.
2. To feel or express an uplifting joy over a success or victory.

1. BOAST *verb*.
2. EXULT.

crowd *noun*
1. An enormous number of persons gathered together: *An enthusiastic crowd surrounded the President.*

2. A very large number of things grouped together: *a crowd of insects.*

3. A number of persons who have come or been gathered together.
4. The common people.
5. A particular social group: *invited only our crowd.*

6. A group of people sharing an interest, activity, or achievement.

1. **Syns:** crush, drove, flock, horde, mass, mob, multitude, swarm, throng.
   Near-syns: army, legion; herd, rabble.
2. **Syns:** army, cloud, drove, flock, host, legion, multitude, rout[1] (*Archaic*), scores.
3. ASSEMBLY.

4. COMMONALTY.
5. **Syns:** bunch (*Informal*), circle, gang, set[2].
6. CIRCLE *noun*.

crowd *verb*
1. To congregate closely around or against: *The fans crowded around the singer.*
2. To fill to excess by compressing or squeezing tightly: *Commuters crowded the bus.*
3. To act on with a steady pushing force: *The passengers crowded each other in the subway.*

1. **Syns:** cram, crush, flock, jam, mob, press, squash, squeeze.
2. **Syns:** cram, jam, jam-pack (*Informal*), load, mob, pack, stuff.
3. **Syns:** compress, constrain, crush, mash, press, push, squash, squeeze.

crowded *adjective*
1. Completely filled.
2. Having all parts near to each other.
3. Affording little room for movement.
4. Excessively filled with detail.

1. FULL.
2. THICK.
3. TIGHT *adjective*.
4. BUSY *adjective*.

crown *verb*
1. To put a topping on.
2. To reach or bring to a climax.

1. TOP *verb*.
2. CLIMAX *verb*.

crown *noun*
1. The highest point or state.
2. The highest point.

1. CLIMAX *noun*.
2. HEIGHT.

crowning *adjective*
Of or constituting a climax.

CLIMACTIC.

crucial *adjective*
1. So serious as to be at the point of crisis.
2. Determining or having the power to determine an outcome.

1. CRITICAL.
2. DECISIVE.

crucible *noun*
A state of pain or anguish that tests one's resiliency and character.

TRIAL *noun*.

crucify *verb*
To subject (another) to extreme physical cruelty, as in punishing.

TORTURE *verb*.

crude *adjective*
1. In a natural state and still not prepared for use: *crude oil; crude ore.*

2. Lacking expert, careful craftsmanship.
3. Displaying a lack of knowledge or skill: *crude attempts to negotiate.*

1. **Syns:** impure, native, raw, unprocessed, unrefined.
   Near-syns: rough; coarse, natural.
   Ants: processed, refined.
2. RUDE.
3. **Syns:** coarse, inexpert.

4. Lacking in delicacy or refinement.
5. Offensive to accepted standards of decency.

cruel *adjective*
1. So intense as to cause extreme suffering: *cruel hurricane winds.*
2. Showing or suggesting a disposition to be violently destructive without scruple or restraint.

cruelty *noun*
A cruel act or an instance of cruel behavior: *the cruelty of an Eastern potentate.*

crumb *noun*
1. A small portion of food.
2. A tiny amount.

crumble *verb*
To reduce or become reduced to pieces or components.

crumby *adjective*

crummy also **crumby** *adjective*
Slang. Of decidedly inferior quality.

crump *verb*
To bite and grind with the teeth.

crumple *verb*
1. To make irregular folds in, esp. by pressing or twisting.
2. To be unable to hold up.

crunch *verb*
1. To bite and grind with the teeth.
2. To rub together noisily.

crusade *noun*
1. A goal or set of interests served with dedication.
2. An organized effort to accomplish a purpose.

crush *verb*
1. To press forcefully so as to break up into a pulpy mass: *crushed mint leaves.*
2. To extract from by applying pressure.
3. To break up into tiny particles: *crushed the iron ore.*

4. To impair severely the spirit, health, effectiveness, etc., of.
5. To bring to an end forcibly as if by imposing a heavy weight.
6. To affect deeply or completely, as with emotion.
7. To congregate closely around or against.
8. To act on with a steady pushing force.

crush *noun*
1. An enormous number of persons gathered together.
2. *Informal.* An extravagant, short-lived romantic attachment.

crust *noun*
Slang. Excessive and arrogant self-confidence.

crusty *adjective*
1. Rudely unceremonious.
2. Offensive to accepted standards of decency.

crutch *noun*
A means or device that keeps something erect, stable, or secure.

cry *verb*
1. To make inarticulate sounds of grief or pain, usu. accompanied by tears: *The child cried after falling down.*

4. COARSE.
5. OBSCENE.

1. **Syns:** ferocious, fierce, savage, vicious.
2. FIERCE.

Syns: barbarity, brutality, ferocity, inhumanity, truculence (*also* truculency), viciousness.

1. BIT[1].
2. BIT[1].

BREAK UP at **break.**
SEE **crummy.**

SHODDY.

CHEW.

1. WRINKLE[1] *verb.*
2. BEND *verb.*

1. CHEW.
2. GRIND *verb.*

1. CAUSE *noun.*
2. DRIVE *noun.*

1. **Syns:** becrush, mash, mush (up), pulp, squash.
2. SQUEEZE *verb.*
3. **Syns:** bray, buck[2], granulate, granulize, grind, mill, powder, pulverize, triturate.
4. BREAK *verb.*
5. SUPPRESS.
6. OVERWHELM.
7. CROWD *verb.*
8. CROWD *verb.*

1. CROWD *noun.*
2. INFATUATION.

PRESUMPTION.

1. ABRUPT.
2. OBSCENE.

SUPPORT *noun.*

1. **Syns:** bawl, blub, blubber, boohoo, howl, keen[2], sob, wail, weep, yowl.

2. To speak or say very loudly.   2. ROAR *verb*.
3. To speak suddenly or sharply, as from surprise or emotion.   3. EXCLAIM.
4. To say (something) with a shout.   4. SHOUT *verb*.
5. To make known vigorously the positive features of (a product).   5. ADVERTISE.

cry *noun*
1. A fit of crying: *had a good cry after the funeral.*   1. *Syns:* bawling, blubbering, boohoos, tears, wailing, weeping. —*Idiom* flood of tears.

2. A rallying term used by proponents of a cause: *"Freedom!" was the cry of the revolutionaries.*   2. *Syn:* motto. —*Idioms* battle cry, call to arms (*or* battle), rallying cry, war cry.
3. The act of demanding.   3. DEMAND *noun*.
4. The current custom.   4. FASHION *noun*.
5. Idle, often sensational and groundless talk about others.   5. GOSSIP *noun*.

crying *adjective*
1. Of immediate import.   1. BURNING.
2. Disgracefully and grossly offensive.   2. OUTRAGEOUS.

crypt *noun*
A burial place or receptacle for human remains.   GRAVE[1].

crystal-clear *adjective*
1. Admitting light so that objects beyond can be seen.   1. TRANSPARENT.
2. Readily seen, perceived, or understood.   2. APPARENT.

crystalline *adjective*
Admitting light so that objects beyond can be seen.   TRANSPARENT.

cuckoo *noun*
An insanely foolish or strange person.   CRACKPOT.

  cuckoo *adjective*
Afflicted with or exhibiting irrationality and mental unsoundness.   INSANE.

cuddle *verb*
1. To lie or press close together, usu. with another person or thing.   1. SNUGGLE *verb*.
2. To touch or stroke affectionately.   2. CARESS *verb*.

cue *noun*
A subtle pointing out.   HINT *noun*.

cuff *noun*
A quick, sharp blow, esp. with the hand.   SLAP *noun*.

  cuff *verb*
To hit with a quick, sharp blow of the hand.   SLAP *verb*.

cuisinier *noun*
A person who prepares food for eating.   COOK *noun*.

cul-de-sac *noun*
A course leading nowhere.   BLIND ALLEY.

cull *verb*
1. To make a choice from a number of alternatives.   1. CHOOSE.
2. To collect (something) bit by bit.   2. GLEAN.

culminate *verb*
To reach or bring to a climax.   CLIMAX *verb*.

culminating *adjective*
Of or constituting a climax.   CLIMACTIC.

culmination *noun*
1. The highest point or state.   1. CLIMAX *noun*.
2. The condition of being fulfilled.   2. FULFILLMENT.

culpability *noun*
Responsibility for an error or crime.   BLAME *noun*.

culpable *adjective*
Deserving blame.   BLAMEWORTHY.

cultivate *verb*
1. To prepare (soil) for the planting and raising of crops.
2. To bring into existence and foster the development of.
3. To promote and sustain the development of.
4. To help bring about.

1. TILL.
2. GROW.
3. NURSE.
4. PROMOTE.

cultivated *adjective*
Characterized by discriminating taste and broad knowledge as a result of development or education.

CULTURED.

cultivation *noun*
Enlightenment and excellent taste resulting from intellectual development.

CULTURE.

cultural *adjective*
Promoting culture: *cultural pursuits such as supporting the local orchestra.*

Syns: civilizing, edifying, enlightening, humanizing, refining.

culture *noun*
1. Enlightenment and excellent taste resulting from intellectual development: *a person of great charm and culture.*
2. The total product of human creativity and intellect at a particular time: *the culture of ancient Greece.*

1. *Syns:* cultivation, polish, refinement.
2. *Syns:* civilization, Kultur (*German*).

culture *verb*
To prepare (soil) for the planting and raising of crops.

TILL.

cultured *adjective*
Characterized by discriminating taste and broad knowledge as a result of development or education: *a cultured man.*

Syns: civilized, cultivated, enlightened, polished, refined, urbane, well-bred.
Near-syns: educated, learned, schooled, taught; genteel.
Ant: uncultured.

cumber *verb*
To place a burden or heavy load on.

CHARGE *verb.*

cumbersome *adjective*
1. Difficult to handle or manage.
2. Unwieldy, esp. due to excess weight.

1. AWKWARD.
2. HEAVY *adjective.*

cumbrous *adjective*
Difficult to handle or manage.

AWKWARD.

cumshaw *noun*
A material favor or gift, usu. money, given in return for service.

GRATUITY.

cumulate *verb*
To bring together so as to increase in mass or number.

ACCUMULATE.

cumulation *noun*
A quantity accumulated.

ACCUMULATION.

cumulative *adjective*
Increasing, as in force, by successive additions.

ACCUMULATIVE.

cumulus *noun*
A quantity accumulated.

ACCUMULATION.

cunning *adjective*
Deceitfully clever.

ARTFUL.

cunning *noun*
1. Deceitful cleverness.
2. The act or practice of deceiving.

1. ART.
2. DECEIT.

cupidity *noun*
Excessive desire for more than one needs or deserves.

GREED.

curative *adjective*
Serving to cure: *curative drugs.*

Syns: curing, healing, polychrestic, remedial, restorative, therapeutic.
Near-syns: beneficial, corrective, medicinal, wholesome.

curative *noun*
Something that corrects or counteracts.

REMEDY *noun*.

curb *verb*
To control, restrict, or arrest.

RESTRAIN.

cure *noun*
1. An agent used to restore health: *had found no cure for cancer.*

1. **Syns:** elixir, medicament, medicant, medication, medicine, nostrum, pharmacon, physic, polychrest, remedy.

2. Something that corrects or counteracts.

2. REMEDY *noun*.

cure *verb*
To rectify an undesirable or unhealthy condition: *cure a cold; cure a sick economy.*

Syns: heal, remedy.

cure-all *noun*
Something believed to cure all human disorders.

PANACEA.

cureless *adjective*
Offering no hope or expectation of improvement.

HOPELESS.

curing *adjective*
Serving to cure.

CURATIVE *adjective*.

curiosity *noun*
1. Mental acquisitiveness: *intellectual curiosity.*

1. **Syns:** inquisitiveness, interest.
   —*Idioms* inquiring mind, thirst for knowledge.

2. Undue interest in the affairs of others: *The neighbors' everlasting curiosity is irritating.*

2. **Syns:** nosiness (*Informal*), prying, snoopiness (*Informal*).

curious *adjective*
1. Eager to acquire knowledge: *was curious about the origins of man.*

1. **Syns:** disquisitive, inquiring (*also* enquiring), inquisitive, investigative, questioning.

2. Unduly interested in the affairs of others: *a curious neighbor.*

2. **Syns:** inquisitive, inquisitorial, inquisitory, nosy (*also* nosey) (*Informal*), prying, snoopy (*Informal*).
   Near-syns: interfering, meddling, tampering; impertinent, intrusive, meddlesome.
   Ant: uncurious.

3. Deviating from the customary.
4. Causing puzzlement; perplexing.

3. ECCENTRIC *adjective*.
4. FUNNY.

curl *verb*
1. To move or proceed on a repeatedly curving course.
2. To have or cause to have a curved or sinuous form or surface.

1. WIND².
2. WAVE.

currency *noun*
Something, as coins, printed bills, etc., used as a medium of exchange.

MONEY.

current *adjective*
1. In existence now.
2. Of or pertaining to recent times or the present.
3. Most generally existing or encountered at a given time.

1. PRESENT¹ *adjective*.
2. MODERN.
3. PREVAILING.

current *noun*
Something suggestive of running water.

FLOW *noun*.

currently *adverb*
At this moment.

NOW *adverb*.

curse *noun*
1. A denunciation invoking a wish or threat of evil or injury: *the dying prisoner's curse against his captors.*

1. **Syns:** anathema, damnation, execration, imprecation, malediction, malison (*Archaic*).
   Near-syns: objurgation; damning, denunciation; blasphemy, profanation, profanity, sacrilege.
   Ant: blessing.

2. A profane or obscene term.
3. A cause of suffering or harm: *Mankind's greatest curse is poverty.*
4. Something or someone believed to bring bad luck.

curse *verb*
1. To invoke evil or injury upon: *cursed my bad luck.*

2. To use profane or obscene language.
3. To bring great harm or suffering to.

cursed also **curst** *adjective*
So annoying or detestable as to deserve condemnation.

cursive *adjective*
Marked by facility, esp. of expression.

cursiveness *noun*
Ready skill in expression.

cursory *adjective*
Lacking in intellectual depth or thoroughness.

curst *adjective*

curt *adjective*
Rudely unceremonious.

curtail *verb*
To decrease, as in length or amount, by or as if by severing or excising.

curtailment *noun*
The act or process of decreasing in length, amount, duration, etc.

curtains *noun*
Slang. The act or fact of dying.

curtilage *noun*
An area partially or entirely enclosed by walls or buildings.

curtsy *noun*
An inclination of the head or body, as in greeting, consent, courtesy, submission, or worship.

curvaceous *adjective*
Having a full, voluptuous figure.

curvation *noun*
Something bent.

curvature *noun*
Something bent.

curve *verb*
1. To swerve from a straight line.
2. To have or cause to have a curved or sinuous form or surface.

curve *noun*
Something bent.

curved *adjective*
1. Deviating from a straight line.
2. Having bends, curves, or angles.

curvesome *adjective*
Having a full, voluptuous figure.

curvilinear *adjective*
Deviating from a straight line.

curving *adjective*
Having bends, curves, or angles.

curvy *adjective*
Having a full, voluptuous figure.

cusp *noun*
A sharp or tapered end.

---

2. SWEAR *noun*
3. *Syns:* affliction, bane, evil, ill, plague, scourge, woe.
4. JINX.

1. *Syns:* accurse (*Rare*), anathematize, damn, execrate (*Archaic*), imprecate, maledict (*Rare*). —*Idiom* call down evil on.
2. SWEAR *verb.*
3. AFFLICT.

DAMNED.

SMOOTH *adjective.*

FLUENCY.

SUPERFICIAL.
SEE **cursed.**

ABRUPT.

CUT BACK.

CUTBACK at **cut back.**

DEATH.

COURT *noun.*

BOW *noun.*

SHAPELY.

BEND *noun.*

BEND *noun.*

1. BEND *verb.*
2. WAVE.

BEND *noun.*

1. BENT *adjective.*
2. CROOKED.

SHAPELY.

BENT *adjective.*

CROOKED.

SHAPELY.

POINT *noun.*

cuspate also **cuspated, cusped** *adjective*
Having an end tapering to a point.   POINTED.

cuspated *adjective*   SEE **cuspate.**

cusped *adjective*   SEE **cuspate.**

cuspidate also **cuspidated** *adjective*
Biol. Having an end tapering to a point.   POINTED.

cuspidated *adjective*   SEE **cuspidate.**

cuss *verb*
Informal. To use profane or obscene language.   SWEAR *verb.*

cuss *noun*
Informal. A profane or obscene term.   SWEAR *noun.*

cussword *noun*
Informal. A profane or obscene term.   SWEAR *noun.*

custodian *noun*
A person who is legally responsible for the person or
property of another considered by law to be
incompetent to manage his affairs.   GUARDIAN.

custody *noun*
The function of watching, guarding, or overseeing.   CARE *noun.*

custom *noun*
1. A habitual way of behaving: *Social custom varies
from country to country.*

    1. *Syns:* habit, habitude, manner,
    practice, praxis, usage, use, way, wont.
    Near-syns: mold, precedent, ritual.

2. The commercial transactions of customers with a
supplier.   2. PATRONAGE.

custom *adjective*
Made according to the specifications of the buyer: *a
custom sports car.*   *Syns:* custom-built, customized, custom-
made, custom-tailored, made-to-order,
tailor-made.

customarily *adverb*
In an expected or customary manner.   USUALLY.

customary *adjective*
Commonly practiced or used: *took his customary route
to work.*   *Syns:* accustomable (*Obs.*), accustomary
(*Archaic*), accustomed, habitual, regular,
usual.

custom-built *adjective*
Made according to the specifications of the buyer.   CUSTOM *adjective.*

customer *noun*
1. One who consumes goods and services.   1. CONSUMER.
2. One who buys goods or services.   2. PATRON.

customized *adjective*
Made according to the specifications of the buyer.   CUSTOM *adjective.*

custom-made *adjective*
Made according to the specifications of the buyer.   CUSTOM *adjective.*

custom-tailored *adjective*
Made according to the specifications of the buyer.   CUSTOM *adjective.*

cut *verb*
1. To penetrate with a sharp edge: *cut my finger with a
razor blade.*

    1. *Syns:* gash, incise, pierce, slash, slit.

2. To separate into parts with or as if with a sharp-
edged instrument: *cut a cake into twelve slices.*

    2. *Syns:* carve, cleave, dissever, sever,
    slice, split.

3. To decrease, as in length or amount, by or as if by
severing or excising.   3. CUT BACK.

4. To bring down, as with a saw or ax: *cut timber.*   4. *Syns:* chop[1], fell[1], hew.

5. To lessen the strength of by or as if by admixture.   5. DILUTE *verb.*

6. To slight (someone) deliberately.   6. SNUB *verb.*

7. *Informal.* To fail to attend on purpose: *cut classes.*

    7. *Syns:* mooch (*Chiefly Brit. Regional*),
    skip. —*Idioms* go A.W.O.L., play hooky
    (*or* truant), skip out on, take French
    leave.

8. To turn aside sharply from a straight course.   8. SWERVE.

cut across *verb*
To pass through or over.   CROSS *verb*.

cut down *verb*
1. To cause to fall, as from a shot or blow.   1. DROP *verb*.
2. To decrease, as in length or amount, by or as if by   2. CUT BACK.
   severing or excising.

cut in *verb*
1. To interject remarks or questions into another's   1. INTERRUPT.
   discourse.
2. To force or come in as an improper or unwanted   2. INTRUDE.
   element.

cut out *verb*
1. *Slang*. To cut short; discontinue.   1. BREAK *verb*.
2. *Slang*. To move or proceed away from a place.   2. GO *verb*.
3. To take the place of (another) against the other's   3. SUPPLANT.
   will.

cut *noun*
1. The result of cutting: *a long cut on his cheek from a* 1. **Syns:** gash, incision, slash, slice, slit,
   duel.   split.
2. A part severed from a whole: *a good cut of beef.*   2. **Syns:** piece, portion, section, segment,
                                                              slice.
3. *Informal*. That which is allotted.   3. ALLOTMENT.
4. A deliberate slight.   4. SNUB *noun*.
5. *Informal*. An unexcused absence: *No cuts are*   5. **Syns:** hooky (*Informal*), skip, truancy.
   allowed in his class.   —*Idiom* French leave.
6. *Informal*. A flippant or sarcastic remark.   6. CRACK *noun*.
7. A class that is defined by the common attribute or   7. KIND^2.
   attributes possessed by all its members.

cut *adjective*
Lower than normal in strength or concentration due to   DILUTE *adjective*.
admixture.

cut across *verb*   SEE **cut**.
cut-and-dried *adjective*
Lacking in interest or originality.   ROUTINE *adjective*.
cutback *noun*   SEE **cut back**.
cut back *verb*
To decrease, as in length or amount, by or as if by   **Syns:** chop^1, clip^1, crop, curtail, cut, cut
severing or excising: *cut back expenses ruthlessly.*   down, lop^1, lower^2, pare, reduce, shear,
                                                           slash, trim.

cutback *noun*
The act or process of decreasing in length, amount,   **Syns:** curtailment, decrease, reduction,
duration, etc.: *a cutback in production.*   slash.
cut down *verb*   SEE **cut**.
cut in *verb*   SEE **cut**.
cut-off *noun*   SEE **cut off**.
cut off *verb*
1. To block the progress of and force to change   1. HEAD OFF at **head**.
   direction.
2. To cause the death of.   2. KILL.
3. To set apart from a group.   3. ISOLATE *verb*.
cut-off *noun*
The act of stopping.   STOP *noun*.
cut out *verb*   SEE **cut**.
cutthroat *noun*
One who murders another.   MURDERER.
cutthroat *adjective*
Eager for bloodshed.   MURDEROUS.
cutting *adjective*
So sharp as to cause mental pain.   BITING.
cutup *noun*   SEE **cut up**.

cut up *verb*
1. *Informal.* To behave in a rowdy or unruly fashion.   1. MISBEHAVE.
2. *Informal.* To find fault with.   2. BLAME *verb*.
cutup *noun*
Informal. A person whose words or actions provoke or   JOKER.
are intended to provoke amusement or laughter.
cycle *noun*
A course, process, or journey that ends where it began.   CIRCLE *noun*.
cyclic also **cyclical** *adjective*
Happening or appearing at regular intervals.   RECURRENT.
cyclopean *adjective*
Of extraordinary size and power.   GIANT *adjective*.
cynic *noun*
A person who expects only the worst from people: *Life's*   *Syns:* man-hater, misanthrope,
experiences had rendered him a cynic.   misanthropist.
cynical *adjective*
Marked by or displaying contemptuous mockery of the   *Syns:* ironic (*also* ironical), sardonic, wry.
motives or virtues of others: *a cynical attitude toward*   *Near-syns:* contemptuous, disdainful,
society.   scornful; derisive, jeering, mocking,
   sneering; sarcastic, satiric.

D

dab¹ *verb*
To spread with a greasy, sticky, or dirty substance.   SMEAR *verb*.
dab *noun*
1. A discolored mark made by smearing.   1. SMEAR *noun*.
2. A tiny amount.   2. BIT¹.
dab² *noun*
Brit. Informal. A person with a high degree of   EXPERT *noun*.
knowledge or skill in a particular field.
dabbler *noun*
One lacking professional skill and ease in a particular   AMATEUR.
pursuit.
dad *noun*
Informal. A male parent.   FATHER *noun*.
daddy *noun*
A male parent.   FATHER *noun*.
daedal *adjective*
Difficult to understand due to intricacy.   COMPLEX *adjective*.
daedalian *adjective*
Difficult to understand due to intricacy.   COMPLEX *adjective*.
daffy *adjective*
Informal. Afflicted with or exhibiting irrationality and   INSANE.
mental unsoundness.
daft *adjective*
Afflicted with or exhibiting irrationality and mental   INSANE.
unsoundness.
dainty *adjective*
1. Appealing to refined taste.   1. DELICATE.
2. Very difficult to please.   2. NICE.
dainty *noun*

Something fine and delicious, esp. a food.   DELICACY

dalliance *noun*
1. A usu. brief romance entered into lightly or   1. FLIRTATION.
frivolously.
2. The practice of flirting.   2. FLIRTATION.

dally *verb*
1. To go or move slowly so that progress is hindered.   1. DELAY *verb*.
2. To make amorous advances without serious   2. FLIRT *verb*.
intentions.
3. To treat lightly or flippantly.   3. FLIRT *verb*.

damage *noun*
1. An act, instance, or consequence of breaking.   1. BREAKAGE.
2. The action or result of inflicting loss or pain.   2. HARM.

damage *verb*
To spoil the soundness or perfection of.   INJURE.

damaging *adjective*
Causing harm or injury.   HARMFUL.

damn *verb*
1. To pronounce judgment against.   1. CONDEMN.
2. To invoke evil or injury upon.   2. CURSE *verb*.
3. To use profane or obscene language.   3. SWEAR *verb*.

damn *noun*
Informal. The least bit: *His opinion isn't worth a damn.*   *Syns:* ace[1], hoot, iota, jot, ounce, rap[2], shred, straw, whit.

damn *adjective*
So annoying or detestable as to deserve condemnation.   DAMNED.

damnation *noun*
A denunciation invoking a wish or threat of evil or   CURSE *noun*.
injury.

damned *adjective*
1. Condemned, esp. to hell: *damned souls.*   1. *Syns:* doomed, lost. —*Idiom* gone to blazes.
2. So annoying or detestable as to deserve   2. *Syns:* accursed, blamed, blankety-blank
condemnation: *The damned car won't start.*   (*Informal*), blasted (*Slang*), blessed, blooming (*Slang*), confounded, cursed (*also* curst), damn, darn, execrable, infernal, ruddy (*Slang*).
3. Completely such, without qualification or exception.   3. UTTER[2].

damp *adjective*
Slightly wet: *damp ground; a damp sponge.*   *Syns:* dank, moist.
Near-syns: dampish; drenched, saturated, soaked, soggy.

dampen *verb*
1. To make moist.   1. WASH.
2. To decrease or dull the sound of.   2. MUFFLE.

dance *verb*
1. To move rhythmically to music, using patterns of   1. *Syns:* foot (it), hoof (*Slang*), step.
steps or gestures: *often dances alone to the radio.*   —*Idioms* cut a rug, trip the light fantastic.
2. To leap and skip about playfully.   2. GAMBOL.

dance *noun*
A party or gathering for dancing: *went to a dance at the*   *Syns:* ball, hop (*Slang*).
country club.

dancer *noun*
A person who dances, esp. professionally: *a ballet*   *Syns:* hoofer (*Slang*), terpsichorean.
dancer.

dandy *adjective*
1. *Informal.* Exceptionally good of its kind.   1. EXCELLENT.
2. *Informal.* Particularly excellent.   2. MARVELOUS.

danger *noun*
Exposure to possible harm, loss, or injury: *High flood waters put the town in danger.*

Syns: endangerment, hazard, imperilment, jeopardy, peril, risk. —*Idiom* thin ice.

danger *verb*
Archaic. To subject to danger or destruction.

ENDANGER.

dangerous *adjective*
1. Involving possible risk, loss, or injury: *a dangerous climb.*

1. **Syns:** adventurous, chancy, hairy (*Slang*), hazardous, jeopardous, parlous (*Archaic*), perilous, risky, treacherous, unsafe, venturous.
   Near-syns: grave, precarious, menacing, threatening, uncertain, unhealthy.
   Ants: safe, secure.

2. Causing or marked by danger, pain, etc.

2. GRIEVOUS.

dangle *verb*
To fasten or be fastened at one point with no support from below.

HANG *verb.*

dank *adjective*
Slightly wet.

DAMP.

dap *verb*
To strike a surface at such an angle as to be deflected.

GLANCE[1] *verb.*

dapple *verb*
To mark with many small spots.

SPECKLE.

dare *verb*
1. To confront boldly and courageously.
2. To call on another to do something requiring boldness: *He dared her to say he was a liar.*

1. DEFY.
2. **Syns:** challenge, defy. —*Idiom* throw down the gauntlet.

dare *noun*
An act of taunting another to do something bold or rash: *I did it on a dare.*

Syns: challenge, stump (*Informal*).

daredevil *noun*
One who engages in exciting, risky pursuits.

ADVENTURER.

daredevil *adjective*
Taking or willing to take risks.

DARING *adjective.*

daring *adjective*
Taking or willing to take risks: *a daring test pilot.*

Syns: adventurous, audacious, bold, daredevil, venturesome, venturous.

daring *noun*
Willingness to take risks: *an officer with nerve and daring.*

Syns: adventurousness, audacity, boldness.

dark *adjective*
1. Deficient in brightness: *kept the sickroom dark and quiet.*

1. **Syns:** dim, dusky, murky (*also* mirky), obscure, tenebrous.
   Near-ants: bright, brilliant, luminous, radiant; illuminated, lighted.
   Ant: light.

2. Of a complexion tending toward brown or black: *a tall, dark man.*
3. Marked by little hopefulness.
4. Characterized by or expressive of a foreboding somberness: *gave me a dark scowl and left the room; dark, angry clouds in the distance.*
5. Having no light.
6. Somewhat black.
7. *Regional.* Without the sense of sight.

2. **Syns:** bistered, black-a-vised, brunet (*also* brunette), dusky, swarthy.
3. GLOOMY.
4. **Syns:** lowering (*also* louring), lowery (*also* loury), overhanging, sullen.
5. BLACK *adjective.*
6. BLACKISH.
7. BLIND *adjective.*

dark *noun*
Absence or deficiency of light: *groping around in the dark for his glasses.*

Syns: darkness, dimness, duskiness, obscurity, tenebrosity.

darken *verb*
To make dark or darker.

SHADE *verb.*

darkness *noun*
Absence or deficiency of light.   DARK *noun*.

darling *noun*
1. A person who is much loved: *Hello, my darling.*   1. **Syns:** beloved, dear, honey, love, sweet, sweetheart, truelove. —*Idiom* light of one's life.

2. One liked or preferred above all others.   2. FAVORITE *noun*.

darling *adjective*
1. Regarded with much love and tenderness: *a darling child.*   1. **Syns:** beloved, dear, loved, precious.

2. *Informal.* Giving great pleasure or delight.   2. DELIGHTFUL.
3. Given special, usu. doting treatment.   3. FAVORITE *adjective*.

darn *adjective*
So annoying or detestable as to deserve condemnation.   DAMNED.

dart *verb*
1. To move swiftly.   1. RUSH *verb*.
2. To pass quickly and lightly through the air.   2. FLY.

dash *verb*
1. To move swiftly.   1. RUSH *verb*.
2. To move swiftly on foot so that both feet leave the ground during each stride.   2. RUN *verb*.
3. To hurl or scatter liquid upon.   3. SPLASH.
4. To spoil or destroy.   4. BLAST *verb*.

dash *noun*
1. A lively, emphatic, eager quality or manner.   1. SPIRIT.
2. A quality of active mental and physical forcefulness.   2. VIGOR.
3. A barely perceivable indication of something.   3. TRACE *noun*.

dashing *adjective*
1. Very brisk, alert, and high-spirited.   1. LIVELY.
2. Being or in accordance with the current fashion.   2. FASHIONABLE.

dastard *noun*
An ignoble, uncourageous person.   COWARD.

dastardliness *noun*
Ignoble lack of courage.   COWARDICE.

dastardly *adjective*
Ignobly lacking in courage.   COWARDLY.

data *noun*
Knowledge about a specific subject or situation.   INFORMATION.

date *noun*
Informal. A commitment to appear at a certain time and place.   ENGAGEMENT.

date *verb*
To be together socially on a regular basis.   SEE.

dated *adjective*
Of a style or method formerly in vogue.   OLD-FASHIONED.

dateless *adjective*
Existing unchanged forever.   AGELESS.

daub *verb*
To spread with a greasy, sticky, or dirty substance.   SMEAR *verb*.

daub *noun*
A discolored mark made by smearing.   SMEAR *noun*.

daunt *verb*
To deprive of courage or the power to act as a result of fear, anxiety, or disgust.   DISMAY *verb*.

dauntless *adjective*
Having or showing courage.   BRAVE *adjective*.

dauntlessness *noun*
The quality of mind enabling one to face danger or hardship resolutely.   COURAGE.

dawdle *verb*
To go or move slowly so that progress is hindered.   DELAY *verb*.

dawn *noun*
1. The first appearance of daylight in the morning: *Farmers often get up before dawn.*

Syns: aurora (*Poetic*), cockcrow, dawning, daybreak, dayspring (*Poetic*), morn (*Poetic*), morning, sunrise, sunup.
—*Idioms* break of day, crack of dawn, first light.

2. The initial stage of a developmental process.

2. BIRTH *noun.*

dawn *verb*
To begin to appear or develop: *A new era in science dawned with the theory of relativity.*

Syns: appear, arise, commence, emerge, originate.

dawn on (or **upon**) *verb*
To come as a realization.

REGISTER *verb.*

dawning *noun*
1. The first appearance of daylight in the morning.
2. The initial stage of a developmental process.

1. DAWN *noun.*
2. BIRTH *noun.*

dawn on (or **upon**) *verb*

SEE **dawn.**

daybreak *noun*
The first appearance of daylight in the morning.

DAWN *noun.*

day(s) *noun*
A particular time notable for its distinctive characteristics.

AGE *noun.*

dayspring *noun*
Poetic. The first appearance of daylight in the morning.

DAWN *noun.*

daze *verb*
1. To confuse with bright light: *The spotlight dazed her, and she shielded her eyes.*

1. **Syns:** bedazzle, blind, dazzle.

2. To stun the senses, as with a heavy blow, a shock, or fatigue: *bewildered and dazed after the bombing.*

2. **Syns:** bedaze, bemuse, benumb, maze (*Archaic*), stupefy.

daze *noun*
A stunned or bewildered condition: *fell flat and lay on the ground in a daze.*

Syns: befuddlement, fog, maze (*Archaic*), muddle, stupor, trance.

dazzle *verb*
To confuse with bright light.

DAZE *verb.*

dazzle *noun*
An intense, blinding light.

GLARE *noun.*

dazzling *adjective*
Extremely bright.

BLAZING.

dead *adjective*
1. No longer alive: *Dead men tell no tales.*

1. **Syns:** asleep, deceased, defunct, demised, departed, extinct, gone, late, lifeless, perished. —*Idioms* at rest, pushing up daisies, with one's fathers.

2. Lacking physical feeling or sensitivity: *Her frostbitten toes felt dead.*
3. No longer in use, force, or operation.
4. *Informal.* Extremely tired.
5. Completely such, without qualification or exception.

2. **Syns:** asleep, benumbed, insensible, insensitive, numb, numbed, unfeeling.
3. VANISHED.
4. EXHAUSTED.
5. UTTER[2].

dead *adverb*
1. To the fullest extent.
2. In a direct line.
3. Without the slightest deviation in any respect.

1. COMPLETELY.
2. DIRECTLY.
3. PRECISELY.

deaden *verb*
1. To render less sensitive: *a topical anesthetic to deaden the pain.*

1. **Syns:** benumb, blunt, desensitize, dull, numb. —*Idiom* take the edge off.

2. To decrease or dull the sound of.

2. MUFFLE.

deadliness *noun*
The quality or condition of causing death.

FATALITY.

deadlock *noun*
An equality of scores, votes, or performances in a contest.

TIE *noun.*

deadly *adjective*
1. Causing or tending to cause death: *Cyanide is a deadly poison.*

    1. **Syns:** deathly, fatal, lethal, mortal, vital (*Archaic*).
    Near-syns: baneful, noxious, pernicious, poisonous, toxic, virulent.

2. Gruesomely suggestive of ghosts or death.
    2. GHASTLY.

3. Extremely destructive or harmful.
    3. VIRULENT.

deadpan *adjective*
Slang. Lacking expression.

    EXPRESSIONLESS.

deafening *adjective*
Marked by extremely high volume and intensity of sound.

    LOUD *adjective*.

deal *verb*
1. To be occupied or concerned: *Astronomy deals with heavenly bodies.*

    1. **Syns:** consider, take up, treat. —*Idiom* have to do with.

2. To give out in portions.
    2. DISTRIBUTE.

3. To mete out by means of some action.
    3. GIVE.

4. To engage in the illicit sale of (narcotics).
    4. PUSH.

deal in *verb*
To offer for sale.

    SELL *verb*.

deal with *verb*
To behave in a specified way toward: *dealt with his assistants as equals.*

    Syns: handle, treat.

deal *noun*
1. *Informal.* An act or state of agreeing between parties regarding a course of action.

    1. AGREEMENT.

2. An indefinite amount or extent: *has a good deal of money; is a great deal thinner.*

    2. **Syns:** lot, quantity.

dealer *noun*
1. A person engaged in buying and selling: *a diamond dealer.*

    1. **Syns:** businessperson, merchandiser, merchant, trader, tradesman, trafficker.

2. A person who sells narcotics illegally.
    2. PUSHER.

deal in *verb*
    SEE **deal.**

deal with *verb*
    SEE **deal.**

dear *noun*
A person who is much loved.

    DARLING *noun*.

dear *adjective*
1. Regarded with much love and tenderness.
    1. DARLING *adjective*.

2. Given special, usu. doting treatment.
    2. FAVORITE *adjective*.

3. Bringing a high price.
    3. COSTLY.

dearth *noun*
The condition of lacking a usual or needed amount.

    ABSENCE.

death *noun*
1. The act or fact of dying: *the hour of her death; the death of a dream.*

    1. **Syns:** curtains (*Slang*), decease, demise, dissolution, extinction, passing, quietus. —*Idioms* eternal rest, Grim Reaper, Pale Horse.

2. A termination of life usu. as the result of an accident or a disaster.

    2. FATALITY.

deathless *adjective*
Not being subject to death.

    IMMORTAL.

deathlessness *noun*
Endless life after death.

    IMMORTALITY.

deathlike *adjective*
Gruesomely suggestive of ghosts or death.

    GHASTLY.

deathly *adjective*
1. Suggestive of death.
    1. DEADLY.

2. Causing or tending to cause death.
    2. DEADLY.

debacle *noun*
An abrupt, disastrous failure.

    COLLAPSE *noun*.

debar *verb*
To keep from being admitted, included, or considered. EXCLUDE.

debark *verb*
To come ashore from a seacraft. LAND *verb*.

debase *verb*
1. To lower in character or quality: *debasing language by misusing it.*
2. To ruin utterly in character or quality.
3. To make impure or inferior by deceptively adding foreign substances.

1. **Syns:** cheapen, degrade, demean², downgrade.
2. CORRUPT *verb*.
3. ADULTERATE.

debased *adjective*
Lowered in character or quality. CORRUPTED.

debatable *adjective*
In doubt or dispute: *a debatable theory.*

Syns: arguable, contested, disputable, disputed, doubtful, moot, mootable, problematical (*also* problematic), questionable, uncertain.
Near-ants: indisputable, unquestionable; certain, confirmed, established, settled, sure.
Ant: undebatable.

debate *verb*
To put forth reasons for or against, often excitedly. ARGUE.

debate *noun*
1. A discussion, often heated, in which a difference of opinion is expressed.
2. The presentation of an argument.

1. ARGUMENT.
2. ARGUMENTATION.

debauch *verb*
1. To ruin utterly in character or quality.
2. To lure or persuade into a sexual relationship.

1. CORRUPT *verb*.
2. SEDUCE.

debauched *adjective*
Lowered in character or quality. CORRUPTED.

debaucher *noun*
A man who seduces women. SEDUCER.

debauching *noun*
The act or an instance of seducing sexually. SEDUCTION.

debauchment *noun*
Obs. The act or an instance of seducing sexually. SEDUCTION.

debilitate *verb*
To lessen or deplete the nerve, energy, or strength of. ENERVATE.

debilitated *adjective*
Depleted of strength or robust health. RUN-DOWN *adjective* at **run down.**

debilitation *noun*
The condition of being infirm or physically weak. INFIRMITY.

debility *noun*
The condition of being infirm or physically weak. INFIRMITY.

debonair also **debonaire** *adjective*
Displaying light-hearted nonchalance. AIRY.

debonaire *adjective* SEE **debonair.**

debt *noun*
1. Something, such as money, owed by one person to another: *a debt of $500; a debt of gratitude.*
2. A condition of owing something to another: *can't seem to get out of debt.*

1. **Syns:** arrear *or* arrears, arrearage, due, indebtedness, liability.
2. **Syns:** arrearage, indebtedness, liability, obligation, obligement.

debunk *verb*
To cause to be no longer believed or valued. DISCREDIT *verb*.

debut also **début** *verb*
To make one's formal entry, as into society. COME OUT at **come.**

decadence *noun*
Descent to a lower level or condition. DETERIORATION.

decamp *verb*
To break loose and leave suddenly, as from confinement or from a difficult or threatening situation.   ESCAPE *verb*.

decampment *noun*
The act or an instance of escaping, as from confinement or difficulty.   ESCAPE *noun*.

decant *verb*
To cause (a liquid) to flow in a steady stream.   POUR.

decay *verb*
To become or cause to become rotten or unsound: *a tooth decaying from neglect.*   **Syns:** break down, decompose, deteriorate, molder, putrefy, putresce, rot, spoil, turn. —*Idioms* go bad, go to pot, go to seed.

decay *noun*
The condition of being decayed: *the complete decay of civilization.*   **Syns:** breakdown, decomposition, deterioration, putrefaction, putrescence, putridness, rot, spoilage.

decayed *adjective*
Impaired because of decay.   BAD.

decaying *adjective*
Showing signs of wear and tear or neglect.   SHABBY.

decease *noun*
The act or fact of dying.   DEATH.

decease *verb*
To cease living.   DIE.

deceased *adjective*
No longer alive.   DEAD *adjective*.

deceit *noun*
The act or practice of deceiving: *A pious man on the Sabbath, during the week he is full of deceit.*   **Syns:** cunning, deceitfulness, deception, double-dealing, duplicity, guile. **Near-ants:** candor, frankness, forthrightness, honesty, openness, straightforwardness, uprightness.

deceitful *adjective*
Given to or marked by deliberate concealment or misrepresentation of the truth.   DISHONEST.

deceitfulness *noun*
The act or practice of deceiving.   DECEIT.

deceive *verb*
To cause to accept what is false, esp. by trickery or misrepresentation: *An inexperienced person is easily deceived.*   **Syns:** bamboozle (*Informal*), beguile, betray, bluff, cozen, delude, double-cross (*Slang*), dupe, fool, four-flush (*Slang*), have, hoodwink, humbug, mislead, take in, trick. —*Idioms* lead astray, play false, pull the wool over someone's eyes, put something over on, take for a ride.

decency *noun*
1. Conformity to recognized standards, as of conduct or appearance: *behaved with decency.*   1. **Syns:** correctness, decorum, propriety, seemliness.
2. A sense of propriety or rightness: *had the decency to resign.*   2. **Syns:** conscience, grace.
3. The condition of being chaste.   3. CHASTITY.

decent *adjective*
1. *Informal.* Proper in appearance: *bought a decent suit of clothes.*   1. **Syns:** presentable, respectable.
2. Of moderately good quality but less than excellent.   2. ACCEPTABLE.
3. Conforming to accepted standards.   3. CORRECT *adjective*.
4. Morally beyond reproach, esp. in sexual conduct.   4. CHASTE.
5. Not lewd or obscene.   5. CLEAN *adjective*.

deception *noun*
1. An action meant to deceive: *guilty of lies and deception.*

2. The act or practice of deceiving.
deceptive *adjective*
Tending to lead one into error.
decide *verb*
1. To make up or cause to make up one's mind: *Have you decided to buy the house?*
2. To make a decision about (a controversy, dispute, etc.) after deliberation, as in a court of law.
decided *adjective*
1. Without any doubt: *The dinner was a decided success.*
2. Not hesitating or wavering.
3. On an unwavering course of action.
4. Clearly, fully, and sometimes emphatically expressed.
decidedness *noun*
Unwavering firmness of character or action.
deciding *adjective*
Determining or having the power to determine an outcome.
decimate *verb*
To kill savagely and indiscriminately.
decimation *noun*
Severe damage or decay rendering something useless or worthless.
decipher *verb*
1. To find the key to.
2. To find a solution for.
3. To make understandable.
decision *noun*
1. A position reached after consideration: *When you've made a decision, please let me know.*
2. Unwavering firmness of character or action: *a woman of extraordinary decision.*

decisive *adjective*
1. Determining or having the power to determine an outcome: *The decisive vote was cast.*
2. Not hesitating or wavering: *took decisive action to end the strike.*
decisiveness *noun*
Unwavering firmness of character or action.
deck *verb*
1. To furnish with decorations.
2. To cause to fall, as from a shot or blow.
  deck out *verb*
  To dress in formal or special clothing.
deck out *verb*
declamation *noun*
1. The art of public speaking.
2. A usu. formal oral communication to an audience.
declamatory *adjective*
1. Of or relating to the art of public speaking.
2. Characterized by language that is elevated and sometimes pompous in style.
declaration *noun*
1. The act of announcing.

1. **Syns:** dodge, imposture, ruse, sell (*Slang*), sleight, stratagem, subterfuge, take-in, trick.
2. DECEIT.

FALLACIOUS.

1. **Syns:** conclude, determine, resolve, settle.
2. JUDGE *verb*.

1. **Syns:** clear, clear-cut, definite, distinct, pronounced, unquestionable.
2. DECISIVE.
3. SET[1] *adjective*.
4. DEFINITE.

DECISION.

DECISIVE.

ANNIHILATE.

RUIN *noun*.

1. BREAK *verb*.
2. RESOLVE *verb*.
3. EXPLAIN.

1. **Syns:** conclusion, determination, resolution.
2. **Syns:** decidedness, decisiveness, determination, firmness, resoluteness, resolution, resolve.

1. **Syns:** conclusive, crucial, deciding, determinative.
2. **Syns:** decided, determined, firm[1], resolute.

DECISION.

1. ADORN.
2. DROP *verb*.

DRESS UP at **dress.**
SEE **deck.**

1. ORATORY.
2. SPEECH.

1. ORATORICAL.
2. SONOROUS.

1. ANNOUNCEMENT.

2. A public statement.

3. The act of asserting positively.

declare *verb*

1. To bring to public notice.

2. To put into words positively and with conviction.

3. To state to be true.

4. To put into words.

déclassé also **declassed** *adjective*

Lacking high station or birth.

declassed *adjective*

declension *noun*

Descent to a lower level or condition.

declination *noun*

1. Descent to a lower level or condition.

2. A marked loss of strength or effectiveness.

decline *verb*

1. To be unwilling to accept, consider, or receive: *always declines offers of help.*

2. To slope downward.

3. To become lower in quality, character, or condition.

4. To lose strength or power.

decline *noun*

1. A downward slope or distance.

2. A usu. swift downward trend, as in prices.

3. Descent to a lower level or condition.

4. A marked loss of strength or effectiveness.

declivity *noun*

A downward slope or distance.

decompose *verb*

1. To reduce or become reduced to pieces or components.

2. To become or cause to become rotten or unsound.

decomposed *adjective*

Impaired because of decay.

decomposition *noun*

The condition of being decayed.

decontaminate *verb*

To render free of microorganisms.

decorate *verb*

To furnish with decorations.

decoration *noun*

1. An emblem of honor worn on one's clothing: *wore all his decorations when he put on his full-dress suit.*

2. Something that adorns.

decorous *adjective*

Conforming to accepted standards.

decorticate *verb*

To remove the skin of.

decorum *noun*

1. Conformity to recognized standards, as of conduct or appearance.

2. Socially correct behavior.

decrease *verb*

To grow or cause to grow gradually less: *Our worries cannot decrease so long as rampant inflation is a fact of life.*

---

2. ANNOUNCEMENT.

3. ASSERTION.

1. ANNOUNCE.

2. ASSERT.

3. CLAIM *verb*.

4. SAY.

LOWLY.

SEE **déclassé**.

DETERIORATION.

1. DETERIORATION.

2. FAILURE.

1. *Syns:* dismiss, nix (*Slang*), refuse, reject, spurn, turn down. —*Idiom* turn thumbs down on.

2. DROP *verb*.

3. DETERIORATE.

4. FADE *verb*.

1. DROP *noun*.

2. FALL *noun*.

3. DETERIORATION.

4. FAILURE.

DROP *noun*.

1. BREAK UP at **break**.

2. DECAY *verb*.

BAD.

DECAY *noun*.

STERILIZE.

ADORN.

1. *Syns:* badge, medal.

2. ADORNMENT.

CORRECT *adjective*.

SKIN *verb*.

1. DECENCY.

2. MANNERS.

Syns: abate, diminish, drain, dwindle, ebb, lessen, let up, peter out, rebate (*Rare*), reduce, tail off, taper off.
Near-ants: amplify, expand, swell; accumulate, amass, augment, enlarge, multiply.
Ant: increase.

decrease *noun*
1. The act or process of decreasing: *a steady decrease in the number of students in the department.*

2. The act or process of decreasing in length, amount, duration, etc.

1. *Syns:* abatement, decrement, diminishment, diminution, letup, reduction.

2. CUTBACK at **cut back.**

decree *noun*
1. A principle governing the affairs of man within or among political units.
2. An authoritative or official decision, esp. one made by a court.

1. LAW *noun.*

2. RULING *noun.*

decree *verb*
To set forth expressly and authoritatively.

DICTATE *verb.*

decrement *noun*
The act or process of decreasing.

DECREASE *noun.*

decrepit *adjective*
1. Not physically strong.
2. Showing signs of wear and tear or neglect.

1. INFIRM.
2. SHABBY.

decrepitude *noun*
The condition of being infirm or physically weak.

INFIRMITY.

decretum *noun*
A principle governing the affairs of man within or among political units.

LAW *noun.*

decry *verb*
To think, represent, or speak of as small or unimportant.

BELITTLE.

decrying *adjective*
Tending or intending to belittle.

DISPARAGING.

decumbent *adjective*
Lying down.

FLAT *adjective.*

decussate *verb*
To pass through or over.

CROSS *verb.*

dedicate *verb*
1. To give over by or as if by vow to a higher purpose.
2. To devote (oneself or one's efforts).

1. DEVOTE.
2. APPLY.

dedicated *adjective*
Given over exclusively to a single use or purpose.

SACRED.

deduce *verb*
To draw a conclusion from evidence or reasoning.

INFER.

deduct *verb*
1. To take away (a quantity) from another quantity: *will deduct the medical costs from her taxable income.*
2. To draw a conclusion from evidence or reasoning.

1. *Syns:* discount, knock off (*Informal*), subtract, take, take off.

2. INFER.

deduction *noun*
1. An amount deducted: *a legitimate tax deduction.*

2. A position arrived at by reasoning from premises or general principles: *The result bore out the deduction he had made.*

1. *Syns:* abatement, discount, rebate, reduction.

2. *Syns:* conclusion, illation, inference, judgment.

deed *noun*
Something done.

ACT *noun.*

deed *verb*
To change the ownership of (property) by means of a legal document.

TRANSFER.

deem *verb*
To have an opinion.

BELIEVE.

de-emphasize *verb*
To make less emphatic or obvious.

SOFT-PEDAL.

deep *adjective*
1. Extending far downward or inward from a surface: *a deep hole; a deep drawer.*
2. Beyond the understanding of an average mind: *a deep mystery.*

3. Resulting from or affecting one's innermost feelings: *a deep love; deep sorrow.*
4. Having one's thoughts fully occupied.
5. Being a sound produced by a relatively small frequency of vibrations.

1. *Syns:* abysmal, profound.
2. *Syns:* abstruse, esoteric, heavy (*Slang*), profound, recondite.
   Near-ants: apparent, clear, distinct, evident, manifest, obvious; lucid.
3. *Syns:* deep-felt, intense, profound, strong.
4. ABSORBED.
5. LOW *adjective.*

deepen *verb*
To increase in intensity or severity.

INTENSIFY.

deep-felt *adjective*
Resulting from or affecting one's innermost feelings.

DEEP *adjective.*

deepness *noun*
1. The extent or measurement downward from a surface.
2. Intellectual penetration or range.

1. DEPTH.
2. DEPTH.

defamation *noun*
The expression of injurious, malicious statements about someone.

LIBEL *noun.*

defamatory *adjective*
Damaging to the reputation.

LIBELOUS.

defame *verb*
To make defamatory statements about.

LIBEL *verb.*

default *noun*
1. *Obs.* The condition of lacking a usual or needed amount.
2. Nonperformance of what ought to be done.

1. ABSENCE.
2. FAILURE.

default *verb*
To not do (something necessary).

FAIL.

defeasance *noun*
An often formal act of putting an end to.

ABOLITION.

defeat *verb*
1. To win a victory over, as in battle or a competition: *The Allies defeated the Axis powers in World War II.*

1. *Syns:* beat, best, bury (*Slang*), clobber (*Slang*), conquer, down (*Informal*), drub (*Slang*), lick (*Slang*), overcome, rout[2], shellac (*Slang*), smear (*Slang*), subdue, thrash, trim (*Informal*), triumph (over), trounce, vanquish, whip (*Informal*), worst. —*Idioms* carry (*or* win) the day, get the better (*or* best) of, go someone one better.

2. To prevent from accomplishing a purpose.

2. FRUSTRATE.

defeat *noun*
The act of defeating or the condition of being defeated: *suffered total defeat by the enemy.*

Syns: beating, clobbering (*Slang*), drubbing (*Slang*), licking (*Informal*), overthrow, rout[2], shellacking (*Slang*), thrashing, trimming (*Informal*), whipping (*Informal*).

defect *noun*
1. Something that mars the appearance or causes inadequacy or failure: *a speech defect.*
2. The condition of lacking a usual or needed amount.
3. The condition or fact of being deficient.

1. *Syns:* blemish, bug (*Slang*), fault, flaw, imperfection, shortcoming.
2. ABSENCE.
3. SHORTAGE.

defect *verb*
To abandon one's cause or party usu. to join another: *defected from the Soviet Union and sought asylum in Switzerland.*

Syns: apostatize, desert[3], rat (*Slang*), run out (*Slang*), tergiversate, turn. —*Idioms* change sides, turn one's coat.

defection *noun*
An instance of defecting from or abandoning a cause: *expected his defection.*

Syns: apostasy, recreancy, tergiversation.

defective *adjective*
1. Having a defect or defects: *bought a book that turned out to be defective.*

1. *Syns:* faulty, flawed, imperfect.
   Near-ants: flawless, impeccable, perfect, unblemished, undamaged, virgin.
   Ant: defectless.

2. Lacking an essential element.

2. DEFICIENT.

defector *noun*
A person who has defected: *a defector from the Soviet Union.*

Syns: apostate, rat (*Slang*), recreant, renegade, runagate (*Archaic*), tergiversator, turncoat.

defend *verb*
1. To keep safe from danger, attack, or harm: *used an alarm system to defend his home against burglars.*
2. To support against arguments, attack, or criticism: *constantly has to defend his opinions and actions.*

1. *Syns:* fend (*Archaic*), guard, protect, safeguard, secure, shield.
2. *Syns:* justify, maintain, vindicate.
   —*Idioms* speak up for, stand up for, stick up for.

defendable *adjective*
Capable of being defended against armed attack.

TENABLE.

defendant *noun*
Law. A person against whom an action is brought.

ACCUSED.

defense *noun*
1. The act or a means of defending: *taking measures for the defense of the country.*
2. A statement that justifies or defends past actions, policies, etc.

1. *Syns:* guard, protection, safeguard, security, shield, ward.
2. APOLOGY.

defenseless *adjective*
Devoid of help or protection.

HELPLESS.

defensible *adjective*
1. Capable of being defended against armed attack.
2. Capable of being justified.

1. TENABLE.
2. JUSTIFIABLE.

defer[1] *verb*
To put off until a later time: *deferred writing the letter until she knew when she would leave.*

Syns: adjourn, delay, hold off, hold up, lay over, postpone, remit, shelve, stay[1], suspend, table, wait (*Informal*), waive.
—*Idioms* put on ice, set aside.

defer[2] *verb*
To conform to the will or judgment of another, esp. out of respect or courtesy: *deferred to his better judgment.*

Syns: bow, submit, yield. —*Idioms* give ground, give place, give way.

deference *noun*
Great respect or high public esteem accorded as a right or as due.

HONOR *noun.*

deferential *adjective*
Marked by courteous submission or respect: *deferential behavior.*

Syns: dutiful, obeisant, respectful.

deferment *noun*
The act of putting off or the condition of being put off.

DELAY *noun.*

deferral *noun*
The act of putting off or the condition of being put off.

DELAY *noun.*

defiance *noun*
1. The disposition boldly to defy or resist authority or an opposing force: *often exhibited defiance toward his parents.*
2. Behavior or an act that is intentionally provocative: *failure to comply that can only be called defiance.*

1. *Syns:* contempt, contumacy, despite, recalcitrance (*also* recalcitrancy), unruliness.
2. *Syns:* challenge, provocation.

defiant *adjective*
Marked by defiance: *a defiant attitude; defiant words.*

Syns: contemptuous, contumacious, recalcitrant, unruly.

deficience *noun*

deficiency also **deficience** *noun*
The condition or fact of being deficient.

deficient *adjective*
1. Lacking an essential element: *deficient in awareness of the world around her.*

2. Not enough to meet a demand or requirement.

deficit *noun*
The condition or fact of being deficient.

defile *verb*
1. To make morally impure.
2. To spoil or mar the sanctity of.
3. *Obs.* To deprive of virginity.

defiled *adjective*
Ceremonially or religiously unfit.

definite *adjective*
1. Clearly, fully, and sometimes emphatically expressed: *a definite statement that he would not run for re-election.*

2. Known positively: *The time of his departure is not definite.*
3. Having distinct limits: *will stay for a short but definite period.*
4. Without any doubt.

definitive *adjective*
Serving the function of deciding or settling with finality: *a definitive biography that answers all the questions.*

deflect *verb*
1. To cause to move, esp. at an angle.
2. To change the direction or course of.

deflorate *verb*
To deprive of virginity.

deflower *verb*
To deprive of virginity.

deform *verb*
To alter and spoil the natural form or appearance of: *Rage deformed his face.*

deformity *noun*
A disfiguring abnormality of shape or form: *scoliosis and other deformities.*

defraud *verb*
To get money or something else from by deceitful trickery.

deft *adjective*
1. Exhibiting or possessing skill and ease in performance.
2. Showing art or skill in performing or doing.
3. Well done or executed.

deftness *noun*
Skillfulness in the use of the hands or body.

defunct *adjective*
1. No longer alive.
2. No longer in use, force, or operation.

SEE **deficiency.**

SHORTAGE.

1. *Syns:* defective, incomplete, lacking, wanting.
   Near-syns: damaged, impaired; faulty, flawed, imperfect; inadequate, insufficient, unsatisfactory.
2. INSUFFICIENT.

SHORTAGE.

1. TAINT *verb.*
2. VIOLATE.
3. VIOLATE.

IMPURE.

1. *Syns:* categorical, clear-cut, decided, explicit, express, positive, precise, specific, unambiguous, unequivocal.
   Near-syns: definitive, incisive; complete, downright, forthright.
   Ants: indefinite, equivocal.
2. *Syns:* certain, positive, sure. —*Idiom* for certain.
3. *Syns:* bounded, determinate, fixed, limited.
4. DECIDED.

Syns: conclusive, determinative, final.

1. BEND *verb.*
2. TURN *verb.*

VIOLATE.

VIOLATE.

Syns: contort, disfigure, distort, misshape, twist.

Syns: disfigurement, malformation.

CHEAT *verb.*

1. DEXTEROUS.

2. ARTFUL.
3. NEAT.

DEXTERITY.

1. DEAD *adjective.*
2. VANISHED.

defy *verb*
1. To confront boldly and courageously: *an innovator who defies tradition at every turn.*

    1. **Syns:** beard, brave, challenge, dare, face, front, outdare. —*Idioms* fly in the face of, hurl defiance at, shake one's fist at, snap one's fingers at, stand up to, thumb one's nose at.

2. To call on another to do something requiring boldness.

    2. DARE *verb.*

3. To refuse or fail to obey.

    3. DISOBEY.

degeneracy *noun*
Descent to a lower level or condition.

    DETERIORATION.

degenerate *adjective*
Utterly reprehensible in nature or behavior.

    CORRUPT *adjective.*

degenerate *verb*
To become lower in quality, character, or condition.

    DETERIORATE.

degeneration *noun*
1. Descent to a lower level or condition.
2. Severe damage or decay rendering something useless or worthless.

    1. DETERIORATION.
    2. RUIN *noun.*

degradation *noun*
The act or an instance of demoting.

    DEMOTION.

degrade *verb*
1. To lower in character or quality.
2. To lower in rank or grade.
3. To deprive of esteem, self-worth, or effectiveness.

    1. DEBASE.
    2. DEMOTE.
    3. HUMBLE *verb.*

degraded *adjective*
Mixed with other substances.

    IMPURE.

degree *noun*
1. One of the units in a course, as on an ascending or descending scale: *moved up slowly and by degrees.*
2. Relative intensity or amount, as of a quality or attribute: *a high degree of accuracy; various degrees of ability.*

    1. **Syns:** grade, level, notch, peg, rung, stage, step.
    2. **Syns:** extent, magnitude, measure, portion, proportion.

dehydrate *verb*
To make or become free of moisture.

    DRY *verb.*

dehydrated *adjective*
Having little or no liquid or moisture.

    DRY *adjective.*

deific *adjective*
Of, from, like, or being a god or God.

    DIVINE[1] *adjective.*

deign *verb*
To descend to a level considered inappropriate to one's dignity.

    CONDESCEND.

deject *verb*
To make sad or gloomy.

    DEPRESS.

dejected *adjective*
In low spirits.

    DEPRESSED.

dejection *noun*
A feeling or spell of dismally low spirits.

    GLOOM.

delay *verb*
1. To cause to be later or slower than expected or desired: *delayed by urgent business.*
2. To go or move slowly so that progress is hindered: *didn't hurry but didn't delay either.*

    1. **Syns:** detain, hang up, hold up, retard, set back, slow (down *or* up).
    2. **Syns:** dally, dawdle, dilly-dally, drag, lag, linger, loiter, poke, procrastinate, tarry, trail. —*Idioms* drag one's feet, mark time, take one's time.

3. To put off until a later time.

    3. DEFER[1].

delay *noun*
1. The condition or fact of being made late or slow: *a delay caused by rush-hour traffic.*

    1. **Syns:** detainment, holdup, lag, retardation.

2. The act of putting off or the condition of being put off: *a delay of 15 minutes.*

delectable *adjective*
1. Giving great pleasure or delight.
2. Highly pleasing, esp. to the sense of taste.

delectate *verb*
To give great or keen pleasure to.

delectation *noun*
1. A feeling of extreme gratification aroused by something good or desired.
2. The condition of responding pleasurably to something.

delegate *noun*
One who stands for another.

delegation *noun*
A diplomatic office or headquarters in a foreign country.

delete *verb*
To take or leave out.

deleterious *adjective*
Causing harm or injury.

deletion *noun*
The act of erasing or the condition of being erased.

deliberate *verb*
1. To consider carefully and at length.
2. To use the faculty of reason.

deliberate *adjective*
1. Done or said on purpose: *a deliberate lie.*

2. Careful and slow in acting, moving, or deciding: *walked with a deliberate step.*
3. Planned, weighed, or estimated in advance.

deliberated *adjective*
Resulting from deliberation and careful thought.

deliberation *noun*
1. An exchange of views in an attempt to reach a decision: *the deliberations of the steering committee.*
2. The act or process of thinking.

deliberative *adjective*
Of, characterized by, or disposed to thought.

delicacy *noun*
Something fine and delicious, esp. a food: *Caviar is a real delicacy.*

delicate *adjective*
1. Appealing to refined taste: *prepared a delicate meal.*

2. So slight as to be difficult to notice or appreciate: *a delicate difference.*
3. Not physically strong.
4. Easily broken or damaged.
5. Showing sensitivity and skill in dealing with others: *too delicate to tell him the gossip we had heard about him.*
6. Able to make or detect effects of great subtlety or precision.
7. Requiring great tact or skill: *a delicate subject.*

2. *Syns:* adjournment, deferment, deferral, postponement, stay[1], suspension.

1. DELIGHTFUL.
2. DELICIOUS.

DELIGHT *verb.*

1. DELIGHT *noun.*

2. ENJOYMENT.

REPRESENTATIVE *noun.*

MISSION.

DROP *verb.*

HARMFUL.

ERASURE.

1. PONDER.
2. REASON *verb.*

1. *Syns:* intended, intentional, voluntary, willful, willing, witting.
2. *Syns:* leisurely, measured, unhurried.

3. CALCULATED.

ADVISED.

1. *Syns:* confabulation, conference, consultation, counsel, parley.
2. THOUGHT.

THOUGHTFUL.

Syns: dainty, goody (*Informal*), morsel, tidbit, treat.

1. *Syns:* choice, dainty, elegant, exquisite, fine[1].
Near-syns: select, superior; delectable, delicious, delightful.
Ants: gross, vulgar.
2. *Syns:* fine[1], finespun, nice, refined, subtle.
3. INFIRM.
4. FRAGILE.
5. *Syns:* diplomatic, discreet, politic, sensitive, tactful.

6. FINE[1].

7. *Syns:* sensitive, ticklish, touch-and-go, touchy, tricky.

delicious *adjective*
1. Highly pleasing, esp. to the sense of taste: *a perfectly delicious pâté.*

1. **Syns:** ambrosial, delectable, heavenly, luscious, savory, scrumptious (*Slang*), tasteful (*Rare*), tasty, toothsome, yummy (*Slang*).

2. Giving great pleasure or delight.

2. DELIGHTFUL.

delight *noun*
A feeling of extreme gratification aroused by something good or desired: *listened to the concert with delight.*

Syns: delectation, enjoyment, joy, pleasure, relish.

delight *verb*
1. To feel or take joy or pleasure.
2. To give great or keen pleasure to: *a view that delights the eye.*

1. REJOICE.
2. **Syns:** cheer, delectate, enchant, gladden, gratify, joy (*Archaic*), please, pleasure, tickle.

delight in *verb*
To like or enjoy enthusiastically, often excessively.

ADORE.

delighted *adjective*
Eagerly compliant.

GLAD.

delightful *adjective*
Giving great pleasure or delight: *a Renoir that is the most delightful painting in the collection.*

Syns: charming, darling (*Informal*), delectable, delicious, enchanting, heavenly, luscious.
Near-ants: distasteful, obnoxious, repellent, repugnant, vile; detestable, disgusting, odious.
Ants: abominable, horrid, wretched.
SEE **delight**.

delight in *verb*
delimit *verb*
1. To fix the limits of.
2. To place a limit on.

1. DETERMINE.
2. LIMIT *verb*.

delimitate *verb*
1. To fix the limits of.
2. To place a limit on.

1. DETERMINE.
2. LIMIT *verb*.

delineate *verb*
To present a lifelike image of.

REPRESENT.

delineation *noun*
1. The act or process of describing in lifelike imagery.
2. A line marking and shaping the outer form of an object.

1. REPRESENTATION.
2. OUTLINE *noun*.

delineative *adjective*
Serving to describe.

DESCRIPTIVE.

delinquency *noun*
Nonperformance of what ought to be done.

FAILURE.

deliquesce *verb*
To change from a solid to a liquid.

MELT.

delirious *adjective*
Marked by extreme excitement, confusion, or agitation.

FRANTIC.

deliver *verb*
1. To relinquish to the possession or control of another.
2. To mete out by means of some action.
3. To give birth to.
4. To extricate, as from danger or confinement.

1. GIVE *verb*.
2. GIVE *verb*.
3. BEAR.
4. RESCUE *verb*.

deliverance *noun*
Extrication from danger or confinement.

RESCUE *noun*.

delivery *noun*
1. The act of delivering or the condition of being delivered: *only one mail delivery a day.*
2. The act or process of bringing forth young.
3. Extrication from danger or confinement.

1. **Syns:** surrender, transfer.

2. BIRTH *noun*.
3. RESCUE *noun*.

delude *verb*
To cause to accept what is false, esp. by trickery or misrepresentation.

DECEIVE.

deluge *verb*
1. To flow over completely.
2. To affect as if by an outpouring of water.

1. FLOOD *verb.*
2. FLOOD *verb.*

deluge *noun*
An abundant, usu. overwhelming flow.

FLOOD *noun.*

delusion *noun*
An erroneous perception of reality.

ILLUSION.

delusive *adjective*
1. Tending to lead one into error.
2. Tending to deceive; of the nature of an illusion.

1. FALLACIOUS.
2. ILLUSORY.

delusory *adjective*
1. Tending to lead one into error.
2. Tending to deceive; of the nature of an illusion.

1. FALLACIOUS.
2. ILLUSORY.

delve *verb*
1. *Archaic.* To break, turn over, or remove (earth, sand, etc.) with or as if with a tool.
2. To go into or through for the purpose of making discoveries or acquiring information.

1. DIG *verb.*

2. EXPLORE.

delving *noun*
A seeking of knowledge, data, or the truth about something.

INQUIRY.

demand *verb*
1. To ask for urgently or insistently: *demanding better working conditions.*

2. To have as a need or prerequisite: *The work of a lawyer demands an analytical mind and patience.*

1. *Syns:* call for, exact, insist on (*or* upon), require, requisition. —*Idiom* cry out for.
2. *Syns:* ask, call for, entail, involve, necessitate, require, take.

demand *noun*
1. The act of demanding: *wouldn't pay up on demand.*

2. Something asked for or needed: *Submit your demands in writing, please.*

1. *Syns:* call, claim, cry, exaction, requisition.
2. *Syns:* exigency (*also* exigence), need, requirement, want.

demanding *adjective*
1. Requiring great effort: *a demanding job.*

1. *Syns:* exacting, exigent, taxing, tough. *Near-syns:* burdensome, grievous, onerous, rigid, rigorous, severe, stern, strict. *Ant:* undemanding.

2. Rigorous and unsparing in treating others.
3. Imposing a severe test of bodily or spiritual strength.

2. SEVERE.
3. BURDENSOME.

demarcate *verb*
To fix the limits of.

DETERMINE.

demean[1] *verb*
To conduct oneself in a specified way.

ACT *verb.*

demean[2] *verb*
1. To lower in character or quality.
2. To deprive of esteem, self-worth, or effectiveness.

1. DEBASE.
2. HUMBLE *verb.*

demeanor *noun*
1. Behavior through which one reveals one's personality.
2. The manner in which one behaves.

1. BEARING.

2. BEHAVIOR.

demented *adjective*
Afflicted with or exhibiting irrationality and mental unsoundness.

INSANE.

dementia *noun*
Serious mental illness or disorder impairing a person's capacity to function normally and safely.

INSANITY.

demise *noun*
The act or fact of dying. DEATH.
demise *verb*
To cease living. DIE.
demised *adjective*
No longer alive. DEAD *adjective*.
demission *noun*
A giving up of a possession, claim, or right. ABDICATION.
demit *verb*
1. To give up a possession, claim, or right. 1. ABDICATE.
2. To withdraw from business or active life. 2. RETIRE.
demobilize *verb*
To release from military duty. DISCHARGE *verb*.
democratic *adjective*
Of, representing, or carried on by people at large. POPULAR.
demolish *verb*
1. To break up so that reconstruction is impossible. 1. DESTROY.
2. To cause the complete ruin or wreckage of. 2. DESTROY.
demonstrate *verb*
1. To make manifest or apparent. 1. SHOW *verb*.
2. To establish as true or genuine. 2. PROVE.
demonstration *noun*
An act of showing or displaying. DISPLAY *noun*.
demoralize *verb*
To ruin utterly in character or quality. CORRUPT *verb*.
demoralizing *adjective*
Morally detrimental. UNWHOLESOME.
demote *verb*
To lower in rank or grade: *was demoted from captain to lieutenant.* **Syns:** break, bump (*Informal*), bust (*Slang*), degrade, downgrade, reduce.
demotion *noun*
The act or an instance of demoting: *received a demotion for insubordination.* **Syns:** degradation, downgrading, reduction.
Near-ants: boost, elevation, lift, raise; advancement, upgrade.
Ant: promotion.

demure *adjective*
Reticent or reserved in manner. MODEST.
demureness *noun*
Reserve in speech, behavior, or dress. MODESTY.
den *noun*
1. A hollow place used as an animal's dwelling. 1. HOLE *noun*.
2. A hiding place. 2. HIDE-OUT.
denial *noun*
1. A refusal to grant the truth of a statement or charge: *The article drew an immediate denial from the mayor.* 1. **Syns:** contradiction, disaffirmation, disclaimer, gainsaying, negation, rejection, traversal (*Law*).
2. A turning down of a request. 2. REFUSAL.
denigrate *verb*
To cast aspersions on. BLACKEN.
denominate *verb*
To give a name or title to. NAME *verb*.
denomination *noun*
1. The word or words by which one is called and identified. 1. NAME *noun*.
2. A system of religious belief. 2. RELIGION.
3. Those who accept and practice a particular religious belief. 3. FAITH.
denotative *adjective*
Serving to designate or indicate. DESIGNATIVE.

denote *verb*
1. To make known or identify, as by signs.
2. To have or convey a particular idea.

1. DESIGNATE.
2. MEAN[1].

denotive *adjective*
Serving to designate or indicate.

DESIGNATIVE.

denounce *verb*
1. To make an accusation against.
2. To find fault with.

1. ACCUSE.
2. BLAME *verb*.

denouncement *noun*
A charging of someone with a misdeed.

ACCUSATION.

denouncer *noun*
One that accuses.

ACCUSER.

dense *adjective*
1. Lacking in intelligence.
2. Growing profusely.

1. STUPID.
2. THICK *adjective*.

density *noun*
The quality, condition, or degree of being thick.

THICKNESS.

denude *verb*
1. To make bare.
2. To remove all the clothing from.

1. BARE *verb*.
2. STRIP[1].

denuded *adjective*
Without the usual covering.

BARE *adjective*.

denunciate *verb*
1. To make an accusation against.
2. To find fault with.

1. ACCUSE.
2. BLAME *verb*.

denunciation *noun*
1. A charging of someone with a misdeed.
2. A finding fault.

1. ACCUSATION.
2. BLAME *noun*.

denunciative *adjective*
Containing, relating to, or involving an accusation.

ACCUSATORIAL.

denunciator *noun*
One that accuses.

ACCUSER.

denunciatory *adjective*
Containing, relating to, or involving an accusation.

ACCUSATORIAL.

deny *verb*
1. To refuse to admit the truth, reality, value, or worth of: *You can't deny that he's an arrogant man.*

1. **Syns:** contradict, contravene, controvert, disaffirm, gainsay, negate, negative, traverse (*Law*).
Near-ants: affirm, assert, aver; avow, confess, confirm, corroborate, substantiate, validate.
Ant: admit.

2. To refuse to recognize or acknowledge.
3. To be unwilling to grant.

2. REPUDIATE.
3. REFUSE.

depart *verb*
1. To move or proceed away from a place.
2. To turn away from a prescribed course of action or conduct.
3. To cease living.

1. GO.
2. DEVIATE *verb*.

3. DIE.

departed *adjective*
No longer alive.

DEAD *adjective*.

departing *adjective*
Of, done, given, or said on departing.

PARTING *adjective*.

department *noun*
A sphere of activity, study, or interest.

AREA.

departure *noun*
1. The act of leaving: *The hour of departure is here.*

1. **Syns:** egress, exit, exodus, going, leaving, withdrawal (*also* withdrawment).

2. A departing from what is prescribed.

2. DEVIATION.

depend *verb*

To fasten or be fastened at one point with no support from below.

HANG *verb.*

depend on (or **upon**) *verb*

1. To place trust or confidence in: *You can depend on me.*

1. **Syns:** bank on (*or* upon) (*Informal*), count on, reckon on (*or* upon), rely on (*or* upon), trust (in).

2. To be determined by or contingent on something unknown, uncertain, or changeable: *Whether he goes back to jail depends on whether he violates parole.*

2. **Syns:** hang on (*or* upon), hinge on (*or* upon), rest on (*or* upon), turn on (*or* upon).

3. To anticipate confidently.

3. EXPECT.

dependable *adjective*

Capable of being depended upon: *a dependable worker who is always punctual.*

Syns: reliable, responsible, solid, trustworthy, trusty.
Near-syns: constant, faithful, loyal, steadfast, steady; assured, confident, secure.
Ant: undependable.
SEE **dependent.**

dependant *adjective*
dependency *noun*

An area subject to rule by an outside power.

POSSESSION.

dependent also **dependant** *adjective*

1. Determined or to be determined by someone or something else: *The result is dependent on many circumstances.*

1. **Syns:** conditional, conditioned, contingent, relative (to), reliant, subject (to).

2. In a position of subordination.

2. SUBORDINATE *adjective.*

dependent *noun*

A person who relies on another for support: *will receive a tax deduction for each dependent.*

Syns: charge, ward.

depend on (or **upon**) *verb*

SEE **depend.**

depict *verb*

To present a lifelike image of.

REPRESENT.

depiction *noun*

The act or process of describing in lifelike imagery.

REPRESENTATION.

depictive *adjective*

Serving to describe.

DESCRIPTIVE.

deplete *verb*

1. To lessen or weaken severely, as by removing something essential: *Our oil supply is depleted.*

1. **Syns:** drain, exhaust, impoverish, sap, use up.

2. To make or become no longer active or productive.

2. DRY UP at **dry.**

depleted *adjective*

Lacking desirable elements or constituents.

POOR.

deplorable *adjective*

Worthy of severe disapproval: *a deplorable lack of manners.*

Syns: disgraceful, opprobrious, shameful, unfortunate.
Near-syns: distressing, dreadful, intolerable, lamentable, miserable, regrettable, sickening, wretched.
Ant: favorable.

deplore *verb*

1. To feel or express strong disapproval of: *deplores all forms of violence.*

1. **Syns:** censure, condemn, reprehend, reprobate.

2. To feel or express sorrow for.

2. REGRET *verb.*

depone *verb*

Archaic. To give evidence or testimony under oath.

TESTIFY.

deponent *noun*

Law. One who testifies, esp. in court.

WITNESS *noun.*

deport *verb*

1. To conduct oneself in a specified way.

1. ACT *verb.*

2. To force to leave a country or place by official decree.

2. BANISH.

deportation *noun*
Enforced removal from one's native country by official decree.

EXILE *noun*.

deportment *noun*
The manner in which one behaves.

BEHAVIOR.

depose *verb*
Law. To give evidence or testimony under oath.

TESTIFY.

deposit *verb*
1. To put down, esp. in layers, by a natural process: *The river deposits silt that forms sandbars.*
2. To place (money) in a bank.

1. *Syns:* lay down, precipitate.

2. BANK[1].

deposit *noun*
1. Matter that settles on a bottom or collects on a surface by a natural process: *a muddy deposit in the riverbed.*
2. A partial or initial payment: *put down a deposit on a mink coat.*

1. *Syns:* dregs, lees, precipitate, precipitation, sediment.

2. *Syn:* down payment.

deposition *noun*
Law. A formal declaration of truth or fact given under oath.

TESTIMONY.

depository *noun*
A place where something is deposited for safekeeping: *found a secure depository for the silver.*

Syns: magazine, repository, store, storehouse.

deprave *verb*
To ruin utterly in character or quality.

CORRUPT *verb*.

depraved *adjective*
1. Utterly reprehensible in nature or behavior.
2. Lowered in character or quality.

1. CORRUPT *adjective*.
2. CORRUPTED.

depravity *noun*
Immoral, degrading acts or habits.

CORRUPTION.

deprecate *verb*
To have or express an unfavorable opinion.

DISAPPROVE.

deprecative *adjective*

SEE **deprecatory**.

deprecatory also **deprecative** *adjective*
Tending or intending to belittle.

DISPARAGING.

depreciate *verb*
1. To become or make less in price or value: *used cars that steadily depreciate; depreciating the U.S. dollar.*

2. To think, represent, or speak of as small or unimportant.

1. *Syns:* cheapen, devaluate, devalue, downgrade, lower[2], mark down, reduce, write down.

2. BELITTLE.

depreciating *adjective*
Tending or intending to belittle.

DISPARAGING.

depreciation *noun*
1. A lowering in price or value: *a depreciation in the value of real estate.*
2. The act or an instance of belittling.

1. *Syns:* devaluation, markdown, reduction.

2. BELITTLEMENT.

depreciative *adjective*
Tending or intending to belittle.

DISPARAGING.

depreciatory *adjective*
Tending or intending to belittle.

DISPARAGING.

depredate *verb*
1. To destroy completely while conquering or occupying.
2. To rob of goods by force, esp. in time of war.

1. DEVASTATE.

2. SACK[2].

depress *verb*
1. To make sad or gloomy: *Returning from the funeral to an empty house depressed her deeply.*
2. To cause to descend.

1. *Syns:* cast down, deject, dispirit, oppress, sadden, weigh down.

2. LOWER[2].

depressed *adjective*
1. In low spirits: *The news left me depressed for several days.*

2. Economically and socially below standard: *a program of aid to depressed areas.*

depressing *adjective*
Tending to cause sadness or low spirits.

depression *noun*
1. An area sunk below its surroundings: *a depression in the road.*
2. A feeling or spell of dismally low spirits.
3. A period of decreased business activity and high unemployment: *All signs pointed to a depression.*

deprival *noun*
The condition of being deprived of what one once had or ought to have.

deprivation *noun*
The condition of being deprived of what one once had or ought to have: *living in poverty and deprivation.*

deprive *verb*
To take or keep something away from: *The poll tax deprived many of their right to vote.*

deprived *adjective*
Economically and socially below standard.

depth *noun*
1. The extent or measurement downward from a surface: *dove to a depth of 100 feet.*
2. Intellectual penetration or range: *showed an amazing depth of knowledge.*

deputy *noun*
One who stands for another.

derange *verb*
1. To make insane: *One survivor of the ordeal was permanently deranged by prolonged confinement in the collapsed mine.*
2. To put out of proper order.
3. To disturb the health or physiological functioning of.

deranged *adjective*
Afflicted with or exhibiting irrationality and mental unsoundness.

derangement *noun*
Serious mental illness or disorder impairing a person's capacity to function normally and safely.

derelict *adjective*
1. Having been given up and left alone.
2. Guilty of neglect; lacking due care or concern.

dereliction *noun*
Nonperformance of what ought to be done.

deride *verb*
To make fun of.

de rigueur *adjective*
French. Conforming to accepted standards.

derision *noun*
Words or actions intended to evoke contemptuous laughter.

---

1. **Syns:** blue (*Informal*), dejected, dispirited, down, downcast, downhearted, dull, gloomy, heavyhearted, low, melancholic, melancholy, sad, saddencd, spiritless, tristful (*Archaic*), unhappy. —*Idioms* down in (*or* at) the mouth, in the depths.
2. **Syns:** backward, deprived, disadvantaged, impoverished, underprivileged.

SAD.

1. **Syns:** basin, concavity, dip, hollow, sag, sink.
2. GLOOM.
3. **Syns:** recession, slump.

DEPRIVATION.

Syns: deprival, dispossession, divestiture, loss, privation.

Syns: bereave, dispossess, divest, rob, strip[1].

DEPRESSED.

1. **Syns:** deepness, drop.

2. **Syns:** deepness, profoundness, profundity.

REPRESENTATIVE *noun.*

1. **Syns:** craze, distract, madden, unbalance, unhinge.

2. DISORDER *verb.*
3. UPSET *verb.*

INSANE.

INSANITY.

1. ABANDONED.
2. NEGLIGENT.

FAILURE.

RIDICULE *verb.*

CORRECT *adjective.*

RIDICULE *noun.*

derivate *adjective*   SEE **derivative.**
derivation *noun*
  1. A point of origination.   1. ORIGIN.
  2. Something derived from another.   2. DERIVATIVE *noun.*
derivational *adjective*
  Stemming from an original source.   DERIVATIVE *adjective.*
derivative also **derivate** *adjective*
  Stemming from an original source: *Derivative problems*   **Syns:** derivational, derived, secondary.
  of economic instability include unemployment and
  devaluation of the dollar.
  derivative *noun*
  Something derived from another: *a televison series that*   **Syns:** by-product, derivation, descendant,
  is a derivative of a novel; an anesthesia that is a curare   offshoot, outgrowth, spin-off.
  derivative.
derive *verb*
  1. To arrive at through reasoning: *derived the formula*   1. **Syns:** educe, evolve, excogitate.
     through a set of equations.
  2. To obtain from another source: *We derive our*   2. **Syns:** draw, get, take.
     surname from Gaelic.
  3. To have as a source.   3. STEM *verb.*
  4. To have hereditary derivation.   4. DESCEND.
derived *adjective*
  1. Stemming from an original source.   1. DERIVATIVE *adjective.*
  2. Proceeding by descent from an ancestor.   2. DESCENDING.
derogate *verb*
  To think, represent, or speak of as small or   BELITTLE.
  unimportant.
derogation *noun*
  The act or an instance of belittling.   BELITTLEMENT.
derogatory *adjective*
  Tending or intending to belittle.   DISPARAGING.
derrière *noun*
  The part of one's back on which one rests in sitting.   BOTTOM *noun.*
descend *verb*
  1. To bring oneself down to a lower level of behavior: 1. **Syns:** sink, stoop.
     Don't descend to his level and be underhanded.
  2. To slope downward.   2. DROP *verb.*
  3. To move downward in response to gravity.   3. FALL *verb.*
  4. To become lower in quality, character, or condition.   4. DETERIORATE.
  5. To have hereditary derivation: *a family that*   5. **Syns:** derive, issue, spring. —*Idiom*
     descends from George III.   trace one's descent.
descendant *noun*
  1. One descended directly from the same parents or   1. **Syns:** child, offspring, scion.
     ancestors: *Elizabeth II is a descendant of George III.*
  2. Something derived from another.   2. DERIVATIVE *noun.*
descendant *adjective*   SEE **descendent.**
descendants *noun*
  Those descended from another: *The Israelis are*   **Syns:** begats (*Slang*), brood, children, get,
  descendants of Abraham.   issue, offspring, posterity, progeny, scions,
                                                                      seed.
descendent also **descendant** *adjective*
  1. Moving down.   1. DESCENDING.
  2. Having a down slope.   2. DESCENDING.
  3. Proceeding by descent from an ancestor.   3. DESCENDING.
descending *adjective*
  1. Moving down: *read the names in descending order;*   1. **Syns:** descendent (*also* descendant),
     the descending escalator.   downward.
  2. Having a down slope: *a descending mountain*   2. **Syns:** descendent (*also* descendant).
     stream.
  3. Proceeding by descent from an ancestor: *a line*   3. **Syns:** derived, descendent (*also*
     descending from kings.   descendant).

descent *noun*
1. A sudden drop to a lower condition or status: *a marked descent in presidential prestige.*
2. The act of dropping from a height.
3. A usu. swift downward trend, as in prices.
4. One's ancestors or their character.

1. *Syns:* comedown, down, downfall, downgrade.
2. FALL *noun.*
3. FALL *noun.*
4. ANCESTRY.

describe *verb*
1. To give a verbal account of: *described the accident for the police officer.*

1. *Syns:* narrate, recite, recount, rehearse, relate, report.
Near-syns: explain, explicate, expound, illustrate; communicate, impart, state.

2. To present a lifelike image of.
2. REPRESENT.

description *noun*
1. The act or process of describing in lifelike imagery.
2. A recounting of past events.
3. A class that is defined by the common attribute or attributes possessed by all its members.

1. REPRESENTATION.
2. STORY.
3. KIND².

descriptive *adjective*
Serving to describe: *descriptive narrative augmenting the photographs.*

Syns: delineative, depictive, graphic, representative.

descry *verb*
1. To perceive, esp. barely or fleetingly.
2. To perceive and fix the identity of.
3. To perceive with a special effort of the senses or the mind.

1. CATCH *verb.*
2. DISCERN.
3. NOTICE *verb.*

desecrate *verb*
To spoil or mar the sanctity of.
VIOLATE.

desecrated *adjective*
Ceremonially or religiously unfit.
IMPURE.

desecration *noun*
An act of disrespect or impiety toward something regarded as sacred.
SACRILEGE.

desegregate *verb*
To open to all people regardless of race.
INTEGRATE *verb.*

desegregation *noun*
The act, process, or result of abolishing racial segregation.
INTEGRATION.

desensitize *verb*
To render less sensitive.
DEADEN.

desert¹ *noun*
A tract of unproductive land.
BARREN *noun.*

desert² *noun*
Something justly deserved.
DUE *noun.*

desert³ *verb*
1. To give up without intending to return or claim again.
2. To abandon one's cause or party usu. to join another.

1. ABANDON *verb.*
2. DEFECT *verb.*

deserted *adjective*
1. Having been given up and left alone.
2. Empty of people.

1. ABANDONED.
2. LONELY.

desertion *noun*
The act of forsaking.
ABANDONMENT.

deserve *verb*
To acquire as a result of one's behavior or effort.
EARN.

deserved *adjective*
Consistent with prevailing or accepted standards or circumstances.
JUST *adjective.*

desiccate *verb*
1. To make or become free of moisture.
2. To make or become no longer active or productive.

1. DRY *verb.*
2. DRY UP at **dry.**

desiccated *adjective*
Having little or no liquid or moisture.

DRY *adjective*.

design *verb*
1. To form a strategy for: *designed an elaborate propaganda campaign.*

1. **Syns:** blueprint, cast, chart, contrive, devise, dope out (*Informal*), draw up, frame, plan, project. —*Idiom* lay plans.

2. To have in mind as a goal or purpose.
3. To work out and arrange the parts or details of: *design a new town.*

2. INTEND.
3. **Syns:** blueprint, lay out, map (out), plan, set out.

design *noun*
1. A method for making, doing, or accomplishing something: *a design for a civic center; a grand design for energy conservation.*
2. An element or component in a decorative composition.
3. What one intends to do or achieve.

1. **Syns:** blueprint, idea, layout, plan, project, schema, scheme, strategy. —*Idiom* game plan.
2. FIGURE *noun*.

3. INTENTION.

designate *verb*
1. To make known or identify, as by signs: *Barriers designated the border crossing.*
2. To give a name or title to.
3. To describe with a word or term.
4. To select for an office or position.
5. To set aside for a specified purpose.

1. **Syns:** denote, indicate, point out, show, specify.
2. NAME *verb*.
3. CALL *verb*.
4. APPOINT.
5. APPROPRIATE *verb*.

designation *noun*
1. The act of appointing to an office or position.
2. The word or words by which one is called and identified.

1. APPOINTMENT.
2. NAME *noun*.

designative *adjective*
Serving to designate or indicate: *applause designative of approval.*

Syns: denotative, denotive, designatory, exhibitive, indicative, indicatory.

designatory *adjective*
Serving to designate or indicate.

DESIGNATIVE.

designee *noun*
A person who is appointed to an office or position.

APPOINTEE.

designing *adjective*
Coldly planning to achieve selfish aims.

CALCULATING.

desirable *adjective*
Arousing erotic desire: *a desirable girl.*

Syns: concupiscible (*Archaic*), desireful (*Archaic*), sexy (*Slang*).

desire *verb*
1. To have a strong longing for: *He gave her everything her heart desired. We only desire peace.*

1. **Syns:** ache, covet, crave, hanker, hone² (for *or* after) (*Regional*), long², pant, yearn for (*or* after), wish.
Near-ants: abhor, detest, hate; reject, repudiate, spurn.

2. To have the desire or inclination to.

2. CHOOSE.

desire *noun*
1. A strong wish for what promises enjoyment or pleasure: *his desire for power; a desire for affection.*

1. **Syns:** appetence (*also* appetency), appetite, appetition, craving, hunger, itch, longing, lust, yearning, yen (*Informal*).

2. Sexual hunger: *mistook physical desire for love.*

2. **Syns:** aphrodisia, concupiscence, eroticism, itch, lust, lustfulness, passion, prurience (*also* pruriency).

desireful *adjective*
Archaic. Arousing erotic desire.

DESIRABLE.

desirous *adjective*
Having a strong urge to obtain or possess something, esp. material wealth, in quantity.

GREEDY.

desist *verb*
1. To come to a cessation.

1. STOP *verb*.

2. To cease trying to accomplish or continue. | **2.** ABANDON *verb*.

desolate *verb*
To destroy completely while conquering or occupying. | DEVASTATE.

desolate *adjective*
Empty of people. | LONELY.

desolating *adjective*
Tending to consume and destroy. | CONSUMPTIVE.

desolation *noun*
A desolate sense of loss. | EMPTINESS.

despair *verb*
To lose all hope: *despaired of ever escaping the prison.* | **Syns:** despond, give up.

despair *noun*
Utter lack of hope: *was in a state of despair just before committing suicide.* | **Syns:** desperateness, desperation, despond, despondency (*also* despondence), hopelessness. —*Idioms* cave of despair, slough of despond.

despairful *adjective*
Having lost all hope. | DESPONDENT.

despairing *adjective*
Having lost all hope. | DESPONDENT.

desperate *adjective*
1. So serious as to be at the point of crisis. | **1.** CRITICAL.
2. Having lost all hope. | **2.** DESPONDENT.
3. Extreme in degree, strength, or effect. | **3.** INTENSE.

desperateness *noun*
Utter lack of hope. | DESPAIR *noun*.

desperation *noun*
Utter lack of hope. | DESPAIR *noun*.

despicable *adjective*
1. Having or proceeding from low moral standards. | **1.** SORDID.
2. So objectionable as to elicit despisal. | **2.** FILTHY.
3. Deserving strong condemnation. | **3.** INFAMOUS.

despisable *adjective*
So objectionable as to elicit despisal. | FILTHY.

despisal *noun*
The feeling of despising: *his despisal of the idle rich.* | **Syns:** contempt, despisement, despite, disdain, scorn.

despise *verb*
1. To regard with utter contempt and disdain: *despised the idle rich.* | **1.** **Syns:** abhor, contemn, contempt (*Archaic*), disdain, scorn, scout[2], sneer (at). —*Idioms* have no use for, look down on (*or* upon), view with a scornful eye, want no part of.

2. To regard with extreme dislike and hostility. | **2.** HATE *verb*.

despisement *noun*
The feeling of despising. | DESPISAL.

despite *noun*
1. The disposition boldly to defy or resist authority or an opposing force. | **1.** DEFIANCE.
2. The feeling of despising. | **2.** DESPISAL.
3. An act that offends a person's sense of pride or dignity. | **3.** INDIGNITY.

despiteful *adjective*
Archaic. Characterized by intense ill will or spite. | MALEVOLENT.

despitefulness *noun*
Archaic. A desire to harm others or to see others suffer. | MALEVOLENCE.

despoil *verb*
To rob of goods by force, esp. in time of war. | SACK[2].

despond *verb*
1. To turn over in the mind, moodily and at length. | **1.** BROOD.
2. To lose all hope. | **2.** DESPAIR *verb*.

despond *noun*
Utter lack of hope.

DESPAIR *noun.*

despondence *noun*

SEE **despondency.**

despondency also **despondence** *noun*
1. Utter lack of hope.
2. A feeling or spell of dismally low spirits.

1. DESPAIR *noun.*
2. GLOOM.

despondent *adjective*
Having lost all hope: *was despondent after the divorce.*

Syns: despairful, despairing, desperate, forlorn, hopeless.
Near-ants: cheerful, glad, happy, joyful, hopeful, optimistic.
Ants: gay, lighthearted.

despot *noun*
1. An absolute ruler, esp. one who is harsh and oppressive.
2. One who imposes or favors absolute obedience to authority.

1. DICTATOR.

2. AUTHORITARIAN *noun.*

despotic *adjective*
1. Having and exercising complete political power and control.
2. Characterized by or favoring absolute obedience to authority.

1. ABSOLUTE *adjective.*

2. AUTHORITARIAN *adjective.*

despotism *noun*
1. A political doctrine advocating the principle of absolute rule.
2. Absolute power, esp. when exercised unjustly or cruelly.

1. ABSOLUTISM.

2. TYRANNY.

destine *verb*
To determine the future of in advance.

FATE *verb.*

destined *adjective*
Governed and decided by or as if by fate.

FATED.

destiny *noun*
That which is inevitably destined.

FATE *noun.*

destitute *adjective*
1. *Obs.* Having been given up and left alone.
2. Lacking a desirable element.
3. Having little or no money or wealth.

1. ABANDONED.
2. EMPTY *adjective.*
3. POOR.

destitution *noun*
The condition of being extremely poor.

POVERTY.

destroy *verb*
1. To cause the complete ruin or wreckage of: *paintings destroyed by fire; drugs that destroyed her health; news that destroyed his hopes.*

2. To break up so that reconstruction is impossible: *destroy a condemned building.*

3. To cause the death of.
4. To take the life of (a person or persons) unlawfully.
5. To collapse or shatter by or as if by breaking.
6. To impair severely the spirit, health, effectiveness, etc., of.

1. *Syns:* demolish, destruct, dynamite, finish, ruin, ruinate (*Regional*), shatter, sink, smash, total, torpedo, undo, wrack, wreck. —*Idiom* put the kibosh on.
2. *Syns:* demolish, destruct, dismantle, knock down, level, pull down, pulverize, raze, rubble, tear down.
3. KILL.
4. MURDER *verb.*
5. BREAK DOWN.
6. BREAK *verb.*

destroyer *noun*
Something that causes total loss or severe impairment of one's health, fortune, honor, hopes, etc.

RUIN *noun.*

destruct *verb*
1. To cause the complete ruin or wreckage of.
2. To break up so that reconstruction is impossible.

1. DESTROY.
2. DESTROY.

destruction *noun*
1. The state of being destroyed: *a tornado that left destruction in its path.*

2. An act, instance, or consequence of breaking.
3. Something that causes total loss or severe impairment of one's health, fortune, honor, hopes, etc.
4. Severe damage or decay rendering something useless or worthless.

destructive *adjective*
1. Having the capability or effect of damaging irreparably: *a destructive ice storm; drugs that are destructive influences on youth.*
2. Causing ruin or destruction.

desuetude *noun*
The quality or state of being obsolete.

desultory *adjective*
1. Without aim, purpose, or intent.
2. Having no particular pattern, purpose, organization, or structure.

detach *verb*
1. To separate one thing from another thing: *detached the side panels from the truck.*

2. To remove from association with: *could not detach himself from his past.*

detached *adjective*
1. Lacking interest in one's surroundings or worldly affairs: *took a detached view of the conflict.*
2. Set away from all others.
3. Not easily excited, even under pressure.
4. Feeling or showing no strong emotional involvement.

detachment *noun*
1. The act or process of detaching: *detachment of a freight car from a train.*
2. The act or an instance of separating one thing from another.
3. Dissociation from one's surroundings or worldly affairs: *viewed the crisis with cold detachment.*
4. The quality or state of being just and unbiased.
5. *Mil.* A unit of troops on special assignment: *an honor-guard detachment.*
6. A group of people organized for a particular purpose.

detail *noun*
1. A small, often specialized element of a whole: *asked to see the details of the contract.*
2. An individually considered portion of a whole.
3. One of the conditions or facts attending an event and having some bearing on it.
4. *Mil.* A unit of troops on special assignment.

detail *verb*
To make specific.

detailed *adjective*
Characterized by attention to detail: *a detailed account of the trip.*

---

1. **Syns:** devastation, havoc, ruin, ruination, wrack, wreck, wreckage. —*Idiom* wrack and ruin.
2. BREAKAGE.
3. RUIN *noun.*

4. RUIN *noun.*

1. **Syns:** pernicious, ruinous, shattering.

2. FATAL.

OBSOLETENESS.

1. AIMLESS.
2. RANDOM.

1. **Syns:** disconnect, disengage, uncouple. **Near-syns:** disjoin, disassemble, dismantle, dismember, part, sever, unfix. **Near-ants:** affix, combine. **Ant:** attach.
2. **Syns:** abstract, disassociate, dissociate, withdraw.

1. **Syns:** aloof, disinterested, incurious, indifferent, unconcerned, uninterested.
2. SOLITARY.
3. COOL *adjective.*
4. NEUTRAL.

1. **Syns:** disconnection, disengagement, separation, uncoupling.
2. DIVISION.

3. **Syns:** aloofness, distance, remoteness.

4. FAIRNESS.
5. **Syn:** detail (*Mil.*).

6. FORCE *noun.*

1. **Syns:** item, particular, punctilio, technicality. —*Idiom* fine print.
2. ELEMENT.
3. CIRCUMSTANCE.

4. DETACHMENT.

STIPULATE.

Syns: blow-by-blow, circumstantial, full, itemized, minute[1], particular, particularized, thorough.

detain *verb*
1. To cause to be later or slower than expected or desired.
2. To take into custody as a prisoner.
3. To maintain restraining control and possession of.

detainment *noun*
The condition or fact of being made late or slow.

detect *verb*
To perceive, esp. barely or fleetingly.

detectable *adjective*
Capable of being noticed or apprehended mentally.

detective *noun*
A person whose work is investigating crimes or obtaining hidden evidence or information: *hired a detective to get the needed facts.*

detention *noun*
A seizing and holding by law.

deter *verb*
1. To persuade (a person) not to do something.
2. To prohibit from occurring by advance planning or action.

deteriorate *verb*
1. To become lower in quality, character, or condition: *a school system rapidly deteriorating; mental health that had deteriorated.*

2. To lose strength or power.
3. To become or cause to become rotten or unsound.

deterioration *noun*
1. Descent to a lower level or condition: *concerned about widespread moral deterioration.*

2. A marked loss of strength or effectiveness.
3. The condition of being decayed.
4. Severe damage or decay rendering something useless or worthless.

determent *noun*
The act of preventing.

determinate *adjective*
1. Having distinct limits.
2. Kept within certain limits.

determination *noun*
1. A position reached after consideration.
2. An authoritative or official decision, esp. one made by a court.
3. Unwavering firmness of character or action.

determinative *adjective*
1. So critically decisive as to affect the future.
2. Determining or having the power to determine an outcome.
3. Serving the function of deciding or settling with finality.

determine *verb*
1. To fix the limits of: *Surveyors determined the property boundaries.*

2. To make up or cause to make up one's mind.

1. DELAY *verb.*

2. ARREST *verb.*
3. HOLD *verb.*

DELAY *noun.*

CATCH *verb.*

PERCEPTIBLE.

Syns: dick (*Slang*), eye (*Informal*), gumshoe (*Slang*), investigator, Javert, sleuth (*Informal*).

ARREST *noun.*

1. DISSUADE.
2. PREVENT.

1. *Syns:* decline, degenerate, descend, disimprove, disintegrate, retrograde, sink, worsen. —*Idioms* get no better fast, go to the bad.
   Near-syns: crumble, decay, decompose, rot; debilitate, undermine, weaken.
   Ant: improve.
2. FADE *verb.*
3. DECAY *verb.*

1. *Syns:* atrophy, decadence, declension, declination, decline, degeneracy, degeneration, disintegration, worsening.
2. FAILURE.
3. DECAY *noun.*
4. RUIN *noun.*

PREVENTION.

1. DEFINITE.
2. RESTRICTED.

1. DECISION.
2. RULING *noun.*

3. DECISION.

1. FATEFUL.
2. DECISIVE.

3. DEFINITIVE.

1. *Syns:* bound^2, delimit, delimitate, demarcate, limit, mark out (*or* off), measure.
2. DECIDE.

3. To obtain knowledge or awareness of something not known before, as through observation, study, etc.

3. DISCOVER.

4. To make a decision about (a controversy, dispute, etc.) after deliberation, as in a court of law.

4. JUDGE *verb*.

determined *adjective*
1. On an unwavering course of action.

1. SET[1] *adjective*.

2. Not hesitating or wavering.

2. DECISIVE.

3. Indicating or possessing determination, resolution, or persistence.

3. FIRM[1].

deterrence *noun*
The act of preventing.

PREVENTION.

deterrent *adjective*
Intended to prevent.

PREVENTIVE.

deterring *adjective*
Intended to prevent.

PREVENTIVE.

detest *verb*
To regard with extreme dislike and hostility.

HATE *verb*.

detestable *adjective*
1. So objectionable as to elicit despisal.

1. FILTHY.

2. Deserving strong condemnation.

2. INFAMOUS.

detestation *noun*
1. Extreme hostility and dislike.

1. HATE *noun*.

2. An object of extreme dislike.

2. HATE *noun*.

detonate *verb*
To release or cause to release energy suddenly and violently, esp. with a loud noise.

EXPLODE.

detonation *noun*
A violent release of confined energy, usu. accompanied by a loud sound and shock waves.

BLAST *noun*.

detour *verb*
To pass around but not through.

SKIRT *verb*.

detract *verb*
To think, represent, or speak of as small or unimportant.

BELITTLE.

detracting *adjective*
1. Tending or intending to belittle.

1. DISPARAGING.

2. Damaging to the reputation.

2. LIBELOUS.

detraction *noun*
1. The expression of injurious, malicious statements about someone.

1. LIBEL *noun*.

2. The act or an instance of belittling.

2. BELITTLEMENT.

detractive *adjective*
Damaging to the reputation.

LIBELOUS.

detractory *adjective*
Damaging to the reputation.

LIBELOUS.

detriment *noun*
1. An unfavorable condition, circumstance, or characteristic.

1. DISADVANTAGE.

2. The action or result of inflicting loss or pain.

2. HARM *noun*.

detrimental *adjective*
Causing harm or injury.

HARMFUL.

de trop *adjective*
French. Being more than is needed, desired, or appropriate.

SUPERFLUOUS.

devaluate *verb*
To become or make less in price or value.

DEPRECIATE.

devaluation *noun*
A lowering in price or value.

DEPRECIATION.

devalue *verb*
To become or make less in price or value.

DEPRECIATE.

devastate *verb*
To destroy completely while conquering or occupying: *The invaders devastated the villages in their path.*

Syns: depredate, desolate, ravage, spoil (*Obs.*), spoliate, strip[1], waste. —*Idiom* lay waste.

devastation *noun*
1. The state of being destroyed.
2. Severe damage or decay rendering something useless or worthless.

1. DESTRUCTION.
2. RUIN *noun.*

develop *verb*
1. To bring (a product, idea, etc.) into being: *developed gasoline from coal.*
2. To be disclosed gradually: *As the plot developed, the story got better.*
3. To disclose bit by bit.
4. To express at greater length or in greater detail.
5. To come gradually to have: *develop a taste for caviar.*
6. To achieve an increment of gradually.
7. To become affected with a disease.
8. To take place.
9. To bring or come to full development.

1. *Syns:* generate, produce.
2. *Syns:* evolve, unfold.
3. ELABORATE *verb.*
4. ELABORATE *verb.*
5. *Syn:* form.
6. GAIN *verb.*
7. CONTRACT *verb.*
8. COME.
9. MATURE *verb.*

developed *adjective*
Having reached full growth and development.

MATURE *adjective.*

developer *noun*
A person instrumental in the growth of something, esp. in its early stages.

BUILDER.

development *noun*
1. A progression from a simple form to a more complex one: *the development of man.*
2. Something significant that happens.
3. The result or product of building up.
4. Steady improvement, as of an individual or a society.

1. *Syns:* evolution, evolvement, growth, progress, unfolding.
2. EVENT.
3. BUILD-UP at **build up.**
4. PROGRESS *noun.*

deviance *noun*
The condition of being abnormal.

ABNORMALITY.

deviancy *noun*
The condition of being abnormal.

ABNORMALITY.

deviant *noun*
One whose sexual behavior differs from the accepted norm: *an aggressive deviant who had to be institutionalized.*

Syns: deviate, pervert.

deviant *adjective*
Departing from the normal.

ABNORMAL.

deviate *verb*
1. To turn away from a prescribed course of action or conduct: *never deviated from the truth.*
2. To turn aside from the main subject in writing or speaking.

1. *Syns:* depart, digress, diverge, err, stray, swerve.
2. DIGRESS.

deviate *noun*
One whose sexual behavior differs from the accepted norm.

DEVIANT *noun.*

deviate *adjective*
Departing from the normal.

ABNORMAL.

deviating *adjective*
1. Departing from the normal.
2. Straying from a proper course or standard.

1. ABNORMAL.
2. ERRANT.

deviation *noun*
1. A departing from what is prescribed: *tolerated no deviation from preflight procedures.*
2. An instance of digressing.
3. The condition of being abnormal.

1. *Syns:* aberration, departure, divergence (*also* divergency), diversion.
2. DIGRESSION.
3. ABNORMALITY.

deviative *adjective*
Departing from the normal. ABNORMAL.

device *noun*
1. Something, as a machine, devised for a particular function: *a new food-processing device.*

   1. **Syns:** apparatus, appliance, contraption, contrivance.
   Near-syns: creation, gadget, gimmick, gismo (*also* gizmo) (*Slang*), invention, machine; doohickey (*Slang*), hickey (*Slang*), thing.

2. Something invented. 2. INVENTION.
3. An indirect, usu. cunning means of gaining an end. 3. TRICK *noun.*
4. An element or component in a decorative composition. 4. FIGURE *noun.*

devilish *adjective*
Perversely bad, cruel, or wicked. FIENDISH.

devious *adjective*
1. Having bends, curves, or angles. 1. CROOKED.
2. Without a fixed or regular course. 2. ERRATIC.
3. Marked by treachery or deceit. 3. UNDERHAND.

deviousness *noun*
Lack of straightforwardness and honesty in action. INDIRECTION.

devise *verb*
1. To form a strategy for. 1. DESIGN *verb.*
2. To use ingenuity in making, developing, or achieving. 2. INVENT.
3. *Law.* To give (property) to another person after one's death. 3. LEAVE[1].

devitalize *verb*
To lessen or deplete the nerve, energy, or strength of. ENERVATE.

devoid *adjective*
1. Containing nothing. 1. EMPTY *adjective.*
2. Lacking a desirable element. 2. EMPTY *adjective.*

devolve *verb*
To come as by lot or inheritance. FALL *verb.*

devote *verb*
1. To give over by or as if by vow to a higher purpose: *a nun who devoted her life to Christ.* 1. **Syns:** consecrate, dedicate, hallow.
2. To devote (oneself or one's efforts). 2. APPLY.

devoted *adjective*
Given over exclusively to a single use or purpose. SACRED.

devotee *noun*
1. One zealously devoted to a religion: *a devotee of Bahaism.* 1. **Syns:** fanatic, sectary, votary.
2. One who ardently admires. 2. ADMIRER.
3. A person who is ardently devoted to a particular subject or activity. 3. ENTHUSIAST.

devotion *noun*
1. Deep and ardent affection. 1. ADORATION.
2. The condition of being closely tied to another by affection or faith. 2. ATTACHMENT.

devour *verb*
1. To take (food) into the body as nourishment. 1. EAT.
2. To eat completely or entirely. 2. CONSUME.
3. To be avidly interested in. 3. EAT UP at **eat.**
4. To do away with completely and destructively. 4. CONSUME.
5. To use up foolishly or needlessly. 5. WASTE *verb.*

devout *adjective*
Deeply concerned with God and the beliefs and practice of religion. HOLY.

dexterity *noun*
1. Skillfulness in the use of the hands or body: *performed with dexterity on the parallel bars.*

1. **Syns:** address, adroitness, deftness, dexterousness, prowess, readiness, skill, sleight.
Near-syns: adeptness, skillfulness, smoothness.
Ant: clumsiness.

2. The quality or state of being agile.

2. AGILITY.

dexterous *adjective*
1. Exhibiting or possessing skill and ease in performance: *dexterous handling of the sports car.*
2. Showing art or skill in performing or doing.

1. **Syns:** adroit, clever, deft, facile, handy, nimble, slick.
2. ARTFUL.

dexterousness *noun*
1. Skillfulness in the use of the hands or body.
2. The quality or state of being agile.

1. DEXTERITY.
2. AGILITY.

diablerie also **diablery** *noun*
1. Annoying yet harmless, usu. playful acts.
2. A wicked act.

1. MISCHIEF.
2. CRIME.

diablery *noun*

SEE **diablerie.**

diabolic also **diabolical** *adjective*
Perversely bad, cruel, or wicked.

FIENDISH.

diagonal *adjective*
Angled at a slant.

BIAS *adjective.*

dial *verb*
Informal. To communicate with (someone) by telephone.

TELEPHONE.

dial *noun*
The marked outer surface of an instrument.

FACE *noun.*

dialect *noun*
1. An often regional form of a language not considered standard: *Cockney is a dialect of English.*

1. **Syns:** argot, cant[2], jargon, lingo, patois, vernacular.
Near-syns: localism, provincialism, regionalism, slang.

2. A system of terms used by a people sharing a history and culture.
3. Specialized expressions indigenous to a particular field, subject, trade, or subculture.

2. LANGUAGE.
3. LANGUAGE.

dialog *noun*

SEE **dialogue.**

dialogue also **dialog** *noun*
Spoken exchange.

CONVERSATION.

diametric *adjective*
Diametrically opposed.

OPPOSITE *adjective.*

diamond *noun*
Someone or something considered exceptionally precious.

TREASURE *noun.*

diaphanous *adjective*
So light and insubstantial as to resemble air or a thin film.

FILMY.

diatribe *noun*
A long, violent, or blustering speech, usu. of censure or denunciation.

TIRADE.

dibs *noun*
Slang. A legitimate or supposed right to demand something as one's rightful due.

CLAIM *noun.*

dick *noun*
Slang. A person whose work is investigating crimes or obtaining hidden evidence or information.

DETECTIVE.

dicker *verb*
To argue about the terms of, as of a sale.

HAGGLE.

dictate *verb*
To set forth expressly and authoritatively: *The victors dictated the surrender terms.*

Syns: decree, fix, impose, lay down, ordain, prescribe. —*Idioms* call the tune (*or* signals *or* shots), lay it on the line.

dictate to *verb*
To command in an arrogant manner.

BOSS *verb.*

dictate *noun*
1. An authoritative indication to be obeyed.
2. A code or set of codes governing action, procedure, etc.

1. COMMAND *noun.*
2. RULE *noun.*

dictate to *verb*

SEE **dictate.**

dictative *adjective*
Tending to dictate.

DICTATORIAL.

dictator *noun*
1. An absolute ruler, esp. one who is harsh and oppressive: *Stalin was a bloody dictator.*

1. *Syns:* Big Brother, despot, führer (*also* fuehrer) (*German*), oppressor, totalitarian, tyrant. —*Idioms* man on horseback, strong man, tinhorn dictator.

2. One who imposes or favors absolute obedience to authority.

2. AUTHORITARIAN *noun.*

dictatorial *adjective*
1. Tending to dictate: *a dictatorial executive who imposed his will on everyone.*

1. *Syns:* authoritarian, bossy, dictative, doctrinaire, dogmatic, domineering, imperious, magisterial, masterful, overbearing, peremptory.

2. Having and exercising complete political power and control.

2. ABSOLUTE.

3. Characterized by or favoring absolute obedience to authority.

3. AUTHORITARIAN *adjective.*

dictatorship *noun*
1. A government in which a single leader or party exercises absolute control over all citizens and every aspect of their lives.

1. ABSOLUTISM.

2. A political doctrine advocating the principle of absolute rule.

2. ABSOLUTISM.

3. Absolute power, esp. when exercised unjustly or cruelly.

3. TYRANNY.

diction *noun*
Choice of words and the way in which they are used.

WORDING.

dictionary *noun*
An alphabetical list of words often defined or translated.

VOCABULARY.

didactic also **didactical** *adjective*
Inclined to teach or moralize excessively.

MORAL *adjective.*

diddle *verb*
1. To pass time without working or in avoiding work.
2. To waste time by engaging in aimless activity.
3. *Slang.* To get money or something else from by deceitful trickery.

1. IDLE *verb.*
2. MESS AROUND at **mess.**
3. CHEAT *verb.*

diddler *noun*
Slang. A person who cheats.

CHEAT *noun.*

die *verb*
1. To cease living: *She died at an early age.*

1. *Syns:* check out (*Slang*), croak (*Slang*), decease, demise, depart, drop, expire, go, kick in (*Slang*), kick off (*Slang*), pass away, pass (on), perish, pop off (*Informal*), succumb. —*Idioms* bite the dust, breathe one's last, cash in one's chips, depart this life, give up the

ghost, go to one's grave, kick the bucket, meet one's end (*or* Maker), pass on to the Great Beyond, take a cab, turn up one's toes.

2. *Theol.* To experience spiritual death: *Those who believe in God shall never die.*

2. Syn: perish.

3. To become inaudible.

3. FADE *verb.*

4. To become less active or intense.

4. SUBSIDE.

die out (or **away**) *verb*
To cease to exist.

DISAPPEAR.

die-hard also **diehard** *noun*
A person who vehemently, often fanatically opposes progress and favors return to a previous condition.

REACTIONARY *noun.*

die-hard also **diehard** *adjective*

1. Vehemently, often fanatically opposing progress or reform.

1. REACTIONARY *adjective.*

2. Firmly, often unreasonably immovable in purpose or will.

2. STUBBORN.

die out (or **away**) *verb*

SEE **die.**

differ *verb*

1. To be unlike or dissimilar: *The two prime ministers differed in every aspect.*

1. Syns: disagree, vary. —*Idiom* be at variance.

2. To be of different opinion: *politicians differing on national health insurance.*

2. Syns: disaccord, disagree, discord, dissent, vary.

difference *noun*

1. The condition of being unlike or dissimilar: *noted the vast difference between liberals and conservatives.*

1. Syns: alterity, discrepancy (*also* discrepance), disparity, dissimilarity, dissimilitude, distinction, divarication, divergence (*also* divergency), unlikeness.

2. The condition or fact of varying.

2. VARIATION.

3. A marked lack of correspondence or agreement.

3. GAP.

different *adjective*

1. Not like another in nature, quality, amount, or form: *two different ways of working; two brothers who could not have been more different.*

1. Syns: disparate, dissimilar, divergent, diverse, unlike, variant, various.
Near-ants: akin, comparable, like, parallel, similar; equal, equivalent.
Ants: alike, identical.

2. Not previously known or used.

2. FRESH.

differentiate *verb*

1. To recognize as being different.

1. DISTINGUISH.

2. To make noticeable or different.

2. DISTINGUISH.

differentiation *noun*
The act or an instance of distinguishing.

DISTINCTION.

difficile *adjective*
Not easy to do, achieve, or master.

DIFFICULT.

difficult *adjective*

1. Not easy to do, achieve, or master: *a difficult problem; a difficult climb.*

1. Syns: difficile, hard, knotty, laborious, serious, slavish, sticky (*Informal*), tall, tough, uphill.
Near-syns: arduous, heavy, labored, severe, strenuous, toilsome.
Ants: easy, simple.

2. Imposing a severe test of bodily or spiritual strength.

2. BURDENSOME.

3. Causing difficulty, trouble, or discomfort.

3. INCONVENIENT.

4. Given to acting in opposition to others.

4. CONTRARY *adjective.*

difficultly *adverb*
With effort.

HARD *adverb.*

difficulty *noun*
1. Something that obstructs progress and requires great effort to overcome: *His chief difficulty was a physical weakness. The negotiators ran into difficulty.*

2. A condition or situation characterized by danger, distress, or annoyance.

diffidence *noun*
Reserve in speech, behavior, or dress.

diffident *adjective*
Reticent or reserved in manner.

diffuse *verb*
To extend over a wide area.

    diffuse *adjective*
    Using or containing an excessive number of words.

dig *verb*
1. To break, turn over, or remove (earth, sand, etc.) with or as if with a tool: *dig for carrots; dig through a trunk for winter clothes.*
2. To make by digging: *dig a well.*
3. To cause to penetrate with force.
4. To thrust against or into: *dug me in the ribs.*
5. *Slang.* To perceive and recognize the meaning of.
6. *Slang.* To receive pleasure from.
7. *Slang.* To have as one's domicile, usu. for an extended period.
8. To go into or through for the purpose of making discoveries or acquiring information.

    dig up (or **out**) *verb*
    To find by investigation.

    dig *noun*
    1. An act of thrusting into or against, as to attract attention: *gave me a sharp dig in the ribs and pointed to the crowd.*
    2. A flippant or sarcastic remark.

digest *verb*
To take in and incorporate, esp. mentally.

digestion *noun*
The process of absorbing and incorporating, esp. mentally.

dignification *noun*
The act of raising to a high position or status or the condition of being so raised.

dignify *verb*
1. To raise to a high position or status.
2. To lend dignity or honor to by an act or favor.

dignitary *noun*
An important, influential person: *State Department dignitaries.*

dignity *noun*
A person's high standing among others.

digress *verb*
1. To turn aside from the main subject in writing or

---

1. *Syns:* asperity, hardship, rigor, vicissitude. —*Idioms* a hard nut to crack, a hard row to hoe, heavy sledding.

2. TROUBLE *noun.*

MODESTY.

MODEST.

SPREAD *verb.*

WORDY.

1. *Syns:* delve (*Archaic*), excavate, grub, shovel, spade.

2. *Syns:* excavate, scoop, shovel, spade.
3. RAM.
4. *Syns:* jab, jog, nudge, poke, prod.
5. UNDERSTAND.
6. ENJOY.
7. LIVE[1].

8. EXPLORE.

UNCOVER.

1. *Syns:* jab, nudge, poke, stab.

2. CRACK *noun.*

ABSORB.

ABSORPTION.

EXALTATION.

1. EXALT.
2. GRACE *verb.*

Syns: big, big shot (*Slang*), big-timer (*Slang*), big wheel (*Slang*), bigwig (*Informal*), character, eminence, heavyweight (*Informal*), leader, lion, luminary, muckamuck (*also* mucketymuck) (*Slang*), nabob, notability, notable, personage, personality, somebody (*Informal*), someone (*Informal*), VIP (*Informal*).

HONOR *noun.*

1. *Syns:* deviate, divagate, diverge,

speaking: *The senator had the annoying habit of digressing from the main theme of his speeches.*
2. To turn away from a prescribed course of action or conduct.

digression *noun*
1. The act of digressing: *His statements on monetary policy, by way of digression, are very misleading.*
2. An instance of digressing: *His aunt used to break off now and then into a brief digression about the old days.*

digressive *adjective*
Marked by or given to digression: *a digressive remark; an author who is habitually digressive.*

digs *noun*
Informal. A building or shelter where one lives.
dig up (or **out**) *verb*
dilapidated *adjective*
1. Showing signs of wear and tear or neglect.
2. Falling to ruin.
dilate *verb*
To express at greater length or in greater detail.
dilatory *adjective*
Proceeding at a rate less than usual or desired.
dilemma *noun*
A difficult, embarrassing situation.
dilettante *noun*
One lacking professional skill and ease in a particular pursuit.
  dilettante *adjective*
  Lacking the required professional skill.
dilettantish *adjective*
Lacking the required professional skill.
dilettantist *adjective*
Lacking the required professional skill.
diligence *noun*
Steady attention and effort, as to one's occupation: *worked with real diligence to finish the audit.*

diligent *adjective*
Characterized by steady attention and effort: *made a diligent search for the missing book.*

dilly-dally *verb*
To go or move slowly so that progress is hindered.
dilute *adjective*
Lower than normal in strength or concentration due to admixture: *dilute wine.*
  dilute *verb*
  To lessen the strength of by or as if by admixture: *The impact of his thesis was diluted by poor organization and bad writing. He always dilutes his drink with a splash of soda.*
diluted *adjective*
Lower than normal in strength or concentration due to admixture.

---

excurse, stray, wander. —*Idiom* go off at (*or* on) a tangent.
2. DEVIATE.

1. **Syns:** aside, divagation, parenthesis.

2. **Syns:** aside, deviation, discursion, divagation, divergence (*also* divergency), ecbole (*Rhet.*), episode, excursion, excursus, irrelevancy, parenthesis, tangent.

Syns: discursive, episodic, excursive, parenthetic (*also* parenthetical), tangential.

HOME.
SEE **dig.**

1. SHABBY.
2. RUINOUS.

ELABORATE *verb.*

SLOW *adjective.*

PREDICAMENT.

AMATEUR.

AMATEURISH.

AMATEURISH.

AMATEURISH.

Syns: application, assiduity, assiduousness, industriousness, industry, sedulousness.

Syns: assiduous, industrious, sedulous, studious.
Near-ants: desultory, laggard, leisurely, slow.
Ant: dilatory.

DELAY *verb.*

Syns: cut, diluted, thin, washy, watered, watered-down, waterish, watery, weak.

Syns: attenuate, cut, thin, water (down), weaken.

DILUTE *adjective.*

dim *verb*
1. To make dim or indistinct.
2. To make or become less keen or responsive.

1. OBSCURE *verb*.
2. DULL *verb*.

dim *adjective*
1. Deficient in brightness.
2. Lacking vividness in color.
3. Covered by or as if by a thin coating or film.
4. Not clearly perceived or perceptible.

1. DARK *adjective*.
2. DULL *adjective*.
3. FILMY.
4. UNCLEAR.

dimensions *noun*
The amount of space occupied by something.

SIZE.

diminish *verb*
To grow or cause to grow gradually less.

DECREASE *verb*.

diminishment *noun*
The act or process of decreasing.

DECREASE *noun*.

diminution *noun*
The act or process of decreasing.

DECREASE *noun*.

diminutive *adjective*
Extremely small.

TINY.

dimness *noun*
Absence or deficiency of light.

DARK *noun*.

dimwit *noun*
Slang. A mentally dull person.

DULLARD.

dimwitted *adjective*
1. Lacking in intelligence.
2. *Slang.* Displaying a complete lack of forethought and good sense.

1. STUPID.
2. MINDLESS.

din *noun*
Sounds or a sound, esp. when loud, confused, or disagreeable.

NOISE *noun*.

ding-a-ling *noun*
Informal. An insanely foolish or strange person.

CRACKPOT.

dingbat *noun*
Informal. An insanely foolish or strange person.

CRACKPOT.

dinge *noun*
A feeling or spell of dismally low spirits.

GLOOM.

dingy *adjective*
Showing signs of wear and tear or neglect.

SHABBY.

dip *verb*
1. To plunge briefly in or into a liquid: *She dipped a piece of bread into her coffee.*
2. To immerse in a coloring solution: *dip Easter eggs.*
3. To take a substance, as liquid, from a container by plunging the hand or a utensil into it: *dipped water from the leaky boat; dipped punch from the bowl.*
4. To slope downward.
5. To undergo a sharp, rapid descent in value or price.
6. *Brit. Slang.* To give or deposit as a pawn.

1. *Syns:* douse, duck, dunk, immerge, immerse, souse, submerge, submerse.
2. *Syns:* color, dye.
3. *Syns:* bail^2, lade, ladle, scoop up.

4. DROP *verb*.
5. FALL *verb*.
6. PAWN^1 *verb*.

dip into *verb*
To look through reading matter casually.

BROWSE.

dip *noun*
1. A usu. swift downward trend, as in prices.
2. An area sunk below its surroundings.
3. The act of swimming.

1. FALL *noun*.
2. DEPRESSION.
3. PLUNGE *noun*.

dip into *verb*

SEE **dip**.

diplomacy *noun*
The ability to say and do the right thing at the right time.

TACT.

diplomatic *adjective*
Showing sensitivity and skill in dealing with others.   DELICATE.
dippy *adjective*
Slang. So senseless as to be laughable.   FOOLISH.
dire *adjective*
  1. So serious as to be at the point of crisis.   1. CRITICAL.
  2. Portending future disaster.   2. FATEFUL.
  3. Causing or able to cause fear.   3. FEARFUL.
direct *adjective*
  1. Proceeding or lying in an uninterrupted line or   1. *Syns:* straight, straightforward,
     course: *a direct path across the fields.*   through.
  2. Speaking or spoken freely and sincerely.   2. FRANK.
  3. Of unbroken descent or lineage: *a direct descendant*   3. *Syn:* lineal.
     of King David.
  4. Marked by the absence of any intervention.   4. IMMEDIATE.
  5. Characterized by a close and thorough acquaintance.   5. INTIMATE[1] *adjective.*
direct *verb*
  1. To have charge of (the affairs of others).   1. ADMINISTER.
  2. To control the course of (an activity).   2. CONDUCT *verb.*
  3. To exercise authority or influence over.   3. CONTROL *verb.*
  4. To give orders to.   4. COMMAND *verb.*
  5. To devote (oneself or one's efforts).   5. APPLY.
  6. To move (a weapon, blow, etc.) in the direction of   6. AIM *verb.*
     someone or something.
  7. To mark (a written communication) with its   7. ADDRESS *verb.*
     destination.
  8. To show the way to.   8. GUIDE *verb.*
direct *adverb*
  1. In a direct line.   1. DIRECTLY.
  2. With precision or absolute conformity.   2. DIRECTLY.
  3. Without the slightest deviation in any respect.   3. PRECISELY.
direction *noun*
  1. Authoritative control over the affairs of others.   1. ADMINISTRATION.
  2. *Archaic.* A written inscription on a deliverable item   2. ADDRESS *noun.*
     giving its destination.
  3. An authoritative indication to be obeyed.   3. COMMAND *noun.*
  4. An act or instance of guiding.   4. GUIDANCE.
  5. The continuous exercise of authority over a political   5. GOVERNMENT.
     unit.
directive *noun*
An authoritative indication to be obeyed.   COMMAND *noun.*
directly *adverb*
  1. In a direct line: *went directly to Atlanta; flew*   1. *Syns:* dead, direct, due, right, straight.
     directly north.
  2. With precision or absolute conformity: *hit him*   2. *Syns:* dead, direct, exactly, fair, flush,
     directly on the kneecap.   just, precisely, right, smack-dab
               (*Slang*), square, straight.
  3. Without delay: *I'll see you at the restaurant directly.*   3. *Syns:* forthwith, immediately, instant
               (*Poetic*), now. —*Idioms* at once, first
               off, right away (*or* off), straight away
               (*or* off).
  4. Without intermediary.   4. IMMEDIATELY.
director *noun*
  1. Someone who directs and supervises workers.   1. BOSS *noun.*
  2. One who is highest in rank or authority.   2. CHIEF *noun.*
  3. A person having administrative or managerial   3. EXECUTIVE.
     authority in an organization.
  4. Something or someone that shows the way.   4. GUIDE *noun.*
direful *adjective*
  1. Portending future disaster.   1. FATEFUL.

2. Causing or able to cause fear. | 2. FEARFUL.

dirt *noun*
1. Foul or dirty matter. | 1. FILTH.
2. Something that is offensive to accepted standards of decency. | 2. OBSCENITY.

dirtiness *noun*
1. The condition or state of being dirty: *the dirtiness of the slum apartment.* | 1. *Syns:* filth, filthiness, foulness, griminess, uncleanliness, uncleanness.
2. Impure condition. | 2. IMPURITY.
3. The quality or state of being obscene. | 3. OBSCENITY.

dirty *adjective*
1. Covered or stained with or as if with dirt or other impurities: *sending the dirty clothes to the laundry.* | 1. *Syns:* black, filthy, grimy, grubby, smutty, soiled, soily, unclean, uncleanly.
Near-syns: contaminated, defiled, dungy, foul, impure, murky, polluted, tainted, squalid.
Ant: clean.
2. Offensive to accepted standards of decency. | 2. OBSCENE.
3. Violently disturbed, as by storms. | 3. ROUGH.

dirty *verb*
1. To make dirty: *dirtied the cuffs of his shirt when he changed his typewriter ribbon.* | 1. *Syns:* befoul, begrime, besoil, black, blacken, smudge, smutch, soil.
2. To cast aspersions on. | 2. BLACKEN.

disable *verb*
1. To render powerless or motionless by inflicting severe injury: *veterans disabled in the war; disabled the tank with a carefully placed grenade.* | 1. *Syns:* cripple, immobilize, incapacitate, knock out (*Informal*), paralyze, prostrate. —*Idioms* lay low, put out of action (*or* commission).
2. To make incapable, as of doing a job. | 2. UNFIT *verb.*

disaccord *noun*
A state of disagreement and disharmony. | CONFLICT *noun.*

disaccord *verb*
1. To fail to be in accord. | 1. CONFLICT *verb.*
2. To be of different opinion. | 2. DIFFER.

disacknowledge *verb*
To refuse to recognize or acknowledge. | REPUDIATE.

disadvantage *noun*
An unfavorable condition, circumstance, or characteristic: *One of the disadvantages of the car is its enormous gas consumption.* | *Syns:* detriment, drawback, handicap, minus, shortcoming.

disadvantaged *adjective*
Economically and socially below standard. | DEPRESSED.

disadvantageous *adjective*
1. Causing difficulty, trouble, or discomfort. | 1. INCONVENIENT.
2. Tending to discourage, retard, or make more difficult. | 2. UNFAVORABLE.

disaffect *verb*
1. To make distant, hostile, or unsympathetic. | 1. ESTRANGE.
2. *Archaic.* To have a feeling of aversion for. | 2. DISLIKE *verb.*

disaffection *noun*
1. An interruption in friendly relations. | 1. BREACH *noun.*
2. An attitude or feeling of aversion. | 2. DISLIKE *noun.*
3. The act of estranging or the condition of being estranged. | 3. ESTRANGEMENT.

disaffirm *verb*
To refuse to admit the truth, reality, value, or worth of. | DENY.

disaffirmation *noun*
A refusal to grant the truth of a statement or charge. | DENIAL.

disagree *verb*
1. To be unlike or dissimilar. | 1. DIFFER.

  2. To be of different opinion.   **2.** DIFFER.

disagreeable *adjective*
  1. Not pleasant or agreeable.   **1.** UNPLEASANT.
  2. Having or showing a bad temper.   **2.** ILL-TEMPERED.

disagreement *noun*
  1. A marked lack of correspondence or agreement.   **1.** GAP.
  2. A discussion, often heated, in which a difference of   **2.** ARGUMENT.
  opinion is expressed.

disallow *verb*
  1. To be unwilling to grant.   **1.** REFUSE.
  2. To refuse to allow.   **2.** FORBID.

disallowance *noun*
  1. A turning down of a request.   **1.** REFUSAL.
  2. A refusal to allow.   **2.** FORBIDDANCE.

disappear *verb*
  1. To pass out of sight either gradually or suddenly: **1.** *Syns:* evanesce, evanish, evaporate,
  The top of the skyscraper disappeared in the fog.   fade, vanish.
  2. To cease to exist: *The ancient Egyptian people*   **2.** *Syns:* die out (*or* away), expire.
  disappeared long ago.

disappearance *noun*
  The act or an example of passing out of sight: *The*   *Syns:* evanescence, evanishment,
  sudden disappearance of the financier is causing   evanition, evaporation, fade-out.
  speculation about his honesty.

disappoint *verb*
  To cause unhappiness by failing to satisfy the hopes,   *Syns:* cast down, discontent, disgruntle,
  desires, or expectations of: *The candidate's speech*   dishearten, dissatisfy, let down.
  disappointed his supporters.

disappointing *adjective*
  Disturbing because of failure to measure up to a   *Syns:* disheartening, dissatisfying, sorry,
  standard or produce the desired results: *disappointing*   unlucky.
  test scores; a disappointing state of affairs.

disappointment *noun*
  Unhappiness caused by the failure of one's hopes,   *Syns:* discontent, discontentment,
  desires, or expectations: *will feel keen disappointment*   disgruntlement, disheartenment,
  when his application is rejected.   dissatisfaction, letdown, regret.

disapprobation *noun*
  Unfavorable opinion or judgment.   DISAPPROVAL.

disapproval *noun*
  Unfavorable opinion or judgment: *couldn't keep the tone*   *Syns:* disapprobation, displeasure.
  of disapproval out of her voice.

disapprove *verb*
  1. To have or express an unfavorable opinion: *Why do*   **1.** *Syns:* deprecate, discountenance,
  you disapprove of the new fashions?   disesteem, disfavor, frown on (*or* upon),
        object[2] (to). —*Idioms* hold no brief for,
        not go for, take a dim view of, take
        exception to.
  2. To be unwilling to grant.   **2.** REFUSE.

disarrange *verb*
  1. To put out of proper order.   **1.** DISORDER *verb*.
  2. To put (the hair or clothes) into a state of disarray.   **2.** TOUSLE.

disarranged *adjective*
  In a condition of disorder.   DISORDERED.

disarrangement *noun*
  A lack of order or regular arrangement.   DISORDER *noun*.

disarray *noun*
  A lack of order or regular arrangement.   DISORDER *noun*.

  disarray *verb*
  To put out of proper order.   DISORDER *verb*.

disassemble *verb*
  To take (something) apart.   TAKE DOWN at **take**.

disassociate *verb*
To remove from association with.

DETACH.

disaster *noun*
An occurrence inflicting widespread destruction and distress: *No sooner had he lost his job than the final disaster struck—his house burned down.*

Syns: calamity, cataclysm, catastrophe, tragedy.
Near-syns: accident, casualty, fatality, mishap, misfortune, woe.

disastrous *adjective*
Causing ruin or destruction.

FATAL.

disavow *verb*
To refuse to recognize or acknowledge.

REPUDIATE.

disbelief *noun*
The refusal or reluctance to believe: *looked at me in pure disbelief.*

Syns: discredit, incredulity, unbelief.

disbelieve *verb*
To give no credence to: *We disbelieve their story as mere rumor.*

Syns: discredit, misbelieve, unbelieve.
—*Idioms* set no store by, take no stock in.

disbelieving *adjective*
Refusing or reluctant to believe.

INCREDULOUS.

disburden *verb*
1. To remove the cargo or load from.
2. To free from something objectionable or undesirable.

1. UNLOAD.
2. RID.

disbursal *noun*
The act of distributing or the condition of being distributed.

DISTRIBUTION.

disburse *verb*
1. To give out in portions or shares.
2. To distribute (money) as payment.

1. DISTRIBUTE.
2. SPEND.

disbursement *noun*
Something expended to obtain a benefit or desired result.

COST *noun.*

discard *verb*
To let go or get rid of as being no longer of use, value, etc.: *plans to discard all the linens in the old trunk.*

Syns: chuck[1] (*Informal*), dispose of, ditch, dump, jettison, junk, scrap[1], shuck (off), throw away, throw out.
Near-syns: abandon, desert, dismiss, forsake, repudiate, spurn.
Ant: retain.

discard *noun*
The act of getting rid of something useless or used up.

DISPOSAL.

discarnate *adjective*
Having no body, form, or substance.

IMMATERIAL.

discern *verb*
1. To perceive and fix the identity of: *We could barely discern a sail on the horizon.*
2. To perceive, esp. barely or fleetingly.
3. To recognize as being different.

1. **Syns:** descry, distinguish, make out, pick out, spot.
2. CATCH *verb.*
3. DISTINGUISH.

discernible *adjective*
Capable of being noticed or apprehended mentally.

PERCEPTIBLE.

discerning *adjective*
1. Characterized by careful and exact evaluation.
2. Possessing or showing sound judgment and keen perception.

1. CRITICAL.
2. WISE[1].

discernment *noun*
Skill in perceiving, discriminating, or judging: *She hires her assistants with such discernment that none ever disappoints her.*

Syns: acumen, astuteness, clear-sightedness, discrimination, eye, keenness, nose, penetration, perceptiveness, percipience, perspicacity, sagacity, sageness, shrewdness, wit.

discharge *verb*
1. To release from military duty: *will be discharged from the army next week.*
2. To set at liberty.
3. To end the employment of.
4. To pass or pour out into: *The Illinois River discharges into the Mississippi.*
5. To carry out the functions, requirements, or terms of.
6. To set right by giving what is due.
7. To free from an obligation or duty.
8. To remove the cargo or load from.
9. To launch with great force.

1. *Syns:* demobilize, muster out, separate.
2. FREE *verb.*
3. DISMISS.
4. *Syns:* emit, empty, flow, issue, vent, void.
5. FULFILL.
6. SETTLE.
7. EXCUSE *verb.*
8. UNLOAD.
9. SHOOT *verb.*

discharge *noun*
The act of dismissing or the condition of being dismissed from employment.

DISMISSAL.

disciple *noun*
One who supports and adheres to another.

FOLLOWER.

disciplinary *adjective*
Inflicting or aiming to inflict punishment.

PUNISHING.

discipline *noun*
1. A penalty imposed for wrongdoing.
2. An area of academic study that is part of a larger body of learning.

1. PUNISHMENT.
2. BRANCH *noun.*

discipline *verb*
1. To subject (one) to a penalty for a wrong.
2. To impart knowledge and skill to.

1. PUNISH.
2. EDUCATE.

disclaim *verb*
To refuse to recognize or acknowledge.

REPUDIATE.

disclaimer *noun*
A refusal to grant the truth of a statement or charge.

DENIAL.

disclose *verb*
1. To make known.
2. To make visible; bring to view.

1. COMMUNICATE.
2. REVEAL.

disclosure *noun*
Something disclosed, esp. something not previously known or realized.

REVELATION.

discolor *verb*
To soil with foreign matter.

STAIN *verb.*

discombobulate *verb*
1. *Slang.* To impair or destroy the composure of.
2. *Slang.* To cause to be unclear in mind or intent.

1. AGITATE.
2. CONFUSE.

discombobulated *adjective*
Slang. Mentally uncertain.

CONFUSED.

discomfiture *noun*
Self-conscious distress.

EMBARRASSMENT.

discomfort *noun*
1. Something that causes difficulty, trouble, or lack of ease.
2. The state or quality of being inconvenient.

1. INCONVENIENCE *noun.*
2. INCONVENIENCE *noun.*

discomfort *verb*
1. To cause inconvenience for.
2. To cause (a person) to be self-consciously distressed.

1. INCONVENIENCE *verb.*
2. EMBARRASS.

discompose *verb*
To impair or destroy the composure of.

AGITATE.

discomposure *noun*
Self-conscious distress.

EMBARRASSMENT.

disconcert *verb*
To cause (a person) to be self-consciously distressed.

EMBARRASS.

disconcerted *adjective*
Distressed and ill at ease.

EMBARRASSED.

disconcertion *noun*
Self-conscious distress.   EMBARRASSMENT.

disconcertment *noun*
Self-conscious distress.   EMBARRASSMENT.

disconnect *verb*
To separate one thing from another thing.   DETACH.

disconnection *noun*
The act or process of detaching.   DETACHMENT.

disconsonant *adjective*
1. Made up of parts or qualities that are disparate or   1. INCONGRUOUS.
   otherwise markedly lacking in consistency.
2. In sharp opposition.   2. CONFLICTING.

discontent *verb*
To cause unhappiness by failing to satisfy the hopes,   DISAPPOINT.
desires, or expectations of.

  discontent *noun*
  Unhappiness caused by the failure of one's hopes,   DISAPPOINTMENT.
  desires, or expectations.

discontentment *noun*
Unhappiness caused by the failure of one's hopes,   DISAPPOINTMENT.
desires, or expectations.

discontinue *verb*
1. To cease trying to accomplish or continue.   1. ABANDON *verb*.
2. To stop suddenly, as a conversation, activity,   2. SUSPEND.
   relationship, etc.
3. To come to a cessation.   3. STOP *verb*.

discontinuity *noun*
A cessation of continuity or regularity.   BREAK *noun*.

discord *noun*
A state of disagreement and disharmony.   CONFLICT *noun*.

  discord *verb*
  1. To fail to be in accord.   1. CONFLICT *verb*.
  2. To be of different opinion.   2. DIFFER.

discordant *adjective*
1. Devoid of harmony and accord.   1. INHARMONIOUS.
2. Characterized by unpleasant discordance of sound.   2. INHARMONIOUS.
3. Made up of parts or qualities that are disparate or   3. INCONGRUOUS.
   otherwise markedly lacking in consistency.
4. Disagreeable to the sense of hearing.   4. HARSH.

discount *verb*
1. To think, represent, or speak of as small or   1. BELITTLE.
   unimportant.
2. To take away (a quantity) from another quantity.   2. DEDUCT.
3. To put out of one's mind as a loss or failure.   3. WRITE OFF at **write**.

  discount *noun*
  An amount deducted.   DEDUCTION.

discountenance *verb*
1. To have or express an unfavorable opinion.   1. DISAPPROVE.
2. To cause (a person) to be self-consciously distressed.   2. EMBARRASS.

discourage *verb*
1. To make less hopeful or enthusiastic: *The magnitude*   1. *Syns:* dishearten, dispirit.
   of the problem discouraged me.
2. To persuade (a person) not to do something.   2. DISSUADE.

discouraging *adjective*
Tending to make less hopeful or enthusiastic: *read a*   *Syns:* disheartening, dispiriting.
discouraging analysis of the current economic situation.

discourse *noun*
1. A formal, lengthy exposition of a topic: *wrote a*   1. *Syns:* disquisition, dissertation,
   discourse on trade deficits.   treatise.
2. The faculty, act, or product of speaking.   2. SPEECH.

  discourse *verb*

To engage in spoken exchange.   CONVERSE[1] *verb*.

discourser *noun*
One given to conversation.   CONVERSATIONALIST.

discourteous *adjective*
Lacking good manners.   RUDE.

discover *verb*
1. To obtain knowledge or awareness of something not   **1. *Syns:*** ascertain, determine, find out,
   known before, as through observation, study, etc.:   hear, learn.
   discovered that the world is round.
2. *Archaic.* To make visible; bring to view.   **2.** REVEAL.
3. *Archaic.* To disclose in a breach of confidence.   **3.** BETRAY.

discovery *noun*
Something that has been discovered: *Radium is one of*   ***Syns:*** find, finding, strike.
the great discoveries of science.

discredit *verb*
1. To cause to be no longer believed or valued: *new*   **1. *Syns:*** debunk, explode, puncture, shoot
   evidence that discredits previous research.   down. —*Idioms* knock the bottom out
                                                          of, shoot full of holes.
2. To prove or show to be false.   **2.** REFUTE.
3. To give no credence to.   **3.** DISBELIEVE.
4. To damage in reputation.   **4.** DISGRACE *verb*.

discredit *noun*
1. Loss of or damage to one's reputation.   **1.** DISGRACE *noun*.
2. The refusal or reluctance to believe.   **2.** DISBELIEF.

discreditable *adjective*
Meriting or causing shame or dishonor.   DISGRACEFUL.

discreet *adjective*
1. Kept within sensible limits.   **1.** CONSERVATIVE *adjective*.
2. Showing sensitivity and skill in dealing with others.   **2.** DELICATE.

discrepance *noun*   SEE **discrepancy**.

discrepancy also **discrepance** *noun*
1. The condition of being unlike or dissimilar. **1.** DIFFERENCE.
2. A marked lack of correspondence or agreement. **2.** GAP.

discrepant *adjective*
1. In sharp opposition.   **1.** CONFLICTING.
2. Made up of parts or qualities that are disparate or   **2.** INCONGRUOUS.
   otherwise markedly lacking in consistency.

discrete *adjective*
1. Distinguished from others by nature or qualities.   **1.** DISTINCT.
2. Being or related to a distinct entity.   **2.** INDIVIDUAL *adjective*.

discretely *adverb*
As a separate unit.   SEPARATELY.

discreteness *noun*
The quality of being individual.   INDIVIDUALITY.

discretion *noun*
Unrestricted freedom to choose.   WILL[1] *noun*.

discretionary *adjective*
1. Based on individual judgment or discretion.   **1.** ARBITRARY.
2. Not compulsory or automatic.   **2.** OPTIONAL.

discriminate *verb*
1. To act on the basis of prejudice: *Some employers*   **1. *Syn:*** prejudice (against).
   used to discriminate against workers for union
   activity.
2. To recognize as being different.   **2.** DISTINGUISH.
3. To make noticeable or different.   **3.** DISTINGUISH.

discriminate *adjective*
Able to recognize small differences or draw fine   DISCRIMINATING.
distinctions.

discriminating *adjective*
1. Able to recognize small differences or draw fine distinctions: *discriminating in his choice of food and wine.*
2. Characterized by careful and exact evaluation.

1. *Syns:* discriminate, discriminative, discriminatory, select, selective.

2. CRITICAL.

discrimination *noun*
1. The ability to distinguish, esp. to recognize small differences or draw fine distinctions: *choice of furniture that shows little artistic discrimination.*
2. The act or an instance of distinguishing.

1. *Syns:* refinement, selectiveness, selectivity.

2. DISTINCTION.

discriminative *adjective*
Able to recognize small differences or draw fine distinctions.

DISCRIMINATING.

discriminatory *adjective*
Able to recognize small differences or draw fine distinctions.

DISCRIMINATING.

disculpate *verb*
To free from a charge or imputation of guilt.

CLEAR *verb.*

discursion *noun*
An instance of digressing.

DIGRESSION.

discursive *adjective*
Marked by or given to digression.

DIGRESSIVE.

discuss *verb*
1. To speak together and exchange ideas and opinions about: *discussing the pros and cons of nuclear power.*

1. *Syns:* hash over (*Informal*), kick around (*Informal*), knock about (*Informal*), knock around (*Informal*), moot, talk over, thrash out, thresh out, toss about (*Informal*), toss around (*Informal*). —*Idiom* go into a huddle.

2. *Rare.* To take (food) into the body as nourishment.

2. EAT.

discussant *noun*
One who participates in a conference.

CONFEREE.

discussion *noun*
1. An exchanging of views.
2. A meeting for the exchange of views.

1. CONFERENCE.
2. CONFERENCE.

discussor *noun*
One who participates in a conference.

CONFEREE.

disdain *noun*
1. The feeling of despising.
2. The quality of being arrogant.

1. DESPISAL.
2. ARROGANCE.

disdain *verb*
To regard with utter contempt and disdain.

DESPISE.

disdainful *adjective*
Overly convinced of one's own superiority and importance.

ARROGANT.

disease *noun*
A pathological condition of mind or body: *a disease of the eyes.*

Syns: affection[2], ailment, complaint, disorder, ill, illness, infirmity, malady, sickness.

disembark *verb*
To come ashore from a seacraft.

LAND *verb.*

disembarrass *verb*
To free from something objectionable or undesirable.

RID.

disembodied *adjective*
Having no body, form, or substance.

IMMATERIAL.

disencumber *verb*
To free from something objectionable or undesirable.

RID.

disengage *verb*
1. To become separated from.
2. To separate one thing from another thing.
3. To free from ties or fasteners.

1. BREAK *verb.*
2. DETACH.
3. UNDO.

4. To free from an entanglement.

4. CLEAR *verb*.

disengaged *adjective*
Freed from contact or connection.

CLEAR *adjective*.

disengagement *noun*
The act or process of detaching.

DETACHMENT.

disentangle *verb*
To free from an entanglement.

CLEAR *verb*.

disesteem *noun*
Loss of or damage to one's reputation.

DISGRACE *noun*.

disesteem *verb*
To have or express an unfavorable opinion.

DISAPPROVE.

disfavor *noun*
An attitude or feeling of aversion.

DISLIKE *noun*.

disfavor *verb*
To have or express an unfavorable opinion.

DISAPPROVE.

disfigure *verb*
To alter and spoil the natural form or appearance of.

DEFORM.

disfigurement *noun*
A disfiguring abnormality of shape or form.

DEFORMITY.

disgorge *verb*
To send forth (confined matter) violently.

ERUPT.

disgrace *noun*
Loss of or damage to one's reputation: *a public official who had to resign in disgrace.*

Syns: discredit, disesteem, dishonor, disrepute, ignominy, obloquy, opprobrium, shame. —*Idioms* bad name (*or* odor), ill repute.
Near-syns: abasement, contempt, debasement, degradation, humiliation, infamy, odium, stigma.
Ants: esteem, respect, reverence.

disgrace *verb*
To damage in reputation: *disgraced his family with his arrest for drug dealing.*

Syns: discredit, dishonor, shame. —*Idioms* be a reproach to, put to the blush.

disgraceful *adjective*
1. Meriting or causing shame or dishonor: *a disgraceful secret that is being withheld from the public; disgraceful behavior.*
2. Worthy of severe disapproval.

1. *Syns:* discreditable, dishonorable, disreputable, ignominious, obloquious, opprobrious, shabby, shameful.
2. DEPLORABLE.

disgracefulness *noun*
The condition of being infamous.

INFAMY.

disgruntle *verb*
To cause unhappiness by failing to satisfy the hopes, desires, or expectations of.

DISAPPOINT.

disgruntlement *noun*
Unhappiness caused by the failure of one's hopes, desires, or expectations.

DISAPPOINTMENT.

disguise *verb*
To change or modify so as to prevent recognition of the true identity or character of: *disguised her interest with a blasé attitude.*

Syns: bemask, camouflage, cloak, cover up, dissemble, dissimulate, mask, masquerade, sleek.
Near-ants: display, exhibit, expose, flaunt, parade; disclose, reveal; discover.

disguise *noun*
1. Clothes or other personal effects, such as make-up, worn to conceal one's identity: *will wear the disguise of a witch to the fancy-dress ball.*
2. A deceptive outward appearance.

1. *Syn:* costume.

2. FAÇADE.

disguisement *noun*
A deceptive outward appearance.

FAÇADE.

disgust *verb*
To offend the senses or feelings of: *The sight of the cockroach scurrying around disgusted her.*

Syns: nauseate, repel, repulse, revolt, sicken. —*Idiom* turn one's stomach.

disgust *noun*
Extreme repugnance excited by something offensive: *behavior that arouses disgust.*

Syns: aversion, loathing, repulsion.

disgusted *adjective*
Out of patience with.

SICK.

disgusting *adjective*
1. Extremely unpleasant to the senses or feelings.
2. So objectionable as to elicit despisal.

1. OFFENSIVE *adjective.*
2. FILTHY.

disharmonic *adjective*
Characterized by unpleasant discordance of sound.

INHARMONIOUS.

disharmonious *adjective*
Characterized by unpleasant discordance of sound.

INHARMONIOUS.

dishearten *verb*
1. To make less hopeful or enthusiastic.
2. To cause unhappiness by failing to satisfy the hopes, desires, or expectations of.

1. DISCOURAGE.
2. DISAPPOINT.

disheartening *adjective*
1. Tending to make less hopeful or enthusiastic.
2. Disturbing because of failure to measure up to a standard or produce the desired results.

1. DISCOURAGING.
2. DISAPPOINTING.

disheartenment *noun*
Unhappiness caused by the failure of one's hopes, desires, or expectations.

DISAPPOINTMENT.

dishevel *verb*
To put (the hair or clothes) into a state of disarray.

TOUSLE.

disheveled *adjective*
Marked by an absence of cleanliness and order.

MESSY.

dishonest *adjective*
1. Given to or marked by deliberate concealment or misrepresentation of the truth: *a sneaky, dishonest manipulator of people; a dishonest answer to the question.*

1. *Syns:* deceitful, lying, mendacious, shifty, untruthful, unveridical.
Near-ants: dependable, reliable, trustworthy, trusty; conscientious, honorable, just, upright; fair, frank, good, open.
Ant: honest.

2. Marked by dishonesty, esp. in matters of public trust.

2. CORRUPT *adjective.*

dishonesty *noun*
1. Lack of integrity: *mistrust him because of his fundamental dishonesty.*
2. Departure from what is legally, ethically, and morally correct.
3. Lack of straightforwardness and honesty in action.

1. *Syn:* improbity.
2. CORRUPTION.
3. INDIRECTION.

dishonor *noun*
Loss of or damage to one's reputation.

DISGRACE *noun.*

dishonor *verb*
To damage in reputation.

DISGRACE *noun.*

dishonorable *adjective*
Meriting or causing shame or dishonor.

DISGRACEFUL.

dishonorableness *noun*
The condition of being infamous.

INFAMY.

disimpassioned *adjective*
Not easily excited, even under pressure.

COOL *adjective.*

disimprove *verb*
To become lower in quality, character, or condition.

DETERIORATE.

disinclination *noun*
1. An attitude or feeling of aversion.
2. The state of not being disposed or inclined.

1. DISLIKE *noun.*
2. INDISPOSITION.

disinclined *adjective*
Not inclined or willing to do or undertake.   INDISPOSED.

disinfect *verb*
To render free of microorganisms.   STERILIZE.

disingenuity *noun*
Lack of sincerity.   INSINCERITY.

disingenuous *adjective*
1. Not being what one purports to be.   1. INSINCERE.
2. Marked by treachery or deceit.   2. UNDERHAND.

disingenuousness *noun*
Lack of sincerity.   INSINCERITY.

disintegrate *verb*
1. To reduce or become reduced to pieces or   1. BREAK UP at **break**.
   components.
2. To become lower in quality, character, or condition.   2. DETERIORATE.

disintegration *noun*
1. Descent to a lower level or condition.   1. DETERIORATION.
2. Severe damage or decay rendering something useless   2. RUIN *noun*.
   or worthless.

disinterest *noun*
1. The quality or state of being just and unbiased.   1. FAIRNESS.
2. Lack of emotion or interest.   2. APATHY.

disinterested *adjective*
1. Lacking interest in one's surroundings or worldly   1. DETACHED.
   affairs.
2. Feeling or showing no strong emotional   2. NEUTRAL.
   involvement.
3. Without emotion or interest.   3. APATHETIC.

disinterestedness *noun*
The quality or state of being just and unbiased.   FAIRNESS.

disjoin *verb*
1. To become or cause to become apart one from   1. DIVIDE.
   another.
2. To crack or split into two or more fragments by   2. BREAK *verb*.
   means of or as a result of force, a blow, or strain.

disjoint *verb*
1. To become or cause to become apart one from   1. DIVIDE.
   another.
2. To crack or split into two or more fragments by   2. BREAK *verb*.
   means of or as a result of force, a blow, or strain.

dislike *verb*
To have a feeling of aversion for: *The two men heartily*   **Syns:** disaffect (*Archaic*), disrelish,
dislike each other.   mislike. —*Idiom* have no use for.

dislike *noun*
An attitude or feeling of aversion: *had a real dislike for*   **Syns:** disaffection, disfavor, disinclination,
canned music.   disrelish, distaste.

dislocate *verb*
1. To alter the settled state or position of.   1. DISTURB.
2. To displace (a bone) from a socket or joint.   2. SLIP *verb*.

disloyal *adjective*
Not true to duty or obligation.   FAITHLESS.

disloyalty *noun*
Betrayal, esp. of a moral obligation.   FAITHLESSNESS.

dismal *adjective*
1. Dark and depressing.   1. GLOOMY.
2. Marked by little hopefulness.   2. GLOOMY.
3. Tending to cause sadness or low spirits.   3. SAD.

dismantle *verb*
1. To take (something) apart.   1. TAKE DOWN at **take**.
2. To break up so that reconstruction is impossible.   2. DESTROY.

dismay *verb*
To deprive of courage or the power to act as a result of fear, anxiety, or disgust: *The news of plummeting stock prices dismayed speculators.*

Syns: appall, consternate, daunt, horrify, shake, shock.

dismay *noun*
A sudden or complete loss of courage in the face of trouble or danger: *looked at me in dismay when she learned she needed surgery.*

Syn: consternation.

dismayed *adjective*
Overcome with intense feeling, as of amazement, horror, or dismay.

SHOCKED.

dismember *verb*
1. To take (something) apart.
2. To deprive of, or of the use of, a limb or bodily member.

1. TAKE DOWN at **take.**
2. CRIPPLE.

dismiss *verb*
1. To end the employment of: *Workers who habitually arrive late are first warned, then dismissed.*

1. *Syns:* boot[1] (*Slang*), bounce (*Slang*), can (*Slang*), cashier, discharge, drop, fire (*Informal*), sack[1] (*Slang*), terminate. —*Idioms* give someone his walking papers, give someone the ax, give someone the gate, give someone the pink slip, let go.

2. To direct or allow to leave: *When the bell rang, the teacher dismissed the class.*

2. *Syn:* send away. —*Idioms* send about one's business, send packing, show the door to.

3. To put out by force.
4. To rid one's mind of: *She thought of chasing the bus but dismissed the idea when another bus came into view.*
5. To cease consideration or treatment of.
6. To be unwilling to accept, consider, or receive.

3. EJECT.
4. *Syns:* banish, cast out, dispel, kiss off (*Slang*), shut out.
5. DROP *verb.*
6. DECLINE *verb.*

dismissal *noun*
1. The act of dismissing or the condition of being dismissed from employment: *deeply resented his dismissal.*
2. The act of ejecting or the state of being ejected.

1. *Syns:* discharge, firing (*Informal*), sack[1] (*Slang*), termination. —*Idioms* the boot, the bounce.
2. EJECTION.

dismount *verb*
To take (something) apart.

TAKE DOWN at **take.**

disobedience *noun*
The condition or practice of not obeying: *Disobedience was quickly punished in that household.*

Syns: insubordination, noncompliance, unruliness.

disobedient *adjective*
Refusing or failing to obey: *a disobedient child.*

Syns: insubordinate, lawless, uncompliant, unruly.

disobey *verb*
To refuse or fail to obey: *disobeying instructions.*

Syns: break, defy, disregard, flout, transgress, violate. —*Idiom* pay no attention (*or* mind) to.

disorder *noun*
1. A lack of order or regular arrangement: *We found the burglarized apartment in disorder.*

1. *Syns:* ballup (*Slang*), chaos, clutter, confusedness, confusion, disarrangement, disarray, disorderliness, disorganization, huddle, jumble, mess, mix-up, muddle, scramble, snafu (*Slang*), snarl[1], topsy-turviness, tumble, turmoil.

2. A lack of civil order or peace: *Looting and disorder prevailed during the blackout.*
3. A pathological condition of mind or body.
4. The condition of being sick.

2. *Syns:* anarchy, lawlessness, misrule.
3. DISEASE.
4. SICKNESS.

disorder *verb*
1. To put out of proper order: *Father warned us not to disorder the books and papers on his desk.*

2. To break up the order or progress of.
3. To put into total disorder.
4. To disturb the health or physiological functioning of.
5. To put (the hair or clothes) into a state of disarray.

disordered *adjective*
1. In a condition of disorder: *disordered schedules; disordered finances.*
2. Characterized by physical confusion.
3. Afflicted with or exhibiting irrationality and mental unsoundness.

disordering *noun*
The act or an example of upsetting.

disorderliness *noun*
A lack of order or regular arrangement.

disorderly *adjective*
1. Lacking regular or logical order: *the disorderly closet of a teen-ager.*
2. Upsetting civil order or peace: *The police moved to disperse the disorderly crowd.*

disorganization *noun*
1. A lack of order or regular arrangement.
2. The act or an example of upsetting.

disorganize *verb*
To put out of proper order.

disorganized *adjective*
In a condition of disorder.

disown *verb*
To refuse to recognize or acknowledge.

disparage *verb*
To think, represent, or speak of as small or unimportant.

disparagement *noun*
The act or an instance of belittling.

disparaging *adjective*
Tending or intending to belittle: *made disparaging comments about the other editors.*

disparate *adjective*
Not like another in nature, quality, amount, or form.

disparity *noun*
1. The condition of being unlike or dissimilar.
2. A marked lack of correspondence or agreement.
3. The condition or fact of being unequal, as in age, rank, or degree.

dispassion *noun*
The quality or state of being just and unbiased.

dispassionate *adjective*
1. Free from bias in judgment.
2. Feeling or showing no strong emotional involvement.

dispassionately *adverb*
In a just way.

---

1. **Syns:** derange, disarrange, disarray, disorganize, disrupt, disturb, jumble, mess up, mix up, muddle, tumble, unsettle, upset.
2. DISRUPT.
3. CONFUSE.
4. UPSET *verb.*
5. TOUSLE.

1. **Syns:** disarranged, disorganized, disrupted.
2. CONFUSED.
3. INSANE.

UPSET *noun.*

DISORDER *noun.*

1. **Syns:** messy, unsystematic.
2. **Syns:** riotous, rowdy, unruly.

1. DISORDER *noun.*
2. UPSET *noun.*

DISORDER *verb.*

DISORDERED.

REPUDIATE.

BELITTLE.

BELITTLEMENT.

Syns: belittling, decrying, deprecatory (*also* deprecative), depreciating, depreciative, depreciatory, derogatory, detracting, pejorative, slighting, uncomplimentary.
Near-ants: extolling, saluting.
Ants: complimenting, praising.

DIFFERENT.

1. DIFFERENCE.
2. GAP.
3. INEQUALITY.

FAIRNESS.

1. FAIR *adjective.*
2. NEUTRAL.

FAIRLY.

dispassionateness *noun*
The quality or state of being just and unbiased.   FAIRNESS.

dispatch *verb*
1. To cause (something) to be conveyed to a destination.   1. SEND.
2. To eat completely or entirely.   2. CONSUME.
3. To cause the death of.   3. KILL.

dispatch *noun*
Rapidness of movement or activity.   HASTE *noun*.

dispel *verb*
1. To rid one's mind of.   1. DISMISS.
2. To separate or cause to separate and go in various directions.   2. SCATTER.
3. To disappear by or as if by rising.   3. LIFT *verb*.

dispensation *noun*
1. The giving of a medication, esp. by prescribed dosage.   1. ADMINISTRATION.
2. The act of distributing or the condition of being distributed.   2. DISTRIBUTION.

dispense *verb*
1. To provide as a remedy.   1. ADMINISTER.
2. To give out in portions or shares.   2. DISTRIBUTE.
3. To free from an obligation or duty.   3. EXCUSE *verb*.

dispensing *noun*
The giving of a medication, esp. by prescribed dosage.   ADMINISTRATION.

disperse *verb*
1. To pass (something) out.   1. DISTRIBUTE.
2. To extend over a wide area.   2. SPREAD *verb*.
3. To disappear by or as if by rising.   3. LIFT *verb*.
4. To separate or cause to separate and go in various directions.   4. SCATTER.

dispirit *verb*
1. To make less hopeful or enthusiastic.   1. DISCOURAGE.
2. To make sad or gloomy.   2. DEPRESS.

dispirited *adjective*
In low spirits.   DEPRESSED.

dispiriting *adjective*
1. Tending to make less hopeful or enthusiastic.   1. DISCOURAGING.
2. Dark and depressing.   2. GLOOMY.

displace *verb*
1. To alter the settled state or position of.   1. DISTURB.
2. To take the place of (another) against the other's will.   2. SUPPLANT.

display *verb*
1. To make a public and usu. ostentatious show of: *displayed her trophies on a pedestal; displaying his trim figure to best advantage.*   1. **Syns:** brandish, disport, exhibit, expose, flash, flaunt, parade, show, show off, sport.
2. To make visible; bring to view.   2. REVEAL.
3. To make manifest or apparent.   3. SHOW *verb*.
4. To be endowed with as a visible characteristic or form.   4. BEAR.
5. To give expression to, as by gestures, facial aspects, or bodily posture.   5. EXPRESS *verb*.

display *noun*
1. An act of showing or displaying: *a display of articles for sale; a display of force.*   1. **Syns:** demonstration, exhibit, exhibition, manifestation, show.
2. An impressive or ostentatious exhibition: *The lottery winner promptly made a display of his new wealth.*   2. **Syns:** array, panoply, parade, pomp, spectacle.

displease *verb*
To be very disagreeable to.   OFFEND.

displeasing *adjective*
Not pleasant or agreeable.　UNPLEASANT.

displeasure *noun*
Unfavorable opinion or judgment.　DISAPPROVAL.

displeasure *verb*
Archaic. To be very disagreeable to.　OFFEND.

disponible *adjective*
Capable of being obtained or used.　AVAILABLE.

disport *verb*
1. To conduct oneself in a specified way.　1. ACT *verb*.
2. To make a public and usu. ostentatious show of.　2. DISPLAY *verb*.
3. To occupy oneself with amusement or diversion.　3. PLAY *verb*.

disport *noun*
Activity engaged in for relaxation and amusement.　PLAY *noun*.

disposal *noun*
1. A way or condition of being arranged.　1. ARRANGEMENT.
2. The act of getting rid of something useless or used up: *Garbage disposal is a municipal function.*　2. *Syns:* discard, dumping, elimination, jettison, riddance.

dispose *verb*
1. To influence or be influenced in a certain direction: *His friendliness disposed me to like him.*　1. *Syns:* bend, bias, incline, predispose, sway.
2. To put into a deliberate order.　2. ARRANGE.

dispose of *verb*
1. To put into correct or conclusive form.　1. SETTLE.
2. To let go or get rid of as being no longer of use, value, etc.　2. DISCARD.

disposed *adjective*
Having or showing a tendency or likelihood.　INCLINED.

dispose of *verb*　SEE **dispose.**

disposition *noun*
1. A person's customary manner of emotional response: *an affectionate disposition.*　1. *Syns:* complexion, humor, kidney, nature, temper, temperament. —*Idiom* frame of mind.
2. A way or condition of being arranged.　2. ARRANGEMENT.
3. An inclination to something.　3. BENT *noun*.
4. The combination of emotional, intellectual, and moral qualities that distinguishes an individual.　4. CHARACTER.
5. A general cast of mind with regard to something.　5. SENTIMENT.

dispossess *verb*
To take or keep something away from.　DEPRIVE.

dispossession *noun*
The condition of being deprived of what one once had or ought to have.　DEPRIVATION.

disproportion *noun*
The condition or fact of being unequal, as in age, rank, or degree.　INEQUALITY.

disprove *verb*
To prove or show to be false.　REFUTE.

disputable *adjective*
In doubt or dispute.　DEBATABLE.

disputation *noun*
The presentation of an argument.　ARGUMENTATION.

disputatious *adjective*
Given to arguing.　ARGUMENTATIVE.

dispute *verb*
1. To take a stand against.　1. CONTEST *verb*.
2. To put forth reasons for or against, often excitedly.　2. ARGUE.

dispute *noun*
A discussion, often heated, in which a difference of opinion is expressed.　ARGUMENT.

disputed *adjective*
In doubt or dispute.   DEBATABLE.

disqualify *verb*
To make incapable, as of doing a job.   UNFIT *verb*.

disquiet *verb*
To impair or destroy the composure of.   AGITATE.

disquiet *noun*
1. A state of discomposure.   1. AGITATION.
2. Anxious concern.   2. ANXIETY.
3. An uneasy or nervous state.   3. RESTLESSNESS.

disquieted *adjective*
In a state of uneasiness.   ANXIOUS.

disquietude *noun*
1. Anxious concern.   1. ANXIETY.
2. An uneasy or nervous state.   2. RESTLESSNESS.

disquisition *noun*
A formal, lengthy exposition of a topic.   DISCOURSE *noun*.

disquisitive *adjective*
Eager to acquire knowledge.   CURIOUS.

disregard *verb*
1. To refuse to pay attention to (a person); treat with contempt.   1. IGNORE.
2. To fail to care for or give proper attention to.   2. NEGLECT *verb*.
3. To avoid the fulfillment of.   3. NEGLECT *verb*.

disregard *noun*
1. An act or instance of neglecting.   1. NEGLECT *noun*.
2. Lack of emotion or interest.   2. APATHY.
3. A lack of consideration for others' feelings.   3. THOUGHTLESSNESS.

disrelish *verb*
To have a feeling of aversion for.   DISLIKE *verb*.

disrelish *noun*
An attitude or feeling of aversion.   DISLIKE *noun*.

disremember *verb*
To fail to remember.   FORGET.

disreputable *adjective*
Meriting or causing shame or dishonor.   DISGRACEFUL.

disrepute *noun*
Loss of or damage to one's reputation.   DISGRACE *noun*.

disrespect *noun*
1. Lack of proper respect: *accused of disrespect for failing to salute the flag.*   1. *Syns:* incivility, irreverence, lese majesty (*also* lèse majesté).
2. The state or quality of being impudent.   2. IMPUDENCE.

disrespectful *adjective*
Having or showing a lack of respect: *It is disrespectful to talk loudly in church.*   *Syns:* irreverent, uncivil.
Near-syns: brusque, curt, gruff; boorish, churlish, ill-mannered, impertinent, impolite, rude.
Ant: respectful.

disrobe *verb*
1. To make bare.   1. BARE *verb*.
2. To remove all the clothing from.   2. STRIP[1].

disrobed *adjective*
Not wearing any clothes.   NUDE.

disrupt *verb*
1. To break up the order or progress of: *Hecklers disrupted the council meeting.*   1. *Syns:* disturb, upset. —*Idiom* play havoc with.
2. To put out of proper order.   2. DISORDER *verb*.

disrupted *adjective*
In a condition of disorder.   DISORDERED.

disruption *noun*
1. A cessation of continuity or regularity.   1. BREAK *noun*.

2. The act or an example of upsetting.   **2.** UPSET *noun*.

disruptive *adjective*
Troubling to the mind or emotions.   DISTURBING.

dissatisfaction *noun*
Unhappiness caused by the failure of one's hopes,   DISAPPOINTMENT.
desires, or expectations.

dissatisfy *verb*
To cause unhappiness by failing to satisfy the hopes,   DISAPPOINT.
desires, or expectations of.

dissatisfying *adjective*
Disturbing because of failure to measure up to a   DISAPPOINTING.
standard or produce the desired results.

dissect *verb*
To separate into parts for study.   ANALYZE.

dissection *noun*
The separation of a whole into its parts for study.   ANALYSIS.

dissemblance *noun*
A display of insincere behavior.   ACT *noun*.

dissemble *verb*
1. To behave affectedly or insincerely.   **1.** ACT *verb*.
2. To change or modify so as to prevent recognition of   **2.** DISGUISE *verb*.
the true identity or character of.
3. *Obs.* To pretend not to see.   **3.** BLINK AT at **blink**.

disseminate *verb*
1. To make (information) generally known.   **1.** ADVERTISE.
2. To pass (something) out.   **2.** DISTRIBUTE.

dissension *noun*
A state of disagreement and disharmony.   CONFLICT *noun*.

dissent *verb*
To be of different opinion.   DIFFER.

dissent *noun*
A state of disagreement and disharmony.   CONFLICT *noun*.

dissenter *noun*
A person who dissents from the doctrine of an   SEPARATIST.
established church.

dissentience *noun*
A state of disagreement and disharmony.   CONFLICT *noun*.

dissertation *noun*
1. A formal, lengthy exposition of a topic.   **1.** DISCOURSE *noun*.
2. A systematic, thorough written presentation of an   **2.** THESIS.
original point of view.

disserve *verb*
To spoil the soundness or perfection of.   INJURE.

disservice *noun*
An act that is not just.   INJUSTICE.

dissever *verb*
To separate into parts with or as if with a sharp-edged   CUT *verb*.
instrument.

dissidence *noun*
A state of disagreement and disharmony.   CONFLICT *noun*.

dissident *noun*
A person who dissents from the doctrine of an   SEPARATIST.
established church.

dissimilar *adjective*
Not like another in nature, quality, amount, or form.   DIFFERENT.

dissimilarity *noun*
The condition of being unlike or dissimilar.   DIFFERENCE.

dissimilitude *noun*
The condition of being unlike or dissimilar.   DIFFERENCE.

dissimulate *verb*
To change or modify so as to prevent recognition of the true identity or character of.   DISGUISE *verb*.

dissipate *verb*
1. To spend (money) excessively and usu. foolishly.   1. WASTE *verb*.
2. To disappear by or as if by rising.   2. LIFT *verb*.
3. To separate or cause to separate and go in various   3. SCATTER.
   directions.

dissociate *verb*
1. To become separated from.   1. BREAK *verb*.
2. To remove from association with.   2. DETACH.

dissolute *adjective*
1. Lacking in moral restraint.   1. ABANDONED.
2. Given to heedless, unrestrained pursuit of pleasure. 2. FAST *adjective*.

dissoluteness *noun*
Excessive freedom; lack of restraint.   LICENSE *noun*.

dissolution *noun*
1. The act or fact of dying.   1. DEATH.
2. Excessive freedom; lack of restraint.   2. LICENSE *noun*.

dissolve *verb*
1. To reduce or become reduced to pieces or   1. BREAK UP at **break.**
   components.
2. To disappear gradually by or as if by dispersal of   2. FADE *verb*.
   particles.
3. To change from a solid to a liquid.   3. MELT.
4. *Motion Pic. & T.V.* To make (a film image)   4. FADE OUT.
   disappear gradually.

dissolve *noun*
Motion Pic. & T.V. The gradual disappearance, esp. of a   FADE-OUT at **fade out.**
film image.

dissonance *noun*
A state of disagreement and disharmony.   CONFLICT *noun*.

dissonant *adjective*
1. Characterized by unpleasant discordance of sound.   1. INHARMONIOUS.
2. Made up of parts or qualities that are disparate or   2. INCONGRUOUS.
   otherwise markedly lacking in consistency.

dissuade *verb*
To persuade (a person) not to do something: *tried to*   **Syns:** deter, discourage, divert. —*Idiom*
dissuade the President from taking military action.   talk out of.
                                                         Ant: persuade.

distaff *noun*
Women in general.   FEMININITY.

distaff *adjective*
Of, relating to, or characteristic of women.   FEMININE.

distance *noun*
1. The fact or condition of being far removed or apart: 1. **Syns:** farness, remoteness.
   Because of its distance Helena was an appropriate
   island of exile.
2. An extent, measured or unmeasured, of linear space: 2. **Syns:** length, piece (*Regional*), space,
   Favorable winds propelled the ship a great distance   stretch, way.
   before sunset.
3. Dissociation from one's surroundings or worldly   3. DETACHMENT.
   affairs.
4. A wide and open area, as of land, sky, or water.   4. EXPANSE.
5. Degree of separation, esp. in time.   5. REMOVE *noun*.

distant *adjective*
1. Far from others in space, time, or relationship: *faint*   1. **Syns:** far, faraway, far-flung, far-off,
   light from distant parts of the universe; crumbled   remote, removed. —*Idiom* at a
   remains of the distant past.   distance.
2. Not friendly, sociable, or warm in manner.   2. COOL *adjective*.

distaste *noun*
An attitude or feeling of aversion. DISLIKE *noun*.

distasteful *adjective*
1. Difficult to accept. **1.** BITTER *adjective*.
2. So unpleasant in flavor as to be inedible. **2.** UNPALATABLE.

distill *verb*
To fall or let fall in drops of liquid. DRIP *verb*.

distinct *adjective*
1. Distinguished from others by nature or qualities: *The design used two compatible but distinct colors.* **1.** *Syns:* discrete, diverse, separate, several, various.
2. Readily seen, perceived, or understood. **2.** APPARENT.
3. Without any doubt. **3.** DECIDED.
4. Clearly defined; not ambiguous. **4.** SHARP *adjective*.

distinction *noun*
1. The act or an instance of distinguishing: *The statistics make no distinction between part-time and full-time employees.* **1.** *Syns:* differentiation, discrimination, separation.
2. The condition of being unlike or dissimilar. **2.** DIFFERENCE.
3. A position of exalted, widely recognized importance. **3.** EMINENCE.
4. A special feature or quality that confers superiority. **4.** VIRTUE.
5. Recognition of achievement or superiority or a sign of this: *graduated with distinction.* **5.** *Syns:* accolade, honor, kudos, laurels.

distinctive *adjective*
Serving to identify or set apart an individual or group: *a bird's distinctive markings; a distinctive behavior pattern.* *Syns:* characteristic, distinguishing, individual, peculiar, typical (*also* typic), vintage.

distinctiveness *noun*
The quality of being individual. INDIVIDUALITY.

distinctness *noun*
The quality of being clear and easy to perceive or understand. CLARITY.

distinguish *verb*
1. To recognize as being different: *could not distinguish fear from cowardice.* **1.** *Syns:* differentiate, discern, discriminate, know, separate, tell.
2. To perceive and fix the identity of. **2.** DISCERN.
3. To perceive with a special effort of the senses or the mind. **3.** NOTICE *verb*.
4. To make noticeable or different: *Simple, clean-cut forms distinguish the work of this architect.* **4.** *Syns:* characterize, differentiate, discriminate, individualize, mark, qualify, set apart, signalize, singularize.
5. To cause to be eminent or recognized: *He distinguished himself as a statesman.* **5.** *Syns:* elevate, ennoble, exalt, honor, signalize.

distinguished *adjective*
Widely known and esteemed. EMINENT.

distinguishing *adjective*
Serving to identify or set apart an individual or group. DISTINCTIVE.

distort *verb*
1. To give an inaccurate view of by representing falsely or misleadingly: *propagandists who distort facts.* **1.** *Syns:* belie, color, falsify, load, misrepresent, misstate, pervert, twist, warp, wrench. —*Idiom* give a false coloring to.
2. To alter and spoil the natural form or appearance of. **2.** DEFORM.

distract *verb*
1. To occupy in an agreeable or pleasing way. **1.** AMUSE *verb*.
2. To make insane. **2.** DERANGE.

distracting *adjective*
Entertaining or pleasing. AMUSING.

distraction *noun*
1. Something, esp. a performance or show, designed to entertain. **1.** AMUSEMENT.

2. The condition of being amused.

distrait *adjective*
So lost in thought as to be unaware of one's surroundings.

distraught *adjective*
Afflicted with or exhibiting irrationality and mental unsoundness.

distress *verb*
1. To cause suffering or painful sorrow to: *The news of the child's death distressed her deeply.*
2. To cause anxious uneasiness in.

distress *noun*
1. A state of physical or mental suffering: *respiratory distress; felt great distress over the death of her father.*
2. Anxious concern.
3. The condition of being in need of immediate assistance: *a swimmer in distress.*

distressed *adjective*
In a state of uneasiness.

distressful *adjective*
Troubling to the mind or emotions.

distressing *adjective*
Troubling to the mind or emotions.

distribute *verb*
1. To give out in portions or shares: *The government distributed land to settlers willing to plant it.*

2. To pass (something) out: *distributing handbills on the street.*
3. To extend over a wide area.
4. To put into a deliberate order.

distribution *noun*
1. The act of distributing or the condition of being distributed: *Attorneys supervised the distribution of the property among the heirs.*
2. A way or condition of being arranged.

distrust *noun*
Lack of trust: *looked at the new device with distrust.*

distrust *verb*
To lack trust or confidence in: *Distrusting banks, he kept his cash in a shoebox.*

distrustful *adjective*
Lacking trust or confidence: *distrustful of strangers.*

disturb *verb*
1. To alter the settled state or position of: *The earthquake disturbed the rocks and started a landslide.*
2. To impair or destroy the composure of.
3. To put out of proper order.
4. To break up the order or progress of.
5. To trouble the nerves or peace of mind of, esp. by repeated vexations.

disturbance *noun*
An interruption of regular procedure or of public peace: *A disturbance at the back of the hall made the speaker pause.*

disturbed *adjective*
In a state of uneasiness.

---

2. AMUSEMENT.

ABSENT-MINDED.

INSANE.

1. *Syns:* afflict, aggrieve, anguish, grieve, pain.
2. WORRY *verb.*

1. *Syns:* affliction, agony, anguish, hurt, misery, pain, woe.

2. ANXIETY.
3. *Syns:* exigency (*also* exigence), trouble.
   —*Idiom* hot water.

ANXIOUS.

DISTURBING.

DISTURBING.

1. *Syns:* deal, disburse, dispense, divide, divvy (*Slang*), dole out, measure out, parcel, portion, share.
2. *Syns:* circulate, disperse, disseminate, hand out.
3. SPREAD *verb.*
4. ARRANGE.

1. *Syns:* apportionment, disbursal, dispensation, division.

2. ARRANGEMENT.

Syns: doubt, doubtfulness, mistrust, suspicion.

Syns: doubt, misdoubt, mistrust, suspect.

Syns: doubtful, doubting, dubious, mistrustful, suspicious, untrusting.

1. *Syns:* agitate, dislocate, displace, move, shake, shift.

2. AGITATE.
3. DISORDER *verb.*
4. DISRUPT.
5. ANNOY.

Syns: agitation, commotion, fuss, rumpus, stir[1], to-do (*Informal*), tumult, turbulence, uproar.

ANXIOUS.

disturbing *adjective*
Troubling to the mind or emotions: *a disturbing turn of events in Southwest Asia.*

Syns: disruptive, distressing, distressful, intrusive, troublesome, unsettling, upsetting.

disunion *noun*
1. The act or an instance of separating one thing from another.
2. The condition of being divided, as in opinion.

1. DIVISION.
2. DIVISION.

disunite *verb*
1. To become or cause to become apart one from another.
2. To make distant, hostile, or unsympathetic.

1. DIVIDE.
2. ESTRANGE.

disuse *noun*
The quality or state of being obsolete.

OBSOLETENESS.

ditch *verb*
To let go or get rid of as being no longer of use, value, etc.

DISCARD.

dither *noun*
A state of discomposure.

AGITATION.

dither *verb*
To be irresolute in acting or doing.

HESITATE.

dithyrambic *adjective*
Fired with intense feeling.

PASSIONATE.

divagate *verb*
To turn aside from the main subject in writing or speaking.

DIGRESS.

divagation *noun*
1. The act of digressing.
2. An instance of digressing.

1. DIGRESSION.
2. DIGRESSION.

divarication *noun*
The condition of being unlike or dissimilar.

DIFFERENCE.

dive *verb*
1. To undergo a sharp, rapid descent in value or price.
2. To move or thrust at, under, or into the midst of with sudden force.

1. FALL *verb*.
2. PLUNGE *verb*.

dive *noun*
1. The act of plunging suddenly downward into or as if into water.
2. A sudden involuntary drop to the ground.
3. A usu. swift downward trend, as in prices.
4. *Slang*. A disreputable or run-down bar or restaurant.

1. PLUNGE *noun*.
2. FALL *noun*.
3. FALL *noun*.
4. JOINT *noun*.

diverge *verb*
1. To separate into branches or branchlike parts.
2. To turn away from a prescribed course of action or conduct.
3. To turn aside from the main subject in writing or speaking.

1. BRANCH *verb*.
2. DEVIATE *verb*.
3. DIGRESS.

divergence also **divergency** *noun*
1. The condition of being unlike or dissimilar.
2. A departing from what is prescribed.
3. The condition of being divided, as in opinion.
4. An instance of digressing.

1. DIFFERENCE.
2. DEVIATION.
3. DIVISION.
4. DIGRESSION.

divergency *noun*

SEE **divergence.**

divergent *adjective*
1. Departing from the normal.
2. Not like another in nature, quality, amount, or form.

1. ABNORMAL.
2. DIFFERENT.

divers *adjective*
1. Not limited to a single class.
2. Consisting of a number of different kinds.

1. GENERAL.
2. VARIOUS.

3. *Archaic.* Consisting of an indefinitely small number that is more than two or three but less than many.   3. SEVERAL.

diverse *adjective*
1. Distinguished from others by nature or qualities.   1. DISTINCT.
2. Not like another in nature, quality, amount, or form.   2. DIFFERENT.
3. Not limited to a single class.   3. GENERAL.
4. Consisting of a number of different kinds.   4. VARIOUS.

diverseness *noun*
The quality of being made of many different elements, forms, kinds, or individuals.   VARIETY.

diversified *adjective*
1. Not limited to a single class.   1. GENERAL.
2. Consisting of a number of different kinds.   2. VARIOUS.

diversion *noun*
1. A departing from what is prescribed.   1. DEVIATION.
2. Something, esp. a performance or show, designed to entertain.   2. AMUSEMENT.
3. The condition of being amused.   3. AMUSEMENT.
4. Activity engaged in for relaxation and amusement.   4. PLAY *noun.*

diversity *noun*
1. A collection of various things.   1. ASSORTMENT.
2. The quality of being made of many different elements, forms, kinds, or individuals.   2. VARIETY.

divert *verb*
1. To change the direction or course of.   1. TURN *verb.*
2. To persuade (a person) not to do something.   2. DISSUADE.
3. To occupy in an agreeable or pleasing way.   3. AMUSE.

diverting *adjective*
Entertaining or pleasing.   AMUSING.

divest *verb*
1. To make bare.   1. BARE *verb.*
2. To take or keep something away from.   2. DEPRIVE.

divestiture *noun*
The condition of being deprived of what one once had or ought to have.   DEPRIVATION.

divide *verb*
1. To make a division into parts, sections, or branches: *Berlin is divided into four sectors.*   1. *Syns:* break up, part, partition, section, segment, separate.
2. To become or cause to become apart one from another: *Many families in Border States were divided over the issue of slavery. A great schism divided the Christian church.*   2. *Syns:* break, detach, disjoin, disjoint, disunite, divorce, separate, split. —*Idioms* part company, set at odds.
3. To give out in portions or shares.   3. DISTRIBUTE.

dividend *noun*
Something given in return for a service or accomplishment.   REWARD *noun.*

divine[1] *adjective*
1. Of, from, like, or being a god or God: *the divine will; divine inspiration.*   1. *Syns:* deific, godlike, godly, heavenly.
2. In the service or worship of God or a god: *divine rites.*   2. *Syns:* holy, religious, sacred.
3. *Informal.* Particularly excellent.   3. MARVELOUS.

divine *noun*
A person ordained for service in a Christian church.   PREACHER.

divine[2] *verb*
1. To know in advance.   1. FORESEE.
2. To tell about or make known (future events) by or as if by supernatural means.   2. PROPHESY.

diviner *noun*
A person who foretells future events by or as if by supernatural means. PROPHET.

divinitory *adjective*
Of or relating to the foretelling of events by or as if by supernatural means. PROPHETICAL.

division *noun*
1. The act or an instance of separating one thing from another: *a division of Church and State.*

2. The act of distributing or the condition of being distributed.

3. One of the parts into which something is divided: *a company with European and U.S. divisions.*

4. The condition of being divided, as in opinion: *a nation rent by wide division over the Vietnam conflict.*

5. A local unit of a business or an auxiliary controlled by such a business.

6. A part of a family, tribe, or other group, or of such a group's language, that is believed to stem from a common ancestor.

7. A component of government that performs a given function.

1. *Syns:* detachment, disunion, divorce, divorcement, partition, separation, split-up.

2. DISTRIBUTION.

3. *Syns:* member, parcel, part, piece, portion, section, segment, subdivision.

4. *Syns:* divergence (*also* divergency), disunion, split.

5. SUBSIDIARY.

6. BRANCH *noun.*

7. BRANCH *noun.*

divorce *verb*
1. To terminate a marriage through legal action: *He divorced his wife.*
2. To become or cause to become apart one from another.

1. *Syn:* unmarry.

2. DIVIDE.

divorce *noun*
The act or an instance of separating one thing from another. DIVISION.

divorcement *noun*
The act or an instance of separating one thing from another. DIVISION.

divulge *verb*
To disclose in a breach of confidence. BETRAY.

divvy *verb*
Slang. To give out in portions or shares. DISTRIBUTE.

divvy *noun*
Slang. That which is allotted. ALLOTMENT.

dizziness *noun*
A sensation of whirling or falling: *suffers dizziness when climbing on ladders.* *Syns:* giddiness, lightheadedness, vertigo, wooziness.

dizzy *adjective*
1. Having a sensation of whirling or falling: *too dizzy to get on the merry-go-round again.*

1. *Syns:* giddy, lightheaded, reeling, vertiginous, woozy. —*Idioms* going around in circles, seeing double. *Near-syns:* befuddled, confused, dazed, dazzled, puzzled; bewildered, confounded; whirling.

2. Producing dizziness or vertigo.
3. *Informal.* Given to lighthearted silliness.
4. Vastly exceeding a normal limit, as in cost.

2. GIDDY.
3. GIDDY.
4. STEEP[1].

dizzy *verb*
To cause to be unclear in mind or intent. CONFUSE.

dizzying *adjective*
1. Producing dizziness or vertigo.
2. Vastly exceeding a normal limit, as in cost.

1. GIDDY.
2. STEEP[1].

do *verb*
1. To begin and carry through to completion. 1. PERFORM.

2. To produce on the stage.   **2.** STAGE *verb*.
3. To play the part of.   **3.** ACT *verb*.
4. To meet a need or requirement.   **4.** SERVE.
5. *Informal.* To spend or complete (time), as a prison   **5.** SERVE.
   term.
6. To conduct oneself in a specified way.   **6.** ACT *verb*.
7. To prepare (food) for eating by the use of heat.   **7.** COOK *verb*.
8. To journey over (a specified distance).   **8.** TRAVERSE *verb*.
9. *Slang.* To get money or something else from by   **9.** CHEAT *verb*.
   deceitful trickery.
10. To progress or perform adequately, esp. in difficult   **10.** MANAGE.
    circumstances.

do for *verb*
To work and care for.   SERVE.

do in *verb*
1. *Slang.* To make extremely tired.   **1.** EXHAUST.
2. *Slang.* To take the life of (a person or persons)   **2.** MURDER *verb*.
   unlawfully.
3. *Informal.* To cause the death of.   **3.** KILL.

do up *verb*
To cover and tie (something), as with paper and string.   WRAP *verb*.

do *noun*
Slang. A large or important social gathering.   PARTY *noun*.

docile *adjective*
Easily managed or handled.   GENTLE *adjective*.

docket *noun*
An organized list of procedures, activities, events, etc.   PROGRAM.

doctor *verb*
1. To give medical aid to.   **1.** TREAT *verb*.
2. To restore to proper condition or functioning.   **2.** FIX *verb*.
3. To make impure or inferior by deceptively adding   **3.** ADULTERATE.
   foreign substances.

doctrinaire *adjective*
1. Devoted to certain doctrines without regard to   **1.** *Syns:* dogmatic, theoretical (*also*
   practicability: *persisted in a doctrinaire faith in the*   theoretic).
   free market even when it wasn't working.
2. Characterized by or favoring absolute obedience to   **2.** AUTHORITARIAN *adjective*.
   authority.
3. Tending to dictate.   **3.** DICTATORIAL.

doctrine *noun*
A principle taught or advanced for belief, as by a   *Syns:* dogma, teaching, tenet.
religious or philosophical group: *the doctrines of the*   *Near-syns:* axiom, canon, fundamental,
church.   instruction, principle; belief, faith.

doddering *adjective*
Exhibiting the mental and physical deterioration often   SENILE.
accompanying old age.

doddery *adjective*
Exhibiting the mental and physical deterioration often   SENILE.
accompanying old age.

dodge *noun*
An action meant to deceive.   DECEPTION.

dodge *verb*
1. To avoid fulfilling or answering completely.   **1.** EVADE.
2. To keep away from.   **2.** AVOID.

doff *verb*
To take from one's own person.   REMOVE *verb*.

do for *verb*   SEE **do**.

dog *verb*
1. To follow closely or persistently: *dogged my footsteps.*   **1.** *Syns:* bloodhound, heel[1], tag, trail.
2. To keep (another) under surveillance by moving   **2.** FOLLOW.
   along behind.

dogged   *adjective*
Tenaciously unwilling to yield.   OBSTINATE.

doggedness   *noun*
The quality or state of being stubbornly unyielding.   OBSTINACY.

dogma   *noun*
A principle taught or advanced for belief, as by a   DOCTRINE.
religious or philosophical group.

dogmatic   *adjective*
1. Devoted to certain doctrines without regard to   1. DOCTRINAIRE.
   practicability.
2. Tending to dictate.   2. DICTATORIAL.

dog-tired   *adjective*
Extremely tired.   EXHAUSTED.

do in   *verb*   SEE **do.**

doing   *noun*
Something done.   ACT *noun.*

doit   *noun*
A tiny amount.   BIT[1].

doldrums   *noun*
A feeling or spell of dismally low spirits.   GLOOM.

dole   *noun*
Assistance, esp. money, food, and other necessities,   RELIEF.
given to the needy or dispossessed.

  dole out   *verb*
  To give out in portions or shares.   DISTRIBUTE.

doleful   *adjective*
1. Full of or expressive of sorrow.   1. SORROWFUL.
2. Causing sorrow.   2. SORROWFUL.

dolefulness   *noun*
A feeling or spell of dismally low spirits.   GLOOM.

dole out   *verb*   SEE **dole.**

dolittle   *noun*
A self-indulgent person who spends time avoiding work   WASTREL.
or other useful activity.

doll   *noun*
Slang. A woman regarded as beautiful.   BEAUTY.

  doll up   *verb*
  Slang. To dress in formal or special clothing.   DRESS UP at **dress.**

doll up   *verb*   SEE **doll.**

dolorous   *adjective*
1. Full of or expressive of sorrow.   1. SORROWFUL.
2. Causing sorrow.   2. SORROWFUL.

dolt   *noun*
A mentally dull person.   DULLARD.

doltish   *adjective*
Lacking in intelligence.   STUPID.

domain   *noun*
A sphere of activity, study, or interest.   AREA.

dome   *noun*
Slang. The uppermost part of the body.   HEAD *noun.*

domestic   *adjective*
1. Of or pertaining to the family or household: *cooking,*   1. **Syns:** familial, family, home, homely,
   cleaning, and other domestic chores.   household.
   Near-ants: civic, public; professional.
2. Trained or bred to live with and be of use to man: *a*   2. **Syns:** domesticated, domesticized, tame.
   domestic cat that reverted to the wild.
3. Of, from, or within a country's own territory: 3. **Syns:** home, internal, national, native.
   domestic political issues; domestic wines.

domesticate   *verb*
To train to live with and be of use to man: *tried to*   **Syns:** domesticize, gentle, master, tame.
domesticate a jaguar.

domesticated *adjective*
Trained or bred to live with and be of use to man.　DOMESTIC.

domesticize *verb*
To train to live with and be of use to man.　DOMESTICATE.

domesticized *adjective*
Trained or bred to live with and be of use to man.　DOMESTIC.

domicile *noun*
A building or shelter where one lives.　HOME.

domicile also **domiciliate** *verb*
1. To provide with often temporary lodging.　1. HARBOR *verb*.
2. To have as one's domicile, usu. for an extended period.　2. LIVE¹.

domiciliate *verb*　SEE **domicile**.

dominance *noun*
1. The condition or fact of being dominant: *a currency of unquestionable dominance in the international money markets.*

1. *Syns:* ascendancy, domination, predominance, pre-eminence (*also* preeminence, preëminence), preponderance (*also* preponderancy), prepotency, supremacy.

2. The act of exercising controlling power or the condition of being so controlled.　2. DOMINATION.

dominant *adjective*
1. Exercising controlling power or influence: *a dominant new dynasty.*

1. *Syns:* commanding, controlling, dominating, dominative, governing, regnant, ruling.

2. Having pre-eminent significance.　2. RULING *adjective*.
3. Most important, influential, or significant.　3. PRIMARY.

dominate *verb*
1. To occupy the pre-eminent position in: *The Yankees dominated the American League for years.*

1. *Syns:* predominate, preponderate, prevail, reign, rule. —*Idioms* have the ascendancy, reign supreme.

2. To exercise authority or influence over.　2. CONTROL *verb*.
3. To command in an arrogant manner.　3. BOSS *verb*.
4. To rise above, esp. so as to afford a view of: *A high water tower dominates the sleepy town.*　4. *Syns:* command, overlook, tower above.

domination *noun*
1. The act of exercising controlling power or the condition of being so controlled: *the former domination of Africa by colonial powers.*

1. *Syns:* command, control, dominance, dominion, mastery, rule, sway.

2. The condition or fact of being dominant.　2. DOMINANCE.
3. The right and power to command, decide, rule, or judge.　3. AUTHORITY.

domineer *verb*
To command in an arrogant manner.　BOSS *verb*.

domineering *adjective*
Tending to dictate.　DICTATORIAL.

dominion *noun*
1. The act of exercising controlling power or the condition of being so controlled.　1. DOMINATION.
2. The right and power to command, decide, rule, or judge.　2. AUTHORITY.
3. Legal right to the possession of a thing.　3. OWNERSHIP.

don *verb*
To put (an article of clothing) on one's person: *donned overalls for the dirty work ahead.*　*Syns:* assume, get on, pull on, put on, slip into, slip on.

donate *verb*
1. To present as a gift to a charity or cause: *donated a painting to the church bazaar.*　1. *Syns:* bestow, contribute, give, hand out.
2. To give in common with others.　2. CONTRIBUTE.

donation *noun*
Something given to a charity or cause: *a donation of $2,000 to the Red Cross.*

Syns: alms, benefaction, beneficence, charity, contribution, gift, handout, offering.

donator *noun*
A person who gives to a charity or cause.

DONOR.

done *adjective*
1. Having reached completion.
2. Having no further relationship.
3. No longer effective, capable, or valuable.

1. COMPLETE *adjective.*
2. THROUGH *adjective.*
3. THROUGH *adjective.*

done for *adjective*
No longer effective, capable, or valuable.

THROUGH *adjective.*

done in *adjective*
Slang. Extremely tired.

EXHAUSTED.

Don Juan *noun*
1. A man amorously attentive to women.
2. A man who philanders.
3. A man who seduces women.

1. GALLANT *noun.*
2. PHILANDERER.
3. SEDUCER.

donnish *adjective*
Characterized by a narrow concern for book learning and formal rules, without knowledge or experience of practical matters.

PEDANTIC.

donnybrook *noun*
A quarrel or fight marked by very noisy, disorderly, and often violent behavior.

BRAWL *noun.*

donor *noun*
A person who gives to a charity or cause: *a generous donor to the Red Cross.*

Syns: benefactor, contributor, donator, giver, grantor, subscriber.

do-nothing *adjective*
Resistant to exertion and activity.

LAZY.

do-nothing *noun*
A self-indulgent person who spends time avoiding work or other useful activity.

WASTREL.

doodad *noun*
Informal. A small, specialized mechanical device.

GADGET.

doodle *verb*
To waste time by engaging in aimless activity.

MESS AROUND at **mess.**

doohickey *noun*
Informal. A small, specialized mechanical device.

GADGET.

doom *noun*
A predestined tragic end.

FATE *noun.*

doom *verb*
1. To predestine to a tragic end.
2. To pronounce judgment against.

1. FATE *verb.*
2. CONDEMN.

doomed *adjective*
Sentenced to terrible, irrevocable punishment.

CONDEMNED.

doomful *adjective*
Portending future disaster.

FATEFUL.

doomsayer *noun*
A prophet of misfortune or disaster.

PESSIMIST.

dope *noun*
1. *Informal.* A narcotic substance, esp. one that is addictive.
2. *Informal.* One deficient in judgment and good sense.

1. DRUG *noun.*
2. FOOL *noun.*

dope *verb*
1. *Informal.* To administer or add a drug to.
2. To make impure or inferior by deceptively adding foreign substances.

1. DRUG *verb.*
2. ADULTERATE.

dope out *verb*
1. *Informal.* To form a strategy for.
2. *Informal.* To find a solution for.

1. DESIGN *verb.*
2. RESOLVE *verb.*

doped *adjective*
  Informal. Stupefied, intoxicated, or otherwise influenced   DRUGGED.
  by the taking of drugs.

dope out *verb*   SEE **dope.**

dopey also **dopy** *adjective*
  Slang. Lacking mental and physical alertness and   LETHARGIC.
  activity.

dopeyness also **dopiness** *noun*
  Slang. A deficiency in mental and physical alertness   LETHARGY.
  and activity.

dopiness *noun*   SEE **dopeyness.**

dopy *adjective*   SEE **dopey.**

dormancy *noun*
  The condition of being temporarily inactive.   ABEYANCE.

dormant *adjective*
  1. Existing in a temporarily inactive and hidden form.   **1.** LATENT.
  2. In a state of temporary inactivity.   **2.** SLEEPING.

dose *verb*
  To administer or add a drug to.   DRUG *verb.*

dot *noun*
  A very small mark.   POINT *noun.*

  dot *verb*
  To mark with many small spots.   SPECKLE.

dotage *noun*
  The condition of being senile.   SENILITY.

dote on *verb*
  To like or enjoy enthusiastically, often excessively.   ADORE.

doting *adjective*
  1. Feeling and expressing affection.   **1.** AFFECTIONATE.
  2. Exhibiting the mental and physical deterioration   **2.** SENILE.
  often accompanying old age.

double *adjective*
  1. Composed of two parts or things: *a double window;*   **1.** *Syns:* biform, binary, dual, duple,
  a double pleat.   duplex, duplicate, geminate, twofold.
  2. Twice as much or as large: *took a double dose of the* **2.** *Syns:* doubled, twofold.
  painkiller.
  3. Characterized by duplicity: *a scoundrel's double*   **3.** *Syns:* double-dealing, double-faced,
  tongue.   Iscariotic *or* Iscariotical, treacherous,
                                                                      two-faced.
  4. Consisting of two identical or similar related things, **4.** TWIN *adjective.*
  parts, or elements.

double *noun*
  1. One exactly resembling another: *ordinary people*   **1.** *Syns:* duplicate, image, picture,
  who happen to be the doubles of celebrities.   portrait, ringer (*Slang*). —*Idiom*
                                                                      spitting image.
  2. One of a matched pair of things.   **2.** MATE *noun.*

double *verb*
  1. To make or become twice as great: *She got a big*   **1.** *Syns:* duplicate, redouble.
  raise that doubled her salary. The price of gold more
  than doubled in the 1970's.
  2. To turn sharply around: *The runner had to double*   **2.** *Syns:* about-face, reverse.
  back to pick up the dropped baton.
  3. To bend together or crease so that one part lies over   **3.** FOLD *verb.*
  another.

double-cross *verb*
  1. *Slang.* To be treacherous.   **1.** BETRAY.
  2. *Slang.* To cause to accept what is false, esp. by   **2.** DECEIVE.
  trickery or misrepresentation.

  double-cross *noun*
  Slang. An act of betraying.   BETRAYAL.

doubled *adjective*
Twice as much or as large.   DOUBLE *adjective.*

double-dealing *adjective*
Characterized by duplicity.   DOUBLE *adjective.*

  double-dealing *noun*
  The act or practice of deceiving.   DECEIT.

double entendre *noun*
An expression or term liable to more than one   AMBIGUITY.
interpretation.

double-faced *adjective*
Characterized by duplicity.   DOUBLE *adjective.*

doublet *noun*
Two items of the same kind together.   COUPLE *noun.*

double-talk *noun*
1. Unintelligible or foolish talk.   1. BABBLE *noun.*
2. Wordy, unclear jargon.   2. GIBBERISH.

doubt *verb*
1. To be uncertain, disbelieving, or skeptical about: 1. *Syns:* mistrust, question. —*Idiom* have
   The new data made the scientists doubt their original   one's doubts.
   assumptions.
2. To lack trust or confidence in.   2. DISTRUST *verb.*

  doubt *noun*
1. A lack of conviction or certainty: *A prior record of* 1. *Syns:* doubtfulness, dubiety,
   perjury cast doubt on his truthfulness. The   dubiousness, incertitude, mistrust,
   commander regarded the battle plan with growing   question, skepticism, suspicion,
   doubt.   uncertainty, wonder.
2. Lack of trust.   2. DISTRUST *noun.*

doubtable *adjective*
Not affording certainty.   AMBIGUOUS.

doubter *noun*
One who habitually or instinctively doubts or   SKEPTIC.
questions.

doubtful *adjective*
1. Experiencing doubt: *I am doubtful about your plans.*   1. *Syns:* dubious, skeptical, uncertain,
                                                              undecided, unsure. —*Idiom* in doubt.
2. Not affording certainty.   2. AMBIGUOUS.
3. Not likely: *It is doubtful that our team will win.*   3. *Syns:* improbable, questionable,
                                                              unlikely.
4. In doubt or dispute.   4. DEBATABLE.
5. Lacking trust or confidence.   5. DISTRUSTFUL.
6. Of dubious character.   6. SHADY.

doubtfulness *noun*
1. A lack of conviction or certainty.   1. DOUBT *noun.*
2. Lack of trust.   2. DISTRUST *noun.*

doubting *adjective*
Lacking trust or confidence.   DISTRUSTFUL.

doubting Thomas *noun*
One who habitually or instinctively doubts or   SKEPTIC.
questions.

doubtless *adverb*
Without question.   ABSOLUTELY.

dough *noun*
Slang. Something, as coins, printed bills, etc., used as a   MONEY.
medium of exchange.

doughty *adjective*
Having or showing courage.   BRAVE *adjective.*

do up *verb*   SEE **do.**

dour *adjective*
1. Cold and forbidding.   1. BLEAK.
2. Broodingly and sullenly unhappy.   2. GLUM.

douse *verb*
1. To plunge briefly in or into a liquid.
2. To make thoroughly wet.
3. To cause to stop burning or giving light.
4. To take from one's own person.

1. DIP *verb*.
2. WET *verb*.
3. EXTINGUISH.
4. REMOVE *verb*.

dovetail *verb*
To conform to another, esp. in size and shape.

FIT *verb*.

dowdy *adjective*
1. Of a style or method formerly in vogue.
2. Quite outmoded.

1. OLD-FASHIONED.
2. TACKY[2].

dower *verb*
To present with a quality, trait, or power.

GIFT *verb*.

down *adjective*
1. In low spirits.
2. Suffering from or affected with an illness.
3. Characterized by reduced economic activity.

1. DEPRESSED.
2. SICK.
3. SLOW *adjective*.

down *verb*
1. To cause to fall, as from a shot or blow.
2. *Informal.* To win a victory over, as in battle or a competition.
3. To cause to pass from the mouth into the stomach.

1. DROP *verb*.
2. DEFEAT *verb*.
3. SWALLOW *verb*.

down *noun*
A sudden drop to a lower condition or status.

DESCENT.

down-and-out *noun*
An impoverished person.

PAUPER *noun*.

down-at-heel or **down-at-the-heel** *adjective*
Showing signs of wear and tear or neglect.

SHABBY.

down-at-the-heel *adjective*

SEE **down-at-heel.**

downcast *adjective*
In low spirits.

DEPRESSED.

downfall *noun*
1. A sudden drop to a lower condition or status.
2. A disastrous, overwhelming defeat or ruin.
3. Something that causes total loss or severe impairment of one's health, fortune, honor, hopes, etc.

1. DESCENT.
2. FALL *noun*.
3. RUIN *noun*.

downgrade *verb*
1. To think, represent, or speak of as small or unimportant.
2. To lower in character or quality.
3. To lower in rank or grade.
4. To become or make less in price or value.

1. BELITTLE.
2. DEBASE.
3. DEMOTE.
4. DEPRECIATE.

downgrade *noun*
A sudden drop to a lower condition or status.

DESCENT.

downgrading *noun*
The act or an instance of demoting.

DEMOTION.

downhearted *adjective*
In low spirits.

DEPRESSED.

down payment *noun*
A partial or initial payment.

DEPOSIT *noun*.

downright *adjective*
1. Completely such, without qualification or exception.
2. Speaking or spoken freely and sincerely.

1. UTTER[2].
2. FRANK.

downslide *noun*
A usu. swift downward trend, as in prices.

FALL *noun*.

downswing *noun*
A usu. swift downward trend, as in prices.

FALL *noun*.

down-to-earth *adjective*
Having or indicating an awareness of things as they really are.

REALISTIC.

downturn *noun*
A usu. swift downward trend, as in prices.

FALL *noun.*

downward *adjective*
Moving down.

DESCENDING.

doze *verb*
To sleep for a brief period.

NAP *verb.*

  doze *noun*
  A brief sleep.

NAP *noun.*

dozy *adjective*
Ready for or needing sleep.

SLEEPY.

drab¹ *adjective*
1. Lacking vividness in color.
2. Lacking liveliness, charm, or surprise.

1. DULL *adjective.*
2. DULL *adjective.*

drab² *noun*
An ugly, frightening old woman.

WITCH *noun.*

draft *noun*
1. Compulsory enrollment in military service: *rioting students opposed to the draft.*
2. The act of drawing or pulling a load.
3. An act of drinking or the amount swallowed.
4. A preliminary plan or version, as of a written work: *finished a first draft of her novel.*

1. *Syns:* conscription, induction, levy.

2. PULL *noun.*
3. DRINK *noun.*
4. *Syns:* outline, rough, skeleton, sketch.

  draft *verb*
  1. To enroll compulsorily in military service: *was drafted into the army for four years.*
  2. To devise and set down: *The committee drafted a national health-insurance program.*
  3. To draw up a preliminary plan or version of: *He drafted his speech quickly, then began to revise.*

1. *Syns:* conscript, induct, levy. —*Idiom* call to the colors.
2. *Syns:* draw up, formulate, frame, lay¹.
3. *Syns:* adumbrate, block out, outline, rough in, rough out, sketch.

drag *noun*
1. An act of drinking or the amount swallowed.
2. *Informal.* An inhalation, as of a cigar, pipe, or cigarette.
3. *Slang.* The power to produce an effect by indirect means.

1. DRINK *noun.*
2. PULL *noun.*

3. INFLUENCE *noun.*

  drag *verb*
  1. To go or move slowly so that progress is hindered.
  2. To advance slowly.
  3. To hang or cause to hang down and be pulled along behind.
  4. To exert force so as to move something toward the source of the force.

1. DELAY *verb.*
2. CRAWL *verb.*
3. TRAIL *verb.*

4. PULL *verb.*

  drag down *verb*
  Slang. To receive, as wages, for one's labor.

EARN.

drag down *verb*

SEE **drag.**

dragging *adjective*
1. Extending tediously beyond a standard duration.
2. Proceeding at a rate less than usual or desired.

1. LONG¹ *adjective.*
2. SLOW *adjective.*

draggle *verb*
To hang or cause to hang down and be pulled along behind.

TRAIL *verb.*

dragoon *verb*
To compel by pressure or threats.

COERCE.

drain *verb*
1. To remove (a liquid) by a steady, gradual process: *We drained the water from the cistern with a siphon.*
2. To use all of.
3. To diminish the strength and energy of.
4. To grow or cause to grow gradually less.
5. To make or become no longer active or productive.

1. *Syns:* draw off, let out, pump, tap².

2. EXHAUST.
3. FATIGUE *verb.*
4. DECREASE *verb.*
5. DRY UP at **dry.**

6. To lessen or weaken severely, as by removing something essential.

6. DEPLETE.

drained *adjective*
1. Extremely tired.
2. Depleted of strength or robust health.

1. EXHAUSTED.
2. RUN-DOWN *adjective* at **run down**.

dram *noun*
1. A tiny amount.
2. A small amount of liquor.

1. BIT[1].
2. DROP *noun*.

dramatic *adjective*
1. Of or pertaining to drama or the theater: *a dramatic performance*.
2. Suggesting drama or a stage performance, as in emotionality or suspense: *made a dramatic entrance in a swirling cape*.

1. **Syns:** dramaturgic, histrionic, theatrical (*also* theatric), thespian.
2. **Syns:** histrionic, melodramatic, sensational, spectacular, theatrical (*also* theatric).

dramaticism *noun*
Showy mannerisms and behavior.

THEATRICALISM.

dramatics *noun*
1. The art and occupation of an actor.
2. Overemotional, exaggerated behavior calculated for effect.

1. ACTING *noun*.
2. THEATRICS.

dramatize *verb*
To produce on the stage.

STAGE *verb*.

dramaturgic *adjective*
Of or pertaining to drama or the theater.

DRAMATIC.

drape *verb*
1. To cover as if with clothes.
2. To sit or lie with the limbs spread out awkwardly.

1. CLOTHE.
2. SPRAWL.

draw *verb*
1. To exert force so as to move something toward the source of the force.
2. To cause (a liquid) to flow in a steady stream.
3. To obtain from another source.
4. To call forth or bring out (something latent, hidden, or unexpressed).
5. To make as income or profit.
6. To direct or impel to oneself by some quality or action.
7. To draw a conclusion from evidence or reasoning.

1. PULL *verb*.
2. POUR.
3. DERIVE.
4. EVOKE.
5. RETURN *verb*.
6. ATTRACT.
7. INFER.

draw down *verb*
To receive, as wages, for one's labor.

EARN.

draw in *verb*
To pull back in.

WITHDRAW.

draw in (or **into**) *verb*
To involve (someone) in an activity.

ENGAGE.

draw off *verb*
To remove (a liquid) by a steady, gradual process.

DRAIN.

draw out *verb*
To make or become longer.

LENGTHEN.

draw up *verb*
1. To form a strategy for.
2. To devise and set down.

1. DESIGN *verb*.
2. DRAFT *verb*.

draw *noun*
1. The act of drawing or pulling a load.
2. The power or quality of attracting.
3. A dominating position, as in a conflict.
4. An equality of scores, votes, or performances in a contest.
5. An inhalation, as of a cigar, pipe, or cigarette.

1. PULL *noun*.
2. ATTRACTION.
3. ADVANTAGE *noun*.
4. TIE *noun*.
5. PULL *noun*.

drawback *noun*

SEE **draw back**.

draw back *verb*
To move back in the face of enemy attack or after a defeat.

RETREAT *verb*.

drawback *noun*
An unfavorable condition, circumstance, or characteristic.

DISADVANTAGE.

draw down *verb*

SEE **draw.**

draw in (or **into**) *verb*

SEE **draw.**

drawn-out *adjective*
Extending tediously beyond a standard duration.

LONG[1] *adjective*.

draw off *verb*

SEE **draw.**

draw out *verb*

SEE **draw.**

draw up *verb*

SEE **draw.**

dread *noun*
1. Great agitation and anxiety caused by the expectation or the realization of danger.
2. The emotion aroused by something awe-inspiring or astounding.

1. FEAR *noun*.

2. WONDER *noun*.

dread *verb*
To be afraid of.

FEAR *verb*.

dreadful *adjective*
1. Causing or able to cause fear.
2. Very bad.

1. FEARFUL.

2. TERRIBLE.

dreadfully *adverb*
Informal. To a high degree.

VERY *adverb*.

dream *noun*
1. An illusory mental image: *bad dreams; can't distinguish dreams from reality.*

1. *Syns:* fancy, fantasy (*also* phantasy), fiction, figment, illusion, phantasm (*also* phantasma), reverie, vision. —*Idiom* figment (*or* creature) of the imagination.

2. A fervent hope, wish, or goal: *the Jews' dream of a national homeland.*
3. A fantastic, impracticable plan or desire.

2. *Syns:* aspiration, ideal.

3. ILLUSION.

dream *verb*
1. To experience dreams or daydreams: *spent her time dreaming instead of working.*
2. To have a fervent hope or aspiration.

1. *Syns:* fantasize, moon, muse[1]. —*Idiom* go woolgathering.

2. ASPIRE.

dream up *verb*
To use ingenuity in making, developing, or achieving.

INVENT.

dreamer *noun*
A person inclined to be imaginative or idealistic but impractical: *Ashley Wilkes was a true dreamer.*

Syns: idealist, utopian, visionary.

dream up *verb*

SEE **dream.**

dreamy *adjective*
1. Given to daydreams or reverie: *a dreamy, quiet child in a world of his own.*
2. *Informal.* Particularly excellent.

1. *Syns:* moony, otherworldly, visionary, woolgathering. —*Idiom* in the clouds.

2. MARVELOUS.

drear *adjective*

SEE **dreary.**

dreary also **drear** *adjective*
1. Arousing no interest or curiosity.
2. Dark and depressing.

1. BORING.

2. GLOOMY.

dregs *noun*
1. Matter that settles on a bottom or collects on a surface by a natural process.
2. A group of persons regarded as the lowest class.

1. DEPOSIT *noun*.

2. TRASH[1] *noun*.

drench *verb*
1. To make thoroughly wet.
2. To rain heavily.

1. WET *verb*.

2. POUR.

drenched *adjective*
Covered with or full of liquid.

WET *adjective*.

dress *verb*
1. To put clothes on: *She dressed her children warmly.*

2. To furnish with decorations.
3. To apply therapeutic materials to (a wound): *used a handkerchief to dress his cut.*
4. To prepare (soil) for the planting and raising of crops.

dress down *verb*
To criticize for a fault or offense.

dress up *verb*
To dress in formal or special clothing: *all dressed up in a new suit.*

dress *noun*
1. Articles worn to cover the body: *expensive dress.*

2. A set or style of clothing: *Edwardian dress.*
3. A one-piece, skirted outer garment for women and children: *long and short dresses.*

dress down *verb*
dress up *verb*
dressy *adjective*
Requiring elegant clothes and fine manners.

dribble *verb*
1. To fall or let fall in drops of liquid.
2. To let saliva run from the mouth.

dribble *noun*
The process or sound of dripping.

driblet *noun*
A quantity of liquid falling or resting in a spherical mass.

drift *verb*
1. To move along with or be carried away by the action of water.
2. To pass smoothly, quietly, and undisturbed on or as if on a slippery surface.
3. To move about at random, esp. over a wide area.
4. To put into a disordered pile.

drift *noun*
1. Something suggestive of running water.
2. A group of things gathered haphazardly.
3. The thread or current of thought uniting or occurring in all the elements of a text or discourse.

drill *noun*
Repetition of an action so as to develop or maintain one's skill.

drill *verb*
1. To subject to forms of exertion in order to train, strengthen, or condition.
2. To instruct in a body of doctrine or belief.

drink *verb*
1. To take into the mouth and swallow (a liquid): *We drank tea and ate biscuits.*

2. To take alcoholic liquor, esp. excessively or habitually: *Strict Hindus do not drink.*

---

1. **Syns:** apparel, array, attire, clad, clothe, garb, garment, invest (*Rare*), tog (*Informal*).
2. ADORN.
3. **Syns:** bandage, bind.

4. TILL.

CALL DOWN at **call.**

Syns: deck out, doll up (*Slang*), slick (up) (*Informal*), tog out (*Informal*), tog up (*Informal*), trick out, trick up.

1. **Syns:** apparel, attire, clothes, clothing, duds (*Informal*), garb, garments, habiliments, raiment, threads (*Slang*), togs (*Informal*).
2. **Syns:** getup, guise, outfit, rig, turnout.
3. **Syns:** frock, gown.

SEE **dress.**
SEE **dress.**

FORMAL.

1. DRIP *verb.*
2. DROOL *verb.*

DRIP *noun.*

DROP *noun.*

1. WASH.

2. SLIDE *verb.*

3. ROVE.
4. HEAP *verb.*

1. FLOW *noun.*
2. HEAP *noun.*
3. THRUST *noun.*

PRACTICE *noun.*

1. EXERCISE *verb.*

2. INDOCTRINATE.

1. **Syns:** imbibe, quaff, sip, sup, swig (*Informal*), toss down, toss off. —*Idiom* wet one's whistle.
2. **Syns:** booze (*Slang*), guzzle, imbibe, liquor up (*Slang*), lush (*Slang*), nip² (*Slang*), soak (*Slang*), tank up (*Slang*), tipple.

3. To salute by raising and drinking from a glass: *We drank to the memory of old friends.*
4. To take in (moisture or liquid): *The parched earth drank in the rain.*

drink *noun*
1. Any liquid that is fit for drinking: *supplied us with food and drink.*
2. An act of drinking or the amount swallowed: *She paused to take a drink from her wine glass.*

drinkable *noun*
Any liquid that is fit for drinking.

drip *verb*
To fall or let fall in drops of liquid: *Water dripped from the leaky faucet.*

drip *noun*
1. The process or sound of dripping: *heard the slow drip of a leaky faucet.*
2. *Slang.* An unpleasant, tiresome person: *an old drip who spoiled all our fun.*

drippy *adjective*
Slang. Affectedly or extravagantly emotional.

drive *verb*
1. To force to move or advance with or as if with blows or pressure: *The fire drove residents from their homes.*
2. To cause to penetrate with force.
3. To fix (an idea) in someone's mind by re-emphasis and repetition.
4. To move or advance against strong resistance.
5. To urge to move along: *driving the cattle to slaughter.*
6. To set or keep going: *a mill driven by wind power.*

7. To run and control (a motor vehicle): *drove the car to work.*
8. To force to work.
9. To exert one's mental or physical powers, usu. under difficulty and to the point of exhaustion.
10. To look for and pursue (game) in order to capture or kill it.

drive *noun*
1. A course affording passage from one place to another.
2. A trip in a motor vehicle: *a Sunday drive.*

3. An organized effort to accomplish a purpose: *a fund-raising drive.*
4. An aggressive readiness to undertake taxing efforts: *a young executive with a lot of drive.*

5. The wish, power, and ability to begin and follow through with a plan or task.

drivel *noun*
1. Saliva running from the mouth.
2. Something that does not have or make sense.

drivel *verb*
To let saliva run from the mouth.

—*Idioms* bend the elbow, hit the bottle, take a drop.
3. **Syns:** pledge, toast. —*Idiom* raise a glass to.
4. **Syns:** absorb, imbibe, soak up, sop (up).

1. **Syns:** beverage, drinkable, liquor, potable.
2. **Syns:** belt (*Slang*), draft, drag, potation, pull, quaff, sip, sup, swig (*Informal*), swill.

DRINK *noun.*

Syns: distill, dribble, drop, trickle, weep.

1. **Syns:** dribble, drop, trickle.

2. **Syns:** bore, clod, jerk (*Slang*), pill (*Slang*), poop (*Slang*).

SENTIMENTAL.

1. **Syns:** propel, push, ram, shove, thrust.

2. RAM.
3. IMPRESS *verb.*

4. PLUNGE *verb.*
5. **Syns:** herd, run.

6. **Syns:** actuate, impel, mobilize, move, propel, run.
7. **Syns:** motor, pilot, tool (*Informal*), wheel.
8. WORK *verb.*
9. LABOR *verb.*

10. HUNT.

1. WAY *noun.*

2. **Syns:** ride, spin (*Informal*), whirl (*Informal*).
3. **Syns:** campaign, crusade, push.

4. **Syns:** enterprise, getup, get-up-and-go (*Informal*), hustle, punch, push (*Informal*), snap (*Informal*), steam, vigor.
5. AMBITION.

1. DROOL *noun.*
2. NONSENSE.

DROOL *verb.*

driveling *adjective*
Lacking the qualities requisite for spiritedness and
originality.   INSIPID.

driver *noun*
A person who operates a motor vehicle: *a reckless*   **Syns:** motorist, operator.
driver.

driving *adjective*
Disposed to action.   VIGOROUS.

droit *noun*
A privilege granted a person by virtue of birth.   BIRTHRIGHT.

droll *adjective*
Arousing laughter.   AMUSING.

drollery *noun*
The quality of being laughable or comical.   HUMOR *noun.*

drollness *noun*
The quality of being laughable or comical.   HUMOR *noun.*

drone¹ *noun*
A self-indulgent person who spends time avoiding work   WASTREL.
or other useful activity.

drone² *verb*
To make a continuous low-pitched droning sound.   HUM *verb.*

drone *noun*
A continuous low-pitched droning sound.   HUM *noun.*

drool *verb*
To let saliva run from the mouth: *Basset hounds drool.*   **Syns:** dribble, drivel, salivate, slaver,
                                                               slobber.

drool *noun*
Saliva running from the mouth: *The nurse wiped the*   **Syns:** drivel, salivation, slaver, slobber.
drool from the patient's face.

droop *verb*
1. To hang limply, loosely, and carelessly.   1. SLOUCH *verb.*
2. To become limp, as from loss of freshness.   2. WILT.

drop *noun*
1. A quantity of liquid falling or resting in a spherical   1. **Syns:** driblet, droplet, globule.
   mass: *Drops of perspiration stood out on her*
   forehead.
2. The process or sound of dripping.   2. DRIP *noun.*
3. A tiny amount.   3. BIT¹.
4. A small amount of liquor: *had only a drop of brandy*   4. **Syns:** dram, nip², sip, shot, slug¹
   left.   (*Informal*), snort (*Slang*), tot¹.
5. The act of dropping from a height.   5. FALL *noun.*
6. A usu. swift downward trend, as in prices.   6. FALL *noun.*
7. A downward slope or distance: *a sheer drop to the*   7. **Syns:** decline, declivity, descent, fall.
   canyon floor.
8. A dominating position, as in a conflict.   8. ADVANTAGE *noun.*
9. The extent or measurement downward from a   9. DEPTH.
   surface.

drop *verb*
1. To go from a more erect posture to a less erect   1. **Syns:** fall, sink, slump.
   posture: *dropped to his knees before the king.*
2. To fall or let fall in drops of liquid.   2. DRIP *verb.*
3. To undergo a sharp, rapid descent in value or   3. FALL *verb.*
   price.
4. To slope downward: *The ocean floor drops sharply*   4. **Syns:** decline, descend, dip, fall, fall
   at the continental shelf.   off, sink.
5. To suddenly lose all health or strength.   5. COLLAPSE *verb.*
6. To cause to fall, as from a shot or blow: *The hunter*   6. **Syns:** bring down, cut down, deck,
   dropped his prey with a single shot. The boxer   down, fell¹, flatten, floor, ground,
   dropped his opponent with a right hook.   knock down, level, prostrate, throw.
                                                               —*Idiom* lay low.

7. To cease consideration or treatment of: *Let's drop the matter.*

8. To decide not to go ahead with (something previously arranged).
9. To end the employment of.
10. To take or leave out: *We have to drop two illustrations from the book for lack of space.*
11. To suffer the loss of: *dropped a lot of money at the race track.*
12. To cease living.
13. To come to the ground suddenly and involuntarily.
14. To move downward in response to gravity.
15. To cause to descend.

drop by *verb*
To go to or seek out the company of in order to socialize.

drop in *verb*
To go to or seek out the company of in order to socialize.

drop by *verb*
drop in *verb*
droplet *noun*
A quantity of liquid falling or resting in a spherical mass.

drop-off *noun*
drop off *verb*
To decline, as in value or quantity, very gradually.
drop-off *noun*
A usu. swift downward trend, as in prices.

drossy *adjective*
Lacking all worth and value.

droughty *adjective*
Having little or no precipitation.

drove *noun*
1. An enormous number of persons gathered together.
2. A very large number of things grouped together.

drown *verb*
To flow over completely.

drowsy *adjective*
Ready for or needing sleep.

drub *verb*
1. To hit heavily and repeatedly.
2. *Slang.* To win a victory over, as in battle or a competition.
3. To render totally ineffective by decisive defeat.
4. To criticize harshly and devastatingly.

drubbing *noun*
1. *Slang.* The act of defeating or the condition of being defeated.
2. *Slang.* A severe defeat.

drudge *verb*
To do tedious, laborious, and sometimes menial work.

drudgery *noun*
Physical exertion that is usu. difficult and exhausting.

drug *noun*
1. A substance used in the treatment of disease: *Aspirin is a common drug for headaches.*
2. A narcotic substance, esp. one that is addictive: *arrested for dealing illictly in drugs.*

drug *verb*

---

7. **Syns:** dismiss, give over, give up, skip. —*Idioms* have done with, wash one's hands of.
8. CANCEL.

9. DISMISS.
10. **Syns:** delete, eliminate, omit, remove.

11. **Syns:** forfeit, lose. —*Idiom* kiss good-by to.
12. DIE.
13. FALL *verb.*
14. FALL *verb.*
15. LOWER^2.

VISIT *verb.*

VISIT *verb.*

SEE **drop.**
SEE **drop.**

DROP *noun.*

SEE **drop off.**

SLIP *verb.*

FALL *noun.*

WORTHLESS.

DRY *adjective.*

1. CROWD *noun.*
2. CROWD *noun.*

FLOOD *verb.*

SLEEPY.

1. BEAT *verb.*
2. DEFEAT *verb.*

3. OVERWHELM.
4. SLAM *verb.*

1. DEFEAT *noun.*

2. TROUNCING.

GRIND *verb.*

LABOR *noun.*

1. **Syns:** medicament, medication, medicine.
2. **Syns:** dope (*Informal*), narcotic, opiate.

To administer or add a drug to: *drugged the patient to induce sleep.*

drugged *adjective*
Stupefied, intoxicated, or otherwise influenced by the taking of drugs: *The drugged bum lay in a heap in the filthy doorway.*

drunk *adjective*
Intoxicated with alcoholic liquor: *too drunk to walk a straight line.*

drunk *noun*
1. A person who is habitually drunk.
2. A drinking bout.

drunkard *noun*
A person who is habitually drunk: *a self-admitted drunkard who refused treatment.*

drunken *adjective*
Intoxicated with alcoholic liquor.

drunkenness *noun*
The condition of being intoxicated with alcoholic liquor: *the drunkenness of an old wino.*

dry *adjective*
1. Having little or no liquid or moisture: *The laundry was dry by morning.*

2. Having little or no precipitation: *a dry climate.*

3. Needing or desiring drink.
4. Having a taste characteristic of that produced by acids.
5. Without addition, decoration, or qualification.
6. With little or no emotion or expression: *dealing out facts in a dry, mechanical way.*
7. Arousing no interest or curiosity.
8. Lacking liveliness, charm, or surprise.
9. Disagreeable to the sense of hearing.

dry *verb*
1. To make or become free of moisture: *drying dishes; a drug that dries out water-laden tissues.*
2. To make or become physically hard.

dry up *verb*
1. To make or become no longer fresh or shapely because of loss of moisture: *The cut flowers wilted and dried up in the hot sun.*

Syns: dope (*Informal*), dose, medicate, narcotize, physic (*Archaic*).

Syns: doped (*Informal*), high (*Slang*), hopped-up (*Slang*), spaced-out (*Slang*), stoned (*Slang*), turned-on (*Slang*), wiped-out (*Slang*), zonked (*Slang*).

Syns: besotted, blind (*Slang*), bombed (*Slang*), boozed (*Slang*), boozy (*Slang*), cock-eyed (*Slang*), crapulent, crapulous, crocked (*Slang*), drunken, high (*Slang*), inebriate, inebriated, lit up (*Slang*), loaded (*Slang*), looped (*Slang*), pickled (*Slang*), pixilated (*Slang*), plastered (*Slang*), potted (*Slang*), sloshed (*Slang*), smashed (*Slang*), sodden (*Slang*), soused (*Slang*), stewed (*Slang*), stinking (*Slang*), stoned (*Slang*), tight (*Slang*), tipsy (*Slang*), zonked (*Slang*). —*Idioms* drunk as a skunk, half-seas over, high as a kite, in one's cups, three sheets to the wind.

1. DRUNKARD.
2. BENDER.

Syns: boozehound (*Slang*), boozer (*Slang*), drunk, inebriate, lush (*Slang*), rummy[1] (*Slang*), soak (*Slang*), sot, souse (*Slang*), sponge (*Slang*), stiff (*Slang*), tippler.

DRUNK *adjective.*

Syns: crapulence, inebriation, inebriety, insobriety, intoxication.

1. *Syns:* anhydrous, arid, bone-dry, dehydrated, desiccated, moistureless, parched, waterless.
2. *Syns:* arid, droughty, rainless, thirsty. *Near-ants:* damp, dank, humid, moist, saturated, soaked, sodden. *Ant:* wet.
3. THIRSTY.
4. SOUR *adjective.*
5. BARE *adjective.*
6. *Syns:* impassive, matter-of-fact, unemotional.
7. BORING.
8. DULL *adjective.*
9. HARSH.

1. *Syns:* dehydrate, desiccate, exsiccate, parch.
2. HARDEN.

1. *Syns:* mummify, mummy, sear, shrivel, wither, wizen.

2. To make or become no longer active or productive: *When he went into exile, his imagination simply dried up.*

2. *Syns:* deplete, desiccate, drain, give out, play out, run out.

dryness *noun*
1. The state or quality of being insipid.
2. The practice of refraining from use of alcoholic liquors.

1. INSIPIDITY.
2. TEMPERANCE.

dry up *verb*

SEE **dry.**

dual *adjective*
1. Composed of two parts or things.
2. Consisting of two identical or similar related things, parts, or elements.

1. DOUBLE *adjective.*
2. TWIN *adjective.*

dub¹ *verb*
To give a name or title to.

NAME *verb.*

dub² *noun*
Slang. A large, ungainly, and dull-witted person.

LUMP¹ *noun.*

dubiety *noun*
A lack of conviction or certainty.

DOUBT *noun.*

dubious *adjective*
1. Lacking trust or confidence.
2. Experiencing doubt.
3. Not affording certainty.
4. Bordering on indelicacy or impropriety.

1. DISTRUSTFUL.
2. DOUBTFUL.
3. AMBIGUOUS.
4. RACY.

dubiously *adverb*
With skepticism.

SKEPTICALLY.

dubiousness *noun*
A lack of conviction or certainty.

DOUBT *noun.*

dubitable *adjective*
Not affording certainty.

AMBIGUOUS.

duck *verb*
1. To plunge briefly in or into a liquid.
2. To avoid fulfilling or answering completely.
3. To keep away from.

1. DIP *verb.*
2. EVADE.
3. AVOID.

ductile *adjective*
Capable of being shaped, bent, or drawn out, as by hammering or pressure.

MALLEABLE.

ductility *noun*
The quality or state of being flexible.

FLEXIBILITY.

dud *noun*
Informal. One that fails completely.

FAILURE.

dudgeon *noun*
Extreme displeasure caused by an insult or slight.

OFFENSE.

duds *noun*
Informal. Articles worn to cover the body.

DRESS *noun.*

due *adjective*
1. Owed as a debt: *The rent is due on the first of each month. The bookkeeper tallied the accounts due.*
2. Consistent with prevailing or accepted standards or circumstances.
3. Known to be about to arrive: *not home, but due shortly.*

1. *Syns:* outstanding, owed, owing, payable, receivable, unpaid, unsettled.
2. JUST *adjective.*
3. *Syns:* anticipated, expected, scheduled.

due *noun*
1. Something justly deserved: *Give the devil his due.*

1. *Syns:* comeuppance (*also* comeupance) (*Informal*), desert² , lumps, recompense, reward, wage(s). —*Idioms* just deserts, what is coming to one, what one has coming.

2. Something, such as money, owed by one person to another.

2. DEBT.

due *adverb*
In a direct line.

DIRECTLY.

duel *verb*
To oppose actively and with force.

RESIST.

dulcet *adjective*
Resembling or having the effect of music, esp. pleasing music.

MELODIOUS.

dulcify *verb*
To ease the anger or agitation of.

PACIFY.

dull *adjective*
1. Lacking responsiveness or alertness: *senses grown dull with fatigue; a dull stupor.*

1. *Syns:* benumbed, insensible, insensitive, numb, unresponsive, wooden.

2. Having only a limited ability to learn and understand.
2. BACKWARD *adjective.*

3. Unwilling or unable to perceive.
3. BLIND *adjective.*

4. In low spirits.
4. DEPRESSED.

5. Characterized by reduced economic activity.
5. SLOW *adjective.*

6. Not physically sharp or keen: *a dull blade.*
6. *Syn:* blunt.

7. Lacking liveliness, charm, or surprise: *a competent but dull performance by a veteran actor.*
7. *Syns:* colorless, drab[1], dry, earthbound (*also* earth-bound), flat, lackluster, lifeless, lusterless, matter-of-fact, spiritless, pedestrian, prosaic, unimaginative, uninspired.

8. Arousing no interest or curiosity.
8. BORING.

9. Lacking vividness in color: *a dull brown.*
9. *Syns:* dim, drab[1], flat, muddy, murky (*also* mirky).
Near-syns: cloudy, hazy; lackluster, lifeless, lusterless.
Ants: clear, vivid.

10. Lacking gloss and luster: *a dull finish on the chest.*
10. *Syns:* flat, lackluster, lusterless, mat (*also* matte).

11. Lacking passion and emotion.
11. INSENSITIVE.

dull *verb*
1. To make or become less sharp-edged: *Misuse will dull the scissors.*
1. *Syns:* blunt, turn. —*Idiom* take the edge off.

2. To make dim or indistinct.
2. OBSCURE *verb.*

3. To make or become less keen or responsive: *afraid that television might dull the minds of viewers.*
3. *Syns:* dim, hebetate, stupefy.

4. To render less sensitive.
4. DEADEN.

dullard *noun*
A mentally dull person: *had to tell the dullard four times to close the door.*

Syns: blockhead (*Slang*), dimwit (*Slang*), dolt, dumbbell (*Slang*), dunce, numskull (*also* numbskull), thickhead.

dullness *noun*
1. The state or quality of being insipid.
1. INSIPIDITY.

2. A deficiency in mental and physical alertness and activity.
2. LETHARGY.

dumb *adjective*
1. Lacking the power or faculty of speech: *A disease in childhood left her deaf and dumb.*
1. *Syns:* aphonic, inarticulate, mute, speechless, voiceless.

2. Temporarily unable or unwilling to speak, as from shock or fear.
2. SPEECHLESS.

3. *Informal.* Lacking in intelligence.
3. STUPID.

dumbbell *noun*
Slang. A mentally dull person.

DULLARD.

dumbfound *verb*

SEE **dumfound.**

dumbfounded *adjective*

SEE **dumfounded.**

dumbness *noun*
The avoidance of speech.

SILENCE *noun.*

dumfound also **dumbfound** *verb*
To overwhelm with surprise, wonder, or bewilderment.

STAGGER.

dumfounded also **dumbfounded** *adjective*
Overcome with intense feeling, as of amazement, horror, or dismay.   SHOCKED.

dump *verb*
1. To let go or get rid of as being no longer of use, value, etc.   1. DISCARD.
2. To get rid of completely by selling, esp. in quantity or at discount.   2. SELL OFF at **sell**.
3. To unburden oneself of by pouring out (one's troubles).   3. UNLOAD.

dumping *noun*
The act of getting rid of something useless or used up.   DISPOSAL.

dumps *noun*
Informal. A feeling or spell of dismally low spirits.   GLOOM.

dumpy *adjective*
Short, heavy, and solidly built.   STOCKY.

dunce *noun*
A mentally dull person.   DULLARD.

dunk *verb*
To plunge briefly in or into a liquid.   DIP *verb*.

duo *noun*
Two persons united, as by marriage.   PAIR.

dupable *adjective*
Easily imposed on or tricked.   EASY.

dupe *noun*
A person who is easily deceived or victimized: *became the dupe of a clever swindler.*

Syns: butt[3], chump[1] (*Slang*), fool, gudgeon (*Slang*), gull, mark, monkey (*Slang*), mug (*Brit.*), patsy (*Slang*), pigeon (*Slang*), pushover (*Informal*), sap[1] (*Slang*), sucker (*Slang*), tool, victim. —*Idioms* easy mark, fall guy.

dupe *verb*
To cause to accept what is false, esp. by trickery or misrepresentation.   DECEIVE.

duple *adjective*
Composed of two parts or things.   DOUBLE *adjective*.

duplex *adjective*
Composed of two parts or things.   DOUBLE *adjective*.

duplicate *noun*
One exactly resembling another.   DOUBLE *noun*.

duplicate *verb*
1. To make a copy of.   1. COPY *verb*.
2. To make or become twice as great.   2. DOUBLE *verb*.

duplicate *adjective*
Composed of two parts or things.   DOUBLE *adjective*.

duplicitous *adjective*
Marked by treachery or deceit.   UNDERHAND.

duplicity *noun*
The act or practice of deceiving.   DECEIT.

duration *noun*
1. Uninterrupted existence or succession.   1. CONTINUATION.
2. The period during which someone or something exists.   2. LIFE.
3. A limited or specific period of time during which something happens, lasts, or extends.   3. TERM *noun*.

duress *noun*
Power used to overcome resistance.   FORCE *noun*.

dusk *noun*
The period between afternoon and nighttime.   EVENING.

duskiness *noun*
Absence or deficiency of light.   DARK *noun*.

dusky *adjective*
1. Deficient in brightness.
2. Of a complexion tending toward brown or black.
3. Somewhat black.

1. DARK *adjective*.
2. DARK *adjective*.
3. BLACKISH.

dust *verb*
1. To scatter or release in drops or small particles.
2. *Slang.* To move swiftly.

1. SPRINKLE *verb*.
2. RUSH *verb*.

dust off *verb*
Slang. To take the life of (a person or persons) unlawfully.

MURDER *verb*.

dusting *noun*
A severe defeat.

TROUNCING.

dust off *verb*

SEE **dust**.

dusty *adjective*
Consisting of small particles.

FINE[1].

Dutch *noun*
Informal. A condition or situation characterized by danger, distress, or annoyance.

TROUBLE *noun*.

dutiful *adjective*
Marked by courteous submission or respect.

DEFERENTIAL.

duty *noun*
1. An act or course of action that is demanded of one, as by position, custom, law, or religion: *It is the duty of the physician to heal the sick.*
2. A piece of work that has been assigned.
3. The condition of being put to use: *a cleanser for heavy kitchen duty.*
4. A compulsory contribution, usu. of money, that is required of persons or groups of persons for the support of a government.

1. *Syns:* charge, commitment, committal, imperative, must, need, obligation, responsibility.
2. TASK *noun*.
3. *Syns:* application, employment, service, use, utilization.
4. TAX *noun*.

dwarf *adjective*
Extremely small.

TINY.

dwell *verb*
1. To have as an inherent basis.
2. To have as one's domicile, usu. for an extended period.

1. CONSIST.
2. LIVE[1].

dwell on (or **upon**) *verb*
To turn over in the mind, moodily and at length.

BROOD.

dwelling *noun*
A building or shelter where one lives.

HOME.

dwell on (or **upon**) *verb*

SEE **dwell**.

dwindle *verb*
To grow or cause to grow gradually less.

DECREASE *verb*.

dye *noun*
Something that imparts color.

COLOR *noun*.

dye *verb*
1. To impart color to.
2. To immerse in a coloring solution.

1. COLOR *verb*.
2. DIP *verb*.

dyestuff *noun*
Something that imparts color.

COLOR *noun*.

dynamic also **dynamical** *adjective*
1. Disposed to action.
2. Possessing, exerting, or displaying energy.
3. Full of or displaying force.

1. VIGOROUS.
2. ENERGETIC.
3. FORCEFUL.

dynamite *verb*
To cause the complete ruin or wreckage of.

DESTROY.

dynamize *verb*
To arouse to action.

ACTIVATE.

dynamo *noun*
Informal. An intensely energetic, enthusiastic person.

dysphoria *noun*
A feeling or spell of dismally low spirits.

EAGER BEAVER.

GLOOM.

E

eager *adjective*
Intensely desirous or interested: *executives eager for profits; eager football fans.*

Syns: agog, anxious, appetent, ardent, athirst, avid, bursting, impatient, keen[1], raring (*Informal*), solicitous, thirsting, thirsty. —*Idioms* champing at the bit, ready and willing.
Near-syns: ambitious, intent, longing, wishful; restive, restless, yearning; enthusiastic, gung ho (*Slang*), hot (*Slang*), nuts (*Slang*).
Ant: listless.

eager beaver *noun*
Informal. An intensely energetic, enthusiastic person: *eager beavers who couldn't wait to get started.*

Syns: dynamo (*Informal*), energumen, go-getter (*Informal*), hustler, live wire (*Slang*).

ear *noun*
The sense by which sound is perceived.

HEARING.

earlier *adverb*
1. At a time in the past: *had heard that rumor earlier.*

1. **Syns:** aforetime (*Archaic*), already, before, beforetime (*Rare*), erstwhile (*Archaic*), formerly, heretofore, once.
2. Up to this time: *straightened out what had earlier been a mess.*
2. **Syns:** heretofore, yet.
3. Until then: *You'll hear from me on Monday and not earlier.*
3. **Syns:** before, beforehand.

earliest *adjective*
Preceding all others in time.

FIRST *adjective.*

early *adjective*
1. At or near the start of a period, development, or series: *early stages of cancer.*
2. Of, existing, or occurring in a distant period: *Early man discovered fire.*
3. Developing, occurring, or appearing before the expected time: *an early death; an early robin.*

1. **Syns:** beginning, first, initial.
2. **Syns:** ancient, antediluvian (*also* antediluvial), primitive, primordial.
3. **Syns:** precocious, premature, untimely.

early *adverb*
Before the expected time: *She arrived early.*

Syns: aforehand (*Chiefly Regional*), ahead, beforehand, betimes. —*Idioms* ahead of time, in advance, with time to spare.

earmark *verb*
To set aside for a specified purpose.

APPROPRIATE *verb.*

earn *verb*
1. To receive, as wages, for one's labor: *earned $20,000 a year.*

1. **Syns:** drag down (*Slang*), draw down, gain, get, make, pull down, win. —*Idioms* earn (*or* make) a living, earn one's keep, make one's way.

2. To acquire as a result of one's behavior or effort: *He has earned our respect through his bravery.*
3. To make as income or profit.

2. *Syns:* deserve, gain, get, merit, rate[1] (*Informal*), win.
3. RETURN *verb.*

earnest *adjective*
1. Marked by sober sincerity.
2. Full of or marked by dignity and seriousness.

1. SERIOUS.
2. GRAVE[2].

earnest *noun*
1. Sober sincerity.
2. Something given to guarantee the repayment of a loan or the fulfillment of an obligation.

1. SERIOUSNESS.
2. PAWN[1] *noun.*

earnestness *noun*
Sober sincerity.

SERIOUSNESS.

earnings *noun*
Payment for work done.

WAGE(S) *noun.*

earshot *noun*
Range of audibility.

HEARING.

earth *noun*
The celestial body where humans live: *The spacecraft orbited the earth.*

Syn: world.

earthbound also **earth-bound** *adjective*
1. Pertaining to or characteristic of the earth or of human life on earth.
2. Lacking liveliness, charm, or surprise.

1. EARTHLY.
2. DULL *adjective.*

earthen *adjective*
1. Consisting of or resembling soil.
2. Pertaining to or characteristic of the earth or of human life on earth.

1. EARTHY.
2. EARTHLY.

earthiness *noun*
A preoccupation with the body and satisfaction of its desires.

PHYSICALITY.

earthlike *adjective*
Consisting of or resembling soil.

EARTHY.

earthquake *noun*
A shaking of the earth.

TREMOR *noun.*

earthly *adjective*
1. Pertaining to or characteristic of the earth or of human life on earth: *totally occupied with earthly pursuits.*

2. Capable of being anticipated, considered, or imagined: *There is no earthly reason for us to go.*

1. *Syns:* earthbound (*also* earth-bound), earthen, earthy, mundane, secular, tellurian, telluric, temporal, terrene, terrestrial, worldly.
2. *Syns:* conceivable, imaginable, likely, mortal, possible, thinkable. —*Idioms* humanly possible, within the bounds (*or* realm *or* range) of possibility.

earthy *adjective*
1. Consisting of or resembling soil: *the earthy smell of the woods after a rain.*
2. Lacking in delicacy or refinement.
3. Pertaining to or characteristic of the earth or of human life on earth.

1. *Syns:* earthen, earthlike, terrene, terrestrial.
2. COARSE.
3. EARTHLY.

ease *noun*
1. Freedom from constraint, embarrassment, or awkwardness: *the ease of her approach to a stranger.*

2. Freedom from labor, responsibility, or strain.
3. The ability to perform without apparent effort: *translated the document with ease.*
4. Steady good fortune or financial security.
5. Freedom, esp. from pain.

1. *Syns:* easiness, informality, naturalness, poise, spontaneity, unrestraint.
2. REST[1] *noun.*
3. *Syns:* easiness, effortlessness, facileness, facility, readiness.
4. PROSPERITY.
5. RELIEF.

ease *verb*

1. To reduce in tension, pressure, or rigidity: *The pull of the current eased as the tide turned. I eased off on the anchor line.*
2. To make less severe or more bearable.
3. To make less difficult: *Use short cuts to ease and speed your work.*

4. To maneuver gently and slowly into place: *ease a pie into the oven.*
5. To advance carefully and gradually.

ease off *verb*
1. To become less active or intense.
2. To moderate or change a position or course of action as a result of pressure.

easeful *adjective*
Affording pleasurable ease.

easiness *noun*
1. Freedom from constraint, embarrassment, or awkwardness.
2. The ability to perform without apparent effort.

ease off *verb*

easy *adjective*
1. Posing no difficulty: *an easy solution to the problem.*

2. Requiring little effort or exertion.
3. Affording pleasurable ease.
4. Unconstrained by rigid standards.
5. Not strict or severe.
6. Easily imposed on or tricked: *an easy target for swindlers.*

7. Sexually promiscuous.
8. Marked by facility, esp. of expression.
9. Enjoying steady good fortune or financial security.
10. Pleasant and friendly.
11. Not steep or abrupt.

easygoing *adjective*
1. Unconstrained by rigid standards: *an easygoing person who never worried.*

2. Pleasant and friendly.

easy-osey also **easy-osie** *adjective*
Scot. Unconstrained by rigid standards.

easy-osie *adjective*

easy street also **Easy Street** *noun*
Slang. Steady good fortune or financial security.

eat *verb*
1. To take (food) into the body as nourishment: *ate a hearty dinner.*

---

1. **Syns:** lax, let up, loose, loosen, relax, slack, slacken, untighten.

2. RELIEVE.
3. **Syns:** expedite, facilitate. —*Idioms* clear (*or* prepare) the way for, grease the wheels, open the door for (*or* to).
4. **Syns:** glide, slide, slip.

5. EDGE *verb*.

1. SUBSIDE.
2. WEAKEN.

COMFORTABLE.

1. EASE *noun*.

2. EASE *noun*.
SEE **ease**.

1. **Syns:** effortless, facile, ready, royal, simple, smooth, snap (*Informal*).
   —*Idioms* easy as ABC, easy as falling off a log, easy as one-two-three, easy as pie, like taking candy from a baby, nothing to it.
   Near-ants: arduous, difficult, troublesome, trying; complex, complicated, intricate.
   Ant: hard.
2. LIGHT^2.
3. COMFORTABLE.
4. EASYGOING.
5. TOLERANT.
6. **Syns:** dupable, exploitable, gullible, naive (*also* naïve, naif, naïf), susceptible.
7. WANTON *adjective*.
8. SMOOTH *adjective*.
9. PROSPEROUS.
10. AMIABLE.
11. GRADUAL.

1. **Syns:** casual, common (*Chiefly Regional*), easy, easy-osey (*also* easy-osie) (*Scot.*), informal, laid-back (*Slang*), relaxed.
2. AMIABLE.

EASYGOING.
SEE **easy-osey**.

PROSPERITY.

1. **Syns:** chow (*Slang*), consume, devour, discuss (*Rare*), fare (*Rare*), grub (*Slang*), ingest, meal, partake (of).
   —*Idioms* break bread, have (*or* take) a bite, take nourishment.

2. To consume gradually, as by chemical reaction,   **2.** BITE *verb.*
friction, etc.

3. To do away with completely and destructively.   **3.** CONSUME.

eat up *verb*

1. To eat completely or entirely.   **1.** CONSUME.

2. *Slang.* To like or enjoy enthusiastically, often   **2.** ADORE.
excessively.

3. *Slang.* To be avidly interested in: *She just eats up*   **3.** *Syns:* devour, feast (on), relish. —*Idiom*
gossip.   eat up with a greasy spoon.

4. To do away with completely and destructively.   **4.** CONSUME.

5. To use all of.   **5.** EXHAUST.

eatable *adjective*
Fit to be eaten.   EDIBLE *adjective.*

eats *noun*
Slang. Something fit to be eaten.   FOOD.

eat up *verb*   SEE **eat.**

eavesdrop *verb*
To observe or listen in secret to obtain information.   SPY *verb.*

ebb *verb*

1. To grow or cause to grow gradually less.   **1.** DECREASE *verb.*

2. To become less active or intense.   **2.** SUBSIDE.

3. To move back or away from a point, limit, or mark.   **3.** RECEDE.

ebb *noun*
The act or process of becoming less active or intense.   WANE *noun.*

ebb *adjective*
Brit. Regional. Measuring little from bottom to top or   SHALLOW *adjective.*
surface.

ebbing *noun*
A marked loss of strength or effectiveness.   FAILURE.

ebon *adjective*
Poetic. Of the darkest achromatic visual value.   BLACK.

ebony *adjective*
Of the darkest achromatic visual value.   BLACK.

ebullient *adjective*
Full of joyful, unrestrained high spirits.   EXUBERANT.

ecbole *noun*
Rhet. An instance of digressing.   DIGRESSION.

eccentric *adjective*
Deviating from the customary: *an eccentric person;*   *Syns:* bizarre, curious, erratic, freakish,
eccentric habits.   idiosyncratic, odd, oddball (*Informal*),
    peculiar, quaint[1], queer, quirky, rum (*also*
    rummy) (*Brit. Slang*), singular, strange,
    unusual, weird.
    Near-syns: irregular, unnatural;
    exceptional, quizzical, wacky (*Slang*);
    fantastic.
    Ants: normal, regular.

eccentric *noun*
An insanely foolish or strange person.   CRACKPOT.

eccentricity *noun*
Peculiar behavior: *Living as a recluse is just one of his*   *Syns:* idiosyncrasy, peculiarity, quirk,
eccentricities.   singularity.

ecclesiastic *noun*
A person ordained for service in a Christian church.   PREACHER.

ecclesiastical *adjective*
Of or relating to a church or to an established religion.   SPIRITUAL.

echinate *adjective*
Full of sharp, needlelike protuberances.   THORNY.

echo *noun*

1. Repetition of sound via reflection from a surface: **1.** *Syns:* rebound, repercussion,
heard an echo of the cry across the canyon.   resounding, reverberation.

2. Imitative reproduction, as of the style of another: *paintings that were echoes of the Impressionists.*

2. *Syns:* reflection, repetition, reflex.

3. One who mindlessly imitates another: *He is but an echo of the king's wishes.*

3. *Syns:* imitator, mimic, parrot.

echo *verb*

1. To send back the sound of: *The canyon echoed her cry.*

1. *Syns:* rebound, re-echo, reflect, repeat, resound, reverberate.

2. To copy (another) slavishly: *corporate minions who merely echoed the style of the president; a composition that echoes Brahms.*

2. *Syns:* image, imitate, mimic, mirror, parrot, reflect, repeat.

echoic *adjective*

Imitating sounds: *The word "cuckoo" is echoic of the bird's call.*

Syns: imitative, onomatopoeic (*also* onomatopoetic).

echoism *noun*

The formation of words in imitation of sounds: *The word "buzz" is an example of echoism.*

Syns: onomatopoeia (*also* onomatopoësis).

eclipse *verb*

To make dim or indistinct.

OBSCURE *verb.*

economical *adjective*

Careful in the use of material resources: *an economical shopper.*

Syns: canny, chary, forehanded, frugal, provident, prudent, saving, Scotch, sparing, stewardly, thrifty, wary.
Near-syns: careful, close, mean, miserly, niggardly, penny-pinching, penurious, stingy.
Ants: extravagant, prodigal.

economize *verb*

To use without wasting: *economize on gas by making fewer trips.*

Syns: Hooverize, save, spare. —*Idiom* keep within compass.

economy *noun*

Careful use of material resources: *One must practice economy when buying food.*

Syns: forehandedness, frugality, providence, prudence, thrift, thriftiness.

ecstasy *noun*

A state of elated bliss.

HEAVEN.

ecumenical *adjective*

So pervasive and all-inclusive as to exist in or affect the whole world.

UNIVERSAL *adjective.*

edacious *adjective*

1. Wanting to eat or drink more than one can reasonably consume.

1. GREEDY.

2. Having an insatiable appetite for an activity or pursuit.

2. VORACIOUS.

edacity *noun*

The quality or condition of being voracious.

VORACITY.

eddy *verb*

To move or cause to move like a rapid rotary current of liquid.

SWIRL.

edge *noun*

1. The cutting part of a sharp instrument: *the edge of a sword.*

1. *Syn:* blade. —*Idiom* cutting edge.

2. A cutting quality: *His voice had an edge to it.*

2. *Syns:* bite, incisiveness, keenness, sharpness, sting. —*Idiom* cutting edge.

3. A fairly narrow line or space forming a boundary.

3. BORDER *noun.*

4. A transitional interval beyond which some new action or different state of affairs is likely to begin or occur.

4. VERGE *noun.*

5. A dominating position, as in a conflict.

5. ADVANTAGE *noun.*

edge *verb*

1. To give a sharp edge to.

1. SHARPEN.

2. To put or form a border on.

2. BORDER *verb.*

3. To advance carefully and gradually: *edged my way across the crowded room.*

3. Syns: ease, sidle.

edge in *verb*
To introduce gradually and slyly.

INSINUATE.

edge in *verb*

SEE **edge.**

edging *noun*
A fairly narrow line or space forming a boundary.

BORDER *noun.*

edgy *adjective*
Feeling or exhibiting nervous tension: *The pilots were edgy before the mission.*

Syns: fidgety, jittery (*Informal*), jumpy, goosey (*also* goosy) (*Informal*), nervous, nervy (*Chiefly Brit.*), restive, restless, skittish, tense, twitchy, uneasy, up tight (*also* uptight) (*Slang*). —*Idioms* a bundle of nerves, all wound up, on edge, on the ragged edge.
Near-syns: excitable, excited, high-strung, irritable, touchy.
Ant: relaxed.

edible *adjective*
Fit to be eaten: *edible fare.*

Syns: comestible, eatable, esculent.

edible(s) *noun*
Something fit to be eaten.

FOOD.

edict *noun*
1. A public statement.
2. A principle governing the affairs of man within or among political units.
3. An authoritative or official decision, esp. one made by a court.

1. ANNOUNCEMENT.
2. LAW *noun.*
3. RULING *noun.*

edification *noun*
The condition of being informed spiritually.

ILLUMINATION.

edifice *noun*
A usu. permanent construction, as a house, store, etc.

BUILDING.

edify *verb*
To enable (one) to understand, esp. in a spiritual sense.

ILLUMINATE.

edifying *adjective*
1. Serving to educate or inform.
2. Promoting culture.

1. EDUCATIONAL.
2. CULTURAL.

educable *adjective*
Capable of being educated: *retarded yet educable children.*

Syns: instructible, teachable.

educand *noun*
One who is being educated.

STUDENT.

educate *verb*
1. To impart knowledge and skill to: *educate our children.*
2. To cause to know about or be aware of.

1. **Syns:** discipline, instruct, teach, train, tutor.
2. INFORM.

educated *adjective*
1. Having an education: *an educated person.*

2. Provided with information; made aware.

1. **Syns:** enlightened, informed, instructed, lettered, literate.
2. INFORMED.

education *noun*
1. The act, process, or art of imparting knowledge and skill: *great advances in public education.*

2. Known facts, ideas, and skill that have been imparted: *received a good education; a man of education.*

1. **Syns:** instruction, pedagogics, pedagogy, schooling, teaching, training, tuition, tutelage, tutoring.
2. **Syns:** erudition, instruction, knowledge, learning, scholarship, science.

educational *adjective*
Serving to educate or inform: *educational TV shows.*

Syns: edifying, educative, enlightening, informative, instructional, instructive.

educationist *noun*
Chiefly D, il. One who educates.

EDUCATOR.

educative *adjective*
Serving to educate.

EDUCATIONAL.

educator *noun*
One who educates: *high-school and college educators.*

Syns: educationist (*Chiefly Brit.*),
instructor, pedagogist, pedagogue, teacher.

educe *verb*
1. To arrive at through reasoning.
2. To call forth or bring out (something latent, hidden, or unexpressed).

1. DERIVE.
2. EVOKE.

eerie also **eery** *adjective*
Of a mysteriously strange and usu. frightening nature.

WEIRD.

eery *adjective*

SEE **eerie.**

effacement *noun*
The act of erasing or the condition of being erased.

ERASURE.

effect *noun*
1. Something brought about by a cause: *The effect of good advertising was increased sales.*

1. *Syns:* aftermath, consequence, corollary, event, fruit, harvest, issue, outcome, precipitate, result, resultant, sequel, sequence, sequent, upshot.
—*Idiom* end product.

2. The power or capacity to produce a desired result: *Our advice had no effect on them.*
3. The condition of being in full force or operation: *The law goes into effect tomorrow.*

2. *Syns:* effectiveness, efficacy, efficiency, influence, potency.
3. *Syns:* actualization, being, realization.

effect *verb*
1. To be the cause of.
2. To carry to a successful conclusion: *effected reunification of the country.*

1. CAUSE *verb.*
2. *Syns:* bring off, carry out, carry through, effectuate, execute, put through, swing (*Slang*). —*Idiom* bring to a happy issue.

3. To compel observance of.

3. ENFORCE.

effective *adjective*
1. Producing or able to produce a desired effect: *an effective reprimand; an antitoxin effective against snakebite.*
2. Acting effectively with minimal waste.
3. Full of or displaying force.
4. In effect: *The law is effective immediately.*

1. *Syns:* effectual, efficacious, efficient, productive, virtuous (*Rare*).
2. EFFICIENT.
3. FORCEFUL.
4. *Syn:* operative.

effectiveness *noun*
1. The power or capacity to produce a desired result.
2. The quality of being efficient.

1. EFFECT *noun.*
2. EFFICIENCY.

effects *noun*
1. One's portable property: *The deceased's effects are here.*

1. *Syns:* belongings, chattels, goods, lares and penates, movables (*also* moveables) (*Law*), possessions, things.

2. Those articles that belong to someone.

2. BELONGINGS.

effectual *adjective*
Producing or able to produce a desired effect.

EFFECTIVE.

effectuate *verb*
1. To carry to a successful conclusion.
2. To be the cause of.

1. EFFECT *verb.*
2. CAUSE *verb.*

effectuation *noun*
The act of beginning and carrying through to completion.

PERFORMANCE.

effeminacy *noun*
The quality of being effeminate: *a man who projected an air of effeminacy.*

Syns: effeminateness, femininity, muliebrity, womanishness.

effeminate *adjective*
Having qualities more appropriate to women than to men: *He had a high, effeminate voice.*

Syns: epicene, feminine, sissified, swish (*Slang*), unmanly, womanish.

effeminate *verb*
To make effeminate: *a perverted schoolmaster who corrupted and effeminated his charges.*

Syns: effeminize, feminize.

effeminateness *noun*
The quality of being effeminate.

EFFEMINACY.

effeminize *verb*
To make effeminate.

EFFEMINATE *verb*.

effervesce *verb*
To form or cause to form foam.

FOAM *verb*.

effervescent *adjective*
Full of joyful, unrestrained high spirits.

EXUBERANT.

efficacious *adjective*
Producing or able to produce a desired effect.

EFFECTIVE.

efficacy *noun*
1. The power or capacity to produce a desired result.
2. The quality of being efficient.

1. EFFECT *noun*.
2. EFFICIENCY.

efficiency *noun*
1. The quality of being efficient: *tested the fuel efficiency of the engine.*
2. The power or capacity to produce a desired result.

1. **Syns:** effectiveness, efficacy, performance, productivity.
2. EFFECT *noun*.

efficient *adjective*
1. Acting effectively with minimal waste: *an efficient motor; an efficient secretary.*
2. Producing or able to produce a desired effect.
3. Showing characteristics advantageous to or of use in business.

1. **Syns:** effective, high-performance, productive, proficient.
2. EFFECTIVE.
3. BUSINESSLIKE.

effloresce *verb*
To bear flowers.

BLOOM *verb*.

efflorescence *noun*
A condition or time of vigor and freshness.

BLOOM *noun*.

effort *noun*
1. The use of energy to do something: *This job isn't worth the effort.*
2. A difficult or tedious undertaking.
3. An earnest try: *Please make an effort to be prompt.*
4. Something completed successfully.

1. **Syns:** endeavor, exertion, pains, strain[1], striving, struggle, trouble, while. —*Idiom* elbow grease.
2. TASK *noun*.
3. **Syns:** attempt, endeavor, essay, trial.
4. ACCOMPLISHMENT.

effortful *adjective*
1. Imposing a severe test of bodily or spiritual strength.
2. Not natural or spontaneous.

1. BURDENSOME.
2. FORCED.

effortless *adjective*
1. Posing no difficulty.
2. Marked by facility, esp. of expression.

1. EASY.
2. SMOOTH *adjective*.

effortlessness *noun*
The ability to perform without apparent effort.

EASE *noun*.

effrontery *noun*
1. The state or quality of being impudent.
2. Excessive and arrogant self-confidence.

1. IMPUDENCE.
2. PRESUMPTION.

effulgent *adjective*
Giving off or reflecting light readily or in large amounts.

BRIGHT.

effuse *verb*
To cause (a liquid) to flow in a steady stream.

POUR.

egg on *verb*
To stir to action or feeling.

PROVOKE.

ego *noun*
1. An individual's awareness of what constitutes his or her essential nature and distinguishes him or her from all others.
2. A sense of one's own dignity or worth.
3. A regarding of oneself with undue favor.

1. SELF.

2. PRIDE *noun.*
3. EGOTISM.

egocentric *adjective*
1. Concerned with the person rather than with society: *an egocentric philosophy advocating the virtue of selfishness.*
2. Concerned only with oneself.

1. *Syns:* egoistic (*also* egoistical), individualist, individualistic.

2. EGOTISTICAL.

egocentric *noun*
A conceited, self-centered person.

EGOTIST.

egocentricity *noun*
Concern only for oneself.

EGOISM.

egocentrism *noun*
Concern only for oneself.

EGOISM.

egoism *noun*
1. Concern only for oneself: *His egoism precluded any thought for the feelings of others.*

2. An exaggerated belief in one's own importance.
3. A regarding of oneself with undue favor.

1. *Syns:* egocentricity, egocentrism, self-absorption, self-centeredness, selfishness.
2. EGOTISM.
3. EGOTISM.

egoist *noun*
A conceited, self-centered person.

EGOTIST.

egoistic *also* **egoistical** *adjective*
1. Concerned with the person rather than with society.
2. Concerned only with oneself.

1. EGOCENTRIC *adjective.*
2. EGOTISTICAL.

egomaniac *noun*
A conceited, self-centered person.

EGOTIST.

egomaniacal *adjective*
Concerned only with oneself.

EGOTISTICAL.

egotism *noun*
1. An exaggerated belief in one's own importance: *a person consumed by egotism.*

2. A regarding of oneself with undue favor: *His incessant boasting is evidence of egotism.*

1. *Syns:* bighead (*Informal*), bigheadedness (*Informal*), egoism, self-importance, swelled head (*Informal*).
2. *Syns:* amour-propre, conceit, ego, egoism, ego trip (*Slang*), narcissism (*also* narcism), pride, vainglory, vainness, vanity.

egotist *noun*
A conceited, self-centered person: *an egotist who constantly aggrandized his abilities.*

Syns: egocentric, egoist, egomaniac, narcissist. —*Idioms* no modest violet, the big It, the only pebble on the beach.

egotistical *or* **egotistic** *adjective*
1. Thinking too highly of oneself: *an egotistical person who thought he was never wrong.*

2. Concerned only with oneself: *an egotistical executive absorbed with his own advancement.*

1. *Syns:* conceited, narcissistic, stuck-up (*Informal*), swellheaded (*Informal*), vainglorious.
2. *Syns:* egocentric, egoistic (*also* egoistical), egomaniacal, self-absorbed, self-centered, selfish, self-seeking, self-serving. —*Idiom* all wrapped up in oneself.

ego trip *noun*
Slang. A regarding of oneself with undue favor.

EGOTISM.

egregious *adjective*
Conspicuously bad or offensive.

FLAGRANT.

egress *noun*
The act of leaving.

DEPARTURE.

eidolon *noun*
A supernatural being.

GHOST *noun.*

ejaculate *verb*
To speak suddenly or sharply, as from surprise or emotion.

EXCLAIM.

ejaculation *noun*
A sudden, sharp utterance.

EXCLAMATION.

eject *verb*
1. To put out by force: *eject a tenant from an apartment.*

1. **Syns:** boot¹ (out) (*Slang*), bounce (*Slang*), bump, chuck¹ (*Informal*), dismiss, evict, expel, kick out (*Slang*), oust, throw out. —*Idioms* give someone his walking papers, give the old heave-ho, send packing, show someone the door, throw out on one's ear.

2. To send forth (confined matter) violently.
3. To catapult oneself from a disabled aircraft: *The pilot ejected at 20,000 feet.*

2. ERUPT.
3. **Syns:** bail out, jump.

ejection *noun*
The act of ejecting or the state of being ejected: *ejection from the apartment.*

Syns: dismissal, ejectment, eviction, expulsion, ouster. —*Idioms* the boot, the bounce, the chuck.

ejectment *noun*
The act of ejecting or the state of being ejected.

EJECTION.

elaborate *adjective*
1. Complexly detailed: *an elaborate bas relief.*
2. Difficult to understand due to intricacy.

1. **Syns:** complicated, fancy, intricate.
2. COMPLEX *adjective.*

elaborate *verb*
1. To express at greater length or in greater detail: *said he was leaving and refused to elaborate. Will you elaborate your point?*
2. To disclose bit by bit: *gradually elaborated the true nature of the plan.*

1. **Syns:** amplify, develop, dilate (on), enlarge (on), expand (on), expatiate (on), labor.
2. **Syns:** develop, evolve. —*Idioms* fill in the details, go into detail.

élan *noun*
A lively, emphatic, eager quality or manner.

SPIRIT.

elapse *verb*
To move toward a termination.

GO *verb.*

elastic *adjective*
1. Capable of withstanding stress without injury.
2. Easily altered or influenced.

1. FLEXIBLE.
2. FLEXIBLE.

elasticity *noun*
1. The quality or state of being flexible.
2. The ability to recover quickly from depression or discouragement.

1. FLEXIBILITY.
2. RESILIENCE.

elate *verb*
To raise the spirits of: *Winning the gold medal elated the team.*

Syns: animate, buoy (up), elevate, exalt, exhilarate, flush, inspire, inspirit, lift, uplift.
Near-ants: discourage, distress, oppress, weary.
Ants: deflate, depress.

elate *adjective*
Feeling great delight and joy.

ELATED.

elated *adjective*
Feeling great delight and joy: *The commanders were elated by the victory.*

Syns: elate, elevated, exalted, exhilarated, flushed, inspired, overjoyed, turned-on (*Slang*), uplifted.
Near-syns: delighted, ecstatic, euphoric, exultant, jubilant.
Ants: deflated, depressed.

elatedness *noun*
High spirits.

ELATION.

elation *noun*
1. High spirits: *felt great elation at winning the regatta.*

2. *Psychiatry.* An exaggerated feeling of well-being and pleasure: *mood swings ranging from elation to depression.*

elbowroom *noun*
Ease of movement.

elder *noun*
1. A person who is older than another.
2. An elderly person.
3. One who stands above another in rank.
elder *adjective*
Of greater age than another.

elderliness *noun*
Old age.

elderly *adjective*
Far along in life or time.

elect *verb*
1. To select by vote for an office: *elect a new president.*
2. To make a choice from a number of alternatives.
elect *noun*
One that is selected: *Only the elect can belong to that club.*

elect *adjective*
Singled out in preference.

election *noun*
The act of choosing.

elective *adjective*
Not compulsory or automatic.

elector *noun*
One who votes: *The electors have cast their ballots.*

electrifying *adjective*
Causing momentary shock.

eleemosynary *adjective*
Of or concerned with charity.

elegance *noun*
Refined, effortless beauty of manner, form, and style: *He noticed her unaffected elegance.*

elegant *adjective*
1. Of such tasteful beauty as to elicit admiration: *an elegant gown; an elegant woman.*
2. Appealing to refined taste.

element *noun*
1. A fundamental, irreducible constituent of a whole: *studied the elements of music.*
2. One of the individual entities contributing to a whole: *the grammatical elements of a sentence; ambition as a key element to success.*
3. An individually considered portion of a whole: *dissected the argument element by element.*

elemental *adjective*
1. Of or being an irreducible element: *elemental aspects of existence such as birth and death.*

2. Of or arising from the most basic structure of an individual.

elementary *adjective*
1. Of or treating the simplest aspects: *an elementary math text.*

---

1. **Syns:** animation, elatedness, euphoria, exaltation, exhilaration, inspiration, lift, uplift.
2. **Syns:** euphoria (*Psychiatry*), exaltation, intoxication.

FREEDOM.

1. SENIOR *noun.*
2. SENIOR *noun.*
3. SUPERIOR *noun.*
SENIOR *adjective.*

AGE *noun.*

OLD.

1. **Syns:** ballot, vote (in).
2. CHOOSE.

Syns: choice, pick, select.

SELECT *adjective.*

CHOICE *noun.*

OPTIONAL.

Syns: balloter, voter.

STARTLING.

BENEVOLENT.

Syns: grace, polish, urbanity.

1. **Syns:** exquisite, graceful.
2. DELICATE.

1. **Syns:** basic, essential, fundamental, rudiment. —*Idiom* part and parcel.
2. **Syns:** component, constituent, factor, ingredient, integrant, part. —*Idiom* building block.
3. **Syns:** article, detail, item, particular, point.

1. **Syns:** basic, elementary, essential, fundamental, primitive, ultimate, underlying.
2. CONSTITUTIONAL *adjective.*

1. **Syns:** basal, basic, beginning, rudimental, rudimentary.

2. Of or being an irreducible element.   2. ELEMENTAL.

elephantine *adjective*
1. Of extraordinary size and power.   1. GIANT *adjective*.
2. Unwieldy, esp. due to excess weight.   2. HEAVY *adjective*.
3. Lacking fluency or gracefulness.   3. PONDEROUS.

elevate *verb*
1. To move (something) to a higher position: *The nurse   1. *Syns:* boost, hoist, lift, pick up, raise,
   elevated the patient's bed. Cranes elevated the crates   take up, uphold, uplift, upraise.
   onto the ship.*
2. To increase markedly in level or intensity, esp. of   2. *Syns:* amplify, heighten, raise.
   sound: *The musician elevated the instrument's
   volume.*
3. To raise in rank.   3. PROMOTE.
4. To raise to a high position or status.   4. EXALT.
5. To cause to be eminent or recognized.   5. DISTINGUISH.
6. To raise the spirits of.   6. ELATE *verb*.

elevated *adjective*
1. Being positioned above a given level: *an elevated   1. *Syns:* lifted, raised, uplifted, upraised,
   train.*   uprisen.
2. Extending to a great height.   2. TALL.
3. Being on a high intellectual or moral level: *elevated   3. *Syns:* high-minded, moral, noble.
   opinions on human rights.*
4. Raised to or occupying a high position or rank.   4. EXALTED.
5. Abnormally increased, esp. in intensity: *an elevated   5. *Syns:* heightened, high, raised.
   fever.*
6. Feeling great delight and joy.   6. ELATED.
7. Exceedingly dignified in form, tone, or style: 7. *Syns:* eloquent, exalted, grand, high,
   elevated prose.   high-flown, lofty.
8. Very broad and noble in character, scope, or grasp.   8. GRAND.

elevation *noun*
1. The distance of something from a given level: *the   1. *Syns:* altitude, height.
   elevation of the land above sea level.*
2. A progression upward in rank.   2. ADVANCEMENT.
3. The act of raising to a high position or status or the   3. EXALTATION.
   condition of being so raised.

elicit *verb*
To call forth or bring out (something latent, hidden, or   EVOKE.
unexpressed).

eligibility *noun*
The quality or state of being eligible.   QUALIFICATION.

eligible *adjective*
1. Satisfying the requirements, as for selection: *eligible   1. *Syns:* fit, fitted, qualified, suitable,
   varsity players; eligible voters.*   worthy.
2. Deemed suitable for marriage: *an eligible bachelor.*   2. *Syns:* marriable (*Archaic*),
                                                                      marriageable.

eligibleness *noun*
The quality or state of being eligible.   QUALIFICATION.

eliminant *adjective*
Of, relating to, or tending to eliminate.   ELIMINATIVE.

eliminate *verb*
1. To get rid of, esp. by banishment or execution: *The   1. *Syns:* eradicate, liquidate, remove,
   dictator has eliminated all opposition.*   purge, wipe out. —*Idioms* do away
                                                                      with, put an end to.
2. To take or leave out.   2. DROP *verb*.
3. *Physiol.* To discharge (wastes or foreign substances)   3. *Syns:* evacuate, excrete, purge (*Med.*).
   from the body: *The kidneys function to eliminate
   bodily wastes.*
4. To keep from being admitted, included, or   4. EXCLUDE.
   considered.

elimination *noun*
1. The act or process of eliminating: *elimination of all opposing voices.*
2. *Physiol.* The act or process of discharging bodily wastes or foreign substances: *The liver aids in the elimination of alcohol from the system.*
3. The act of getting rid of something useless or used up.

1. **Syns:** clearance, eradication, liquidation, purge, removal, riddance.
2. **Syns:** evacuation, excretion, purgation.

3. DISPOSAL.

eliminative *adjective*
Of, relating to, or tending to eliminate: *the eliminative organs of the body; drugs serving eliminative functions.*

Syns: cathartic, eliminant, eliminatory, evacuant, evacuative, excretory, purgative.

eliminatory *adjective*
Of, relating to, or tending to eliminate.

ELIMINATIVE.

elite also **élite** *noun*
1. That which is superlative.
2. People of the highest social level.

1. BEST *noun.*
2. SOCIETY.

elitist also **élitist** *adjective*
Characteristic of or resembling a snob.

SNOBBISH.

elitist also **élitist** *noun*
One who despises people or things he regards as inferior, esp. because of social or intellectual pretension.

SNOB.

elixir *noun*
An agent used to restore health.

CURE *noun.*

elocution *noun*
The art of public speaking.

ORATORY.

elocutionary *adjective*
Of or relating to the art of public speaking.

ORATORICAL.

elongate *verb*
To make or become longer.

LENGTHEN.

elongate *adjective*
Having great physical length.

LONG[1] *adjective.*

elongated *adjective*
Having great physical length.

LONG[1] *adjective.*

elongation *noun*
The act of making something longer or the condition of being made longer.

EXTENSION.

eloquence *noun*
Vivid, effective, or persuasive communication in speech or artistic performance: *gave the oration with eloquence.*

Syns: eloquentness, expression, expressiveness, expressivity, facundity.

eloquent *adjective*
1. Fluently persuasive and forceful: *an eloquent rebuttal.*

1. **Syns:** articulate, facund, fluent, silver-tongued, smooth-spoken.
   Near-syns: glib, vocal, voluble; forceful, powerful; impassioned, passionate.

2. Effectively conveying meaning, feeling, or mood.
3. Exceedingly dignified in form, tone, or style.

2. EXPRESSIVE.
3. ELEVATED.

eloquentness *noun*
Vivid, effective, or persuasive communication in speech or artistic performance.

ELOQUENCE.

elucidate *verb*
To make clear or clearer.

CLARIFY.

elucidation *noun*
Something that serves to explain or clarify.

EXPLANATION.

elucidative *adjective*
Serving to explain.

EXPLANATORY.

elude *verb*
1. To keep away from.
2. To get away from (a pursuer).

1. AVOID.
2. LOSE.

3. To fail to be fixed by the mind, memory, or senses.

3. ESCAPE *verb.*

elusion   *noun*
Rare. The act, an instance, or a means of avoiding.

ESCAPE *noun.*

elusive   *adjective*
Characterized by or exhibiting evasion.

EVASIVE.

emaciated   *adjective*
Physically haggard.

WASTED.

emanate   *verb*
To have as a source.

STEM *verb.*

emancipate   *verb*
To set at liberty.

FREE *verb.*

emancipated   *adjective*
At liberty; not imprisoned or enslaved.

FREE *adjective.*

emancipation   *noun*
The state of not being in confinement or servitude.

LIBERTY.

embark   *verb*
To go about the initial step in doing (something).

START *verb.*

embarrass   *verb*
  1. To cause (a person) to be self-consciously distressed: *Personal questions embarrass me.*

  1. *Syns:* abash, chagrin, confound, confuse, discomfort, disconcert, discountenance, faze, mortify, put out, rattle (*Informal*). —*Idioms* put on the spot, put to the blush.
  Near-syns: agitate, bother, discompose, fluster, perturb, vex.

  2. To make complex, intricate, or perplexing.

  2. COMPLICATE *verb.*

embarrassed   *adjective*
Distressed and ill at ease: *I am embarrassed by my child's misbehavior.*

Syns: abashed, chagrined, confounded, disconcerted, mortified, put-out, rattled (*Informal*).

embarrassing   *adjective*
Causing self-conscious distress: *asked embarrassing questions about the divorce.*

Syns: awkward, incommodious, mortifying.

embarrassment   *noun*
  1. Self-conscious distress: *a face red with embarrassment; financial embarrassment.*

  1. *Syns:* abashment, chagrin, confusion, discomfiture, discomposure, disconcertion, disconcertment.

  2. A condition of going or being beyond what is needed, desired, or appropriate.

  2. EXCESS *noun.*

embed also **imbed**   *verb*
To implant so deeply as to make change nearly impossible.

FIX *verb.*

embellish   *verb*
  1. To furnish with decorations.
  2. To endow with beauty and elegance by way of a notable addition.

  1. ADORN.
  2. GRACE *verb.*

embellishment   *noun*
Something that adorns.

ADORNMENT.

embitter   *verb*
To make or become bitter: *Their hard life has embittered them.*

Syns: bitter, sour.

embittered   *adjective*
Bitingly hostile.

RESENTFUL.

emblem   *noun*
An object associated with and serving to identify something else.

SYMBOL *noun.*

emblematic also **emblematical**   *adjective*
Serving as a symbol.

SYMBOLIC.

embodiment *noun*
A physical entity typifying an abstraction: *a soldier who was the very embodiment of courage.*

Syns: incarnation, personification, prosopopeia (*also* prosopopoeia) (*Rhet.*), substantiation.

embody *verb*
1. To represent (an abstraction) in or as if in bodily form: *The general embodies the spirit of revolution and freedom.*

1. *Syns:* exteriorize, externalize, incarnate, manifest, materialize, objectify, personalize, personify, substantiate.
   Near-syns: actualize, realize; symbolize, typify; exemplify, illustrate, represent.
   Ant: disembody.

2. To make a part of a united whole: *a judicial system embodying much of Roman law.*
3. To serve as the image of.
4. To have as an integral part.

2. *Syns:* combine, incorporate, integrate.
3. REPRESENT.
4. CONTAIN.

embolden *verb*
To impart courage, inspiration, and resolution to.

ENCOURAGE.

embrace *verb*
1. To put one's arms around affectionately: *She embraced her husband.*

1. *Syns:* bosom (*Archaic*), clasp, clinch (*Slang*), clip² (*Brit. Regional*), enfold (*also* infold), hold, hug, press, squeeze.

2. To have as an integral part.
3. To take, as another's idea, and make one's own.
4. To receive (something given or offered) willingly and gladly.

2. CONTAIN.
3. ADOPT.
4. ACCEPT.

embrace *noun*
The act of embracing: *held his wife in a tight embrace.*

Syns: clasp, clinch (*Slang*), hug, squeeze.

embracement *noun*
A ready taking up of something.

ADOPTION.

embracing *noun*
A ready taking up of something.

ADOPTION.

embrangle *verb*
To draw in in such a way that extrication is difficult.

INVOLVE.

embroil *verb*
To draw in in such a way that extrication is difficult.

INVOLVE.

embroilment *noun*
The condition of being entangled or implicated.

ENTANGLEMENT.

embrue *verb*

SEE **imbrue.**

embrued *adjective*

SEE **imbrued.**

embryo *noun*
A source of further growth and development.

GERM.

emend *verb*
1. To make right what is wrong.
2. To prepare a new version of.

1. CORRECT *verb.*
2. REVISE.

emendate *verb*
To prepare a new version of.

REVISE.

emendation *noun*
The act or process of revising.

REVISION.

emendatory *adjective*
Tending to correct.

CORRECTIVE *adjective.*

emerge *verb*
1. To begin to appear or develop.
2. To come into view.

1. DAWN *verb.*
2. APPEAR.

emergency *noun*
A highly volatile, dangerous situation requiring immediate remedial action.

CRISIS.

emergency *adjective*
Used or held in reserve.

AUXILIARY *adjective.*

emigrant *noun*
One who emigrates: *an island full of Southeast Asian emigrants.*

Syns: immigrant, migrant, transmigrant.

emigrate *verb*
To leave one's native land and to settle in another: *In 1908 he emigrated to America from Italy.*

Syns: immigrate, migrate, transmigrate.

emigration *noun*
Departure from one's native land to settle in another: *a steady emigration of Soviet Jews to Israel.*

Syns: exodus, immigration, migration, transmigration.

émigré *noun*
1. One forced to emigrate, usu. for political reasons: *Paris was the new home for many White Russian émigrés.*
2. A person coming from another country.

1. *Syns:* exile, expatriate, expellee.

2. FOREIGNER.

eminence *noun*
1. A position of exalted, widely recognized importance: *a man of eminence in medicine.*

1. *Syns:* distinction, eminency (*Obs.*), glory, illustriousness, luster, mark, notability, note, pre-eminence (*also* preeminence, preëminence), prestige, prominence (*also* prominency), renown.

2. An important, influential person.
3. A natural land elevation.

2. DIGNITARY.
3. HILL *noun.*

eminency *noun*
1. Something at which a person excels.
2. *Obs.* A position of exalted, widely recognized importance.

1. FORTE.
2. EMINENCE.

eminent *adjective*
Widely known and esteemed: *an eminent statesman and scholar.*

Syns: celebrated, distinguished, famed, famous, great, illustrious, lustrous, notable, noted, pre-eminent (*also* preeminent, preëminent), prestigious, prominent, redoubtable, renowned.
Near-syns: august, exalted, important, lofty, noble; well-known.
Ants: unesteemed, unknown.

eminently *adverb*
To a high degree.

VERY *adverb.*

emit *verb*
1. To discharge material, as vapor or fumes, usu. suddenly and violently: *a geyser emitting steam.*

1. *Syns:* give, give forth, give off, give out, issue, let off, let out, release, send forth, throw off, vent.

2. To pass or pour out into.
3. To send out heat, light, or energy.

2. DISCHARGE *verb.*
3. SHED.

emolument *noun*
Payment for work done.

WAGE(S) *noun.*

emote *verb*
To make an emotional display.

EMOTIONALIZE.

emotion *noun*
A complex and usu. strong subjective response, as love, hate, etc.: *a person of emotion, not reason.*

Syns: affection[1], affectivity, feeling, sentiment.

emotionable *adjective*
Readily stirred by emotion.

EMOTIONAL.

emotional *adjective*
1. Readily stirred by emotion: *an emotional person who cried a lot.*
2. Relating to, arising from, or appealing to the emotions: *an emotional appeal for help.*

1. *Syns:* emotionable, feeling, sensitive, sentient.
2. *Syns:* affective, emotive, moving.

emotionalize *verb*
To make an emotional display: *a mother emotionalizing over her sick child.*

Syns: emote, gush.

emotionless *adjective*
1. Not affected by or showing emotion.
2. Lacking all friendliness and warmth.

1. COLD *adjective*.
2. COLD *adjective*.

emotive *adjective*
Relating to, arising from, or appealing to the emotions.

EMOTIONAL.

empathetic *adjective*
Cognizant of and comprehending the needs, feelings, problems, and views of others.

UNDERSTANDING.

empathize *verb*
1. To associate or affiliate oneself closely with a person or group.
2. To understand or be sensitive to another's feelings or ideas.

1. IDENTIFY.

2. SYMPATHIZE.

empathy *noun*
A very close relationship between persons, esp. one resulting in mutual understanding or affection.

SYMPATHY.

emphasis *noun*
Special weight placed upon something considered important: *a strong emphasis on foreign languages.*

Syns: accent, accentuation, stress.

emphasize *verb*
To accord emphasis to: *a school emphasizing academic discipline.*

Syns: accent, accentuate, feature, italicize, play up (*Informal*), point up, stress, underline, underscore. —*Idioms* bear down hard on (*or* upon), lay stress on (*or* upon).

emphatic *adjective*
1. Expressed or performed with emphasis: *My answer is an emphatic "No"!*
2. Bold and definite in character: *an emphatic gesture of disapproval.*

1. *Syns:* accented, accentuated, forceful, resounding, underlined, underscored.
2. *Syns:* assertive, forceful, insistent.
   Near-ants: insipid, unassertive, undecided, weak, wishy-washy (*Informal*).
   Ant: unemphatic.

emphatically *adverb*
In a direct, positive manner.

FLATLY.

emplacement *noun*
The place where a person or thing is located.

POSITION *noun*.

employ *verb*
1. To obtain the use or services of: *employed a new secretary.*
2. To put into action or use.

1. *Syns:* engage, hire, retain, take on.
   —*Idiom* put on the payroll.
2. USE *verb*.

employ *noun*
1. *Archaic.* Activity pursued as a livelihood.
2. The state of being employed.

1. BUSINESS.
2. EMPLOYMENT.

employable *adjective*
1. Available for use.
2. In a condition to be used.

1. OPEN *adjective*.
2. USABLE.

employe also **employé** *noun*

SEE **employee.**

employed *adjective*
1. Having a job: *statistics on employed women.*
2. Involved in activity or work.

1. *Syns:* hired, jobholding, working.
2. BUSY *adjective*.

employee also **employe, employé** *noun*
One who is employed by another: *a company of 100 employees.*

Syns: hireling, jobholder, worker.

employer *noun*
One that employs persons for wages: *The employer must withhold Social Security taxes.*

Syn: hirer.

employment *noun*
1. The act of employing for wages: *investigated the company's methods of employment.*
2. The act of putting into play.

1. *Syns:* engagement, engaging, hire, hiring.
2. EXERCISE *noun*.

3. The condition of being put to use.

4. A specific use.

5. The state of being employed: *No person in our employment will betray trade secrets.*

6. Activity pursued as a livelihood.

empoison *verb*

Archaic. To have a destructive effect on.

emporium *noun*

A retail establishment where merchandise is sold.

empower *verb*

1. To give the means, ability, or opportunity to do.

2. To give authority to.

emprise also **emprize** *noun*

An exciting, often hazardous undertaking.

emprize *verb*

emptiness *noun*

1. Total absence of matter: *The emptiness of the city in early morning is depressing.*

2. Total lack of ideas, meaning, or substance: *the emptiness of political rhetoric.*

3. A desolate sense of loss: *He felt only emptiness after she left him.*

4. Empty, unfilled space.

empty *adjective*

1. Containing nothing: *an empty cupboard; an empty apartment.*

2. Lacking value, use, or substance: *an empty life.*

3. Lacking intelligent thought or content.

4. Lacking a desirable element: *writing empty of insight; a person empty of feeling.*

empty *verb*

1. To remove the contents of: *emptied the cellar of combustible materials.*

2. To pass or pour out into.

empty-headed *adjective*

1. Lacking intelligent thought or content.

2. Given to lighthearted silliness.

emulate *verb*

To take as a model.

emulative *adjective*

Copying another in an inferior or obsequious way.

emulous *adjective*

1. Given to competition.

2. Full of ambition.

enable *verb*

1. To give the means, ability, or opportunity to do: *Modern medicine has enabled us to prolong life.*

2. To give authority to.

enact *verb*

1. To cause to be by official action: *laws enacted by Congress.*

2. To put in force by legal authority.

3. To play the part of.

4. To produce on the stage.

---

3. DUTY.

4. APPLICATION.

5. *Syns:* employ, hire.

6. BUSINESS.

POISON *verb*.

STORE *noun*.

1. ENABLE.

2. AUTHORIZE.

ADVENTURE *noun*.

SEE **emprise.**

1. *Syns:* vacancy, vacuity, vacuum.

2. *Syns:* barrenness, blankness, hollowness, vacancy, vacuity.

3. *Syns:* blankness, desolation, hollowness, vacuum, void.

4. NOTHINGNESS.

1. *Syns:* bare, clear, devoid (of), stark, vacant, vacuous, void.
Near-syns: abandoned, barren, deserted, forsaken, uninhabited, vacated.
Ant: full.

2. *Syns:* hollow, idle, nugatory, otiose, vacant, vain.

3. VACANT.

4. *Syns:* barren (of), destitute (of), devoid (of), innocent (of), void (of), wanting.
—*Idiom* in want of.

1. *Syns:* clean out, clear, evacuate, vacate, void.

2. DISCHARGE *verb*.

1. VACANT.

2. GIDDY *adjective*.

FOLLOW.

IMITATIVE.

1. COMPETITIVE.

2. AMBITIOUS.

1. *Syns:* empower, permit.

2. AUTHORIZE.

1. *Syns:* constitute, establish, legislate, make.

2. ESTABLISH.

3. ACT *verb*.

4. STAGE *verb*.

enactment *noun*
The formal product of a legislative or judicial body.   LAW.

enamored *adjective*
Affected with intense romantic attraction.   INFATUATED.

enceinte *adjective*
Carrying a developing fetus within the uterus.   PREGNANT.

enchant *verb*
1. To act upon with or as if with magic.   1. CHARM *verb*.
2. To please greatly or irresistibly.   2. CHARM *verb*.
3. To give great or keen pleasure to.   3. DELIGHT *verb*.

enchanting *adjective*
1. Giving great pleasure or delight.   1. DELIGHTFUL.
2. Pleasing to the eye or mind.   2. ATTRACTIVE.

enchantment *noun*
The power or quality of attracting.   ATTRACTION.

enchantress *noun*
1. A woman who practices magic.   1. WITCH *noun*.
2. A usu. unscrupulous woman who seduces or exploits   2. SEDUCTRESS.
men.

encircle *verb*
To shut in on all sides.   SURROUND.

enclose *verb*
1. To confine within a limited area: *convicts enclosed*   1. **Syns:** cage, coop (in *or* up), fence (in),
within prison walls; cattle enclosed in feedlots.   hem (in *or* about *or* around), immure,
   mew (up), mure (*Rare*), pen² , shut in,
   wall (in *or* up).

2. To shut in on all sides.   2. SURROUND.
3. To surround and advance upon.   3. CLOSE IN at **close¹** .

enclosure *noun*
An area partially or entirely enclosed by walls or   COURT *noun*.
buildings.

encompass *verb*
1. To have as an integral part.   1. CONTAIN *verb*.
2. To shut in on all sides.   2. SURROUND.

encounter *verb*
1. To come up against: *They encountered enormous*   1. **Syns:** confront, face, meet¹ , run into.
obstacles in the peace talks.
2. To meet face-to-face, esp. defiantly.   2. CONFRONT.
3. To come together face to face by arrangement.   3. MEET¹ *verb*.
4. To enter into conflict with.   4. ENGAGE.

encounter *noun*
1. A face-to-face, usu. hostile meeting.   1. CONFRONTATION.
2. A brief, hostile exposure to or contact with   2. BRUSH *noun*.
something, as danger, opposition, etc.

encourage *verb*
1. To impart strength and confidence to: *The doctor's*   1. **Syns:** buck up (*Informal*), cheer (up),
report has encouraged me.   enhearten, hearten, nerve, perk².
2. To impart courage, inspiration, and resolution to: 2. **Syns:** animate, cheer (on), embolden,
encouraged the students to try harder.   inspirit, inspire, motivate, stimulate.
3. To help bring about.   3. PROMOTE.
4. To lend supportive approval to: *The government*   4. **Syns:** countenance, favor, smile on (*or*
encouraged the peace initiative.   upon).

encouragement *noun*
1. Something that encourages: *The prospect of a bonus*   1. **Syns:** inspiration, motivation,
is encouragement to produce a good product.   stimulation.
2. A tendency to cause or bring on.   2. INVITATION.

encouraging *adjective*
Inspiring confidence or hope: *Increased trade with*   **Syns:** cheering, heartening, hopeful,
China is an encouraging sign.   likely, promising, roseate, rose-colored,
   rosy.

encumber *verb*
1. To place a burden or heavy load on.
2. To interfere with the progress of.

end *noun*
1. A demarcation point or boundary beyond which something does not extend or occur: *Buffalo lies at the eastern end of Lake Erie. I am at the end of my patience.*
2. A concluding or terminating: *the end of the fighting.*

3. The last part: *the end of the performance.*

4. The hindmost part of something.
5. What one intends to do or achieve.
6. Residual matter: *broken candle ends.*

end *verb*
To bring or come to a natural or proper end.

endanger *verb*
To subject to danger or destruction: *Drunken driving endangers lives.*

endangerment *noun*
Exposure to possible harm, loss, or injury.

endeavor *verb*
To make an attempt to do or make.

endeavor *noun*
1. An effort to do or make something.
2. The use of energy to do something.
3. An earnest try.

ended *adjective*
Having reached completion.

endemic *adjective*
1. Existing, born, or produced naturally in a land or region.
2. Belonging to one because of the place or circumstances of one's birth.

ending *noun*
1. A concluding or terminating.
2. The last part.

endless *adjective*
1. Having no ends or limits: *an endless stretch of sandy beach; endless patience.*

2. Enduring for all time: *endless truths.*

3. Existing or occurring without interruption or end.

Near-ants: disheartening, dismal, dreary, gloomy, pessimistic; hopeless.
Ant: discouraging.

1. CHARGE *verb*.
2. HINDER.

1. *Syns:* bound(s), confine(s), limit, limitation.

2. *Syns:* cease, cessation, close[1], closing, closure, completion, conclusion, consummation, ending, finish, period, stop, termination, terminus, wind-up (*Informal*), wrap-up. —*Idioms* end of the line, stopping point.

3. *Syns:* close[1], conclusion, ending, finale, finish, last[1], termination, wind-up (*Informal*), wrap-up.

4. TAIL *noun*.
5. INTENTION.
6. *Syns:* butt[4], fragment, scrap[1], shard, remnant.

CLOSE[1] *verb*.

Syns: danger (*Archaic*), imperil, jeopard, jeopardize, jeopardy, menace, peril, risk.

DANGER *noun*.

ATTEMPT *verb*.

1. ATTEMPT *noun*.
2. EFFORT.
3. EFFORT.

COMPLETE *adjective*.

1. INDIGENOUS.

2. NATIVE *adjective*.

1. END *noun*.
2. END *noun*.

1. *Syns:* boundless, immeasurable, infinite, limitless, measureless, unbounded, unlimited.
Near-syns: bottomless, countless, incalculable, indefinite, inexhaustible, vast.
Ant: finite.

2. *Syns:* amaranthine, ceaseless, eternal, eterne (*Archaic*), everlasting, immortal, never-ending, perpetual, unending, world-without-end.

3. CONTINUAL.

endlessness *noun*
The quality or state of having no end: *the endlessness of human suffering.*

Syns: eternality, eternalness, eternity, everlastingness, foreverness, perpetuity, world-without-end.

endmost *adjective*
Bringing up the rear.

LAST[1] *adjective.*

endorse *verb*
1. To establish as true or genuine.
2. To affix one's signature to.

1. PROVE.
2. SIGN *verb.*

endow *verb*
To present with a quality, trait, or power.

GIFT *verb.*

endowed *adjective*
Having talent.

GIFTED.

endue *verb*
To present with a quality, trait, or power.

GIFT *verb.*

endurable *adjective*
Capable of being tolerated.

BEARABLE.

endurance *noun*
1. The quality or power of withstanding hardship or stress: *lacked the endurance needed for long-distance running.*
2. Uninterrupted existence or succession.

1. **Syn:** stamina. —*Idiom* staying power.

2. CONTINUATION.

endure *verb*
1. To carry on through despite hardships: *enduring an Arctic winter.*
2. To put up with: *couldn't endure such insolence.*

3. To withstand stress or difficulty.
4. To remain in existence or in a certain state for an indefinitely long time: *stone buildings that endure for centuries.*

1. **Syns:** sweat out, tough out.

2. **Syns:** abide, accept, bear, brook[2], go, lump[2] (*Informal*), stand (for), stomach, suffer, support, sustain, swallow, take, tolerate. —*Idioms* take it, take it lying down.

3. BEAR UP at **bear.**
4. **Syns:** abide, continue, go on, hold out, last[2], persist.

enduring *adjective*
Existing or remaining in the same state for an indefinitely long time.

CONTINUING.

enemy *noun*
One who is hostile to or opposes the purposes or interests of another: *lost his job because he made enemies of his colleagues.*

Syns: foe, opponent.

energetic *adjective*
1. Possessing, exerting, or displaying energy: *an energetic worker; an energetic attempt to win the race.*

2. Disposed to action.

1. **Syns:** active, dynamic (*also* dynamical), forceful, kinetic, lively, peppy (*Informal*), sprightly, strenuous, vigorous.
Near-ants: apathetic, inert, lethargic, limp, listless, passive, spiritless.
Ants: inactive, unenergetic.

2. VIGOROUS.

energize *verb*
To arouse to action.

ACTIVATE.

energizing *adjective*
Producing or stimulating physical, mental, or emotional vigor.

TONIC *adjective.*

energumen *noun*
An intensely energetic, enthusiastic person.

EAGER BEAVER.

energy *noun*
Capacity or power for work or vigorous activity: *We all lacked the energy to do the dishes. He ran about with furious energy.*

Syns: animation, force, get-up-and-go (*Informal*), go (*Informal*), might, pep (*Informal*), potency, puissance,

enervate *verb*
To lessen or deplete the nerve, energy, or strength of: *enervated by the humidity; enervated by the crisis.*

enervated *adjective*
Depleted of strength or robust health.

enfeeble *verb*
To lessen or deplete the nerve, energy, or strength of.

enfeebled *adjective*
Depleted of strength or robust health.

enfold also **infold** *verb*
1. To put one's arms around affectionately.
2. To cover completely and closely, as with clothing or bandages.
3. To surround and cover completely so as to obscure.

enforce *verb*
To compel observance of: *Policemen enforce the law.*

engage *verb*
1. To get and hold the attention of: *The striking billboard engaged many passers-by.*
2. To obtain the use or services of.
3. To cause to be busy or in use.
4. To make busy.
5. To assume an obligation.
6. To come or bring together and interlock: *The teeth of the two gear wheels engaged smoothly.*
7. To involve (someone) in an activity: *engaged him in conversation.*
8. To involve oneself in (an activity).
9. To enter into conflict with: *Armored units advanced and engaged the enemy.*

10. To claim in advance.

engaged *adjective*
1. Pledged to marry: *gave a party for the engaged couple.*
2. Involved in activity or work.

engagement *noun*
1. The act or condition of being pledged to marry: *announced their engagement at a party.*
2. A commitment to appear at a certain time and place: *had several engagements for the weekend.*
3. A hostile encounter between opposing military forces.
4. The act of employing for wages.

engaging *adjective*
Pleasing to the eye or mind.

engaging *noun*
The act of employing for wages.

engender *verb*
1. To be the cause of.
2. To cause to come into existence.
3. To give rise to a particular development.

engineer *verb*
To make, achieve, or get through contrivance or guile.

---

sprightliness, steam, strength, vigor, vim, zip (*Informal*).

Syns: attenuate, debilitate, devitalize, enfeeble, sap[2], undo, undermine, unnerve, weaken.

RUN-DOWN *adjective* at **run down.**

ENERVATE.

RUN-DOWN *adjective* at **run down.**

1. EMBRACE *verb.*
2. WRAP UP.

3. WRAP *verb.*

Syns: carry out, effect, execute, implement, invoke. —*Idioms* put into action, put in force, put (*or* set) in motion.

1. **Syns:** involve, occupy.

2. EMPLOY *verb.*
3. TIE UP.
4. BUSY *verb.*
5. PLEDGE *verb.*
6. **Syns:** intermesh, mesh.

7. **Syns:** draw in (*or* into), entangle.

8. PARTICIPATE.
9. **Syns:** encounter, meet[1], take on (*Informal*). —*Idiom* do (*or* join) battle with.
10. BOOK *verb.*

1. **Syns:** affianced, betrothed, intended, plighted.
2. BUSY *adjective.*

1. **Syns:** betrothal, betrothment, espousal, troth.
2. **Syns:** appointment, assignation, date (*Informal*), rendezvous, tryst.
3. COMBAT *noun.*

4. EMPLOYMENT.

ATTRACTIVE.

EMPLOYMENT.

1. CAUSE *verb.*
2. PRODUCE.
3. GENERATE.

WANGLE.

engird *verb*
To encircle with or as if with a band.   BAND[1] *verb*.

engirdle *verb*
To encircle with or as if with a band.   BAND[1] *verb*.

englut *verb*
To swallow (food or drink) greedily or rapidly in large   GULP *verb*.
amounts.

engorge *verb*
To swallow (food or drink) greedily or rapidly in large   GULP *verb*.
amounts.

engorgement *noun*
The condition of being full to or beyond satisfaction.   SATIATION.

engrave *verb*
1. To cut (a design or inscription) into a hard surface,   1. *Syns:* etch, grave[3], incise.
   esp. for printing: *engraved a copper plate for making*
   calling cards.
2. To produce a deep impression on: *The scene of the*   2. *Syns:* etch, fix, grave[3], impress,
   accident was engraved in his memory ever after.   imprint, inscribe, stamp.

engross *verb*
1. To occupy the full attention of.   1. ABSORB.
2. To make busy.   2. BUSY *verb*.
3. To form letters, characters, or words on a surface   3. WRITE.
   with an instrument.

engrossed *adjective*
Having one's thoughts fully occupied.   ABSORBED.

engrossing *adjective*
Catching and holding the full attention.   ABSORBING.

engrossment *noun*
Total occupation of the attention or of the mind.   ABSORPTION.

engulf *verb*
1. To flow over completely.   1. FLOOD *verb*.
2. To affect deeply or completely, as with emotion.   2. OVERWHELM.

enhance *verb*
1. To endow with beauty and elegance by way of a   1. GRACE *verb*.
   notable addition.
2. To look good on or with.   2. FLATTER.
3. To increase or seek to increase the importance or   3. PROMOTE.
   reputation of by favorable publicity.
4. To increase in intensity or severity.   4. INTENSIFY.

enhancement *noun*
Something added to another for embellishment or   ACCOMPANIMENT.
completion.

enhearten *verb*
To impart strength and confidence to.   ENCOURAGE.

enigma *noun*
Anything that arouses curiosity or perplexes because it   MYSTERY.
is unexplained, inexplicable, or secret.

enjoin *verb*
1. To give orders to.   1. COMMAND *verb*.
2. To refuse to allow.   2. FORBID.

enjoy *verb*
1. To receive pleasure from: *enjoy good food.*   1. *Syns:* dig (*Slang*), like[1], relish, savor.
2. To be possessed of.   2. COMMAND *verb*.
3. To have the use or benefit of: *Women did not enjoy*   3. *Syns:* have, hold, possess.
   the right to vote until early in this century.
4. To recognize the worth, quality, importance, etc., of.   4. APPRECIATE.
5. To regard with great pleasure or approval.   5. ADMIRE.

enjoyable *adjective*
Affording enjoyment: *The movie proved so enjoyable*   *Syns:* gratifying, pleasant, pleasing,
that we saw it twice.   pleasurable.

enjoyment *noun*
1. The condition of responding pleasurably to something: *A sudden headache put an end to her enjoyment of the party.*
2. A feeling of extreme gratification aroused by something good or desired.
3. Recognition of worth, quality, importance, etc.

enkindle *verb*
1. To cause to burn or undergo combustion.
2. To arouse the emotions of; make ardent.

enlarge *verb*
1. To make or become greater or larger.
2. To express at greater length or in greater detail.

enlargement *noun*
1. The act of increasing or rising.
2. The act of increasing in dimensions, scope, or inclusiveness.
3. The amount by which something is increased.
4. The result or product of building up.

enlighten *verb*
1. To enable (one) to understand, esp. in a spiritual sense.
2. To cause to know about or be aware of.

enlightened *adjective*
1. Characterized by discriminating taste and broad knowledge as a result of development or education.
2. Having an education.
3. Provided with information; made aware.

enlightening *adjective*
1. Promoting culture.
2. Serving to educate or inform.

enlightenment *noun*
The condition of being informed spiritually.

enlist *verb*
To become a member of.

enliven *verb*
1. To make alive.
2. To make lively or animated.

enlivening *adjective*
Serving to enliven.

enmesh *verb*
1. To gain control of or an advantage over by or as if by trapping.
2. To draw in in such a way that extrication is difficult.

enmeshment *noun*
The condition of being entangled or implicated.

enmity *noun*
Deep-seated hatred, as between longtime opponents or rivals: *felt bitter enmity toward the oppressor.*

ennoble *verb*
1. To cause to be eminent or recognized.
2. To raise to a high position or status.

ennui *verb*
To fatigue with dullness or tedium.

ennui *noun*
The condition of being bored.

1. *Syns:* delectation, pleasure.
2. DELIGHT *noun.*
3. APPRECIATION.

1. LIGHT[1] *verb.*
2. FIRE *verb.*

1. INCREASE *verb.*
2. ELABORATE *verb.*

1. INCREASE *noun.*
2. EXPANSION.
3. INCREASE *noun.*
4. BUILD-UP at **build up.**

1. ILLUMINATE.
2. INFORM.

1. CULTURED.
2. EDUCATED.
3. INFORMED.

1. CULTURAL.
2. EDUCATIONAL.

ILLUMINATION.

JOIN.

1. QUICKEN.
2. LIGHT[1] *verb.*

STIMULATING.

1. CATCH *verb.*
2. INVOLVE.

ENTANGLEMENT.

Syns: animosity, animus, antagonism, antipathy, hostility.
Near-ants: amicablilty, cordiality, friendliness; empathy, goodwill, sympathy, understanding.
Ant: amity.

1. DISTINGUISH.
2. EXALT.

BORE *verb.*

BOREDOM.

enormity *noun*
1. The quality of passing all moral bounds: *the enormity of the crime of matricide.*
2. A monstrous offense or evil.
3. The quality or state of being flagrant.

1. **Syns:** atrociousness, atrocity, heinousness, monstrousness.
2. OUTRAGE *noun.*
3. FLAGRANCY.

enormous *adjective*
1. Of extraordinary size and power.
2. *Archaic.* Disgracefully and grossly offensive.

1. GIANT *adjective.*
2. OUTRAGEOUS.

enormousness *noun*
The quality of being enormous: *the enormousness of the blue whale.*

Syns: hugeness, immensity, magnitude, tremendousness, vastness.

enough *adjective*
Being what is needed without being in excess.

SUFFICIENT.

enough *noun*
An adequate quantity: *Give me enough to eat.*

Syns: adequacy, sufficiency, sufficient.

enounce *verb*
To declare by way of a systematic statement.

STATE *verb.*

enquire *verb*
SEE **inquire.**

enquirer *noun*
SEE **inquirer.**

enquiring *adjective*
SEE **inquiring.**

enquiry *noun*
SEE **inquiry.**

enrage *verb*
To cause to feel or show anger.

ANGER *verb.*

enraged *adjective*
1. Feeling or showing anger.
2. Full of or marked by extreme anger.

1. ANGRY.
2. FURIOUS.

enrapture *verb*
To move or excite greatly.

CARRY AWAY at **carry.**

enrich *verb*
To make fertile.

FERTILIZE.

enrichment *noun*
Something added to another for embellishment or completion.

ACCOMPANIMENT.

enroll *verb*
1. To become a member of.
2. To register in or as if in a book.

1. JOIN.
2. LIST[1] *verb.*

ensanguine *verb*
To cover with blood.

BLOODY *verb.*

ensanguined *adjective*
Of or covered with blood.

BLOODY *adjective.*

ensconce *verb*
1. To place securely in a position or condition.
2. To put or keep out of sight.

1. ESTABLISH.
2. HIDE[1] *verb.*

ensemble *adverb*
French. In, into, or as a single body.

TOGETHER *adverb.*

enshroud *verb*
1. To surround and cover completely so as to obscure.
2. To prevent (something) from being known.

1. WRAP *verb.*
2. COVER *verb.*

ensign *noun*
Fabric used esp. as a symbol.

FLAG[1] *noun.*

enslave *verb*
To make a slave of: *The Romans often enslaved their conquered enemies.*

Syns: enthrall, subject, subjugate.
Near-ants: free, liberate.
Ant: emancipate.

enslavement *noun*
A state of subjugation to an owner or master.

SLAVERY.

ensnare *verb*
1. To gain control of or an advantage over by or as if by trapping.
2. To draw in in such a way that extrication is difficult.

1. CATCH *verb.*

2. INVOLVE.

ensnarement *noun*
The condition of being entangled or implicated.　ENTANGLEMENT.

ensnarl *verb*
1. To twist together so that separation is difficult.　1. ENTANGLE.
2. To draw in in such a way that extrication is
difficult.　2. INVOLVE.

ensorcel *verb*
To act upon with or as if with magic.　CHARM *verb*.

ensue *verb*
To occur as a consequence.　FOLLOW.

ensuing *adjective*
Occurring right after another.　FOLLOWING *adjective*.

ensure also **insure** *verb*
To render certain.　GUARANTEE *verb*.

enswathe *verb*
To cover completely and closely, as with clothing or
bandages.　WRAP UP.

entail *verb*
1. To have as an accompaniment, condition, or
consequence.　1. CARRY.
2. To have as a need or prerequisite.　2. DEMAND *verb*.

entangle *verb*
1. To twist together so that separation is difficult: *The*　1. *Syns:* ensnarl, foul, intertangle, snarl[1],
cat batted and entangled the spool of thread.　tangle.
2. To draw in in such a way that extrication is　2. INVOLVE.
difficult.
3. To make complex, intricate, or perplexing.　3. COMPLICATE.
4. To gain control of or an advantage over by or as if　4. CATCH *verb*.
by trapping.
5. To involve (someone) in an activity.　5. ENGAGE.

entanglement *noun*
1. The condition of being entangled or implicated: *old*　1. *Syns:* embroilment, enmeshment,
romantic entanglements.　ensnarement, involvement.
2. Something that is intricately and often　2. TANGLE *noun*.
bewilderingly complex.

enter *verb*
1. To come or go into (a place): *The bull entered the*　1. *Syns:* come in, go in, ingress,
arena. He opened the door and entered. The ship　penetrate, put in (*Naut.*). —*Idioms*
entered the harbor.　gain entrance (*or* entry), set foot in.
2. To become a member of.　2. JOIN.
3. To place on a list or in a record.　3. POST *verb*.
4. To go about the initial step in doing (something).　4. START *verb*.

enterprise *noun*
1. An exciting, often hazardous undertaking.　1. ADVENTURE *noun*.
2. A commercial organization.　2. COMPANY *noun*.
3. The wish, power, and ability to begin and follow　3. AMBITION.
through with a plan or task.
4. An aggressive readiness to undertake taxing efforts.　4. DRIVE *noun*.
5. Something undertaken, esp. something requiring　5. PROJECT *noun*.
extensive planning and work.

enterprising *adjective*
Disposed to action.　VIGOROUS.

entertain *verb*
1. To occupy in an agreeable or pleasing way.　1. AMUSE.
2. To think about seriously.　2. CONSIDER.
3. To receive (an idea) and take it into consideration.　3. HEAR OF at **hear**.

entertainment *noun*
Something, esp. a performance or show, designed to　AMUSEMENT.
entertain.

enthrall *verb*
1. To act upon with or as if with magic.　1. CHARM *verb*.

2. To make a slave of.

2. ENSLAVE.

3. To compel the attention, interest, imagination, etc., of.

3. GRIP *verb*.

enthralling *adjective*
Catching and holding the full attention.

ABSORBING.

enthrallment *noun*
Total occupation of the attention or of the mind.

ABSORPTION.

enthuse *verb*
Informal. To show enthusiasm: *He enthused over my new stereo.*

Syns: carry on, rave, rhapsodize.

enthusiasm *noun*
  1. Passionate devotion to or interest in a cause, subject, etc.: *His enthusiasm for butterfly collecting persisted throughout life.*
  2. A subject or activity that inspires lively interest: *Mahjong was one of the enthusiasms of the 1920's.*

  1. *Syns:* ardor, fervor, fire, passion, zeal, zealousness.

  2. *Syns:* craze, mania, passion, rage.

enthusiast *noun*
A person who is ardently devoted to a particular subject or activity: *roller-skating enthusiasts.*

Syns: bug (*Slang*), devotee, fan[2] (*Informal*), fanatic, fiend (*Slang*), freak (*Slang*), maniac, nut (*Slang*), zealot.

enthusiastic *adjective*
Showing or having enthusiasm: *enthusiastic applause; enthusiastic about the new movie.*

Syns: ardent, crazy (*Informal*), fervent, glowing, gung ho (*Slang*), keen[1], mad (*Informal*), nutty (*Informal*), warm, zealous.
Near-ants: apathetic, detached, indifferent, uninterested.
Ant: unenthusiastic.

entice *verb*
To beguile or draw into a wrong or foolish course of action.

TEMPT.

enticement *noun*
Something that attracts, esp. with the promise of pleasure or reward.

LURE *noun*.

enticer *noun*
One that seduces.

SEDUCER.

enticing *adjective*
  1. Pleasing to the eye or mind.
  2. Tending to seduce.

  1. ATTRACTIVE.
  2. SEDUCTIVE.

entire *adjective*
  1. Lacking nothing essential or normal.
  2. Including every constituent or individual.
  3. In excellent condition.
  4. Not more or less.

  1. COMPLETE *adjective*.
  2. WHOLE *adjective*.
  3. GOOD *adjective*.
  4. ROUND.

entirely *adverb*
  1. To the fullest extent.
  2. All the way.
  3. To the exclusion of anyone or anything else.

  1. COMPLETELY.
  2. CLEAR *adverb*.
  3. SOLELY.

entireness *noun*
The state of being entirely whole.

COMPLETENESS.

entirety *noun*
  1. The state of being entirely whole.
  2. An amount or quantity from which nothing is left out or held back.

  1. COMPLETENESS.
  2. WHOLE *noun*.

entitle *verb*
  1. To give a name or title to.
  2. To give authority to.

  1. NAME *verb*.
  2. AUTHORIZE.

entity *noun*
  1. The fact or state of existing.
  2. One that exists independently.

  1. EXISTENCE.
  2. THING.

3. An organized array of individual elements and parts forming and working as a unit.   3. SYSTEM *noun*.

entomb *verb*
To place (a corpse) in or as if in a grave.   BURY.

entombment *noun*
An act of placing a body in a grave or tomb.   BURIAL.

entourage *noun*
A group of attendants or followers.   RETINUE.

entrance¹ *noun*
1. The act of entering: *Courtiers stood awaiting the entrance of the king.*   1. ***Syns:*** entry, ingress (*also* ingression).
2. The state of being allowed entry.   2. ADMISSION.
3. The right to enter or make use of.   3. ADMISSION.

entrance² *verb*
1. To act upon with or as if with magic.   1. CHARM *verb*.
2. To please greatly or irresistibly.   2. CHARM *verb*.

entrancing *adjective*
Pleasing to the eye or mind.   ATTRACTIVE.

entrap *verb*
To gain control of or an advantage over by or as if by trapping.   CATCH *verb*.

entreat *verb*
To make an earnest or urgent request.   APPEAL *verb*.

entreaty *noun*
An earnest or urgent request.   APPEAL *noun*.

entrée *noun*
The right to enter or make use of.   ADMISSION.

entrench *verb*
To implant so deeply as to make change nearly impossible.   FIX *verb*.

entrenched *adjective*
Firmly established by long standing.   CONFIRMED.

entrust *also* **intrust** *verb*
1. To give over to another for care, use, or performance: *entrusted the task to his aides; entrust one's soul to God.*   1. ***Syns:*** commend, commit, confide, consign, hand over, relegate, turn over. —*Idiom* give in trust (*or* charge).
2. To place a trust upon: *entrusted his aides with the task.*   2. ***Syns:*** charge, trust.

entry *noun*
1. The act of entering.   1. ENTRANCE¹.
2. The right to enter or make use of.   2. ADMISSION.
3. An item inserted, as in a diary, register, or reference book: *There were no entries in her journal for the next week.*   3. ***Syns:*** insertion, posting.

entwine *verb*
To move or proceed on a repeatedly curving course.   WIND².

enucleate *verb*
Archaic. To make understandable.   EXPLAIN.

enumerate *verb*
1. To name or specify one by one: *Town meetings give ordinary citizens a chance to enumerate their complaints.*   1. ***Syns:*** itemize, list¹, numerate, tick off.
2. To note (items) one by one so as to get a total.   2. COUNT *verb*.

enunciate *verb*
1. To produce or make (speech sounds).   1. PRONOUNCE.
2. To declare by way of a systematic statement.   2. STATE *verb*.

envelop *verb*
1. To surround and advance upon.   1. CLOSE IN at **close¹**.
2. To shut in on all sides.   2. SURROUND.
3. To surround and cover completely so as to obscure.   3. WRAP *verb*.

4. To cover completely and closely, as with clothing or bandages.

4. WRAP UP.

envenom *verb*
To have a destructive effect on.

POISON *verb*.

envious *adjective*
Resentfully or painfully desirous of another's advantages: *envious of his brother's luck with women.*

Syns: covetous, green-eyed, invidious (*Obs.*), jealous.
Near-syns: grasping, greedy, resentful; desirous, longing, yearning.

enviousness *noun*
Resentful or painful desire for another's advantages.

ENVY *noun*.

environ *verb*
To shut in on all sides.

SURROUND.

environment *noun*
1. A surrounding area: *visited the new national capital and its backwoods environment.*
2. The totality of surrounding conditions and circumstances affecting growth or development: *plants able to survive in the desert environment; a social environment that encouraged racial prejudice.*
3. Existing surroundings that affect an activity.

1. *Syns:* environs, locale, locality, surroundings, vicinity.
2. *Syns:* ambiance (*also* ambience), atmosphere, climate, medium, milieu, mise en scène (*French*), surroundings, world.
3. CONDITIONS.

environs *noun*
1. The boundary surrounding a certain area.
2. A surrounding area.
3. The periphery of a city or town.

1. LIMIT *noun*.
2. ENVIRONMENT.
3. SKIRTS.

envisage *verb*
To form mental images of.

IMAGINE.

envision *verb*
1. To know in advance.
2. To form mental images of.

1. FORESEE.
2. IMAGINE.

envy *noun*
Resentful or painful desire for another's advantages: *The rich boy's fine clothing and toys provoked envy among his poorer classmates.*

Syns: covetousness, enviousness, invidiousness (*Obs.*), jealousy.

envy *verb*
To feel envy for: *She envied her friend's good fortune.*

Syns: begrudge, covet, grudge.

enwrap *verb*
1. To surround and cover completely so as to obscure.
2. To cover completely and closely, as with clothing or bandages.

1. WRAP *verb*.
2. WRAP UP.

eon *also* **aeon** *noun*
A long time.

AGE *noun*.

ephemeral *adjective*
Lasting or existing only for a short time.

TRANSITORY.

epicene *adjective*
Having qualities more appropriate to women than to men.

EFFEMINATE *adjective*.

epicure *noun*
Archaic. A person devoted to pleasure and luxury.

SYBARITE.

epicurean *adjective*
1. Characterized by or devoted to pleasure and luxury as a lifestyle.
2. Pertaining to, suggestive of, or appealing to sense gratification.

1. SYBARITIC.
2. SENSUOUS.

epidemic *noun*
A sudden increase in something, as the occurrence of a disease.

OUTBREAK.

epidermis *noun*
The tissue forming the external covering of the body.

SKIN *noun*.

epigrammic *also* **epigrammical** *adjective*
Precisely meaningful and tersely cogent.

PITHY.

episode *noun*
1. An instance of digressing.   1. DIGRESSION.
2. Something significant that happens.   2. EVENT.

episodic *adjective*
Marked by or given to digression.   DIGRESSIVE.

epistle *noun*
A written communication directed to another.   LETTER.

epithet *noun*
A profane or obscene term.   SWEAR *noun*.

epitome *noun*
A short summary prepared by cutting down a larger   SYNOPSIS.
work.

epitomize *verb*
1. To recapitulate the salient facts of.   1. REVIEW *verb*.
2. To serve as the image of.   2. REPRESENT.

epoch *noun*
A particular time notable for its distinctive   AGE *noun*.
characteristics.

equable *adjective*
Having no variations.   EVEN[1] *adjective*.

equal *adjective*
1. Agreeing exactly in value, quantity, or effect: *The*   1. *Syns:* equivalent, even[1], identical,
   meter is equal to 39.37 inches.   same, tantamount. —*Idioms* on a par,
                                                              one and the same.
2. Having the necessary strength or ability: *not equal*   2. *Syns:* competent, qualified, up
   to the task.   (*Informal*).
3. Just to all parties: *All citizens are entitled to equal*   3. *Syns:* equitable, even[1], evenhanded,
   treatment in courts of law.   fair.

equal *noun*
One that is very similar to another in rank or position.   PEER[2].

equal *verb*
1. To be equal or alike.   1. COMPARE.
2. To do or make something equal to: *He equaled the*   2. *Syns:* match, meet[1], tie.
   world's record in the mile run.
3. To be equivalent or tantamount.   3. AMOUNT *verb*.
4. To make equal.   4. EQUALIZE.

equality *noun*
The state of being equivalent.   EQUIVALENCE.

equalize *verb*
1. To make equal: *The goal of the program was to*   1. *Syns:* equal, equate, even[1], level,
   equalize economic opportunities for the poor.   square.
2. To put in balance.   2. BALANCE *verb*.

equanimity *noun*
1. A stable, calm state of the emotions.   1. BALANCE *noun*.
2. Lack of emotional agitation.   2. CALM *noun*.

equate *verb*
1. To make equal.   1. EQUALIZE.
2. To represent as similar.   2. LIKEN.

equilibrium *noun*
A stable state characterized by the cancellation of all   BALANCE *noun*.
forces by equal opposing forces.

equip *verb*
To supply what is needed for some activity or purpose.   FURNISH.

equipment *noun*
Things needed for a task, journey, or other purpose.   OUTFIT *noun*.

equipoise *noun*
A stable state characterized by the cancellation of all   BALANCE *noun*.
forces by equal opposing forces.

equitable *adjective*
1. Just to all parties.   1. EQUAL *adjective*.
2. Free from bias.   2. FAIR *adjective*.

equitableness *noun*
1. The quality or state of being just and unbiased.
2. The state, action, or principle of treating all persons equally in accordance with the law.

1. FAIRNESS.
2. JUSTICE.

equitably *adverb*
In a just way.

FAIRLY.

equity *noun*
The state, action, or principle of treating all persons equally in accordance with the law.

JUSTICE.

equivalence also **equivalency** *noun*
The state of being equivalent: *Einstein asserted the equivalence of mass and energy.*

Syns: equality, par, parity, sameness.

equivalency *noun*

SEE **equivalence.**

equivalent *adjective*
1. Agreeing exactly in value, quantity, or effect.
2. Possessing the same or almost the same characteristics.

1. EQUAL *adjective.*
2. LIKE[2].

equivalent *noun*
One that is very similar to another in rank or position.

PEER[2].

equivocal *adjective*
1. Liable to more than one interpretation.
2. Not affording certainty.
3. Deliberately ambiguous or vague.
4. Of dubious character.

1. AMBIGUOUS.
2. AMBIGUOUS.
3. EVASIVE.
4. SHADY.

equivocality *noun*
An expression or term liable to more than one interpretation.

AMBIGUITY.

equivocalness *noun*
The quality or state of being ambiguous.

VAGUENESS.

equivocate *verb*
1. To use evasive or deliberately vague language: *The candidate had to equivocate on several issues he knew little about.*

1. *Syns:* hedge, pussyfoot (*Slang*), shuffle, tergiversate, waffle (*Informal*), weasel. —*Idioms* beat about (*or* around) the bush, mince words.

2. To stray from truthfulness or sincerity: *By concealing the facts he was equivocating, if not actually lying.*

2. *Syns:* palter, prevaricate.

equivocating *adjective*
Deliberately ambiguous or vague.

EVASIVE.

equivocation *noun*
1. The use or an instance of equivocal language: *a speech full of equivocation.*
2. An expression or term liable to more than one interpretation.
3. Plausible but invalid reasoning.

1. *Syns:* ambiguity, equivoque (*also* equivoke), tergiversation.
2. AMBIGUITY.
3. FALLACY.

equivoke *noun*

SEE **equivoque.**

equivoque also **equivoke** *noun*
1. An expression or term liable to more than one interpretation.
2. The use or an instance of equivocal language.

1. AMBIGUITY.
2. EQUIVOCATION.

era *noun*
A particular time notable for its distinctive characteristics.

AGE *noun.*

eradicate *verb*
1. To get rid of, esp. by banishment or execution.
2. To destroy all traces of.

1. ELIMINATE.
2. ANNIHILATE.

eradication *noun*
1. The act or process of eliminating.
2. Utter destruction.

1. ELIMINATION.
2. ANNIHILATION.

erase *verb*
1. To remove or invalidate by or as if by running a line through or wiping clean.
2. To destroy all traces of.
3. *Slang.* To take the life of (a person or persons) unlawfully.

1. CANCEL.

2. ANNIHILATE.
3. MURDER *verb*.

erasure *noun*
The act of erasing or the condition of being erased: *the erasure of his name from the roster.*

Syns: cancellation, deletion, effacement, expunction, obliteration.

erect *adjective*
Directed or pointed upward: *erect posture; a frightened cat's erect hair.*

Syns: raised, upraised, upright, upstanding.

erect *verb*
1. To raise upright: *We erected the Christmas tree and decorated it.*
2. To make or form (a structure).

1. *Syns:* pitch, put up, raise, rear[2], set up, upraise, uprear.
2. BUILD.

erector *noun*
A person or business that makes or builds something.

BUILDER.

eristic *adjective*
Given to arguing.

ARGUMENTATIVE.

erode *verb*
To consume gradually, as by chemical reaction, friction, etc.

BITE *verb*.

erotic *adjective*
1. Of, concerning, or promoting sexual love or desire: *erotic art.*

1. *Syns:* amative, amatory, amorous, aphrodisiac, sexual, sexy (*Slang*).
Near-syns: ardent, fervent, fervid, impassioned, passionate; lecherous, lewd, prurient, salacious, sensual; carnal, earthy.

2. Feeling or devoted to sexual love or desire: *a highly erotic nature.*

2. *Syns:* amorous, concupiscent, horny (*Slang*), libidinous, lustful, passionate, prurient, sexy (*Slang*).

eroticism *noun*
Sexual hunger.

DESIRE *noun*.

err *verb*
1. To make an error or mistake: *must have erred while adding up the bill.*

1. *Syns:* miscue, mistake, slip, slip up (*Informal*), stumble, trip. —*Idiom* pull a boner.

2. To turn away from a prescribed course of action or conduct.

2. DEVIATE *verb*.

errable *adjective*
Liable to err.

FALLIBLE.

errand *noun*
An assignment one is sent to carry out.

MISSION.

errant *adjective*
1. Traveling about, esp. in search of adventure: *a knight errant.*
2. Straying from a proper course or standard: *Errant pupils are no longer whipped but are put to remedial work.*
3. Liable to err.

1. *Syns:* itinerant, roaming, roving, wandering.
2. *Syns:* aberrant, deviating, erring.

3. FALLIBLE.

erratic *adjective*
1. Without a fixed or regular course: *the erratic movements of a lost animal.*

1. *Syns:* devious, stray, wandering.
Near-ants: fixed, stable, static, unmoving; deliberate, planned.

2. Following no predictable pattern.
3. Deviating from the customary.

2. CAPRICIOUS.
3. ECCENTRIC *adjective*.

erratum *noun*
An act or thought that unintentionally deviates from what is correct, right, or true.

ERROR.

erring *adjective*
Straying from a proper course or standard.

erroneous *adjective*
1. Containing an error or errors: *erroneous information.*

2. Devoid of truth.

erroneousness *noun*
An erroneous or false idea.

error *noun*
1. An act or thought that unintentionally deviates from what is correct, right, or true: *an error in logic; a printer's error.*
2. An erroneous or false idea.
3. A wrong calculation.

errorless *adjective*
Having no errors.

ersatz *adjective*
Fraudulently or deceptively imitative.

    ersatz *noun*
An inferior substitute imitating an original.

erstwhile *adjective*
Having been such previously.

    erstwhile *adverb*
Archaic. At a time in the past.

eruct *verb*
To send forth (confined matter) violently.

erudite *adjective*
Having or showing profound knowledge and scholarship.

erudition *noun*
Known facts, ideas, and skill that have been imparted.

erupt *verb*
1. To send forth (confined matter) violently: *The geyser erupts steam periodically.*
2. To become manifest suddenly and in full force.

eruption *noun*
1. The act of emerging violently from limits or restraints: *the eruption of lava and ash from a volcano.*
2. A sudden, violent expression, as of emotion.

escalate *verb*
To become greater in number, amount, or intensity.

escape *verb*
1. To break loose and leave suddenly, as from confinement or from a difficult or threatening situation: *escaped from a prison cell.*

2. To keep away from.
3. To fail to be fixed by the mind, memory, or senses: *His name escapes me at the moment.*

    escape *noun*
1. The act or an instance of escaping, as from confinement or difficulty: *The thief made his escape by crawling through an air-conditioning duct.*

ERRANT.

1. **Syns:** fallacious, false, inaccurate, incorrect, mistaken, off, unsound, untrue, wrong. —*Idioms* all wet, in error, off base, off (*or* wide of) the mark, off the track.
Near-syns: defective, specious.
Ants: accurate, correct.
2. FALSE.

FALLACY.

1. **Syns:** erratum, lapse, miscue, misstep, mistake, slip, slip-up (*Informal*), trip.

2. FALLACY.
3. MISCALCULATION.

ACCURATE.

COUNTERFEIT *adjective.*

COPY *noun.*

LATE *adjective.*

EARLIER.

ERUPT.

LEARNED.

EDUCATION.

1. **Syns:** belch, disgorge, eject, eruct, expel, extravasate (*Geol.*), spew.
2. BREAK OUT.

1. **Syns:** explosion, outbreak, outburst.

2. OUTBURST.

RISE *verb.*

1. **Syns:** abscond, absquatulate (*Slang*), break out, bunk[3] (*Brit.*), decamp, flee, fly, get away, run away, skip. —*Idioms* cut and run, do a bunk (*Brit.*), fly the coop, give the slip, slip the cable, take flight, take it on the lam.
2. AVOID.
3. **Syns:** elude, slip away (from).

1. **Syns:** break, breakout, decampment, escapement, flight, getaway, slip (*Slang*).

2. The act, an instance, or a means of avoiding: *Bankruptcy seemed the only escape from his creditors.*

2. *Syns:* avoidance, elusion (*Rare*), evasion.

3. Freedom from worry, care, or unpleasantness: *The movie is suitable for those seeking lighthearted escape.*

3. *Syns:* forgetfulness, oblivion.

escaped *adjective*
Fleeing or having fled, as from home, confinement, captivity, justice, etc.

FUGITIVE *adjective*.

escapee *noun*
One who flees, as from home, confinement, captivity, justice, etc.

FUGITIVE *noun*.

escapement *noun*
The act or an instance of escaping, as from confinement or difficulty.

ESCAPE *noun*.

eschew *verb*
To keep away from.

AVOID.

escort *verb*
1. To be with or go with (another).
2. To show the way to.

1. ACCOMPANY.
2. GUIDE *verb*.

esculent *adjective*
Fit to be eaten.

EDIBLE.

esculent *noun*
Something fit to be eaten.

FOOD.

esoteric *adjective*
Beyond the understanding of an average mind.

DEEP *adjective*.

especial *adjective*
Of, relating to, or intended for a distinctive thing or group.

SPECIAL.

espousal *noun*
1. A ready taking up of something.
2. The act or condition of being pledged to marry.
3. The act or ceremony by which two people become husband and wife.

1. ADOPTION.
2. ENGAGEMENT.
3. WEDDING.

espouse *verb*
1. To take, as another's idea, and make one's own.
2. To join or be joined in marriage.

1. ADOPT.
2. MARRY.

esprit *noun*
1. A strong sense of enthusiasm and dedication to a common goal that unites a group.
2. A lively, emphatic, eager quality or manner.

1. MORALE.
2. SPIRIT.

esprit de corps *noun*
A strong sense of enthusiasm and dedication to a common goal that unites a group.

MORALE.

espy *verb*
1. To perceive, esp. barely or fleetingly.
2. To perceive with a special effort of the senses or the mind.

1. CATCH *verb*.
2. NOTICE *verb*.

essay *noun*
1. A relatively brief discourse written esp. as an exercise.
2. An earnest try.
3. An effort to do or make something.
4. A procedure that ascertains effectiveness, value, proper function, or other quality.

1. COMPOSITION.
2. EFFORT.
3. ATTEMPT *noun*.
4. TEST *noun*.

essay *verb*
1. To make an attempt to do or make.
2. To subject to a procedure that ascertains effectiveness, value, proper function, or other quality.

1. ATTEMPT *verb*.
2. TEST *verb*.

essence *noun*
1. A basic trait or set of traits that define and establish the character of something: *Free enterprise is the essence of capitalism.*
2. The most central and material part.

1. **Syns:** being, essentia, essentiality, nature, pith, quintessence, quintessential, texture.
2. HEART.

essentia *noun*
A basic trait or set of traits that define and establish the character of something.

ESSENCE.

essential *adjective*
1. Constituting or forming part of the essence of something: *We have meat and the other essential ingredients for beef stew.*
2. Incapable of being dispensed with: *Fresh vegetables are essential to good nutrition.*

3. Of or being an irreducible element.

1. **Syns:** basic, constitutional, constitutive, fundamental, integral, vital.

2. **Syns:** imperative, indispensable, necessary, necessitous, required, requisite.
3. ELEMENTAL.

essential *noun*
1. A fundamental, irreducible constituent of a whole.
2. Something indispensable.

1. ELEMENT.
2. CONDITION *noun*.

essentiality *noun*
A basic trait or set of traits that define and establish the character of something.

ESSENCE.

essentially *adverb*
In regard to the essence of a matter: *Essentially what the bargain hunter wants is something for nothing.*

Syns: basically, fundamentally. —*Idioms* at bottom, at heart, au fond (*French*), in essence.

establish *verb*
1. To place securely in a position or condition: *It took time to establish himself socially in the community.*
2. To bring into existence formally.
3. To cause to be by official action.
4. To put in force by legal authority: *a bill establishing import quotas on certain classes of goods.*
5. To establish as true or genuine.
6. To take or serve as the basis for.

1. **Syns:** ensconce, fix, install, seat, settle.

2. FOUND.
3. ENACT.
4. **Syns:** constitute, enact, promulgate.

5. PROVE.
6. BASE[1] *verb*.

establishment *noun*
1. A commercial organization.
2. The act of founding or establishing.

1. COMPANY *noun*.
2. FOUNDATION.

establishmentarian *adjective*
Conforming to established practice or standards.

CONVENTIONAL.

estate *noun*
1. Something, as land and assets, legally possessed.
2. *Law.* Usu. extensive real estate.

1. HOLDING(S).
2. LAND *noun*.

esteem *noun*
A feeling of deference, approval, and liking: *a professor held in great esteem.*

Syns: account, admiration, appreciation, consideration, estimation, favor, honor, regard, respect.

esteem *verb*
1. To have a high opinion of.
2. To look upon in a particular way.
3. To recognize the worth, quality, importance, etc., of.

1. ADMIRE.
2. REGARD *verb*.
3. APPRECIATE.

esthetic *adjective*

SEE **aesthetic**.

estimable *adjective*
1. Deserving admiration.
2. Deserving honor or respect.

1. ADMIRABLE.
2. HONORABLE.

estimate *verb*
1. To make a judgment as to the worth or value of: *How do you estimate that man's abilities?*

1. **Syns:** appraise, assay, assess, calculate, evaluate, gauge (*also* gage), judge, rate[1], size up (*Informal*), valuate, value. —*Idiom* take the measure of.

2. To calculate approximately: *Police estimated the crowd at six thousand.*

estimate *noun*
1. The act or result of judging the worth or value of something or someone: *a correct estimate of the enemy's resources.*
2. A rough or tentative calculation: *The contractor gave us an estimate of the cost of the work.*

estimation *noun*
1. The act or result of judging the worth or value of something or someone.
2. A rough or tentative calculation.
3. A feeling of deference, approval, and liking.

estrange *verb*
To make distant, hostile, or unsympathetic: *They were once friends, but political differences estranged them.*

estrangement *noun*
1. The act of estranging or the condition of being estranged: *a critical attitude that caused their permanent estrangement.*
2. An interruption in friendly relations.

estrus also **oestrus** *noun*
A regular period of sexual excitement in female mammals.

etceteras *noun*
Articles too small or numerous to be specified.

etch *verb*
1. To cut (a design or inscription) into a hard surface, esp. for printing.
2. To produce a deep impression on.

eternal *adjective*
1. Without beginning or end: *God is conceived as an eternal, changeless being.*
2. Enduring for all time.
3. Existing unchanged forever.
4. Existing or occurring without interruption or end.

eternality *noun*
The quality or state of having no end.

eternalize *verb*
To cause to last endlessly.

eternalness *noun*
The quality or state of having no end.

eterne *adjective*
1. *Archaic.* Existing unchanged forever.
2. *Archaic.* Enduring for all time.

eternity *noun*
1. The totality of time without beginning or end: *At death we are launched back into eternity.*
2. The quality or state of having no end.
3. A long time.
4. Endless life after death.

eternize *verb*
To cause to last endlessly.

ethereal *adjective*
So light and insubstantial as to resemble air or a thin film.

ethic *noun*
A principle of right or good conduct or a body of such principles: *the Protestant ethic.*

2. Syns: approximate, call, place, put, reckon, set[1].

1. Syns: appraisal, appraisement, assessment, estimation, evaluation, judgment, valuation.
2. Syns: approximation, estimation.

1. ESTIMATE *noun*.
2. ESTIMATE *noun*.
3. ESTEEM *noun*.

Syns: alienate, disaffect, disunite. —*Idiom* set at odds.

1. Syns: alienation, disaffection.

2. BREACH *noun*.

HEAT *noun*.

ODDS AND ENDS.

1. ENGRAVE.
2. ENGRAVE.

1. Syns: illimitable, infinite, sempiternal.
2. ENDLESS.
3. AGELESS.
4. CONTINUAL.

ENDLESSNESS.

IMMORTALIZE.

ENDLESSNESS.

1. AGELESS.
2. ENDLESS.

1. Syns: forever, foreverness, infinity, sempiternity.
2. ENDLESSNESS.
3. AGE *noun*.
4. IMMORTALITY.

IMMORTALIZE.

FILMY.

Syns: morality, morals, mores.

ethical *adjective*
In accordance with principles of right or good conduct: *Taking credit for someone else's work is not ethical.*

Syns: moral, principled, proper, right, righteous, right-minded.

ethicalness *noun*
The moral quality of a course of action.

ETHICS.

ethics *noun*
The moral quality of a course of action: *I question the ethics of reviewing a performance without attending it.*

Syns: ethicalness, propriety, righteousness, rightness.

ethos *noun*
The thought processes characteristic of an individual or group.

PSYCHOLOGY.

etiolate *verb*
To lose normal coloration; turn pale.

PALE *verb.*

etiquette *noun*
Socially correct behavior.

MANNERS.

eulogize *verb*
To honor (God) in religious worship.

PRAISE *verb.*

euphonic *adjective*
Resembling or having the effect of music, esp. pleasing music.

MELODIOUS.

euphonious *adjective*
Resembling or having the effect of music, esp. pleasing music.

MELODIOUS.

euphoria *noun*
1. High spirits.
2. *Psychiatry.* An exaggerated feeling of well-being and pleasure.

1. ELATION.
2. ELATION.

evacuant *adjective*
Of, relating to, or tending to eliminate.

ELIMINATIVE.

evacuate *verb*
1. To remove the contents of.
2. To discharge (wastes or foreign substances) from the body.

1. EMPTY *verb.*
2. ELIMINATE.

evacuation *noun*
The act or process of discharging bodily wastes or foreign substances.

ELIMINATION.

evacuative *adjective*
Of, relating to, or tending to eliminate.

ELIMINATIVE.

evade *verb*
1. To avoid fulfilling or answering completely: *The mayor neatly evaded questions about the scandal.*
2. To keep away from.
3. To get away from (a pursuer).

1. *Syns:* dodge, duck, sidestep.
2. AVOID.
3. LOSE.

evaluate *verb*
To make a judgment as to the worth or value of.

ESTIMATE *verb.*

evaluation *noun*
The act or result of judging the worth or value of something or someone.

ESTIMATE *noun.*

evanesce *verb*
To pass out of sight either gradually or suddenly.

DISAPPEAR.

evanescence *noun*
The act or an example of passing out of sight.

DISAPPEARANCE.

evanescent *adjective*
Lasting or existing only for a short time.

TRANSITORY.

evangelical *adjective*
Of missionaries or their work.

MISSIONARY *adjective.*

evangelist *noun*
A person doing religious or charitable work in a foreign country.

MISSIONARY *noun.*

evangelize *verb*
To deliver (a sermon or sermons), esp. as a vocation.

PREACH.

evanish *verb*
To pass out of sight either gradually or suddenly.

DISAPPEAR.

evanishment *noun*
The act or an example of passing out of sight.

DISAPPEARANCE.

evanition *noun*
The act or an example of passing out of sight.

DISAPPEARANCE.

evaporate *verb*
1. To pass off as vapor, esp. due to being heated: *The scalded milk began to evaporate.*
2. To pass out of sight either gradually or suddenly.

1. **Syns:** boil away, vaporize, volatilize.

2. DISAPPEAR.

evaporation *noun*
The act or an example of passing out of sight.

DISAPPEARANCE.

evasion *noun*
The act, an instance, or a means of avoiding.

ESCAPE *noun.*

evasive *adjective*
1. Characterized by or exhibiting evasion: *timid, evasive animals.*
2. Deliberately ambiguous or vague: *His evasive answer to the question led us to believe he had something to hide.*

1. **Syns:** elusive, slippery.

2. **Syns:** equivocal, equivocating, hedging, pussyfooting (*Slang*), shifty.
Near-ants: categorical, definite, explicit, forthright, unambiguous.
Ants: direct, frank.

eve *noun*
Poetic. The period between afternoon and nighttime.

EVENING.

even[1] *adjective*
1. Having no irregularities, roughness, or indentations: *even boards. Ivory has a hard, even surface.*
2. On the same plane or line: *The top of the boy's head was even with his father's chin.*
3. Having no variations: *an even rate of speed.*

1. **Syns:** flat, flush, level, planate, plane, smooth, straight.
2. **Syns:** flush, level.
3. **Syns:** constant, equable, regular, steady, unchanging, uniform, unvarying.

4. Not easily excited, even under pressure.
5. Agreeing exactly in value, quantity, or effect.
6. Just to all parties.
7. Owing or being owed nothing: *Pay me back and we'll be even.*
8. Being an exact amount or number: *an even dollar.*

4. COOL *adjective.*
5. EQUAL *adjective.*
6. EQUAL *adjective.*
7. **Syns:** quit, square.
8. **Syns:** exact, square. —*Idiom* on the nose.

9. Neither favorable nor unfavorable.

9. FAIR *adjective.*

even *verb*
1. To make even, smooth, or level: *evened the ground with a bulldozer.*
2. To make equal.

1. **Syns:** flatten, flush, level, plane, smooth.
2. EQUALIZE.

even *adverb*
1. To a more extreme degree: *an even worse condition.*
2. At the very time: *Even now he persists in a suicidal course.*
3. Not just this but also: *unhappy, even weeping; a horrible, even unspeakable act.*
4. In the same manner: *He can study hard even as his classmates do.*

1. **Syns:** still, yet.
2. **Syn:** already.
3. **Syns:** indeed, truly, verily. —*Idiom* not to mention.
4. **Syns:** exactly, just, precisely. —*Idiom* as well.

even[2] *noun*
Archaic. The period between afternoon and nighttime.

EVENING.

evenhanded *adjective*
Just to all parties.

EQUAL *adjective.*

evening *noun*
The period between afternoon and nighttime: *usually eat dinner at seven in the evening.*

Syns: dusk, eve (*Poetic*), even[2] (*Archaic*), eventide (*Poetic*), gloaming (*Poetic*), nightfall, twilight, vesper (*Archaic*).

event *noun*
1. Something significant that happens: *The chief event of the year for Edna was a trip to China and Japan.*

    1. **Syns:** circumstance, development, episode, happening, incident, news, occasion, occurrence, thing.

2. Something that happens.
3. Something brought about by a cause.
4. Something having real, demonstrable existence.

    2. CIRCUMSTANCE.
    3. EFFECT *noun.*
    4. FACT.

even-tempered *adjective*
Not easily excited, even under pressure.

    COOL *adjective.*

eventide *noun*
Poetic. The period between afternoon and nighttime.

    EVENING.

eventual *adjective*
Capable of being but not yet in existence.

    POTENTIAL *adjective.*

eventuality *noun*
Something that may occur or be done.

    POSSIBILITY.

everlasting *adjective*
1. Existing or occurring without interruption or end.
2. Enduring for all time.

    1. CONTINUAL.
    2. ENDLESS.

everlastingness *noun*
1. The quality or state of having no end.
2. Endless life after death.

    1. ENDLESSNESS.
    2. IMMORTALITY.

everyday *adjective*
1. Of or suitable for ordinary days or routine occasions: *an everyday suit; everyday chores.*
2. Occurring quite often.

    1. **Syns:** commonplace, mundane, prosaic, quotidian, workaday, workday.
    2. COMMON *adjective.*

evict *verb*
To put out by force.

    EJECT.

eviction *noun*
The act of ejecting or the state of being ejected.

    EJECTION.

evidence *noun*
1. That which confirms.
2. Something visible or evident that gives grounds for believing in the existence or presence of something else.

    1. CONFIRMATION.
    2. SIGN *noun.*

evidence *verb*
To make manifest or apparent.

    SHOW *verb.*

evident *adjective*
Readily seen, perceived, or understood.

    APPARENT.

evidently *adverb*
On the surface.

    APPARENTLY.

evil *adjective*
1. Morally objectionable: *repented of his evil deeds.*

    1. **Syns:** bad, black, immoral, iniquitous, nefarious, peccant, reprobate, sinful, vicious, wicked, wrong.
    Near-syns: baneful, pernicious, vile; base, damnable, noxious.
    Ant: good.

2. Causing harm or injury.
3. Extremely unpleasant to the senses or feelings.
4. Bringing, predicting, or characterized by misfortune.
5. Characterized by intense ill will or spite.

    2. HARMFUL.
    3. OFFENSIVE *adjective.*
    4. BAD *adjective.*
    5. MALEVOLENT.

evil *noun*
1. That which is morally bad or objectionable: *a villain whose heart is blackened with evil.*

    1. **Syns:** sin, wickedness, wrong.

2. Whatever is destructive or harmful: *The reconstruction of the burned city showed that good can come out of evil.*

    2. **Syns:** bad, badness, ill.

3. A cause of suffering or harm.
4. A wicked act.

    3. CURSE *noun.*
    4. CRIME.

evildoing *noun*
A wicked act.

    CRIME.

evince *verb*
To make manifest or apparent.

SHOW *verb*.

evocative *adjective*
Tending to bring something, as a memory, mood, or image, subtly or indirectly to mind.

SUGGESTIVE.

evoke *verb*
To call forth or bring out (something latent, hidden, or unexpressed): *a clown whose wry face always evokes laughter and applause.*

Syns: draw, educe, elicit.

evolution *noun*
1. A progression from a simple form to a more complex one.
2. A calculated change in position.

1. DEVELOPMENT.
2. MOVEMENT.

evolve *verb*
1. To be disclosed gradually.
2. To disclose bit by bit.
3. To arrive at through reasoning.

1. DEVELOP.
2. ELABORATE *verb*.
3. DERIVE.

evolvement *noun*
A progression from a simple form to a more complex one.

DEVELOPMENT.

evulse *verb*
To remove from a fixed position.

PULL *verb*.

exact *adjective*
1. Conforming to fact.
2. Not deviating from correctness, accuracy, or completeness.
3. Being an exact amount or number.
4. Strictly distinguished from others.
5. Conforming completely to established rule.

1. ACCURATE.
2. CLOSE[1] *adjective*.
3. EVEN[1] *adjective*.
4. PRECISE.
5. STRICT.

exact *verb*
1. To ask for urgently or insistently.
2. To obtain by coercion or intimidation.
3. To establish and apply as compulsory.

1. DEMAND *verb*.
2. EXTORT.
3. IMPOSE.

exacting *adjective*
1. Imposing a severe test of bodily or spiritual strength.
2. Rigorous and unsparing in treating others.
3. Requiring great effort.
4. Very difficult to please.

1. BURDENSOME.
2. SEVERE.
3. DEMANDING.
4. NICE.

exaction *noun*
1. The act of demanding.
2. A fixed amount of money charged for a privilege or service.

1. DEMAND *noun*.
2. TOLL[1].

exactitude *noun*
1. Freedom from error.
2. Correspondence with fact or truth.

1. ACCURACY.
2. VERACITY.

exactly *adverb*
1. Without the slightest deviation in any respect.
2. In the same manner.

1. PRECISELY.
2. EVEN[1] *adverb*.

exactness *noun*
1. Freedom from error.
2. Correspondence with fact or truth.

1. ACCURACY.
2. VERACITY.

exaggerate *verb*
To make (something) seem greater than is actually the case: *Some anglers tend to exaggerate the size of the fish they catch.*

Syns: hyperbolize, inflate, magnify, overcharge, overstate, stretch. —*Idioms* blow up out of proportion, lay it on thick, stretch the truth.

exaggeration *noun*
The act or an instance of exaggerating: *The tabloid*

Syns: hyperbole, hyperbolism,

headline *"World War Imminent"* turned out to be a gross exaggeration.

exalt *verb*
1. To raise to a high position or status: *best sellers that exalt physical fitness as a cure-all for modern ills.*

2. To cause to be eminent or recognized.
3. To raise the spirits of.
4. To pay tribute or homage to.
5. To honor (God) in religious worship.

exaltation *noun*
1. The act of raising to a high position or status or the condition of being so raised: *the exaltation of materialism.*
2. High spirits.
3. *Psychiatry.* An exaggerated feeling of well-being and pleasure.
4. The honoring of God, as in worship.

exalted *adjective*
1. Raised to or occupying a high position or rank: *dared not hope to see such an exalted personage as the queen herself.*

2. Exceedingly dignified in form, tone, or style.
3. Very broad and noble in character, scope, or grasp.
4. Feeling great delight and joy.

exam *noun*
1. *Informal.* A set of questions or exercises designed to determine knowledge or skill.
2. *Informal.* A medical inquiry into a patient's state of health.

examination *noun*
1. The act of examining carefully: *A close examination of the knife revealed traces of human blood.*
2. A close or systematic study.
3. A set of questions or exercises designed to determine knowledge or skill.
4. A medical inquiry into a patient's state of health: *went for an eye examination.*

examine *verb*
1. To look at carefully or critically: *An expert examined the handwriting and declared it a forgery.*

2. To study closely or systematically.
3. To put a question to (someone).
4. To subject to a test of knowledge or skill.
5. To subject to a procedure that ascertains effectiveness, value, proper function, or other quality.

example *noun*
1. One that is representative of a group or class: *Hungary is an example of a landlocked nation.*
2. One that is worthy of imitation or duplication.
3. An instance that warns or discourages prospective imitators: *Let this punishment be an example to all shoplifters.*
4. A closely similar case in existence or in the past.

---

magnification, overstatement. —*Idiom* tall talk.

1. **Syns:** aggrandize, apotheosize, dignify, elevate, ennoble, glorify, magnify, uplift. —*Idiom* put on a pedestal.
2. DISTINGUISH.
3. ELATE *verb.*
4. HONOR *verb.*
5. PRAISE *verb.*

1. **Syns:** aggrandizement, apotheosis, dignification, elevation, glorification, sublimation.
2. ELATION.
3. ELATION.

4. PRAISE *noun.*

1. **Syns:** august, elevated, grand, high-ranking, lofty, sublime.
   Near-syns: first, leading, outstanding; eminent, extraordinary, illustrious, noble, prominent.
   Ants: abject, ignoble.
2. ELEVATED.
3. GRAND.
4. ELATED.

1. TEST *noun.*

2. EXAMINATION.

1. **Syns:** check, checkup, inspection, perusal, scrutiny, study.
2. ANALYSIS.
3. TEST *noun.*

4. **Syns:** checkup, exam (*Informal*).

1. **Syns:** case (*Slang*), check, con, go over, inspect, peruse, scrutinize, study, survey, traverse, view. —*Idiom* give a going over.
2. ANALYZE.
3. ASK.
4. TEST *verb.*
5. TEST *verb.*

1. **Syns:** case, illustration, instance, representative, sample, specimen.
2. MODEL *noun.*
3. **Syns:** caution, lesson, warning.

4. PRECEDENT.

example *verb*
To demonstrate and clarify with examples.

INSTANCE *verb.*

exasperate *verb*
To trouble the nerves or peace of mind of, esp. by repeated vexations.

ANNOY.

exasperation *noun*
The feeling of being annoyed.

ANNOYANCE.

excavate *verb*
1. To break, turn over, or remove (earth, sand, etc.) with or as if with a tool.
2. To make by digging.

1. DIG *verb.*

2. DIG *verb.*

exceed *verb*
1. To go beyond the limits of: *In sending the pupil home the teacher exceeded his authority.*
2. To be greater or better than.

1. *Syns:* overreach, overrun, overstep, surpass.
2. SURPASS.

excel *verb*
To be greater or better than.

SURPASS.

excellence *noun*
1. The quality of being exceptionally good of its kind: *her excellence at both the violin and the keyboard.*
2. A special feature or quality that confers superiority.

1. *Syns:* fineness, superbness, superiority.

2. VIRTUE.

excellent *adjective*
Exceptionally good of its kind: *an excellent portrait, showing her just as she is; excellent wines.*

Syns: A-one (*Informal*), banner, blue-ribbon, boss (*Slang*), brag, bully (*Informal*), capital, champion, dandy (*Informal*), fine[1], first-class, first-rate, great, prime, quality, sovereign, splendid, super (*Slang*), superb, superior, swell (*Informal*), terrific (*Informal*), tiptop, top, topflight, topnotch (*Informal*).
Near-ants: bad, inferior, low, substandard; commonplace, mediocre, ordinary; shoddy, sorry; execrable, despicable, wretched.
Ant: poor.

except *verb*
1. To keep from being admitted, included, or considered.
2. To express opposition by argument.

1. EXCLUDE.

2. OBJECT[2].

exceptionable *adjective*
Arousing disapproval.

OBJECTIONABLE.

exceptional *adjective*
1. Far above others in quality or excellence.
2. Far beyond what is usual, normal, or customary.

1. OUTSTANDING.
2. RARE.

exceptionally *adverb*
1. In a manner or to a degree that is unusual.
2. To a high degree.

1. UNUSUALLY.
2. VERY *adverb.*

excess *noun*
1. A condition of going or being beyond what is needed, desired, or appropriate: *baggage in excess of the weight limit; an excess of qualified job applicants.*
2. An amount or quantity beyond what is needed, desired, or appropriate.
3. Immoderate indulgence, as in food or drink: *warned by his doctor to avoid excess.*

1. *Syns:* embarrassment, excessiveness, overabundance, plethora, superabundance, superfluity, surfeit, surplus.
2. SURPLUS *noun.*

3. *Syns:* intemperance, overindulgence.

excess *adjective*
Being more than is needed, desired, or appropriate.

SUPERFLUOUS.

excessive *adjective*
Exceeding a normal or reasonable limit: *excessive taxes; an excessive amount of salt.*

Syns: exorbitant, extravagant, extreme, immoderate, inordinate, overmuch, undue.
—*Idioms* out of all bounds, out of sight.

Near-ants: meager, narrow, scant, scanty, skimpy, sparse, stingy.
Ant: deficient.

excessiveness *noun*
A condition of going or being beyond what is needed, desired, or appropriate.

EXCESS *noun*.

exchange *verb*
1. To give and receive: *The delegates exchanged ideas at an informal dinner.*
2. To give up in return for something else.

1. *Syns:* bandy, interchange.
2. CHANGE *verb*.

exchange *noun*
The act of exchanging or substituting.

CHANGE *noun*.

excite *verb*
1. To stir to action or feeling.
2. To elicit a strong emotional response from.

1. PROVOKE.
2. INSPIRE.

excited *adjective*
Feeling a very strong emotion.

THRILLED.

excitement *noun*
Intensity of feeling or reaction.

HEAT *noun*.

exclaim *verb*
To speak suddenly or sharply, as from surprise or emotion: *"Watch out!" she exclaimed.*

Syns: blurt (out), cry, ejaculate, rap out.

exclamation *noun*
A sudden, sharp utterance: *an exclamation of astonishment.*

Syns: blurt, ejaculation, outcry.

exclude *verb*
To keep from being admitted, included, or considered: *a club that excluded certain people from membership.*

Syns: bar, count out, debar, eliminate, except, keep out, rule out.

exclusive *adjective*
1. Not divided among or shared with others: *exclusive publishing rights; your exclusive function.*
2. Not diffused or dispersed.
3. Singled out in preference.
4. Catering to, used by, or admitting only the wealthy or socially superior: *an exclusive hotel; an exclusive neighborhood.*

1. *Syns:* single, sole.
2. CONCENTRATED.
3. SELECT *adjective*.
4. *Syns:* fancy, posh (*Informal*), ritzy (*Slang*), swank (*also* swanky).
   Near-syns: chic, dapper, dashing, fashionable, smart.
   Ant: unexclusive.

excogitate *verb*
1. To think about seriously.
2. To arrive at through reasoning.

1. CONSIDER.
2. DERIVE.

excoriate *verb*
1. To make (the skin) raw by or as if by friction.
2. To criticize harshly and devastatingly.

1. CHAFE.
2. SLAM *verb*.

excorticate *verb*
To remove the skin of.

SKIN *verb*.

excrete *verb*
To discharge (wastes or foreign substances) from the body.

ELIMINATE.

excretion *noun*
The act or process of discharging bodily wastes or foreign substances.

ELIMINATION.

excretory *adjective*
Of, relating to, or tending to eliminate.

ELIMINATIVE.

excruciate *verb*
To bring great harm or suffering to.

AFFLICT.

excruciating *adjective*
Extraordinarily painful or distressing.

TORMENTING.

exculpate *verb*
1. To free from a charge or imputation of guilt.
2. To grant forgiveness for a fault, offense, or injury.

1. CLEAR *verb*.
2. FORGIVE.

exculpation *noun*
The act or an instance of forgiving. FORGIVENESS.

excurse *verb*
To turn aside from the main subject in writing or DIGRESS.
speaking.

excursion *noun*
1. An instance of digressing. 1. DIGRESSION.
2. A setting out or venturing forth. 2. TRIP *noun*.

excursionist *noun*
One who travels for pleasure. TOURIST.

excursive *adjective*
Marked by or given to digression. DIGRESSIVE.

excursus *noun*
An instance of digressing. DIGRESSION.

excusable *adjective*
1. Admitting of forgiveness or pardon. 1. PARDONABLE.
2. Capable of being justified. 2. JUSTIFIABLE.

excuse *verb*
1. To free from an obligation or duty: *The teacher* 1. *Syns:* absolve, discharge, dispense,
excused the sick boy from the day's remaining exempt, let off, relieve, spare.
classes.
2. To grant forgiveness for a fault, offense, or injury. 2. FORGIVE.
3. To show to be just, right, or valid. 3. JUSTIFY.

excuse *noun*
1. An explanation offered to justify an action or make 1. *Syns:* alibi (*Informal*), plea, pretext.
it better understood: *used a prior engagement as an*
excuse to leave early.
2. A statement of acknowledgment expressing regret 2. APOLOGY.
or asking pardon.

exec *noun*
Informal. A person having administrative or EXECUTIVE.
managerial authority in an organization.

execrable *adjective*
So annoying or detestable as to deserve condemnation. DAMNED.

execrate *verb*
1. To use profane or obscene language. 1. SWEAR *verb*.
2. *Archaic.* To invoke evil or injury upon. 2. CURSE *verb*.
3. To regard with extreme dislike and hostility. 3. HATE *verb*.

execration *noun*
A denunciation invoking a wish or threat of evil or CURSE *noun*.
injury.

execute *verb*
1. To oversee the provision or execution of. 1. ADMINISTER.
2. To carry to a successful conclusion. 2. EFFECT *verb*.
3. To compel observance of. 3. ENFORCE.
4. To carry out the functions, requirements, or terms 4. FULFILL.
of.
5. To perform according to one's artistic conception. 5. INTERPRET.
6. To begin and carry through to completion. 6. PERFORM.

execution *noun*
1. One's artistic conception as shown by the rendering 1. INTERPRETATION.
of a dramatic role, musical composition, etc.
2. The act of beginning and carrying through to 2. PERFORMANCE.
completion.

executive *noun*
A person having administrative or managerial *Syns:* administrant, administrator,
authority in an organization: *a brash young executive* director, exec (*Informal*), manager, officer,
in the advertising business. official.

executive *adjective*
Of, for, or relating to administration or administrators. ADMINISTRATIVE.

exegesis *noun*
1. Critical explanation or analysis.
2. Something that serves to explain or clarify.

1. COMMENTARY.
2. EXPLANATION.

exegetic *adjective*
Serving to explain.

EXPLANATORY.

exemplar *noun*
One that is worthy of imitation or duplication.

MODEL *noun.*

exemplary *adjective*
1. Beyond reproach: *has lived an exemplary life.*

1. **Syns:** blameless, good, lily-white, irreprehensible, irreproachable, unblamable.
Near-syns: admirable, commendable, praiseworthy, worthy; innocent, pure, righteous, virtuous.
Ant: reprehensible.

2. Conforming to an ultimate form of perfection or excellence.

2. IDEAL *adjective.*

exemplify *verb*
1. To serve as the image of.
2. To demonstrate and clarify with examples.

1. REPRESENT.
2. INSTANCE *verb.*

exempt *verb*
To free from an obligation or duty.

EXCUSE *verb.*

exercise *noun*
1. The act of putting into play: *Conformity is stifling to any free exercise of intellect.*
2. Energetic physical action.
3. Repetition of an action so as to develop or maintain one's skill.

1. **Syns:** application, employment, exertion, operation, play, usage, use.
2. ACTIVITY.
3. PRACTICE *noun.*

exercise *verb*
1. To put into action or use.
2. To bring to bear steadily or forcefully: *exercised a strong influence on his generation.*
3. To subject to forms of exertion in order to train, strengthen, or condition: *He exercised every morning at a local gym. The teacher exercised the child by assigning extra problems.*
4. To carry out the functions, requirements, or terms of.

1. USE *verb.*
2. **Syns:** exert, ply, put out, throw, wield.
3. **Syns:** drill, practice, work out.

4. FULFILL.

exercising *noun*
Energetic physical action.

ACTIVITY.

exert *verb*
To bring to bear steadily or forcefully.

EXERCISE *verb.*

exertion *noun*
1. Energetic physical action.
2. The use of energy to do something.
3. The act of putting into play.

1. ACTIVITY.
2. EFFORT.
3. EXERCISE *noun.*

exhalation *noun*
Air breathed out, evidenced by vapor, odor, or heat.

BREATH.

exhale *verb*
To expel air in the process of respiration.

BREATHE.

exhaust *verb*
1. To use all of: *Faced with the heavy expenses of city life, he soon had exhausted his money.*

1. **Syns:** consume, drain, eat up, finish, play out, polish off (*Informal*), run through, spend, use up.

2. To lessen or weaken severely, as by removing something essential.

2. DEPLETE.

3. To make extremely tired: *The long day of work in the fields exhausted us.*

3. **Syns:** bush (*Slang*), do in (*Slang*), fag (out) (*Slang*), gruel, knock out (*Informal*), poop (out) (*Slang*), tire out, tucker (*Informal*), wear out. —*Idioms* run ragged, take it out of.

4. To be depleted.

exhausted *adjective*
Extremely tired: *exhausted after a long day at the office.*

exhausting *adjective*
Causing fatigue.

exhaustion *noun*
The condition of being extremely tired: *labored to exhaustion.*

exhaustive *adjective*
Covering all aspects with painstaking accuracy.

exhaustively *adverb*
In a complete manner.

exhibit *verb*
1. To make manifest or apparent.
2. To be endowed with as a visible characteristic or form.
3. To make a public and usu. ostentatious show of.

exhibit *noun*
1. An act of showing or displaying.
2. A large public display, as of goods, works of art, etc.

exhibition *noun*
1. A large public display, as of goods, works of art, etc.: *went to an exhibition of old prints at the museum.*
2. An act of showing or displaying.

exhibitive *adjective*
Serving to designate or indicate.

exhilarant *adjective*
Providing inspiration.

exhilarate *verb*
To raise the spirits of.

exhilarated *adjective*
Feeling great delight and joy.

exhilarating *adjective*
Providing inspiration.

exhilaration *noun*
High spirits.

exhort *verb*
To impel to action.

exigence *noun*

exigency also **exigence** *noun*
1. A condition in which something necessary or desirable is required or wanted.
2. A decisive point.
3. The condition of being in need of immediate assistance.
4. Something asked for or needed.

exigent *adjective*
1. Of immediate import.
2. Imposing a severe test of bodily or spiritual strength.
3. So serious as to be at the point of crisis.
4. Requiring great effort.

4. GO *verb.*

Syns: all in (*Informal*), beat (*Informal*), bleary, bushed (*Slang*), dead (*Informal*), dog-tired, done in (*Slang*), drained, fagged (out) (*Slang*), fatigued, pooped (out) (*Slang*), tired out, tuckered (out) (*Informal*), wearied, weariful, weary, worn, worn-down, worn-out. —*Idioms* all in, ready to drop.

TIRING.

Syns: fatigue, lassitude, tire, tiredness, weariness.

THOROUGH *adjective.*

COMPLETELY.

1. SHOW *verb.*
2. BEAR.

3. DISPLAY *verb.*

1. DISPLAY *noun.*
2. EXHIBITION.

1. **Syns:** exhibit, exposition, show.

2. DISPLAY *noun.*

DESIGNATIVE.

INSPIRING.

ELATE *verb.*

ELATED.

INSPIRING.

ELATION.

URGE *verb.*
SEE **exigency.**

1. NEED *noun.*

2. CRISIS *noun.*
3. DISTRESS *noun.*

4. DEMAND *noun.*

1. BURNING.
2. BURDENSOME.

3. CRITICAL.
4. DEMANDING.

exiguous *adjective*
Conspicuously deficient in quantity, fullness, or extent.　MEAGER.

exile *noun*
1. Enforced removal from one's native country by official decree: *Convicted revolutionaries were given the choice of imprisonment or exile.*

2. One forced to emigrate, usu. for political reasons.

exile *verb*
To force to leave a country or place by official decree.

1. ***Syns:*** banishment, deportation, expatriation, ostracism.
   Near-syns: displacement, exclusion, expulsion.
2. ÉMIGRÉ.

BANISH.

exist *verb*
1. To have being or actuality: *a town that has existed since the Middle Ages.*
2. To have reality or life.
3. To have as an inherent basis.

1. ***Syns:*** be, subsist.

2. BE.
3. CONSIST.

existence *noun*
1. The fact or state of existing: *questioning the existence of God; laws in existence for centuries.*
2. The state or fact of having reality.
3. One that exists independently.
4. The period during which someone or something exists.

1. ***Syns:*** actuality, being, entity.

2. ACTUALITY.
3. THING.
4. LIFE.

existent *adjective*
1. In existence now.
2. Occurring or existing in act or fact.
3. Having existence or life.

1. PRESENT[1] *adjective.*
2. ACTUAL.
3. ALIVE.

existent *noun*
One that exists independently.

THING.

existing *adjective*
1. In existence now.
2. Having existence or life.
3. Occurring or existing in act or fact.

1. PRESENT[1] *adjective.*
2. ALIVE.
3. ACTUAL.

exit *noun*
The act of leaving.

DEPARTURE.

exit *verb*
To move or proceed away from a place.

GO *verb.*

exodus *noun*
1. The act of leaving.
2. Departure from one's native land to settle in another.

1. DEPARTURE.
2. EMIGRATION.

exonerate *verb*
To free from a charge or imputation of guilt.

CLEAR *verb.*

exorbitant *adjective*
Exceeding a normal or reasonable limit.

EXCESSIVE.

exotic *adjective*
Of, from, or characteristic of another place or part of the world.

FOREIGN.

expand *verb*
1. To move or arrange so as to cover a larger area.
2. To make or become greater or larger.
3. To make or become more comprehensive or inclusive.
4. To express at greater length or in greater detail.

1. SPREAD *verb.*
2. INCREASE *verb.*
3. EXTEND.

4. ELABORATE *verb.*

expanse *noun*
A wide and open area, as of land, sky, or water: *crossed the vast expanse of the prairie.*

Syns: breadth, distance, expansion, reach, space, spread, stretch, sweep.

expansible *adjective*
Capable of being extended or expanded.

EXTENSIBLE.

expansile *adjective*
Capable of being extended or expanded.

EXTENSIBLE.

expansion *noun*
1. The act of increasing in dimensions, scope, or inclusiveness: *the gradual westward expansion of the empire.*
2. A wide and open area, as of land, sky, or water.

1. ***Syns:*** amplification, enlargement, extension, spread.
2. EXPANSE.

expansive *adjective*
1. Large in expanse.
2. Covering a wide scope.
3. Disposed to be open, sociable, and talkative.

1. BROAD.
2. GENERAL.
3. OUTGOING.

expatiate *verb*
To express at greater length or in greater detail.

ELABORATE *verb.*

expatriate *verb*
To force to leave a country or place by official decree.

BANISH.

expatriate *noun*
One forced to emigrate, usu. for political reasons.

ÉMIGRÉ.

expatriation *noun*
Enforced removal from one's native country by official decree.

EXILE *noun.*

expect *verb*
1. To anticipate confidently: *The weatherman expects rain for the weekend.*

2. To oblige to do or not do by force of authority, propriety, or custom.

1. ***Syns:*** anticipate, await, bargain on (*or* for), count on (*Informal*), depend on (*or* upon), figure on, look for.
2. REQUIRE.

expectance *noun*

SEE **expectancy.**

expectancy also **expectance** *noun*
1. The condition of looking forward to something, esp. with eagerness.
2. Something expected.

1. ANTICIPATION.

2. EXPECTATION.

expectant *adjective*
1. Having or marked by expectation: *An expectant pause followed her question.*
2. Carrying a developing fetus within the uterus.

1. ***Syns:*** anticipant, anticipative, anticipatory.
2. PREGNANT.

expectation *noun*
1. Something expected: *That he would succeed was his confident expectation.*
2. The condition of looking forward to something, esp. with eagerness.

1. ***Syns:*** anticipation, expectancy (*also* expectance), prospect.
2. ANTICIPATION.

expected *adjective*
Known to be about to arrive.

DUE *adjective.*

expecting *adjective*
Carrying a developing fetus within the uterus.

PREGNANT.

expedience *noun*

SEE **expediency.**

expediency also **expedience** *noun*
1. Something used temporarily or reluctantly when other means are not available.
2. That to which one turns for help when in desperation.

1. MAKESHIFT.

2. RESORT *noun.*

expedient *noun*
1. Something used temporarily or reluctantly when other means are not available.
2. That to which one turns for help when in desperation.

1. MAKESHIFT.

2. RESORT *noun.*

expedient *adjective*
1. Worth doing, esp. for practical reasons.
2. Suited to one's end or purpose.

1. ADVISABLE.
2. CONVENIENT.

expedite *verb*
1. To make less difficult.
2. To increase the speed of.

1. EASE *verb.*
2. SPEED UP at **speed.**

expedition *noun*
Rapidity of movement or activity.

HASTE *noun.*

expeditiousness *noun*
Rapidness of movement or activity.   HASTE *noun*.

expel *verb*
1. To force to leave a country or place by official   1. BANISH.
   decree.
2. To put out by force.   2. EJECT.
3. To send forth (confined matter) violently.   3. ERUPT.

expellee *noun*
One forced to emigrate, usu. for political reasons.   ÉMIGRÉ.

expend *verb*
1. To distribute (money) as payment.   1. SPEND.
2. To be depleted.   2. GO *verb*.

expenditure *noun*
Something expended to obtain a benefit or desired   COST *noun*.
result.

expense *noun*
1. Something expended to obtain a benefit or desired   1. COST *noun*.
   result.
2. A loss sustained in the accomplishment of or as the   2. COST *noun*.
   result of something.

expensive *adjective*
Bringing a high price.   COSTLY.

experience *verb*
1. To participate in or partake of personally: *experience*   1. **Syns:** go through, have, know, meet
   a change of heart; must experience a toboggan ride   with, prove (*Archaic*), see, suffer,
   to know what it is like.   taste, undergo. —*Idiom* run up
                                                              against.
2. To be physically aware of through the senses.   2. FEEL *verb*.
3. To undergo an emotional reaction.   3. FEEL *verb*.

experience *noun*
Personal knowledge derived from participation or   ACQUAINTANCE.
observation.

experienced *adjective*
Skilled or knowledgeable through long practice: *An*   **Syns:** old, practiced, seasoned, versed,
experienced carpenter never splinters wood.   veteran. —*Idiom* knowing the ropes.

experiment *noun*
An operation employed to resolve an uncertainty.   TEST *noun*.
experiment *verb*
To engage in experiments.   TEST *verb*.

experimental *adjective*
Constituting a tentative model for future experiment or   PILOT *adjective*.
development.

experimentation *noun*
An operation employed to resolve an uncertainty.   TEST *noun*.

expert *noun*
A person with a high degree of knowledge or skill in a   **Syns:** ace[2] (*Informal*), adept, authority,
particular field: *Only an expert can detect certain art* crackerjack (*also* crackajack) (*Slang*),
forgeries.   dab[2] (*Brit. Informal*), master, proficient,
                                                          whiz (*also* whizz) (*Slang*), wizard.
                                                          —*Idiom* past master.
                                                          Near-syns: artist, maven, pro (*Informal*),
                                                          professional, specialist, virtuoso.
                                                          Ant: amateur.

expert *adjective*
Having or demonstrating a high degree of knowledge   **Syns:** adept, crack, crackerjack (*also*
or skill: *an expert marksman.*   crackajack) (*Slang*), master, masterful,
                                                          masterly, proficient.

expertise *noun*
Natural or acquired facility in a specific activity.   ABILITY.

expertism *noun*
Natural or acquired facility in a specific activity.   ABILITY.

expertness *noun*
Natural or acquired facility in a specific activity.   ABILITY.

expiative *adjective*
Serving to purify of sin.   PURGATIVE.

expire *verb*
1. To expel air in the process of respiration.   1. BREATHE.
2. To cease living.   2. DIE.
3. To cease to exist.   3. DISAPPEAR.
4. To move toward a termination.   4. GO *verb*.
5. To become void, esp. through passage of time or an   5. LAPSE *verb*.
   omission.

explain *verb*
1. To make understandable: *The poet read, pausing*   1. ***Syns:*** construe, decipher, enucleate
   occasionally to explain a rare word or obscure   (*Archaic*), explicate, expound,
   symbol.   illustrate, interpret, spell out. —*Idiom*
                                                                      put into plain English.
2. To find a solution for.   2. RESOLVE *verb*.
3. To offer reasons for or a cause of.   3. ACCOUNT FOR at **account**.

explain away *verb*
To show to be just, right, or valid.   JUSTIFY.

explainable *adjective*
Capable of being accounted for: *Her mistakes are*   ***Syns:*** accountable, explicable.
explainable in terms of inexperience.

explain away *verb*   SEE **explain**.

explanation *noun*
1. Something that serves to explain or clarify: *wrote*   1. ***Syns:*** clarification, construction,
   for an explanation of a complicated tax law.   elucidation, exegesis, explication,
                                                                      exposition, illumination, interpretation.
2. A statement of causes or motives.   2. ACCOUNT *noun*.

explanative *adjective*
Serving to explain.   EXPLANATORY.

explanatory *adjective*
Serving to explain: *issued the declaration with some*   ***Syns:*** elucidative, exegetic, explanative,
explanatory remarks.   explicative, explicatory, expositive,
                                                                   expository, hermeneutic, interpretive.

expletive *noun*
1. A profane or obscene term.   1. SWEAR *noun*.
2. *Rare.* Something that completes another.   2. COMPLEMENT *noun*.

explicable *adjective*
Capable of being accounted for.   EXPLAINABLE.

explicate *verb*
To make understandable.   EXPLAIN.

explication *noun*
Something that serves to explain or clarify.   EXPLANATION.

explicative *adjective*
Serving to explain.   EXPLANATORY.

explicatory *adjective*
Serving to explain.   EXPLANATORY.

explicit *adjective*
Clearly, fully, and sometimes emphatically expressed.   DEFINITE.

explode *verb*
1. To release or cause to release energy suddenly and   1. ***Syns:*** blast, blow[1], blow up, burst,
   violently, esp. with a loud noise: *The bomb exploded*   detonate, fire, fulminate, go off, touch
   in midair. The dynamite was exploded with an   off.
   electric fuse.
2. To come open or fly apart suddenly and violently, as   2. BURST *verb*.
   from internal pressure.
3. To be or become angry.   3. ANGER *verb*.
4. To become manifest suddenly and in full force.   4. BREAK OUT.

5. To increase or expand suddenly, rapidly, or without control: *feared that without natural checks on growth the population would explode.*

6. To cause to be no longer believed or valued.

exploit *verb*
1. To put into action or use.
2. To take advantage of unfairly.
3. To control to one's own advantage by artful or indirect means.

exploit *noun*
A great or heroic deed.

exploitable *adjective*
Easily imposed on or tricked.

exploration *noun*
The act or an instance of exploring or investigating: *the exploration of the Arctic; an exploration of the mentality of a criminal.*

explore *verb*
To go into or through for the purpose of making discoveries or acquiring information: *explored the upper Amazon; exploring the chances for a compromise.*

explosion *noun*
1. A violent release of confined energy, usu. accompanied by a loud sound and shock waves.
2. A sudden sharp, explosive noise.
3. A sudden, violent expression, as of emotion.
4. The act of emerging violently from limits or restraints.

expose *verb*
1. To lay open, as to something undesirable or injurious: *Cracks around the windows exposed us to a frigid draft.*
2. To make visible; bring to view.
3. To make bare.
4. To disclose in a breach of confidence.
5. To make a public and usu. ostentatious show of.

exposé *noun*
Something disclosed, esp. something not previously known or realized.

exposed *adjective*
1. Without the usual covering.
2. Having no protecting or concealing cover.

exposition *noun*
1. A large public display, as of goods, works of art, etc.
2. Something that serves to explain or clarify.

expositive *adjective*
Serving to explain.

expository *adjective*
Serving to explain.

expostulate *verb*
To express opposition by argument.

expostulation *noun*
The act of expressing strong or reasoned opposition.

exposure *noun*
The condition of being laid open to something undesirable or injurious: *exposure to ridicule.*

expound *verb*
To make understandable.

---

5. *Syns:* mushroom, snowball.

6. DISCREDIT *verb*.

1. USE *verb*.
2. ABUSE *verb*.
3. MANIPULATE.

FEAT.

EASY.

Syns: investigation, probe, reconnaissance.

Syns: delve (into), dig (into), inquire (*also* enquire) (into), investigate, look into, probe, reconnoiter, scout[1].

1. BLAST *noun*.

2. REPORT *noun*.
3. OUTBURST.
4. ERUPTION.

1. *Syns:* subject, uncover. —*Idiom* open the door to.

2. REVEAL.
3. BARE *verb*.
4. BETRAY.
5. DISPLAY *verb*.

REVELATION.

1. BARE *adjective*.
2. OPEN *adjective*.

1. EXHIBITION.
2. EXPLANATION.

EXPLANATORY.

EXPLANATORY.

OBJECT[2].

OBJECTION.

Syns: liability, openness, susceptibility, vulnerability, vulnerableness.

EXPLAIN.

express *verb*

1. To give expression to, as by gestures, facial aspects, or bodily posture: *a smirk that expressed smug self-satisfaction; expressing indifference with a shrug.*
2. To put into words.
3. To utter publicly.
4. To convey in language or words of a particular form.
5. To extract from by applying pressure.

1. **Syns:** communicate, convey, display, manifest.

2. SAY *verb.*
3. AIR *verb.*
4. PHRASE *verb.*

5. SQUEEZE *verb.*

express *adjective*

1. Clearly, fully, and sometimes emphatically expressed.
2. Fixed and distinct from others.

1. DEFINITE.

2. SPECIFIC.

expression *noun*

1. The act or an instance of expressing in words: *His views found expression in a series of essays.*
2. Something that takes the place of words in communicating a thought or feeling: *squeezed her hand as an expression of affection.*
3. A word or group of words forming a unit and conveying meaning: *used an idiomatic expression.*
4. Vivid, effective, or persuasive communication in speech or artistic performance.
5. A disposition of the facial features that conveys meaning, feeling, or mood: *Her kindly expression showed that we were not to take her harsh words too seriously.*

1. **Syns:** articulation, statement, utterance, vent, voice.
2. **Syns:** gesture, indication, sign, token.

3. **Syns:** locution, phrase.

4. ELOQUENCE.

5. **Syns:** aspect, cast, countenance, face, look, visage.

expressionless *adjective*

Lacking expression: *the expressionless face of the weary cashier.*

Syns: blank, deadpan (*Slang*), inexpressive, pokerfaced.

expressive *adjective*

Effectively conveying meaning, feeling, or mood: *expressive hands; an expressive gesture.*

Syns: eloquent, meaning, meaningful, significant.

expressiveness *noun*

Vivid, effective, or persuasive communication in speech or artistic performance.

ELOQUENCE.

expressivity *noun*

Vivid, effective, or persuasive communication in speech or artistic performance.

ELOQUENCE.

expropriate *verb*

To take quick and forcible possession of.

SEIZE.

expropriation *noun*

The act of taking quick and forcible possession of.

SEIZURE.

expunction *noun*

The act of erasing or the condition of being erased.

ERASURE.

expunge *verb*

To remove or invalidate by or as if by running a line through or wiping clean.

CANCEL.

expurgate *verb*

1. To examine (material) and remove parts considered harmful or improper for publication or transmission.
2. To free from sin, guilt, or defilement.

1. CENSOR.

2. PURIFY.

expurgation *noun*

A freeing from sin, guilt, or defilement.

PURIFICATION.

expurgatorial *adjective*

SEE **expurgatory.**

expurgatory also **expurgatorial** *adjective*

Serving to purify of sin.

PURGATIVE.

exquisite *adjective*

1. Appealing to refined taste.
2. Of such tasteful beauty as to elicit admiration.

1. DELICATE.
2. ELEGANT.

exsiccate *verb*
To make or become free of moisture.   DRY *verb.*

extant *adjective*
1. Having existence or life.   1. ALIVE.
2. Occurring or existing in act or fact.   2. ACTUAL.

extemporaneous *adjective*
Spoken, performed, or composed with little or no   *Syns:* ad-lib (*Informal*), extemporary,
preparation or forethought: *added a few*   extempore, impromptu, improvised,
extemporaneous remarks to his prepared speech;   offhand, off-the-cuff (*Informal*), snap,
extemporaneous decisions.   spur-of-the-moment, unrehearsed.

extemporary *adjective*
Spoken, performed, or composed with little or no   EXTEMPORANEOUS.
preparation or forethought.

extempore *adjective*
Spoken, performed, or composed with little or no   EXTEMPORANEOUS.
preparation or forethought.

extemporization *noun*
Something improvised.   IMPROVISATION.

extemporize *verb*
To compose or recite without preparation.   IMPROVISE.

extend *verb*
1. To make or become more comprehensive or   1. *Syns:* broaden, expand, widen.
   inclusive: *extended the nation's boundaries; extended*
   the right to vote to include all adult citizens.
2. To move or arrange so as to cover a larger area.   2. SPREAD *verb.*
3. To make or become longer.   3. LENGTHEN.
4. To make or become greater or larger.   4. INCREASE *verb.*
5. To put before another for acceptance.   5. OFFER *verb.*
6. To proceed on a certain course or for a certain   6. *Syns:* carry, go, lead, reach, run,
   distance: *The coast extends northward from here.*   stretch.
   God's love extends to the smallest creatures.
7. To change or fluctuate within limits.   7. GO *verb.*

extended *adjective*
1. Having great physical length.   1. LONG[1] *adjective.*
2. Large in expanse.   2. BROAD.
3. Covering a wide scope.   3. GENERAL.

extendible *adjective*
Capable of being extended or expanded.   EXTENSIBLE.

extensible *adjective*
Capable of being extended or expanded: *an extensible*   *Syns:* expansible, expansile, extendible,
ladder; a frog's extensible tongue.   extensile, stretch, stretchable.

extensile *adjective*
Capable of being extended or expanded.   EXTENSIBLE.

extension *noun*
1. The act of making something longer or the   1. *Syns:* elongation, production (*Geom.*),
   condition of being made longer: *the extension of the*   prolongation, protraction.
   ladder.
2. The act of increasing in dimensions, scope, or   2. EXPANSION.
   inclusiveness.
3. An area within which something or someone exists,   3. RANGE *noun.*
   acts, or has influence or power.
4. A part added to a main structure: *building an*   4. *Syns:* annex, arm, wing.
   extension to the library.

extensive *adjective*
1. Large in expanse.   1. BROAD *adjective.*
2. Covering a wide scope.   2. GENERAL.
3. Notably above average in amount, size, or scope.   3. BIG *adjective.*

extent *noun*
1. The measure of how far or long something goes in   1. *Syns:* length, reach, span, stretch.
   space, time, or degree: *the indefinite extent of outer*
   space; was at fault to a considerable extent.

2. The amount of space occupied by something.　　2. SIZE.

3. An area within which something or someone exists, acts, or has influence or power.　　3. RANGE *noun*.

4. The quality or state of being large in amount, extent, or importance.　　4. SIZE.

5. Relative intensity or amount, as of a quality or attribute.　　5. DEGREE.

extenuate *verb*

1. To conceal or make light of a fault or offense: *a breach of trust that could be neither forgiven nor extenuated*.　　1. **Syns:** gloss over, gloze over, palliate, whitewash.

2. *Archaic*. To make physically thin or thinner.　　2. THIN *verb*.

exteriorize *verb*

To represent (an abstraction) in or as if in bodily form.　　EMBODY.

exterminate *verb*

To destroy all traces of.　　ANNIHILATE.

extermination *noun*

Utter destruction.　　ANNIHILATION.

externalize *verb*

To represent (an abstraction) in or as if in bodily form.　　EMBODY.

extinct *adjective*

1. No longer alive.　　1. DEAD *adjective*.

2. No longer in use, force, or operation.　　2. VANISHED.

extinction *noun*

1. The act or fact of dying.　　1. DEATH.

2. Utter destruction.　　2. ANNIHILATION.

extinguish *verb*

1. To cause to stop burning or giving light: *extinguished the fire with a pail of water; extinguished all lamps*.　　1. **Syns:** douse, put out, quench, snuff[2] (out).

2. To bring to an end forcibly as if by imposing a heavy weight.　　2. SUPPRESS.

3. To destroy all traces of.　　3. ANNIHILATE.

extinguishment *noun*

1. An often formal act of putting an end to.　　1. ABOLITION.

2. Utter destruction.　　2. ANNIHILATION.

extirpate *verb*

To destroy all traces of.　　ANNIHILATE.

extirpation *noun*

Utter destruction.　　ANNIHILATION.

extol *verb*

1. To pay tribute or homage to.　　1. HONOR *verb*.

2. To honor (God) in religious worship.　　2. PRAISE *verb*.

extort *verb*

To obtain by coercion or intimidation: *bullies who extort money and favors from smaller children*.　　**Syns:** exact, gouge, shake down (*Informal*), squeeze, wrench, wrest, wring.

extra *adjective*

1. Being an addition.　　1. ADDITIONAL.

2. Being more than is needed, desired, or appropriate.　　2. SUPERFLUOUS.

extra *adverb*

To a high degree.　　VERY *adverb*.

extract *verb*

1. To collect (something) bit by bit.　　1. GLEAN.

2. To remove from a fixed position.　　2. PULL *verb*.

extraction *noun*

One's ancestors or their character.　　ANCESTRY.

extramundane *adjective*

Of, coming from, or relating to forces or beings that exist outside the natural world.　　SUPERNATURAL.

extraneous *adjective*

1. Not part of the essential nature of a thing.　　1. FOREIGN.

2. Not relevant or pertinent to the subject; not applicable.

2. IRRELEVANT.

extraordinarily *adverb*
In a manner or to a degree that is unusual.

UNUSUALLY.

extraordinary *adjective*
Far beyond what is usual, normal, or customary.

RARE.

extrasensory *adjective*
Of, coming from, or relating to forces or beings that exist outside the natural world.

SUPERNATURAL.

extravagance also **extravagancy** *noun*
1. Excessive or imprudent expenditure: *a small income that made comfort difficult and extravagance impossible.*
2. Something costly and unnecessary.

1. **Syns:** lavishness, prodigality, profligacy, squander, waste, wastefulness.
2. LUXURY.

extravagancy *noun*

SEE **extravagance.**

extravagant *adjective*
1. Characterized by excessive or imprudent spending: *an extravagant fellow who soon squandered his fortune.*
2. Exceeding a normal or reasonable limit.
3. Given to or marked by unrestrained abundance.

1. **Syns:** lavish, prodigal, profligate, spendthrift, wasteful.
2. EXCESSIVE.
3. PROFUSE.

extravasate *verb*
Geol. To send forth (confined matter) violently.

ERUPT.

extreme *adjective*
1. Most distant or remote from a center: *comets whose orbits reach the extreme limits of the solar system.*

2. Of the greatest or highest degree: *taking extreme care; extreme heat.*
3. Holding esp. political views that deviate drastically and fundamentally from conventional or traditional beliefs: *the party of the extreme right.*

4. Exceeding a normal or reasonable limit.

1. **Syns:** farthermost, farthest, furthermost, furthest, outermost, outmost, ultimate, utmost, uttermost.
2. **Syns:** utmost, uttermost.
3. **Syns:** extremist, fanatical (*also* fanatic), far-out (*Slang*), rabid, radical, revolutionary, ultra.
   Near-ants: conservative, moderate, restrained, sensible, sound.
4. EXCESSIVE.

extreme *noun*
1. Either of the two points at the ends of a spectrum or range: *experienced the extremes of joy and despair.*
2. The ultimate point to which an action, thought, discussion, or policy is carried.

1. **Syns:** extremity, limit.

2. LENGTH.

extremist *noun*
One who holds extreme views or advocates extreme measures: *Extremists of both the left and right opposed a moderate solution.*

Syns: fanatic, radical, revolutionary (*also* revolutionist), ultra.

extremist *adjective*
Holding esp. political views that deviate drastically and fundamentally from conventional or traditional beliefs.

EXTREME *adjective.*

extremity *noun*
1. Either of the two points at the ends of a spectrum or range.
2. A highly volatile, dangerous situation requiring immediate remedial action.

1. EXTREME *noun.*

2. CRISIS.

extricate *verb*
To free from an entanglement.

CLEAR *verb.*

extrinsic *adjective*
Not part of the essential nature of a thing.

FOREIGN.

extroverted *adjective*
Disposed to be open, sociable, and talkative.

OUTGOING.

exuberant *adjective*
1. Full of joyful, unrestrained high spirits: *bright and varied colors that expressed her exuberant personality.*

    1. ***Syns:*** ebullient, effervescent, high-spirited, sparkling, vivacious.

2. Given to or marked by unrestrained abundance.

    2. PROFUSE.

exude *verb*
To flow or leak out slowly.

    OOZE.

exult *verb*
1. To feel or express an uplifting joy over a success or victory: *The victorious army exulted in its capture of the town.*

    1. ***Syns:*** crow, glory, jubilate, triumph.

2. To feel or take joy or pleasure.

    2. REJOICE.

exultance also **exultancy** *noun*
The act or condition of feeling an uplifting joy over a success or victory.

    EXULTATION.

exultancy *noun*

    SEE **exultance.**

exultant *adjective*
Feeling or expressing an uplifting joy over a success or victory: *The goal posts were torn down by exultant spectators after the game.*

    Syns: jubilant, triumphant.

exultation *noun*
The act or condition of feeling an uplifting joy over a success or victory: *The winning candidate's headquarters was full of the exultation of victory.*

    Syns: exultance (*also* exultancy), jubilance, jubilation, triumph.

exuviate *verb*
Zool. To cast off by natural process.

    SHED.

eye *noun*
1. An organ of vision: *She has blue eyes.*

    1. ***Syns:*** blinker (*Slang*), orb (*Poetic*).

2. An act of directing the eyes on an object.

    2. LOOK *noun.*

3. The act of observing, often for an extended time.

    3. WATCH *noun.*

4. Skill in perceiving, discriminating, or judging.

    4. DISCERNMENT.

5. *Informal.* A person whose work is investigating crimes or obtaining hidden evidence or information.

    5. DETECTIVE.

6. A length of line folded over and joined at the ends so as to form a curve or circle.

    6. LOOP *noun.*

7. The most intensely active central part.

    7. THICK *noun.*

eye *verb*
1. To direct the eyes on an object.

    1. LOOK *verb.*

2. To look at or on attentively or carefully.

    2. WATCH *verb.*

3. To look intently and fixedly.

    3. GAZE *verb.*

eye-catching *adjective*
Readily attracting notice.

    NOTICEABLE.

eyeless *adjective*
Without the sense of sight.

    BLIND *adjective.*

eye opener *noun*
Something disclosed, esp. something not previously known or realized.

    REVELATION.

eyes *noun*
1. The faculty of seeing.

    1. VISION.

2. The position from which something is observed or considered.

    2. POINT OF VIEW.

eyesight *noun*
The faculty of seeing.

    VISION.

eyewash *noun*
Something that does not have or make sense.

    NONSENSE.

eyewitness *noun*
Someone who sees something occur.

    WITNESS.

F

fable *noun*
1. A narrative not based on fact.
2. A traditional story or tale dealing with ancestors, heroes, supernatural events, etc., that has no proven factual basis but attempts to explain beliefs, practices, or natural phenomena.
3. An entertaining and often oral account of a real or fictitious occurrence.

1. FICTION.
2. MYTH.

3. YARN.

fabric *noun*
A distinctive, complex underlying pattern or structure.

TEXTURE.

fabricate *verb*
1. To create by forming, combining, or altering materials.
2. To use ingenuity in making, developing, or achieving.
3. To impart a false character to (something) by alteration.

1. MAKE.

2. INVENT.

3. FAKE *verb*.

fabricator *noun*
One who tells lies.

LIAR.

fabulous *adjective*
1. So remarkable as to elicit disbelief: *the fabulous endurance of a marathon runner.*

2. Of or existing only in myths.
3. *Informal.* Particularly excellent.

1. **Syns:** amazing, astonishing, astounding, fantastic (*also* fantastical), incredible, marvelous (*also* marvellous), miraculous, phenomenal, prodigious, stupendous, unbelievable, wonderful, wondrous.
2. MYTHICAL.
3. MARVELOUS.

façade *also* **facade** *noun*
1. *Archit.* The forward outer surface of a building: *the famous façade of the Supreme Court building.*
2. A deceptive outward appearance: *put on a façade of respectability.*

1. **Syns:** face, front, frontage, frontal, frontispiece (*Archit.*).
2. **Syns:** cloak, color, coloring, cover, disguise, disguisement, face, front, gloss, guise, mask, masquerade, pretense, pretext, put-on (*Slang*), semblance, show, veil, veneer, window-dressing (*also* window dressing).
   —*Idiom* false colors.

face *noun*
1. The front surface of the head: *turned her face toward the camera; cattle with white faces.*

2. A disposition of the facial features that conveys meaning, feeling, or mood.
3. A facial contortion indicating displeasure, disgust, pain, etc.: *made a face at the teacher.*

4. An outward appearance: *The face of the city has changed.*
5. A deceptive outward appearance.
6. The forward outer surface of a building.
7. The outer layer covering something: *the face of the earth.*

1. **Syns:** countenance, features, kisser (*Slang*), map (*Slang*), mug (*Slang*), muzzle, pan (*Slang*), puss (*Slang*), visage.
2. EXPRESSION.

3. **Syns:** grimace, mop (*Archaic*), moue, mouth, mow (*also* mowe), mug (*Slang*). —*Idiom* wry face (*or* mouth).
4. **Syns:** aspect, countenance, look, physiognomy, surface, view, visage.
5. FAÇADE.
6. FAÇADE.
7. **Syns:** surface, top.

8. The marked outer surface of an instrument: *the face of a clock.*

8. *Syn:* dial.

9. The level of credit or respect at which one is regarded by others: *They hushed up the scandal to save face.*

9. *Syns:* prestige, standing, status.

10. Excessive and arrogant self-confidence.

10. PRESUMPTION.

face *verb*

1. To have the face or front turned in a specific direction: *Face the class. The house faces the ocean.*

1. *Syns:* front, look on (*or* upon).

2. To come up against.

2. ENCOUNTER *verb*.

3. To meet face-to-face, esp. defiantly.

3. CONFRONT.

4. To confront boldly and courageously.

4. DEFY.

5. To furnish with a covering of a different material: *a house faced with rock veneer.*

5. *Syns:* clad, sheathe, side, skin.

facelift *noun*

SEE **face lifting**.

face lifting also **facelift** *noun*

The act of making new or as if new again.

RENEWAL.

face-off *noun*

A face-to-face, usu. hostile meeting.

CONFRONTATION.

facet *noun*

The particular angle from which something is considered.

PHASE.

facetious *adjective*

Intended to excite laughter or amusement.

HUMOROUS.

facile *adjective*

1. Exhibiting or possessing skill and ease in performance.

1. DEXTEROUS.

2. Moving or performing quickly, lightly, and easily.

2. NIMBLE.

3. Posing no difficulty.

3. EASY.

4. Characterized by ready but often insincere or superficial discourse.

4. GLIB.

facileness *noun*

The ability to perform without apparent effort.

EASE *noun*.

facilitate *verb*

To make less difficult.

EASE *verb*.

facility *noun*

1. The ability to perform without apparent effort.

1. EASE *noun*.

2. Ready skill in expression.

2. FLUENCY.

3. Anything that increases physical comfort.

3. AMENITY.

facsimile *noun*

1. Something closely resembling another.

1. COPY *noun*.

2. A representation of a person or thing.

2. LIKENESS.

fact *noun*

1. Something having real, demonstrable existence: *distinguish between fact and fiction.*

1. *Syns:* event, phenomenon.

2. The quality of being factual.

2. ACTUALITY.

3. One of the conditions or facts attending an event and having some bearing on it.

3. CIRCUMSTANCE.

faction *noun*

A group of individuals united in a common cause.

COMBINE *noun*.

factitious *adjective*

Marked by unnaturalness, pretension, and often a slavish love of fads.

PLASTIC.

factor *noun*

1. One of the conditions or facts attending an event and having some bearing on it.

1. CIRCUMSTANCE.

2. One of the individual entities contributing to a whole.

2. ELEMENT.

facts *noun*

Knowledge about a specific subject or situation.

INFORMATION.

factual *adjective*
Based on fact.   ACTUAL.

factuality *noun*
The quality of being factual.   ACTUALITY.

factualness *noun*
The quality of being factual.   ACTUALITY.

facultative *adjective*
Not compulsory or automatic.   OPTIONAL.

faculty *noun*
1. Conferred power: *The states now have the faculty to redefine their penal codes.*
2. Physical, mental, financial, or legal power to perform.
3. An innate capability.

1. **Syns:** authority, competence (*also* competency) (*Law*), right.
2. ABILITY.
3. TALENT.

facund *adjective*
Fluently persuasive and forceful.   ELOQUENT.

facundity *noun*
Vivid, effective, or persuasive communication in speech or artistic performance.   ELOQUENCE.

facy *adjective*
Brit. Regional. Rude and disrespectful.   IMPUDENT.

fad *noun*
The current custom.   FASHION *noun.*

fade *verb*
1. To lose strength or power: *His health and vitality faded after fifty.*

1. **Syns:** decline, deteriorate, fail, fizzle (out) (*Informal*), flag[2], languish, wane, waste (away), weaken. —*Idioms* go downhill, hit the skids, sink into a decline.

2. To pass out of sight either gradually or suddenly.
3. To become inaudible: *The sound of his footsteps gradually faded.*
4. To disappear gradually by or as if by dispersal of particles: *The rainbow faded. The riders faded into the distance. Our hopes for peace are fading.*

2. DISAPPEAR.
3. **Syns:** die (away, out, *or* down), fade out.
4. **Syns:** dissolve, melt (away). —*Idiom* do a fade-out.

fade *noun*
Motion Pic.&T.V. The gradual disappearance, esp. of a film image.   FADE-OUT at **fade out.**

fadeaway *noun*
Motion Pic.&T.V. The gradual disappearance, esp. of a film image.   FADE-OUT at **fade out.**

faded *adjective*
Showing signs of wear and tear or neglect.   SHABBY.

fade-out *noun*   SEE **fade out.**

fade out *verb*
1. *Motion Pic.&T.V.* To make (a film image) disappear gradually: *The camera faded out the last shot.*
2. To become inaudible.

1. **Syn:** dissolve (*Motion Pic.&T.V.*).
2. FADE *verb.*

fade-out *noun*
1. *Motion Pic.&T.V.* The gradual disappearance, esp. of a film image: *ended the love scene with a classic fade-out.*
2. The act or an example of passing out of sight.

1. **Syns:** dissolve (*Motion Pic.&T.V.*), fade (*Motion Pic.&T.V.*), fadeaway (*Motion Pic.&T.V.*).
2. DISAPPEARANCE.

fag *noun*
Physical exertion that is usu. difficult and exhausting.   LABOR *noun.*

fag *verb*
1. To exert one's mental or physical powers, usu. under difficulty and to the point of exhaustion.
2. *Slang.* To make extremely tired.

1. LABOR *verb.*
2. EXHAUST.

fagged *adjective*
Slang. Extremely tired.   EXHAUSTED.

fail *verb*
1. To prove deficient or insufficient: *The heating-oil supply failed in mid-winter.*
2. To be unsuccessful: *The attack failed.*

3. To lose strength or power.
4. To undergo sudden financial failure.
5. To cease functioning properly: *The brakes failed.*
6. To make or become unusable or inoperative.
7. To receive less than a passing grade: *failed the course.*
8. To not do (something necessary): *The defendant failed to appear in court. You have failed to meet your payments.*

failing *noun*
A liking or personal preference for something.

fail-safe *adjective*
Designed so as to be impervious to human error or misuse.

failure *noun*
1. The condition of not achieving the desired end: *the candidate's failure to win the election.*
2. One that fails completely: *The play was a failure. I am a failure as a writer.*

3. The condition or fact of being deficient.
4. A cessation of proper mechanical functions: *a power failure.*
5. Nonperformance of what ought to be done: *Failure to pay taxes can result in a stiff fine.*
6. A marked loss of strength or effectiveness: *experienced failure of physical stamina in his later years.*
7. The condition of being financially insolvent: *bank failures in 1929.*

fain *adjective*
Archaic. Disposed to accept or agree.

fainéance *noun*

fainéancy also **fainéance** *noun*
The quality or state of being lazy.

fainéant *adjective*
Resistant to exertion and activity.

fainéant *noun*
A self-indulgent person who spends time avoiding work or other useful activity.

faint *adjective*
1. So lacking in strength as to be barely audible: *faint cries for help.*

2. Not clearly perceived or perceptible.
3. Free from severity or violence, as in movement.

faint *verb*
To suffer temporary loss of consciousness.

faint *noun*
A temporary loss of consciousness.

faint-hearted *adjective*
Ignobly lacking in courage.

1. **Syns:** give out, run out. —*Idioms* fall (*or* run) short, run dry.
2. **Syns:** fall down (*Informal*), fall through, flop (*Informal*), flummox (*Slang*). —*Idioms* fail of success, fall short of success.
3. FADE *verb*.
4. COLLAPSE *verb*.
5. **Syns:** break down, conk out, give out.
6. BREAK *verb*.
7. **Syns:** flunk (*Informal*), wash out (of).
8. **Syns:** default, neglect, omit.

WEAKNESS.

FOOLPROOF.

1. **Syns:** insuccess, unsuccess, unsuccessfulness.
2. **Syns:** bomb (*Slang*), bust (*Slang*), dud (*Informal*), fiasco, flop (*Informal*), lemon (*Informal*), loser, washout.
3. SHORTAGE.
4. **Syns:** breakdown, outage.
5. **Syns:** default, delinquency, dereliction, neglect, nonfeasance (*Law*), omission.
6. **Syns:** declination, decline, deterioration, ebbing, weakening.
7. **Syns:** bankruptcy, bust (*Slang*), insolvency.

WILLING.

SEE **fainéancy.**

LAZINESS.

LAZY.

WASTREL.

1. **Syns:** feeble, muted, weak.
   Near-syns: hushed, inaudible, low, muffled, soft, stifled, thin.
   Ants: clear, loud, strong.
2. UNCLEAR.
3. GENTLE *adjective*.

BLACK OUT.

BLACKOUT at **black out.**

COWARDLY.

faint-heartedness   *noun*
Ignoble lack of courage.

COWARDICE.

faintly   *adverb*
In a barely audible way: *whispered faintly from her sickbed.*

Syns: feebly, weakly.

fair   *adjective*
1. Having light hair: *Mother and daughter are very fair.*
2. Of a moderately white color: *fair skin.*

3. Having qualities that delight the eye.
4. Free from clouds, mist, etc.
5. Indicative of future success.
6. Neither favorable nor unfavorable: *had a fair chance to survive.*
7. Free from bias in judgment: *a fair judge.*

1. *Syns:* blond (*also* blonde), fair-haired, towheaded.
2. *Syns:* alabaster (*also* alabastrine), albescent, ivory, light[1], pale.
3. BEAUTIFUL.
4. CLEAR *adjective.*
5. FAVORABLE.
6. *Syns:* balanced, even[1], fifty-fifty (*Informal*), sporting (*Informal*).
7. *Syns:* dispassionate, equitable, fair-minded, impartial, indifferent, just, liberal, nonpartisan, objective, square, unbiased, unprejudiced. —*Idiom* fair and square.
   Near-ants: biased, partial, partisan, prejudicial; unjust.
   Ant: unfair.

8. Just to all parties.
9. According to the rules.
10. Of moderately good quality but less than excellent.

8. EQUAL *adjective.*
9. SPORTSMANLIKE.
10. ACCEPTABLE.

fair   *adverb*
In a fair, sporting manner: *play fair.*

Syns: cleanly, correctly, fairly, properly.

fair-haired   *adjective*
1. Having light hair.
2. Given special, usu. doting treatment.

1. FAIR *adjective.*
2. FAVORITE *adjective.*

fairish   *adjective*
Of moderately good quality but less than excellent.

ACCEPTABLE.

fairly   *adverb*
1. In a just way: *settled the dispute fairly.*
2. In a fair, sporting manner.
3. In truth.
4. To some extent: *felt fairly well but not terrific.*

1. *Syns:* dispassionately, equitably, justly.
2. FAIR *adverb.*
3. REALLY.
4. *Syns:* pretty, rather. —*Idiom* more or less.

fair-minded   *adjective*
Free from bias in judgment.

FAIR *adjective.*

fair-mindedness   *noun*
The quality or state of being just and unbiased.

FAIRNESS.

fairness   *noun*
The quality or state of being just and unbiased: *a judge noted for his scrupulous fairness.*

Syns: detachment, disinterest, disinterestedness, dispassion, dispassionateness, equitableness, fair-mindedness, impartiality, justice, justness, nonpartisanship, objectiveness, objectivity.

faith   *noun*
1. Those who accept and practice a particular religious belief: *All faiths participated in the ecumenical service.*
2. A system of religious belief.
3. Absolute certainty in the trustworthiness of another.
4. Mental acceptance of the truth or actuality of something.

1. *Syns:* church, communion, creed, denomination, persuasion, sect.

2. RELIGION.
3. CONFIDENCE.
4. BELIEF.

faithful   *adjective*
1. Adhering firmly and devotedly, as to a person, a cause, or a duty: *a faithful party member; a faithful spouse.*

1. *Syns:* allegiant, constant, fast, firm[1], loyal, liege, resolute, staunch, steadfast, steady, true.

2. Conforming to fact.
3. Not deviating from correctness, accuracy, or completeness.
4. Worthy of belief because of precision, faithfulness to an original, etc.

faithless *adjective*
Not true to duty or obligation: *a faithless spouse; a faithless quisling.*

faithlessness *noun*
Betrayal, esp. of a moral obligation: *the faithlessness of a cheating spouse.*

fake *verb*
1. To impart a false character to (something) by alteration: *fake the results of an experiment.*
2. To make a fraudulent copy of.
3. *Slang.* To compose or recite without preparation.
4. To contrive and present as genuine: *You're not really hurt; you're faking.*

5. To behave affectedly or insincerely.
6. To take on or give a false appearance of.

fake *noun*
1. One who is not what he claims to be: *He's not a doctor; he's a fake.*

2. A fraudulent imitation.

fake *adjective*
Fraudulently or deceptively imitative.

faker *noun*
One who is not what he claims to be.

fall *verb*
1. To move downward in response to gravity: *Apples fell from the tree.*
2. To slope downward.
3. To go from a more erect posture to a less erect posture.
4. To come to the ground suddenly and involuntarily: *I stumbled and fell.*

5. To undergo a sharp, rapid descent in value or price: *That stock fell 40 points in one day of trading.*

6. To become less active or intense.
7. To undergo capture, defeat, or ruin.
8. To undergo moral deterioration: *Society has fallen into decay. Lucifer is the fallen angel.*
9. To take place at a set time.
10. To come as by lot or inheritance: *Child support often falls to the father. The estate fell to the eldest son.*

Near-ants: disloyal, false, perfidious, traitorous, treacherous, treasonous; capricious, fickle, whimsical.
Ants: faithless, unfaithful.
2. ACCURATE.
3. CLOSE[1] *adjective.*

4. AUTHENTIC.

Syns: disloyal, false, false-hearted, perfidious, recreant, traitorous, treacherous, unfaithful, untrue.

Syns: disloyalty, falseness, falsity, infidelity, perfidiousness, perfidy, unfaithfulness.

1. **Syns:** fabricate, falsify, fictionalize.

2. COUNTERFEIT *verb.*
3. IMPROVISE.
4. **Syns:** feign, pretend, simulate.
   —*Idioms* make believe, make out like, put on an act.
5. ACT *verb.*
6. ASSUME.

1. **Syns:** charlatan, faker, fraud, humbug, impostor, mountebank, phony (*also* phoney) (*Informal*), pretender, quack.
   Near-syns: beguiler, deceiver, shyster, trickster; bluffer, cheat, four-flusher; imitator, mimic.
2. COUNTERFEIT *noun.*

COUNTERFEIT *adjective.*

FAKE *noun.*

1. **Syns:** descend, drop.

2. DROP *verb.*
3. DROP *verb.*

4. **Syns:** drop, go down, pitch, plunge, spill, sprawl, topple, tumble. —*Idiom* take a fall (*or* header *or* plunge *or* spill *or* tumble).

5. **Syns:** dip, dive, drop, nose-dive, plummet, plunge, sink, skid, slump, tumble. —*Idiom* take a sudden downturn (*or* downtrend).

6. SUBSIDE.
7. SURRENDER *verb.*
8. **Syns:** sink, slip, vitiate. —*Idiom* go bad (*or* wrong).
9. COME.
10. **Syns:** devolve, pass.

fall down *verb*
Informal. To be unsuccessful.

fall off *verb*
1. To slope downward.
2. To become less active or intense.
3. To decline, as in value or quantity, very gradually.

fall on (or **upon**) *verb*
To set upon with violent force.

fall through *verb*
To be unsuccessful.

fall *noun*
1. The act of dropping from a height: *the fall of Skylab to the earth.*
2. A sudden involuntary drop to the ground: *had a bad fall on the ice.*
3. A disastrous, overwhelming defeat or ruin: *the fall of the Iranian dynasty.*
4. A usu. swift downward trend, as in prices: *a fall in stock prices.*

5. A downward slope or distance.

fallacious *adjective*
1. Containing fundamental errors in reasoning: *a fallacious syllogism; fallacious logic.*

2. Containing an error or errors.
3. Tending to lead one into error: *the fallacious expectation that the streets were paved with gold.*

fallaciousness *noun*
An erroneous or false idea.

fallacy *noun*
1. An erroneous or false idea: *an educational philosophy grounded on fallacy.*

2. Plausible but invalid reasoning: *The fallacy of the hypothesis negates the conclusions.*

fallback *noun*

fall back *verb*
1. To move in a reverse direction.
2. To move back in the face of enemy attack or after a defeat.

fallback *noun*
The moving back of a military force in the face of enemy attack or after a defeat.

fall down *verb*

fall guy *noun*
Slang. One who is made an object of blame.

fallible *adjective*
Liable to err: *The President is fallible too.*

fall off *verb*

fall on (or **upon**) *verb*

fall through *verb*

false *adjective*
1. Devoid of truth: *The rumor is false.*

FAIL.

1. DROP.
2. SUBSIDE.
3. SLIP *verb*.

ATTACK *verb*.

FAIL.

1. **Syns:** descent, drop.

2. **Syns:** dive, header (*Slang*), nose-dive, pitch, plunge, spill, sprawl, tumble.

3. **Syns:** collapse, downfall, toppling, Waterloo.

4. **Syns:** decline, descent, dip, dive, downslide, downswing, downturn, drop, drop-off, plunge, skid, slide, slump, tumble.

5. DROP *noun*.

1. **Syns:** false, illogical, invalid, sophistic, specious, spurious.
   Near-syns: absurd, irrational, meaningless, unreasonable.
   Ants: sound, valid.

2. ERRONEOUS.
3. **Syns:** deceptive, delusive, delusory, misleading.

FALLACY.

1. **Syns:** erroneousness, error, fallaciousness, falsehood, falseness, falsity, untruth.

2. **Syns:** casuistry, equivocation, sophism, sophistry, speciousness, spuriousness.

SEE **fall back.**

1. BACK *verb*.
2. RETREAT *verb*.

RETREAT *noun*.

SEE **fall.**

SCAPEGOAT.

Syns: errable, errant.

SEE **fall.**

SEE **fall.**

SEE **fall.**

1. **Syns:** counterfactual, erroneous, inaccurate, incorrect, specious, truthless, unsound, untruthful, wrong.
   —*Idiom* way off the mark.
   Near-syns: deceptive, delusive,

2. Containing an error or errors.
3. Containing fundamental errors in reasoning.
4. Not true to duty or obligation.
5. Fraudulently or deceptively imitative.

false-hearted *adjective*
Not true to duty or obligation.

falsehood *noun*
1. An erroneous or false idea.
2. An untrue declaration.
3. The practice of lying.

falseness *noun*
1. An erroneous or false idea.
2. Betrayal, esp. of a moral obligation.

falsifier *noun*
One who tells lies.

falsify *verb*
1. To give an inaccurate view of by representing falsely or misleadingly.
2. To impart a false character to (something) by alteration.
3. To make untrue declarations.
4. To make a fraudulent copy of.

falsity *noun*
1. An erroneous or false idea.
2. Betrayal, esp. of a moral obligation.
3. An untrue declaration.

falter *verb*
1. To be irresolute in acting or doing.
2. To walk unsteadily.

faltering *adjective*
Given to or exhibiting hesitation.

fame *noun*
1. Wide recognition for one's deeds: *a star whose fame was worldwide.*

2. Unfavorable, usu. unsavory renown.

famed *adjective*
1. Widely known and esteemed.
2. Widely known and discussed.

familial *adjective*
Of or pertaining to the family or household.

familiar *adjective*
1. Having good knowledge of: *familiar with the roads here; familiar with that case.*

2. Occurring quite often.
3. Indicating intimacy and mutual trust.
4. Very closely associated: *familiar companions.*

5. Having or exhibiting excessive and arrogant self-confidence.

familiar *noun*
A person whom one knows well, likes, and trusts.

---

distorted, fallacious, misleading; dishonest, mendacious.
Ant: true.
2. ERRONEOUS.
3. FALLACIOUS.
4. FAITHLESS.
5. COUNTERFEIT *adjective*.

FAITHLESS.

1. FALLACY.
2. LIE² *noun*.
3. MENDACITY.

1. FALLACY.
2. FAITHLESSNESS.

LIAR.

1. DISTORT.

2. FAKE *verb*.

3. LIE² *verb*.
4. COUNTERFEIT *verb*.

1. FALLACY.
2. FAITHLESSNESS.
3. LIE² *noun*.

1. HESITATE.
2. LURCH *verb*.

HESITANT.

1. ***Syns:*** celebrity, famousness, notoriety, renown, reputation, repute.
Near-ants: disgrace, dishonor, disrepute, ignominy, odium, shame.
Ant: obscurity.
2. NOTORIETY.

1. EMINENT.
2. FAMOUS.

DOMESTIC.

1. ***Syns:*** acquainted, conversant, up on (*Informal*), versant, versed.
Near-syns: abreast, au courant, informed; aware, conscious, mindful.
Ant: unfamiliar.
2. COMMON *adjective*.
3. CONFIDENTIAL.
4. ***Syns:*** chummy (*Informal*), close¹, friendly, intimate¹, thick (*Informal*), tight (*Slang*). —*Idiom* hand and glove.
5. PRESUMPTUOUS.

FRIEND.

familiarity *noun*
1. Excessive and arrogant self-confidence.
2. Personal knowledge derived from participation or observation.

familiarize *verb*
Archaic. To make familiar through constant practice or use.

family *noun*
1. A group of people sharing common ancestry: *The British royal family includes descendants of Queen Victoria.*
2. A group of usu. related people living together as a unit: *a family of three.*
3. One's ancestors or their character.

family *adjective*
Of or pertaining to the family or household.

famished *adjective*
Desiring or craving food.

famous *adjective*
1. Widely known and discussed: *a famous newscaster.*

2. Widely known and esteemed.
3. *Archaic.* Known widely and unfavorably.

famousness *noun*
Wide recognition for one's deeds.

fan[1] *verb*
Slang. To examine the person or personal effects of in order to find something lost or concealed.

fan out *verb*
To move or arrange so as to cover a larger area.

fan[2] *noun*
1. *Informal.* One who ardently admires.
2. *Informal.* A person who is ardently devoted to a particular subject or activity.

fanatic *noun*
1. A person who is ardently devoted to a particular subject or activity.
2. One zealously devoted to a religion.
3. One who holds extreme views or advocates extreme measures.

fanatic *adjective*

fanatical also **fanatic** *adjective*
Holding esp. political views that deviate drastically and fundamentally from conventional or traditional beliefs.

fancied *adjective*
Existing only in the imagination.

fancier *noun*
One who ardently admires.

fanciful *adjective*
1. Appealing to fancy: *fanciful Baroque fountains in the park.*
2. Existing only in the imagination.
3. Consisting or suggestive of fiction.

fancy *noun*
1. An impulsive, often illogical turn of mind: *had a sudden fancy to take up hang gliding.*

1. PRESUMPTION.
2. ACQUAINTANCE.

ACCUSTOM.

1. *Syns:* clan, house, kindred, lineage, stock, tribe. —*Idioms* kith and kin, one's own flesh and blood.
2. *Syns:* house, household, ménage.
3. ANCESTRY.

DOMESTIC.

RAVENOUS.

1. *Syns:* famed, leading, notorious, popular, well-known.
Near-ants: obscure, unheard-of, unimportant, unpopular.
Ant: unknown.
2. EMINENT.
3. NOTORIOUS.

FAME.

SEARCH *verb.*

SPREAD *verb.*

1. ADMIRER.
2. ENTHUSIAST.

1. ENTHUSIAST.
2. DEVOTEE.
3. EXTREMIST.

SEE **fanatical.**

EXTREME *adjective.*

IMAGINARY.

ADMIRER.

1. *Syns:* fancy, fantastic (*also* fantastical), imaginative, whimsical.
2. IMAGINARY.
3. FICTITIOUS.

1. *Syns:* bee, boutade, caprice, conceit, freak, humor, impulse, megrim, notion, vagary, whim, whimsy (*also* whimsey). —*Idiom* bee in one's bonnet.

Near-syns: characteristic, foible, habit, mannerism, trait; mood, temper, vein.

2. The power of the mind to form images.   2. IMAGINATION.
3. An illusory mental image.   3. DREAM *noun.*
4. A desire for a particular thing or activity.   4. LIKING.
5. *Obs.* Deep and ardent affection.   5. ADORATION.

fancy *verb*
1. To form mental images of.   1. IMAGINE.
2. To find agreeable.   2. LIKE[1].

fancy *adjective*
1. Appealing to fancy.   1. FANCIFUL.
2. Complexly detailed.   2. ELABORATE *adjective.*
3. Catering to, used by, or admitting only the wealthy 3. EXCLUSIVE.
   or socially superior.

fancy-dress *adjective*
Requiring elegant clothes and fine manners.   FORMAL.

fanfaron *noun*
Obs. One given to boasting.   BRAGGART.

fanfaronade *noun*
An act of boasting.   BOAST *noun.*

fanny *noun*
Slang. The part of one's back on which one rests in BOTTOM *noun.*
sitting.

fan out *verb*   SEE **fan**[1].

fans *noun*
Informal. The body of persons who admire a public   PUBLIC *noun.*
personality, esp. an entertainer.

fantasize *verb*
1. To form mental images of.   1. IMAGINE.
2. To experience dreams or daydreams.   2. DREAM *verb.*

fantastic also **fantastical** *adjective*
1. Conceived or done with no reference to reality or   1. *Syns:* antic, bizarre, far-fetched,
   common sense: *a fantastic alibi.*   grotesque.
2. Existing only in the imagination.   2. IMAGINARY.
3. Appealing to fancy.   3. FANCIFUL.
4. Consisting or suggestive of fiction.   4. FICTITIOUS.
5. So remarkable as to elicit disbelief.   5. FABULOUS.
6. Following no predictable pattern.   6. CAPRICIOUS.
7. So senseless as to be laughable.   7. FOOLISH.

fantasy also **phantasy** *noun*
1. An illusory mental image.   1. DREAM *noun.*
2. A fantastic, impracticable plan or desire.   2. ILLUSION.
3. The power of the mind to form images.   3. IMAGINATION.
4. Any fictitious idea accepted as part of an ideology by 4. MYTH.
   an uncritical group; a received idea.

far *adjective*
Far from others in space, time, or relationship.   DISTANT.

far *adverb*
To a considerable extent.   CONSIDERABLY.

faraway *adjective*
1. Far from others in space, time, or relationship.   1. DISTANT.
2. So lost in thought as to be unaware of one's   2. ABSENT-MINDED.
   surroundings.

farce *noun*
A false, derisive, or impudent imitation of something. MOCKERY.

farcer *noun*   SEE **farceur.**

farceur also **farcer** *noun*
A person whose words or actions provoke or are   JOKER.
intended to provoke amusement or laughter.

farcical *adjective*
Deserving laughter.   LAUGHABLE.

fare   *verb*
1. To progress or perform adequately, esp. in difficult circumstances.
2. *Rare.* To take (food) into the body as nourishment.
3. *Archaic.* To move along a particular course.
fare   *noun*
Something fit to be eaten.
farewell   *adjective*
Of, done, given, or said on departing.
farewell   *noun*
A separation of two or more people.
far-fetched   *adjective*
Conceived or done with no reference to reality or common sense.
far-flung   *adjective*
Far from others in space, time, or relationship.
farness   *noun*
The fact or condition of being far removed or apart.
far-off   *adjective*
Far from others in space, time, or relationship.
far-out   *adjective*
Slang. Holding esp. political views that deviate drastically and fundamentally from conventional or traditional beliefs.
far-reaching   *adjective*
Covering a wide scope.
far-sighted   *adjective*
Characterized by foresight.
far-sightedness   *noun*
Unusual or creative discernment or perception.
farthermost   *adjective*
Most distant or remote from a center.
farthest   *adjective*
Most distant or remote from a center.
fascinate   *verb*
1. To compel the attention, interest, imagination, etc., of.
2. To please greatly or irresistibly.
fascinating   *adjective*
Pleasing to the eye or mind.
fascination   *noun*
The power or quality of attracting.
fashion   *noun*
1. The current custom: *Shorter dresses are now the fashion.*

2. A distinctive way of expressing oneself.
3. The manner in which something is done.
fashion   *verb*
1. To create by forming, combining, or altering materials.
2. To make or become suitable to a particular situation or use.
fashionable   *adjective*
Being or in accordance with the current fashion: *a fashionable fur; a fashionable little restaurant.*

1. MANAGE.

2. EAT.
3. GO *verb.*

FOOD.

PARTING *adjective.*

PARTING *noun.*

FANTASTIC.

DISTANT.

DISTANCE.

DISTANT.

EXTREME *adjective.*

GENERAL.

VISIONARY *adjective.*

VISION.

EXTREME *adjective.*

EXTREME *adjective.*

1. GRIP *verb.*

2. CHARM *verb.*

ATTRACTIVE.

ATTRACTION.

1. **Syns:** craze, cry, fad, furor, mode, rage, style, thing, ton, trend, vogue.
—*Idioms* the in thing, the last word, the latest thing.
Near-syns: bandwagon, drift; convention, form.
2. STYLE *noun.*
3. WAY.

1. MAKE.

2. ADAPT.

Syns: à la mode, chic, classy (*Slang*), dashing, in (*Slang*), modish, posh (*Informal*), sharp (*Slang*), smart, snappy (*Informal*), stylish, swank (*also swanky*), swish (*Chiefly Brit.*), tonish, tony (*also* toney), trendy (*Informal*), trig, with-it (*Slang*). —*Idioms* all the rage, right up to the minute.

fast *adjective*
1. Characterized by great celerity: *a fast freight train; a fast pace.*

1. **Syns:** breakneck, celeritous, fleet[1], hell-for-leather (*Informal*), quick, rapid, speedy, swift. —*Idioms* fleet as the wind, quick as lightning (*or* thought), swift as an arrow.

2. Accomplished in very little time.
3. Given to heedless, unrestrained pursuit of pleasure: *led a fast but short life devoted to booze, girls, and gambling.*
4. Sexually promiscuous.
5. Persistently holding to something.
6. Firmly settled or positioned.
7. Adhering firmly and devotedly, as to a person, a cause, or a duty.
8. Permanently resistive to fading: *a fast dye.*

2. QUICK.
3. **Syns:** dissolute, gay, rakehell, rakish, wild. —*Idiom* fast and loose.

4. WANTON *adjective.*
5. TIGHT *adjective.*
6. SURE.
7. FAITHFUL.

8. **Syn:** indelible.

fast *adverb*
1. In a firm way.
2. In a rapid way: *Run—fast! I need the statistics fast. The fire is spreading fast.*

1. TIGHT *adverb.*
2. **Syns:** apace, flat-out (*Informal*), hell-for-leather (*Informal*), lickety-split, posthaste, pronto (*Informal*), quick. —*Idioms* full tilt, in a flash, in nothing flat, lightning fast, like a bat out of hell, like a blue streak, like a flash, like a house on fire, like a shot, like a streak, like greased lightning, like wildfire.

fasten *verb*
1. To make secure: *fasten your seat belts.*

1. **Syns:** anchor, catch, fix, moor, secure. —*Idiom* make fast.

2. To join one thing to another.
3. To make fast or firmly fixed by means of a cord, rope, etc.
4. To implant so deeply as to make change nearly impossible.
5. To ascribe (a misdeed, error, etc.) to.

2. ATTACH.
3. TIE *verb.*

4. FIX *verb.*

5. FIX *verb.*

fastener *noun*
A device for fastening or for checking motion.

CATCH *noun.*

fastidious *adjective*
Very difficult to please.

NICE.

fastigium *noun*
The highest point.

HEIGHT.

fat *adjective*
1. Having too much flesh: *a fat person.*

1. **Syns:** corpulent, fatty, fleshy, gross, obese, overblown, overweight, porcine, portly, stout, weighty.
Near-ants: emaciated, gaunt, lanky, lean, scrawny, skinny, slender, slim.
Ant: thin.

2. Having the qualities of fat.
3. Affording profit.
4. *Slang.* Small in degree, esp. of probability.
5. Relatively great in extent from one surface to the opposite.

2. FATTY *adjective.*
3. PROFITABLE.
4. REMOTE.
5. THICK *adjective.*

fat *noun*
1. Adipose tissue: *soap made of animal fat.*

1. **Syn:** suet.

2. An amount or quantity beyond what is needed, desired, or appropriate.

2. SURPLUS *noun*.

fatal *adjective*
1. Causing ruin or destruction: *Trusting the enemy was a fatal error.*

2. Causing or tending to cause death.
3. So critically decisive as to affect the future.

1. *Syns:* calamitous, cataclysmic (*also* cataclysmal), catastrophic, destructive, disastrous, fateful, ruinous.
2. DEADLY.
3. FATEFUL.

fatality *noun*
1. The quality or condition of causing death: *The fatality of cancer is on the upswing.*
2. A termination of life, usu. as the result of an accident or a disaster: *ten fatalities in the crash.*

1. *Syns:* deadliness, lethality, lethalness, mortality.
2. *Syns:* casualty, death.

fate *noun*
1. That which is inevitably destined: *His fate was to become a king.*

1. *Syns:* destiny, kismet, lot, portion, predestination.
Near-ants: accident, chance, fortune, hap, happenstance, hazard, luck.

2. A predestined tragic end: *Execution is often the fate of dissidents.*

2. *Syns:* doom, foredoom (*Rare*).

fate *verb*
1. To determine the future of in advance: *The gods fated the ascendancy of Athens.*

1. *Syns:* destine, foredestine, foreordain, predestinate, predestine, predetermine, preordain.

2. To predestine to a tragic end: *This escape plan is fated to fail.*

2. *Syns:* doom, foredoom.

fated *adjective*
1. Governed and decided by or as if by fate: *his fated lot.*
2. Sentenced to terrible, irrevocable punishment.

1. *Syns:* destined, fateful, foreordained, predestined, predetermined.
2. CONDEMNED.

fateful *adjective*
1. So critically decisive as to affect the future: *the fateful Yalta Conference.*
2. Governed and decided by or as if by fate.
3. Causing ruin or destruction.
4. Portending future disaster: *fateful warnings of a nuclear holocaust.*

1. *Syns:* fatal, determinative, momentous.
2. FATED.
3. FATAL.
4. *Syns:* apocalyptic (*also* apocalyptical), baleful, baneful, dire, direful, doomful, fire-and-brimstone, grave^2, hellfire, ominous, unlucky.

father *noun*
1. A male parent: *He was the father of nine children. I have to ask Father.*
2. One that creates, founds, or originates.
3. A person from whom one is descended.

1. *Syns:* dad (*Informal*), daddy, sire.
2. ORIGINATOR.
3. ANCESTOR.

father *verb*
1. To be the biological father of: *a man who fathered nine children.*
2. To cause to come into existence.

1. *Syns:* beget, breed, get, procreate, sire.
2. PRODUCE.

fatherless *adjective*
Born out of wedlock.

ILLEGITIMATE.

fatherlike *adjective*
Like a father.

FATHERLY.

fatherly *adjective*
Like a father: *He took a fatherly interest in his late brother's children.*

Syns: fatherlike, paternal.

fathom *verb*
1. To perceive directly with the intellect.
2. To perceive and recognize the meaning of.

1. KNOW.
2. UNDERSTAND.

fathomable *adjective*
Capable of being readily understood.

UNDERSTANDABLE.

fatidic also **fatidical** *adjective*
Of or relating to the foretelling of events by or as if by supernatural means. PROPHETIC.

fatigue *noun*
The condition of being extremely tired. EXHAUSTION.

fatigue *verb*
To diminish the strength and energy of: *The long flight fatigued me.*

Syns: drain, tire, wear, wear down, wear out, weary.
Near-ants: assuage, refresh, rejuvenate, relieve, renew.

fatigued *adjective*
Extremely tired. EXHAUSTED.

fatiguing *adjective*
Causing fatigue. TIRING.

fatty *adjective*
1. Having the qualities of fat: *a fatty residue in the ham boiler.*
2. Having too much flesh.

1. *Syns:* fat, greasy, oily, oleaginous, unctuous.
2. FAT *adjective*.

fatuous *adjective*
Displaying a complete lack of forethought and good sense. MINDLESS.

fault *noun*
1. Something that mars the appearance or causes inadequacy or failure.
2. A liking or personal preference for something.
3. Responsibility for an error or crime.

1. DEFECT *noun*.
2. WEAKNESS.
3. BLAME *noun*.

fault *verb*
To find fault with. BLAME *verb*.

faultfinder *noun*
1. A person who finds fault, often severely and willfully.
2. A person who habitually complains or grumbles.

1. CRITIC.
2. GROUCH *noun*.

faultfinding *adjective*
Inclined to judge too severely. CRITICAL.

faultless *adjective*
1. Supremely excellent in quality or nature.
2. Free from guilt or blame.

1. PERFECT *adjective*.
2. INNOCENT *adjective*.

faulty *adjective*
Having a defect or defects. DEFECTIVE.

favor *noun*
1. A kindly act: *do a favor for a friend.*
2. Favorable regard.
3. A feeling of deference, approval, and liking.
4. A charitable deed.
5. Something beneficial.
6. Favorable, preferential bias: *curried favor with the congressman.*
7. An act requiring special generosity.

1. *Syns:* benefit (*Archaic*), grace, indulgence, kindness, service. —*Idiom* good turn.
2. ACCEPTANCE.
3. ESTEEM *noun*.
4. BENEVOLENCE.
5. ADVANTAGE *noun*.
6. *Syns:* favoritism, partiality, partialness, preference.
7. COURTESY.

favor *verb*
1. To perform a service or a courteous act.
2. To be favorably disposed toward.
3. To lend supportive approval to.
4. To be similar to, as in appearance: *John favors his father.*
5. To treat with inordinate gentleness and care: *The wounded soldier favored his right leg.*
6. To show partiality toward (someone): *The jurors seemed to favor the defendant. Some fathers favor sons over daughters.*

1. OBLIGE.
2. APPROVE.
3. ENCOURAGE.
4. *Syns:* feature (*Informal*), liken (to), resemble, take after.
5. *Syn:* spare. —*Idiom* handle (*or* treat) with kid gloves.
6. *Syn:* prefer. —*Idiom* play favorites.

7. To lend dignity or honor to by an act or favor.

7. GRACE *verb*.

favorable *adjective*
1. Indicative of future success: *a favorable economic climate for investment; favorable omens.*

1. *Syns:* auspicious, benign, bright, brilliant, fair, fortunate, good, propitious.
Near-ants: baleful, malign, sinister; calamitous, catastrophic, disastrous, fatal, ruinous, unlucky.
Ant: unfavorable.

2. Occurring at a fitting or advantageous time.
3. Affording benefit.
4. To one's liking.
5. Disposed to favor one over another: *We received favorable treatment after the payoff.*
6. Giving assent: *received a favorable reply to the request.*

2. OPPORTUNE.
3. BENEFICIAL.
4. AGREEABLE.
5. *Syns:* partial, preferential.

6. *Syns:* affirmative, affirmatory, assenting, positive.

favored *adjective*
1. Being a favorite.
2. Given special, usu. doting treatment.

1. FAVORITE *adjective*.
2. FAVORITE *adjective*.

favorite *adjective*
1. Given special, usu. doting treatment: *His favorite daughter could do no wrong.*

2. Being a favorite: *her favorite song.*

1. *Syns:* beloved, blue-eyed, darling, dear, fair-haired, favored, loved, pet¹, precious.
2. *Syns:* favored, popular, preferred, well-liked.

favorite *noun*
1. One liked or preferred above all others: *He is the current matinee favorite.*
2. A competitor regarded as the most likely winner: *the favorite in the Kentucky Derby.*

1. *Syns:* darling, pet¹. —*Idiom* apple of one's eye.
2. *Syns:* pot (*Brit. Slang*), shoo-in (*Informal*).

favoritism *noun*
Favorable, preferential bias.

FAVOR *noun*.

fawn *verb*
To support slavishly every opinion or suggestion of a superior: *an assistant who fawned on the president and fulfilled his every desire.*

Syns: apple-polish (*Informal*), bootlick, brown-nose (*Slang*), cotton, grovel, honey (up), kowtow, slaver, truckle. —*Idioms* curry favor, dance attendance, kiss someone's feet, lick someone's boots, slobber all over, suck up to.

faze *verb*
To cause (a person) to be self-consciously distressed.

EMBARRASS.

fealty *noun*
Faithfulness or devotion to a person, a cause, obligations, or duties.

FIDELITY.

fear *noun*
Great agitation and anxiety caused by the expectation or the realization of danger: *a fear of heights; felt great fear during the hijacking.*

Syns: affright (*Archaic*), alarm, consternation, dread, fearfulness, fright, funk², horror, panic, terror, trepidation. —*Idioms* cold feet (*or* sweat), fear and trembling.

fear *verb*
To be afraid of: *feared the steep climb; feared her attacker.*

Syns: apprehend, dread. —*Idioms* be in fear and trembling, have one's heart in one's mouth.

fearful *adjective*
1. Causing or able to cause fear: *spent a fearful night as a hostage; fearful stillness before the tornado.*

1. *Syns:* alarming, appalling, awful, dire, direful, dreadful, fearsome, formidable, frightening, frightful, ghastly, redoubtable, scary (*Informal*), terrible, tremendous.

2. Filled with fear or terror.

3. Very bad.

fearfulness *noun*

Great agitation and anxiety caused by the expectation or the realization of danger.

fearless *adjective*

Having or showing courage.

fearlessness *noun*

The quality of mind enabling one to face danger or hardship resolutely.

fearsome *adjective*

1. Causing or able to cause fear.

2. Filled with fear or terror.

feasible *adjective*

Capable of occurring or being done.

feast *noun*

A large meal elaborately prepared or served: *staged a traditional Hawaiian feast for the mainland visitors.*

feast *verb*

To be avidly interested in.

feat *noun*

1. A great or heroic deed: *acrobatic feats.*

2. Something completed successfully.

3. A clever, dexterous act.

feather *noun*

A class that is defined by the common attribute or attributes possessed by all its members.

featherbrained *adjective*

Given to lighthearted silliness.

featly *adjective*

Moving or performing quickly, lightly, and easily.

feature *noun*

1. A prominent article in a periodical: *a front-page feature on the assassination.*

2. A distinctive element.

feature *verb*

1. To accord emphasis to.

2. *Informal.* To be similar to, as in appearance.

3. *Informal.* To form mental images of.

features *noun*

The front surface of the head.

febrile *adjective*

Being at a higher temperature than is normal or desirable.

feckless *adjective*

1. Lacking or marked by a lack of care.

2. Lacking or showing a lack of a sense of responsibility.

fecund *adjective*

1. Capable of reproducing.

2. Characterized by great productivity.

fecundate *verb*

To make fertile.

fecundity *noun*

The quality or state of being fertile.

federate *verb*

To be formally associated, as by treaty.

---

2. AFRAID.

3. TERRIBLE.

FEAR *noun.*

BRAVE *adjective.*

COURAGE.

1. FEARFUL.

2. AFRAID.

POSSIBLE.

Syns: banquet, feed (*Informal*), junket, spread.

EAT UP at **eat.**

1. *Syns:* achievement, exploit, gest *or* geste (*Archaic*), masterstroke, stunt, tour de force (*French*).

2. ACCOMPLISHMENT.

3. TRICK *noun.*

KIND².

GIDDY.

NIMBLE.

1. *Syns:* lead (*Jour.*), leader (*Chiefly Brit.*). —*Idiom* feature story.

2. QUALITY *noun.*

1. EMPHASIZE.

2. FAVOR *verb.*

3. IMAGINE.

FACE *noun.*

HOT *adjective.*

1. CARELESS.

2. IRRESPONSIBLE.

1. FERTILE.

2. FERTILE.

FERTILIZE.

FERTILITY.

ALLY *verb.*

federated *adjective*
Closely connected by or as if by a treaty.   ALLIED.

federation *noun*
1. An association, esp. of nations for a common cause.   1. ALLIANCE.
2. A group of people united in a relationship and   2. UNION.
   having some interest, activity, or purpose in
   common.

fed up *adjective*
Out of patience with.   SICK.

fee *noun*
1. Payment for work done.   1. WAGE(S) *noun.*
2. A fixed amount of money charged for a privilege or   2. TOLL[1].
   service.

feeble *adjective*
1. So lacking in strength as to be barely audible.   1. FAINT *adjective.*
2. Not physically strong.   2. INFIRM.
3. Having little substance or significance; not solidly   3. TENUOUS.
   based.

feeble-minded *adjective*
1. Lacking in intelligence.   1. STUPID.
2. So senseless as to be laughable.   2. FOOLISH.

feebleness *noun*
The condition of being infirm or physically weak.   INFIRMITY.

feebly *adverb*
In a barely audible way.   FAINTLY.

feed *verb*
1. To sustain (a living organism) with food.   1. NOURISH.
2. To help bring about.   2. PROMOTE.
3. To maintain existence in a certain way.   3. LIVE[1].

feed *noun*
Informal. A large meal elaborately prepared or served.   FEAST.

feel *verb*
1. To be physically aware of through the senses: *felt a* 1. *Syns:* experience, have.
   sharp pain.
2. To bring into contact with, esp. by means of the   2. TOUCH *verb.*
   hands or fingers, so as to give or receive a physical
   sensation.
3. To undergo an emotional reaction: *The team felt the*   3. *Syns:* experience, have, know, savor,
   first flush of victory.   taste.
4. To be intuitively aware of.   4. PERCEIVE.
5. To view in a certain way: *I feel that this is the*   5. *Syns:* believe, hold, sense, think.
   wrong approach. We feel it advisable to wait. She felt
   he was entirely mistaken.
6. To experience or express compassion: *I feel for the*   6. *Syns:* ache (for), commiserate (with),
   families of the crash victims.   compassionate, pity, sympathize (with),
                                                              yearn. —*Idiom* be sorry for.
7. To reach about or search blindly or uncertainly.   7. GROPE.

feel out *verb*
To test the attitude of: *Let's feel out his opinion on that* *Syns:* probe, sound[1]. —*Idioms* put out
issue first.   feelers, send up a trial balloon.

feel *noun*
1. The faculty or ability to perceive tactile stimulation. 1. TOUCH *noun.*
2. A particular sensation conveyed by means of   2. TOUCH *noun.*
   physical contact.
3. A general impression produced by a predominant   3. AIR *noun.*
   quality or characteristic.

feeler *noun*
Something, as a remark, used to determine the attitude   *Syn:* probe. —*Idiom* trial balloon.
of another: *put out peace feelers.*

feeling *noun*
1. Intuitive cognition: *I have a feeling that she's going to leave him.*

2. A complex and usu. strong subjective response, as love, hate, etc.
3. An act of touching.
4. A particular sensation conveyed by means of physical contact.
5. The faculty or ability to perceive tactile stimulation.
6. A general impression produced by a predominant quality or characteristic.
7. Something believed or accepted as true by a person.
8. The quality or condition of being emotionally and intuitively sensitive.
9. The capacity for or an act of responding to a stimulus.
10. A general cast of mind with regard to something.

feeling *adjective*
Readily stirred by emotion.

feel out *verb*

feign *verb*
1. To behave affectedly or insincerely.
2. To take on or give a false appearance of.
3. To contrive and present as genuine.

feigned *adjective*
Not genuine or sincere.

feint *noun*
An indirect, usu. cunning means of gaining an end.

felicitous *adjective*
Suitable for a particular person, condition, occasion, or place.

feline *adjective*
So slow, deliberate, and secret as to escape observation.

fell[1] *verb*
1. To bring down, as with a saw or ax.
2. To cause to fall, as from a shot or blow.

fell[2] *adjective*
Showing or suggesting a disposition to be violently destructive without scruple or restraint.

fell[3] *noun*
The skin of an animal.

fellow *noun*
1. A member of the human race.
2. One that is very similar to another in rank or position.
3. One of a matched pair of things.
4. One who is united in a relationship with another.

fellowship *noun*
1. A pleasant association among people.
2. A group of people united in a relationship and having some interest, activity, or purpose in common.

felon *noun*
Law. One who commits a crime.

felony *noun*
Law. A serious breaking of the public law.

1. **Syns:** hunch, idea, impression, intuition, suspicion. —*Idioms* funny (*or* intuitive) feeling, sneaking suspicion.
2. EMOTION.
3. TOUCH *noun.*
4. TOUCH *noun.*
5. TOUCH *noun.*
6. AIR *noun.*
7. BELIEF.
8. SENSITIVENESS.
9. SENSATION.
10. SENTIMENT.

EMOTIONAL.

SEE **feel.**

1. ACT *verb.*
2. ASSUME.
3. FAKE *verb.*

ARTIFICIAL.

TRICK *noun.*

APPROPRIATE *adjective.*

STEALTHY.

1. CUT *verb.*
2. DROP *verb.*

FIERCE.

HIDE[2] *noun.*

1. HUMAN BEING.
2. PEER[2].
3. MATE *noun.*
4. ASSOCIATE *noun.*

1. COMPANY *noun.*
2. UNION.

CRIMINAL *noun.*

CRIME.

female *adjective*
Of, relating to, or characteristic of women.   FEMININE.

femaleness *noun*
The quality or condition of being feminine.   FEMININITY.

feminality *noun*
The quality or condition of being feminine.   FEMININITY.

femineity *noun*
The quality or condition of being feminine.   FEMININITY.

feminie *noun*
Women in general.   FEMININITY.

feminine *adjective*
1. Of, relating to, or characteristic of women: *a*   1. **Syns:** distaff, female, muliebral,
   musical, feminine laugh; the feminine side of the   womanly.
   family.
2. Having qualities more appropriate to women than to   2. EFFEMINATE *adjective.*
   men.

feminineness *noun*
The quality or condition of being feminine.   FEMININITY.

femininity *noun*
1. The quality or condition of being feminine: *a woman*   1. **Syns:** femaleness, feminality,
   whose attitude and appearance projected true   femineity, feminineness, womanity,
   femininity.   womanliness, womanness.
2. Women in general: *laws disadvantageous to*   2. **Syns:** distaff, feminie, muliebrity,
   femininity.   womankind, womenfolk. —*Idiom* the
                                                                 fair (*or* weaker) sex.
3. The quality of being effeminate.   3. EFFEMINACY.

feminize *verb*
To make effeminate.   EFFEMINATE *verb.*

femme fatale *noun*
French. A usu. unscrupulous woman who seduces or   SEDUCTRESS.
exploits men.

fen *noun*
A usu. low-lying area of soft, waterlogged ground and   SWAMP.
standing water.

fenagle *verb*   SEE **finagle.**

fence *verb*
1. To separate with or as if with a wall.   1. WALL *verb.*
2. To confine within a limited area.   2. ENCLOSE.
3. To surround and advance upon.   3. CLOSE IN at **close**[1].

fend *verb*
1. To progress or perform adequately, esp. in difficult   1. MANAGE.
   circumstances.
2. *Archaic.* To keep safe from danger, attack, or harm.   2. DEFEND.

fend off *verb*
To turn or drive away.   PARRY.

fend off *verb*   SEE **fend.**

feral *adjective*
1. Of or relating to beasts of prey.   1. SAVAGE.
2. Showing or suggesting a disposition to be violently   2. FIERCE.
   destructive without scruple or restraint.

ferment *verb*
To be in a state of emotional or mental turmoil.   BOIL *verb.*

ferment *noun*
1. An agent that stimulates or precipitates a reaction,   1. CATALYST.
   development, or change.
2. A state of uneasiness and usu. resentment brewing   2. UNREST.
   to an eventual explosion.

ferocious *adjective*
1. Showing or suggesting a disposition to be violently   1. FIERCE.
   destructive without scruple or restraint.
2. So intense as to cause extreme suffering.   2. CRUEL.

3. Eager for bloodshed.

3. MURDEROUS.

ferocity *noun*
1. A cruel act or an instance of cruel behavior.
2. Exceptionally great concentration, power, or force, esp. in activity.

1. CRUELTY.
2. INTENSITY.

fertile *adjective*
1. Capable of reproducing: *a woman still fertile after 50; a fertile egg.*
2. Characterized by great productivity: *fertile farm land; a brain fertile with unique ideas.*
3. Able to use the means at one's disposal to meet situations effectively.

1. *Syns:* fecund, productive, proliferous (*Biol.*), prolific, spawning.
2. *Syns:* fecund, fruitful, productive, prolific, rich.
3. RESOURCEFUL.

fertility *noun*
The quality or state of being fertile: *increased the fertility of the soil with chemical nutrients.*

Syns: fecundity, fruitfulness, productivity, richness.

fertilize *verb*
To make fertile: *fertilized the fields.*

Syns: enrich, fecundate.

fervency *noun*
Powerful, intense emotion.

PASSION.

fervent *adjective*
1. Showing or having enthusiasm.
2. Fired with intense feeling.

1. ENTHUSIASTIC.
2. PASSIONATE.

fervid *adjective*
1. Characterized by intense emotion and activity: *a fervid arms race; a man of fervid artistic imagination.*
2. Fired with intense feeling.

1. *Syns:* burning, fevered, feverish, heated, hectic.
2. PASSIONATE.

fervidity *noun*
Powerful, intense emotion.

PASSION.

fervidness *noun*
Powerful, intense emotion.

PASSION.

fervor *noun*
1. Powerful, intense emotion.
2. Passionate devotion to or interest in a cause, subject, etc.
3. Intensity of feeling or reaction.
4. *Poetic.* Intense warmth.

1. PASSION.
2. ENTHUSIASM.
3. HEAT *noun.*
4. HEAT *noun.*

Fescennine *adjective*
Offensive to accepted standards of decency.

OBSCENE.

fess up *verb*
Slang. To recognize, often reluctantly, the reality or truth of.

ACKNOWLEDGE.

festinate *verb*
To move swiftly.

RUSH *verb.*

festive *adjective*
1. Characterized by joyful exuberance.
2. Marked by festal celebration.
3. Providing joy and pleasure.

1. GAY *adjective.*
2. MERRY.
3. GLAD.

festivity *noun*
1. The act of showing happy satisfaction in an event.
2. A large or important social gathering.
3. Joyful, exuberant activity.

1. CELEBRATION.
2. PARTY *noun.*
3. GAIETY.

fetch *verb*
1. To cause to come along with oneself.
2. *Informal.* To achieve a certain price.

1. BRING.
2. BRING.

fetching *adjective*
Pleasing to the eye or mind.

ATTRACTIVE.

fete also **fête** *noun*
A large or important social gathering.

PARTY *noun.*

fetid *adjective*
Having an unpleasant odor.

SMELLY.

fetish *noun*
1. An irrational preoccupation.
2. A small object worn or kept for its supposed magical power.

1. THING.
2. CHARM *noun.*

fetter *verb*
To restrict the activity or free movement of.

HAMPER.

fetters *noun*
Something that physically confines the legs or arms.

BONDS.

fettle *noun*
A state of sound readiness.

TRIM *noun.*

fevered *adjective*
1. Being at a higher temperature than is normal or desirable.
2. Characterized by intense emotion and activity.

1. HOT *adjective.*
2. FERVID.

feverish *adjective*
1. Being at a higher temperature than is normal or desirable.
2. Characterized by intense emotion and activity.

1. HOT *adjective.*
2. FERVID.

feverous *adjective*
Being at a higher temperature than is normal or desirable.

HOT *adjective.*

fiasco *noun*
One that fails completely.

FAILURE.

fib *verb*
To make untrue declarations.

LIE² *verb.*

fib *noun*
An untrue declaration.

LIE² *noun.*

fibber *noun*
One who tells lies.

LIAR.

fibbery *noun*
The practice of lying.

MENDACITY.

fiber *noun*
1. A very fine, continuous strand.
2. A distinctive, complex underlying pattern or structure.
3. Moral or ethical strength.

1. THREAD *noun.*
2. TEXTURE.
3. CHARACTER.

fibril also **fibrilla** *noun*
A very fine, continuous strand.

THREAD *noun.*

fibrilla *noun*

SEE **fibril.**

fibster *noun*
One who tells lies.

LIAR.

fickle *adjective*
Following no predictable pattern.

CAPRICIOUS.

fiction *noun*
1. A narrative not based on fact: *short stories and other fiction.*

2. An illusory mental image.
3. An untrue declaration.
4. Any fictitious idea accepted as part of an ideology by an uncritical group; a received idea.

1. **Syns:** fable, story.
   Near-syns: fantasy, figment, invention; anecdote, narrative, tale, yarn.
   Ant: nonfiction.
2. DREAM *noun.*
3. LIE² *noun.*
4. MYTH.

fictional *adjective*
Consisting or suggestive of fiction.

FICTITIOUS.

fictionalize *verb*
To impart a false character to (something) by alteration.

FAKE *verb.*

fictitious *adjective*
Consisting or suggestive of fiction: *fictional characters in a novel.*

Syns: fanciful, fantastic (*also* fantastical), fictional, fictive, invented, made-up.

fictive *adjective*
Consisting or suggestive of fiction.
FICTITIOUS.

fiddle *verb*
1. To move one's fingers or hands in a nervous or aimless fashion: *fiddled with her papers; fiddling around with the dials of the television set.*
2. To handle something idly, ignorantly, or destructively.

1. *Syns:* fidget, fool, monkey, play, putter (around), tinker, toy, trifle, twiddle.

2. TAMPER.

fiddle away *verb*
To pass (time) without working or in avoiding work.
IDLE *verb.*

fiddle away *verb*
SEE **fiddle.**

fiddle-faddle *noun*
Slang. Something lacking substance or depth.
FROTH *noun.*

fidelity *noun*
1. Faithfulness or devotion to a person, a cause, obligations, or duties: *The captain expected the full fidelity of his crew.*
2. Correspondence with fact or truth.

1. *Syns:* allegiance, constancy, fealty, loyalty, steadfastness.

2. VERACITY.

fidget *verb*
To move one's fingers or hands in a nervous or aimless fashion.
FIDDLE.

fidgets *noun*
A state of nervous restlessness or agitation.
JITTERS.

fidgety *adjective*
Feeling or exhibiting nervous tension.
EDGY.

field *noun*
A sphere of activity, study, or interest.
AREA.

fiend *noun*
1. A perversely bad, cruel, or wicked person: *a fiend who tormented and killed his prisoners.*

2. *Slang.* A person who is ardently devoted to a particular subject or activity.

1. *Syns:* archfiend, beast, ghoul, monster, ogre, tiger, vampire. —*Idiom* devil incarnate.

2. ENTHUSIAST.

fiendish *adjective*
Perversely bad, cruel, or wicked: *took fiendish pleasure in torturing his victims.*

Syns: devilish, diabolic (*also* diabolical), ghoulish, hellish (*Informal*), infernal, ogreish, satanic (*also* satanical).
Near-syns: demoniac, malevolent, malignant, sinister; barbaric, cruel, heinous, monstrous, savage, vicious.

fierce *adjective*
1. Showing or suggesting a disposition to be violently destructive without scruple or restraint: *a fierce interrogator; fierce cannibals.*
2. Eager for bloodshed.
3. Extreme in degree, strength, or effect.
4. Intensely violent in sustained velocity.
5. Intensely sustained, esp. in activity.
6. So intense as to cause extreme suffering.

1. *Syns:* barbarous, bestial, cruel, fell[2], feral, ferocious, inhuman, savage, truculent, vicious, wolfish.
2. MURDEROUS.
3. INTENSE.
4. HIGH.
5. HEAVY *adjective.*
6. CRUEL.

fiercely *adverb*
In a violent, strenuous way.
HARD *adverb.*

fierceness *noun*
Exceptionally great concentration, power, or force, esp. in activity.
INTENSITY.

fiery *adjective*
1. On fire.
2. Marked by much heat.
3. Full of or characterized by a lively, emphatic, eager quality.
4. Fired with intense feeling.

1. BLAZING.
2. HOT *adjective.*
3. SPIRITED.
4. PASSIONATE.

fifty-fifty   *adjective*
Informal. Neither favorable nor unfavorable.

FAIR *adjective.*

fight   *verb*
1. To take a stand against.
2. To engage in a quarrel.
3. To strive in opposition to.
4. To oppose actively and with force.

1. CONTEST *verb.*
2. ARGUE.
3. CONTEND.
4. RESIST.

fight   *noun*
1. A physical conflict involving two or more: *a disagreement that is bound to lead to a fight; saw a dreadful fight with knives and fists.*
2. A discussion, often heated, in which a difference of opinion is expressed.
3. The power or will to fight: *There's a lot of fight left in her.*

1. *Syns:* fisticuffs, fray, run-in, scrap², scuffle, tussle.

2. ARGUMENT.

3. *Syns:* bellicosity, belligerence, belligerency, combativeness, contentiousness, pugnacity, pugnaciousness, scrap².

fighter   *noun*
One who engages in a combat or struggle: *a fighter for freedom.*

Syns: combatant, soldier, warrior.

fighting   *adjective*
Of or engaged in warfare.

BELLIGERENT.

figment   *noun*
1. An illusory mental image.
2. Any fictitious idea accepted as part of an ideology by an uncritical group; a received idea.

1. DREAM *noun.*
2. MYTH.

figure   *noun*
1. The external outline of a thing.
2. An element or component in a decorative composition: *a tapestry with a floral figure.*

1. FORM *noun.*
2. *Syns:* design, device, motif, motive, pattern.

figure   *verb*
1. To ascertain by mathematics.
2. To combine (figures) to form a sum.
3. *Informal.* To have an opinion.

1. CALCULATE.
2. ADD.
3. BELIEVE.

figure on   *verb*
To anticipate confidently.

EXPECT.

figure out   *verb*
1. To find a solution for.
2. *Informal.* To arrive at an answer to (a mathematical problem).

1. RESOLVE *verb.*
2. WORK *verb.*

figure on   *verb*

SEE **figure.**

figure out   *verb*

SEE **figure.**

figures   *noun*
Arithmetic calculations: *a good head for figures; has no facility for figures.*

Syns: arithmetic, computation, numbers.

figuring   *noun*
The act, process, or result of calculating.

CALCULATION.

filament   *noun*
A very fine, continuous strand.

THREAD *noun.*

filch   *verb*
To take (another's property) without permission.

STEAL *verb.*

file   *noun*
A group of people or things arranged in a row.

LINE *noun.*

fill   *verb*
1. To make or become full; put into as much as can be held: *fill a theater; filled a sack with grain.*
2. To plug up something, as a hole, space, or container: *fill a tooth; filled the cracks with cement.*
3. To supply fully or completely.
4. To occupy the whole of; be found throughout: *The smell of flowers filled the room.*

1. *Syns:* charge, freight, heap, load, pack, pile.
2. *Syns:* block, choke, clog, close¹, congest, plug, stop (up).
3. SATISFY.
4. *Syns:* imbue, permeate, pervade, suffuse.

fill out *verb*
To fill in what is lacking and make perfect.   COMPLEMENT *verb.*

fille de joie *noun*
French. A woman who engages in sexual intercourse   PROSTITUTE.
for payment.

fillet *noun*
A thin strip of material or color.   BAND[1] *noun.*

fill-in *noun*   SEE **fill in.**

fill in *verb*
To act as a substitute.   SUBSTITUTE *verb.*

fill-in *noun*
One that takes the place of another.   SUBSTITUTE *noun.*

fillip *noun*
Something that causes and encourages a given   STIMULUS.
response.

fill out *verb*   SEE **fill.**

film *noun*
A thick, heavy atmospheric condition offering reduced   HAZE *noun.*
visibility due to the presence of suspended particles.

filmy *adjective*
1. So light and insubstantial as to resemble air or a   1. ***Syns:*** aerial, aery, airy, diaphanous,
   thin film: *a filmy chiffon dress.*   ethereal, gauzy, gossamer (*also*
                                                                  gossamery), sheer[2], transparent,
                                                                  vaporous (*also* vapory).
2. Covered by or as if by a thin coating or film: *filmy* 2. ***Syns:*** beclouded, blurred, dim, hazy,
   lights in the distance.   misty.

filth *noun*
1. Foul or dirty matter: *Flies carry filth.*   1. ***Syns:*** dirt, grime, muck.
2. The condition or state of being dirty.   2. DIRTINESS.
3. Something that is offensive to accepted standards of   3. OBSCENITY.
   decency.

filthiness *noun*
1. The condition or state of being dirty.   1. DIRTINESS.
2. The quality or state of being obscene.   2. OBSCENITY.

filthy *adjective*
1. Heavily soiled; very dirty or unclean: *a filthy pair of* 1. ***Syns:*** foul, nasty, squalid, vile.
   shoes.
2. Covered or stained with or as if with dirt or other   2. DIRTY *adjective.*
   impurities.
3. Offensive to accepted standards of decency.   3. OBSCENE.
4. So objectionable as to elicit despisal: *a filthy trick.* 4. ***Syns:*** abhorrent, contemptible,
                                                              despicable, despisable, detestable,
                                                              disgusting, foul, loathsome, low, lousy
                                                              (*Slang*), mean[2], nasty, obnoxious,
                                                              odious, reprehensible, repugnant,
                                                              rotten, shabby, sorry, vile, wretched.
                                                              Near-ants: agreeable, appealing,
                                                              attractive, pleasant; favorable,
                                                              welcome.

finagle also **fenagle** *verb*
1. *Informal.* To take clever or cunning steps to achieve 1. MANEUVER *verb.*
   one's goals.
2. *Informal.* To make, achieve, or get through   2. WANGLE.
   contrivance or guile.

final *adjective*
1. Of or relating to a terminative condition, stage, or   1. LAST[1] *adjective.*
   point.
2. Coming after all others.   2. LAST[1] *adjective.*
3. Serving the function of deciding or settling with   3. DEFINITIVE.
   finality.

finale *noun*
The last part.

finally *adverb*
1. In conclusion.
2. After a considerable length of time, usu. after a delay.

finance *verb*
To supply capital to or for: *finance the renovation of an old house.*

finances *noun*
The monetary resources of a government, organization, or individual.

financial *adjective*
Of or relating to finances or those who deal in finances: *a financial adviser.*

financier *noun*
One who is occupied with or expert in large-scale financial affairs: *an internationally famous financier.*

find *verb*
1. To look for and discover: *Help me find my glasses.*
2. To find or meet by chance.

find out *verb*
To obtain knowledge or awareness of something not known before, as through observation, study, etc.

find *noun*
Something that has been discovered.

finding *noun*
Something that has been discovered.

find out *verb*

fine¹ *adjective*
1. Able to make or detect effects of great subtlety or precision: *a fine eye for color.*
2. Exceptionally good of its kind.
3. So slight as to be difficult to notice or appreciate.
4. Appealing to refined taste.
5. Free from clouds, mist, etc.
6. Consisting of small particles: *fine buckwheat flour.*

fine² *noun*
A sum of money levied as punishment for an offense: *a fine for overtime parking. Failure to file an income-tax return results in a fine set by law.*

fine *verb*
To impose a fine on: *fined them a large sum for failing to comply with the law.*

fineness *noun*
The quality of being exceptionally good of its kind.

finespun *adjective*
So slight as to be difficult to notice or appreciate.

finesse *verb*
1. To make, achieve, or get through contrivance or guile.
2. To outmaneuver (an opponent), esp. with the aid of some extra resource.

finest *noun*
A member of a law-enforcement agency.

finger *verb*
1. To bring into contact with, esp. by means of the hands or fingers, so as to give or receive a physical sensation.

END *noun.*

1. LAST¹ *adverb.*
2. AT LAST at **last¹**.

Syns: back, bankroll (*Slang*), capitalize, fund, grubstake, stake (*Informal*), subsidize. —*Idiom* put up money for.

FUNDS.

Syns: fiscal, monetary, pecuniary.

Syns: capitalist, moneyman (*Informal*).

1. *Syns:* locate, pinpoint, spot.
2. COME ACROSS at **come**.

DISCOVER.

DISCOVERY.

DISCOVERY.
SEE **find**.

1. *Syns:* delicate, nice, subtle.

2. EXCELLENT.
3. DELICATE.
4. DELICATE.
5. CLEAR *adjective.*
6. *Syns:* dusty, powdery, pulverous, pulverulent, small (*Brit. Regional*).

Syns: amercement, mulct, penalty.

Syns: amerce, mulct, penalize.

EXCELLENCE.

DELICATE.

1. WANGLE.

2. TRUMP *verb.*

POLICEMAN.

1. TOUCH *verb.*

2. To establish the identification of.

finical *adjective*
Very difficult to please.

finicky *adjective*
Very difficult to please.

finish *verb*
1. To bring or come to a natural or proper end.
2. To use all of.
3. To cause the complete ruin or wreckage of.
4. To cause the death of.
5. To take the life of (a person or persons) unlawfully.
6. To be depleted.
7. To complete a race or competition in a specified position.

finish off *verb*
Informal. To cause the death of.

finish *noun*
1. The last part.
2. A concluding or terminating.

finished *adjective*
1. Very proficient as a result of practice and study.
2. Having reached completion.
3. Having no further relationship.
4. No longer effective, capable, or valuable.

finish off *verb*

fink *noun*
Slang. One who gives incriminating information about others.

fink *verb*
Slang. To give incriminating information about others, esp. to the authorities.

fink out *verb*
Slang. To abandon a former position or commitment.

fink out *verb*

fire *noun*
1. The visible signs of combustion: *a huge fire at the refinery.*
2. Powerful, intense emotion.
3. Passionate devotion to or interest in a cause, subject, etc.
4. Liveliness and vivacity of imagination: *poetry of divine fire.*
5. Exceptional brightness and clarity, as of a cut and polished stone: *a diamond with extraordinary fire.*

fire *verb*
1. To arouse the emotions of; make ardent: *fired by righteous indignation.*
2. To cause to burn or undergo combustion.
3. To release or cause to release energy suddenly and violently, esp. with a loud noise.
4. To discharge a gun or firearm.
5. To send through the air with a motion of the hand or arm.
6. To launch with great force.
7. *Informal.* To end the employment of.

fire-and-brimstone *adjective*
1. Portending future disaster.
2. Fired with intense feeling.

fired up *adjective*
Feeling a very strong emotion.

---

2. PLACE *verb.*

NICE.

NICE.

1. CLOSE[1] *verb.*
2. EXHAUST.
3. DESTROY.
4. KILL.
5. MURDER *verb.*
6. GO *verb.*
7. RUN *verb.*

KILL.

1. END *noun.*
2. END *noun.*

1. ACCOMPLISHED.
2. COMPLETE *adjective.*
3. THROUGH *adjective.*
4. THROUGH *adjective.*
SEE **finish.**

INFORMER.

INFORM.

BACK DOWN at **back.**
SEE **fink.**

1. *Syns:* blaze[1], conflagration, flame(s), flare-up.
2. PASSION.
3. ENTHUSIASM.

4. *Syns:* genius, inspiration.

5. *Syns:* brilliance (*also* brilliancy), luminosity, radiance.

1. *Syns:* animate, enkindle, impassion, inspire, kindle, stir[1] (up).
2. LIGHT[1] *verb.*
3. EXPLODE.

4. SHOOT.
5. THROW.

6. SHOOT *verb.*
7. DISMISS.

1. FATEFUL.
2. PASSIONATE.

THRILLED.

firing *noun*
Informal. The act of dismissing or the condition of being dismissed.

DISMISSAL.

firm[1] *adjective*
1. Unyielding to pressure or force: *firm muscles.*
2. Not easily moved or shaken.
3. Persistently holding to something.
4. Indicating or possessing determination, resolution, or persistence: *a firm intention to do the right thing.*

5. Not hesitating or wavering.
6. In a definite and final form; not likely to change: *a firm price.*

1. **Syns:** hard, incompressible, solid.
2. SOUND[2].
3. TIGHT *adjective.*
4. **Syns:** determined, resolute, tough, unbending, uncompromising, unyielding.
5. DECISIVE.
6. **Syns:** certain, fixed, flat, set[1], settled, straight.
   Near-syns: definite, exact, explicit, specific; established, prevailing.
   Ant: variable.

7. Adhering firmly and devotedly, as to a person, a cause, or a duty.
8. Firmly settled or positioned.

7. FAITHFUL.
8. SURE.

firm[2] *noun*
A commercial organization.

COMPANY *noun.*

firmament *noun*
The celestial regions as seen from the earth.

AIR *noun.*

firmness *noun*
1. Unwavering firmness of character or action.
2. Reliability in withstanding pressure, force, or stress.
3. The condition of being free from defects or flaws.

1. DECISION.
2. STABILITY.
3. SOUNDNESS.

first *adjective*
1. Preceding all others in time: *America's first space flight.*

1. **Syns:** earliest, initial, maiden, original, pioneer, primary, prime.
   Near-syns: early, primordial, pristine.
   Ant: last.

2. Most important, influential, or significant.
3. At or near the start of a period, development, or series.

2. PRIMARY.
3. EARLY *adjective.*

first-class *adjective*
1. Of fine quality.
2. Exceptionally good of its kind.

1. CHOICE *adjective.*
2. EXCELLENT.

firsthand *adjective*
1. Marked by the absence of any intervention.
2. Characterized by a close and thorough acquaintance.

1. IMMEDIATE.
2. INTIMATE[1] *adjective.*

first-rate *adjective*
Exceptionally good of its kind.

EXCELLENT.

fiscal *adjective*
Of or relating to finances or those who deal in finances.

FINANCIAL.

fish *verb*
To try to obtain, usu. by subtleness and cunning.

HINT *verb.*

fishwife *noun*
A person, esp. a woman, who habitually uses loud, abusive language.

SCOLD *noun.*

fishy *adjective*
Of dubious character.

SHADY.

fissure *noun*
1. A usu. narrow partial opening caused by splitting and rupture.
2. An interruption in friendly relations.

1. CRACK *noun.*
2. BREACH *noun.*

fissure *verb*
To undergo partial breaking.

CRACK *verb.*

fisticuffs *noun*
A physical conflict involving two or more.

FIGHT *noun.*

fit *verb*

1. To conform to another, esp. in size and shape: *two boards that fit together; a shoe that fits.*
2. To be in keeping with: *a dress that fits the occasion.*

3. To make or become suitable to a particular situation or use.
4. To have a proper or suitable place.
5. To be compatible or in correspondence.
6. To cause to be ready, as for use, consumption, or a special purpose.

fit up (or **out**) *verb*

1. To supply what is needed for some activity or purpose.
2. To provide with furniture.

fit *noun*

1. A sudden, violent expression, as of emotion.
2. An angry outburst.

fit *adjective*

1. Suitable for a particular person, condition, occasion, or place.
2. Suited to one's end or purpose.
3. Satisfying the requirements, as for selection.
4. Having good health.

fitful *adjective*

Happening or appearing now and then.

fitness *noun*

1. A state of sound readiness.
2. The quality or state of being eligible.

fitted *adjective*

Satisfying the requirements, as for selection.

fitting *adjective*

1. Consistent with prevailing or accepted standards or circumstances.
2. Suitable for a particular person, condition, occasion, or place.

fitting *noun*

A piece of equipment for comfort or convenience.

fit up (or **out**) *verb*

fix *verb*

1. To ascribe (a misdeed, error, etc.) to: *fixed the blame on me.*
2. To produce a deep impression on.
3. To implant so deeply as to make change nearly impossible: *Racial prejudice was fixed in their minds.*
4. To become or cause to become stuck or lodged.
5. To make secure.
6. To place securely in a position or condition.
7. To set forth expressly and authoritatively.
8. To put into correct or conclusive form.
9. To alter (parts of a device) for proper functioning.
10. To join one thing to another.
11. To come to an agreement about.
12. To restore to proper condition or functioning: *fix some torn clothes.*

13. To cause to be ready, as for use, consumption, or a special purpose.
14. To render incapable of reproducing sexually.

---

1. **Syn:** dovetail.

2. **Syns:** become, befit, conform to, correspond to, go with, match, suit.
   —*Idiom* hit the spot.
3. ADAPT.

4. BELONG.
5. AGREE.
6. PREPARE.

1. FURNISH.

2. FURNISH.

1. ERUPTION.
2. TEMPER *noun.*

1. APPROPRIATE *adjective.*

2. CONVENIENT.
3. ELIGIBLE.
4. HEALTHY.

INTERMITTENT.

1. TRIM *noun.*
2. QUALIFICATION.

ELIGIBLE.

1. JUST *adjective.*

2. APPROPRIATE *adjective.*

FURNISHING.
SEE **fit.**

1. **Syns:** affix, assign, blame, fasten, impute, pin on, place, saddle (on).
2. ENGRAVE.
3. **Syns:** embed (*also* imbed), entrench, fasten, infix, ingrain, lodge, root[1].
4. CATCH *verb.*
5. FASTEN.
6. ESTABLISH.
7. DICTATE.
8. SETTLE.
9. ADJUST.
10. ATTACH.
11. ARRANGE.
12. **Syns:** doctor, fix up (*Informal*), mend, overhaul, patch, repair, revamp, right.
    —*Idiom* set right.
13. PREPARE.

14. STERILIZE.

15. *Informal.* To exact revenge for.

16. To prearrange the outcome of (a contest) unlawfully: *fix a football game; fix an election.*

17. To give, offer, or promise a bribe to.

fix up *verb*

1. *Informal.* To improve in appearance, esp. by refurbishing: *fix up old toys by repainting them; decorators fixing up an old house.*

2. *Informal.* To restore to proper condition or functioning.

fix *noun*

1. A difficult, embarrassing situation.

2. Money, property, or a favor given, offered, or promised to a person in a position of trust as an inducement to dishonest behavior.

fixation *noun*

Psychol. An irrational preoccupation.

fixed *adjective*

1. Firmly in position: *There are no fixed objects in space.*

2. Not diffused or dispersed.

3. Having distinct limits.

4. Kept within certain limits.

5. On an unwavering course of action.

6. In a definite and final form; not likely to change.

fix up *verb*

fizz *noun*

A mass of bubbles in or on the surface of a liquid.

fizz *verb*

1. To form or cause to form foam.

2. To make a sharp sibilant sound.

fizzle *verb*

1. *Informal.* To lose strength or power.

2. To make a sharp sibilant sound.

flabbergast *verb*

To overwhelm with surprise, wonder, or bewilderment.

flabby *adjective*

Lacking in stiffness or firmness.

flaccid *adjective*

Lacking in stiffness or firmness.

flag¹ *noun*

Fabric used esp. as a symbol: *salute our country's flag.*

flag *verb*

To communicate by means of such devices as lights or signs.

flag² *verb*

1. To lose strength or power.

2. To become limp, as from loss of freshness.

flagging *adjective*

Proceeding at a rate less than usual or desired.

flagitious *adjective*

Utterly reprehensible in nature or behavior.

flagrance *noun*

flagrancy or **flagrance** *noun*

The quality or state of being flagrant: *the flagrancy of his crimes.*

---

15. AVENGE.

16. *Syn:* tamper (with). —*Idiom* pack the deck.

17. BRIBE *verb.*

1. *Syns:* smarten (up), spruce (up).

2. FIX *verb.*

1. PREDICAMENT.

2. BRIBE *noun.*

THING.

1. *Syns:* immobile, immovable, stationary, steadfast, unmovable, unmoving.

2. CONCENTRATED.

3. DEFINITE.

4. RESTRICTED.

5. SET¹ *adjective.*

6. FIRM¹.

SEE **fix.**

FOAM *noun.*

1. FOAM *verb.*

2. HISS *verb.*

1. FADE *verb.*

2. HISS *verb.*

STAGGER.

LIMP *adjective.*

LIMP *adjective.*

Syns: banderole (*also* banderol, bannerol), banner, colors, ensign, jack, oriflamme (*also* auriflamme), pennant, pennon, standard, streamer.

SIGNAL *verb.*

1. FADE *verb.*

2. WILT.

SLOW *adjective.*

CORRUPT *adjective.*

SEE **flagrancy.**

Syns: atrociousness, atrocity, enormity, flagrantness, grossness, outrageousness, rankness.

flagrant *adjective*
1. Conspicuously bad or offensive: *a flagrant attempt at price fixing; flagrant debauchery.*

    1. **Syns:** arrant, capital, egregious, glaring, gross, rank^2.
    Near-syns: bold, brazen, conspicuous, obvious; reprehensible, shameful, shocking, wicked.

2. Disgracefully and grossly offensive.

    2. OUTRAGEOUS.

flagrantness *noun*
The quality or state of being flagrant.

    FLAGRANCY.

flail *verb*
To swing about or strike at wildly.

    THRASH.

flair *noun*
An innate capability.

    TALENT.

flamboyant *adjective*
1. Elaborately and heavily ornamented.
2. Marked by outward, often extravagant display.

    1. ORNATE.
    2. SHOWY.

flame *verb*
To undergo combustion.

    BURN *verb*.

flame(s) *noun*
The visible signs of combustion.

    FIRE *noun*.

flaming *adjective*
1. On fire.
2. Fired with intense feeling.

    1. BLAZING.
    2. PASSIONATE.

flank *noun*
One of two or more contrasted parts or places identified by its location with respect to a center.

    SIDE.

flap *verb*
1. To move (wings, arms, etc.) up and down: *The gull flapped its heavy wings.*
2. To move or cause to move about while being fixed at one edge: *a naval ensign flapping in the breeze; flapped the signal flags.*
3. To move through the air with or as if with wings.

    1. **Syns:** beat, flitter, flop, flutter, waggle, wave.
    2. **Syns:** flitter, flutter, fly, wave.

    3. FLY.

flap *noun*
Slang. A state of discomposure.

    AGITATION.

flare *verb*
1. To undergo combustion.
2. To react explosively or suddenly.
3. To become manifest suddenly and in full force.

    1. BURN *verb*.
    2. FLY.
    3. BREAK OUT.

flare-up *noun*

    SEE **flare up.**

flare up *verb*
To be or become angry.

    ANGER *verb*.

flare-up *noun*
1. The visible signs of combustion.
2. A sudden, violent expression, as of emotion.

    1. FIRE *noun*.
    2. OUTBURST.

flaring *adjective*
On fire.

    BLAZING.

flash *verb*
1. To emit light suddenly in rays or sparks: *Jagged streaks of lightning flashed. Diamond tiaras were flashing in the candlelight.*

    1. **Syns:** coruscate, glance^1, gleam, glimmer, glint, glisten, glister (*Poetic*), glitter, scintillate, shimmer, spangle, sparkle, twinkle.

2. To shine with intermittent gleams.
3. To make a public and usu. ostentatious show of.
4. To move swiftly.

    2. BLINK *verb*.
    3. DISPLAY *verb*.
    4. RUSH *verb*.

flash *noun*
1. A sudden quick light.
2. A very brief time: *was gone in a flash.*

    1. BLINK *noun*.
    2. **Syns:** crack, instant, jiffy (*also* jiff) (*Informal*), minute^2, moment, second^1, tick (*Brit. Informal*), trice, twinkle,

3. Sparkling, brilliant light.

flashy *adjective*
Tastelessly showy.

flat *adjective*
1. Lying down: *I am flat on my back in bed.*

2. Having no irregularities, roughness, or indentations.
3. Completely such, without qualification or exception.
4. In a definite and final form; not likely to change.
5. Lacking liveliness, charm, or surprise.
6. Having lost tang or effervescence: *a flat champagne.*
7. Lacking an appetizing flavor: *a flat, starchy meal.*

8. Lacking vividness in color.
9. Lacking gloss and luster.

flat *adverb*
1. In a direct, positive manner.
2. To the fullest extent.

flatfoot *noun*
Slang. A member of a law-enforcement agency.

flatly *adverb*
In a direct, positive manner: *denied it flatly.*

flatness *noun*
The state or quality of being insipid.

flat-out *adjective*
Completely such, without qualification or exception.

flat-out *adverb*
1. *Informal.* In a rapid way.
2. *Regional.* In a direct, positive manner.

flatten *verb*
1. To cause to fall, as from a shot or blow.
2. To make even, smooth, or level.

flatter *verb*
1. To compliment excessively and ingratiatingly: *sycophants who flattered the king's mistress.*

2. To look good on or with: *a gown that flatters the figure.*

flatterer *noun*
One who flatters another excessively.

flattering *adjective*
Pleasingly suited to the wearer.

flattery *noun*
Excessive, ingratiating praise: *a person blinded by flattery.*

flatulent *adjective*
Filled up with or as if with something insubstantial.

flaunt *verb*
To make a public and usu. ostentatious show of.

---

twinkling, wink. —*Idioms* split second, the twinkling of an eye.
3. GLITTER *noun.*

GAUDY.

1. **Syns:** decumbent, horizontal, procumbent, prone, prostrate, recumbent.
2. EVEN[1] *adjective.*
3. UTTER[2].
4. FIRM[1].
5. DULL *adjective.*
6. **Syn:** stale.
7. **Syns:** flavorless, insipid, tasteless. **Near-ants:** appetizing, delectable, delicious, flavorsome, piquant, savory, tasty.
8. DULL *adjective.*
9. DULL *adjective.*

1. FLATLY.
2. COMPLETELY.

POLICEMAN.

Syns: emphatically, flat, flat-out (*Regional*), positively.

INSIPIDITY.

UTTER[2].

1. FAST *adverb.*
2. FLATLY.

1. DROP *verb.*
2. EVEN[1] *verb.*

1. **Syns:** adulate, blandish, butter up (*Informal*), glaver (*Obs.*), honey, oil (*Informal*), slaver, soft-soap (*Informal*), sweet-talk (*Informal*).
2. **Syns:** become, compliment, enhance, suit. —*Idiom* put in the best light.

SYCOPHANT.

BECOMING.

Syns: adulation, blandishment, blarney, incense[2], oil (*Informal*), slaver (*Archaic*). —*Idioms* honeyed words, soft soap. **Near-ants:** censure, condemnation, criticism; contempt, disdain, disparagement, reprobation, scorn. **Ant:** excoriation.

INFLATED.

DISPLAY *verb.*

flavor *noun*
1. A distinctive property of a substance affecting the gustatory sense: *meat permeated with the flavor of garlic.*
2. A distinctive yet intangible quality deemed typical of a given thing: *a city imbued with the flavor of the Orient.*
3. A substance that imparts taste.

flavor *verb*
1. To impart flavor to: *flavored the sauce with herbs and wine.*
2. To have a particular flavor or suggestion of something.

flavoring *noun*
A substance that imparts taste: *lemon flavoring.*

flavorless *adjective*
Lacking an appetizing flavor.

flavorlessness *noun*
The state or quality of being insipid.

flaw *noun*
Something that mars the appearance or causes inadequacy or failure.

flawed *adjective*
Having a defect or defects.

flawless *adjective*
1. Free from flaws or blemishes.
2. In excellent condition.
3. Supremely excellent in quality or nature.

flay *verb*
To criticize harshly and devastatingly.

fleck *verb*
To mark with many small spots.

fledgling *noun*
One who is just starting to learn or do something.

flee *verb*
To break loose and leave suddenly, as from confinement or from a difficult or threatening situation.

fleecy *adjective*
Covered with hair.

fleeing *adjective*
Lasting or existing only for a short time.

fleer *verb*
To smile or laugh scornfully or derisively.

fleer at *verb*
To make fun of.

fleer *noun*
A facial expression conveying scorn or derision.

fleer at *verb*

fleet[1] *verb*
To move swiftly.

fleet *adjective*
Characterized by great celerity.

fleet[2] *adjective*
Chiefly Regional. Measuring little from bottom to top or surface.

fleeting *adjective*
Lasting or existing only for a short time.

fleetness *noun*
Rapidness of movement or activity.

Fleet Street *noun*
Brit. Journalists and journalism in general.

1. *Syns:* relish, sapor, savor, smack[2], taste, twang.

2. *Syns:* aroma, atmosphere, savor, smack[2].

3. FLAVORING.

1. *Syn:* season.

2. SMACK[2] *verb.*

Syns: condiment, flavor, seasoning.

FLAT *adjective.*

INSIPIDITY.

DEFECT *noun.*

DEFECTIVE.

1. CLEAR *adjective.*
2. GOOD *adjective.*
3. PERFECT *adjective.*

SLAM *verb.*

SPECKLE.

BEGINNER.

ESCAPE *verb.*

HAIRY.

TRANSITORY.

SNEER *verb.*

RIDICULE *verb.*

SNEER *noun.*

SEE **fleer.**

RUSH *verb.*

FAST *adjective.*

SHALLOW *adjective.*

TRANSITORY.

HASTE *noun.*

PRESS *noun.*

flesh *noun*
The human race.   MANKIND.
fleshless *adjective*
Having little flesh or fat on the body.   THIN *adjective*.
fleshliness *noun*
A preoccupation with the body and satisfaction of its   PHYSICALITY.
desires.
fleshly *adjective*
1. Of or pertaining to the human body.   1. BODILY.
2. Relating to the desires and appetites of the body.   2. PHYSICAL.
fleshy *adjective*
Having too much flesh.   FAT *adjective*.
flexibility *noun*
The quality or state of being flexible: *measured the*   **Syns:** ductility, elasticity, flexibleness,
flexibility of the aluminum.   flexure (*Obs.*), give (*Informal*),
                                                           malleability, plasticity, pliability,
                                                           pliableness, pliancy, resilience (*also*
                                                           resiliency), springiness, suppleness.

flexible also **flexile** *adjective*
1. Easily altered or influenced: *the flexible mind of the* 1. **Syns:** elastic, malleable, plastic,
   diplomat.   pliable, pliant.
2. Capable of being shaped, bent, or drawn out, as by   2. MALLEABLE.
   hammering or pressure.
3. Capable of withstanding stress without injury: *a*   3. **Syns:** elastic, plastic, resilient, springy,
   flexible girder.   supple.
flexibleness *noun*
The quality or state of being flexible.   FLEXIBILITY.
flexile *adjective*   SEE **flexible.**
flexuose *adjective*   SEE **flexuous.**
flexuous also **flexuose** *adjective*
1. Capable of being shaped, bent, or drawn out, as by   1. MALLEABLE.
   hammering or pressure.
2. Repeatedly curving in alternate directions.   2. WINDING.
flexure *noun*
Obs. The quality or state of being flexible.   FLEXIBILITY.
flick *noun*
Light and momentary contact with another person or   BRUSH *noun*.
thing.
flick *verb*
To make light and momentary contact with.   BRUSH *verb*.
flicker *verb*
1. To shine with intermittent gleams.   1. BLINK *verb*.
2. To move quickly and intermittently in a nervous,   2. FLUTTER *verb*.
   excited way.
flicker *noun*
A sudden quick light.   BLINK *noun*.
flight *noun*
The act or an instance of escaping, as from confinement   ESCAPE *noun*.
or difficulty.
flighty *adjective*
Given to lighthearted silliness.   GIDDY.
flimflam *verb*
Slang. To get money or something else from by   CHEAT *verb*.
deceitful trickery.
flimflam *noun*
Slang. An act of cheating.   CHEAT *noun*.
flimflammer *noun*
Slang. A person who cheats.   CHEAT *noun*.
flimsy *adjective*
1. Having little substance or significance; not solidly   1. TENUOUS.
   based.

2. Not plausible or believable. — 2. IMPLAUSIBLE.

flinch *verb*
To draw away involuntarily, usu. due to fear or disgust: *flinched at the sight of the carnage.*

Syns: blench[1], quail, recoil, shrink, shy[1], squinch, start, wince.
Near-syns: avoid, elude, escape, evade, shun; retreat, withdraw.

fling *noun*
1. An act of throwing.
2. A period of uncontrolled self-indulgence.
3. *Informal.* A brief trial.
fling *verb*
To send through the air with a motion of the hand or arm.

1. THROW *noun.*
2. BINGE.
3. TRY *noun.*
THROW *verb.*

flip *verb*
1. To throw (a coin) in order to decide something.
2. To look through reading matter casually.
flip *adjective*
1. *Informal.* Characterized by ready but often insincere or superficial discourse.
2. *Informal.* Rude and disrespectful.

1. TOSS.
2. BROWSE.
1. GLIB.
2. IMPUDENT.

flirt *verb*
1. To make amorous advances without serious intentions: *a girl who flirted with all the boys.*
2. To treat lightly or flippantly: *a stunt pilot who flirted with death.*
flirt *noun*
A woman who leads men on: *Scarlett O'Hara—the epitome of a flirt.*

1. *Syns:* coquet, dally, toy, trifle.
2. *Syns:* dally (with), play (with), toy (with), trifle (with).
Syns: coquette, vamp.

flirtation *noun*
1. The practice of flirting: *Dancing and flirtation were their chief amusements.*
2. A usu. brief romance entered into lightly or frivolously: *It's not love; it's just another flirtation.*

1. *Syns:* coquetry, dalliance.
2. *Syn:* dalliance.

flirtatious *adjective*
Given to flirting: *a flirtatious belle.*
flirty *adjective*
Given to flirting.

Syns: coquettish, coy, flirty.
FLIRTATIOUS.

flit *verb*
1. To move quickly and intermittently in a nervous, excited way.
2. To move through the air with or as if with wings.
3. To move swiftly.

1. FLUTTER *verb.*
2. FLY.
3. RUSH *verb.*

flitter *verb*
1. To move quickly and intermittently in a nervous, excited way.
2. To move (wings, arms, etc.) up and down.
3. To move or cause to move about while being fixed at one edge.

1. FLUTTER *verb.*
2. FLAP *verb.*
3. FLAP *verb.*

float *verb*
1. To move along with or be carried away by the action of water.
2. To pass quickly and lightly through the air.

1. WASH *verb.*
2. FLY.

flock *noun*
1. An enormous number of persons gathered together.
2. A very large number of things grouped together.
flock *verb*
To congregate closely around or against.

1. CROWD *noun.*
2. CROWD *noun.*
CROWD *verb.*

flog *verb*
To punish with blows or lashes.
BEAT *verb.*

flogging *noun*
A punishment dealt with blows or lashes.
BEATING.

flood *noun*
1. An abundant, usu. overwhelming flow: *a flood following the storm; a flood of tears.*

 1. **Syns:** alluvion, cataclysm, cataract, deluge, freshet, inundation, Niagara, overflow, spate, torrent.

2. Something suggestive of running water.

 2. FLOW *noun.*

flood *verb*
1. To flow over completely: *The storm flooded our basement. Tears flooded my face.*

 1. **Syns:** deluge, drown, engulf, flush, inundate, overflow, submerge, whelm.

2. To affect as if by an outpouring of water: *The White House was flooded with angry telegrams.*

 2. **Syns:** deluge, overwhelm, whelm.

3. To come or go in large numbers.

 3. POUR.

floor *verb*
1. To cause to fall, as from a shot or blow.

 1. DROP *verb.*

2. To overwhelm with surprise, wonder, or bewilderment.

 2. STAGGER.

floozey *noun*

 SEE **floozy.**

floozy also **floozey** *noun*
Slang. A vulgar, promiscuous woman who flouts propriety.

 SLUT.

flop *verb*
1. To drop or sink heavily and noisily: *He flopped into the chair with a groan.*

 1. **Syns:** flump, plop, plump^2, plunk.

2. To move (wings, arms, etc.) up and down.

 2. FLAP *verb.*

3. To hang limply, loosely, and carelessly.

 3. SLOUCH *verb.*

4. *Informal.* To be unsuccessful.

 4. FAIL.

5. *Slang.* To go to bed.

 5. RETIRE.

flop *noun*
Informal. One that fails completely.

 FAILURE.

floppy *adjective*
Lacking in stiffness or firmness.

 LIMP *adjective.*

florescence *noun*
A condition or time of vigor and freshness.

 BLOOM *noun.*

floret *noun*
The showy reproductive structure of a plant.

 BLOOM *noun.*

florid *adjective*
1. Of a healthy, reddish color.

 1. RUDDY.

2. Elaborately and heavily ornamented.

 2. ORNATE.

flounce *verb*
To walk with exaggerated or unnatural motions expressive of self-importance or self-display.

 STRUT.

flounder *verb*
To move about in an indolent or clumsy manner.

 WALLOW.

flourish *verb*
1. To grow rapidly and luxuriantly: *Most flowers flourish in full sunlight.*

 1. **Syns:** bloom, blossom, thrive.

2. To fare well.

 2. PROSPER.

3. To be in one's prime: *an artist who flourished in the late 14th century.*

 3. **Syns:** flower, shine. —*Idioms* cut a figure, make a splash.

4. To wield boldly and dramatically: *a drum major flourishing his baton.*

 4. **Syns:** brandish, sweep, wave.

flourishing *adjective*
Improving, growing, or succeeding steadily: *a flourishing business.*

 Syns: booming, coming (*Informal*), healthy, prospering, prosperous, roaring, robust, thrifty, thriving. —*Idiom* going strong.
 Near-ants: decreasing, deteriorating, failing, languishing.
 Ant: declining.

flout *verb*
To refuse or fail to obey.

 DISOBEY.

flow *verb*
1. To move freely as a liquid: *blood flowing through the veins.*
2. To come forth or emit in abundance: *Food parcels for the tornado victims flowed in. Tears flowed.*
3. To pass or pour out into.
4. To have as a source.
5. To overflow with.
6. To proceed with ease, esp. of expression: *Churchill's resplendent prose flowed on and on.*

flow *noun*
Something suggestive of running water: *a flow of sympathy; a steady flow of complaints.*

flower *noun*
1. The showy reproductive structure of a plant.
2. A condition or time of vigor and freshness.
3. That which is superlative.
4. People of the highest social level.

flower *verb*
1. To bear flowers.
2. To be in one's prime.

flowing *adjective*
Marked by facility, esp. of expression.

fluency *noun*
Ready skill in expression: *achieved fluency in Russian.*

fluent *adjective*
1. Fluently persuasive and forceful.
2. Marked by facility, esp. of expression.

fluff *noun*
Informal. A minor mistake.

fluid *adjective*
1. Capable of or liable to change.
2. Changing easily, as in expression.
3. Marked by facility, esp. of expression.

fluidity *noun*
Ready skill in expression.

fluke *noun*
An unexpected random event.

fluky *adjective*
Occurring unexpectedly.

flummox *verb*
1. *Slang.* To be unsuccessful.
2. *Slang.* To make incapable of finding something to think, do, or say.

flump *verb*
To drop or sink heavily and noisily.

flunk *verb*
Informal. To receive less than a passing grade.

flurry *verb*
To impair or destroy the composure of.

flurry *noun*
1. A state of discomposure.
2. Agitated, excited movement and activity.

flush *verb*
1. To make even, smooth, or level.
2. To raise the spirits of.
3. To flow over completely.
4. To become red in the face.

flush *noun*
1. A condition or time of vigor and freshness.
2. A fresh, rosy complexion.

---

1. *Syns:* circulate, course, run, stream.

2. *Syns:* course, gush, pour, rush, stream, surge, well[1].
3. DISCHARGE *verb.*
4. STEM *verb.*
5. TEEM[1].
6. *Syns:* glide, roll, sail.

Syns: current, drift, flood, flux, rush, spate, stream, tide.

1. BLOOM *noun.*
2. BLOOM *noun.*
3. BEST *noun.*
4. SOCIETY.

1. BLOOM *verb.*
2. FLOURISH.

SMOOTH *adjective.*

Syns: cursiveness, facility, fluidity.

1. ELOQUENT.
2. SMOOTH *adjective.*

LAPSE *noun.*

1. CHANGEABLE.
2. MOBILE.
3. SMOOTH *adjective.*

FLUENCY.

CHANCE *noun.*

ACCIDENTAL *adjective.*

1. FAIL.
2. NONPLUS.

FLOP *verb.*

FAIL.

AGITATE.

1. AGITATION.
2. STIR[1] *noun.*

1. EVEN[1] *verb.*
2. ELATE *verb.*
3. FLOOD *verb.*
4. BLUSH *verb.*

1. BLOOM *noun.*
2. BLOOM *noun.*

3. A feeling of pervasive emotional warmth.

3. GLOW *noun.*

flush *adjective*
1. On the same plane or line.
2. Having no irregularities, roughness, or indentations.
3. Of a healthy, reddish color.
4. Possessing a large amount of money, land, or other material possessions.

1. EVEN[1] *adjective.*
2. EVEN[1] *adjective.*
3. RUDDY.
4. RICH.

flushed *adjective*
1. Feeling great delight and joy.
2. Of a healthy, reddish color.

1. ELATED.
2. RUDDY.

fluster *verb*
To impair or destroy the composure of.

AGITATE.

fluster *noun*
A state of discomposure.

AGITATION.

flutter *verb*
1. To move quickly and intermittently in a nervous, excited way: *The children fluttered around the birthday cake.*
2. To move (wings, arms, etc.) up and down.
3. To move or cause to move about while being fixed at one edge.
4. To move through the air with or as if with wings.

1. *Syns:* flicker, flit, flitter, hover.
Near-syns: fluctuate, oscillate, vibrate; flap, quiver, shake, tremble, wobble.
2. FLAP *verb.*
3. FLAP *verb.*

4. FLY.

flutter *noun*
A state of discomposure.

AGITATION.

flux *noun*
Something suggestive of running water.

FLOW *noun.*

flux *verb*
To change from a solid to a liquid.

MELT.

fly *verb*
1. To move through the air with or as if with wings: *Gulls flew over the beach.*
2. To pass quickly and lightly through the air: *Storm clouds flew past us.*
3. To move or cause to move about while being fixed at one edge.
4. To break loose and leave suddenly, as from confinement or from a difficult or threatening situation.
5. To move swiftly.
6. To react explosively or suddenly: *flew into a towering rage.*
7. *Informal.* To move swiftly on foot so that both feet leave the ground during each stride.
8. To leave hastily.

1. *Syns:* flap, flit, flutter, sail, wing.
2. *Syns:* dart, float, sail, shoot, skim.
3. FLAP *verb.*
4. ESCAPE *verb.*

5. RUSH *verb.*
6. *Syn:* flare (up).
7. RUN *verb.*

8. RUN *verb.*

flying *adjective*
Accomplished in very little time.

QUICK.

foam *noun*
A mass of bubbles in or on the surface of a liquid: *Foam rose on the beer.*

Syns: fizz, froth, head, lather, spume, suds, yeast.

foam *verb*
To form or cause to form foam: *The beer foamed in the glass.*

Syns: bubble, cream, effervesce, fizz, froth, lather, spume.

foamy *adjective*
Consisting of or resembling foam: *Winds churned the sea into a foamy spray.*

Syns: frothy, lathery, spumy, sudsy.

fob *verb*
To offer or put into circulation (an inferior or spurious item).

FOIST.

focalize *verb*
To direct toward a common center.

CONCENTRATE.

focus *noun*
A point of origin from which ideas, influences, etc., emanate.

CENTER *noun.*

focus *verb*
1. To devote (oneself or one's efforts).
2. To direct toward a common center.

1. APPLY.
2. CONCENTRATE.

foe *noun*
One who is hostile to or opposes the purposes or interests of another.

ENEMY.

fog *noun*
1. A thick, heavy atmospheric condition offering reduced visibility due to the presence of suspended particles.
2. A stunned or bewildered condition.

1. HAZE *noun.*

2. DAZE *noun.*

fog *verb*
To make dim or indistinct.

OBSCURE *verb.*

foggy *adjective*
Not clearly perceived or perceptible.

UNCLEAR.

fogy *noun*
An old-fashioned person who is reluctant to change or innovate.

SQUARE *noun.*

foible *noun*
A liking or personal preference for something.

WEAKNESS.

foil *verb*
To prevent from accomplishing a purpose.

FRUSTRATE.

foist *verb*
1. To offer or put into circulation (an inferior or spurious item): *tried to foist damaged merchandise on his customers.*
2. To force (another) to accept a burden.
3. To introduce gradually and slyly.

1. *Syns:* fob (off), palm off, pass off.

2. IMPOSE.
3. INSINUATE.

fold *noun*
A line made by the doubling of one part over another: *the folds of a curtain.*

Syns: crease, crinkle, pleat, plica, plication, ply, rimple, ruck², wrinkle¹.

fold *verb*
1. To bend together or crease so that one part lies over another: *folded the paper in thirds.*
2. *Informal.* To undergo sudden financial failure.
3. *Informal.* To be unable to hold up.
4. *Informal.* To give way mentally and emotionally.
5. *Informal.* To give in from or as if from a gradual loss of strength.

1. *Syns:* double, pleat, plicate, ruck².

2. COLLAPSE *verb.*
3. BEND.
4. BREAK DOWN.
5. SUCCUMB.

folklore *noun*
A body of traditional beliefs and notions accumulated about a particular subject.

LORE.

follow *verb*
1. To move behind (another) in the same direction: *She followed me into the room.*

2. To keep (another) under surveillance by moving along behind: *The police followed the suspect home.*
3. To take as a model: *He tried to follow his father's high standards.*

4. To act in conformity with: *follow the rules; was just following orders.*

5. To occur after (another) in time: *The reign of Elizabeth II followed George VI's.*

1. *Syns:* heel¹, pursue, trail. —*Idioms* camp on the heel of, follow in the trail of, follow on the heel of.
2. *Syns:* bedog, bird-dog, dog, shadow, tail (*Informal*), trail, track.
3. *Syns:* copy, emulate, model, pattern (on, upon, *or* after). —*Idioms* follow in the footsteps of, follow suit, follow the example of.
4. *Syns:* abide by, adhere (to), comply (with), conform (to), keep, mind, obey, observe.
5. *Syns:* follow on, succeed, supervene. —*Idiom* follow on the heels of.

6. To occur as a consequence: *If you do that, it follows that you will be caught.*

6. ***Syns:*** attend, ensue, result.

7. To perceive and recognize the meaning of.

7. UNDERSTAND.

follow on *verb*
To occur after (another) in time.

FOLLOW.

follow through *verb*
To strengthen the effect of (an action) by further action.

FOLLOW UP.

follow up *verb*
To strengthen the effect of (an action) by further action: *followed up the barrage with an assault.*

Syns: follow through (on), pursue.

follower *noun*
One who supports and adheres to another: *Lenin's followers.*

Syns: adherent, cohort, disciple, henchman, partisan, satellite, supporter.

following *adjective*
Occurring right after another: *On the following day he quit.*

Syns: coming, ensuing, next.

following *noun*
1. A group of attendants or followers.
2. The body of persons who admire a public personality, esp. an entertainer.

1. RETINUE.
2. PUBLIC *noun.*

follow on *verb*
follow through *verb*
follow up *verb*

SEE **follow.**
SEE **follow.**
SEE **follow.**

folly *noun*
Foolish behavior.

FOOLISHNESS.

foment *verb*
To induce or elicit (a reaction or emotion).

AROUSE.

fomenter *noun*
One who agitates, esp. politically.

AGITATOR.

fond *adjective*
Feeling and expressing affection.

AFFECTIONATE.

fondle *verb*
To touch or stroke affectionately.

CARESS *verb.*

fondness *noun*
1. The condition of being closely tied to another by affection or faith.
2. A liking or personal preference for something.

1. ATTACHMENT.
2. TASTE *noun.*

food *noun*
1. Something fit to be eaten: *delicious food.*

1. ***Syns:*** bread, chow (*Slang*), chuck² (*Regional*), comestible, eats (*Slang*), edible(s), esculent, fare, foodstuff, grub (*Slang*), meat, nurture, peck², provisions, sustenance. —*Idioms* daily bread, meat and drink.

2. That which sustains the mind or spirit: *a passion that found its food in music.*

2. ***Syns:*** aliment, nourishment, nutriment, pablum, pap, sustenance.

foodstuff *noun*
Something fit to be eaten.

FOOD.

fool *noun*
1. One deficient in judgment and good sense: *acted like a fool over her.*

1. ***Syns:*** ass, dope (*Informal*), goose (*Informal*), idiot, imbecile, jackass, jerk (*Slang*), mooncalf, nincompoop, ninny, nitwit (*Informal*), numskull (*also* numbskull), schmo (*also* schmoe) (*Slang*), schmuck (*Slang*), simple, simpleton, tomfool, turkey (*Slang*).

2. A person who is easily deceived or victimized.
3. A mentally deficient person: *had the mentality of a fool.*

2. DUPE *noun.*
3. ***Syns:*** ament, cretin, gander¹ (*Informal*), half-wit, idiot, imbecile, moron, natural, simpleton.

fool *verb*

1. To cause to accept what is false, esp. by trickery or misrepresentation.
2. *Informal.* To make jokes; behave playfully.
3. To move one's fingers or hands in a nervous or aimless fashion.
4. To handle something idly, ignorantly, or destructively.

fool around *verb*
1. *Informal.* To waste time by engaging in aimless activity.
2. *Informal.* To be sexually unfaithful to another.

fool away *verb*
To spend (money) excessively and usu. foolishly.

fool around *verb*
fool away *verb*
foolery *noun*
Foolish behavior.

foolhardy *adjective*
Characterized by unthinking boldness and haste.

foolish *adjective*
1. So senseless as to be laughable: *a foolish land-speculation scheme.*

2. Displaying a complete lack of forethought and good sense.

foolishness *noun*
Foolish behavior: *The utter foolishness of that marketing plan is embarrassing.*

foolproof *adjective*
Designed so as to be impervious to human error or misuse: *a foolproof detonator.*

foot *verb*
1. To go on foot.
2. To move rhythmically to music, using patterns of steps or gestures.
3. To combine (figures) to form a sum.

foot *noun*
The lowest or supporting part or structure.

footfall *noun*
The act or manner of going on foot.

footing *noun*
1. Anything on which something immaterial, such as an argument or charge, rests.
2. An established position from which to operate or deal with others.
3. The lowest or supporting part or structure.
4. Positioning of one individual vis-à-vis others.

footstep *noun*
The act or manner of going on foot.

1. DECEIVE.
2. JOKE *verb.*
3. FIDDLE.
4. TAMPER.

1. MESS AROUND at **mess.**
2. PHILANDER *verb.*

WASTE *verb.*
SEE **fool.**
SEE **fool.**
FOOLISHNESS.

RASH[1].

1. **Syns:** absurd, balmy (*Slang*), cock-eyed (*Slang*), crazy, dippy (*Slang*), fantastic (*also* fantastical), feeble-minded, harebrained, idiotic, insane, jerky (*Slang*), loony (*also* luny) (*Informal*), loopy (*Informal*), lunatic, mad, nonsensical, preposterous, sappy (*Slang*), silly, softheaded, tomfool, unearthly, wacky (*also* whacky) (*Slang*), zany.
Near-ants: judicious, sagacious, sage; discreet, prudent, savvy (*Slang*), shrewd.
Ants: sensible, wise.
2. MINDLESS.

Syns: absurdity, craziness, folly, foolery, idiocy, insanity, lunacy, preposterousness, senselessness, silliness, tomfoolery.

Syn: fail-safe.

1. WALK *verb.*
2. DANCE *verb.*

3. ADD.

BASE[1] *noun.*

TREAD *noun.*

1. BASIS.

2. BASIS.

3. BASE[1] *noun.*
4. PLACE *noun.*

TREAD *noun.*

foozle *noun*
A stupid, clumsy mistake.   BLUNDER *noun*.

foozler *noun*
A stupid, clumsy person.   BLUNDERER.

forage *verb*
To make a thorough search of.   SCOUR.

foray *noun*
An act of invading, esp. by military forces.   INVASION.

foray *verb*
To enter in order to attack, plunder, destroy, or   INVADE.
conquer.

forbear *verb*
To hold oneself back.   REFRAIN.

forbearance *noun*
1. Forbearing or lenient treatment.   1. TOLERANCE.
2. The capacity of enduring hardship or inconvenience 2. PATIENCE.
   without complaint.

forbearant *adjective*
Archaic. Not strict or severe.   TOLERANT.

forbearing *adjective*
1. Not strict or severe.   1. TOLERANT.
2. Enduring or capable of enduring hardship or   2. PATIENT.
   inconvenience without complaint.

forbid *verb*
To refuse to allow: *The law forbids tax evasion. The*   ***Syns:*** ban, disallow, enjoin, inhibit,
guard forbade them entry.   interdict, outlaw, prohibit, proscribe.
                                                           Near-syns: exclude, preclude, prevent,
                                                           restrain; check, halt, stop; hinder, impede,
                                                           obstruct.
                                                           Ants: allow, permit.

forbiddance *noun*
A refusal to allow: *protested that nation's forbiddance of*   ***Syns:*** ban, disallowance, interdiction,
racial mingling.   prohibition, proscription, taboo (*also*
                                                               tabu).

forbidden *adjective*
Not allowed: *Smoking is forbidden.*   ***Syns:*** banned, impermissible, prohibited,
                                                               taboo (*also* tabu), verboten.

forbidding *adjective*
So disagreeably austere as to discourage approach: *a*   ***Syns:*** inhospitable, unhospitable,
forbidding look; forbidding castle walls.   uninviting.

force *noun*
1. Power used to overcome resistance: *used force to*   1. ***Syns:*** coercion, constraint, duress,
   obtain a confession.   pressure, strength, violence.
2. Effective means of influencing, compelling, or   2. MUSCLE *noun*.
   punishing.
3. The capacity to exert an influence: *The force of the*   3. ***Syns:*** forcefulness, magnetism, power,
   speaker's personality moved the crowd to an ovation.   vigor, vitality.
4. Capacity or power for work or vigorous activity.   4. ENERGY.
5. A group of people organized for a particular purpose: 5. ***Syns:*** body, corps, crew, detachment,
   a work force; a police force.   team, unit.
6. The strong effect exerted by one person or thing on   6. IMPACT *noun*.
   another.

force *verb*
1. To cause (a person or thing) to act or move in spite   1. ***Syns:*** coerce, compel, constrain, make,
   of resistance: *Tear gas forced the fugitives out of*   oblige, pressure.
   their hiding place.
2. To compel (another) to participate in or submit to a   2. RAPE.
   sexual act.
3. To compel by pressure or threats.   3. COERCE.

forced *adjective*
1. Done under force: *roads built with forced labor.*   1. ***Syns:*** coerced, compulsory, constrained.

2. Not natural or spontaneous: *She greeted us with a forced smile.*

forceful *adjective*
1. Full of or displaying force: *a forceful speaker.*

2. Bold and definite in character.
3. Possessing, exerting, or displaying energy.
4. Expressed or performed with emphasis.

forcefully *adverb*
With intense energy and force.

forcefulness *noun*
The capacity to exert an influence.

forcible *adjective*
Accomplished by force: *forcible seizure of American sailors.*

forcibly *adverb*
With intense energy and force.

fore *noun*
The part of an object, person, etc., facing the viewer.

forearm *verb*
To prepare (oneself) for action.

forebear *noun*
A person from whom one is descended.

forebode *verb*
To give warning signs of (impending peril).

forecast *verb*
To tell about or make known (future events) in advance, esp. by means of special knowledge or inference.

forecast *noun*
The act of predicting.

foredestine *verb*
To determine the future of in advance.

foredoom *verb*
To predestine to a tragic end.

foredoom *noun*
Rare. A predestined tragic end.

foredoomed *adjective*
Sentenced to terrible, irrevocable punishment.

forefather *noun*
A person from whom one is descended.

forefend *verb*
foregather *verb*
forego *verb*
foregoing *adjective*
1. Next before the present one.
2. Just gone by or elapsed.

forehand *noun*
A dominating position, as in a conflict.

forehanded *adjective*
Careful in the use of material resources.

forehandedness *noun*
Careful use of material resources.

foreign *adjective*
1. Of, from, or characteristic of another place or part of the world: *foreign species of plants; a foreign accent.*
2. Not part of the essential nature of a thing: *Jealousy is foreign to his nature.*

---

2. *Syns:* effortful, labored, strained.

1. *Syns:* dynamic (*also* dynamical), effective, powerful, strong, vigorous.
2. EMPHATIC.
3. ENERGETIC.
4. EMPHATIC.

HARD *adverb.*

FORCE *noun.*

Syns: coercive, strong-arm (*Informal*), violent.

HARD *adverb.*

FRONT *noun.*

GIRD.

ANCESTOR.

THREATEN.

PREDICT.

PREDICTION.

FATE *verb.*

FATE *verb.*

FATE *noun.*

CONDEMNED.

ANCESTOR.
SEE **forfend.**
SEE **forgather.**
SEE **forgo.**

1. LAST[1] *adjective.*
2. PAST *adjective.*

ADVANTAGE *noun.*

ECONOMICAL.

ECONOMY.

1. *Syns:* alien, exotic, outlandish (*Archaic*), strange.
2. *Syns:* alien, extraneous, extrinsic.
Near-syns: incompatible, inconsistent, inconsonant.
Ant: germane.

foreigner *noun*
A person coming from another country: *a foreigner who came to the U.S. in 1910.*

Syns: alien, émigré, newcomer, outlander, outsider, stranger.

foreknow *verb*
To know in advance.

FORESEE.

foreman *noun*
Someone who directs and supervises workers.

BOSS *noun*.

foremost *adjective*
1. Most important, influential, or significant.
2. Having or exercising authority.

1. PRIMARY.
2. PRINCIPAL.

forenoon *noun*
The time of day from sunrise to noon.

MORNING.

forensics *noun*
The presentation of an argument.

ARGUMENTATION.

foreordain *verb*
To determine the future in advance.

FATE *verb*.

foreordained *adjective*
Governed and decided by or as if by fate.

FATED.

forepart *noun*
The part of an object, person, etc., facing the viewer.

FRONT *noun*.

forerun *verb*
To come, exist, or occur prior to in time.

PRECEDE.

foresee *verb*
To know in advance: *difficulties that no one could foresee.*

Syns: anticipate, divine[2], envision, foreknow, see.
Near-syns: forebode, forecast, foretell, predict, presage, prophesy.

foreshadow *verb*
1. To give an indication of something in advance.
2. To give reason for expecting.

1. ADUMBRATE.
2. PROMISE *verb*.

foresight *noun*
1. Unusual or creative discernment or perception.
2. The exercise of good judgment or common sense in practical matters.

1. VISION.
2. PRUDENCE.

forestall *verb*
To prohibit from occurring by advance planning or action.

PREVENT.

forestalling *noun*
The act of preventing.

PREVENTION.

forestalling *adjective*
Intended to prevent.

PREVENTIVE.

forestallment *noun*
The act of preventing.

PREVENTION.

foreswear *verb*

SEE **forswear**.

foresworn *adjective*

SEE **forsworn**.

foretaste *noun*
A limited or anticipatory experience.

TASTE *noun*.

foretell *verb*
1. To tell about or make known (future events) by or as if by supernatural means.
2. To tell about or make known (future events) in advance, esp. by means of special knowledge or inference.

1. PROPHESY.
2. PREDICT.

foreteller *noun*
A person who foretells future events by or as if by supernatural means.

PROPHET.

foretelling *noun*
1. Something that is foretold by or as if by supernatural means.
2. The act of predicting.

1. PROPHECY.
2. PREDICTION.

forethink *verb*
To consider and plan in advance.   PREMEDITATE.

forethought *noun*
The exercise of good judgment or common sense in   PRUDENCE.
practical matters.

foretoken *noun*
A phenomenon that serves as a sign or warning of   OMEN.
some future good or evil.

  foretoken *verb*
  To give reason for expecting.   PROMISE *verb.*

forever *noun*
The totality of time without beginning or end.   ETERNITY.

foreverness *noun*
1. The quality or state of having no end.   **1.** ENDLESSNESS.
2. The totality of time without beginning or end.   **2.** ETERNITY.

forewarn *verb*
1. To notify (someone) of imminent danger or risk.   **1.** WARN.
2. To give warning signs of (impending peril).   **2.** THREATEN.

forewarning *noun*
1. Advice to beware, as of a person or thing.   **1.** WARNING *noun.*
2. An indication of impending danger or harm.   **2.** THREAT.

foreword *noun*
A short section of preliminary remarks.   INTRODUCTION.

forfeit *verb*
To suffer the loss of.   DROP *verb.*

forfend also **forefend** *verb*
To prohibit from occurring by advance planning or   PREVENT.
action.

forgather also **foregather** *verb*
To come together.   ASSEMBLE.

forge[1] *verb*
1. To shape, break, or flatten with repeated blows.   **1.** BEAT *verb.*
2. To create by forming, combining, or altering   **2.** MAKE.
   materials.
3. To make a fraudulent copy of.   **3.** COUNTERFEIT *verb.*

forge[2] *verb*
To move or advance against strong resistance.   PLUNGE *verb.*

forgery *noun*
A fraudulent imitation.   COUNTERFEIT *noun.*

forget *verb*
To fail to remember: *I always forget his name.*   **Syn:** disremember. —*Idiom* draw a blank.

forgetful *adjective*
Unable to remember: *Anyone who's that forgetful*   **Syn:** amnesiac.
should write things down.

forgetfulness *noun*
Freedom from worry, care, or unpleasantness.   ESCAPE *noun.*

forgivable *adjective*
Admitting of forgiveness or pardon.   PARDONABLE.

forgive *verb*
To grant forgiveness for a fault, offense, or injury: *It*   **Syns:** condone, excuse, exculpate, pardon,
was an insulting remark, but I forgave him.   remit. —*Idiom* forgive and forget.
                                                             Near-ants: castigate, chasten, chastise,
                                                             discipline; admonish, rebuke, reprimand;
                                                             blame, censure, criticize.

forgiveness *noun*
The act or an instance of forgiving: *forgiveness for all*   **Syns:** absolution, amnesty, condonation,
our sins.   exculpation, pardon, remission.

forgo also **forego** *verb*
To let (something) go.   RELINQUISH.

fork *noun*
Something resembling or structurally analogous to a tree branch. BRANCH *noun.*

fork *verb*
To separate into branches or branchlike parts. BRANCH *verb.*

fork out *verb*
Informal. To distribute (money) as payment. SPEND.

fork out *verb* SEE **fork.**

forlorn *adjective*
1. Having been given up and left alone. 1. ABANDONED.
2. Empty of people. 2. LONELY.
3. Having lost all hope. 3. DESPONDENT.

form *noun*
1. The external outline of a thing: *a cake in the form of a guitar.* 1. *Syns:* cast, configuration, figure, format, pattern, shape.
2. A model for making a mold: *Concrete is poured into forms.* 2. *Syns:* cast, matrix.
3. A conventional social gesture or act without intrinsic purpose. 3. RITUAL *noun.*
4. An accepted way of doing something. 4. CONVENTION.
5. A state of sound readiness. 5. TRIM *noun.*
6. A document used in applying, as for a job. 6. APPLICATION.

form *verb*
1. To be the constituent parts of. 1. CONSTITUTE.
2. To give form to by or as if by pressing and kneading: *used his hands to form the clay into a statue.* 2. *Syns:* model, mold, shape.
3. To come gradually to have. 3. DEVELOP.

formal *adjective*
1. Requiring elegant clothes and fine manners: *a formal dance.* 1. *Syns:* dressy, fancy-dress, full-dress.
2. Of or characterized by ceremony. 2. RITUAL *adjective.*
3. Fond of or given to ceremony. 3. CEREMONIOUS.

formalistic *adjective*
Characterized by a narrow concern for book learning and formal rules, without knowledge or experience of practical matters. PEDANTIC.

formality *noun*
1. A conventional social gesture or act without intrinsic purpose. 1. RITUAL *noun.*
2. Strict observance of social conventions. 2. CEREMONY.

format *noun*
The external outline of a thing. FORM *noun.*

formation *noun*
A way or condition of being arranged. ARRANGEMENT.

former *adjective*
1. Having been such previously. 1. LATE *adjective.*
2. Just gone by or elapsed. 2. PAST *adjective.*

formerly *adverb*
At a time in the past. EARLIER.

formicate *verb*
1. To overflow with. 1. TEEM[1].
2. To experience a repugnant tingling sensation. 2. CRAWL *verb.*

formidable *adjective*
1. Causing or able to cause fear. 1. FEARFUL.
2. Imposing a severe test of bodily or spiritual strength. 2. BURDENSOME.

formless *adjective*
Having no distinct shape. SHAPELESS.

formulaic *adjective*
Lacking in interest or originality. ROUTINE *adjective.*

formulate *verb*
1. To devise and set down.
2. To use ingenuity in making, developing, or achieving.
3. To convey in language or words of a particular form.

1. DRAFT *verb*.
2. INVENT.
3. PHRASE *verb*.

forsake *verb*
To give up without intending to return or claim again.

ABANDON *verb*.

forsaken *adjective*
Having been given up and left alone.

ABANDONED.

forswear also **foreswear** *verb*
1. To cease trying to accomplish or continue.
2. To make untrue declarations.

1. ABANDON *verb*.
2. LIE² *verb*.

forsworn or **foresworn** *adjective*
Marked by lying under oath.

PERJURIOUS.

forte *noun*
Something at which a person excels: *She's all right as a cook, but writing is her forte.*

Syns: bag (*Slang*), eminency, medium, métier, specialty, thing (*Slang*). —*Idioms* long suit, strong point (*or* suit).
Near-syns: ability, competence, effectiveness, expertise.

forthcoming *adjective*
In the relatively near future.

COMING.

forthright *adjective*
1. Speaking or spoken freely and sincerely.
2. Executed without pretense or obfuscation.

1. FRANK.
2. PLAIN *adjective*.

forthwith *adverb*
Without delay.

DIRECTLY.

fortify *verb*
1. To make firmer in a particular conviction or habit.
2. To prepare (oneself) for action.

1. CONFIRM.
2. GIRD.

fortitude *noun*
The quality of mind enabling one to face danger or hardship resolutely.

COURAGE.

fortitudinous *adjective*
Having or showing courage.

BRAVE *adjective*.

fortuitous *adjective*
Occurring unexpectedly.

ACCIDENTAL *adjective*.

fortuitousness *noun*
The quality shared by random, unintended, or unpredictable events or this quality regarded as the cause of such events.

CHANCE *noun*.

fortuity *noun*
1. The quality shared by random, unintended, or unpredictable events or this quality regarded as the cause of such events.
2. An unexpected random event.

1. CHANCE *noun*.
2. CHANCE *noun*.

fortunate *adjective*
1. Indicative of future success.
2. Characterized by luck or good fortune.

1. FAVORABLE.
2. HAPPY.

fortunateness *noun*
Success attained as a result of chance.

LUCK.

fortune *noun*
1. A large sum of money: *made a fortune in gold mining.*

1. ***Syns:*** boodle (*Slang*), bundle (*Slang*), mint, pile (*Slang*), wad (*Informal*). —*Idioms* pretty penny, tidy sum.

2. All property or goods having economic value.
3. A great amount of accumulated money and precious possessions.
4. The quality shared by random, unintended, or unpredictable events or this quality regarded as the cause of such events.

2. RESOURCES.
3. RICHES.

4. CHANCE *noun*.

5. Success attained as a result of chance. | **5.** LUCK.

forward *verb*
1. To cause to move forward or upward, as toward a goal. | **1.** ADVANCE *verb*.
2. To cause (something) to be conveyed to a destination. | **2.** SEND.

forward *adjective*
1. Ahead of current trends or customs. | **1.** ADVANCED.
2. Rude and disrespectful. | **2.** IMPUDENT.

forwardness *noun*
The state or quality of being impudent. | IMPUDENCE.

fossil *noun*
An old-fashioned person who is reluctant to change or innovate. | SQUARE *noun*.

foster *verb*
1. To cause to move forward or upward, as toward a goal. | **1.** ADVANCE *verb*.
2. To help bring about. | **2.** PROMOTE.
3. To promote and sustain the development of. | **3.** NURSE.

foul *adjective*
1. Heavily soiled; very dirty or unclean. | **1.** FILTHY.
2. So objectionable as to elicit despisal. | **2.** FILTHY.
3. Having an unpleasant odor. | **3.** SMELLY.
4. Extremely unpleasant to the senses or feelings. | **4.** OFFENSIVE *adjective*.
5. Offensive to accepted standards of decency. | **5.** OBSCENE.
6. Deserving strong condemnation. | **6.** INFAMOUS.

foul *verb*
1. To make physically impure. | **1.** CONTAMINATE.
2. To twist together so that separation is difficult. | **2.** ENTANGLE.

foul up *verb*
Slang. To harm irreparably through inept handling; make a mess of. | BOTCH.

foulness *noun*
1. The condition or state of being dirty. | **1.** DIRTINESS.
2. Impure condition. | **2.** IMPURITY.

foul-smelling *adjective*
Having an unpleasant odor. | SMELLY.

foul up *verb* | SEE **foul**.

found *verb*
1. To bring into existence formally: *My grandfather founded the university.* | **1.** *Syns:* constitute, create, establish, institute, organize, originate, set up, start.
2. To take or serve as the basis for. | **2.** BASE[1] *verb*.

foundation *noun*
1. The act of founding or establishing: *the foundation of a scholarship fund.* | **1.** *Syns:* creation, establishment, institution.
2. The lowest or supporting part or structure. | **2.** BASE[1] *noun*.
3. A fundamental principle or underlying concept. | **3.** BASIS.
4. Anything on which something immaterial, such as an argument or charge, rests. | **4.** BASIS.
5. A justifying fact or consideration. | **5.** BASIS.

foundational *adjective*
Arising from or going to the root or source. | RADICAL *adjective*.

founder[1] *noun*
One that creates, founds, or originates. | ORIGINATOR.

founder[2] *verb*
To go beneath the surface or to the bottom of a liquid. | SINK *verb*.

fount *noun*
A point of origination. | ORIGIN.

fountain *noun*
A point of origination. | ORIGIN.

fountainhead *noun*
A point of origination.

ORIGIN.

four-flush *verb*
Slang. To cause to accept what is false, esp. by trickery or misrepresentation.

DECEIVE.

fourth estate *noun*
Journalists and journalism in general.

PRESS *noun.*

foxiness *noun*
Deceitful cleverness.

ART.

foxy *adjective*
Deceitfully clever.

ARTFUL.

fracas *noun*
A quarrel or fight marked by very noisy, disorderly, and often violent behavior.

BRAWL *noun.*

fractional *adjective*
Pertaining to or affecting only a part; not total.

PARTIAL.

fractious *adjective*
Not submitting to discipline or control.

UNRULY.

fractiousness *noun*
The quality or condition of being unruly.

UNRULINESS.

fracturable *adjective*
Easily broken or damaged.

FRAGILE.

fracture *verb*
To crack or split into two or more fragments by means of or as a result of force, a blow, or strain.

BREAK *verb.*

fragile *adjective*
1. Easily broken or damaged: *a fragile piece of glassware.*

1. **Syns:** breakable, brittle, delicate, fracturable, frangible.
Near-ants: strong, sturdy, tenacious, tough.
Ants: indestructible, unbreakable.

2. Not physically strong.

2. INFIRM.

fragility *noun*
The condition of being infirm or physically weak.

INFIRMITY.

fragment *noun*
1. A tiny amount.
2. Residual matter.

1. BIT[1].
2. END *noun.*

fragment *verb*
To reduce or become reduced to pieces or components.

BREAK UP at **break.**

fragmentary *adjective*
Pertaining to or affecting only a part; not total.

PARTIAL.

fragmentize *verb*
To reduce or become reduced to pieces or components.

BREAK UP at **break.**

fragrance *noun*
A sweet or pleasant odor: *the fragrance of a fresh rose.*

Syns: aroma, bouquet, perfume, redolence, scent.

fragrant *adjective*
Having a pleasant odor: *a fragrant bouquet of lilacs.*

Syns: aromatic, perfumed, redolent, scented.
Near-syns: balmy, delicious, delightful, savory, sweet.
Ants: fetid, smelly.

frail *adjective*
Not physically strong.

INFIRM.

frailty *noun*
1. The condition of being infirm or physically weak.
2. A liking or personal preference for something.

1. INFIRMITY.
2. WEAKNESS.

frame *verb*
1. To devise and set down.
2. To form a strategy for.

1. DRAFT *verb.*
2. DESIGN *verb.*

3. To create by forming, combining, or altering materials.

3. MAKE.

frangible *adjective*
Easily broken or damaged.

FRAGILE.

frank *adjective*
Speaking or spoken freely and sincerely: *a frank statement of his objections.*

Syns: candid, direct, downright, forthright, honest, open, plainspoken, straight, straightforward, straight-from-the-shoulder (*Informal*), undisguised.
Near-syns: blunt, outspoken, uninhibited; fair, impartial, just, unprejudiced; natural, simple; brash, brazen.
Ant: reticent.

frantic *adjective*
Marked by extreme excitement, confusion, or agitation: *frantic with worry; a frantic scramble for seats.*

Syns: delirious, frenetic, frenzied, mad, madding (*Obs.*), rabid, wild.

frantically *adverb*
In a violent, strenuous way.

HARD *adverb*.

fraternity *noun*
A group of people united in a relationship and having some interest, activity, or purpose in common.

UNION.

fraternize *verb*
To keep company.

ASSOCIATE *verb*.

fraud *noun*
1. An act of cheating.
2. One who is not what he claims to be.

1. CHEAT *noun*.
2. FAKE *noun*.

fraudulent *adjective*
Fraudulently or deceptively imitative.

COUNTERFEIT *adjective*.

fray *noun*
1. A quarrel or fight marked by very noisy, disorderly, and often violent behavior.
2. A physical conflict involving two or more.

1. BRAWL *noun*.

2. FIGHT *noun*.

freak *noun*
1. A person or animal that is abnormally formed: *freaks exhibited in the circus sideshow.*
2. An impulsive, often illogical turn of mind.
3. *Slang.* A person who is ardently devoted to a particular subject or activity.

1. *Syns:* monster, monstrosity, oddity.

2. FANCY *noun*.
3. ENTHUSIAST.

freakish *adjective*
1. Resembling a freak: *a person of freakish appearance.*

2. Deviating from the customary.
3. Following no predictable pattern.

1. *Syns:* bizarre, freaky, grotesque, monstrous.
2. ECCENTRIC *adjective*.
3. CAPRICIOUS.

freaky *adjective*
Resembling a freak.

FREAKISH.

freckle *verb*
To mark with many small spots.

SPECKLE.

free *adjective*
1. Costing nothing: *a free ticket to the ball game.*

2. At liberty; not imprisoned or enslaved: *Slaves became free with Lincoln's Emancipation Proclamation.*
3. Able to move about at will without bounds or restraint.
4. Done by one's own choice.
5. Having political independence: *Jamaica is now a free country.*
6. Freed from contact or connection.
7. Characterized by bounteous giving.
8. Lacking literal exactness.

1. *Syns:* complimentary, cost-free, gratis, gratuitous, on-the-house (*Slang*).
2. *Syns:* emancipated, liberated, manumitted, released.

3. LOOSE *adjective*.

4. VOLUNTARY *adjective*.
5. *Syns:* autonomous, independent, sovereign.
6. CLEAR *adjective*.
7. GENEROUS.
8. LOOSE *adjective*.

9. Not spoken for or occupied.

9. UNRESERVED.

10. Speaking or spoken without reserve.

10. OUTSPOKEN.

free *verb*
To set at liberty: *freeing a man from prison.*

Syns: discharge, emancipate, liberate, loose, manumit, release, spring (*Slang*). —*Idiom* let loose.
SEE **freebie.**

freebee *noun*
freebie also **freebee** *noun*
Slang. A free ticket entitling one to transportation or admission.

PASS *noun.*

freedom *noun*
  1. The condition of being politically free: *granted the colony its freedom.*

1. ***Syns:*** autonomy, independence, liberty, sovereignty.

  2. The state of not being in confinement or servitude.

2. LIBERTY.

  3. Ease of movement: *a coat that gives the wearer plenty of freedom.*

3. ***Syns:*** elbowroom, latitude, play, swing.

  4. Departure from normal rules or procedures.

4. LIBERTY.

free-for-all *noun*
A quarrel or fight marked by very noisy, disorderly, and often violent behavior.

BRAWL *noun.*

freehanded *adjective*
Characterized by bounteous giving.

GENEROUS.

freehandedness *noun*
The quality or state of being generous.

GENEROSITY.

freeloader *noun*
Slang. One who depends on another for support without reciprocating.

PARASITE.

freeloading *adjective*
Slang. Of or characteristic of a parasite.

PARASITIC.

free-speaking *adjective*
Speaking or spoken without reserve.

OUTSPOKEN.

free-spoken *adjective*
  1. Given to conversation.

1. TALKATIVE.

  2. Speaking or spoken without reserve.

2. OUTSPOKEN.

freeway *noun*
A course affording passage from one place to another.

WAY *noun.*

freezing *adjective*
Very cold.

FRIGID.

freight *noun*
Something carried physically.

BURDEN *noun.*

freight *verb*
  1. To place a burden or heavy load on.

1. CHARGE *verb.*

  2. To make or become full; put into as much as can be held.

2. FILL.

  3. To cause to be filled with a particular mood or tone.

3. CHARGE *verb.*

frenetic *adjective*
Marked by extreme excitement, confusion, or agitation.

FRANTIC.

frenzied *adjective*
Marked by extreme excitement, confusion, or agitation.

FRANTIC.

frenziedly *adverb*
In a violent, strenuous way.

HARD *adverb.*

frequent *verb*
To visit regularly: *We frequented the park on Saturday mornings.*

Syns: hang around (*Informal*), hang out (*Slang*), haunt, resort to.

frequent *adjective*
Occurring quite often.

COMMON *adjective.*

frequently *adverb*
For the most part.

USUALLY.

fresh *adjective*
  1. Not previously known or used: *fresh evidence; a fresh coat of paint.*

1. ***Syns:*** brand-new, different, new.

2. Being an addition.

3. Bright and clear; not dull or faded: *the fresh complexion of a young girl.*

4. *Informal.* Rude and disrespectful.

5. Showing marked departure from previous practice.

freshen *verb*

1. To impart renewed energy and strength to (a person).

2. To make neat and trim; make presentable.

freshet *noun*

An abundant, usu. overwhelming flow.

freshman *noun*

One who is just starting to learn or do something.

freshness *noun*

The quality of being novel.

fret *verb*

1. To turn over in the mind, moodily and at length.

2. To worry over trifles.

3. To trouble the nerves or peace of mind of, esp. by repeated vexations.

4. To make (the skin) raw by or as if by friction.

fretful *adjective*

1. Being unable to endure irritation or opposition.

2. Easily annoyed.

fribbling *adjective*

Given to lighthearted silliness.

friction *noun*

A state of disagreement and disharmony.

friend *noun*

1. A person whom one knows well, likes, and trusts: *He's been my friend since high school.*

2. A person whom one knows casually.

3. A person who supports or champions an activity, institution, etc.

friendliness *noun*

The quality of being pleasant and friendly.

friendly *adjective*

1. Of or befitting a friend or friends: *a friendly letter; friendly cooperation.*

2. Very closely associated.

3. Easily approached.

4. Exhibiting accord in feeling or action.

friendship *noun*

The condition of being friends: *Our friendship has survived many arguments.*

fright *noun*

1. Great agitation and anxiety caused by the expectation or the realization of danger.

2. An unsightly object.

fright *verb*

Archaic. To fill with fear.

frighten *verb*

To fill with fear: *The explosion frightened me. A small child frightens easily.*

---

2. ADDITIONAL.

3. *Syns:* blooming, creamy, glowing, peaches-and-cream.

4. IMPUDENT.

5. NEW *adjective.*

1. REFRESH.

2. TIDY *verb.*

FLOOD *noun.*

BEGINNER.

NOVELTY.

1. BROOD.

2. FUSS *verb.*

3. ANNOY.

4. CHAFE.

1. IMPATIENT.

2. IRRITABLE.

GIDDY.

CONFLICT *noun.*

1. *Syns:* amigo (*Spanish*), confidant, familiar, intimate[1], mate, sidekick (*Slang*).

2. ACQUAINTANCE.

3. PATRON.

AMIABILITY.

1. *Syns:* amiable, amicable, chummy (*Informal*), congenial, convivial, neighborly, sympathetic, warmhearted.

2. FAMILIAR *adjective.*

3. APPROACHABLE.

4. HARMONIOUS.

Syns: brotherhood, comradeship, intimacy.

1. FEAR *noun.*

2. MESS *noun.*

FRIGHTEN.

Syns: affright (*Archaic*), alarm, fright (*Archaic*), panic, scare, scarify (*Regional*), shake up (*Informal*), startle, terrify, terrorize. —*Idioms* make one's blood run cold, make one's hair stand on end, scare silly (*or* spitless *or* stiff), scare the daylights out of.

frightened *adjective*
Filled with fear or terror. AFRAID.

frightening *adjective*
Causing or able to cause fear. FEARFUL.

frightful *adjective*
1. Causing or able to cause fear.
2. Very bad.
3. Too awful to be described.

1. FEARFUL.
2. TERRIBLE.
3. UNSPEAKABLE.

frightfulness *noun*
The quality or condition of being ugly. UGLINESS.

frigid *adjective*
1. Very cold: *a frigid January day.*

1. *Syns:* arctic, bitter, boreal, freezing, frore (*Archaic*), frory (*Archaic*), frosty, gelid, glacial, icy, polar, wintry.

2. Deficient in or lacking sexual desire: *a frigid person unable to respond to love.*
3. Lacking all friendliness and warmth.

2. *Syns:* ardorless, cold, inhibited, passionless, unresponsive.
3. COLD *adjective.*

frill *noun*
Something costly and unnecessary. LUXURY.

fringe *noun*
1. A fairly narrow line or space forming a boundary.
2. The periphery of a city or town.

1. BORDER *noun.*
2. SKIRTS.

fringe *verb*
To put or form a border on. BORDER *verb.*

frippery *noun*
Something lacking substance or depth. FROTH *noun.*

frisk *verb*
1. To leap and skip about playfully.
2. To examine the person or personal effects of in order to find something lost or concealed.

1. GAMBOL.
2. SEARCH *verb.*

frisk *noun*
A thorough search of a place or person. SHAKEDOWN at **shake down.**

fritter away *verb*
To spend (money) excessively and usu. foolishly. WASTE *verb.*

frivolity *noun*
Something lacking substance or depth. FROTH *noun.*

frivolous *adjective*
Given to lighthearted silliness. GIDDY.

frock *noun*
A one-piece, skirted outer garment for women and children. DRESS *noun.*

frolic *verb*
1. To leap and skip about playfully.
2. To behave riotously.

1. GAMBOL.
2. REVEL *verb.*

frolic *noun*
A mischievous act. PRANK.

front *noun*
1. The part of an object, person, etc., facing the viewer: *a blouse with tucks down the front; spilled gravy down his front.*

1. *Syns:* fore, forepart.

2. The forward outer surface of a building.
3. A deceptive outward appearance.

2. FAÇADE.
3. FAÇADE.

front *verb*
1. To have the face or front turned in a specific direction.
2. To confront boldly and courageously.
3. To meet face-to-face, esp. defiantly.

1. FACE *verb.*
2. DEFY.
3. CONFRONT.

frontage *noun*
The forward outer surface of a building. FAÇADE.

frontal *noun*
The forward outer surface of a building. FAÇADE.

frontispiece *noun*
Archit. The forward outer surface of a building.   FAÇADE.

front-runner *noun*
A leading contestant.   LEADER.

frore *adjective*
Archaic. Very cold.   FRIGID.

frory *adjective*
Archaic. Very cold.   FRIGID.

frosty *adjective*
1. Very cold.   1. FRIGID.
2. Not friendly, sociable, or warm in manner.   2. COOL *adjective*.

froth *noun*
1. Something lacking substance or depth: *The play was*   1. **Syns:** fiddle-faddle (*Slang*), frippery,
   nothing but froth.   frivolity, trivia, triviality.
2. A mass of bubbles in or on the surface of a liquid.   2. FOAM *noun*.
   froth *verb*
   To form or cause to form foam.   FOAM *verb*.

frothy *adjective*
1. Amusing but essentially empty and frivolous: *a*   1. **Syn:** light[2].
   frothy new comedy.
2. Consisting of or resembling foam.   2. FOAMY.
3. Given to lighthearted silliness.   3. GIDDY.

froward *adjective*
Given to acting in opposition to others.   CONTRARY *adjective*.

frown *verb*
To wrinkle one's brow, as in thought, puzzlement, or   **Syns:** glare, glower, lower[1] (*also* lour),
displeasure: *frowns when he's angry.*   scowl. —*Idiom* look black.
   frown on (or **upon**) *verb*
   To have or express an unfavorable opinion.   DISAPPROVE.
   frown *noun*
   The act of wrinkling the brow, as in thought,   **Syns:** glare, glower, lower[1] (*also* lour),
   puzzlement, or displeasure: *With a frown, she refused to*   scowl. —*Idiom* black look.
   shake hands.

frown on (or **upon**) *verb*   SEE **frown.**

frowsy *adjective*
Smelling of mildew or decay.   MOLDY.

frugal *adjective*
Careful in the use of material resources.   ECONOMICAL.

frugality *noun*
Careful use of material resources.   ECONOMY.

fruit *noun*
1. The produce gathered from the land.   1. HARVEST *noun*.
2. Something brought about by a cause.   2. EFFECT *noun*.

fruitage *noun*
The produce gathered from the land.   HARVEST *noun*.

fruitfulness *noun*
The quality or state of being fertile.   FERTILITY.

fruition *noun*
The condition of being fulfilled.   FULFILLMENT.

fruitless *adjective*
Having no useful result.   FUTILE.

fruitlessness *noun*
The condition or quality of being useless or ineffective.   FUTILITY.

fruity *adjective*
Slang. Afflicted with or exhibiting irrationality and   INSANE.
mental unsoundness.

frumpish *adjective*
Quite outmoded.   TACKY[2].

frustrate *verb*
To prevent from accomplishing a purpose: *A poor memory frustrated his efforts to become an actor.*

Syns: baffle, balk, check, checkmate, defeat, foil, stymie, thwart. —*Idiom* cut the ground from under.
Near-syns: block, hinder, impede, obstruct; disappoint, ruin, wreck; halt, interrupt.
Near-ants: accomplish, fulfill.
Ant: expedite.

fuddle *verb*
To cause to be unclear in mind or intent.

CONFUSE.

fuddy-duddy *noun*
An old-fashioned person who is reluctant to change or innovate.

SQUARE *noun.*

fudge *verb*
To proceed or perform in an unsteady, faltering manner.

MUDDLE.

fuehrer *noun*

SEE **führer.**

fugacious *adjective*
Lasting or existing only for a short time.

TRANSITORY.

fugitive *noun*
One who flees, as from home, confinement, captivity, justice, etc.: *a fugitive from a Cuban jail.*

Syns: escapee, refugee, runaway.

fugitive *adjective*
1. Fleeing or having fled, as from home, confinement, captivity, justice, etc.: *a manhunt for fugitive convicts.*
2. Lasting or existing only for a short time.

1. *Syns:* escaped, runaway.

2. TRANSITORY.

führer also **fuehrer** *noun*
German. An absolute ruler, esp. one who is harsh and oppressive.

DICTATOR.

fulfill *verb*
1. To carry out the functions, requirements, or terms of: *fulfilling her official duties; fulfilled my side of the bargain.*
2. To supply fully or completely.

1. *Syns:* discharge, execute, exercise, implement, perform. —*Idiom* live up to.
2. SATISFY.

fulfilled *adjective*
Having achieved satisfaction, as of one's goal: *She felt fulfilled when she reached the top of her profession.*

Syns: content, gratified, happy, satisfied.

fulfillment *noun*
The condition of being fulfilled: *dreams that could never reach fulfillment.*

Syns: consummation, culmination, fruition, realization.

full *adjective*
1. Completely filled: *a full pail; a room full of people.*

1. *Syns:* brimful, brimming, bursting, chockablock, chock-full (*also* chuck-full, choke-full), crammed, crowded, jam-full, jammed, jam-packed (*Informal*), loaded, packed, replete, stuffed, trig (*Brit. Regional*).
Near-ants: bare, barren, blank, vacant, vacuous, void.
Ant: empty.

2. Lacking nothing essential or normal.
3. Of full measure; not narrow or restricted: *a full skirt.*
4. Not deviating from correctness, accuracy, or completeness.
5. Characterized by attention to detail.
6. Not more or less.

2. COMPLETE *adjective.*
3. *Syns:* ample, capacious, voluminous, wide.
4. CLOSE[1] *adjective.*
5. DETAILED.
6. ROUND.

full-blooded *adjective*
1. Of pure breeding stock.
2. Of a healthy, reddish color.

1. THOROUGHBRED *adjective.*
2. RUDDY.

full-blown *adjective*
Having reached full growth and development.

MATURE *adjective*.

full-dress *adjective*
1. Requiring elegant clothes and fine manners.
2. Covering all aspects with painstaking accuracy.

1. FORMAL.
2. THOROUGH *adjective*.

full-fledged *adjective*
Having reached full growth and development.

MATURE *adjective*.

full-grown *adjective*
Having reached full growth and development.

MATURE *adjective*.

full-strength *adjective*
Not diluted or mixed with other substances.

STRAIGHT *adjective*.

fully *adverb*
1. To the fullest extent.
2. All the way.

1. COMPLETELY.
2. CLEAR *adverb*.

fulminate *verb*
To release or cause to release energy suddenly and violently, esp. with a loud noise.

EXPLODE.

fulmination *noun*
1. A violent release of confined energy, usu. accompanied by a loud sound and shock waves.
2. A long, violent, or blustering speech, usu. of censure or denunciation.

1. BLAST *noun*.
2. TIRADE.

fulsome *adjective*
Affectedly and self-servingly earnest.

UNCTUOUS.

fumble *verb*
1. To harm irreparably through inept handling; make a mess of.
2. To reach about or search blindly or uncertainly.
3. To proceed or perform in an unsteady, faltering manner.

1. BOTCH.
2. GROPE.
3. MUDDLE.

fumble *noun*
A stupid, clumsy mistake.

BLUNDER *noun*.

fumbler *noun*
A stupid, clumsy person.

BLUNDERER.

fume *verb*
To be or become angry.

ANGER *verb*.

fume *noun*
A condition of excited distress.

STATE *noun*.

fun *noun*
1. Activity engaged in for relaxation and amusement.
2. Actions taken as a joke.
3. Joyful, exuberant activity.

1. PLAY *noun*.
2. PLAY *noun*.
3. GAIETY.

fun *verb*
1. To make jokes; behave playfully.
2. To tease or mock good-humoredly.

1. JOKE *verb*.
2. JOKE *verb*.

function *noun*
1. The proper activity of a person or thing: *the function of a teacher; the function of a carburetor.*
2. A large or important social gathering.

1. *Syns:* job, purpose, role.
2. PARTY *noun*.

function *verb*
1. To function effectively.
2. To react in a specified way: *He functioned well in the crisis.*
3. To perform the duties of another.

1. WORK *verb*.
2. *Syns:* act, behave, operate, take, work.
3. ACT FOR at **act**.

functional *adjective*
Serving or capable of serving a useful purpose.

PRACTICAL.

functioning *noun*
The way in which a machine or other thing performs or functions.

BEHAVIOR.

functioning *adjective*
In action or full operation.

ACTIVE.

fund *verb*
To supply capital to or for.   FINANCE.

fundament *noun*
The lowest or supporting part or structure.   BASE[1] *noun.*

fundamental *adjective*
1. Of or being an irreducible element.   1. ELEMENTAL.
2. Arising from or going to the root or source.   2. RADICAL *adjective.*
3. Constituting or forming part of the essence of   3. ESSENTIAL *adjective.*
   something.

fundamental *noun*
1. A fundamental principle or underlying concept.   1. BASIS.
2. A broad and basic rule or truth.   2. LAW *noun.*
3. A fundamental, irreducible constituent of a whole.   3. ELEMENT *noun.*

fundamentalist *noun*
One who strongly favors retention of the existing order.   CONSERVATIVE *noun.*

fundamentally *adverb*
In regard to the essence of a matter.   ESSENTIALLY.

funds *noun*
The monetary resources of a government, organization,   *Syns:* capital, finances, moneys.
or individual: *state government funds; had insufficient
funds to pay for the elaborate banquet.*

funk[1] *verb*
To have or give off a foul odor.   SMELL *verb.*

funk[2] *noun*
1. Great agitation and anxiety caused by the   1. FEAR *noun.*
   expectation or the realization of danger.
2. *Chiefly Brit.* Ignoble lack of courage.   2. COWARDICE.
3. *Chiefly Brit.* A feeling or spell of dismally low   3. GLOOM.
   spirits.
4. *Chiefly Brit.* An ignoble, uncourageous person.   4. COWARD.

funniness *noun*
The quality of being laughable or comical.   HUMOR *noun.*

funny *adjective*
1. Causing puzzlement; perplexing: *That's a funny way*   1. *Syns:* curious, kooky (*Slang*), odd,
   to behave when you're paid a compliment.   peculiar, queer, strange, weird.
2. Arousing laughter.   2. AMUSING.
3. Intended to excite laughter or amusement.   3. HUMOROUS.
4. Deserving laughter.   4. LAUGHABLE.
5. Agreeably curious, esp. in an old-fashioned or   5. QUAINT[1].
   unusual way.

funny *noun*
Informal. Words or actions intended to excite laughter   JOKE *noun.*
or amusement.

fur *noun*
The skin of an animal.   HIDE[2] *noun.*

furbish *verb*
1. To give a gleaming luster to, usu. through friction.   1. GLOSS *verb.*
2. To make new or as if new again.   2. RENEW.

furious *adjective*
1. Full of or marked by extreme anger: *He was furious*   1. *Syns:* enraged, inflamed, infuriated,
   when I criticized him   rabid, raging, ranting, raving.
                                                                   —Idioms foaming at the mouth, in a
                                                                   towering rage.
2. Feeling or showing anger.   2. ANGRY.
3. Intensely violent in sustained velocity.   3. HIGH.
4. Intensely sustained, esp. in activity.   4. HEAVY *adjective.*

furiously *adverb*
In a violent, strenuous way.   HARD *adverb.*

furlough *noun*
A regularly scheduled period spent away from work or   VACATION.
duty, often in recreation.

furnish *verb*
1. To supply what is needed for some activity or purpose: *furnished their new house.*

  1. **Syns:** accouter, appoint, equip, fit up (*or* out), gear, outfit, rig (out *or* up), turn out.
  Near-syns: give, provide, provision, supply.

2. To relinquish to the possession or control of another.

  2. GIVE *verb.*

furnishing *noun*
A piece of equipment for comfort or convenience: *a chair or other furnishing.*

Syns: appointment, chattel, fitting, movable (*also* moveable).

furor *noun*
1. Violent or unrestrained anger.
2. The current custom.

  1. FURY.
  2. FASHION *noun.*

furrow *noun*
An indentation or seam on the skin, esp. on the face.

LINE *noun.*

furry *adjective*
Covered with hair.

HAIRY.

further *adjective*
1. Going beyond what currently exists: *without further ado.*

  1. **Syns:** additional, subsequent, ulterior.

2. Being an addition.

  2. ADDITIONAL.

further *verb*
To cause to move forward or upward, as toward a goal.

ADVANCE *verb.*

further *adverb*
In addition.

ADDITIONALLY.

furtherance *noun*
Forward movement.

ADVANCE *noun.*

furthermore *adverb*
In addition.

ADDITIONALLY.

furthermost *adjective*
Most distant or remote from a center.

EXTREME *adjective.*

furthest *adjective*
Most distant or remote from a center.

EXTREME *adjective.*

furtive *adjective*
1. So slow, deliberate, and secret as to escape observation.

  1. STEALTHY.

2. Trickily secret.

  2. SLY *adjective.*

furtiveness *noun*
The act of proceeding slowly, deliberately, and secretly to escape observation.

STEALTH.

fury *noun*
1. Violent or unrestrained anger: *He smashed the glass in his fury.*

  1. **Syns:** choler, furor, ire, rage, wrath, wrathfulness.

2. Exceptionally great concentration, power, or force, esp. in activity.

  2. INTENSITY.

3. A person, esp. a woman, who habitually uses loud, abusive language.

  3. SCOLD *noun.*

fuse *verb*
1. To change from a solid to a liquid.
2. To put together into one mass so that the constituent parts are more or less homogeneous.

  1. MELT.
  2. MIX *verb.*

fused *adjective*
Joined together into a whole.

COMBINED.

fusillade *noun*
A concentrated outpouring, as of missiles, words, or blows.

BARRAGE *noun.*

fusion *noun*
Something produced by mixing.

MIXTURE.

fuss *noun*
1. Busy and useless activity: *Can't we give a party without a lot of fuss?*

  1. **Syns:** ado, to-do (*Informal*).

2. Needless trouble.

3. An interruption of regular procedure or of public peace.

fuss *verb*

1. To be nervously or uselessly active: *She fussed in the kitchen all afternoon.*
2. To worry over trifles: *no need to fuss about a bad dream.*
3. To scold or find fault constantly.

fussy *adjective*

1. Excessively filled with detail.
2. Very difficult to please.

fustian *adjective*

Characterized by language that is elevated and sometimes pompous in style.

fusty *adjective*

1. Smelling of mildew or decay.
2. Of a style or method formerly in vogue.

futile *adjective*

Having no useful result: *a futile effort to engage him in conversation.*

futility *noun*

The condition or quality of being useless or ineffective: *a war that was an exercise in futility.*

future *noun*

1. Time that is yet to be: *We'll face that problem some time in the future.*
2. Chance of success or advancement: *a job with no future.*

future *adjective*

Being or occurring in the time ahead: *postponed the meeting to a future date.*

fuzz *noun*

Slang. A member of a law-enforcement agency.

fuzzy *adjective*

Not clearly perceived or perceptible.

---

2. BOTHER *noun*.

3. DISTURBANCE.

1. **Syns:** bustle, mess around (*Slang*), pother, putter (around).
2. **Syns:** chafe, fret, stew, take on.

3. NAG.

1. BUSY *adjective*.
2. NICE.

SONOROUS.

1. MOLDY.
2. OLD-FASHIONED.

Syns: barren, bootless, fruitless, ineffective, ineffectual, unavailing, unsuccessful, useless, vain. —*Idiom* in vain.
Near-syns: abortive, empty, hollow, idle, unproductive, unsatisfactory.

Syns: fruitlessness, ineffectiveness, ineffectuality, ineffectualness, inefficacy, uselessness.

1. **Syns:** by-and-by, hereafter. —*Idiom* time to come.
2. **Syns:** outlook, prospect.

Syns: coming, later, subsequent.

POLICEMAN.

UNCLEAR.

G

gab *verb*

Informal. To talk volubly, persistently, and usu. inconsequentially.

gab *noun*

Informal. Incessant and usu. inconsequential talk.

gabble *verb*

To talk rapidly, incoherently, or indistinctly.

CHATTER *verb*.

CHATTER *noun*.

BABBLE *verb*.

gabble *noun*
Unintelligible or foolish talk.

BABBLE *noun*.

gabby *adjective*
Given to conversation.

TALKATIVE.

gad about (or **around**) *verb*
To move about at random, esp. over a wide area.

ROVE.

gadget *noun*
Informal. A small, specialized mechanical device: *a gadget for peeling potatoes.*

Syns: concern (*Informal*), contraption, contrivance, doodad (*Informal*), doohickey (*Informal*), gimmick (*Slang*), gismo (*also* gizmo) (*Slang*), jigger, thing, thingamabob (*also* thingumabob) (*Informal*), thingamajig (*also* thingumajig) (*Informal*), widget (*Informal*).

gag *noun*
Informal. Words or actions intended to excite laughter or amusement.

JOKE *noun*.

gag *verb*
To hold (something requiring an outlet) in check.

REPRESS.

gaga *adjective*
1. *Slang.* Given to lighthearted silliness.
2. *Slang.* Afflicted with or exhibiting irrationality and mental unsoundness.

1. GIDDY.
2. INSANE.

gage *noun & verb*

SEE **gauge.**

gaiety *noun*
1. A state of joyful exuberance: *the gaiety of the holidays; a house that rang with the gaiety of children.*
2. Joyful, exuberant activity: *a weekend of unrestrained gaiety.*

1. *Syns:* glee, gleefulness, hilarity, jocularity, jocundity, jollity, joviality, jovialness, merriment, mirth.
2. *Syns:* festivity, fun, jollity, merriment, merrymaking, revel, reveling, revelry, whoopee (*Slang*).

gain *verb*
1. To achieve an increment of gradually: *gain weight; gain speed.*
2. To reach a goal or objective.
3. To make as income or profit.
4. To acquire as a result of one's behavior or effort.
5. To receive, as wages, for one's labor.
6. To come into possession of.
7. To obtain possession or control of.
8. To regain one's health.

1. *Syns:* build up, develop, increase.
2. ARRIVE AT at **arrive.**
3. RETURN *verb*.
4. EARN.
5. EARN.
6. GET.
7. CAPTURE.
8. RECOVER.

gain *noun*
1. Something earned, won, or otherwise acquired: *a net gain of $5 per share.*
2. Something beneficial.

1. *Syns:* profit, return.
2. ADVANTAGE *noun*.

gainsay *verb*
To refuse to admit the truth, reality, value, or worth of.

DENY.

gainsaying *noun*
A refusal to grant the truth of a statement or charge.

DENIAL.

gala *noun*
A large or important social gathering.

PARTY *noun*.

gala *adjective*
Marked by festal celebration.

MERRY.

gale *noun*
Archaic. A natural movement or current of air.

WIND¹ *noun*.

gall¹ *noun*
The quality or state of feeling bitter.

RESENTMENT.

gall *verb*
1. To make (the skin) raw by or as if by friction.

1. CHAFE.

2. To trouble the nerves or peace of mind of, esp. by repeated vexations.

2. ANNOY.

gall² *noun*
  1. The state or quality of being impudent.
  2. Excessive and arrogant self-confidence.

  1. IMPUDENCE.
  2. PRESUMPTION.

gallant *adjective*
  1. Respectfully attentive, esp. to women: *gallant conduct.*
  2. Having or showing courage.
  3. Characterized by elaborate but usu. formal courtesy.

  1. *Syns:* chivalric, chivalrous, courtly.
  2. BRAVE *adjective.*
  3. GRACIOUS.

gallant *noun*
A man amorously attentive to women: *a flirtatious gallant keeping an eye out for pretty young things.*

Syns: amorist, Casanova, Don Juan, Lothario, Romeo. —*Idioms* gay blade, lady's man (*also* ladies' man).

gallantry *noun*
  1. Respectful attention, esp. toward women: *true gentlemen, noted for gallantry.*
  2. The quality of mind enabling one to face danger or hardship resolutely.
  3. The quality or state of being heroic.

  1. *Syns:* chivalrousness, chivalry, courtliness.
  2. COURAGE.
  3. HEROISM.

gallimaufry *noun*
A collection of various things.

ASSORTMENT.

galling *adjective*
Troubling the nerves or peace of mind, as by repeated vexations.

VEXATIOUS.

gallivant *verb*
To move about at random, esp. over a wide area.

ROVE.

gallumph *verb*

SEE **galumph.**

galumph or **gallumph** *verb*
To move heavily.

LUMP¹ *verb.*

galvanize *verb*
  1. To arouse to action.
  2. To stir to action or feeling.

  1. ACTIVATE.
  2. PROVOKE.

gamble *verb*
  1. To take a risk in the hope of gaining advantage: *gambled in cotton futures.*
  2. To make a bet on.
  3. To put up as a stake in a game or speculation: *gambled her half of the estate against his.*

  1. *Syns:* speculate, venture.

  2. BET *verb.*
  3. *Syns:* bet, go, lay¹, risk, set¹, stake, venture, wager. —*Idiom* put one's money on.

gamble *noun*
  1. A venture depending on chance: *His gamble was that the market would rise.*
  2. A possibility of danger or harm.

  1. *Syns:* bet, speculation, wager.

  2. RISK *noun.*

gambler *noun*
One who bets.

BETTOR.

gambol *verb*
To leap and skip about playfully: *children gamboling on the lawn.*

Syns: caper, cavort, dance, frisk, frolic, prance, rollick, romp.
Near-syns: bound, leap, spring; skip, tumble.

game *verb*
To make a bet on.

BET *verb.*

game *noun*
Actions taken as a joke.

PLAY *noun.*

game *adjective*
  1. Having or showing courage.
  2. *Informal.* Disposed to accept or agree.

  1. BRAVE *adjective.*
  2. WILLING.

gamester *noun*
One who bets.

BETTOR.

gander[1] *noun*
Informal. A mentally deficient person.

FOOL *noun.*

gander[2] *noun*
Slang. A quick look.

GLANCE[1] *noun.*

gang *noun*
1. An organized group of criminals, hoodlums, or wrongdoers: *the City Hall gang; a gang of car thieves.*
2. A particular social group.

1. **Syns:** band[2], mob (*Informal*), pack, ring[1].
2. CROWD *noun.*

gang up *verb*
Informal. To assemble or join in a group.

BAND[2] *verb.*

gangling *adjective*
Tall, thin, and awkwardly built: *danced reluctantly with a gangling youth.*

Syns: gangly, lanky, loose-jointed, rangy, spindling, spindly.
Near-syns: bony, lank, lean, scrawny, skinny, slim, tall, thin.
Ant: squat.

gangly *adjective*
Tall, thin, and awkwardly built.

GANGLING.

gang up *verb*

SEE **gang.**

gaol *noun*
Chiefly Brit. A place for the confinement of persons in lawful detention.

JAIL *noun.*

gaoler *noun*
Chiefly Brit. A guard or keeper of a prison.

JAILER.

gap *noun*
1. An interval during which continuity is suspended: *an 18-minute gap in the taped conversation.*
2. An opening, esp. in a solid structure.
3. A marked lack of correspondence or agreement: *a gap between revenue and spending; the generation gap.*

1. **Syns:** breach, break, hiatus, interim, lacuna, void.
2. BREACH *noun.*
3. **Syns:** difference, disagreement, discrepancy (*also* discrepance), disparity, incongruity, inconsistency.

gap *verb*
Regional. To open wide.

YAWN.

gape *verb*
1. To look intently and fixedly.
2. To open the mouth wide with a deep inward breath, as when tired or bored.
3. To open wide.

1. GAZE *verb.*
2. YAWN.

3. YAWN.

gape *noun*
An intent, fixed look.

GAZE *noun.*

gaping *adjective*
Open wide.

YAWNING.

garb *noun*
Articles worn to cover the body.

DRESS *noun.*

garb *verb*
To put clothes on.

DRESS *verb.*

garden *adjective*
Being of no special quality or type.

ORDINARY *adjective.*

garden-variety *adjective*
Being of no special quality or type.

ORDINARY *adjective.*

gargantuan *adjective*
Of extraordinary size and power.

GIANT *adjective.*

garish *adjective*
Tastelessly showy.

GAUDY.

garment *verb*
To put clothes on.

DRESS *verb.*

garments *noun*
Articles worn to cover the body.

DRESS *noun.*

garner *verb*
1. To bring together so as to increase in mass or number.
2. To collect (something) bit by bit.
3. To collect ripe crops.

1. ACCUMULATE.

2. GLEAN.

3. GATHER.

garner *noun*
A quantity accumulated.

ACCUMULATION.

garnish *verb*
To furnish with decorations.

ADORN.

garnishment *noun*
Something that adorns.

ADORNMENT.

garniture *noun*
Something that adorns.

ADORNMENT.

garrulous *adjective*
Given to conversation.

TALKATIVE.

gas *noun*
Slang. Something or someone uproariously funny or absurd.

SCREAM *noun.*

gas *verb*
Slang. To talk volubly, persistently, and usu. inconsequentially.

CHATTER *verb.*

gasconade *verb*
To talk with excessive pride.

BOAST *verb.*

gasconade *noun*
An act of boasting.

BOAST *noun.*

gash *verb*
To penetrate with a sharp edge.

CUT *verb.*

gash *noun*
The result of cutting.

CUT *noun.*

gasp *verb*
1. To utter in a breathless manner: *gasped a warning and fainted.*
2. To breathe hard.

1. *Syns:* heave, pant.

2. PANT.

gate *noun*
The amount of money collected as admission, esp. to a sporting event.

TAKE *noun.*

gate money *noun*
The amount of money collected as admission, esp. to a sporting event.

TAKE *noun.*

gather *verb*
1. To collect ripe crops: *gather peaches.*
2. To bring together.
3. To come together.
4. To bring together so as to increase in mass or number.
5. To come or bring into a group or groups.
6. To collect (something) bit by bit.
7. To draw a conclusion from evidence or reasoning.

1. *Syns:* garner, harvest, reap.

2. ASSEMBLE.

3. ASSEMBLE.

4. ACCUMULATE.

5. GROUP *verb.*

6. GLEAN.

7. INFER.

gathering *noun*
1. The act or fact of coming together.
2. A number of persons who have come or been gathered together.
3. The act or process of bringing in a crop.

1. JUNCTION.

2. ASSEMBLY.

3. HARVEST *noun.*

gauche *adjective*
Clumsily lacking in the ability to do or perform.

UNSKILLFUL.

gaudy *adjective*
Tastelessly showy: *a gaudy disco; gaudy clothes.*

Syns: chintzy, flashy, garish, glaring, loud, meretricious, tacky[2], tawdry, tinsel.
Near-syns: ostentatious, pretentious, showy; glittery, shiny, tasteless; cheap, crude, vulgar.

gauge also **gage** *noun*
A means by which individuals are compared and
judge.
    STANDARD *noun.*

gauge also **gage** *verb*
1. To ascertain the dimensions, quantity, or capacity
of.
    1. MEASURE *verb.*
2. To make a judgment as to the worth or value of.
    2. ESTIMATE *verb.*

gaum *noun*
Regional. A large, ungainly, and dull-witted person.
    LUMP[1] *noun.*

gaunt *adjective*
1. Having little flesh or fat on the body.
    1. THIN *adjective.*
2. Physically haggard.
    2. WASTED.

gaunt *verb*
To make physically thin or thinner.
    THIN *verb.*

gauzy *adjective*
So light and insubstantial as to resemble air or a thin
film.
    FILMY.

gawk *noun*
A large, ungainly, and dull-witted person.
    LUMP[1] *noun.*

gawk *verb*
Informal. To look intently and fixedly.
    GAZE *verb.*

gawky *adjective*
Lacking dexterity and grace in physical movement.
    AWKWARD.

gay *adjective*
1. Characterized by joyful exuberance: *a gay*
companion; a gay Christmas party.
    1. *Syns:* blithe, blithesome, boon[2], festive,
gleeful, jocund, jolly, jovial,
lighthearted, merry, mirthful.
2. Providing joy and pleasure.
    2. GLAD.
3. Full of color.
    3. COLORFUL.
4. Given to heedless, unrestrained pursuit of pleasure.
    4. FAST *adjective.*
5. Pertaining to, characteristic of, or exhibiting sexual
desire for others of one's own sex: *the Gay Rights*
Movement.
    5. *Syns:* homophile, homosexual.

gaze *verb*
1. To look intently and fixedly: *gazed in awe at the*
Alps.
    1. *Syns:* eye, gape, gawk (*Informal*),
glare, goggle, ogle, peer[1], stare, yawp
(*also* yaup) (*Regional*). —*Idioms* gaze
open-mouthed, rivet the eyes on.
2. To direct the eyes on an object.
    2. LOOK *verb.*

gaze *noun*
1. An intent, fixed look: *was disconcerted by his*
penetrating gaze.
    1. *Syns:* gape, peer[1], stare.
2. An act of directing the eyes on an object.
    2. LOOK *noun.*

gear *noun*
Things needed for a task, journey, or other purpose.
    OUTFIT *noun.*

gear *verb*
To supply what is needed for some activity or purpose.
    FURNISH.

gee *verb*
Informal. To be compatible or in correspondence.
    AGREE.

gelastic *adjective*
Deserving laughter.
    LAUGHABLE.

gelatinize *verb*
To change or be changed from a liquid into a soft,
semisolid, or solid mass.
    COAGULATE.

gelatinous *adjective*
Having so many constituent particles in suspension as
to be condensed, often viscous.
    THICK *adjective.*

geld *verb*
To render incapable of reproducing sexually.
    STERILIZE.

gelding *noun*
The act or an instance of making one incapable of reproducing sexually.

STERILIZATION.

gelid *adjective*
Very cold.

FRIGID.

gelt *noun*
Slang. Something, as coins, printed bills, etc., used as a medium of exchange.

MONEY.

gem *noun*
Someone or something considered exceptionally precious.

TREASURE *noun.*

geminate *adjective*
Composed of two parts or things.

DOUBLE *adjective.*

gendarme *noun*
Slang. A member of a law-enforcement agency.

POLICEMAN.

genealogy *noun*
1. A written record of ancestry: *studied her family's genealogy.*
2. One's ancestors or their character.

1. **Syns:** begats (*Slang*), pedigree. —*Idiom* family tree.
2. ANCESTRY.

general *adjective*
1. Belonging or pertaining to the whole: *a general change in society.*
2. Covering a wide scope: *general discontent.*

1. **Syns:** common, generic, universal.
2. **Syns:** all-inclusive, all-round (*also* all-around), broad, broad-spectrum, comprehensive, expansive, extended, extensive, far-ranging, far-reaching, global, inclusive, large, overall, sweeping, wide-ranging, wide-reaching, widespread.

3. Belonging to, shared by, or applicable to all alike.
4. To be expected.
5. Not limited to a single class: *general merchandise.*

3. COMMON *adjective.*
4. COMMON *adjective.*
5. **Syns:** divers, diverse, diversified, sundry.

6. Of, representing, or carried on by people at large.

6. POPULAR.

generalize *verb*
To make universal.

UNIVERSALIZE.

generate *verb*
1. To give rise to a particular development: *strict policies generating employee discontent.*

1. **Syns:** breed, cause, engender, hatch, induce, provoke, spawn, stir[1] (up), touch off.

2. To cause to come into existence.
3. To bring (a product, idea, etc.) into being.

2. PRODUCE.
3. DEVELOP.

generic *adjective*
Belonging or pertaining to the whole.

GENERAL.

generosity *noun*
The quality or state of being generous: *a philanthropist whose generosity was famed.*

Syns: big-heartedness, freehandedness, generousness, great-heartedness, liberality, magnanimity, magnanimousness, munificence, openhandedness.

generous *adjective*
1. Willing to give of oneself and one's possessions: *He is a generous contributor. That's generous of you.*

1. **Syns:** big, big-hearted, great-hearted, large-hearted, magnanimous, unselfish. **Near-ants:** base, ignoble, mean, selfish, self-serving; hypocritical, thoughtless, unkind. **Ant:** ungenerous.

2. Characterized by bounteous giving: *a generous divorce settlement; was generous with her money.*

2. **Syns:** free, freehanded, handsome, liberal, munificent, openhanded, unsparing, unstinting.

3. Characterized by abundance: *a generous serving of potatoes.*

generousness *noun*
The quality or state of being generous.

genesis *noun*
1. The act or process of bringing or being brought into existence.
2. The initial stage of a developmental process.

genial *adjective*
1. Characterized by kindness and warm, unaffected courtesy.
2. Pleasant and friendly.

geniality *noun*
The quality of being pleasant and friendly.

genius *noun*
1. An innate capability.
2. Liveliness and vivacity of imagination.

genteel *adjective*
1. Marked by excessive concern for propriety and good form: *a genteel abhorrence of plain speaking.*

2. Characterized by good manners.

gentility *noun*
People of the highest social level.

gentle *adjective*
1. Of a kindly, considerate character: *a gentle mother.*

2. Free from severity or violence, as in movement: *a gentle summer breeze.*

3. Easily managed or handled: *a gentle horse.*
4. Not steep or abrupt.
5. Of small intensity.

gentle *verb*
1. To ease the anger or agitation of.
2. To make (an animal) docile: *gentled a wild horse.*
3. To train to live with and be of use to man.

gentry *noun*
People of the highest social level.

genuflection *noun*
An inclination of the head or body, as in greeting, consent, courtesy, submission, or worship.

genuine *adjective*
1. Devoid of any hypocrisy or pretense: *genuine grief.*

2. Not counterfeit or copied.

genuinely *adverb*
In point of fact.

genuineness *noun*
The quality of being authentic.

---

3. *Syns:* abundant, ample, bounteous, bountiful, copious, liberal, plenteous, plentiful.

GENEROSITY.

1. BEGINNING *noun.*

2. BIRTH *noun.*

1. GRACIOUS.

2. AMIABLE.

AMIABILITY.

1. TALENT.

2. FIRE *noun.*

1. *Syns:* bluenosed, missish, old-maidish, precise, prim, prissy, proper, prudish, puritanical, strait-laced, stuffy (*Informal*), tight-laced, Victorian. —*Idiom* prim and proper.
2. COURTEOUS.

SOCIETY.

1. *Syns:* mild, soft, softhearted, tender[1], tenderhearted.
2. *Syns:* balmy, bland, delicate, faint, mild, smooth, soft.
   Near-ants: coarse, harsh; fierce, forceful, intense, rough, severe, violent.
   Ant: savage.
3. *Syns:* docile, meek, mild, tame.
4. GRADUAL.
5. LIGHT[2].

1. PACIFY.
2. *Syns:* break, bust (*Slang*), tame.
3. DOMESTICATE.

SOCIETY.

BOW *noun.*

1. *Syns:* heartfelt, heart-whole, hearty, honest, real, sincere, true, unaffected, unfeigned.
   Near-syns: dependable, reliable, trustworthy, veritable.
   Ants: insincere, ungenuine.
2. AUTHENTIC.

ACTUALLY.

AUTHENTICITY.

germ *noun*

1. *Med.* A minute organism usu. producing disease: *influenza germs.*
2. A source of further growth and development: *germs of doubt; the germ of a new idea.*

1. **Syns:** bug (*Informal*), microbe, microorganism (*also* micro-organism).
2. **Syns:** bud, embryo, kernel, nucleus, seed, spark.

germane *adjective*

Related to the matter at hand.

RELEVANT.

germaneness *noun*

The fact of being related to the matter at hand.

RELEVANCE.

gest or **geste** *noun*

1. *Archaic.* Behavior through which one reveals one's personality.
2. *Archaic.* A great or heroic deed.

1. BEARING.

2. FEAT.

gestation *noun*

The condition of carrying a developing fetus within the uterus.

PREGNANCY.

geste *noun*

SEE **gest.**

gesticulate *verb*

To make bodily motions so as to convey an idea or complement speech.

GESTURE *verb.*

gesticulation *noun*

An expressive, meaningful bodily movement.

GESTURE *noun.*

gesture *noun*

1. An expressive, meaningful bodily movement: *made an emphatic gesture of disapproval.*
2. Something that takes the place of words in communicating a thought or feeling.

1. **Syns:** gesticulation, indication, motion, sign, signal.
2. EXPRESSION.

gesture *verb*

To make bodily motions so as to convey an idea or complement speech: *gestured to me to be quiet; gestured as she described the accident.*

Syns: gesticulate, motion, sign, signal, signalize. —*Idiom* give the high sign.

get *verb*

1. To come into possession of: *Where did you get that expensive car?*
2. To succeed in communicating with.
3. To receive, as wages, for one's labor.
4. To acquire as a result of one's behavior or effort.
5. To cause to be in a certain state or to undergo a particular experience or action: *got ready; get the car washed; got her angry.*
6. To become affected with a disease.
7. To gain knowledge or mastery of by study.
8. *Informal.* To perceive and recognize the meaning of.
9. *Informal.* To perceive, esp. barely or fleetingly.
10. To obtain from another source.
11. To be the biological father of.
12. To gain possession of, esp. after a struggle or chase.
13. To obtain possession or control of.
14. To come to be.
15. *Informal.* To evoke a usu. strong mental or emotional response from.
16. To trouble the nerves or peace of mind of, esp. by repeated vexations.
17. *Regional & Informal.* To leave hastily.

1. **Syns:** acquire, come by, gain, land, obtain, pick up, procure, secure, win.
2. REACH.
3. EARN.
4. EARN.
5. **Syns:** have, make.

6. CONTRACT *verb.*
7. LEARN.
8. UNDERSTAND.

9. CATCH *verb.*
10. DERIVE.
11. FATHER *verb.*
12. TAKE *verb.*

13. CAPTURE.
14. BECOME.
15. AFFECT[1].

16. ANNOY.

17. RUN *verb.*

get about *verb*

To become known far and wide: *The news got about very quickly.*

Syns: circulate, get around, go around, spread, travel. —*Idiom* make the rounds.

get across *verb*

To make known.

COMMUNICATE.

get ahead *verb*
To gain wealth or fame.   SUCCEED.

get along *verb*
1. To live or act together in harmony: *a family that got*   1. *Syns:* cotton (*Informal*), get on,
   along well.   harmonize. —*Idiom* hit it off.
2. To progress or perform adequately, esp. in difficult   2. MANAGE.
   circumstances.
3. To go forward, esp. toward a conclusion.   3. COME.
4. To grow old.   4. AGE *verb*.

get around *verb*
1. To become known far and wide.   1. GET ABOUT.
2. To keep away from.   2. AVOID.
3. To evade, as a topic, esp. by circumlocution.   3. SKIRT *verb*.

get behind *verb*
To aid the cause of by approving or favoring.   SUPPORT *verb*.

get by *verb*
To progress or perform adequately, esp. in difficult   MANAGE.
circumstances.

get in *verb*
To come to a particular place.   ARRIVE.

get off *verb*
Informal. To go about the initial step in doing   START *verb*.
(something).

get on *verb*
1. To grow old.   1. AGE *verb*.
2. To live or act together in harmony.   2. GET ALONG.
3. To put (an article of clothing) on one's person.   3. DON.
4. To gain wealth or fame.   4. SUCCEED.

get out *verb*
1. To leave hastily.   1. RUN *verb*.
2. To be made public.   2. COME OUT.

get to *verb*
To reach a goal or objective.   ARRIVE AT at **arrive**.

get together *verb*
1. To come together.   1. ASSEMBLE.
2. To bring together.   2. ASSEMBLE.
3. To come to an understanding or to terms.   3. AGREE.

get *noun*
A group consisting of those descended directly from the   PROGENY.
same parents or ancestors.

get about *verb*   SEE **get.**
get across *verb*   SEE **get.**
get ahead *verb*   SEE **get.**
get along *verb*   SEE **get.**
get around *verb*   SEE **get.**
getaway *noun*   SEE **get away.**
get away *verb*
1. To break loose and leave suddenly, as from   1. ESCAPE *verb*.
   confinement or from a difficult or threatening
   situation.
2. To move or proceed away from a place.   2. GO *verb*.

getaway *noun*
The act or an instance of escaping, as from confinement   ESCAPE *noun*.
or difficulty.

get behind *verb*   SEE **get.**
get by *verb*   SEE **get.**
get in *verb*   SEE **get.**
get off *verb*   SEE **get.**
get on *verb*   SEE **get.**
get out *verb*   SEE **get.**

gettable *adjective*
Capable of being obtained or used.

AVAILABLE.

get to *verb*

SEE **get.**

get together *verb*

SEE **get.**

getup *noun*

SEE **get up.**

get up *verb*
1. To leave one's bed: *got up at seven.*

1. *Syns:* arise, pile out, rise, roll out, turn out, uprise. —*Idiom* rise and shine.

2. To adopt a standing posture: *The football player got up after being tackled.*

2. *Syns:* rise, stand up, uprise, upspring. —*Idiom* get to one's feet.

getup *noun*
A set or style of clothing.

DRESS *noun.*

get-up-and-go *noun*
1. *Informal.* An aggressive readiness to undertake taxing efforts.

1. DRIVE *noun.*

2. *Informal.* Capacity or power for work or vigorous activity.

2. ENERGY.

gewgaw *noun*
A small, showy article.

NOVELTY.

ghastly *adjective*
1. Shockingly repellent: *the ghastly sight of starving refugee children.*

1. *Syns:* grim, grisly, gruesome, hideous, horrible, horrid, lurid, macabre.
Near-syns: appalling, awful, disgusting, dreadful, frightening, nauseating, sickening, terrible.

2. Causing or able to cause fear.

2. FEARFUL.

3. Gruesomely suggestive of ghosts or death: *A ghastly figure loomed up. The dying man had a ghastly pallor.*

3. *Syns:* cadaverous, corpselike, deadly, deathlike, deathly, ghostlike, ghostly, mortuary, spectral.

4. Very bad.

4. TERRIBLE.

ghost *noun*
1. A supernatural being: *thought she saw the ghost of her great-grandmother.*

1. *Syns:* apparition, bogle, bogy (*also* bogey, bogie), bugbear (*Archaic*), eidolon, haunt (*Regional*), phantasm (*also* phantasma), phantom, revenant, shade, shadow, specter, spectrum, spirit, spook, umbra, visitant, wraith.

2. A slight amount.

2. SHADE *noun.*

ghost *verb*
To write for and credit authorship to another: *She ghosted the queen's autobiography.*

Syns: ghostwrite, spook (*Slang*).

ghostlike *adjective*
Gruesomely suggestive of ghosts or death.

GHASTLY.

ghostly *adjective*
Gruesomely suggestive of ghosts or death.

GHASTLY.

ghostwrite *verb*
To write for and credit authorship to another.

GHOST *verb.*

ghoul *noun*
A perversely bad, cruel, or wicked person.

FIEND.

ghoulish *adjective*
Perversely bad, cruel, or wicked.

FIENDISH.

giant *noun*
One that is extraordinarily large and powerful: *a giant of a linebacker; a literary giant; a giant among corporations.*

Syns: behemoth, Goliath, jumbo, leviathan, mammoth, monster, titan, whopper.

giant *adjective*
Of extraordinary size and power: *a giant football player; a giant interlocking conglomerate.*

Syns: Antaean, behemothic, Brobdingnagian, Bunyanesque, colossal, cyclopean, elephantine, enormous, gargantuan, gigantean, gigantesque, gigantic, herculean, heroic, huge,

immense, jumbo, leviathan, mammoth,
massive, massy (*Archaic*), mastodonic,
mighty, monster, monstrous, monumental,
mountainous, planetary, prodigious,
pythonic, stupendous, titan, titanic,
tremendous, vast, walloping (*Informal*),
whopping.

BABBLE *verb*.

gibber *verb*
To talk rapidly, incoherently, or indistinctly.

gibberish *noun*
1. Wordy, unclear jargon: *couldn't understand government gibberish.*

2. Unintelligible or foolish talk.
3. Esoteric, formulaic, and often incomprehensible speech relating to the occult: *the gibberish of witches.*

1. **Syns:** abracadabra, double talk, gobbledygook (*also* gobbledegook), jabberwocky (*also* jabberwock), mumbo jumbo.
2. BABBLE *noun*.
3. **Syns:** abracadabra, hocus-pocus, mumbo jumbo.

gibbet *verb*
To execute by suspending by the neck.

HANG *verb*.

gibe at *verb*
To make fun of.

RIDICULE *verb*.

giddiness *noun*
A sensation of whirling or falling.

DIZZINESS.

giddy *adjective*
1. Given to lighthearted silliness: *giddy youngsters.*

1. **Syns:** birdbrained (*Slang*), dizzy (*Informal*), empty-headed, featherbrained, flighty, fribbling, frivolous, frothy, gaga (*Slang*), harebrained, lightheaded, scatterbrained, silly, skittish. —*Idiom* giddy as a goose.
Near-ants: contemplative, earnest, pensive, sedate, serious, sober, solemn, thoughtful.

2. Producing dizziness or vertigo: *a giddy height.*
3. Having a sensation of whirling or falling.

2. **Syns:** dizzy, dizzying, vertiginous.
3. DIZZY *adjective*.

gift *noun*
1. Something bestowed freely: *The platter was a wedding gift.*
2. Something given to a charity or cause.
3. An innate capability.

1. **Syns:** handsel (*also* hansel) (*Chiefly Brit.*), present[2], presentation.
2. DONATION.
3. TALENT.

gift *verb*
1. *Chiefly Brit.* To make a gift of.
2. To present with a quality, trait, or power: *The Lord has gifted us with good health.*

1. GIVE.
2. **Syns:** dower, endow, endue, gird, invest.

gifted *adjective*
Having talent: *a gifted pianist.*

Syns: endowed, talented.

gig *noun*
Slang. A post of employment.

POSITION *noun*.

gigantean *adjective*
Of extraordinary size and power.

GIANT *adjective*.

gigantesque *adjective*
Of extraordinary size and power.

GIANT *adjective*.

gigantic *adjective*
Of extraordinary size and power.

GIANT *adjective*.

giggle *verb*
To laugh in a stifled way: *children giggling in class.*

Syns: snicker (*also* snigger), tehee *or* tee-hee, titter.

giggle *noun*

A stifled laugh: *had a fit of giggles.*

gild *verb*
1. To give a deceptively attractive appearance to.
2. To make superficially more acceptable or appealing.

gimcrack *noun*
A small, showy article.

gimmick *noun*
1. *Slang.* A small, specialized mechanical device.
2. *Slang.* An indirect, usu. cunning means of gaining an end.
3. *Slang.* A clever, unexpected new trick or method.

ginger *noun*
Informal. A lively, emphatic, eager quality or manner.

gingerliness *noun*
Careful forethought to avoid harm or risk.

gingerly *adjective*
Trying attentively to avoid danger, risk, or error.

gip *verb*

gird *verb*
1. To prepare (oneself) for action: *soldiers girding themselves for the forthcoming battle.*

2. To encircle with or as if with a band.
3. To shut in on all sides.
4. To present with a quality, trait, or power.

girdle *verb*
1. To encircle with or as if with a band.
2. To shut in on all sides.

gismo also **gizmo** *noun*
Slang. A small, specialized mechanical device.

gist *noun*
The most central and material part.

give *verb*
1. To make a gift of: *gave the children candy; was given an expensive watch.*
2. To relinquish to the possession or control of another: *gave them the cottage for a week; give me the scissors.*
3. To present as a gift to a charity or cause.
4. To let have as a favor or privilege.
5. To cause (a disease) to pass to another or others.
6. To mete out by means of some action: *give a spanking.*
7. To discharge material, as vapor or fumes, usu. suddenly and violently.
8. To set aside or distribute as a share.
9. To distribute (money) as payment.
10. To devote (oneself or one's efforts).
11. To organize and carry out (an activity).
12. To produce on the stage.
13. To be unable to hold up.
14. To fall in.

give back *verb*
1. To send, put, or carry back to a former location.
2. To put (someone) in the possession of a prior position or office.

give forth *verb*

Syns: snicker (*also* snigger), tehee *or* teehee, titter.

1. COLOR *verb*.
2. SWEETEN.

NOVELTY.

1. GADGET.
2. TRICK *noun*.
3. WRINKLE[2].

SPIRIT.

CAUTION *noun*.

WARY.

SEE **gyp.**

1. *Syns:* brace[2], forearm, fortify, ready, steel, strengthen. —*Idiom* gird one's loins.
   Near-syns: bolster, harden, reinforce; prepare, support, sustain.
2. BAND[1] *verb*.
3. SURROUND.
4. GIFT *verb*.

1. BAND[1] *verb*.
2. SURROUND.

GADGET.

HEART.

1. *Syns:* bestow, gift (*Chiefly Brit.*), give away, hand out, present[2].
2. *Syns:* deliver, furnish, hand, hand over, provide, supply, transfer, turn over.
3. DONATE.
4. GRANT *verb*.
5. COMMUNICATE.
6. *Syns:* administer, deal (out), deliver.
7. EMIT.
8. ALLOT.
9. SPEND.
10. APPLY.
11. HAVE.
12. STAGE *verb*.
13. BEND *verb*.
14. CAVE IN at **cave.**

1. RETURN *verb*.
2. RESTORE.

To discharge material, as vapor or fumes, usu. suddenly and violently. EMIT.

give in *verb*
To cease opposition: *finally saw that he had lost the election and gave in.* *Syns:* concede, yield.

give off *verb*
To discharge material, as vapor or fumes, usu. suddenly and violently. EMIT.

give out *verb*
1. To suddenly lose all health or strength. 1. COLLAPSE *verb.*
2. To cease functioning properly. 2. FAIL.
3. To lose so much strength and power as to become ineffective or motionless. 3. RUN DOWN.
4. To prove deficient or insufficient. 4. FAIL.
5. To make or become no longer active or productive. 5. DRY UP at **dry.**
6. To discharge material, as vapor or fumes, usu. suddenly and violently. 6. EMIT.

give over *verb*
1. To cease consideration or treatment of. 1. DROP *verb.*
2. To yield (oneself) unrestrainedly, as to a particular impulse: *gave herself over to uncontrolled sobbing.* 2. *Syns:* abandon, give up, surrender.

give up *verb*
1. To cease trying to accomplish or continue. 1. ABANDON *verb.*
2. To cease consideration or treatment of. 2. DROP *verb.*
3. To lose all hope. 3. DESPAIR *verb.*
4. To yield (oneself) unrestrainedly, as to a particular impulse. 4. GIVE OVER.
5. To cut short; discontinue. 5. BREAK *verb.*

give *noun*
Informal. The quality or state of being flexible. FLEXIBILITY.

give-and-take *noun*
A settlement of differences through mutual concession. COMPROMISE *noun.*

giveaway *noun* SEE **give away.**

give away *verb*
1. To make a gift of. 1. GIVE *verb.*
2. To disclose in a breach of confidence. 2. BETRAY.

giveaway *noun*
Informal. Something offered or bought at a low price. BARGAIN *noun.*

give back *verb* SEE **give.**
give forth *verb* SEE **give.**
give in *verb* SEE **give.**
given *adjective*
Having or showing a tendency or likelihood. INCLINED.
give off *verb* SEE **give.**
give out *verb* SEE **give.**
give over *verb* SEE **give.**
giver *noun*
A person who gives to a charity or cause. DONOR.
give up *verb* SEE **give.**
gizmo *noun* SEE **gismo.**
glacial *adjective*
1. Lacking all friendliness and warmth. 1. COLD *adjective.*
2. Very cold. 2. FRIGID.

glad *adjective*
1. Providing joy and pleasure: *a glad occasion; glad tidings.* 1. *Syns:* cheerful, cheery, festive, gay, joyful, joyous, pleasing.
2. Eagerly compliant: *I am glad to help.* 2. *Syns:* delighted, happy, pleased, proud (*Chiefly Regional*), ready, tickled.
3. Marked by festal celebration. 3. MERRY.

gladden *verb*
To give great or keen pleasure to. DELIGHT *verb.*

gladness *noun*
A condition of supreme well-being and good spirits. HAPPINESS.

gladsome *adjective*
Marked by festal celebration. MERRY.

glamor *noun* SEE **glamour.**

glamorous also **glamourous** *adjective*
Pleasing to the eye or mind. ATTRACTIVE.

glamour also **glamor** *noun*
The power or quality of attracting. ATTRACTION.

glamourous *adjective* SEE **glamorous.**

glance¹ *verb*
1. To strike a surface at such an angle as to be deflected: *bullets glancing off the armor plating.*

2. To make light and momentary contact with, as in passing.

3. To emit light suddenly in rays or sparks.
4. To look briefly and quickly.
5. To look through reading matter casually.

glance at (or **over** or **through**) *verb*
To look through reading matter casually.

glance *noun*
1. A quick look: *took a glance at the book.*

2. A sudden quick light.
3. Light and momentary contact with another person or thing.

1. *Syns:* carom (*also* carrom) (off), dap, glint (*Archaic*), graze, ricochet, skim, skip.
2. BRUSH *verb.*

3. FLASH *verb.*
4. GLIMPSE *verb.*
5. BROWSE.

BROWSE.

1. *Syns:* blink, gander² (*Slang*), glimpse, peek, peep, squiz (*Austral. & New Zeal.*).
2. BLINK *noun.*
3. BRUSH *noun.*

glance² *verb*
To give a gleaming luster to, usu. through friction. GLOSS *verb.*

glance at (or **over** or **through**) *verb* SEE **glance¹.**

glare *verb*
1. To stare fixedly and angrily: *glared at me with obvious resentment.*
2. To wrinkle one's brow, as in thought, puzzlement, or displeasure.
3. To look intently and fixedly.
4. To be projected with blinding intensity: *a desert sun that glared mercilessly.*
5. To be obtrusively conspicuous: *errors glaring from the page.*

1. *Syns:* glower, lower¹ (*also* lour), scowl. —*Idiom* look daggers.
2. FROWN *verb.*

3. GAZE *verb.*
4. *Syns:* beat (down), blare, blaze¹.

5. *Syns:* stand out, stick out. —*Idioms* hit someone in the eye, hit (*or* stare) someone in the face, stick out like a sore thumb.

glare *noun*
1. A fixed, angry stare: *looked at me with a ferocious glare.*
2. The act of wrinkling the brow, as in thought, puzzlement, or displeasure.
3. An intense, blinding light: *Sunglasses will decrease the glare.*

1. *Syns:* glower, scowl.

2. FROWN *noun.*

3. *Syns:* blare, blaze¹, dazzle.

glaring *adjective*
1. Extremely bright.
2. Tastelessly showy.
3. Conspicuously bad or offensive.

1. BLAZING.
2. GAUDY.
3. FLAGRANT.

glassy *adjective*
Having a high, radiant sheen. GLOSSY.

glaver *verb*
Obs. To compliment excessively and ingratiatingly. FLATTER.

glaze *noun*
A radiant brightness or glow, usu. due to light reflected from a smooth surface. GLOSS *noun.*

glaze *verb*
To give a gleaming luster to, usu. through friction.

GLOSS *verb*.

gleam *noun*
A sudden quick light.

BLINK *noun*.

gleam *verb*
1. To emit a bright light.
2. To emit light suddenly in rays or sparks.
3. To shine brightly and steadily but without a flame.

1. BEAM *verb*.
2. FLASH *verb*.
3. GLOW *verb*.

gleaming *adjective*
Having a high, radiant sheen.

GLOSSY.

glean *verb*
1. To gather (grain) left by reapers: *gleaned a huge wheat crop*.
2. To collect (something) bit by bit: *gleaned the true facts through long investigation*.

1. **Syns:** crop (*Brit. Regional*), harvest, reap.
2. **Syns:** cull, extract, garner, gather, pick up.

glee *noun*
A state of joyful exuberance.

GAIETY.

gleeful *adjective*
Characterized by joyful exuberance.

GAY *adjective*.

gleefulness *noun*
A state of joyful exuberance.

GAIETY.

glib *adjective*
Characterized by ready but often insincere or superficial discourse: *glib commercials; a glib denial*.

Syns: facile, flip (*Informal*), glossy, silver-tongued, slick, vocative, voluble.
Near-syns: articulate, eloquent, fluent, talkative, vocal; chattering, gibbering.

glide *verb*
1. To move smoothly, continuously, and effortlessly: *sharks gliding about in search of prey*.
2. To move silently and furtively.
3. To proceed with ease, esp. of expression.
4. To maneuver gently and slowly into place.

1. **Syns:** glissade, lapse (*Poetic*), slick, slide, slip, slither.
2. SNEAK *verb*.
3. FLOW *verb*.
4. EASE *verb*.

glimmer *noun*
A sudden quick light.

BLINK *noun*.

glimmer *verb*
1. To shine with intermittent gleams.
2. To emit light suddenly in rays or sparks.

1. BLINK *verb*.
2. FLASH *verb*.

glimpse *verb*
To look briefly and quickly: *glimpsed at the photos but quickly pushed them away*.

Syns: glance¹, glint, peek, peep.

glimpse *noun*
A quick look.

GLANCE¹ *noun*.

glint *noun*
1. A radiant brightness or glow, usu. due to light reflected from a smooth surface.
2. Sparkling, brilliant light.
3. A sudden quick light.

1. GLOSS *noun*.

2. GLITTER *noun*.
3. BLINK *noun*.

glint *verb*
1. To look briefly and quickly.
2. To emit light suddenly in rays or sparks.
3. *Archaic*. To strike a surface at such an angle as to be deflected.

1. GLIMPSE *verb*.
2. FLASH *verb*.
3. GLANCE¹ *verb*.

glissade *verb*
To move smoothly, continuously, and effortlessly.

GLIDE.

glisten *verb*
To emit light suddenly in rays or sparks.

FLASH *verb*.

glisten *noun*
Sparkling, brilliant light.

GLITTER *noun*.

glistening *adjective*
Having a high, radiant sheen.

GLOSSY.

glister *verb*
Poetic. To emit light suddenly in rays or sparks.   FLASH *verb*.

glister *noun*
Poetic. Sparkling, brilliant light.   GLITTER *noun*.

glitter *noun*
1. Sparkling, brilliant light: *the glitter of diamonds.*   1. **Syns:** flash, glint, glisten, glister (*Poetic*), scintillation, shimmer, sparkle.

2. Brilliant, showy splendor: *the opulence and glitter of the Romanov court.*   2. **Syns:** brilliance (*also* brilliancy), glory, magnificence, resplendence *or* resplendency, sparkle, sumptuousness.

3. A small, sparkling decoration: *Christmas costumes decorated with glitter.*   3. **Syns:** sequin, spangle.

glitter *verb*
To emit light suddenly in rays or sparks.   FLASH *verb*.

gloaming *noun*
Poetic. The period between afternoon and nighttime.   EVENING.

global *adjective*
1. Covering a wide scope.   1. GENERAL.
2. So pervasive and all-inclusive as to exist in or affect the whole world.   2. UNIVERSAL *adjective*.

globoid *adjective*
Having the shape of a curve everywhere equidistant from a fixed point.   ROUND.

globular *adjective*
Having the shape of a curve everywhere equidistant from a fixed point.   ROUND.

globule *noun*
A quantity of liquid falling or resting in a spherical mass.   DROP *noun*.

gloom *noun*
A feeling or spell of dismally low spirits: *could not dispel his gloom after the funeral.*   **Syns:** blues (*Informal*), dejection, depression, despondency (*also* despondence), dinge, doldrums, dolefulness, dumps (*Informal*), dysphoria, funk[2] (*Chiefly Brit.*), glumness, heavy-heartedness, melancholy, mopes, mournfulness, sadness, suds (*Informal*), unhappiness.

gloom *verb*
To make dim or indistinct.   OBSCURE *verb*.

glooming *adjective*
Dark and depressing.   GLOOMY.

gloomy *adjective*
1. Dark and depressing: *a gloomy, rainy day.*   1. **Syns:** Acheronian, Acherontic, black, bleak, blue, cheerless, cold, dismal, dispiriting, dreary (*also* drear), glooming, glum (*Brit. Regional*), joyless, somber (*also* sombre), tenebrific.
Near-ants: bright, cheerful, happy, light, optimistic, sunny.
Ants: gloomless, radiant.

2. In low spirits.   2. DEPRESSED.
3. Tending to cause sadness or low spirits.   3. SAD.
4. Broodingly and sullenly unhappy.   4. GLUM.
5. Marked by little hopefulness: *gloomy predictions of a recession.*   5. **Syns:** dark, dismal, pessimistic.

glorification *noun*
1. The act of raising to a high position or status or the condition of being so raised.   1. EXALTATION.

2. The honoring of God, as in worship.

glorify *verb*
1. To raise to a high position or status.
2. To pay tribute or homage to.
3. To honor (God) in religious worship.

glorious *adjective*
1. Marked by extraordinary elegance, beauty, and splendor: *the glorious palace of Versailles.*

2. Particularly excellent.

glory *noun*
1. Something meriting the highest praise or regard: *the glory that was Rome; the glory of the Presidency.*
2. A position of exalted, widely recognized importance.
3. Brilliant, showy splendor.

    glory *verb*
To feel or express an uplifting joy over a success or victory.

gloss *noun*
1. A radiant brightness or glow, usu. due to light reflected from a smooth surface: *the gloss of satin and pearls by candlelight.*
2. A deceptive outward appearance.

    gloss *verb*
1. To give a gleaming luster to, usu. through friction: *gloss furniture with wax.*
2. To give a deceptively attractive appearance to.

    gloss over *verb*
To conceal or make light of a fault or offense.

gloss over *verb*

glossy *adjective*
1. Having a high, radiant sheen: *glossy beads.*

2. Characterized by ready but often insincere or superficial discourse.

glow *verb*
1. To shine brightly and steadily but without a flame: *red-hot coals glowing in the grate; lights glowing from windows.*
2. To emit a bright light.

    glow *noun*
1. A fresh, rosy complexion.
2. A feeling of pervasive emotional warmth: *saw the glow of first love in her eyes; felt the glow of victory.*

glower *verb*
1. To wrinkle one's brow, as in thought, puzzlement, or displeasure.
2. To stare fixedly and angrily.

    glower *noun*
1. The act of wrinkling the brow, as in thought, puzzlement, or displeasure.
2. A fixed, angry stare.

glowing *adjective*
1. Of a healthy, reddish color.
2. Showing or having enthusiasm.
3. Bright and clear; not dull or faded.

---

2. PRAISE *noun.*

1. EXALT.
2. HONOR *verb.*
3. PRAISE *verb.*

1. *Syns:* gorgeous, magnificent, proud, resplendent, splendorous *or* splendrous, sublime, superb.
    Near-syns: brilliant, effulgent, lustrous, shining, stunning; imposing, impressive, lavish, majestic, noble; beautiful, elegant, exclusive, splendid.
2. MARVELOUS.

1. *Syns:* grandeur, grandiosity, grandness, greatness, majesty, splendor.
2. EMINENCE.
3. GLITTER *noun.*

EXULT.

1. *Syns:* glaze, glint, luster, polish, sheen, shine.

2. FAÇADE.

1. *Syns:* buff, burnish, furbish, glance[2], glaze, polish, shine, sleek.
2. COLOR *verb.*

EXTENUATE.
SEE **gloss.**

1. *Syns:* glassy, gleaming, glistening, lustrous, polished, shining, shiny.
    Near-ants: dull, flat, lackluster, mat.
2. GLIB.

1. *Syns:* gleam, incandesce.

2. BEAM *verb.*

1. BLOOM *noun.*
2. *Syns:* blush, flush, radiance.

1. FROWN *verb.*

2. GLARE *verb.*

1. FROWN *noun.*

2. GLARE *noun.*

1. RUDDY.
2. ENTHUSIASTIC.
3. FRESH.

gloze *verb*
To give a deceptively attractive appearance to.
gloze over *verb*
To conceal or make light of a fault or offense.
gloze over *verb*
gluey *adjective*
Having the property of adhering.
glum *adjective*
1. Broodingly and sullenly unhappy: *a glum, petulant loser.*

2. *Brit. Regional.* Dark and depressing.
glumness *noun*
A feeling or spell of dismally low spirits.
glut *verb*
To satisfy to the full or to excess.
glut *noun*
An amount or quantity beyond what is needed, desired, or appropriate.
glutinous *adjective*
Having a heavy, gluey quality.
glutted *adjective*
Filled to satisfaction or excess.
gluttonous *adjective*
Wanting to eat or drink more than one can reasonably consume.
gnash *verb*
1. To seize, as food, with the teeth.
2. To rub together noisily.
gnaw *verb*
1. To seize, as food, with the teeth.
2. To consume gradually, as by chemical reaction, friction, etc.
gnawing *adjective*
Marked by severity or intensity.
go *verb*
1. To move along a particular course: *We were going along a narrow road.*

2. To move or proceed away from a place: *We must go now.*

3. To proceed in a specified direction.
4. To function effectively.
5. To proceed on a certain course or for a certain distance.
6. To be in keeping with.
7. To have a proper or suitable place.
8. To cease living.
9. To be unable to hold up.
10. To fall in.

COLOR *verb.*

EXTENUATE.

SEE **gloze.**

STICKY.

1. *Syns:* chuff (*Regional*), chuffy (*Brit. Regional*), dour, gloomy, morose, mumpish, saturnine, sour, sulky, sullen, surly.
Near-ants: glad, happy, joyful, lighthearted, merry, mirthful.
Ant: cheerful.
2. GLOOMY.

GLOOM.

SATIATE.

SURPLUS *noun.*

VISCOUS.

SATIATED.

GREEDY.

1. BITE *verb.*
2. GRIND *verb.*

1. BITE *verb.*
2. BITE *verb.*

SHARP *adjective.*

1. *Syns:* fare (*Archaic*), journey, pass, proceed, push on, repair, travel, wend (*Archaic*).
2. *Syns:* blow[1] (*Slang*), cut out (*Slang*), depart, exit, get away, get off, go away, leave[1], pull out, push off (*Informal*), quit, remove (*Poetic*), retire, run, run along, shove off (*Slang*), split (*Slang*), take off (*Slang*), withdraw. —*Idioms* beat it, hit the road, take one's leave.
3. BEAR.
4. WORK *verb.*
5. EXTEND.

6. FIT *verb.*
7. BELONG.
8. DIE.
9. BEND *verb.*
10. CAVE IN at **cave.**

11. To be depleted: *All my money is gone.*

11. *Syns:* consume, exhaust, expend, finish, run through, spend, use (up), wash up. —*Idiom* go down the drain. *Near-syns:* deplete, fritter (away), overspend, squander, waste.

12. To move toward a termination: *The pain is going now.*

12. *Syns:* elapse, go away, go by, expire, pass, pass away.

13. To change or fluctuate within limits: *The prices go from $20 to $50.*

13. *Syns:* extend, range, run, vary.

14. To fare well.

14. PROSPER.

15. To turn out well.

15. SUCCEED.

16. To put up as a stake in a game or speculation.

16. GAMBLE *verb.*

17. To make an offer of: *was willing to go $50 for the antique teapot.*

17. *Syns:* bid, offer.

18. To have recourse to when in need.

18. RESORT TO at **resort.**

go along *verb*
To agree to cooperate or participate.

PLAY ALONG at **play.**

go around *verb*
1. To become known far and wide.
2. To pass around but not through.

1. GET ABOUT at **get.**
2. SKIRT *verb.*

go at *verb*
1. To start work on vigorously.
2. To set upon with violent force.

1. ATTACK *verb.*
2. ATTACK *verb.*

go away *verb*
1. To move or proceed away from a place.
2. To move toward a termination.

1. GO.
2. GO.

go by *verb*
To move toward a termination.

GO.

go down *verb*
1. To come to the ground suddenly and involuntarily.
2. To undergo capture, defeat, or ruin.

1. FALL *verb.*
2. SURRENDER *verb.*

go for *verb*
1. *Informal.* To recognize the worth, quality, importance, etc., of.
2. To be favorably disposed toward.
3. *Slang.* To regard (something) as true or real.
4. To require a specified price.

1. APPRECIATE.

2. APPROVE.
3. BELIEVE.
4. COST *verb.*

go in *verb*
To come or go into (a place).

ENTER.

go off *verb*
To release or cause to release energy suddenly and violently, esp. with a loud noise.

EXPLODE.

go on *verb*
1. *Informal.* To talk volubly, persistently, and usu. inconsequentially.
2. To remain in existence or in a certain state for an indefinitely long time.
3. To continue without halting.

1. CHATTER *verb.*

2. ENDURE.

3. CARRY ON at **carry.**

go over *verb*
1. To turn out well.
2. To look at carefully or critically.
3. To recapitulate the salient facts of.

1. SUCCEED.
2. EXAMINE.
3. REVIEW *verb.*

go through *verb*
To participate in or partake of personally.

EXPERIENCE *verb.*

go under *verb*
1. To undergo capture, defeat, or ruin.
2. To undergo sudden financial failure.

1. SURRENDER *verb.*
2. COLLAPSE *verb.*

go up *verb*
To move upward on or along.

ASCEND.

go with *verb*
To be in keeping with.

FIT *verb.*

go *noun*
1. *Informal.* A brief trial.
2. A limited, often assigned period of activity, duty, or opportunity.
3. An often prolonged period, as of illness.
4. *Informal.* Capacity or power for work or vigorous activity.

go *adjective*
Informal. In a state of preparedness.

goad *verb*
To stir to action or feeling.

goal *noun*
1. Something strongly desired.
2. What one intends to do or achieve.

go along *verb*
go around *verb*
go at *verb*
goat *noun*
One who is made an object of blame.

go away *verb*
gob¹ *noun*
1. *Informal.* An indeterminately great amount or number.
2. An irregularly shaped mass of indefinite size.

gob² *noun*
Slang. The opening in the body through which food is ingested.

gob³ *noun*
A person engaged in sailing or working on a ship.

gobble *verb*
To swallow (food or drink) greedily or rapidly in large amounts.

gobble *noun*
An act of swallowing.

gobbledegook *noun*
gobbledygook also **gobbledegook** *noun*
Wordy, unclear jargon.

go-between *noun*
Someone who acts as an intermediate agent in a transaction: *He was the go-between in negotiations with the kidnappers.*

go by *verb*
godforsaken also **Godforsaken** *adjective*
Empty of people.

godlike *adjective*
Of, from, like, or being a god or God.

godly *adjective*
1. Of, from, like, or being a god or God.
2. Deeply concerned with God and the beliefs and practice of religion.

go down *verb*
go for *verb*
go-getter *noun*
Informal. An intensely energetic, enthusiastic person.

go-getting *adjective*
Marked by boldness and assertiveness.

goggle *verb*
To look intently and fixedly.

go in *verb*
going *noun*
The act of leaving.

---

1. TRY *noun.*
2. TURN *noun.*

3. SIEGE *noun.*
4. ENERGY.

READY *adjective.*

PROVOKE.

1. AMBITION.
2. INTENTION.

SEE **go.**
SEE **go.**
SEE **go.**

SCAPEGOAT.

SEE **go.**

1. HEAP *noun.*

2. LUMP¹ *noun.*

MOUTH.

SAILOR.

GULP *verb.*

SWALLOW *noun.*
SEE **gobbledygook.**

GIBBERISH.

Syns: broker, interagent, interceder, intercessor, intermediary, intermediate, intermediator, mediator, middleman.
SEE **go.**

LONELY.

DIVINE¹ *adjective.*

1. DIVINE¹ *adjective.*
2. HOLY.

SEE **go.**
SEE **go.**

EAGER BEAVER.

AGGRESSIVE.

GAZE *verb.*

SEE **go.**

DEPARTURE.

going *adjective*
In action or full operation.   ACTIVE.

goldbrick *verb*
Slang. To pass time without working or in avoiding   IDLE *verb.*
work.

golden ager *noun*
An elderly person.   SENIOR *noun.*

Goliath *noun*
One that is extraordinarily large and powerful.   GIANT *noun.*

gone *adjective*
1. Not present.   1. ABSENT.
2. No longer in one's possession.   2. LOST.
3. No longer alive.   3. DEAD.
4. Carrying a developing fetus within the uterus. 4. PREGNANT.
5. *Slang.* Affected with intense romantic attraction. 5. INFATUATED.

good *adjective*
1. Well above average: *a good student; good*   1. *Syns:* high-grade, nice.
   workmanship.
2. Having pleasant, desirable qualities: *a good chap.* 2. *Syns:* bonny (*Scot.*), braw (*Scot.*),
                                     goodly, nice. —*Idiom* good as gold.
3. Suited to one's end or purpose.   3. CONVENIENT.
4. In excellent condition: *a good tooth.*   4. *Syns:* entire, flawless, intact, perfect,
                                     sound^2, unblemished, unbroken,
                                     undamaged, unhurt, unimpaired,
                                     uninjured, unmarred, whole.
                                   Near-ants: damaged, defective, flawed,
                                   impaired, imperfect, marred, unsound;
                                   blemished, broken, tarnished.
                                   Ant: bad.
5. Affording benefit.   5. BENEFICIAL.
6. Having the ability to perform well.   6. ABLE.
7. Not counterfeit or copied.   7. AUTHENTIC.
8. Notably above average in amount, size, or scope. 8. BIG.
9. Not more or less.   9. ROUND.
10. To one's liking.   10. AGREEABLE.
11. Indicative of future success.   11. FAVORABLE.
12. Beyond reproach.   12. EXEMPLARY.
13. Characterized by kindness and concern for others. 13. BENEVOLENT.

good *noun*
1. A state of health, happiness, and prospering. 1. WELFARE.
2. The quality or state of being morally sound: *Good* 2. *Syns:* goodness, morality, probity,
   triumphed over evil.   rectitude, righteousness, rightness,
                                     uprightness, virtue, virtuousness.
3. Something that contributes to or increases one's 3. INTEREST *noun.*
   well-being.

good-by or **good-bye** *noun*
A separation of two or more people.   PARTING *noun.*

good-by or **good-bye** *adjective*
Of, done, given, or said on departing.   PARTING *adjective.*

good-bye *noun & adjective*   SEE **good-by.**

good-for-nothing *noun*
A self-indulgent person who spends time avoiding work WASTREL.
or other useful activity.

good-for-nothing *adjective*
Lacking all worth and value.   WORTHLESS.

good-hearted *adjective*
Having or showing a tender, considerate, and helping KIND^1.
nature.

goodish *adjective*
Of moderately good quality but less than excellent. ACCEPTABLE.

good-looking *adjective*
Having qualities that delight the eye. BEAUTIFUL.

goodly *adjective*
1. Having pleasant, desirable qualities. **1.** GOOD *adjective*.
2. Somewhat big. **2.** SIZABLE.

good-natured *adjective*
Pleasant and friendly. AMIABLE.

goodness *noun*
The quality or state of being morally sound. GOOD *noun*.

goods *noun*
1. Products bought and sold in commerce: *inventoried* **1.** *Syns:* commodities, line, merchandise,
   all the goods in the store. wares.
2. Those articles that belong to someone. **2.** BELONGINGS.
3. One's portable property. **3.** EFFECTS.

good-tempered *adjective*
Pleasant and friendly. AMIABLE.

good will *noun*
Kindly, charitable interest in others. BENEVOLENCE.

goody *noun*
Informal. Something fine and delicious, esp. a food. DELICACY.

gooey *adjective*
1. *Informal.* Having the property of adhering. **1.** STICKY.
2. *Informal.* Affectedly or extravagantly emotional. **2.** SENTIMENTAL.

goof *noun*
Slang. A stupid, clumsy mistake. BLUNDER *noun*.

goof off *verb*
Slang. To pass time without working or in avoiding IDLE *verb*.
work.

goof up *verb*
Slang. To harm irreparably through inept handling; BOTCH.
make a mess of.

go off *verb* SEE **go.**

goof off *verb* SEE **goof.**

goof up *verb* SEE **goof.**

go on *verb* SEE **go.**

goon *noun*
Slang. A person who treats others violently and THUG.
roughly, esp. for hire.

goose *noun*
Informal. One deficient in judgment and good sense. FOOL *noun*.

goose-pimply *adjective*
Experiencing a repugnant tingling sensation. CRAWLY.

goosey also **goosy** *adjective*
Informal. Feeling or exhibiting nervous tension. EDGY.

goosy *adjective* SEE **goosey.**

go over *verb* SEE **go.**

gordian *adjective*
Difficult to understand due to intricacy. COMPLEX *adjective*.

gore *noun*
The fluid circulated by the heart through the vascular BLOOD *noun*.
system.

gorge *verb*
To satisfy to the full or to excess. SATIATE.

gorged *adjective*
Filled to satisfaction or excess. SATIATED.

gorgeous *adjective*
1. Having qualities that delight the eye. **1.** BEAUTIFUL.
2. Marked by extraordinary elegance, beauty, and **2.** GLORIOUS.
   splendor.

gorilla *noun*
Slang. A person who treats others violently and roughly, esp. for hire.

THUG.

gory *adjective*
Of or covered with blood.

BLOODY *adjective.*

gossamer also **gossamery** *adjective*
So light and insubstantial as to resemble air or a thin film.

FILMY.

gossamery *adjective*

SEE **gossamer.**

gossip *noun*
1. Idle, often sensational and groundless talk about others: *a tabloid full of gossip. According to gossip, they eloped.*

1. ***Syns:*** buzz, cry, hearsay, murmur, report, rumor, scuttlebutt (*Slang*), tattle, tittle-tattle, whispering, word. ***Near-syns:*** account, chronicle, conversation, grapevine, story, tale; banter, chatter, prattle.

2. A person habitually engaged in idle talk about others: *Our local gossip claimed we were getting a divorce.*

2. ***Syns:*** gossiper, gossipmonger, mumblenews, newsmonger, quidnunc, rumorer, rumormonger, scandalmonger, tabby, talebearer, tattle, tattler, tattletale, telltale, yenta (*Slang*).

gossip *verb*
To engage in or spread gossip: *gossiped about the President's private life.*

Syns: buzz, blab, noise (about *or* abroad), rumor, talk, tattle, tittle-tattle. —*Idiom* tell tales out of school.

gossiper *noun*
A person habitually engaged in idle talk about others.

GOSSIP *noun.*

gossipmonger *noun*
A person habitually engaged in idle talk about others.

GOSSIP *noun.*

gossipy *adjective*
Inclined to gossip: *a gossipy old crone.*

Syns: blabby, talebearing, taletelling.

go through *verb*

SEE **go.**

gouge *verb*
1. To obtain by coercion or intimidation.
2. *Informal.* To exploit (another) by charging too much for something.

1. EXTORT.
2. SKIN *verb.*

go under *verb*

SEE **go.**

go up *verb*

SEE **go.**

govern *verb*
1. To exercise the authority of a sovereign: *Catherine the Great thought she governed in an enlightened manner.*

1. ***Syns:*** overrule, reign, rule, sway. —*Idioms* wear the crown, wield the scepter. ***Near-syns:*** admininster, control, direct, manage; command, regulate, supervise.

2. To have charge of (the affairs of others).
3. To exercise authority or influence over.
4. To keep the mechanical operation of (a device) within proper parameters: *a valve governing fuel intake.*

2. ADMINISTER.
3. CONTROL *verb.*
4. ***Syns:*** control, regulate.

governable *adjective*
Capable of being governed: *a docile, governable people; a financial situation that while bad was still governable.*

Syns: administrable, controllable, handleable, manageable.

governance *noun*
1. A system by which a political unit is controlled.
2. The continuous exercise of authority over a political unit.

1. GOVERNMENT.
2. GOVERNMENT.

governing *adjective*
Exercising controlling power or influence.

DOMINANT.

government *noun*
1. A system by which a political unit is controlled: *The United States has a democratic form of government.*

1. ***Syns:*** governance, regime, rule.

2. Authoritative control over the affairs of others.   **2.** ADMINISTRATION.

3. The continuous exercise of authority over a political unit: *was active in the government of the province.*   **3.** *Syns:* administration, control, direction, governance, rule.

governmental *adjective*

Of or relating to government: *governmental agencies.*   *Syns:* gubernatorial, regulatory.

go with *verb*   SEE **go.**

gown *noun*

A one-piece, skirted outer garment for women and children.   DRESS *noun.*

grab *verb*

1. To take quick and forcible possession of.   **1.** SEIZE.

2. To get hold of (something moving).   **2.** CATCH *verb.*

3. To take firmly with the hand and maintain a hold on.   **3.** GRASP *verb.*

4. *Informal.* To compel the attention, interest, imagination, etc., of.   **4.** GRIP *verb.*

grab *noun*

The act of catching, esp. a sudden taking and holding.   CATCH *noun.*

grabble *verb*

To reach about or search blindly or uncertainly.   GROPE.

grabby *adjective*

Informal. Having a strong urge to obtain or possess something, esp. material wealth, in quantity.   GREEDY.

grace *noun*

1. Kind, forgiving, or compassionate treatment of or disposition toward others: *forgiven by the grace of the king.*   **1.** *Syns:* caritas, charity, clemency, leniency (*also* lenience), lenity, mercifulness, mercy.

2. Kindly, charitable interest in others.   **2.** BENEVOLENCE.

3. A kindly act.   **3.** FAVOR *noun.*

4. A sense of propriety or rightness.   **4.** DECENCY.

5. Temporary immunity from penalties: *a day of grace before enforcing the new law.*   **5.** *Syns:* respite, reprieve.

6. Refined, effortless beauty of manner, form, and style.   **6.** ELEGANCE.

7. A short prayer said at meals: *said grace before dinner.*   **7.** *Syns:* benediction, blessing, thanks, thanksgiving.

grace *verb*

1. To lend dignity or honor to by an act or favor: *The prime minister graced our gathering with his august presence.*   **1.** *Syns:* dignify, favor, honor.

2. To endow with beauty and elegance by way of a notable addition: *Magnificent gold candlesticks graced an already opulent table.*   **2.** *Syns:* adorn, beautify, embellish, enhance, ornament, set off.

graceful *adjective*

1. Of such tasteful beauty as to elicit admiration.   **1.** ELEGANT.

2. Marked by facility, esp. of expression.   **2.** SMOOTH *adjective.*

graceless *adjective*

Lacking dexterity and grace in physical movement.   AWKWARD.

gracious *adjective*

1. Characterized by kindness and warm, unaffected courtesy: *a gracious attitude toward everyone.*   **1.** *Syns:* affable, congenial, cordial, genial, sociable.
Near-ants: boorish, churlish, discourteous, rude, unsociable; blunt, brusque, curt, gruff, surly.
Ant: ungracious.

2. Characterized by elaborate but usu. formal courtesy: *gracious old-world manners.*   **2.** *Syns:* chivalrous, courtly, gallant, knightly, stately.

gradation *noun*

1. The degree of vividness of a color, as when modified by the addition of black or white pigment.   **1.** SHADE *noun.*

2. A slight variation between nearly identical entities.   **2.** SHADE *noun.*

gradational *adjective*
Proceeding very slowly by degrees.

GRADUAL.

grade *noun*
1. One of the units in a course, as on an ascending or descending scale.
2. An upward slope.
3. Degree of excellence.
4. A division of persons or things by quality, rank, or grade.

1. DEGREE.
2. ASCENT.
3. QUALITY.
4. CLASS *noun*.

grade *verb*
To assign to a class or classes.

CLASS *verb*.

gradient *noun*
1. An upward slope.
2. Deviation from a particular direction.

1. ASCENT.
2. INCLINATION.

gradual *adjective*
1. Proceeding very slowly by degrees: *a gradual shift in Sino-Soviet policy.*
2. Not steep or abrupt: *a gradual slope.*

1. *Syns:* gradational, piecemeal, step-by-step.
2. *Syns:* easy, gentle, moderate.

graft *noun*
Money, property, or a favor given, offered, or promised to a person in a position of trust as an inducement to dishonest behavior.

BRIBE *noun*.

grain *noun*
A tiny amount.

BIT[1].

grainy *adjective*
Consisting of or covered with large particles.

COARSE.

grand *adjective*
1. Large and impressive in size, scope, or extent: *The view of the Winter Palace is indeed grand.*

1. *Syns:* august, baronial, grandiose, imposing, lordly, magnific (*Obs.*), magnificent, majestic, noble, princely, regal, royal, stately, sublime, superb.
   Near-ants: humble, lowly, measly, paltry, petty, puny, trifling, trivial, unimpressive.

2. Marked by magnificently lavish ceremony and display: *The inaugural ball is a truly grand occasion.*
3. Very broad and noble in character, scope, or grasp: *the Secretary of State's grand design for peace.*
4. Exceedingly dignified in form, tone, or style.
5. Raised to or occupying a high position or rank.

2. *Syns:* impressive, regal, splendid, stately.
3. *Syns:* astral, elevated, exalted, lofty.
4. ELEVATED.
5. EXALTED.

grandeur *noun*
Something meriting the highest praise or regard.

GLORY *noun*.

grandiloquent *adjective*
Characterized by language that is elevated and sometimes pompous in style.

SONOROUS.

grandiose *adjective*
1. Large and impressive in size, scope, or extent.
2. Characterized by an exaggerated show of dignity or self-importance.

1. GRAND.
2. POMPOUS.

grandiosity *noun*
Something meriting the highest praise or regard.

GLORY *noun*.

grandness *noun*
Something meriting the highest praise or regard.

GLORY *noun*.

grant *verb*
1. To let have as a favor or privilege: *granted them a hearing.*

1. *Syns:* accord, award, concede, give, vouchsafe.
   Near-syns: bestow, confer, donate, present; allow, permit.

2. To give formally or officially.

3. To recognize, often reluctantly, the reality or truth of.

4. To change the ownership of (property) by means of a legal document.

grant *noun*

1. Something, as a gift, granted for a definite purpose: *the foundation's grant for medical research.*

2. A making over of legal ownership or title: *the court's grant of the property to her.*

grantor *noun*

A person who gives to a charity or cause.

granular *adjective*

Consisting of or covered with large particles.

granulate *verb*

To break up into tiny particles.

granulize *verb*

To break up into tiny particles.

graphic *adjective*

1. Of or pertaining to representation by means of writing: *graphic communication.*

2. Of or pertaining to representation by drawings or pictures: *a textbook's graphic aids.*

3. Described verbally in sharp and accurate detail: *a graphic account of the battle.*

4. Serving to describe.

grapple *noun*

An act or means of holding something.

grapple *verb*

To contend with an opponent, esp. by attempting to throw him.

grasp *verb*

1. To take firmly with the hand and maintain a hold on: *grasped the handrail of the moving escalator.*

2. To perceive and recognize the meaning of.

grasp *noun*

1. An act or means of holding something.

2. The ability or power to seize or attain: *a goal within their grasp.*

3. Intellectual hold: *a grasp of practical politics.*

4. Firm control.

grasping *adjective*

Having a strong urge to obtain or possess something, esp. material wealth, in quantity.

grate *verb*

To bring or come into sliding, abrasive contact, often with a harsh, grating sound.

grateful *adjective*

1. Showing or feeling gratitude: *a grateful glance; grateful for your understanding.*

2. Affording pleasure or comfort: *the grateful quiet of evening.*

gratefulness *noun*

A being grateful.

gratified *adjective*

Having achieved satisfaction, as of one's goal.

---

2. CONFER.

3. ACKNOWLEDGE.

4. TRANSFER.

1. **Syns:** appropriation, subsidy, subvention.

2. **Syns:** conveyance (*Law*), transfer.

DONOR.

COARSE.

CRUSH *verb.*

CRUSH *verb.*

1. **Syns:** calligraphic, scriptural, written.

2. **Syns:** illustrative, photographic, pictographic, pictorial.

3. **Syns:** lifelike, photographic, pictorial, picturesque, realistic, vivid.
   Near-syns: definite, explicit, precise; cogent, convincing, telling; revealing, striking.

4. DESCRIPTIVE.

HOLD *noun.*

WRESTLE.

1. **Syns:** clasp, clench, clinch, clutch, grab, grip, hang on, seize.

2. UNDERSTAND.

1. HOLD *noun.*

2. **Syns:** capacity, compass, range, reach, scope.

3. **Syns:** apprehension, comprehension, grip, mastery, savvy (*Slang*), understanding.

4. GRIP *noun.*

GREEDY.

SCRAPE *verb.*

1. **Syns:** appreciative, obliged, thankful.

2. **Syns:** congenial, gratifying, satisfying, welcome.

APPRECIATION.

FULFILLED.

gratify *verb*
1. To give great or keen pleasure to.
2. To comply with the wishes or ideas of (another).

1. DELIGHT *verb*.
2. HUMOR *verb*.

gratifying *adjective*
1. To one's liking.
2. Affording enjoyment.
3. Affording pleasure or comfort.

1. AGREEABLE.
2. ENJOYABLE.
3. GRATEFUL.

grating *adjective*
Disagreeable to the sense of hearing.

HARSH.

gratis *adjective*
Costing nothing.

FREE *adjective*.

gratitude *noun*
A being grateful.

APPRECIATION.

gratuitous *adjective*
1. Costing nothing.
2. Not required, necessary, or warranted by the circumstances of the case.

1. FREE *adjective*.
2. WANTON.

gratuity *noun*
A material favor or gift, usu. money, given in return for service: *Gratuities must be reported with taxable income.*

Syns: cumshaw, lagniappe (*Informal*), largess (*also* largesse), perk[1] (*Slang*), perquisite, tip[3].
Near-syns: alms, benefaction, contribution, donation, offering, reward.

gravamen *noun*
The most central and material part.

HEART.

grave[1] *noun*
A burial place or receptacle for human remains: *graves decorated with floral pieces.*

Syns: catacomb, cinerarium, crypt, mausoleum, ossuary, sepulcher, sepulture (*Archaic*), tomb, vault[1].

grave[2] *adjective*
1. Having great consequence or weight: *a grave problem.*
2. Causing or marked by danger, pain, etc.
3. Portending future disaster.
4. Full of or marked by dignity and seriousness: *had a grave expression when he told me I needed surgery.*

1. *Syns:* heavy, momentous, serious, severe, weighty.
2. GRIEVOUS.
3. FATEFUL.
4. *Syns:* earnest, sedate, serious, sober, solemn, somber (*also* sombre), staid.
Near-ants: flip, flippant, light, laughable.
Ant: gay.

grave[3] *verb*
1. To cut (a design or inscription) into a hard surface, esp. for printing.
2. To produce a deep impression on.

1. ENGRAVE.
2. ENGRAVE.

gravid *adjective*
Carrying a developing fetus within the uterus.

PREGNANT.

gravidation *noun*
Obs. The condition of carrying a developing fetus within the uterus.

PREGNANCY.

gravidity *noun*
The condition of carrying a developing fetus within the uterus.

PREGNANCY.

gravitate *verb*
To fall or drift down to the bottom.

SETTLE.

gravity *noun*
1. The condition of being grave and of involving serious consequences: *the gravity of her accusation.*
2. High seriousness of manner or bearing: *the gravity of courtroom procedure.*
3. *Rare.* The state or quality of being physically heavy.

1. *Syns:* momentousness, seriousness, severity, weightiness.
2. *Syns:* sobriety, solemnness, solemnity, somberness.
3. HEAVINESS.

gray matter *noun*
Informal. The seat of the faculty of intelligence and reason.

HEAD *noun*.

graze *verb*
1. To make light and momentary contact with, as in passing.
2. To strike a surface at such an angle as to be deflected.

1. BRUSH *verb*.
2. GLANCE[1] *verb*.

graze *noun*
Light and momentary contact with another person or thing.

BRUSH *noun*.

greasy *adjective*
Having the qualities of fat.

FATTY *adjective*.

great *adjective*
1. Notably above average in amount, size, or scope.
2. Exceptionally good of its kind.
3. Widely known and esteemed.

1. BIG.
2. EXCELLENT.
3. EMINENT.

greater *adjective*
1. Much more than half.
2. Being at a height or level above another.

1. BEST *adjective*.
2. HIGHER.

great-hearted *adjective*
Willing to give of oneself and one's possessions.

GENEROUS.

great-heartedness *noun*
The quality or state of being generous.

GENEROSITY.

greatness *noun*
1. The quality or state of being large in amount, extent, or importance.
2. Something meriting the highest praise or regard.
3. *Archaic.* The condition of carrying a developing fetus within the uterus.

1. SIZE.
2. GLORY *noun*.
3. PREGNANCY.

greed *noun*
Excessive desire for more than one needs or deserves: *the greed of speculators that feeds on small investors.*

Syns: acquisitiveness, avarice, avariciousness, avidity, covetousness, cupidity, rapacity.

greedy *adjective*
1. Having a strong urge to obtain or possess something, esp. material wealth, in quantity: *foreclosures that enriched greedy landowners.*

1. **Syns:** acquisitive, avaricious, avid, covetous, desirous, grabby (*Informal*), grasping, hungry, rapacious.
   Near-syns: envious, grudging, jealous; eager, selfish; immoderate, unrestrained.
   Ant: generous.

2. Wanting to eat or drink more than one can reasonably consume: *a greedy boy hunched over an overfilled plate.*

2. **Syns:** edacious, gluttonous, hoggish, piggish, ravenous, voracious.

green *adjective*
1. Being in an early period of growth or development.
2. Lacking experience and the knowledge gained from it.

1. YOUNG.
2. INEXPERIENCED.

green *noun*
A tract of cultivated land belonging to and used by a community.

COMMON *noun*.

greenbacks *noun*
Something, as coins, printed bills, etc., used as a medium of exchange.

MONEY.

green-eyed *adjective*
Resentfully or painfully desirous of another's advantages.

ENVIOUS.

greenness *noun*
1. The time of life between childhood and maturity.

1. YOUTH.

2. Lack of experience and the knowledge gained from it.

greet *verb*
1. To address in a friendly and respectful way: *greeted each guest individually.*
2. To present with a specified reaction: *greeted our proposal with scorn.*

greeting *noun*
An expression, in words or gestures, marking a meeting of persons: *had a friendly greeting for all.*

gregarious *adjective*
1. Of, characterized by, or inclined to living together in communities.
2. Disposed to be open, sociable, and talkative.

grief *noun*
Mental anguish or pain caused by loss or despair: *showing grief openly at the funeral.*

grievance *noun*
1. A circumstance regarded as a cause for protest or complaint: *legislation aimed at the remedy of basic grievances.*
2. An expression of dissatisfaction.

grieve *verb*
1. To feel, show, or express grief: *grieved deeply over the death of her husband.*

2. To cause suffering or painful sorrow to.

grievous *adjective*
1. Causing or marked by danger, pain, etc.: *sustained a grievous wound.*
2. Causing sorrow or regret.
3. Difficult to accept.

grill *verb*
Informal. To question thoroughly and relentlessly to verify facts.

grim *adjective*
1. Having or showing uncompromising determination or resolution in purpose or action: *a grim will to succeed.*

2. Shockingly repellent.
3. Cold and forbidding.

grimace *noun*
A facial contortion indicating displeasure, disgust, pain, etc.

grimace *verb*
To contort one's face to indicate displeasure, disgust, pain, etc.: *grimaced like a monkey when he saw the bills.*

grime *noun*
Foul or dirty matter.

griminess *noun*
The condition or state of being dirty.

grimy *adjective*
Covered or stained with or as if with dirt or other impurities.

grin *verb*
To curve the lips upward in expressing amusement, pleasure, or happiness.

grin *noun*

---

2. INEXPERIENCE.

1. Syns: hail², salute, welcome.

2. Syns: meet¹, react to, respond to.

Syns: salutation, salute, welcome.

1. SOCIAL.

2. OUTGOING.

Syns: heartache, heartbreak, sorrow, woe.

1. Syns: beef (*Informal*), gripe (*Informal*), kick (*Informal*). —*Idiom* bone to pick.

2. COMPLAINT.

1. Syns: lament, mourn, sorrow, suffer. **Near-syns:** bemoan, bewail, cry, wail, weep. **Ant:** rejoice.

2. DISTRESS *verb.*

1. Syns: dangerous, grave², serious, severe.
2. SORROWFUL.
3. BITTER *adjective.*

INTERROGATE.

1. Syns: implacable, hard-shell (*also* hard-shelled), inexorable, intransigent, merciless, remorseless, unbending, unrelenting, unyielding.
2. GHASTLY.
3. BLEAK.

FACE *noun.*

Syns: mop (*Archaic*), mouth, mow, mug (*Slang*). —*Idioms* make (*or* pull) a face, make faces.

FILTH.

DIRTINESS.

DIRTY *adjective.*

SMILE *verb.*

A facial expression marked by an upward curving of the lips.

SMILE *noun.*

grind *verb*

1. To rub together noisily: *ground his teeth in rage.*
2. To break up into tiny particles.
3. To do tedious, laborious, and sometimes menial work: *grinding away to support his family.*
4. To study hard, esp. when pressed for time.

1. **Syns:** crunch, gnash.
2. CRUSH *verb.*
3. **Syns:** drudge, grub, plod, slave, slog, toil.
4. BONE UP at **bone.**

grind *noun*

Informal. A habitual, laborious, often tiresome course of action: *tired of the daily grind—to work and straight home again.*

Syns: groove, routine, rut, treadmill.
—*Idiom* the beaten path.

grip *noun*

1. Firm control: *has a good grip on her emotions; seems to have lost his grip on reality.*
2. An act or means of holding something.
3. Intellectual hold.
4. A strong or powerful influence.
5. A violent, excruciating seizure of pain.

1. **Syns:** grasp, handle, hold.
2. HOLD *noun.*
3. GRASP *noun.*
4. HOLD *noun.*
5. THROE.

grip *verb*

1. To take firmly with the hand and maintain a hold on.
2. To compel the attention, interest, imagination, etc., of: *a scene that gripped the entire audience.*

1. GRASP *verb.*
2. **Syns:** arrest, catch up, enthrall, fascinate, grab (*Informal*), hold, mesmerize, rivet, spellbind, transfix.

gripe *verb*

Informal. To express negative feelings, esp. of dissatisfaction or resentment.

COMPLAIN.

gripe *noun*

1. *Informal.* An expression of dissatisfaction.
2. *Informal.* A circumstance regarded as a cause for protest or complaint.

1. COMPLAINT.
2. GRIEVANCE.

griper *noun*

Informal. A person who habitually complains or grumbles.

GROUCH *noun.*

gripping *adjective*

Catching and holding the full attention.

ABSORBING.

grisly *adjective*

Shockingly repellent.

GHASTLY.

gritty *adjective*

Consisting of or covered with large particles.

COARSE.

grobian *noun*

An unrefined, rude person.

BOOR.

groom *verb*

To make neat and trim; make presentable.

TIDY *verb.*

groove *noun*

A habitual, laborious, often tiresome course of action.

GRIND *noun.*

groove on *verb*

Slang. To like or enjoy enthusiastically, often excessively.

ADORE.

groove on *verb*

SEE **groove.**

groovy *adjective*

Slang. Particularly excellent.

MARVELOUS.

grope *verb*

To reach about or search blindly or uncertainly: *groping for the light switch; groped for the answer to the question.*

Syns: feel (around), fumble, grabble, poke around.

gross *adjective*

1. Including every constituent or individual.
2. Lacking in delicacy or refinement.
3. Conspicuously bad or offensive.

1. WHOLE *adjective.*
2. COARSE.
3. FLAGRANT.

4. Having too much flesh.

5. Offensive to accepted standards of decency.

gross *noun*

An amount or quantity from which nothing is left out or held back.

gross *verb*

To make as income or profit.

grossness *noun*

The quality or state of being flagrant.

grotesque *adjective*

1. Resembling a freak.

2. Conceived or done with no reference to reality or common sense.

grouch *verb*

To express negative feelings, esp. of dissatisfaction or resentment.

grouch *noun*

A person who habitually complains or grumbles: *Her upstairs neighbor is an old grouch who bangs on the floor at the smallest noise.*

grouchy *adjective*

Having or showing a bad temper.

ground *noun*

1. Anything on which something immaterial, such as an argument or charge, rests.

2. The lowest or supporting part or structure.

3. A basis for an action or decision.

4. A fact or circumstance that gives logical support to an assertion, claim, or proposal.

ground *verb*

1. To take or serve as the basis for.

2. To cause to fall, as from a shot or blow.

groundless *adjective*

Having no basis or foundation in fact.

groundlessly *adverb*

Without basis or foundation in fact.

groundwork *noun*

1. The lowest or supporting part or structure.

2. Anything on which something immaterial, such as an argument or charge, rests.

group *noun*

1. A number of individuals making up or considered a unit: *a group of men standing on the corner; a group of islands off the coast of Alaska.*

2. A number of persons who have come or been gathered together.

3. A usu. small number of individuals: *The waiter asked how many were in the group.*

group *verb*

1. To come or bring into a group or groups: *travelers grouping with their tour guide in the hotel lobby.*

2. To assign to a class or classes.

3. To put into a deliberate order.

4. To distribute into groups according to kinds.

grouping *noun*

A way or condition of being arranged.

---

4. FAT *adjective*.

5. OBSCENE.

WHOLE *noun*.

RETURN *verb*.

FLAGRANCY.

1. FREAKISH.

2. FANTASTIC.

COMPLAIN.

Syns: bellyacher (*Slang*), complainer, crab (*Informal*), crank (*Informal*), faultfinder, griper (*Informal*), grouser (*Informal*), growler, grumbler, grump, kicker (*Informal*), sorehead (*Slang*), sourpuss (*Slang*).

ILL-TEMPERED.

1. BASIS.

2. BASE^1 *noun*.

3. CAUSE *noun*.

4. REASON *noun*.

1. BASE^1 *verb*.

2. DROP *verb*.

BASELESS.

UNFOUNDEDLY.

1. BASE^1 *noun*.

2. BASIS.

1. **Syns:** array, batch, body, bunch (*Informal*), bundle, clump, cluster, clutch, collection, knot, lot, set^2.

2. ASSEMBLY.

3. **Syns:** band^2, bevy, bunch (*Informal*), party.

1. **Syns:** aggroup, assemble, cluster, collect, gather.

2. CLASS *verb*.

3. ARRANGE.

4. ASSORT.

ARRANGEMENT.

grouse *verb*
Informal. To express negative feelings, esp. of COMPLAIN.
dissatisfaction or resentment.

grouser *noun*
Informal. A person who habitually complains or GROUCH *noun.*
grumbles.

grow *verb*
1. To bring into existence and foster the development   1. **Syns:** breed, cultivate, produce,
   of: *grows orchids as a hobby; a farm where corn and*   propagate, raise.
   apples are grown.   **Near-syns:** foster, nurse, nurture, rear,
                                                             tend.
2. To bring or come to full development.   2. MATURE *verb.*
3. To make or become greater or larger.   3. INCREASE *verb.*
4. To come to be.   4. BECOME.

growl *verb*
To make a continuous deep, reverberating sound.   RUMBLE *verb.*

growler *noun*
A person who habitually complains or grumbles.   GROUCH *noun.*

grown *adjective*
Having reached full growth and development.   MATURE *adjective.*

grown-up *adjective*
Having reached full growth and development.   MATURE *adjective.*

growth *noun*
1. A progression from a simple form to a more complex   1. DEVELOPMENT.
   one.
2. The act of increasing or rising.   2. INCREASE *noun.*

grub *verb*
1. To break, turn over, or remove (earth, sand, etc.)   1. DIG *verb.*
   with or as if with a tool.
2. To do tedious, laborious, and sometimes menial   2. GRIND *verb.*
   work.
3. *Slang.* To take (food) into the body as nourishment. 3. EAT.

grub *noun*
Slang. Something fit to be eaten.   FOOD.

grubby *adjective*
Covered or stained with or as if with dirt or other   DIRTY *adjective.*
impurities.

grubstake *verb*
To supply capital to or for.   FINANCE.

grudge *verb*
To feel envy for.   ENVY *verb.*

gruel *verb*
To make extremely tired.   EXHAUST.

gruesome *adjective*
Shockingly repellent.   GHASTLY.

gruff *adjective*
1. Low and grating in sound.   1. HOARSE.
2. Rudely unceremonious.   2. ABRUPT.

grumble *verb*
1. To complain in low, indistinct tones.   1. MUTTER *verb.*
2. To express negative feelings, esp. of dissatisfaction 2. COMPLAIN.
   or resentment.
3. To make a continuous deep, reverberating sound.   3. RUMBLE *verb.*

grumble *noun*
1. A low, indistinct utterance of complaint.   1. MUTTER *noun.*
2. An expression of dissatisfaction.   2. COMPLAINT.

grumbler *noun*
A person who habitually complains or grumbles.   GROUCH *noun.*

grump *noun*
A person who habitually complains or grumbles.   GROUCH *noun.*

grumpy *adjective*
Having or showing a bad temper.   ILL-TEMPERED.

grunt *verb*
To complain in low, indistinct tones.   MUTTER *verb*.

grunt *noun*
A low, indistinct utterance of complaint.   MUTTER *noun*.

guarantee *noun*
1. An assumption of responsibility, as one given by a   1. *Syns:* surety, warrant, warranty.
   manufacturer, for the quality, worth, or durability of   *Near-syns:* bond, pledge, promise,
   a product: *a stereo with a one-year guarantee.*   security, token; oath, vow, word.
2. A declaration that one will or will not do a certain   2. PROMISE *noun*.
   thing.
3. A statement that expresses a commitment on the   3. WORD *noun*.
   part of its maker as to its truthfulness or to the
   fulfillment of its conditions.

guarantee *verb*
1. To render certain: *His family connections guarantee   1. *Syns:* assure, cinch (*Slang*), ensure
   his success in business.*   (*also* insure), secure, warrant.
2. To assume responsibility for the quality, worth, or   2. *Syns:* certify, guaranty, warrant.
   durability of: *The factory guaranteed the dishwasher
   for three years.*
3. To give a promise of payment to (a creditor).   3. SECURE *verb*.

guarantor *noun*
One who assumes financial responsibility for another.   SPONSOR.

guaranty *noun*
1. Something given to guarantee the repayment of a   1. PAWN[1] *noun*.
   loan or the fulfillment of an obligation.
2. One who assumes financial responsibility for   2. SPONSOR.
   another.

guaranty *verb*
To assume responsibility for the quality, worth, or   GUARANTEE *verb*.
durability of.

guard *verb*
To keep safe from danger, attack, or harm.   DEFEND.

guard *noun*
1. A person or special body of persons assigned to   1. *Syns:* lookout, picket, sentry, ward,
   provide protection, keep watch over, etc.: *a bank   watch.
   guard; the palace guard.*
2. The act or a means of defending.   2. DEFENSE.

guardian *noun*
A person who is legally responsible for the person or   *Syns:* conservator (*Law*), custodian,
property of another considered by law to be   keeper, warden.
incompetent to manage his affairs: *was appointed as the
child's guardian under the parents' will.*

guardianship *noun*
The function of watching, guarding, or overseeing.   CARE *noun*.

gubernatorial *adjective*
Of or relating to government.   GOVERNMENTAL.

gudgeon *noun*
Slang. A person who is easily deceived or victimized.   DUPE *noun*.

guerdon *noun*
Poetic. Something given in return for a service or   REWARD *noun*.
accomplishment.

guerdon *verb*
Poetic. To bestow a reward on.   REWARD *verb*.

guess *verb*
To draw an inference on the basis of inconclusive   *Syns:* conjecture, infer, presume, suppose,
evidence or insufficient information: *We can only guess   surmise.
that he had a motive for the crime.*   *Near-syns:* assume, believe, expect,
                                                              imagine, judge, suspect; gather, glean,
                                                              understand.

guess *noun*
A judgment, estimate, or opinion arrived at by
guessing: *All this is merely a guess on my part.*

Syns: conjecture, presumption,
supposition, surmise.

guest *noun*
A person or persons visiting one.

COMPANY *noun.*

guffaw *verb*
To express great amusement or mirth.

BREAK UP at **break.**

guggling *adjective*
Emitting a murmuring sound felt to resemble a laugh.

LAUGHING.

guidance *noun*
An act or instance of guiding: *a tax program
administered under the guidance of the Secretary of the
Treasury.*

Syns: direction, lead, leadership,
management.

guide *noun*
Something or someone that shows the way: *Let your
conscience be your guide. Her designer friend is her
guide in choosing clothes.*

Syns: conductor, director, lead, leader,
mentor, pilot.

guide *verb*
To show the way to: *Sailors once used the stars to guide
them. He guided me to my seat.*

Syns: conduct, direct, escort, lead, pilot,
route, shepherd, show, steer, usher.
Near-ants: distract, perplex; beguile,
deceive, delude, mislead, misroute.
Ant: misguide.

guild *noun*
A group of people united in a relationship and having
some interest, activity, or purpose in common.

UNION.

guile *noun*
1. The act or practice of deceiving.
2. Deceitful cleverness.

1. DECEIT.
2. ART.

guileful *adjective*
1. Deceitfully clever.
2. Marked by treachery or deceit.

1. ARTFUL.
2. UNDERHAND.

guileless *adjective*
Free from guile, cunning, or deceit.

ARTLESS.

guilt *noun*
Responsibility for an error or crime.

BLAME *noun.*

guiltless *adjective*
Free from guilt or blame.

INNOCENT *adjective.*

guilty *adjective*
Deserving blame.

BLAMEWORTHY.

guise *noun*
1. A set or style of clothing.
2. A deceptive outward appearance.

1. DRESS *noun.*
2. FAÇADE.

gull *noun*
A person who is easily deceived or victimized.

DUPE *noun.*

gull *verb*
To get money or something else from by deceitful
trickery.

CHEAT *verb.*

gullible *adjective*
Easily imposed on or tricked.

EASY.

gulosity *noun*
The quality or condition of being voracious.

VORACITY.

gulp *verb*
To swallow (food or drink) greedily or rapidly in large
amounts: *Too busy to take a full hour, she had to gulp
down her lunch.*

Syns: bolt, englut, engorge, gobble, guttle,
guzzle, ingurgitate, swill, wolf.

gulp *noun*
An act of swallowing.

SWALLOW *noun.*

gummy *adjective*
Having the property of adhering.

STICKY.

gumption *noun*
1. The ability to make sensible decisions.
2. *Informal.* The wish, power, and ability to begin and follow through with a plan or task.

1. COMMON SENSE.
2. AMBITION.

gumshoe *noun*
Slang. A person whose work is investigating crimes or obtaining hidden evidence or information.

DETECTIVE.

gumshoe *verb*
Slang. To move silently and furtively.

SNEAK *verb*.

gum up *verb*
Slang. To harm irreparably through inept handling; make a mess of.

BOTCH.

gun *verb*
To wound or kill with a firearm.

SHOOT *verb*.

gung ho *adjective*
Slang. Showing or having enthusiasm.

ENTHUSIASTIC.

gurge *verb*
To move or cause to move like a rapid rotary current of liquid.

SWIRL.

gurgle *verb*
To flow or move with a low, slapping sound.

WASH.

gurgling *adjective*
Emitting a murmuring sound felt to resemble a laugh.

LAUGHING.

gush *verb*
1. To come forth or emit in abundance.
2. To make an emotional display.

1. FLOW *verb*.
2. EMOTIONALIZE.

gushy *adjective*
Affectedly or extravagantly emotional.

SENTIMENTAL.

gust *noun*
1. A sudden, violent expression, as of emotion.
2. A natural movement or current of air.

1. OUTBURST.
2. WIND[1] *noun*.

gusto *noun*
Spirited enjoyment.

ZEST.

gusty *adjective*
Exposed to or characterized by the presence of freely circulating air or wind.

AIRY.

gut *adjective*
Slang. Of, pertaining to, or arising from one's mental or spiritual being.

INNER.

gutless *adjective*
Ignobly lacking in courage.

COWARDLY.

gutlessness *noun*
Ignoble lack of courage.

COWARDICE.

guts *noun*
Slang. The quality of mind enabling one to face danger or hardship resolutely.

COURAGE.

gutsy *adjective*
Informal. Having or showing courage.

BRAVE *adjective*.

guttle *verb*
To swallow (food or drink) greedily or rapidly in large amounts.

GULP *verb*.

gutty *adjective*
Having or showing courage.

BRAVE *adjective*.

guzzle *verb*
1. To take alcoholic liquor, esp. excessively or habitually.
2. To swallow (food or drink) greedily or rapidly in large amounts.

1. DRINK *verb*.
2. GULP *verb*.

gyp also **gip** *verb*
Informal. To get money or something else from by deceitful trickery.

CHEAT *verb*.

gyp *noun*
1. *Informal.* An act of cheating.
2. *Informal.* A person who cheats.

1. CHEAT *noun*.
2. CHEAT *noun*.

gypper *noun*
Informal. A person who cheats.

CHEAT *noun*.

gyrate *verb*
1. To move or cause to move in circles or around an axis or center.
2. To rotate rapidly.

1. TURN *verb*.
2. SPIN *verb*.

gyration *noun*
Circular movement around a point or about an axis.

REVOLUTION.

gyre *noun*
A closed plane curve everywhere equidistant from a fixed point or something shaped like this.

CIRCLE *noun*.

gyves *noun*
Archaic. Something that physically confines the legs or arms.

BONDS.

H

habiliments *noun*
Articles worn to cover the body.

DRESS *noun*.

habit *noun*
1. An activity done without thinking: *has a habit of pulling his ear.*

2. A habitual way of behaving.
3. Clothing worn by members of a religious order: *a nun dressed in her habit.*
4. *Rare.* Bodily type.

1. *Syns:* characteristic, pattern, trait. *Near-syns:* bent, inclination, manner, practice, style, tendency.
2. CUSTOM *noun*.
3. *Syns:* robes, vestments.

4. CONSTITUTION.

habit *verb*
Archaic. To live in (a place).

INHABIT.

habitable *adjective*
Fit to live in.

LIVABLE.

habitat *noun*
The natural environment of an animal or plant.

HOME.

habitation *noun*
A building or shelter where one lives.

HOME.

habitual *adjective*
1. Familiar through repetition.
2. Subject to a disease or habit for a long time.

1. ACCUSTOMED.
2. CHRONIC.

habituate *verb*
To make familiar through constant practice or use.

ACCUSTOM.

habituated *adjective*
Subject to a disease or habit for a long time.

CHRONIC.

habitude *noun*
A habitual way of behaving.

CUSTOM *noun*.

habitus *noun*
Bodily type.

CONSTITUTION.

hackneyed *adjective*
Without freshness or appeal due to overuse.

TRITE.

hag *noun*
1. An ugly, frightening old woman.
2. A woman who practices magic.

1. WITCH *noun*.
2. WITCH *noun*.

haggard *adjective*
Pale and exhausted because of worry, sleeplessness, etc.: *always looks haggard in the morning*.

Syns: careworn, gaunt, hollow-eyed, toilworn, wan, worn.
Near-syns: exhausted, fatigued, tired, wearied, worn-out.

haggle *verb*
To argue about the terms, as of a sale: *preferred being overcharged to haggling*.

Syns: bargain, dicker, higgle, huckster, palter.
Near-syns: barter, deal, trade; bicker, quibble, squabble, stickle, wrangle.

ha-ha *noun*
Slang. Words or actions intended to excite laughter or amusement.

JOKE *noun*.

hail¹ *noun*
A concentrated outpouring, as of missiles, words, or blows.

BARRAGE *noun*.

hail² *verb*
1. To have as one's home or place of origin.
2. To address in a friendly and respectful way.
3. To pay tribute or homage to.

1. COME.
2. GREET.
3. HONOR *verb*.

hair *noun*
A slight amount.

SHADE *noun*.

hair-raising *adjective*
Causing great horror.

HORRIBLE.

hairy *adjective*
1. Covered with hair: *a hairy animal; a hairy chest.*

2. *Slang.* Involving possible risk, loss, or injury.

1. *Syns:* fleecy, furry, hirsute, pilose, woolly.
2. DANGEROUS.

halcyon *adjective*
Motionless and undisturbed.

STILL *adjective*.

hale *adjective*
Having good health.

HEALTHY.

haleness *noun*
The condition of being physically and mentally sound.

HEALTH.

halfhearted *adjective*
Lacking warmth, interest, enthusiasm, or involvement.

TEPID.

half-wit *noun*
A mentally deficient person.

FOOL *noun*.

half-witted *adjective*
Lacking in intelligence.

STUPID.

halloa *verb & noun*

SEE **halloo.**

halloo also **halloa** *verb*
To speak or say very loudly.

ROAR *verb*.

halloo also **halloa** *noun*
A loud cry.

SHOUT *noun*.

hallow *verb*
1. To make sacred by a religious rite.
2. To give over by or as if by vow to a higher purpose.

1. SANCTIFY.
2. DEVOTE.

hallowed *adjective*
1. Regarded with particular reverence or respect.
2. Given over exclusively to a single use or purpose.

1. HOLY.
2. SACRED.

hallowedness *noun*
The quality of being holy or sacred.

HOLINESS.

hallucination *noun*
1. An illusion of perceiving something that does not really exist: *LSD-induced hallucinations.*
2. An erroneous perception of reality.

1. *Syns:* phantasmagoria (*also* phantasmagory*), trip (*Slang*).
2. ILLUSION.

hallucinatory *adjective*
Of, pertaining to, or in the nature of an illusion;   ILLUSIVE.
lacking reality.

halt¹ *verb*
1. To come to a cessation.   1. STOP *verb*.
2. To prevent the occurrence or continuation of a   2. STOP *verb*.
   movement, action, or operation.
3. To bring or come to a forced end.   3. BREAK UP at **break**.

halt *noun*
1. The act of stopping.   1. STOP *noun*.
2. The condition of being stopped.   2. STOP *noun*.

halt² *verb*
1. To walk in a lame way.   1. LIMP *verb*.
2. To be irresolute in acting or doing.   2. HESITATE.

halting *adjective*
Given to or exhibiting hesitation.   HESITANT.

hammer *verb*
1. To hit heavily and repeatedly with violent blows.   1. BEAT *verb*.
2. To shape, break, or flatten with repeated blows.   2. BEAT *verb*.
3. *Brit. Regional.* To intrude involuntary repetitions   3. STAMMER *verb*.
   and pauses into one's speech.

hamper *verb*
1. To restrict the activity or free movement of: 1. *Syns:* fetter, hamstring, handcuff,
   Hampered by leg irons, the escaped convicts were   hobble, hog-tie (*also* hogtie), leash,
   soon overtaken.   manacle, shackle, tie down, trammel.
                                                               Near-ants: free, liberate, loose, release,
                                                               unencumber, unfetter, unleash,
                                                               unrestrain, unshackle.
                                                               Ant: aid.
2. To interfere with the progress of.   2. HINDER.

hamper *noun*
Anything that impedes or prevents entry or passage.   BAR *noun*.

hamstring *verb*
To restrict the activity or free movement of.   HAMPER *verb*.

hand *verb*
1. To relinquish to the possession or control of another. 1. GIVE *verb*.
2. To cause to be transferred from one to another.   2. PASS *verb*.

hand down *verb*
1. To convey (something) from one generation to the   1. *Syns:* bequeath, hand on, pass (along
   next: *The farm was handed down from father to son.*   or on), transmit.
2. To deliver (an indictment or verdict).   2. RETURN *verb*.

hand on *verb*
To convey (something) from one generation to the next.   HAND DOWN.

hand over *verb*
1. To give up a possession, claim, or right.   1. ABDICATE.
2. To give over to another for care, use, or   2. ENTRUST.
   performance.
3. To relinquish to the possession or control of another. 3. GIVE *verb*.

hand *noun*
1. The act or an instance of helping.   1. HELP *noun*.
2. One who labors.   2. LABORER.
3. *Informal.* Approval expressed by clapping.   3. APPLAUSE.
4. The particular angle from which something is   4. PHASE.
   considered.
5. One of two or more contrasted parts or places   5. SIDE.
   identified by its location with respect to a center.

handcuff *verb*
To restrict the activity or free movement of.   HAMPER *verb*.

hand down *verb*   SEE **hand**.

handicap *noun*
1. An unfavorable condition, circumstance, or characteristic.
2. A factor conducive to superiority and success.

1. DISADVANTAGE.

2. ADVANTAGE *noun.*

handle *verb*
1. To use with or as if with the hands: *He handles an ax like a born woodsman.*
2. To offer for sale.
3. To bring into contact with, esp. by means of the hands or fingers, so as to give or receive a physical sensation.
4. To behave in a specified way toward.
5. To control or direct the functioning of.

1. *Syns:* manipulate, ply, wield.

2. SELL *verb.*
3. TOUCH *verb.*

4. DEAL WITH at **deal.**
5. OPERATE.

handle *noun*
1. Firm control.
2. *Slang.* The word or words by which one is called and identified.

1. GRIP *noun.*
2. NAME *noun.*

handleable *adjective*
Capable of being governed.

GOVERNABLE.

hand on *verb*

SEE **hand.**

handout *noun*

SEE **hand out.**

hand out *verb*
1. To pass (something) out.
2. To present as a gift to a charity or cause.
3. To make a gift of.

1. DISTRIBUTE.
2. DONATE.
3. GIVE *verb.*

handout *noun*
1. Something given to a charity or cause.
2. Assistance, esp. money, food, and other necessities, given to the needy or dispossessed.

1. DONATION.
2. RELIEF.

hand over *verb*

SEE **hand.**

handsel also **hansel** *noun*
Chiefly Brit. Something bestowed freely.

GIFT *noun.*

handsome *adjective*
1. Having qualities that delight the eye.
2. Characterized by bounteous giving.

1. BEAUTIFUL.
2. GENEROUS.

handy *adjective*
1. Exhibiting or possessing skill and ease in performance.
2. Being within easy reach.
3. Serving or capable of serving a useful purpose.

1. DEXTEROUS.

2. CONVENIENT.
3. PRACTICAL.

hang *verb*
1. To fasten or be fastened at one point with no support from below: *hang decorations on a Christmas tree; clothes hanging in a closet.*
2. To execute by suspending by the neck: *a murderer sentenced to be hanged.*

3. To incline downward or over: *hung his head in shame; children hanging from bus windows.*
4. To remain stationary over a place or object: *black clouds hanging in the sky.*
5. To be imminent.

1. *Syns:* dangle, depend (from), sling, suspend.

2. *Syns:* gibbet, noose, stretch (*Archaic*), string up (*Informal*), swing (*Informal*), turn off (*Rare*).
3. *Syns:* beetle, bend (over), jut, lean[1] (over), overhang.
4. *Syns:* hover, poise.

5. THREATEN.

hang around *verb*
Informal. To visit regularly.

FREQUENT *verb.*

hang on *verb*
1. To take firmly with the hand and maintain a hold on.
2. To continue without halting despite difficulties or setbacks.

1. GRASP *verb.*

2. CARRY ON at **carry.**

hang on (or **upon**) *verb*

To be determined by or contingent on something unknown, uncertain, or changeable.

DEPEND ON at **depend**.

hang *noun*
Informal. The proper method for doing, using, or handling something: *get the hang of using a food processor.*

Syns: knack, swing (*Informal*), trick.

hang around *verb*

SEE **hang**.

hanger-on *noun*
One who depends on another for support without reciprocating.

PARASITE.

hanging *adjective*
Hung or appearing to be hung from a support: *a hanging plant.*

Syns: pendulous, pensile, suspended.

hang on *verb*

SEE **hang**.

hang on (or **upon**) *verb*

SEE **hang**.

hangout *noun*

SEE **hang out**.

hang out *verb*
1. *Slang.* To visit regularly.
2. *Slang.* To keep company.

1. FREQUENT *verb*.
2. ASSOCIATE *verb*.

hangout *noun*
Informal. A frequently visited place.

HAUNT *noun*.

hangup *noun*

SEE **hang up**.

hang up *verb*
To cause to be later or slower than expected or desired.

DELAY *verb*.

hangup *noun*
Informal. An exaggerated concern.

COMPLEX *noun*.

hanker *verb*
To have a strong longing for.

DESIRE *verb*.

hansel *noun*

SEE **handsel**.

hap¹ *verb*
1. *Archaic.* To take place.
2. *Archaic.* To take place by chance.

1. COME.
2. CHANCE *verb*.

hap *noun*
1. *Archaic.* The quality shared by random, unintended, or unpredictable events or this quality regarded as the cause of such events.
2. *Archaic.* An unexpected random event.

1. CHANCE *noun*.

2. CHANCE *noun*.

hap² *noun*
Regional. A garment wrapped about a person.

WRAP *noun*.

hap *verb*
Regional. To put on warm clothes.

WRAP UP.

haphazard *adjective*
Having no particular pattern, purpose, organization, or structure.

RANDOM.

hapless *adjective*
Involving or undergoing chance misfortune.

UNFORTUNATE *adjective*.

happen *verb*
1. To take place.
2. To take place by chance.

1. COME.
2. CHANCE *verb*.

happen on (or **upon**) *verb*
To find or meet by chance.

COME ACROSS at **come**.

happenchance *noun*

SEE **happenstance**.

happening *noun*
1. Something that happens.
2. Something significant that happens.

1. CIRCUMSTANCE.
2. EVENT.

happen on (or **upon**) *verb*

SEE **happen**.

happenstance also **happenchance** *noun*
An unexpected random event.

CHANCE *noun*.

happiness *noun*
A condition of supreme well-being and good spirits: *felt great happiness on her wedding day.*

Syns: beatitude, blessedness, cheer, cheerfulness, gladness, joy.

happy   *adjective*
1. Characterized by luck or good fortune: *a happy outcome to a tense situation.*

2. Being in or showing good spirits.
3. Eagerly compliant.
4. Having achieved satisfaction, as of one's goal.
5. Marked by festal celebration.

1. *Syns:* fortunate, lucky, providential. *Near-syns:* auspicious, benign, favorable; advantageous, beneficial, profitable. *Ants:* unfortunate; unhappy.
2. CHEERFUL.
3. GLAD.
4. FULFILLED.
5. MERRY.

harangue   *verb*
To speak in a loud, pompous, or prolonged manner.

RANT.

harangue   *noun*
A long, violent, or blustering speech, usu. of censure or denunciation.

TIRADE.

harass   *verb*
1. To trouble persistently from or as if from all sides.
2. To disturb by repeated attacks.
3. To make a surprise attack on.

1. BESIEGE.
2. ANNOY.
3. RAID *verb.*

harassment   *noun*
The act of annoying.

ANNOYANCE.

harbor   *noun*
Something that physically protects, esp. from danger.

COVER *noun*

harbor   *verb*
1. To give refuge to: *harbored escaped convicts.*
2. To provide with often temporary lodging: *harbored the migrant workers in barracks.*

3. To hold and turn over in the mind.

1. *Syns:* haven (*Rare*), house, shelter.
2. *Syns:* accommodate, bed, berth, bestow (*Archaic*), billet, board, bunk[1], domicile (*also* domiciliate), house, put up, quarter, room.
3. BEAR.

harborage   *noun*
Something that physically protects, esp. from danger.

COVER *noun.*

hard   *adjective*
1. Physically toughened so as to have great endurance: *a lean, hard farmer who was used to 14-hour days.*

2. Having or indicating an awareness of things as they really are.
3. Unyielding to pressure or force.
4. Not easy to do, achieve, or master.
5. Imposing a severe test of bodily or spiritual strength.
6. Cold and forbidding.
7. Causing sharp, often prolonged discomfort.
8. Bitingly hostile.
9. Conveying great physical force.
10. Based on fact.
11. Containing alcohol: *hard liquor.*
12. Indulging in drink to an excessive degree.
13. Lacking passion and emotion.

1. *Syns:* casehardened, hard-bitten, hardened, hardfisted, hardhanded, hardy, rugged, tough. —*Idiom* hard (*or* tough) as nails.
2. REALISTIC.
3. FIRM[1].
4. DIFFICULT.
5. BURDENSOME.
6. BLEAK.
7. BITTER *adjective.*
8. RESENTFUL.
9. SEVERE.
10. ACTUAL.
11. *Syns:* alcoholic, spirituous, strong.
12. HEAVY *adjective.*
13. INSENSITIVE.

hard   *adverb*
1. With intense energy and force: *hit the baseball hard.*

2. In such a way as to inflict hardship or difficulty: *Things went hard for her after the divorce.*
3. In a violent, strenuous way: *fought hard; storm winds blowing hard.*
4. With effort: *breathing hard in the oxygen tent.*
5. To a point near in time, space, or relation.

1. *Syns:* forcefully, forcibly, vigorously. —*Idioms* hammer and tongs, tooth and nail, with might and main.
2. *Syns:* bad (*Informal*), badly, sour (*Informal*).
3. *Syns:* fiercely, frantically, frenziedly, furiously.
4. *Syns:* arduously, difficultly, heavily.
5. CLOSE[1] *adverb.*

hard-bitten *adjective*
Physically toughened so as to have great endurance.   HARD *adjective*.

hard-boiled *adjective*
1. *Informal.* Totally lacking in compassion.   1. COLD-BLOODED.
2. Having or indicating an awareness of things as they   2. REALISTIC at **real**.
really are.

harden *verb*
1. To make or become physically hard: *a cement that*   1. *Syns:* cake, concrete, congeal, dry,
hardens in 30 seconds.   indurate, petrify, set¹, solidify.
2. To make firmer in a particular conviction or habit.   2. CONFIRM.
3. To make resistant to hardship, esp. through   3. *Syns:* acclimate, acclimatize,
continued exposure: *Life in the outback quickly*   caseharden, climatize, indurate, season,
hardened the settlers.   stiffen, toughen.

hardened *adjective*
1. Physically toughened so as to have great endurance.   1. HARD *adjective*.
2. Totally lacking in compassion.   2. COLD-BLOODED.

hard-eyed *adjective*
Having or indicating an awareness of things as they   REALISTIC.
really are.

hardfisted *adjective*
1. Ungenerously or pettily reluctant to spend money.   1. STINGY.
2. Physically toughened so as to have great endurance.   2. HARD *adjective*.

hardhanded *adjective*
Physically toughened so as to have great endurance.   HARD *adjective*.

hardheaded *adjective*
1. Tenaciously unwilling to yield.   1. OBSTINATE.
2. Having or indicating an awareness of things as they   2. REALISTIC.
really are.

hardheadedness *noun*
The quality or state of being stubbornly unyielding.   OBSTINACY.

hardhearted *adjective*
Totally lacking in compassion.   COLD-BLOODED.

hard-hitting *adjective*
Marked by boldness and assertiveness.   AGGRESSIVE.

hardly *adverb*
By a very little; almost not.   BARELY.

hard-shell also **hard-shelled** *adjective*
1. Having or showing uncompromising determination   1. GRIM.
or resolution in purpose or action.
2. Firmly established by long standing.   2. CONFIRMED.

hard-shelled *adjective*   SEE **hard-shell**.

hardship *noun*
Something that obstructs progress and requires great   DIFFICULTY.
effort to overcome.

hardy *adjective*
1. Physically toughened so as to have great endurance.   1. HARD *adjective*.
2. Capable of exerting considerable effort or of   2. STRONG.
withstanding considerable stress or hardship.

harebrain *noun*
An insanely foolish or strange person.   CRACKPOT.

harebrained *adjective*
1. So senseless as to be laughable.   1. FOOLISH.
2. Given to lighthearted silliness.   2. GIDDY.

hark *verb*
1. To perceive by ear, usu. attentively.   1. HEAR.
2. To make an effort to hear something.   2. LISTEN.

harken *verb*   SEE **hearken**.

harlot *noun*
A woman who engages in sexual intercourse for   PROSTITUTE.
payment.

harm *noun*
The action or result of inflicting loss or pain: *did harm to the hostages.*

Syns: damage, detriment, hurt, injury, mischief, outrage.
Near-ants: aid, benefit, charity, favor, service.

harm *verb*
To spoil the soundness or perfection of.

INJURE.

harmful *adjective*
Causing harm or injury: *The sun's rays can be harmful when exposure is excessive.*

Syns: bad, damaging, deleterious, detrimental, evil, hurtful, injurious.

harmless *adjective*
1. Devoid of hurtful qualities: *asked a few harmless questions.*

1. **Syns:** innocent, innocuous, inoffensive, unoffensive.
   Near-ants: baleful, baneful, dangerous, destructive, injurious; deadly, fatal, poisonous, toxic, virulent.
   Ant: harmful.

2. Incapable of inflicting injury: *a harmless garter snake.*
3. Free from guilt or blame.

2. **Syns:** hurtless, innocuous.

3. INNOCENT *adjective.*

harmonic *adjective*
Characterized by harmony of sound.

harmonious *adjective*
1. Exhibiting accord in feeling or action: *a harmonious relationship between father and son.*
2. Having components pleasingly combined.
3. Characterized by harmony of sound: *a harmonious piano-violin duet.*

HARMONIOUS.

1. **Syns:** amicable, amical, congenial, friendly.
2. SYMMETRICAL.
3. **Syns:** consonant, harmonic, musical, symphonic.

harmonize *verb*
1. To bring into accord: *a leader who harmonized numerous factions into a solid front.*

1. **Syns:** accommodate, attune, conform, coordinate (*also* co-ordinate), integrate, proportion, reconcile, reconciliate, tune.

2. To combine and adapt in order to attain a particular effect: *harmonized the wall hangings with the room decor.*
3. To come to an understanding or to terms.
4. To be compatible or in correspondence.
5. To live or act together in harmony.

2. **Syns:** arrange, blend, coordinate (*also* co-ordinate), integrate, orchestrate, synthesize, unify.
3. AGREE.
4. AGREE.
5. GET ALONG at **get**.

harmony *noun*
1. Pleasing agreement, as of musical sounds: *three-part harmony.*
2. Satisfying arrangement marked by even distribution of elements, as in a design.
3. Harmonious mutual understanding.
4. The state of individuals who are in utter agreement: *family harmony.*

1. **Syns:** accord, concert, concord, consonance (*Mus.*), tune.
2. PROPORTION.

3. AGREEMENT.
4. **Syns:** concord, rapport, unity. —*Idiom* meeting of minds.
   Near-syns: affinity, empathy, kinship, peace, tranquility.
   Ants: discord, disharmony.

harpy *noun*
A person, esp. a woman, who habitually uses loud, abusive language.

SCOLD *noun.*

harrow *verb*
To rob of goods by force, esp. in time of war.

SACK[2].

harrowing *adjective*
Extraordinarily painful or distressing.

TORMENTING.

harry *verb*
1. To trouble persistently from or as if from all sides.
2. To disturb by repeated attacks.
3. To make a surprise attack on.

1. BESIEGE.
2. ANNOY.
3. RAID *verb.*

harsh *adjective*
1. Disagreeable to the sense of hearing: *He had a harsh, parade-ground voice.*

    1. **Syns:** discordant, dry, grating, hoarse, jarring, rasping, raspy, raucous, rough, rugged, squawky, strident.
    Near-ants: agreeable, harmonious, mellow, melodious, musical, resonant, soft, sonorous.

2. Having a coarse, irregular surface.
3. Having a noticeably sharp, pungent taste or smell.
4. Cold and forbidding.
5. Causing sharp, often prolonged discomfort.

    2. ROUGH.
    3. BITTER *adjective.*
    4. BLEAK.
    5. BITTER *adjective.*

harshness *noun*
The fact or condition of being rigorous and unsparing.

    SEVERITY.

harum-scarum *adjective*
Characterized by unthinking boldness and haste.

    RASH[1].

haruspex also **aruspex** *noun*
A person who foretells future events by or as if by supernatural means.

    PROPHET.

harvest *noun*
1. The act or process of bringing in a crop: *Thanksgiving culminates the harvest.*
2. The produce gathered from the land: *a huge cucumber harvest.*
3. Something brought about by a cause.

    1. **Syns:** cropping, gathering, harvesting, reaping.
    2. **Syns:** crop, fruit, fruitage, yield.
    3. EFFECT *noun.*

harvest *verb*
1. To collect ripe crops.
2. To gather (grain) left by reapers.

    1. GATHER.
    2. GLEAN.

harvesting *noun*
The act or process of bringing in a crop.

    HARVEST *noun.*

hash *noun*
A ruinous state of disorder.

    BOTCH *noun.*

hash over *verb*
Informal. To speak together and exchange ideas and opinions about.

    DISCUSS.

hash over *verb*

    SEE **hash.**

hassle *noun*
A discussion, often heated, in which a difference of opinion is expressed.

    ARGUMENT.

hassle *verb*
To engage in a quarrel.

    ARGUE.

haste *noun*
1. Rapidity of movement or activity: *left the room in great haste.*

    1. **Syns:** celerity, dispatch, expedition, expeditiousness, fleetness, hurry, hustle (*Informal*), rapidity, speed, speediness, swiftness.

2. Careless, headlong action: *Haste makes waste.*

    2. **Syns:** hastiness, hurriedness, precipitance (*also* precipitancy), precipitation, rashness, rush.
    Near-ants: care, carefulness, circumspection, deliberation, patience.
    Ant: unhurriedness.

haste *verb*
Poetic. To move swiftly.

    RUSH *verb.*

hasten *verb*
1. To move swiftly.
2. To increase the speed of.

    1. RUSH *verb.*
    2. SPEED UP at **speed.**

hastiness *noun*
Careless, headlong action.

    HASTE *noun.*

hasty *adjective*
1. Accomplished in very little time.
2. Characterized by unthinking boldness and haste.

    1. QUICK *adjective.*
    2. RASH[1].

3. Happening quickly and without warning.
4. Lacking due thought or consideration.

hatch *verb*
1. To cause to come into existence.
2. To give rise to a particular development.
3. To use ingenuity in making, developing, or achieving.

hate *verb*
To regard with extreme dislike and hostility: *hated the enemy.*

hate *noun*
1. Extreme hostility and dislike: *looked at me with undisguised hate.*

2. An object of extreme dislike: *A pet hate of mine is laziness.*

hateable *adjective*
Eliciting or deserving hate.
hateful *adjective*
1. Eliciting or deserving hate: *a hateful child who tortures animals.*
2. *Rare.* Characterized by intense ill will or spite.
3. Arousing deep-seated dislike.
hatred *noun*
Extreme hostility and dislike.
haughtiness *noun*
The quality of being arrogant.
haughty *adjective*
Overly convinced of one's own superiority and importance.
haul *noun*
1. Something carried physically.
2. The act of drawing or pulling a load.
haul *verb*
To exert force so as to move something toward the source of the force.
haunt *verb*
1. To recur to continually: *The fear of failure haunted him.*
2. To visit regularly.
haunt *noun*
1. A frequently visited place: *His favorite haunt is the clubhouse.*
2. *Regional.* A supernatural being.
3. The natural environment of an animal or plant.
hauteur *noun*
The quality of being arrogant.
haut monde *noun*
French. People of the highest social level.
have *verb*
1. To keep at one's disposal: *I have a savings account. We have property on the shore.*
2. To have the use or benefit of.
3. To be possessed of.
4. To participate in or partake of personally.

3. ABRUPT.
4. PRECIPITATE *adjective.*

1. PRODUCE.
2. GENERATE.
3. INVENT.

Syns: abominate, despise, detest, execrate, loathe.
Near-syns: abhor, contemn, deprecate, disdain, dislike, reprove, resent, scorn.
Ant: love.

1. **Syns:** abhorrence, abomination, detestation, hatred, loathing, repugnance (*also* repugnancy), repulsion, revulsion.
2. **Syns:** abomination, anathema, bête noire (*French*), bugbear, detestation. —*Idiom* black beast.

HATEFUL.

1. **Syns:** abominable, hateable, horrid, odious.
2. MALEVOLENT.
3. ANTIPATHETIC.

HATE *noun.*

ARROGANCE.

ARROGANT.

1. BURDEN *noun.*
2. PULL *noun.*

PULL *verb.*

1. **Syns:** obsess, torment, trouble, weigh on (*or* upon).
2. FREQUENT *verb.*

1. **Syns:** hangout (*Informal*), rendezvous, resort. —*Idiom* stamping ground.
2. GHOST *noun.*
3. HOME.

ARROGANCE.

SOCIETY.

1. **Syns:** hold, own, possess, retain.

2. ENJOY.
3. COMMAND *verb.*
4. EXPERIENCE *verb.*

5. To cause to accept what is false, esp. by trickery or misrepresentation.

6. To have within.

7. To have as an integral part.

8. To be endowed with as a visible characteristic or form.

9. To be physically aware of through the senses.

10. To cause to be in a certain state or to undergo a particular experience or action.

11. To undergo an emotional reaction.

12. To neither forbid nor prevent.

13. To organize and carry out (an activity): *have a dinner party; have a parade.*

14. To hold on one's person.

15. To involve oneself in (an activity).

16. To engage in sexual relations with.

17. To give birth to.

have at *verb*
To set upon with violent force.

have at *verb*

haven *noun*
1. Something that physically protects, esp. from danger.

2. An institution that provides care and shelter.

haven *verb*
Rare. To give refuge to.

have-not *noun*
An impoverished person.

havings *noun*
Scot. The manner in which one behaves.

havior *noun*
Regional. The manner in which one behaves.

havoc *noun*
The state of being destroyed.

havoc *verb*
Rare. To rob of goods by force, esp. in time of war.

hawk *verb*
To travel about selling goods.

hazard *verb*
1. To run the risk of: *hazard frostbite in the cold.*

2. To expose to possible loss or damage.

3. To have the courage to put forward, as an idea, esp. when rebuff or criticism is likely.

hazard *noun*
1. The quality shared by random, unintended, or unpredictable events or this quality regarded as the cause of such events.

2. Exposure to possible harm, loss, or injury.

3. A possibility of danger or harm.

hazardous *adjective*
Involving possible risk, loss, or injury.

haze *noun*
A thick, heavy atmospheric condition offering reduced visibility due to the presence of suspended particles: *a haze of cigar smoke.*

haze *verb*
To make dim or indistinct.

hazy *adjective*
1. Not clearly perceived or perceptible.

2. Covered by or as if by a thin coating or film.

5. DECEIVE.

6. CONTAIN *verb.*

7. CONTAIN *verb.*

8. BEAR.

9. FEEL *verb.*

10. GET *verb.*

11. FEEL *verb.*

12. PERMIT *verb.*

13. *Syns:* give, hold, stage.

14. CARRY *verb.*

15. PARTICIPATE.

16. TAKE *verb.*

17. BEAR.

ATTACK *verb.*

SEE **have.**

1. COVER *noun.*

2. HOME.

HARBOR *verb.*

PAUPER.

BEHAVIOR.

BEHAVIOR.

DESTRUCTION.

SACK².

PEDDLE.

1. *Syns:* adventure, chance, risk, venture.

2. RISK *verb.*

3. PRESUME.

1. CHANCE *noun.*

2. DANGER.

3. RISK *noun.*

DANGEROUS.

Syns: brume, film, fog, mist, murk (*also* mirk), smaze.
Near-syns: cloud, smog, smoke, vapor; soup (*Slang*).

OBSCURE *verb.*

1. UNCLEAR.

2. FILMY.

3. Heavy, dark, or dense, esp. with impurities.

3. TURBID.

head *noun*

1. The uppermost part of the body: *He had a handsome oval head.*

1. **Syns:** bean (*Slang*), block (*Slang*), conk (*Slang*), dome (*Slang*), noddle, noggin (*Slang*), noodle (*Slang*), nut (*Slang*), pate, poll.

2. The seat of the faculty of intelligence and reason: *used her head and found the solution.*

2. **Syns:** brain, gray matter (*Informal*), mind, upper story (*Informal*), upperworks (*Informal*).

3. *Slang.* A person of great mental ability.
4. An innate capability.
5. Lack of emotional agitation.
6. Someone who directs and supervises workers.
7. One who is highest in rank or authority.
8. A mass of bubbles in or on the surface of a liquid.
9. A decisive point.
10. *Informal.* A term or terms in large type introducing a text: *The head was set in 24-point type.*

3. MIND *noun.*
4. TALENT.
5. CALM *noun.*
6. BOSS *noun.*
7. CHIEF *noun.*
8. FOAM *noun.*
9. CRISIS.
10. **Syns:** heading, headline.

head *verb*

1. To have charge of (the affairs of others).
2. To proceed in a specified direction.
3. To move (a weapon, blow, etc.) in the direction of someone or something.

1. ADMINISTER.
2. BEAR.
3. AIM *verb.*

head off *verb*

1. To block the progress of and force to change direction: *A posse headed off the robbers at the pass.*
2. To prohibit from occurring by advance planning or action.

1. **Syns:** cut off, intercept.

2. PREVENT.

head *adjective*

Having or exercising authority

PRINCIPAL.

header *noun*

1. *Slang.* A sudden involuntary drop to the ground.
2. *Informal.* The act of plunging suddenly downward into or as if into water.

1. FALL *noun.*
2. PLUNGE *noun.*

heading *noun*

1. The compass direction in which a ship or aircraft moves: *checked the heading of the enemy destroyer.*
2. A term or terms in large type introducing a text.

1. **Syns:** bearing, course, vector.

2. HEAD *noun.*

headline *noun*

A term or terms in large type introducing a text.

HEAD *noun.*

headlong *adjective*

Characterized by unthinking boldness and haste.

RASH[1].

headman *noun*

One who is highest in rank or authority.

CHIEF *noun.*

head off *verb*

SEE **head.**

headquarters *noun*

1. A center of organization, supply, or activity.
2. A place of concentrated activity, influence, or importance.

1. BASE[1] *noun.*
2. CENTER *noun.*

headshaker *noun*

One who habitually or instinctively doubts or questions.

SKEPTIC.

head start *noun*

A factor conducive to superiority and success.

ADVANTAGE *noun.*

headstrong *adjective*

Tenaciously unwilling to yield.

OBSTINATE.

headway *noun*

Forward movement.

ADVANCE *noun.*

heal *verb*

To rectify an undesirable or unhealthy condition.

CURE *verb.*

heal-all *noun*
Something believed to cure all human disorders.

PANACEA.

healing *adjective*
Serving to cure.

CURATIVE *adjective.*

health *noun*
The condition of being physically and mentally sound: *A proper diet is essential to good health.*

Syns: haleness, healthiness, heartiness, soundness, wholeness.

healthful *adjective*
1. Promoting good health: *Jogging is a healthful exercise.*
2. *Rare.* Having good health.

1. ***Syns:*** healthsome, healthy, hygienic, salubrious, salutary, wholesome.
2. HEALTHY.

healthiness *noun*
The condition of being physically and mentally sound.

HEALTH.

healthsome *adjective*
Promoting good health.

HEALTHFUL.

healthy *adjective*
1. Having good health: *a healthy child.*

1. ***Syns:*** bunkum[2] (*Regional*), fit, hale, healthful (*Rare*), hearty, right, sound[2], well[2], whole, wholesome. —*Idioms* fit as a fiddle, hale and hearty, in fine fettle, sound as a dollar.
Near-syns: agile, fleet, nimble; lusty, robust; thriving, vigorous; strong, sturdy, tough.
Near-ants: sickly; ill.
Ant: unhealthy.

2. Promoting good health.
3. Notably above average in amount, size, or scope.
4. Improving, growing, or succeeding steadily.

2. HEALTHFUL.
3. BIG *adjective.*
4. FLOURISHING.

heap *noun*
1. A group of things gathered haphazardly: *a heap of ironing on the table; a heap of beer cans.*

1. ***Syns:*** agglomeration, bank[2], drift, hill, mass, mess, mound, mountain, pile, pyramid, ruck[1], shock, stack, tumble.

2. *Informal.* A great deal: *learned a heap from him; a heap of troubles.*

2. ***Syns:*** barrel (*Informal*), lot, mass, mountain, much, pack, peck[1] (*Informal*), pile (*Informal*), plenty, power (*Regional*), sight (*Chiefly Regional*), wealth, world.

3. *Informal.* An indeterminately great amount or number: *has a heap of money; had heaps of good ideas.*

3. ***Syns:*** bushel (*Informal*), gob[1] (*Informal*), jillion (*Informal*), load (*Informal*), lot, million, multiplicity, oodle (*Informal*), passel (*Regional*), peck[1] (*Informal*), ream, scad (*Informal*), slew (*also* slue) (*Informal*), trillion, wad (*Informal*), zillion (*Informal*).

heap *verb*
1. To put into a disordered pile: *heaped the rags on the garage floor.*
2. To fill to overflowing: *heaped his plate with food.*
3. To give in great abundance.

1. ***Syns:*** bank[2], drift, hill, lump[1], mound, pile (up), stack.
2. ***Syns:*** lade, load, pile.
3. SHOWER *verb.*

hear *verb*
1. To perceive by ear, usu. attentively: *Hear my advice before you act.*

1. ***Syns:*** attend, hark, hearken (*also* harken) (*Poetic & Archaic*), heed, listen. —*Idioms* bend an ear, give a hear to, give an ear to, lend one's ear.

2. To obtain knowledge or awareness of something not known before, as through observation, study, etc.

2. DISCOVER.

hear of *verb*
To receive (an idea) and take it into consideration: *I won't even hear of apologizing!*

Syns: entertain, think of. —*Idiom* turn a willing ear.

hearing *noun*
1. The sense by which sound is perceived: *keen hearing*.
2. Range of audibility: *Don't say that within their hearing!*
3. A chance to be heard: *At least give me a hearing*.
4. *Law*. The examination and deciding upon evidence, charges, and claims in court.

1. **Syns:** audition, ear.

2. **Syns:** earshot, sound[1].

3. **Syns:** audience, audition.

4. TRIAL *noun*.

hearken *also* **harken** *verb*
1. *Poetic & Archaic*. To make an effort to hear something.
2. *Poetic & Archaic*. To perceive by ear, usu. attentively.

1. LISTEN.

2. HEAR.

hear of *verb*

SEE **hear**.

hearsay *noun*
Idle, often sensational and groundless talk about others.

GOSSIP *noun*.

heart *noun*
1. *Anat*. The circulatory organ of the body: *The patient's heart stopped*.
2. The seat of a person's innermost emotions and feelings: *knew in my heart that I had failed*.

3. The quality of mind enabling one to face danger or hardship resolutely.
4. The most central and material part: *the heart of the matter*.

5. A place of concentrated activity, influence, or importance.
6. A point of origin from which ideas, influences, etc., emanate.

1. **Syn:** ticker (*Slang*).

2. **Syns:** bosom, breast, soul. —*Idioms* bottom of one's heart, cockles of one's heart, one's heart of hearts.

3. COURAGE.

4. **Syns:** core, essence, gist, gravamen, kernel, marrow, meat, nub, pith, quintessence, root[1], soul, spirit, stuff, substance.

5. CENTER *noun*.

6. CENTER *noun*.

heartache *noun*
Mental anguish or pain caused by loss or despair.

GRIEF.

heartbreak *noun*
Mental anguish or pain caused by loss or despair.

GRIEF.

hearten *verb*
To impart strength and confidence to.

ENCOURAGE.

heartening *adjective*
Inspiring confidence or hope.

ENCOURAGING.

heartfelt *adjective*
Devoid of any hypocrisy or pretense.

GENUINE.

heartiness *noun*
The condition of being physically and mentally sound.

HEALTH.

heartless *adjective*
Totally lacking in compassion.

COLD-BLOODED.

heart-whole *adjective*
Devoid of any hypocrisy or pretense.

GENUINE.

hearty *adjective*
1. Devoid of any hypocrisy or pretense.
2. Having good health.

1. GENUINE.
2. HEALTHY.

heat *noun*
1. Intense warmth: *the summer's heat*.

2. Intensity of feeling or reaction: *retorted with some heat when cross-examined*.
3. A regular period of sexual excitement in female mammals: *a cat in heat*.
4. *Slang*. A member of a law-enforcement agency.

1. **Syns:** fervor (*Poetic*), hot (*Regional*), hotness, torridness.
2. **Syns:** excitement, fervor, warmth.
3. **Syns:** estrus (*also* oestrus), rut, season.
4. POLICEMAN.

heat *verb*

To make hot: *The broiling sun heated the sand.*
heat up   *verb*
To make hot.

heated   *adjective*
1. Marked by much heat.
2. Characterized by intense emotion and activity.

heat up   *verb*

heave   *verb*
1. To move vigorously from side to side or up and down.
2. To send through the air with a motion of the hand or arm.
3. To utter in a breathless manner.
4. To breathe hard.

heave   *noun*
1. An instance of lifting or being lifted.
2. *Informal.* An act of throwing.

heaven   *noun*
A state of elated bliss: *I was in heaven while living in Hawaii.*

heaven(s)   *noun*
The celestial regions as seen from the earth.

heavenly   *adjective*
1. Of or relating to heaven: *heavenly angels.*

2. Giving great pleasure or delight.
3. Of or relating to the heavens: *The moon and the stars are heavenly bodies.*
4. *Informal.* Particularly excellent.
5. Highly pleasing, esp. to the sense of taste.
6. Of, from, like, or being a god or God.

heavily   *adverb*
1. With effort.
2. In a weary way.

heaviness   *noun*
1. The state or quality of being physically heavy: *dieted to lose excess heaviness.*

2. *Archaic.* The condition of carrying a developing fetus within the uterus.

heavy   *adjective*
1. Having a relatively great weight: *a heavy piano.*

2. Large in number or yield: *heavy amounts of paperwork; a heavy crop of asparagus.*
3. Intensely sustained, esp. in activity: *heavy artillery fire.*
4. Conveying great physical force.
5. Violently disturbed, as by storms.
6. Intensely violent in sustained velocity.
7. Indulging in drink to an excessive degree: *a heavy drinker.*
8. Having great consequence or weight.

Syns: heat up, hot (up) (*Chiefly Brit.*).

HEAT *verb.*

1. HOT *adjective.*
2. FERVID.
SEE **heat.**

1. TOSS *verb.*
2. THROW *verb.*
3. GASP.
4. PANT.

1. LIFT *noun.*
2. THROW *noun.*

Syns: ecstasy, paradise, rapture, transport.
—*Idioms* cloud nine, seventh heaven.
Near-syns: bliss, felicity, happiness; delight, elation, exuberance; euphoria, exhilaration, intoxication, rhapsody.
Ant: hell.

AIR *noun.*

1. *Syns:* celestial, paradisaical *or* paradisiacal.
2. DELIGHTFUL.
3. *Syns:* celestial, empyrean.

4. MARVELOUS.
5. DELICIOUS.
6. DIVINE[1] *adjective.*

1. HARD *adverb.*
2. WEARILY.

1. *Syns:* avoirdupois (*Informal*), gravity (*Rare*), heftiness, massiveness, ponderosity, ponderousness, weight, weightiness.
2. PREGNANCY.

1. *Syns:* burdensome, heavyweight, hefty, massive, ponderous, weighty.
Near-ants: airy, manageable, weightless.
Ant: light.
2. *Syns:* abundant, copious, substantial, voluminous.
3. *Syns:* concentrated, fierce, furious, heightened, intense, intensive.
4. SEVERE.
5. ROUGH.
6. HIGH.
7. *Syns:* hard, two-fisted (*Informal*).

8. GRAVE[2].

9. Imposing a severe test of bodily or spiritual strength.

9. BURDENSOME.

10. Not readily digested because of richness: *a heavy meal; heavy dough.*

10. *Syn:* rich.

11. Growing profusely.

11. THICK *adjective.*

12. Having a solid, compact build: *a heavy wrestler.*

12. *Syns:* heavyset, hefty, thick, thickbodied, thickset.

13. Unwieldy, esp. due to excess weight: *heavy Victorian furniture.*

13. *Syns:* cumbersome, elephantine, lumpish, ponderous.

14. Burdened by a weighty load: *trees heavy with peaches.*

14. *Syns:* heavy-laden, loaded (down).

15. *Slang.* Beyond the understanding of an average mind.

15. DEEP *adjective.*

16. Having so many constituent particles in suspension as to be condensed, often viscous.

16. THICK *adjective.*

17. *Archaic.* Carrying a developing fetus within the uterus.

17. PREGNANT.

heavy *noun*
A mean, worthless character in a story or play: *played the heavy in a western.*

Syns: scoundrel, villain.

heavy-handed *adjective*
1. Clumsily lacking in the ability to do or perform.
2. Lacking fluency or gracefulness.

1. UNSKILLFUL.
2. PONDEROUS.

heavy-hearted *adjective*
In low spirits.

DEPRESSED.

heavy-heartedness *noun*
A feeling or spell of dismally low spirits.

GLOOM.

heavy-laden *adjective*
Burdened by a weighty load.

HEAVY *adjective.*

heavyset *adjective*
Having a solid, compact build.

HEAVY *adjective.*

heavyweight *adjective*
1. Having a relatively great weight.
2. *Informal.* Being among the leaders of a particular class.

1. HEAVY *adjective.*
2. BIG-LEAGUE.

heavyweight *noun*
Informal. An important, influential person.

DIGNITARY.

hebetate *verb*
To make or become less keen or responsive.

DULL *verb.*

hebetude *noun*
A deficiency in mental and physical alertness and activity.

LETHARGY.

hebetudinous *adjective*
1. Lacking mental and physical alertness and activity.
2. Lacking in intelligence.

1. LETHARGIC.
2. STUPID.

hecatomb *noun*
A living creature slain and offered to a deity as part of a religious rite.

SACRIFICE *noun.*

heckle *verb*
To torment with persistent insult or ridicule.

BAIT *verb.*

hectic *adjective*
1. Characterized by intense emotion and activity.
2. Being at a higher temperature than is normal or desirable.

1. FERVID.
2. HOT *adjective.*

hector *verb*
1. To torment with persistent insult or ridicule.
2. To domineer or drive into compliance by the use of threats, force, etc.

1. BAIT *verb.*
2. INTIMIDATE.

hector *noun*
One who is habitually cruel to smaller or weaker people.

BULLY *noun.*

hedge *verb*
1. To shut in on all sides.
2. To surround and advance upon.
3. To evade, as a topic, esp. by circumlocution.
4. To use evasive or deliberately vague language.

1. SURROUND.
2. CLOSE IN at **close**[1].
3. SKIRT *verb*.
4. EQUIVOCATE.

hedging *adjective*
Deliberately ambiguous or vague.

EVASIVE.

hedonic *adjective*
Characterized by or devoted to pleasure and luxury as a lifestyle.

SYBARITIC.

hedonist *noun*
A person devoted to pleasure and luxury.

SYBARITE.

hedonistic *adjective*
Characterized by or devoted to pleasure and luxury as a lifestyle.

SYBARITIC.

heebie-jeebies *noun*
Slang. A state of nervous restlessness or agitation.

JITTERS.

heed *noun*
1. Cautious attentiveness.
2. The act of noting, observing, or taking into account.

1. CARE *noun*.
2. NOTICE *noun*.

heed *verb*
To perceive by ear, usu. attentively.

HEAR.

heedful *adjective*
1. Cautiously attentive.
2. Concentrating the mental powers on something.
3. Tending toward awareness and appreciation.

1. CAREFUL.
2. ATTENTIVE.
3. MINDFUL.

heedfulness *noun*
1. Cautious attentiveness.
2. Concentration of the mental powers on something.

1. CARE *noun*.
2. ATTENTION.

heedless *adjective*
1. Lacking or marked by a lack of care.
2. Showing no concern, attention, or regard.

1. CARELESS.
2. MINDLESS.

heedlessness *noun*
A careless, often reckless disregard for consequences.

ABANDON *noun*.

heehaw *noun*
An act of laughing.

LAUGH *noun*.

heehaw *verb*
To express amusement, mirth, or scorn by smiling and emitting loud, inarticulate sounds.

LAUGH *verb*.

heel[1] *verb*
1. To follow closely or persistently.
2. To move behind (another) in the same direction.

1. DOG *verb*.
2. FOLLOW.

heel[2] *verb*
To depart or cause to depart from true vertical or horizontal.

INCLINE *verb*.

heftiness *noun*
The state or quality of being physically heavy.

HEAVINESS.

hefty *adjective*
1. Having a relatively great weight.
2. Having a solid, compact build.
3. Conveying great physical force.

1. HEAVY *adjective*.
2. HEAVY *adjective*.
3. SEVERE.

height *noun*
1. The highest point: *scaled the mountain to its very height.*
2. The distance of something from a given level.
3. The highest point or state.

1. *Syns:* apex, crest, crown, fastigium, peak, roof, summit, top, vertex.
2. ELEVATION.
3. CLIMAX *noun*.

heighten *verb*
1. To increase markedly in level or intensity, esp. of sound.
2. To increase in intensity or severity.
3. To become greater in number, amount, or intensity.

1. ELEVATE.
2. INTENSIFY.
3. RISE *verb*.

heightened *adjective*
1. Abnormally increased, esp. in intensity.
2. Intensely sustained, esp. in activity.

1. ELEVATED.
2. HEAVY *adjective*.

heinous *adjective*
Disgracefully and grossly offensive.

OUTRAGEOUS.

heinousness *noun*
The quality of passing all moral bounds.

ENORMITY.

heir *verb*
Chiefly Regional. To receive (property) from one who has died.

INHERIT.

heist *verb*
Slang. To take property or possessions from (a person, company, etc.) unlawfully and usu. forcibly.

ROB.

heist *noun*
Slang. The act or crime of taking another's property unlawfully and by force.

ROBBERY.

hell *noun*
Excruciating punishment: *subjected the concentration-camp inmates to pure hell.*

Syns: persecution, torment, torture.
—*Idioms* living hell, tortures of the damned.

hell *verb*
1. *Informal.* To move swiftly.
2. *Informal.* To behave riotously.

1. RUSH *verb*.
2. REVEL *verb*.

hellfire *adjective*
Portending future disaster.

FATEFUL.

hell-for-leather *adjective*
Informal. Characterized by great celerity.

FAST *adjective*.

hell-for-leather *adverb*
Informal. In a rapid way.

FAST *adverb*.

hellish *adjective*
Informal. Perversely bad, cruel, or wicked.

FIENDISH.

helotry *noun*
A state of subjugation to an owner or master.

SLAVERY.

help *verb*
1. To give support or assistance: *The lifeguard helped the exhausted swimmer.*

1. **Syns:** abet, aid, assist, benefact, help out, succor. —*Idioms* give (*or* lend) a hand, give a leg up.
   Near-syns: benefit, bolster, boost, champion, expedite, facilitate, support.
   Ants: hinder, impede.

2. To advance to a more desirable state.

2. IMPROVE.

help out *verb*
To give support or assistance.

HELP *verb*.

help *noun*
1. The act or an instance of helping: *Welfare provides help for the needy.*
2. A person who helps.

1. **Syns:** aid, assist, assistance, hand, relief, succor, support.
2. HELPER.

helper *noun*
A person who helps: *After a year as a helper he was made foreman.*

Syns: aid, assistant, attendant, help.

helpful *adjective*
1. Affording support or assistance: *helpful advice.*

1. **Syns:** aidant, aiding, assistive, serviceable, supportive.
   Near-syns: beneficial, benevolent, constructive, effective, practical, useful.
   Ant: unhelpful.

2. Affording benefit.

2. BENEFICIAL.

helping *noun*
An individual quantity of food.

SERVING.

helping *adjective*
Giving or able to give help or support.

AUXILIARY *adjective*.

helpless *adjective*
1. Unable to manage for oneself: *The dying patient was helpless in his attempt to speak.*
2. Devoid of help or protection: *helpless hostages.*

1. *Syns:* impotent, incapable, paralyzed, powerless.
2. *Syns:* aidless, defenseless, unprotected.

helplessly *adverb*
Without regard to desire or inclination: *a nation drifting helplessly toward anarchy.*

Syns: inextricably, perforce, willy-nilly.

help out *verb*

SEE **help.**

helter-skelter *adjective*
Characterized by physical confusion.

CONFUSED.

hem *verb*
1. To shut in on all sides.
2. To surround and advance upon.
3. To confine within a limited area.

1. SURROUND.
2. CLOSE IN at **close**[1].
3. ENCLOSE.

henchman *noun*
One who supports and adheres to another.

FOLLOWER.

henpeck *verb*
To scold or find fault constantly.

NAG.

herald *verb*
To make known the presence or arrival of.

USHER IN at **usher.**

herculean *adjective*
Of extraordinary size and power.

GIANT *adjective.*

herd *verb*
To urge to move along.

DRIVE *verb.*

hereafter *noun*
Time that is yet to be.

FUTURE *noun.*

hereditary *adjective*
1. Of or from one's ancestors.
2. Possessed at birth.

1. ANCESTRAL.
2. INNATE.

heretic *noun*
A person who dissents from the doctrine of an established church.

SEPARATIST.

heretofore *adverb*
1. At a time in the past.
2. Up to this time.

1. EARLIER.
2. EARLIER.

heritage *noun*
1. Something immaterial, as a style or philosophy, that is passed from one generation to another: *The heritage of ancient Rome is reflected in Western architecture.*
2. Any special privilege accorded a firstborn.

1. *Syns:* inheritance, legacy, tradition.

2. BIRTHRIGHT.

hermeneutic *adjective*
Serving to explain.

EXPLANATORY.

hermetic *adjective*
Solitary and shut off from society.

SECLUDED.

hero *noun*
1. A person revered esp. for noble courage: *Sergeant York was one of the heroes of World War I.*
2. A famous person.

1. *Syn:* paladin. —*Idiom* man of the hour.

2. CELEBRITY.

heroic *adjective*
1. Having or showing courage.
2. Of extraordinary size and power.

1. BRAVE *adjective.*
2. GIANT *adjective.*

heroism *noun*
The quality or state of being heroic: *a rescue that was an act of heroism.*

Syns: gallantry, prowess, valiancy (*also* valiance), valor, valorousness.

hesitancy *noun*
The act or an instance of hesitating.

HESITATION.

hesitant *adjective*
Given to or exhibiting hesitation: *A hesitant leader is an ineffective one.*

Syns: faltering, halting, hesitating, indecisive, irresolute, pendulous, tentative, timid, uncertain, undecisive,

vacillant, vacillating (*also* vacillatory), wavering, wobbly.
Near-ants: certain, decisive, firm, fixed, resolute, resolved, sure; definite, positive, unwavering.

hesitate *verb*
To be irresolute in acting or doing: *The witness hesitated before answering the question.*

Syns: dither, falter, halt[2], pause, shilly-shally, stagger, vacillate, waver.

hesitating *adjective*
Given to or exhibiting hesitation.

HESITANT.

hesitation *noun*
The act or an instance of hesitating: *Hesitation in foreign-policy decision-making can be disastrous.*

Syns: hesitancy, indecision, indecisiveness, irresolution, shilly-shally, to-and-fro, vacillation, wavering.

Hessian *noun*
A free-lance fighter.

MERCENARY *noun*.

heterogeneity *noun*
The quality of being made of many different elements, forms, kinds, or individuals.

VARIETY.

heterogeneous *adjective*
Consisting of a number of different kinds.

VARIOUS.

hew *verb*
To bring down, as with a saw or ax.

CUT *verb*.

hex *noun*
1. Something or someone believed to bring bad luck.
2. A woman who practices magic.

1. JINX.
2. WITCH *noun*.

hiatus *noun*
An interval during which continuity is suspended.

GAP.

hick *adjective*
Informal. Of or pertaining to the countryside.

COUNTRY *adjective*.

hidden *adjective*
1. Concealed from view.
2. Screened from the view of oncoming drivers.
3. Lying beyond what is obvious or avowed.

1. SECLUDED.
2. BLIND *adjective*.
3. ULTERIOR.

hide[1] *verb*
1. To put or keep out of sight: *They hid the stolen jewels in an abandoned mine shaft.*

2. To conceal in obscurity.
3. To prevent (something) from being known.
4. To cut off from sight.

1. ***Syns:*** bury, bush up (*Chiefly Regional*), cache, conceal, ensconce, occult, plant (*Informal*), secrete, stash.
2. OBSCURE *verb*.
3. COVER *verb*.
4. BLOCK OUT at **block**.

hide *noun*
1. A hiding place.
2. *Brit.* A shelter for concealing hunters.

1. HIDE-OUT.
2. BLIND *noun*.

hide[2] *noun*
The skin of an animal: *trappers selling hides.*

Syns: fell[3], fur, jacket, pelt[1].

hide *verb*
To punish with blows or lashes.

BEAT *verb*.

hideaway *noun*
A hiding place.

HIDE-OUT.

hidebound *adjective*
Not tolerant of the beliefs, opinions, etc., of others.

INTOLERANT.

hideous *adjective*
1. Extremely displeasing to the eye.
2. Shockingly repellent.

1. UGLY *adjective*.
2. GHASTLY.

hideousness *noun*
The quality or condition of being ugly.

UGLINESS.

hide-out *noun*
A hiding place: *The robbers' hide-out was deep in the desert.*

Syns: covert, den, hide[1], hideaway, lair.

hide out *verb*

To shut oneself up in secrecy.

hide out *verb*

hiding *noun*
A punishment dealt with blows or lashes.

hierarch *noun*
One who is highest in rank or authority.

hifalutin *adjective*

higgle *verb*
To argue about the terms of, as of a sale.

higgledy-piggledy *adjective*
Characterized by physical confusion.

high *adjective*
1. Having a rather great upward projection: *a high building; high French windows.*
2. Extending to a great height.
3. Elevated in pitch: *a high voice; high notes.*

4. Exceedingly dignified in form, tone, or style.
5. Bringing a high price.
6. Long past: *high antiquity.*

7. Intensely violent in sustained velocity: *high winds.*
8. Abnormally increased, esp. in intensity.
9. *Slang.* Intoxicated with alcoholic liquor.
10. *Slang.* Stupefied, intoxicated, or otherwise influenced by the taking of drugs.

high *noun*
Slang. A strong, pleasant feeling of excitement or stimulation.

high-and-mighty *adjective*
Overly convinced of one's own superiority and importance.

highball *verb*
To move swiftly.

highborn *adjective*
Of high birth or social position.

highbred *adjective*
1. Of high birth or social position.
2. Of pure breeding stock.

highbrow *adjective*
Informal. Appealing to or engaging the intellect.

higher *adjective*
1. Being at a rank above another: *The clerk had to consult with a higher official.*
2. Being at a height or level above another: *a higher rock stratum.*

higher-up *noun*
1. One who stands above another in rank.
2. *Informal.* A person or group having the right and power to command, decide, rule, or judge.

highest *adjective*
1. Pre-eminent in rank or position: *rumors that were denied at the highest levels.*

2. Of, being, located at, or forming the top.

highest-ranking *adjective*
Pre-eminent in rank or position.

HOLE UP at **hole.**
SEE **hide-out.**

BEATING.

CHIEF *noun.*
SEE **highfalutin.**

HAGGLE.

CONFUSED.

1. **Syns:** altitudinous, long[1] (*Rare*), tall.

2. TALL.
3. **Syns:** acute (*Mus.*), argute, high-pitched, piercing, piping, shrieky, shrill, shrilly, treble.

4. ELEVATED.
5. COSTLY.
6. **Syns:** ancient, immemorial, remote, removed.

7. **Syns:** fierce, furious, heavy, strong.
8. ELEVATED.
9. DRUNK *adjective.*
10. DRUGGED.

THRILL *noun.*

ARROGANT.

RUSH *verb.*

NOBLE.

1. NOBLE.
2. THOROUGHBRED *adjective.*

INTELLECTUAL *adjective.*

1. **Syns:** senior, superior.

2. **Syns:** greater, over, superior.

1. SUPERIOR *noun.*
2. AUTHORITY.

1. **Syns:** astral, highest-ranking, stratospheric, top-drawer (*Informal*), top-ranking.
   Near-ants: humble, low, lowly, minor, pedestrian, unimportant.
   Ant: lowest.
2. TOP *adjective.*

HIGHEST.

highfalutin or **hifalutin** also **highfaluting** *adjective*
1. *Informal.* Characterized by an exaggerated show of dignity or self-importance.
2. *Informal.* Characterized by language that is elevated and sometimes pompous in style.

1. POMPOUS.

2. SONOROUS.

highfaluting *adjective*

SEE **highfalutin.**

high-flown *adjective*
1. Exceedingly dignified in form, tone, or style.
2. Characterized by language that is elevated and sometimes pompous in style.

1. ELEVATED.
2. SONOROUS.

high-grade *adjective*
Well above average.

GOOD *adjective.*

high-hat *noun*
Slang. One who despises people or things he regards as inferior, esp. because of social or intellectual pretension.

SNOB.

high-hat *adjective*
Slang. Characteristic of or resembling a snob.

SNOBBISH.

highjack *verb*

SEE **hijack.**

high-minded *adjective*
Being on a high intellectual or moral level.

ELEVATED.

high-performance *adjective*
Acting effectively with minimal waste.

EFFICIENT.

high-pitched *adjective*
Elevated in pitch.

HIGH.

high-priced *adjective*
Bringing a high price.

COSTLY.

high-ranking *adjective*
Raised to or occupying a high position or rank.

EXALTED.

high-sounding *adjective*
Characterized by language that is elevated and sometimes pompous in style.

SONOROUS.

high-spirited *adjective*
1. Full of joyful, unrestrained high spirits.
2. Full of or characterized by a lively, emphatic, eager quality.

1. EXUBERANT.
2. SPIRITED.

hightail *verb*
Slang. To leave hastily.

RUN *verb.*

highty-tighty *adjective*

SEE **hoity-toity.**

highway *noun*
A course affording passage from one place to another.

WAY *noun.*

hijack also **highjack** *verb*
Informal. To compel by pressure or threats.

COERCE.

hike *noun*
1. A usu. brief and regular journey on foot, esp. for exercise.
2. The act of increasing or rising.
3. The amount by which something is increased.

1. CONSTITUTIONAL *noun.*

2. INCREASE *noun.*
3. INCREASE *noun.*

hike *verb*
To increase in amount.

RAISE *verb.*

hilarious *adjective*
Extremely funny.

PRICELESS.

hilarity *noun*
A state of joyful exuberance.

GAIETY.

hill *noun*
1. A natural land elevation: *The palace stood on a hill overlooking a lake.*
2. A group of things gathered haphazardly.

1. *Syns:* eminence, projection, prominence (*also* prominency), rise.
2. HEAP *noun.*

hill *verb*
To put into a disordered pile.

HEAP *verb.*

hind *adjective*
Located in the rear.

BACK *adjective.*

hinder *verb*
To interfere with the progress of: *Demands on both sides hindered resolution of the conflict.*

Syns: bog (down), encumber, hamper, hold back, impede, obstruct, overslaugh, retard. —*Idiom* get in the way of.
SEE **hindmost.**

hindermost *adjective*
hindmost also **hindermost** *adjective*
1. Located in the rear.
2. Bringing up the rear.

1. BACK *adjective.*
2. LAST[1] *adjective.*

hindrance *noun*
Anything that impedes or prevents entry or passage.

BAR *noun.*

hinge on (or **upon**) *verb*
To be determined by or contingent on something unknown, uncertain, or changeable.

DEPEND ON at **depend.**

hint *noun*
1. A subtle pointing out: *Give me a hint to the solution of this puzzle.*

1. **Syns:** clue (*also* clew), cue, indication, intimation, suggestion.
   Near-syns: inkling, notion, wind; advice, tip; innuendo, insinuation.

2. A subtle quality underlying or felt to underlie a situation, action, or person: *wanted to avoid any hint of nepotism.*
3. A barely perceivable indication of something.
4. A slight amount.

2. **Syns:** implication, inkling, innuendo, suspicion, undertone.
3. TRACE *noun.*
4. SHADE *noun.*

hint *verb*
1. To convey an idea by indirect, subtle means: *hinted at a breakthrough in negotiations.*

1. **Syns:** imply, innuendo, insinuate, intimate[2], suggest. —*Idiom* drop a hint.

2. To try to obtain, usu. by subtleness and cunning: *kept hinting for an invitation to the party.*

2. **Syns:** angle, fish.

hip *adjective*
Slang. Marked by comprehension, cognizance, and perception.

AWARE.

hire *verb*
1. To engage the temporary use of (something) for a fee: *hired a bus for the school trip.*
2. To obtain the use or services of.

1. **Syns:** charter, lease, let, rent[1].
2. EMPLOY *verb.*

hire *noun*
1. Payment for work done.
2. The act of employing for wages.
3. The state of being employed.

1. WAGE(S).
2. EMPLOYMENT.
3. EMPLOYMENT.

hired *adjective*
Having a job.

EMPLOYED.

hireling *noun*
1. One who is employed by another.
2. A free-lance fighter.

1. EMPLOYEE.
2. MERCENARY *noun.*

hirer *noun*
One that employs persons for wages.

EMPLOYER.

hiring *noun*
The act of employing for wages.

EMPLOYMENT.

hirsute *adjective*
Covered with hair.

HAIRY.

hiss *verb*
To make a sharp sibilant sound: *The coiled snake hissed and then struck. Air hissed from the tire.*

Syns: fizz, fizzle, sibilate, sizzle, swish, whisk, whiz (*also* whizz), whoosh.

hiss *noun*
Any derisive sound of disapproval: *Hisses filled the auditorium.*

Syns: bazoo, bird (*Slang*), boo, Bronx cheer (*Slang*), catcall, hoot, raspberry (*Slang*), razz (*Slang*).

historic *adjective*
Having great significance.

IMPORTANT.

history *noun*
1. A chronological record of past events: *the history of Western Europe.*
2. A recounting of past events.
3. Past events surrounding a person or thing: *He has a history of heart disease.*

1. **Syns:** annals, chronicle.

2. STORY.

3. **Syns:** background, past. —*Idiom* past history.

histrionic *adjective*
Of or pertaining to drama or the theater.

DRAMATIC.

histrionics *noun*
Overemotional, exaggerated behavior calculated for effect.

THEATRICS.

hit *verb*
1. To deliver (a powerful blow) suddenly and sharply: *The boxer hit his opponent on the jaw.*

1. **Syns:** bash (*Informal*), belt (*Slang*), biff (*Slang*), bop (*Informal*), catch, clip¹ (*Informal*), clobber (*Slang*), clout, knock, paste (*Slang*), pop, slam, slog, slug² (*Slang*), smack¹, smash, smite, sock (*Slang*), strike, swat, wallop (*Informal*), whack, wham. —*Idioms* let someone have it, sock it to someone.

2. *Slang.* To take property or possessions from (a person, company, etc.) unlawfully and usu. forcibly.
3. To enter a person's mind.
4. *Slang.* To take the life of (a person or persons) unlawfully.
5. To set upon with violent force.

2. ROB.

3. OCCUR.
4. MURDER *verb.*

5. ATTACK *verb.*

hit back *verb*
To return like for like, esp. to return an unfriendly or hostile action with a similar one.

RETALIATE.

hit on (or **upon**) *verb*
1. To come upon, esp. suddenly or unexpectedly.
2. To reach a goal or objective.

1. TAKE *verb.*
2. ARRIVE AT at **arrive.**

hit *noun*
1. A sudden sharp, powerful stroke.
2. A dazzling, often sudden instance of success: *a Broadway hit.*

1. BLOW².
2. **Syns:** bang, boff, sleeper (*Informal*), smash (*Informal*), ten-strike (*Informal*), wow (*Informal*). —*Idioms* bell ringer, smash hit.

3. *Slang.* An inhalation, as of a cigar, pipe, or cigarette.

3. PULL *noun.*

hit back *verb*

SEE **hit.**

hitch *verb*
1. To walk in a lame way.
2. *Slang.* To join or be joined in marriage.

1. LIMP *verb.*
2. MARRY.

hitch *noun*
1. A limited, often assigned period of activity, duty, or opportunity.
2. A term of service, as in the military or in prison.

1. TURN *noun.*

2. TIME *noun.*

hit on (or **upon**) *verb*

SEE **hit.**

hit-or-miss *adjective*
Having no particular pattern, purpose, organization, or structure.

RANDOM.

hive *verb*
To bring together so as to increase in mass or number.

ACCUMULATE.

hoard *verb*
To store up (supplies or money), usu. well beyond one's needs: *was arrested for hoarding coffee and selling it on the black market.*

Syns: lay up, squirrel, stash, stockpile, treasure.
Near-ants: consume, exhaust, expend, spend, use; dispel, disperse, scatter, strew; decrease, diminish, lessen.

hoard *noun*
A supply stored or hidden for future use: *kept a hoard of food in his bomb shelter.*

Syns: backlog, hoarding, inventory, reserve, reservoir, stock, stockpile, store, treasure. —*Idiom* nest egg.

hoarding *noun*
A supply stored or hidden for future use.

HOARD *noun.*

hoarse *adjective*
1. Low and grating in sound: *spoke in a hoarse whisper.*
2. Disagreeable to the sense of hearing.

1. **Syns:** croaking, croaky, gruff, husky, roupy (*Chiefly Scot.*).
2. HARSH.

hoary *adjective*
Belonging to, existing, or occurring in times long past.

OLD.

hobble *verb*
1. To walk in a lame way.
2. To restrict the activity or free movement of.

1. LIMP *verb.*
2. HAMPER *verb.*

hobnob *verb*
To keep company.

ASSOCIATE *verb.*

hock *verb*
Informal. To give or deposit as a pawn.

PAWN[1] *verb.*

hocus-pocus *noun*
Esoteric, formulaic, and often incomprehensible speech relating to the occult.

GIBBERISH.

hodgepodge *noun*
A collection of various things.

ASSORTMENT.

hoggish *adjective*
Wanting to eat or drink more than one can reasonably consume.

GREEDY.

hog-tie also **hogtie** *verb*
To restrict the activity or free movement of.

HAMPER.

hoi polloi *noun*
A group of persons regarded as the lowest class.

TRASH[1] *noun.*

hoist *verb*
To move (something) to a higher position.

ELEVATE.

hoist *noun*
An instance of lifting or being lifted.

LIFT *noun.*

hoity-toity also **highty-tighty** *adjective*
Overly convinced of one's own superiority and importance.

ARROGANT.

hold *verb*
1. To have and maintain in one's possession: *holds a controlling interest in the company.*
2. To have the use or benefit of.
3. To put one's arms around affectionately.
4. To have within.
5. To keep at one's disposal.
6. To maintain restraining control and possession of: *holding a material witness in protective custody.*
7. To be possessed of.
8. To compel the attention, interest, imagination, etc.
9. To sustain the weight of.
10. To have an opinion.
11. To view in a certain way.
12. To put into words positively and with conviction.
13. To organize and carry out (an activity).
14. To have the room or capacity for.

1. **Syns:** hold back, keep, keep back, reserve, retain, withhold.
2. ENJOY.
3. EMBRACE *verb.*
4. CONTAIN.
5. HAVE.
6. **Syns:** detain, hold up.
7. COMMAND *verb.*
8. GRIP *verb.*
9. SUPPORT *verb.*
10. BELIEVE.
11. FEEL *verb.*
12. ASSERT.
13. HAVE.
14. ACCOMMODATE.

hold back *verb*
1. To have and maintain in one's possession.
2. To interfere with the progress of.
3. To control, restrict, or arrest.
4. To hold (something requiring an outlet) in check.

1. HOLD *verb.*
2. HINDER.
3. RESTRAIN.
4. REPRESS.

hold down *verb*

1. To control, restrict, or arrest.
2. To hold (something requiring an outlet) in check.

hold in *verb*
To control, restrict, or arrest.

hold off *verb*
1. To put off until a later time.
2. To hold oneself back.

hold out *verb*
To remain in existence or in a certain state for an indefinitely long time.

hold *noun*
1. An act or means of holding something: *Keep a firm hold on your purse.*
2. A strong or powerful influence: *had a real hold on my emotions.*

hold back *verb*
hold down *verb*
holder *noun*
A person who has legal title to property.

hold in *verb*
holding(s) *noun*
Something, as land and assets, legally possessed: *The company has vast holdings in South Africa.*

hold off *verb*
hold out *verb*
holdup *noun*
hold up *verb*
1. To withstand stress or difficulty.
2. To cause to be later or slower than expected or desired.
3. To put off until a later time.
4. To maintain restraining control and possession of.
5. To take property or possessions from (a person, company, etc.) unlawfully and usu. forcibly.
6. *Slang.* To exploit (another) by charging too much for something.
7. To prove valid under scrutiny.

holdup *noun*
1. The condition or fact of being made late or slow.
2. The act or crime of taking another's property unlawfully and by force.

hole *noun*
1. A space in an otherwise solid mass: *a hole in the ground.*
2. An opening, esp. in a solid structure.
3. An open space allowing passage: *rats running through a hole in the baseboard.*
4. A hollow place used as an animal's dwelling: *chipmunk holes.*
5. An ugly, squalid dwelling: *refugees subsisting in filthy holes.*
6. A difficult, embarrassing situation.

hole *verb*
To make a hole or other opening in.

hole up *verb*
To shut oneself up in secrecy: *The bandits holed up in a sleazy motel.*

hole up *verb*
holiday *noun*
A regularly scheduled period spent away from work or duty, often in recreation.

---

1. RESTRAIN.
2. REPRESS.

RESTRAIN.

1. DEFER[1].
2. REFRAIN.

ENDURE.

1. *Syns:* clasp, clench, clutch, grapple, grasp, grip.
2. *Syn:* grip.

SEE **hold.**
SEE **hold.**

OWNER.
SEE **hold.**

Syns: estate, possessions, property.

SEE **hold.**
SEE **hold.**
SEE **hold up.**

1. BEAR UP at **bear.**
2. DELAY *verb.*

3. DEFER[1].
4. HOLD *verb.*
5. ROB.

6. SKIN *verb.*

7. WASH.

1. DELAY *noun.*
2. ROBBERY.

1. *Syns:* cavity, hollow, vacuity, void.

2. BREACH *noun.*
3. *Syns:* aperture, opening, orifice, outlet, vent.
4. *Syns:* burrow, den, lair.

5. *Syns:* hovel, hut, shanty.

6. PREDICAMENT.

BREACH *verb.*

Syns: hide out, lair, lay low. —*Idioms* go underground, lie low.
SEE **hole.**

VACATION.

holiness *noun*
The quality of being holy or sacred: *the holiness of a religious shrine.*

Syns: blessedness, hallowedness, sacredness, sanctity.

holler *verb*
1. To speak or say very loudly.
2. To say (something) with a shout.

1. ROAR *verb.*
2. SHOUT *verb.*

holler *noun*
A loud cry.

SHOUT *noun.*

hollow *adjective*
1. Curving inward: *a tired face with hollow cheeks.*
2. Lacking value, use, or substance.

1. **Syns:** cavernous, concave, indented.
2. EMPTY *adjective*

hollow *noun*
1. A space in an otherwise solid mass.
2. An area sunk below its surroundings.

1. HOLE *noun.*
2. DEPRESSION.

hollow-eyed *adjective*
Pale and exhausted because of worry, sleeplessness, etc.

HAGGARD.

hollowness *noun*
1. Total lack of ideas, meaning, or substance.
2. A desolate sense of loss.

1. EMPTINESS.
2. EMPTINESS.

holy *adjective*
1. Deeply concerned with God and the beliefs and practice of religion: *saints and other holy men.*
2. Regarded with particular reverence or respect: *the Holy Grail.*
3. In the service or worship of God or a god.

1. **Syns:** devout, godly, pietistic, pious, religious.
2. **Syns:** blessed, hallowed, sacred, sacrosanct, sanctified.
3. DIVINE[1] *adjective.*

homage *noun*
Great respect or high public esteem.

HONOR *noun.*

home *noun*
1. A building or shelter where one lives: *a modest home on the edge of town.*

2. The natural environment of an animal or plant: *Florida is the home of the alligator.*
3. An institution that provides care and shelter: *a home for wayward boys; a home for the aged.*

1. **Syns:** abode, digs (*Informal*), domicile, dwelling, habitation, house, lodgings, place.
2. **Syns:** habitat, haunt. —*Idiom* stamping ground.
3. **Syns:** asylum, haven, hospice, refuge, retreat.

home *adjective*
1. Of or pertaining to the family or household.
2. Of, from, or within a country's own territory.

1. DOMESTIC.
2. DOMESTIC.

homely *adjective*
1. Of or pertaining to the family or household.
2. Not handsome or beautiful.
3. Of a plain and unsophisticated nature.

1. DOMESTIC.
2. PLAIN *adjective.*
3. RUSTIC *adjective.*

homespun *adjective*
Of a plain and unsophisticated nature.

RUSTIC *adjective.*

homicidal *adjective*
Eager for bloodshed.

MURDEROUS.

homicide *noun*
1. The crime of murdering someone.
2. One who murders another.

1. MURDER *noun.*
2. MURDERER.

homilize *verb*
To deliver (a sermon or sermons), esp. as a vocation.

PREACH.

hominoid *adjective*
Resembling a man or human being.

MANLIKE.

homo *noun*
A member of the human race.

HUMAN BEING.

homophile *adjective*
Pertaining to, characteristic of, or exhibiting sexual desire for others of one's own sex.

GAY *adjective.*

Homo sapiens *noun*
The human race.

MANKIND.

homosexual   *adjective*
Pertaining to, characteristic of, or exhibiting sexual
desire for others of one's own sex.

GAY *adjective*.

honcho   *noun*
Informal. One who is highest in rank or authority.

CHIEF *noun*.

hone¹   *verb*
To give a sharp edge to.

SHARPEN.

hone²   *verb*
Regional. To have a strong longing for.

DESIRE *verb*.

honed   *adjective*
Having a fine edge, as for cutting.

SHARP *adjective*.

honest   *adjective*
1. Having or marked by uprightness in principle and
   action: *an honest man; an honest business.*

1. **Syns:** honorable, incorruptible,
   righteous, straight-shooting (*Informal*),
   true, upright, upstanding. —*Idiom* on
   the up and up.
   Near-syns: conscientious, forthright,
   just, open, right, scrupulous,
   trustworthy, truthful, veracious.
   Ant: dishonest.

2. Devoid of any hypocrisy or pretense.
3. Speaking or spoken freely and sincerely.

2. GENUINE.
3. FRANK.

honesty   *noun*
1. The quality of being honest: *a man respected for his
   honesty.*

1. **Syns:** honor, incorruptibility (*also*
   incorruptibleness), integrity, rectitude,
   uprightness.

2. Moral or ethical strength.

2. CHARACTER.

honey   *verb*
1. To compliment excessively and ingratiatingly.
2. To support slavishly every opinion or suggestion of a
   superior.
3. To make superficially more acceptable or appealing.

1. FLATTER.
2. FAWN.

3. SWEETEN.

honey   *noun*
A person who is much loved.

DARLING *noun*.

honky-tonk   *noun*
Slang. A disreputable or run-down bar or restaurant.

JOINT *noun*.

honor   *noun*
1. Great respect or high public esteem accorded as a
   right or as due: *Only a head of state receives the
   honor of a 21-gun salute.*

1. **Syns:** deference, homage, obeisance.

2. A feeling of deference, approval, and liking.
3. Recognition of achievement or superiority or a sign
   of this.
4. A person's high standing among others: *had to fight
   to protect his honor.*

2. ESTEEM *noun*.
3. DISTINCTION.

4. **Syns:** dignity, prestige, reputation,
   repute, status. —*Idiom* good name (*or*
   report).

5. The quality of being honest.

5. HONESTY.

honor   *verb*
1. To have a high opinion of.
2. To pay tribute or homage to: *a country honoring its
   heroes.*

1. ADMIRE.
2. **Syns:** acclaim, celebrate, exalt, extol,
   glorify, hail², laud, magnify,
   panegyrize, praise, venerate. —*Idiom*
   sing someone's praises.

3. To cause to be eminent or recognized.
4. To lend dignity or honor to by an act or favor.

3. DISTINGUISH.
4. GRACE *verb*.

honorable   *adjective*
1. Deserving honor or respect: *Teaching is an
   honorable occupation.*

1. **Syns:** creditable, estimable, reputable,
   respectable, worthy.
   Near-syns: august, noble, revered,
   venerable, worshipful.
   Ant: dishonorable.

2. Having or marked by uprightness in principle and
action.   **2.** HONEST.

honorarium *noun*
Something given in return for a service or   REWARD *noun*.
accomplishment.

hood *noun*
Slang. A person who treats others violently and   THUG.
roughly, esp. for hire.

hoodlum *noun*
A person who treats others violently and roughly, esp.   THUG.
for hire.

hoodoo *noun*
Something or someone believed to bring bad luck.   JINX.

hoodwink *verb*
To cause to accept what is false, esp. by trickery or   DECEIVE.
misrepresentation.

hooey *noun*
Slang. Something that does not have or make sense.   NONSENSE.

hoof *verb*
1. *Informal.* To go on foot.   **1.** WALK *verb*.
2. *Slang.* To move rhythmically to music, using   **2.** DANCE *verb*.
patterns of steps or gestures.

hoofer *noun*
Slang. A person who dances, esp. professionally.   DANCER.

hoo-hah *noun*
Slang. A condition of intense public interest or   SENSATION.
excitement.

hook *verb*
Slang. To take (another's property) without permission.   STEAL *verb*.

hook *noun*
A device for fastening or for checking motion.   CATCH *noun*.

hooker *noun*
Slang. A woman who engages in sexual intercourse for   PROSTITUTE.
payment.

hookup *noun*
Informal. A logical or natural association between two   RELATION.
or more things.

hooky *noun*
Informal. An unexcused absence.   CUT *noun*.

hooligan *noun*
A person who treats others violently and roughly, esp.   THUG.
for hire.

hoosegow *noun*
Slang. A place for the confinement of persons in lawful   JAIL *noun*.
detention.

hoot *noun*
1. A tiny amount.   **1.** BIT[1].
2. The least bit.   **2.** DAMN *noun*.
3. Any derisive sound of disapproval.   **3.** HISS *noun*.
4. *Slang.* Something or someone uproariously funny or   **4.** SCREAM *noun*.
absurd.

Hooverize *verb*
To use without wasting.   ECONOMIZE.

hop *noun*
1. A light bounding movement.   **1.** SKIP *noun*.
2. *Slang.* A party or gathering for dancing.   **2.** DANCE *noun*.

hop *verb*
To bound lightly.   SKIP *verb*.

hope *verb*
To have a fervent hope or aspiration.   ASPIRE.

hopeful *adjective*
Inspiring confidence or hope.   ENCOURAGING.
hopeful *noun*
1. One who aspires.   **1.** ASPIRANT.
2. A person who applies for or seeks a job or position.   **2.** APPLICANT.
hopeless *adjective*
1. Offering no hope or expectation of improvement: *an*   **1.** **Syns:** cureless, impossible, incurable,
illness that seemed hopeless.   irremediable, irreparable.
                                                                              Near-ants: curable, redeemable,
                                                                              remediable, reparable.
                                                                              Ant: hopeful.
2. Having lost all hope.   **2.** DESPONDENT.
hopelessness *noun*
Utter lack of hope.   DESPAIR *noun.*
hopped-up *adjective*
Slang. Stupefied, intoxicated, or otherwise influenced by   DRUGGED.
the taking of drugs.
horde *noun*
An enormous number of persons gathered together.   CROWD *noun.*
horizon *noun*
The extent of one's perception, understanding,   KEN.
knowledge, or vision.
horizontal *adjective*
Lying down.   FLAT *adjective.*
horn in *verb*
1. To force or come in as an improper or unwanted   **1.** INTRUDE.
element.
2. *Slang.* To intervene officiously or indiscreetly in the   **2.** MEDDLE.
affairs of others.
horny *adjective*
Slang. Feeling or devoted to sexual love or desire.   EROTIC.
horrendous *adjective*
Very bad.   TERRIBLE.
horrible *adjective*
1. Causing great horror: *a horrible scream.*   **1.** **Syns:** bloodcurdling, hair-raising,
                                                                              horrid, horrific, horrifying, terrific,
                                                                              terrifying.
2. Very bad.   **2.** TERRIBLE.
3. Shockingly repellent.   **3.** GHASTLY.
horrid *adjective*
1. Causing great horror.   **1.** HORRIBLE.
2. Shockingly repellent.   **2.** GHASTLY.
3. Eliciting or deserving hate.   **3.** HATEFUL.
horrific *adjective*
Causing great horror.   HORRIBLE.
horrified *adjective*
Overcome with intense feeling, as of amazement,   SHOCKED.
horror, or dismay.
horrify *verb*
To deprive of courage or the power to act as a result of   DISMAY *verb.*
fear, anxiety, or disgust.
horrifying *adjective*
Causing great horror.   HORRIBLE.
horror *noun*
1. A feeling of fear and repugnance: *experienced horror*   **1.** **Syns:** abhorrence, aversion, repulsion,
at the sight of blood.   revulsion.
2. Great agitation and anxiety caused by the   **2.** FEAR *noun.*
expectation or the realization of danger.
horrorstruck *adjective*
Overcome with intense feeling, as of amazement,   SHOCKED.
horror, or dismay.

horse around *verb*
Informal. To behave in a rowdy or unruly fashion. MISBEHAVE.

horseplay *verb*
To behave in a rowdy or unruly fashion. MISBEHAVE.

hospice *noun*
An institution that provides care and shelter. HOME.

host *noun*
A very large number of things grouped together. CROWD *noun.*

hostile *adjective*
1. Feeling or showing unfriendliness: *had a hostile attitude toward authority.*

1. **Syns:** inimicable, inimical, unfriendly.
   Near-syns: argumentative, bellicose, belligerent, contentious, contrary, militant; dour, disapproving.
   Ant: friendly.

2. Having or showing an eagerness to fight. 2. BELLIGERENT.

hostilities *noun*
A state of open, prolonged fighting. CONFLICT *noun.*

hostility *noun*
1. A state of mind brought on by something that is antipathetic. 1. ANTIPATHY.
2. Hostile behavior. 2. AGGRESSION.
3. Warlike or hostile attitude or nature. 3. BELLIGERENCE.
4. Deep-seated hatred, as between longtime opponents or rivals. 4. ENMITY.

hot *adjective*
1. Marked by much heat: *a hot oven; a hot day.*

1. **Syns:** ardent, baking, blistering, boiling, broiling, burning, fiery, heated, red-hot, scalding, scorching, sizzling, sultry, sweltering, torrid.
   Near-ants: arctic, chilly, cool, freezing, frigid, frosty, icy.
   Ant: cold.

2. Being at a higher temperature than is normal or desirable: *a hot forehead.* 2. **Syns:** febrile, fevered, feverish, feverous, hectic, pyretic.
3. Slang. Particularly excellent. 3. MARVELOUS.
4. Informal. Of great current interest: *a hot topic.* 4. **Syns:** live^2, red-hot.

hot *noun*
Regional. Intense warmth. HEAT *noun.*

hot *verb*
Chiefly Brit. To make hot. HEAT *verb.*

hot-blooded *adjective*
Fired with intense feeling. PASSIONATE.

hotfoot *verb*
Slang. To leave hastily. RUN *verb.*

hotheaded *adjective*
Characterized by unthinking boldness and haste. RASH^1.

hotness *noun*
Intense warmth. HEAT *noun.*

hot-tempered *adjective*
Easily annoyed. TESTY.

hot water *noun*
Slang. A condition or situation characterized by danger, distress, or annoyance. TROUBLE *noun.*

hound *verb*
1. To trouble persistently from or as if from all sides. 1. BESIEGE.
2. To torment with persistent insult or ridicule. 2. BAIT *verb.*

house *noun*
1. A building or shelter where one lives. 1. HOME.
2. A group of people sharing common ancestry. 2. FAMILY.
3. A group of usu. related people living together as a unit. 3. FAMILY.

4. A commercial organization.

4. COMPANY *noun*.

house *verb*
1. To give refuge to.
2. To provide with often temporary lodging.

1. HARBOR *verb*.
2. HARBOR *verb*.

housebreak *verb*
To enter forcibly and illegally.

BREAK IN at **break.**

house-cleaning *noun*
A thorough or drastic reorganization.

SHAKEUP at **shake up.**

household *noun*
A group of usu. related people living together as a unit.

FAMILY.

household *adjective*
Of or pertaining to the family or household.

DOMESTIC.

housing *noun*
Dwellings in general.

SHELTER *noun*.

hovel *noun*
An ugly, squalid dwelling.

HOLE *noun*.

hover *verb*
1. To move quickly and intermittently in a nervous, excited way.

1. FLUTTER *verb*.

2. To remain stationary over a place or object.

2. HANG *verb*.

howl *verb*
1. To utter or emit a long, mournful, plaintive sound: *a dog howling at the moon.*

1. *Syns:* bay², ululate, wail, yowl.
   Near-syns: bark, cry, whimper, yelp.

2. To make inarticulate sounds of grief or pain, usu. accompanied by tears.

2. CRY *verb*.

3. To cry loudly, as a healthy child does from pain or distress.

3. BAWL.

4. *Slang.* To express great amusement or mirth.

4. BREAK UP at **break.**

howl *noun*
1. A long, mournful cry: *heard the howl of a wolf.*

1. *Syns:* moan, ululation, wail, yowl.

2. *Slang.* Something or someone uproariously funny or absurd.

2. SCREAM *noun*.

hub *noun*
A point of origin from which ideas, influences, etc., emanate.

CENTER *noun*.

hubbub *noun*
Sounds or a sound, esp. when loud, confused, or disagreeable.

NOISE *noun*.

huckster *verb*
1. To travel about selling goods.
2. To argue about the terms of, as of a sale.

1. PEDDLE.
2. HAGGLE.

huddle *verb*
To stoop low with the limbs pulled in close to the body.

CROUCH.

huddle *noun*
A lack of order or regular arrangement.

DISORDER *noun*.

hue *noun*
1. The property by which the sense of vision can distinguish between objects, as a red apple and a green apple, that are very similar or identical in form or size.

1. COLOR *noun*.

2. The degree of vividness of a color, as when modified by the addition of black or white pigment.

2. SHADE *noun*.

3. A shade of a color, esp. a pale or delicate variation.

3. TINT *noun*.

huff *noun*
1. Extreme displeasure caused by an insult or slight.
2. An angry outburst.

1. OFFENSE.
2. TEMPER *noun*.

huff *verb*
To breathe hard.

PANT.

hug *verb*
To put one's arms around affectionately.

EMBRACE *verb*.

hug *noun*

The act of embracing. — EMBRACE *noun.*

huge *adjective*
Of extraordinary size and power. — GIANT *adjective.*

hugeness *noun*
The quality of being enormous. — ENORMOUSNESS.

huggermugger or **hugger-mugger** *adjective*
Existing or operating in a way so as to ensure complete concealment and confidentiality. — SECRET *adjective.*

  huggermugger or **hugger-mugger** *noun*
  The habit, practice, or policy of keeping secrets. — SECRECY.

  huggermugger or **hugger-mugger** *adverb*
  In a secret way. — SECRETLY.

hugger-muggery *noun*
The habit, practice, or policy of keeping secrets. — SECRECY.

hulk *noun*
A large, ungainly, and dull-witted person. — LUMP[1] *noun.*

  hulk *verb*
  To move heavily. — LUMP[1] *verb.*

hulking *adjective*
Having a large body, esp. in girth. — BULKY.

hulky *adjective*
Having a large body, esp. in girth. — BULKY.

hullaballoo *noun* — SEE **hullabaloo.**

hullabaloo also **hullaballoo** *noun*
1. Sounds or a sound, esp. when loud, confused, or disagreeable. — 1. NOISE *noun.*
2. Offensively loud and insistent utterances, esp. of disapproval. — 2. VOCIFERATION.

hum *verb*
To make a continuous low-pitched droning sound: *The radio hummed briefly after being turned on.* — *Syns:* bombinate, bumble[2], burr (*also* bur), buzz, drone[2], whir, whiz (*also* whizz).

  hum *noun*
  A continuous low-pitched droning sound: *the steady hum of a roomful of sewing machines.* — *Syns:* bombination, bumble[2], burr (*also* bur), buzz, drone[2], whir, whiz (*also* whizz).

human *adjective*
1. Of or characteristic of human beings or mankind: *the caprices of human conduct.* — 1. *Syn:* mortal.
2. Concerned with human welfare and the alleviation of suffering. — 2. HUMANITARIAN.

  human *noun*
  A member of the human race. — HUMAN BEING.

human being *noun*
A member of the human race: *freedom for all human beings.* — *Syns:* being, body (*Informal*), creature, fellow, homo, human, individual, life, man, mortal, party (*Informal*), person, personage, soul.

humane *adjective*
1. Characterized by kindness and concern for others. — 1. BENEVOLENT.
2. Concerned with human welfare and the alleviation of suffering. — 2. HUMANITARIAN.

humanitarian *adjective*
1. Concerned with human welfare and the alleviation of suffering: *The governor spared the prisoner out of humanitarian considerations.* — 1. *Syns:* charitable, compassionate, human, humane, merciful.
2. Characterized by kindness and concern for others. — 2. BENEVOLENT.

humanity *noun*
The human race. — MANKIND.

humanizing *adjective*
Promoting culture. — CULTURAL.

humankind *noun*
The human race.   MANKIND.

humanoid *adjective*
Resembling a man or human being.   MANLIKE.

humble *adjective*
1. Having or expressing feelings of humility: *had a   1. **Syns:** lowly, meek, modest,
   humble opinion of his own aptitude.*   unassuming, unpresuming.
                                                                   Near-ants: arrogant, disdainful,
                                                                   haughty, lordly, overbearing,
                                                                   pretentious, proud, snobbish, uppish,
                                                                   uppity (*Informal*); egotistic, vain.
                                                                   Ant: conceited.
2. Of little distinction: *my humble abode.*   2. **Syns:** lowly, mean², modest, simple,
                                                                   undistinguished, unpretentious.
3. Lacking high station or birth.   3. LOWLY.

humble *verb*
To deprive of esteem, self-worth, or effectiveness: **Syns:** abase, bemean, degrade, demean²,
humbled his opponent in the debate.   humiliate. —*Idioms* bring low, take down
                                                            a peg or two.

humbleness *noun*
Lack of vanity or self-importance.   MODESTY.

humbug *verb*
To cause to accept what is false, esp. by trickery or   DECEIVE.
misrepresentation.

humbug *noun*
One who is not what he claims to be.   FAKE *noun.*

humdrum *adjective*
Arousing no interest or curiosity.   BORING.

humdrum *noun*
A tiresome lack of variety.   MONOTONY.

humid *adjective*
Damp and warm.   STICKY.

humiliate *verb*
To deprive of esteem, self-worth, or effectiveness.   HUMBLE *verb.*

humility *noun*
Lack of vanity or self-importance.   MODESTY.

Humist *noun*
One who habitually or instinctively doubts or   SKEPTIC.
questions.

humor *noun*
1. The quality of being laughable or comical: *finally   1. **Syns:** comedy, comicality (*also*
   saw the humor of the situation.*   comicalness), drollery, drollness,
                                                                   funniness, humorousness, wit,
                                                                   wittiness.
2. A person's customary manner of emotional response.   2. DISPOSITION.
3. An impulsive, often illogical turn of mind.   3. FANCY *noun.*
4. A temporary state of mind or feeling.   4. MOOD.

humor *verb*
To comply with the wishes or ideas of (another):   **Syns:** cater to, gratify, indulge, oblige.
humored the cook and stayed out of the kitchen.   —*Idioms* give in (*or* way) to, go along
                                                            with.

humorist *noun*
A person whose words or actions provoke or are   JOKER.
intended to provoke amusement or laughter.

humorous *adjective*
1. Intended to excite laughter or amusement: 1. **Syns:** facetious, funny, jesting, jocose,
   humorous comments.   jocular, witty.
                                                                   Near-ants: serious, sober, solemn,
                                                                   unamusing.

2. Arousing laughter.

2. AMUSING.

humorousness *noun*

The quality of being laughable or comical.

HUMOR *noun.*

humorsome *adjective*

Given to changeable emotional states, esp. of anger or gloom.

MOODY.

hump *noun*

An unevenness or elevation on a surface.

BUMP *noun.*

hump *verb*

To incline the body.

STOOP.

hunch *verb*

1. To incline the body.
2. To stoop low with the limbs pulled in close to the body.

1. STOOP.
2. CROUCH.

hunch *noun*

1. An irregularly shaped mass of indefinite size.
2. Intuitive cognition.

1. LUMP¹ *noun.*
2. FEELING.

hunger *noun*

1. A desire for food or drink.
2. A strong wish for what promises enjoyment or pleasure.

1. APPETITE.
2. DESIRE *noun.*

hunger *verb*

To have a greedy, obsessive desire.

LUST *verb.*

hungry *adjective*

1. Desiring or craving food.
2. Having a strong urge to obtain or possess something, esp. material wealth, in quantity.

1. RAVENOUS.
2. GREEDY.

hunk *noun*

1. An irregularly shaped mass of indefinite size.
2. A large, ungainly, and dull-witted person.

1. LUMP¹ *noun.*
2. LUMP¹ *noun.*

hunker *verb*

1. To stoop low with the limbs pulled in close to the body.
2. To sit on one's heels.

1. CROUCH.
2. SQUAT *verb.*

hunks *noun*

A stingy person.

MISER.

hunky-dory *adjective*

Slang. Particularly excellent.

MARVELOUS.

hunt *verb*

To look for and pursue (game) in order to capture or kill it: *We hunt deer in November.*

Syns: drive, stalk, run.

hunt down *verb*

To pursue and locate.

RUN DOWN.

hunt up *verb*

To try to find.

SEEK.

hunt down *verb*

SEE **hunt.**

hunt up *verb*

SEE **hunt.**

hurdle *noun*

1. The act of jumping.
2. Anything that impedes or prevents entry or passage.

1. JUMP *noun.*
2. BAR *noun.*

hurdle *verb*

1. To move off the ground by a muscular effort of the legs and feet.
2. To pass by or over safely or successfully.

1. JUMP *verb.*
2. CLEAR *verb.*

hurl *verb*

To send through the air with a motion of the hand or arm.

THROW *verb.*

hurl *noun*

An act of throwing.

THROW *noun.*

hurried *adjective*

1. Accomplished in very little time.

1. QUICK *adjective.*

2. Happening quickly and without warning.
3. Characterized by unexpected hastiness.

hurriedness *noun*
Careless, headlong action.

hurry *verb*
1. To move swiftly.
2. To increase the speed of.

hurry *noun*
Rapidness of movement or activity.

hurry-up *adjective*
Designed to meet emergency needs as quickly as possible.

hurt *verb*
1. To cause physical damage to: *hurt his eye when he broke his glasses.*
2. To have or cause a feeling of physical pain or discomfort: *Does your back still hurt?*
3. To spoil the soundness or perfection of.

hurt *noun*
1. The action or result of inflicting loss or pain.
2. A state of physical or mental suffering.

hurtful *adjective*
1. Causing harm or injury.
2. Marked by, causing, or experiencing physical pain.

hurtle *verb*
To launch with great force.

hurtless *adjective*
Incapable of inflicting injury.

husband *verb*
To protect (an asset) from loss or destruction.

husbandry *noun*
The careful guarding of an asset.

hush *verb*
1. To cause to become silent.
2. To prevent (something) from being known.
3. To hold (something requiring an outlet) in check.

hush up *verb*
To keep from beng published or transmitted.

hush *noun*
1. An absence of motion or disturbance.
2. The absence of sound or noise.

hush *adjective*
Marked by, done with, or making no sound or noise.

hushed *adjective*
Not irritating, strident, or loud.

hush-hush *adjective*
1. *Informal.* Known about by very few.
2. *Informal.* Existing or operating in a way so as to ensure complete concealment and confidentiality.

hush up *verb*

hussy *noun*
A vulgar, promiscuous woman who flouts propriety.

hustle *noun*
1. An aggressive readiness to undertake taxing efforts.
2. *Informal.* Rapidness of movement or activity.

hustle *verb*
Informal. To move swiftly.

hustler *noun*
An intensely energetic, enthusiastic person.

hut *noun*
An ugly, squalid dwelling.

---

2. ABRUPT.
3. ABRUPT.

HASTE *noun.*

1. RUSH *verb.*
2. SPEED UP at **speed.**

HASTE *noun.*

CRASH *adjective.*

1. **Syns:** injure, wound.

2. **Syns:** ache, pain.

3. INJURE.

1. HARM *noun.*
2. DISTRESS *noun.*

1. HARMFUL.
2. PAINFUL.

SHOOT *verb.*

HARMLESS.

CONSERVE *verb.*

CONSERVATION.

1. SILENCE *verb.*
2. COVER *verb.*
3. REPRESS.

CENSOR.

1. STILLNESS.
2. SILENCE *noun.*

SILENT.

SOFT.

1. CONFIDENTIAL.
2. SECRET *adjective.*

SEE **hush.**

SLUT.

1. DRIVE *noun.*
2. HASTE *noun.*

RUSH *verb.*

EAGER BEAVER.

HOLE *noun.*

hygienic *adjective*
Promoting good health.   HEALTHFUL.
hymeneal *adjective*
Of, relating to, or typical of marriage.   MARITAL.
hype *verb*
Slang. To increase or seek to increase the importance   PROMOTE.
or reputation of by favorable publicity.
hype *noun*
Slang. A systematic effort to increase the importance or PROMOTION.
reputation of by favorable publicity.
hyperbole *noun*
The act or an instance of exaggerating.   EXAGGERATION.
hyperbolism *noun*
The act or an instance of exaggerating.   EXAGGERATION.
hyperbolize *verb*
To make (something) seem greater than is actually the   EXAGGERATE.
case.
hypercritic *noun*
A person who finds fault, often severely and willfully.   CRITIC.
hypercritical *adjective*
Inclined to judge too severely.   CRITICAL.
hypernormal *adjective*
Greatly exceeding or departing from the normal course   PRETERNATURAL.
of nature.
hypnotic *adjective*
Inducing sleep.   SLEEPY.
hypnotic *noun*
Something that induces sleep.   SOPORIFIC *noun.*
hypocrisy *noun*
A show or expression of feelings or beliefs one does not   **Syns:** hypocriticalness, pecksniffery,
actually hold or possess: *the hypocrisy of condemning*   pharisaism (*also* phariseeism), sanctimony
graft when you're taking kickbacks.   (*also* sanctimoniousness), tartuffery, two-
                                                           facedness.
                                                           Near-syns: cant, glibness; insincerity; self-
                                                           righteousness, sham; pietism, religiosity.

hypocrite *noun*
A person who practices hypocrisy: *a hypocrite who prays* **Syns:** pharisee, phony (*also* phoney)
on Sunday and cheats customers on Monday.   (*Informal*), tartuffe (*also* tartufe).
hypocritical *adjective*
Of or practicing hypocrisy: *hypocritical praise; a*   **Syns:** pecksniffian, pharisaic (*also*
hypocritical rogue.   pharisaical), sanctimonious, tartuffian,
                                                           two-faced.
hypocriticalness *noun*
A show or expression of feelings or beliefs one does not   HYPOCRISY.
actually hold or possess.
hypogeal also **hypogean, hypogeous** *adjective*
Located or operating beneath the earth's surface.   UNDERGROUND *adjective.*
hypogean *adjective*   SEE **hypogeal.**
hypogeous *adjective*   SEE **hypogeal.**
hypothecate *verb*
To give or deposit as a pawn.   PAWN[1] *verb.*
hypothesis *noun*
A belief used as the basis for action.   THEORY.
hypothetical also **hypothetic** *adjective*
1. Presumed to be true, real, or genuine, esp. on   1. SUPPOSED.
   inconclusive grounds.
2. Existing only in concept and not in reality.   2. THEORETICAL.

I

icy *adjective*
1. Very cold.
2. Lacking all friendliness and warmth.

idea *noun*
1. That which exists in the mind as the product of careful mental activity: *a novel idea about energy conservation.*
2. Intuitive cognition.
3. Something believed or accepted as true by a person.
4. A method for making, doing, or accomplishing something.
5. The gist of a specific action or situation: *What's the idea of shouting?*

ideal *noun*
1. One that is worthy of imitation or duplication.
2. A fervent hope, wish, or goal.

ideal *adjective*
1. Conforming to an ultimate form of perfection or excellence: *the ideal vacation.*

2. Existing only in concept and not in reality.
3. Showing a tendency to envision things in perfect but unrealistic form.

idealist *noun*
A person inclined to be imaginative or idealistic but impractical.

idealistic *adjective*
1. Showing a tendency to envision things in perfect but unrealistic form: *an idealistic but disastrously naive approach to foreign policy.*
2. Not compatible with reality: *an idealistic view of controlling inflation.*

identic *adjective*
Archaic. Being one and not another or others.

identical *adjective*
1. Being one and not another or others.
2. Agreeing exactly in value, quantity, or effect.
3. Strictly distinguished from others.

identicalness *noun*
The quality or condition of being exactly the same as something else.

identify *verb*
1. To associate or affiliate oneself closely with a person or group: *couldn't identify with the play's hero.*
2. To establish the identification of.
3. To come or bring together in one's mind or imagination.
4. To set off by or as if by a mark indicating ownership or manufacture.

identity *noun*
1. The set of behavioral or personal characteristics by which an individual is recognizable: *watching a child develop its own identity.*

---

1. FRIGID.
2. COLD *adjective.*

1. **Syns:** concept, conception, image, perception, thought.

2. FEELING.
3. BELIEF.
4. DESIGN *noun.*

5. **Syns:** import, meaning, point, purport, significance (*also* significancy).

1. MODEL *noun.*
2. DREAM *noun.*

1. **Syns:** exemplary, model, perfect, supreme.
   Near-syns: appropriate, exact, express, fit, precise, proper, right, suitable, superlative.
2. THEORETICAL.
3. IDEALISTIC.

DREAMER.

1. **Syns:** ideal, utopian, visionary.

2. **Syns:** quixotic, romantic, starry-eyed, unrealistic, utopian, visionary.

SAME.

1. SAME.
2. EQUAL *adjective.*
3. PRECISE.

SAMENESS.

1. **Syns:** empathize, relate (to), sympathize.
2. PLACE *verb.*
3. ASSOCIATE *verb.*

4. MARK *verb.*

1. **Syns:** individualism, individuality, personality, selfhood.

2. The quality or condition of being exactly the same as something else. — **2.** SAMENESS.

idiocy *noun*
1. Foolish behavior. — **1.** FOOLISHNESS.
2. Something that does not have or make sense. — **2.** NONSENSE.

idiom *noun*
Specialized expressions indigenous to a particular field, subject, trade, or subculture. — LANGUAGE.

idiosyncrasy *noun*
Peculiar behavior. — ECCENTRICITY.

idiosyncratic *adjective*
Deviating from the customary. — ECCENTRIC *adjective*.

idiot *noun*
1. One deficient in judgment and good sense. — **1.** FOOL *noun*.
2. A mentally deficient person. — **2.** FOOL *noun*.

idiotic *adjective*
So senseless as to be laughable. — FOOLISH.

idle *adjective*
1. Not occupied or put to use: *idle machines*. — **1.** *Syns:* inactive, unemployed, unused, vacant.
2. Marked by a lack of action or activity. — **2.** INACTIVE.
3. Resistant to exertion and activity. — **3.** LAZY.
4. Having no basis or foundation in fact. — **4.** BASELESS.
5. Lacking value, use, or substance. — **5.** EMPTY *adjective*.

idle *verb*
1. To pass time without working or in avoiding work: *He idled while his parents slaved*. — **1.** *Syns:* bum (around) (*Informal*), diddle, goldbrick (*Slang*), goof off (*Slang*), laze, lazy, loaf, loiter, lounge, shirk.
2. To pass (time) without working or in avoiding work: *idled the hours away*. — **2.** *Syns:* fiddle away, trifle, waste, while (away), wile (away).
3. To cause to cease regular activity. — **3.** TIE UP.

idleness *noun*
1. A lack of action or activity. — **1.** INACTION.
2. The quality or state of being lazy. — **2.** LAZINESS.

idler *noun*
A self-indulgent person who spends time avoiding work or other useful activity. — WASTREL.

idolization *noun*
The act of adoring, esp. reverently. — ADORATION.

idolize *verb*
To regard with great awe and devotion. — ADORE.

iffy *adjective*
Informal. Not affording certainty. — AMBIGUOUS.

ignis fatuus *noun*
An erroneous perception of reality. — ILLUSION.

ignite *verb*
To cause to burn or undergo combustion. — LIGHT[1] *verb*.

ignited *adjective*
On fire. — BLAZING.

ignoble *adjective*
1. Having or proceeding from low moral standards. — **1.** SORDID.
2. Lacking high station or birth. — **2.** LOWLY.

ignominious *adjective*
Meriting or causing shame or dishonor. — DISGRACEFUL.

ignominy *noun*
Loss of or damage to one's reputation. — DISGRACE *noun*.

ignorance *noun*
1. The condition of being ignorant; lack of knowledge or learning: *Ignorance is unusual in modern Western society*. — **1.** *Syns:* benightedness, illiteracy, nescience.

2. The condition of being uninformed: *her ignorance of the new tax structure.*

ignorant *adjective*
1. Without education or knowledge: *ignorant youths who dropped out of school.*

2. Exhibiting lack of education or knowledge: *ignorant nomads at odds with a machine-age culture.*
3. Not aware or informed: *ignorant of the change in plans.*

ignore *verb*
1. To refuse to pay attention to (a person); treat with contempt: *greeted her but ignored me.*
2. To pretend not to see.

ilk *noun*
A class that is defined by the common attribute or attributes possessed by all its members.

ill *adjective*
1. Suffering from or affected with an illness.
2. Bringing, predicting, or characterized by misfortune.

ill *noun*
1. A pathological condition of mind or body.
2. A cause of suffering or harm.
3. Whatever is destructive or harmful.

ill-advised *adjective*
Not wise.

illation *noun*
A position arrived at by reasoning from premises or general principles.

ill-behaved *adjective*
Misbehaving, often in a troublesome way.

ill-bred *adjective*
1. Lacking in delicacy or refinement.
2. Lacking good manners.

ill-chosen *adjective*
Characterized by inappropriateness and gracelessness, esp. in expression.

ill-considered *adjective*
1. Lacking due thought or consideration.
2. Not wise.

illegal *adjective*
1. Prohibited by law: *an illegal tax deduction.*

2. Of, involving, or being a crime.

illegality *noun*
1. The state or quality of being illegal: *the illegality of a labor contract.*
2. A serious breaking of the public law.

illegitimacy *noun*
1. The condition of being of illegitimate birth: *His illegitimacy made him the target of cruel jokes.*

2. **Syns:** innocence, nescience, unfamiliarity.

1. **Syns:** illiterate, nescient, uneducated, unlearned, unschooled, untaught. **Near-ants:** educated, erudite, knowledgeable, literate, schooled, smart, trained. **Ant:** learned.
2. **Syns:** backward, benighted, primitive, unenlightened.
3. **Syns:** innocent, oblivious, unacquainted, unaware, unconscious, unenlightened, unfamiliar, uninformed, unknowing, unwitting. —*Idiom* in the dark.

1. **Syns:** disregard, neglect, slight, snub. —*Idiom* give someone the go-by.
2. BLINK AT at **blink.**

KIND[2].

1. SICK.
2. BAD.

1. DISEASE.
2. CURSE *noun.*
3. EVIL *noun.*

UNWISE.

DEDUCTION.

NAUGHTY.

1. COARSE.
2. RUDE.

UNFORTUNATE *adjective.*

1. PRECIPITATE *adjective.*
2. UNWISE.

1. **Syns:** illegitimate, illicit, lawless, outlawed, unlawful, wrongful. **Near-syns:** banned, forbidden, prohibited, unauthorized; fraudulent; felonious. **Ant:** legal.
2. CRIMINAL *adjective.*

1. **Syns:** illegitimacy, illicitness, unlawfulness.
2. CRIME.

1. **Syn:** bastardy.

2. The state or quality of being illegal.   **2.** ILLEGALITY.

illegitimate *adjective*
   1. Born out of wedlock: *her illegitimate son.*   **1.** *Syns:* baseborn, bastard, fatherless, misbegotten, natural, spurious, unlawful.

   2. Prohibited by law.   **2.** ILLEGAL.
   3. Of, involving, or being a crime.   **3.** CRIMINAL *adjective.*

ill-fated *adjective*
Involving or undergoing chance misfortune.   UNFORTUNATE *adjective.*

ill-favored *adjective*
   1. Arousing disapproval.   **1.** OBJECTIONABLE.
   2. Extremely displeasing to the eye.   **2.** UGLY *adjective.*

illiberal *adjective*
Not tolerant of the beliefs, opinions, etc., of others.   INTOLERANT.

illicit *adjective*
   1. Of, involving, or being a crime.   **1.** CRIMINAL *adjective.*
   2. Prohibited by law.   **2.** ILLEGAL.
   3. Contrary to accepted, esp. moral conventions.   **3.** UNLAWFUL.

illicitness *noun*
The state or quality of being illegal.   ILLEGALITY.

illimitable *adjective*
Without beginning or end.   ETERNAL.

illiteracy *noun*
The condition of being ignorant; lack of knowledge or learning. IGNORANCE.

illiterate *adjective*
Without education or knowledge.   IGNORANT.

ill-judged *adjective*
Not wise.   UNWISE.

ill-kempt *adjective*
Marked by an absence of cleanliness and order.   MESSY.

ill-looking *adjective*
Extremely displeasing to the eye.   UGLY *adjective.*

ill-mannered *adjective*
Lacking good manners.   RUDE.

illness *noun*
   1. A pathological condition of mind or body.   **1.** DISEASE.
   2. The condition of being sick.   **2.** SICKNESS.

illogical *noun*
   1. Not governed by or predicated on reason.   **1.** UNREASONABLE.
   2. Containing fundamental errors in reasoning.   **2.** FALLACIOUS.

ill-starred *adjective*
Involving or undergoing chance misfortune.   UNFORTUNATE *adjective.*

ill-suited *adjective*
Not suited to a given purpose.   UNFIT *adjective.*

ill-tempered *adjective*
Having or showing a bad temper: *ill-tempered employees; an ill-tempered reply.*

Syns: bad-tempered, cantankerous, crabbed, crabby, cranky, cross, disagreeable, grouchy, grumpy, irascible, irritable, mean² (*Informal*), nasty, peevish, petulant, querulous, ratty (*Chiefly Brit.*), runty (*Regional*), snappish, surly, testy, ugly (*Informal*), waspish.
Near-ants: calm easygoing, good-natured, kindly, tolerant, tranquil; amiable, friendly.

ill-timed *adjective*
Not occurring at a favorable time.   INCONVENIENT.

illume *verb*
   1. *Poetic.* To provide, cover, or fill with light.   **1.** ILLUMINATE.

2. *Poetic.* To enable (one) to understand, esp. in a spiritual sense.

2. ILLUMINATE.

illuminate *verb*
1. To provide, cover, or fill with light: *A bonfire illuminated the clearing.*
2. To make clear or clearer.
3. To enable (one) to understand, esp. in a spiritual sense: *a sermon that illuminated me.*

1. *Syns:* illume (*Poetic*), illumine, light[1], lighten.
2. CLARIFY.
3. *Syns:* edify, enlighten, illume (*Poetic*), illumine, instruct.

illumination *noun*
1. The act of physically illuminating or the condition of being filled with light: *presided at the illumination of the nation's official Christmas tree.*
2. Electromagnetic radiation that makes vision possible.
3. The condition of being informed spiritually: *illumination experienced through meditation.*
4. Something that serves to explain or clarify.

1. *Syns:* light[1], lighting.

2. LIGHT[1] *noun.*

3. *Syns:* edification, enlightenment, instruction.
4. EXPLANATION.

illumine *verb*
1. To provide, cover, or fill with light.
2. To enable (one) to understand, esp. in a spiritual sense.

1. ILLUMINATE.
2. ILLUMINATE.

ill-use *verb*
To hurt or injure by maltreatment.

ABUSE *verb.*

illusion *noun*
1. An erroneous perception of reality: *optical illusions caused by trick mirrors.*

2. A fantastic, impracticable plan or desire: *had grand illusions of changing the world.*

3. An illusory mental image.

1. *Syns:* delusion, hallucination, ignis fatuus, mirage, phantasm (*also* phantasma), will-o'-the-wisp.
2. *Syns:* bubble, chimera, dream, fantasy (*also* phantasy), pipe dream, rainbow. —*Idiom* castle in the air.
3. DREAM *noun.*

illusive *adjective*
1. Of, pertaining to, or in the nature of an illusion; lacking reality: *the mental patient's illusive perceptions.*
2. Tending to deceive; of the nature of an illusion.

1. *Syns:* chimerical (*also* chimeric), hallucinatory, illusory.

2. ILLUSORY.

illusory *adjective*
1. Tending to deceive; of the nature of an illusion: *illusory wage gains.*
2. Of, pertaining to, or in the nature of an illusion; lacking reality.

1. *Syns:* delusive, delusory, illusive.

2. ILLUSIVE.

illustrate *verb*
1. To demonstrate and clarify with examples.
2. To make understandable.
3. To serve as the image of.

1. INSTANCE *verb.*
2. EXPLAIN.
3. REPRESENT.

illustration *noun*
One that is representative of a group or class.

EXAMPLE.

illustrative *adjective*
Of or pertaining to representation by drawings or pictures.

GRAPHIC.

illustrious *adjective*
Widely known and esteemed.

EMINENT.

illustriousness *noun*
A position of exalted, widely recognized importance.

EMINENCE.

ill will *noun*
A desire to harm others or to see others suffer.

MALEVOLENCE.

image *noun*
1. The character projected by someone to the public: *a politician concerned about his image.*
2. One exactly resembling another.

1. *Syns:* appearance, impression.

2. DOUBLE *noun.*

3. That which exists in the mind as the product of careful mental activity.

4. A representation of a person or thing.

5. Something that is reflected.

image *verb*

1. To present a lifelike image of.

2. To copy (another) slavishly.

3. To form mental images of.

4. To make a copy of.

5. To send back or form an image of.

imaginable *adjective*

Capable of being anticipated, considered, or imagined.

imaginary *adjective.*

Existing only in the imagination: *an imaginary playmate.*

imagination *noun*

The power of the mind to form images: *Children have great imagination in playing.*

imaginative *adjective*

Appealing to fancy.

imaginativeness *noun*

The power of the mind to form images.

imagine *verb*

To form mental images of: *imagined that she had seen the murder; couldn't imagine what it was like.*

imagined *adjective*

Existing only in the imagination.

imbecile *noun*

1. A mentally deficient person.

2. One deficient in judgment and good sense.

imbed *verb*

imbibe *verb*

1. To take in (moisture or liquid).

2. To take into the mouth and swallow (a liquid).

3. To take alcoholic liquor, esp. excessively or habitually.

4. To take in and incorporate, esp. mentally.

imbrue also **embrue** *verb*

To cover with blood.

imbrued also **embrued** *adjective*

Of or covered with blood.

imbue *verb*

To occupy the whole of; be found throughout.

imitate *verb*

1. To copy (the manner or expression of another), esp. in an exaggerated or mocking way: *He imitated the teacher behind her back.*

2. To make a copy of.

3. To copy (another) slavishly.

imitation *noun*

1. The act, practice, or art of copying the manner or expression of another.

2. A usu. amusing caricature of another.

3. An inferior substitute imitating an original.

imitation *adjective*

Made to imitate something else.

---

3. IDEA.

4. LIKENESS.

5. REFLECTION.

1. REPRESENT.

2. ECHO *verb*.

3. IMAGINE.

4. COPY *verb*.

5. REFLECT.

EARTHLY.

Syns: chimerical (*also* chimeric), conceptual, fancied, fanciful, fantastic (*also* fantastical), imagined, notional, unreal.

Syns: fancy, fantasy (*also* phantasy), imaginativeness. —*Idiom* flight of fancy.

FANCIFUL.

IMAGINATION.

Syns: conceive, envisage, envision, fancy, fantasize, feature (*Informal*), image, picture, see, think, vision, visualize.

IMAGINARY.

1. FOOL *noun*.

2. FOOL *noun*.

SEE **embed.**

1. DRINK *verb*.

2. DRINK *verb*.

3. DRINK *verb*.

4. ABSORB.

BLOODY *verb*.

BLOODY *adjective*.

FILL.

1. **Syns:** ape, burlesque, mimic, mock, parody, take off (*Informal*), travesty. —*Idiom* do a takeoff on.

2. COPY *verb*.

3. ECHO *verb*.

1. MIMICRY.

2. TAKEOFF at **take off.**

3. COPY *noun*.

ARTIFICIAL.

imitative   *adjective*
1. Copying another in an inferior or obsequious way: *executives imitative of their president; a forgery imitative of a Rembrandt.*
2. Imitating sounds.

1. **Syns:** apish, emulative, slavish.

2. ECHOIC.

imitator   *noun*
One who mindlessly imitates another.

ECHO *noun.*

immaculate   *adjective*
Free from dirt, stain, or impurities.

CLEAN *adjective.*

immaterial   *adjective*
1. Having no body, form, or substance: *immaterial apparitions.*

1. **Syns:** asomatous, bodiless, discarnate, disembodied, incorporeal, insubstantial, metaphysical (*also* metaphysic), nonphysical, spiritual, unbodied, uncorporal, unsubstantial.

2. Not relevant or pertinent to the subject; not applicable.

2. IRRELEVANT.

immature   *adjective*
1. Of or characteristic of a child, esp. in immaturity.
2. Being in an early period of growth or development.

1. CHILDISH.

2. YOUNG *adjective.*

immeasurable   *adjective*
1. Having no ends or limits.
2. Too great to be calculated.

1. ENDLESS.

2. INCALCULABLE.

immediate   *adjective*
1. Marked by the absence of any intervention: *The police had immediate evidence of a plot.*
2. Not far from another in space, time, or relation.

1. **Syns:** direct, firsthand, primary.

2. CLOSE[1] *adjective.*

immediately   *adverb*
1. Without intermediary: *Their yard is immediately behind ours.*
2. Without delay.

1. **Syn:** directly.

2. DIRECTLY.

immemorial   *adjective*
Long past.

HIGH *adjective.*

immense   *adjective*
Of extraordinary size and power.

GIANT *adjective.*

immensity   *noun*
The quality of being enormous.

ENORMOUSNESS.

immerge   *verb*
To plunge briefly in or into a liquid.

DIP *verb.*

immerse   *verb*
1. To plunge briefly in or into a liquid.
2. To occupy the full attention of.

1. DIP *verb.*

2. ABSORB.

immersed   *adjective*
Having one's thoughts fully occupied.

ABSORBED.

immigrant   *noun*
One who emigrates.

EMIGRANT.

immigrate   *verb*
To leave one's native land and to settle in another.

EMIGRATE.

immigration   *noun*
Departure from one's native land to settle in another.

EMIGRATION.

imminence   *noun*
The act or fact of coming near.

APPROACH *noun.*

imminent   *adjective*
About to occur at any moment.

MOMENTARY.

immission   *noun*
Archaic. The state of being allowed entry.

ADMISSION.

immit   *verb*
Archaic. To serve as a means of entrance for.

ADMIT.

immobile   *adjective*
1. Firmly in position.
2. Not moving.

1. FIXED.

2. MOTIONLESS.

immobilize *verb*
1. To render powerless or motionless by inflicting severe injury.
2. To cause to cease regular activity.

1. DISABLE.
2. TIE UP.

immoderate *adjective*
Exceeding a normal or reasonable limit.

EXCESSIVE.

immolate *verb*
To offer as a sacrifice.

SACRIFICE *verb*.

immolation *noun*
A living creature slain and offered to a deity as part of a religious rite.

SACRIFICE *noun*.

immoral *adjective*
1. Not chaste or moral.
2. Morally objectionable.

1. IMPURE.
2. EVIL *adjective*.

immorality *noun*
Immoral, degrading acts or habits.

CORRUPTION.

immortal *adjective*
1. Not being subject to death: *prayed for his immortal soul.*
2. Enduring for all time.

1. *Syns:* deathless, undying.

2. ENDLESS.

immortality *noun*
Endless life after death: *believed in the immortality of the soul.*

Syns: afterlife, deathlessness, eternity, everlastingness, world-without-end.
—*Idiom* everlasting life.

immortalize *verb*
To cause to last endlessly: *a colossal statue that immortalizes the memory of our fallen heroes.*

Syns: eternalize, eternize, perpetuate.

immovable *adjective*
Firmly in position.

FIXED.

immune *adjective*
Having the capacity to withstand.

RESISTANT *adjective*.

immunity *noun*
The capacity to withstand.

RESISTANCE.

immure *verb*
1. To confine within a limited area.
2. To put in jail.

1. ENCLOSE.
2. JAIL *verb*.

immutable *adjective*
Incapable of changing or being modified.

INFLEXIBLE.

imp *noun*
One who causes minor trouble or damage.

MISCHIEF.

impact *noun*
1. The strong effect exerted by one person or thing on another: *The impact of the oil embargo is still being felt by the consumer.*
2. The capacity to create a powerful effect.
3. Violent, forcible contact between two or more things.

1. *Syns:* force, repercussion.

2. WALLOP *noun*.
3. COLLISION.

impact *verb*
To evoke a usu. strong mental or emotional response from.

AFFECT[1].

impair *verb*
To spoil the soundness or perfection of.

INJURE.

impairment *noun*
An act, instance, or consequence of breaking.

BREAKAGE.

impalpable *adjective*
Incapable of being apprehended by the mind or the senses.

IMPERCEPTIBLE.

impart *verb*
To make known.

COMMUNICATE.

impartial *adjective*
1. Free from bias in judgment.

1. FAIR *adjective*.

2. Not inclining toward or actively taking either side in a matter under dispute.

2. NEUTRAL.

impartiality *noun*
The quality or state of being just and unbiased.

FAIRNESS.

impassable *adjective*
Incapable of being negotiated or overcome.

INSUPERABLE.

impassible *adjective*
Not capable of being affected or impressed.

INSENSITIVE.

impassion *verb*
To arouse the emotions of; make ardent.

FIRE *verb.*

impassioned *adjective*
Fired with intense feeling.

PASSIONATE.

impassive *adjective*
1. With little or no emotion or expression.
2. Without emotion or interest.
3. Not capable of being affected or impressed.

1. DRY *adjective.*
2. APATHETIC.
3. INSENSITIVE.

impassivity *noun*
Lack of emotion or interest.

APATHY.

impatient *adjective*
1. Being unable to endure irritation or opposition: *an impatient person who could not abide incompetence.*

1. *Syns:* chafing, fretful.
   Near-syns: anxious, edgy, irritable, jittery, nervous; abrupt, hasty, impetuous; uncontrolled, undisciplined.
   Ant: patient.

2. Intensely desirous or interested.
3. Not able or willing to tolerate or endure with equanimity.

2. EAGER.
3. INTOLERANT.

impeccable *adjective*
Supremely excellent in quality or nature.

PERFECT *adjective.*

impecunious *adjective*
Having little or no money or wealth.

POOR.

impecuniousness *noun*
The condition of being extremely poor.

POVERTY.

impede *verb*
1. To interfere with the progress of.
2. To stop or prevent passage of.

1. HINDER.
2. OBSTRUCT.

impediment *noun*
Anything that impedes or prevents entry or passage.

BAR *noun.*

impel *verb*
1. To set or keep going.
2. To stir to action or feeling.

1. DRIVE *verb.*
2. PROVOKE.

impend *verb*
To be imminent.

THREATEN.

impending *adjective*
About to occur at any moment.

MOMENTARY.

impenetrable *adjective*
Incapable of being grasped by the intellect or understanding.

INCOMPREHENSIBLE.

impenitent *adjective*
Devoid of remorse.

REMORSELESS.

imperative *adjective*
1. Imposed on one by authority, command, or convention.
2. Of immediate import.
3. Incapable of being dispensed with.

1. REQUIRED.
2. BURNING.
3. ESSENTIAL *adjective.*

imperative *noun*
An act or course of action that is demanded of one, as by position, custom, law, or religion.

DUTY.

imperceptible *adjective*
1. Incapable of being apprehended by the mind or the senses: *imperceptible variations in the patient's breathing. Color is imperceptible to the touch.*

1. **Syns:** impalpable, imponderable, inappreciable, indiscernible, indistinguishable, insensible, intangible, invisible, unappreciable, undistinguishable, unnoticeable, unobservable.
Near-syns: faint, inconspicuous, indistinct, obscure, vague; ethereal, ephemeral; insignificant, slight, trivial.
Ant: perceptible.

2. So minute as to be undiscernible: *imperceptible particles in liquid suspension.*

2. **Syns:** infinitesimal, microscopic.

imperfect *adjective*
Having a defect or defects. DEFECTIVE.

imperfection *noun*
Something that mars the appearance or causes inadequacy or failure. DEFECT *noun.*

imperil *verb*
To subject to danger or destruction. ENDANGER.

imperilment *noun*
Exposure to possible harm, loss, or injury. DANGER *noun.*

imperious *adjective*
Tending to dictate. DICTATORIAL.

impermanent *adjective*
Intended, used, or present for a limited time. TEMPORARY.

impermissible *adjective*
Not allowed. FORBIDDEN.

impersonal *adjective*
Feeling or showing no strong emotional involvement. NEUTRAL.

impersonate *verb*
1. To play the part of. 1. ACT *verb.*
2. To represent oneself in a given character or as other than what one is. 2. POSE *verb.*

impersonator *noun*
A performer skilled at copying the manner or expression of another. MIMIC *noun.*

impertinence *noun*
The state or quality of being impudent. IMPUDENCE.

impertinent *adjective*
1. Rude and disrespectful. 1. IMPUDENT.
2. Not relevant or pertinent to the subject; not applicable. 2. IRRELEVANT.

imperturbability *noun*
The state or quality of being nonchalant. NONCHALANCE.

imperturbable *adjective*
Not easily excited, even under pressure. COOL *adjective.*

impervious *adjective*
Having the capacity to withstand. RESISTANT *adjective.*

imperviousness *noun*
The capacity to withstand. RESISTANCE.

impetuous *adjective*
1. Lacking due thought or consideration. 1. PRECIPITATE *adjective.*
2. Characterized by unthinking boldness and haste. 2. RASH[1].

impetus *noun*
Something that causes and encourages a given response. STIMULUS.

impignorate *verb*
To give or deposit as a pawn. PAWN[1] *verb.*

impishness *noun*
Annoying yet harmless, usu. playful acts.   MISCHIEF.

implacable *adjective*
Having or showing uncompromising determination or   GRIM.
resolution in purpose or action.

implausible *adjective*
Not plausible or believable: *an implausible alibi.*   **Syns:** flimsy, improbable, inconceivable,
incredible, shaky, thick, thin,
unbelievable, unconceivable,
unconvincing, unsubstantial, weak.
Near-syns: doubtful, dubious, fishy
(*Informal*), questionable, shady, suspect,
tenuous.
Ant: plausible.

implement *verb*
1. To put into action or use.   1. USE *verb.*
2. To compel observance of.   2. ENFORCE.
3. To carry out the functions, requirements, or terms   3. FULFILL.
of.

implement *noun*
A device used to do work or perform a task.   TOOL.

implementation *noun*
A specific use.   APPLICATION.

implicate *verb*
To draw in in such a way that extrication is difficult.   INVOLVE.

implication *noun*
A subtle quality underlying or felt to underlie a   HINT *noun.*
situation, action, or person.

implicit *adjective*
1. Conveyed indirectly without words or speech: *Those*   1. **Syns:** implied, inferred, tacit,
companies reached an implicit agreement to fix   undeclared, understood, unexpressed,
prices.   unsaid, unspoken, unuttered, wordless.
—*Idiom* taken for granted.
Near-ants: categorical, declared,
expressed, spoken, unequivocal.
Ant: explicit.

2. Involved in the essential nature of something but   2. **Syns:** practical, virtual.
not shown or developed: *Suspicion is implicit in that*
tone of voice.
3. Having no reservations: *I have implicit trust in you.*   3. **Syns:** unconditional, undoubting,
unhesitating, unquestioning,
unreserved, wholehearted.

implied *adjective*
Conveyed indirectly without words or speech.   IMPLICIT.

imploration *noun*
An earnest or urgent request.   APPEAL *noun.*

implore *verb*
To make an earnest or urgent request.   APPEAL *verb.*

imply *verb*
1. To lead to by logical inference: *War implies loss of*   1. **Syns:** indicate, point to, suggest.
life. His aims imply a good deal of effort.
2. To convey an idea by indirect, subtle means.   2. HINT *verb.*

impolite *adjective*
Lacking good manners.   RUDE.

impolitic *adjective*
1. Lacking sensitivity and skill in dealing with others.   1. TACTLESS.
2. Not wise.   2. UNWISE.

imponderable *adjective*
Incapable of being apprehended by the mind or the   IMPERCEPTIBLE.
senses.

import *noun*
1. The general sense or significance, as of an action, statement, etc.: *The import of his words did not register until much later.*
2. The quality or state of being important.
3. That which is signified by a word or expression.

import *verb*
1. To be of significance or importance.
2. To have or convey a particular idea.

importance *noun*
The quality or state of being important: *Energy conservation is a matter of great importance.*

important *adjective*
1. Having great significance: *an important news story.*

2. Having or exercising influence.

importunate *adjective*
Of immediate import.

importune *verb*
To trouble persistently from or as if from all sides.

impose *verb*
1. To establish and apply as compulsory: *imposed a tax on imported oil.*
2. To set forth expressly and authoritatively.
3. To cause to undergo or bear, as something unwelcome or damaging.
4. To force (another) to accept a burden: *Don't try to impose that hard job on me!*
5. To take advantage of unfairly.

imposing *adjective*
Large and impressive in size, scope, or extent.

imposition *noun*
An excessive, unwelcome burden: *Unannounced house guests are an imposition on the hostess.*

impossible *adjective*
1. Not capable of happening or being done: *impossible dreams; an impossible plan.*

2. Offering no hope or expectation of improvement.
3. Given to acting in opposition to others.
4. Not capable of being endured or tolerated.
5. Not to be believed.

impost *noun*
1. A compulsory contribution, usu. of money, that is required of persons or groups of persons for the support of a government.
2. Something carried physically.

impostor *noun*
One who is not what he claims to be.

imposture *noun*
An action meant to deceive.

---

1. **Syns:** amount, burden, drift, purport, substance. —*Idioms* sum and substance, sum total.
2. IMPORTANCE.
3. MEANING *noun*.

1. COUNT *verb*.
2. MEAN[1].

Syns: concern, concernment, consequence, import, moment, significance (*also* significancy), weight, weightiness.

1. **Syns:** big, consequential, considerable, historic, large, material, meaningful, momentous, significant, substantial, weighty.
2. INFLUENTIAL.

BURNING.

BESIEGE.

1. **Syns:** assess, exact, levy, put.

2. DICTATE *verb*.
3. INFLICT.

4. **Syns:** foist, inflict, saddle, stick (*Slang*).
5. ABUSE *verb*.

GRAND.

Syns: infliction, intrusion.

1. **Syns:** impracticable, impractical, irrealizable, unattainable, unfeasible, unrealizable, unthinkable, unworkable. —*Idioms* beyond the bounds of possibility (*or* reason), out of the question.
   Near-ants: attainable, feasible, practicable, practical, probable, rational, realizable, reasonable.
   Ant: possible.
2. HOPELESS.
3. CONTRARY.
4. UNBEARABLE.
5. INCREDIBLE.

1. TAX *noun*.

2. BURDEN *noun*.

FAKE *noun*.

DECEPTION.

impotence *noun*
The condition or state of being incapable of
accomplishing or effecting anything.

INEFFECTUALITY.

impotent *adjective*
1. Unable to manage for oneself.
2. Not capable of accomplishing anything.

1. HELPLESS.
2. INEFFECTUAL.

impoverish *verb*
1. To reduce to financial insolvency.
2. To lessen or weaken severely, as by removing
   something essential.

1. RUIN *verb*.
2. DEPLETE.

impoverished *adjective*
1. Having little or no money or wealth.
2. Economically and socially below standard.
3. Lacking desirable elements or constituents.

1. POOR.
2. DEPRESSED.
3. POOR.

impoverishment *noun*
The condition of being extremely poor.

POVERTY.

impracticable *adjective*
1. Incapable of being used or availed of to advantage:
   chose an impracticable route through the desert.

2. Not capable of happening or being done.

1. *Syns:* impractical, unnegotiable,
   unserviceable, unusable, unworkable,
   useless.
2. IMPOSSIBLE.

impractical *adjective*
1. Incapable of dealing efficiently with practical
   matters: *a complex, impractical solution to the
   problem.*
2. Incapable of being used or availed of to advantage.
3. Not capable of happening or being done.

1. *Syns:* ivory-tower, ivory-towered, ivory-
   towerish.

2. IMPRACTICABLE.
3. IMPOSSIBLE.

imprecate *verb*
1. To invoke evil or injury upon.
2. To use profane or obscene language.

1. CURSE *verb*.
2. SWEAR *verb*.

imprecation *noun*
A denunciation invoking a wish or threat of evil or
injury.

CURSE *noun*.

impregnable *adjective*
Incapable of being conquered, overrun, or subjugated.

INVINCIBLE.

impregnate *verb*
To cause to be filled with a particular mood or tone.

CHARGE *verb*.

impress *verb*
1. To fix (an idea) in someone's mind by re-emphasis
   and repetition: *impressed the necessity of water safety
   in the minds of the children.*
2. To produce a deep impression on.
3. To evoke a usu. strong mental or emotional response
   from.

1. *Syns:* drive, inculcate, pound.

2. ENGRAVE.
3. AFFECT[1].

impress *noun*
The visible effect made on a surface by pressure.

IMPRESSION.

impressed *adjective*
Emotionally aroused.

AFFECTED[1].

impressible *adjective*
Able to receive and respond to external stimuli.

SENSITIVE.

impression *noun*
1. The visible effect made on a surface by pressure:
   saw the impression of a heavy boot in the sand.
2. Intuitive cognition.
3. *Print.* The entire number of copies of a publication
   printed from a single typesetting: *the third
   impression of a book.*
4. The character projected by someone to the public.

1. *Syns:* impress, imprint, indent,
   indentation, print, stamp.
2. FEELING.
3. *Syn:* printing.

4. IMAGE *noun*.

impressionable *adjective*
Able to receive and respond to external stimuli.

SENSITIVE.

impressionistic *adjective*
Tending to bring something, as a memory, mood, or image, subtly or indirectly to mind.

SUGGESTIVE.

impressive *adjective*
1. Exciting a deep, usu. somber response.
2. Marked by magnificently lavish ceremony and display.

1. AFFECTING.
2. GRAND.

imprint *verb*
To produce a deep impression on.

ENGRAVE.

imprint *noun*
The visible effect made on a surface by pressure.

IMPRESSION.

imprison *verb*
1. To enclose so as to hinder or prohibit escape: *We were imprisoned in the house during the blizzard.*
2. To put in jail.

1. *Syns:* closet, confine, isolate, shut up.

2. JAIL *verb.*

improbable *adjective*
1. Not likely.
2. Not plausible or believable.

1. DOUBTFUL.
2. IMPLAUSIBLE.

improbity *noun*
1. Departure from what is legally, ethically, and morally correct.
2. Lack of integrity.

1. CORRUPTION.

2. DISHONESTY.

impromptu *adjective*
Spoken, performed, or composed with little or no preparation or forethought.

EXTEMPORANEOUS.

impromptu *noun*
Something improvised.

IMPROVISATION.

improper *adjective*
1. Not suited to circumstances: *wore improper attire for church.*

1. *Syns:* inappropriate, inapt, inept, incongruous, malapropos, unapt, unbecoming, unbefitting, unfitting, unseemly, unsuitable. —*Idiom* out of place.
   Near-ants: appropriate, apt, becoming, befitting, felicitous, fitting, opportune, pertinent, suitable, timely.
   Ant: proper.

2. Not in keeping with conventional mores: *nothing improper about going alone; used improper language when drunk.*

2. *Syns:* indecent, indecorous, indelicate, unbecoming, unbefitting, unseemly, untoward. —*Idiom* out of line.

impropriety *noun*
1. The condition of being improper: *the impropriety of speaking one's mind at the wrong time.*

1. *Syns:* inappropriateness, unfitness, unseemliness, unsuitability, unsuitableness.

2. An improper act or statement: *barred from the club after his improprieties at the dance.*

2. *Syns:* indecency, indecorum, indelicacy.

improve *verb*
1. To advance to a more desirable state: *Practice will improve your golf game.*
2. To regain one's health.

1. *Syns:* ameliorate, amend, better[1], help, meliorate, upgrade.
2. RECOVER.

improvement *noun*
1. Something that improves: *made improvements in the working conditions.*
2. Steady improvement, as of an individual or a society.

1. *Syns:* amelioration, amendment, betterment, melioration, upgrading.
2. PROGRESS *noun.*

improvident *adjective*
1. Reckless esp. in the use of material resources: *ended his life as a pauper due to his improvident lifestyle.*
2. Not wise.

1. *Syns:* thriftless, unthrifty.

2. UNWISE.

improvisation *noun*
Something improvised: *The President's speech to Congress was a skillful improvisation.*

Syns: ad-lib (*Informal*), extemporization, impromptu.

improvise *verb*
To compose or recite without preparation: *He had to improvise the monologue on camera.*

Syns: ad-lib (*Informal*), extemporize, fake (*Slang*), make up. —*Idiom* wing it.

improvised *adjective*
Spoken, performed, or composed with little or no preparation or forethought.

EXTEMPORANEOUS.

imprudent *adjective*
Not wise.

UNWISE.

impudence also **impudency** *noun*
The state or quality of being impudent: *made to apologize for his impudence.*

Syns: audacity, boldness, brazenness, cheek, disrespect, effrontery, forwardness, gall[2], impertinence, insolence (*also* insolency), nerve (*Informal*), rudeness, sauce (*Informal*), sauciness.

impudency *noun*

SEE **impudence.**

impudent *adjective*
Rude and disrespectful: *was reproved for being impudent; made an impudent remark; an impudent child who never obeyed.*

Syns: audacious, bold, boldacious (*Brit. Regional*), boldfaced, brazen, cheeky, contumelious, facy (*Brit. Regional*), flip (*Informal*), forward, fresh (*Informal*), impertinent, insolent, malapert, nervy (*Informal*), pert, presumptuous, sassy, saucy, smart, smart-alecky (*Informal*), wise[1].
Near-syns: arrogant, brash, discourteous, disdainful, disrespectful, impolite, rude, uncivil.
Near-ants: courteous, polite.
Ant: respectful.

impulse *noun*
1. An impulsive, often illogical turn of mind.
2. Something that causes and encourages a given response.

1. FANCY *noun.*
2. STIMULUS.

impulsive *adjective*
1. Lacking due thought or consideration.
2. Characterized by unthinking boldness and haste.
3. Acting or happening without apparent forethought, prompting, or planning.

1. PRECIPITATE *adjective.*
2. RASH[1].
3. SPONTANEOUS.

impure *adjective*
1. Ceremonially or religiously unfit: *communion vessels made impure by vandalism.*
2. Not chaste or moral: *confessed to thinking impure thoughts.*
3. In a natural state and still not prepared for use.
4. Mixed with other substances: *impure gold.*

1. *Syns:* contaminated, defiled, desecrated, polluted, unclean.
2. *Syns:* immoral, unchaste, unclean, uncleanly.
3. CRUDE.
4. *Syns:* adulterated, alloyed, degraded.

impurity *noun*
1. Impure condition: *Smog increases the impurity of the air.*
2. One that contaminates.

1. *Syns:* dirtiness, foulness, pollution, uncleanness, unwholesomeness.
2. CONTAMINANT.

imputation *noun*
1. A charging of someone with a misdeed.
2. The act of attributing.

1. ACCUSATION.
2. ATTRIBUTION.

impute *verb*
1. To regard as belonging to or resulting from another.
2. To ascribe (a misdeed, error, etc.) to.

1. ATTRIBUTE *verb.*
2. FIX *verb.*

in *adjective*
Slang. Being or in accordance with the current fashion.

FASHIONABLE.

inability *noun*
Lack of ability or capacity: *has a real inability to follow a diet.*

Syns: incapability, incapacity, powerlessness.

inaccessible *adjective*
1. Unable to be reached: *His house is distant and inaccessible.*
2. Not accessible or handy.

1. *Syns:* unapproachable, unattainable, unreachable. —*Idioms* beyond reach, out of the way.
2. INCONVENIENT.

inaccurate *adjective*
1. Containing an error or errors.
2. Devoid of truth.

1. ERRONEOUS.
2. FALSE.

inaction *noun*
A lack of action or activity: *Danger forced him out of his inaction.*

Syns: idleness, inactivity, inertness, lethargy, stagnation, torpor.

inactive *adjective*
1. Marked by a lack of action or activity: *an inactive volcano; an invalid leading an inactive life.*
2. In a state of temporary inactivity.
3. Not occupied or put to use.

1. *Syns:* idle, inert, inoperative.

2. SLEEPING.
3. IDLE *adjective.*

inactivity *noun*
A lack of action or activity.

INACTION.

inadequacy *noun*
The condition or state of being incapable of accomplishing or effecting anything.

INEFFECTUALITY.

inadequate *adjective*
1. Lacking capability: *felt inadequate to the task.*

2. Not enough to meet a demand or requirement.
3. Not capable of accomplishing anything.

1. *Syns:* incapable, incompetent, unequal, unfit, unqualified.
2. INSUFFICIENT.
3. INEFFECTUAL.

inadmissible *adjective*
Arousing disapproval.

OBJECTIONABLE.

inadvertent *adjective*
1. Occurring unexpectedly.
2. Not intended.

1. ACCIDENTAL *adjective.*
2. UNINTENTIONAL.

inalterable *adjective*
Incapable of changing or being modified.

INFLEXIBLE.

inane *adjective*
Lacking the qualities requisite for spiritedness and originality.

INSIPID.

inaneness *noun*
The state or quality of being insipid.

INSIPIDITY.

inanity *noun*
The state or quality of being insipid.

INSIPIDITY.

inapplicable *adjective*
Not relevant or pertinent to the subject; not applicable.

IRRELEVANT.

inappreciable *adjective*
Incapable of being apprehended by the mind or the senses.

IMPERCEPTIBLE.

inappropriate *adjective*
1. Not suited to a given purpose.
2. Not suited to circumstances.
3. Characterized by inappropriateness and gracelessness, esp. in expression.

1. UNFIT *adjective.*
2. IMPROPER.
3. UNFORTUNATE *adjective.*

inappropriateness *noun*
The condition of being improper.

IMPROPRIETY.

inapt *adjective*
1. Not suited to circumstances.
2. Not suited to a given purpose.
3. Lacking the qualities, as efficiency or skill, required to produce desired results.

1. IMPROPER.
2. UNFIT *adjective.*
3. INEFFICIENT.

inarguable *adjective*
Established beyond a doubt.   CERTAIN.

inarticulate *adjective*
Lacking the power or faculty of speech.   DUMB.

inattentive *adjective*
So lost in thought as to be unaware of one's   ABSENT-MINDED.
surroundings.

inaugural *noun*
The act or process of formally admitting a person to   INITIATION.
membership or office.

inaugurate *verb*
1. To go about the initial step in doing (something).   **1.** START *verb*.
2. To bring into currency, use, fashion, or practice.   **2.** INTRODUCE.
3. To admit formally into membership or office, as with **3.** INITIATE *verb*.
   ritual.

inauguration *noun*
1. The act or process of bringing or being brought into **1.** BEGINNING *noun*.
   existence.
2. The act or process of formally admitting a person to **2.** INITIATION.
   membership or office.

inauspicious *adjective*
Bringing, predicting, or characterized by misfortune.   BAD.

inborn *adjective*
1. Forming an essential element.   **1.** BUILT-IN.
2. Of or arising from the most basic structure of an   **2.** CONSTITUTIONAL *adjective*.
   individual.
3. Possessed at birth.   **3.** INNATE.

inbred *adjective*
1. Forming an essential element.   **1.** BUILT-IN.
2. Of or arising from the most basic structure of an   **2.** CONSTITUTIONAL *adjective*.
   individual.

incalculable *adjective*
Too great to be calculated: *an incalculable number of*   **Syns:** countless, immeasurable,
mosquitoes.   incomputable, inestimable, infinite,
                                                innumerable, measureless, uncountable.
                                                Near-syns: boundless, enormous, limitless,
                                                vast.
                                                Ant: infinitesimal.

incandesce *verb*
1. To emit a bright light.   **1.** BEAM *verb*.
2. To shine brightly and steadily but without a flame.   **2.** GLOW *verb*.

incandescent *adjective*
Giving off or reflecting light readily or in large   BRIGHT.
amounts.

incapability *noun*
1. The condition or state of being incapable of   **1.** INEFFECTUALITY.
   accomplishing or effecting anything.
2. Lack of ability or capacity.   **2.** INABILITY.

incapable *adjective*
1. Unable to manage for oneself.   **1.** HELPLESS.
2. Lacking capability.   **2.** INADEQUATE.
3. Lacking the qualities, as efficiency or skill, required **3.** INEFFICIENT.
   to produce desired results.

incapacitate *verb*
To render powerless or motionless by inflicting severe   DISABLE.
injury.

incapacity *noun*
Lack of ability or capacity.   INABILITY.

incarcerate *verb*
To put in jail.   JAIL *verb*.

incarnate *verb*
To represent (an abstraction) in or as if in bodily form.   EMBODY.

incarnation *noun*
A physical entity typifying an abstraction.   EMBODIMENT.

incautious *adjective*
Lacking or showing a lack of a sense of responsibility.   IRRESPONSIBLE.

incense¹ *verb*
To cause to feel or show anger.   ANGER *verb*.

incense² *noun*
Excessive, ingratiating praise.   FLATTERY.

incensed *adjective*
Feeling or showing anger.   ANGRY.

incentive *noun*
Something that causes and encourages a given   STIMULUS.
response.

inception *noun*
1. The initial stage of a developmental process.   **1.** BIRTH *noun*.
2. The act or process of bringing or being brought into   **2.** BEGINNING *noun*.
   existence.

inceptive *adjective*
Indicating the start of something.   BEGINNING *adjective*.

incertitude *noun*
A lack of conviction or certainty.   DOUBT *noun*.

incessant *adjective*
Existing or occurring without interruption or end.   CONTINUAL.

inch *verb*
To advance slowly.   CRAWL *verb*.

inchoate *adjective*
Having no distinct shape.   SHAPELESS.

incident *noun*
1. Something that happens.   **1.** CIRCUMSTANCE.
2. Something significant that happens.   **2.** EVENT.

incident *adjective*
Archaic. Not part of the real or essential nature of a   ACCIDENTAL *adjective*.
thing.

incidental *adjective*
Not part of the real or essential nature of a thing.   ACCIDENTAL *adjective*.

incise *verb*
1. To penetrate with a sharp edge.   **1.** CUT *verb*.
2. To cut (a design or inscription) into a hard surface,   **2.** ENGRAVE.
   esp. for printing.

incision *noun*
The result of cutting.   CUT *noun*.

incisive *adjective*
1. Having or suggesting keen, discerning intellect: *an*   **1.** *Syns:* acute, biting, clear-cut,
   incisive analysis of the problem.   penetrating, perceptive, probing, sharp,
   shrewd, trenchant.
   Near-ants: dull, slow; bloated, diffuse,
   prolix, verbose, windy.
   Ant: unincisive.

2. So sharp as to cause mental pain.   **2.** BITING.

incisiveness *noun*
A cutting quality.   EDGE *noun*.

incitation *noun*
Something that incites esp. a violent response.   STIMULUS.

incite *verb*
To stir to action or feeling.   PROVOKE.

incitement *noun*
Something that incites esp. a violent response.   STIMULUS.

incivility *noun*
Lack of proper respect.   DISRESPECT.

inclination *noun*
  1. Deviation from a particular direction: *an inclination of 45° from the horizontal.*
  2. An innate capability.
  3. A liking or personal preference for something.

  1. **Syns:** cant[1], gradient, incline, slope, slant, tilt.
  2. TALENT.
  3. TASTE *noun.*

incline *verb*
  1. To depart or cause to depart from true vertical or horizontal: *The flagpole inclines toward the roof.*
  2. To influence or be influenced in a certain direction.
  3. To have a tendency or inclination.

  1. **Syns:** cant[1], heel[2], lean[1], list[2], rake[2], slant, slope, tilt, tip[2].
  2. DISPOSE.
  3. TEND[1].

  incline *noun*
  Deviation from a particular direction.

  INCLINATION.

inclined *adjective*
  1. Departing from true vertical or horizontal: *an inclined plane.*
  2. Having or showing a tendency or likelihood: *inclined to take offense easily.*
  3. Disposed to accept or agree.

  1. **Syns:** canted, pitched, sloped, sloping, tilted, tilting, tipped.
  2. **Syns:** apt, disposed, given, liable, likely, prone, susceptible.
  3. WILLING.

include *verb*
  To have as an integral part.

  CONTAIN.

inclusive *adjective*
  Covering a wide scope.

  GENERAL.

incomer *noun*
  One that arrives.

  ARRIVAL.

incommode *verb*
  To cause inconvenience for.

  INCONVENIENCE *verb.*

incommodious *adjective*
  1. Causing self-conscious distress.
  2. Causing difficulty, trouble, or discomfort.

  1. EMBARRASSING.
  2. INCONVENIENT.

incommunicable *adjective*
  1. Tending to keep one's thoughts and emotions to oneself.
  2. That cannot be described.

  1. RESERVED.
  2. UNSPEAKABLE.

incomparable *adjective*
  Without equal or rival.

  UNIQUE.

incompatible *adjective*
  Made up of parts or qualities that are disparate or otherwise markedly lacking in consistency.

  INCONGRUOUS.

incompetent *adjective*
  1. Totally incapable of doing a job: *weed out a few incompetent employees.*
  2. Lacking capability.
  3. Lacking the qualities, as efficiency or skill, required to produce desired results.

  1. **Syns:** unfit, unqualified.
  2. INADEQUATE.
  3. INEFFICIENT.

incomplete *adjective*
  Lacking an essential element.

  DEFICIENT.

incompliance or **incompliancy** *noun*
  The quality or state of being stubbornly unyielding.

  OBSTINACY.

incompliancy *noun*

  SEE **incompliance.**

incompliant *adjective*
  Tenaciously unwilling to yield.

  OBSTINATE.

incomprehensible *adjective*
  Incapable of being grasped by the intellect or understanding: *spoke an incomprehensible dialect; a decision that is incomprehensible to me.*

  Syns: impenetrable, unfathomable, uncomprehensible, unintelligible.

incompressible *adjective*
  Unyielding to pressure or force.

  FIRM[1].

incomputable *adjective*
  Too great to be calculated.

  INCALCULABLE.

inconceivable *adjective*
  1. Not plausible or believable.

  1. IMPLAUSIBLE.

2. Not to be believed.

2. INCREDIBLE.

incongruent *adjective*
1. In sharp opposition.
2. Made up of parts or qualities that are disparate or otherwise markedly lacking in consistency.

1. CONFLICTING.
2. INCONGRUOUS.

incongruity *noun*
A marked lack of correspondence or agreement.

GAP.

incongruous *adjective*
1. Made up of parts or qualities that are disparate or otherwise markedly lacking in consistency: *a hodgepodge of incongruous literary styles.*

1. *Syns:* disconsonant, discordant, discrepant, dissonant, incompatible, incongruent, inconsistent.
Near-syns: alien, extraneous, foreign; bizarre, fantastic, grotesque, weird.

2. In sharp opposition.
3. Not suited to circumstances.

2. CONFLICTING.
3. IMPROPER.

inconquerable *adjective*
Incapable of being conquered, overrun, or subjugated.

INVINCIBLE.

inconscient *adjective*
So lost in thought as to be unaware of one's surroundings.

ABSENT-MINDED.

inconscious *adjective*
Lacking consciousness.

UNCONSCIOUS.

inconsequence *noun*
1. Lack of importance.
2. Contemptible unimportance.

1. INDIFFERENCE.
2. PETTINESS.

inconsequent *adjective*
Contemptibly unimportant.

PETTY.

inconsequential *adjective*
1. Not of great importance.
2. Contemptibly unimportant.

1. LITTLE.
2. PETTY.

inconsiderable *adjective*
Contemptibly unimportant.

PETTY.

inconsiderate *adjective*
Devoid of consideration for others' feelings.

THOUGHTLESS.

inconsiderateness *noun*
A lack of consideration for others' feelings.

THOUGHTLESSNESS.

inconsideration *noun*
A lack of consideration for others' feelings.

THOUGHTLESSNESS.

inconsistency *noun*
A marked lack of correspondence or agreement.

GAP.

inconsistent *adjective*
1. Following no predictable pattern.
2. In sharp opposition.
3. Made up of parts or qualities that are disparate or otherwise markedly lacking in consistency.

1. CAPRICIOUS.
2. CONFLICTING.
3. INCONGRUOUS.

inconsonant *adjective*
Devoid of harmony and accord.

INHARMONIOUS.

inconspicuous *adjective*
Not readily noticed or seen: *an inconspicuous flaw; a disgraced President who lived an inconspicuous life as a private citizen.*

Syns: obscure, unconspicuous, unnoticeable, unobtrusive. —*Idiom* having (or keeping) a low profile.
Near-ants: apparent, bold, distinct, noticeable, prominent, showy, striking.
Ant: conspicuous.

inconstant *adjective*
Following no predictable pattern.

CAPRICIOUS.

incontestable *adjective*
Established beyond a doubt.

CERTAIN.

incontinence *noun*
A complete surrender of inhibitions.

ABANDON *noun.*

incontinent *adjective*
Lacking in moral restraint. ABANDONED.

incontrovertible *adjective*
Established beyond a doubt. CERTAIN.

inconvenience *noun*
1. The state or quality of being inconvenient: *the inconvenience caused by poor lighting.*
2. Something that causes difficulty, trouble, or lack of ease: *Rising before dawn was an inconvenience.*

1. *Syns:* discomfort, inconveniency, trouble.
2. *Syn:* discomfort.

inconvenience *verb*
To cause inconvenience for: *inconvenienced her by arriving late.*

Syns: discomfort, incommode, put out, trouble.

inconveniency *noun*
The state or quality of being inconvenient. INCONVENIENCE *noun.*

inconvenient *adjective*
1. Not accessible or handy: *an inconvenient location for a shop.*
2. Difficult to handle or manage.
3. Causing difficulty, trouble, or discomfort: *Being without modern plumbing was inconvenient.*

4. Not occurring at a favorable time: *an inconvenient appointment.*

1. *Syns:* inaccessible, unhandy.
2. AWKWARD.
3. *Syns:* difficult, disadvantageous, discomforting, incommodious, troublesome.
4. *Syns:* ill-timed, inopportune, untimely.

incorporate *verb*
1. To construct or include as an integral or permanent part.
2. To make a part of a united whole.

1. BUILD IN at **build.**
2. EMBODY.

incorporated *adjective*
Constructed as a nondetachable part of a larger unit. BUILT-IN.

incorporeal *adjective*
Having no body, form, or substance. IMMATERIAL.

incorrect *adjective*
1. Containing an error or errors.
2. Devoid of truth.

1. ERRONEOUS.
2. FALSE.

incorruptibility also **incorruptibleness** *noun*
The quality of being honest. HONESTY.

incorruptible *adjective*
Having or marked by uprightness in principle and action. HONEST.

incorruptibleness *noun* SEE **incorruptibility.**

increase *verb*
1. To make or become greater or larger: *increased her income; difficulties that seemed to increase daily.*

1. *Syns:* aggrandize, amplify, augment, beef up (*Slang*), build up, enlarge, expand, extend, grow, magnify, mount, multiply, run up, snowball, swell, upsurge, wax.

2. To achieve an increment of gradually.
3. To become greater in number, amount, or intensity.

2. GAIN *verb.*
3. RISE *verb.*

increase *noun*
1. The act of increasing or rising: *seasonal increases in sales; property values showing an increase; an increase in enemy infiltration.*
2. The amount by which something is increased: *a wage increase of $50 per month.*
3. The result or product of building up.

1. *Syns:* augmentation, boost, enlargement, growth, hike, jump, multiplication, rise, upswing, upturn.
2. *Syns:* advance, boost, enlargement, hike, increment, jump, raise, rise.
3. BUILD-UP at **build up.**

incredible *adjective*
1. Not to be believed: *an incredible blunder; a weapon of incredible power.*

1. *Syns:* impossible, inconceivable, preposterous, unbelievable, unimaginable, unthinkable. —*Idioms* beyond belief, contrary to all reason.

2. So remarkable as to elicit disbelief.

2. FABULOUS.

3. Not plausible or believable.   **3.** IMPLAUSIBLE.

incredulity *noun*
The refusal or reluctance to believe.   DISBELIEF.

incredulous *adjective*
Refusing or reluctant to believe: *trying to reassure*   **Syns:** disbelieving, leery (*Informal*),
incredulous customers.   questioning, skeptical, unbelieving.

increment *noun*
1. The result or product of building up.   **1.** BUILD-UP at **build up.**
2. The amount by which something is increased.   **2.** INCREASE *noun.*

incriminate *verb*
To make an accusation against.   ACCUSE.

incriminating *adjective*
Containing, relating to, or involving an accusation.   ACCUSATORIAL.

incrimination *noun*
A charging of someone with a misdeed.   ACCUSATION.

incriminative *adjective*
Containing, relating to, or involving an accusation.   ACCUSATORIAL.

incriminator *noun*
One that accuses.   ACCUSER.

inculcate *verb*
1. To fix (an idea) in someone's mind by re-emphasis   **1.** IMPRESS *verb.*
and repetition.
2. To instruct in a body of doctrine or belief.   **2.** INDOCTRINATE.

inculpate *verb*
To make an accusation against.   ACCUSE.

incumbency *noun*
The holding of something, such as a position.   TENURE.

incur *verb*
To take upon oneself.   ASSUME.

incurable *adjective*
Offering no hope or expectation of improvement.   HOPELESS.

incurious *adjective*
Lacking interest in one's surroundings or worldly   DETACHED.
affairs.

incursion *noun*
An act of invading, esp. by military forces.   INVASION.

indebted *adjective*
Owing something, as gratitude or appreciation, to   OBLIGED.
another.

indebtedness *noun*
Something, such as money, owed by one person to   DEBT.
another.

indecency *noun*
1. The quality or state of being obscene.   **1.** OBSCENITY.
2. An improper act or statement.   **2.** IMPROPRIETY.

indecent *adjective*
1. Offensive to accepted standards of decency.   **1.** OBSCENE.
2. Not in keeping with conventional mores.   **2.** IMPROPER.

indecision *noun*
The act or an instance of hesitating.   HESITATION.

indecisive *adjective*
1. Not affording certainty.   **1.** AMBIGUOUS.
2. Given to or exhibiting hesitation.   **2.** HESITANT.

indecisiveness *noun*
The act or an instance of hesitating.   HESITATION.

indecorous *adjective*
Not in keeping with conventional mores.   IMPROPER.

indecorum *noun*
An improper act or statement.   IMPROPRIETY.

indeed *adverb*
1. Not just this but also.   **1.** EVEN[1] *adverb.*

2. In truth.

3. In point of fact.

indefatigable   *adjective*
Having or showing a capacity for protracted effort, regardless of difficulty or frustration.

indefectible   *adjective*
Supremely excellent in quality or nature.

indefensible   *adjective*
Impossible to excuse, pardon, or justify.

indefinable   *adjective*
That cannot be described.

indefinite   *adjective*
1. Lacking precise limits: *plans to be away for an indefinite period.*

2. Marked by lack of firm decision or commitment; of questionable outcome: *vacation plans that are still indefinite.*
3. Not clearly perceived or perceptible.

indefiniteness   *noun*
The quality or state of being ambiguous.

indelible   *adjective*
Permanently resistive to fading.

indelicacy   *noun*
An improper act or statement.

indelicate   *adjective*
1. Not in keeping with conventional mores.
2. Lacking sensitivity and skill in dealing with others.

indemnification   *noun*
Something to make up for loss or damage.

indemnificatory   *adjective*
Affording compensation.

indemnify   *verb*
To give compensation to.

indemnity   *noun*
Something to make up for loss or damage.

indent   *noun*
The visible effect made on a surface by pressure.

indentation   *noun*
The visible effect made on a surface by pressure.

indented   *adjective*
Curving inward.

independence   *noun*
1. The capacity to manage one's own affairs, make one's own judgments, and provide for oneself: *showed her independence by getting a job and moving out.*
2. The condition of being politically free.

independent   *adjective*
1. Free from the influence, guidance, or control of others: *an independent mind.*
2. Having political independence.
3. Able to support oneself financially: *a job that made her independent.*

indescribable   *adjective*
That cannot be described.

indeterminate   *adjective*
1. Not affording certainty.

---

2. REALLY.

3. ACTUALLY.

TIRELESS.

PERFECT *adjective*.

INEXCUSABLE.

UNSPEAKABLE.

1. **Syns:** indeterminate, inexact, undetermined.
Near-syns: broad, general, indistinct, loose, obscure, unclear, undefined, unmeasured, unspecific, vague.
Ant: definite.

2. **Syns:** open, uncertain, undecided, undetermined, unresolved, unsettled, unsure, vague. —*Idiom* up in the air.

3. UNCLEAR.

VAGUENESS.

FAST *adjective*.

IMPROPRIETY.

1. IMPROPER.
2. TACTLESS.

COMPENSATION.

COMPENSATORY.

COMPENSATE.

COMPENSATION.

IMPRESSION.

IMPRESSION.

HOLLOW *adjective*.

1. **Syns:** self-determination, self-reliance, self-sufficiency.

2. FREEDOM.

1. **Syns:** self-contained, self-reliant, self-sufficient.
2. FREE *adjective*.
3. **Syns:** self-sufficient, self-supporting.

UNSPEAKABLE.

1. AMBIGUOUS.

2. Lacking precise limits.

index *noun*
Something visible or evident that gives grounds for
believing in the existence or presence of something else.

indicate *verb*
  1. To give grounds for believing in the existence or
     presence of: *High unemployment usually indicates a
     sick economy.*
  2. To make known or identify, as by signs.
  3. To lead to by logical inference.
  4. To give reason for expecting.
  5. To give a precise indication of, as on a register or
     scale.

indication *noun*
  1. Something visible or evident that gives grounds for
     believing in the existence or presence of something
     else.
  2. A subtle pointing out.
  3. Something that takes the place of words in
     communicating a thought or feeling.
  4. An expressive, meaningful bodily movement.

indicative *adjective*
  1. Serving to designate or indicate.
  2. Serving as a symbol.

indicator *noun*
Something visible or evident that gives grounds for
believing in the existence or presence of something else.

indicatory *adjective*
Serving to designate or indicate.

indict *verb*
To make an accusation against.

indicter *noun*

indictment *noun*
Law. A charging of someone with a misdeed.

indictor also **indicter** *noun*
One that accuses.

indifference *noun*
  1. Lack of importance: *Their approval is a matter of
     complete indifference to me.*
  2. Lack of emotion or interest.

indifferent *adjective*
  1. Free from bias in judgment.
  2. Of moderately good quality but less than excellent.
  3. Without emotion or interest.
  4. Lacking interest in one's surroundings or worldly
     affairs.

indigence also **indigency** *noun*
The condition of being extremely poor.

indigency *noun*

indigenous *adjective*
  1. Existing, born, or produced naturally in a land or
     region: *plants indigenous to the New World; a
     disease indigenous to the Far East.*
  2. Of or arising from the most basic structure of an
     individual.

indigent *adjective*
Having little or no money or wealth.

  indigent *noun*
  An impoverished person.

indigestible *adjective*
Difficult to accept.

---

2. INDEFINITE.

SIGN *noun.*

  1. *Syns:* argue, attest, bespeak, betoken,
     mark, point to, testify, witness.
  2. DESIGNATE.
  3. IMPLY.
  4. PROMISE *verb.*
  5. SHOW *verb.*

  1. SIGN *noun.*

  2. HINT *noun.*
  3. EXPRESSION.

  4. GESTURE *noun.*

  1. DESIGNATIVE.
  2. SYMBOLIC.

SIGN *noun.*

DESIGNATIVE.

ACCUSE.
SEE **indictor.**

ACCUSATION.

ACCUSER.

  1. *Syns:* inconsequence, insignificance
     (*also* insignificancy), unimportance.
  2. APATHY.

  1. FAIR.
  2. ACCEPTABLE.
  3. APATHETIC.
  4. DETACHED.

POVERTY.
SEE **indigence.**

  1. *Syns:* endemic, native.

  2. CONSTITUTIONAL *adjective.*

POOR.

PAUPER *noun.*

BITTER *adjective.*

indignant *adjective*
Feeling or showing anger.   ANGRY.

indignation *noun*
A strong feeling of displeasure or hostility.   ANGER *noun.*

indignity *noun*
An act that offends a person's sense of pride or dignity: ***Syns:*** affront, contumely, despite, insult,
suffered the indignity of being ignored by his own   offense, outrage. —*Idiom* slap in the face.
children.

indirect *adjective*
1. Not taking a direct or straight line or course: *made*   1. ***Syns:*** anfractuous, circuitous, circular,
   an indirect approach to the painful subject.   oblique, roundabout, tortuous.
2. Marked by treachery or deceit.   2. UNDERHAND.

indirection *noun*
Lack of straightforwardness and honesty in action: ***Syns:*** chicanery, craft, craftiness,
achieve a goal by indirection.   deviousness, dishonesty, shadiness,
                                                         slyness, sneakiness, trickery, trickiness,
                                                         underhandedness.

indiscernible *adjective*
Incapable of being apprehended by the mind or the   IMPERCEPTIBLE.
senses.

indiscriminate *adjective*
Having no particular pattern, purpose, organization, or RANDOM.
structure.

indispensable *adjective*
Incapable of being dispensed with.   ESSENTIAL *adjective.*

indisposed *adjective*
1. Not inclined or willing to do or undertake: 1. ***Syns:*** averse, disinclined, loath (*also*
   indisposed to interfere in their quarrel.   loth), reluctant, unwilling.
2. Affected or tending to be affected with minor health 2. SICKLY.
   problems.

indisposition *noun*
1. A minor illness, esp. one of a temporary nature: *lost* 1. ***Syns:*** ailment, complaint, rockiness.
   a day's work because of an indisposition.
2. The condition of being sick.   2. SICKNESS.
3. The state of not being disposed or inclined: *The*   3. ***Syns:*** averseness, disinclination,
   slowness of her response revealed an indisposition to   reluctance, unwillingness.
   help.

indisputable *adjective*
1. In agreement or correspondence with fact.   1. ACTUAL.
2. Established beyond a doubt.   2. CERTAIN.

indistinct *adjective*
Not clearly perceived or perceptible.   UNCLEAR.

indistinctive *adjective*
Without definite or distinctive characteristics.   NEUTRAL.

indistinguishable *adjective*
Incapable of being apprehended by the mind or the   IMPERCEPTIBLE.
senses.

indite *verb*
1. To form letters, characters, or words on a surface   1. WRITE.
   with an instrument.
2. To form by artistic effort.   2. COMPOSE.

individual *adjective*
1. Being or related to a distinct entity: *the individual* 1. ***Syns:*** discrete, separate, single,
   words that make up a sentence.   singular.
2. Serving to identify or set apart an individual or   2. DISTINCTIVE.
   group.
3. Belonging to, pertaining to, or affecting a particular 3. PERSONAL.
   person.
4. Of, relating to, or intended for a distinctive thing or 4. SPECIAL.
   group.

individual *noun*

1. One that exists independently.

2. A member of the human race.

individualism *noun*

The set of behavioral or personal characteristics by which an individual is recognizable.

individualist *adjective*

Concerned with the person rather than with society.

individualistic *adjective*

Concerned with the person rather than with society.

individuality *noun*

1. The quality of being individual: *a slowly emerging sense of individuality.*

2. The set of behavioral or personal characteristics by which an individual is recognizable.

individualize *verb*

To make noticeable or different.

indocile *adjective*

Not submitting to discipline or control.

indoctrinate *verb*

1. To instruct in a body of doctrine or belief: *lectures intended to indoctrinate patriotism in soldiers.*

2. To teach to accept a system of thought uncritically: *prisoners indoctrinated by a system of rewards and punishments.*

indolence *noun*

The quality or state of being lazy.

indolent *adjective*

Resistant to exertion and activity.

indomitable *adjective*

1. Incapable of being negotiated or overcome.

2. Not submitting to discipline or control.

indubitable *adjective*

1. Established beyond a doubt.

2. Not counterfeit or copied.

induce *verb*

1. To succeed in causing (a person) to act in a certain way.

2. To give rise to a particular development.

3. To be the cause of.

inducement *noun*

1. A tendency to cause or bring on.

2. Something that attracts, esp. with the promise of pleasure or reward.

induct *verb*

1. To enroll compulsorily in military service.

2. To admit formally into membership or office, as with ritual.

induction *noun*

1. Compulsory enrollment in military service.

2. The act or process of formally admitting a person to membership or office.

inductive *adjective*

Prior to or preparing for the main matter, action, or business.

indulge *verb*

1. To treat with indulgence and often overtender care.

2. To involve oneself in (an activity).

3. To grant or have what is demanded by (a need or desire).

4. To comply with the wishes or ideas of (another).

5. To take extravagant pleasure.

---

1. THING.

2. HUMAN BEING.

IDENTITY.

EGOCENTRIC *adjective.*

EGOCENTRIC *adjective.*

1. *Syns:* discreteness, distinctiveness, particularity, separateness, singularity.

2. IDENTITY.

DISTINGUISH.

UNRULY.

1. *Syns:* drill, inculcate, instill.

2. *Syns:* brainwash, propagandize.

LAZINESS.

LAZY *adjective.*

1. INSUPERABLE.

2. UNRULY.

1. CERTAIN.

2. AUTHENTIC.

1. PERSUADE.

2. GENERATE.

3. CAUSE *verb.*

1. INVITATION.

2. LURE *noun.*

1. DRAFT *verb.*

2. INITIATE *verb.*

1. DRAFT *noun.*

2. INITIATION.

PRELIMINARY.

1. BABY *verb.*

2. PARTICIPATE.

3. SATISFY.

4. HUMOR *verb.*

5. LUXURIATE.

indulgence *noun*
1. A kindly act.
2. Forbearing or lenient treatment.
3. An act requiring special generosity.

1. FAVOR *noun.*
2. TOLERANCE.
3. COURTESY.

indulgent *adjective*
1. Not strict or severe.
2. Ready to do favors for another.

1. TOLERANT.
2. OBLIGING.

indurate *verb*
1. To make resistant to hardship, esp. through continued exposure.
2. To make or become physically hard.

1. HARDEN.
2. HARDEN.

industrious *adjective*
Characterized by steady attention and effort.

DILIGENT.

industriousness *noun*
Steady attention and effort, as to one's occupation.

DILIGENCE.

industry *noun*
1. Commercial, industrial, or professional activity in general.
2. Steady attention and effort, as to one's occupation.

1. BUSINESS.
2. DILIGENCE.

indwelling *adjective*
Of or arising from the most basic structure of an individual.

CONSTITUTIONAL *adjective.*

inebriate *verb*
To make drunk: *a brandy that inebriates with one sip.*

Syn: intoxicate.

inebriate *adjective*
Intoxicated with alcoholic liquor.

DRUNK *adjective.*

inebriate *noun*
A person who is habitually drunk.

DRUNKARD.

inebriated *adjective*
Intoxicated with alcoholic liquor.

DRUNK *adjective.*

inebriation *noun*
The condition of being intoxicated with alcoholic liquor.

DRUNKENNESS.

inebriety *noun*
The condition of being intoxicated with alcoholic liquor.

DRUNKENNESS.

ineffable *adjective*
That cannot be described.

UNSPEAKABLE.

ineffective *adjective*
1. Not having the desired effect.
2. Having no useful result.

1. INEFFECTUAL.
2. FUTILE.

ineffectiveness *noun*
1. The condition or quality of being useless or ineffective.
2. The condition or state of being incapable of accomplishing or effecting anything.

1. FUTILITY.
2. INEFFECTUALITY.

ineffectual *adjective*
1. Not having the desired effect: *an ineffectual remedy for inflation.*
2. Having no useful purpose.
3. Having no useful result.
4. Not capable of accomplishing anything: *an ineffectual leader.*

1. *Syns:* ineffective, inefficacious, inefficient.
2. USELESS.
3. FUTILE.
4. *Syns:* impotent, inadequate, powerless, weak.

ineffectuality *noun*
1. The condition or state of being incapable of accomplishing or effecting anything: *showed her ineffectuality in getting the cooperation of the community.*
2. The condition or quality of being useless or ineffective.

1. *Syns:* impotence, inadequacy, incapability, ineffectiveness, ineffectualness, inefficacy, powerlessness.
2. FUTILITY.

ineffectualness *noun*
1. The condition or quality of being useless or ineffective.

1. FUTILITY.

2. The condition or state of being incapable of accomplishing or effecting anything.

2. INEFFECTUALITY.

inefficacious *adjective*
Not having the desired effect.

INEFFECTUAL.

inefficacy *noun*
1. The condition or state of being incapable of accomplishing or effecting anything.

1. INEFFECTUALITY.

2. The condition or quality of being useless or ineffective.

2. FUTILITY.

inefficient *adjective*
1. Lacking the qualities, as efficiency or skill, required to produce desired results: *inefficient workers*.

1. **Syns:** inapt, incapable, incompetent, inept, inexpert, unapt, unskilled, unskillful, unworkmanlike.

2. Not having the desired effect.

2. INEFFECTUAL.

inelastic *adjective*
Not changing shape or bending.

RIGID.

inelegant *adjective*
Lacking style and good taste.

TACKY².

inenarrable *adjective*
That cannot be described.

UNSPEAKABLE.

inept *adjective*
1. Not suited to circumstances.
2. Lacking dexterity and grace in physical movement.
3. Lacking the qualities, as efficiency or skill, required to produce desired results.
4. Clumsily lacking in the ability to do or perform.
5. Characterized by inappropriateness and gracelessness, esp. in expression.

1. IMPROPER.
2. AWKWARD.
3. INEFFICIENT.

4. UNSKILLFUL.
5. UNFORTUNATE *adjective*.

inequality *noun*
1. The condition or fact of being unequal, as in age, rank, or degree: *the inequality between the rich and the poor.*

1. **Syns:** disparity, disproportion.

2. Lack of smoothness or regularity.

2. IRREGULARITY.

inequitable *adjective*
Not fair, right, or just.

UNFAIR.

inequitableness *noun*
Lack of justice.

INJUSTICE.

inequity *noun*
Lack of justice.

INJUSTICE.

inert *adjective*
Marked by a lack of action or activity.

INACTIVE.

inertness *noun*
A lack of action or activity.

INACTION.

inescapable *adjective*
Sure to happen.

CERTAIN.

inessential *adjective*
Not necessary.

UNNECESSARY.

inestimable *adjective*
1. Too great to be calculated.
2. Of great value.

1. INCALCULABLE.
2. VALUABLE.

inevitable *adjective*
Sure to happen.

CERTAIN.

inexact *adjective*
1. Lacking literal exactness.
2. Lacking precise limits.

1. LOOSE *adjective*.
2. INDEFINITE.

inexcusable *adjective*
Impossible to excuse, pardon, or justify: *an inexcusable insult.*

Syns: indefensible, unforgivable, unjustifiable, unpardonable.

inexhaustibility *noun*
The state or quality of being infinite.

INFINITY.

inexhaustible   *adjective*
Having or showing a capacity for protracted effort, regardless of difficulty or frustration.

TIRELESS.

inexorable   *adjective*
1. Firmly, often unreasonably immovable in purpose or will.
2. Having or showing uncompromising determination or resolution in purpose or action.

1. STUBBORN.

2. GRIM.

inexpensive   *adjective*
Low in price.

CHEAP.

inexperience   *noun*
Lack of experience and the knowledge gained from it: *will make allowances for her inexperience.*

Syns: greenness, inexpertness.

inexperienced   *adjective*
Lacking experience and the knowledge gained from it: *Inexperienced employees are seldom paid more than the minimum wage.*

Syns: green, inexpert, raw, unpracticed, unseasoned, untried, unversed.

inexpert   *adjective*
1. Displaying a lack of knowledge or skill.
2. Lacking the qualities, as efficiency or skill, required to produce desired results.
3. Lacking experience and the knowledge gained from it.

1. CRUDE.
2. INEFFICIENT.

3. INEXPERIENCED.

inexpertness   *noun*
Lack of experience and the knowledge gained from it.

INEXPERIENCE.

inexplicable   *adjective*
That cannot be explained: *an inexplicable burst of anger.*

Syns: unaccountable, unexplainable.

inexpressible   *adjective*
That cannot be described.

UNSPEAKABLE.

inexpressive   *adjective*
Lacking expression.

EXPRESSIONLESS.

inextricably   *adverb*
Without regard to desire or inclination.

HELPLESSLY.

infallible   *adjective*
Such as could not possibly fail or disappoint.

SURE.

infamous   *adjective*
1. Deserving strong condemnation: *guilty of an infamous crime.*

2. Known widely and unfavorably.

1. *Syns:* abhorrent, despicable, detestable, foul, perfidious, reprehensible, shocking, vile.
2. NOTORIOUS.

infamy   *noun*
1. The condition of being infamous: *President Roosevelt said that December 7, 1941, was a day that would live in infamy.*
2. Unfavorable, usu. unsavory renown.

1. *Syns:* disgracefulness, dishonorableness, odiousness, perfidy, shamefulness, villainy, wickedness.
2. NOTORIETY.

infancy   *noun*
Law. The state or period of being under legal age.

MINORITY.

infant   *noun*
1. A very young child.
2. *Law.* One who is not yet legally of age.

1. BABY *noun.*
2. MINOR *noun.*

infant   *adjective*
Being in an early period of growth or development.

YOUNG *adjective.*

infantile   *adjective*
1. Of or like a baby.
2. Of or characteristic of a child, esp. in immaturity.

1. BABYISH.
2. CHILDISH.

infatuated   *adjective*
Affected with intense romantic attraction: *a prince infatuated with a chorus girl.*

Syns: beguiled, bewitched, captivated, enamored, gone (*Slang*), mashed (*Slang*), smitten.

infatuation *noun*
An extravagant, short-lived romantic attachment: *an infatuation with her geography professor.*

infect *verb*
1. To have a destructive effect on.
2. To make morally impure.

infectious *adjective*
Capable of transmission by infection.

infecund *adjective*
Unable to produce offspring.

infecundity *noun*
The state or condition of being unable to reproduce sexually.

infelicitous *adjective*
Characterized by inappropriateness and gracelessness, esp. in expression.

infer *verb*
1. To draw a conclusion from evidence or reasoning: *Am I to infer that you're not going?*
2. To draw an inference on the basis of inconclusive evidence or insufficient information.

inference *noun*
A position arrived at by reasoning from premises or general principles.

inferior *adjective*
1. Of mediocre quality: *The inferior cloth quickly disintegrated.*

2. Of subordinate standing or importance.

inferior *noun*
One belonging to a lower class or rank.

infernal *adjective*
1. So annoying or detestable as to deserve condemnation.
2. Perversely bad, cruel, or wicked.

inferred *adjective*
1. Conveyed indirectly without words or speech.
2. Based on inference, not fact.

infertile *adjective*
1. Unable to produce offspring.
2. Lacking or unable to produce growing plants or crops.

infertility *noun*
The state or condition of being unable to reproduce sexually.

infidelity *noun*
Betrayal, esp. of a moral obligation.

infiltrate *verb*
To introduce gradually and slyly.

infinite *adjective*
1. Too great to be calculated.
2. Without beginning or end.
3. Having no ends or limits.

Near-syns: bedeviled, dotty, enraptured, enthralled, fixated, obsessed, possessed.

Syns: béguin (*French*), crush (*Informal*), passion.

1. POISON *verb*.
2. TAINT *verb*.

COMMUNICABLE.

BARREN *adjective*.

STERILITY.

UNFORTUNATE *adjective*.

1. *Syns:* conclude, deduce, deduct, draw, gather, judge.
2. GUESS *verb*.

DEDUCTION.

1. *Syns:* common, low-grade, low-quality, mean^2, miserable, second-class, second-rate, substandard.
Near-syns: average, base, fair, hack, mediocre, middling (*Informal*), ordinary, shoddy, worthless; cheap, inexpensive.
Ant: superior.
2. MINOR *adjective*.

SUBORDINATE *noun*.

1. DAMNED.
2. FIENDISH.

1. IMPLICIT.
2. PRESUMPTIVE.

1. BARREN *adjective*.
2. BARREN *adjective*.

STERILITY.

FAITHLESSNESS.

INSINUATE.

1. INCALCULABLE.
2. ETERNAL.
3. ENDLESS.

infiniteness *noun*
The state or quality of being infinite.   INFINITY.

infinitesimal *adjective*
So minute as to be undiscernible.   IMPERCEPTIBLE.

infinity *noun*
1. The state or quality of being infinite: *Nature's*   1. **Syns:** boundlessness, inexhaustibility,
   variety is close to infinity.   infiniteness, limitlessness.
2. The totality of time without beginning or end.   2. ETERNITY.

infirm *adjective*
1. Not physically strong: *too infirm to resume his daily*   1. **Syns:** decrepit, delicate, feeble, fragile,
   walks.   frail, insubstantial, puny, unsound,
                                                                            unsubstantial, weak, weakly.
2. *Rare.* Lacking stability.   2. INSECURE.

infirmity *noun*
1. The condition of being infirm or physically weak: 1. **Syns:** debilitation, debility, decrepitude,
   Infirmity often comes with old age.   feebleness, fragility, frailty,
                                                                            unsoundness, weakliness, weakness.
2. A pathological condition of mind or body.   2. DISEASE.
3. The condition of being sick.   3. SICKNESS.
4. A liking or personal preference for something.   4. WEAKNESS.

infix *verb*
To implant so deeply as to make change nearly   FIX *verb.*
impossible.

inflame *verb*
1. To cause to become sore or inflamed.   1. IRRITATE.
2. To stir to action or feeling.   2. PROVOKE.

inflamed *adjective*
Full of or marked by extreme anger.   FURIOUS.

inflammation *noun*
An instance of irritating, as of a part of the body.   IRRITATION.

inflate *verb*
To make (something) seem greater than is actually the   EXAGGERATE.
case.

inflated *adjective*
Filled up with or as if with something insubstantial: **Syns:** flatulent, overblown, tumescent,
has a highly inflated ego.   tumid, turgid, windy (*Chiefly Scot.*).
                                                              Near-syns: bombastic, flowery, grandiose,
                                                              ostentatious, pompous, pretentious,
                                                              verbose, wordy.

inflatus *noun*
Divine guidance and motivation imparted directly.   INSPIRATION.

inflection *noun*
A particular vocal quality that indicates some emotion   TONE.
or feeling.

inflexible *adjective*
1. Incapable of changing or being modified: *inflexible*   1. **Syns:** immutable, inalterable,
   standards of performance.   invariable, ironclad, rigid, stiff,
                                                                            unalterable, unchangeable, unpliant,
                                                                            unyielding.
2. Not changing shape or bending.   2. RIGID.
3. Firmly, often unreasonably immovable in purpose or   3. STUBBORN.
   will.

inflict *verb*
1. To cause to undergo or bear, as something   1. **Syns:** impose, play, visit, wreak.
   unwelcome or damaging: *inflicting punishment; a*
   storm that inflicted widespread destruction; inflicted
   an intolerable responsibility on me when he made me
   his executor.
2. To force (another) to accept a burden.   2. IMPOSE.

infliction *noun*
An excessive, unwelcome burden.   IMPOSITION.

influence *noun*
1. The power to produce an effect by indirect means: *a special-interest group with influence on Capitol Hill.*
2. The power or capacity to produce a desired result.

influence *verb*
1. To have an effect or impact upon: *Don't let him influence your decision.*
2. To evoke a usu. strong mental or emotional response from.

influential *adjective*
Having or exercising influence: *one of our more influential citizens.*

infold *verb*

inform *verb*
1. To cause to know about or be aware of: *Inform everyone of the change in schedule. Was he informed of his rights?*
2. To give incriminating information about others, esp. to the authorities: *The thief informed on his accomplice.*

informal *adjective*
1. Not formal or ceremonious: *an informal gathering of close friends; wore informal attire.*
2. Unconstrained by rigid standards.
3. In the style of conversation.

informality *noun*
1. Lack or avoidance of formality: *a candlelight supper served with charming informality.*
2. Freedom from constraint, embarrassment, or awkwardness.

informant *noun*
One who gives incriminating information about others.

information *noun*
1. Knowledge about a specific subject or situation: *gathering information for a biography.*
2. That which is known; the sum of what has been perceived, discovered, or inferred.

informative *adjective*
Serving to educate or inform.

informed *adjective*
1. Provided with information; made aware: *able to give an informed opinion; one of our best-informed officials.*
2. Having an education.

informer *noun*
One who gives incriminating information about others: *He's a paid informer.*

infra *adverb*
At a subsequent time.

infraction *noun*
An act or instance of breaking a law or regulation or of nonfulfillment of an obligation, promise, etc.

infrequent *adjective*
Rarely occurring or appearing: *Our parties are infrequent these days. He is an infrequent visitor.*

---

1. **Syns:** clout (*Informal*), drag (*Slang*), leverage, pull (*Slang*), sway, weight.
2. EFFECT *noun.*

1. **Syns:** bias, prejudice, sway.

2. AFFECT[1].

Syns: consequential, important, powerful, weighty.

SEE **enfold.**

1. **Syns:** acquaint, advise, apprise (*also* apprize) (of), educate, enlighten, notify, tell.
2. **Syns:** fink (*Slang*), rat (*Slang*), sing (*Slang*), snitch (*Slang*), squeal (*Slang*), stool (*Slang*), talk, tattle. —*Idiom* blow the whistle.

1. **Syns:** simple, unceremonious, unpretentious.
2. EASYGOING.
3. CONVERSATIONAL.

1. **Syns:** casualness, naturalness, simplicity, unceremoniousness.
2. EASE *noun.*

INFORMER.

1. **Syns:** data, facts, intelligence.

2. KNOWLEDGE.

EDUCATIONAL.

1. **Syns:** advised, educated, enlightened, instructed, knowledgeable.

2. EDUCATED.

Syns: fink (*Slang*), informant, rat (*Slang*), snitch (*also* snitcher) (*Slang*), squealer (*Slang*), stoolie (*Slang*), stool pigeon (*Slang*), tattler, tattletale, tipster.

LATER *adverb.*

BREACH *noun.*

Syns: occasional, rare, scarce, sporadic, uncommon, unusual. —*Idiom* few and far between.

infrequently *adverb*
At rare intervals: *I now go to Europe infrequently if at all.*

Syns: little, rarely, seldom. —*Idioms* hardly (*or* scarcely) ever, once in a blue moon.

infringement *noun*
An act or instance of breaking a law or regulation or of nonfulfillment of an obligation, promise, etc.

BREACH *noun.*

infuriate *verb*
To cause to feel or show anger.

ANGER *verb.*

infuriated *adjective*
Full of or marked by extreme anger.

FURIOUS.

ingenerate *adjective*
1. Of or arising from the most basic structure of an individual.
2. Possessed at birth.

1. CONSTITUTIONAL *adjective.*

2. INNATE.

ingenerate *verb*
To be the cause of.

CAUSE *verb.*

ingenious *adjective*
1. Characterized by or productive of new things or new ideas.
2. Able to use the means at one's disposal to meet situations effectively.

1. INVENTIVE.

2. RESOURCEFUL.

ingénue *noun*
A guileless, unsophisticated person.

INNOCENT *noun.*

ingenuity *noun*
The power or ability to invent.

INVENTION.

ingenuous *adjective*
Free from guile, cunning, or deceit.

ARTLESS.

ingest *verb*
1. To cause to pass from the mouth into the stomach.
2. To take (food) into the body as nourishment.

1. SWALLOW *verb.*

2. EAT.

ingestion *noun*
An act of swallowing.

SWALLOW *noun.*

ingrain *verb*
To implant so deeply as to make change nearly impossible.

FIX *verb.*

ingrained *adjective*
1. Firmly established by long standing.
2. Of or arising from the most basic structure of an individual.

1. CONFIRMED.
2. CONSTITUTIONAL *adjective.*

ingratiating *adjective*
Purposefully contrived to gain favor.

INSINUATING.

ingratiative *adjective*
Purposefully contrived to gain favor.

INSINUATING.

ingredient *noun*
One of the individual entities contributing to a whole.

ELEMENT.

ingress *verb*
To come or go into (a place).

ENTER.

ingress also **ingression** *noun*
1. The state of being allowed entry.
2. The right to enter or make use of.
3. The act of entering.

1. ADMISSION.
2. ADMISSION.
3. ENTRANCE[1].

ingression *noun*

SEE **ingress.**

ingurgitate *verb*
To swallow (food or drink) greedily or rapidly in large amounts.

GULP *verb.*

inhabit *verb*
To live in (a place): *Nomads inhabited the steppes.*

Syns: habit (*Archaic*), occupy, people, populate.

inhabitable *adjective*
Fit to live in.

LIVABLE.

inhalation *noun*
1. The act of breathing in.   **1.** INSPIRATION.
2. Air breathed in.   **2.** BREATH.

inhale *verb*
To draw air into the lungs in the process of respiration.   BREATHE.

inharmonic also **inharmonical** *adjective*
Characterized by unpleasant discordance of sound.   INHARMONIOUS.

inharmonious *adjective*
1. Characterized by unpleasant discordance of sound: **1.** *Syns:* cacophonous (*also* cacophonic,
   an inharmonious performance by the student band.   cacophonical), discordant, disharmonic,
                                                                    disharmonious, dissonant, inharmonic
                                                                    (*also* inharmonical), rude,
                                                                    unharmonious, unmusical.
2. Devoid of harmony and accord: *He had an*   **2.** *Syns:* discordant, inconsonant,
   inharmonious relationship with his mother.   uncongenial, unharmonious.

inharmony *noun*
A state of disagreement and disharmony.   CONFLICT *noun.*

inhere *verb*
To have as an inherent basis.   CONSIST.

inherent *adjective*
1. Of or arising from the most basic structure of an   **1.** CONSTITUTIONAL *adjective.*
   individual.
2. Forming an essential element.   **2.** BUILT-IN.

inherit *verb*
To receive (property) from one who has died: *inherited*   *Syns:* come into, heir (*Chiefly Regional*).
the farm from his late father.

inheritance *noun*
1. Any special privilege accorded a firstborn.   **1.** BIRTHRIGHT.
2. Something immaterial, as a style or philosophy, that   **2.** HERITAGE.
   is passed from one generation to another.

inherited *adjective*
1. Possessed at birth.   **1.** INNATE.
2. Of or from one's ancestors.   **2.** ANCESTRAL.

inhibit *verb*
1. To refuse to allow.   **1.** FORBID.
2. To check the freedom and spontaneity of.   **2.** CONSTRAIN.
3. To control, restrict, or arrest.   **3.** RESTRAIN.

inhibited *adjective*
Deficient in or lacking sexual desire.   FRIGID.

inhospitable *adjective*
So disagreeably austere as to discourage approach.   FORBIDDING.

inhospitableness *noun*
Lack of cordiality and hospitableness.   UNWELCOME *noun.*

inhospitality *noun*
Lack of cordiality and hospitableness.   UNWELCOME *noun.*

inhuman *adjective*
Showing or suggesting a disposition to be violently   FIERCE.
destructive without scruple or restraint.

inhumanity *noun*
A cruel act or an instance of cruel behavior.   CRUELTY.

inhumation *noun*
An act of placing a body in a grave or tomb.   BURIAL.

inhume *verb*
To place (a corpse) in or as if in a grave.   BURY.

inimicable *adjective*
Feeling or showing unfriendliness.   HOSTILE.

inimical *adjective*
Feeling or showing unfriendliness.   HOSTILE.

iniquitous *adjective*
Morally objectionable.   EVIL *adjective.*

iniquity *noun*
1. A wicked act.
2. *Scot. Law.* Lack of justice.

1. CRIME.
2. INJUSTICE.

initial *adjective*
1. Indicating the start of something.
2. At or near the start of a period, development, or series.
3. Preceding all others in time.

1. BEGINNING *adjective.*
2. EARLY *adjective.*
3. FIRST *adjective.*

initiate *verb*
1. To admit formally into membership or office, as with ritual: *initiated pledges into the fraternity.*
2. To go about the initial step in doing (something).
3. To bring into currency, use, fashion, or practice.

1. *Syns:* inaugurate, induct, install, instate, invest.
2. START *verb.*
3. INTRODUCE.

initiate *noun*
One who is just starting to learn or do something.

BEGINNER.

initiation *noun*
1. The act or process of formally admitting a person to membership or office: *the initiation of new sorority pledges.*
2. The act or process of bringing or being brought into existence.

1. *Syns:* inaugural, inauguration, induction, installation, instatement, investiture.
2. BEGINNING *noun.*

initiative *noun*
The wish, power, and ability to begin and follow through with a plan or task.

AMBITION.

injudicious *adjective*
Not wise.

UNWISE.

injunction *noun*
An authoritative indication to be obeyed.

COMMAND *noun.*

injure *verb*
1. To spoil the soundness or perfection of: *a President who injured his credibility by lying.*

2. To cause physical damage to.

1. *Syns:* blemish, damage, disserve, harm, hurt, impair, mar, prejudice, tarnish, vitiate.
2. HURT *verb.*

injurious *adjective*
1. Causing harm or injury.
2. Serving to corrupt.
3. Damaging to the reputation.

1. HARMFUL.
2. CORRUPTIVE.
3. LIBELOUS.

injury *noun*
1. The action or result of inflicting loss or pain.
2. An act that is not just.

1. HARM *noun.*
2. INJUSTICE.

injust *adjective*
Obs. Not fair, right, or just.

UNFAIR.

injustice *noun*
1. Lack of justice: *an attorney general who saw injustice and tried to remedy it.*

2. An act that is not just: *By lying he did himself and others an injustice.*

1. *Syns:* inequitableness, inequity, iniquity (*Scot. Law*), unfairness, unjustness, wrong.
2. *Syns:* disservice, injury, wrong.
—*Idiom* raw deal.

inkhorn *adjective*
Characterized by a narrow concern for book learning and formal rules, without knowledge or experience of practical matters.

PEDANTIC.

inkling *noun*
A subtle quality underlying or felt to underlie a situation, action, or person.

HINT *noun.*

inky *adjective*
1. Of the darkest achromatic visual value.
2. Having no light.

1. BLACK.
2. BLACK.

inlying *adjective*
Located farther in.

INNER.

innate *adjective*
1. Possessed at birth: *innate cardiovascular abnormalities; innate talent.*

2. Of or arising from the most basic structure of an individual.
3. Forming an essential element.

innative *adjective*
Possessed at birth.

inner *adjective*
1. Located farther in: *an inner room.*

2. Of, pertaining to, or arising from one's mental or spiritual being: *has inner conflicts.*

3. Being closer to a center of power and influence: *the inner circles of the CIA.*

innerve *verb*
To stir to action or feeling.

innings *noun*
A limited, often assigned period of activity, duty, or opportunity.

innocence *noun*
The condition of being uninformed.

innocent *adjective*
1. Free from evil and corruption: *innocent little children.*

2. Free from guilt or blame: *innocent of all charges; innocent parties to the scandal.*

3. Devoid of hurtful qualities.
4. Within, allowed by, or sanctioned by the law.
5. Free from guile, cunning, or deceit.
6. Lacking a desirable element.
7. Not aware or informed.

innocent *noun*
1. A pure, uncorrupted person: *a woman who had the beguiling look of a young innocent.*
2. A guileless, unsophisticated person: *a foreign-policy adviser who was a mere innocent in dealing with the Soviets.*

3. A young person between birth and puberty.
4. One who is just starting to learn or do something.

innocuous *adjective*
1. Devoid of hurtful qualities.
2. Incapable of inflicting injury.
3. Lacking the qualities requisite for spiritedness and originality.

innovation *noun*
A new, unusual thing.

innovative *adjective*
1. Characterized by or productive of new things or new ideas.
2. Showing marked departure from previous practice.

innuendo *noun*
1. A subtle quality underlying or felt to underlie a situation, action, or person.

1. **Syns:** congenital, hereditary, inborn, ingenerate, inherited, innative, native, natural.
2. CONSTITUTIONAL *adjective.*

3. BUILT-IN.

INNATE.

1. **Syns:** inlying, inside, interior, internal, intestine (*Obs.*).
2. **Syns:** gut (*Slang*), interior, internal, intestine, intimate[1], inward, visceral, viscerous.
3. **Syn:** inside (*Slang*).

PROVOKE.

TURN *noun.*

IGNORANCE.

1. **Syns:** angelic (*also* angelical), clean, lily-white, pure, unblemished, undefiled, uncorrupted, unstained, unsullied, untainted, virginal. —*Idiom* pure as the driven snow.
2. **Syns:** blameless, clean (*Slang*), faultless, guiltless, harmless. —*Idiom* in the clear.
3. HARMLESS.
4. LAWFUL.
5. ARTLESS.
6. EMPTY *adjective.*
7. IGNORANT.

1. **Syns:** angel, lamb, virgin.

2. **Syns:** babe (*Slang*), child, ingénue, naive (*also* naïve, naif, naïf), unsophisticate. —*Idiom* babe in the woods.
3. CHILD.
4. BEGINNER.

1. HARMLESS.
2. HARMLESS.
3. INSIPID.

NOVELTY.

1. INVENTIVE.

2. NEW *adjective.*

1. HINT *noun.*

2. An artful, indirect hint.

2. INSINUATION.

innuendo *verb*
To convey an idea by indirect, subtle means.

HINT *verb.*

innumerable *adjective*
Too great to be calculated.

INCALCULABLE.

inobtrusive *adjective*
Not showy or obtrusive.

QUIET.

inoffensive *adjective*
Devoid of hurtful qualities.

HARMLESS.

inoperative *adjective*
Marked by a lack of action or activity.

INACTIVE.

inopportune *adjective*
Not occurring at a favorable time.

INCONVENIENT.

inordinate *adjective*
Exceeding a normal or reasonable limit.

EXCESSIVE.

inquest *noun*
A seeking of knowledge, data, or the truth about something.

INQUIRY.

inquietude *noun*
An uneasy or nervous state.

RESTLESSNESS.

inquire also **enquire** *verb*
1. To go into or through for the purpose of making discoveries or acquiring information.
2. To put a question to (someone).

1. EXPLORE.

2. ASK.

inquirer also **enquirer** *noun*
One who inquires: *avoided reporters and other inquirers.*

Syns: inquisitor, querier, questioner.

inquiring also **enquiring** *adjective*
Eager to acquire knowledge.

CURIOUS.

inquiry also **enquiry** *noun*
1. A seeking of knowledge, data, or the truth about something: *an inquiry as to the cause of the patient's death.*
2. A request for data: *The company receives many inquiries about the cost of books.*

1. *Syns:* delving, inquest, inquisition, investigation, probe, quest.

2. *Syns:* interrogation, interrogatory (*Law*), query, question.

inquisition *noun*
A seeking of knowledge, data, or the truth about something.

INQUIRY.

inquisitive *adjective*
1. Eager to acquire knowledge.
2. Unduly interested in the affairs of others.

1. CURIOUS.
2. CURIOUS.

inquisitiveness *noun*
Mental acquisitiveness.

CURIOSITY.

inquisitor *noun*
1. One who conducts an official inquiry, usu. with no regard for human rights: *The captured spy was tortured by his inquisitors.*
2. One who inquires.

1. *Syns:* interrogator, questioner.

2. INQUIRER.

inquisitorial *adjective*
Unduly interested in the affairs of others.

CURIOUS.

inquisitory *adjective*
Unduly interested in the affairs of others.

CURIOUS.

inroad *noun*
An act of invading, esp. by military forces.

INVASION.

insalubrious *adjective*
Not sustaining or promoting health.

UNWHOLESOME.

insalutary *adjective*
Not sustaining or promoting health.

UNWHOLESOME.

insane *adjective*
1. Afflicted with or exhibiting irrationality and mental unsoundness: *The assassin was diagnosed insane by two psychiatrists.*

1. **Syns:** batty (*Slang*), bedlamite, bonkers (*Slang*), brainsick, buggy (*Slang*), bughouse (*Slang*), bugs (*Slang*), cracked, crackers (*Chiefly Brit. Slang*), cracky (*Chiefly Brit. Slang*), crazed, crazy, cuckoo, daffy (*Informal*), daft, demented, deranged, disordered, distraught, fruity (*Slang*), gaga (*Slang*), loco (*Slang*), loony (*also* luny) (*Informal*), lunatic, mad, maniac, maniacal, mental (*Chiefly Brit.*), mindless, moonstruck (*also* moonstricken), non compos mentis (*Law*), nuts (*Slang*), nutty (*Informal*), off, screwy (*Slang*), touched, unbalanced, unsound, wacky (*also* whacky) (*Slang*), witless, wrong. —*Idioms* around the bend, crazy as a loon, mad as a hatter, not all there, nutty as a fruitcake, off one's rocker, out of one's head (*or* mind), sick in the head, stark raving mad, unsound of mind.

2. So senseless as to be laughable.

2. FOOLISH.

insaneness *noun*
Serious mental illness or disorder impairing a person's capacity to function normally and safely.

INSANITY.

insanity *noun*
1. Serious mental illness or disorder impairing a person's capacity to function normally and safely: *Wild fears and suspicions were the first signs of his approaching insanity.*

1. **Syns:** aberration, alienation, brainsickness, craziness, dementia, derangement, insaneness, lunacy, madness, mania, psychopathy, unbalance.

2. Foolish behavior.

2. FOOLISHNESS.

inscribe *verb*
1. To affix one's signature to.
2. To form letters, characters, or words on a surface with an instrument.
3. To register in or as if in a book.
4. To produce a deep impression on.

1. SIGN *verb*.
2. WRITE.
3. LIST[1] *verb*.
4. ENGRAVE.

insecure *adjective*
1. Inadequately protected: *Without the military police the air base would be insecure.*

1. **Syns:** unguarded, unprotected, unsafe.

2. Lacking stability: *an insecure peace; an insecure ally.*

2. **Syns:** infirm (*Rare*), insubstantial, shaky, tottery, unstable, unsteady, unsure, weak, wobbly.

insecurity *noun*
The quality or condition of being erratic and undependable.

INSTABILITY.

insensate *adjective*
Lacking passion and emotion.

INSENSITIVE.

insensibility *noun*
Lack of emotion or interest.

APATHY.

insensible *adjective*
1. Lacking consciousness.
2. Lacking responsiveness or alertness.
3. Lacking physical feeling or sensitivity.
4. Without emotion or interest.
5. Incapable of being apprehended by the mind or the senses.

1. UNCONSCIOUS.
2. DULL *adjective*.
3. DEAD *adjective*.
4. APATHETIC.
5. IMPERCEPTIBLE.

6. Lacking passion and emotion.

insensitive *adjective*
1. Lacking passion and emotion: *turned an insensitive ear to our pleas.*

2. Lacking physical feeling or sensitivity.
3. Lacking responsiveness or alertness.
4. Not capable of being affected or impressed: *I am totally insensitive to flattery.*

insert *verb*
1. To place on a list or in a record.
2. To put or set into, between, or among another or other things.

insertion *noun*
An item inserted, as in a diary, register, or reference book.

inside *adjective*
1. Located farther in.
2. *Slang.* Being closer to a center of power and influence.
3. Characterized by a close and thorough acquaintance.
4. *Slang.* Known about by very few.

insight *noun*
1. The power to discern the true nature of a person or situation.
2. Deep, thorough, or mature understanding.

insignificance also **insignificancy** *noun*
Lack of importance.

insignificancy *noun*

insignificant *adjective*
Not of great importance.

insincere *adjective*
1. Not being what one purports to be: *insincere flattery; an insincere person not to be trusted.*
2. Not genuine or sincere.

insincerity *noun*
Lack of sincerity: *was shocked by their insincerity.*

insinuate *verb*
1. To introduce gradually and slyly: *A spy has insinuated himself into government circles. She insinuated her beliefs into every policy discussion.*
2. To convey an idea by indirect, subtle means.

insinuating *adjective*
1. Provoking a change of outlook and esp. gradual doubt and suspicion: *made insinuating remarks about his competence.*
2. Purposefully contrived to gain favor: *the insinuating smiles of corporate courtiers.*

insinuation *noun*
An artful, indirect hint: *made ugly insinuations that he had cheated on the exam.*

insinuative *adjective*
Provoking a change of outlook and esp. gradual doubt and suspicion.

insipid *adjective*
1. Lacking the qualities requisite for spiritedness and originality: *an insipid soap opera.*

6. INSENSITIVE.

1. **Syns:** anesthetic, bloodless, dull, hard, insensate, insensible. —*Idiom* as hard as nails.
2. DEAD *adjective*.
3. DULL *adjective*.
4. **Syns:** impassible, impassive, insusceptible, unimpressionable, unsusceptible.

1. POST *verb*.
2. INTRODUCE.

ENTRY.

1. INNER.
2. INNER.
3. INTIMATE[1] *adjective*.
4. CONFIDENTIAL.

1. INSTINCT *noun*.

2. WISDOM.

INDIFFERENCE.
SEE **insignificance**.

LITTLE.

1. **Syns:** ambidextrous, disingenuous, left-handed, mala fide (*Latin*).
2. ARTIFICIAL.

Syns: disingenuity, disingenuousness, uncandor.

1. **Syns:** edge in, foist, infiltrate, wind[2] (into), work (into), worm.

2. HINT *verb*.

1. **Syns:** insinuative, suggestive.

2. **Syns:** ingratiating, ingratiative, saccharine, sugary.

Syn: innuendo.

INSINUATING.

1. **Syns:** banal, bland, driveling, inane, innocuous, jejune, namby-pamby, vapid, washy, waterish, watery, wishy-washy (*Informal*).

2. Lacking an appetizing flavor.

insipidity *noun*
The state or quality of being insipid: *the insipidity of the play; the insipidity of her cooking.*

insipidness *noun*
The state or quality of being insipid.

insist *verb*
1. To take and maintain a stand obstinately: *He still insisted on the truth of his story.*
2. To solicit insistently: *The prime minister insisted that the king abdicate. You insisted upon my going to the party.*

insist on (or **upon**) *verb*
To ask for urgently or insistently.

insistence also **insistency** *noun*
1. The state or quality of being insistent: *The attorney's insistence on learning the truth saved his client.*
2. Urgent solicitation: *We signed this contract only at your insistence.*

insistency *noun*

insistent *adjective*
1. Obstinately maintaining a stand: *insistent denials of all guilt.*
2. Bold and definite in character.

insist on (or **upon**) *verb*

insobriety *noun*
The condition of being intoxicated with alcoholic liquor.

insolence also **insolency** *noun*
1. The state or quality of being impudent.
2. The quality of being arrogant.

insolency *noun*

insolent *adjective*
1. Rude and disrespectful.
2. Overly convinced of one's own superiority and importance.

insolvency *noun*
The condition of being financially insolvent.

insorb *verb*
To take in and incorporate, esp. mentally.

inspect *verb*
1. To look at carefully or critically.
2. To study closely or systematically.
3. To examine the person or personal effects of in order to find something lost or concealed.

inspection *noun*
1. The act of examining carefully.
2. A close or systematic study.

inspiration *noun*
1. *Theol.* Divine guidance and motivation imparted directly: *received inspiration through prayer and contemplation.*
2. Something that encourages.
3. High spirits.
4. The act of breathing in: *counted the rate of the patient's inspirations.*

Near-syns: feeble, flat, sapless, subdued, tame, unspirited, vacuous.
2. FLAT *adjective*.

Syns: banality, blandness, colorlessness, dullness, dryness, flatness, flavorlessness, inaneness, inanity, insipidness, jejunity, vapidity.

INSIPIDITY.

1. *Syns:* persevere, persist.

2. *Syns:* press, pressure, prod, urge.

DEMAND *verb*.

1. *Syns:* perseverance, persistence (*also* persistency).

2. *Syns:* instance (*Archaic*), plying, pressing, prodding, urgence, urgency, urging.
SEE **insistence**.

1. *Syns:* perseverant, persevering, persistent, persisting, unremitting.
2. EMPHATIC.
SEE **insist**.

DRUNKENNESS.

1. IMPUDENCE.
2. ARROGANCE.
SEE **insolence**.

1. IMPUDENT.
2. ARROGANT.

FAILURE.

ABSORB.

1. EXAMINE.
2. ANALYZE.
3. SEARCH *verb*.

1. EXAMINATION.
2. ANALYSIS.

1. *Syns:* afflation, afflatus, inflatus.

2. ENCOURAGEMENT.
3. ELATION.
4. *Syns:* afflation, inhalation.

5. A sudden, exciting thought: *had an inspiration to change lifestyles.*
6. Liveliness and vivacity of imagination.

inspirational *adjective*
Providing inspiration.

inspire *verb*
1. To elicit a strong emotional response from: *a woman capable of inspiring a man's devotion; conduct inspiring only disgust.*
2. To arouse the emotions of; make ardent.
3. To impart courage, inspiration, and resolution to.
4. To raise the spirits of.
5. To draw air into the lungs in the process of respiration.

inspired *adjective*
1. Emotionally aroused.
2. Feeling great delight and joy.

inspiring *adjective*
Providing inspiration: *an inspiring sermon.*

inspirit *verb*
1. To impart courage, inspiration, and resolution to.
2. To raise the spirits of.

inspissate *verb*
To make thick or thicker, esp. through evaporation or condensation.

instability *noun*
1. The quality or condition of being erratic and undependable: *the instability of the bond market; the instability of the new government.*
2. The quality or condition of being physically unsteady.

install *verb*
1. To place securely in a position or condition.
2. To place in proper position or location.
3. To admit formally into membership or office, as with ritual.

installation *noun*
1. A center of organization, supply, or activity.
2. The act or process of formally admitting a person to membership or office.

instance *verb*
1. To demonstrate and clarify with examples: *The author's true intent is instanced in these quotations.*
2. To refer to by name.

instance *noun*
1. One that is representative of a group or class.
2. A legal proceeding to demand justice or enforce a right.
3. *Archaic.* Urgent solicitation.

instant *noun*
1. A particular interval of time that is limited and often crucial: *At the very instant the general fell ill, the enemy attacked.*
2. A very brief time.

instant *adjective*
Of immediate import.

instant *adverb*
Poetic. Without delay.

---

5. *Syns:* brainstorm, brain wave.

6. FIRE *noun.*

INSPIRING.

1. *Syns:* arouse, excite, prompt, provoke, stimulate, stir[1]. —*Idiom* stir the blood of.
2. FIRE *verb.*
3. ENCOURAGE.
4. ELATE.
5. BREATHE.

1. AFFECTED[1].
2. ELATED.

Syns: exhilarant, exhilarating, inspirational, intoxicating, rousing, stirring.

1. ENCOURAGE.
2. ELATE.

THICKEN.

1. *Syns:* insecurity, precariousness, shakiness, unstability, unstableness.

2. UNSTABLENESS.

1. ESTABLISH.
2. POSITION *verb.*
3. INITIATE *verb.*

1. BASE[1] *noun.*
2. INITIATION.

1. *Syns:* example, exemplify, illustrate.

2. NAME *verb.*

1. EXAMPLE *noun.*
2. LAWSUIT.

3. INSISTENCE.

1. *Syns:* juncture, moment, point.

2. FLASH *noun.*

BURNING.

DIRECTLY.

instate *verb*
To admit formally into membership or office, as with ritual.

INITIATE *verb*.

instatement *noun*
The act or process of formally admitting a person to membership or office.

INITIATION.

instigate *verb*
To stir to action or feeling.

PROVOKE.

instigation *noun*
Something that incites esp. a violent response.

STIMULUS.

instigator *noun*
One who agitates, esp. politically.

AGITATOR.

instill *verb*
To instruct in a body of doctrine or belief.

INDOCTRINATE.

instinct *noun*
1. The power to discern the true nature of a person or situation: *Instinct warned me never to trust him.*

1. *Syns:* anschauung (*German*), insight, intuitiveness, intuition. —*Idiom* sixth sense.

2. An innate capability.

2. TALENT.

instinctive *adjective*
1. Derived from or prompted by a natural tendency or impulse: *The cornered animal drew back with instinctive fear. My instinctive feeling is that he's a crook.*

1. *Syns:* instinctual, intuitive, visceral.

2. Acting or happening without apparent forethought, prompting, or planning.

2. SPONTANEOUS.

instinctual *adjective*
Derived from or prompted by a natural tendency or impulse.

INSTINCTIVE.

institute *verb*
1. To bring into existence formally.
2. To bring into currency, use, fashion, or practice.

1. FOUND.
2. INTRODUCE.

institute *noun*
A principle governing the affairs of man within or among political units.

LAW *noun*.

institution *noun*
The act of founding or establishing.

FOUNDATION.

institutionalize *verb*
To place officially in confinement.

COMMIT.

instruct *verb*
1. To impart knowledge and skill to.
2. To enable (one) to understand, esp. in a spiritual sense.
3. To give orders to.

1. EDUCATE.
2. ILLUMINATE.

3. COMMAND *verb*.

instructed *adjective*
1. Having an education.
2. Provided with information; made aware.

1. EDUCATED.
2. INFORMED.

instructible *adjective*
Capable of being educated.

EDUCABLE.

instruction *noun*
1. The act, process, or art of imparting knowledge and skill.
2. Known facts, ideas, and skill that have been imparted.
3. An authoritative indication to be obeyed.
4. The condition of being informed spiritually.

1. EDUCATION.

2. EDUCATION.

3. COMMAND *noun*.
4. ILLUMINATION.

instructional *adjective*
Serving to educate.

EDUCATIONAL.

instructive *adjective*
Serving to educate.

EDUCATIONAL.

instructor *noun*
One who educates. — EDUCATOR.

instrument *noun*
1. A device used to do work or perform a task. — 1. TOOL.
2. That by which something is accomplished or some end achieved. — 2. MEANS.
3. A person used or controlled by others. — 3. PAWN².

instrumentality *noun*
That by which something is accomplished or some end achieved. — MEANS.

instrumentation *noun*
That by which something is accomplished or some end achieved. — MEANS.

insubordinate *adjective*
Refusing or failing to obey. — DISOBEDIENT.

insubordination *noun*
The condition or practice of not obeying. — DISOBEDIENCE.

insubstantial *adjective*
1. Having no body, form, or substance. — 1. IMMATERIAL.
2. Lacking stability. — 2. INSECURE.
3. Not physically strong. — 3. INFIRM.
4. Having little substance or significance; not solidly based. — 4. TENUOUS.

insuccess *noun*
The condition of not achieving the desired end. — FAILURE.

insufferable *adjective*
Not capable of being endured or tolerated. — UNBEARABLE.

insufficience *noun* — SEE **insufficiency.**

insufficiency also **insufficience** *noun*
The condition or fact of being deficient. — SHORTAGE.

insufficient *adjective*
Not enough to meet a demand or requirement: *Men cannot work on insufficient rations.* — **Syns:** deficient, inadequate, scanty, scarce, short, shy¹, skimpy, wanting.

insular *adjective*
1. Far from centers of human population. — 1. REMOTE.
2. Having the restricted outlook often characteristic of geographic isolation. — 2. LOCAL *adjective.*

insulate *verb*
To set apart from a group. — ISOLATE *verb.*

insult *verb*
To cause resentment or hurt by callous, rude behavior: *The drunken guest insulted the hostess.* — **Syns:** affront, offend, outrage. —*Idioms* add insult to injury, give offense to.

insult *noun*
An act that offends a person's sense of pride or dignity. — INDIGNITY.

insuperable *adjective*
1. Incapable of being negotiated or overcome: *were confronted with insuperable problems.* — 1. **Syns:** impassable, indomitable, insurmountable, unsurmountable.
2. Incapable of being conquered, overrun, or subjugated. — 2. INVINCIBLE.

insupportable *adjective*
Not capable of being endured or tolerated. — UNBEARABLE.

insure *verb* — SEE **ensure.**

insurgence *noun*
Organized opposition intended to change or overthrow existing authority. — REBELLION.

insurgency *noun*
Organized opposition intended to change or overthrow existing authority. — REBELLION.

insurgent *adjective*
In open revolt against a government or ruling authority. — REBELLIOUS.

insurgent *noun*
A person who rebels.   REBEL *noun*.

insurmountable *adjective*
Incapable of being negotiated or overcome.   INSUPERABLE.

insurrect *verb*
To refuse allegiance to and oppose by force a government or ruling authority.   REBEL *verb*.

insurrection *noun*
Organized opposition intended to change or overthrow existing authority.   REBELLION.

insurrectionist *noun*
A person who rebels.   REBEL *noun*.

insusceptible *adjective*
Not capable of being affected or impressed.   INSENSITIVE.

intact *adjective*
1. Lacking nothing essential or normal.   1. COMPLETE *adjective*.
2. In excellent condition.   2. GOOD *adjective*.

intangible *adjective*
Incapable of being apprehended by the mind or the senses.   IMPERCEPTIBLE.

integral *adjective*
1. Lacking nothing essential or normal.   1. COMPLETE *adjective*.
2. Constituting or forming part of the essence of something.   2. ESSENTIAL *adjective*.

integral *noun*
An organized array of individual elements and parts forming and working as a unit.   SYSTEM.

integrant *noun*
One of the individual entities contributing to a whole.   ELEMENT.

integrate *verb*
1. To make into a whole by joining a system of parts: *a political party that had integrated both liberal and conservative elements.*   1. *Syns:* articulate, concatenate, unify.
2. To open to all people regardless of race: *worked to integrate the schools.*   2. *Syn:* desegregate.
3. To make a part of a united whole.   3. EMBODY.
4. To construct or include as an integral or permanent part.   4. BUILD IN.
5. To bring into accord.   5. HARMONIZE.
6. To combine and adapt in order to attain a particular effect.   6. HARMONIZE.

integrate *noun*
An organized array of individual elements and parts forming and working as a unit.   SYSTEM.

integration *noun*
The act, process, or result of abolishing racial segregation: *school integration.*   *Syn:* desegregation.

integrity *noun*
1. Moral or ethical strength.   1. CHARACTER.
2. The quality of being honest.   2. HONESTY.
3. The condition of being free from defects or flaws.   3. SOUNDNESS.
4. The state of being entirely whole.   4. COMPLETENESS.

integument *noun*
The tissue forming the external covering of the body.   SKIN *noun*.

intellect *noun*
1. The faculty of thinking, reasoning, and acquiring and applying knowledge.   1. INTELLIGENCE.
2. A person of great mental ability.   2. MIND *noun*.

intellective *adjective*
Relating to or performed by the mind.   MENTAL.

intellectual *adjective*
1. Appealing to or engaging the intellect: *an intellectual discussion.*
2. Relating to or performed by the mind.
3. Having or showing intelligence, often of a high order.

intellectual *noun*
A person of great mental ability.

intelligence *noun*
1. The faculty of thinking, reasoning, and acquiring and applying knowledge: *A woman of her intelligence would make a good Supreme Court justice.*
2. New information, esp. about recent events and happenings.
3. Knowledge about a specific subject or situation.

intelligent *adjective*
1. Having or showing intelligence, often of a high order: *an intelligent child; a book for an intelligent readership.*
2. Mentally quick and original.
3. Consistent with reason and intellect.

intelligible *adjective*
Capable of being readily understood.

intemperance *noun*
Immoderate indulgence, as in food or drink.

intend *verb*
1. To have in mind as a goal or purpose: *We intend to sell the house.*

2. To have or convey a particular idea.

intended *noun*
A person to whom one is engaged to be married: *took his intended to meet his mother.*

intended *adjective*
1. Done or said on purpose.
2. Pledged to marry.

intense *adjective*
1. Extreme in degree, strength, or effect: *an intense struggle of wills.*
2. Intensely sustained, esp. in activity.
3. Resulting from or affecting one's innermost feelings.

intensify *verb*
To increase in intensity or severity: *intensified their efforts; pain that intensified every minute.*

intensity *noun*
Exceptionally great concentration, power, or force, esp. in activity: *a hurricane of staggering intensity.*

intensive *adjective*
1. Not diffused or dispersed.
2. Covering all aspects with painstaking accuracy.
3. Intensely sustained, esp. in activity.

intensively *adverb*
In a complete manner.

intent *noun*
1. What one intends to do or achieve.
2. That which is signified by a word or expression.
3. The thread or current of thought uniting or occurring in all the elements of a text or discourse.
4. That which is signified by a word or expression.

intent *adjective*

---

1. **Syns:** cerebral, highbrow (*Informal*), sophisticated, thoughtful.
2. MENTAL.
3. INTELLIGENT.

MIND *noun.*

1. **Syns:** brain(s) (*Informal*), brainpower (*Informal*), intellect, mentality, mind, smarts (*Slang*), sense, understanding, wit.
2. NEWS.

3. INFORMATION.

1. **Syns:** brainy (*Informal*), brilliant, intellectual, knowing, knowledgeable.

2. CLEVER.
3. LOGICAL.

UNDERSTANDABLE.

EXCESS *noun.*

1. **Syns:** aim, contemplate, design, mean[1], mind (*Chiefly Regional*), plan, propose, project, purpose.
2. MEAN[1].

Syns: betrothed, affianced.

1. DELIBERATE *adjective.*
2. ENGAGED.

1. **Syns:** desperate, fierce, furious, terrible, vehement, violent.
2. HEAVY *adjective.*
3. DEEP *adjective.*

Syns: aggravate, deepen, enhance, heighten, mount, redouble.

Syns: ferocity, fierceness, fury, pitch, severity, vehemence, violence.

1. CONCENTRATED.
2. THOROUGH.
3. HEAVY *adjective.*

COMPLETELY.

1. INTENTION.
2. MEANING.
3. THRUST *noun.*

4. MEANING.

1. Having one's thoughts fully occupied.
2. On an unwavering course of action.
3. Concentrating the mental powers on something.

1. ABSORBED.
2. SET[1] *adjective.*
3. ATTENTIVE.

intention *noun*
What one intends to do or achieve: *It was not my intention to offend you.*

Syns: aim, design, end, goal, intent, mark, meaning, plan, point, purpose, target, view. —*Idiom* end in view.

intentional *adjective*
1. Done or said on purpose.
2. Planned, weighed, or estimated in advance.

1. DELIBERATE *adjective.*
2. CALCULATED.

inter *verb*
To place (a corpse) in or as if in a grave.

BURY.

interagent *noun*
Someone who acts as an intermediate agent in a transaction.

GO-BETWEEN.

interceder *noun*
Someone who acts as an intermediate agent in a transaction.

GO-BETWEEN.

intercept *verb*
To block the progress of and force to change direction.

HEAD OFF at **head.**

intercessor *noun*
Someone who acts as an intermediate agent in a transaction.

GO-BETWEEN.

interchange *verb*
1. To give up in return for something else.
2. To give and receive.

1. CHANGE *verb.*
2. EXCHANGE.

interchange *noun*
The act of exchanging or substituting.

CHANGE *noun.*

intercommunication *noun*
1. A situation allowing exchange of ideas or messages.
2. The exchange of ideas by writing, speech, or signals.

1. TOUCH *noun.*
2. COMMUNICATION.

interconnection *noun*
A logical or natural association between two or more things.

RELATION.

intercourse *noun*
The exchange of ideas by writing, speech, or signals.

COMMUNICATION.

interdependence *noun*
A logical or natural association between two or more things.

RELATION.

interdict *verb*
To refuse to allow.

FORBID.

interdict *noun*
A coercive measure intended to ensure compliance or conformity.

SANCTION *noun.*

interdiction *noun*
1. A refusal to allow.
2. A coercive measure intended to ensure compliance or conformity.

1. FORBIDDANCE.
2. SANCTION *noun.*

interest *noun*
1. Something that contributes to or increases one's well-being: *always considered the interest of his clients.*
2. Mental acquisitiveness.
3. A being personally interested in.
4. A right or legal share in something: *own a half interest in a computer company.*

1. *Syns:* advantage, benefit, good, profit.

2. CURIOSITY.
3. CONCERN *noun.*
4. *Syns:* claim, portion, stake, title.

interest *verb*
To arouse the interest and attention of: *Archaeology has always interested me.*

Syns: attract, intrigue, turn on (*Slang*). —*Idiom* get going.

interested *adjective*
Having concern.

CONCERNED.

interestedness *noun*
A being personally interested in.   CONCERN *noun*.

interfere *verb*
To intervene officiously or indiscreetly in the affairs of   MEDDLE.
others.

interference *noun*
The act or an instance of interfering.   MEDDLING *noun*.

interfering *adjective*
Given to intruding in other people's affairs.   MEDDLING *adjective*

interim *adjective*
1. Temporarily assuming the duties of another.   1. TEMPORARY.
2. Intended, used, or present for a limited time.   2. TEMPORARY.

interim *noun*
An interval during which continuity is suspended.   GAP.

interior *adjective*
1. Located farther in.   1. INNER.
2. Of, pertaining to, or arising from one's mental or   2. INNER.
spiritual being.

interject *verb*
To put or set into, between, or among another or other   INTRODUCE.
things.

interlard *adjective*
To put or set into, between, or among another or other   INTRODUCE.
things.

interlope *verb*
To force or come in as an improper or unwanted   INTRUDE.
element.

intermediary *noun*
1. Someone who acts as an intermediate agent in a   1. GO-BETWEEN.
transaction.
2. That by which something is accomplished or some   2. MEANS.
end achieved.

intermediate *adjective*
Not extreme.   MIDDLE *adjective*.

intermediate *noun*
Someone who acts as an intermediate agent in a   GO-BETWEEN.
transaction.

intermediator *noun*
Someone who acts as an intermediate agent in a   GO-BETWEEN.
transaction.

interment *noun*
An act of placing a body in a grave or tomb.   BURIAL.

intermesh *verb*
To come or bring together and interlock.   ENGAGE.

interminable *adjective*
Existing or occurring without interruption or end.   CONTINUAL.

intermingle *verb*
To put together into one mass so that the constituent   MIX *verb*.
parts are more or less homogeneous.

intermission *noun*
1. A pause or interval, as from work or duty.   1. BREAK *noun*.
2. The condition of being temporarily inactive.   2. ABEYANCE.

intermittent *adjective*
Happening or appearing now and then: *intermittent*   ***Syns:*** fitful, occasional, periodic (*also*
showers; intermittent outbreaks of violence.   periodical), sporadic.

intermix *verb*
To put together into one mass so that the constituent   MIX *verb*.
parts are more or less homogeneous.

intermutual *adjective*
Belonging to, shared by, or applicable to all alike.   COMMON *adjective*.

intern *verb*
To put in jail.   JAIL *verb*.

internal *adjective*
1. Located farther in.   **1.** INNER.
2. Of, from, or within a country's own territory.   **2.** DOMESTIC.
3. Of, pertaining to, or arising from one's mental or   **3.** INNER.
   spiritual being.

interpolate *verb*
To put or set into, between, or among another or other   INTRODUCE.
things.

interpose *verb*
To put or set into, between, or among another or other   INTRODUCE.
things.

interpret *verb*
1. To perform according to one's artistic conception: **1.** *Syns:* execute, play, render.
   How did she interpret the role of Lady Macbeth?
2. To make understandable.   **2.** EXPLAIN.
3. To understand in a particular way: *We didn't know*   **3.** *Syns:* construe, read, take.
   how to interpret her remark.

interpretation *noun*
1. One's artistic conception as shown by the rendering   **1.** *Syns:* execution, performance, reading,
   of a dramatic role, musical composition, etc.: *a*   realization, rendition.
   bizarre interpretation of Beethoven's "Appassionata"
   Sonata.
2. Something that serves to explain or clarify.   **2.** EXPLANATION.
3. Critical explanation or analysis.   **3.** COMMENTARY.

interpretive *adjective*
Serving to explain.   EXPLANATORY.

interrelation *noun*
A logical or natural association between two or more   RELATION.
things.

interrelationship *noun*
A logical or natural association between two or more   RELATION.
things.

interrogate *verb*
1. To question thoroughly and relentlessly to verify   **1.** *Syns:* cross-examine, cross-interrogate,
   facts: *interrogated the captured soldier.*   cross-question, grill (*Informal*), third-
                                                                             degree. —*Idioms* give someone the
                                                                             third degree, put on the grill.
2. To put a question to (someone).   **2.** ASK.

interrogation *noun*
A request for data.   INQUIRY.

interrogator *noun*
One who conducts an official inquiry, usu. with no   INQUISITOR.
regard for human rights.

interrogatory *noun*
Law. A request for data.   INQUIRY.

interrupt *verb*
1. To interject remarks or questions into another's   **1.** *Syns:* break in, chime in, chip in, cut
   discourse: *Hecklers interrupted the speech.*   in.
2. To stop suddenly, as a conversation, activity,   **2.** SUSPEND.
   relationship, etc.

interruption *noun*
A cessation of continuity or regularity.   BREAK *noun*.

intersect *verb*
To pass through or over.   CROSS *verb*.

intertangle *verb*
To twist together so that separation is difficult.   ENTANGLE.

intervention *noun*
The act or an instance of interfering.   MEDDLING *noun*.

intestine *adjective*
1. Of, pertaining to, or arising from one's mental or spiritual being.
2. *Obs.* Located farther in.

1. INNER.

2. INNER.

intimacy *noun*
The condition of being friends.

FRIENDSHIP.

intimate¹ *adjective*
1. Characterized by a close and thorough acquaintance: *has an intimate knowledge of drug dealing.*
2. Very closely associated.
3. Indicating intimacy and mutual trust.

1. *Syns:* direct, firsthand, inside, personal.

2. FAMILIAR *adjective.*
3. CONFIDENTIAL.

intimate *noun*
A person whom one knows well, likes, and trusts.

FRIEND.

intimate *adjective*
Of, pertaining to, or arising from one's mental or spiritual being.

INNER.

intimate² *verb*
To convey an idea by indirect, subtle means.

HINT *verb.*

intimation *noun*
1. A subtle pointing out.
2. A slight amount.

1. HINT *noun.*
2. SHADE *noun.*

intimidate *verb*
To domineer or drive into compliance by the use of threats, force, etc.: *mob members intimidating local merchants.*

Syns: bludgeon, browbeat, bulldoze, bully, bullyrag, cow, hector, strong-arm (*Informal*), threaten.

intimidation *noun*
An expression of the intent to hurt or punish another.

THREAT.

intimidator *noun*
One who is habitually cruel to smaller or weaker people.

BULLY *noun.*

intolerable *adjective*
Not capable of being endured or tolerated.

UNBEARABLE.

intolerance *noun*
Irrational suspicion or hatred of a particular group, race, or religion.

PREJUDICE *noun.*

intolerant *adjective*
1. Not tolerant of the beliefs, opinions, etc., of others: *an intolerant old-line conservative.*

1. *Syns:* bigoted, close-minded, hidebound, illiberal, narrow, narrow-minded, small-minded.
Near-syns: biased, inflexible, obdurate, prejudiced, unsympathetic.
Ant: tolerant.

2. Not able or willing to tolerate or endure with equanimity: *intolerant of everything unfamiliar.*

2. *Syns:* impatient, unforbearing.

intonation *noun*
A particular vocal quality that indicates some emotion or feeling.

TONE.

intoxicate *verb*
To make drunk.

INEBRIATE.

intoxicating *adjective*
Providing inspiration.

INSPIRING.

intoxication *noun*
1. The condition of being intoxicated with alcoholic liquor.
2. An exaggerated feeling of well-being and pleasure.

1. DRUNKENNESS.

2. ELATION.

intractability *noun*
The quality or state of being stubbornly unyielding.

OBSTINACY.

intractable *adjective*
Tenaciously unwilling to yield.

OBSTINATE.

intransigence or **intransigency** *noun*
The quality or state of being stubbornly unyielding.

OBSTINACY.

intransigency *noun*   SEE **intransigence.**

intransigent *adjective*
1. Having or showing uncompromising determination   1. GRIM.
   or resolution in purpose or action.
2. Tenaciously unwilling to yield.   2. OBSTINATE.

intrepid *adjective*
Having or showing courage.   BRAVE *adjective.*

intrepidity *noun*
The quality of mind enabling one to face danger or   COURAGE.
hardship resolutely.

intricacy *noun*
Something complex.   COMPLEXITY.

intricate *adjective*
1. Difficult to understand due to intricacy.   1. COMPLEX *adjective.*
2. Complexly detailed.   2. ELABORATE *adjective.*

intrigue *noun*
1. A secret plan to achieve an evil or illegal end.   1. PLOT *noun.*
2. The series of events and relationships forming the   2. PLOT *noun.*
   basis of a composition.

intrigue *verb*
1. To work out a secret plan to achieve an evil or   1. PLOT *verb.*
   illegal end.
2. To arouse the interest and attention of.   2. INTEREST *verb.*

intrinsic *adjective*
1. Forming an essential element.   1. BUILT-IN.
2. Of or arising from the most basic structure of an   2. CONSTITUTIONAL *adjective.*
   individual.

introduce *verb*
1. To bring into currency, use, fashion, or practice: 1. *Syns:* inaugurate, initiate, institute,
   Automobiles were introduced for commercial use in   launch, originate, usher in.
   the twentieth century.
2. To make known socially.   2. ACQUAINT.
3. To put or set into, between, or among another or   3. *Syns:* insert, interject, interlard,
   other things: *introduced some suspense into the*   interpolate, interpose.
   novel.
4. To put forward a topic for discussion.   4. BROACH.
5. To begin (something) with preliminary or prefatory   5. *Syns:* lead, precede, preface, usher in.
   material: *introduced the poem with a dedication.*
6. To make known the presence or arrival of.   6. USHER IN at **usher.**

introduction *noun*
1. A short section of preliminary remarks: *explains his*   1. *Syns:* foreword, overture, preamble,
   work methods in the introduction.   preface, prelude, prolegomenon,
                                                              prologue.
2. The state of being allowed entry.   2. ADMISSION.

introductory *adjective*
1. Serving to introduce a subject, person, etc.: *a few*   1. *Syns:* prefatory (*also* prefatorial),
   introductory remarks before the program.   preliminary, preparatory,
                                                              prolegomenous.
2. Indicating the start of something.   2. BEGINNING *adjective.*
3. Prior to or preparing for the main matter, action, or   3. PRELIMINARY.
   business.

intromission *noun*
The state of being allowed entry.   ADMISSION.

intromit *verb*
To serve as a means of entrance for.   ADMIT.

intrude *verb*
To force or come in as an improper or unwanted   *Syns:* butt in, cut in, horn in, interlope,
element: *won't make the mistake of intruding myself on*   obtrude.
your guests.

intrusion *noun*
An excessive, unwelcome burden.   IMPOSITION.

intrusive *adjective*
1. Given to intruding in other people's affairs.
2. Troubling to the mind or emotions.

1. MEDDLING *adjective*.
2. DISTURBING.

intrust *verb*

SEE **entrust.**

intuit *verb*
To be intuitively aware of.

PERCEIVE.

intuition *noun*
1. Intuitive cognition.
2. The power to discern the true nature of a person or situation.

1. FEELING.
2. INSTINCT.

intuitive *adjective*
Derived from or prompted by a natural tendency or impulse.

INSTINCTIVE.

intuitiveness *noun*
The power to discern the true nature of a person or situation.

INSTINCT.

inumbrate *verb*
To shelter, esp. from light.

SHADE *verb*.

inundate *verb*
To flow over completely.

FLOOD *verb*.

inundation *noun*
An abundant, usu. overwhelming flow.

FLOOD *noun*.

inure *verb*
To make familiar through constant practice or use.

ACCUSTOM.

inutile *adjective*
1. Having no useful purpose.
2. Lacking all worth and value.

1. USELESS.
2. WORTHLESS.

invade *verb*
To enter in order to attack, plunder, destroy, or conquer: *The Nazis invaded Czechoslovakia.*

Syns: foray (into), overrun, raid, swarm over.

invalid *adjective*
Containing fundamental errors in reasoning.

FALLACIOUS.

invalidate *verb*
To put an end to formally and with authority.

ABOLISH.

invalidation *noun*
An often formal act of putting an end to.

ABOLITION.

invaluable *adjective*
Of great value.

VALUABLE.

invariable *adjective*
1. Remaining continually unchanged.
2. Incapable of changing or being modified.

1. CONSISTENT.
2. INFLEXIBLE.

invasion *noun*
An act of invading, esp. by military forces: *the Roman invasion of Britain.*

Syns: foray, incursion, inroad, raid.

invective *noun*
1. Harsh, often insulting language.
2. A profane or obscene term.

1. VITUPERATION.
2. SWEAR *noun*.

invective *adjective*
Of, relating to, or characterized by verbal abuse.

ABUSIVE.

inveigh *verb*
To express opposition by argument.

OBJECT[2].

inveigle *verb*
To beguile or draw into a wrong or foolish course of action.

TEMPT.

inveiglement *noun*
Something that attracts, esp. with the promise of pleasure or reward.

LURE *noun*.

inveigler *noun*
One that seduces.

SEDUCER.

invent *verb*
To use ingenuity in making, developing, or achieving: *a gang that invented a remote-control bomb. Gutenberg invented movable type.*

Syns: concoct, contrive, cook up (*Informal*), devise, dream up, fabricate, formulate, hatch, make up, think up. —*Idiom* come up with.

invented *adjective*
Consisting or suggestive of fiction.

FICTITIOUS.

invention *noun*
1. Something invented: *The cotton gin was a vitally important invention for the South's economy.*
2. The power or ability to invent: *a dress designer of amazing invention.*
3. Any fictitious idea accepted as part of an ideology by an uncritical group; a received idea.

1. **Syns:** brain child (*Informal*), contrivance, device.
2. **Syns:** creativity, ingenuity, inventiveness, originality.
3. MYTH.

inventive *adjective*
1. Characterized by or productive of new things or new ideas: *an inventive mind; inventive solutions to the energy problem.*
2. Showing marked departure from previous practice.
3. Able to use the means at one's disposal to meet situations effectively.

1. **Syns:** creative, ingenious, innovative, original.

2. NEW *adjective*.
3. RESOURCEFUL.

inventiveness *noun*
The power or ability to invent.

INVENTION.

inventor *noun*
One that creates, founds, or originates.

ORIGINATOR.

inventory *noun*
A supply stored or hidden for future use.

HOARD *noun*.

inveracity *noun*
An untrue declaration.

LIE[2] *noun*.

inverse *verb*
To change to the opposite position, direction, or course.

REVERSE *verb*.

inversion *noun*
The act of changing or being changed from one position, direction, or course to the opposite.

REVERSAL.

invert *verb*
To change to the opposite position, direction, or course.

REVERSE *verb*.

inverted *adjective*
Overturned completely.

UPSIDE-DOWN.

invest *verb*
1. To present with a quality, trait, or power.
2. *Rare.* To put clothes on.
3. To admit formally into membership or office, as with ritual.
4. To cover completely and closely, as with clothing or bandages.
5. To surround and cover completely so as to obscure.
6. *Mil.* To surround with hostile troops.

1. GIFT *verb*.
2. DRESS *verb*.
3. INITIATE *verb*.

4. WRAP UP.

5. WRAP *verb*.
6. BESIEGE.

investigate *verb*
1. To go into or through for the purpose of making discoveries or acquiring information.
2. To study closely or systematically.

1. EXPLORE.

2. ANALYZE.

investigation *noun*
1. A seeking of knowledge, data, or the truth about something.
2. The act or an instance of exploring or investigating.
3. A close or systematic study.

1. INQUIRY.

2. EXPLORATION.
3. ANALYSIS.

investigative *adjective*
Eager to acquire knowledge.

CURIOUS.

investigator *noun*
A person whose work is investigating crimes or obtaining hidden evidence or information.

DETECTIVE.

investiture *noun*
The act or process of formally admitting a person to membership or office.
INITIATION.

inveterate *adjective*
1. Firmly established by long standing.
2. Existing or remaining in the same state for an indefinitely long time.
3. Subject to a disease or habit for a long time.

1. CONFIRMED.
2. CONTINUING.

3. CHRONIC.

invidious *adjective*
1. Damaging to the reputation.
2. *Obs.* Resentfully or painfully desirous of another's advantages.

1. LIBELOUS.
2. ENVIOUS.

invidiousness *noun*
Obs. Resentful or painful desire for another's advantages.
ENVY *noun.*

invigorating *adjective*
Producing or stimulating physical, mental, or emotional vigor.
TONIC *adjective.*

invincible *adjective*
Incapable of being conquered, overrun, or subjugated: *an invincible foe; an invincible fortress.*
Syns: impregnable, inconquerable, insuperable, unconquerable.

inviolability *noun*
The quality or condition of being safe from assault, trespass, or violation.
SANCTITY.

inviolable *adjective*
Protected from violation or abuse by custom, law, or feelings of reverence.
SACRED.

invisible *adjective*
Incapable of being apprehended by the mind or the senses.
IMPERCEPTIBLE.

invitation *noun*
1. A spoken or written request for someone to take part or be present: *sent out the wedding invitations.*
2. A tendency to cause or bring on: *Reckless driving is an invitation to disaster.*

1. *Syn:* bid.

2. *Syns:* encouragement, inducement.

invite *verb*
1. To request that someone take part in or be present at a particular occasion: *Let's invite them to dinner.*
2. To solicit (danger) playfully and provocatively, often unwittingly.

1. *Syns:* ask, bid.

2. COURT *verb.*

inviting *adjective*
Tending to seduce.
SEDUCTIVE.

invocate *verb*
Archaic. To offer a reverent petition to God or a god.
PRAY.

invocation *noun*
The act of praying.
PRAYER.

invoice *noun*
A precise list of fees or charges.
ACCOUNT *noun.*

invoice *verb*
To present a statement of fees or charges to.
BILL[1] *verb.*

invoke *verb*
To compel observance of.
ENFORCE.

involute *adjective*
Difficult to understand due to intricacy.
COMPLEX *adjective.*

involve *verb*
1. To draw in in such a way that extrication is difficult: *a local skirmish that could involve the major powers.*

2. To have as a need or prerequisite.
3. To be pertinent.
4. To have as an integral part.

1. *Syns:* catch up, embrangle, embroil, enmesh, ensnare, ensnarl, entangle, implicate, suck in (*Informal*).
2. DEMAND *verb.*
3. APPLY.
4. CONTAIN *verb.*

5. To have as an accompaniment, condition, or consequence.

5. CARRY.

6. To get and hold the attention of.

6. ENGAGE.

involved *adjective*
1. Difficult to understand due to intricacy.

1. COMPLEX *adjective*.

2. Having concern.

2. CONCERNED.

involvement *noun*
1. The condition of being entangled or implicated.

1. ENTANGLEMENT.

2. The act or fact of participating.

2. PARTICIPATION.

inward *adjective*
Of, pertaining to, or arising from one's mental or spiritual being.

INNER.

iota *noun*
1. A tiny amount.

1. BIT[1].

2. The least bit.

2. DAMN *noun*.

irascibility *noun*
A tendency to become angry or irritable.

TEMPER *noun*.

irascible *adjective*
1. Easily annoyed.

1. TESTY.

2. Having or showing a bad temper.

2. ILL-TEMPERED.

irascibleness *noun*
A tendency to become angry or irritable.

TEMPER *noun*.

irate *adjective*
Feeling or showing anger.

ANGRY.

irateness *noun*
A strong feeling of displeasure or hostility.

ANGER *noun*.

ire *noun*
1. Violent or unrestrained anger.

1. FURY.

2. A strong feeling of displeasure or hostility.

2. ANGER *noun*.

ire *verb*
To cause to feel or show anger.

ANGER *verb*.

ireful *adjective*
Feeling or showing anger.

ANGRY.

irenic *adjective*
Inclined or disposed to peace; not quarrelsome or unruly.

PEACEABLE.

irk *verb*
To trouble the nerves or peace of mind of, esp. by repeated vexations.

ANNOY.

irksome *adjective*
1. Arousing no interest or curiosity.

1. BORING.

2. Troubling the nerves or peace of mind, as by repeated vexations.

2. VEXATIOUS.

iron *verb*
To smooth by applying heat and pressure.

PRESS *verb*.

iron *adjective*
Firmly, often unreasonably immovable in purpose or will.

STUBBORN.

ironbound *adjective*
Having a coarse, irregular surface.

ROUGH.

ironclad *adjective*
Incapable of changing or being modified.

INFLEXIBLE.

ironic also **ironical** *adjective*
Marked by or displaying contemptuous mockery of the motives or virtues of others.

CYNICAL.

irons *noun*
Something that physically confines the legs or arms.

BONDS.

irradiant *adjective*
Giving off or reflecting light readily or in large amounts.

BRIGHT.

irradiate *verb*
To send out heat, light, or energy.   SHED.
irradicable *adjective*
Firmly established by long standing.   CONFIRMED.
irrational *adjective*
1. Lacking rational direction or purpose.   1. MINDLESS.
2. Not governed by or predicated on reason.   2. UNREASONABLE.
irrationality *noun*
The absence of reason.   UNREASON.
irrealizable *adjective*
Not capable of happening or being done.   IMPOSSIBLE.
irrefutable *adjective*
Established beyond a doubt.   CERTAIN.
irregular *adjective*
Not straight, uniform, or symmetrical: *an irregular*   ***Syns:*** asymmetric (*also* asymmetrical),
coastline; irregular teeth.   crooked, jagged, uneven.
irregularity *noun*
Lack of smoothness or regularity: *the irregularity of the* ***Syns:*** asymmetry, crookedness, inequality,
terrain.   jaggedness, roughness, unevenness.
irrelevancy *noun*
An instance of digressing.   DIGRESSION.
irrelevant *adjective*
Not relevant or pertinent to the subject; not applicable: ***Syns:*** extraneous, immaterial,
tells us about the weather, which is irrelevant to the   impertinent, inapplicable. —*Idioms* beside
question we asked.   the point, neither here nor there, off
                                                           target.
                                                           Near-ants: applicable, appropriate,
                                                           germane, pertinent; consequential,
                                                           important, material, significant.
                                                           Ant: relevant.

irremediable *adjective*
Offering no hope or expectation of improvement.   HOPELESS.
irreparable *adjective*
Offering no hope or expectation of improvement.   HOPELESS.
irreprehensible *adjective*
Beyond reproach.   EXEMPLARY.
irreproachable *adjective*
Beyond reproach.   EXEMPLARY.
irresolute *adjective*
Given to or exhibiting hesitation.   HESITANT.
irresolution *noun*
The act or an instance of hesitating.   HESITATION.
irresponsible *adjective*
Lacking or showing a lack of a sense of responsibility: ***Syns:*** feckless, incautious, reckless.
irresponsible actions.
irreverence *noun*
Lack of proper respect.   DISRESPECT.
irreverent *adjective*
Having or showing a lack of respect.   DISRESPECTFUL.
irreversible *adjective*
That cannot be revoked or undone.   IRREVOCABLE.
irrevocable *adjective*
That cannot be revoked or undone: *My decision is*   ***Syns:*** irreversible, unalterable. —*Idiom*
irrevocable.   beyond recall.
irritable *adjective*
1. Easily annoyed: *Hot, sticky weather always makes*   1. ***Syns:*** fretful, peevish, petulant,
   me irritable.   prickish, querulent, querulous,
                                                              snappish, snappy, waspish. —*Idiom* out
                                                              of sorts.
2. Having or showing a bad temper.   2. ILL-TEMPERED.

irritant *noun*
Something that annoys.   ANNOYANCE.

irritate *verb*
1. To cause to become sore or inflamed: *Smoke irritates*   1. **Syns:** burn, inflame, sting.
   my eyes.
2. To trouble the nerves or peace of mind of, esp. by   2. ANNOY.
   repeated vexations.

irritating *adjective*
Troubling the nerves or peace of mind, as by repeated   VEXATIOUS.
vexations.

irritation *noun*
1. An instance of irritating, as of a part of the body: 1. **Syns:** inflammation, soreness.
   Aspirin sometimes causes stomach irritation.
2. Something that annoys.   2. ANNOYANCE.
3. The feeling of being annoyed.   3. ANNOYANCE.

Iscariotic or **Iscariotical** *adjective*
1. Characterized by duplicity.   1. DOUBLE *adjective.*
2. Involving or constituting treason.   2. TREASONOUS.

isochronal also **isochronic, isochronous** *adjective*
Happening or appearing at regular intervals.   RECURRENT.

isochronic *adjective*   SEE **isochronal.**

isochronous *adjective*   SEE **isochronal.**

isolate *verb*
1. To set apart from a group: *trying to isolate a*   1. **Syns:** close off, cut off, insulate,
   suspected carcinogen.   seclude, segregate, separate, sequester.
2. To enclose so as to hinder or prohibit escape.   2. IMPRISON.

isolate *adjective*
Set away from all others.   SOLITARY.

isolated *adjective*
1. Set away from all others.   1. SOLITARY.
2. Far from centers of human population.   2. REMOTE.
3. Confined to a particular location or site.   3. LOCAL *adjective.*

isolation *noun*
1. The act or process of isolating: *the isolation of cancer*   1. **Syns:** segregation, separation,
   patients.   sequestration.
2. The quality or state of being alone.   2. ALONENESS.

issue *verb*
1. To pass or pour out into.   1. DISCHARGE *verb.*
2. To discharge material, as vapor or fumes, usu.   2. EMIT.
   suddenly and violently.
3. To come into view.   3. APPEAR.
4. To present for circulation, exhibit, or sale.   4. PUBLISH.
5. To have as a source.   5. STEM *verb.*
6. To have hereditary derivation.   6. DESCEND.

issue *noun*
1. Something brought about by a cause.   1. EFFECT *noun.*
2. A situation that presents difficulty, uncertainty, or   2. PROBLEM.
   perplexity.
3. The act or process of publishing printed matter.   3. PUBLICATION.
4. A group consisting of those descended directly from   4. PROGENY.
   the same parents or ancestors.

italicize *verb*
To accord emphasis to.   EMPHASIZE.

itch *noun*
1. A strong wish for what promises enjoyment or   1. DESIRE *noun.*
   pleasure.
2. Sexual hunger.   2. DESIRE *noun.*

itch for *verb*
To have a greedy, obsessive desire.   LUST *verb.*

itch for *verb*   SEE **itch.**

item *noun*
1. A usu. brief detail of news or information: *The morning paper has an item about their divorce.*
2. A small, often specialized element of a whole.
3. An individually considered portion of a whole.
4. Something having material existence.

item *adverb*
In addition.

itemize *verb*
To name or specify one by one.

itemized *adjective*
Characterized by attention to detail.

iterate *verb*
To state again.

iteration *noun*
The act or process of repeating.

iterative *adjective*
Characterized by repetition.

itinerant *adjective*
1. Traveling about, esp. in search of adventure.
2. Leading the life of a person without a fixed domicile; moving from place to place.
3. Moving from one area to another in search of work.

ivory *adjective*
Of a moderately white color.

ivory-tower *adjective*
Incapable of dealing efficiently with practical matters.

ivory-towered *adjective*
Incapable of dealing efficiently with practical matters.

ivory-towerish *adjective*
Incapable of dealing efficiently with practical matters.

1. *Syns:* bit, paragraph, piece, squib, story.
2. DETAIL *noun*.
3. ELEMENT.
4. OBJECT¹.

ADDITIONALLY.

ENUMERATE.

DETAILED.

REPEAT.

REPETITION.

REPETITIVE.

1. ERRANT.
2. NOMADIC.

3. MIGRANT *adjective*.

FAIR *adjective*.

IMPRACTICAL.

IMPRACTICAL.

IMPRACTICAL.

J

jab *verb*
To thrust against or into.

jab *noun*
1. An act of thrusting into or against, as to attract attention.
2. A flippant or sarcastic remark.

jabber *verb*
1. To talk rapidly, incoherently, or indistinctly.
2. To talk volubly, persistently, and usu. inconsequentially.

jabber *noun*
1. Unintelligible or foolish talk.
2. Incessant and usu. inconsequential talk.

jabberwock *noun*

jabberwocky also **jabberwock** *noun*
1. Wordy, unclear jargon.
2. Unintelligible or foolish talk.

DIG *verb*.

1. DIG *noun*.

2. CRACK *noun*.

1. BABBLE *verb*.
2. CHATTER *verb*.

1. BABBLE *noun*.
2. CHATTER *noun*.
SEE **jabberwocky**.

1. GIBBERISH.
2. BABBLE *noun*.

jack *noun*
1. Fabric used esp. as a symbol.   1. FLAG¹ *noun.*
2. *Slang.* Something, as coins, printed bills, etc., used   2. MONEY.
   as a medium of exchange.
3. *Informal.* A person engaged in sailing or working on   3. SAILOR.
   a ship.

jack *verb*
To increase in amount.   RAISE *verb.*

jackass *noun*
One deficient in judgment and good sense.   FOOL *noun.*

jacket *noun*
The skin of an animal.   HIDE² *noun.*

jackleg *adjective*
Informal. Lacking the required professional skill.   AMATEURISH.

jack-tar *noun*
Informal. A person engaged in sailing or working on a   SAILOR.
ship.

jade *noun*
A vulgar, promiscuous woman who flouts propriety.   SLUT.

jag *noun*
Slang. A period of uncontrolled self-indulgence.   BINGE.

jagged *adjective*
1. Having a coarse, irregular surface.   1. ROUGH.
2. Not straight, uniform, or symmetrical.   2. IRREGULAR.

jaggedness *noun*
Lack of smoothness or regularity.   IRREGULARITY.

jail *noun*
A place for the confinement of persons in lawful   *Syns:* brig, calaboose (*Slang*), can (*Slang*),
detention: *was sent to jail for murder.*   clink (*Slang*), cooler (*Slang*), coop
                                                                         (*Slang*), gaol (*Chiefly Brit.*), hoosegow
                                                                         (*Slang*), joint (*Slang*), jug (*Slang*), keep,
                                                                         lockup (*Informal*), pen³ (*Slang*),
                                                                         penitentiary, pokey¹ (*Slang*), prison,
                                                                         slammer (*Slang*), stir² (*Slang*). —*Idioms*
                                                                         big house (*also* Big House), house of
                                                                         correction (*or* detention), rock pile.

jail *verb*
To put in jail: *will jail the suspect for attempted robbery.*   *Syns:* confine, immure, imprison,
                                                                         incarcerate, intern, lock up.

jailer also **jailor** *noun*
A guard or keeper of a prison: *a jailer in the state*   *Syns:* gaoler (*Chiefly Brit.*), turnkey,
penitentiary.   warden, warder (*Brit.*). —*Idiom* The Man.

jailor *noun*   SEE **jailer.**

jam *verb*
1. To fill to excess by compressing or squeezing tightly.   1. CROWD *verb.*
2. To congregate closely around or against.   2. CROWD *verb.*

jam *noun*
Informal. A difficult, embarrassing situation.   PREDICAMENT.

jam-full *adjective*
Completely filled.   FULL.

jammed *adjective*
Completely filled.   FULL.

jam-pack *verb*
Informal. To fill to excess by compressing or squeezing   CROWD *verb.*
tightly.

jam-packed *adjective*
Informal. Completely filled.   FULL.

jape *noun*
Words or actions intended to excite laughter or   JOKE *noun.*
amusement.

jar *verb*
To fail to be in accord.   CONFLICT *verb.*

jar *noun*
Violent, forcible contact between two or more things.   COLLISION.

jargon *noun*
1. Specialized expressions indigenous to a particular   1. LANGUAGE.
   field, subject, trade, or subculture.
2. An often regional form of a language not considered   2. DIALECT.
   standard.

jarring *adjective*
Disagreeable to the sense of hearing.   HARSH.

jaundice *verb*
To cause to have a prejudiced view.   BIAS *verb.*

jaunt *noun*
A setting out or venturing forth.   TRIP *noun.*

jaunty *adjective*
Displaying light-hearted nonchalance.   AIRY.

Javert *noun*
A person whose work is investigating crimes or   DETECTIVE.
obtaining hidden evidence or information.

jaw *verb*
Slang. To talk volubly, persistently, and usu.   CHATTER *verb.*
inconsequentially.

jealous *adjective*
1. Fearful of the loss of position or affection: *a jealous*   1. ***Syns:*** clutching, possessive.
   husband.   ***Near-syns:*** covetous, grasping,
                                                                grudging, mistrustful, questioning,
                                                                suspicious.
2. Resentfully or painfully desirous of another's   2. ENVIOUS.
   advantages.

jealousy *noun*
Resentful or painful desire for another's advantages.   ENVY *noun.*

jeer at *verb*
To make fun of.   RIDICULE *verb.*

jejune *adjective*
Lacking the qualities requisite for spiritedness and   INSIPID.
originality.

jejunity *noun*
The state or quality of being insipid.   INSIPIDITY.

jell *verb*
To change or be changed from a liquid into a soft,   COAGULATE.
semisolid, or solid mass.

jeopard *verb*
To subject to danger or destruction.   ENDANGER.

jeopardize *verb*
To subject to danger or destruction.   ENDANGER.

jeopardous *adjective*
Involving possible risk, loss, or injury.   DANGEROUS.

jeopardy *noun*
Exposure to possible harm, loss, or injury.   DANGER.

jeopardy *verb*
To subject to danger or destruction.   ENDANGER.

jeremiad *noun*
A long, violent, or blustering speech, usu. of censure or   TIRADE.
denunciation.

jerk *verb*
1. To move or cause to move with a sudden, abrupt   1. ***Syns:*** lurch, snap, tug, twitch, wrench,
   motion: *jerked the window open. His head jerked*   yank (*Informal*).
   forward onto his chest.   ***Near-syns:*** drag, lug; pull; fling, throw,
                                                               toss.
2. To proceed with sudden, abrupt movements.   2. BUMP *verb.*

jerk *noun*
1. A sudden pull: *opened the door with a jerk.*

1. **Syns:** lurch, snap, tug, twitch, wrench, yank (*Informal*).

2. *Slang.* One deficient in judgment and good sense.
3. *Slang.* An unpleasant, tiresome person.

2. FOOL *noun.*
3. DRIP *noun.*

jerky *adjective*
Slang. So senseless as to be laughable.

FOOLISH.

jest *verb*
1. To make jokes; behave playfully.
2. To tease or mock good-humoredly.

1. JOKE *verb.*
2. JOKE *verb.*

jest *noun*
1. Words or actions intended to excite laughter or amusement.
2. An object of amusement or laughter.

1. JOKE *noun.*
2. JOKE *noun.*

jester *noun*
A person whose words or actions provoke or are intended to provoke amusement or laughter.

JOKER.

jesting *adjective*
Intended to excite laughter or amusement.

HUMOROUS.

jet[1] *adjective*
Of the darkest achromatic visual value.

BLACK *adjective.*

jet[2] *noun*
A sudden, swift stream of ejected liquid.

SPURT *noun.*

jet *verb*
To eject or be ejected in a sudden, swift stream.

SPURT *noun.*

jet-black *adjective*
Of the darkest achromatic visual value.

BLACK *adjective.*

jettison *noun*
The act of getting rid of something useless or used up.

DISPOSAL.

jettison *verb*
To let go or get rid of as being no longer of use, value, etc.

DISCARD.

jetty *adjective*
Of the darkest achromatic visual value.

BLACK *adjective.*

jibe *verb*
Informal. To be compatible or in correspondence.

AGREE.

jiff *noun*

SEE **jiffy.**

jiffy also **jiff** *noun*
Informal. A very brief time.

FLASH *noun.*

jig *noun*
Slang. An indirect, usu. cunning means of gaining an end.

TRICK *noun.*

jigger *noun*
A small, specialized mechanical device.

GADGET.

jiggle *verb*
To cause to move to and fro with short, jerky movements.

SHAKE *verb.*

jillion *noun*
Informal. An indeterminately great amount or number.

HEAP *noun.*

jim-jams *noun*
Slang. A state of nervous restlessness or agitation.

JITTERS.

jimmies *noun*
Slang. A state of nervous restlessness or agitation.

JITTERS.

jinx *noun*
Informal. Something or someone believed to bring bad luck: *His teammates considered him a jinx.*

Syns: curse, hex, hoodoo.
Near-syns: charm, evil eye, spell, sign, whammy (*Slang*).

jitters *noun*
Informal. A state of nervous restlessness or agitation: *got the jitters at the thought of going to the dentist.*

Syns: all-overs (*Chiefly Regional*), fidgets, heebie-jeebies (*Slang*), jim-jams (*Slang*), jimmies (*Slang*), jumps (*Informal*),

shakes, shivers, tremble(s), whim-whams
(*also* wim-wams), willies (*Slang*).

jittery *adjective*
Informal. Feeling or exhibiting nervous tension.   EDGY.

jive *verb*
Slang. To tease or mock good-humoredly.   JOKE *verb*.

job *noun*
1. Activity pursued as a livelihood.   1. BUSINESS.
2. A post of employment.   2. POSITION *noun*.
3. The proper activity of a person or thing.   3. FUNCTION *noun*.
4. A piece of work that has been assigned.   4. TASK *noun*.
5. A difficult or tedious undertaking.   5. TASK *noun*.

jobholder *noun*
One who is employed by another.   EMPLOYEE.

jobholding *adjective*
Having a job.   EMPLOYED.

jobless *adjective*
Out of work.   WORKLESS.

jockey *verb*
To take clever or cunning steps to achieve one's goals.   MANEUVER *verb*.

jocular *adjective*
Intended to excite laughter or amusement.   HUMOROUS.

jocularity *noun*
A state of joyful exuberance.   GAIETY.

jocund *adjective*
Characterized by joyful exuberance.   GAY *adjective*.

jocundity *noun*
A state of joyful exuberance.   GAIETY.

jog *verb*
1. To thrust against or into.   1. DIG *verb*.
2. To move with a steady, easy gait faster than a walk   2. TROT *verb*.
   but slower than a run.

jog *noun*
A person's steady, easy gait that is faster than a walk   TROT *noun*.
but slower than a run.

joggle *verb*
To cause to move to and fro with short, jerky   SHAKE *verb*.
movements.

join *verb*
1. To become a member of: *wants to join the tennis*   1. **Syns:** enlist (in), enroll (in), enter,
   club.   muster (in), sign up (*or* on).
2. To bring or come together into a united whole.   2. COMBINE *verb*.
3. To unite or be united in a relationship.   3. ASSOCIATE *verb*.
4. *Informal.* To be contiguous or next to.   4. ADJOIN.

joined *adjective*
Informal. Sharing a common boundary.   ADJOINING.

joining *noun*
A point or position at which two or more things are   JOINT *noun*.
joined.

joint *noun*
1. A point or position at which two or more things are   1. **Syns:** connection, coupling, joining,
   joined: *a gas leak at the joint in the pipe.*   junction, juncture, seam, union.
                                                                      Near-syns: articulation; abutment;
                                                                      bond, link, tie.
2. *Slang.* A disreputable or run-down bar or   2. **Syns:** dive (*Slang*), honky-tonk
   restaurant: *a cheap, sleazy joint.*   (*Slang*).
3. *Slang.* A place for the confinement of persons in   3. JAIL *noun*.
   lawful detention.

joint *adjective*
Belonging to, shared by, or applicable to all alike.   COMMON *adjective*.

jointly *adverb*
In, into, or as a single body.

TOGETHER *adverb.*

joke *noun*
1. Words or actions intended to excite laughter or amusement: *opened the speech with a joke.*

1. **Syns:** funny (*Informal*), gag (*Informal*), ha-ha (*Slang*), jape, jest, quip, witticism.
   Near-syns: banter, crack, raillery, wisecrack; burlesque, caricature, parody, satire; humor, sarcasm, wit.

2. A mischievous act.
3. An object of amusement or laughter: *The employees consider their inept boss a joke.*
4. *Slang.* Something or someone uproariously funny or absurd.

2. PRANK.
3. **Syns:** butt[3], jest, laughingstock, mockery.
4. SCREAM *noun.*

joke *verb*
1. To make jokes; behave playfully: *joking with his friends.*
2. To tease or mock good-humoredly: *joked him about his shyness with girls.*

1. **Syns:** clown (around) (*Informal*), fool (around) (*Informal*), fun, jest.
2. **Syns:** banter, chaff, fun, jest, jive (*Slang*), josh, kid (*Informal*), rag (*Slang*), razz (*Slang*), rib (*Slang*), ride (*Informal*).

joker *noun*
A person whose words or actions provoke or are intended to provoke amusement or laughter: *His uncle is quite a joker.*

Syns: card (*Informal*), clown, comedian, comic, cutup (*Informal*), farceur (*also* farcer), humorist, jester, jokester, wag[2], wit, zany.

jokester *noun*
A person whose words or actions provoke or are intended to provoke amusement or laughter.

JOKER.

jollity *noun*
1. Joyful, exuberant activity.
2. A state of joyful exuberance.

1. GAIETY.
2. GAIETY.

jolly *adjective*
Characterized by joyful exuberance.

GAY *adjective.*

jolt *verb*
1. To proceed with sudden, abrupt movements.
2. To cause to experience a sudden, momentary shock.

1. BUMP *verb.*
2. STARTLE *verb.*

jolt *noun*
1. Something that jars the mind or emotions.
2. Violent, forcible contact between two or more things.

1. SHOCK *noun.*
2. COLLISION.

jolting *adjective*
Causing momentary shock.

STARTLING.

josh *verb*
To tease or mock good-humoredly.

JOKE *verb.*

jot *noun*
1. A tiny amount.
2. The least bit.

1. BIT[1].
2. DAMN *noun.*

journey *verb*
1. To make or go on a journey: *journeying to Spain; journeyed through the mountains.*
2. To move along a particular course.

1. **Syns:** pass, peregrinate, travel, trek, trip (*Rare*). —*Idiom* hit the road.
2. GO *verb.*

joust *noun*
Any competition or test of opposing wills likened to the sport in which knights fought with lances.

TILT *noun.*

jovial *adjective*
Characterized by joyful exuberance.

GAY *adjective.*

joviality *noun*
A state of joyful exuberance.

GAIETY.

jovialness *noun*
A state of joyful exuberance.

GAIETY.

joy *noun*
1. A condition of supreme well-being and good spirits.
2. A feeling of extreme gratification aroused by something good or desired.

1. HAPPINESS.
2. DELIGHT *noun*.

joy *verb*
1. *Archaic.* To give great or keen pleasure to.
2. To feel or take joy or pleasure.

1. DELIGHT *verb*.
2. REJOICE.

joyful *adjective*
1. Providing joy and pleasure.
2. Marked by festal celebration.

1. GLAD.
2. MERRY.

joyless *adjective*
Tending to cause sadness or low spirits.

SAD.

joyous *adjective*
1. Providing joy and pleasure.
2. Marked by festal celebration.

1. GLAD.
2. MERRY.

jubilance *noun*
The act or condition of feeling an uplifting joy over a success or victory.

EXULTATION.

jubilant *adjective*
Feeling or expressing an uplifting joy over a success or victory.

EXULTANT.

jubilate *verb*
To feel or express an uplifting joy over a success or victory.

EXULT.

jubilation *noun*
The act or condition of feeling an uplifting joy over a success or victory.

EXULTATION.

Judas *noun*
One who betrays.

BETRAYER.

judge *verb*
1. To make a decision about (a controversy, dispute, etc.) after deliberation, as in a court of law: *The jury judged the merits of the case.*
2. To draw a conclusion from evidence or reasoning.
3. To make a judgment as to the worth or value of.

1. *Syns:* adjudge, adjudicate, arbitrate, decide, decree, determine, referee, rule, umpire.
2. INFER.
3. ESTIMATE *verb*.

judge *noun*
1. A public official who decides cases brought before a court of law in order to administer justice: *a judge in the appellate court.*
2. A person, usu. appointed, who decides the issues or results, or supervises the conduct, of a competition or conflict: *a judge in the skating championships.*

1. *Syns:* justice, magistrate.

2. *Syns:* arbiter, arbitrator, ref (*Slang*), referee, ump (*Slang*), umpire.
Near-syns: conciliator, counselor, intermediary, mediator, negotiator, peacemaker.

3. A person who evaluates and reports on the worth of something.

3. CRITIC.

judgment *noun*
1. The ability to make sensible decisions.
2. A position arrived at by reasoning from premises or general principles.
3. The act or result of judging the worth or value of something or someone.
4. An authoritative or official decision, esp. one made by a court.
5. A judicial decision, esp. one setting the punishment to be inflicted on a convicted person.

1. COMMON SENSE.
2. DEDUCTION.

3. ESTIMATE *noun*.

4. RULING *noun*.

5. SENTENCE *noun*.

judgmental *adjective*
Based on individual judgment or discretion.

ARBITRARY.

judicious *adjective*
Possessing, proceeding from, or exhibiting good judgment and prudence.

SANE.

jug *noun*
Slang. A place for the confinement of persons in lawful
detention.   JAIL *noun.*

juju *noun*
A small object worn or kept for its supposed magical
power.   CHARM *noun.*

jumble *verb*
1. To put out of proper order.   1. DISORDER *verb.*
2. To put into total disorder.   2. CONFUSE.
3. To mix together so as to change the order of   3. SHUFFLE.
   arrangement.

jumble *noun*
1. A lack of order or regular arrangement.   1. DISORDER *noun.*
2. A collection of various things.   2. ASSORTMENT.

jumbled *adjective*
Characterized by physical confusion.   CONFUSED.

jumbo *noun*
One that is extraordinarily large and powerful.   GIANT *noun.*

jumbo *adjective*
Of extraordinary size and power.   GIANT *adjective.*

jump *verb*
1. To move off the ground by a muscular effort of the   1. *Syns:* hurdle, leap, spring, vault^2.
   legs and feet: *jumped three feet into the air.*
2. To move suddenly and involuntarily: *always jumps*   2. *Syns:* bolt, start, startle.
   when the telephone rings.
3. To increase in amount.   3. RAISE *verb.*
4. To raise in rank.   4. PROMOTE.
5. To catapult oneself from a disabled aircraft.   5. EJECT.

jump *noun*
1. The act of jumping: *gave a jump for joy.*   1. *Syns:* hurdle, leap, spring, vault^2.
2. A sudden lively movement.   2. BOUNCE *noun.*
3. A sudden and involuntary movement: *woke up with*   3. *Syns:* bolt, start, startle.
   a jump.
4. A progression upward in rank.   4. ADVANCEMENT.
5. A dominating position, as in a conflict.   5. ADVANTAGE *noun.*
6. The act of increasing or rising.   6. INCREASE *noun.*
7. The amount by which something is increased.   7. INCREASE *noun.*

jumps *noun*
Informal. A state of nervous restlessness or agitation.   JITTERS.

jumpy *adjective*
Feeling or exhibiting nervous tension.   EDGY.

junction *noun*
1. The act or fact of coming together: *St. Louis is near*   1. *Syns:* concourse, concursion, confluence,
   the junction of the Mississippi and Missouri rivers.   convergence, gathering, meeting.
2. A point or position at which two or more things are   2. JOINT *noun.*
   joined.

juncture *noun*
1. A decisive point.   1. CRISIS.
2. A particular interval of time that is limited and   2. INSTANT *noun.*
   often crucial.
3. A point or position at which two or more things are   3. JOINT *noun.*
   joined.

jungle *noun*
Something that is intricately and often bewilderingly
complex.   TANGLE *noun.*

junior *noun*
One belonging to a lower class or rank.   SUBORDINATE *noun.*

junk *verb*
To let go or get rid of as being no longer of use, value,   DISCARD.
etc.

junket *noun*
1. A setting out or venturing forth.
2. A large meal elaborately prepared or served.

1. TRIP *noun*.
2. FEAST.

jurisdiction *noun*
The right and power to command, decide, rule, or judge.

AUTHORITY.

jus *noun*
Latin. The formal product of a legislative or judicial body.

LAW *noun*.

just *adjective*
1. Consistent with prevailing or accepted standards or circumstances: *Many believe that execution is never a just punishment.*

1. **Syns:** appropriate, deserved, due, merited, right, rightful, suitable.
Near-ants: improper; inapplicable, inappropriate; cruel, excessive, harsh, unsuitable, unwarranted.
Ant: unjust.

2. Free from bias in judgment.
3. Based on good judgment, reasoning, or evidence.

2. FAIR *adjective*.
3. SOUND.

just *adverb*
1. Only a moment ago: *just walked in.*
2. By a very little; almost not.
3. Nothing more than.
4. In the same manner.
5. Without exception; in its entirety.

1. **Syns:** newly, recently.
2. BARELY.
3. MERELY.
4. EVEN[1] *adverb*.
5. PURELY.

justice *noun*
1. The state, action, or principle of treating all persons equally in accordance with the law: *Justice prevailed at the trial.*
2. The quality or state of being just and unbiased.
3. A public official who decides cases brought before a court of law in order to administer justice.

1. **Syns:** equitableness, equity. —*Idiom* due process.

2. FAIRNESS.
3. JUDGE *noun*.

justifiable *adjective*
Capable of being justified: *a justifiable reaction.*

Syns: defensible, excusable, tenable.
Near-syns: admissible, allowable, condonable, legitimate, pardonable, reasonable.
Ant: unjustifiable.

justification *noun*
1. A statement that justifies or defends past actions, policies, etc.
2. A justifying fact or consideration.
3. That which provides a reason or justification.
4. A statement of causes or motives.

1. APOLOGY.
2. BASIS.
3. CAUSE *noun*.
4. ACCOUNT *noun*.

justify *verb*
1. To show to be just, right, or valid: *He lamely tried to justify his mistaken conduct.*
2. To present evidence in support of.
3. To be a proper or sufficient occasion for.
4. To assure the certainty or validity of.
5. To support against arguments, attack, or criticism.
6. To offer reasons for or a cause of.

1. **Syns:** excuse, explain away, rationalize, vindicate. —*Idiom* make a case for.
2. BACK *verb*.
3. CALL FOR at **call**.
4. CONFIRM.
5. DEFEND.
6. ACCOUNT FOR at **account**.

justly *adverb*
In a just way.

FAIRLY.

justness *noun*
The quality or state of being just and unbiased.

FAIRNESS.

jut *verb*
1. To curve outward past the normal or usual limit.
2. To incline downward or over.

1. BULGE *verb*.
2. HANG *verb*.

jut *noun*
A part that protrudes or extends outward.

BULGE *noun*.

juvenescence *noun*
The time of life between childhood and maturity.

YOUTH.

juvenile *adjective*
1. Of or characteristic of a child, esp. in immaturity.
2. Being in an early period of growth or development.

1. CHILDISH.
2. YOUNG *adjective*.

juvenile *noun*
A young person between birth and puberty.

CHILD.

juvenility *noun*
1. The time of life between childhood and maturity.
2. Young people collectively.

1. YOUTH.
2. YOUNG *noun*.

juxtapose *verb*
To be contiguous or next to.

ADJOIN.

juxtaposed *adjective*
Sharing a common boundary.

ADJOINING.

K

kaput *adjective*
Slang. No longer effective, capable, or valuable.

THROUGH *adjective*.

keel over *verb*
To suffer temporary loss of consciousness.

BLACK OUT.

keen[1] *adjective*
1. Mentally quick and original.
2. Possessing or displaying perceptions of great accuracy and sensitivity.
3. Having a fine edge, as for cutting.
4. Intensely desirous or interested.
5. Showing or having enthusiasm.
6. *Slang.* Particularly excellent.

1. CLEVER.
2. ACUTE.

3. SHARP *adjective*.
4. EAGER.
5. ENTHUSIASTIC.
6. MARVELOUS

keen[2] *verb*
To make inarticulate sounds of grief or pain, usu. accompanied by tears.

CRY *verb*.

keenness *noun*
1. Skill in perceiving, discriminating, or judging.
2. A cutting quality.

1. DISCERNMENT.
2. EDGE *noun*.

keep *verb*
1. To persevere in some condition, action, or belief: *keep quiet; kept a busy schedule.*
2. To mark (a day or event) with ceremonies of respect, festivity, or rejoicing.
3. To act in conformity with.
4. To control, restrict, or arrest.
5. To hold oneself back.
6. To have and maintain in one's possession.
7. To reserve for the future.
8. To have or put in a customary place: *keeps the pots in the kitchen.*
9. To supply with the necessities of life.
10. To have for sale.
11. To remain fresh and unspoiled: *The soufflé won't keep.*

1. *Syns:* maintain, retain, stay with.

2. CELEBRATE.

3. FOLLOW.
4. RESTRAIN.
5. REFRAIN.
6. HOLD *verb*.
7. SAVE.
8. *Syns:* stash, store.

9. SUPPORT *verb*.
10. CARRY.
11. *Syns:* last[2], stay[1].

keep back *verb*
1. To have and maintain in one's possession.
2. To control, restrict, or arrest.

1. HOLD *verb*.
2. RESTRAIN.

keep off *verb*
To turn or drive away.   PARRY.
keep on *verb*
To continue without halting.   CARRY ON at **carry.**
keep out *verb*
To keep from being admitted, included, or considered.   EXCLUDE.
keep up *verb*
To keep in a condition of good repair, efficiency, or use.   MAINTAIN.
keep *noun*
1. The means needed to support life.   1. LIVING *noun.*
2. A place for the confinement of persons in lawful   2. JAIL *noun.*
   detention.
keep back *verb*   SEE **keep.**
keeper *noun*
A person who is legally responsible for the person or   GUARDIAN.
property of another considered by law to be
incompetent to manage his affairs.
keeping *noun*
The function of watching, guarding, or overseeing.   CARE *noun.*
keep off *verb*   SEE **keep.**
keep on *verb*   SEE **keep.**
keep out *verb*   SEE **keep.**
keepsake *noun*
Something that causes one to remember.   REMEMBRANCE.
keep up *verb*   SEE **keep.**
ken *noun*
The extent of one's perception, understanding,   *Syns:* horizon, purview, range, reach,
knowledge, or vision: *The speaker went into technical*   scope.
details beyond the ken of the audience.   *Near-syns:* ability, acumen,
                                                                 comprehension, grasp, perception,
                                                                 understanding.

ken *verb*
1. *Archaic.* To apprehend (images) by use of the eyes.   1. SEE.
2. *Scot.* To perceive and recognize the meaning of.   2. UNDERSTAND.
kernel *noun*
1. A fertilized plant ovule capable of germinating.   1. SEED *noun.*
2. A source of further growth and development.   2. GERM.
3. The most central and material part.   3. HEART.
key *noun*
A means or method of entering into or achieving   TICKET *noun.*
something desired.
key *adjective*
1. Dominant in importance or influence.   1. PIVOTAL.
2. Most important, influential, or significant.   2. PRIMARY.
kibitzer *noun*
Informal. A person given to intruding in other people's   MEDDLER.
affairs.
kick *verb*
1. *Slang.* To cut short; discontinue.   1. BREAK *verb.*
2. *Informal.* To express negative feelings, esp. of   2. COMPLAIN.
   dissatisfaction or resentment.
3. *Informal.* To express opposition by argument.   3. OBJECT².
kick around *verb*
Informal. To speak together and exchange ideas and   DISCUSS.
opinions about.
kick in *verb*
1. *Slang.* To give in common with others.   1. CONTRIBUTE.
2. *Slang.* To cease living.   2. DIE.
kick out *verb*
Slang. To put out by force.   EJECT.
kick *noun*

1. *Slang.* A temporary concentration of interest: *He's on a science-fiction kick.*
2. *Slang.* A stimulating or intoxicating effect: *quite a kick in that martini.*
3. *Slang.* A strong, pleasant feeling of excitement or stimulation.
4. *Informal.* A circumstance regarded as a cause for protest or complaint.
5. A clever, unexpected new trick or method.
6. *Informal.* The act of expressing strong or reasoned opposition.

1. **Syns:** binge (*Slang*), thing (*Slang*), trip (*Slang*).
2. **Syns:** punch (*Informal*), sting (*Informal*), wallop.
3. THRILL *noun.*
4. GRIEVANCE.
5. WRINKLE².
6. OBJECTION.

kick around *verb*

SEE **kick.**

kicker *noun*
1. *Informal.* A person who habitually complains or grumbles.
2. A clever, unexpected new trick or method.

1. GROUCH *noun.*
2. WRINKLE².

kick in *verb*

SEE **kick.**

kickoff *noun*

SEE **kick off.**

kick off *verb*
1. *Slang.* To cease living.
2. *Informal.* To go about the initial step in doing (something).

1. DIE.
2. START *verb.*

kickoff *noun*
Informal. The act or process of bringing or being brought into existence.

BEGINNING *noun.*

kick out *verb*

SEE **kick.**

kid *noun*
Informal. A young person between birth and puberty.

CHILD.

kid *verb*
Informal. To tease or mock good-humoredly.

JOKE *verb.*

kidnap *verb*
To seize and detain (a person) unlawfully: *Terrorists kidnapped the ambassador.*

Syns: abduct, carry off, snatch (*Slang*), spirit away.
Near-syns: cajole, coax; decoy, entice, inveigle, lure, seduce; shanghai, waylay.

kidney *noun*
A person's customary manner of emotional response.

DISPOSITION.

kill *verb*
1. To cause the death of: *Famine killed thousands.*

1. **Syns:** carry off, cut off, destroy, dispatch, do in (*Informal*), finish, finish off (*Informal*), slay, zap (*Slang*).
   —*Idioms* lay low, put an end to, put to sleep.
   Near-syns: massacre, slaughter; annihilate, exterminate, ruin, sacrifice.

2. To take the life of (a person or persons) unlawfully.
3. *Slang.* To decide not to go ahead with (something previously arranged).

2. MURDER *verb.*
3. CANCEL.

killer *noun*
One who murders another.

MURDERER.

killing *noun*
The crime of murdering someone.

MURDER *noun.*

killing *adjective*
1. *Slang.* Arousing laughter.
2. *Informal.* Extremely funny.

1. AMUSING.
2. PRICELESS.

kilter *noun*
A state of sound readiness.

TRIM *noun.*

kin *noun*
1. One's relatives collectively: *His kin thought he was dead.*
2. A person connected to another person by blood.

1. **Syns:** kindred, kinsfolk (*also* kinfolk).
2. RELATIVE *noun.*

kind[1] *adjective*
Having or showing a tender, considerate, and helping nature: *a kind person; a kind gesture.*

Syns: benign, benignant, good-hearted, kindhearted, kindly.
Near-syns: altruistic, benevolent, charitable, compassionate, cordial, genial, supportive, sympathetic, tender, warm.
Ant: unkind.

kind[2] *noun*
A class that is defined by the common attribute or attributes possessed by all its members: *the kind of people who dress for dinner; flowers of every kind.*

Syns: breed, cast, cut, description, feather, ilk, lot, manner, mold, nature, order, persuasion, sort, species, stamp, stripe, type, variety.
Near-syns: brand, character, class, form, specimen; category, group.

kindhearted *adjective*
Having or showing a tender, considerate, and helping nature.

KIND[1].

kindle *verb*
1. To cause to burn or undergo combustion.
2. To arouse the emotions of; make ardent.
3. To induce or elicit (a reaction or emotion).
4. To stir to action or feeling.

1. LIGHT[1] *verb.*
2. FIRE *verb.*
3. AROUSE.
4. PROVOKE.

kindliness *noun*
Kindly, charitable interest in others.

BENEVOLENCE.

kindly *adjective*
Having or showing a tender, considerate, and helping nature.

KIND[1].

kindness *noun*
1. The quality or state of being kind: *impossible to repay their kindness.*
2. A kindly act.
3. A charitable deed.

1. *Syn:* benignity (*also* benignancy).
2. FAVOR *noun.*
3. BENEVOLENCE.

kindred *noun*
1. A group of people sharing common ancestry.
2. One's relatives collectively.

1. FAMILY.
2. KIN.

kindred *adjective*
Connected by or as if by kinship or common origin.

RELATED.

kinetic *adjective*
Possessing, exerting, or displaying energy.

ENERGETIC.

kinfolk *noun*

SEE **kinsfolk.**

kinsfolk also **kinfolk** *noun*
One's relatives collectively.

KIN.

kinsman *noun*
A person connected to another person by blood.

RELATIVE *noun.*

kinswoman *noun*
A person connected to another person by blood.

RELATIVE *noun.*

kismet *noun*
That which is inevitably destined.

FATE *noun.*

kiss *verb*
1. To touch or caress with the lips, esp. as a sign of passion or affection: *I kissed her good-bye.*
2. To make light and momentary contact with, as in passing.

1. *Syns:* buss, osculate, peck[2], smack[1], smooch.
2. BRUSH *verb.*

kiss off *verb*
Slang. To rid one's mind of.

DISMISS.

kiss *noun*
The act or an instance of kissing: *gave me a kiss.*

Syns: buss, peck[2], smack[1], smacker, smooch.

kisser *noun*
Slang. The front surface of the head.

FACE *noun.*

kiss off *verb*

SEE **kiss.**

klutz *noun*
Slang. A large, ungainly, and dull-witted person.   LUMP[1] *noun.*

klutzy *adjective*
Slang. Lacking dexterity and grace in physical   AWKWARD.
movement.

knack *noun*
1. Natural or acquired facility in a specific activity.   **1.** ABILITY.
2. An innate capability.   **2.** TALENT.
3. A skill in doing or performing that is attained by   **3.** ART.
    study, practice, or observation.
4. The proper method for doing, using, or handling   **4.** HANG *noun.*
    something.

knead *verb*
To handle in a way so as to mix, form, and shape.   WORK *verb.*

knell *verb*
To give forth or cause to give forth a clear, resonant   RING[2].
sound.

knickknack *noun*
A small, showy article.   NOVELTY.

knifelike *adjective*
Marked by severity or intensity.   SHARP.

knightly *adjective*
Characterized by elaborate but usu. formal courtesy.   GRACIOUS.

knob *noun*
1. A part that protrudes or extends outward.   **1.** BULGE *noun.*
2. An unevenness or elevation on a surface.   **2.** BUMP *noun.*
3. A small raised area of skin resulting from a light   **3.** BUMP *noun.*
    blow, an insect sting, etc.

knock *verb*
1. To deliver (a powerful blow) suddenly and sharply.   **1.** HIT *verb.*
2. To make a noise by striking.   **2.** TAP[1] *verb.*
3. *Slang.* To think, represent, or speak of as small or   **3.** BELITTLE.
    unimportant.

knock around *verb*
1. To injure or damage, as by abuse or heavy wear.   **1.** BATTER.
2. *Informal.* To speak together and exchange ideas and   **2.** DISCUSS.
    opinions.

knock down *verb*
1. To cause to fall, as from a shot or blow.   **1.** DROP *verb.*
2. To break up so that reconstruction is impossible.   **2.** DESTROY.

knock off *verb*
1. *Informal.* To take away (a quantity) from another   **1.** DEDUCT.
    quantity.
2. *Slang.* To take the life of (a person or persons)   **2.** MURDER *verb.*
    unlawfully.
3. *Slang.* To take property or possessions from (a   **3.** ROB.
    person, company, etc.) unlawfully and usu. forcibly.

knock over *verb*
1. To turn or cause to turn from a vertical or   **1.** OVERTURN.
    horizontal position.
2. *Slang.* To take property or possessions from (a   **2.** ROB.
    person, company, etc.) unlawfully and usu. forcibly.

knock *noun*
An audible blow.   TAP[1] *noun.*

knockabout *adjective*   SEE **knock about.**

knock about *verb*
1. To injure or damage, as by abuse or heavy wear.   **1.** BATTER.
2. *Informal.* To speak together and exchange ideas and   **2.** DISCUSS.
    opinions about.

knockabout *adjective*
Marked by vigorous physical exertion.   ROUGH.

knock around *verb*   SEE **knock.**

knock down *verb*   SEE **knock.**

knocker *noun*
Slang. A person who finds fault, often severely and   CRITIC.
willfully.

knock off *verb*   SEE **knock.**

knockout *noun*   SEE **knock out.**

knock out *verb*
1. *Informal.* To make extremely tired.   1. EXHAUST.
2. *Informal.* To render powerless or motionless by 2. DISABLE.
   inflicting severe injury.

knockout *noun*
Slang. A woman regarded as beautiful.   BEAUTY.

knock over *verb*   SEE **knock.**

knot *noun*
1. A part that protrudes or extends outward.   1. BULGE *noun.*
2. That which unites or binds.   2. BOND *noun.*
3. A small raised area of skin resulting from a light 3. BUMP *noun.*
   blow, an insect sting, etc.
4. A number of individuals making up or considered a 4. GROUP *noun.*
   unit.
5. Something that is intricately and often   5. TANGLE *noun.*
   bewilderingly complex.

knot *verb*
To make fast or firmly fixed by means of a cord, rope, TIE *verb.*
etc.

knotty *adjective*
1. Difficult to understand due to intricacy.   1. COMPLEX *adjective.*
2. Not easy to do, achieve, or master.   2. DIFFICULT.

know *verb*
1. To perceive directly with the intellect: *He knows* 1. **Syns:** apprehend, comprehend, fathom,
   quantum mechanics.   grasp, understand.
                                                        Near-syns: acknowledge, appreciate,
                                                        discern, discriminate, distinguish,
                                                        realize.
2. To undergo an emotional reaction.   2. FEEL *verb.*
3. To recognize as being different.   3. DISTINGUISH.
4. To perceive to be identical with something held in 4. RECOGNIZE.
   the memory.
5. To participate in or partake of personally.   5. EXPERIENCE *verb.*

knowable *adjective*
Capable of being readily understood.   UNDERSTANDABLE.

know-how *noun*
1. *Informal.* Natural or acquired facility in a specific 1. ABILITY.
   activity.
2. *Informal.* A skill in doing or performing that is 2. ART.
   attained by study, practice, or observation.

knowing *adjective*
1. Having or showing intelligence, often of a high   1. INTELLIGENT.
   order.
2. Marked by comprehension, cognizance, and   2. AWARE.
   perception.
3. Possessing or showing sound judgment and keen   3. WISE[1].
   perception.
4. Having or showing a clever awareness and   4. SHREWD.
   resourcefulness.

know-it-all *noun*
Informal. One who is obnoxiously self-assertive and SMART ALECK.
arrogant.

knowledge *noun*
1. That which is known; the sum of what has been perceived, discovered, or inferred: *new additions to our knowledge about the universe.*

2. Known facts, ideas, and skill that have been imparted.

knowledgeable *adjective*
1. Having or showing intelligence, often of a high order.
2. Provided with information; made aware.

kook *noun*
Slang. An insanely foolish or strange person.

kooky *adjective*
Slang. Causing puzzlement; perplexing.

kowtow *noun*
An inclination of the head or body, as in greeting, consent, courtesy, submission, or worship.

kowtow *verb*
To support slavishly every opinion or suggestion of a superior.

kudize *verb*
Informal. To express warm approval of.

kudos *noun*
1. Recognition of achievement or superiority or a sign of this.
2. An expression of warm approval.

Kultur *noun*
German. The total product of human creativity and intellect at a particular time.

1. **Syns:** information, lore, wisdom. **Near-syns:** abstract, compendium, corpus; data, evidence, facts; intelligence, news, science.
2. EDUCATION.

1. INTELLIGENT.

2. INFORMED.

CRACKPOT.

FUNNY.

BOW *noun.*

FAWN.

PRAISE *verb.*

1. DISTINCTION.

2. PRAISE *noun.*

CULTURE.

L

label *noun*
An identifying or descriptive slip.

label *verb*
1. To attach a ticket to.
2. To describe with a word or term.
3. To set off by or as if by a mark indicating ownership or manufacture.

labor *noun*
1. Physical exertion that is usu. difficult and exhausting: *a life full of labor and little rest.*

2. The act or process of bringing forth young.
labor *verb*
1. To exert one's mental or physical powers, usu. under

TICKET *noun.*

1. TICKET *verb.*
2. CALL *verb.*
3. MARK *verb.*

1. **Syns:** bullwork, drudgery, fag, moil, sweat, toil, travail, work. —*Idioms* lick (*or* stroke) of work, sweat of one's brow. **Near-ants:** amusement, entertainment, leisure, recreation, repose, rest.
2. BIRTH *noun.*

1. **Syns:** drive, fag, moil, strain[1], strive,

difficulty and to the point of exhaustion: *The child labored over his homework. My father labored all his life to support us.*

2. To force to work.
3. To express at greater length or in greater detail.
4. *Archaic.* To prepare (soil) for the planting and raising of crops.

labored *adjective*
1. Not natural or spontaneous.
2. Lacking fluency or gracefulness.

laborer *noun*
One who labors: *migrant farm laborers.*

laborious *adjective*
1. Imposing a severe test of bodily or spiritual strength.
2. Not easy to do, achieve, or master.

labyrinth *noun*
Something that is intricately and often bewilderingly complex.

labyrinthine *adjective*
Difficult to understand due to intricacy.

lachrymose *adjective*
Filled with or shedding tears.

lack *verb*
To be without what is needed, required, or essential: *a house that lacks indoor plumbing; a school that lacks discipline.*

lack *noun*
1. The condition of lacking a usual or needed amount.
2. The condition or fact of being deficient.

lackadaisical *adjective*
Lacking energy and vitality.

lacking *adjective*
1. Deficient in a usual or needed amount.
2. Lacking an essential element.

lackluster *adjective*
1. Lacking gloss and luster.
2. Lacking liveliness, charm, or surprise.

laconic *adjective*
Marked by or consisting of few words.

lacuna *noun*
An interval during which continuity is suspended.

lade *verb*
1. To place a burden or heavy load on.
2. To take a substance, as liquid, from a container by plunging the hand or a utensil into it.
3. To fill to overflowing.

la-de-da *adjective*

la-di-da also **la-de-da** *adjective*
Informal. Artificially genteel.

ladies' man *noun*

ladle *verb*
To take a substance, as liquid, from a container by plunging the hand or a utensil into it.

ladykiller *noun*
Slang. A man who philanders.

---

sweat, toil, travail, tug, work. —*Idiom* break one's back (*or* neck).

2. WORK *verb.*
3. ELABORATE *verb.*
4. TILL.

1. FORCED.
2. PONDEROUS.

Syns: coolie (*also* cooly), hand, operative, roustabout, worker, workhand, workingman, workman. —*Idiom* beast of burden.

1. BURDENSOME.

2. DIFFICULT.

TANGLE *noun.*

COMPLEX *adjective.*

TEARFUL.

Syns: need, require, want.

1. ABSENCE.
2. SHORTAGE.

LANGUID.

1. ABSENT.
2. DEFICIENT.

1. DULL *adjective.*
2. DULL *adjective.*

BRIEF.

GAP.

1. CHARGE *verb.*
2. DIP *verb.*

3. HEAP *verb.*
SEE **la-di-da.**

AFFECTED[2].
SEE **lady's man.**

DIP *verb.*

PHILANDERER.

lady's man also **ladies' man**   *noun*
A man who philanders.
PHILANDERER.

lag   *verb*
To go or move slowly so that progress is hindered.
DELAY *verb.*

lag   *noun*
1. One that lags.
2. The condition or fact of being made late or slow.

1. LAGGARD *noun.*
2. DELAY *noun.*

lag   *adjective*
Rare. Of or relating to a terminative condition, stage, or point.
LAST¹ *adjective.*

laggard   *noun*
One that lags: *That child is a real laggard on field trips. The company was a laggard in the drive to conserve energy.*

Syns: lag, lingerer, loiterer, poke, slowpoke (*Informal*), straggler. —*Idiom* slow coach.
Near-ants: eager beaver (*Informal*), go-getter (*Informal*), hustler, live wire (*Informal*).

laggard   *adjective*
Proceeding at a rate less than usual or desired.
SLOW *adjective.*

lagging   *adjective*
1. Not progressing and developing as fast as others, as in economic and social aspects.
2. Proceeding at a rate less than usual or desired.

1. BACKWARD *adjective.*
2. SLOW *adjective.*

lagniappe   *noun*
Informal. A material favor or gift, usu. money, given in return for service.
GRATUITY.

laid-back   *adjective*
Slang. Unconstrained by rigid standards.
EASYGOING.

laid up   *adjective*
Informal. Suffering from or affected with an illness.
SICK.

lair   *noun*
1. A hollow place used as an animal's dwelling.
2. A hiding place.

1. HOLE *noun.*
2. HIDE-OUT.

lair   *verb*
To shut oneself up in secrecy.
HOLE UP at **hole.**

lamb   *noun*
A pure, uncorrupted person.
INNOCENT *noun.*

lambaste   *verb*
1. *Slang.* To hit heavily and repeatedly.
2. *Slang.* To criticize for a fault or offense.

1. BEAT *verb.*
2. CALL DOWN at **call.**

lambasting   *noun*
Slang. A severe defeat.
TROUNCING.

lambent   *adjective*
Giving off or reflecting light readily or in large amounts.
BRIGHT.

lament   *verb*
To feel, show, or express grief.
GRIEVE.

lamentable   *adjective*
Causing sorrow or regret.
SORROWFUL.

lamia   *noun*
A woman who practices magic.
WITCH *noun.*

lamina   *noun*
A thin outer covering of an object.
SKIN *noun.*

lampoon   *noun*
A work, as a novel or play, that exposes folly by the use of humor or irony.
SATIRE.

lancinating   *adjective*
Marked by severity or intensity.
SHARP.

land   *noun*
1. *Law.* Usu. extensive real estate: *an English noble who owned land in Scotland.*
1. *Syns:* acres, estate, property.

2. An organized geopolitical unit.

land *verb*
1. To come to rest on the ground: *The jet landed. When I fell, I landed on my back.*
2. To come ashore from a seacraft: *The D-day invasion forces landed on the Normandy beaches.*
3. To come into possession of.

language *noun*
1. A system of terms used by a people sharing a history and culture: *Polish, Russian, and Serbo-Croatian are Slavic languages.*
2. Specialized expressions indigenous to a particular field, subject, trade, or subculture: *Chemical engineers speak their own language. The language of the social sciences is often unintelligible to the uninitiated.*

languid *adjective*
1. Lacking energy and vitality: *gave a languid wave of her hand.*

2. Showing weariness: *was obviously languid after her long nap.*

languidness *noun*
A deficiency in mental and physical alertness and activity.

languish *verb*
1. To waste away from longing or grief: *When her husband was killed, she languished and died.*
2. To lose strength or power.

languishing *adjective*
Lacking energy and vitality.

languor *noun*
A deficiency in mental and physical alertness and activity.

languorous *adjective*
1. Lacking energy and vitality.
2. Showing weariness.

lanky *adjective*
Tall, thin, and awkwardly built.

lap *verb*
1. To flow against or along.
2. To flow or move with a low, slapping sound.

lapse *noun*
1. A minor mistake: *a brief lapse of memory.*

2. An act or thought that unintentionally deviates from what is correct, right, or true.
3. A slipping from a higher or better condition to a lower or poorer one: *a lapse into senility; another lapse into vulgarity.*

lapse *verb*
1. To become less active or intense.
2. To slip from a higher or better condition to a former, usu. lower or poorer one.
3. *Law.* To become void, esp. through passage of time or an omission: *The insurance policy lapsed because we failed to renew it.*

---

2. STATE *noun*.

1. *Syns:* alight[1], light[2], set down, settle, touch down.
2. *Syns:* debark, disembark.

3. GET.

1. *Syns:* dialect, speech, tongue, vernacular.

2. *Syns:* cant[2], dialect, idiom, jargon, lexicon, terminology, vernacular, vocabulary.

1. *Syns:* lackadaisical, languishing, languorous, limp, lymphatic, spiritless.
Near-syns: apathetic, enervated, inactive, lethargic, passive, phlegmatic, slothful, sluggish, torpid.
Ants: active, spirited, vivacious.
2. *Syns:* languorous, leaden, listless.

LETHARGY.

1. *Syns:* pine (away), wither.

2. FADE *verb*.

LANGUID.

LETHARGY.

1. LANGUID.
2. LANGUID.

GANGLING.

1. WASH.
2. WASH.

1. *Syns:* fluff (*Informal*), slip (*Informal*), slip-up (*Informal*).
2. ERROR.

3. *Syns:* backslide, backsliding, recidivation, recidivism, relapse.

1. SUBSIDE.
2. RELAPSE *verb*.

3. *Syns:* expire, run out.

4. *Poetic.* To move smoothly, continuously, and effortlessly.

larcener *noun*
A person who steals: *a larcener who specializes in automobiles.*

larcenist *noun*
A person who steals.

larcenous *adjective*
Tending to larceny: *larcenous white-collar workers who stole supplies.*

larceny *noun*
The crime of taking someone else's property without consent: *convicted of larceny.*

lardy-dardy *adjective*
Slang. Artificially genteel.

lares and penates *noun*
One's portable property.

large *adjective*
1. Notably above average in amount, size, or scope.
2. Having great significance.
3. Covering a wide scope.

large-hearted *adjective*
Willing to give of oneself and one's possessions.

largeish *adjective*

largeness *noun*
The quality or state of being large in amount, extent, or importance.

larger *adjective*
Much more than half.

large-scale *adjective*
Notably above average in amount, size, or scope.

largess also **largesse** *noun*
A material favor or gift, usu. money, given in return for service.

largesse *noun*

largest *adjective*
Much more than half.

largish also **largeish** *adjective*
Somewhat big.

lark *noun*
A mischievous act.

lash *verb*
1. To move to and fro vigorously and usu. repeatedly.
2. To criticize harshly and devastatingly.

lassitude *noun*
1. The condition of being extremely tired.
2. Lack of emotion or interest.
3. A deficiency in mental and physical alertness and activity.

last¹ *adjective*
1. Coming after all others: *the last act.*

2. Of or relating to a terminative condition, stage, or point: *the last days of Pompeii; a last farewell; last rites.*
3. Bringing up the rear: *the last car in the gas line.*

4. Next before the present one: *last night.*

last *noun*

---

4. GLIDE *verb.*

Syns: larcenist, purloiner, stealer, thief.

LARCENER.

Syns: sticky-fingered, thieving, thievish.

Syns: conveyance (*Archaic*), lifting (*Informal*), pinching (*Slang*), purloining, steal, stealing, theft, thievery, thieving.

AFFECTED².

EFFECTS.

1. BIG *adjective.*
2. IMPORTANT.
3. GENERAL.

GENEROUS.
SEE **largish.**

SIZE.

BEST *adjective.*

BIG *adjective.*

GRATUITY.

SEE **largess.**

BEST *adjective.*

SIZABLE.

PRANK.

1. WAG¹.
2. SLAM *verb.*

1. EXHAUSTION.
2. APATHY.
3. LETHARGY.

1. *Syns:* closing, concluding, final, terminal.
2. *Syns:* final, lag (*Rare*), latter, terminal, ultimate.
3. *Syns:* endmost, hindmost (*also* hindermost), lattermost, rearmost.
4. *Syns:* foregoing, latter, preceding, previous.

The last part.

at last *adverb*

After a considerable length of time, usu. after a delay: *We arrived at last.*

last *adverb*

In conclusion: *Last, we ask you to find this defendant guilty.*

last² *verb*
1. To remain in existence or in a certain state for an indefinitely long time.
2. To exist in spite of adversity.
3. To remain fresh and unspoiled.

lasting *adjective*

Existing or remaining in the same state for an indefinitely long time.

lastly *adverb*

In conclusion.

late *adjective*
1. Not being on time: *was late for the appointment; sent late condolences.*
2. Having been such previously: *the company's late president, now retired; the late capital of that nation.*

3. No longer alive.

late *adverb*
1. Not on time: *arrived late.*
2. So as to fall behind schedule.
3. Not long ago: *As late as last night the hostages had not been released.*

lately *adverb*

Not long ago.

latency *noun*

The condition of being temporarily inactive.

lateness *noun*

The quality or condition of not being on time: *Please forgive the lateness of my arrival.*

latent *adjective*
1. Existing in a temporarily inactive and hidden form: *latent cancer.*

2. Capable of being but not yet in existence.

later *adjective*
1. Following something else in time: *Later developments vindicated my predictions.*
2. Being or occurring in the time ahead.

later *adverb*

At a subsequent time: *I'll finish later. Later we left the club and went home.*

lather *noun*
1. Moisture excreted through the pores of the skin.
2. A mass of bubbles in or on the surface of a liquid.
3. *Slang.* A state of discomposure.

lather *verb*
1. To excrete moisture through the pores of the skin.
2. To form or cause to form foam.

lathery *adjective*

Consisting of or resembling foam.

END *noun*.

Syns: finally, ultimately. —*Idiom* at long last.

Syns: conclusively, finally, lastly.

1. ENDURE.
2. SURVIVE.
3. KEEP *verb*.

CONTINUING.

LAST¹ *adverb*.

1. **Syns:** behindhand, belated, overdue, tardy.
2. **Syns:** erstwhile, former, old, once, one-time (*also* onetime), past, previous, quondam, sometime, whilom.
3. DEAD *adjective*.

1. **Syns:** behind, behindhand.
2. SLOW *adverb*.
3. **Syns:** lately, latterly, recently. —*Idiom* of late.

LATE *adverb*.

ABEYANCE.

Syns: belatedness, tardiness.

1. **Syns:** abeyant, dormant, quiescent, remissive, remittent.
   Near-syns: concealed, hidden; idle, inactive; unacknowledged.
   Ant: patent.
2. POTENTIAL *adjective*.

1. **Syns:** after, posterior, postliminary, subsequent, subsequential.
2. FUTURE *adjective*.

Syns: after, afterward (*also* afterwards), afterwhile, infra, latterly, next. —*Idioms* after a while, by and by, later on.

1. SWEAT *noun*.
2. FOAM *noun*.
3. AGITATION.

1. SWEAT *verb*.
2. FOAM *verb*.

FOAMY.

latitude *noun*
1. Ease of movement.
2. Suitable opportunity to accept or allow something.
3. Departure from normal rules or procedures.

1. FREEDOM.
2. ROOM.
3. LIBERTY.

latter *adjective*
1. Of or relating to a terminative condition, stage, or point.
2. Next before the present one.

1. LAST¹ *adjective*.
2. LAST¹ *adjective*.

latter-day *adjective*
Of or pertaining to recent times or the present.

MODERN.

latterly *adverb*
1. Not long ago.
2. At a subsequent time.

1. LATE *adverb*.
2. LATER *adverb*.

lattermost *adjective*
Bringing up the rear.

LAST¹ *adjective*.

laud *verb*
1. To pay tribute or homage to.
2. To express warm approval of.
3. To honor (God) in religious worship.

1. HONOR *verb*.
2. PRAISE *verb*.
3. PRAISE *verb*.

laudable *adjective*
Deserving admiration.

ADMIRABLE.

laudation *noun*
1. An expression of warm approval.
2. The honoring of God, as in worship.

1. PRAISE *noun*.
2. PRAISE *noun*.

laugh *verb*
To express amusement, mirth, or scorn by smiling and emitting loud, inarticulate sounds: *laughed at the comedian.*

Syns: cachinnate, cackle, heehaw.
—*Idioms* die laughing, laugh one's head off, roll in the aisles, split one's sides.

laugh at *verb*
To make fun of.

RIDICULE *verb*.

laugh *noun*
1. An act of laughing: *gave a hearty laugh.*

2. *Informal.* Something or someone uproariously funny or absurd.

1. *Syns:* cachinnation, cackle, heehaw, laughter.
2. SCREAM *noun*.

laughable *adjective*
1. Deserving laughter: *a laughable matter.*

2. Arousing laughter.

1. *Syns:* comic, comical, farcical, funny, gelastic, laughing, ludicrous, ridiculous, risible.
2. AMUSING.

laugh at *verb*

SEE **laugh**.

laughing *adjective*
1. Emitting a murmuring sound felt to resemble a laugh: *laughing brooks.*
2. Deserving laughter.

1. *Syns:* babbling, burbling, guggling, gurgling, rippling.
2. LAUGHABLE.

laughingstock *noun*
An object of amusement or laughter.

JOKE *noun*.

laughter *noun*
An act of laughing.

LAUGH *noun*.

launch *verb*
1. To go about the initial step in doing (something).
2. To bring into currency, use, fashion, or practice.

1. START *verb*.
2. INTRODUCE.

launching *noun*
The act or process of bringing or being brought into existence.

BEGINNING *noun*.

laurels *noun*
Recognition of achievement or superiority or a sign of this.

DISTINCTION.

lave *verb*
To flow against or along.

WASH.

lavish *adjective*
1. Characterized by excessive or imprudent spending.
2. Characterized by extravagant, ostentatious magnificence.
3. Given to or marked by unrestrained abundance.
lavish *verb*
To give in great abundance.
lavishness *noun*
Excessive or imprudent expenditure.
law *noun*
1. The formal product of a legislative or judicial body: *federal and state laws.*

2. A principle governing the affairs of man within or among political units: *the law of nations; maritime law.*
3. A broad and basic rule or truth: *the laws of decency; the laws of physics.*
4. *Informal.* A member of a law-enforcement agency.
law *verb*
Chiefly Regional. To institute or subject to legal proceedings.
lawbreaker *noun*
One who commits a crime.
lawcourt *noun*
A judicial assembly.
lawful *adjective*
Within, allowed by, or sanctioned by the law: *lawful entry; a lawful marriage.*
lawfulness *noun*
The state or quality of being within the law.
lawless *adjective*
1. Refusing or failing to obey.
2. Of, involving, or being a crime.
3. Contrary to accepted, esp. moral conventions.
4. Prohibited by law.
lawlessness *noun*
A lack of civil order or peace.
lawsuit *noun*
A legal proceeding to demand justice or enforce a right: *The lawsuit was heard in the superior court.*
lax *verb*
To reduce in tension, pressure, or rigidity.
lax *adjective*
1. Not strict or severe.
2. Not tautly bound to something else.
3. Guilty of neglect; lacking due care or concern.
laxity *noun*
The state or quality of being negligent.
laxness *noun*
The state or quality of being negligent.
lay¹ *verb*
1. To place in a designated setting: *The novel is laid in Italy.*
2. To deposit in a specified position.
3. To arrange tableware upon (a table) in preparation for a meal.
4. *Mil.* To move (a weapon, blow, etc.) in the direction of someone or something.
5. To make a bet on.
6. To put up as a stake in a game or speculation.

1. EXTRAVAGANT.
2. LUXURIOUS.

3. PROFUSE.

SHOWER *verb*.

EXTRAVAGANCE.

1. **Syns:** act, assize (*Eng. Hist.*), enactment, jus (*Latin*), legislation, lex, measure, statute.

2. **Syns:** canon, decree, decretum, edict, institute, ordinance, precept, prescription, regulation, rule.
3. **Syns:** axiom, fundamental, principle, theorem, universal.
4. POLICEMAN.

SUE.

CRIMINAL *noun*.

COURT *noun*.

Syns: innocent, legal, legit (*Slang*), legitimate, licit.

LEGALITY.

1. DISOBEDIENT.
2. CRIMINAL *adjective*.
3. UNLAWFUL.
4. ILLEGAL.

DISORDER *noun*.

Syns: action (*Law*), case (*Law*), cause (*Law*), instance, suit (*Law*).

EASE *verb*.

1. TOLERANT.
2. LOOSE *adjective*.
3. NEGLIGENT.

NEGLIGENCE.

NEGLIGENCE.

1. **Syn:** set¹.

2. SET¹ *verb*.
3. SET¹ *verb*.

4. AIM *verb*.

5. BET *verb*.
6. GAMBLE *verb*.

7. To devise and set down.   **7.** DRAFT *verb*.

8. To regard as belonging to or resulting from another.   **8.** ATTRIBUTE *verb*.

9. To bring forward and quote for formal consideration.   **9.** PRESENT² *verb*.

lay aside   *verb*

To reserve for the future.   SAVE.

lay away   *verb*

1. To reserve for the future.   **1.** SAVE.

2. To place (money) in a bank.   **2.** BANK¹.

3. *Informal.* To place (a corpse) in or as if in a grave.   **3.** BURY.

lay by   *verb*

To reserve for the future.   SAVE.

lay down   *verb*

1. To set forth expressly and authoritatively.   **1.** DICTATE *verb*.

2. To put down, esp. in layers, by a natural process.   **2.** DEPOSIT *verb*.

3. To let (something) go.   **3.** RELINQUISH.

4. To make a bet on.   **4.** BET *verb*.

lay for   *verb*

Informal. To wait concealed in order to attack (someone): *The terrorists lay in the bushes for the busload of soldiers.*   ***Syns:*** ambuscade, ambush. —*Idioms* lay wait for, lie in wait for.

lay in   *verb*

To reserve for the future.   SAVE.

lay into   *verb*

To punish with blows or lashes.   BEAT *verb*.

lay low   *verb*

To shut oneself up in secrecy.   HOLE UP at **hole.**

lay off   *verb*

1. *Slang.* To cease trying to accomplish or continue.   **1.** ABANDON *verb*.

2. *Slang.* To come to a cessation.   **2.** STOP *verb*.

lay open   *verb*

To make visible; bring to view.   REVEAL.

lay up   *verb*

1. To accumulate and set aside for future use.   **1.** STOCKPILE *verb*.

2. To store up (supplies or money), usu. well beyond one's needs.   **2.** HOARD *verb*.

lay²   *adjective*

Not religious in subject matter, form, or use.   PROFANE.

lay aside   *verb*   SEE **lay¹**.

lay away   *verb*   SEE **lay¹**.

lay by   *verb*   SEE **lay¹**.

lay down   *verb*   SEE **lay¹**.

lay for   *verb*   SEE **lay¹**.

lay in   *verb*   SEE **lay¹**.

lay into   *verb*   SEE **lay¹**.

lay low   *verb*   SEE **lay¹**.

lay off   *verb*   SEE **lay¹**.

lay open   *verb*   SEE **lay¹**.

layout   *noun*   SEE **lay out.**

lay out   *verb*

1. To work out and arrange the parts or details of.   **1.** DESIGN *verb*.

2. To plan the details or arrangements of.   **2.** ARRANGE.

3. To show graphically the direction or location of.   **3.** PLOT *verb*.

4. *Informal.* To distribute (money) as payment.   **4.** SPEND *verb*.

layout   *noun*

1. A method for making, doing, or accomplishing something.   **1.** DESIGN *noun*.

2. A way or condition of being arranged.   **2.** ARRANGEMENT.

lay over   *verb*

To put off until a later time.   DEFER¹.

lay up   *verb*   SEE **lay¹**.

laze *verb*
To pass time without working or in avoiding work.

IDLE *verb.*

laze *noun*
The quality or state of being lazy.

LAZINESS.

laziness *noun*
The quality or state of being lazy: *Laziness and carelessness have no place in editorial work.*

Syns: fainéancy (*also* fainéance), idleness, indolence, laze, loafing, shiftlessness, sloth, slothfulness, sluggishness.

lazy *adjective*
Resistant to exertion and activity: *a lazy procrastinator.*

Syns: do-nothing, fainéant, idle, indolent, shiftless, slothful, trifling (*Chiefly Regional*). —*Idioms* bone lazy, born tired, lazy as Ludlam's dog.
Near-ants: active, animated, diligent, energetic, hardworking, industrious, spry, vigorous, vivacious.
Ant: productive.

lazy *verb*
To pass time without working or in avoiding work.

IDLE *verb.*

lazybones *noun*
Slang. A self-indulgent person who spends time avoiding work or other useful activity.

WASTREL.

leach *verb*
To flow or leak out slowly.

OOZE.

lead *verb*
1. To have authoritative charge of: *This man has led his troops well.*
2. To show the way to.
3. To begin (something) with preliminary or prefatory material.
4. To convince (another) to adopt a particular faith or belief.
5. To go through (life) in a certain way: *She has led a full and varied life.*
6. To proceed on a certain course or for a certain distance.

1. **Syns:** captain, command, officer.
2. GUIDE *verb.*
3. INTRODUCE.
4. CONVERT *verb.*
5. **Syns:** live[1], pass, pursue.
6. EXTEND.

lead to *verb*
To be the cause of.

CAUSE *verb.*

lead *noun*
1. Something or someone that shows the way.
2. An act or instance of guiding.
3. A piece of information useful in a search: *had picked up a strong lead in the hunt for the killer.*
4. The capacity to lead others: *a young captain who took the lead in battle.*
5. The main performer in a theatrical production: *was the lead in the play.*
6. *Jour.* A prominent article in a periodical.

1. GUIDE *noun.*
2. GUIDANCE.
3. **Syns:** clue (*also* clew), scent.
4. **Syns:** command, leadership.
5. **Syns:** principal, protagonist, star.
6. FEATURE *noun.*

leaden *adjective*
Showing weariness.

LANGUID.

leader *noun*
1. A leading contestant: *the leader in the marathon.*
2. Something or someone that shows the way.
3. One who is highest in rank or authority.
4. A professional politician who controls a party or political machine.
5. *Chiefly Brit.* A prominent article in a periodical.
6. An important, influential person.

1. **Syns:** front-runner, number one (*Informal*).
2. GUIDE *noun.*
3. CHIEF *noun.*
4. BOSS *noun.*
5. FEATURE *noun.*
6. DIGNITARY.

leadership *noun*
1. The capacity to lead others.

1. LEAD *noun.*

2. An act or instance of guiding.

2. GUIDANCE.

leading *adjective*

1. Most important, influential, or significant.

1. PRIMARY.

2. Widely known and discussed.

2. FAMOUS.

leadoff *noun*

SEE **lead off.**

lead off *verb*

Informal. To go about the initial step in doing (something).

START *verb.*

leadoff *noun*

The act or process of bringing or being brought into existence.

BEGINNING *noun.*

lead to *verb*

SEE **lead.**

leaf *verb*

To look through reading matter casually.

BROWSE.

league *noun*

1. An association, esp. of nations for a common cause.

1. ALLIANCE.

2. A group of athletic teams that play each other.

2. CONFERENCE.

3. *Informal.* A division of persons or things by quality, rank, or grade.

3. CLASS *noun.*

4. A group of people united in a relationship and having some interest, activity, or purpose in common.

4. UNION.

league *verb*

1. To be formally associated, as by treaty.

1. ALLY *verb.*

2. To assemble or join in a group.

2. BAND^2 *verb.*

leaguer *noun*

One nation associated with another in a common cause.

ALLY *noun.*

leak *verb*

To be made public.

COME OUT.

lean^1 *verb*

1. To depart or cause to depart from true vertical or horizontal.

1. INCLINE *verb.*

2. To incline downward or over.

2. HANG *verb.*

3. To have a tendency or inclination.

3. TEND^1.

lean^2 *adjective*

1. Having little flesh or fat on the body.

1. THIN *adjective.*

2. Marked by or consisting of few words.

2. BRIEF.

3. Characterized by an economy of artistic expression.

3. TIGHT *adjective.*

lean *verb*

To make physically thin or thinner.

THIN *verb.*

leaning *noun*

An inclination to something.

BENT *noun.*

leap *verb*

1. To move off the ground by a muscular effort of the legs and feet.

1. JUMP *verb.*

2. To move in a lively way.

2. BOUNCE *verb.*

leap *noun*

1. The act of jumping.

1. JUMP *noun.*

2. A sudden lively movement.

2. BOUNCE *noun.*

learn *verb*

1. To gain knowledge or mastery of by study: *learn French.*

1. *Syns:* get, master, pick up.

2. To obtain knowledge or awareness of something not known before, as through observation, study, etc.

2. DISCOVER.

3. To commit to memory.

3. MEMORIZE.

learned *adjective*

Having or showing profound knowledge and scholarship: *a learned man.*

Syns: erudite, scholarly, scholastic, wise^1.
Near-syns: academic, bookish, pedantic; cultivated, cultured, educated, lettered, literate, sagacious.
Ants: ignorant, uneducated, unlearned.

learner *noun*
One who is being educated.   STUDENT.

learning *noun*
Known facts, ideas, and skill that have been imparted.   EDUCATION.

lease *verb*
To engage the temporary use of (something) for a fee.   HIRE *verb*.

leash *verb*
To restrict the activity or free movement of.   HAMPER.

leave¹ *verb*
1. To give (property) to another person after one's   1. **Syns:** bequeath (*Law*), devise (*Law*),
   death: *My aunt left me a house and $100.*   legate, will².
2. To move or proceed away from a place.   2. GO *verb*.
3. To give up without intending to return or claim   3. ABANDON *verb*.
   again.
4. To relinquish one's engagement in or occupation   4. QUIT.
   with.

    leave off *verb*
    1. To cut short; discontinue.   1. BREAK *verb*.
    2. To come to a cessation.   2. STOP *verb*.

leave² *noun*
1. A regularly scheduled period spent away from work   1. VACATION.
   or duty, often in recreation.
2. Approval for an action, esp. as granted by one in   2. PERMISSION.
   authority.

    leave *verb*
    To neither forbid nor prevent.   PERMIT *verb*.

leaven *noun*
An agent that stimulates or precipitates a reaction,   CATALYST.
development, or change.

leavening *noun*
An agent that stimulates or precipitates a reaction,   CATALYST.
development, or change.

leave off *verb*   SEE **leave¹**.

leave-taking *noun*
A separation of two or more people.   PARTING *noun*.

leaving *noun*
The act of leaving.   DEPARTURE.

leavings *noun*
What remains after a part has been used or subtracted.   BALANCE *noun*.

lecher *noun*
An immoral or licentious man.   WANTON *noun*.

lecture *verb*
To talk to (an audience) formally.   ADDRESS *verb*.

    lecture *noun*
    A usu. formal oral communication to an audience.   SPEECH.

leech *noun*
One who depends on another for support without   PARASITE.
reciprocating.

leery *adjective*
Informal. Refusing or reluctant to believe.   INCREDULOUS.

lees *noun*
Matter that settles on a bottom or collects on a surface   DEPOSIT *noun*.
by a natural process.

leeway *noun*
1. Suitable opportunity to accept or allow something.   1. ROOM.
2. Departure from normal rules or procedures.   2. LIBERTY.

left-handed *adjective*
Not being what one purports to be.   INSINCERE.

leftover *adjective*
That remains, esp. after a part has been removed.   REMAINING.

legacy *noun*
1. Any special privilege accorded a firstborn.
2. Something immaterial, as a style or philosophy, that is passed from one generation to another.

1. BIRTHRIGHT.
2. HERITAGE.

legal *adjective*
Within, allowed by, or sanctioned by the law.

LAWFUL.

legality *noun*
The state or quality of being within the law: *The legality of your actions is suspect.*

Syns: lawfulness, legitimacy, legitimateness, licitness.

legalize *verb*
To make lawful: *tried to legalize marijuana.*

Syns: legitimate, legitimatize, legitimize.

legate *verb*
To give (property) to another person after one's death.

LEAVE[1].

legation *noun*
A diplomatic office or headquarters in a foreign country.

MISSION.

legend *noun*
1. A traditional story or tale dealing with ancestors, heroes, supernatural events, etc., that has no proven factual basis but attempts to explain beliefs, practices, or natural phenomena.
2. A body of traditional beliefs and notions accumulated about a particular subject.

1. MYTH.

2. LORE.

legendary *adjective*
Of or existing only in myths.

MYTHICAL.

legerdemain *noun*
The use of skillful tricks and deceptions to produce entertainingly baffling effects.

MAGIC *noun.*

legion *noun*
A very large number of things grouped together.

CROWD *noun.*

legion *adjective*
Amounting to or consisting of a large, indefinite number.

MANY.

legislate *verb*
To cause to be by official action.

ENACT.

legislation *noun*
The formal product of a legislative or judicial body.

LAW *noun.*

legit *adjective*
Slang. Within, allowed by, or sanctioned by the law.

LAWFUL.

legitimacy *noun*
1. The quality of being authentic.
2. The state or quality of being within the law.

1. AUTHENTICITY.
2. LEGALITY.

legitimate *adjective*
1. Within, allowed by, or sanctioned by the law.
2. Being so legitimately.

1. LAWFUL.
2. TRUE.

legitimate *verb*
To make lawful.

LEGALIZE.

legitimateness *noun*
The state or quality of being within the law.

LEGALITY.

legitimatize *verb*
To make lawful.

LEGALIZE.

legitimize *verb*
To make lawful.

LEGALIZE.

leisure *noun*
Freedom from labor, responsibility, or strain.

REST[1] *noun.*

leisurely *adjective*
Careful and slow in acting, moving, or deciding.

DELIBERATE *adjective.*

lemon *noun*
Informal. One that fails completely.

FAILURE.

lend *verb*
To supply (money), esp. on credit: *refused to lend her any cash.*

length *noun*
1. The ultimate point to which an action, thought, discussion, or policy is carried: *will go to any length to free the hostages.*
2. An extent, measured or unmeasured, of linear space.
3. The measure of how far or long something goes in space, time, or degree.

lengthen *verb*
To make or become longer: *lengthened the table by inserting a leaf; relapses that lengthened her convalescence.*

lengthy *adjective*
1. Having great physical length.
2. Extending tediously beyond a standard duration.

lenience *noun*

leniency also **lenience** *noun*
1. Kind, forgiving, or compassionate treatment of or disposition toward others.
2. Forbearing or lenient treatment.

lenient *adjective*
Not strict or severe.

lenity *noun*
Kind, forgiving, or compassionate treatment of or disposition toward others.

lentitude *noun*
Archaic. A deficiency in mental and physical alertness and activity.

lese majesty also **lèse majesté** *noun*
Lack of proper respect.

lessen *verb*
1. To grow or cause to grow gradually less.
2. To make less severe or more bearable.

lesser *adjective*
Of subordinate standing or importance.

lesson *noun*
An instance that warns or discourages prospective imitators.

let *verb*
1. To neither forbid nor prevent.
2. To give one's consent to.
3. To afford an opportunity for.
4. To engage the temporary use of (something) for a fee.

let in *verb*
To serve as a means of entrance for.

let off *verb*
1. To discharge material, as vapor or fumes, usu. suddenly and violently.
2. To free from an obligation or duty.

let out *verb*
1. To discharge material, as vapor or fumes, usu. suddenly and violently.
2. To disclose in a breach of confidence.
3. To remove (a liquid) by a steady, gradual process.

letdown *noun*

let down *verb*
1. To cause to descend.

Syns: advance, loan.

1. *Syns:* extreme, limit.

2. DISTANCE.
3. EXTENT.

Syns: draw out, elongate, extend, produce (*Geom.*), prolong, prolongate, protract, spin out, stretch (out).

1. LONG[1] *adjective.*
2. LONG[1] *adjective.*
SEE **leniency.**

1. GRACE *noun.*

2. TOLERANCE.

TOLERANT.

GRACE *noun.*

LETHARGY.

DISRESPECT.

1. DECREASE *verb.*
2. RELIEVE.

MINOR *adjective.*

EXAMPLE.

1. PERMIT *verb.*
2. PERMIT *verb.*
3. PERMIT *verb.*
4. HIRE *verb.*

ADMIT.

1. EMIT.
2. EXCUSE *verb.*

1. EMIT.
2. BETRAY.
3. DRAIN.
SEE **let down.**

1. LOWER[2].

2. To cause unhappiness by failing to satisfy the hopes, desires, or expectations of.   **2.** DISAPPOINT.

letdown *noun*
Unhappiness caused by the failure of one's hopes, desires, or expectations.   DISAPPOINTMENT.

lethal *adjective*
Causing or tending to cause death.   DEADLY.

lethargic *adjective*
1. Lacking mental and physical alertness and activity: *lethargic, overtranquilized patients.*

1. *Syns:* dopey (*also* dopy) (*Slang*), hebetudinous, sluggish, stupid, torpid. *Near-syns:* dilatory, lackadaisical, languid, languorous, listless, slow; comatose, slumberous, soporific. *Ant:* energetic.

2. Without emotion or interest.   **2.** APATHETIC.

lethargy *noun*
1. A deficiency in mental and physical alertness and activity: *The overmedicated patient sank into a state of lethargy.*

1. *Syns:* dopeyness (*also* dopiness) (*Slang*), dullness, hebetude, languidness, languor, lassitude, lentitude (*Archaic*), sluggishness, stupor, torpidity, torpidness, torpor.

2. Lack of emotion or interest.   **2.** APATHY.
3. A lack of action or activity.   **3.** INACTION.

let in *verb*   SEE **let.**
let off *verb*   SEE **let.**
let out *verb*   SEE **let.**

letter *noun*
1. A written communication directed to another: *I wrote a letter to my son.*

1. *Syns:* epistle, missive, note.

2. The literal meaning of something: *the letter of the law.*

2. *Syns:* literality, literalness.

lettered *adjective*
Having an education.   EDUCATED.

lettuce *noun*
Slang. Something, as coins, printed bills, etc., used as a medium of exchange.   MONEY.

letup *noun*   SEE **let up.**

let up *verb*
1. To grow or cause to grow gradually less.   **1.** DECREASE *verb.*
2. To become less active or intense.   **2.** SUBSIDE.
3. To reduce in tension, pressure, or rigidity.   **3.** EASE *verb.*

letup *noun*
1. The act or process of decreasing.   **1.** DECREASE *noun.*
2. The act or process of becoming less active or intense.   **2.** WANE *noun.*

level *adjective*
1. On the same plane or line.   **1.** EVEN[1] *adjective.*
2. Having no irregularities, roughness, or indentations.   **2.** EVEN[1] *adjective.*

level *noun*
One of the units in a course, as on an ascending or descending scale.   DEGREE.

level *verb*
1. To make even, smooth, or level.   **1.** EVEN[1] *verb.*
2. To make equal.   **2.** EQUALIZE.
3. To move (a weapon, blow, etc.) in the direction of someone or something.   **3.** AIM *verb.*
4. To break up so that reconstruction is impossible.   **4.** DESTROY.
5. To cause to fall, as from a shot or blow.   **5.** DROP *verb.*

levelheaded *adjective*
Possessing, proceeding from, or exhibiting good judgment and prudence.   SANE.

leverage *noun*
The power to produce an effect by indirect means.   INFLUENCE *noun.*

leviathan *noun*
One that is extraordinarily large and powerful.   GIANT *noun.*

leviathan *adjective*
Of extraordinary size and power.   GIANT *adjective.*

levy *noun*
1. A compulsory contribution, usu. of money, that is   1. TAX *noun.*
   required of persons or groups of persons for the
   support of a government.
2. Compulsory enrollment in military service.   2. DRAFT *noun.*

levy *verb*
1. To establish and apply as compulsory.   1. IMPOSE.
2. To enroll compulsorily in military service.   2. DRAFT *verb.*

lewd *adjective*
Offensive to accepted standards of decency.   OBSCENE.

lewdness *noun*
The quality or state of being obscene.   OBSCENITY.

lex *noun*
The formal product of a legislative or judicial body.   LAW *noun.*

lexicon *noun*
1. An alphabetical list of words often defined or   1. VOCABULARY.
   translated.
2. All the words of a language.   2. VOCABULARY.
3. Specialized expressions indigenous to a particular   3. LANGUAGE.
   field, subject, trade, or subculture.

liability *noun*
1. Something, such as money, owed by one person to   1. DEBT.
   another.
2. A condition of owing something to another.   2. DEBT.
3. The condition of being laid open to something   3. EXPOSURE.
   undesirable or injurious.

liable *adjective*
1. Legally obligated: *a bill to make parents liable for a*   1. **Syns:** accountable, answerable,
   child's vandalism.   responsible.
2. Having or showing a tendency or likelihood.   2. INCLINED.
3. Tending to incur: *liable to asthma attacks.*   3. **Syns:** open, prone, subject, susceptible,
                                                                         vulnerable.

liar *noun*
One who tells lies: *a notorious liar whom no one*   **Syns:** Ananias, fabricator, falsifier, fibber,
believed.   fibster, perjurer, prevaricator, storyteller.
                                                                     —*Idiom* false witness.

libel *noun*
The expression of injurious, malicious statements about   **Syns:** aspersion, calumny, defamation,
someone: *Those remarks about the senator's taking*   detraction, scandal, slander. —*Idioms*
payoffs are libel.   character assassination, malicious
                                                                       falsehood.

libel *verb*
To make defamatory statements about: *libeled his rival*   **Syns:** asperse, calumniate, defame,
on the Senate floor.   malign, scandal, scandalize, slander, slur,
                                                                       spatter, tear down, vilify. —*Idioms* cast
                                                                       aspersions on, sling mud on.

libelous *adjective*
Damaging to the reputation: *libelous remarks for which*   **Syns:** backbiting, calumnious, defamatory,
we brought suit.   detracting, detractive, detractory,
                                                                       injurious, invidious, maligning,
                                                                       scandalous, slanderous, vilifying.
                                                                     Near-syns: debasing, derogatory,
                                                                       disparaging, perjorative, vituperative;
                                                                       contumelious, malevolent, malignant.

liberal   *adjective*
1. Favoring civil liberties and social progress: *holds liberal political opinions.*
2. Not narrow or conservative in thought, expression, or conduct.
3. Free from bias in judgment.
4. Characterized by bounteous giving.
5. Characterized by abundance.

1. **Syns:** liberalistic, progressive.

2. BROAD.

3. FAIR.
4. GENEROUS.
5. GENEROUS.

liberal   *noun*
A person with liberal political opinions: *The liberals will debate the conservatives.*

Syns: liberalist, progressive.

liberalist   *noun*
A person with liberal political opinions.

LIBERAL *noun.*

liberalistic   *adjective*
Favoring civil liberties and social progress.

LIBERAL *adjective.*

liberality   *noun*
The quality or state of being generous.

GENEROSITY.

liberate   *verb*
To set at liberty.

FREE *verb.*

liberated   *adjective*
At liberty; not imprisoned or enslaved.

FREE *adjective.*

liberation   *noun*
The state of not being in confinement or servitude.

LIBERTY.

libertine   *adjective*
Sexually promiscuous.

WANTON *adjective.*

libertine   *noun*
An immoral or licentious man.

WANTON *noun.*

libertinism   *noun*
Excessive freedom; lack of restraint.

LICENSE *noun.*

liberty   *noun*
1. The state of not being in confinement or servitude: *a prisoner given his liberty when he received his parole.*
2. The condition of being politically free.
3. Departure from normal rules or procedures: *too much liberty in her translation of Homer.*

1. **Syns:** emancipation, freedom, liberation, manumission.

2. FREEDOM.
3. **Syns:** freedom, latitude, leeway, license.

libidinous   *adjective*
Feeling or devoted to sexual love or desire.

EROTIC.

license   *noun*
1. Legal permission to do something: *You need a license to operate a car.*
2. Departure from normal rules or procedures.
3. Excessive freedom; lack of restraint: *Unrestricted behavior can turn to license.*
4. Approval for an action, esp. as granted by one in authority.

1. **Syns:** permit, warrant. —*Idiom* piece of paper.
2. LIBERTY.
3. **Syns:** dissoluteness, dissolution, libertinism, licentiousness, profligacy.
4. PERMISSION.

license   *verb*
To give authority to.

AUTHORIZE.

licentious   *adjective*
Lacking in moral restraint.

ABANDONED.

licentiousness   *noun*
Excessive freedom; lack of restraint.

LICENSE *noun.*

licit   *adjective*
Within, allowed by, or sanctioned by the law.

LAWFUL.

licitness   *noun*
The state or quality of being within the law.

LEGALITY.

lick   *verb*
1. *Slang.* To win a victory over, as in battle or a competition.
2. *Slang.* To punish with blows or lashes.

1. DEFEAT *verb.*

2. BEAT *verb.*

lick   *noun*

A sudden sharp, powerful stroke.

lickety-split *adverb*
In a rapid way.

licking *noun*
1. *Informal.* The act of defeating or the condition of being defeated.
2. *Slang.* A severe defeat.
3. *Slang.* A punishment dealt with blows or lashes.

lie¹ *verb*
1. To be or place oneself in a prostrate or recumbent position: *He lay under the oak tree and read.*
2. To take repose by sleeping, lying quietly, or the like.
3. To have as an inherent basis.

  lie down *verb*
  1. To be or place oneself in a prostrate or recumbent position.
  2. To take repose by sleeping, lying quietly, or the like.

lie² *noun*
An untrue declaration: *spread lies about the star's personal life.*

lie *verb*
To make untrue declarations: *lied about his whereabouts on the night of the murder.*

lie down *verb*

liege *adjective*
Adhering firmly and devotedly, as to a person, a cause, or a duty.

lieu *noun*
The function or position customarily occupied by another.

lieutenant *noun*
A person who holds a position auxiliary to another and assumes some of his responsibilities.

life *noun*
1. The period during which someone or something exists: *his brief, unhappy life; a warranty good for the life of the car.*
2. A member of the human race.
3. A lively, emphatic, eager quality or manner.

lifeless *adjective*
1. No longer alive.
2. Lacking liveliness, charm, or surprise.

lifelike *adjective*
1. Accurately representing what is depicted or described.
2. Described verbally in sharp and accurate detail.

lifetime *noun*
The period during which someone or something exists.

lift *verb*
1. To disappear by or as if by rising: *waiting for the fog to lift.*
2. To move (something) to a higher position.
3. To take back or remove: *lifted the ban on smoking.*
4. To raise the spirits of.
5. To rise up in flight.
6. To move from a lower to a higher position.

BLOW².

FAST *adverb.*

1. DEFEAT *noun.*
2. TROUNCING.
3. BEATING.

1. *Syns:* lie down, recline, repose, stretch out.
2. REST¹ *verb.*
3. CONSIST.

1. LIE¹.
2. REST¹ *verb.*

Syns: canard, falsehood, falsity, fib, fiction, inveracity, misrepresentation, misstatement, prevarication, story, tale, untruth, whopper. —*Idioms* barefaced lie, cock-and-bull story, fish story, tall story (*or* tale).

Syns: falsify, fib, forswear (*also* foreswear), perjure, prevaricate.
SEE **lie¹**.

FAITHFUL.

PLACE *noun.*

ASSISTANT.

1. *Syns:* duration, existence, lifetime, term. —*Idiom* one's born days.
2. HUMAN BEING.
3. SPIRIT.

1. DEAD *adjective.*
2. DULL *adjective.*

1. REALISTIC.
2. GRAPHIC.

LIFE.

1. *Syns:* dispel, disperse, dissipate, scatter.
2. ELEVATE.
3. *Syns:* recall, repeal, rescind, reverse, revoke.
4. ELATE.
5. TAKE OFF.
6. RISE.

7. *Informal.* To take (another's property) without permission.

7. STEAL.

lift *noun*

1. An instance of lifting or being lifted: *Give me a lift onto the saddle.*

1. *Syns:* boost, heave, hoist.

2. High spirits.

2. ELATION.

3. A strong, pleasant feeling of excitement or stimulation.

3. THRILL *noun*.

lifted *adjective*

Being positioned above a given level.

ELEVATED.

lifting *noun*

Informal. The crime of taking someone else's property without consent.

LARCENY.

liftoff *noun*

The act of rising in flight.

TAKEOFF at **take off.**

ligament *noun*

That which unites or binds.

BOND *noun*.

ligature *noun*

That which unites or binds.

BOND *noun*.

light¹ *noun*

1. Electromagnetic radiation that makes vision possible: *enough light so we could read.*

1. *Syns:* illumination, luminosity.

2. The act of physically illuminating or the condition of being filled with light.

2. ILLUMINATION.

3. A way of considering a matter: *now sees the problem in a new light.*

3. *Syns:* angle, aspect, slant, standpoint, viewpoint. —*Idioms* frame of reference, vantage point.

4. *Poetic.* The faculty of seeing.

4. VISION.

light *verb*

1. To provide, cover, or fill with light.

1. ILLUMINATE.

2. To cause to burn or undergo combustion: *Light the fire.*

2. *Syns:* enkindle, fire, ignite, kindle, torch (*Slang*). —*Idioms* set fire to, set on fire (*or* afire).

3. To make lively or animated: *smiles lighting their faces.*

3. *Syns:* animate, brighten, enliven.

light *adjective*

Of a moderately white color.

FAIR *adjective*.

light² *adjective*

1. Having little weight; not heavy: *a light suitcase; a light jacket.*

1. *Syns:* lightweight, weightless. —*Idiom* light as a feather.
Near-ants: big, bulky burdensome, cumbersome, huge, massive, ponderous, unwieldy, weighty.
Ant: heavy.

2. Of small intensity: *a light breeze; a light tap at the door.*

2. *Syns:* gentle, moderate, slight, soft.

3. Free from care or worry: *a light heart; a light mood.*

3. *Syns:* blithe, carefree, debonair, lighthearted, sprightly.

4. Requiring little effort or exertion: *light chores; light exercise.*

4. *Syns:* easy, moderate.

5. Amusing but essentially empty and frivolous.

5. FROTHY.

6. Sexually promiscuous.

6. WANTON *adjective*.

light *verb*

To come to rest on the ground.

LAND *verb*.

light on (or **upon**) *verb*

To find or meet by chance.

COME ACROSS at **come.**

lighten *verb*

1. To provide, cover, or fill with light.

1. ILLUMINATE.

2. To make less severe or more bearable.

2. RELIEVE.

lightheaded *adjective*

1. Having a sensation of whirling or falling.

1. DIZZY *adjective*.

2. Given to lighthearted silliness.

lightheadedness *noun*
A sensation of whirling or falling.

lighthearted *adjective*
1. Being in or showing good spirits.
2. Characterized by joyful exuberance.
3. Free from care or worry.

lighting *noun*
The act of physically illuminating or the condition of being filled with light.

light on (or **upon**) *verb*

lightweight *adjective*
Having little weight; not heavy.

like¹ *verb*
1. To find agreeable: *Do you like this kind of music?*
2. To receive pleasure from.
3. To have the desire or inclination to.

like² *adjective*
Possessing the same or almost the same characteristics: *two sisters of like opinions.*

likeliness *noun*
The likelihood of a given event occurring.

likely *adjective*
1. Inspiring confidence or hope.
2. Having or showing a tendency or likelihood.
3. Based on probability or presumption.
4. Capable of being anticipated, considered, or imagined.

liken *verb*
1. To represent as similar: *Some liken politics to a game of chess.*
2. To be similar to, as in appearance.

likeness *noun*
1. A representation of a person or thing: *The photo is a very good likeness of you.*
2. The quality or state of being alike: *the amazing likeness between Edward and his brother.*

liking *noun*
1. A desire for a particular thing or activity: *Maybe this will be more to your liking.*
2. Recognition of worth, quality, importance, etc.

lilliputian *adjective*
Extremely small.

lily-livered *adjective*
Ignobly lacking in courage.

lily-white *adjective*
1. Beyond reproach.
2. Free from evil and corruption.

limit *noun*
1. The boundary surrounding a certain area: *a house outside the city limits.*

---

2. GIDDY.

DIZZINESS.

1. CHEERFUL.
2. GAY *adjective*.
3. LIGHT².

ILLUMINATION.

SEE **light²**.

LIGHT².

1. ***Syns:*** conceit (*Rare*), fancy, take to.
2. ENJOY.
3. CHOOSE.

Syns: alike, analogous, comparable, corresponding, equivalent, parallel, similar, uniform.
Near-syns: akin, close, consonant, equal, related, resembling.
Ant: unlike.

CHANCE *noun*.

1. ENCOURAGING.
2. INCLINED.
3. PRESUMPTIVE.
4. EARTHLY.

1. ***Syns:*** analogize, assimilate, compare, equate, match, parallel.
2. FAVOR *verb*.

1. ***Syns:*** copy, facsimile, image, replica.

2. ***Syns:*** affinity, alikeness, analogy, comparison, resemblance, similarity, similitude.
Near-ants: contrast, dissimilarity, distinction, divergence, inconsistency, unsimilarity.
Ants: difference, unlikeness.

1. ***Syns:*** fancy, mind, pleasure, will¹.

2. APPRECIATION.

TINY.

COWARDLY.

1. EXEMPLARY.
2. INNOCENT *adjective*.

1. ***Syns:*** bound(s), confine(s), environs, precinct(s).

2. A demarcation point or boundary beyond which something does not extend or occur.

3. The greatest amount or number allowed: *a speed limit of 30 miles an hour.*

4. Either of the two points at the ends of a spectrum or range.

5. The ultimate point to which an action, thought, discussion, or policy is carried.

limit *verb*

1. To place a limit on: *limiting the number of free coupons; research limited to the laboratory.*

2. To fix the limits of.

limitation *noun*

1. A demarcation point or boundary beyond which something does not extend or occur.

2. The act of limiting or condition of being limited.

3. Something that limits or restricts.

4. The greatest amount or number allowed.

limited *adjective*

1. Having distinct limits.

2. Confined to a particular location or site.

3. Having the restricted outlook often characteristic of geographic isolation.

4. Not broad or elevated in scope or understanding.

5. Kept within certain limits.

6. Not total, unlimited, or wholehearted.

limitless *adjective*

Having no ends or limits.

limitlessness *noun*

The state or quality of being infinite.

limn *verb*

To present a lifelike image of.

limp *verb*

1. To walk in a lame way: *The quarterback limped off the field.*

2. To proceed or perform in an unsteady, faltering manner.

limp *adjective*

1. Lacking in stiffness or firmness: *a limp shirt collar.*

2. Lacking energy and vitality.

limpid *adjective*

1. Admitting light so that objects beyond can be seen.

2. Free from what obscures or dims.

limpidity *noun*

The quality of being clear and easy to perceive or understand.

line *noun*

1. A group of people or things arranged in a row: *a long line at the bus stop.*

2. Activity pursued as a livelihood.

3. Products bought and sold in commerce.

4. An indentation or seam on the skin, esp. on the face: *needed more and more make-up to hide the lines.*

5. An official or prescribed plan or course of action: *adhering to the party line.*

6. A method used in dealing with something.

7. One's ancestors or their character.

line *verb*

To place in or form a line or lines: *lines his pencils on the table.*

2. END *noun*.

3. *Syns:* ceiling, limitation, maximum.

4. EXTREME *noun*.

5. LENGTH.

1. *Syns:* circumscribe, confine, delimit, delimitate, restrict.

2. DETERMINE.

1. END *noun*.

2. RESTRICTION.

3. RESTRICTION.

4. LIMIT *noun*.

1. DEFINITE.

2. LOCAL *adjective*.

3. LOCAL *adjective*.

4. NARROW.

5. RESTRICTED.

6. QUALIFIED.

ENDLESS.

INFINITY.

REPRESENT.

1. *Syns:* halt², hitch, hobble.

2. MUDDLE.

1. *Syns:* flabby, flaccid, floppy.

2. LANGUID.

1. TRANSPARENT.

2. CLEAR *adjective*.

CLARITY.

1. *Syns:* column, file, queue, rank¹, row¹, string, tier.

2. BUSINESS.

3. GOODS.

4. *Syns:* crease, crinkle, furrow, wrinkle¹.

5. *Syns:* policy, procedure, program.

6. APPROACH *noun*.

7. ANCESTRY.

Syns: align, line up, range.

lineage *noun*
1. A group of people sharing common ancestry.
2. One's ancestors or their character.
lineal *adjective*
Of unbroken descent or lineage.
line-up also **lineup** *noun*
line up *verb*
To place in or form a line or lines.
line-up also **lineup** *noun*
1. A way or condition of being arranged.
2. An organized list of procedures, activities, events, etc.
3. A list of candidates proposed or endorsed by a political party.
linger *verb*
1. To continue to be in a place.
2. To stop temporarily and remain, as if reluctant to leave.
3. To go or move slowly so that progress is hindered.
lingerer *noun*
One that lags.
lingering *adjective*
Of long duration.
lingo *noun*
An often regional form of a language not considered standard.
link *verb*
1. To bring or come together into a united whole.
2. To come or bring together in one's mind or imagination.
3. To unite or be united in a relationship.
link *noun*
1. That which unites or binds.
2. A logical or natural association between two or more things.
linkage *noun*
That which unites or binds.
lion *noun*
An important, influential person.
lip *verb*
To flow against or along.
liquefy *verb*
To change from a solid to a liquid.
liquidate *verb*
1. To destroy all traces of.
2. To get rid of, esp. by banishment or execution.
3. To take the life of (a person or persons) unlawfully.
4. To set right by giving what is due.
liquidation *noun*
1. The act or process of eliminating.
2. Utter destruction.
liquor *noun*
Any liquid that is fit for drinking.
liquor up *verb*
Slang. To take alcoholic liquor, esp. excessively or habitually.
liquor up *verb*
list¹ *verb*
1. To register in or as if in a book: *list names on the honor roll.*

1. FAMILY.
2. ANCESTRY.

DIRECT *adjective.*

SEE **line up.**

LINE *verb.*

1. ARRANGEMENT.
2. PROGRAM.

3. TICKET *noun.*

1. REMAIN.
2. PAUSE *verb.*

3. DELAY *verb.*

LAGGARD *noun.*

CHRONIC.

DIALECT.

1. COMBINE *verb.*
2. ASSOCIATE *verb.*

3. ASSOCIATE *verb.*

1. BOND *noun.*
2. RELATION.

BOND *noun.*

DIGNITARY.

WASH.

MELT.

1. ANNIHILATE.
2. ELIMINATE.
3. MURDER *verb.*
4. SETTLE.

1. ELIMINATION.
2. ANNIHILATION.

DRINK *noun.*

DRINK *verb.*

SEE **liquor.**

1. *Syns:* book, catalogue (*also* catalog), enroll, inscribe. —*Idiom* set (*or* write) down.

2. To name or specify one by one.

list *noun*
A series of names, words, etc., printed or written down: *keeps a list of her friends' birthdays.*

list² *verb*
To depart or cause to depart from true vertical or horizontal.

list³ *verb*
Poetic. To make an effort to hear something.

listen *verb*
1. To make an effort to hear something: *He's such a fine violinist that everyone listens carefully.*

2. To perceive by ear, usu. attentively.

listless *adjective*
1. Without emotion or interest.
2. Showing weariness.

listlessness *noun*
Lack of emotion or interest.

literal *adjective*
Employing the very same words as another: *a literal transcription of the witnesses' reports.*

literality *noun*
The literal meaning of something.

literalness *noun*
The literal meaning of something.

literate *adjective*
Having an education.

litigable *adjective*
Subject to a lawsuit: *not enough evidence to make the case litigable.*

litigate *verb*
To institute or subject to legal proceedings.

litigious *adjective*
Given to arguing.

litter *noun*
The offspring, as of an animal, bird, etc., that are the result of one breeding season.

little *adjective*
1. Notably below average in amount, size, or scope: *bought a little sports car.*
2. Not of great importance: *Every little thing upsets him.*

3. Not broad or elevated in scope or understanding.
4. Not yet large in size due to incomplete growth.

little *adverb*
At rare intervals.

lit up *adjective*
Slang. Intoxicated with alcoholic liquor.

liturgical *adjective*
Of or characterized by ceremony.

liturgy *noun*
A formal act or set of acts prescribed by ritual.

livable also **liveable** *adjective*
Fit to live in: *a livable apartment house.*

---

2. ENUMERATE.

Syns: catalogue (*also* catalog), register, roll, roster, schedule.

INCLINE *verb.*

LISTEN.

1. ***Syns:*** hark, hearken (*also* harken) (*Poetic & Archaic*), list³ (*Poetic*). —*Idioms* bend (*or* lend) an ear, give ear to.
2. HEAR.

1. APATHETIC.
2. LANGUID.

APATHY.

Syns: verbal, verbatim, word-for-word. —*Idiom* true to the letter.

LETTER.

LETTER.

EDUCATED.

Syns: prosecutable, triable.

SUE.

ARGUMENTATIVE.

YOUNG *noun.*

1. ***Syns:*** bantam, petite, small, smallish.

2. ***Syns:*** inconsequential, insignificant, trivial, unimportant. —*Idiom* of no account.
Near-syns: casual, incidental, inconsiderable, light, meaningless, minor, minute, petty, small, trifling, unessential.

3. NARROW.
4. SMALL.

INFREQUENTLY.

DRUNK *adjective.*

RITUAL *adjective.*

CEREMONY.

Syns: habitable, inhabitable, lodgeable.

live¹ *verb*
1. To have as one's domicile, usu. for an extended period: *had lived in Europe for ten years.*
2. To have reality or life.
3. To go through (life) in a certain way.
4. To maintain existence in a certain way: *lived on fast foods and sodas; a propaganda machine that lived on lies.*

live² *adjective*
1. Marked by or exhibiting life.
2. In action or full operation.
3. Of great current interest.

liveable *adjective*

livelihood *noun*
The means needed to support life.

liveliness *noun*
A lively, emphatic, eager quality or manner.

lively *adjective*
1. Very brisk, alert, and high-spirited: *a lively personality.*

2. Possessing, exerting, or displaying energy.
3. Disposed to action.

liven *verb*
To make alive.

live wire *noun*
Slang. An intensely energetic, enthusiastic person.

livid *adjective*
Lacking color.

living *adjective*
1. Having existence or life.
2. Marked by or exhibiting life.

living *noun*
The means needed to support life: *earned a comfortable living by selling real estate.*

load *noun*
1. A quantity of explosives put into a weapon: *a high-powered rifle capable of firing heavy loads; missiles armed with multiple nuclear loads.*
2. Something carried physically.
3. *Informal.* An indeterminately great amount or number.

load *verb*
1. To make or become full; put into as much as can be held.
2. To place a burden or heavy load on.
3. To put (explosive material) into a weapon: *load a rifle.*
4. To fill to excess by compressing or squeezing tightly.

Near-syns: bearable, occupiable, tenantable; cozy, snug.
Ant: unlivable.

1. *Syns:* abide, bide, dig (*Slang*), domicile (*also* domiciliate), dwell, reside.
2. BE.
3. LEAD *verb.*
4. *Syns:* feed, subsist.

1. ALIVE.
2. ACTIVE.
3. HOT *adjective.*
SEE **livable.**

LIVING *noun.*

SPIRIT.

1. *Syns:* animate, animated, bouncy, chipper, dashing, peppy (*Informal*), pert, spirited, vivacious. —*Idioms* bright-eyed and bushy-tailed, full of life.
Near-syns: agile, alert, blithe, brisk, buoyant, effervescent, jolly, joyful, merry, mirthful, quick, sprightly, spry, vigorous.
Ants: dull, lethargic.
2. ENERGETIC.
3. VIGOROUS.

QUICKEN.

EAGER BEAVER.

PALE *adjective.*

1. ALIVE.
2. ALIVE.

Syns: alimentation, alimony, bread, keep, livelihood, maintenance, salt, subsistence, support, sustenance, upkeep. —*Idiom* bread and butter.

1. *Syn:* charge.

2. BURDEN *noun.*
3. HEAP *noun.*

1. FILL.

2. CHARGE *verb.*
3. *Syns:* arm, charge.

4. CROWD *verb.*

5. To give an inaccurate view of by representing falsely or misleadingly.   5. DISTORT.

6. To make impure or inferior by deceptively adding foreign substances.   6. ADULTERATE.

7. To fill to overflowing.   7. HEAP *verb.*

loaded *adjective*
1. *Slang.* Intoxicated with alcoholic liquor.   1. DRUNK *adjective.*
2. Burdened by a weighty load.   2. HEAVY *adjective.*
3. Completely filled.   3. FULL.
4. *Slang.* Possessing a large amount of money, land, or other material possessions.   4. RICH.

loaf *verb*
To pass time without working or in avoiding work.   IDLE *verb.*

loafer *noun*
A self-indulgent person who spends time avoiding work or other useful activity.   WASTREL.

loafing *noun*
The quality or state of being lazy.   LAZINESS.

loan *verb*
To supply (money), esp. on credit.   LEND.

loath also **loth** *adjective*
Not inclined or willing to do or undertake.   INDISPOSED.

loathe *verb*
To regard with extreme dislike and hostility.   HATE *verb.*

loathing *noun*
1. Extreme repugnance excited by something offensive.   1. DISGUST *noun.*
2. Extreme hostility and dislike.   2. HATE *noun.*

loathsome *adjective*
1. Extremely unpleasant to the senses or feelings.   1. OFFENSIVE *adjective.*
2. So objectionable as to elicit despisal.   2. FILTHY.

local *adjective*
1. Confined to a particular location or site: *local problems of no concern to the federal government; a local infection.*   1. *Syns:* isolated, limited, localized, restricted.
2. Having the restricted outlook often characteristic of geographic isolation: *took a local, not a global, view of the monetary crisis.*   2. *Syns:* insular, limited, narrow, narrow-minded, parochial, provincial, small-town.

locale *noun*
1. A particular geographic area.   1. LOCALITY.
2. A surrounding area.   2. ENVIRONMENT.
3. The place where an action or event occurs.   3. SCENE.

locality *noun*
1. A particular geographic area: *wanted to live in a locality near the city.*   1. *Syns:* locale, location, place.
2. A part of the earth's surface.   2. AREA.
3. A surrounding site: *searched for the stolen car in the locality of the waterfront.*   3. *Syns:* area, neighborhood, vicinity.
4. A rather small part of a geographic unit considered in regard to its inhabitants or distinctive characteristics.   4. NEIGHBORHOOD.
5. A surrounding area.   5. ENVIRONMENT.

localized *adjective*
Confined to a particular location or site.   LOCAL *adjective.*

locate *verb*
1. To place in proper position or location.   1. POSITION *verb.*
2. To look for and discover.   2. FIND *verb.*

location *noun*
1. A particular geographic area.   1. LOCALITY.
2. A particular portion of space chosen for something.   2. POINT *noun.*
3. The place where a person or thing is located.   3. POSITION *noun.*

4. One's place and direction relative to one's surroundings.

4. BEARING.

lock *verb*
To shut in with or as if with bars.

BAR *verb*.

lockup *noun*

SEE **lock up.**

lock up *verb*
To put in jail.

JAIL *verb*.

lockup *noun*
Informal. A place for the confinement of persons in lawful detention.

JAIL *noun*.

loco *adjective*
Slang. Afflicted with or exhibiting irrationality and mental unsoundness.

INSANE.

locus *noun*
1. The place where a person or thing is located.
2. A particular portion of space chosen for something.

1. POSITION *noun*.
2. POINT *noun*.

locution *noun*
A word or group of words forming a unit and conveying meaning.

EXPRESSION.

lodge *verb*
1. To become or cause to become stuck or lodged.
2. To implant so deeply as to make change nearly impossible.

1. CATCH *verb*.
2. FIX *verb*.

lodgeable *adjective*
Fit to live in.

LIVABLE.

lodging *noun*
Dwellings in general.

SHELTER *noun*.

lodgings *noun*
A building or shelter where one lives.

HOME.

loftiest *adjective*
Of, being, located at, or forming the top.

TOP *adjective*.

loftiness *noun*
The quality of being arrogant.

ARROGANCE.

lofty *adjective*
1. Imposingly high: *The cathedral's central feature is its magnificent lofty spire.*
2. Extending to a great height.
3. Raised to or occupying a high position or rank.
4. Very broad and noble in character, scope, or grasp.
5. Exceedingly dignified in form, tone, or style.
6. Overly convinced of one's own superiority and importance.

1. *Syns:* aerial, airy, sky-high, skyscraping, towering.
2. TALL.
3. EXALTED.
4. GRAND.
5. ELEVATED.
6. ARROGANT.

logic *noun*
1. Exact, valid, and rational reasoning: *used logic to solve life's problems.*
2. What is sound or reasonable.

1. *Syns:* ratiocination, rationality, reason.
2. SENSE *noun*.

logical *adjective*
1. Consistent with reason and intellect: *gave the class a logical explanation for the phenomena.*
2. Able to reason validly: *a logical mind.*

1. *Syns:* consequent, intelligent, rational, reasonable, sensible.
2. *Syns:* analytic (*also* analytical), ratiocinative, rational.
Near-syns: clear, cogent, convincing, discerning, discriminating, lucid, perspicacious, perspicuous, reasonable.
Ant: illogical.

loiter *verb*
1. To go or move slowly so that progress is hindered.
2. To pass time without working or in avoiding work.

1. DELAY *verb*.
2. IDLE *verb*.

loiterer *noun*
One that lags.

LAGGARD *noun*.

loll *verb*
1. To sit or lie with the limbs spread out awkwardly.
2. To hang limply, loosely, and carelessly.
3. To take on or move with an awkward, slovenly posture.

1. SPRAWL.
2. SLOUCH *verb*.
3. SLOUCH *verb*.

lone *adjective*
1. Alone in a given category: *This dolmen is the lone example of prehistoric monuments in our village.*

2. Set away from all others.
3. Without a spouse.

1. *Syns:* one, only, particular, separate, single, sole, solitary, unique. —*Idioms* first and last, one and only.
2. SOLITARY.
3. SINGLE *adjective*.

lonelihood *noun*
The quality or state of being alone.

ALONENESS.

loneliness *noun*
The quality or state of being alone.

ALONENESS.

lonely *adjective*
1. Empty of people: *a dark, lonely road.*

2. Lacking the company of others.
3. Far from centers of human population.
4. Dejected due to the awareness of being alone: *a lonely, unwanted child relegated to foster homes.*

1. *Syns:* deserted, desolate, forlorn, godforsaken (*also* Godforsaken), lonesome, unfrequented.
2. ALONE *adjective*.
3. REMOTE.
4. *Syns:* forlorn, lonesome, lorn (*Poetic*). *Near-syns:* abandoned, depressed, deserted, forsaken, friendless, homeless, wretched.

loneness *noun*
The quality or state of being alone.

ALONENESS.

lonesome *adjective*
1. Far from centers of human population.
2. Dejected due to the awareness of being alone.
3. Empty of people.
4. Lacking the company of others.

1. REMOTE.
2. LONELY.
3. LONELY.
4. ALONE *adjective*.

long¹ *adjective*
1. Having great physical length: *a long distance.*

2. Extending tediously beyond a standard duration: *a long, boring play.*

3. *Rare.* Having a rather great upward projection.
4. Having many syllables: *long words.*

1. *Syns:* elongate, elongated, extended, lengthy.
2. *Syns:* dragging, drawn-out, lengthy, long-drawn (*also* long-drawn-out), overlong, prolonged, protracted.
3. HIGH.
4. *Syns:* multisyllabic, polysyllabic, sesquipedalian.

long *noun*
A long time.

AGE *noun*.

long² *verb*
To have a strong longing for.

DESIRE *verb*.

long-drawn also **long-drawn-out** *adjective*
Extending tediously beyond a standard duration.

LONG¹ *adjective*.

long-drawn-out *adjective*

SEE **long-drawn**.

longing *noun*
1. A fervent hope, wish, or goal.
2. A strong wish for what promises enjoyment or pleasure.

1. DREAM *noun*.
2. DESIRE *noun*.

long-lasting *adjective*
Existing or remaining in the same state for an indefinitely long time.

CONTINUING.

long-lived *adjective*
Existing or remaining in the same state for an indefinitely long time.

CONTINUING.

long-standing *adjective*
Existing or remaining in the same state for an indefinitely long time.

CONTINUING.

long-suffering *adjective*
Enduring or capable of enduring hardship or inconvenience without complaint. PATIENT.

long-suffering *noun*
The capacity of enduring hardship or inconvenience without complaint. PATIENCE.

longwinded *adjective*
Using or containing an excessive number of words. WORDY.

look *verb*
1. To use the power of vision: *Look before you cross the street.*
2. To direct the eyes on an object: *She looked at the child with a smile.*
3. To have the appearance of.
4. To be sure that: *Look that you don't arrive too late.*

1. **Syns:** observe, perceive, watch.

2. **Syns:** consider, contemplate, eye, gaze (at, on, *or* upon), regard, view.
3. APPEAR.
4. **Syns:** mind, see, watch.
   Near-syns: attend, beware, heed, notice, observe, tend.

look after *verb*
To have the care and supervision of. TEND[2].

look for *verb*
1. To anticipate confidently.
2. To try to find.

1. EXPECT.
2. SEEK.

look in *verb*
To go to or seek out the company of in order to socialize. VISIT *verb.*

look into *verb*
To go into or through for the purpose of making discoveries or acquiring information. EXPLORE.

look on (or **upon**) *verb*
To have the face or front turned in a specific direction. FACE *verb.*

look over *verb*
To view broadly or from a height. SURVEY *verb.*

look up *verb*
To go to or seek out the company of in order to socialize. VISIT *verb.*

look *noun*
1. An act of directing the eyes on an object: *took a close look at the merchandise.*
2. A disposition of the facial features that conveys meaning, feeling, or mood.
3. An outward appearance.

1. **Syns:** eye, gaze, regard, sight, view.

2. EXPRESSION.

3. FACE *noun.*

look(s) *noun*
The way something or someone looks. APPEARANCE.

look after *verb* SEE **look.**

looker *noun*
Slang. A woman regarded as beautiful. BEAUTY.

looker-on *noun*
Someone who observes. WATCHER.

look for *verb* SEE **look.**
look in *verb* SEE **look.**
look into *verb* SEE **look.**
look on (or **upon**) *verb* SEE **look.**
lookout *noun* SEE **look out.**
look out *verb*
To be careful: *Look out for ice on the steps.*

Syns: beware, mind, watch out. —*Idioms* be on guard, be on the lookout, keep an eye peeled, take care (*or* heed).

lookout *noun*
1. The act of carefully watching: *kept a constant lookout for enemy aircraft.*

1. **Syns:** surveillance, vigil, vigilance, watch. —*Idiom* watch and ward.

2. A high structure commanding a wide view: *a concentration camp surrounded with high fences and lookouts.*

2. **Syns:** observatory, outlook, overlook.

3. A person or special body of persons assigned to provide protection, keep watch over, etc.

3. GUARD *noun.*

4. Something that concerns or involves one personally.

4. BUSINESS.

5. That which is or can be seen.

5. VIEW *noun.*

look over *verb*

SEE **look.**

look up *verb*

SEE **look.**

loom *verb*
1. To come into view.
2. To be imminent.

1. APPEAR.
2. THREATEN.

loon *noun*
An insanely foolish or strange person.

CRACKPOT.

loony also **luny** *adjective*
1. *Informal.* So senseless as to be laughable.
2. *Informal.* Afflicted with or exhibiting irrationality and mental unsoundness.

1. FOOLISH.
2. INSANE.

loony also **luny** *noun*
An insanely foolish or strange person.

CRACKPOT.

loop *noun*
A length of line folded over and joined at the ends so as to form a curve or circle: *a loop of ribbon.*

Syns: eye, ring[1].

looped *adjective*
Slang. Intoxicated with alcoholic liquor.

DRUNK *adjective.*

loopy *adjective*
Informal. So senseless as to be laughable.

FOOLISH.

loose *adjective*
1. Able to move about at will without bounds or restraint: *The fence is down and the cattle are loose. Two escaped convicts are loose.*
2. Not tautly bound to something else: *a loose anchor line.*

1. **Syns:** free, unconfined, unrestrained.
   —*Idioms* at liberty, free as a bird, on the loose.
2. **Syns:** lax, relaxed, slack.
   Near-ants: bound, checked, restrained, rigid, taut, tethered, tied.
   Ant: tight.

3. Sexually promiscuous.
4. Lacking literal exactness: *a loose translation.*

3. WANTON *adjective.*
4. **Syns:** free, inexact.

loose *verb*
1. To set at liberty.
2. To free from ties or fasteners.
3. To reduce in tension, pressure, or rigidity.
4. To launch with great force.

1. FREE *verb.*
2. UNDO.
3. EASE *verb.*
4. SHOOT *verb.*

loose-jointed *adjective*
Tall, thin, and awkwardly built.

GANGLING.

loosen *verb*
1. To free from ties or fasteners.
2. To reduce in tension, pressure, or rigidity.

1. UNDO.
2. EASE *verb.*

loot *verb*
1. To rob on a large scale: *The rioting mob looted many stores.*
2. To rob of goods by force, esp. in time of war.

1. **Syns:** plunder, ransack.

2. SACK[2].

loot *noun*
Goods or property seized unlawfully, esp. by a victor in wartime.

PLUNDER *noun.*

lop[1] *verb*
1. To decrease, as in length or amount, by or as if by severing or excising.
2. To make short or shorter by or as if by cutting.

1. CUT BACK.

2. TRUNCATE.

lop[2] *verb*
1. To hang limply, loosely, and carelessly.

1. SLOUCH *verb.*

2. To take on or move with an awkward, slovenly posture.

lope *verb*
 1. To move with a steady, easy gait faster than a walk but slower than a run.
 2. To bound lightly.

 lope *noun*
 A person's steady, easy gait that is faster than a walk but slower than a run.

loquacious *adjective*
 Given to conversation.

lordliness *noun*
 The quality of being arrogant.

lordly *adjective*
 1. Large and impressive in size, scope, or extent.
 2. Exercising authority.
 3. Overly convinced of one's own superiority and importance.

lore *noun*
 1. A body of traditional beliefs and notions accumulated about a particular subject: *World War II lore; sea lore.*

 2. That which is known; the sum of what has been perceived, discovered, or inferred.

lorn *adjective*
 1. *Poetic.* Having been given up and left alone.
 2. *Poetic.* Dejected due to the awareness of being alone.

lose *verb*
 1. To be unable to find: *I've lost my keys.*
 2. To suffer the loss of.
 3. To fail to take advantage of: *lost a good chance to explain.*

 4. To get away from (a pursuer): *The hunted criminal managed to lose the police in traffic.*

loser *noun*
 1. One that fails completely.
 2. A person living under very unhappy circumstances.

loss *noun*
 1. The act or an instance of losing something: *was troubled by the loss of her keys.*
 2. The condition of being deprived of what one once had or ought to have.

lost *adjective*
 1. No longer in one's possession: *My keys are lost.*
 2. Sentenced to terrible, irrevocable punishment.
 3. No longer in use, force, or operation.

lot *noun*
 1. A piece of land: *bought a cemetery lot.*
 2. That which is inevitably destined.
 3. That which is allotted.
 4. A great deal.
 5. An indeterminately great amount or number.
 6. An indefinite amount or extent.
 7. A class that is defined by the common attribute or attributes possessed by all its members.
 8. A number of individuals making up or considered a unit.

lot *verb*
 To set aside or distribute as a share.

---

2. SLOUCH *verb.*

1. TROT *verb.*

2. SKIP *verb.*

TROT *noun.*

TALKATIVE.

ARROGANCE.

1. GRAND.
2. AUTHORITATIVE.
3. ARROGANT.

1. *Syns:* folklore, legend, myth, mythology, mythos, tradition. *Near-syns:* custom, folkway; epic, fable, saga, superstition, tale.
2. KNOWLEDGE.

1. ABANDONED.
2. LONELY.

1. *Syns:* mislay, misplace.
2. DROP *verb.*
3. *Syns:* miss, waste. —*Idioms* let slip by, let slip through one's fingers, lose out on.
4. *Syns:* elude, evade, shake (off), throw off. —*Idiom* give someone the slip.

1. FAILURE.
2. UNFORTUNATE *noun.*

1. *Syns:* mislaying, misplacement, misplacing.
2. DEPRIVATION.

1. *Syns:* gone, missing.
2. CONDEMNED.
3. VANISHED.

1. *Syns:* parcel, plot, tract.
2. FATE *noun.*
3. ALLOTMENT.
4. HEAP *noun.*
5. HEAP *noun.*
6. DEAL *noun.*
7. KIND^2.

8. GROUP *noun.*

ALLOT.

loth *adjective*   SEE **loath.**

Lothario *noun*
A man amorously attentive to women.   GALLANT *noun.*

loud *adjective*
1. Marked by extremely high volume and intensity of   1. **Syns:** blaring, deafening, roaring,
   sound: *loud yells; a loud rock band.*   stentorian, stentorious.
                                                            Near-syns: booming, earsplitting,
                                                            ringing, thunderous; harsh, raucous,
                                                            strident; resonant, resounding.
                                                            Ants: low, soft.
2. Tastelessly showy.   2. GAUDY.

loudmouthed *adjective*
Offensively loud and insistent.   VOCIFEROUS.

lounge *verb*
To pass time without working or in avoiding work.   IDLE *verb.*

lour *verb & noun*   SEE **lower**[1].

louring *adjective*   SEE **lowering.**

loury *adjective*   SEE **lowery.**

louse up *verb*
Slang. To harm irreparably through inept handling;   BOTCH.
make a mess of.

lousy *adjective*
1. *Slang.* Of decidedly inferior quality.   1. SHODDY.
2. *Slang.* So objectionable as to elicit despisal.   2. FILTHY.

lout *noun*
A large, ungainly, and dull-witted person.   LUMP[1] *noun.*

lovable *adjective*
Easy to love.   ADORABLE.

love *noun*
1. The passionate affection and desire felt by lovers for 1. **Syns:** amorousness, amour, passion.
   each other: *Their love knew no bounds.*
2. Deep and ardent affection.   2. ADORATION.
3. A person who is much loved.   3. DARLING *noun.*
4. An intimate sexual relationship between two people: 4. **Syns:** affair, amour, love affair,
   couldn't discuss this latest illicit love.   romance.
5. A strong, enthusiastic liking for something: *a love of* 5. **Syns:** love affair, passion.
   the sea.
6. The condition of being closely tied to another by   6. ATTACHMENT.
   affection or faith.

love *verb*
1. To feel deep, devoted love for.   1. ADORE.
2. To like or enjoy enthusiastically, often excessively. 2. ADORE.

love affair *noun*
1. An intimate sexual relationship between two people.   1. LOVE *noun.*
2. A strong, enthusiastic liking for something.   2. LOVE *noun.*

loved *adjective*
1. Regarded with much love and tenderness.   1. DARLING *adjective.*
2. Given special, usu. doting treatment.   2. FAVORITE *adjective.*

lovely *adjective*
1. Having qualities that delight the eye.   1. BEAUTIFUL.
2. Pleasing to the eye or mind.   2. ATTRACTIVE.

lovely *noun*
A woman regarded as beautiful.   BEAUTY.

lover *noun*
1. A person's regular sexual partner: *He has been her*   1. **Syn:** paramour.
   lover for years.
2. One who ardently admires.   2. ADMIRER.

loving *adjective*
Feeling and expressing affection.   AFFECTIONATE.

low *adjective*
1. Cut to reveal the wearer's neck, chest, and back: *a revealingly low bodice.*
2. Of subordinate standing or importance.
3. So objectionable as to elicit despisal.
4. Having or proceeding from low moral standards.
5. In low spirits.
6. Low in price.
7. *Mus.* Being a sound produced by a relatively small frequency of vibrations: *The instrument was capable of very low pitches.*
8. Not irritating, strident, or loud.
9. Affected or tending to be affected with minor health problems.

1. **Syns:** low-cut, low-necked (*also* low-neck), plunging.
2. MINOR *adjective.*
3. FILTHY.
4. SORDID.
5. DEPRESSED.
6. CHEAP.
7. **Syns:** alto (*Mus.*), bass, deep, low-pitched.
8. SOFT.
9. SICKLY.

low *noun*
A very low level, position, or degree: *The stock market has reached an all-time low.*

Syn: bottom. —*Idiom* rock bottom.

low-cost *adjective*
Low in price.

CHEAP.

low-cut *adjective*
Cut to reveal the wearer's neck, chest, and back.

LOW *adjective.*

low-down *adjective*
Having or proceeding from low moral standards.

SORDID.

lower[1] *also* **lour** *verb*
1. To wrinkle one's brow, as in thought, puzzlement, or displeasure.
2. To stare fixedly and angrily.
3. To be imminent.

1. FROWN *verb.*
2. GLARE *verb.*
3. THREATEN.

lower *also* **lour** *noun*
The act of wrinkling the brow, as in thought, puzzlement, or displeasure.

FROWN *noun.*

lower[2] *verb*
1. To cause to descend: *The pilot lowered the flaps.*
2. To become or make less in price or value.
3. To decrease, as in length or amount, by or as if by severing or excising.

1. **Syns:** depress, drop, let down, take down.
2. DEPRECIATE.
3. CUT BACK.

lower *adjective*
Of subordinate standing or importance.

MINOR *adjective.*

lowering *also* **louring** *adjective*
Characterized by or expressive of a foreboding somberness.

DARK *adjective.*

lowermost *adjective*
Opposite to or farthest from the top.

BOTTOM *adjective.*

lowery *also* **loury** *adjective*
Characterized by or expressive of a foreboding somberness.

DARK *adjective.*

lowest *adjective*
Opposite to or farthest from the top.

BOTTOM *adjective.*

low-grade *adjective*
Of mediocre quality.

INFERIOR.

low-key *also* **low-keyed** *adjective*
Not irritating, strident, or loud.

SOFT.

low-keyed *adjective*

SEE **low-key.**

lowly *adjective*
1. Lacking high station or birth: *a lowly peasant; the lowly masses.*

2. Having or expressing feelings of humility.
3. Of little distinction.

1. **Syns:** base[2], baseborn, common, déclassé (*also* declassed), humble, ignoble, mean[2], ordinary, plebeian, unwashed, vulgar.
2. HUMBLE *adjective.*
3. HUMBLE *adjective.*

low-neck *adjective*   SEE **low-necked.**
low-necked also **low-neck** *adjective*
  Cut to reveal the wearer's neck, chest, and back.   LOW *adjective.*
low-pitched *adjective*
  Being a sound produced by a relatively small frequency   LOW *adjective.*
  of vibrations.
low-priced *adjective*
  Low in price.   CHEAP.
low-quality *adjective*
  Of mediocre quality.   INFERIOR.
loyal *adjective*
  Adhering firmly and devotedly, as to a person, a cause,   FAITHFUL *adjective.*
  or a duty.
loyalty *noun*
  1. Faithfulness or devotion to a person, a cause,   1. FIDELITY.
    obligations, or duties.
  2. The condition of being closely tied to another by   2. ATTACHMENT.
    affection or faith.
lubricious *adjective*
  1. Following no predictable pattern.   1. CAPRICIOUS.
  2. So smooth and glassy as to offer insecure hold or   2. SLICK *adjective.*
    footing.
lucent *adjective*
  Giving off or reflecting light readily or in large   BRIGHT.
  amounts.
lucid *adjective*
  1. Free from what obscures or dims.   1. CLEAR *adjective.*
  2. Of sound mind; mentally healthy.   2. SANE.
lucidity *noun*
  1. The quality of being clear and easy to perceive or   1. CLARITY.
    understand.
  2. A healthy mental state.   2. SANITY.
lucidness *noun*
  A healthy mental state.   SANITY.
luck *noun*
  1. Success attained as a result of chance: *It was just*   1. *Syns:* fortunateness, fortune, luckiness.
    my luck to find the money.   —*Idiom* good luck (*or* fortune).
  2. The quality shared by random, unintended, or   2. CHANCE *noun.*
    unpredictable events or this quality regarded as the
    cause of such events.
  luck *verb*
  To expose to possible loss or damage.   RISK *verb.*
luckiness *noun*
  Success attained as a result of chance.   LUCK *noun.*
luckless *adjective*
  Involving or undergoing chance misfortune.   UNFORTUNATE *adjective.*
lucky *adjective*
  Characterized by luck or good fortune.   HAPPY.
lucrative *adjective*
  Affording profit.   PROFITABLE.
lucre *noun*
  Something, as coins, printed bills, etc., used as a   MONEY.
  medium of exchange.
lucubrate *verb*
  To apply one's mind to the acquisition of knowledge.   STUDY *verb.*
lucubration *noun*
  Archaic. A careful considering of a matter.   ADVISEMENT.
ludicrous *adjective*
  Deserving laughter.   LAUGHABLE.
lug *verb*
  To move while supporting.   CARRY *verb.*

lug *noun*
Slang. A large, ungainly, and dull-witted person.   LUMP[1] *noun.*

lug(s) *noun*
Artificial behavior adopted to impress others.   AFFECTATION.

lugubrious *adjective*
Causing sorrow.   SORROWFUL.

lukewarm *adjective*
Lacking warmth, interest, enthusiasm, or involvement.   TEPID.

lull *verb*
To make or become calm.   CALM *verb.*

lull *noun*
An absence of motion or disturbance.   STILLNESS.

lumber *verb*
To move heavily.   LUMP[1] *verb.*

lumbering *adjective*
Lacking dexterity and grace in physical movement.   AWKWARD.

luminary *noun*
1. A famous person.   1. CELEBRITY.
2. An important, influential person.   2. DIGNITARY.

luminosity *noun*
1. Electromagnetic radiation that makes vision   1. LIGHT[1] *noun.*
   possible.
2. Exceptional brightness and clarity, as of a cut and   2. FIRE *noun.*
   polished stone.

luminous *adjective*
Giving off or reflecting light readily or in large   BRIGHT.
amounts.

lummox *noun*
A large, ungainly, and dull-witted person.   LUMP[1] *noun.*

lump[1] *noun*
1. An irregularly shaped mass of indefinite size: *a*   1. *Syns:* chunk, clod, clump, gob[1], hunch,
   lump of sugar; lumps of dirt all over the floor.   hunk, nugget, wad.
2. A small raised area of skin resulting from a light   2. BUMP *noun.*
   blow, an insect sting, etc.
3. An unevenness or elevation on a surface.   3. BUMP *noun.*
4. A large, ungainly, and dull-witted person: *a dumb*   4. *Syns:* bohunk (*Slang*), clod, dub[2]
   lump of a man.   (*Slang*), gaum (*Regional*), gawk, hulk,
                                                                       hunk, klutz (*Slang*), lout, lug (*Slang*),
                                                                       lummox, meatball (*Slang*), meathead
                                                                       (*Slang*), oaf, ox.

lump *verb*
1. To put into a disordered pile.   1. HEAP *verb.*
2. To move heavily: *linebackers lumping across the*   2. *Syns:* clump, galumph *or* gallumph,
   field.   hulk, lumber, stump.

lump[2] *verb*
Informal. To put up with.   ENDURE.

lumpish *adjective*
1. Unwieldy, esp. due to excess weight.   1. HEAVY *adjective.*
2. Lacking dexterity and grace in physical movement.   2. AWKWARD.

lumps *noun*
Something justly deserved.   DUE *noun.*

lunacy *noun*
1. Serious mental illness or disorder impairing a   1. INSANITY.
   person's capacity to function normally and safely.
2. Foolish behavior.   2. FOOLISHNESS.

lunatic *adjective*
1. Afflicted with or exhibiting irrationality and mental   1. INSANE.
   unsoundness.
2. So senseless as to be laughable.   2. FOOLISH.

lunatic *noun*
An insanely foolish or strange person.   CRACKPOT.

lunge *verb*
1. To move or advance against strong resistance.
2. To move or thrust at, under, or into the midst of with sudden force.

1. PLUNGE *verb.*
2. PLUNGE *verb.*

luny *adjective & noun*

SEE **loony.**

lurch *verb*
1. To lean suddenly, unsteadily, and erratically from the vertical axis: *The deck lurched back and forth in the heavy swells.*
2. To move awkwardly or clumsily.
3. To walk unsteadily: *The drunk lurched out of the bar and into the alley.*
4. To move or cause to move with a sudden, abrupt motion.

1. *Syns:* cant[1], pitch, roll, seesaw, tilt, yaw.
2. BLUNDER *verb.*
3. *Syns:* falter, reel, stagger, stammer, stumble, teeter, totter, weave, wobble.
4. JERK *verb.*

lurch *noun*
A sudden pull.

JERK *noun.*

lure *noun*
1. Something that attracts, esp. with the promise of pleasure or reward: *Her beauty was an irresistible lure to men.*
2. Something that leads one into a place or situation from which escape is difficult: *The lure of fast money drew him into gambling.*
3. The power or quality of attracting.

1. *Syns:* allurement, come-on, enticement, inducement, inveiglement, seduction, temptation.
2. *Syns:* bait, snare, trap.

3. ATTRACTION.

lure *verb*
1. To direct or impel to oneself by some quality or action.
2. To beguile or draw into a wrong or foolish course of action.

1. ATTRACT.

2. TEMPT.

lurid *adjective*
1. Shockingly repellent.
2. Lacking color.

1. GHASTLY.
2. PALE *adjective.*

lurk *verb*
To move silently and furtively.

SNEAK *verb.*

luscious *adjective*
1. Highly pleasing, esp. to the sense of taste.
2. Giving great pleasure or delight.

1. DELICIOUS.
2. DELIGHTFUL.

lush *noun*
Slang. A person who is habitually drunk.

DRUNKARD.

lush *verb*
Slang. To take alcoholic liquor, esp. excessively or habitually.

DRINK *verb.*

lush *adjective*
1. Growing profusely.
2. Given to or marked by unrestrained abundance.
3. Characterized by extravagant, ostentatious magnificence.

1. THICK *adjective.*
2. PROFUSE.
3. LUXURIOUS.

lust *verb*
To have a greedy, obsessive desire: *an executive who lusted only for power and money.*

Syns: crave, hunger (after *or* for), itch for, thirst.

lust *noun*
1. Sexual hunger.
2. A strong wish for what promises enjoyment or pleasure.

1. DESIRE *noun.*
2. DESIRE *noun.*

luster *noun*
1. A radiant brightness or glow, usu. due to light reflected from a smooth surface.
2. A position of exalted, widely recognized importance.

1. GLOSS *noun.*

2. EMINENCE.

lusterless *adjective*
1. Lacking liveliness, charm, or surprise.
2. Lacking gloss and luster.

1. DULL *adjective.*
2. DULL *adjective.*

lustful *adjective*
1. Feeling or devoted to sexual love or desire.
2. *Archaic.* Full of vigor.

  1. EROTIC.
  2. LUSTY.

lustfulness *noun*
Sexual hunger.

  DESIRE *noun.*

lustral *adjective*
Serving to purify of sin.

  PURGATIVE.

lustrate *verb*
To free from sin, guilt, or defilement.

  PURIFY.

lustration *noun*
A freeing from sin, guilt, or defilement.

  PURIFICATION.

lustrative *adjective*
Serving to purify of sin.

  PURGATIVE.

lustratory *adjective*
Serving to purify of sin.

  PURGATIVE.

lustrous *adjective*
1. Having a high, radiant sheen.
2. Giving off or reflecting light readily or in large amounts.
3. Widely known and esteemed.

  1. GLOSSY.
  2. BRIGHT.
  3. EMINENT.

lusty *adjective*
1. Full of vigor: *a healthy, lusty man who worked and played hard.*
2. Having great physical strength.

  1. *Syns:* lustful (*Archaic*), red-blooded, robust, vigorous, vital.
  2. STRONG.

luxuriant *adjective*
1. Growing profusely.
2. Given to or marked by unrestrained abundance.
3. Characterized by extravagant, ostentatious magnificence.

  1. THICK *adjective.*
  2. PROFUSE.
  3. LUXURIOUS.

luxuriate *verb*
To take extravagant pleasure: *Oh, to luxuriate in the warmth of a Pacific island!*

  Syns: bask, indulge, revel, roll, rollick, wallow.

luxurious *adjective*
Characterized by extravagant, ostentatious magnificence: *The shipping magnate's luxurious yacht featured a lapis lazuli table.*

  Syns: lavish, lush, luxuriant, opulent, palatial, plush, plushy (*Informal*), rich.
  Near-syns: deluxe, elaborate, extravagant, grandiloquent, grandiose, ostentatious, posh, pretentious, showy; costly, exclusive, expensive, majestic, stately.
  Ants: austere, meager.

luxury *noun*
Something costly and unnecessary: *a fur coat that is a real luxury.*

  Syns: extravagance (*also* extravagancy), frill.

lying *adjective*
Given to or marked by deliberate concealment or misrepresentation of the truth.

  DISHONEST.

lying-in *noun*
The act or process of bringing forth young.

  BIRTH *noun.*

lymphatic *adjective*
Lacking energy and vitality.

  LANGUID.

lyric *adjective*
Of, pertaining to, or having the characteristics of poetry.

  POETIC.

lyricism *noun*
Something likened to verse, as in form or style.

  POETRY.

M

macabre *adjective*
1. Shockingly repellent.
2. Susceptible to or marked by preoccupation with unwholesome matters.

1. GHASTLY.
2. MORBID.

machinate *verb*
To work out a secret plan to achieve an evil or illegal end.

PLOT *verb*.

machination *noun*
A secret plan to achieve an evil or illegal end.

PLOT *noun*.

macho *adjective*
Of, characteristic of, or befitting the male sex.

MANLY.

macrocosm *noun*
The totality of all existing things.

UNIVERSE.

macrocosmos *noun*
The totality of all existing things.

UNIVERSE.

mad *adjective*
1. Afflicted with or exhibiting irrationality and mental unsoundness.
2. *Informal.* Showing or having enthusiasm.
3. Feeling or showing anger.
4. So senseless as to be laughable.
5. Marked by extreme excitement, confusion, or agitation.

1. INSANE.
2. ENTHUSIASTIC.
3. ANGRY.
4. FOOLISH.
5. FRANTIC.

mad-brained *adjective*
Characterized by unthinking boldness and haste.

RASH[1].

madcap *adjective*
Characterized by unthinking boldness and haste.

RASH[1].

madden *verb*
1. To make insane.
2. To cause to feel or show anger.

1. DERANGE.
2. ANGER *verb*.

maddened *adjective*
Feeling or showing anger.

ANGRY.

madding *adjective*
Obs. Marked by extreme excitement, confusion, or agitation.

FRANTIC.

made-to-order *adjective*
Made according to the specifications of the buyer.

CUSTOM *adjective*.

made-up *adjective*
1. Consisting or suggestive of fiction.
2. Being fictitious and not real.

1. FICTITIOUS.
2. ASSUMED.

mad-headed *adjective*
Characterized by unthinking boldness and haste.

RASH[1].

madness *noun*
Serious mental illness or disorder impairing a person's capacity to function normally and safely.

INSANITY.

Maecenas *noun*
A person who supports or champions an activity, institution, etc.

PATRON.

magazine *noun*
A place where something is deposited for safekeeping.

DEPOSITORY.

magic *noun*
1. The use of supernatural powers to influence or predict events: *By magic the door opened at the command of the long-bearded old man.*

1. *Syns:* conjuration, conjury, sorcery, sortilege, thaumaturgy, theurgy, witchcraft, witchery, witching, wizardry.

Near-syns: abracadabra, alchemy, augury, enchantment, exorcism, fortune-telling, mumbo jumbo, occultism, soothsaying, voodooism.

2. The use of skillful tricks and deceptions to produce entertainingly baffling effects: *a show of magic for children.*

2. **Syns:** conjuration, conjury, legerdemain, prestidigitation. —*Idiom* sleight of hand.

magic also **magical** *adjective*
1. Having or brought about by supernatural powers: *a magic wand; a magic transformation.*

1. **Syns:** thaumaturgic, wizardly.

2. Pertaining to magic.

2. WITCHING *adjective.*
SEE **magic.**

magical *adjective*

magisterial *adjective*
Tending to dictate.

DICTATORIAL.

magistrate *noun*
A public official who decides cases brought before a court of law in order to administer justice.

JUDGE *noun.*

magnanimity *noun*
The quality or state of being generous.

GENEROSITY.

magnanimous *adjective*
Willing to give of oneself and one's possessions.

GENEROUS.

magnanimousness *noun*
The quality or state of being generous.

GENEROSITY.

magnetic *adjective*
Pleasing to the eye or mind.

ATTRACTIVE.

magnetism *noun*
1. The capacity to exert an influence.
2. The power or quality of attracting.

1. FORCE *noun.*
2. ATTRACTION.

magnetize *verb*
To direct or impel to oneself by some quality or action.

ATTRACT.

magnific *adjective*
Obs. Large and impressive in size, scope, or extent.

GRAND.

magnification *noun*
1. The act or an instance of exaggerating.
2. The honoring of God, as in worship.

1. EXAGGERATION.
2. PRAISE *noun.*

magnificence *noun*
Brilliant, showy splendor.

GLITTER *noun.*

magnificent *adjective*
1. Large and impressive in size, scope, or extent.
2. Far above others in quality or excellence.
3. Marked by extraordinary elegance, beauty, and splendor.

1. GRAND.
2. OUTSTANDING.
3. GLORIOUS.

magnify *verb*
1. To make or become greater or larger.
2. To become greater in number, amount, or intensity.
3. To raise to a high position or status.
4. To pay tribute or homage to.
5. To honor (God) in religious worship.
6. To make (something) seem greater than is actually the case.

1. INCREASE *verb.*
2. RISE *verb.*
3. EXALT.
4. HONOR *verb.*
5. PRAISE *verb.*
6. EXAGGERATE.

magniloquent *adjective*
Characterized by language that is elevated and sometimes pompous in style.

SONOROUS.

magnitude *noun*
1. Great extent, amount, or dimension.
2. The quality or state of being large in amount, extent, or importance.
3. The amount of space occupied by something.
4. Relative intensity or amount, as of a quality or attribute.
5. The quality of being enormous.

1. BULK.
2. SIZE.

3. SIZE.
4. DEGREE.

5. ENORMOUSNESS.

magnum opus *noun*
An outstanding and ingenious work.

MASTERPIECE.

maiden *adjective*
Preceding all others in time.

FIRST.

maim *verb*
To deprive of, or of the use of, a limb or bodily member.

CRIPPLE.

main *adjective*
Most important, influential, or significant.

PRIMARY.

maintain *verb*
1. To keep in a condition of good repair, efficiency, or use: *maintained fitness with daily exercise.*
2. To persevere in some condition, action, or belief.
3. To put into words positively and with conviction.
4. To supply with the necessities of life.
5. To support against arguments, attack, or criticism.
6. To state to be true.
7. To sustain the weight of.

1. *Syns:* keep up, preserve, sustain.
2. KEEP *verb.*
3. ASSERT.
4. SUPPORT *verb.*
5. DEFEND.
6. CLAIM *verb.*
7. SUPPORT *verb.*

maintenance *noun*
The means needed to support life.

LIVING *noun.*

majestic *adjective*
Large and impressive in size, scope, or extent.

GRAND.

majesty *noun*
Something meriting the highest praise or regard.

GLORY *noun.*

major *adjective*
1. Most important, influential, or significant.
2. Being among the leaders of a particular class.

1. PRIMARY *adjective.*
2. BIG-LEAGUE.

major-league *adjective*
Being among the leaders of a particular class.

BIG-LEAGUE.

make *verb*
1. To create by forming, combining, or altering materials: *made a house from logs; making a sandwich.*

2. To be the cause of.
3. To cause to come into existence.
4. To cause to be by official action.
5. To cause to be ready, as for use, consumption, or a special purpose.
6. To cause to be in a certain state or to undergo a particular experience or action.
7. To cause (a person or thing) to act or move in spite of resistance.
8. To be the constituent parts of.
9. To receive, as wages, for one's labor.
10. To select for an office or position.
11. To journey over (a specified distance).
12. To proceed in a specified direction.

1. *Syns:* assemble, build, construct, fabricate, fashion, forge[1], frame, manufacture, mold, produce, put together, shape.
2. CAUSE *verb.*
3. PRODUCE.
4. ENACT.
5. PREPARE.

6. GET *verb.*

7. FORCE *verb.*

8. CONSTITUTE.
9. EARN.
10. APPOINT.
11. TRAVERSE.
12. BEAR.

make out *verb*
1. To perceive and fix the identity of.
2. To perceive and recognize the meaning of.
3. *Informal.* To progress or perform adequately, esp. in difficult circumstances.
4. *Slang.* To fare well.

1. DISCERN.
2. UNDERSTAND.
3. MANAGE.

4. PROSPER.

make over *verb*
To change the ownership of (property) by means of a legal document.

TRANSFER *verb.*

make-believe *noun*
The presentation of something false as true.

PRETENSE.

make out *verb*

SEE **make.**

make over *verb*

SEE **make.**

maker *noun*
1. A person or business that makes or builds something.
2. One that creates, founds, or originates.

1. BUILDER.

2. ORIGINATOR.

makeshift *noun*
Something used temporarily or reluctantly when other means are not available: *Lacking a bat, the boys used a broom handle as a makeshift.*

Syns: expediency (*also* expedience), expedient, shift, stopgap.

make-up also **makeup** *noun*

SEE **make up.**

make up *verb*
1. To use ingenuity in making, developing, or achieving.
2. To be the constituent parts of.
3. To act as an equalizing weight or force to.
4. To compose or recite without preparation.

1. INVENT.

2. CONSTITUTE.
3. BALANCE *verb.*
4. IMPROVISE.

make-up also **makeup** *noun*
The combination of emotional, intellectual, and moral qualities that distinguishes an individual.

CHARACTER.

maladroit *adjective*
1. Clumsily lacking in the ability to do or perform.
2. Lacking sensitivity and skill in dealing with others.

1. UNSKILLFUL.

2. TACTLESS.

malady *noun*
A pathological condition of mind or body.

DISEASE.

mala fide *adjective*
Latin. Not being what one purports to be.

INSINCERE.

malapert *adjective*
Rude and disrespectful.

IMPUDENT.

malapert *noun*
One who is obnoxiously self-assertive and arrogant.

SMART ALECK.

malapropos *adjective*
Not suited to circumstances.

IMPROPER.

malarkey also **malarky** *noun*
Slang. Something that does not have or make sense.

NONSENSE.

malarky *noun*

SEE **malarkey.**

male *adjective*
Of, characteristic of, or befitting the male sex.

MANLY.

maledict *verb*
Rare. To invoke evil or injury upon.

CURSE *verb.*

malediction *noun*
A denunciation invoking a wish or threat of evil or injury.

CURSE *noun.*

malefactor *noun*
One who commits a crime.

CRIMINAL *noun.*

malevolence *noun*
A desire to harm others or to see others suffer: *Out of sheer malevolence he refused to help lost travelers who knocked on his door to ask directions.*

Syns: despitefulness (*Archaic*), ill will, malice, maliciousness, malignancy (*also* malignance), malignity, spite, spitefulness.

malevolent *adjective*
Characterized by intense ill will or spite: *a malevolent hatred of anyone who dared to challenge him.*

Syns: bitchy (*Slang*), black, black-hearted, despiteful (*Archaic*), evil, hateful (*Rare*), malicious, malign, malignant, mean^2, nasty, poisonous, spiteful, venomous, vicious, wicked.
Near-ants: beneficent, benevolent, charitable, friendly, kind, selfless, thoughtful.

malformation *noun*
A disfiguring abnormality of shape or form.

DEFORMITY.

malfunction *verb*
To work improperly due to mechanical difficulties: *The bank's accounting system came to a halt when the central computer malfunctioned.*

Syns: act up (*Informal*), misbehave.

malice *noun*
A desire to harm others or to see others suffer.

MALEVOLENCE.

malicious *adjective*
Characterized by intense ill will or spite.

MALEVOLENT.

maliciousness *noun*
A desire to harm others or to see others suffer.

MALEVOLENCE.

malign *verb*
To make defamatory statements about.

LIBEL *verb.*

malign *adjective*
1. Strongly suggestive of great harm, menace, or evil: *the executioner's malign hood.*
2. Characterized by intense ill will or spite.

1. **Syns:** baleful, sinister.

2. MALEVOLENT.

malignance *noun*

SEE **malignancy.**

malignancy also **malignance** *noun*
A desire to harm others or to see others suffer.

MALEVOLENCE.

malignant *adjective*
1. Characterized by intense ill will or spite.
2. Extremely destructive or harmful.

1. MALEVOLENT.
2. VIRULENT.

maligning *adjective*
Damaging to the reputation.

LIBELOUS.

malignity *noun*
A desire to harm others or to see others suffer.

MALEVOLENCE.

malism *noun*
The doctrine that this world is evil.

PESSIMISM.

malison *noun*
Archaic. A denunciation invoking a wish or threat of evil or injury.

CURSE *noun.*

malleability *noun*
The quality or state of being flexible.

FLEXIBILITY.

malleable *adjective*
1. Capable of being shaped, bent, or drawn out, as by hammering or pressure: *Gold and copper are malleable metals.*

2. Easily altered or influenced.

1. **Syns:** ductile, flexible (*also* flexile), flexuous (*also* flexuose), moldable, plastic, pliable, pliant, supple, workable.

2. FLEXIBLE.

malodorous *adjective*
Having an unpleasant odor.

SMELLY.

maltreat *verb*
To hurt or injure by maltreatment.

ABUSE *verb.*

maltreatment *noun*
Physically harmful treatment.

ABUSE *noun.*

mammoth *noun*
One that is extraordinarily large and powerful.

GIANT *noun.*

mammoth *adjective*
Of extraordinary size and power.

GIANT *adjective.*

man *noun*
1. A member of the human race.
2. The human race.

1. HUMAN BEING.
2. MANKIND.

Man *noun*
Slang. A member of a law-enforcement agency.

POLICEMAN.

manacle *verb*
To restrict the activity or free movement of.

HAMPER.

manacles *noun*
Something that physically confines the legs or arms.

BONDS.

manage *verb*
1. To progress or perform adequately, esp. in difficult circumstances: *The trail looked steep, but the lone hiker assured his friends that he could manage.*

2. To have charge of (the affairs of others).
3. To control the course of (an activity).

1. **Syns:** do, fare, fend, get along, get by, make out (*Informal*), muddle through (*Chiefly Brit.*), shift, stagger (on *or* along). —*Idioms* make do, make shift.
2. ADMINISTER.
3. CONDUCT *verb*.

manageable *adjective*
Capable of being governed.

GOVERNABLE.

management *noun*
1. Authoritative control over the affairs of others.
2. The careful guarding of an asset.
3. An act or instance of guiding.

1. ADMINISTRATION.
2. CONSERVATION.
3. GUIDANCE.

manager *noun*
1. Someone who directs and supervises workers.
2. A person having administrative or managerial authority in an organization.

1. BOSS *noun*.
2. EXECUTIVE.

managerial *adjective*
Of, for, or relating to administration or administrators.

ADMINISTRATIVE.

mandate *noun*
An authoritative indication to be obeyed.

COMMAND *noun*.

mandatory *adjective*
Imposed on one by authority, command, or convention.

REQUIRED.

maneuver *noun*
1. A calculated change in position.
2. An indirect, usu. cunning means of gaining an end.
3. A method of deploying troops and equipment in combat.

1. MOVEMENT.
2. TRICK *noun*.
3. TACTIC[1].

maneuver *verb*
1. To direct the course of carefully: *maneuvered the great ship into the dock.*
2. To go or cause to go from one place to another.
3. To take clever or cunning steps to achieve one's goals: *schemed and maneuvered to get promoted.*
4. To control to one's own advantage by artful or indirect means.

1. **Syns:** navigate, pilot, steer. —*Idiom* back and fill.
2. MOVE *verb*.
3. **Syns:** finagle (*also* fenagle) (*Informal*), jockey. —*Idiom* pull strings (*or* wires).
4. MANIPULATE.

manful *adjective*
Of, characteristic of, or befitting the male sex.

MANLY.

mangle *verb*
1. To injure or damage, as by abuse or heavy wear.
2. To smooth by applying heat and pressure.

1. BATTER.
2. PRESS *verb*.

mangy *adjective*
Showing signs of wear and tear or neglect.

SHABBY.

manhandle *verb*
To be rough or brutal with.

SLAP AROUND at **slap**.

man-hater *noun*
A person who expects only the worst from people.

CYNIC.

mania *noun*
1. Serious mental illness or disorder impairing a person's capacity to function normally and safely.
2. A subject or activity that inspires lively interest.
3. An irrational preoccupation.

1. INSANITY.
2. ENTHUSIASM.
3. THING.

maniac *noun*
A person who is ardently devoted to a particular subject or activity.

ENTHUSIAST.

maniac *adjective*
Afflicted with or exhibiting irrationality and mental unsoundness.

INSANE.

maniacal *adjective*
Afflicted with or exhibiting irrationality and mental unsoundness.

INSANE.

manifest *verb*
1. To make manifest or apparent.
2. To represent (an abstraction) in or as if in bodily form.
3. To give expression to, as by gestures, facial aspects, or bodily posture.

1. SHOW *verb*.
2. EMBODY.

3. EXPRESS *verb*.

manifest *adjective*
Readily seen, perceived, or understood.

APPARENT.

manifestation *noun*
1. An act of showing or displaying.
2. Something visible or evident that gives grounds for believing in the existence or presence of something else.

1. DISPLAY *noun*.
2. SIGN *noun*.

manifesto *noun*
A public statement.

ANNOUNCEMENT.

manipulate *verb*
1. To control to one's own advantage by artful or indirect means: *She manipulates people into helping her by pretending to be overworked.*

1. *Syns:* exploit, maneuver, play. *Near-syns:* beguile, cajole, lure; conduct, control, direct, engineer, manage.

2. To use with or as if with the hands.
3. To handle in a way so as to mix, form, and shape.

2. HANDLE *verb*.
3. WORK *verb*.

mankind *noun*
The human race: *A nuclear war might destroy all mankind.*

Syns: flesh, Homo sapiens, humanity, humankind, man, universe, world.

manlike *adjective*
Resembling a man or human being: *reports of a furry, manlike creature living in the forest.*

Syns: anthropoid, anthropomorphic, anthropomorphous, hominoid, humanoid.

manly *adjective*
Of, characteristic of, or befitting the male sex: *manly self-reliance; paying manly attentions to the ladies.*

Syns: macho, male, manful, masculine, virile.

manmade *adjective*
1. Made by human beings, not nature.
2. Made to imitate something else.

1. ARTIFICIAL.
2. ARTIFICIAL.

manner *noun*
1. A habitual way of behaving.
2. Behavior through which one reveals one's personality.
3. A class that is defined by the common attribute or attributes possessed by all its members.
4. A distinctive way of expressing oneself.

1. CUSTOM *noun*.
2. BEARING.

3. KIND[2] *noun*.

4. STYLE *noun*.

mannered *adjective*
Artificially genteel.

AFFECTED[2].

mannerism *noun*
Artificial behavior adopted to impress others.

AFFECTATION.

mannerly *adjective*
Characterized by good manners.

COURTEOUS.

manners *noun*
Socially correct behavior: *minding his manners.*

Syns: decorum, etiquette, mores, proprieties. —*Idioms* good form, p's and q's.
Near-syns: amenities, civilities, formalities, protocol; bearing, behavior, demeanor, deportment, mien.

manslaying *noun*
The crime of murdering someone.

MURDER *noun*.

mantic *adjective*
Of or relating to the foretelling of events by or as if by supernatural means.

PROPHETIC.

mantle *verb*
1. To cover as if with clothes.

1. CLOTHE.

2. To become red in the face.

man-to-man *adjective*
Executed without pretense or obfuscation.

manufacture *verb*
To create by forming, combining, or altering materials.

manufactured *adjective*
Made by human beings, not nature.

manufacturer *noun*
A person or business that makes or builds something.

manumission *noun*
The state of not being in confinement or servitude.

manumit *verb*
To set at liberty.

manumitted *adjective*
At liberty; not imprisoned or enslaved.

many *adjective*
Amounting to or consisting of a large, indefinite number: *Many sails dotted the horizon.*

many-sided *adjective*
Having many aspects, uses, or abilities.

map *noun*
Slang. The front surface of the head.

  map *verb*
  1. To work out and arrange the parts or details of.
  2. To show graphically the direction or location of, as by using coordinates.

mar *verb*
To spoil the soundness or perfection of.

maraud *verb*
To make a surprise attack on.

marbles *noun*
Slang. A healthy mental state.

march¹ *verb*
  1. To walk with long steps, esp. in a vigorous manner.
  2. To go forward, esp. toward a conclusion.

  march *noun*
  Forward movement.

march² *noun*
The line or area separating geopolitical units.

marchland *noun*
The line or area separating geopolitical units.

margin *noun*
  1. A fairly narrow line or space forming a boundary.
  2. The least possible quantity or degree.
  3. Suitable opportunity to accept or allow something.

  margin *verb*
  To put or form a border on.

marine *adjective*
  1. Of or relating to the seas or oceans: *marine life; marine exploration.*
  2. Of or relating to sea navigation.

mariner *noun*
A person engaged in sailing or working on a ship.

marital *adjective*
Of, relating to, or typical of marriage: *the marital bond; marital difficulties.*

---

2. BLUSH *verb.*

PLAIN *adjective.*

MAKE.

ARTIFICIAL.

BUILDER.

LIBERTY.

FREE *verb.*

FREE *adjective.*

Syns: legion, multitudinous, myriad, numerous, voluminous. —*Idiom* quite a few.
Near-ants: only, sole; scant, sparse.
Ant: few.

VERSATILE.

FACE *noun.*

1. DESIGN *verb.*
2. PLOT *verb.*

INJURE.

RAID *verb.*

SANITY.

1. STRIDE.
2. COME.

ADVANCE *noun.*

BORDER *noun.*

BORDER *noun.*

1. BORDER *noun.*
2. MINIMUM *noun.*
3. ROOM.

BORDER *verb.*

1. ***Syns:*** maritime, oceanic, pelagic, thalassic.
2. NAUTICAL.

SAILOR.

Syns: conjugal, connubial, hymeneal, married, matrimonial, nuptial, spousal, wedded.

maritime *adjective*
1. Of or relating to the seas or oceans.
2. Of or relating to sea navigation.

1. MARINE.
2. NAUTICAL.

mark *noun*
1. A name or other device placed on merchandise to signify its ownership or manufacture: *The maker's mark was nearly invisible.*
2. Something visible or evident that gives grounds for believing in the existence or presence of something else.
3. A distinctive element.
4. The act of noting, observing, or taking into account.
5. A means by which individuals are compared and judged.
6. A position of exalted, widely recognized importance.
7. What one intends to do or achieve.
8. Something strongly desired.
9. One that is fired at, attacked, or abused.
10. A person who is easily deceived or victimized.

1. *Syns:* brand, colophon, trademark.

2. SIGN *noun.*

3. QUALITY *noun.*
4. NOTICE *noun.*

5. STANDARD *noun.*

6. EMINENCE.

7. INTENTION.
8. AMBITION.
9. TARGET.
10. DUPE *noun.*

mark *verb*
1. To give grounds for believing in the existence or presence of.
2. To make manifest or apparent.
3. To make noticeable or different.
4. To set off by or as if by a mark indicating ownership or manufacture: *marked each product with the company seal.*
5. To perceive with a special effort of the senses or the mind.
6. To indicate (time or rhythm), as with repeated gestures or sounds.
7. To give a precise indication of, as on a register or scale.
8. To make a target of.

1. INDICATE.

2. SHOW *verb.*
3. DISTINGUISH.
4. *Syns:* brand, identify, label, tag.

5. NOTICE *verb.*

6. BEAT *verb.*

7. SHOW *verb.*

8. TARGET *verb.*

mark out (or **off**) *verb*
To fix the limits of.

DETERMINE.

markdown *noun*

SEE **mark down.**

mark down *verb*
To become or make less in price or value.

DEPRECIATE.

markdown *noun*
A lowering in price or value.

DEPRECIATION.

marked *adjective*
Readily attracting notice.

NOTICEABLE.

marker *noun*
An identifying or descriptive slip.

TICKET *noun.*

market *verb*
To offer for sale.

SELL *verb.*

marketability *noun*
Market appeal.

SELL *noun.*

marketableness *noun*
Market appeal.

SELL *noun.*

mark out (or **off**) *verb*

SEE **mark.**

marriable *adjective*
Archaic. Deemed suitable for marriage.

ELIGIBLE.

marriage *noun*
1. The state of being united as husband and wife: *seldom quarreled during their long marriage.*
2. The act or ceremony by which two people become husband and wife.

1. *Syns:* conjugality, connubiality, matrimony, wedlock.
2. WEDDING.

marriageable *adjective*
Deemed suitable for marriage.   ELIGIBLE.

married *adjective*
Of, relating to, or typical of marriage.   MARITAL.

marrow *noun*
The most central and material part.   HEART.

marrowy *adjective*
Precisely meaningful and tersely cogent.   PITHY.

marry *verb*
1. To join or be joined in marriage: *married his high-*   1. **Syns:** espouse, hitch (*Slang*), mate,
   school sweetheart; a brief courtship, after which they   wed. —*Idiom* tie the knot.
   married.
2. To bring or come together into a united whole.   2. COMBINE *verb.*

marsh *noun*
A usu. low-lying area of soft, waterlogged ground and   SWAMP.
standing water.

marshal *verb*
1. To bring together.   1. ASSEMBLE.
2. To put into a deliberate order.   2. ARRANGE.
3. To assemble, prepare, or put into operation, as for   3. MOBILIZE.
   war or a similar emergency.

marshland *noun*
A usu. low-lying area of soft, waterlogged ground and   SWAMP.
standing water.

martial *adjective*
1. Of, pertaining to, or inclined toward war.   1. MILITARY.
2. Pertaining to, characteristic of, or performed by   2. MILITARY.
   troops.

martinet *noun*
One who imposes or favors absolute obedience to   AUTHORITARIAN *noun.*
authority.

marvel *noun*
One that evokes great surprise and admiration: *such*   **Syns:** miracle, phenomenon, prodigy,
natural marvels as the Grand Canyon; a prose style that   sensation, stunner, wonder, wonderment.
is a marvel of precision.   —*Idioms* one for the books, the eighth
                                                            wonder of the world.

marvel *verb*
To have a feeling of great awe and rapt admiration.   WONDER *verb.*

marveling *noun*
The emotion aroused by something awe-inspiring or   WONDER *noun.*
astounding.

marvellous *adjective*   SEE **marvelous.**

marvelous also **marvellous** *adjective*
1. Particularly excellent: *had a marvelous time in*   1. **Syns:** cool (*Slang*), dandy (*Informal*),
   Europe.   divine[1] (*Informal*), dreamy (*Informal*),
                                                               fabulous (*Informal*), glorious, groovy
                                                               (*Slang*), heavenly (*Informal*), hot
                                                               (*Slang*), hunky-dory (*Slang*), keen[1]
                                                               (*Slang*), neat (*Slang*), nifty (*Slang*),
                                                               ripping, sensational, splendid, super
                                                               (*Informal*), superb, swell (*Informal*),
                                                               terrific, tremendous (*Informal*),
                                                               wonderful. —*Idiom* out of this world.
                                                               Near-ants: dreary, dull, ho-hum,
                                                               humdrum, monotonous, so-so, tedious;
                                                               dissatisfying, inferior, poor, unpleasant.
2. So remarkable as to elicit disbelief.   2. FABULOUS.

masculine *adjective*
Of, characteristic of, or befitting the male sex.   MANLY.

mash *verb*
1. To press forcefully so as to break up into a pulpy mass.
2. To act on with a steady pushing force.

1. CRUSH *verb*.

2. CROWD *verb*.

mashed *adjective*
Slang. Affected with intense romantic attraction.

INFATUATED.

mask *noun*
A deceptive outward appearance.

FAÇADE.

mask *verb*
1. To change or modify so as to prevent recognition of the true identity or character of.
2. To prevent (something) from being known.

1. DISGUISE *verb*.

2. COVER *verb*.

masquerade *noun*
1. A display of insincere behavior.
2. A deceptive outward appearance.

1. ACT *noun*.

2. FAÇADE.

masquerade *verb*
1. To change or modify so as to prevent recognition of the true identity or character of.
2. To represent oneself in a given character or as other than what one is.

1. DISGUISE *verb*.

2. POSE *verb*.

mass *noun*
1. A separate and distinct portion of matter.
2. Great extent, amount, or dimension.
3. The greatest part or portion.
4. A great deal.
5. An enormous number of persons gathered together.
6. A group of things gathered haphazardly.
7. A quantity accumulated.

1. BODY *noun*.
2. BULK.
3. WEIGHT *noun*.
4. HEAP *noun*.
5. CROWD *noun*.
6. HEAP *noun*.
7. ACCUMULATION.

massacre *noun*
The savage killing of many victims: *a massacre during the revolution.*

Syns: blood bath, bloodletting, bloodshed, butchery, carnage, pogrom, slaughter.

massacre *verb*
1. To kill savagely and indiscriminately.
2. *Informal.* To render totally ineffective by decisive defeat.

1. ANNIHILATE.

2. OVERWHELM.

massacrer *noun*
One who murders another.

MURDERER.

masses *noun*
The common people.

COMMONALTY.

massive *adjective*
1. Extremely large; having great mass.
2. Of extraordinary size and power.
3. Having a relatively great weight.

1. BULKY.
2. GIANT *adjective*.
3. HEAVY *adjective*.

massiveness *noun*
The state or quality of being physically heavy.

HEAVINESS.

massy *adjective*
Archaic. Of extraordinary size and power.

GIANT *adjective*.

master *noun*
1. One who is highest in rank or authority.
2. One that conquers.
3. A person who has legal title to property.
4. A person with a high degree of knowledge or skill in a particular field.
5. A first form from which varieties arise or imitations are made.

1. CHIEF *noun*.
2. CONQUEROR.
3. OWNER.
4. EXPERT *noun*.

5. ORIGINAL *noun*.

master *verb*
1. To gain knowledge or mastery of by study.
2. To get the better of.
3. To train to live with and be of use to man.

1. LEARN.
2. TRIUMPH *verb*.
3. DOMESTICATE.

master *adjective*

Having or demonstrating a high degree of knowledge or skill.

EXPERT *adjective*.

masterful *adjective*
1. Exercising authority.
2. Tending to dictate.
3. Having or demonstrating a high degree of knowledge or skill.
4. Showing art or skill in performing or doing.

1. AUTHORITATIVE.
2. DICTATORIAL.
3. EXPERT *adjective*.
4. ARTFUL.

masterly *adjective*
1. Having or demonstrating a high degree of knowledge or skill.
2. Showing art or skill in performing or doing.

1. EXPERT *adjective*.
2. ARTFUL.

masterpiece *noun*
An outstanding and ingenious work: *a novel that is a real masterpiece.*

Syns: chef d'oeuvre (*French*), magnum opus, masterwork, tour de force (*French*).

masterstroke *noun*
A great or heroic deed.

FEAT.

masterwork *noun*
An outstanding and ingenious work.

MASTERPIECE.

mastery *noun*
1. The act of exercising controlling power or the condition of being so controlled.
2. The right and power to command, decide, rule, or judge.
3. Intellectual hold.
4. Natural or acquired facility in a specific activity.

1. DOMINATION.
2. AUTHORITY.
3. GRASP *noun*.
4. ABILITY.

masticate *verb*
To bite and grind with the teeth.

CHEW.

mastodonic *adjective*
Of extraordinary size and power.

GIANT *adjective*.

mat also **matte** *adjective*
Lacking gloss and luster.

DULL *adjective*.

match *noun*
1. One of a matched pair of things.
2. Something closely resembling or analogous to something else.

1. MATE *noun*.
2. PARALLEL *noun*.

match *verb*
1. To be compatible or in correspondence.
2. To be equal or alike.
3. To do or make something equal to.
4. To be in keeping with.
5. To represent as similar.
6. To place in opposition or be in opposition to.

1. AGREE.
2. COMPARE.
3. EQUAL *verb*.
4. FIT.
5. LIKEN.
6. OPPOSE.

matchless *adjective*
Without equal or rival.

UNIQUE.

mate *noun*
1. One of a matched pair of things: *The mate of this glove is missing.*
2. A husband or wife.
3. A person whom one knows well, likes, and trusts.
4. One who keeps company with another.

1. *Syns:* companion, double, fellow, match, twin.
2. SPOUSE.
3. FRIEND.
4. ASSOCIATE *noun*.

mate *verb*
1. To join or be joined in marriage.
2. To engage in sexual relations with.

1. MARRY.
2. TAKE *verb*.

material *noun*
1. That from which things are or can be made: *built a crude shelter out of materials at hand; a novelist in search of material.*
2. That which occupies space and can be perceived by the senses.

1. *Syns:* matter, stuff, substance. —*Idiom* grist for one's mill.
2. MATTER *noun*.

3. The basic substance or essential elements of character that qualify a person for a specified role.

material *adjective*
1. Composed of or relating to things that occupy space and can be perceived by the senses.
2. Having great significance.
3. Related to the matter at hand.

materialistic *adjective*
Of or preoccupied with material rather than spiritual or intellectual things: *the materialistic goal of amassing property.*

materiality *noun*
1. That which occupies space and can be perceived by the senses.
2. Something that exists.

materialization *noun*
The act of coming into view.

materialize *verb*
1. To come into view.
2. To make real or actual.
3. To represent (an abstraction) in or as if in bodily form.

materials *noun*
Things needed for a task, journey, or other purpose.

materiel or **matériel** *noun*
Things needed for a task, journey, or other purpose.

matrimonial *adjective*
Of, relating to, or typical of marriage.

matrimony *noun*
The state of being united as husband and wife.

matrix *noun*
A model for making a mold.

matte *adjective*

matter *noun*
1. That which occupies space and can be perceived by the senses: *a universe consisting of matter and energy.*
2. That from which things are or can be made.
3. Something to be done, considered, or dealt with: *There are several matters left before we can adjourn.*
4. What a speech, piece of writing, or artistic work is about.

matter *verb*
To be of significance or importance.

matter-of-course *adjective*
To be expected.

matter-of-fact *adjective*
1. Lacking liveliness, charm, or surprise.
2. With little or no emotion or expression.
3. Having or indicating an awareness of things as they really are.

maturate *verb*
To bring or come to full development.

mature *adjective*
Having reached full growth and development: *mature fruit, ready for picking.*

---

3. TIMBER.

1. PHYSICAL.

2. IMPORTANT.
3. RELEVANT.

Syns: mundane, sensual, temporal, worldly.
Near-syns: carnal, earthly, earthy, secular.

1. MATTER *noun.*

2. ACTUALITY.

APPEARANCE.

1. APPEAR.
2. REALIZE.
3. EMBODY.

OUTFIT *noun.*

OUTFIT *noun.*

MARITAL.

MARRIAGE.

FORM *noun.*
SEE **mat.**

1. *Syns:* material, materiality, substance.

2. MATERIAL *noun.*
3. *Syns:* affair, thing.

4. SUBJECT *noun.*

COUNT *verb.*

COMMON *adjective.*

1. DULL *adjective.*
2. DRY *adjective.*
3. REALISTIC.

MATURE *verb.*

Syns: adult, big, developed, full-blown, full-fledged, full-grown, grown, grown-up, ripe. —*Idiom* of age.
Near-ants: green, undeveloped, unripe; juvenile, puerile, youthful.
Ant: immature.

mature *verb*
To bring or come to full development: *He matured the wine in vats in his cellar. As a teen-ager she matured slowly.*

Syns: age, develop, grow, maturate, mellow, ripe (*Chiefly Regional*), ripen.

matured *adjective*
Brought to full flavor and richness by aging.

AGED.

maudlin *adjective*
Affectedly or extravagantly emotional.

SENTIMENTAL.

maudlinism *noun*
The quality or condition of being affectedly or overly emotional.

SENTIMENTALITY.

maul *verb*
To injure or damage, as by abuse or heavy wear.

BATTER.

mausoleum *noun*
A burial place or receptacle for human remains.

GRAVE[1].

mawkish *adjective*
Affectedly or extravagantly emotional.

SENTIMENTAL.

mawkishness *noun*
The quality or condition of being affectedly or overly emotional.

SENTIMENTALITY.

maxim *noun*
A usu. pithy and familiar statement expressing an observation or principle generally accepted as wise or true.

PROVERB.

maximal *adjective*
Greatest in quantity or highest in degree that has been or can be attained.

MAXIMUM *adjective*.

maximum *adjective*
Greatest in quantity or highest in degree that has been or can be attained: *An inflated balloon reaches its maximum size just before bursting.*

Syns: maximal, top, topmost, upside (*Informal*), ultimate, utmost.
Near-ants: least, lowest, slightest, smallest, tiniest.
Ant: minimum.

maximum *noun*
1. The greatest quantity or highest degree attainable: *Desert temperatures are at a maximum in late afternoon and then fall sharply.*
2. The greatest amount or number allowed.

1. *Syns:* ceiling, climax, crest, outside, peak, top, ultimate. —*Idiom* ne plus ultra.
2. LIMIT *noun*.

maybe *adverb*
Possibly but not certainly: *Maybe it will rain, and maybe not.*

Syns: perchance, perhaps.

maze *verb*
Archaic. To stun the senses, as with a heavy blow, a shock, or fatigue.

DAZE *verb*.

maze *noun*
1. Something that is intricately and often bewilderingly complex.
2. *Archaic.* A stunned or bewildered condition.

1. TANGLE *noun*.
2. DAZE *noun*.

mazuma *noun*
Slang. Something, as coins, printed bills, etc., used as a medium of exchange.

MONEY.

meager *adjective*
1. Conspicuously deficient in quantity, fullness, or extent: *a meager diet of rice and broth; a meager living.*

1. *Syns:* exiguous, measly (*Slang*), poor, puny, scant, scanty, skimpy, spare, sparse, stingy.
Near-ants: adequate, ample, appreciable, considerable, enough, sufficient; bountiful, copious, plentiful, surplus.

2. Having little flesh or fat on the body.

meal *verb*

To take (food) into the body as nourishment.

mean¹ *verb*

1. To have or convey a particular idea: *We discussed what the poem meant. A red light means to stop.*
2. To have in mind as a goal or purpose.

mean² *adjective*

1. Of mediocre quality.
2. Lacking high station or birth.
3. Having or proceeding from low moral standards.
4. Characterized by intense ill will or spite.
5. So objectionable as to elicit despisal.
6. Ungenerously or pettily reluctant to spend money.
7. Not broad or elevated in scope or understanding.
8. *Slang.* Hard to treat, manage, or cope with.
9. *Informal.* Having or showing a bad temper.
10. *Informal.* Affected or tending to be affected with minor health problems.
11. Of little distinction.

mean³ *noun*

Something, as a type, number, quantity, or degree, that represents a midpoint between extremes on a scale of valuation.

mean *adjective*

Not extreme.

meander *verb*

1. To move about at random, esp. over a wide area.
2. To walk at a leisurely pace.
3. To move or proceed on a repeatedly curving course.

meandering *adjective*

Repeatedly curving in alternate directions.

meandrous *adjective*

Repeatedly curving in alternate directions.

meaning *noun*

1. That which is signified by a word or expression: *Synonyms are words having the same meaning.*

2. What one intends to do or achieve.

meaning *adjective*

Effectively conveying meaning, feeling, or mood.

meaningful *adjective*

1. Effectively conveying meaning, feeling, or mood.
2. Having great significance.
3. Conveying hidden or unexpressed meaning.

meaningless *adjective*

Lacking rational direction or purpose.

means *noun*

1. That by which something is accomplished or some end achieved: *We built a rope bridge and by this means crossed the gorge.*

2. All property or goods having economic value.

measliness *noun*

Slang. Contemptible unimportance.

---

2. THIN *adjective*.

EAT.

1. **Syns:** add up to, connote, denote, import, intend, signify, spell¹.
2. INTEND.

1. INFERIOR.
2. LOWLY.
3. SORDID.
4. MALEVOLENT.
5. FILTHY.
6. STINGY.
7. NARROW.
8. TROUBLESOME.
9. ILL-TEMPERED.
10. SICKLY.

11. HUMBLE *adjective*.

AVERAGE *noun*.

MIDDLE *adjective*.

1. ROVE.
2. STROLL *verb*.
3. WIND².

WINDING.

WINDING.

1. **Syns:** acceptation, acception, import, intent, message, purport, sense, significance (*also* significancy), signification, value.
2. INTENTION.

EXPRESSIVE.

1. EXPRESSIVE.
2. IMPORTANT.
3. PREGNANT.

MINDLESS.

1. **Syns:** agency, agent, instrument, instrumentality, instrumentation, intermediary, mechanism, medium, organ.
   Near-syns: apparatus, equipment, fashion, manner, method, mode, system, vehicle, way.
2. RESOURCES.

PETTINESS.

measly *adjective*
1. *Slang.* Conspicuously deficient in quantity, fullness, or extent.
2. *Slang.* Contemptibly unimportant.

1. MEAGER.
2. PETTY.

measure *noun*
1. The amount of space occupied by something.
2. Relative intensity or amount, as of a quality or attribute.
3. The act or process of ascertaining dimensions, quantity, or capacity.
4. A means by which individuals are compared and judged.
5. That which is allotted.
6. The formal product of a legislative or judicial body.
7. An action calculated to achieve an end.
8. The regular recurrence of strong and weak elements, such as stressed and unstressed notes in music.
9. Avoidance of extremes of opinion, feeling, or personal conduct.

1. SIZE.
2. DEGREE.
3. MEASUREMENT.
4. STANDARD *noun*.
5. ALLOTMENT.
6. LAW *noun*.
7. MOVE *noun*.
8. RHYTHM.
9. MODERATION.

measure *verb*
1. To ascertain the dimensions, quantity, or capacity of: *measured the room with a yardstick.*

2. To fix the limits of.

1. *Syns:* gauge (*also* gage), mete (*Archaic*). —*Idiom* take the measure of.
2. DETERMINE.

measure out *verb*
To give out in portions or shares.

DISTRIBUTE.

measure up *verb*
To be equal or alike.

COMPARE.

measured *adjective*
1. Careful and slow in acting, moving, or deciding.
2. Marked by a regular rhythm.

1. DELIBERATE *adjective*.
2. RHYTHMICAL.

measureless *adjective*
1. Having no ends or limits.
2. Too great to be calculated.

1. ENDLESS.
2. INCALCULABLE.

measurement *noun*
The act or process of ascertaining dimensions, quantity, or capacity: *equipment used in the measurement of the speed of light.*

Syns: measure, mensuration, metrology.

measure out *verb*

SEE **measure.**

measure up *verb*

SEE **measure.**

meat *noun*
1. Something fit to be eaten.
2. The most central and material part.

1. FOOD.
2. HEART.

meatball *noun*
Slang. A large, ungainly, and dull-witted person.

LUMP[1] *noun*.

meathead *noun*
Slang. A large, ungainly, and dull-witted person.

LUMP[1] *noun*.

meaty *adjective*
Precisely meaningful and tersely cogent.

PITHY.

mechanical *adjective*
Performed or performing automatically and impersonally.

PERFUNCTORY.

mechanism *noun*
That by which something is accomplished or some end achieved.

MEANS.

medal *noun*
An emblem of honor worn on one's clothing.

DECORATION.

meddle *verb*
1. To intervene officiously or indiscreetly in the affairs of others: *tried to keep her mother-in-law from meddling in her life.*

2. To handle something idly, ignorantly, or destructively.

1. *Syns:* butt in (*Slang*), horn in (*Slang*), interfere.
   Near-ants: avoid, eschew, ignore, neglect, overlook.

2. TAMPER.

meddler *noun*
1. A person given to intruding in other people's affairs: *A hopeless meddler, she took sides in every family quarrel on the block.*
2. A person who snoops.

1. *Syns:* busybody, buttinsky (*Slang*), kibitzer (*Informal*), pragmatic, quidnunc.

2. SNOOP *noun.*

meddlesome *adjective*
Given to intruding in other people's affairs.

MEDDLING *adjective.*

meddling *noun*
The act or an instance of interfering: *constant meddling in the colony's internal politics.*

Syns: interference, intervention.

meddling *adjective*
Given to intruding in other people's affairs: *a meddling mother who can't let her daughter lead a life of her own.*

Syns: interfering, intrusive, meddlesome, obtrusive, officious.

media *noun*
Journalists and journalism in general.

PRESS *noun.*

medial *adjective*
1. At, in, near, or being the center.
2. Not extreme.

1. CENTRAL.
2. MIDDLE *adjective.*

median *noun*
Something, as a type, number, quantity, or degree, that represents a midpoint between extremes on a scale of valuation.

AVERAGE *noun.*

median *adjective*
1. At, in, near, or being the center.
2. Not extreme.

1. CENTRAL.
2. MIDDLE *adjective.*

mediator *noun*
Someone who acts as an intermediate agent in a transaction.

GO-BETWEEN.

medicament *noun*
1. An agent used to restore health.
2. A substance used in the treatment of disease.

1. CURE *noun.*
2. DRUG *noun.*

medicant *noun*
An agent used to restore health.

CURE *noun.*

medicate *verb*
To administer or add a drug to.

DRUG *verb.*

medication *noun*
1. An agent used to restore health.
2. A substance used in the treatment of disease.

1. CURE *noun.*
2. DRUG *noun.*

medicine *noun*
1. An agent used to restore health.
2. A substance used in the treatment of disease.

1. CURE *noun.*
2. DRUG *noun.*

meditate *verb*
To consider carefully and at length.

PONDER.

meditation *noun*
The act or process of thinking.

THOUGHT.

meditative *adjective*
1. Of, characterized by, or disposed to thought.
2. Suggestive of or expressing deep, often melancholy thoughtfulness.

1. THOUGHTFUL.
2. PENSIVE.

medium *noun*
1. Something, as a type, number, quantity, or degree, that represents a midpoint between extremes on a scale of valuation.

1. AVERAGE *noun.*

2. That by which something is accomplished or some end achieved.

2. MEANS.

3. The totality of surrounding conditions and circumstances affecting growth or development.

3. ENVIRONMENT.

4. Something at which a person excels.

4. FORTE.

5. A settlement of differences through mutual concession.

5. COMPROMISE *noun*.

medium-priced *adjective*
Suited to or within the means of ordinary people.

POPULAR.

medley *noun*
A collection of various things.

ASSORTMENT.

meek *adjective*
1. Easily managed or handled.
2. Having or expressing feelings of humility.

1. GENTLE *adjective*.
2. HUMBLE *adjective*.

meet[1] *verb*
1. To come together face-to-face by arrangement: *met with the child's teacher; met him for lunch.*
2. To come up against.
3. To enter into conflict with.
4. To be contiguous or next to.
5. To come together.
6. To do or make something equal to.
7. To supply fully or completely.
8. To present with a specified reaction.

1. *Syns:* encounter, rendezvous.
2. ENCOUNTER *verb*.
3. ENGAGE.
4. ADJOIN.
5. CLOSE[1] *verb*.
6. EQUAL *verb*.
7. SATISFY.
8. GREET.

meet with *verb*
To participate in or partake of personally.

EXPERIENCE *verb*.

meet *noun*
A trial of skill or ability.

COMPETITION.

meet[2] *adjective*
1. Suitable for a particular person, condition, occasion, or place.
2. *Archaic.* Suited to one's end or purpose.

1. APPROPRIATE *adjective*.
2. CONVENIENT.

meeting *noun*
1. The act or fact of coming together.
2. A number of persons who have come or been gathered together.
3. A formal assemblage of the members of a group.

1. JUNCTION.
2. ASSEMBLY.
3. CONVENTION.

meeting *adjective*
Sharing a common boundary.

ADJOINING.

meet with *verb*

SEE **meet**.

megacosm *noun*
The totality of all existing things.

UNIVERSE.

megrim *noun*
An impulsive, often illogical turn of mind.

FANCY *noun*.

melancholic *adjective*
In low spirits.

DEPRESSED.

melancholy *adjective*
1. In low spirits.
2. Tending to cause sadness or low spirits.

1. DEPRESSED.
2. SAD.

melancholy *noun*
A feeling or spell of dismally low spirits.

GLOOM.

mélange also **melange** *noun*
A collection of various things.

ASSORTMENT.

meld *verb*
To bring or come together into a united whole.

COMBINE *verb*.

melded *adjective*
Joined together into a whole.

COMBINED.

melding *noun*
The result of combining.

COMBINATION.

melee also **mêlée**   *noun*
A quarrel or fight marked by very noisy, disorderly, and often violent behavior.   BRAWL *noun*.

meliorate   *verb*
To advance to a more desirable state.   IMPROVE.

melioration   *noun*
1. Something that improves.
2. Steady improvement, as of an individual or a society.

1. IMPROVEMENT.
2. PROGRESS *noun*.

mellow   *adjective*
1. Brought to full flavor and richness by aging.
2. Having or producing a full, deep, or rich sound.

1. AGED.
2. RESONANT.

mellow   *verb*
To bring or come to full development.   MATURE *verb*.

melodia   *noun*
A pleasing succession of musical tones forming a usu. brief aesthetic unit.   MELODY.

melodic   *adjective*
Resembling or having the effect of music, esp. pleasing music.   MELODIOUS.

melodious   *adjective*
1. Having or producing a pleasing melody: *a melodious and lilting passage in the scherzo; the melodious flute.*

2. Resembling or having the effect of music, esp. pleasing music: *As she recited she varied the pitch in a richly melodious voice.*

1. *Syns:* ariose, melodic, musical, tuneful.

2. *Syns:* dulcet, euphonic, euphonious, melodic, musical, tuneful.

melodramatic   *adjective*
Suggesting drama or a stage performance, as in emotionality or suspense.   DRAMATIC.

melodramatics   *noun*
Overemotional, exaggerated behavior calculated for effect.   THEATRICS.

melody   *noun*
A pleasing succession of musical tones forming a usu. brief aesthetic unit: *picked out a simple melody on his guitar.*   *Syns:* air, aria, melodia, note (*Poetic*), strain², tune.

melt   *verb*
1. To change from a solid to a liquid: *Plastic bowls will melt in the oven. We melted the butter in a saucepan.*
2. To disappear gradually by or as if by dispersal of particles.

1. *Syns:* deliquesce, dissolve, flux, fuse, liquefy, run, thaw.
2. FADE *verb*.

member   *noun*
One of the parts into which something is divided.   DIVISION.

memento   *noun*
Something that causes one to remember.   REMEMBRANCE.

memoir   *noun*
A narrative of experiences undergone by the writer.   COMMENTARY.

memorial   *noun*
Something, as a structure or custom, serving to honor or keep alive a memory: *The poet's house is preserved as a memorial.*   *Syns:* commemoration, monument, remembrance.

memorial   *adjective*
Serving to honor or keep alive a memory: *a memorial ceremony at the graves of the war dead.*   *Syn:* commemorative.

memorialize   *verb*
To honor or keep alive the memory of: *A plaque at the base of the bridge memorialized the workmen killed in its construction.*   *Syn:* commemorate.

memorize   *verb*
To commit to memory: *memorized her lines for the play.*   *Syns:* con, learn.

memory *noun*
1. The power of retaining and recalling past experience: *a poor memory for names.*

2. An act or instance of remembering: *The old friends traded memories of school days.*

1. *Syns:* recall, recollection, remembrance, reminiscence.
   Near-syns: awareness, cognizance, consciousness, mind, retention.
2. *Syns:* recollection, remembrance, reminiscence.

menace *verb*
1. To subject to danger or destruction.
2. To be imminent.

1. ENDANGER.
2. THREATEN.

menace *noun*
1. One regarded as an imminent danger.
2. An expression of the intent to hurt or punish another.

1. THREAT.
2. THREAT.

menacing *adjective*
Expressing, indicating, or warning of an impending danger or misfortune.

THREATENING.

ménage *noun*
A group of usu. related people living together as a unit.

FAMILY.

mend *verb*
1. To make right what is wrong.
2. To restore to proper condition or functioning.
3. To regain one's health.

1. CORRECT *verb.*
2. FIX *verb.*
3. RECOVER.

mendacious *adjective*
Given to or marked by deliberate concealment or misrepresentation of the truth.

DISHONEST.

mendaciousness *noun*
The practice of lying.

MENDACITY.

mendacity *noun*
The practice of lying: *The prosecutor exposed the witness's mendacity by making her contradict herself.*

Syns: falsehood, fibbery, mendaciousness, perjury, truthlessness, untruthfulness, unveracity.
Near-syns: caviling, dodging, equivocation, hedging, prevarication, quibbling.
Ant: veracity.

mendicancy *noun*
The condition of being a beggar.

BEGGARY.

mendicant *noun*
One who begs habitually or for a living.

BEGGAR *noun.*

mendicity *noun*
The condition of being a beggar.

BEGGARY.

menial *adjective*
Excessively eager to serve or obey.

SERVILE.

mensuration *noun*
The act or process of ascertaining dimensions, quantity, or capacity.

MEASUREMENT.

mental *adjective*
1. Relating to or performed by the mind: *mental arithmetic; such mental events as dreams.*
2. *Chiefly Brit.* Afflicted with or exhibiting irrationality and mental unsoundness.

1. *Syns:* cerebral, intellective, intellectual, psychic (*also* psychical), psychological.
2. INSANE.

mentality *noun*
1. The faculty of thinking, reasoning, and acquiring and applying knowledge.
2. The thought processes characteristic of an individual or group.

1. INTELLIGENCE.
2. PSYCHOLOGY.

mention *verb*
1. To call or direct attention to (an occurrence, situation, etc.).
2. To refer to by name.

1. REFER.
2. NAME *verb.*

mentor *noun*
1. One who advises another, esp. officially or professionally.
2. Something or someone that shows the way.

1. ADVISER.

2. GUIDE *noun.*

mephitic or **mephitical** *adjective*
1. Having an unpleasant odor.
2. Capable of injuring or killing by poison.

1. SMELLY.
2. POISONOUS.

mercenary *adjective*
Ruthlessly seeking personal advantage.
mercenary *noun*
A free-lance fighter: *mercenaries fighting in Africa.*

CORRUPT *adjective.*

Syns: adventurer, Hessian, hireling.
—*Idiom* soldier of fortune.

merchandise *noun*
Products bought and sold in commerce.
merchandise *verb*
To offer for sale.

GOODS.

SELL *verb.*

merchandiser *noun*
A person engaged in buying and selling.

DEALER.

merchant *noun*
A person engaged in buying and selling.
merchant *verb*
To offer for sale.

DEALER.

SELL.

merciful *adjective*
1. Not strict or severe.
2. Concerned with human welfare and the alleviation of suffering.

1. TOLERANT.
2. HUMANITARIAN.

mercifulness *noun*
Kind, forgiving, or compassionate treatment of or disposition toward others.

GRACE *noun.*

merciless *adjective*
1. Having or showing no mercy: *a merciless Gestapo interrogator.*
2. Having or showing uncompromising determination or resolution in purpose or action.

1. *Syns:* pitiless, remorseless, unmerciful.
—*Idiom* without an ounce of pity.
2. GRIM.

mercurial *adjective*
Following no predictable pattern.

CAPRICIOUS.

mercy *noun*
Kind, forgiving, or compassionate treatment of or disposition toward others.

GRACE *noun.*

mere *adjective*
1. Being what is specified and nothing more: *a mere mortal.*
2. Just sufficient.

1. *Syns:* bare, very.

2. BARE *adjective.*

merely *adverb*
Nothing more than: *Merely thinking of home makes me nostalgic.*

Syns: just, only.

meretricious *adjective*
Tastelessly showy.

GAUDY.

merge *verb*
To put together into one mass so that the constituent parts are more or less homogeneous.

MIX *verb.*

meridian *noun*
The highest point or state.

CLIMAX *noun.*

merit *noun*
1. A level of superiority that is usu. high: *a book of merit.*

2. A special feature or quality that confers superiority.
merit *verb*
To acquire as a result of one's behavior or effort.

1. *Syns:* caliber, quality, stature, value, virtue, worth.
Near-syns: excellence, perfection, superiority, superlativeness, virtuosity.
2. VIRTUE.

EARN.

meritable *adjective*
Deserving admiration.

ADMIRABLE.

merited *adjective*
Consistent with prevailing or accepted standards or circumstances.

JUST *adjective*.

meritorious *adjective*
Deserving admiration.

ADMIRABLE.

merriment *noun*
1. A state of joyful exuberance.
2. Joyful, exuberant activity.

1. GAIETY.
2. GAIETY.

merry *adjective*
1. Marked by festal celebration: *had a merry Christmas.*
2. Characterized by joyful exuberance.

1. **Syns:** festive, gala, glad, gladsome, happy, joyful, joyous.
2. GAY *adjective*.

merrymaking *noun*
1. The act of showing happy satisfaction in an event.
2. Joyful, exuberant activity.

1. CELEBRATION.
2. GAIETY.

mesh *noun*
1. An open fabric woven of strands that are interlaced and knotted at usu. regular intervals.
2. Something that is intricately and often bewilderingly complex.

1. WEB *noun*.
2. TANGLE *noun*.

mesh *verb*
To come or bring together and interlock.

ENGAGE.

mesmerize *verb*
To compel the attention, interest, imagination, etc., of.

GRIP *verb*.

mess *noun*
1. An unsightly object: *That old abandoned house is a mess.*
2. A group of things gathered haphazardly.
3. A lack of order or regular arrangement.
4. A ruinous state of disorder.
5. An individual quantity of food.

1. **Syns:** fright, monstrosity, sight, ugliness, ugly.
2. HEAP *noun*.
3. DISORDER *noun*.
4. BOTCH *noun*.
5. SERVING.

mess *verb*
1. To handle something idly, ignorantly, or destructively.
2. To put (the hair or clothes) into a state of disarray.

1. TAMPER.
2. TOUSLE.

mess around (or **about**) *verb*
1. *Informal.* To waste time by engaging in aimless activity: *While the diplomats were messing around, the world moved to the brink of war.*
2. *Slang.* To be nervously or uselessly active.
3. *Informal.* To be sexually unfaithful to another.

1. **Syns:** diddle, doodle, fool around (*Informal*), puddle, putter.
2. FUSS *verb*.
3. PHILANDER *verb*.

message *noun*
1. Something communicated, as information.
2. That which is signified by a word or expression.

1. COMMUNICATION.
2. MEANING *noun*.

mess around (or **about**) *verb*

SEE **mess**.

messenger *noun*
A person who carries messages or is sent on errands.

BEARER.

mess-up *noun*

SEE **mess up**.

mess up *verb*
1. To put out of proper order.
2. To put into total disorder.
3. To harm irreparably through inept handling; make a mess of.

1. DISORDER *verb*.
2. CONFUSE.
3. BOTCH *verb*.

mess-up *noun*
A ruinous state of disorder.

BOTCH *noun*.

messy *adjective*
1. Marked by an absence of cleanliness and order: *a messy house; messy attire.*

1. **Syns:** disheveled, ill-kempt, mussy, slipshod, slobbery, sloppy, slovenly, unkempt, untidy.

2. Indifferent to correctness, accuracy, or neatness.   **2.** CARELESS.
3. Lacking regular or logical order.   **3.** DISORDERLY.

metamorphize *verb*
To change into a different form, substance, or state.   CONVERT.

metamorphose *verb*
1. To change into a different form, substance, or state.   **1.** CONVERT.
2. To bring about a radical change in.   **2.** REVOLUTIONIZE.

metamorphosis *noun*
The process or result of giving a different form or   CHANGE *noun*.
appearance.

metanoia *noun*
A fundamental change in one's beliefs.   CONVERSION.

metaphysical also **metaphysic** *adjective*
1. Having no body, form, or substance.   **1.** IMMATERIAL.
2. Of, coming from, or relating to forces or beings that   **2.** SUPERNATURAL.
exist outside the natural world.

mete *verb*
1. To set aside or distribute as a share.   **1.** ALLOT.
2. *Archaic.* To ascertain the dimensions, quantity, or   **2.** MEASURE *verb*.
capacity of.

meter *noun*
The regular recurrence of strong and weak elements,   RHYTHM.
such as stressed and unstressed notes in music.

method *noun*
1. Systematic arrangement and design: *tried to find*   **1.** *Syns:* order, orderliness, pattern, plan,
some sort of method in this madness.   system.
2. A systematic body of procedures and techniques   **2.** *Syn:* methodology.
characteristic of a field or discipline: *the scientific*
method.
3. The manner in which something is done.   **3.** WAY.

methodical also **methodic** *adjective*
Arranged or proceeding in a set, systematized pattern: *Syns:* orderly, regular, systematic (*also*
methodical, cogently expressed arguments.   systematical).

methodize *verb*
To arrange in an orderly manner: *developed a set of*   *Syns:* order, organize, systematize,
emergency procedures and methodized them.   systemize.

methodology *noun*
A systematic body of procedures and techniques   METHOD *noun*.
characteristic of a field or discipline.

meticulous *adjective*
1. Showing or marked by attentiveness to all aspects   **1.** CAREFUL.
or details.
2. Very difficult to please.   **2.** NICE.

meticulousness *noun*
Attentiveness to detail.   THOROUGHNESS.

métier *noun*
Something at which a person excels.   FORTE.

metrical also **metric** *adjective*
Marked by a regular rhythm.   RHYTHMICAL.

metrology *noun*
The act or process of ascertaining dimensions, quantity,   MEASUREMENT.
or capacity.

metropolis *noun*
A large and important town.   CITY *noun*.

metropolitan *adjective*
Of, in, or belonging to a city.   CITY *adjective*.

metropolitanize *verb*
To imbue with city ways, manners, and customs.   CITIFY.

mettle *noun*
The quality of mind enabling one to face danger or   COURAGE.
hardship resolutely.

mettlesome *adjective*
1. Having or showing courage.
2. Full of or characterized by a lively, emphatic, eager quality.

1. BRAVE *adjective*.
2. SPIRITED.

mew *verb*
To confine within a limited area.

ENCLOSE.

microbe *noun*
A minute organism usu. producing disease.

GERM.

microorganism also **micro-organism** *noun*
A minute organism usu. producing disease.

GERM.

microscopic *adjective*
So minute as to be undiscernible.

IMPERCEPTIBLE.

mid *adjective*
1. At, in, near, or being the center.
2. Not extreme.

1. CENTRAL.
2. MIDDLE *adjective*.

mid-course *noun*
A settlement of differences through mutual concession.

COMPROMISE *noun*.

middle *adjective*
1. Not extreme: *took the middle course in the negotiations*.

2. At, in, near, or being the center.

1. *Syns:* central, intermediate, mean³, medial, median, mid, middle-of-the-road, middle-road, midway.

2. CENTRAL.

middle *noun*
A point or area equidistant from all sides of something.

CENTER *noun*.

middleman *noun*
Someone who acts as an intermediate agent in a transaction.

GO-BETWEEN.

middle-of-the-road *adjective*
Not extreme.

MIDDLE *adjective*.

middle-road *adjective*
Not extreme.

MIDDLE *adjective*.

midget *adjective*
Extremely small.

TINY.

midpoint *noun*
A point or area equidistant from all sides of something.

CENTER *noun*.

midst *noun*
1. A point or area equidistant from all sides of something.
2. The most intensely active central part.

1. CENTER *noun*.
2. THICK *noun*.

midway *adjective*
Not extreme.

MIDDLE *adjective*.

mien *noun*
1. The way something or someone looks.
2. Behavior through which one reveals one's personality.

1. APPEARANCE.
2. BEARING.

miff *noun*
Extreme displeasure caused by an insult or slight.

OFFENSE.

might *noun*
1. Physical, mental, financial, or legal power to perform.
2. The right and power to command, decide, rule, or judge.
3. The state or quality of being physically strong.

1. ABILITY.

2. AUTHORITY.

3. STRENGTH.

mighty *adjective*
1. Of extraordinary size and power.
2. Exercising authority.
3. Having or able to exert great power.

1. GIANT *adjective*.
2. AUTHORITATIVE.
3. POWERFUL.

mighty *adverb*
Informal. To a high degree.

VERY *adverb*.

migrant *noun*
One who emigrates.

EMIGRANT.

migrant *adjective*
1. Moving from one habitat to another on a seasonal basis.
2. Moving from one area to another in search of work: *migrant farm workers*.

1. MIGRATORY.

2. *Syns:* itinerant, migratory.

migrate *verb*
1. To change habitat seasonally: *geese migrating from Canada to Florida every fall*.
2. To leave one's native land and to settle in another.

1. *Syn:* transmigrate.

2. EMIGRATE.

migration *noun*
Departure from one's native land to settle in another.

EMIGRATION.

migrational *adjective*
Moving from one habitat to another on a seasonal basis.

MIGRATORY.

migrative *adjective*
Moving from one habitat to another on a seasonal basis.

MIGRATORY.

migratory *adjective*
1. Moving from one habitat to another on a seasonal basis: *Swallows are migratory birds*.
2. Moving from one area to another in search of work.

1. *Syns:* migrant, migrational, migrative, mobile, transmigratory.
2. MIGRANT *adjective*.

mild *adjective*
1. Free from extremes in temperature: *a mild climate*.
2. Of a kindly, considerate character.
3. Easily managed or handled.
4. Free from severity or violence, as in movement.

1. *Syns:* moderate, temperate.
2. GENTLE *adjective*.
3. GENTLE *adjective*.
4. GENTLE *adjective*.

milden *verb*
To ease the anger or agitation of.

PACIFY.

milieu *noun*
The totality of surrounding conditions and circumstances affecting growth or development.

ENVIRONMENT.

militant *adjective*
Inclined to act in a hostile way.

AGGRESSIVE.

militaristic *adjective*
Of, pertaining to, or inclined toward war.

MILITARY *adjective*.

militarize *verb*
To assemble, equip, and train for war: *In World War II the Soviet population was totally militarized*.

Syn: mobilize.

military *adjective*
1. Pertaining to, characteristic of, or performed by troops: *saluted with military precision; military science and tactics*.
2. Of, pertaining to, or inclined toward war: *military actions on the border*.

1. *Syns:* martial, soldierly.

2. *Syns:* bellicose, martial, militaristic, warlike.

milksop *noun*
A person who behaves in a childish, weak, or spoiled way.

BABY *noun*.

mill *noun*
A building or complex in which an industry is located.

WORKS.

mill *verb*
To break up into tiny particles.

CRUSH *verb*.

million *noun*
An indeterminately great amount or number.

HEAP *noun*.

millstone *noun*
A duty or responsibility that is a source of anxiety, worry, or hardship.

BURDEN *noun*.

milquetoast *noun*
A person who behaves in a childish, weak, or spoiled way.

BABY *noun*.

mime *noun*
A performer skilled at copying the manner or expression of another.

MIMIC *noun.*

mimetism *noun*
The act, practice, or art of copying the manner or expression of another.

MIMICRY.

mimic *noun*
1. A performer skilled at copying the manner or expression of another: *a renowned mimic whose take-offs on the President were hilarious.*

1. **Syns:** impersonator, mime.

2. One who mindlessly imitates another.

2. ECHO *noun.*

mimic *verb*
1. To copy (the manner or expression of another), esp. in an exaggerated or mocking way.

1. IMITATE.

2. To copy (another) slavishly.

2. ECHO *verb.*

mimicry *noun*
The act, practice, or art of copying the manner or expression of another: *an actor who was an expert at mimicry.*

Syns: apery, aping, imitation, mimetism.

mind *noun*
1. A person of great mental ability: *He is one of the greatest minds of this century.*

1. **Syns:** brain (*Slang*), head (*Slang*), intellect, intellectual, thinker.

2. The faculty of thinking, reasoning, and acquiring and applying knowledge.

2. INTELLIGENCE.

3. The seat of the faculty of intelligence and reason.

3. HEAD *noun.*

4. The thought processes characteristic of an individual or group.

4. PSYCHOLOGY.

5. Something believed or accepted as true by a person.

5. BELIEF.

6. A healthy mental state.

6. SANITY.

7. A desire for a particular thing or activity.

7. LIKING.

mind *verb*
1. To act in conformity with.

1. FOLLOW.

2. To have the care and supervision of.

2. TEND[2].

3. To be careful.

3. LOOK OUT.

4. To be sure that.

4. LOOK *verb.*

5. To perceive with a special effort of the senses or the mind.

5. NOTICE *verb.*

6. To have an objection.

6. CARE *verb.*

7. *Chiefly Regional.* To have in mind as a goal or purpose.

7. INTEND.

8. *Rare.* To renew (an image or thought) in the mind.

8. REMEMBER.

mind-blowing *adjective*
Slang. Of such a character as to overwhelm.

STAGGERING.

mind-boggling *adjective*
Slang. Of such a character as to overwhelm.

STAGGERING.

minded *adjective*
Disposed to accept or agree.

WILLING.

mindful *adjective*
1. Tending toward awareness and appreciation: *a person mindful of the feelings of others.*

1. **Syns:** conscious, heedful, observant, observative, observing, thoughtful.
Near-syns: alert, attentive, aware, conscientious, keen, sharp, vigilant, watchful.
Ants: heedless, mindless.

2. Marked by comprehension, cognizance, and perception.

2. AWARE.

3. Cautiously attentive.

3. CAREFUL.

mindless *adjective*
1. Displaying a complete lack of forethought and good sense: *The wrecked car is the handiwork of my mindless teen-age son.*

1. **Syns:** brainless, dimwitted (*Slang*), fatuous, foolish, senseless, silly, simple, unintelligent, weak-minded, witless.

2. Afflicted with or exhibiting irrationality and mental unsoundness.

3. Lacking rational direction or purpose: *Mindless violence is always shocking.*

4. Showing no concern, attention, or regard: *plunged on, mindless of the danger.*

mingle *verb*
1. To put together into one mass so that the constituent parts are more or less homogeneous.
2. To take part in social activities.

miniature *noun*
A small-scale representation of something.
miniature *adjective*
Extremely small.

minim *noun*
A tiny amount.

minimal *adjective*
Comprising the least possible: *was exposed to minimal radiation; the minimal accepted dosage.*

minimize *verb*
To think, represent, or speak of as small or unimportant.

minimum *noun*
The least possible quantity or degree: *systems that reduced the probability of error to a minimum.*
minimum *adjective*
Comprising the least possible.

minister *noun*
A person ordained for service in a Christian church.
minister *verb*
To work and care for.
minister to *verb*
To have the care and supervision of.

ministerial *adjective*
Of, for, or relating to administration or administrators.

minister to *verb*

ministry *noun*
A diplomatic office or headquarters in a foreign country.

minor *adjective*
1. Of subordinate standing or importance: *minor government officials.*

2. *Law.* Not yet a legal adult: *left his estate to one minor child.*
minor *noun*
Law. One who is not yet legally of age: *was arrested for contributing to the delinquency of a minor.*

minority *noun*
The state or period of being under legal age: *an heir still in his minority.*

minor-league *adjective*
Of subordinate standing or importance.

---

2. INSANE.

3. *Syns:* irrational, meaningless, pointless, purposeless, senseless.
—*Idiom* without rhyme or reason.

4. *Syns:* heedless, unheeding, unmindful.

1. MIX *verb.*

2. SOCIALIZE.

MODEL *noun.*

TINY.

BIT[1].

Syns: minimum, smallest.
Near-syns: basic, essential, fundamental, littlest, slightest, tiniest.
Ant: maximal.

BELITTLE.

Syn: margin.

MINIMAL.

PREACHER.

SERVE.

TEND[2].

ADMINISTRATIVE.
SEE **minister.**

MISSION.

1. *Syns:* inferior, lesser, low, lower[2], minor-league, petty, secondary, small, small-fry (*Informal*), small-time (*Informal*), under.
Near-syns: average, fair, insignificant, mediocre, middling (*Informal*), second-rate, trivial, unimportant.
Ant: major.

2. *Syn:* underage[2].

Syns: child, infant (*Law*).

Syns: infancy (*Law*), nonage.

MINOR *adjective.*

mint *noun*
A large sum of money.   FORTUNE.

minus *noun*
An unfavorable condition, circumstance, or   DISADVANTAGE.
characteristic.

minute¹ *adjective*
Characterized by attention to detail.   DETAILED.

minute² *noun*
A very brief time.   FLASH *noun*.

minutiae *noun*
Unimportant matters or concerns.   TRIVIA.

miracle *noun*
1. An event inexplicable by the laws of nature: *Many* 1. **Syn:** wonder.
   miracles are attributed to Our Lady of Lourdes.
2. One that evokes great surprise and admiration.   2. MARVEL.

miraculous *adjective*
1. Of, coming from, or relating to forces or beings that 1. SUPERNATURAL.
   exist outside the natural world.
2. So remarkable as to elicit disbelief.   2. FABULOUS.

mirage *noun*
An erroneous perception of reality.   ILLUSION.

mire *noun*
A usu. low-lying area of soft, waterlogged ground and   SWAMP.
standing water.

mirk *noun & verb*   SEE **murk.**
mirky *adjective*   SEE **murky.**

mirror *noun*
One that is worthy of imitation or duplication.   MODEL *noun*.
   mirror *verb*
1. To send back or form an image of.   1. REFLECT.
2. To copy (another) slavishly.   2. ECHO *verb*.

mirth *noun*
A state of joyful exuberance.   GAIETY.

mirthful *adjective*
Characterized by joyful exuberance.   GAY *adjective*.

miry *adjective*
Covered or soiled with mud.   MUDDY *adjective*.

misadventure *noun*
An unexpected and usu. undesirable event.   ACCIDENT.

misanthrope *noun*
A person who expects only the worst from people.   CYNIC.

misanthropist *noun*
A person who expects only the worst from people.   CYNIC.

misapplication *noun*
Wrong, often corrupt use.   ABUSE *noun*.

misapply *verb*
To use wrongly and improperly.   ABUSE *verb*.

misapprehend *verb*
To understand incorrectly.   MISUNDERSTAND.

misapprehension *noun*
A failure to understand correctly.   MISUNDERSTANDING.

misappropriate *verb*
To use wrongly and improperly.   ABUSE *verb*.

misappropriation *noun*
Wrong, often corrupt use.   ABUSE *noun*.

misbegotten *adjective*
Born out of wedlock.   ILLEGITIMATE.

misbehave *verb*
1. To behave in a rowdy or unruly fashion: *The*   1. **Syns:** act up (*Informal*), carry on, cut
   children had to be disciplined because they   up (*Informal*), horse around
   misbehaved.   (*Informal*), horseplay.

2. To work improperly due to mechanical difficulties. 2. MALFUNCTION.

misbehavior *noun*
Improper, often rude behavior: *was soundly thrashed for his misbehavior in church.* **Syns:** misconduct, misdoing, naughtiness, wrongdoing.

misbelieve *verb*
To give no credence to. DISBELIEVE.

miscalculate *verb*
To calculate wrongly: *The pilot miscalculated the air speed.* **Syns:** misestimate, misjudge, misreckon.

miscalculation *noun*
A wrong calculation: *The cost overrun is due to a miscalculation of production time.* **Syns:** error, misjudgment, misreckoning.

miscarry *verb*
1. To go wrong: *The marketing strategy miscarried and sales suffered.* **1. Syns:** misfire, miss. —*Idioms* fall short, go amiss (*or* astray), miss the mark.
2. To bring forth a nonviable fetus prematurely: *The mother miscarried during the first trimester.* **2. Syns:** abort, cast (*Brit. & Vet. Med.*), slip (*Vet. Med.*).

miscellaneous *adjective*
Consisting of a number of different kinds. VARIOUS.

miscellany *noun*
A collection of various things. ASSORTMENT.

mischance *noun*
An unexpected and usu. undesirable event. ACCIDENT.

mischief *noun*
1. Annoying yet harmless, usu. playful acts: *The mischief that toddlers can get into is endless.* **1. Syns:** diablerie (*also* diablery), impishness, prankishness, roguery, roguishness, sportiveness.
2. The action or result of inflicting loss or pain. 2. HARM *noun*.
3. One who causes minor trouble or damage: *The child was a real mischief in school.* **3. Syns:** imp, prankster, rascal, rogue, scamp.

misconceive *verb*
To understand incorrectly. MISUNDERSTAND.

misconception *noun*
A failure to understand correctly. MISUNDERSTANDING.

misconduct *noun*
Improper, often rude behavior. MISBEHAVIOR.

misconstrue *verb*
To understand incorrectly. MISUNDERSTAND.

miscreant *adjective*
Utterly reprehensible in nature or behavior. CORRUPT *adjective*.

miscue *noun*
1. An act or thought that unintentionally deviates from what is correct, right, or true. 1. ERROR.
2. A stupid, clumsy mistake. 2. BLUNDER *noun*.
miscue *verb*
To make an error or mistake. ERR.

misdeed *noun*
1. A serious breaking of the public law. 1. CRIME.
2. A wicked act. 2. CRIME.

misdeem *verb*
1. To take (one thing) mistakenly for another. 1. CONFUSE.
2. To make a mistake in judging. 2. MISJUDGE.

misdoing *noun*
Improper, often rude behavior. MISBEHAVIOR.

misdoubt *verb*
To lack trust or confidence in. DISTRUST *verb*.

mise en scène *noun*
1. The properties, backdrops, and other objects arranged for a dramatic presentation. 1. SCENE.
2. *French.* The totality of surrounding conditions and circumstances affecting growth or development. 2. ENVIRONMENT.

misemploy *verb*
To use wrongly and improperly.

ABUSE *verb*.

misemployment *noun*
Wrong, often corrupt use.

ABUSE *noun*.

miser *noun*
A stingy person: *a miser who wouldn't spend a penny on his family.*

Syns: cheapskate (*also* cheap skate) (*Slang*), chuff, hunks, muckworm, niggard, Scrooge, skinflint (*Slang*), stiff (*Slang*), tightwad (*Slang*). —*Idiom* penny pincher.

miserable *adjective*
1. Suffering from usu. prolonged anguish: *miserable, half-starved prisoners.*

1. **Syns:** woebegone (*also* wobegone) (*Archaic*), woeful (*also* woful), wretched.

2. *Informal.* Having a painful ailment: *was just miserable with a bad cold.*
3. Of mediocre quality.

2. **Syns:** afflicted, suffering, wretched.

3. INFERIOR *adjective*.

miserable *noun*
A person living under very unhappy circumstances.

UNFORTUNATE *noun*.

miserly *adjective*
Ungenerously or pettily reluctant to spend money.

STINGY.

misery *noun*
1. A state of prolonged anguish and privation: *The misery of the starving refugees is heartbreaking.*

1. **Syns:** suffering, unhappiness, woe, wretchedness.
   Near-syns: agony, anguish, depression, despair, despondency, grief, sadness, squalor.
   Ants: contentment, happiness.

2. A state of physical or mental suffering.
3. *Informal.* A sensation of physical discomfort occurring as the result of disease or injury.

2. DISTRESS *noun*.
3. PAIN *noun*.

misestimate *verb*
1. To make a mistake in judging.
2. To calculate wrongly.

1. MISJUDGE.
2. MISCALCULATE.

misfire *verb*
To go wrong.

MISCARRY.

misfortunate *adjective*
Involving or undergoing chance misfortune.

UNFORTUNATE *adjective*.

misfortune *noun*
1. Bad fortune: *Be brave in times of misfortune. She had the misfortune to marry a faithless man.*
2. An unexpected and usu. undesirable event.

1. **Syns:** adversity, unluck (*Chiefly Regional*), unluckiness.
2. ACCIDENT.

misgiving *noun*
A feeling of uncertainty about the fitness or correctness of an action.

QUALM.

mishandle *verb*
1. To hurt or injure by maltreatment.
2. To use wrongly and improperly.
3. To harm irreparably through inept handling; make a mess of.

1. ABUSE *verb*.
2. ABUSE *verb*.
3. BOTCH.

mishandling *noun*
Wrong, often corrupt use.

ABUSE *noun*.

mishap *noun*
An unexpected and usu. undesirable event.

ACCIDENT.

mishmash *noun*
A collection of various things.

ASSORTMENT.

misinterpret *verb*
To understand incorrectly.

MISUNDERSTAND.

misinterpretation *noun*
A failure to understand correctly.

MISUNDERSTANDING.

misjudge *verb*
1. To make a mistake in judging: *I misjudged his true character.*
2. To calculate wrongly.

1. **Syns:** misdeem, misestimate, misread.

2. MISCALCULATE.

misjudgment *noun*
A wrong calculation.

MISCALCULATION.

mislay *verb*
To be unable to find.

LOSE.

mislaying *noun*
The act or an instance of losing something.

LOSS.

mislead *verb*
To cause to accept what is false, esp. by trickery or misrepresentation.

DECEIVE.

mislike *verb*
To have a feeling of aversion for.

DISLIKE *verb*.

mismanage *verb*
To harm irreparably through inept handling; make a mess of.

BOTCH.

misplace *verb*
To be unable to find.

LOSE.

misplacement *noun*
The act or an instance of losing something.

LOSS.

misplacing *noun*
The act or an instance of losing something.

LOSS.

misread *verb*
To make a mistake in judging.

MISJUDGE.

misreckon *verb*
To calculate wrongly.

MISCALCULATE.

misreckoning *noun*
A wrong calculation.

MISCALCULATION.

misrepresent *verb*
To give an inaccurate view of by representing falsely or misleadingly.

DISTORT.

misrepresentation *noun*
An untrue declaration.

LIE² *noun*.

misrule *noun*
A lack of civil order or peace.

DISORDER *noun*.

miss *verb*
1. To go wrong.
2. To fail to take advantage of.

1. MISCARRY.
2. LOSE.

miss *noun*
Regional. The condition of lacking a usual or needed amount.

ABSENCE.

misshape *verb*
To alter and spoil the natural form or appearance of.

DEFORM.

missing *adjective*
1. Not present.
2. No longer in one's possession.

1. ABSENT.
2. LOST.

mission *noun*
1. An assignment one is sent to carry out: *on a mission of mercy.*
2. An inner urge to pursue an activity or perform a service.
3. A diplomatic office or headquarters in a foreign country: *the Soviet mission to the U.N.*

1. **Syns:** commission, errand, office, task.

2. VOCATION.

3. **Syns:** delegation, legation, post, ministry.

missionary *noun*
A person doing religious or charitable work in a foreign country: *missionaries spreading the faith.*

Syns: apostle, evangelist, missioner.
—*Idioms* field preacher, propagator of the faith.

missionary *adjective*

Of missionaries or their work: *off to Africa on a missionary assignment.*

missioner *noun*
A person doing religious or charitable work in a foreign country.

missish *adjective*
Marked by excessive concern for propriety and good form.

missive *noun*
A written communication directed to another.

misstate *verb*
To give an inaccurate view of by representing falsely or misleadingly.

misstatement *noun*
An untrue declaration.

misstep *noun*
An act or thought that unintentionally deviates from what is correct, right, or true.

mist *noun*
A thick, heavy atmospheric condition offering reduced visibility due to the presence of suspended particles.

mist *verb*
To make dim or indistinct.

mistake *noun*
An act or thought that unintentionally deviates from what is correct, right, or true.

mistake *verb*
1. To make an error or mistake.
2. To take (one thing) mistakenly for another.
3. To understand incorrectly.

mistaken *adjective*
Containing an error or errors.

mistreat *verb*
To hurt or injure by maltreatment.

mistreatment *noun*
Physically harmful treatment.

mistrust *noun*
1. Lack of trust.
2. A lack of conviction or certainty.

mistrust *verb*
1. To lack trust or confidence in.
2. To be uncertain, disbelieving, or skeptical about.

mistrustful *adjective*
Lacking trust or confidence.

misty *adjective*
1. Covered by or as if by a thin coating or film.
2. Not clearly perceived or perceptible.

misunderstand *verb*
To understand incorrectly: *completely misunderstood the instructions.*

misunderstanding *noun*
A failure to understand correctly: *a misunderstanding about what he was to do.*

misusage *noun*
Physically harmful treatment.

misuse *verb*
1. To hurt or injure by maltreatment.
2. To use wrongly and improperly.

misuse *noun*
Wrong, often corrupt use.

Syns: apostolic, evangelical.

MISSIONARY *noun.*

GENTEEL.

LETTER.

DISTORT.

LIE[2] *noun.*

ERROR.

HAZE *noun.*

OBSCURE *verb.*

ERROR.

1. ERR.
2. CONFUSE *verb.*
3. MISUNDERSTAND.

ERRONEOUS.

ABUSE *verb.*

ABUSE *noun.*

1. DISTRUST *noun.*
2. DOUBT *noun.*

1. DISTRUST *verb.*
2. DOUBT *verb.*

DISTRUSTFUL.

1. FILMY.
2. UNCLEAR.

Syns: misapprehend, misconceive, misconstrue, misinterpret, mistake.

Syns: misapprehension, misconception, misinterpretation. —*Idiom* false impression.

ABUSE *noun.*

1. ABUSE *verb.*
2. ABUSE *verb.*

ABUSE *noun.*

mite *noun*
A tiny amount.   BIT[1].

mitigate *verb*
To make less severe or more bearable.   RELIEVE.

mitigation *noun*
Freedom, esp. from pain.   RELIEF.

mix *verb*
To put together into one mass so that the constituent   *Syns:* admix, amalgamate, blend, combine,
parts are more or less homogeneous: *mixing eggs,*   commingle, commix, compound, fuse,
butter, and sugar into a batter.   intermingle, intermix, merge, mingle,
                                                             stir[1].

mix *noun*
Something produced by mixing.   MIXTURE.

mixed *adjective*
Consisting of a number of different kinds.   VARIOUS.

mixed-up *adjective*
Characterized by physical confusion.   CONFUSED.

mixture *noun*
Something produced by mixing: *a mixture of flour and*   *Syns:* admixture, amalgam,
milk; yarn that is a mixture of wool and nylon.   amalgamation, blend, compound, fusion,
                                                             mix.

mix-up *noun*   SEE **mix up.**

mix up *verb*
1. To cause to be unclear in mind or intent.   1. CONFUSE.
2. To take (one thing) mistakenly for another.   2. CONFUSE.
3. To put out of proper order.   3. DISORDER *verb.*
4. To make complex, intricate, or perplexing.   4. COMPLICATE.

mix-up *noun*
A lack of order or regular arrangement.   DISORDER *noun.*

moan *noun*
A long, mournful cry.   HOWL *noun.*

mob *noun*
1. An enormous number of persons gathered together.   1. CROWD *noun.*
2. The common people.   2. COMMONALTY.
3. *Informal.* An organized group of criminals,   3. GANG.
   hoodlums, or wrongdoers.

mob *verb*
1. To congregate closely around or against.   1. CROWD *verb.*
2. To fill to excess by compressing or squeezing tightly.   2. CROWD *verb.*

mobile *adjective*
1. Capable of moving or being moved from place to   1. *Syns:* movable (*also* moveable),
   place: *a mobile home; a mobile hospital.*   moving, transportable, traveling.
2. Changing easily, as in expression: *a mobile face.*   2. *Syns:* changeable, fluid, plastic.
3. Moving from one habitat to another on a seasonal   3. MIGRATORY.
   basis.

mobilize *verb*
1. To assemble, prepare, or put into operation, as for   1. *Syns:* marshal, muster, organize, rally.
   war or a similar emergency: *mobilized the troops;*
   trying to mobilize public opinion.
2. To set or keep going.   2. DRIVE *verb.*
3. To assemble, equip, and train for war.   3. MILITARIZE.

mock *verb*
1. To copy (the manner or expression of another), esp.   1. IMITATE.
   in an exaggerated or mocking way.
2. To make fun of.   2. RIDICULE.

mock *noun*
A false, derisive, or impudent imitation of something.   MOCKERY.

mock *adjective*
Made to imitate something else.   ARTIFICIAL.

mockery *noun*
1 A false, derisive, or impudent imitation of something: *The trial was a mockery of justice.*

2. An object of amusement or laughter.
3. Words or actions intended to evoke contemptuous laughter.

mod *adjective*
Informal. Modern.

mode *noun*
1. Manner of being or form of existence.
2. A distinctive way of expressing oneself.
3. The current custom.

model *noun*
1. A small-scale representation of something: *a model of a proposed skyscraper; a model of an oldtime sailing vessel.*
2. One that is worthy of imitation or duplication: *My aunt was a model of ladylike behavior.*

model *verb*
1. To give form to.
2. To take as a model.

model *adjective*
1. Conforming to an ultimate form of perfection or excellence.
2. Having the nature of, constituting, or serving as a type.

moderate *adjective*
1. Not excessive or extreme in amount, degree, or force: *drives at moderate speeds; antiques for sale at moderate prices.*

2. Kept within sensible limits.
3. Not steep or abrupt.
4. Requiring little effort or exertion.
5. Of small intensity.
6. Free from extremes in temperature.

moderate *verb*
1. To make or become less severe or extreme: *In later years he moderated his views.*
2. To become less active or intense.

moderateness *noun*
Avoidance of extremes of opinion, feeling, or personal conduct.

moderation *noun*
Avoidance of extremes of opinion, feeling, or personal conduct: *was advised to eat and drink with moderation.*

modern *adjective*
Of or pertaining to recent times or the present: *a course in modern history; studies modern languages.*

modern *noun*
A person of the present age.

modern-day *adjective*
Of or pertaining to recent times or the present.

1. *Syns:* burlesque, caricature, farce, mock, parody, sham, travesty.
   Near-syns: derision, imitation, joke, satire.
2. JOKE *noun.*
3. RIDICULE *noun.*

CONTEMPORARY *adjective.*

1. CONDITION *noun.*
2. STYLE *noun.*
3. FASHION *noun.*

1. *Syn:* miniature. —*Idiom* pocket edition.

2. *Syns:* beau ideal, example, exemplar, ideal, mirror, paradigm, pattern, phenomenon, standard.

1. FORM *verb.*
2. FOLLOW.

1. IDEAL *adjective.*

2. TYPICAL.

1. *Syns:* modest, reasonable, temperate.
   Near-ants: excessive, extravagant, extreme, immodest, inordinate, intemperate, radical, unreasonable.
   Ant: immoderate.
2. CONSERVATIVE *adjective.*
3. GRADUAL.
4. LIGHT².
5. LIGHT².
6. MILD.

1. *Syns:* mute, soften, subdue, tame, temper, tone down.
2. SUBSIDE.

MODERATION.

Syns: measure, moderateness, temperance.

Syns: current, latter-day, modern-day.
Near-ants: antiquated, antique, old-fashioned, old hat (*Informal*), outdated, outmoded, outworn.
Ant: old-time.

CONTEMPORARY *noun.*

MODERN *adjective.*

modernize *verb*
To make modern in appearance or style: *modernized their colonial house.*

Syns: refurbish, rejuvenate, renovate, restore, revamp, update.

modest *adjective*

1. Reticent or reserved in manner: *too modest to speak up for herself.*

1. *Syns:* backward, bashful, coy, demure, diffident, retiring, self-effacing, shy[1], timid.
Near-ants: aggressive, assertive, brash, brazen, forward, intrusive, pushy (*Informal*).
Ant: bold.

2. Having or expressing feelings of humility.

2. HUMBLE *adjective.*

3. Not elaborate or showy, as in appearance or style: *a modest little house; a modest gift.*

3. *Syns:* plain, simple, unostentatious, unpretentious.

4. Not excessive or extreme in amount, degree, or force.

4. MODERATE *adjective.*

5. Morally beyond reproach, esp. in sexual conduct.

5. CHASTE.

6. Not lewd or obscene.

6. CLEAN *adjective.*

modesty *noun*

1. Reserve in speech, behavior, or dress: *a woman of unaffected modesty.*

1. *Syns:* demureness, diffidence, reticence.

2. Lack of vanity or self-importance: *The President never lost his modesty.*

2. *Syns:* humbleness, humility.

3. Lack of ostentation or pretension: *amazed at the modesty of their lifestyle.*

3. *Syns:* plainness, simplicity, unostentatiousness, unpretentiousness.

4. The condition of being chaste.

4. CHASTITY.

modicum *noun*
A tiny amount.

BIT[1].

modification *noun*
The process or result of making or becoming different.

CHANGE *noun.*

modified *adjective*
Not total, unlimited, or wholehearted.

QUALIFIED.

modify *verb*
To make or become different.

CHANGE *verb.*

modish *adjective*
Being or in accordance with the current fashion.

FASHIONABLE.

modus *noun*
The manner in which something is done.

WAY.

modus operandi *noun*

1. *Latin.* The manner in which something is done.

1. WAY.

2. *Latin.* A method used in dealing with something.

2. APPROACH *noun.*

moil *verb*

1. To be in a state of emotional or mental turmoil.

1. BOIL *verb.*

2. To exert one's mental or physical powers, usu. under difficulty and to the point of exhaustion.

2. LABOR *verb.*

moil *noun*
Physical exertion that is usu. difficult and exhausting.

LABOR *noun.*

moist *adjective*
Slightly wet.

DAMP.

moisten *verb*
To make moist.

WASH.

moistureless *adjective*
Having little or no liquid or moisture.

DRY *adjective.*

mold *noun*
A class that is defined by the common attribute or attributes possessed by all its members.

KIND[2].

mold *verb*

1. To give form to by or as if by pressing and kneading.

1. FORM *verb.*

2. To create by forming, combining, or altering materials.

2. MAKE.

moldable *adjective*
Capable of being shaped, bent, or drawn out, as by
hammering or pressure.   MALLEABLE.

molder *verb*
To become or cause to become rotten or unsound.   DECAY *verb*.

moldy *adjective*
Smelling of mildew or decay: *We held our noses against*   ***Syns:*** frowsy, fusty, musty, putrid, rank².
the moldy air in the cluttered attic.

molecule *noun*
A tiny amount.   BIT¹.

moll *noun*
Slang. A woman who engages in sexual intercourse for   PROSTITUTE.
payment.

mollify *verb*
To ease the anger or agitation of.   PACIFY.

mollycoddle *noun*
A person who behaves in a childish, weak, or spoiled   BABY *noun*.
way.

mollycoddle *verb*
To treat with indulgence and often overtender care.   BABY *verb*.

molt *verb*
To cast off by natural process.   SHED.

moment *noun*
1. A very brief time.   1. FLASH *noun*.
2. A particular interval of time that is limited and   2. INSTANT *noun*.
   often crucial.
3. The quality or state of being important.   3. IMPORTANCE.

momentary *adjective*
1. About to occur at any moment: *We awaited her*   1. ***Syns:*** imminent, impending, proximate.
   momentary return.
2. Lasting or existing only for a short time.   2. TRANSITORY.

momentous *adjective*
1. Having great significance.   1. IMPORTANT.
2. So critically decisive as to affect the future.   2. FATEFUL.
3. Having great consequence or weight.   3. GRAVE².

momentousness *noun*
The condition of being grave and of involving serious   GRAVITY.
consequences.

momus *noun*
A person who finds fault, often severely and willfully.   CRITIC.

monetary *adjective*
Of or relating to finances or those who deal in finances. FINANCIAL.

money *noun*
Something, as coins, printed bills, etc., used as a   ***Syns:*** brass (*Brit. Slang*), bread (*Slang*),
medium of exchange: *counted out the money and paid*   bucks (*Slang*), cabbage (*Slang*), cash,
the waiter.   currency, dough (*Slang*), gelt (*Slang*),
                                                          greenbacks, jack (*Slang*), lettuce (*Slang*),
                                                          lucre, mazuma (*Slang*), moola *or* moolah
                                                          (*Slang*), pelf, scratch (*Slang*), wampum.
                                                          —*Idioms* green stuff, long green.

moneyed *adjective*
Possessing a large amount of money, land, or other   RICH.
material possessions.

moneymaking *adjective*
Affording profit.   PROFITABLE.

moneyman *noun*
Informal. One who is occupied with or expert in large-   FINANCIER.
scale financial affairs.

moneys *noun*
The monetary resources of a government, organization,   FUNDS.
or individual.

monicker *noun* SEE **moniker**.

moniker or **monicker** *noun*
Slang. The word or words by which one is called and NAME *noun*.
identified.

monition *noun*
Advice to beware, as of a person or thing. WARNING *noun*.

monitory *adjective*
Giving warning. CAUTIONARY.

monkey *noun*
Slang. A person who is easily deceived or victimized. DUPE *noun*.

  monkey *verb*
  1. To move one's fingers or hands in a nervous or **1.** FIDDLE.
  aimless fashion.
  2. *Informal.* To handle something idly, ignorantly, or **2.** TAMPER.
  destructively.

monkeyshine *noun*
A mischievous act. PRANK.

monocracy *noun*
A government in which a single leader or party ABSOLUTISM.
exercises absolute control over all citizens and every
aspect of their lives.

monocratic *adjective*
Having and exercising complete political power and ABSOLUTE.
control.

monopolize *verb*
  1. To occupy the full attention of. **1.** ABSORB.
  2. To cause to be busy or in use. **2.** TIE UP.

monopoly *noun*
Exclusive control or possession: *efforts to break the* **Syn:** corner.
monopoly of the utility companies.

monotone *noun*
A tiresome lack of variety. MONOTONY.

monotonous *adjective*
Arousing no interest or curiosity. BORING.

monotony *noun*
A tiresome lack of variety: *the monotony of his office* **Syns:** humdrum, monotone, sameness,
routine. tediousness, tedium.
  Near-syns: boredom, ennui, routine,
  uniformity.
  Ant: diversity.

monster *noun*
  1. A person or animal that is abnormally formed. **1.** FREAK.
  2. One that is extraordinarily large and powerful. **2.** GIANT *noun*.
  3. A perversely bad, cruel, or wicked person. **3.** FIEND.

  monster *adjective*
  Of extraordinary size and power. GIANT *adjective*.

monstrosity *noun*
  1. A monstrous offense or evil. **1.** OUTRAGE *noun*.
  2. A person or animal that is abnormally formed. **2.** FREAK.
  3. An unsightly object. **3.** MESS *noun*.

monstrous *adjective*
  1. Beyond all reason. **1.** OUTRAGEOUS.
  2. Disgracefully and grossly offensive. **2.** OUTRAGEOUS.
  3. Of extraordinary size and power. **3.** GIANT *adjective*.
  4. Resembling a freak. **4.** FREAKISH.

monstrousness *noun*
The quality of passing all moral bounds. ENORMITY.

monument *noun*
Something, as a structure or custom, serving to honor MEMORIAL *noun*.
or keep alive a memory.

monumental *adjective*
Of extraordinary size and power.

mooch *verb*
1. *Slang.* To ask or ask for as charity.
2. *Chiefly Brit. Regional.* To fail to attend on purpose.

moocher *noun*
Slang. One who begs habitually or for a living.

mood *noun*
1. A temporary state of mind or feeling: *Bad weather puts her in a gloomy mood.*

2. A general impression produced by a predominant quality or characteristic.
3. A prevailing quality, as of thought, behavior, or attitude.

moody *adjective*
Given to changeable emotional states, esp. of anger or gloom: *The pressures of work make her moody.*

moola or **moolah** *noun*
Slang. Something, as coins, printed bills, etc., used as a medium of exchange.

moolah *noun*

moon *verb*
To experience dreams or daydreams.

mooncalf *noun*
One deficient in judgment and good sense.

moonstricken *adjective*

moonstruck also **moonstricken** *adjective*
Afflicted with or exhibiting irrationality and mental unsoundness.

moony *adjective*
Given to daydreams or reverie.

moor *verb*
1. To make secure.
2. To join one thing to another.

moot *verb*
1. To put forward a topic for discussion.
2. To speak together and exchange ideas and opinions about.

moot *adjective*
In doubt or dispute.

mootable *adjective*
In doubt or dispute.

mop *noun*
Archaic. A facial contortion indicating displeasure, disgust, pain, etc.

mop *verb*
Archaic. To contort one's face to indicate displeasure, disgust, pain, etc.

mope *verb*
1. To be sullenly aloof or withdrawn, as in silent resentment or protest.
2. To turn over in the mind, moodily and at length.

mopes *noun*
A feeling or spell of dismally low spirits.

GIANT *adjective*.

1. BEG.
2. CUT *verb*.

BEGGAR *noun*.

1. *Syns:* humor, spirits, temper, vein.
  —*Idiom* frame of mind.
  Near-syns: character, disposition, emotion, feeling, mind, temperament, tone.
2. AIR *noun*.
3. TEMPER *noun*.

Syns: humorsome, notional, temperamental.
Near-syns: capricious, excitable, fanciful, fickle, inconstant, jittery, mercurial, whimsical.

MONEY.

SEE **moola.**

DREAM *verb*.

FOOL *noun*.

SEE **moonstruck.**

INSANE.

DREAMY.

1. FASTEN.
2. ATTACH.

1. BROACH.
2. DISCUSS.

DEBATABLE.

DEBATABLE.

FACE *noun*.

GRIMACE *verb*.

1. SULK.
2. BROOD.

GLOOM.

moppet *noun*
A young person between birth and puberty.   CHILD.

moral *adjective*
1. Inclined to teach or moralize excessively: *a tiresomely moral lecture.*
2. In accordance with principles of right or good conduct.
3. Being on a high intellectual or moral level.

1. *Syns:* didactic (*also* didactical), moralizing, preachy.
2. ETHICAL.
3. ELEVATED.

moral *noun*
The principle taught by a fable, parable, etc.: *The moral is not to waste one's youth.*

Syns: lesson, precept.

morale *noun*
A strong sense of enthusiasm and dedication to a common goal that unites a group: *The morale of the troops is superb.*

Syns: esprit, esprit de corps.

morality *noun*
1. A principle of right or good conduct or a body of such principles.
2. The quality or state of being morally sound.

1. ETHIC.
2. GOOD *noun*.

moralize *verb*
To indulge in moral reflection, usu. pompously: *loves to moralize.*

Syns: preach, sermonize.

morals *noun*
A principle of right or good conduct or a body of such principles.

ETHIC.

morass *noun*
1. Something that is intricately and often bewilderingly complex.
2. A usu. low-lying area of waterlogged ground and standing water.

1. TANGLE *noun*.
2. SWAMP.

morbid *adjective*
Susceptible to or marked by preoccupation with unwholesome matters: *a morbid fascination with concentration-camp tortures.*

Syns: macabre, sick, sickly, unhealthy, unwholesome.
Near-syns: melancholic, morose, sullen.

mordacious *adjective*
So sharp as to cause mental pain.

BITING.

mordacity *noun*
Ironic, bitter humor designed to wound.

SARCASM.

mordancy *noun*
Ironic, bitter humor designed to wound.

SARCASM.

mordant *adjective*
1. So sharp as to cause mental pain.
2. Given to or expressing sarcasm.

1. BITING.
2. SARCASTIC.

more *adjective*
Being an addition.

ADDITIONAL.

more *adverb*
1. In addition.
2. To a greater extent.

1. ADDITIONALLY.
2. BETTER[1] *adverb*.

mores *noun*
1. A principle of right or good conduct or a body of such principles.
2. Socially correct behavior.

1. ETHIC *noun*.
2. MANNERS.

morn *noun*
Poetic. The first appearance of daylight in the morning.

DAWN *noun*.

morning *noun*
1. The time of day from sunrise to noon: *worked all morning, then lunched.*
2. The first appearance of daylight in the morning.

1. *Syn:* forenoon.
2. DAWN *noun*.

moron *noun*
A mentally deficient person.

FOOL *noun*.

morose *adjective*
Broodingly and sullenly unhappy.   GLUM.

morsel *noun*
1. A small portion of food.   1. BIT[1].
2. A light meal.   2. BITE *noun*.
3. Something fine and delicious, esp. a food.   3. DELICACY.

mort *noun*
Rare. The physical frame of a dead person or animal.   BODY *noun*.

mortal *adjective*
1. Of or characteristic of human beings or mankind.   1. HUMAN *adjective*.
2. Causing or tending to cause death.   2. DEADLY.
3. Capable of being anticipated, considered, or   3. EARTHLY.
   imagined.

mortal *noun*
A member of the human race.   HUMAN BEING.

mortality *noun*
The quality or condition of causing death.   FATALITY.

mortgage *verb*
To give or deposit as a pawn.   PAWN[1] *verb*.

mortified *adjective*
Distressed and ill at ease.   EMBARRASSED.

mortify *verb*
To cause (a person) to be self-consciously distressed.   EMBARRASS.

mortifying *adjective*
Causing self-conscious distress.   EMBARRASSING.

mortuary *adjective*
Gruesomely suggestive of ghosts or death.   GHASTLY.

mosey *verb*
Informal. To walk at a leisurely pace.   STROLL *verb*.

mossback *noun*
1. An old-fashioned person who is reluctant to change   1. SQUARE *noun*.
   or innovate.
2. A person who vehemently, often fanatically opposes   2. REACTIONARY *noun*.
   progress and favors return to a previous condition.

most *adverb*
To a high degree.   VERY *adverb*.

motif *noun*
An element or component in a decorative composition.   FIGURE *noun*.

motion *noun*
1. The act or process of moving: *made a sudden motion* 1. *Syns:* move, movement, stir[1].
   in his sleep.
2. An expressive, meaningful bodily movement.   2. GESTURE *noun*.

motion *verb*
To make bodily motions so as to convey an idea or   GESTURE *verb*.
complement speech.

motionless *adjective*
Not moving: *sitting motionless at the desk.*   *Syns:* immobile, stationary, still, stock-
                                                         still.

motivate *verb*
1. To impart courage, inspiration, and resolution to.   1. ENCOURAGE.
2. To stir to action or feeling.   2. PROVOKE.

motivation *noun*
1. Something that encourages.   1. ENCOURAGEMENT.
2. A basis for an action or decision.   2. CAUSE *noun*.

motive *noun*
1. A basis for an action or decision.   1. CAUSE *noun*.
2. An element or component in a decorative   2. FIGURE *noun*.
   composition.

motley *adjective*
1. Consisting of a number of different kinds.   1. VARIOUS.
2. Having many different colors.   2. MULTICOLORED.

motor *verb*
To run and control (a motor vehicle).   DRIVE *verb*.

motorist *noun*
A person who operates a motor vehicle.   DRIVER.

mottle *verb*
To mark with many small spots.   SPECKLE.

motto *noun*
A rallying term used by proponents of a cause.   CRY *noun*.

moue *noun*
A facial contortion indicating displeasure, disgust, pain, etc.   FACE *noun*.

mound *noun*
A group of things gathered haphazardly.   HEAP *noun*.

mound *verb*
To put into a disordered pile.   HEAP *verb*.

mount *verb*
1. To move from a lower to a higher position.   1. RISE *verb*.
2. To move upward on or along.   2. ASCEND.
3. To make or become greater or larger.   3. INCREASE *verb*.
4. To increase in intensity or severity.   4. INTENSIFY.
5. To attain a higher status, rank, or condition.   5. RISE *verb*.
6. To become greater in number, amount, or intensity.   6. RISE *verb*.

mountain *noun*
1. A group of things gathered haphazardly.   1. HEAP *noun*.
2. A great deal.   2. HEAP *noun*.

mountainous *adjective*
Of extraordinary size and power.   GIANT *adjective*.

mountebank *noun*
One who is not what he claims to be.   FAKE *noun*.

mounting *noun*
1. The act of moving upward on or along.   1. ASCENT.
2. The act of rising or moving upward.   2. RISE *noun*.

mourn *verb*
To feel, show, or express grief.   GRIEVE.

mournful *adjective*
1. Full of or expressive of sorrow.   1. SORROWFUL.
2. Causing sorrow or regret.   2. SORROWFUL.

mournfulness *noun*
A feeling or spell of dismally low spirits.   GLOOM.

mouse *noun*
Slang. A bruise surrounding the eye.   BLACK EYE.

mouse *verb*
To move silently and furtively.   SNEAK *verb*.

mouth *noun*
1. The opening in the body through which food is ingested: *put a spoonful of ice cream in his mouth*.   1. *Syns:* gob[2] (*Slang*), puss (*Slang*), trap (*Slang*).
2. A facial contortion indicating displeasure, disgust, pain, etc.   2. FACE *noun*.
3. *Informal*. A person who speaks on behalf of another or others.   3. SPEAKER.

mouth *verb*
1. To speak in a loud, pompous, or prolonged manner.   1. RANT.
2. To contort one's face to indicate displeasure, disgust, pain, etc.   2. GRIMACE *verb*.

mouthful *noun*
A small portion of food.   BIT[1].

mouthpiece *noun*
Informal. A person who speaks on behalf of another or others.   SPEAKER.

mouthwatering *adjective*
Enticingly in sight, yet often out of reach.   TANTALIZING.

movable also **moveable** *adjective*
Capable of moving or being moved from place to place.   MOBILE.
movable also **moveable** *noun*
A piece of equipment for comfort or convenience.   FURNISHING.
movables also **moveables** *noun*
Law. One's portable property.   EFFECTS.
move *verb*
1. To go or cause to go from one place to another: *moved away from the railing; moved the lamp closer.*   1. *Syns:* maneuver, remove, shift, transfer.
2. To make a slight movement.   2. STIR[1] *verb.*
3. To impart movement to.   3. STIR[1] *verb.*
4. To alter the settled state or position of.   4. DISTURB.
5. To go forward, esp. toward a conclusion.   5. COME *verb.*
6. To change one's residence, place of business, etc.: *We moved here last October.*   6. *Syns:* relocate, remove, transfer.
7. To set or keep going.   7. DRIVE *verb.*
8. To stir to action or feeling.   8. PROVOKE.
9. To evoke a usu. strong mental or emotional response from.   9. AFFECT[1].
move *noun*
1. The act or process of moving.   1. MOTION *noun.*
2. The act or process of moving from one place to another.   2. REMOVAL.
3. A calculated change in position.   3. MOVEMENT.
4. An action calculated to achieve an end: *Changing jobs was a wise move.*   4. *Syns:* maneuver, measure, procedure, step, tactic[1].
moveable *adjective & noun*   SEE **movable.**
moveables *noun*   SEE **movables.**
moved *adjective*
Emotionally aroused.   AFFECTED[1].
movement *noun*
1. A calculated change in position: *troop movements; the movements of a dance.*   1. *Syns:* evolution, maneuver, move, turn.
2. The act or process of moving.   2. MOTION *noun.*
moving *adjective*
1. Capable of moving or being moved from place to place.   1. MOBILE.
2. Exciting a deep, usu. somber response.   2. AFFECTING.
3. Relating to, arising from, or appealing to the emotions.   3. EMOTIONAL.
mow *verb*
To contort one's face to indicate displeasure, disgust, pain, etc.   GRIMACE *verb.*
mow also **mowe** *noun*
A facial contortion indicating displeasure, disgust, pain, etc.   FACE *noun.*
mowe *noun*   SEE **mow.**
moxie *noun*
Slang. The quality of mind enabling one to face danger or hardship resolutely.   COURAGE.
Mrs. Grundy *noun*
A person who is too much concerned with being proper, modest, or righteous.   PRUDE.
much *noun*
A great deal.   HEAP *noun.*
muchly *adverb*
To a high degree.   VERY *adverb.*
mucilaginous *adjective*
Having a heavy, gluey quality.   VISCOUS.
muck *noun*
1. A viscous, usu. offensively dirty substance.   1. SLIME.

2. Foul or dirty matter.   **2.** FILTH.

muck *verb*
To soil with mud.   MUDDY *verb*.

muck up *verb*
To harm irreparably through inept handling; make a   BOTCH.
mess of.

muckamuck also **mucketymuck** *noun*
Slang. An important, influential person.   DIGNITARY.

mucker *noun*
An unrefined, rude person.   BOOR.

mucketymuck *noun*   SEE **muckamuck.**

muck up *verb*   SEE **muck.**

muckworm *noun*
A stingy person.   MISER.

mucky *adjective*
   1. Damp and warm.   **1.** STICKY.
   2. Of, pertaining to, or covered with slime.   **2.** SLIMY.

mucro *noun*
Biol. A sharp or tapered end.   POINT *noun*.

mucronate *adjective*
Biol. Having an end tapering to a point.   POINTED.

mucronation *noun*
Biol. A sharp or tapered end.   POINT *noun*.

muddle *verb*
   1. To proceed or perform in an unsteady, faltering   **1.** *Syns:* fudge, fumble, limp, shuffle,
   manner: *He muddled through the lesson, clearly*   stagger, stumble.
   unprepared.
   2. To put out of proper order.   **2.** DISORDER *verb*.
   3. To put into total disorder.   **3.** CONFUSE.
   4. To harm irreparably through inept handling; make a   **4.** BOTCH *verb*.
   mess of.

muddle through *verb*
Chiefly Brit. To progress or perform adequately, esp. in   MANAGE.
difficult circumstances.

muddle *noun*
   1. A lack of order or regular arrangement.   **1.** DISORDER *noun*.
   2. A stunned or bewildered condition.   **2.** DAZE *noun*.
   3. A ruinous state of disorder.   **3.** BOTCH *noun*.

muddled *adjective*
Characterized by physical confusion.   CONFUSED.

muddle through *verb*   SEE **muddle.**

muddy *adjective*
   1. Covered or soiled with mud: *a muddy road; muddy*   **1.** *Syns:* bemired, miry.
   shoes.
   2. Lacking vividness in color.   **2.** DULL *adjective*.
   3. Having sediment or foreign particles stirred up or   **3.** TURBID.
   suspended.

muddy *verb*
To soil with mud: *muddied the clean floor.*   *Syns:* bemire, bemud (*Archaic*), muck
                                                                (up).

mudslinging *noun*
An attempt to destroy someone's reputation.   SMEAR *noun*.

muff *verb*
To harm irreparably through inept handling; make a   BOTCH *verb*.
mess of.

muffle *verb*
   1. To decrease or dull the sound of: *The trumpeter*   **1.** *Syns:* dampen, deaden, mute, stifle.
   muffled his horn to give a blues quality to his   *Near-ants:* amplify, enhance, heighten,
   playing.   increase, magnify, reinforce,
                                                                strengthen.
   2. To hold (something requiring an outlet) in check.   **2.** REPRESS.

mug *noun*
1. *Slang.* The front surface of the head.
2. *Slang.* A facial contortion indicating displeasure, disgust, pain, etc.
3. *Brit.* A person who is easily deceived or victimized.
4. A rough, violent person who engages in destructive actions.

mug *verb*
Slang. To contort one's face to indicate displeasure, disgust, pain, etc.

muggy *adjective*
Damp and warm.

mulct *verb*
1. To get money or something else from by deceitful trickery.
2. To impose a fine on.

mulct *noun*
A sum of money levied as punishment for an offense.

muleheaded *adjective*
Tenaciously unwilling to yield.

muley *adjective*
Tenaciously unwilling to yield.

muliebral *adjective*
Of, relating to, or characteristic of women.

muliebrity *noun*
1. Women in general.
2. The quality of being effeminate.

mulish *adjective*
Tenaciously unwilling to yield.

mulishness *noun*
The quality or state of being stubbornly unyielding.

mull¹ *noun*
A ruinous state of disorder.

mull² *verb*
To consider carefully and at length.

multicolored *adjective*
Having many different colors: *a cheerful multicolored bedspread.*

multifaceted *adjective*
Having many aspects, uses, or abilities.

multifarious *adjective*
Consisting of a number of different kinds.

multifariousness *noun*
The quality of being made of many different elements, forms, kinds, or individuals.

multiformity *noun*
The quality of being made of many different elements, forms, kinds, or individuals.

multiloquent *adjective*
Given to conversation.

multiplication *noun*
1. The result or product of building up.
2. The act of increasing or rising.
3. The process by which an organism produces others of its kind.

multiplicity *noun*
1. An indeterminately great amount or number.
2. The quality of being made of many different elements, forms, kinds, or individuals.

---

1. FACE *noun.*
2. FACE *noun.*

3. DUPE *noun.*
4. TOUGH *noun.*

GRIMACE *verb.*

STICKY.

1. CHEAT *verb.*

2. FINE² *verb.*

FINE² *noun.*

OBSTINATE.

OBSTINATE.

FEMININE.

1. FEMININITY.
2. EFFEMINACY.

OBSTINATE.

OBSTINACY.

BOTCH *noun.*

PONDER.

Syns: motley, polychromatic (*also* polychromic, polychromous), polychrome, varicolored, variegated, versicolor (*also* versicolored).

VERSATILE.

VARIOUS.

VARIETY.

VARIETY.

TALKATIVE.

1. BUILD-UP at **build up.**
2. INCREASE *noun.*
3. REPRODUCTION.

1. HEAP *noun.*
2. VARIETY.

multiply *verb*
1. To make or become greater or larger.
2. To become greater in number, amount, or intensity.
3. To produce sexually or asexually others of one's kind.

1. INCREASE *verb*.
2. RISE *verb*.
3. REPRODUCE.

multisyllabic *adjective*
Having many syllables.

LONG[1] *adjective*.

multitude *noun*
1. An enormous number of persons gathered together.
2. A very large number of things grouped together.

1. CROWD *noun*.
2. CROWD *noun*.

multitudinous *adjective*
Amounting to or consisting of a large, indefinite number.

MANY.

multivocal *adjective*
Offensively loud and insistent.

VOCIFEROUS.

mum *adjective*
Temporarily unable or unwilling to speak, as from shock or fear.

SPEECHLESS.

mumble *verb*
To speak or utter indistinctly, as by lowering the voice or partially closing the mouth.

MUTTER *verb*.

mumble *noun*
A low, indistinct, and often continuous sound.

MURMUR *noun*.

mumblenews *noun*
A person habitually engaged in idle talk about others.

GOSSIP *noun*.

mumbo jumbo *noun*
1. Wordy, unclear jargon.
2. Esoteric, formulaic, and often incomprehensible speech relating to the occult.

1. GIBBERISH.
2. GIBBERISH.

mummify *verb*
To make or become no longer fresh or shapely because of loss of moisture.

DRY UP at **dry**.

mummy *verb*
To make or become no longer fresh or shapely because of loss of moisture.

DRY UP at **dry**.

mumpish *adjective*
Broodingly and sullenly unhappy.

GLUM.

mun *verb*
Brit. Regional. To be required or compelled to do.

MUST.

munch *verb*
To bite and grind with the teeth.

CHEW.

mundane *adjective*
1. Pertaining to or characteristic of the earth or of human life on earth.
2. Of or suitable for ordinary days or routine occasions.
3. Of or preoccupied with material rather than spiritual or intellectual things.

1. EARTHLY.
2. EVERYDAY.
3. MATERIALISTIC.

municipal *adjective*
Of, in, or belonging to a city.

CITY *adjective*.

municipality *noun*
A large and important town.

CITY *noun*.

munificence *noun*
The quality or state of being generous.

GENEROSITY.

munificent *adjective*
Characterized by bounteous giving.

GENEROUS.

murder *verb*
To take the life of (a person or persons) unlawfully: *murdered his parents.*

Syns: bump off (*Slang*), destroy, do in (*Slang*), dust off (*Slang*), erase (*Slang*), finish, hit (*Slang*), kill, knock off (*Slang*), liquidate, off (*Slang*), put away, rub out

(*Slang*), slay, waste (*Slang*), wipe out
(*Informal*), zap (*Slang*).

murder   *noun*
The crime of murdering someone: *convicted of first-
degree murder.*

Syns: blood, bump-off (*Slang*), homicide,
killing, manslaying, slaying.

murderer   *noun*
One who murders another: *arrested the murderer.*

Syns: butcher, Cain, cutthroat, homicide,
killer, manslayer, massacrer, slaughterer,
slayer, triggerman (*Slang*). —*Idiom* hit
man.

murderous   *adjective*
Eager for bloodshed: *a murderous pirate.*

Syns: bloodthirsty, bloody, cutthroat,
ferocious, fierce, homicidal, sanguinary,
sanguineous, slaughterous.
Near-syns: deadly, destructive,
devastating, ruinous, savage, villainous;
criminal, psychopathic, psychotic.

mure   *verb*
Rare. To confine within a limited area.

ENCLOSE.

murk also **mirk**   *noun*
A thick, heavy atmospheric condition offering reduced
visibility due to the presence of suspended particles.

HAZE *noun.*

murk also **mirk**   *verb*
To make dim or indistinct.

OBSCURE *verb.*

murky also **mirky**   *adjective*
1. Lacking vividness in color.
2. Deficient in brightness.
3. Heavy, dark, or dense, esp. with impurities.

1. DULL *adjective.*
2. DARK *adjective.*
3. TURBID.

murmur   *noun*
1. A low, indistinct, and often continuous sound: *the
   murmur of the sea; the approving murmurs of the
   listeners.*
2. A low, indistinct utterance of complaint.
3. Idle, often sensational and groundless talk about
   others.

1. *Syns:* mumble, sigh, sough,
   susurration, whisper.

2. MUTTER *noun.*
3. GOSSIP *noun.*

murmur   *verb*
1. To make a low, continuous, and indistinct sound:
   The wind murmured through the trees.
2. To speak or utter indistinctly, as by lowering the
   voice or partially closing the mouth.
3. To express negative feelings, esp. of dissatisfaction
   or resentment.
4. To complain in low, indistinct tones.

1. *Syns:* sigh, sough, whisper.

2. MUTTER *verb.*

3. COMPLAIN.

4. MUTTER *verb.*

muscle   *noun*
1. Effective means of influencing, compelling, or
   punishing: *putting muscle in law enforcement.*
2. The state or quality of being physically strong.

1. *Syns:* clout (*Informal*), force, power,
   weight.
2. STRENGTH.

muscle   *verb*
To force one's way into a place or situation: *muscled his
way through the crowd; muscled into our conversation.*

Syns: push, shove, strong-arm.

muscular   *adjective*
Characterized by marked muscular development;
powerfully built: *a muscular boxer; a strong, muscular
physique.*

Syns: brawny, burly, robust, sinewy,
sturdy.

muse¹   *verb*
1. To consider carefully and at length.
2. To experience dreams or daydreams.

1. PONDER.
2. DREAM *verb.*

muse   *noun*
The condition of being so lost in solitary thought as to
be unaware of one's surroundings.

TRANCE.

muse² *noun*
Someone who writes verse. POET.

museful *adjective*
Of, characterized by, or disposed to thought. THOUGHTFUL.

mush *verb*
To press forcefully so as to break up into a pulpy mass. CRUSH *verb*.

mush *noun*
Informal. The quality or condition of being affectedly or overly emotional. SENTIMENTALITY.

mushiness *noun*
Informal. The quality or condition of being affectedly or overly emotional. SENTIMENTALITY.

mushroom *verb*
To increase or expand suddenly, rapidly, or without control. EXPLODE.

mushy *adjective*
1. Yielding easily to pressure or weight; not firm. 1. SOFT.
2. *Informal.* Affectedly or extravagantly emotional. 2. SENTIMENTAL.

musical *adjective*
1. Characterized by harmony of sound. 1. HARMONIOUS.
2. Resembling or having the effect of music, esp. pleasing music. 2. MELODIOUS.

musician *noun*
One who plays a musical instrument. PLAYER.

musicianer *noun*
One who plays a musical instrument. PLAYER.

musico *noun*
One who plays a musical instrument. PLAYER.

musing *adjective*
Suggestive of or expressing deep, often melancholy thoughtfulness. PENSIVE.

muskeg *noun*
A usu. low-lying area of soft, waterlogged ground and standing water. SWAMP.

muss *verb*
To put (the hair or clothes) into a state of disarray. TOUSLE.

muss *noun*
A ruinous state of disorder. BOTCH *noun*.

mussy *adjective*
Marked by an absence of cleanliness and order. MESSY.

must *verb*
To be required or compelled to do: *You simply must answer that letter.* **Syns:** need, mun (*Brit. Regional*).
—*Idioms* have got to, have to, must needs.

must *noun*
1. Something indispensable. 1. CONDITION *noun*.
2. An act or course of action that is demanded of one, as by position, custom, law, or religion. 2. DUTY.

muster *verb*
1. To come together. 1. ASSEMBLE.
2. To bring together. 2. ASSEMBLE.
3. To demand to appear, come, or assemble. 3. CALL *verb*.
4. To become a member of. 4. JOIN.
5. To assemble, prepare, or put into operation, as for war or a similar emergency. 5. MOBILIZE.

muster out *verb*
To release from military duty. DISCHARGE *verb*.

muster *noun*
A number of persons who have come or been gathered together. ASSEMBLY.

muster out *verb* SEE **muster**.

musty *adjective*
1. Smelling of mildew or decay.
2. Without freshness or appeal due to overuse.

1. MOLDY.
2. TRITE.

mutable *adjective*
Capable of or liable to change.

CHANGEABLE.

mutate *verb*
1. To change into a different form, substance, or state.
2. To make or become different.

1. CONVERT.
2. CHANGE *verb*.

mutation *noun*
The process or result of making or becoming different.

CHANGE *noun*.

mute *adjective*
1. Lacking the power or faculty of speech.
2. Temporarily unable or unwilling to speak, as from shock or fear.

1. DUMB.
2. SPEECHLESS.

mute *verb*
1. To decrease or dull the sound of.
2. To make or become less severe or extreme.

1. MUFFLE.
2. MODERATE *verb*.

muted *adjective*
So lacking in strength as to be barely audible.

FAINT *adjective*.

muteness *noun*
The avoidance of speech.

SILENCE *noun*.

mutilate *verb*
To deprive of, or of the use of, a limb or bodily member.

CRIPPLE.

mutineer *noun*
A person who rebels.

REBEL *noun*.

mutineer *verb*
Archaic. To refuse allegiance to and oppose by force a government or ruling authority.

REBEL *verb*.

mutinize *verb*
Archaic. To refuse allegiance to and oppose by force a government or ruling authority.

REBEL *verb*.

mutinous *adjective*
In open revolt against a government or ruling authority.

REBELLIOUS.

mutiny *noun*
Organized opposition intended to change or overthrow existing authority.

REBELLION.

mutiny *verb*
To refuse allegiance to and oppose by force a government or ruling authority.

REBEL *verb*.

mutter *verb*
1. To speak or utter indistinctly, as by lowering the voice or partially closing the mouth: *Don't mutter—speak up.*
2. To complain in low, indistinct tones: *The crowd muttered in disapproval.*

1. *Syns:* mumble, murmur, whisper.
    —*Idiom* swallow one's words.
2. *Syns:* grumble, grunt, murmur, rumble.

mutter *noun*
A low, indistinct utterance of complaint: *a mutter of angry voices.*

Syns: grumble, grunt, murmur, rumble.

mutual *adjective*
1. Having the same relationship each to the other: *mutual affections.*
2. Belonging to, shared by, or applicable to all alike.

1. *Syns:* reciprocal, reciprocative.
2. COMMON.

muzzle *noun*
The front surface of the head.

FACE *noun*.

myriad *adjective*
Amounting to or consisting of a large, indefinite number.

MANY.

mysterious *adjective*
Difficult to explain or understand: *He has some mysterious power over women.*

Syns: arcane, cabalistic, mystic, mystical, mystifying, unaccountable, unexplainable, unfathomable.
Near-syns: abstruse, esoteric, occult, recondite; ambiguous, cryptic, enigmatic, equivocal, inexplicable, inscrutable, obscure, strange.
Ants: comprehensible, explainable.

mystery *noun*
Anything that arouses curiosity or perplexes because it is unexplained, inexplicable, or secret: *Her whereabouts remains a mystery. The location of the lost continent of Atlantis is one of history's great unsolved mysteries.*

Syns: conundrum, enigma, puzzle, puzzlement, puzzler, riddle. —*Idiom* question mark.

mystic *adjective*
Difficult to explain or understand.

MYSTERIOUS.

mystical *adjective*
Difficult to explain or understand.

MYSTERIOUS.

mystifying *adjective*
Difficult to explain or understand.

MYSTERIOUS.

myth *noun*
1. A traditional story or tale dealing with ancestors, heroes, supernatural events, etc., that has no proven factual basis but attempts to explain beliefs, practices, or natural phenomena: *The myth told how mankind was given the gift of fire by the gods.*
2. A body of traditional beliefs and notions accumulated about a particular subject.
3. Any fictitious idea accepted as part of an ideology by an uncritical group; a received idea: *The myth of a pure Aryan race was largely the product of Nazi propaganda.*

1. **Syns:** fable, legend.

2. LORE.

3. **Syns:** creation, fantasy (*also* phantasy), fiction, figment, invention.

mythical also **mythic** *adjective*
Of or existing only in myths: *the mythical unicorn; the mythical golden cities of Cibola.*

Syns: fabulous, legendary, mythological (*also* mythologic).

mythological also **mythologic** *adjective*
Of or existing only in myths.

MYTHICAL.

mythology *noun*
A body of traditional beliefs and notions accumulated about a particular subject.

LORE.

mythos *noun*
A body of traditional beliefs and notions accumulated about a particular subject.

LORE.

N

nab *verb*
1. To get hold of (something moving).
2. *Slang.* To take into custody as a prisoner.

1. CATCH *verb.*
2. ARREST *verb.*

nab *noun*
1. *Slang.* A seizing and holding by law.
2. *Slang.* A member of a law-enforcement agency.

1. ARREST *noun.*
2. POLICEMAN.

nabob *noun*
An important, influential person.   DIGNITARY.

nag *verb*
To scold or find fault constantly: *always nagging me*   ***Syns:*** carp (at), fuss (at), henpeck, peck[2],
about something or other.   pick (on).

naif also **naïf** *adjective & noun*   SEE **naive**.

nail *verb*
Slang. To gain possession of, esp. after a struggle or   TAKE *verb*.
chase.

naive also **naïve, naif, naïf** *adjective*
1. Free from guile, cunning, or deceit.   1. ARTLESS.
2. Easily imposed on or tricked.   2. EASY.

   naive also **naïve, naif, naïf** *noun*
A guileless, unsophisticated person.   INNOCENT *noun*.

naked *adjective*
1. Not wearing any clothes.   1. NUDE.
2. Without the usual covering.   2. BARE *adjective*.

nakedness *noun*
The state of being without clothes.   NUDITY.

namby-pamby *adjective*
Lacking the qualities requisite for spiritedness and   INSIPID.
originality.

name *noun*
1. The word or words by which one is called and   1. ***Syns:*** appellation, appellative,
   identified: *gave his son two names; recalled the name*   cognomen, denomination, designation,
   of the book.   handle (*Slang*), moniker *or* monicker
                                                                                               (*Slang*), nomen, style, tag (*Slang*).
                                                                                               Near-syns: alias, byword, epithet, label,
                                                                                               nickname, nom de plume, pseudonym,
                                                                                               rubric, title.
2. Public estimation of someone.   2. REPUTATION.
3. A famous person.   3. CELEBRITY.

   name *verb*
1. To give a name or title to: *named the baby after his*   1. ***Syns:*** baptize, call, christen,
   father.   denominate, designate, dub[1], entitle,
                                                                                               style, term, title.
2. To select for an office or position.   2. APPOINT.
3. To refer to by name: *She spoke of her previous jobs,*   3. ***Syns:*** cite, instance, mention, specify.
   naming several.

nameless *adjective*
1. Unknown by name.   1. OBSCURE *adjective*.
2. Having an unknown name or author.   2. ANONYMOUS.

namelessness *noun*
The quality or state of being obscure.   OBSCURITY.

namely *adverb*
That is to say: *You must improve your manners,*   ***Syns:*** scilicet, videlicet. —*Idiom* to wit.
namely, your eating habits.

naming *noun*
The act of appointing to an office or position.   APPOINTMENT.

nap *noun*
A brief sleep: *takes a nap after lunch.*   ***Syns:*** catnap, doze, siesta.

   nap *verb*
To sleep for a brief period: *napped for an hour before*   ***Syns:*** catnap, doze (off), nod (off), siesta.
dinner.   —*Idiom* catch (*or* grab) forty winks.

narcism *noun*   SEE **narcissism**.

narcissism also **narcism** *noun*
A regarding of oneself with undue favor.   EGOTISM.

narcissist *noun*
A conceited, self-centered person.   EGOTIST.

narcissistic *adjective*
1. Thinking too highly of oneself.   1. EGOTISTICAL.

2. Unduly preoccupied with one's own appearance.

narcotic *noun*

1. A narcotic substance, esp. one that is addictive.

2. Something that induces sleep.

narcotic *adjective*

Inducing sleep.

narcotize *verb*

To administer or add a drug to.

narrate *verb*

To give a verbal account of.

narrative *noun*

A recounting of past events.

narrow *adjective*

1. Not broad or elevated in scope or understanding: *unappreciated by the narrow provincials of her home town.*

2. Affording little room for movement.

3. Not tolerant of the beliefs, opinions, etc., of others.

4. Having the restricted outlook often characteristic of geographic isolation.

5. *Regional.* Ungenerously or pettily reluctant to spend money.

narrow *verb*

To render narrow or narrower.

narrow-minded *adjective*

1. Having the restricted outlook often characteristic of geographic isolation.

2. Not broad or elevated in scope or understanding.

3. Not tolerant of the beliefs, opinions, etc., of others.

nascence also **nascency** *noun*

The initial stage of a developmental process.

nascency *noun*

nasty *adjective*

1. So objectionable as to elicit despisal.

2. Offensive to accepted standards of decency.

3. Extremely unpleasant to the senses or feelings.

4. Heavily soiled; very dirty or unclean.

5. Characterized by intense ill will or spite.

6. Having or showing a bad temper.

nation *noun*

An organized geopolitical unit.

national *noun*

A person owing loyalty to and entitled to the protection of a given state.

national *adjective*

1. Of, from, or within a country's own territory.

2. Of, concerning, or affecting the community or the people.

nationalize *verb*

To place under government or group ownership or control.

native *adjective*

1. Belonging to one because of the place or circumstances of one's birth: *our native land; her native language.*

2. Possessed at birth.

3. Existing, born, or produced naturally in a land or region.

4. Of, from, or within a country's own territory.

5. In a primitive state; not domesticated or cultivated.

6. In a natural state and still not prepared for use.

---

2. VAIN.

1. DRUG *noun.*

2. SOPORIFIC *noun.*

SLEEPY.

DRUG *verb.*

DESCRIBE.

STORY.

1. *Syns:* limited, little, mean², narrow-minded, paltry, petty, small, small-minded.

2. TIGHT *adjective.*

3. INTOLERANT.

4. LOCAL *adjective.*

5. STINGY.

CONSTRICT.

1. LOCAL *adjective.*

2. NARROW.

3. INTOLERANT.

BIRTH *noun.*

SEE **nascense.**

1. FILTHY.

2. OBSCENE.

3. OFFENSIVE *adjective.*

4. FILTHY.

5. MALEVOLENT.

6. ILL-TEMPERED.

STATE *noun.*

CITIZEN.

1. DOMESTIC.

2. PUBLIC *adjective.*

SOCIALIZE.

1. *Syns:* aboriginal, autochthonous (*also* autochthonal, autochthonic), endemic, indigenous.

2. INNATE.

3. INDIGENOUS.

4. DOMESTIC.

5. WILD *adjective.*

6. CRUDE.

natural   *adjective*
1. Produced by nature; not artificial or manmade: *natural foods.*
2. Forming an essential element.
3. Possessed at birth.
4. Free from guile, cunning, or deceit.
5. Born out of wedlock.
6. In a primitive state; not domesticated or cultivated.
7. Accurately representing what is depicted or described.
8. Of a plain and unsophisticated nature.

natural   *noun*
A mentally deficient person.

naturalistic   *adjective*
Accurately representing what is depicted or described.

naturally   *adverb*
In an expected or customary manner.

naturalness   *noun*
1. Freedom from constraint, embarrassment, or awkwardness.
2. Lack or avoidance of formality.

nature   *noun*
1. The combination of emotional, intellectual, and moral qualities that distinguishes an individual.
2. A person's customary manner of emotional response.
3. A basic trait or set of traits that define and establish the character of something.
4. A class that is defined by the common attribute or attributes possessed by all its members.
5. The totality of all existing things.

naughtiness   *noun*
Improper, often rude behavior.

naughty   *adjective*
Misbehaving, often in a troublesome way: *a naughty child.*

nauseate   *verb*
To offend the senses or feelings of.

nauseating   *adjective*
1. Extremely unpleasant to the senses or feelings.
2. Too awful to be described.

nautical   *adjective*
Of or relating to sea navigation: *nautical charts and instruments.*

navigable   *adjective*
Capable of being passed, traversed, or crossed.

navigate   *verb*
To direct the course of carefully.

navigational   *adjective*
Of or relating to sea navigation.

navigator   *noun*
A person engaged in sailing or working on a ship.

nay   *noun*
1. A negative vote or voter.
2. A negative response.

nay   *adverb*
1. Not so.
2. Not just this but also.

---

1. **Syns:** organic, unadulterated. —*Idiom* pure as the driven snow.
2. BUILT-IN.
3. INNATE.
4. ARTLESS.
5. ILLEGITIMATE.
6. WILD *adjective.*
7. REALISTIC.
8. RUSTIC *adjective.*

FOOL *noun.*

REALISTIC.

USUALLY.

1. EASE *noun.*
2. INFORMALITY.

1. CHARACTER.
2. DISPOSITION.
3. ESSENCE.
4. KIND².
5. UNIVERSE.

MISBEHAVIOR.

Syns: bad, ill-behaved, out-of-line (*Informal*).
Near-syns: contrary, disobedient, intractable, mischievous, recalcitrant, refractory, rowdy, unruly.

DISGUST *verb.*

1. OFFENSIVE *adjective.*
2. UNSPEAKABLE.

Syns: marine, maritime, navigational.

PASSABLE.

MANEUVER *verb.*

NAUTICAL.

SAILOR.

1. NO *noun.*
2. NO *noun.*

1. NO *adverb.*
2. EVEN¹ *adverb.*

near *adjective*
Not far from another in space, time, or relation.

CLOSE[1] *adjective.*

near *verb*
To come near in space or time.

APPROACH *verb.*

near *adverb*
To a point near in time, space, or relation.

CLOSE[1] *adverb.*

near-at-hand *adjective*
1. Not far from another in space, time, or relation.
2. Being within easy reach.

1. CLOSE[1] *adjective.*
2. CONVENIENT.

nearby *adjective*
1. Not far from another in space, time, or relation.
2. Being within easy reach.

1. CLOSE[1] *adjective.*
2. CONVENIENT.

nearby *adverb*
To a point near in time, space, or relation.

CLOSE[1] *adverb.*

nearly *adverb*
Near to in quantity or amount.

APPROXIMATELY.

nearness *noun*
The act or fact of coming near.

APPROACH *noun.*

neat *adjective*
1. In good order or clean condition: *a neat room; a neat appearance.*

1. *Syns:* orderly, shipshape, snug, spic-and-span, spruce, taut, tidy, tight (*Regional*), trig, trim, well-groomed.
—*Idiom* neat as a pin.
Near-ants: dirty, foul, messy; disordered, sloppy, slovenly, unkempt.
Ants: disorderly, untidy.

2. Not diluted or mixed with other substances.
3. *Slang.* Particularly excellent.
4. Well done or executed: *a neat turn of phrase.*

2. STRAIGHT *adjective.*
3. MARVELOUS.
4. *Syns:* adept, adroit, deft, skillful.

neaten *verb*
1. To make or keep (an area) clean and orderly.
2. To make neat and trim; make presentable.

1. TIDY *verb.*
2. TIDY *verb.*

nebbish *noun*
Slang. A totally insignificant person.

NONENTITY.

nebulous *adjective*
Liable to more than one interpretation.

AMBIGUOUS.

necessary *adjective*
1. Incapable of being dispensed with.
2. Imposed on one by authority, command, or convention.

1. ESSENTIAL *adjective.*
2. REQUIRED.

necessitate *verb*
To have as a need or prerequisite.

DEMAND *verb.*

necessitous *adjective*
1. Incapable of being dispensed with.
2. Having little or no money or wealth.

1. ESSENTIAL *adjective.*
2. POOR.

necessity *noun*
1. Something indispensable.
2. A condition in which something necessary or desirable is required or wanted.
3. That which provides a reason or justification.

1. CONDITION *noun.*
2. NEED *noun.*
3. CAUSE *noun.*

neck-and-neck *adjective*
Informal. Nearly equivalent or even.

CLOSE[1] *adjective.*

need *noun*
1. A condition in which something necessary or desirable is required or wanted: *patients in need of nursing.*
2. An act or course of action that is demanded of one, as by position, custom, law, or religion.
3. Something asked for or needed.
4. The condition of being extremely poor.

1. *Syns:* exigency (*also* exigence), necessity.

2. DUTY.

3. DEMAND *noun.*
4. POVERTY.

need *verb*

1. To be without what is needed, required, or essential.   **1.** LACK *verb*.
2. To be required or compelled to do.   **2.** MUST *verb*.

neediness *noun*
The condition of being extremely poor.   POVERTY.

needle *noun*
A sharp, pointed object.   PRICK *noun*.

needle *verb*
Informal. To torment with persistent insult or ridicule.   BAIT *verb*.

needless *adjective*
Not necessary.   UNNECESSARY.

needy *adjective*
Having little or no money or wealth.   POOR.

ne'er-do-well *noun*
A self-indulgent person who spends time avoiding work   WASTREL.
or other useful activity.

nefarious *adjective*
1. Utterly reprehensible in nature or behavior.   **1.** CORRUPT *adjective*.
2. Morally objectionable.   **2.** EVIL *adjective*.

negate *verb*
1. To put an end to formally and with authority.   **1.** ABOLISH.
2. To refuse to admit the truth, reality, value, or worth   **2.** DENY.
of.

negation *noun*
1. An often formal act of putting an end to.   **1.** ABOLITION.
2. A refusal to grant the truth of a statement or   **2.** DENIAL.
charge.

negative *adjective*
Tending to discourage, retard, or make more difficult.   UNFAVORABLE.

negative *verb*
1. To refuse to admit the truth, reality, value, or worth   **1.** DENY.
of.
2. To prevent or forbid authoritatively.   **2.** VETO *verb*.

neglect *verb*
1. To fail to care for or give proper attention to: **1.** *Syns:* disregard, slight.
neglected her children.
2. To refuse to pay attention to (a person); treat with   **2.** IGNORE.
contempt.
3. To avoid the fulfillment of: *neglected their duty.*   **3.** *Syns:* disregard, shirk, slack. —*Idiom*
let slide.
4. To not do (something necessary).   **4.** FAIL.

neglect *noun*
1. An act or instance of neglecting: *parents' neglect of*   **1.** *Syns:* disregard, oversight, slight.
their responsibility; property ruined through neglect.
2. Nonperformance of what ought to be done.   **2.** FAILURE.

neglectful *adjective*
Guilty of neglect; lacking due care or concern.   NEGLIGENT.

negligence *noun*
The state or quality of being negligent: *mine operators*   *Syns:* laxity, laxness, remissness,
charged with negligence.   slackness.

negligent *adjective*
Guilty of neglect; lacking due care or concern: *negligent*   *Syns:* derelict, lax, neglectful, remiss,
ship's officers who disregarded warnings about icebergs.   slack.
   Near-ants: careful, considerate, heedful,
   mindful, thoughtful.
   Ant: attentive.

negligible *adjective*
1. Contemptibly unimportant.   **1.** PETTY.
2. Small in degree, esp. of probability.   **2.** REMOTE.

negotiable *adjective*
Capable of being passed, traversed, or crossed.   PASSABLE.

negotiate *verb*
1. To come to an agreement about.
2. To pass by or over safely or successfully.

1. ARRANGE.
2. CLEAR *verb*.

negotiation *noun*
The act or process of dealing with another to reach an agreement.

TALK *noun*.

neighbor *verb*
To be contiguous or next to.

ADJOIN.

neighborhood *noun*
1. A rather small part of a geographic unit considered in regard to its inhabitants or distinctive characteristics: *a well-known Italian neighborhood.*
2. A part of the earth's surface.
3. *Informal.* Approximate size or amount: *priced in the neighborhood of fifty dollars.*
4. A surrounding site.

1. *Syns:* area, locality, quarter.

2. AREA.
3. *Syns:* order, range, vicinity.

4. LOCALITY.

neighboring *adjective*
Sharing a common boundary.

ADJOINING.

neighborly *adjective*
Of or befitting a friend or friends.

FRIENDLY.

neonate *noun*
A very young child.

BABY *noun*.

neophyte *noun*
One who is just starting to learn or do something.

BEGINNER.

nephalism *noun*
The practice of refraining from use of alcoholic liquors.

TEMPERANCE.

nerve *noun*
1. *Informal.* The state or quality of being impudent.
2. *Informal.* Excessive and arrogant self-confidence.
3. The quality of mind enabling one to face danger or hardship resolutely.

1. IMPUDENCE.
2. PRESUMPTION.
3. COURAGE.

nerve *verb*
To impart strength and confidence to.

ENCOURAGE.

nervous *adjective*
1. Feeling or exhibiting nervous tension.
2. In a state of uneasiness.

1. EDGY.
2. ANXIOUS.

nervy *adjective*
1. *Informal.* Having or exhibiting excessive and arrogant self-confidence.
2. *Informal.* Rude and disrespectful.
3. *Chiefly Brit.* Feeling or exhibiting nervous tension.

1. PRESUMPTUOUS.

2. IMPUDENT.
3. EDGY.

nescience *noun*
1. The condition of being ignorant; lack of knowledge or learning.
2. The condition of being uninformed.

1. IGNORANCE.

2. IGNORANCE.

nescient *adjective*
Without education or knowledge.

IGNORANT.

nestle *verb*
To lie or press close together, usu. with another person or thing.

SNUGGLE *verb*.

Nestor *noun*
A usu. elderly man noted for wisdom, knowledge, and judgment.

SAGE *noun*.

net¹ *verb*
To gain possession of, esp. after a struggle or chase.

TAKE *verb*.

net *noun*
An open fabric woven of strands that are interlaced and knotted at usu. regular intervals.

WEB *noun*.

net² *verb*
To make as income or profit.

RETURN *verb*.

nethermost *adjective*
Opposite to or farthest from the top.   BOTTOM *adjective.*

netting *noun*
An open fabric woven of strands that are interlaced and   WEB *noun.*
knotted at usu. regular intervals.

nettle *verb*
To trouble the nerves or peace of mind of, esp. by   ANNOY.
repeated vexations.

nettlesome *adjective*
1. Troubling the nerves or peace of mind, as by   1. VEXATIOUS.
   repeated vexations.
2. So replete with interlocking points and   2. THORNY.
   complications as to be painfully irritating.

network *noun*
1. An open fabric woven of strands that are interlaced   1. WEB *noun.*
   and knotted at usu. regular intervals.
2. A group of things that are linked or interconnected   2. WEB *noun.*
   as if by weaving.

neuter *verb*
To render incapable of reproducing sexually.   STERILIZE.

neuter *adjective*
Not inclining toward or actively taking either side in a   NEUTRAL.
matter under dispute.

neutral *adjective*
1. Not inclining toward or actively taking either side   1. **Syns:** impartial, neuter, nonaligned,
   in a matter under dispute: *strove to be neutral in the*   nonpartisan, unbiased, uncommitted,
   cold war.   uninvolved, unprejudiced. —*Idiom* on
                                                                      the fence.
2. Without definite or distinctive characteristics: *His*   2. **Syns:** bland, colorless, indistinctive.
   neutral personality contrasted with her flamboyant
   one.
3. Feeling or showing no strong emotional   3. **Syns:** detached, disinterested,
   involvement: *a neutral approach to a controversial*   dispassionate, impersonal.
   issue.   **Near-syns:** aloof, calm, collected,
                                                                      composed, cool, indifferent, nonchalant,
                                                                      uncommitted.
                                                                      Ant: biased.

neutralize *verb*
1. To make ineffective by applying an opposite force or   1. CANCEL.
   amount.
2. To make up for the defects of.   2. COMPENSATE.

never-ending *adjective*
Enduring for all time.   ENDLESS.

new *adjective*
1. Showing marked departure from previous practice: *a*   1. **Syns:** fresh, innovative, inventive,
   new style of painting.   newfangled, novel, original, unfamiliar,
                                                                      unprecedented.
                                                                      Near-ants: dated, hackneyed, old hat
                                                                      (*Informal*), outdated, outmoded, trite,
                                                                      unoriginal, worn, worn-out.
                                                                      Ant: old.
2. In existence now.   2. PRESENT[1] *adjective.*
3. Not previously known or used.   3. FRESH.
4. Being an addition.   4. ADDITIONAL.

new *adverb*
Once more: *new-remembered pleasures.*   **Syns:** afresh, again, anew.

newborn *noun*
A very young child.   BABY *noun.*

newcomer *noun*
A person coming from another country.   FOREIGNER.

newfangle *noun*
Archaic. A new, unusual thing. NOVELTY.

newfangled *adjective*
Showing marked departure from previous practice. NEW *adjective*.

newly *adverb*
Only a moment ago. JUST *adverb*.

newness *noun*
The quality of being novel. NOVELTY.

news *noun*
1. New information, esp. about recent events and
happenings: *just got the news of the hurricane.*
2. Something significant that happens.

   1. *Syns:* advice(s), intelligence, tidings,
word.
   2. EVENT.

newsmonger *noun*
A person habitually engaged in idle talk about others. GOSSIP *noun*.

next *adjective*
1. Sharing a common boundary.
2. Occurring right after another.

   1. ADJOINING.
   2. FOLLOWING *adjective*.

next *adverb*
At a subsequent time. LATER *adverb*.

nexus *noun*
That which unites or binds. BOND *noun*.

Niagara *noun*
An abundant, usu. overwhelming flow. FLOOD *noun*.

nice *adjective*
1. Very difficult to please: *was nice to a fault about his
appearance.*

   1. *Syns:* choosy, dainty, exacting,
fastidious, finical, finicky, fussy,
meticulous, particular, persnickety,
picky.
Near-syns: discerning, discriminating,
squeamish; careful, punctilious,
scrupulous.

2. To one's liking.
3. Morally beyond reproach, esp. in sexual conduct.
4. Conforming to accepted standards.
5. So slight as to be difficult to notice or appreciate.
6. Able to make or detect effects of great subtlety or
precision.
7. Having pleasant, desirable qualities.

   2. AGREEABLE.
   3. CHASTE.
   4. CORRECT *adjective*.
   5. DELICATE.
   6. FINE[1].
   7. GOOD *adjective*.

niche *noun*
The proper or designated location. PLACE *noun*.

nictitate *verb*
To open and close the eyes rapidly. BLINK *verb*.

nictitation *noun*
A brief closing of the eyes. BLINK *noun*.

nifty *adjective*
Slang. Particularly excellent. MARVELOUS.

niggard *noun*
A stingy person. MISER.

niggard *adjective*
Ungenerously or pettily reluctant to spend money. STINGY.

niggardly *adjective*
Ungenerously or pettily reluctant to spend money. STINGY.

niggle *verb*
To raise unnecessary or trivial objections. QUIBBLE.

niggling *adjective*
Contemptibly unimportant. PETTY.

nigh *adverb*
To a point near in time, space, or relation. CLOSE[1] *adverb*.

nigh *adjective*
Not far from another in space, time, or relation. CLOSE[1] *adjective*.

night *noun*
The period of time between sunset and sunrise: *will return tomorrow night.*
  night *adjective*
Of or occurring during the night.

Syns: nighttide, nighttime.

NIGHTLY.

nightfall *noun*
The period between afternoon and nighttime.

EVENING.

nightly *adjective*
Of or occurring during the night: *nightly prowlings.*

Syns: night, nocturnal.

nighttide *noun*
The period of time between sunset and sunrise.

NIGHT *noun.*

nighttime *noun*
The period of time between sunset and sunrise.

NIGHT *noun.*

nihility *noun*
Absence of anything perceptible.

NOTHINGNESS.

nil *noun*
No thing; not anything.

NOTHING *noun.*

nimble *adjective*
1. Moving or performing quickly, lightly, and easily: *nimble feet.*

1. **Syns:** active, agile, brisk, facile, featly, quick, spry.
   Near-ants: dull, slow, sluggish, soporific; inactive, inert, passive; leaden, lethargic.

2. Mentally acute and resourceful.
3. Exhibiting or possessing skill and ease in performance.

2. AGILE.
3. DEXTEROUS.

nimbleness *noun*
The quality or state of being agile.

AGILITY.

nincompoop *noun*
One deficient in judgment and good sense.

FOOL *noun.*

ninny *noun*
One deficient in judgment and good sense.

FOOL *noun.*

nip¹ *verb*
1. To grasp at (something) eagerly, forcibly, and abruptly with the jaws.
2. *Slang.* To take (another's property) without permission.
3. *Brit. Slang.* To move swiftly.

1. SNAP *verb.*
2. STEAL.
3. RUSH *verb.*

nip² *noun*
A small amount of liquor.
  nip *verb*
To take alcoholic liquor, esp. excessively or habitually.

DROP *noun.*

DRINK *verb.*

nippy *adjective*
Marked by a low temperature.

COLD *adjective.*

nit-pick *verb*
Informal. To raise unnecessary or trivial objections.

QUIBBLE.

nitwit *noun*
Informal. One deficient in judgment and good sense.

FOOL *noun.*

nix *verb*
1. *Slang.* To be unwilling to accept, consider, or receive.
2. *Slang.* To prevent or forbid authoritatively.
  nix *noun*
Slang. No thing; not anything.
  nix *adverb*
Slang. Not so.

1. DECLINE *verb.*
2. VETO.

NOTHING *noun.*

NO *adverb.*

no *noun*
1. A negative response: *The proposal produced only noes.*
2. A negative vote or voter: *The noes carried the day.*
  no *adverb*

1. **Syns:** nay, refusal, rejection.
2. **Syn:** nay.

Not so: *No, I won't be there.*

noble *adjective*
1. Of high birth or social position: *a noble family; noble ladies of the court.*

2. Being on a high intellectual or moral level.
3. Large and impressive in size, scope, or extent.

nobody *pronoun*
No person: *Nobody stayed after the lecture.*

nobody *noun*
A totally insignificant person.

nocturnal *adjective*
Of or occurring during the night.

nod *noun*
1. An inclination of the head or body, as in greeting, consent, courtesy, submission, or worship.
2. The act or process of accepting.

nod *verb*
To sleep for a brief period.

nodding *adjective*
Ready for or needing sleep.

noddle *noun*
The uppermost part of the body.

noggin *noun*
Slang. The uppermost part of the body.

no-good *noun*
A self-indulgent person who spends time avoiding work or other useful activity.

no-good *adjective*
Lacking all worth and value.

noise *noun*
1. Sounds or a sound, esp. when loud, confused, or disagreeable: *deafened by the noise in the subway.*

2. The sensation caused by vibrating wave motion that is perceived by the organs of hearing.

noise *verb*
1. To spread as news: *It was noised about that he would be appointed to the post.*
2. To engage in or spread gossip.
3. To make (information) generally known.

noiseless *adjective*
Marked by, done with, or making no sound or noise.

noisome *adjective*
Having an unpleasant odor.

nomadic *adjective*
Leading the life of a person without a fixed domicile; moving from place to place: *a nomadic tribe.*

nomen *noun*
The word or words by which one is called and identified.

nominate *verb*
To select for an office or position.

nomination *noun*
The act of appointing to an office or position.

nominee *noun*
A person who is appointed to an office or position.

Syns: nay, nix (*Slang*), nope (*Slang*).
—*Idioms* nothing doing, no way.

1. **Syns:** aristocratic, blue-blooded, highborn, highbred, patrician, thoroughbred, well-born.
2. ELEVATED.
3. GRAND.

Syn: no one.

NONENTITY.

NIGHTLY.

1. BOW *noun.*

2. ACCEPTANCE.

NAP *verb.*

SLEEPY.

HEAD *noun.*

HEAD *noun.*

WASTREL.

WORTHLESS.

1. **Syns:** babel, clamor, din, hubbub, hullabaloo (*also* hullaballoo), pandemonium, racket, rumpus, tumult, uproar.
2. SOUND[1].

1. **Syns:** bruit (about), report.

2. GOSSIP *verb.*
3. ADVERTISE.

SILENT.

SMELLY.

Syns: itinerant, peripatetic, roaming, roving, vagabond, vagrant, wandering.
Near-syns: ambulatory, moving, rambling, ranging, shifting, wayfaring.

NAME *noun.*

APPOINT.

APPOINTMENT.

APPOINTEE.

nonage *noun*
The state or period of being under legal age. MINORITY.

nonaligned *adjective*
Not inclining toward or actively taking either side in a NEUTRAL.
matter under dispute.

nonappearance *noun*
Failure to be present. ABSENCE.

nonattendance *noun*
Failure to be present. ABSENCE.

nonchalance *noun*
The state or quality of being nonchalant: *An assumed* **Syns:** cool (*Slang*), imperturbability, sang-
nonchalance concealed his agitation. froid.

nonchalant *adjective*
Not easily excited, even under pressure. COOL *adjective.*

noncommittal *adjective*
Tending to keep one's thoughts and emotions to oneself. RESERVED.

noncompliance *noun*
The condition or practice of not obeying. DISOBEDIENCE.

non compos mentis *adjective*
Law. Afflicted with or exhibiting irrationality and INSANE.
mental unsoundness.

nonconformist *noun*
A person who dissents from the doctrine of an SEPARATIST.
established church.

nonentity *noun*
A totally insignificant person: *a colorless nonentity* **Syns:** cipher, nebbish (*Slang*), nobody,
overlooked by everyone. nothing, pip-squeak, shrimp (*Slang*), zero,
zilch (*Slang*).

nonessential *adjective*
Not necessary. UNNECESSARY.

nonesuch *noun*
A person or thing so excellent as to have no equal or NONPAREIL *noun.*
match.

nonexistence *noun*
Absence of anything perceptible. NOTHINGNESS.

nonfeasance *noun*
Law. Nonperformance of what ought to be done. FAILURE.

no-nonsense *adjective*
Marked by sober sincerity. SERIOUS.

nonpareil *noun*
A person or thing so excellent as to have no equal or **Syns:** nonesuch, paragon, phoenix.
match: *the nonpareil of singers.*

nonpareil *adjective*
Without equal or rival. UNIQUE.

nonpartisan *adjective*
1. Free from bias in judgment. 1. FAIR *adjective.*
2. Not inclining toward or actively taking either side 2. NEUTRAL.
   in a matter under dispute.

nonpartisanship *noun*
The quality or state of being just and unbiased. FAIRNESS.

nonphysical *adjective*
Having no body, form, or substance. IMMATERIAL.

nonplus *verb*
To make incapable of finding something to think, do, or **Syns:** beat (*Slang*), confound, flummox
say: *was nonplussed by their audacity.* (*Slang*), stick (*Informal*), stump
(*Informal*). —*Idiom* put someone at a loss.

nonprofessional *noun*
One lacking professional skill and ease in a particular AMATEUR.
pursuit.

nonresistant *adjective*
Submitting without objection or resistance. PASSIVE.

nonresisting *adjective*
Submitting without objection or resistance.   PASSIVE.

nonsense *noun*
1. Something that does not have or make sense: *was completely ignorant and held views that were utter nonsense.*

   1. *Syns:* applesauce (*Slang*), balderdash, baloney (*also* boloney) (*Slang*), bilge, blather, bull (*Slang*), bunk² (*Slang*), bunkum¹ (*also* buncombe), claptrap, crap (*Slang*), drivel, eyewash, hooey (*Slang*), idiocy, malarkey (*also* malarky) (*Slang*), piffle, pishposh, poppycock, rigmarole (*also* rigamarole), stuff, tomfoolery, tommyrot (*Informal*), trash¹, twaddle.

2. Unintelligible or foolish talk.   2. BABBLE *noun*.

nonsensical *adjective*
So senseless as to be laughable.   FOOLISH.

nonstop *adjective*
Existing or occurring without interruption or end.   CONTINUAL.

noodle *noun*
Slang. The uppermost part of the body.   HEAD *noun*.

no one *pronoun*
No person.   NOBODY *pronoun*.

noose *verb*
To execute by suspending by the neck.   HANG *verb*.

nope *adverb*
Slang. Not so.   NO *adverb*.

norm *noun*
Something, as a type, number, quantity, or degree, that represents a midpoint between extremes on a scale of valuation.   AVERAGE *noun*.

normal *adjective*
To be expected.   COMMON *adjective*.

normally *adverb*
In an expected or customary manner.   USUALLY.

nose *noun*
1. The structure on the human face that contains the nostrils and organs of smell and forms the beginning of the respiratory tract: *a snub nose.*

   1. *Syns:* beak (*Informal*), nozzle (*Slang*), proboscis, schnozzle (*Slang*), smeller (*Informal*), snoot (*Slang*), snout (*Slang*).

2. The sense by which odors are perceived.   2. SMELL *noun*.
3. Skill in perceiving, discriminating, or judging.   3. DISCERNMENT.

nose *verb*
1. To perceive with the olfactory sense.   1. SMELL *verb*.
2. To look into or inquire about curiously, inquisitively, or in a meddlesome fashion.   2. SNOOP *verb*.

nose out *verb*
Slang. To pursue and locate.   RUN DOWN.

nose-dive *noun*
1. A sudden involuntary drop to the ground.   1. FALL *noun*.
2. The act of plunging suddenly downward into or as if into water.   2. PLUNGE *noun*.

nose-dive *verb*
To undergo a sharp, rapid descent in value or price.   FALL *verb*.

nose out *verb*   SEE **nose**.

nosey *adjective*   SEE **nosy**.

nosiness *noun*
Informal. Undue interest in the affairs of others.   CURIOSITY.

nostrum *noun*
An agent used to restore health.   CURE *noun*.

nosy *also* **nosey** *adjective*
Informal. Unduly interested in the affairs of others.   CURIOUS.

notability *noun*
1. A position of exalted, widely recognized importance.
2. An important, influential person.

1. EMINENCE.
2. DIGNITARY.

notable *adjective*
Widely known and esteemed.

EMINENT.

notable *noun*
1. An important, influential person.
2. A famous person.

1. DIGNITARY.
2. CELEBRITY.

notably *adverb*
To a high degree.

VERY *adverb*.

notation *noun*
A brief record written as an aid to the memory.

NOTE *noun*.

notch *verb*
To gain (a point or points) in a game or contest.

SCORE *verb*.

notch *noun*
One of the units in a course, as on an ascending or descending scale.

DEGREE.

note *noun*
1. A brief record written as an aid to the memory: *made a note of what was said.*
2. A written communication directed to another.
3. An expression of fact or opinion.
4. Critical explanation or analysis.
5. A position of exalted, widely recognized importance.
6. The act of noting, observing, or taking into account.
7. *Poetic.* A pleasing succession of musical tones forming a usu. brief aesthetic unit.

1. *Syns:* memo, memorandum, notation.
2. LETTER.
3. COMMENT *noun*.
4. COMMENTARY.
5. EMINENCE.
6. NOTICE *noun*.
7. MELODY.

note *verb*
1. To perceive with a special effort of the senses or the mind.
2. To make observations.

1. NOTICE *verb*.
2. COMMENT *verb*.

noted *adjective*
Widely known and esteemed.

EMINENT.

nothing *noun*
1. No thing; not anything: *I have nothing to say. The fire left us with nothing.*
2. The quality or state of being obscure.
3. A totally insignificant person.
4. Absence of anything perceptible.

1. *Syns:* aught (*Archaic*), nil, nix (*Slang*), zilch (*Slang*).
2. OBSCURITY.
3. NONENTITY.
4. NOTHINGNESS.

nothing *adjective*
Slang. Lacking all worth and value.

WORTHLESS.

nothingness *noun*
1. Absence of anything perceptible: *Hiroshima was reduced to nothingness by the atomic bomb.*
2. Empty, unfilled space: *looked out into the nothingness of the Arctic night.*

1. *Syns:* nihility, nonexistence, nothing, vacuity.
2. *Syns:* barrenness, emptiness, void.

notice *noun*
1. The act of noting, observing, or taking into account: *took notice of the youth's performance and promoted him.*
2. A public statement.
3. Evaluative and critical discourse.

1. *Syns:* attention, cognizance, heed, mark, note, observance, observation, regard, remark.
2. ANNOUNCEMENT.
3. REVIEW *noun*.

notice *verb*
To perceive with a special effort of the senses or the mind: *noticed a change in the old man's expression.*

Syns: descry, distinguish, espy, mark, mind, note, observe, remark, see.

noticeable *adjective*
1. Readily attracting notice: *a noticeable swelling in her right leg; a noticeable increase in East-West tension.*

1. *Syns:* arresting, arrestive, conspicuous, eye-catching, marked, observable, outstanding, pointed, prominent, remarkable, salient, signal, striking.
—*Idiom* sticking out like a sore thumb.

Near-syns: evident, evocative, manifest, obvious, palpable, patent, sensational, spectacular; notable, noteworthy, notorious.
Ant: unnoticeable.

2. Readily seen, perceived, or understood.   2. APPARENT.
3. Capable of being noticed or apprehended mentally.   3. PERCEPTIBLE.

notify *verb*
To cause to know about or be aware of.   INFORM.

notion *noun*
1. An impulsive, often illogical turn of mind.   1. FANCY *noun.*
2. Something believed or accepted as true by a person. 2. BELIEF.

notional *adjective*
1. Existing only in the imagination.   1. IMAGINARY.
2. Given to changeable emotional states, esp. of anger   2. MOODY.
   or gloom.

notoriety *noun*
1. Unfavorable, usu. unsavory renown: *a disbarred*   1. *Syns:* fame, infamy, notoriousness.
   lawyer of great notoriety.
2. Wide recognition for one's deeds.   2. FAME.

notorious *adjective*
1. Known widely and unfavorably: *a notorious crook.*   1. *Syns:* common, famous (*Archaic*),
                                                         infamous.
2. Widely known and discussed.   2. FAMOUS.

notoriousness *noun*
Unfavorable, usu. unsavory renown.   NOTORIETY.

nourish *verb*
1. To sustain (a living organism) with food: *Well-*   1. *Syn:* feed.
   balanced meals nourished the growing children.
2. To promote and sustain the development of.   2. NURSE.

nourishing *adjective*
Providing nourishment.   NUTRITIOUS.

nourishment *noun*
That which sustains the mind or spirit.   FOOD.

novel *adjective*
1. Showing marked departure from previous practice.   1. NEW *adjective.*
2. Not usual or ordinary.   2. UNUSUAL.

novelty *noun*
1. The quality of being novel: *He tired of the game*   1. *Syns:* freshness, newness, originality.
   after the novelty wore off.
2. A new, unusual thing: *Edison's light bulb was at*   2. *Syns:* innovation, newfangle (*Archaic*).
   first merely an interesting novelty.
3. A small, showy article: *a novelty store that sold*   3. *Syns:* bauble, bibelot, gewgaw,
   rings, key chains, and post cards to tourists.   gimcrack, knickknack, toy, trifle,
                                                         trinket, whatnot.

novice *noun*
1. An entrant who has not yet taken the final vows of   1. *Syn:* novitiate (*also* noviciate) (*Eccles.*).
   a religious order: *a novice in a convent.*
2. One who is just starting to learn or do something.   2. BEGINNER.

noviciate *noun*   SEE **novitiate.**

novitiate also **noviciate** *noun*
1. One who is just starting to learn or do something.   1. BEGINNER.
2. *Eccles.* An entrant who has not yet taken the final   2. NOVICE.
   vows of a religious order.

now *noun*
The current time: *Now is the time that tries men's*   *Syns:* nowadays, present[1], today.
souls.

now *adjective*
In existence now.   PRESENT[1] *adjective.*

now *adverb*

1. At the present; these days: *Air travel is much faster now with the supersonic transports.*
2. At this moment: *I'm on the phone now.*

3. Without delay.
4. At times: *a ballet that was now adagio, now allegro.*

1. *Syns:* nowadays, today. —*Idiom* in this day and age.
2. *Syns:* actually, currently. —*Idiom* just (*or* right) now.
3. DIRECTLY.
4. *Syns:* betimes, periodically. —*Idioms* ever and again, ever and anon, now and again, now and then.

nowadays *noun*
The current time.
nowadays *adverb*
At the present; these days.

NOW *noun.*

NOW *adverb.*

noxious *adjective*
Extremely destructive or harmful.

VIRULENT.

nozzle *noun*
Slang. The structure on the human face that contains the nostrils and organs of smell and forms the beginning of the respiratory tract.

NOSE *noun.*

nuance *noun*
A slight variation between nearly identical entities.

SHADE *noun.*

nub *noun*
1. An unevenness or elevation on a surface.
2. The most central and material part.

1. BUMP *noun.*
2. HEART.

nucleus *noun*
A source of further growth and development.

GERM.

nude *adjective*
1. Not wearing any clothes: *nude models.*

1. *Syns:* au naturel, bare, disrobed, naked, stripped, unclad, unclothed, undressed. —*Idioms* bare as a newborn babe, in one's birthday suit, in the altogether (*or* buff *or* raw), naked as a jaybird, stark naked, without a stitch.
2. BARE *adjective.*

2. Without the usual covering.
nudeness *noun*
The state of being without clothes.

NUDITY.

nudge *verb*
To thrust against or into.
nudge *noun*
An act of thrusting into or against, as to attract attention.

DIG *verb.*

DIG *noun.*

nudity *noun*
The state of being without clothes: *The artist found nudity an appealing subject.*

Syns: bareness, nakedness, nudeness, undress.

nugatory *adjective*
Lacking value, use, or substance.

EMPTY *adjective.*

nugget *noun*
An irregularly shaped mass of indefinite size.

LUMP[1] *noun.*

nuisance *noun*
Something that annoys.

ANNOYANCE.

nullification *noun*
An often formal act of putting an end to.

ABOLITION.

nullify *verb*
To put an end to formally and with authority.

ABOLISH.

numb *verb*
1. To render less sensitive.
2. To render helpless, as by emotion.
numb *adjective*
1. Lacking responsiveness or alertness.
2. Lacking physical feeling or sensitivity.

1. DEADEN.
2. PARALYZE.

1. DULL *adjective.*
2. DEAD *adjective.*

numbed *adjective*
Lacking physical feeling or sensitivity.

DEAD *adjective.*

number *verb*
1. To note (items) one by one so as to get a total.
2. To come to in number or quantity.

1. COUNT *verb*.
2. AMOUNT *verb*.

number-one *adjective*
Informal. Most important, influential, or significant.

PRIMARY.

number one *noun*
Informal. A leading contestant.

LEADER.

numbers *noun*
Arithmetic calculations.

FIGURES.

numbskull *noun*

SEE **numskull**.

numerate *verb*
1. To note (items) one by one so as to get a total.
2. To name or specify one by one.

1. COUNT *verb*.
2. ENUMERATE.

numeration *noun*
A noting of items one by one.

COUNT *noun*.

numerous *adjective*
Amounting to or consisting of a large, indefinite number.

MANY.

numinous *adjective*
Of or concerned with the spirit rather than the body or material things.

SPIRITUAL.

numskull also **numbskull** *noun*
1. A mentally dull person.
2. One deficient in judgment and good sense.

1. DULLARD.
2. FOOL *noun*.

nuptial *noun*
The act or ceremony by which two people become husband and wife.

WEDDING.

nuptial *adjective*
Of, relating to, or typical of marriage.

MARITAL.

nurse *verb*
1. To promote and sustain the development of: *agitators who nursed discontent into open revolution.*
2. To hold and turn over in the mind.

1. *Syns:* cultivate, foster, nourish, nurture.
2. BEAR.

nursling *noun*
A very young child.

BABY *noun*.

nurture *verb*
To promote and sustain the development of.

NURSE.

nurture *noun*
Something fit to be eaten.

FOOD.

nut *noun*
1. Slang. An insanely foolish or strange person.
2. Slang. A person who is ardently devoted to a particular subject or activity.
3. Slang. The uppermost part of the body.

1. CRACKPOT.
2. ENTHUSIAST.
3. HEAD *noun*.

nutrient *adjective*
Providing nourishment.

NUTRITIOUS.

nutriment *noun*
That which sustains the mind or spirit.

FOOD.

nutritional *adjective*
Of or relating to food or nutrition.

NUTRITIVE.

nutritious *adjective*
Providing nourishment: *served the children nutritious and satisfying meals.*

Syns: nourishing, nutrient, nutritive.
Near-syns: healthful, nutrimental, salubrious, wholesome.
Ant: unnourishing.

nutritive *adjective*
1. Of or relating to food or nutrition: *the nutritive system of a plant.*
2. Providing nourishment.

1. *Syns:* alimentary, nutritional.
2. NUTRITIOUS.

nuts *adjective*
Slang. Afflicted with or exhibiting irrationality and mental unsoundness.   INSANE.

nutty *adjective*
1. *Informal.* Showing or having enthusiasm.   1. ENTHUSIASTIC.
2. *Informal.* Afflicted with or exhibiting irrationality and mental unsoundness.   2. INSANE.

nuzzle *verb*
To lie or press close together, usu. with another person or thing.   SNUGGLE *verb.*

oaf *noun*
A large, ungainly, and dull-witted person.   LUMP[1] *noun.*

oath *noun*
A profane or obscene term.   SWEAR *noun.*

obdurate *adjective*
1. Firmly, often unreasonably immovable in purpose or will.   1. STUBBORN.
2. Totally lacking in compassion.   2. COLD-BLOODED.

obedience *noun*
1. The quality or state of willingly carrying out the wishes of others: *The commander wanted absolute obedience from the troops.*   1. *Syns:* acquiescence, compliance (*also* compliancy), submission.
2. An act of willingly carrying out the wishes of others: *obedience of the law.*   2. *Syns:* conformance, conformity, obeyance, observance.

obedient *adjective*
Willing to carry out the wishes of others: *an obedient child.*   *Syns:* amenable, biddable, compliant, complying, conformable, submissive, tractable. —*Idiom* toeing the mark (*or* line).
Near-ants: headstrong, impertinent, insubordinate, intractable, rebellious, recalcitrant, refractory, sassy, ungovernable, unruly.
Ant: disobedient.

obeisance *noun*
1. An inclination of the head or body, as in greeting, consent, courtesy, submission, or worship.   1. BOW *noun.*
2. Great respect or high public esteem accorded as a right or as due.   2. HONOR *noun.*

obeisant *adjective*
Marked by courteous submission or respect.   DEFERENTIAL.

obese *adjective*
Having too much flesh.   FAT *adjective.*

obey *verb*
To act in conformity with.   FOLLOW.

obeyance *noun*
An act of willingly carrying out the wishes of others.   OBEDIENCE.

obfuscate *verb*
To make dim or indistinct.   OBSCURE *verb.*

obiter dictum *noun*
An expression of fact or opinion.

object[1] *noun*
1. Something having material existence: *Place the object directly beneath the lens.*
2. One that exists independently.
3. A separate and distinct portion of matter.
4. Something strongly desired.

object[2] *verb*
1. To express opposition by argument: *The defense attorney objected to that line of questioning.*

2. To have an objection.
3. To have or express an unfavorable opinion.

objectify *verb*
To represent (an abstraction) in or as if in bodily form.

objection *noun*
The act of expressing strong or reasoned opposition: *The forest was cut down despite the objections of conservationists.*

objectionable *adjective*
Arousing disapproval: *objectionable behavior.*

objective *noun*
Something strongly desired.

objective *adjective*
1. Composed of or relating to things that occupy space and can be perceived by the senses.
2. Free from bias in judgment.
3. Having or indicating an awareness of things as they really are.

objectiveness *noun*
The quality or state of being just and unbiased.

objectivity *noun*
The quality or state of being just and unbiased.

objectless *adjective*
1. Without aim, purpose, or intent.
2. Having no particular pattern, purpose, organization, or structure.

oblation *noun*
1. A presentation made to a deity as an act of worship.
2. A charitable deed.

obligate *verb*
To be morally bound to do.

obligated *adjective*
Owing something, as gratitude or appreciation, to another.

obligation *noun*
1. An act or course of action that is demanded of one, as by position, custom, law, or religion.
2. A condition of owing something to another.

obligatory *adjective*
Imposed on one by authority, command, or convention.

oblige *verb*
1. To perform a service or a courteous act: *You will oblige me if you will keep this matter quiet.*
2. To cause (a person or thing) to act or move in spite of resistance.

COMMENT *noun.*

1. **Syns:** article, item, thing.

2. THING.
3. BODY *noun.*
4. AMBITION.

1. **Syns:** except, expostulate, inveigh, kick (*Informal*), protest, remonstrate, squawk (*Informal*). —*Idiom* raise a squawk, take exception to.
2. CARE *verb.*
3. DISAPPROVE.

EMBODY.

Syns: challenge, expostulation, kick (*Informal*), protest, protestation, remonstrance, remonstration, squawk (*Informal*).

Syns: exceptionable, ill-favored, inadmissible, unacceptable, undesirable, unwanted, unwelcome.

AMBITION.

1. PHYSICAL.

2. FAIR.
3. REALISTIC.

FAIRNESS.

FAIRNESS.

1. AIMLESS.
2. RANDOM.

1. OFFERING.
2. BENEVOLENCE.

COMMIT.

OBLIGED.

1. DUTY.

2. DEBT.

REQUIRED.

1. **Syns:** accommodate, convenience, favor.

2. FORCE *verb.*

3. To comply with the wishes or ideas of (another).

3. HUMOR *verb*.

obliged *adjective*
  1. Owing something, as gratitude or appreciation, to another: *I felt obliged to help him after he had helped me.*
  2. Showing or feeling gratitude.

1. *Syns:* beholden, bound³, bounden, indebted, obligated. —*Idiom* under obligation.
2. GRATEFUL.

obligement *noun*
  A condition of owing something to another.

DEBT.

obliging *adjective*
  Ready to do favors for another: *an obliging person, always willing to help.*

Syns: accommodating, agreeable, complaisant, indulgent.

oblique *adjective*
  1. Angled at a slant.
  2. Not taking a direct or straight line or course.

1. BIAS *adjective*.
2. INDIRECT.

obliterate *verb*
  To destroy all traces of.

ANNIHILATE.

obliteration *noun*
  1. The act of erasing or the condition of being erased.
  2. Utter destruction.

1. ERASURE.
2. ANNIHILATION.

oblivion *noun*
  Freedom from worry, care, or unpleasantness.

ESCAPE *noun*.

oblivious *adjective*
  Not aware or informed.

IGNORANT.

obloquious *adjective*
  1. Of, relating to, or characterized by verbal abuse.
  2. Meriting or causing shame or dishonor.

1. ABUSIVE.
2. DISGRACEFUL.

obloquy *noun*
  1. A long, violent, or blustering speech, usu. of censure or denunciation.
  2. Harsh, often insulting language.
  3. Loss of or damage to one's reputation.

1. TIRADE.

2. VITUPERATION.
3. DISGRACE *noun*.

obnoxious *adjective*
  So objectionable as to elicit despisal.

FILTHY.

obscene *adjective*
  1. Offensive to accepted standards of decency: *obscene jokes.*

1. *Syns:* barnyard, coarse, crude, crusty, dirty, Fescennine, filthy, foul, gross, indecent, lewd, nasty, profane, rank², raunchy (*Slang*), raw, rocky, scatological (*also* scatologic), scurrilous, smutty.
  Near-syns: bawdy, earthy, sultry; foulmouthed, vulgar; lascivious, salacious, scabrous; lurid, pornographic.

  2. Beyond all reason.

2. OUTRAGEOUS.

obsceneness *noun*
  The quality or state of being obscene.

OBSCENITY.

obscenity *noun*
  1. The quality or state of being obscene: *a campaign to eradicate obscenity from films.*

  2. Something that is offensive to accepted standards of decency: *four-letter words and other obscenities.*

1. *Syns:* dirtiness, filthiness, indecency, lewdness, obsceneness, raunchiness (*Slang*).
2. *Syns:* dirt, filth, profanity, smut.

obscure *verb*
  1. To make dim or indistinct: *Swirling snow obscured the road. Smog had obscured an otherwise clear view.*

1. *Syns:* adumbrate, becloud, bedim, befog, blear, blur, cloud, dim, dull, eclipse, fog, gloom, haze, mist, murk (*also* mirk), obfuscate, overcast, overshadow, shadow.

Near-syns: cloak, conceal, cover, hide, mask, overcloud, screen, shade, shroud, veil.
Ants: illuminate, illumine.

2. To conceal in obscurity: *details obscured in a maze of legal jargon.*

2. **Syns:** hide[1], submerge.

3. To cut off from sight.

3. BLOCK OUT at **block.**

obscure *adjective*
1. Deficient in brightness.
2. Not clearly perceived or perceptible.
3. Far from centers of human population.
4. Not readily noticed or seen.
5. Unknown by name: *an obscure writer; an obscure disease.*
6. Liable to more than one interpretation.

1. DARK *adjective.*
2. UNCLEAR.
3. REMOTE.
4. INCONSPICUOUS.
5. **Syns:** nameless, unheard-of.

6. AMBIGUOUS.

obscured *adjective*
Lying beyond what is obvious or avowed.

ULTERIOR.

obscurity *noun*
1. The quality or state of being obscure: *a Third World leader who rose from obscurity to notoriety.*
2. The quality or state of being ambiguous.
3. Absence or deficiency of light.

1. **Syns:** anonymity, namelessness, nothing.
2. VAGUENESS.
3. DARK *noun.*

obsequious *adjective*
Excessively eager to serve or obey.

SERVILE.

observable *adjective*
1. Capable of being noticed or apprehended mentally.
2. Readily attracting notice.

1. PERCEPTIBLE.
2. NOTICEABLE.

observance *noun*
1. An act of willingly carrying out the wishes of others.
2. The act of observing a day or event with ceremonies.
3. A formal act or set of acts prescribed by ritual.
4. The act of noting, observing, or taking into account.
5. The act of observing, often for an extended time.

1. OBEDIENCE.

2. CELEBRATION.
3. CEREMONY.
4. NOTICE *noun.*
5. WATCH *noun.*

observant *adjective*
1. Vigilantly attentive.
2. Concentrating the mental powers on something.
3. Tending toward awareness and appreciation.

1. ALERT *adjective.*
2. ATTENTIVE.
3. MINDFUL.

observation *noun*
1. The act of noting, observing, or taking into account.
2. The act of observing, often for an extended time.
3. An expression of fact or opinion.

1. NOTICE *noun.*
2. WATCH *noun.*
3. COMMENT *noun.*

observative *adjective*
Tending toward awareness and appreciation.

MINDFUL.

observatory *noun*
A high structure commanding a wide view.

LOOKOUT.

observe *verb*
1. To perceive with a special effort of the senses or the mind.
2. To use the power of vision.
3. To look at or on attentively or carefully.
4. To make observations.
5. To act in conformity with.
6. To mark (a day or event) with ceremonies of respect, festivity, or rejoicing.

1. NOTICE *verb.*

2. LOOK *verb.*
3. WATCH *verb.*
4. COMMENT *verb.*
5. FOLLOW.
6. CELEBRATE.

observer *noun*
Someone who observes.

WATCHER.

observing *adjective*
Tending toward awareness and appreciation.

MINDFUL.

obsess *verb*
1. To recur to continually.

1. HAUNT *verb.*

2. To dominate the mind or thoughts of.

obsession *noun*
An irrational preoccupation.

obsolesce *verb*
To make or become obsolete: *As surgical procedures obsolesce they are no longer used.*

obsolescence *noun*
The process of becoming obsolete: *Building new roads retards the obsolescence of our highway system.*

obsolete *adjective*
No longer in use: *obsolete weaponry; obsolete Middle English words.*

obsolete *verb*
To make or become obsolete.

obsolete *noun*
Something that is obsolete.

obsoleteness *noun*
The quality or state of being obsolete: *words that had fallen into obsoleteness.*

obsoletion *noun*
1. The quality or state of being obsolete.
2. The process of becoming obsolete.

obsoletism *noun*
1. Something that is obsolete: *The word "pervicacy" is now an obsoletism.*
2. The quality or state of being obsolete.

obstacle *noun*
Anything that impedes or prevents entry or passage.

obstinacy also **obstinance** *noun*
The quality or state of being stubbornly unyielding: *The prime minister's obstinacy was a hindrance to the peace talks.*

obstinance *noun*
obstinate *adjective*
1. Tenaciously unwilling to yield: *an obstinate man who never apologized.*

2. Difficult to alleviate or cure.

obstreperous *adjective*
1. Not submitting to discipline or control.
2. Offensively loud and insistent.

obstreperousness *noun*
The quality or condition of being unruly.

obstruct *verb*
1. To stop or prevent passage of: *obstructed the vote by filibustering.*
2. To interfere with the progress of.
3. To cut off from sight.

2. POSSESS.

THING.

Syns: obsolete, outdate, superannuate.

Syn: obsoletion.

Syn: superseded. —*Idioms* in mothballs, on the shelf.

OBSOLESCE.

OBSOLETISM.

Syns: desuetude, disuse, obsoletion, obsoletism.

1. OBSOLETENESS.
2. OBSOLESCENCE.

1. **Syn:** obsolete.

2. OBSOLETENESS.

BAR *noun*.

Syns: bullheadedness, doggedness, hardheadedness, incompliance *or* incompliancy, intractability, intransigence *or* intransigency, mulishness, pertinacity, perverseness, perversity, pigheadedness, refractoriness, stubbornness, willfulness.
SEE **obstinacy**.

1. **Syns:** bulldogged, bulldoggish, bulldoggy, bullheaded, close-minded, dogged, hardheaded, headstrong, incompliant, intractable, intransigent, muleheaded, muley, mulish, pertinacious, perverse, pigheaded, refractory, stiff-necked, stubborn, tenacious, tough, willful.
Near-ants: acquiescent, compliant, obliging, yielding; agreeable, cooperative; fawning, obsequious, servile.
Ants: pliable, pliant.
2. STUBBORN.

1. UNRULY.
2. VOCIFEROUS.

UNRULINESS.

1. **Syns:** bar, block, impede, overslaugh.
—*Idiom* stand in the way of.
2. HINDER.
3. BLOCK OUT at **block.**

obstruction *noun*
Anything that impedes or prevents entry or passage.   BAR *noun*.

obtain *verb*
To come into possession of.   GET.

obtainable *adjective*
Capable of being obtained or used.   AVAILABLE.

obtrude *verb*
To force or come in as an improper or unwanted
element.   INTRUDE.

obtrusive *adjective*
Given to intruding in other people's affairs.   MEDDLING *adjective*.

obtuse *adjective*
Lacking in intelligence.   STUPID.

obviate *verb*
To prohibit from occurring by advance planning or
action.   PREVENT.

obviation *noun*
The act of preventing.   PREVENTION.

obvious *adjective*
1. Readily seen, perceived, or understood.   1. APPARENT.
2. Easily seen through due to a lack of subtlety.   2. UNSUBTLE.

occasion *noun*
1. The general point at which an event occurs: *We met*   1. *Syn:* time. —*Idiom* point in time.
   on several occasions.
2. Something significant that happens.   2. EVENT.
3. A favorable or advantageous combination of   3. OPPORTUNITY.
   circumstances.
4. That which provides a reason or justification.   4. CAUSE *noun*.
5. A large or important social gathering.   5. PARTY *noun*.

occasion *verb*
1. To be a proper or sufficient occasion for.   1. CALL FOR at **call**.
2. To be the cause of.   2. CAUSE *verb*.

occasional *adjective*
1. Rarely occurring or appearing.   1. INFREQUENT.
2. Happening or appearing now and then.   2. INTERMITTENT.

occult *verb*
To put or keep out of sight.   HIDE[1] *verb*.

occupancy *noun*
The holding of something, such as a position.   TENURE.

occupation *noun*
1. Activity pursued as a livelihood.   1. BUSINESS.
2. The holding of something, such as a position.   2. TENURE.

occupied *adjective*
Involved in activity or work.   BUSY *adjective*.

occupy *verb*
1. To seize and move into by force: *Terrorists have*   1. *Syn:* take over.
   attacked and occupied the embassy.
2. To live in (a place).   2. INHABIT.
3. To make busy.   3. BUSY *verb*.
4. To get and hold the attention of.   4. ENGAGE.
5. To cause to be busy or in use.   5. TIE UP.

occur *verb*
1. To enter a person's mind: *It occurred to him that he*   1. *Syns:* hit, strike. —*Idiom* cross one's
   was on the wrong street.   mind.
2. To take place.   2. COME.
3. To take place at a set time.   3. COME.

occurrence *noun*
1. Something that happens.   1. CIRCUMSTANCE.
2. Something significant that happens.   2. EVENT.
3. The condition or fact of being present.   3. PRESENCE.

oceanic *adjective*
Of or relating to the seas or oceans.   MARINE.

odd *adjective*
1. Occurring unexpectedly.   1. ACCIDENTAL *adjective*.
2. Deviating from the customary.   2. ECCENTRIC *adjective*.
3. Causing puzzlement; perplexing.   3. FUNNY.
4. Agreeably curious, esp. in an old-fashioned or   4. QUAINT[1].
   unusual way.

oddball *adjective*
1. *Informal.* Deviating from the customary.   1. ECCENTRIC *adjective*.
2. *Informal.* Agreeably curious, esp. in an old-fashioned 2. QUAINT[1].
   or unusual way.

oddity *noun*
1. A person who is appealingly odd or curious.   1. CHARACTER.
2. A person or animal that is abnormally formed.   2. FREAK.

oddments *noun*
Articles too small or numerous to be specified.   ODDS AND ENDS.

odds *noun*
1. A factor conducive to superiority and success.   1. ADVANTAGE *noun*.
2. The likelihood of a given event occurring.   2. CHANCE *noun*.

odds and ends *noun*
Articles too small or numerous to be specified: *a box in*   ***Syns:*** etceteras, oddments, sundries.
the closet in which she kept odds and ends.

odious *adjective*
1. Eliciting or deserving hate.   1. HATEFUL.
2. So objectionable as to elicit despisal.   2. FILTHY.

odiousness *noun*
The condition of being infamous.   INFAMY.

odor *noun*
The quality of something that may be perceived by the   SMELL *noun*.
olfactory sense.

oestrus *noun*   SEE **estrus**.

off *adjective*
1. Containing an error or errors.   1. ERRONEOUS.
2. Small in degree, esp. of probability.   2. REMOTE.
3. Afflicted with or exhibiting irrationality and mental   3. INSANE.
   unsoundness.
4. Characterized by reduced economic activity.   4. SLOW *adjective*.
off *verb*
Slang. To take the life of (a person or persons)   MURDER *verb*.
unlawfully.

offbeat *adjective*
Informal. Not usual or ordinary.   UNUSUAL.

off-color *adjective*
1. Bordering on indelicacy or impropriety.   1. RACY.
2. Affected or tending to be affected with minor health   2. SICKLY.
   problems.

offend *verb*
1. To be very disagreeable to: *Bad manners offend me.*   1. ***Syns:*** displease, displeasure (*Archaic*),
                                                              turn off (*Slang*). —*Idioms* give offense,
                                                              not set right (*or* well) with.

2. To cause resentment or hurt by callous, rude   2. INSULT *verb*.
   behavior.
3. To violate a moral or divine law: *offended against*   3. ***Syns:*** sin, transgress, trespass.
   the word of the Lord.

offender *noun*
One who commits a crime.   CRIMINAL *noun*.

offense *noun*
1. Extreme displeasure caused by an insult or slight: 1. ***Syns:*** dudgeon, huff, miff, pique,
   took offense at the least provocation.   resentment, umbrage. —*Idiom* ruffled
                                                              feathers.

2. An act that offends a person's sense of pride or dignity.
3. A wicked act.
4. A serious breaking of the public law.
5. The act of attacking.

offensive   *adjective*
1. Extremely unpleasant to the senses or feelings: *offensive odors; offensive language.*

2. Not pleasant or agreeable.
3. Inclined to act in a hostile way.

offensive   *noun*
The act of attacking.

offer   *verb*
1. To put before another for acceptance: *offering us cookies; offered his sympathy to the widow; offered us his help.*
2. To advance, as an idea, for consideration.
3. To make (something) readily available: *a college offering a broad curriculum.*
4. To make an offer of.
5. To make an attempt to do or make.

offer   *noun*
1. Something offered: *made him an offer of $4,000 for the car; had numerous job offers.*
2. An effort to do or make something.

offering   *noun*
1. A presentation made to a deity as an act of worship: *made sacrifices and other offerings to the gods.*
2. Something given to a charity or cause.
3. A living creature slain and offered to a deity as part of a religious rite.

offhand   *adjective*
Spoken, performed, or composed with little or no preparation or forethought.

office   *noun*
1. A post of employment.
2. *Eccles.* A formal act or set of acts prescribed by ritual.
3. An assignment one is sent to carry out.

officer   *noun*
1. A member of a law-enforcement agency.
2. A person having administrative or managerial authority in an organization.

officer   *verb*
To have authoritative charge of.

office(s)   *noun*
A charitable deed.

official   *adjective*
Having or arising from authority.

official   *noun*
1. A person or group having the right and power to command, decide, rule, or judge.
2. A person having administrative or managerial authority in an organization.

---

2. INDIGNITY.

3. CRIME.
4. CRIME.
5. ATTACK *noun.*

1. **Syns:** atrocious, disgusting, evil, foul, loathsome, nasty, nauseating, repellent, repulsive, revolting, sickening, ugly, unwholesome, vile. **Near-syns:** appalling, awful, detestable, dreadful, frightful, ghastly, grim, grisly, grotesque, gruesome, monstrous, objectionable, obscene, repugnant. **Ant:** inoffensive.

2. UNPLEASANT.
3. AGGRESSIVE.

ATTACK *noun.*

1. **Syns:** extend, present[2], proffer, tender[2], volunteer. —*Idioms* come forward with, lay at someone's feet.
2. PROPOSE.
3. **Syns:** afford, provide. —*Idiom* place (or put) at one's disposal.
4. GO *verb.*
5. ATTEMPT *verb.*

1. **Syns:** bid, proffer, proposal, tender[2].

2. ATTEMPT *noun.*

1. **Syn:** oblation.

2. DONATION.
3. SACRIFICE *noun.*

EXTEMPORANEOUS.

1. POSITION *noun.*
2. CEREMONY.

3. MISSION.

1. POLICEMAN.
2. EXECUTIVE *noun.*

LEAD *verb.*

BENEVOLENCE.

AUTHORITATIVE.

1. AUTHORITY.

2. EXECUTIVE *noun.*

officiate *verb*
To perform the duties of another.   ACT FOR at **act.**

officious *adjective*
Given to intruding in other people's affairs.   MEDDLING *adjective.*

offish *adjective*
1. Affected or tending to be affected with minor health   1. SICKLY.
   problems.
2. Not friendly, sociable, or warm in manner.   2. COOL *adjective.*

offset *verb*
1. To act as an equalizing weight or force to.   1. BALANCE *verb.*
2. To make up for the defects of.   2. COMPENSATE.

offset *noun*
Something to make up for loss or damage.   COMPENSATION.

offshoot *noun*
1. A young stemlike growth arising from a plant.   1. SHOOT *noun.*
2. Something resembling or structurally analogous to a   2. BRANCH *noun.*
   tree branch.
3. A part of a family, tribe, or other group, or of such a 3. BRANCH *noun.*
   group's language, that is believed to stem from a
   common ancestor.

offspring *noun*
1. One descended directly from the same parents or   1. DESCENDANT *noun.*
   ancestors.
2. A group consisting of those descended directly from   2. PROGENY.
   the same parents or ancestors.

off-the-cuff *adjective*
Informal. Spoken, performed, or composed with little or EXTEMPORANEOUS.
no preparation or forethought.

ogle *verb*
To look intently and fixedly.   GAZE *verb.*

ogre *noun*
A perversely bad, cruel, or wicked person.   FIEND.

ogreish *adjective*
Perversely bad, cruel, or wicked.   FIENDISH.

oil *noun*
Informal. Excessive, ingratiating praise.   FLATTERY.

oil *verb*
Informal. To compliment excessively and ingratiatingly. FLATTER.

oily *adjective*
1. Having the qualities of fat.   1. FATTY *adjective.*
2. Affectedly and self-servingly earnest.   2. UNCTUOUS.

O.K. or **OK** *adjective*
Informal. Of moderately good quality but less than   ACCEPTABLE.
excellent.

O.K. or **OK** *adverb*
Informal. It is so; as you say or ask.   YES *adverb.*

okeydoke also **okeydokey** *adverb*
Slang. It is so; as you say or ask.   YES *adverb.*

okeydokey *adverb*   SEE **okeydoke.**

old *adjective*
1. Far along in life or time: *an old lady in her nineties.* 1. *Syns:* advanced, aged, elderly, olden
                                                              (*Archaic & Poetic*), oldish, senior.
                                                              —*Idiom* getting on (*or* along) in years.
2. Belonging to, existing, or occurring in times long   2. *Syns:* ancient, aged, age-old, ante-
   past: *an old castle; an old tale.*   diluvian (*also* antediluvial), antique,
                                                              hoary, olden (*Archaic & Poetic*),
                                                              timeworn, venerable. —*Idioms* old as
                                                              Methuselah, old as time, old as the hills.
                                                              Near-ants: contemporary, current,
                                                              recent.
                                                              Ant: new.

3. Existing or remaining in the same state for an indefinitely long time.

3. CONTINUING.

4. Of a style or method formerly in vogue.

4. OLD-FASHIONED.

5. Skilled or knowledgeable through long practice.

5. EXPERIENCED.

6. Having been such previously.

6. LATE *adjective*.

olden *adjective*
1. *Archaic & Poetic.* Far along in life or time.

1. OLD.

2. *Archaic & Poetic.* Belonging to, existing, or occurring in times long past.

2. OLD.

olden *verb*
To grow old.

AGE *verb*.

older *adjective*
Of greater age than another.

SENIOR *adjective*.

oldfangled *adjective*
Of a style or method formerly in vogue.

OLD-FASHIONED.

old-fashioned *adjective*
Of a style or method formerly in vogue: *an old-fashioned refrigerator.*

Syns: antiquated, antique, archaic, bygone, dated, dowdy, fusty, old, oldfangled, old-time, outdated, outmoded, out-of-date, passé, stale, vintage.
Near-ants: contemporary, current, modernistic, modish, newfangled, recent, timely, trendy, up-to-date.
Ants: modern, new, new-fashioned.

oldish *adjective*
Far along in life or time.

OLD.

old maid *noun*
A person who is too much concerned with being proper, modest, or righteous.

PRUDE.

old-maidish *adjective*
Marked by excessive concern for propriety and good form.

GENTEEL.

oldster *noun*
Informal. An elderly person.

SENIOR *noun*.

old-time *adjective*
Of a style or method formerly in vogue.

OLD-FASHIONED.

old-timer *noun*
1. *Informal.* An elderly person.

1. SENIOR *noun*.

2. *Informal.* One who has had long experience in a given activity or capacity.

2. VETERAN *noun*.

oleaginous *adjective*
1. Having the qualities of fat.

1. FATTY *adjective*.

2. Affectedly and self-servingly earnest.

2. UNCTUOUS.

olfaction *noun*
The sense by which odors are perceived.

SMELL *noun*.

olio *noun*
A collection of various things.

ASSORTMENT.

omen *noun*
A phenomenon that serves as a sign or warning of some future good or evil: *The crash seemed to be an omen of trouble to come.*

Syns: augury, bodement, foretoken, portent, presage, prognostic, prognostication. —*Idiom* writing (or handwriting) on the wall.
Near-syns: forewarning, herald, hint, indication, inkling, mark, precursor, premonition, presentiment, shadow, sign, symptom, token.

ominous *adjective*
Portending future disaster.

FATEFUL.

omission *noun*
Nonperformance of what ought to be done.

FAILURE.

omit *verb*
1. To take or leave out.
2. To not do (something necessary).

1. DROP *verb*.
2. FAIL.

omnipresent *adjective*
Ever present in all places.

UNIVERSAL *adjective*.

omnivorous *adjective*
Having an insatiable appetite for an activity or pursuit.

VORACIOUS.

on-again-off-again *adjective*
Lacking consistency or regularity in quality or performance.

UNEVEN.

once *adjective*
Having been such previously.

LATE *adjective*.

once *adverb*
At a time in the past.

EARLIER.

once-over *noun*
Informal. A thorough search of a place or person.

SHAKEDOWN at **shake down**.

one *adjective*
Alone in a given category.

LONE.

one-dimensional *adjective*
Lacking in intellectual depth or thoroughness.

SUPERFICIAL.

oneness *noun*
1. The state of being entirely whole.
2. The quality or condition of being exactly the same as something else.
3. An identity or coincidence of interests, purposes, or sympathies among the members of a group.
4. The condition of being one.
5. The quality or condition of being unique.

1. COMPLETENESS.
2. SAMENESS.
3. UNITY.
4. UNITY.
5. UNIQUENESS.

onerous *adjective*
Imposing a severe test of bodily or spiritual strength.

BURDENSOME.

one-sided *adjective*
Exhibiting bias.

BIASED.

one-sidedness *noun*
An inclination for or against that inhibits impartial judgment.

BIAS *noun*.

one-time also **onetime** *adjective*
Having been such previously.

LATE *adjective*.

one-up *verb*
Slang. To outmaneuver (an opponent), esp. with the aid of some extra resource.

TRUMP *verb*.

ongoing *noun*
Forward movement.

ADVANCE *noun*.

only *adjective*
1. Without equal or rival.
2. Alone in a given category.

1. UNIQUE.
2. LONE.

only *adverb*
1. To the exclusion of anyone or anything else.
2. Nothing more than.

1. SOLELY.
2. MERELY.

onomatopoeia also **onomatopoësis** *noun*
The formation of words in imitation of sounds.

ECHOISM.

onomatopoeic also **onomatopoetic** *adjective*
Imitating sounds.

ECHOIC.

onomatopoësis *noun*
onomatopoetic *adjective*

SEE **onomatopoeia**.
SEE **onomatopoeic**.

onrush *noun*
The act of attacking.

ATTACK *noun*.

onset *noun*
1. The initial stage of a developmental process.
2. The act of attacking.

1. BIRTH *noun*.
2. ATTACK *noun*.

onslaught *noun*
The act of attacking.

ATTACK *noun*.

on-the-house *adjective*
Slang. Costing nothing.   FREE *adjective*.

onus *noun*
1. A duty or responsibility that is a source of anxiety,   1. BURDEN *noun*.
   worry, or hardship.
2. A difficult or tedious undertaking.   2. TASK *noun*.
3. Responsibility for an error or crime.   3. BLAME *noun*.
4. A mark of discredit or disgrace.   4. STAIN *noun*.

onyx *adjective*
Of the darkest achromatic visual value.   BLACK.

oodle *noun*
Informal. An indeterminately great amount or number.   HEAP *noun*.

oomph *noun*
Slang. A lively, emphatic, eager quality or manner.   SPIRIT.

ooze *verb*
To flow or leak out slowly: *blood oozing from a cut.*   **Syns:** bleed, exude, leach, percolate, seep,
                                                            transpire, transude, weep.

ooze *noun*
A viscous, usu. offensively dirty substance.   SLIME.

oozy *adjective*
Of, pertaining to, or covered with slime.   SLIMY.

ope *verb*
To become or cause to become open.   OPEN *verb*.

open *adjective*
1. Having no protecting or concealing cover: *cooking*   1. **Syns:** exposed, uncovered,
   over an open fire.   unprotected.
2. Tending to incur.   2. LIABLE.
3. Not restricted or confined to few: *open enrollment;*   3. **Syns:** open-door, public, unrestricted.
   open competition.
4. Free from obstructions.   4. CLEAR *adjective*.
5. Available for use: *Only two possibilities remain*   5. **Syns:** accessible, employable,
   open.   operative, practicable, usable.
                                                               Near-ants: inaccessible, inoperable,
                                                               inoperative, unemployable, unusable.
                                                               Ant: closed.
6. Not spoken for or occupied.   6. UNRESERVED.
7. Speaking or spoken freely and sincerely.   7. FRANK.
8. Not affording certainty.   8. AMBIGUOUS.
9. Marked by lack of firm decision or commitment; of   9. INDEFINITE.
   questionable outcome.
10. Ready and willing to receive favorably, as new   10. RECEPTIVE.
    ideas.

open *verb*
1. To become or cause to become open: *The door*   1. **Syns:** ope, unclose, undo.
   suddenly opened. Let's open the package.
2. To move or arrange so as to cover a larger area.   2. SPREAD.
3. To go about the initial step in doing (something).   3. START *verb*.
4. To rid of obstructions.   4. CLEAR *verb*.

open-door *adjective*
Not restricted or confined to few.   OPEN *adjective*.

open-eyed *adjective*
Vigilantly attentive.   ALERT *adjective*.

openhanded *adjective*
Characterized by bounteous giving.   GENEROUS.

openhandedness *noun*
The quality or state of being generous.   GENEROSITY.

opening *noun*
1. The act or process of bringing or being brought into   1. BEGINNING *noun*.
   existence.
2. The initial stage of a developmental process.   2. BIRTH *noun*.

3. An open space allowing passage.

4. A favorable or advantageous combination of circumstances.

open-minded *adjective*
1. Not narrow or conservative in thought, expression, or conduct.
2. Ready and willing to receive favorably, as new ideas.

openness *noun*
The condition of being laid open to something undesirable or injurious.

operate *verb*
1. To control or direct the functioning of: *operate the movie projector.*
2. To control the course of (an activity).
3. To react in a specified way.
4. To function effectively.

operation *noun*
1. The act of putting into play.
2. A specific use.
3. The way in which a machine or other thing performs or functions.

operative *noun*
1. One who labors.
2. A person who secretly observes others to obtain information.

operative *adjective*
1. In action or full operation.
2. Available for use.
3. In effect.

operator *noun*
1. A person who operates a motor vehicle.
2. One who speculates for quick profits.

opiate *noun*
1. A narcotic substance, esp. one that is addictive.
2. Something that induces sleep.

opine *verb*
To have an opinion.

opinion *noun*
Something believed or accepted as true by a person.

opponent *noun*
1. One that opposes another in a battle, contest, controversy, or debate: *legislation that found rabid opponents in Congress.*
2. One who resists.
3. One who is hostile to or opposes the purposes or interests of another.
4. One that competes.

opportune *adjective*
Occurring at a fitting or advantageous time: *Wait for the opportune moment.*

opportunity *noun*
A favorable or advantageous combination of circumstances: *a job with opportunities for advancement.*

3. HOLE *noun.*

4. OPPORTUNITY.

1. BROAD.

2. RECEPTIVE.

EXPOSURE.

1. **Syns:** handle, run, use, work.

2. CONDUCT *verb.*
3. FUNCTION.
4. WORK *verb.*

1. EXERCISE *noun.*
2. APPLICATION.
3. BEHAVIOR.

1. LABORER.
2. SPY *noun.*

1. ACTIVE.
2. OPEN *adjective.*
3. EFFECTIVE.

1. DRIVER.
2. SPECULATOR.

1. DRUG *noun.*
2. SOPORIFIC *noun.*

BELIEVE.

BELIEF.

1. **Syns:** adversary, antagonist, opposer, opposition.

2. RESISTER.
3. ENEMY.

4. COMPETITOR.

Syns: auspicious, favorable, propitious, prosperous, seasonable, timely, well-timed.
Near-ants: improper, inappropriate, inauspicious, unfavorable, unsuitable, untimely.
Ant: inopportune.

Syns: break (*Informal*), chance, occasion, opening, shot (*Informal*).

oppose *verb*
1. To place in opposition or be in opposition to: *oppose a liberal and a conservative in the debate; two armies opposing each other.*

1. **Syns:** counter, match, pit, play off.
—*Idioms* bump heads with, meet head-on, set (*or* be) at odds, set (*or* be) at someone's throat, trade blows (*or* punches).

2. To take a stand against.

2. CONTEST *verb.*

opposed *adjective*
Acting against or in opposition.

OPPOSING.

opposer *noun*
One that opposes another in a battle, contest, controversy, or debate.

OPPONENT.

opposing *adjective*
1. Acting against or in opposition: *opposing forces; opposing interests.*
2. Diametrically opposed.

1. **Syns:** adverse, antagonistic, antipathetic, opposed.
2. OPPOSITE *adjective.*

opposite *adjective*
1. Diametrically opposed: *The democrat and the autocrat hold opposite political views.*

1. **Syns:** antipodal, antipodean, antithetical (*also* antithetic), contradictory, contrary, converse², counter, diametric, opposing, polar, reverse.
Near-ants: akin, alike, analogous, equal, equivalent, like, parallel, related, similar.
Ant: same.

2. Characterized by a natural or innate opposition.

2. CONTRARY *adjective.*

opposite *noun*
That which is diametrically opposed to another: *Love and hate are opposites.*

Syns: antipode, antipole, antithesis, contra, contradictory, contraposition, contrary, converse², counter, polarity, reverse.

opposition *noun*
1. The condition of being in conflict: *the basic opposition of good and evil.*

1. **Syns:** antagonism, antithesis, contradistinction, contraposition, contrariety, contrary, polarity.

2. One that opposes another in a battle, contest, controversy, or debate.

2. OPPONENT.

3. The act of resisting.

3. RESISTANCE.

oppress *verb*
1. To make sad or gloomy.
2. To do a wrong to; treat unjustly.

1. DEPRESS.
2. WRONG *verb.*

oppressive *adjective*
Imposing a severe test of bodily or spiritual strength.

BURDENSOME.

oppressor *noun*
An absolute ruler, esp. one who is harsh and oppressive.

DICTATOR.

opprobrious *adjective*
1. Of, relating to, or characterized by verbal abuse.
2. Meriting or causing shame or dishonor.
3. Worthy of severe disapproval.

1. ABUSIVE.
2. DISGRACEFUL.
3. DEPLORABLE.

opprobrium *noun*
Loss of or damage to one's reputation.

DISGRACE *noun.*

oppugn *verb*
To strive in opposition to.

CONTEND.

opt for *verb*
To make a choice from a number of alternatives.

CHOOSE.

optic *adjective*
Serving, resulting from, or pertaining to the sense of sight.

VISUAL.

optical   *adjective*
Serving, resulting from, or pertaining to the sense of sight.

VISUAL.

optimal   *adjective*
Surpassing all others in quality.

BEST *adjective*.

optimism   *noun*
A tendency to expect a favorable outcome or to dwell on hopeful aspects: *didn't let the bad news shake his optimism.*

Syns: Pollyannaism, sanguineness, sanguinity.

optimist   *noun*
One who expects a favorable outcome or dwells on hopeful aspects: *was an optimist about his team's chances for the pennant.*

Syns: Pangloss, Pollyanna.

optimistic   *adjective*
Expecting a favorable outcome or dwelling on hopeful aspects: *an optimistic estimate of future oil discoveries.*

Syns: Panglossian, Pollyannaish, roseate, rosy, sanguine, upbeat (*Informal*).
—*Idioms* looking on the bright side, looking through rose-colored glasses.
Near-syns: assured, cheerful, confident, merry, mirthful, sunny; hopeful, idealistic, positive.
Ant: pessimistic.

optimum   *adjective*
Surpassing all others in quality.

BEST *adjective*.

option   *noun*
1. The act of choosing.
2. The power or right of choosing.

1. CHOICE *noun*.
2. CHOICE *noun*.

optional   *adjective*
Not compulsory or automatic: *Radios and whitewall tires are optional features in new cars.*

Syns: discretionary, elective, facultative.

opulent   *adjective*
1. Characterized by extravagant, ostentatious magnificence.
2. Given to or marked by unrestrained abundance.

1. LUXURIOUS.
2. PROFUSE.

opus   *noun*
1. Something that is the result of creative effort.
2. An issue of printed material offered for sale or distribution.

1. COMPOSITION.
2. PUBLICATION.

oracle   *noun*
Something that is foretold by or as if by supernatural means.

PROPHECY.

oracular   *adjective*
Of or relating to the foretelling of events by or as if by supernatural means.

PROPHETIC.

oral   *adjective*
1. Expressed or transmitted in speech: *an oral message; home remedies known by oral tradition.*
2. Produced by the voice.

1. *Syns:* spoken, unwritten, verbal, word-of-mouth.
2. VOCAL.

oration   *noun*
A usu. formal oral communication to an audience.

SPEECH.

orator   *noun*
A public speaker: *known as a silver-tongued orator.*

Syn: rhetorician.

oratorical   *adjective*
Of or relating to the art of public speaking: *The candidate's oratorical gifts helped him win.*

Syns: declamatory, elocutionary, rhetorical.

oratory   *noun*
The art of public speaking: *Political leaders must be skilled at oratory.*

Syns: declamation, elocution, rhetoric.

orb *noun*
1. *Archaic.* A closed plane curve everywhere equidistant from a fixed point or something shaped like this.
2. *Poetic.* An organ of vision.

1. CIRCLE *noun*.

2. EYE *noun*.

orbit *noun*
1. A course, process, or journey that ends where it began or repeats itself.
2. A sphere of activity, study, or interest.
3. An area within which something or someone exists, acts, or has influence or power.

1. CIRCLE *noun*.

2. AREA.
3. RANGE *noun*.

orchestrate *verb*
To combine and adapt in order to attain a particular effect.

HARMONIZE.

orchid(s) *noun*
An expression of admiration or congratulation.

COMPLIMENT *noun*.

ordain *verb*
To set forth expressly and authoritatively.

DICTATE *verb*.

ordeal *noun*
A state of pain or anguish that tests one's resiliency and character.

TRIAL *noun*.

order *noun*
1. A way in which things follow each other in space or time: *The child could recite the months of the year in the proper order.*
2. A way or condition of being arranged.
3. Systematic arrangement and design.
4. A state of sound readiness.
5. A number of things placed or occurring one after the other.
6. A division of persons or things by quality, rank, or grade.
7. A class that is defined by the common attribute or attributes possessed by all its members.
8. A group of people united in a relationship and having some interest, activity, or purpose in common.
9. A subdivision of a larger group.
10. Approximate size or amount.
11. An authoritative indication to be obeyed.

1. *Syns:* consecution, procession, sequence, succession.

2. ARRANGEMENT.
3. METHOD.
4. TRIM *noun*.
5. SERIES.

6. CLASS *noun*.

7. KIND².

8. UNION.

9. CLASS *noun*.
10. NEIGHBORHOOD.
11. COMMAND *noun*.

order *verb*
1. To put into a deliberate order.
2. To arrange in an orderly manner.
3. To give orders to.
4. To command in an arrogant manner.

1. ARRANGE.
2. METHODIZE.
3. COMMAND *verb*.
4. BOSS *verb*.

ordering *noun*
A way or condition of being arranged.

ARRANGEMENT.

orderliness *noun*
Systematic arrangement and design.

METHOD.

orderly *adjective*
1. Arranged or proceeding in a set, systematized pattern.
2. In good order or clean condition.

1. METHODICAL.

2. NEAT.

ordinance *noun*
A principle governing the affairs of man within or among political units.

LAW *noun*.

ordinariness *noun*
The quality or condition of being usual.

USUALNESS.

ordinary *adjective*
1. Being of no special quality or type: *an ordinary response; an ordinary rodent.*

1. *Syns:* average, common, commonplace, garden, garden-variety, plain, run-of-the-mill, stock, unexceptional.
   Near-ants: aberrant, divergent, eccentric, excellent, exceptional, notable, noteworthy, remarkable, singular.
   Ant: extraordinary.

2. To be expected.
3. Occurring quite often.
4. Lacking high station or birth.

2. COMMON *adjective.*
3. COMMON *adjective.*
4. LOWLY.

ordinary *noun*
A regular or customary matter, condition, or course of events.

USUAL *noun.*

organ *noun*
1. That by which something is accomplished or some end achieved.
2. A component of government that performs a given function.

1. MEANS.
2. BRANCH *noun.*

organic *adjective*
Produced by nature; not artificial or manmade.

NATURAL *adjective.*

organization *noun*
A group of people united in a relationship and having some interest, activity, or purpose in common.

UNION.

organize *verb*
1. To bring into existence formally.
2. To put into a deliberate order.
3. To arrange in an orderly manner.
4. To assemble, prepare, or put into operation, as for war or a similar emergency.

1. FOUND.
2. ARRANGE.
3. METHODIZE.
4. MOBILIZE.

orgy *noun*
A period of uncontrolled self-indulgence.

BINGE.

orientation *noun*
One's place and direction relative to one's surroundings.

BEARING.

orifice *noun*
An open space allowing passage.

HOLE *noun.*

oriflamme also **auriflamme** *noun*
Fabric used esp. as a symbol.

FLAG[1] *noun.*

origin *noun*
1. A point of origination: *The word "vodka" is of Russian origin. The origin of the American Revolution lay in France.*
2. The initial stage of a developmental process.
3. One's ancestors or their character.

1. *Syns:* derivation, fount, fountain, fountainhead, provenance, provenience, root[1], rootstock, source, spring, well[1].
2. BIRTH *noun.*
3. ANCESTRY.

original *adjective*
1. Not derived from something else: *an original play, not an adaptation.*
2. Preceding all others in time.
3. Not counterfeit or copied.
4. Characterized by or productive of new things or new ideas.
5. Showing marked departure from previous practice.
6. Arising from or going to the root or source.

1. *Syns:* primary, prime, primitive.
2. FIRST *adjective.*
3. AUTHENTIC.
4. INVENTIVE.
5. NEW *adjective.*
6. RADICAL *adjective.*

original *noun*
1. A first form from which varieties arise or imitations are made: *Copies of the portrait lack the vivid colors of the original.*

1. *Syns:* archetype, master, protoplast (*Rare*), prototype.

2. A person who is appealingly odd or curious.   **2.** CHARACTER.

originality   *noun*
  1. The power or ability to invent.   **1.** INVENTION.
  2. The quality of being novel.   **2.** NOVELTY.

originate   *verb*
  1. To come into being.   **1.** BEGIN.
  2. To begin to appear or develop.   **2.** DAWN *verb*.
  3. To cause to come into existence.   **3.** PRODUCE.
  4. To have as a source.   **4.** STEM *verb*.
  5. To have as one's home or place of origin.   **5.** COME.
  6. To bring into existence formally.   **6.** FOUND.
  7. To bring into currency, use, fashion, or practice.   **7.** INTRODUCE.

originator   *noun*
One that creates, founds, or originates: *the originator of*   **Syns:** architect, author, creator, father,
the atomic bomb; the originator of the new company.   founder[1], inventor, maker, patriarch.

orison   *noun*
A formula of words used in praying.   PRAYER.

ornament   *verb*
  1. To furnish with decorations.   **1.** ADORN.
  2. To endow with beauty and elegance by way of a   **2.** GRACE *verb*.
     notable addition.

ornament   *noun*
Something that adorns.   ADORNMENT.

ornamentation   *noun*
Something that adorns.   ADORNMENT.

ornate   *adjective*
Elaborately and heavily ornamented: *an ornate hall*   **Syns:** baroque, flamboyant, florid, rococo.
with a marble portal, arched ceilings, wrought-iron   **Near-syns:** elaborate, eloquent, grandiose,
balconies, and plentiful statuary.   luxuriant, luxurious, opulent, pretentious,
                                                                     sumptuous.
                                                                     Near-ants: chaste, Spartan.
                                                                     Ant: austere.

ornery   *adjective*
Given to acting in opposition to others.   CONTRARY *adjective*.

orotund   *adjective*
  1. Having or producing a full, deep, or rich sound.   **1.** RESONANT.
  2. Characterized by language that is elevated and   **2.** SONOROUS.
     sometimes pompous in style.

orthodox   *adjective*
  1. Adhering to beliefs or practices approved by   **1.** **Syns:** canonical, received, sanctioned,
     authority or tradition: *held an orthodox view of*   time-honored.
     papal infallibility; an orthodox putting stance.   **Near-ants:** heretical, heterodox,
                                                                                   unacknowledged, unauthoritative,
                                                                                   unauthorized, uncanonical,
                                                                                   unsanctioned.
                                                                                   Ant: unorthodox.

  2. Conforming to established practice or standards.   **2.** CONVENTIONAL.
  3. Generally approved or agreed upon.   **3.** ACCEPTED.
  4. Strongly favoring retention of the existing order.   **4.** CONSERVATIVE *adjective*.

oscillate   *verb*
To move rhythmically back and forth suspended or as if   SWING *verb*.
suspended from above.

osculate   *verb*
To touch or caress with the lips, esp. as a sign of   KISS *verb*.
passion or affection.

ossuary   *noun*
A burial place or receptacle for human remains.   GRAVE[1].

ostensible   *adjective*
Appearing as such but not necessarily so.   APPARENT.

ostentation   *noun*
Boastful self-importance.   PRETENTIOUSNESS.

ostentatious *adjective*
Marked by outward, often extravagant display.   SHOWY.

ostracism *noun*
Enforced removal from one's native country by official   EXILE *noun.*
decree.

ostracize *verb*
1. To exclude from normal social or professional   1. BLACKBALL.
activities.
2. To force to leave a country or place by official   2. BANISH.
decree.

other *adjective*
Being an addition.   ADDITIONAL.

otherworldly *adjective*
1. Given to daydreams or reverie.   1. DREAMY.
2. Of or concerned with the spirit rather than the body   2. SPIRITUAL.
or material things.

otiose *adjective*
Lacking value, use, or substance.   EMPTY *adjective.*

ounce *noun*
1. A tiny amount.   1. BIT[1].
2. The least bit.   2. DAMN *noun.*

oust *verb*
To put out by force.   EJECT.

ouster *noun*
The act of ejecting or the state of being ejected.   EJECTION.

out *adjective*
Informal. In a state of sleep.   SLEEPING.

out *verb*
To be made public.   COME OUT at **come.**

outage *noun*
A cessation of proper mechanical functions.   FAILURE.

out-and-out *adjective*
Completely such, without qualification or exception.   UTTER[2].

outbreak *noun*
1. A sudden increase in something, as the occurrence   1. *Syns:* epidemic, plague, rash[2].
of a disease: *an outbreak of influenza.*
2. A sudden, violent expression, as of emotion.   2. OUTBURST.
3. The act of emerging violently from limits or   3. ERUPTION.
restraints.

outburst *noun*
1. A sudden, violent expression, as of emotion: *calmed*   1. *Syns:* access, blowup, burst, eruption,
down and apologized for his intemperate outburst.   explosion, fit, flare-up, gust, outbreak.
2. The act of emerging violently from limits or   2. ERUPTION.
restraints.

outcome *noun*
Something brought about by a cause.   EFFECT *noun.*

outcry *noun*
1. A sudden, sharp utterance.   1. EXCLAMATION.
2. Offensively loud and insistent utterances, esp. of   2. VOCIFERATION.
disapproval.

outdate *verb*
To make or become obsolete.   OBSOLESCE.

outdated *adjective*
Of a style or method formerly in vogue.   OLD-FASHIONED.

outdo *verb*
To be greater or better than.   SURPASS.

outermost *adjective*
Most distant or remote from a center.   EXTREME *adjective.*

outfit *noun*
1. Things needed for a task, journey, or other purpose: *Goggles are an essential part of a skier's outfit.*

1. *Syns:* accouterments, apparatus, equipment, gear, materials, materiel *or* matériel, paraphernalia, rig, tackle, turnout.

2. A set or style of clothing.
3. A commercial organization.

2. DRESS *noun.*
3. COMPANY *noun.*

outfit *verb*
To supply what is needed for some activity or purpose.

FURNISH.

outgoing *adjective*
Disposed to be open, sociable, and talkative: *a friendly and outgoing young man.*

Syns: communicable, communicative, expansive, extroverted, gregarious, unreserved.
Near-ants: aloof, bashful, detached, diffident, indifferent, introverted, reserved, restrained, retiring, shy.

outgrowth *noun*
Something derived from another.

DERIVATIVE *noun.*

outlander *noun*
A person coming from another country.

FOREIGNER.

outlandish *adjective*
Archaic. Of, from, or characteristic of another place or part of the world.

FOREIGN.

outlast *verb*
To live, exist, or remain longer than: *A stone house will outlast any number of wooden ones.*

Syns: outlive, outwear, survive.

outlaw *verb*
To refuse to allow.

FORBID.

outlawed *adjective*
Prohibited by law.

ILLEGAL.

outlay *noun*
Something expended to obtain a benefit or desired result.

COST *noun.*

outlay *verb*
To distribute (money) as payment.

SPEND.

outlet *noun*
1. An open space allowing passage.
2. A retail establishment where merchandise is sold.

1. HOLE *noun.*
2. STORE *noun.*

outline *noun*
1. A line marking and shaping the outer form of an object: *We saw the outline of a deer among the trees.*
2. A preliminary plan or version, as of a written work.

1. *Syns:* contour, delineation, profile, silhouette.
2. DRAFT *noun.*

outline *verb*
To draw up a preliminary plan or version of.

DRAFT *verb.*

outlive *verb*
To live, exist, or remain longer than.

OUTLAST.

outlook *noun*
1. That which is or can be seen.
2. A high structure commanding a wide view.
3. The position from which something is observed or considered.
4. A frame of mind affecting one's thoughts or behavior.
5. The act of predicting.
6. The likelihood of a given event occurring.
7. Chance of success or advancement.

1. VIEW *noun.*
2. LOOKOUT.
3. POINT OF VIEW.
4. POSTURE *noun.*
5. PREDICTION.
6. CHANCE *noun.*
7. FUTURE *noun.*

outlying *adjective*
Distant from a center of activity.

BACK *adjective.*

outmaneuver *verb*
To get the better of by cleverness or cunning.

OUTWIT.

outmatch *verb*
To be greater or better than.   SURPASS.

outmoded *adjective*
Of a style or method formerly in vogue.   OLD-FASHIONED.

outmost *adjective*
Most distant or remote from a center.   EXTREME *adjective*.

out-of-date *adjective*
1. Of a style or method formerly in vogue.   1. OLD-FASHIONED.
2. Quite outmoded.   2. TACKY[2].

out-of-line *adjective*
Informal. Misbehaving, often in a troublesome way.   NAUGHTY.

out-of-the-way *adjective*
Far from centers of human population.   REMOTE.

output *noun*
The amount or quantity produced.   YIELD *noun*.

outrage *noun*
1. A monstrous offense or evil: *the outrages committed in the Nazi death camps.*   1. *Syns:* atrocity, enormity, monstrosity.
2. Something that offends one's sense of propriety, fairness, or justice.   2. CRIME.
3. The action or result of inflicting loss or pain.   3. HARM *noun*.
4. An act that offends a person's sense of pride or dignity.   4. INDIGNITY.

outrage *verb*
1. To do a wrong to; treat unjustly.   1. WRONG *verb*.
2. To cause resentment or hurt by callous, rude behavior.   2. INSULT *verb*.
3. To compel (another) to participate in or submit to a sexual act.   3. RAPE.

outrageous *adjective*
1. Disgracefully and grossly offensive: *outrageous violations of the Geneva Convention.*   1. *Syns:* atrocious, crying, enormous (*Archaic*), flagrant, heinous, monstrous, scandalous, shocking.
Near-syns: egregious, gross, insidious, nefarious, notorious, noxious, vile, villainous, wicked.
2. Beyond all reason: *charged an outrageous sum to repair the clock.*   2. *Syns:* monstrous, obscene, preposterous, ridiculous, shocking, unconscionable, unreasonable. —*Idioms* out of bounds, out of sight.
Near-ants: acceptable, bearable, endurable, normal, reasonable, supportable, tolerable, understandable.

outrageousness *noun*
The quality or state of being flagrant.   FLAGRANCY.

outright *adjective*
Completely such, without qualification or exception.   UTTER[2].

outset *noun*
The initial stage of a developmental process.   BIRTH *noun*.

outshine *verb*
To be greater or better than.   SURPASS.

outside *adjective*
Small in degree, esp. of probability.   REMOTE.

outside *noun*
The greatest quantity or highest degree attainable.   MAXIMUM *noun*.

outsider *noun*
A person coming from another country.   FOREIGNER.

outskirts *noun*
The periphery of a city or town.   SKIRTS.

outsmart *verb*
To get the better of by cleverness or cunning.   OUTWIT.

outspoken *adjective*
Speaking or spoken without reserve: *She's outspoken but not rude.*

Syns: free, free-speaking, free-spoken, vocal.

outstanding *adjective*
1. Far above others in quality or excellence: *outstanding athletes; outstanding accomplishments.*

1. *Syns:* exceptional, magnificent, preeminent (*also* preeminent, preëminent), standout, surpassing, towering, transcendent.
   Near-ants: atrocious, awful, deplorable, dismal, inferior, mediocre, poor, substandard; base, lowly.

2. Most important, influential, or significant.
3. Readily attracting notice.
4. Owed as a debt.

2. PRIMARY.
3. NOTICEABLE.
4. DUE *adjective.*

outstretch *verb*
1. To extend, esp. an appendage.
2. To move or arrange so as to cover a larger area.

1. REACH.
2. SPREAD *verb.*

outstrip *verb*
To be greater or better than.

SURPASS.

outthink *verb*
To get the better of by cleverness or cunning.

OUTWIT.

outward *adjective*
Appearing as such but not necessarily so.

APPARENT.

outwear *verb*
To live, exist, or remain longer than.

OUTLAST.

outweigh *verb*
To make up for the defects of.

COMPENSATE.

outwit *verb*
To get the better of by cleverness or cunning: *The police outwitted the master criminal.*

Syns: outmaneuver, outsmart, outthink, overreach.
Near-syns: bamboozle (*Informal*), dupe, hoax, hoodwink, outfox, outguess, trick.

oval *adjective*
Resembling an egg in shape: *an oval table; an oval face.*

Syns: ovate, oviform, ovoid (*also* ovoidal).

ovate *adjective*
Resembling an egg in shape.

OVAL.

ovation *noun*
Approval expressed by clapping.

APPLAUSE.

over *adjective*
Being at a height or level above another.

HIGHER.

over *adverb*
1. Too much.
2. To an end or conclusion.
3. From one end to the other.

1. UNDULY.
2. THROUGH *adverb.*
3. THROUGH *adverb.*

overabundance *noun*
A condition of going or being beyond what is needed, desired, or appropriate.

EXCESS *noun.*

overage *noun*
An amount or quantity beyond what is needed, desired, or appropriate.

SURPLUS *noun.*

overall *adjective*
Covering a wide scope.

GENERAL.

overbearing *adjective*
1. Overly convinced of one's own superiority and importance.
2. Tending to dictate.

1. ARROGANT.
2. DICTATORIAL.

overbearingness *noun*
The quality of being arrogant.

ARROGANCE.

overblown *adjective*
1. Having too much flesh.
2. Filled up with or as if with something insubstantial.

1. FAT *adjective.*
2. INFLATED.

overcast *verb*
1. To extend over the surface of.
2. To make dim or indistinct.

    1. COVER *verb*.
    2. OBSCURE *verb*.

overcharge *verb*
1. To exploit (another) by charging too much for something.
2. To make (something) seem greater than is actually the case.

    1. SKIN *verb*.

    2. EXAGGERATE.

overcome *verb*
1. To win a victory over, as in battle or a competition.
2. To get the better of.
3. To affect deeply or completely, as with emotion.

    1. DEFEAT *verb*.
    2. TRIUMPH *verb*.
    3. OVERWHELM.

overconfidence *noun*
Excessive and arrogant self-confidence.

    PRESUMPTION.

overconfident *adjective*
Having or exhibiting excessive and arrogant self-confidence.

    PRESUMPTUOUS.

overcritical *adjective*
Inclined to judge too severely.

    CRITICAL.

overdue *adjective*
Not being on time.

    LATE *adjective*.

overflow *verb*
To flow over completely.

    FLOOD *verb*.

  overflow *noun*
1. An amount or quantity beyond what is needed, desired, or appropriate.
2. An abundant, usu. overwhelming flow.

    1. SURPLUS *noun*.

    2. FLOOD *noun*.

overflowing *adjective*
1. Full of animation and activity.
2. Full to the point of flowing over.

    1. ALIVE.
    2. BIG *adjective*.

overhang *verb*
1. To curve outward past the normal or usual limit.
2. To incline downward or over.
3. To be imminent.

    1. BULGE *verb*.
    2. HANG *verb*.
    3. THREATEN.

overhanging *adjective*
1. Expressing, indicating, or warning of an impending danger or misfortune.
2. Characterized by or expressive of a foreboding somberness.

    1. THREATENING.

    2. DARK *adjective*.

overhaul *verb*
1. To restore to proper condition or functioning.
2. To catch up with and move past.

    1. FIX *verb*.
    2. PASS *verb*.

  overhaul *noun*
A thorough or drastic reorganization.

    SHAKEUP at **shake up.**

overindulge *verb*
To treat with indulgence and often overtender care.

    BABY *verb*.

overindulgence *noun*
Immoderate indulgence, as in food or drink.

    EXCESS *noun*.

overjoyed *adjective*
Feeling great delight and joy.

    ELATED.

overlay *verb*
To extend over the surface of.

    COVER *verb*.

overlong *adjective*
Extending tediously beyond a standard duration.

    LONG[1] *adjective*.

overlook *verb*
1. To rise above, esp. so as to afford a view of.
2. To view broadly or from a height.
3. To direct and watch over the work and performance of others.

    1. DOMINATE.
    2. SURVEY *verb*.
    3. SUPERVISE.

  overlook *noun*
A high structure commanding a wide view.

    LOOKOUT.

overmuch *adjective*
Exceeding a normal or reasonable limit. EXCESSIVE.

overmuch *noun*
An amount or quantity beyond what is needed, desired, SURPLUS *noun*.
or appropriate.

overmuch *adverb*
Too much. UNDULY.

overpower *verb*
1. To render totally ineffective by decisive defeat. 1. OVERWHELM.
2. To affect deeply or completely, as with emotion. 2. OVERWHELM.

overpowering *adjective*
Awesomely or forbiddingly intense. TOWERING.

overreach *verb*
1. To go beyond the limits of. 1. EXCEED.
2. To get the better of by cleverness or cunning. 2. OUTWIT.

overrule *verb*
To exercise the authority of a sovereign. GOVERN.

overrun *verb*
1. To go beyond the limits of. 1. EXCEED.
2. To enter in order to attack, plunder, destroy, or 2. INVADE.
conquer.

overrun *noun*
An amount or quantity beyond what is needed, desired, SURPLUS *noun*.
or appropriate.

oversee *verb*
1. To view broadly or from a height. 1. SURVEY *verb*.
2. To direct and watch over the work and performance 2. SUPERVISE.
of others.

overseer *noun*
Someone who directs and supervises workers. BOSS *noun*.

overshadow *verb*
To make dim or indistinct. OBSCURE *verb*.

oversight *noun*
An act or instance of neglecting. NEGLECT *noun*.

oversize also **oversized** *adjective*
Extremely large; having great mass. BULKY.

oversized *adjective* SEE **oversize**.

overslaugh *verb*
1. To stop or prevent passage of. 1. OBSTRUCT.
2. To interfere with the progress of. 2. HINDER.

oversleep *verb*
To sleep longer than intended. SLEEP IN at **sleep**.

overstate *verb*
To make (something) seem greater than is actually the EXAGGERATE.
case.

overstatement *noun*
The act or an instance of exaggerating. EXAGGERATION.

overstep *verb*
To go beyond the limits of. EXCEED.

overstock *noun*
An amount or quantity beyond what is needed, desired, SURPLUS *noun*.
or appropriate.

oversupply *noun*
An amount or quantity beyond what is needed, desired, SURPLUS *noun*.
or appropriate.

overtake *verb*
1. To come up even with (another). 1. CATCH UP at **catch**.
2. To catch up with and move past. 2. PASS *verb*.

overthrow *verb*
1. To bring about the downfall of: *Religious zealots* 1. *Syns:* bring down, overturn, subvert,
succeeded in overthrowing the government. topple, tumble, unhorse.

2. To turn or cause to turn from a vertical or horizontal position.

2. OVERTURN.

overthrow *noun*
The act of defeating or the condition of being defeated.

DEFEAT *noun.*

overture *noun*
A short section of preliminary remarks.

INTRODUCTION.

overture(s) *noun*
Preliminary actions intended to elicit a favorable response.

ADVANCES.

overturn *verb*
1. To turn or cause to turn from a vertical or horizontal position: *Rough seas overturned several sailboats.*

1. **Syns:** knock over, overthrow, topple, turn over, upset.

2. To bring about the downfall of.

2. OVERTHROW.

overview *noun*
A general or comprehensive view or treatment.

SURVEY *noun.*

overweening *adjective*
Overly convinced of one's own superiority and importance.

ARROGANT.

overweight *adjective*
Having too much flesh.

FAT *adjective.*

overwhelm *verb*
1. To render totally ineffective by decisive defeat: *All resistance was overwhelmed by the blitzkrieg attack. Our team overwhelmed the visitors 20 to 1.*

1. **Syns:** annihilate (*Informal*), blast (*Slang*), clobber (*Slang*), cream (*Slang*), drub, massacre (*Informal*), overpower, shellac (*Slang*), smear (*Slang*), smother, steamroller, thrash, trounce, wallop (*Informal*).

2. To affect deeply or completely, as with emotion: *Grief overwhelmed the bereaved parents.*

2. **Syns:** crush, engulf, overcome, overpower, prostrate.

3. To affect as if by an outpouring of water.

3. FLOOD *verb.*

overwhelming *adjective*
1. Awesomely or forbiddingly intense.
2. Of such a character as to overwhelm.

1. TOWERING.
2. STAGGERING.

oviform *adjective*
Resembling an egg in shape.

OVAL.

ovoid also **ovoidal** *adjective*
Resembling an egg in shape.

OVAL.

ovoidal *adjective*

SEE **ovoid.**

owed *adjective*
Owed as a debt.

DUE *adjective.*

owing *adjective*
Owed as a debt.

DUE *adjective.*

own *verb*
1. To keep at one's disposal.
2. To recognize, often reluctantly, the reality or truth of.

1. HAVE.
2. ACKNOWLEDGE.

owner *noun*
A person who has legal title to property: *the owner of a large estate.*

Syns: holder, master, possessor, proprietor.

ownership *noun*
1. Legal right to the possession of a thing: *Ownership of the factory passed to the nephew.*
2. The fact of possessing.

1. **Syns:** dominion, possession, proprietorship, title.
2. POSSESSION.

ox *noun*
A large, ungainly, and dull-witted person.

LUMP[1] *noun.*

P

pablum *noun*
That which sustains the mind or spirit.   FOOD.

pace *noun*
Rate of motion or performance.   SPEED *noun*.
pace *verb*
To go on foot.   WALK *verb*.

pacific also **pacifical** *adjective*
Inclined or disposed to peace; not quarrelsome or
unruly.   PEACEABLE.

pacifist also **pacifistic** *adjective*
Inclined or disposed to peace; not quarrelsome or
unruly.   PEACEABLE.

pacifistic *adjective*   SEE **pacifist.**

pacify *verb*
To ease the anger or agitation of: *She managed to
pacify the irate customer by offering a full refund.*
Syns: appease, assuage, calm, calm down,
conciliate, dulcify, gentle, milden, mollify,
placate, propitiate, soften, soothe, sweeten.
—Idiom pour oil on troubled waters.
Near-syns: allay, alleviate, mitigate,
moderate, relieve, smooth, temper.
Ant: anger.

pack *verb*
1. To fill to excess by compressing or squeezing tightly.   1. CROWD *verb*.
2. To make or become full; put into as much as can be
held.   2. FILL.
3. *Informal.* To hold on one's person.   3. CARRY *verb*.
pack *noun*
1. An organized group of criminals, hoodlums, or
wrongdoers.   1. GANG.
2. A great deal.   2. HEAP *noun*.

package *verb*
To cover and tie (something), as with paper and string.   WRAP *verb*.

packed *adjective*
1. Having all parts near to each other.   1. THICK *adjective*.
2. Completely filled.   2. FULL.

pact *noun*
1. An act or state of agreeing between parties
regarding a course of action.   1. AGREEMENT.
2. A formal, usu. written settlement between nations.   2. TREATY.

paddy *noun*
Slang. A member of a law-enforcement agency.   POLICEMAN.

pain *noun*
1. A sensation of physical discomfort occurring as the
result of disease or injury: *a pain in my left ankle.*   1. **Syns:** ache, misery (*Informal*), pang,
smart, soreness, stitch, throe, twinge.
2. A state of physical or mental suffering.   2. DISTRESS *noun*.
3. One that makes another totally miserable by
causing sharp pain and irritation.   3. THORN *noun*.
pain *verb*
1. To have or cause a feeling of physical pain or
discomfort.   1. HURT *verb*.
2. To cause suffering or painful sorrow to.   2. DISTRESS *verb*.

painful *adjective*
1. Marked by, causing, or experiencing physical pain: *a
painful back injury.*   1. **Syns:** aching, afflictive, hurtful,
smarting, sore.
Near-syns: agonizing, excruciating,

hurting, jabbing, piercing, sharp, shooting, tormenting, torturous.
Ant: painless.

2. Difficult to accept.

2. BITTER.

pains *noun*
1. Attentiveness to detail.
2. The use of energy to do something.

1. THOROUGHNESS.
2. EFFORT.

painstaking *adjective*
Showing or marked by attentiveness to all aspects or details.

CAREFUL.

painstaking *noun*
Attentiveness to detail.

THOROUGHNESS.

pair *noun*
1. Two persons united, as by marriage: *toasted the happy pair.*
2. Two items of the same kind together.

1. ***Syns:*** couple, duo, twosome.

2. COUPLE *noun.*

paired *adjective*
Consisting of two identical or similar related things, parts, or elements.

TWIN *adjective.*

pal *noun*
Informal. One who keeps company with another.

ASSOCIATE *noun.*

paladin *noun*
A person revered esp. for noble courage.

HERO.

palatial *adjective*
Characterized by extravagant, ostentatious magnificence.

LUXURIOUS.

palaver *noun*
Incessant and usu. inconsequential talk.

CHATTER *noun.*

palaver *verb*
To talk volubly, persistently, and usu. inconsequentially.

CHATTER *verb.*

pale *adjective*
1. Lacking color: *a pale face.*

1. ***Syns:*** ashen, ashy, blanched, bloodless, cadaverous, colorless, livid, lurid, pallid, pasty, sallow, wan, waxen.
Near-syns: doughy, deathlike, ghastly, ghostly, gray, hoary, sick, sickly, white.

2. Being weak in quality or substance: *a pale, uninspiring campaign speech.*

2. ***Syns:*** anemic, bloodless, pallid, waterish, watery.
Near-ants: effective, effectual, strong, substantial; bright, colorful, spirited.
Ant: brilliant.

3. Of a moderately white color.

3. FAIR *adjective.*

pale *verb*
To lose normal coloration; turn pale: *He paled when he read the telegram.*

Syns: blanch (*also* blench), bleach, etiolate, wan.

palinode *verb*
To disavow (something previously written or said) irrevocably and usu. formally.

RETRACT.

palinode *noun*
A formal statement of disavowal.

RETRACTION.

pall *verb*
To fatigue with dullness or tedium.

BORE *verb.*

palliate *verb*
1. To make less severe or more bearable.
2. To give a deceptively attractive appearance to.
3. To conceal or make light of a fault or offense.

1. RELIEVE.
2. COLOR *verb.*
3. EXTENUATE.

pallid *adjective*
1. Being weak in quality or substance.
2. Lacking color.

1. PALE *adjective.*
2. PALE *adjective.*

palm off *verb*
To offer or put into circulation (an inferior or spurious item). — FOIST.

palp *verb*
To bring into contact with, esp. by means of the hands or fingers, so as to give or receive a physical sensation. — TOUCH *verb*.

palpability *noun*
The quality or condition of being discernible by touch. — TANGIBILITY.

palpable *adjective*
1. Discernible by touch. — 1. TANGIBLE.
2. Capable of being noticed or apprehended mentally. — 2. PERCEPTIBLE.

palpate *verb*
To bring into contact with, esp. by means of the hands or fingers, so as to give or receive a physical sensation. — TOUCH *verb*.

palpation *noun*
An act of touching. — TOUCH *noun*.

palpitate *verb*
To make rhythmic contractions, sounds, or movements. — BEAT *verb*.

palter *verb*
1. To stray from truthfulness or sincerity. — 1. EQUIVOCATE.
2. To argue about the terms of, as of a sale. — 2. HAGGLE.

paltriness *noun*
Contemptible unimportance. — PETTINESS.

paltry *adjective*
1. Of decidedly inferior quality. — 1. SHODDY.
2. Not broad or elevated in scope or understanding. — 2. NARROW.
3. Contemptibly unimportant. — 3. PETTY.

pamper *verb*
To treat with indulgence and often overtender care. — BABY *verb*.

pan *verb*
Informal. To find fault with. — BLAME *verb*.

pan out *verb*
Informal. To turn out well. — SUCCEED.

pan *noun*
Slang. The front surface of the head. — FACE *noun*.

panacea *noun*
Something believed to cure all human disorders: *Money is not the panacea for human suffering.* — *Syns:* catholicon, cure-all, heal-all.

pandemic *adjective*
So pervasive and all-inclusive as to exist in or affect the whole world. — UNIVERSAL *adjective*.

pandemonium *noun*
Sounds or a sound, esp. when loud, confused, or disagreeable. — NOISE *noun*.

panegyrize *verb*
1. To pay tribute or homage to. — 1. HONOR *verb*.
2. To honor (God) in religious worship. — 2. PRAISE *verb*.

pang *noun*
1. A sensation of physical discomfort occurring as the result of disease or injury. — 1. PAIN *noun*.
2. A sudden, sharp, painful feeling. — 2. PRICK *noun*.

Pangloss *noun*
One who expects a favorable outcome or dwells on hopeful aspects. — OPTIMIST.

Panglossian *adjective*
Expecting a favorable outcome or dwelling on hopeful aspects. — OPTIMISTIC.

panhandle *verb*
Slang. To ask or ask for as charity. — BEG.

panhandler *noun*
Slang. One who begs habitually or for a living. — BEGGAR *noun*.

panic *noun*
1. Great agitation and anxiety caused by the expectation or the realization of danger.
2. *Slang.* Something or someone uproariously funny or absurd.

1. FEAR *noun.*

2. SCREAM *noun.*

panic *verb*
To fill with fear.

FRIGHTEN.

panoply *noun*
An impressive or ostentatious exhibition.

DISPLAY *noun.*

pan out *verb*

SEE **pan.**

pant *verb*
1. To breathe hard: *was panting after climbing six flights.*
2. To utter in a breathless manner.
3. To have a strong longing for.

1. *Syns:* blow[1], gasp, heave, huff, puff.

2. GASP.

3. DESIRE *verb.*

pap *noun*
That which sustains the mind or spirit.

FOOD.

paper *noun*
A relatively brief discourse written esp. as an exercise.

COMPOSITION.

pappy *adjective*
Yielding easily to pressure or weight; not firm.

SOFT.

par *noun*
1. The state of being equivalent.
2. Something, as a type, number, quantity, or degree, that represents a midpoint between extremes on a scale of valuation.

1. EQUIVALENCE.

2. AVERAGE *noun.*

parade *noun*
1. A formal military inspection.
2. An impressive or ostentatious exhibition.

1. REVIEW *noun.*

2. DISPLAY *noun.*

parade *verb*
To make a public and usu. ostentatious show of.

DISPLAY *verb.*

paradigm *noun*
One that is worthy of imitation or duplication.

MODEL *noun.*

paradigmatic *adjective*
Having the nature of, constituting, or serving as a type.

TYPICAL.

paradisaical or **paradisiacal** *adjective*
Of or relating to heaven.

HEAVENLY.

paradise *noun*
A state of elated bliss.

HEAVEN.

paradisiacal *adjective*

SEE **paradisaical.**

paragon *noun*
A person or thing so excellent as to have no equal or match.

NONPAREIL *noun.*

paragraph *noun*
A usu. brief detail of news or information.

ITEM.

parallel *adjective*
1. Lying in the same plane and not intersecting: *Railroad tracks are parallel.*
2. Possessing the same or almost the same characteristics.

1. *Syns:* coextensive, collateral, concurrent. —*Idiom* side by side.

2. LIKE[2].

parallel *noun*
Something closely resembling or analogous to something else: *The rank of army captain is the parallel of the rank of navy lieutenant.*

Syns: analogon, analogue, congener, correlate, correspondent, counterpart, countertype, match.

parallel *verb*
1. To be equal or alike.
2. To represent as similar.

1. COMPARE.

2. LIKEN.

paralyze *verb*
1. To render helpless, as by emotion: *Sudden fear paralyzed him.*

1. ***Syns:*** benumb, numb, stun, stupefy.
—*Idioms* cut the ground from under, knock the props out from under.
Near-syns: appall, bemuse, daze, dazzle, dismay, petrify; astonish, astound, flabbergast; bewilder, confound, dumbfound.
Ant: galvanize.

2. To render powerless or motionless by inflicting severe injury.

2. DISABLE.

paralyzed *adjective*
Unable to manage for oneself.

HELPLESS.

paramount *adjective*
Most important, influential, or significant.

PRIMARY.

paramour *noun*
A person's regular sexual partner.

LOVER.

paraphernalia *noun*
Things needed for a task, journey, or other purpose.

OUTFIT *noun.*

paraphrase *noun*
A restating of something in other, esp. simpler, words: *will write a paraphrase of the Latin text.*

Syns: rendering, restatement, rewording, translation, version.

paraphrase *verb*
To express the meaning of in other, esp. simpler, words: *paraphrased a passage from the Bible.*

Syns: rephrase, restate, reword, translate.

parasite *noun*
One who depends on another for support without reciprocating: *a king surrounded by parasites.*

Syns: barnacle, bloodsucker, freeloader (*Slang*), hanger-on, leech, sponge.

parasitic also **parasitical** *adjective*
Of or characteristic of a parasite: *leads a parasitic existence.*

Syns: bloodsucking, freeloading (*Slang*).

parboil *verb*
To cook (food) in liquid heated to the point of steaming.

BOIL *verb.*

parcel *noun*
1. One of the parts into which something is divided.
2. A piece of land.

1. DIVISION.
2. LOT *noun.*

parcel *verb*
To give out in portions or shares.

DISTRIBUTE.

parch *verb*
To make or become free of moisture.

DRY *verb.*

parched *adjective*
1. Having little or no liquid or moisture.
2. Needing or desiring drink.

1. DRY *adjective.*
2. THIRSTY.

pardon *verb*
To grant forgiveness for a fault, offense, or injury.

FORGIVE.

pardon *noun*
The act or an instance of forgiving.

FORGIVENESS.

pardonable *adjective*
Admitting of forgiveness or pardon: *a pardonable offense; spoke with pardonable pride.*

Syns: condonable, excusable, forgivable, venial.

pare *verb*
To decrease, as in length or amount, by or as if by severing or excising.

CUT BACK.

parent *verb*
To cause to come into existence.

PRODUCE.

parentage *noun*
One's ancestors or their character.

ANCESTRY.

parenthesis *noun*
1. The act of digressing.
2. An instance of digressing.

1. DIGRESSION.
2. DIGRESSION.

parenthetic also **parenthetical** *adjective*
Marked by or given to digression.   DIGRESSIVE.

parity *noun*
The state of being equivalent.   EQUIVALENCE.

parlance *noun*
Choice of words and the way in which they are used.   WORDING.

parley *noun*
1. Spoken exchange.   1. CONVERSATION.
2. The act or process of dealing with another to reach   2. TALK *noun*.
   an agreement.
3. An exchange of views in an attempt to reach a   3. DELIBERATION.
   decision.

  parley *verb*
  To meet and exchange views to reach a decision.   CONFER.

parlous *adjective*
Archaic. Involving possible risk, loss, or injury.   DANGEROUS.

parochial *adjective*
Having the restricted outlook often characteristic of   LOCAL *adjective*.
geographic isolation.

parody *noun*
1. A usu. amusing caricature of another.   1. TAKEOFF at **take off**.
2. A false, derisive, or impudent imitation of   2. MOCKERY.
   something.

  parody *verb*
  To copy (the manner or expression of another), esp. in   IMITATE.
  an exaggerated or mocking way.

paroxysm *noun*
1. A condition of anguished struggle and disorder.   1. THROE.
2. A violent, excruciating seizure of pain.   2. THROE.

parrot *noun*
One who mindlessly imitates another.   ECHO *noun*.

  parrot *verb*
  To copy (another) slavishly.   ECHO *verb*.

parry *verb*
To turn or drive away: *He stood, sword in hand, ready*   ***Syns:*** beat off, fend off, keep off, repel,
to parry his opponent.   repulse, ward off.

parsimonious *adjective*
Ungenerously or pettily reluctant to spend money.   STINGY.

parson *noun*
A person ordained for service in a Christian church.   PREACHER.

part *noun*
1. One's proper or expected function in a common   1. ***Syns:*** piece, role (*also* rôle), share.
   effort: *Everyone must do his part.*
2. One of the individual entities contributing to a   2. ELEMENT.
   whole.
3. One of the parts into which something is divided.   3. DIVISION.
4. That which is allotted.   4. ALLOTMENT.
5. A particular subdivision of a written work.   5. SECTION *noun*.
6. One of two or more opposing opinions, actions, or   6. SIDE.
   attitudes, as in a disagreement.

  part *verb*
  1. To make a division into parts, sections, or branches. 1. DIVIDE.
  2. To terminate a relationship or association by or as if 2. SEPARATE *verb*.
     by leaving one another.

  part *adjective*
  Pertaining to or affecting only a part; not total.   PARTIAL.

partake *verb*
1. To have a share in (an act, result, etc.); have a hand   1. CONTRIBUTE.
   in.
2. To involve oneself in (an activity).   2. PARTICIPATE.
3. To take (food) into the body as nourishment.   3. EAT.

partial *adjective*
1. Pertaining to or affecting only a part; not total: *a partial solution; partial success.*
2. Disposed to favor one over another.
3. Exhibiting bias.

1. *Syns:* fractional, fragmentary, part.
2. FAVORABLE.
3. BIASED.

partiality *noun*
1. An inclination for or against that inhibits impartial judgment.
2. An inclination to something.
3. Favorable, preferential bias.
4. A liking or personal preference for something.

1. BIAS *noun.*
2. BENT *noun.*
3. FAVOR *noun.*
4. TASTE *noun.*

partialness *noun*
Favorable, preferential bias.

FAVOR *noun.*

participant *noun*
One who participates: *prizes for all participants in the tournament.*

Syns: actor, party.

participate *verb*
To involve oneself in (an activity): *participated in a lively conversation.*

Syns: carry on, engage, have, indulge, partake. —*Idiom* take part.

participation *noun*
The act or fact of participating: *trying to increase participation in the political process.*

Syns: involvement, sharing.

particle *noun*
A tiny amount.

BIT[1].

particular *noun*
1. One of the conditions or facts attending an event and having some bearing on it.
2. A small, often specialized element of a whole.
3. An individually considered portion of a whole.

1. CIRCUMSTANCE.
2. DETAIL *noun.*
3. ELEMENT.

particular *adjective*
1. Of, relating to, or intended for a distinctive thing or group.
2. Characterized by attention to detail.
3. Alone in a given category.
4. Very difficult to please.

1. SPECIAL.
2. DETAILED.
3. LONE.
4. NICE.

particularity *noun*
The quality of being individual.

INDIVIDUALITY.

particularize *verb*
To make specific.

STIPULATE.

particularized *adjective*
Characterized by attention to detail.

DETAILED.

parting *noun*
A separation of two or more people: *feeling sad at their parting.*

Syns: adieu, farewell, good-by *or* good-bye, leave-taking.

parting *adjective*
Of, done, given, or said on departing: *parting words; a parting gift.*

Syns: departing, farewell, good-by *or* good-bye, valedictory.

partisan *noun*
One who supports and adheres to another.

FOLLOWER.

partisan *adjective*
Exhibiting bias.

BIASED.

partition *noun*
1. A solid structure that encloses an area or separates one area from another.
2. The act or an instance of separating one thing from another.

1. WALL *noun.*
2. DIVISION.

partition *verb*
1. To separate with or as if with a wall.
2. To make a division into parts, sections, or branches.

1. WALL *verb.*
2. DIVIDE.

partner *noun*
1. One who is united in a relationship with another.
2. A husband or wife.

1. ASSOCIATE *noun*.
2. SPOUSE.

partnership *noun*
The state of being associated.

ASSOCIATION.

parturiency *noun*
The condition of carrying a developing fetus within the uterus.

PREGNANCY.

parturient *adjective*
Carrying a developing fetus within the uterus.

PREGNANT.

parturition *noun*
The act or process of bringing forth young.

BIRTH *noun*.

party *noun*
1. A large or important social gathering: *a party at the White House.*

2. A group of performers.
3. A usu. small number of individuals.
4. A group of individuals united in a common cause.
5. One who participates.
6. *Informal.* A member of the human race.

1. *Syns:* affair, bash (*Slang*), do (*Slang*), festivity, fete (*also* fête), function, gala, occasion, soiree (*also* soirée).
2. BAND² *noun*.
3. GROUP *noun*.
4. COMBINE *noun*.
5. PARTICIPANT.
6. HUMAN BEING.

pass *verb*
1. To catch up with and move past: *cars passing us on all sides.*
2. To be greater or better than.
3. To use time in a particular way.
4. To go through (life) in a certain way.
5. To move along a particular course.
6. To journey over (a specified distance).
7. To cause to be transferred from one to another: *Pass your plate for seconds. Did you pass the word along?*
8. To give or convey (something) from one generation to the next.
9. To come as by lot or inheritance.
10. To take place.
11. To make known.
12. To cause (a disease) to pass to another or others.
13. To be accepted or approved: *The motion passed by a wide margin.*
14. To accept officially: *The Senate voted to pass the resolution.*
15. To move toward a termination.
16. To cease living.
17. To represent oneself in a given character or as other than what one is.

1. *Syns:* overhaul, overtake.
2. SURPASS.
3. SPEND.
4. LEAD *verb*.
5. GO *verb*.
6. TRAVERSE *verb*.
7. *Syns:* convey, hand (over), transmit.

8. HAND DOWN at **hand.**

9. FALL *verb*.
10. COME.
11. COMMUNICATE.
12. COMMUNICATE.
13. *Syns:* carry, clear.

14. *Syns:* adopt, approve.

15. GO *verb*.
16. DIE.
17. POSE *verb*.

pass away *verb*
1. To cease living.
2. To move toward a termination.

1. DIE.
2. GO *verb*.

pass off *verb*
To offer or put into circulation (an inferior or spurious item).

FOIST.

pass out *verb*
Informal. To suffer temporary loss of consciousness.

BLACK OUT.

pass over *verb*
To pretend not to see.

BLINK AT at **blink.**

pass *noun*
1. A free ticket entitling one to transportation or admission: *a movie pass for students.*
2. A decisive point.

1. *Syns:* comp (*Informal*), freebie (*also* freebee) (*Slang*).
2. CRISIS.

passable *adjective*
1. Capable of being passed, traversed, or crossed: *The highways are passable for the first time since the blizzard.*
2. Of moderately good quality but less than excellent.

passage *noun*
1. The process or an instance of passing from one form, state, or stage to another.
2. A particular subdivision of a written work.

pass away *verb*

passé *adjective*
Of a style or method formerly in vogue.

passel *noun*
Regional. An indeterminately great amount or number.

passing *adjective*
Lasting or existing only for a short time.

passing *noun*
The act or fact of dying.

passion *noun*
1. Powerful, intense emotion: *a sermon filled with passion; shows no passion in his acting.*

2. The passionate affection and desire felt by lovers for each other.
3. An extravagant, short-lived romantic attachment.
4. Sexual hunger.
5. Passionate devotion to or interest in a cause, subject, etc.
6. A subject or activity that inspires lively interest.
7. A strong, enthusiastic liking for something.
8. An angry outburst.

passionate *adjective*
1. Fired with intense feeling: *a passionate rebuttal.*

2. Feeling or devoted to sexual love or desire.

passionless *adjective*
Deficient in or lacking sexual desire.

passive *adjective*
Submitting without objection or resistance: *remained passive when sentence was passed.*

pass off *verb*
pass out *verb*
pass over *verb*
past *adjective*
1. Just gone by or elapsed: *lunched together several times during the past year.*

2. Having been such previously.

past *noun*

---

1. *Syns:* navigable, negotiable.

2. ACCEPTABLE.

1. TRANSITION.

2. SECTION *noun.*

SEE **pass.**

OLD-FASHIONED.

HEAP *noun.*

TRANSITORY.

DEATH.

1. *Syns:* ardor, fervency, fervidity, fervidness, fervor, fire. —*Idiom* fire and brimstone.
Near-syns: dedication, devotion, eagerness, ecstasy, enrapturement, flame, fury, rage, rapture, transport, zeal.

2. LOVE *noun.*

3. INFATUATION.
4. DESIRE *noun.*
5. ENTHUSIASM.

6. ENTHUSIASM.
7. LOVE *noun.*
8. TEMPER *noun.*

1. *Syns:* ardent, blazing, burning, dithyrambic, fervent, fervid, fiery, fire-and-brimstone, flaming, hot-blooded, impassioned, perfervid, red-hot, scorching, torrid.
2. EROTIC.

FRIGID.

Syns: acquiescent, nonresistant, nonresisting, resigned, submissive, yielding.
Near-syns: accepting, bearing, compliant, docile, enduring, patient, tractable.
SEE **pass.**
SEE **pass.**
SEE **pass.**

1. *Syns:* antecedent, anterior, foregoing, former, precedent, preceding, previous, prior.
2. LATE *adjective.*

1. A former period of time or of one's life: *You can't relive the past.*

    1. *Syns:* yesterday, yesteryear, yore.
    —*Idioms* bygone days, days gone by, the good old days, the old days.

2. Past events surrounding a person or thing.

    2. HISTORY.

paste *verb*
Slang. To deliver (a powerful blow) suddenly and sharply.

HIT *verb.*

paste *noun*
Slang. A sudden sharp, powerful stroke.

BLOW².

pastoral *adjective*
Of or pertaining to the countryside.

COUNTRY *adjective.*

pasty *adjective*
Lacking color.

PALE *adjective.*

patch *verb*
To restore to proper condition or functioning.

FIX *verb.*

patchwork *noun*
A collection of various things.

ASSORTMENT.

patchy *adjective*
Lacking consistency or regularity in quality or performance.

UNEVEN.

pate *noun*
The uppermost part of the body.

HEAD *noun.*

patent *adjective*
1. Easily seen through due to a lack of subtlety.
2. Readily seen, perceived, or understood.

    1. UNSUBTLE.
    2. APPARENT.

paternal *adjective*
Like a father.

FATHERLY.

path *noun*
A course affording passage from one place to another.

WAY.

pathetic *adjective*
Arousing or deserving pity.

PITIFUL.

patience *noun*
The capacity of enduring hardship or inconvenience without complaint: *needed real patience not to respond to his insults.*

Syns: forbearance, long-suffering, resignation.
Ant: impatience.

patient *adjective*
Enduring or capable of enduring hardship or inconvenience without complaint: *a quiet and patient mother of four.*

Syns: forbearing, long-suffering, resigned.

patois *noun*
An often regional form of a language not considered standard.

DIALECT.

patriarch *noun*
One that creates, founds, or originates.

ORIGINATOR.

patrician *adjective*
Of high birth or social position.

NOBLE.

patriciate *noun*
People of the highest social level.

SOCIETY.

patrimonial *adjective*
Of or from one's ancestors.

ANCESTRAL.

patrimony *noun*
Any special privilege accorded a firstborn.

BIRTHRIGHT.

patrol *verb*
To maintain or keep in order with or as if with police.

POLICE *verb.*

patrolman *noun*
A member of a law-enforcement agency.

POLICEMAN.

patron *noun*
1. A person who supports or champions an activity, institution, etc.: *a patron of the arts.*

    1. *Syns:* angel (*Informal*), backer, benefactor, contributor, friend, Maecenas, sponsor, supporter.

2. One who buys goods or services: *a regular patron known to all the dealers.*

patronage *noun*
1. Aid or support given by a patron: *hoped to gain the patronage of the rich and influential.*
2. The commercial transactions of customers with a supplier: *a shop with a large patronage.*
3. Customers or patrons collectively: *sending announcements of the sale to the patronage.*
4. The political appointments or jobs that are at the disposal of those in power: *dispensed patronage to the party regulars in her ward.*

patronization *noun*
1. Aid or support given by a patron.
2. Superciliously indulgent treatment, esp. of those considered inferior.

patronize *verb*
1. To act as a patron to: *patronized all the worthy causes in the community.*
2. To treat in a superciliously indulgent manner.

patronizing *noun*
Superciliously indulgent treatment, esp. of those considered inferior.

patronizing *adjective*
Exhibiting condescension.

patsy *noun*
1. *Slang.* A person who is easily deceived or victimized.
2. *Slang.* One who is made an object of blame.

pattern *noun*
1. One that is worthy of imitation or duplication.
2. An element or component in a decorative composition.
3. The external outline of a thing.
4. An activity done without thinking.
5. Systematic arrangement and design.

pattern *verb*
To take as a model.

paucity *noun*
The condition or fact of being deficient.

pauper *noun*
An impoverished person: *The revolution spawned a new generation of paupers when personal property was nationalized.*

pauper *verb*
To reduce to financial insolvency.

pause *verb*
1. To stop temporarily and remain, as if reluctant to leave: *paused for a while at a small café.*
2. To be irresolute in acting or doing.

pause *noun*
A cessation of continuity or regularity.

pawn[1] *noun*
Something given to guarantee the repayment of a loan or the fulfillment of an obligation: *left her jewels as pawns for her brother's debt.*

pawn *verb*
To give or deposit as a pawn: *pawned his typewriter for the price of a meal.*

---

2. **Syns:** buyer, client, customer, purchaser.

1. **Syns:** aegis, auspices, backing, sponsorship, patronization.
2. **Syns:** business, custom, trade, traffic.
3. **Syn:** clientele.

4. **Syns:** pork (*Slang*), spoils.

1. PATRONAGE.
2. CONDESCENSION.

1. **Syns:** sponsor, support.
2. CONDESCEND.

CONDESCENSION.

CONDESCENDING.

1. DUPE *noun.*
2. SCAPEGOAT.

1. MODEL *noun.*
2. FIGURE *noun.*
3. FORM *noun.*
4. HABIT.
5. METHOD.

FOLLOW.

SHORTAGE.

Syns: beggar, down-and-out, have-not, indigent.

RUIN *verb.*

1. **Syns:** abide, bide, linger, tarry, wait.
2. HESITATE.

BREAK *noun.*

Syns: earnest, guaranty, pledge, security, token, warrant.

Syns: dip (*Brit. Slang*), hock (*Informal*), hypothecate, impignorate, mortgage, pignorate, pledge, pop (*Brit. Slang*).

pawn² *noun*
A person used or controlled by others: *was a pawn in the struggle for political control.*

Syns: cat's-paw (*also* cats-paw), instrument, puppet, stooge, tool.

pay *verb*
1. To give payment to in return for goods or services rendered: *was prepared to pay him $100 for the chair.*
2. To give compensation to.
3. To set right by giving what is due.
4. To distribute (money) as payment.
5. To make as income or profit.

1. *Syns:* compensate, recompense, remunerate.
2. COMPENSATE.
3. SETTLE.
4. SPEND.
5. RETURN *verb*.

pay back *verb*
To exact revenge for.

AVENGE.

pay *noun*
Payment for work done.

WAGE(S) *noun*.

payable *adjective*
Owed as a debt.

DUE *adjective*.

pay back *verb*

SEE **pay.**

payment *noun*
Something given in exchange for goods or services rendered: *required immediate payment for the delivery.*

Syns: compensation, consideration, recompense, remuneration.

pay off *verb*
1. *Informal.* To give, offer, or promise a bribe to.
2. To exact revenge for.

1. BRIBE *verb*.
2. AVENGE.

payoff *noun*
1. *Informal.* Money, property, or a favor given, offered, or promised to a person in a position of trust as an inducement to dishonest behavior.
2. *Informal.* The highest point or state.

1. BRIBE *noun*.

2. CLIMAX *noun*.

payoff *noun*

SEE **pay off.**

payola *noun*
Slang. Money, property, or a favor given, offered, or promised to a person in a position of trust as an inducement to dishonest behavior.

BRIBE *noun*.

peaceable *adjective*
Inclined or disposed to peace; not quarrelsome or unruly: *met in a peaceable spirit.*

Syns: irenic, pacific (*also* pacifical), pacifist (*also* pacifistic), peaceful.
Near-syns: amiable, amicable, complaisant, friendly, neighborly, nonviolent, tranquil.
Near-ants: acrimonious, contentious, pugnacious.
Ant: warlike.

peaceful *adjective*
Inclined or disposed to peace; not quarrelsome or unruly.

PEACEABLE.

peaches-and-cream *adjective*
Bright and clear; not dull or faded.

FRESH.

peacock *verb*
To walk with exaggerated or unnatural motions expressive of self-importance or self-display.

STRUT.

peak *noun*
1. The highest point.
2. The highest point or state.
3. The greatest quantity or highest degree attainable.

1. HEIGHT.
2. CLIMAX *noun*.
3. MAXIMUM *noun*.

peak *adjective*
Of or constituting a climax.

CLIMACTIC.

peak *verb*
To reach or bring to a climax.

CLIMAX *verb*.

peaked *adjective*
Of or associated with sickness.

SICKLY.

peaky *adjective*
Of or associated with sickness.   SICKLY.

peal *verb*
To give forth or cause to give forth a clear, resonant   RING².
sound.

peanuts *noun*
Slang. A small or trifling amount of money: *sold his*   **Syns:** chicken feed (*Slang*), two bits
car for peanuts.   (*Informal*).

pearl *noun*
Someone or something considered exceptionally   TREASURE *noun.*
precious.

peccant *adjective*
Morally objectionable.   EVIL *adjective.*

peck¹ *noun*
1. *Informal.* An indeterminately great amount or   1. HEAP *noun.*
number.
2. *Informal.* A great deal.   2. HEAP *noun.*

peck² *noun*
1. Something fit to be eaten.   1. FOOD.
2. The act or an instance of kissing.   2. KISS *noun.*
    peck *verb*
1. To touch or caress with the lips, esp. as a sign of   1. KISS *verb.*
passion or affection.
2. To scold or find fault constantly.   2. NAG.

pecksniffery *noun*
A show or expression of feelings or beliefs one does not   HYPOCRISY.
actually hold or possess.

pecksniffian *adjective*
Of or practicing hypocrisy.   HYPOCRITICAL.

peculiar *adjective*
1. Deviating from the customary.   1. ECCENTRIC *adjective.*
2. Serving to identify or set apart an individual or   2. DISTINCTIVE.
group.
3. Causing puzzlement; perplexing.   3. FUNNY.

peculiarity *noun*
1. A distinctive element.   1. QUALITY.
2. Peculiar behavior.   2. ECCENTRICITY.

pecuniary *adjective*
Of or relating to finances or those who deal in finances.   FINANCIAL.

pedagogics *noun*
The act, process, or art of imparting knowledge and   EDUCATION.
skill.

pedagogist *noun*
One who educates.   EDUCATOR.

pedagogue *noun*
One who educates.   EDUCATOR.

pedagogy *noun*
The act, process, or art of imparting knowledge and   EDUCATION.
skill.

pedantic also **pedantical** *adjective*
Characterized by a narrow concern for book learning   **Syns:** academic, bookish, booky, donnish,
and formal rules, without knowledge or experience of   formalistic, inkhorn, quodlibetic,
practical matters: *a pedantic attention to details.*   scholastic.
    Near-syns: didactic, dry, dull, erudite,
    learned, schooled, schoolish.
    Ant: unpedantic.

peddle *verb*
1. To travel about selling goods: *loaded the trunk with*   1. **Syns:** hawk, huckster, vend.
apples and went peddling.
2. To offer for sale.   2. SELL *verb.*
3. To engage in the illicit sale of (narcotics).   3. PUSH *verb.*

pedestrian *adjective*
Lacking liveliness, charm, or surprise. DULL *adjective.*

pedigree *noun*
1. A written record of ancestry. 1. GENEALOGY.
2. One's ancestors or their character. 2. ANCESTRY.

peek *verb*
To look briefly and quickly. GLIMPSE *verb.*

peek *noun*
A quick look. GLANCE¹ *noun.*

peel *noun*
The outer covering of a fruit. SKIN *noun.*

peel *verb*
To remove the skin of. SKIN *verb.*

peep *verb*
To look briefly and quickly. GLIMPSE *verb.*

peep *noun*
A quick look. GLANCE¹ *noun.*

peer¹ *verb*
To look intently and fixedly. GAZE *verb.*

peer *noun*
An intent, fixed look. GAZE *noun.*

peer² *noun*
One that is very similar to another in rank or position: ***Syns:*** coequal, colleague, compeer, equal,
doctors' competency reviewed by their peers. She is the equivalent, fellow.
peer of any tennis player on the professional circuit.

peerless *adjective*
Without equal or rival. UNIQUE.

peeve *verb*
To trouble the nerves or peace of mind of, esp. by ANNOY.
repeated vexations.

peeve *noun*
Something that annoys. ANNOYANCE.

peevish *adjective*
1. Easily annoyed. 1. IRRITABLE.
2. Having or showing a bad temper. 2. ILL-TEMPERED.

peewee *adjective*
Extremely small. TINY.

peg *noun*
One of the units in a course, as on an ascending or DEGREE.
descending scale.

pejorative *adjective*
Tending or intending to belittle. DISPARAGING.

pelagic *adjective*
Of or relating to the seas or oceans. MARINE.

pelf *noun*
Something, as coins, printed bills, etc., used as a MONEY.
medium of exchange.

pellucid *adjective*
Free from what obscures or dims. CLEAR *adjective.*

pelt¹ *noun*
The skin of an animal. HIDE² *noun.*

pelt² *verb*
To move swiftly. RUSH *verb.*

pen¹ *verb*
To be the author of (a published work or works). PUBLISH.

pen² *verb*
To confine within a limited area. ENCLOSE.

pen³ *noun*
Slang. A place for the confinement of persons in lawful JAIL *noun.*
detention.

penalize *verb*
To impose a fine on.

FINE[2] *verb*.

penalty *noun*
1. A sum of money levied as punishment for an offense.
2. A coercive measure intended to ensure compliance or conformity.

1. FINE[2] *noun*.
2. SANCTION *noun*.

penchant *noun*
An inclination to something.

BENT *noun*.

pendulous *adjective*
1. Hung or appearing to be hung from a support.
2. Given to or exhibiting hesitation.

1. HANGING.
2. HESITANT.

penetrate *verb*
1. To pass into or through by overcoming resistance: *Enemy sappers penetrated our defenses. The cold penetrated his bones.*
2. To come or go into (a place).

1. *Syns:* break (through), perforate, pierce, puncture.
2. ENTER.

penetrating *adjective*
1. So sharp as to cause mental pain.
2. Characterized by careful and exact evaluation.
3. Having or suggesting keen, discerning intellect.

1. BITING.
2. CRITICAL.
3. INCISIVE.

penetration *noun*
Skill in perceiving, discriminating, or judging.

DISCERNMENT.

penitence also **penitency** *noun*
A feeling of regret for one's sins or misdeeds: *didn't know how to express his penitence.*

Syns: attrition, compunction, contriteness, contrition, remorse, remorsefulness, repentance, rue.
Near-syns: anguish, angst, debasement, distress, grief, humiliation, regret, sadness, sorrow; qualm, scruple.
SEE **penitence**.

penitency *noun*

penitent *adjective*
1. Feeling or expressing regret for one's sins or misdeeds.
2. Expressing or inclined to express an apology.

1. REMORSEFUL.
2. APOLOGETIC.

penitential *adjective*
Feeling or expressing regret for one's sins or misdeeds.

REMORSEFUL.

penitentiary *noun*
A place for the confinement of persons in lawful detention.

JAIL *noun*.

pennant *noun*
Fabric used esp. as a symbol.

FLAG[1] *noun*.

penniless *adjective*
Having little or no money or wealth.

POOR.

pennon *noun*
Fabric used esp. as a symbol.

FLAG[1] *noun*.

penny-pinching *adjective*
Ungenerously or pettily reluctant to spend money.

STINGY.

pensile *adjective*
Hung or appearing to be hung from a support.

HANGING.

pension *verb*
To remove from active service.

RETIRE.

pensive *adjective*
1. Suggestive of or expressing deep, often melancholy thoughtfulness: *a pensive expression.*

1. *Syns:* meditative, musing, tristful (*Archaic*), wistful.
Near-ants: alert, aware, excited, extroverted, outgoing.

2. Of, characterized by, or disposed to thought.

2. THOUGHTFUL.

penumbra *noun*
Comparative darkness that results from the blocking of light rays.

SHADE *noun*.

penurious *adjective*
1. Ungenerously or pettily reluctant to spend money.   1. STINGY.
2. Having little or no money or wealth.   2. POOR.

penury *noun*
The condition of being extremely poor.   POVERTY.

people *noun*
Persons as an organized body.   PUBLIC *noun.*

  people *verb*
  To live in (a place).   INHABIT.

pep *noun*
1. *Informal.* Capacity or power for work or vigorous   1. ENERGY.
   activity.
2. *Informal.* A lively, emphatic, eager quality or   2. SPIRIT.
   manner.

pepper *verb*
1. To direct a barrage at.   1. BARRAGE *verb.*
2. To mark with many small spots.   2. SPECKLE.

peppery *adjective*
1. Full of or characterized by a lively, emphatic, eager   1. SPIRITED.
   quality.
2. Easily annoyed.   2. TESTY.

peppy *adjective*
1. *Informal.* Very brisk, alert, and high-spirited.   1. LIVELY.
2. *Informal.* Possessing, exerting, or displaying energy.   2. ENERGETIC.
3. Disposed to action.   3. VIGOROUS.

perambulate *verb*
To walk at a leisurely pace.   STROLL *verb.*

perambulation *noun*
An act of walking, esp. for pleasure.   WALK *noun.*

perceivable *adjective*
1. Capable of being noticed or apprehended mentally.   1. PERCEPTIBLE.
2. Capable of being seen.   2. VISIBLE.

perceive *verb*
1. To be intuitively aware of: *could easily perceive her*   1. *Syns:* apprehend (*Obs.*), feel, intuit,
   unexpressed hostility.   sense. —*Idioms* feel in one's bones, get
                                                                 vibrations.
2. To apprehend (images) by use of the eyes.   2. SEE.
3. To use the power of vision.   3. LOOK *verb.*

perceptible *adjective*
1. Capable of being noticed or apprehended mentally: 1. *Syns:* appreciable, detectable,
   speaks with a perceptible edge in her voice when   discernible, noticeable, observable,
   angry; underwent a perceptible change in outlook.   palpable, perceivable.
                                                                 Near-ants: impalpable, indiscernible,
                                                                 intangible, invisible, unappreciable,
                                                                 undetectable, unnoticeable.
                                                                 Ant: imperceptible.
2. Capable of being seen.   2. VISIBLE.

perception *noun*
1. That which exists in the mind as the product of   1. IDEA.
   careful mental activity.
2. The condition of being aware.   2. AWARENESS.

perceptive *adjective*
1. Having or suggesting keen, discerning intellect.   1. INCISIVE.
2. Possessing or displaying perceptions of great   2. ACUTE.
   accuracy and sensitivity.

perceptiveness *noun*
Skill in perceiving, discriminating, or judging.   DISCERNMENT.

perch *verb*
To place or be placed on a narrow or insecure surface.   BALANCE *verb.*

perchance *adverb*
Possibly but not certainly.   MAYBE.

percipience *noun*
Skill in perceiving, discriminating, or judging. DISCERNMENT.

percolate *verb*
To flow or leak out slowly. OOZE.

percussion *noun*
Violent, forcible contact between two or more things. COLLISION.

perdurable *adjective*
Existing or remaining in the same state for an CONTINUING.
indefinitely long time.

peregrinate *verb*
1. To make or go on a journey. 1. JOURNEY *verb*.
2. To move about at random, esp. over a wide area. 2. ROVE.

peremptory *adjective*
Tending to dictate. DICTATORIAL.

perennial *adjective*
Existing or remaining in the same state for an CONTINUING.
indefinitely long time.

perfect *adjective*
1. Supremely excellent in quality or nature: *a perfect* 1. **Syns:** absolute, consummate, faultless,
   diamond; a perfect performance. flawless, impeccable, indefectible,
   unflawed.
2. Lacking nothing essential or normal. 2. COMPLETE *adjective*.
3. Conforming to an ultimate form of perfection or 3. IDEAL *adjective*.
   excellence.
4. Free from extraneous elements. 4. PURE *adjective*.
5. Completely such, without qualification or exception. 5. UTTER².
6. Not more or less. 6. ROUND.
7. In excellent condition. 7. GOOD *adjective*.
8. Without imperfections or blemishes. 8. CLEAN *adjective*.

perfect *verb*
To bring to perfection or completion: *The architect* **Syns:** polish, refine, smooth. —*Idiom*
worked to perfect his design. smooth off the rough edges.

perfection *noun*
A special feature or quality that confers superiority. VIRTUE.

perfervid *adjective*
Fired with intense feeling. PASSIONATE.

perfidious *adjective*
1. Not true to duty or obligation. 1. FAITHLESS.
2. Deserving strong condemnation. 2. INFAMOUS.

perfidiousness *noun*
1. Willful betrayal of fidelity, confidence, or trust. 1. TREACHERY.
2. Betrayal, esp. of a moral obligation. 2. FAITHLESSNESS.

perfidy *noun*
1. Willful betrayal of fidelity, confidence, or trust. 1. TREACHERY.
2. Betrayal, esp. of a moral obligation. 2. FAITHLESSNESS.
3. The condition of being infamous. 3. INFAMY.

perforate *verb*
1. To make a hole or other opening in. 1. BREACH *verb*.
2. To pass into or through by overcoming resistance. 2. PENETRATE.

perforation *noun*
1. An opening, esp. in a solid structure. 1. BREACH *noun*.
2. A small mark or hole made by a sharp, pointed 2. PRICK *noun*.
   object.

perforce *adverb*
Without regard to desire or inclination. HELPLESSLY.

perform *verb*
1. To begin and carry through to completion: *perform* 1. **Syns:** do, execute, prosecute, pull off
   an acrobatic feat. (*Informal*).
2. To carry out the functions, requirements, or terms 2. FULFILL.
   of.
3. To play the part of. 3. ACT *verb*.

4. To produce on the stage.

4. STAGE *verb*.

performance *noun*
1. The act of beginning and carrying through to completion: *in the performance of his duty.*
2. The quality of being efficient.
3. The way in which a machine or other thing performs or functions.
4. One's artistic conception as shown by the rendering of a dramatic role, musical composition, etc.

1. *Syns:* effectuation, execution, prosecution.
2. EFFICIENCY.
3. BEHAVIOR.

4. INTERPRETATION.

performer *noun*
One who plays a musical instrument.

PLAYER.

perfume *noun*
A sweet or pleasant odor.

FRAGRANCE.

perfume *verb*
To fill with a pleasant odor.

SCENT *verb*.

perfumed *adjective*
Having a pleasant odor.

FRAGRANT.

perfunctory *adjective*
Performed or performing automatically and impersonally: *gave me a perfunctory nod as he passed.*

Syns: automatic, mechanical.
Near-syns: impersonal, indifferent, involuntary, routine, stock, unconcerned, uninterested, wooden; cursory, quick, superficial.

perhaps *adverb*
Possibly but not certainly.

MAYBE.

perhaps *noun*
Abstract reasoning.

THEORY.

periapt *noun*
A small object worn or kept for its supposed magical power.

CHARM *noun*.

peril *noun*
Exposure to possible harm, loss, or injury.

DANGER.

peril *verb*
To subject to danger or destruction.

ENDANGER.

perilous *adjective*
Involving possible risk, loss, or injury.

DANGEROUS.

perimeter *noun*
1. A line around a closed figure or area.
2. *Mil.* A fairly narrow line or space forming a boundary.

1. CIRCUMFERENCE.
2. BORDER *noun*.

period *noun*
1. A specific length of time characterized by the occurrence of certain conditions or events: *a period of sunshine.*
2. A particular time notable for its distinctive characteristics.
3. An interval regarded as a distinct evolutionary or developmental unit: *Picasso's blue period.*
4. A span designated for a given activity.
5. A concluding or terminating.

1. *Syns:* season, span, term.

2. AGE *noun*.

3. *Syns:* phase, stage.

4. TIME *noun*.
5. END *noun*.

periodic also **periodical** *adjective*
1. Happening or appearing now and then.
2. Happening or appearing at regular intervals.

1. INTERMITTENT.
2. RECURRENT.

periodically *adverb*
At times.

NOW *adverb*.

peripatetic *adjective*
Leading the life of a person without a fixed domicile; moving from place to place.

NOMADIC.

periphery *noun*
1. A fairly narrow line or space forming a boundary.
2. A line around a closed figure or area.

1. BORDER *noun*.
2. CIRCUMFERENCE.

periphrastic *adjective*
Using or containing an excessive number of words.   WORDY.
perish *verb*
1. To cease living.   1. DIE.
2. To experience spiritual death.   2. DIE.
perished *adjective*
No longer alive.   DEAD *adjective*.
perjure *verb*
To make untrue declarations.   LIE² *verb*.
perjured *adjective*
Marked by lying under oath.   PERJURIOUS.
perjurer *noun*
One who tells lies.   LIAR.
perjurious *adjective*
Marked by lying under oath: *perjurious witnesses;*   *Syns:* forsworn (*also* foresworn), perjured.
perjurious testimony.
perjury *noun*
The practice of lying.   MENDACITY.
perk¹ *noun*
Slang. A material favor or gift, usu. money, given in   GRATUITY.
return for service.
perk² *verb*
To impart strength and confidence to.   ENCOURAGE.
  perk up *verb*
  To regain one's health.   RECOVER.
perk up *verb*   SEE **perk²**.
permeate *verb*
1. To cause to be filled with a particular mood or tone.   1. CHARGE *verb*.
2. To occupy the whole of; be found throughout.   2. FILL.
permissible *adjective*
Capable of being allowed: *It is permissible to smoke*   *Syns:* admissible, allowable.
here.   *Near-ants:* banned, forbidden, outlawed,
                                                                prohibited, unauthorized, verboten.
                                                                Ant: impermissible.

permission *noun*
Approval for an action, esp. as granted by one in   *Syns:* allowance, authorization, consent,
authority: *gave them permission to smoke.*   leave², license, permit, sanction.
permit *verb*
1. To neither forbid nor prevent: *just permits the*   1. *Syns:* allow, have, leave², let, suffer,
   children to run wild.   tolerate.
2. To give one's consent to: *permitted me to leave the*   2. *Syns:* allow, authorize, consent, let,
   office early.   sanction.
3. To afford an opportunity for: *a job that permits me to*   3. *Syns:* admit, allow, let.
   advance.
4. To give the means, ability, or opportunity to do.   4. ENABLE.
permit *noun*
1. Approval for an action, esp. as granted by one in   1. PERMISSION.
   authority.
2. Legal permission to do something.   2. LICENSE *noun*.
permutation *noun*
The process or result of making or becoming different.   CHANGE *noun*.
pernicious *adjective*
1. Extremely destructive or harmful.   1. VIRULENT.
2. Having the capability or effect of damaging   2. DESTRUCTIVE.
   irreparably.
perorate *verb*
To speak in a loud, pompous, or prolonged manner.   RANT.
perpendicular *adjective*
At right angles to the horizon or to level ground.   VERTICAL.
perpetrate *verb*
To be responsible for or guilty of (an error or crime).   COMMIT.

perpetual *adjective*
1. Existing or occurring without interruption or end.   1. CONTINUAL.
2. Enduring for all time.   2. ENDLESS.

perpetuate *verb*
To cause to last endlessly.   IMMORTALIZE.

perpetuity *noun*
The quality or state of having no end.   ENDLESSNESS.

perplex *verb*
1. To cause to be unclear in mind or intent.   1. CONFUSE.
2. To make complex, intricate, or perplexing.   2. COMPLICATE.

perplexing *adjective*
Difficult to understand due to intricacy.   COMPLEX *adjective*.

perquisite *noun*
1. A privilege granted a person by virtue of birth.   1. BIRTHRIGHT.
2. A material favor or gift, usu. money, given in return for service.   2. GRATUITY.

persecute *verb*
To do a wrong to; treat unjustly.   WRONG *verb*.

persecution *noun*
Excruciating punishment.   HELL *noun*.

perseverance *noun*
The state or quality of being insistent.   INSISTENCE.

perseverant *adjective*
Obstinately maintaining a stand.   INSISTENT.

persevere *verb*
1. To take and maintain a stand obstinately.   1. INSIST.
2. To continue without halting.   2. CARRY ON at **carry**.

persevering *adjective*
Obstinately maintaining a stand.   INSISTENT.

persist *verb*
1. To take and maintain a stand obstinately.   1. INSIST.
2. To exist in spite of adversity.   2. SURVIVE.
3. To remain in existence or in a certain state for an indefinitely long time.   3. ENDURE.
4. To continue without halting.   4. CARRY ON at **carry**.

persistence also **persistency** *noun*
1. The state or quality of being insistent.   1. INSISTENCE.
2. Uninterrupted existence or succession.   2. CONTINUATION.
3. An uninterrupted course.   3. CONTINUANCE.

persistency *noun*   SEE **persistence**.

persistent *adjective*
1. Obstinately maintaining a stand.   1. INSISTENT.
2. Of long duration.   2. CHRONIC.
3. Difficult to alleviate or cure.   3. STUBBORN.

persisting *adjective*
Obstinately maintaining a stand.   INSISTENT.

persnickety *adjective*
Very difficult to please.   NICE.

person *noun*
A member of the human race.   HUMAN BEING.

persona *noun*
A person portrayed in fiction or drama.   CHARACTER.

personage *noun*
1. A member of the human race.   1. HUMAN BEING.
2. An important, influential person.   2. DIGNITARY.
3. A famous person.   3. CELEBRITY.
4. A person portrayed in fiction or drama.   4. CHARACTER.

personal *adjective*
1. Belonging to, pertaining to, or affecting a particular person: *personal loyalties*.   1. *Syn:* individual.

2. Belonging or confined to a particular person or group as opposed to the public or the government.　**2.** PRIVATE.

3. Of or pertaining to the human body.　**3.** BODILY.

4. Based on individual judgment or discretion.　**4.** ARBITRARY.

5. Characterized by a close and thorough acquaintance.　**5.** INTIMATE[1] *adjective*.

personality *noun*
1. The set of behavioral or personal characteristics by which an individual is recognizable.　**1.** IDENTITY.

2. An important, influential person.　**2.** DIGNITARY.

personalize *verb*
To represent (an abstraction) in or as if in bodily form.　EMBODY.

personification *noun*
A physical entity typifying an abstraction.　EMBODIMENT.

personify *verb*
1. To represent (an abstraction) in or as if in bodily form.　**1.** EMBODY.

2. To serve as the image of.　**2.** REPRESENT.

perspective *noun*
That which is or can be seen.　VIEW *noun*.

perspicacious *adjective*
Having or showing a clever awareness and resourcefulness in practical matters.　SHREWD.

perspicacity *noun*
Skill in perceiving, discriminating, or judging.　DISCERNMENT.

perspicuity *noun*
The quality of being clear and easy to perceive or understand.　CLARITY.

perspire *verb*
To excrete moisture through the pores of the skin.　SWEAT *verb*.

perspiring *adjective*
Producing or covered with sweat.　SWEATY.

persuade *verb*
1. To succeed in causing (a person) to act in a certain way: *persuaded the President to deregulate the airlines. Nothing could persuade her to forgive him.*　**1.** *Syns:* argue into, bring, bring around, convince, get, induce, prevail on (*or* upon), sell (on), talk into.

2. To convince (another) to adopt a particular faith or belief.　**2.** CONVERT.

3. To cause (another) to believe something.　**3.** CONVINCE.

persuasion *noun*
1. Something believed or accepted as true by a person.　**1.** BELIEF.

2. A system of religious belief.　**2.** RELIGION.

3. Those who accept and practice a particular religious belief.　**3.** FAITH.

4. A class that is defined by the common attribute or attributes possessed by all its members.　**4.** KIND[2].

persuasive *adjective*
Serving to convince.　CONVINCING.

pert *adjective*
1. Rude and disrespectful.　**1.** IMPUDENT.

2. Very brisk, alert, and high-spirited.　**2.** LIVELY.

pertain *verb*
1. To be the property of a person or thing.　**1.** BELONG.

2. To be pertinent.　**2.** APPLY.

pertinacious *adjective*
1. Tenaciously unwilling to yield.　**1.** OBSTINATE.

2. Difficult to alleviate or cure.　**2.** STUBBORN.

pertinacity *noun*
The quality or state of being stubbornly unyielding.　OBSTINACY.

pertinence also **pertinency** *noun*
1. The fact of being related to the matter at hand.　**1.** RELEVANCE.

2. A connecting relation.　**2.** CONCERN *noun*.

pertinency *noun*   SEE **pertinence.**
pertinent *adjective*
Related to the matter at hand.   RELEVANT.
perturb *verb*
To impair or destroy the composure of.   AGITATE.
perturbation *noun*
A state of discomposure.   AGITATION.
perusal *noun*
The act of examining carefully.   EXAMINATION.
peruse *verb*
To look at carefully or critically.   EXAMINE.
pervade *verb*
1. To cause to be filled with a particular mood or tone.   1. CHARGE *verb*.
2. To occupy the whole of; be found throughout.   2. FILL.
perverse *adjective*
1. Given to acting in opposition to others.   1. CONTRARY *adjective*.
2. Tenaciously unwilling to yield.   2. OBSTINATE.
3. Utterly reprehensible in nature or behavior.   3. CORRUPT *adjective*.
perverseness *noun*
The quality or state of being stubbornly unyielding.   OBSTINACY.
perversion *noun*
Wrong, often corrupt use.   ABUSE *noun*.
perversity *noun*
The quality or state of being stubbornly unyielding.   OBSTINACY.
pervert *verb*
1. To use wrongly and improperly.   1. ABUSE *verb*.
2. To ruin utterly in character or quality.   2. CORRUPT.
3. To give an inaccurate view of by representing falsely   3. DISTORT.
   or misleadingly.
  pervert *noun*
  One whose sexual behavior differs from the accepted   DEVIANT *noun*.
  norm.
perverted *adjective*
Lowered in character or quality.   CORRUPTED.
pesky *adjective*
Hard to treat, manage, or cope with.   TROUBLESOME.
pessimism *noun*
The doctrine that this world is evil: *a philosophy*   **Syn:** malism.
grounded on pessimism.

pessimist *noun*
A prophet of misfortune or disaster: *pessimists*   **Syns:** Cassandra, crepehanger, doomsayer,
predicting a nuclear holocaust.   worrywart (*Informal*). —Idioms calamity
                                                     howler, prophet of doom and gloom.
                                                     Near-syns: crybaby, cynic, defeatist,
                                                     killjoy, misanthrope; fussbudget, doubting
                                                     Thomas.
                                                     Ant: optimist.

pessimistic *adjective*
Marked by little hopefulness.   GLOOMY.
pester *verb*
1. To trouble persistently from or as if from all sides.   1. BESIEGE.
2. To disturb by repeated attacks.   2. ANNOY.
pestering *noun*
The act of annoying.   ANNOYANCE.
pestilent *adjective*
Extremely destructive or harmful.   VIRULENT.
pestilential *adjective*
Extremely destructive or harmful.   VIRULENT.
pet¹ *verb*
To touch or stroke affectionately.   CARESS *verb*.
  pet *noun*

One liked or preferred above all others.   FAVORITE *noun*.

pet   *adjective*
Given special, usu. doting treatment.   FAVORITE *adjective*.

pet²   *verb*
To be sullenly aloof or withdrawn, as in silent resentment or protest.   SULK.

petechia   *noun*
A mark on the skin indicative of a disease, as typhus.   STIGMA.

peter out   *verb*
To grow or cause to grow gradually less.   DECREASE *verb*.

petite   *adjective*
Notably below average in amount, size, or scope.   LITTLE.

petition   *noun*
An application to a higher authority, as for sanction or a decision.   APPEAL *noun*.

petition   *verb*
1. To make application to a higher authority.   1. APPEAL *verb*.
2. To ask for employment, acceptance, or admission.   2. APPLY.
3. To bring an appeal or request to the attention of.   3. ADDRESS *verb*.

petitioner   *noun*
1. One that asks a higher authority for something, as a favor or redress.   1. APPEALER.
2. A person who applies for or seeks a job or position.   2. APPLICANT.

petrified   *adjective*
Filled with fear or terror.   AFRAID.

petrify   *verb*
1. To make or become physically hard.   1. HARDEN.
2. To render (another) speechless or incapable of action.   2. WITHER.

pettifog   *verb*
To raise unnecessary or trivial objections.   QUIBBLE.

pettiness   *noun*
Contemptible unimportance: *The pettiness of his criticism is incredible.*   *Syns:* inconsequence, measliness (*Slang*), paltriness, smallness, triviality, trivialness.

petty   *adjective*
1. Contemptibly unimportant: *the petty concerns of bored socialites.*   1. *Syns:* inconsequent, inconsequential, inconsiderable, measly (*Slang*), negligible, niggling, paltry, picayune, piddling, small, small-minded, trifling, trivial, unconsequential, unconsidered.
Near-syns: fastidious, fussy, insignificant, irrelevant, little, picky (*Informal*), puny.
Near-ants: important, momentous, vital.
2. Of subordinate standing or importance.   2. MINOR *adjective*.
3. Not broad or elevated in scope or understanding.   3. NARROW.

petulant   *adjective*
1. Easily annoyed.   1. IRRITABLE.
2. Having or showing a bad temper.   2. ILL-TEMPERED.

phantasm also **phantasma**   *noun*
1. An illusory mental image.   1. DREAM *noun*.
2. A supernatural being.   2. GHOST *noun*.
3. An erroneous perception of reality.   3. ILLUSION.

phantasma   *noun*   SEE **phantasm.**

phantasmagoria also **phantasmagory**   *noun*
An illusion of perceiving something that does not really exist.   HALLUCINATION.

phantasmagory   *noun*   SEE **phantasmagoria.**

phantasy   *noun*   SEE **fantasy.**

phantom *noun*
A supernatural being.   GHOST *noun*.

pharisaic also **pharisaical** *adjective*
Of or practicing hypocrisy.   HYPOCRITICAL.

pharisaism also **phariseeism** *noun*
A show or expression of feelings or beliefs one does not   HYPOCRISY.
actually hold or possess.

pharisee *noun*
A person who practices hypocrisy.   HYPOCRITE.

phariseeism *noun*   SEE **pharisaism**.

pharmacon *noun*
An agent used to restore health.   CURE *noun*.

phase *noun*
1. The particular angle from which something is   **1. *Syns:*** aspect, facet, hand, respect, side.
    considered: *examined the problem from the practical*
    phase.
2. An interval regarded as a distinct evolutionary or   **2.** PERIOD.
    developmental unit.

phenomenal *adjective*
1. So remarkable as to elicit disbelief.   **1.** FABULOUS.
2. Composed of or relating to things that occupy space   **2.** PHYSICAL.
    and can be perceived by the senses.

phenomenon *noun*
1. Something having real, demonstrable existence.   **1.** FACT.
2. One that is worthy of imitation or duplication.   **2.** MODEL *noun*.
3. One that evokes great surprise and admiration.   **3.** MARVEL.

philander *verb*
To be sexually unfaithful to another: *a husband well*   ***Syns:*** cheat, fool around (*Informal*), mess
known for philandering.   around (*Informal*), play around
     (*Informal*), womanize.

philander *noun*
A man who philanders.   PHILANDERER.

philanderer *noun*
A man who philanders: *Edward VII was a notorious*   ***Syns:*** Casanova, Don Juan, ladykiller
philanderer.   (*Slang*), lady's man (*also* ladies' man),
     philander, wolf (*Slang*), womanizer.
     —*Idioms* man on the make, skirt chaser.

philanthropic also **philanthropical** *adjective*
Of or concerned with charity.   BENEVOLENT.

philanthropy *noun*
A charitable deed.   BENEVOLENCE.

philippic *noun*
A long, violent, or blustering speech, usu. of censure or   TIRADE.
denunciation.

Philistine also **philistine** *noun*
An unrefined, rude person.   BOOR.

Philistine also **philistine** *adjective*
Lacking in delicacy or refinement.   COARSE.

philosopher *noun*
A person who seeks reason and truth by thinking and   THINKER.
meditation.

phlegm *noun*
Lack of emotion or interest.   APATHY.

phlegmatic *adjective*
Without emotion or interest.   APATHETIC.

phoenix *noun*
A person or thing so excellent as to have no equal or   NONPAREIL *noun*.
match.

phone *verb*
To communicate with (someone) by telephone.   TELEPHONE.

phoney *adjective & noun*
SEE **phony.**

phony also **phoney** *adjective*
1. *Informal.* Fraudulently or deceptively imitative.
2. *Informal.* Not genuine or sincere.

1. COUNTERFEIT *adjective.*
2. ARTIFICIAL.

phony also **phoney** *noun*
1. *Informal.* A fraudulent imitation.
2. *Informal.* One who is not what he claims to be.
3. *Informal.* A person who practices hypocrisy.

1. COUNTERFEIT *noun.*
2. FAKE *noun.*
3. HYPOCRITE.

photographic *adjective*
1. Of or pertaining to representation by drawings or pictures.
2. Described verbally in sharp and accurate detail.

1. GRAPHIC.
2. GRAPHIC.

phrase *verb*
To convey in language or words of a particular form: *He phrased the promise so as to give himself an escape.*

Syns: couch, express, formulate, put, word.

phrase *noun*
1. A word or group of words forming a unit and conveying meaning.
2. Choice of words and the way in which they are used.

1. EXPRESSION.
2. WORDING.

phraseology *noun*
Choice of words and the way in which they are used.

WORDING.

phrasing *noun*
Choice of words and the way in which they are used.

WORDING.

phthisic also **phthisical** *adjective*
Path. Pertaining to or afflicted with tuberculosis.

TUBERCULAR.

phthisic *noun*
Path. A contagious disease producing lesions esp. of the lungs.

TUBERCULOSIS.

phthisis also **phthisic** *noun*
Path. A contagious disease producing lesions esp. of the lungs.

TUBERCULOSIS.

phylactery *noun*
Archaic. A small object worn or kept for its supposed magical power.

CHARM *noun.*

physic *noun*
An agent used to restore health.

CURE *noun.*

physic *verb*
Archaic. To administer or add a drug to.

DRUG *verb.*

physical *adjective*
1. Composed of or relating to things that occupy space and can be perceived by the senses: *a physical barrier; physical changes in the landscape.*
2. Of or pertaining to the human body.
3. Relating to the desires and appetites of the body: *It was purely physical attraction.*

1. *Syns:* concrete, corporeal, material, objective, phenomenal, sensible, substantial, tangible.
2. BODILY.
3. *Syns:* animal, carnal, fleshly, sensual.

physicality *noun*
A preoccupation with the body and satisfaction of its desires: *was struck by his sheer physicality.*

Syns: animalism, animality, carnality, earthiness, fleshliness, sensuality.

physiognomy *noun*
An outward appearance.

FACE *noun.*

physique *noun*
Bodily type.

CONSTITUTION.

picayune *adjective*
Contemptibly unimportant.

PETTY.

pick *noun*
1. That which is superlative.
2. One that is selected.

1. BEST *noun.*
2. ELECT *noun.*

pick *verb*
1. To make a choice from a number of alternatives.
2. To scold or find fault constantly.

1. CHOOSE.
2. NAG.

pick off *verb*

To wound or kill with a firearm.   SHOOT *verb.*
pick out *verb*
To perceive and fix the identity of.   DISCERN.
picket *noun*
A person or special body of persons assigned to provide   GUARD *noun.*
protection, keep watch over, etc.
pickle *noun*
Informal. A difficult, embarrassing situation.   PREDICAMENT.
pickled *adjective*
Slang. Intoxicated with alcoholic liquor.   DRUNK *adjective.*
pick-me-up *noun*
Informal. A medicine that restores or increases vigor.   TONIC *noun.*
pick off *verb*   SEE **pick.**
pick out *verb*   SEE **pick.**
pick up *verb*
1. To collect (something) bit by bit.   1. GLEAN.
2. To come into possession of.   2. GET.
3. To take into custody as a prisoner.   3. ARREST *verb.*
4. To go on after an interruption.   4. CONTINUE.
5. To move (something) to a higher position.   5. ELEVATE.
6. To gain knowledge or mastery of by study.   6. LEARN.
   pickup *noun*
   A seizing and holding by law.   ARREST *noun.*
pickup *noun*   SEE **pick up.**
picky *adjective*
Very difficult to please.   NICE.
pictographic *adjective*
Of or pertaining to representation by drawings or   GRAPHIC.
pictures.
pictorial *adjective*
1. Of or pertaining to representation by drawings or   1. GRAPHIC.
   pictures.
2. Described verbally in sharp and accurate detail.   2. GRAPHIC.
picture *verb*
1. To present a lifelike image of.   1. REPRESENT.
2. To form mental images of.   2. IMAGINE.
   picture *noun*
1. The act or process of describing in lifelike imagery.   1. REPRESENTATION.
2. One exactly resembling another.   2. DOUBLE *noun.*
picturesque *adjective*
1. Evoking strong mental images through   1. COLORFUL.
   distinctiveness.
2. Described verbally in sharp and accurate detail.   2. GRAPHIC.
piddling *adjective*
Contemptibly unimportant.   PETTY.
piece *noun*
1. One of the parts into which something is divided.   1. DIVISION.
2. A part severed from a whole.   2. CUT *noun.*
3. A small portion of food.   3. BIT[1].
4. Something that is the result of creative effort.   4. COMPOSITION.
5. *Regional.* An extent, measured or unmeasured, of   5. DISTANCE.
   linear space.
6. A usu. brief detail of news or information.   6. ITEM.
7. One's proper or expected function in a common   7. PART *noun.*
   effort.
piecemeal *adjective*
Proceeding very slowly by degrees.   GRADUAL.
pierce *verb*
1. To make a hole or other opening in.   1. BREACH *verb.*
2. To pass into or through by overcoming resistance.   2. PENETRATE.
3. To penetrate with a sharp edge.   3. CUT *verb.*

piercing *adjective*
1. Marked by severity or intensity.
2. Elevated in pitch.

1. SHARP *adjective*.
2. HIGH.

pietistic *adjective*
Deeply concerned with God and the beliefs and practice of religion.

HOLY.

piffle *noun*
Something that does not have or make sense.

NONSENSE.

pig *noun*
Slang. A member of a law-enforcement agency.

POLICEMAN.

pigeon *noun*
Slang. A person who is easily deceived or victimized.

DUPE *noun*.

pigeonhole *verb*
1. To distribute into groups according to kinds.
2. To assign to a class or classes.

1. ASSORT.
2. CLASS *verb*.

piggish *adjective*
Wanting to eat or drink more than one can reasonably consume.

GREEDY.

pigheaded *adjective*
Tenaciously unwilling to yield.

OBSTINATE.

pigheadedness *noun*
The quality or state of being stubbornly unyielding.

OBSTINACY.

pigment *noun*
Something that imparts color.

COLOR *noun*.

pigmy *adjective*

SEE **pygmy**.

pignorate *verb*
To give or deposit as a pawn.

PAWN[1] *verb*.

pile *noun*
1. A group of things gathered haphazardly.
2. *Informal.* A great deal.
3. *Slang.* A large sum of money.
4. A usu. permanent construction, as a house, store, etc.

1. HEAP *noun*.
2. HEAP *noun*.
3. FORTUNE.
4. BUILDING.

pile *verb*
1. To put into a disordered pile.
2. To fill to overflowing.

1. HEAP *verb*.
2. HEAP *verb*.

pile in *verb*
Informal. To go to bed.

RETIRE.

pile out *verb*
To leave one's bed.

GET UP at **get**.

pile in *verb*

SEE **pile**.

pile out *verb*

SEE **pile**.

pile up *verb*
1. To bring together so as to increase in mass or number.
2. To undergo wrecking.
3. To damage, disable, or destroy (a seacraft).

1. ACCUMULATE.
2. CRASH *verb*.
3. WRECK *verb*.

pileup *noun*
A wrecking of a vehicle.

CRASH *noun*.

pileup *noun*

SEE **pile up**.

pilfer *verb*
To take (another's property) without permission.

STEAL *verb*.

pill *noun*
Slang. An unpleasant, tiresome person.

DRIP *noun*.

pillage *verb*
To rob of goods by force, esp. in time of war.

SACK[2].

pillage *noun*
Goods or property seized unlawfully, esp. by a victor in wartime.

PLUNDER *noun*.

pilose *adjective*
Covered with hair.

HAIRY.

pilot *noun*
Something or someone that shows the way.   GUIDE *noun*.

pilot *verb*
1. To run and control (a motor vehicle).   **1.** DRIVE *verb*.
2. To show the way to.   **2.** GUIDE *verb*.
3. To direct the course of carefully.   **3.** MANEUVER *verb*.

pilot *adjective*
Constituting a tentative model for future experiment or   *Syns:* experimental, test, trial.
development: *a pilot project in urban renewal.*

pinch *verb*
1. To be severely sparing in order to economize.   **1.** SCRIMP.
2. *Slang.* To take into custody as a prisoner.   **2.** ARREST *verb*.
3. *Slang.* To take (another's property) without   **3.** STEAL *verb*.
   permission.

pinch *noun*
A seizing and holding by law.   ARREST *noun*.

pinchbeck *noun*
An inferior substitute imitating an original.   COPY *noun*.

pinch-hit *verb*
Informal. To act as a substitute.   SUBSTITUTE *verb*.

pinch hitter *noun*
Informal. One that takes the place of another.   SUBSTITUTE *noun*.

pinching *adjective*
Ungenerously or pettily reluctant to spend money.   STINGY.

pinching *noun*
Slang. The crime of taking someone else's property   LARCENY.
without consent.

pine *verb*
To waste away from longing or grief.   LANGUISH.

pinnacle *noun*
The highest point or state.   CLIMAX *noun*.

pin on *verb*
To ascribe (a misdeed, error, etc.) to.   FIX *verb*.

pinpoint *noun*
A very small mark.   POINT *noun*.

pinpoint *verb*
1. To establish the identification of.   **1.** PLACE *verb*.
2. To look for and discover.   **2.** FIND *verb*.

pint-size also **pint-sized** *adjective*
Extremely small.   TINY.

pint-sized *adjective*   SEE **pint-size.**

pioneer *noun*
A person instrumental in the growth of something, esp.   BUILDER.
in its early stages.

pioneer *adjective*
Preceding all others in time.   FIRST *adjective*.

pious *adjective*
Deeply concerned with God and the beliefs and practice   HOLY.
of religion.

pip *noun*
A fertilized plant ovule capable of germinating.   SEED *noun*.

pipe dream *noun*
A fantastic, impracticable plan or desire.   ILLUSION.

pip-squeak *noun*
A totally insignificant person.   NONENTITY.

piquant *adjective*
Affecting the organs of taste or smell with a strong and   PUNGENT.
often harsh sensation.

pique *noun*
Extreme displeasure caused by an insult or slight.   OFFENSE.

pique *verb*

To stir to action or feeling.　　　　　　　　　　　PROVOKE.

pirate *noun*
One who illicitly reproduces the artistic work of
another: *a pirate who lifted a chapter from another
writer's book.*

Syns: cribber (*Informal*), plagiarist.
—*Idiom* literary pirate.

pirate *verb*
To reproduce (the artistic work of another) illicitly: *She
pirated another director's ideas and used them in the
play.*

Syns: crib (*Informal*), plagiarize.

pirouette *verb*
To rotate rapidly.　　　　　　　　　　　　　　　SPIN *verb.*

pishposh *noun*
Something that does not have or make sense.　　　NONSENSE.

pit *noun*
1. A place known for its great filth or corruption:
*Upright citizens considered the red-light district to be
a pit.*
2. A fertilized plant ovule capable of germinating.

1. *Syns:* cesspit, cesspool, sink. —*Idiom*
Augean stable.

2. SEED *noun.*

pit *verb*
To place in opposition or be in opposition to.　　　OPPOSE.

pitch *verb*
1. To send through the air with a motion of the hand
or arm.
2. To put (seeds) into the ground for growth.
3. To move or advance against strong resistance.
4. To raise upright.
5. To lean suddenly, unsteadily, and erratically from
the vertical axis.
6. To move vigorously from side to side or up and
down.
7. To come to the ground suddenly and involuntarily.

1. THROW *verb.*

2. SEED *verb.*
3. PLUNGE *verb.*
4. ERECT *verb.*
5. LURCH *verb.*

6. TOSS *verb.*

7. FALL *verb.*

pitch into *verb*
Informal. To set upon with violent force.　　　ATTACK *verb.*

pitch *noun*
1. An act of throwing.
2. A sudden involuntary drop to the ground.
3. Exceptionally great concentration, power, or force,
esp. in activity.
4. *Slang.* A systematic effort to increase the
importance or reputation of by favorable publicity.

1. THROW *noun.*
2. FALL *noun.*
3. INTENSITY.

4. PROMOTION.

pitch-black *adjective*
Of the darkest achromatic visual value.　　　　　BLACK *adjective.*

pitch-dark *adjective*
Having no light.　　　　　　　　　　　　　　　BLACK *adjective.*

pitched *adjective*
Departing from true vertical or horizontal.　　　INCLINED.

pitch into *verb*　　　　　　　　　　　　　　SEE **pitch.**

pitchy *adjective*
Of the darkest achromatic visual value.　　　　　BLACK *adjective.*

piteous *adjective*
1. Arousing or deserving pity.
2. *Archaic.* Feeling or expressing pity.

1. PITIFUL.
2. PITYING.

pitfall *noun*
A source of danger or difficulty not easily foreseen and
avoided: *The possibility of being kidnapped is one of the
pitfalls of being wealthy.*

Syns: booby trap, trap.
Near-syns: danger, deadfall,
entanglement, hazard, peril, risk, web;
bait, lure, snare, snarl.

pith *noun*
1. The most central and material part.
2. A basic trait or set of traits that define and
establish the character of something.

1. HEART.
2. ESSENCE.

pithy   *adjective*
Precisely meaningful and tersely cogent: *gave a pithy evaluation of the President's foreign policy.*

Syns: aphoristic, brass-tacks, compact[1], epigrammic (*also* epigrammical), marrowy, meaty. —*Idiom* down to brass tacks.
Near-ants: flat, flatulent, inflated, insubstantial, tumid, turgid, verbose, wordy.
Ant: diffuse.

pitiful   *adjective*
1. Arousing or deserving pity: *a pitiful abandoned baby.*

1. *Syns:* commiserable, pathetic, piteous, pitiable, poor, rueful, ruthful (*Archaic*).
Near-syns: affecting, arresting, moving, touching; forsaken, miserable, woeful, wretched.

2. *Archaic.* Feeling or expressing pity.

2. PITYING.

pitiless   *adjective*
Having or showing no mercy.

MERCILESS.

pity   *noun*
1. Sympathetic, sad concern for someone in misfortune: *felt great pity for the hostages.*
2. A great disappointment or regrettable fact.

1. *Syns:* commiseration, compassion, sympathy.
2. SHAME *noun.*

pity   *verb*
To experience or express compassion.

FEEL *verb.*

pitying   *adjective*
Feeling or expressing pity: *didn't give a single pitying thought for the wounded.*

Syns: compassionate, piteous (*Archaic*), pitiful (*Archaic*), ruthful (*Archaic*), sympathetic.

pivot   *verb*
1. To turn or cause to turn in place, as on a hinge or fixed point, tracing an arclike path.
2. To change the direction or course of.
3. To move, as a gun, laterally.

1. SWING *verb.*

2. TURN *verb.*
3. TRAVERSE *verb.*

pivotal   *adjective*
Dominant in importance or influence: *the pivotal piece of evidence in the case; the pivotal character in the play.*

Syns: cardinal, central, key.

pixilated   *adjective*
Slang. Intoxicated with alcoholic liquor.

DRUNK *adjective.*

placate   *verb*
To ease the anger or agitation of.

PACIFY.

place   *noun*
1. The function or position customarily occupied by another: *I was sent on the trip in her place.*
2. A particular geographic area.
3. A building or shelter where one lives.
4. A particular position in a designated order of importance: *secured a top place in the executive echelon.*
5. Positioning of one individual vis-à-vis others: *A person in your place should know better.*
6. The proper or designated location: *everything in its place.*
7. A particular portion of space chosen for something.
8. A post of employment.

1. *Syns:* lieu, room (*Archaic*), stead.

2. LOCALITY.
3. HOME.
4. *Syns:* berth, billet, slot, spot.

5. *Syns:* footing, position, rank[1], situation, standing, station, status.
6. *Syn:* niche.

7. POINT *noun.*
8. POSITION *noun.*

place   *verb*
1. To establish the identification of: *He looks familiar, but I can't place him.*
2. To deposit in a specified position.
3. To assign to a class or classes.
4. To calculate approximately.
5. To ascribe (a misdeed, error, etc.) to.

1. *Syns:* finger, identify, pinpoint, recognize. —*Idiom* put one's finger on.
2. SET[1] *verb.*
3. CLASS *verb.*
4. ESTIMATE *verb.*
5. FIX *verb.*

6. To complete a race or competition in a specified
position.

placement *noun*
The place where a person or thing is located.

placid *adjective*
1. Motionless and undisturbed.
2. Not excited or emotionally agitated.

placidity *noun*
An absence of motion or disturbance.

plagiarist *noun*
One who illicitly reproduces the artistic work of
another.

plagiarize *verb*
To reproduce (the artistic work of another) illicitly.

plague *noun*
1. A cause of suffering or harm.
2. A sudden increase in something, as the occurrence
of a disease.
3. Something that annoys.

plague *verb*
1. To disturb by repeated attacks.
2. To trouble persistently from or as if from all sides.
3. To bring great harm or suffering to.

plaguey *adjective*

plaguy also **plaguey** *adjective*
Informal. Troubling the nerves or peace of mind, as by
repeated vexations.

plain *adjective*
1. Executed without pretense or obfuscation: *plain
dealings with our allies.*

2. Readily seen, perceived, or understood.
3. Easily seen through due to a lack of subtlety.
4. Free from extraneous elements.
5. Being of no special quality or type.
6. Without addition, decoration, or qualification.
7. Not diluted or mixed with other substances.
8. Not handsome or beautiful: *a plain face.*

9. Not elaborate or showy, as in appearance or style.

plainness *noun*
1. The quality of being clear and easy to perceive or
understand.
2. Lack of ostentation or pretension.

plainspoken *adjective*
Speaking or spoken freely and sincerely.

plaintiff *noun*
Law. One that makes a formal complaint, esp. in court.

plaintive *adjective*
Full of or expressive of sorrow.

plan *noun*
1. A method for making, doing, or accomplishing
something.
2. Systematic arrangement and design.
3. What one intends to do or achieve.
4. A method used in dealing with something.

plan *verb*

---

6. RUN *verb*.

POSITION *noun*.

1. STILL *adjective*.
2. CALM *adjective*.

STILLNESS.

PIRATE *noun*.

PIRATE *verb*.

1. CURSE *noun*.
2. OUTBREAK *noun*.

3. ANNOYANCE.

1. ANNOY.
2. BESIEGE.
3. AFFLICT.
SEE **plaguy**.

VEXATIOUS.

1. *Syns:* forthright, man-to-man,
straightforward, straight-shooting,
undissembling, unmannered,
unreserved. —*Idioms* plain and open,
shooting straight from the hip.
2. APPARENT.
3. UNSUBTLE.
4. PURE *adjective*.
5. ORDINARY *adjective*.
6. BARE *adjective*.
7. STRAIGHT *adjective*.
8. *Syns:* homely, unattractive, uncomely,
unlovely. —*Idioms* not much for looks,
not much to look at, plain as a mud
fence, short on looks.

9. MODEST.

1. CLARITY.

2. MODESTY.

FRANK.

COMPLAINANT.

SORROWFUL.

1. DESIGN *noun*.

2. METHOD.
3. INTENTION.
4. APPROACH *noun*.

1. To form a strategy for.   1. DESIGN *verb*.
2. To work out and arrange the parts or details of.   2. DESIGN *verb*.
3. To have in mind as a goal or purpose.   3. INTEND.

planate *adjective*
Having no irregularities, roughness, or indentations.   EVEN[1] *adjective*.

plane *adjective*
Having no irregularities, roughness, or indentations.   EVEN[1] *adjective*.
plane *verb*
To make even, smooth, or level.   EVEN[1] *verb*.

planetary *adjective*
1. Of extraordinary size and power.   1. GIANT *adjective*.
2. So pervasive and all-inclusive as to exist in or affect   2. UNIVERSAL *adjective*.
   the whole world.

plangent *adjective*
Having or producing a full, deep, or rich sound.   RESONANT.

plant *verb*
1. To put (seeds) into the ground for growth.   1. SEED *verb*.
2. *Informal.* To put or keep out of sight.   2. HIDE[1] *verb*.
plant *noun*
A building or complex in which an industry is located.   WORKS.

plaster *verb*
To spread with a greasy, sticky, or dirty substance.   SMEAR *verb*.

plastered *adjective*
Slang. Intoxicated with alcoholic liquor.   DRUNK *adjective*.

plastic *adjective*
1. Marked by unnaturalness, pretension, and often a   1. **Syns:** artificial, factitious, synthetic.
   slavish love of fads: *the plastic world of Madison
   Avenue hype; plastic, superficial socialites.*
2. Capable of withstanding stress without injury.   2. FLEXIBLE.
3. Easily altered or influenced.   3. FLEXIBLE.
4. Capable of being shaped, bent, or drawn out, as by   4. MALLEABLE.
   hammering or pressure.
5. Changing easily, as in expression.   5. MOBILE.

plasticity *noun*
The quality or state of being flexible.   FLEXIBILITY.

platform *noun*
A temporary framework with a floor, used by workmen.   STAGE *noun*.

platitude *noun*
A trite expression or idea.   CLICHÉ *noun*.

platitudinous *adjective*
Without freshness or appeal due to overuse.   TRITE.

plaudit *noun*
1. An expression of warm approval.   1. PRAISE *noun*.
2. Approval expressed by applauding.   2. APPLAUSE.

plausibility *noun*
Appearance of truth or authenticity.   VERISIMILITUDE.

plausible *adjective*
Worthy of being believed.   BELIEVABLE.

play *verb*
1. To occupy oneself with amusement or diversion: 1. **Syns:** disport, recreate, sport.
   children playing after school.
2. To treat lightly or flippantly.   2. FLIRT *verb*.
3. To be performed: *"The Mousetrap" is still playing in*   3. **Syns:** run, show.
   London.
4. To make music: *The pianist played in Carnegie Hall.*   4. **Syn:** perform.
5. To perform according to one's artistic conception.   5. INTERPRET.
6. To move one's fingers or hands in a nervous or   6. FIDDLE.
   aimless fashion.
7. To control to one's own advantage by artful or   7. MANIPULATE.
   indirect means.
8. To make a bet on.   8. BET *verb*.

9. To cause to undergo or bear, as something unwelcome or damaging.

9. INFLICT.

play along *verb*
Informal. To agree to cooperate or participate: *I played along and drove the getaway car.*

Syn: go along (with).

play around *verb*
Informal. To be sexually unfaithful to another.

PHILANDER.

play down *verb*
Informal. To make less emphatic or obvious.

SOFT-PEDAL.

play off *verb*
To place in opposition or be in opposition to.

OPPOSE.

play out *verb*
1. To cause (a line) to become longer and less taut: *played out the anchor line.*
2. To use all of.
3. To make or become no longer active or productive.
4. To lose so much strength and power as to become ineffective or motionless.

1. *Syns:* unroll, unwind.

2. EXHAUST.
3. DRY UP at **dry.**
4. RUN DOWN.

play up *verb*
Informal. To accord emphasis to.

EMPHASIZE.

play *noun*
1. Activity engaged in for relaxation and amusement: *Children need time for play.*
2. Actions taken as a joke: *It was done all in play.*

3. An indirect, usu. cunning means of gaining an end.
4. The act of putting into play.
5. Ease of movement.
6. Suitable opportunity to accept or allow something.

1. *Syns:* disport, diversion, fun, recreation, sport.
2. *Syns:* fun, game, sport. —*Idiom* fun and games.
3. TRICK *noun.*
4. EXERCISE *noun.*
5. FREEDOM.
6. ROOM.

play-act *verb*
1. To play the part of.
2. To behave affectedly or insincerely.

1. ACT *verb.*
2. ACT *verb.*

play-acting *noun*
1. A display of insincere behavior.
2. The art and occupation of an actor.

1. ACT *noun.*
2. ACTING *noun.*

play along *verb*

SEE **play.**

play around *verb*

SEE **play.**

play down *verb*

SEE **play.**

player *noun*
1. One who plays a musical instrument: *The players in the orchestra were tuning up.*
2. A theatrical performer.
3. One who bets.

1. *Syns:* musician, musicianer, musico, performer.
2. ACTOR.
3. BETTOR.

playing *noun*
The art and occupation of an actor.

ACTING *noun.*

play off *verb*

SEE **play.**

play out *verb*

SEE **play.**

plaything *noun*
An object for children to play with.

TOY *noun.*

play up *verb*

SEE **play.**

plea *noun*
1. An earnest or urgent request.
2. An explanation offered to justify an action or make it better understood.

1. APPEAL *noun.*
2. EXCUSE *noun.*

plead with *verb*
To make an earnest or urgent request.

APPEAL *verb.*

pleasant *adjective*
1. To one's liking.
2. Affording enjoyment.

1. AGREEABLE.
2. ENJOYABLE.

pleasantness *noun*
The quality of being pleasant and friendly.

AMIABILITY.

pleasantries *noun*
Courteous acts that contribute to smoothness and ease in dealings and social relationships.   AMENITIES.

please *verb*
1. To be satisfactory to: *This job pleases me.*   1. **Syns:** satisfy, suit.
2. To give great or keen pleasure to.   2. DELIGHT *verb*.
3. To have the desire or inclination to.   3. CHOOSE.

pleased *adjective*
Eagerly compliant.   GLAD.

pleasing *adjective*
1. Affording enjoyment.   1. ENJOYABLE.
2. To one's liking.   2. AGREEABLE.
3. Providing joy and pleasure.   3. GLAD.

pleasurable *adjective*
1. To one's liking.   1. AGREEABLE.
2. Affording enjoyment.   2. ENJOYABLE.

pleasure *noun*
1. A feeling of extreme gratification aroused by something.   1. DELIGHT *noun*.
2. A desire for a particular thing or activity.   2. LIKING.
3. The condition of responding pleasurably to something.   3. ENJOYMENT.
4. Unrestricted freedom to choose.   4. WILL[1] *noun*.

pleasure *verb*
To give great or keen pleasure to.   DELIGHT *verb*.

pleat *noun*
A line made by the doubling of one part over another.   FOLD *noun*.

pleat *verb*
To bend together or crease so that one part lies over another.   FOLD *verb*.

plebeian *adjective*
Lacking high station or birth.   LOWLY.

plebeians *noun*
The common people.   COMMONALTY.

plebs *noun*
The common people.   COMMONALTY.

pledge *verb*
1. To guarantee by a solemn promise: *The couple pledged their undying love.*   1. **Syns:** covenant, plight[2], promise, swear, vow. —*Idioms* give one's word of honor, solemnly swear.
2. To be morally bound to do.   2. COMMIT.
3. To assume an obligation: *The benefactor pledged to pay the girl's way through school.*   3. **Syns:** contract, engage, promise, undertake.
4. To give or deposit as a pawn.   4. PAWN[1] *verb*.
5. To salute by raising and drinking from a glass.   5. DRINK *verb*.
6. To give a promise of payment to (a creditor).   6. SECURE *verb*.

pledge *noun*
1. A declaration that one will or will not do a certain thing.   1. PROMISE *noun*.
2. Something given to guarantee the repayment of a loan or the fulfillment of an obligation.   2. PAWN[1] *noun*.
3. The act of drinking to someone.   3. TOAST.

plenitude *noun*
Prosperity and a sufficiency of life's necessities.   PLENTY *noun*.

plenteous *adjective*
Characterized by abundance.   GENEROUS.

plenteousness *noun*
Prosperity and a sufficiency of life's necessities.   PLENTY *noun*.

plentiful *adjective*
Characterized by abundance.   GENEROUS.

plenty *noun*
1. Prosperity and a sufficiency of life's necessities: *America is a land of plenty.*
2. A great deal.

1. *Syns:* abundance, bounteousness, bountifulness, plenitude, plenteousness.
2. HEAP *noun.*

pleonastic *adjective*
1. Characterized by excessive and obfuscatory wordiness.
2. Using or containing an excessive number of words.

1. TAUTOLOGICAL.
2. WORDY.

plethora *noun*
A condition of going or being beyond what is needed, desired, or appropriate.

EXCESS *noun.*

pliability *noun*
The quality or state of being flexible.

FLEXIBILITY.

pliable *adjective*
1. Easily altered or influenced.
2. Capable of being shaped, bent, or drawn out, as by hammering or pressure.

1. FLEXIBLE.
2. MALLEABLE.

pliableness *noun*
The quality or state of being flexible.

FLEXIBILITY.

pliancy *noun*
The quality or state of being flexible.

FLEXIBILITY.

pliant *adjective*
1. Easily altered or influenced.
2. Capable of being shaped, bent, or drawn out, as by hammering or pressure.

1. FLEXIBLE.
2. MALLEABLE.

plica *noun*
A line made by the doubling of one part over another.

FOLD *noun.*

plicate *verb*
To bend together or crease so that one part lies over another.

FOLD *verb.*

plication *noun*
A line made by the doubling of one part over another.

FOLD *noun.*

plight[1] *noun*
A difficult, embarrassing situation.

PREDICAMENT.

plight[2] *verb*
To guarantee by a solemn promise.

PLEDGE *verb.*

plighted *adjective*
Pledged to marry.

ENGAGED.

plod *verb*
1. To walk heavily, slowly, and with difficulty: *Troops loaded with heavy packs plodded through the rice paddies.*

2. To do tedious, laborious, and sometimes menial work.

1. *Syns:* slog, slop, toil, trash[2] (*Brit. Regional*), trudge, wade.
Near-syns: stamp, stomp, tramp, trample, trod.
2. GRIND *verb.*

plop *verb*
To drop or sink heavily and noisily.

FLOP *verb.*

plot *noun*
1. The series of events and relationships forming the basis of a composition: *a novel with a complex plot and subplot.*
2. A piece of land.
3. A secret plan to achieve an evil or illegal end: *a plot to hijack an airliner.*

1. *Syns:* intrigue, story. —*Idiom* story line.
2. LOT *noun.*
3. *Syns:* cabal, collusion, connivance (*also* connivence), conspiracy, intrigue, machination, scheme.

plot *verb*
1. To show graphically the direction or location of, as by using coordinates: *The navigator plotted the bomber's course.*

1. *Syns:* chart, lay out, map (out).

2. To work out a secret plan to achieve an evil or illegal end: *Revolutionaries plotted the overthrow of the government.*

2. *Syns:* collude, connive, conspire, intrigue, machinate, practice (against *or* with) (*Obs.*), scheme.

plow *verb*
To spade or dig (soil) to bring the undersoil to the surface.

TURN *verb.*

ploy *noun*
An indirect, usu. cunning means of gaining an end.

TRICK *noun.*

pluck *noun*
The quality of mind enabling one to face danger or hardship resolutely.

COURAGE.

pluck *verb*
To remove from a fixed position.

PULL *verb.*

plucky *adjective*
Having or showing courage.

BRAVE *adjective.*

plug *verb*
1. To plug up something, as a hole, space, or container.
2. *Informal.* To increase or seek to increase the importance or reputation of by favorable publicity.
3. *Informal.* To make known vigorously the positive features of (a product).
4. *Slang.* To wound or kill with a firearm.

1. FILL.
2. PROMOTE.

3. ADVERTISE.

4. SHOOT *verb.*

plum *noun*
1. Something given in return for a service or accomplishment.
2. A person or thing worth catching.

1. REWARD *noun.*

2. CATCH *noun.*

plumb *adjective*
At right angles to the horizon or to level ground.

VERTICAL.

plummet *verb*
To undergo a sharp, rapid descent in value or price.

FALL *verb.*

plump¹ *adjective*
Well-rounded and usu. short in physique: *a plump lady.*

Syns: chubby, plumpish, plumpy, podgy, puddy, pudgy, roly-poly, rotund, round, tubby, zaftig *or* zoftig. —*Idiom* plump as a dumpling (*or* partridge).

plump² *verb*
To drop or sink heavily and noisily.

FLOP *verb.*

plump for *verb*
To aid the cause of by approving or favoring.

SUPPORT *verb.*

plump for *verb*

SEE **plump²**.

plumpish *adjective*
Well-rounded and usu. short in physique.

PLUMP¹.

plumpy *adjective*
Well-rounded and usu. short in physique.

PLUMP¹.

plunder *noun*
Goods or property seized unlawfully, esp. by a victor in wartime: *The marauders ransacked the castle and carried their plunder back to their tents.*

Syns: boodle (*Slang*), booty, loot, pillage, prize, spoils.
Near-syns: acquisition, grab, haul, pickings, take.

plunder *verb*
1. To rob on a large scale.
2. To rob of goods by force, esp. in time of war.

1. LOOT *verb.*
2. SACK².

plunge *verb*
1. To move or thrust at, under, or into the midst of with sudden force: *The duck plunged under water. The senator plunged into the crowd to shake hands.*
2. To move or advance against strong resistance: *He bent his head and plunged into the wind.*
3. To cause to penetrate with force.
4. To come to the ground suddenly and involuntarily.
5. To undergo a sharp, rapid descent in value or price.

1. ***Syns:*** dive, lunge, wade in (*or* into).

2. ***Syns:*** drive, forge², lunge, pitch.

3. RAM.
4. FALL *verb.*
5. FALL *verb.*

plunge *noun*
1. The act of plunging suddenly downward into or as if into water: *took a plunge off the high board into the lake.*
2. The act of swimming: *longed for a refreshing plunge in the pool after work.*
3. A sudden involuntary drop to the ground.
4. A usu. swift downward trend, as in prices.

1. **Syns:** dive, header (*Informal*), nosedive, swoop.
2. **Syns:** dip, swim.
3. FALL *noun.*
4. FALL *noun.*

plunging *adjective*
Cut to reveal the wearer's neck, chest, and back.

LOW *adjective.*

plunk *verb*
To drop or sink heavily and noisily.

FLOP *verb.*

plus *verb*
To join so as to form a larger or more comprehensive entity.

ADD.

plus *adjective*
Involving addition.

ADDITIVE.

plush *adjective*
Characterized by extravagant, ostentatious magnificence.

LUXURIOUS.

plushy *adjective*
Informal. Characterized by extravagant, ostentatious magnificence.

LUXURIOUS.

ply *noun*
A line made by the doubling of one part over another.

FOLD *noun.*

ply *verb*
1. To use with or as if with the hands.
2. To bring to bear steadily or forcefully.

1. HANDLE.
2. EXERCISE *verb.*

plying *noun*
Urgent solicitation.

INSISTENCE.

pneuma *noun*
The vital principle or animating force within living beings.

SPIRIT.

pneumatic *adjective*
Of or relating to air.

AIRY.

podgy *adjective*
Well-rounded and usu. short in physique.

PLUMP[1].

poem *noun*
1. A metrical composition: *read Byron's poems.*
2. Something likened to verse, as in form or style.

1. **Syns:** poesy (*Archaic*), poetry, rhyme (*also* rime), verse.
2. POETRY.

poesy *noun*
Archaic. A metrical composition.

POEM.

poet *noun*
Someone who writes verse: *Pushkin is Russia's greatest poet.*

Syns: bard, muse[2].

poetic also **poetical** *adjective*
Of, pertaining to, or having the characteristics of poetry: *poetic works; poetic diction.*

Syn: lyric.

poetry *noun*
1. Something likened to verse, as in form or style: *Her dance movements were sheer poetry.*
2. A metrical composition.

1. **Syns:** lyricism, poem.
2. POEM.

pogrom *noun*
The savage killing of many victims.

MASSACRE *noun.*

poignant *adjective*
1. Exciting a deep, usu. somber response.
2. *Archaic.* Affecting the organs of taste or smell with a strong and often harsh sensation.

1. AFFECTING.
2. PUNGENT.

point *noun*
1. A sharp or tapered end: *the point of a stiletto; the point of a yucca leaf.*

2. A very small mark: *A point of light fell on the screen.*
3. A particular portion of space chosen for something: *The beginning is a good point at which to start.*
4. A transitional interval beyond which some new action or different state of affairs is likely to begin or occur.
5. A particular interval of time that is limited and often crucial.
6. What one intends to do or achieve.
7. The gist of a specific action or situation.
8. What a speech, piece of writing, or artistic work is about.
9. A course of reasoning.
10. An individually considered portion of a whole.

point *verb*
1. To move (a weapon, blow, etc.) in the direction of someone or something.
2. To mark with punctuation: *pointed the text.*

point out *verb*
1. To make known or identify, as by signs.
2. To call or direct attention to (an occurrence, situation, etc.).

point to *verb*
1. To lead to by logical inference.
2. To give grounds for believing in the existence or presence of.

point up *verb*
To accord emphasis to.

pointed *adjective*
1. Having an end tapering to a point: *pointed yucca leaves; a pointed quill; pointed bamboo stakes.*

2. Readily attracting notice.

pointer *noun*
An item of advance or inside information given as a guide to action.

pointless *adjective*
Lacking rational direction or purpose.

point of view *noun*
The position from which something is observed or considered: *You must live in China for some time to understand the Chinese point of view on world affairs.*

point out *verb*
point to *verb*
point up *verb*

pointy *adjective*
Having an end tapering to a point.

poise *noun*
1. A stable, calm state of the emotions.
2. Freedom from constraint, embarrassment, or awkwardness.

poise *verb*
1. To place or be placed on a narrow or insecure surface.

---

1. **Syns:** acumination (*Biol.*), apex, cusp, mucro (*Biol.*), mucronation (*Biol.*), tip[1].
2. **Syns:** dot, pinpoint, spot.

3. **Syns:** location, locus, place, spot.

4. VERGE *noun.*

5. INSTANT *noun.*

6. INTENTION.
7. IDEA.
8. SUBJECT *noun.*

9. ARGUMENT.
10. ELEMENT.

1. AIM *verb.*

2. **Syn:** punctuate.

1. DESIGNATE.
2. REFER.

1. IMPLY.
2. INDICATE.

EMPHASIZE.

1. **Syns:** acicular, aciculate, acuminate (*Biol.*), acuminous (*Biol.*), acute, cuspate (*also* cuspated, cusped), cuspidate (*also* cuspidated) (*Biol.*), mucronate (*Biol.*), pointy, sharp.
2. NOTICEABLE.

TIP[3] *noun.*

MINDLESS.

Syns: angle, eyes, outlook, slant, standpoint, view, viewpoint.

SEE **point.**
SEE **point.**
SEE **point.**

POINTED.

1. BALANCE *noun.*
2. EASE *noun.*

1. BALANCE *verb.*

2. To remain stationary over a place or object.

2. HANG *verb*.

poison *noun*
1. Anything that is injurious, destructive, or fatal: *Rhubarb leaves contain a deadly poison. Her life was ruined by the poison of pernicious gossip.*
2. One that contaminates.

1. *Syns:* bane, contagion, toxin, venom, virus.

2. CONTAMINANT.

poison *verb*
1. To have a destructive effect on: *Jealousy poisoned their love.*
2. To make physically impure.

1. *Syns:* canker, empoison (*Archaic*), envenom, infect.

2. CONTAMINATE.

poison *adjective*
Capable of injuring or killing by poison.

POISONOUS.

poisonous *adjective*
1. Capable of injuring or killing by poison: *a poisonous snake; poisonous chemicals; a poisonous atmosphere in the office.*

1. *Syns:* mephitic *or* mephitical, poison, toxic, toxicant, venomous, virulent. *Near-syns:* baleful, baneful, deadly, deleterious, detrimental, fatal, lethal, noxious, pernicious.

2. Characterized by intense ill will or spite.

2. MALEVOLENT.

poke *verb*
1. To cause to stick out: *A seal poked its head out of the water.*
2. To thrust against or into.
3. To go or move slowly so that progress is hindered.
4. To look into or inquire about curiously, inquisitively, or in a meddlesome fashion.

1. *Syns:* push, shove, thrust.

2. DIG *verb*.
3. DELAY *verb*.
4. SNOOP *verb*.

poke around *verb*
To reach about or search blindly or uncertainly.

GROPE.

poke *noun*
1. An act of thrusting into or against, as to attract attention.
2. One that lags.

1. DIG *noun*.

2. LAGGARD *noun*.

poke around *verb*

SEE **poke.**

pokerfaced *adjective*
Lacking expression.

EXPRESSIONLESS.

pokey¹ *noun*
Slang. A place for the confinement of persons in lawful detention.

JAIL *noun*.

pokey² *adjective*

SEE **poky.**

poky also **pokey** *adjective*
Informal. Proceeding at a rate less than usual or desired.

SLOW *adjective*.

polar *adjective*
1. Very cold.
2. Diametrically opposed.

1. FRIGID.
2. OPPOSITE *adjective*.

polarity *noun*
1. The condition of being in conflict.
2. That which is diametrically opposed to another.

1. OPPOSITION.
2. OPPOSITE *noun*.

polemic *noun*
A discussion, often heated, in which a difference of opinion is expressed.

ARGUMENT.

polemical *adjective*
Given to arguing.

ARGUMENTATIVE.

police *verb*
1. To maintain or keep in order with or as if with police: *plainclothesmen policing the campus.*
2. To make or keep (an area) clean and orderly.

1. *Syn:* patrol.

2. TIDY *verb*.

police *noun*
A member of a law-enforcement agency.

POLICEMAN.

policeman *noun*
A member of a law-enforcement agency: *Policemen direct traffic.*

Syns: bluebottle (*Brit.*), bluecoat, bobby (*Brit. Slang*), bull (*Slang*), constable (*Brit.*), cop (*Informal*), copper (*Slang*), finest, flatfoot (*Slang*), fuzz (*Slang*), gendarme (*Slang*), heat (*Slang*), law (*Informal*), Man (*Slang*), nab (*Slang*), officer, paddy (*Slang*), patrolman, peeler (*Obs. Brit. Slang*), pig (*Slang*), police, rozzer (*Brit. Slang*), trap (*Brit.*). —*Idioms* John Law, peace officer, police officer.

policy *noun*
An official or prescribed plan or course of action. LINE *noun.*

polish *verb*
1. To give a gleaming luster to, usu. through friction.   1. GLOSS *verb.*
2. To bring to perfection or completion.   2. PERFECT *verb.*
3. To improve by making minor changes or additions.   3. TOUCH UP at **touch.**

polish off *verb*
1. *Informal.* To use all of.   1. EXHAUST.
2. *Informal.* To eat completely or entirely.   2. CONSUME.

polish *noun*
1. A radiant brightness or glow, usu. due to light reflected from a smooth surface.   1. GLOSS *noun.*
2. Enlightenment and excellent taste resulting from intellectual development.   2. CULTURE.
3. Refined, effortless beauty of manner, form, and style.   3. ELEGANCE.

polished *adjective*
1. Having a high, radiant sheen.   1. GLOSSY.
2. Characterized by discriminating taste and broad knowledge as a result of development or education.   2. CULTURED.

polish off *verb*   SEE **polish.**

polite *adjective*
1. Characterized by good manners.   1. COURTEOUS.
2. Fond of or given to ceremony.   2. CEREMONIOUS.

politeness *noun*
Well-mannered behavior toward others.   COURTESY.

politic *adjective*
Showing sensitivity and skill in dealing with others.   DELICATE.

polity *noun*
An organized geopolitical unit.   STATE *noun.*

poll *noun*
The uppermost part of the body.   HEAD *noun.*

pollutant *noun*
One that contaminates.   CONTAMINANT.

pollute *verb*
1. To make physically impure.   1. CONTAMINATE.
2. To make morally impure.   2. TAINT *verb.*

polluted *adjective*
Ceremonially or religiously unfit.   IMPURE.

pollution *noun*
1. The state of being contaminated.   1. CONTAMINATION.
2. Impure condition.   2. IMPURITY.

Pollyanna *noun*
One who expects a favorable outcome or dwells on hopeful aspects.   OPTIMIST.

Pollyannaish *adjective*
Expecting a favorable outcome or dwelling on hopeful aspects.   OPTIMISTIC.

Pollyannaism *noun*
A tendency to expect a favorable outcome or to dwell on hopeful aspects.   OPTIMISM.

poltroon *noun*
Archaic. An ignoble, uncourageous person.   COWARD.

poltroonery *noun*
Ignoble lack of courage.   COWARDICE.

polychrest *noun*
An agent used to restore health.   CURE *noun.*

polychrestic *adjective*
Serving to cure.   CURATIVE *adjective.*

polychromatic also **polychromic, polychromous**
adjective
Having many different colors.   MULTICOLORED.

polychrome *adjective*
Having many different colors.   MULTICOLORED.

polychromic *adjective*   SEE **polychromatic.**

polychromous *adjective*   SEE **polychromatic.**

polymorphism *noun*
Biol. The quality of being made of many different elements, forms, kinds, or individuals.   VARIETY.

polysyllabic *adjective*
Having many syllables.   LONG[1] *adjective.*

pomp *noun*
An impressive or ostentatious exhibition.   DISPLAY *noun.*

pomposity *noun*
Boastful self-importance.   PRETENTIOUSNESS.

pompous *adjective*
Characterized by an exaggerated show of dignity or self-importance: *a pompous old fool.*

Syns: bloated, grandiose, highfalutin *or* hifalutin (*also* highfaluting) (*Informal*), pretentious, puffed-up, puffy, self-important, stuffy.
Near-ants: humble, meek, mild, modest, simple, unassuming; natural, plain.

ponder *verb*
To consider carefully and at length: *pondered the problem as he drove along. The jurors pondered the defendant's testimony.*

Syns: cerebrate, chew over, cogitate, contemplate, deliberate, meditate, mull[2], muse[1], reflect (on), revolve, ruminate, think over, think through, turn over, weigh. —*Idioms* cudgel one's brains, put on one's thinking cap.
Near-syns: brood, consider, debate, dwell, examine, reason, speculate, think.

ponderosity *noun*
The state or quality of being physically heavy.   HEAVINESS.

ponderous *adjective*
1. Lacking fluency or gracefulness: *a ponderous history of Bronze Age agriculture.*

1. *Syns:* elephantine, heavy-handed, labored.
   Near-syns: flat, insipid, vacuous, vapid; dim, dreary, dry, dull, ho-hum, humdrum, lifeless; belabored, boring, monotonous.

2. Having a relatively great weight.   2. HEAVY *adjective.*
3. Unwieldy, esp. due to excess weight.   3. HEAVY *adjective.*

ponderousness *noun*
The state or quality of being physically heavy.   HEAVINESS.

pool *noun*
A combination of businesses closely interconnected for common profit.   COMBINE *noun.*

poop *verb*
Slang. To make extremely tired.   EXHAUST.

poop out *verb*
Slang. To lose so much strength and power as to become ineffective or motionless.   RUN DOWN.

poop *noun*
Slang. An unpleasant, tiresome person.

pooped *adjective*
Slang. Extremely tired.

EXHAUSTED.

poop out *verb*

SEE **poop.**

poor *adjective*
1. Having little or no money or wealth: *too poor to eat regularly.*

DRIP *noun.*

1. **Syns:** broke (*Informal*), busted (*Slang*), destitute, impecunious, impoverished, indigent, necessitous, needy, penniless, penurious, poverty-stricken, strapped (*Informal*). —*Idioms* down and out, hard up, on one's uppers.
   Near-ants: affluent, comfortable, moneyed, opulent, prosperous, wealthy, well-fixed (*Informal*), well-heeled (*Slang*), well-off, well-to-do.
   Ant: rich.

2. Lacking desirable elements or constituents: *poor soil.*
3. Of decidedly inferior quality.
4. Conspicuously deficient in quantity, fullness, or extent.
5. Arousing or deserving pity.

2. **Syns:** depleted, impoverished.

3. SHODDY.
4. MEAGER.

5. PITIFUL.

poorly *adjective*
Affected or tending to be affected with minor health problems.

SICKLY.

pop *verb*
1. To make a sudden sharp, explosive noise.
2. To come open or fly apart suddenly and violently, as from internal pressure.
3. To deliver (a powerful blow) suddenly and sharply.
4. *Brit. Slang.* To give or deposit as a pawn.

1. CRACK *verb.*
2. BURST *verb.*

3. HIT *verb.*
4. PAWN[1] *verb.*

pop in *verb*
To go to or seek out the company of in order to socialize.

VISIT *verb.*

pop off *verb*
Informal. To cease living.

DIE.

pop *noun*
A sudden sharp, explosive noise.

REPORT *noun.*

pop in *verb*

SEE **pop.**

pop off *verb*

SEE **pop.**

poppycock *noun*
Something that does not have or make sense.

NONSENSE.

populace *noun*
The common people.

COMMONALTY.

popular *adjective*
1. Of, representing, or carried on by people at large: *held popular elections.*

1. **Syns:** democratic, general, public.

2. Being a favorite.
3. Suited to or within the means of ordinary people: *seats available at popular prices.*
4. Widely known and discussed.

2. FAVORITE *adjective.*
3. **Syns:** medium-priced, modest, reasonable.
4. FAMOUS.

populate *verb*
To live in (a place).

INHABIT.

porcine *adjective*
Having too much flesh.

FAT *adjective.*

pork *noun*
Slang. The political appointments or jobs that are at the disposal of those in power.

PATRONAGE.

port *noun*
Archaic. Behavior through which one reveals one's personality. — BEARING.

portent *noun*
A phenomenon that serves as a sign or warning of some future good or evil. — OMEN.

portion *verb*
1. To set aside or distribute as a share.
2. To give out in portions or shares.
   1. ALLOT.
   2. DISTRIBUTE.

portion *noun*
1. That which is allotted.
2. One of the parts into which something is divided.
3. A part severed from a whole.
4. That which is inevitably destined.
5. A right or legal share in something.
6. An individual quantity of food.
   1. ALLOTMENT.
   2. DIVISION.
   3. CUT *noun*.
   4. FATE *noun*.
   5. INTEREST *noun*.
   6. SERVING.

portly *adjective*
Having too much flesh. — FAT *adjective*.

portrait *noun*
One exactly resembling another. — DOUBLE *noun*.

portraiture *noun*
The act or process of describing in lifelike imagery. — REPRESENTATION.

portray *verb*
1. To play the part of.
2. To present a lifelike image of.
   1. ACT *verb*.
   2. REPRESENT.

portrayal *noun*
The act or process of describing in lifelike imagery. — REPRESENTATION.

pose *verb*
1. To assume a particular position, as for a portrait: *The family posed in front of the fireplace.*
2. To assume an exaggerated or unnatural attitude or pose.
3. To behave affectedly or insincerely.
4. To represent oneself in a given character or as other than what one is: *The confidence man posed as a wealthy count.*

5. To seek an answer to (a question).
6. To advance, as an idea, for consideration.
   1. *Syns:* posture, sit.
   2. POSTURE *verb*.
   3. ACT *verb*.
   4. *Syns:* attitudinize, impersonate, masquerade, pass, posture. —*Idiom* pass oneself off as.
     Near-syns: fake, feign, pretend, profess, purport.
   5. ASK.
   6. PROPOSE.

pose *noun*
1. The way in which a person holds or carries his body.
2. The way in which one is placed or arranged.
3. A display of insincere behavior.
   1. POSTURE *noun*.
   2. POSITION *noun*.
   3. ACT *noun*.

posh *adjective*
1. *Informal.* Catering to, used by, or admitting only the wealthy or socially superior.
2. *Informal.* Being or in accordance with the current fashion.
   1. EXCLUSIVE.
   2. FASHIONABLE.

posit *verb*
To take for granted without proof. — SUPPOSE.

position *noun*
1. The place where a person or thing is located: *The positions of the guards are reassigned each day. The position of the boxwood is undesirable.*
2. The way in which one is placed or arranged: *in a sitting position.*
3. One's place and direction relative to one's surroundings.
4. Positioning of one individual vis-à-vis others.
   1. *Syns:* emplacement, location, locus, placement, site, situation.
   2. *Syns:* attitude, pose, posture.
   3. BEARING.
   4. PLACE *noun*.

5. A post of employment: *a top position with a brokerage firm.*

6. Something believed or accepted as true by a person.

7. A frame of mind affecting one's thoughts or behavior.

position *verb*

To place in proper position or location: *positioned the shrubs in a circle.*

positive *adjective*

1. Of a constructive nature: *positive suggestions for improving our service.*

2. Having no doubt.

3. Established beyond a doubt.

4. Known positively.

5. *Informal.* Completely such, without qualification or exception.

6. Clearly, fully, and sometimes emphatically expressed.

7. Giving assent.

positively *adverb*

1. Without question.

2. In a direct, positive manner.

3. In truth.

possess *verb*

1. To dominate the mind or thoughts of: *Delusions of omnipotence possessed him.*

2. To keep at one's disposal.

3. To hold on one's person.

4. To have the use or benefit of.

5. To be possessed of.

6. To be endowed with as a visible characteristic or form.

possession *noun*

1. The fact of possessing: *Possession of the property is being contested.*

2. An area subject to rule by an outside power: *Cuba was once a possession of Spain.*

3. Legal right to the possession of a thing.

possessions *noun*

1. Those articles that belong to someone.

2. One's portable property.

3. Something, as land and assets, legally possessed.

possessive *adjective*

1. Having or showing a tendency to control or dominate: *a possessive mother.*

2. Fearful of the loss of position or affection.

possessor *noun*

A person who has legal title to property.

possessory *adjective*

Having or showing a tendency to control or dominate.

possibility *noun*

Something that may occur or be done: *Rain is a possibility for the weekend.*

possible *adjective*

1. Capable of occurring or being done: *There are four possible solutions to the problem.*

---

5. *Syns:* appointment, berth, billet, gig (*Slang*), job, office, place, situation, slot, spot.

6. BELIEF.

7. POSTURE *noun*.

Syns: install, locate, put, set[1], site, situate.

1. *Syns:* affirmative, upbeat (*Informal*).

2. SURE.

3. CERTAIN.

4. DEFINITE.

5. UTTER[2].

6. DEFINITE.

7. FAVORABLE.

1. ABSOLUTELY.

2. FLATLY.

3. REALLY.

1. *Syn:* obsess.

2. HAVE.

3. CARRY *verb*.

4. ENJOY.

5. COMMAND *verb*.

6. BEAR.

1. *Syns:* ownership, proprietorship, title.

2. *Syns:* colony, dependency, province, territory.

3. OWNERSHIP.

1. BELONGINGS.

2. EFFECTS.

3. HOLDING(S).

1. *Syn:* possessory.

2. JEALOUS.

OWNER.

POSSESSIVE.

Syns: contingency, eventuality.

1. *Syns:* feasible, practicable, viable, workable. —*Idiom* within reach.
Near-ants: fruitless, futile, hopeless, impracticable, improbable.
Ant: impossible.

2. Capable of favorable development: *a possible source of cheap fuel.*
3. Likely to happen or to be true.
4. Capable of being but not yet in existence.
5. Capable of being anticipated, considered, or imagined.

post *verb*
1. To place on a list or in a record: *posted all payments in the ledger.*
2. To make a bet on.
3. To appoint and send to a particular place.
4. To gain (a point or points) in a game or contest.

post *noun*
1. An assigned position.
2. A diplomatic office or headquarters in a foreign country.

posterior *adjective*
1. Located in the rear.
2. Following something else in time.

posterior *noun*
1. The part or area farthest from the front.
2. The part of one's back on which one rests in sitting.

posterity *noun*
A group consisting of those descended directly from the same parents or ancestors.

postern *adjective*
Located in the rear.

posthaste *adverb*
In a rapid way.

posthumous *adjective*
Occurring or done after death: *posthumous publication of his memoirs.*

posting *noun*
1. An item inserted, as in a diary, register, or reference book.
2. An assigned position.

postliminary *adjective*
Following something else in time.

post-mortem *adjective*
Occurring or done after death.

post-obit also **post-obituary** *adjective*
Occurring or done after death.

post-obituary *adjective*

postpone *verb*
To put off until a later time.

postponement *noun*
The act of putting off or the condition of being put off.

postulate *verb*
To take for granted without proof.

postulate *noun*
Something taken to be true without proof.

postulation *noun*
Something taken to be true without proof.

posture *noun*
1. The way in which a person holds or carries his body: *learning good posture.*
2. A frame of mind affecting one's thoughts or behavior: *a posture of defenseless womanhood.*
3. Manner of being or form of existence.
4. The way in which one is placed or arranged.

posture *verb*

---

2. *Syn:* potential.
3. PROBABLE.
4. POTENTIAL *adjective.*
5. EARTHLY.

1. *Syns:* enter, insert, record, register.
2. BET *verb.*
3. STATION *verb.*
4. SCORE *verb.*

1. STATION *noun.*
2. MISSION.

1. BACK *adjective.*
2. LATER *adjective.*

1. BACK *noun.*
2. BOTTOM *noun.*

PROGENY.

BACK *adjective.*

FAST *adverb.*

Syns: post-mortem, post-obit (*also* post-obituary).

1. ENTRY.

2. STATION *noun.*

LATER *adjective.*

POSTHUMOUS.

POSTHUMOUS.
SEE **post-obit.**

DEFER[1].

DELAY *noun.*

SUPPOSE.

ASSUMPTION.

ASSUMPTION.

1. *Syns:* attitude, carriage, pose, stance.
2. *Syns:* attitude, outlook, position, stance.
3. CONDITION *noun.*
4. POSITION *noun.*

1. To assume an exaggerated or unnatural attitude or pose: *postured whenever a photographer came near.*
2. To assume a particular position, as for a portrait.
3. To represent oneself in a given character or as other than what one is.

pot *noun*
1. *Card Games.* Something valuable risked on an uncertain outcome.
2. *Brit. Slang.* A competitor regarded as the most likely winner.

potable *noun*
Any liquid that is fit for drinking.

potation *noun*
An act of drinking or the amount swallowed.

potency *noun*
1. Capacity or power for work or vigorous activity.
2. The power or capacity to produce a desired result.
3. The state or quality of being physically strong.

potent *adjective*
1. Having or able to exert great power.
2. Having great physical strength.
3. Having a high concentration of the distinguishing ingredient.

potential *adjective*
1. Capable of being but not yet in existence: *a potential buyer; a potential threat.*
2. Capable of favorable development.

potential *noun*
The inherent capacity for growth or development: *a potential for artistry that has never been realized.*

potentiality *noun*
The inherent capacity for growth or development.

pother *noun*
Needless trouble.

pother *verb*
1. To be nervously or uselessly active.
2. To be troubled.

potted *adjective*
Slang. Intoxicated with alcoholic liquor.

pouch *verb*
To curve outward past the normal or usual limit.

pound *verb*
1. To hit heavily and repeatedly.
2. To shape, break, or flatten with repeated blows.
3. To fix (an idea) in someone's mind by re-emphasis and repetition.

pound *noun*
A sudden sharp, powerful stroke.

pounding *noun*
A repeated stroke or blow, esp. one that produces a sound.

pour *verb*
1. To cause (a liquid) to flow in a steady stream: *pouring milk from the carton.*
2. To come forth or emit in abundance.
3. To rain heavily: *It started to pour just as I left for work.*

4. To come or go in large numbers: *The army poured into enemy territory.*

---

1. *Syns:* attitudinize, pose. —*Idiom* strike an attitude.
2. POSE *verb.*
3. POSE *verb.*

1. BET *noun.*

2. FAVORITE *noun.*

DRINK *noun.*

DRINK *noun.*

1. ENERGY.
2. EFFECT *noun.*
3. STRENGTH.

1. POWERFUL.
2. STRONG.
3. STRONG.

1. *Syns:* eventual, latent, possible.

2. POSSIBLE.

Syn: potentiality.

POTENTIAL *noun.*

BOTHER *noun.*

1. FUSS *verb.*
2. WORRY *verb.*

DRUNK *adjective.*

BULGE *verb.*

1. BEAT *verb.*
2. BEAT *verb.*
3. IMPRESS *verb.*

BLOW[2].

BEAT *noun.*

1. *Syns:* decant, draw (off), effuse.

2. FLOW *verb.*
3. *Syns:* drench, teem[2]. —*Idioms* come down in buckets (*or* sheets *or* torrents), rain cats and dogs.
4. *Syns:* flood, swarm, teem[1], throng, troop.

pout *verb*
1. To be sullenly aloof or withdrawn, as in silent resentment or protest.
2. To curve outward past the normal or usual limit.

1. SULK.

2. BULGE *verb*.

poverty *noun*
The condition of being extremely poor: *government aid to those living in poverty.*

Syns: beggary, destitution, impecuniousness, impoverishment, indigence (*also* indigency), need, neediness, penury, privation, want.
—*Idiom* distressed (*or* reduced *or* straitened) circumstances.
Near-ants: affluence, comfort, luxury, prosperity, riches.
Ant: wealth.

poverty-stricken *adjective*
Having little or no money or wealth.

POOR.

powder *verb*
1. To break up into tiny particles.
2. To scatter or release in drops or small particles.

1. CRUSH *verb*.
2. SPRINKLE *verb*.

powdery *adjective*
Consisting of small particles.

FINE[1].

power *noun*
1. The state or quality of being physically strong.
2. The capacity to exert an influence.
3. The right and power to command, decide, rule, or judge.
4. Effective means of influencing, compelling, or punishing.
5. *Regional.* A great deal.

1. STRENGTH.
2. FORCE *noun*.
3. AUTHORITY.

4. MUSCLE *noun*.

5. HEAP *noun*.

powerful *adjective*
1. Having or able to exert great power: *a powerful nation.*

1. **Syns:** mighty, potent, puissant.
Near-syns: able, competent, effective; authoritative, dominant, forceful, influential; dynamic, energetic, vigorous.
Ant: powerless.

2. Full of or displaying force.
3. Exercising authority.
4. Conveying great physical force.
5. Having or exercising influence.
6. Having great physical strength.

2. FORCEFUL.
3. AUTHORITATIVE.
4. SEVERE.
5. INFLUENTIAL.
6. STRONG.

powerfulness *noun*
The state or quality of being physically strong.

STRENGTH.

powerless *adjective*
1. Unable to manage for oneself.
2. Not capable of accomplishing anything.

1. HELPLESS.
2. INEFFECTUAL.

powerlessness *noun*
1. The condition or state of being incapable of accomplishing or effecting anything.
2. Lack of ability or capacity.

1. INEFFECTUALITY.

2. INABILITY.

powwow *noun*
A meeting for the exchange of views.

CONFERENCE.

powwow *verb*
To meet and exchange views to reach a decision.

CONFER.

practic *adjective*
Having or indicating an awareness of things as they really are.

REALISTIC.

practicable *adjective*
1. Available for use.
2. Capable of occurring or being done.
3. Serving or capable of serving a useful purpose.

1. OPEN *adjective*.
2. POSSIBLE.
3. PRACTICAL.

practical   *adjective*
1. Serving or capable of serving a useful purpose. *A wrist watch is one piece of jewelry that is practical.*
2. Having or indicating an awareness of things as they really are.
3. Resulting from experience or practice: *has a practical knowledge of the shoe business.*
4. Involved in the essential nature of something but not shown or developed.

1. **Syns:** functional, handy, practicable, serviceable, useful, utilitarian.
2. REALISTIC.
3. **Syns:** practiced, veteran.
4. IMPLICIT.

practice   *verb*
1. To do or perform repeatedly so as to master: *practice the shot-put; practice the violin.*
2. To subject to forms of exertion in order to train, strengthen, or condition.
3. To work at, esp. as a profession: *practices law.*
4. To put into action or use.
5. *Obs.* To work out a secret plan to achieve an evil or illegal end.

1. **Syn:** rehearse.
2. EXERCISE *verb.*
3. **Syn:** pursue.
4. USE *verb.*
5. PLOT *verb.*

practice   *noun*
1. Repetition of an action so as to develop or maintain one's skill: *It takes years of practice to play the cello.*
2. A habitual way of behaving.
3. A working at a profession or occupation: *began the practice of medicine.*

1. **Syns:** drill, exercise, rehearsal, study, training.
2. CUSTOM *noun.*
3. **Syn:** pursuit.

practiced   *adjective*
1. Very proficient as a result of practice and study.
2. Skilled or knowledgeable through long practice.
3. Resulting from experience or practice.

1. ACCOMPLISHED.
2. EXPERIENCED.
3. PRACTICAL.

praelect   *verb*

SEE **prelect.**

praetorian   *adjective*
Ruthlessly seeking personal advantage.

CORRUPT *adjective.*

praetorian   *noun*
One who strongly favors retention of the existing order.

CONSERVATIVE *noun.*

pragmatic   *noun*
A person given to intruding in other people's affairs.

MEDDLER.

pragmatic also **pragmatical**   *adjective*
Having or indicating an awareness of things as they really are.

REALISTIC.

praise   *noun*
1. An expression of warm approval: *emphatic in their praise of his performance.*

2. An expression of admiration or congratulation.
3. The honoring of God, as in worship: *a hymn of praise.*

1. **Syns:** acclaim, acclamation, applause, commendation, compliment(s), kudos, laudation, plaudit.
2. COMPLIMENT *noun.*
3. **Syns:** exaltation, glorification, laudation, magnification.

praise   *verb*
1. To express warm approval of: *His partner praises him to the skies.*
2. To pay a compliment to.
3. To honor (God) in religious worship: *Praise God, from whom all blessings flow.*

1. **Syns:** acclaim, applaud, commend, compliment, kudize (*Informal*), laud.
2. COMPLIMENT *verb.*
3. **Syns:** eulogize, exalt, extol, glorify, laud, magnify, panegyrize. —*Idiom* pay homage to.
   Near-syns: bless, celebrate, consecrate, dignify, distinguish, ennoble, honor, proclaim.
   Near-ants: blame, revile.
   Ant: dispraise.

4. To pay tribute or homage to.

4. HONOR *verb.*

praiseworthy   *adjective*
Deserving admiration.

ADMIRABLE.

prance *verb*
To leap and skip about excitedly.

GAMBOL.

prank *noun*
A mischievous act: *Halloween pranks.*

Syns: antic, caper, frolic, joke, lark, monkeyshine, shenanigan, tomfoolery, trick. —*Idiom* high jinks.
Near-syns: escapade, horseplay, skylarking; gambol, play, sport.

prankishness *noun*
Annoying yet harmless, usu. playful acts.

MISCHIEF.

prankster *noun*
One who causes minor trouble or damage.

MISCHIEF.

prate *verb*
1. To talk rapidly, incoherently, or indistinctly.
2. To talk volubly, persistently, and usu. inconsequentially.

1. BABBLE *verb.*
2. CHATTER *verb.*

prate *noun*
1. Unintelligible or foolish talk.
2. Incessant and usu. inconsequential talk.

1. BABBLE *noun.*
2. CHATTER *noun.*

prattle *verb*
1. To talk rapidly, incoherently, or indistinctly.
2. To talk volubly, persistently, and usu. inconsequentially.

1. BABBLE *verb.*
2. CHATTER *verb.*

prattle *noun*
1. Unintelligible or foolish talk.
2. Incessant and usu. inconsequential talk.

1. BABBLE *noun.*
2. CHATTER *noun.*

praxis *noun*
A habitual way of behaving.

CUSTOM *noun.*

pray *verb*
1. To offer a reverent petition to God or a god: *praying for a bountiful harvest.*
2. To make an earnest or urgent request.

1. **Syns:** invocate (*Archaic*), supplicate.
2. APPEAL *verb.*

prayer *noun*
1. The act of praying: *hands clasped in prayer.*
2. A formula of words used in praying: *Hear my prayer, oh Lord!*
3. One who humbly entreats.
4. An earnest or urgent request.

1. **Syns:** invocation, supplication.
2. **Syns:** collect[2], orison, rogation.
3. SUPPLICANT.
4. APPEAL *noun.*

prayerful *adjective*
Deeply concerned with God and the beliefs and practice of religion: *a prayerful and exemplary life.*

Syns: devotional, devout, godly, pious.

preach *verb*
1. To deliver (a sermon or sermons), esp. as a vocation: *preached the gospel.*
2. To indulge in moral reflection, usu. pompously.

1. **Syns:** evangelize, homilize, sermonize.
2. MORALIZE.

preacher *noun*
A person ordained for service in a Christian church: *a marriage performed by a preacher.*

Syns: churchman, clergyman, cleric, clerical, clerk (*Archaic*), divine[1], ecclesiastic, minister, parson, reverend (*Informal*).

preachy *adjective*
Inclined to teach or moralize excessively.

MORAL *adjective.*

preamble *noun*
A short section of preliminary remarks.

INTRODUCTION.

precariousness *noun*
1. The quality or condition of being erratic and undependable.
2. The quality or condition of being physically unsteady.

1. INSTABILITY.
2. UNSTABLENESS.

precaution *noun*
1. Careful forethought to avoid harm or risk.

1. CAUTION *noun.*

2. The exercise of good judgment or common sense in practical matters.

precede *verb*
1. To come, exist, or occur prior to in time: *Her birthday precedes mine.*

2. To begin (something) with preliminary or prefatory material.

precedence also **precedency** *noun*
The act, condition, or right of preceding: *Her career takes precedence over her family.*

precedency *noun*

precedent *noun*
A closely similar case in existence or in the past: *a ruling without precedent in legal history.*

precedent *adjective*
1. Going before.
2. Just gone by or elapsed.

preceding *adjective*
1. Going before.
2. Next before the present one.
3. Just gone by or elapsed.

precept *noun*
1. A principle governing the affairs of man within or among political units.
2. The principle taught by a fable, parable, etc.

precinct(s) *noun*
The boundary surrounding a certain area.

precious *adjective*
1. Of great value.
2. Regarded with much love and tenderness.
3. Given special, usu. doting treatment.
4. Artificially genteel.
5. Pretentiously artistic.

precipitance also **precipitancy** *noun*
Careless, headlong action.

precipitancy *noun*

precipitant *adjective*
1. Happening quickly and without warning.
2. Characterized by unthinking boldness and haste.

precipitate *verb*
1. To cause to happen suddenly or unexpectedly: *The heckling precipitated a riot.*
2. To put down, esp. in layers, by a natural process.

precipitate *adjective*
1. Happening quickly and without warning.
2. Lacking due thought or consideration: *forced to make a precipitate decision.*
3. Characterized by unthinking boldness and haste.
4. So sharply inclined as to be almost perpendicular.

precipitate *noun*
1. Matter that settles on a bottom or collects on a surface by a natural process.
2. Something brought about by a cause.

precipitation *noun*
1. Matter that settles on a bottom or collects on a surface by a natural process.
2. Careless, headlong action.

---

2. PRUDENCE.

1. Syns: antecede, antedate, forerun, predate.
Near-syns: announce, foreshadow, herald, presage.
Ants: follow, succeed.

2. INTRODUCE.

Syns: antecedence, priority. —*Idiom* right of way.
SEE **precedence.**

Syns: antecedent, example.

1. ADVANCE *adjective.*
2. PAST *adjective.*

1. ADVANCE *adjective.*
2. LAST[1] *adjective.*
3. PAST *adjective.*

1. LAW *noun.*

2. MORAL *noun.*

LIMIT *noun.*

1. VALUABLE.
2. DARLING *adjective.*
3. FAVORITE *adjective.*
4. AFFECTED[2].
5. ARTY.

HASTE *noun.*
SEE **precipitance.**

1. ABRUPT.
2. RASH[1].

1. Syns: bring on, prompt, spur.

2. DEPOSIT *verb.*

1. ABRUPT.
2. Syns: hasty, ill-considered, impetuous, impulsive, rash[1], reckless.
3. RASH[1].
4. STEEP[1].

1. DEPOSIT *noun.*

2. EFFECT *noun.*

1. DEPOSIT *noun.*

2. HASTE *noun.*

precipitous *adjective*
1. Characterized by unthinking boldness and haste.
2. So sharply inclined as to be almost perpendicular.

1. RASH[1].
2. STEEP[1].

precise *adjective*
1. Strictly distinguished from others: *at that precise moment.*
2. Clearly, fully, and sometimes emphatically expressed.
3. Conforming to fact.
4. Marked by excessive concern for propriety and good form.

1. *Syns:* exact, identical, very.

2. DEFINITE.

3. ACCURATE.
4. GENTEEL.

precisely *adverb*
1. Without the slightest deviation in any respect: *precisely at 3:00 A.M.*

2. With precision or absolute conformity.
3. In the same manner.

1. *Syns:* bang (*Informal*), dead, direct, directly, exactly, right, smack[1] (*Informal*), square, straight.
2. DIRECTLY.
3. EVEN[1] *adverb.*

preciseness *noun*
Freedom from error.

ACCURACY.

precision *noun*
Freedom from error.

ACCURACY.

preclude *verb*
To prohibit from occurring by advance planning or action.

PREVENT.

preclusion *noun*
The act of preventing.

PREVENTION.

precocious *adjective*
1. Developing, occurring, or appearing before the expected time.
2. Ahead of current trends or customs.

1. EARLY *adjective.*

2. ADVANCED.

precondition *noun*
Something indispensable.

CONDITION *noun.*

preconsider *verb*
To consider and plan in advance.

PREMEDITATE.

precursor *noun*
A forerunner.

ANCESTOR.

predate *verb*
To come, exist, or occur prior to in time.

PRECEDE.

predecessor *noun*
A forerunner.

ANCESTOR.

predeliberate *verb*
To consider and plan in advance.

PREMEDITATE.

predestinate *verb*
To determine the future of in advance.

FATE *verb.*

predestination *noun*
That which is inevitably destined.

FATE *noun.*

predestine *verb*
To determine the future of in advance.

FATE *verb.*

predestined *adjective*
Governed and decided by or as if by fate.

FATED.

predetermine *verb*
1. To determine the future of in advance.
2. To consider and plan in advance.

1. FATE *verb.*
2. PREMEDITATE.

predetermined *adjective*
Governed and decided by or as if by fate.

FATED.

predicament *noun*
A difficult, embarrassing situation: *got into a real predicament when he wrecked his fiancée's car.*

Syns: bind (*Informal*), box[1], corner, dilemma, fix, hole, jam (*Informal*), pickle (*Informal*), plight[1], quagmire, scrape (*Slang*), soup (*Slang*), spot (*Informal*).

—*Idioms* deep water, hot spot, hot water, a spot of trouble, trouble in paradise.
Near-syns: Dutch, trouble; emergency, pinch, strait.

predicate *verb*
To take or serve as the basis for.

BASE[1] *verb*.

predict *verb*
To tell about or make known (future events) in advance, esp. by means of special knowledge or inference: *predicting the collapse of the government.*

Syns: adumbrate, call, forecast, foretell, prognosticate.
Near-syns: announce, declare, proclaim, prophesy, soothsay; anticipate, divine, foreknow, foresee, forewarn, warn.

prediction *noun*
The act of predicting: *listened to the weather predictions.*

Syns: forecast, foretelling, outlook, prognosis, prognostication, projection.

predictive *adjective*
Of or relating to prediction: *the weather forecaster's predictive methods.*

Syns: prognostic, prognosticative.

predilection *noun*
An inclination to something.

BENT *noun*.

predispose *verb*
To influence or be influenced in a certain direction.

DISPOSE.

predisposition *noun*
1. An inclination to something.
2. A liking or personal preference for something.

1. BENT *noun*.
2. TASTE *noun*.

predominance *noun*
The condition or fact of being dominant.

DOMINANCE.

predominant *adjective*
Having pre-eminent significance.

RULING *adjective*.

predominate *verb*
To occupy the pre-eminent position in.

DOMINATE.

pre-eminence also **preeminence, preëminence** *noun*
1. The condition or fact of being dominant.
2. A position of exalted, widely recognized importance.

1. DOMINANCE.
2. EMINENCE.

pre-eminent also **preeminent, preëminent** *adjective*
1. Most important, influential, or significant.
2. Far above others in quality or excellence.
3. Widely known and esteemed.

1. PRIMARY.
2. OUTSTANDING.
3. EMINENT.

pre-empt also **preempt, preëmpt** *verb*
To lay claim to for oneself or as one's right.

ASSUME.

pre-emption also **preemption, preëmption** *noun*
The act of taking something for oneself.

USURPATION.

preen *verb*
To be proud of (oneself) because of some accomplishment, achievement, etc.

PRIDE *verb*.

preface *noun*
A short section of preliminary remarks.

INTRODUCTION.

preface *verb*
To begin (something) with preliminary or prefatory material.

INTRODUCE.

prefatorial *adjective*

SEE **prefatory**.

prefatory also **prefatorial** *adjective*
1. Prior to or preparing for the main matter, action, or business.
2. Serving to introduce a subject, person, etc.

1. PRELIMINARY.
2. INTRODUCTORY.

prefer *verb*
To show partiality toward (someone).

FAVOR *verb*.

preferable *adjective*
Of greater excellence than another.

BETTER[1] *adjective*.

preference *noun*
1. The act of choosing.

1. CHOICE *noun*.

2. Favorable, preferential bias.

preferential *adjective*
Disposed to favor one over another.

preferred *adjective*
Being a favorite.

prefigure *verb*
1. To give an indication of something in advance.
2. To give reason for expecting.

pregnable *adjective*
Open to attack and capture because of a lack of protection.

pregnancy *noun*
The condition of carrying a developing fetus within the uterus: *a difficult pregnancy.*

pregnant *adjective*
1. Carrying a developing fetus within the uterus: *She's three months pregnant.*

2. Conveying hidden or unexpressed meaning: *a pregnant silence.*

prejudice *noun*
1. Irrational suspicion or hatred of a particular group, race, or religion: *prejudice against women.*
2. An inclination for or against that inhibits impartial judgment.

prejudice *verb*
1. To cause to have a prejudiced view.
2. To act on the basis of prejudice.
3. To spoil the soundness or perfection of.
4. To have an effect or impact upon.

prejudiced *adjective*
Exhibiting bias.

prejudicial *adjective*
Exhibiting bias.

prelect also **praelect** *verb*
To talk to (an audience) formally.

prelection *noun*
A usu. formal oral communication to an audience.

preliminary *adjective*
1. Prior to or preparing for the main matter, action, or business: *a preliminary statement.*

2. Serving to introduce a subject, person, etc.
3. Not perfected, elaborated, or completed.

prelude *noun*
A short section of preliminary remarks.

premature *adjective*
Developing, occurring, or appearing before the expected time.

premeditate *verb*
To consider and plan in advance: *She premeditated her strategy down to the last step.*

premeditated *adjective*
Planned, weighed, or estimated in advance.

premier *adjective*
Most important, influential, or significant.

---

2. FAVOR *noun.*

FAVORABLE.

FAVORITE *adjective.*

1. ADUMBRATE.
2. PROMISE *verb.*

VULNERABLE.

Syns: gestation, gravidation (*Obs.*), gravidity, greatness (*Archaic*), heaviness (*Archaic*), parturiency.

1. **Syns:** enceinte, expectant, expecting, gone, gravid, heavy (*Archaic*), parturient. —*Idioms* big (*or* heavy) with child, in a family way, with child.
2. **Syns:** meaningful, significant, suggestive.

1. **Syns:** bigotry, intolerance.

2. BIAS *noun.*

1. BIAS *verb.*
2. DISCRIMINATE *verb.*
3. INJURE.
4. INFLUENCE *verb.*

BIASED.

BIASED.

ADDRESS *verb.*

SPEECH.

1. **Syns:** inductive, introductory, prefatory (*also* prefatorial), preparatory, prolegomenous.
Near-syns: elemental, elementary, primary; basic, fundamental.
Ant: postliminary.
2. INTRODUCTORY.
3. ROUGH.

INTRODUCTION.

EARLY *adjective.*

Syns: forethink, preconsider, predeliberate, predetermine.

CALCULATED.

PRIMARY.

premise *noun*
Something taken to be true without proof.   ASSUMPTION.
premise *verb*
To take for granted without proof.   SUPPOSE.
preoccupation *noun*
1. Total occupation of the attention or of the mind.   **1.** ABSORPTION.
2. An exaggerated concern.   **2.** COMPLEX *noun*.
preoccupied *adjective*
1. Having one's thoughts fully occupied.   **1.** ABSORBED.
2. So lost in thought as to be unaware of one's   **2.** ABSENT-MINDED.
   surroundings.
preoccupy *verb*
To occupy the full attention of.   ABSORB.
preordain *verb*
To determine the future of in advance.   FATE *verb*.
preparation *noun*
The condition of being made ready beforehand: *Syns:* preparedness, readiness.
adequate preparation in case of disaster or accident.
preparations *noun*
Plans made in preparation for some undertaking.   ARRANGEMENTS.
preparatory *adjective*
1. Serving to introduce a subject, person, etc.   **1.** INTRODUCTORY.
2. Prior to or preparing for the main matter, action, or   **2.** PRELIMINARY.
   business.
prepare *verb*
1. To cause to be ready, as for use, consumption, or a   **1.** *Syns:* fit, fix, make, ready.
   special purpose: *preparing dinner.*
2. To plan the details or arrangements of.   **2.** ARRANGE.
prepared *adjective*
In a state of preparedness.   READY *adjective*.
preparedness *noun*
The condition of being made ready beforehand.   PREPARATION.
preponderance also **preponderancy** *noun*
1. The condition or fact of being dominant.   **1.** DOMINANCE.
2. The greatest part or portion.   **2.** WEIGHT *noun*.
preponderancy *noun*   SEE **preponderance**.
preponderate *verb*
To occupy the pre-eminent position in.   DOMINATE.
prepossess *verb*
To cause to have a prejudiced view.   BIAS *verb*.
prepossessed *adjective*
Exhibiting bias.   BIASED.
prepossessing *adjective*
Pleasing to the eye or mind.   ATTRACTIVE.
prepossession *noun*
1. An inclination for or against that inhibits impartial   **1.** BIAS *noun*.
   judgment.
2. An exaggerated concern.   **2.** COMPLEX *noun*.
preposterous *adjective*
1. So senseless as to be laughable.   **1.** FOOLISH.
2. Beyond all reason.   **2.** OUTRAGEOUS.
preposterousness *noun*
Foolish behavior.   FOOLISHNESS.
prepotency *noun*
The condition or fact of being dominant.   DOMINANCE.
prepotent *adjective*
Having pre-eminent significance.   RULING *adjective*.
prerequisite *noun*
Something indispensable.   CONDITION *noun*.
prerogative *noun*
1. A privilege granted a person by virtue of birth.   **1.** BIRTHRIGHT.

2. The right and power to command, decide, rule, or judge.

2. AUTHORITY.

presage *verb*
1. To give an indication of something in advance.
2. To give reason for expecting.
3. To make known the presence or arrival of.

1. ADUMBRATE.
2. PROMISE *verb.*
3. USHER IN at **usher.**

presage *noun*
A phenomenon that serves as a sign or warning of some future good or evil.

OMEN.

prescience *noun*
Unusual or creative discernment or perception.

VISION.

prescient *adjective*
Characterized by foresight.

VISIONARY *adjective.*

prescribe *verb*
To set forth expressly and authoritatively.

DICTATE *verb.*

prescript *noun*
A code or set of codes governing action, procedure, etc.

RULE *noun.*

prescription *noun*
A principle governing the affairs of man within or among political units.

LAW *noun.*

presence *noun*
1. The condition or fact of being present: *A reddish dust indicated the presence of termites.*
2. Behavior through which one reveals one's personality.

1. *Syn:* occurrence.
2. BEARING.

present[1] *noun*
The current time.

NOW *noun.*

present *adjective*
In existence now: *present trends; the present generation.*

Syns: contemporary, current, existent, existing, new, now, present-day.
Near-ants: bygone, erstwhile, gone, late, old, once, onetime, sometime.
Ant: past.

present[2] *verb*
1. To bring forward and quote for formal consideration: *a brief that presented all the precedents to the court for review.*
2. To make known socially.
3. To produce on the stage.
4. To make a gift of.
5. To give formally or officially.
6. To put before another for acceptance.
7. To move (a weapon, blow, etc.) in the direction of someone or something.

1. *Syns:* adduce, advance, allege (*Archaic*), cite, lay[1].
2. ACQUAINT.
3. STAGE *verb.*
4. GIVE *verb.*
5. CONFER.
6. OFFER *verb.*
7. AIM *verb.*

present *noun*
Something bestowed freely.

GIFT *noun.*

presentable *adjective*
Proper in appearance.

DECENT.

presentation *noun*
1. The instance or occasion of being presented for the first time to society: *the presentation of this season's debutantes.*
2. Something bestowed freely.
3. The act of conferring, as of an honor.

1. *Syn:* coming-out (*Informal*).
2. GIFT *noun.*
3. CONFERMENT.

present-day *adjective*
In existence now.

PRESENT[1] *adjective.*

preserval *noun*
The careful guarding of an asset.

CONSERVATION.

preservation *noun*
The careful guarding of an asset.

CONSERVATION.

preservative *adjective*
Able to preserve: *Arizona has a dry, preservative climate.*

Syns: conservative, conservatory, preservatory, protective.

preservatory *adjective*
Able to preserve.

PRESERVATIVE.

preserve *verb*
1. To protect (an asset) from loss or destruction.
2. To keep in a condition of good repair, efficiency, or use.
3. To prepare (food) for storage and future use.

1. CONSERVE *verb*.
2. MAINTAIN.

3. CONSERVE *verb*.

preserve *noun*
Public land kept for a special purpose.

RESERVATION.

press *verb*
1. To smooth by applying heat and pressure: *press shirts.*
2. To exert pressure.
3. To act on with a steady pushing force.
4. To extract from by applying pressure.
5. To solicit insistently.
6. To impel to action.
7. To congregate closely around or against.
8. To put one's arms around affectionately.
9. To do or achieve by forcing obstacles out of one's way.

1. **Syns:** iron, mangle.

2. BEAR.
3. CROWD *verb*.
4. SQUEEZE *verb*.
5. INSIST.
6. URGE *verb*.
7. CROWD *verb*.
8. EMBRACE *verb*.
9. PUSH *verb*.

press *noun*
Journalists and journalism in general: *The press covered the President's speech. We advocate freedom of the press.*

Syns: Fleet Street (*Brit.*), fourth estate, media.

pressing *adjective*
Of immediate import.

BURNING.

pressing *noun*
Urgent solicitation.

INSISTENCE.

pressure *noun*
1. The act, condition, or effect of exerting force on someone or something: *Excessive pressure on the job caused her breakdown. The engine pylon sheared off under pressure in the wind tunnel.*
2. Power used to overcome resistance.

1. **Syns:** strain[1], stress, tension.

2. FORCE *noun*.

pressure *verb*
1. To solicit insistently.
2. To cause (a person or thing) to act or move in spite of resistance.
3. To maintain normal air pressure in.

1. INSIST.
2. FORCE *verb*.

3. PRESSURIZE.

pressurize *verb*
To maintain normal air pressure in: *The cockpit is pressurized for high-altitude flying.*

Syn: pressure.

prestidigitation *noun*
The use of skillful tricks and deceptions to produce entertainingly baffling effects.

MAGIC *noun*.

prestige *noun*
1. The level of credit or respect at which one is regarded by others.
2. A person's high standing among others.
3. A position of exalted, widely recognized importance.

1. FACE *noun*.

2. HONOR *noun*.
3. EMINENCE.

prestigious *adjective*
Widely known and esteemed.

EMINENT.

presumable *adjective*
Based on probability or presumption.

PRESUMPTIVE.

presume *verb*
1. To have the courage to put forward, as an idea, esp. when rebuff or criticism is likely: *I wouldn't even presume to explain his motives.*
2. To take for granted without proof.
3. To draw an inference on the basis of inconclusive evidence or insufficient information.
4. To take advantage of unfairly.

1. **Syns:** hazard, pretend, venture.

2. SUPPOSE.
3. GUESS *verb.*

4. ABUSE *verb.*

presumed *adjective*
Based on inference, not fact.

PRESUMPTIVE.

presuming *adjective*
Having or exhibiting excessive and arrogant self-confidence.

PRESUMPTUOUS.

presumption *noun*
1. Excessive and arrogant self-confidence: *has the presumption to accept the invitation for me.*

1. **Syns:** assumption, brashness, brass (*Informal*), brazenness, cheek, cheekiness, crust (*Slang*), effrontery, face, familiarity, gall², nerve (*Informal*), overconfidence, presumptuousness, temerity, uppitiness (*Informal*).

2. The quality of being arrogant.
3. Something taken to be true without proof.
4. A judgment, estimate, or opinion arrived at by guessing.

2. ARROGANCE.
3. ASSUMPTION.
4. GUESS *noun.*

presumptive *adjective*
1. Based on probability or presumption: *the heiress presumptive to the throne.*
2. Based on inference, not fact: *The enemy's presumptive intentions cannot yet be verified.*
3. *Archaic.* Having or exhibiting excessive and arrogant self-confidence.

1. **Syns:** assumptive, likely, presumable, probable. —*Idiom* taken for granted.
2. **Syns:** assumed, conjectured, inferred, presumed, supposed.
3. PRESUMPTUOUS.

presumptuous *adjective*
1. Having or exhibiting excessive and arrogant self-confidence: *a disrespectful, presumptuous pip-squeak.*

1. **Syns:** assuming, assumptive, brash, brassy (*Informal*), brazen, cheeky, familiar, nervy (*Informal*), overconfident, presuming, presumptive (*Archaic*), pushy (*Informal*), uppity (*also* uppish) (*Informal*).
Near-ants: appropriate, fitting, proper; dutiful, humble, respectful, submissive.

2. Overly convinced of one's own superiority and importance.
3. Rude and disrespectful.

2. ARROGANT.

3. IMPUDENT.

presumptuousness *noun*
Excessive and arrogant self-confidence.

PRESUMPTION.

presuppose *verb*
To take for granted without proof.

SUPPOSE.

presupposition *noun*
Something taken to be true without proof.

ASSUMPTION.

pretend *verb*
1. To behave affectedly or insincerely.
2. To contrive and present as genuine.
3. To take on or give a false appearance of.
4. To have the courage to put forward, as an idea, esp. when rebuff or criticism is likely.

1. ACT *verb.*
2. FAKE *verb.*
3. ASSUME.
4. PRESUME.

pretend *adjective*
Informal. Made to imitate something else.

ARTIFICIAL.

pretended *adjective*
Not genuine or sincere.

ARTIFICIAL.

pretender *noun*
1. One who is not what he claims to be.
2. One who sets forth a claim to a royal title.

1. FAKE *noun.*
2. CLAIMANT.

pretense *noun*
1. The presentation of something false as true: *Their protestations of innocence were sheer pretense.*

1. *Syns:* charade, make-believe, pretension.
   Near-syns: affectation, air, mannerism, pose; deceit, deception, fake, fraud, imposture, sham.
   Ant: sincerity.

2. A deceptive outward appearance.
3. Artificial behavior adopted to impress others.
4. A display of insincere behavior.
5. A professed rather than a real reason: *a secret agent who entered the country on the pretense of being a diplomat.*
6. A legitimate or supposed right to demand something as one's rightful due.

2. FAÇADE.
3. AFFECTATION.
4. ACT *noun.*
5. *Syns:* cover, pretension, pretext.

6. CLAIM *noun.*

pretension *noun*
1. The presentation of something false as true.
2. A professed rather than a real reason.
3. A legitimate or supposed right to demand something as one's rightful due.
4. Boastful self-importance.

1. PRETENSE.
2. PRETENSE.
3. CLAIM *noun.*
4. PRETENTIOUSNESS.

pretentious *adjective*
1. Characterized by an exaggerated show of dignity or self-importance.
2. Artificially genteel.
3. Marked by outward, often extravagant display.
4. Pretentiously artistic.

1. POMPOUS.
2. AFFECTED[2].
3. SHOWY.
4. ARTY.

pretentiousness *noun*
Boastful self-importance: *The rock star's press conference was the height of pretentiousness.*

Syns: ostentation, pomposity, pretension.

preternatural *adjective*
1. Greatly exceeding or departing from the normal course of nature: *a hurricane of preternatural force and violence.*
2. Departing from the normal.
3. Of, coming from, or relating to forces or beings that exist outside the natural world.

1. *Syns:* hypernormal, supernatural, unnatural.
2. ABNORMAL.
3. SUPERNATURAL.

preternaturalness *noun*
The condition of being abnormal.

ABNORMALITY.

pretext *noun*
1. An explanation offered to justify an action or make it better understood.
2. A professed rather than a real reason.
3. A deceptive outward appearance.

1. EXCUSE *noun.*
2. PRETENSE.
3. FAÇADE.

pretty *adjective*
1. Having qualities that delight the eye.
2. Pleasing to the eye or mind.

1. BEAUTIFUL.
2. ATTRACTIVE.

pretty *adverb*
To some extent.

FAIRLY.

prevail *verb*
1. To get the better of.
2. To occupy the pre-eminent position in.

1. TRIUMPH *verb.*
2. DOMINATE.

prevail on (or **upon**) *verb*
To succeed in causing (a person) to act in a certain way.

PERSUADE.

prevailing *adjective*
1. Most generally existing or encountered at a given time: *The prevailing view is that war is imminent.*

1. *Syns:* current, prevalent, regnant, rife, widespread.
   Near-syns: common, familiar, general,

2. Having pre-eminent significance.

prevail on (or **upon**) *verb*

prevalence *noun*
The quality or condition of being usual.

prevalent *adjective*
Most generally existing or encountered at a given time.

prevaricate *verb*
1. To stray from truthfulness or sincerity.
2. To make untrue declarations.

prevarication *noun*
An untrue declaration.

prevaricator *noun*
One who tells lies.

prevent *verb*
To prohibit from occurring by advance planning or action: *Crisis management is an unreliable way of preventing war. Mass inoculations prevented an epidemic.*

preventative *adjective*

prevention *noun*
The act of preventing: *prevention of war through balance of power.*

preventive also **preventative** *adjective*
1. Intended to prevent: *took preventive measures to avoid a conflict.*
2. *Med.* Defending against disease: *preventive dentistry.*

previous *adjective*
1. Next before the present one.
2. Just gone by or elapsed.
3. Having been such previously.

prey *noun*
One that is made to suffer injury, loss, or death.

price *noun*
1. An amount paid or to be paid for a purchase.
2. A loss sustained in the accomplishment of or as the result of something.

priceless *adjective*
1. Extremely funny: *That joke is just priceless!*

2. Of great value.

prick *noun*
1. A sudden, sharp, painful feeling: *felt a prick of remorse.*
2. A small mark or hole made by a sharp, pointed object: *looked for telltale needle pricks in the suspected addict's arm.*
3. A sharp, pointed object: *the pricks on a cactus.*

prick *verb*
To impel to action

prickish *adjective*
Easily annoyed.

prickle *noun*
1. A sharp, pointed object.
2. A sudden, sharp, painful feeling.

prickly *adjective*
1. Full of sharp, needlelike protuberances.
2. So replete with interlocking points and complications as to be painfully irritating.

---

ordinary; dominant, popular, predominant, rampant.

2. RULING *adjective*.

SEE **prevail**.

USUALNESS.

PREVAILING.

1. EQUIVOCATE.
2. LIE² *verb*.

LIE² *noun*.

LIAR.

Syns: avert, deter, forestall, forfend (*also* forefend), head off, obviate, preclude, rule out, stave off, turn aside, ward (off).
—*Idiom* nip in the bud.

SEE **preventive**.

Syns: determent, deterrence, forestalling, forestallment, obviation, preclusion.

1. *Syns:* deterrent, deterring, forestalling.

2. *Syns:* prophylactic, protective.

1. LAST¹ *adjective*.
2. PAST *adjective*.
3. LATE *adjective*.

VICTIM.

1. COST *noun*.
2. COST *noun*.

1. *Syns:* hilarious, killing (*Informal*), rich (*Informal*), screaming (*Slang*), sidesplitting, slaying (*Slang*).
2. VALUABLE.

1. *Syns:* pang, prickle, stab, sting.

2. *Syns:* perforation, puncture, stab.

3. *Syns:* needle, prickle, thorn.

URGE *verb*.

IRRITABLE.

1. PRICK *noun*.
2. PRICK *noun*.

1. THORNY.
2. THORNY.

pride *noun*
1. A sense of one's own dignity or worth: *had to respond to save his pride.*
2. A regarding of oneself with undue favor.
3. The quality of being arrogant.

    pride *verb*
To be proud of (oneself) because of some accomplishment, achievement, etc.: *prides herself on her organizational ability.*

prideful *adjective*
Properly valuing oneself, one's honor, or one's dignity.

prier also **pryer** *noun*
A person who snoops.

prim *adjective*
Marked by excessive concern for propriety and good form.

primary *adjective*
1. Most important, influential, or significant: *the primary duty of an employee; the primary leader of the opposition.*

2. Preceding all others in time.
3. Arising from or going to the root or source.
4. Not derived from something else.
5. Marked by the absence of any intervention.
6. Of or pertaining to early stages in the evolution of human culture.

prime *noun*
1. *Rare.* The time of life between childhood and maturity.
2. A condition or time of vigor and freshness.

    prime *adjective*
1. Of fine quality.
2. Exceptionally good of its kind.
3. Most important, influential, or significant.
4. Preceding all others in time.
5. Not derived from something else.

primed *adjective*
In a state of preparedness.

primeval *adjective*
Of or pertaining to early stages in the evolution of human culture.

primitive *adjective*
1. Of or pertaining to early stages in the evolution of human culture: *a primitive society.*
2. Of, existing, or occurring in a distant period.
3. Lacking expert, careful craftsmanship.
4. Not derived from something else.
5. Of or being an irreducible element.
6. Exhibiting lack of education or knowledge.
7. Not civilized.

primordial *adjective*
Of, existing, or occurring in a distant period.

princely *adjective*
Large and impressive in size, scope, or extent.

principal *adjective*
1. Having or exercising authority: *the principal carpenter on that job.*
2. Most important, influential, or significant.

1. ***Syns:*** amour-propre, ego, self-esteem, self-regard, self-respect.
2. EGOTISM.
3. ARROGANCE.

Syns: congratulate, preen.

PROUD.

SNOOP *noun.*

GENTEEL.

1. ***Syns:*** capital, cardinal, chief, dominant, first, foremost, key, leading, main, major, number-one (*Informal*), outstanding, paramount, pre-eminent (*also* preeminent, preëminent), premier, prime, principal, top.
2. FIRST *adjective.*
3. RADICAL *adjective.*
4. ORIGINAL *adjective.*
5. IMMEDIATE.
6. PRIMITIVE.

1. YOUTH.

2. BLOOM *noun.*

1. CHOICE *adjective.*
2. EXCELLENT.
3. PRIMARY.
4. FIRST *adjective.*
5. ORIGINAL *adjective.*

READY *adjective.*

PRIMITIVE.

1. ***Syns:*** primary, primeval.

2. EARLY *adjective.*
3. RUDE.
4. ORIGINAL *adjective.*
5. ELEMENTAL.
6. IGNORANT.
7. UNCIVILIZED.

EARLY *adjective.*

GRAND.

1. ***Syns:*** boss, chief, foremost, head.

2. PRIMARY.

principal *noun*
The main performer in a theatrical production.   LEAD *noun*.

principle *noun*
A broad and basic rule or truth.   LAW *noun*.

principled *adjective*
In accordance with principles of right or good conduct.   ETHICAL.

principles *noun*
Moral or ethical strength.   CHARACTER.

print *noun*
1. The visible effect made on a surface by pressure.   1. IMPRESSION.
2. A visible sign or mark of the passage of someone or   2. TRACK *noun*.
   something.

printing *noun*
1. The act or process of publishing printed matter.   1. PUBLICATION.
2. The entire number of copies of a publication printed   2. IMPRESSION.
   from a single typesetting.

prior *adjective*
1. Going before.   1. ADVANCE *adjective*.
2. Just gone by or elapsed.   2. PAST *adjective*.

priority *noun*
The act, condition, or right of preceding.   PRECEDENCE.

prison *noun*
A place for the confinement of persons in lawful   JAIL *noun*.
detention.

prissy *adjective*
Marked by excessive concern for propriety and good   GENTEEL.
form.

private *adjective*
1. Belonging or confined to a particular person or   1. *Syns:* personal, privy.
   group as opposed to the public or the government:
   private property.
2. Known about by very few.   2. CONFIDENTIAL.

privation *noun*
1. The condition of being deprived of what one once   1. DEPRIVATION.
   had or ought to have.
2. The condition of being extremely poor.   2. POVERTY.

privileged *adjective*
Law. Of or being information available only to   CONFIDENTIAL.
authorized persons.

privy *adjective*
1. Belonging or confined to a particular person or   1. PRIVATE.
   group as opposed to the public or the government.
2. *Archaic.* Known about by very few.   2. CONFIDENTIAL.
3. *Obs.* Indicating intimacy and mutual trust.   3. CONFIDENTIAL.

prize *noun*
1. That which is superlative.   1. BEST *noun*.
2. Something given in return for a service or   2. REWARD *noun*.
   accomplishment.
3. A memento received as a symbol of excellence or   3. TROPHY.
   victory.
4. Goods or property seized unlawfully, esp. by a victor   4. PLUNDER *noun*.
   in wartime.
5. A person or thing worth catching.   5. CATCH *noun*.
6. Someone or something considered exceptionally   6. TREASURE *noun*.
   precious.

prize *verb*
1. To recognize the worth, quality, importance, etc., of.   1. APPRECIATE.
2. To have the highest regard for.   2. CHERISH.

probability *noun*
The likelihood of a given event occurring.   CHANCE *noun*.

probable *adjective*
1. Likely to happen or to be true: *The probable consequences are frightening.*

2. Based on probability or presumption.

probe *noun*
1. The act or an instance of exploring or investigating.
2. Something, as a remark, used to determine the attitude of another.
3. A seeking of knowledge, data, or the truth about something.

probe *verb*
1. To go into or through for the purpose of making discoveries or acquiring information.
2. To test the attitude of.

probing *adjective*
Having or suggesting keen, discerning intellect.

probity *noun*
1. The quality or state of being morally sound.
2. Moral or ethical strength.

problem *noun*
A situation that presents difficulty, uncertainty, or perplexity: *dealing with the unemployment problem.*

problematical also **problematic** *adjective*
1. Not affording certainty.
2. In doubt or dispute.

proboscis *noun*
The structure on the human face that contains the nostrils and organs of smell and forms the beginning of the respiratory tract.

procedure *noun*
1. A method used in dealing with something.
2. An official or prescribed plan or course of action.

proceed *verb*
1. To go forward, esp. toward a conclusion.
2. To have as a source.
3. To move along a particular course.

procession *noun*
A way in which things follow each other in space or time.

proclaim *verb*
1. To bring to public notice.
2. To make known the presence or arrival of.
3. To make manifest or apparent.

proclamation *noun*
1. The act of announcing.
2. A public statement.

proclivity *noun*
An inclination to something.

procrastinate *verb*
To go or move slowly so that progress is hindered.

procreant *adjective*
Biol. Of or pertaining to reproduction.

procreate *verb*
1. To produce sexually or asexually others of one's kind.
2. To be the biological father of.
3. To cause to come into existence.

1. **Syns:** conceivable, possible.
   Near-ants: doubtful, dubious, incredible, questionable, unlikely.
   Ant: improbable.
2. PRESUMPTIVE.

1. EXPLORATION.
2. FEELER.
3. INQUIRY.

1. EXPLORE.
2. FEEL OUT at **feel.**

INCISIVE.

1. GOOD *noun.*
2. CHARACTER.

Syns: issue, question. —*Idioms* can of worms, hornet's nest.

1. AMBIGUOUS.
2. DEBATABLE.

NOSE *noun.*

1. APPROACH *noun.*
2. LINE *noun.*

1. COME.
2. STEM *verb.*
3. GO *verb.*

ORDER *noun.*

1. ANNOUNCE.
2. USHER IN at **usher.**
3. SHOW *verb.*

1. ANNOUNCEMENT.
2. ANNOUNCEMENT.

BENT *noun.*

DELAY *verb.*

REPRODUCTIVE.

1. REPRODUCE.
2. FATHER *verb.*
3. PRODUCE.

procreation *noun*
The process by which an organism produces others of its kind.   REPRODUCTION.

procreative *adjective*
Of or pertaining to reproduction.   REPRODUCTIVE.

procumbent *adjective*
Lying down.   FLAT *adjective*.

procurable *adjective*
Capable of being obtained or used.   AVAILABLE.

procure *verb*
To come into possession of.   GET.

prod *verb*
1. To thrust against or into.   1. DIG *verb*.
2. To solicit insistently.   2. INSIST.
3. To impel to action.   3. URGE *verb*.

prod *noun*
1. An act or instance of using force so as to propel ahead.   1. PUSH *noun*.
2. Something that causes and encourages a given response.   2. STIMULUS.

prodding *noun*
Urgent solicitation.   INSISTENCE.

prodigal *adjective*
1. Characterized by excessive or imprudent spending.   1. EXTRAVAGANT.
2. Given to or marked by unrestrained abundance.   2. PROFUSE.

prodigal *noun*
A person who spends money or resources wastefully.   WASTREL.

prodigality *noun*
Excessive or imprudent expenditure.   EXTRAVAGANCE.

prodigious *adjective*
1. Of extraordinary size and power.   1. GIANT *adjective*.
2. So remarkable as to elicit disbelief.   2. FABULOUS.

prodigy *noun*
One that evokes great surprise and admiration.   MARVEL.

produce *verb*
1. To cause to come into existence: *produce an alternative energy plan*.   1. *Syns:* create, engender, father, generate, hatch, make, originate, parent, procreate, sire, spawn. —*Idioms* bring to pass, give birth (*or* rise) to.
2. To bring (a product, idea, etc.) into being.   2. DEVELOP.
3. To bring forth (a product).   3. BEAR.
4. To form by artistic effort.   4. COMPOSE.
5. To create by forming, combining, or altering materials.   5. MAKE.
6. To bring into existence and foster the development of.   6. GROW.
7. To be the cause of.   7. CAUSE *verb*.
8. To make as income or profit.   8. RETURN *verb*.
9. *Geom.* To make or become longer.   9. LENGTHEN.

product *noun*
1. Something produced by human effort: *the product of an active imagination*.   1. *Syn:* production.
2. The amount or quantity produced.   2. YIELD *noun*.

production *noun*
1. Something that is the result of creative effort.   1. COMPOSITION.
2. Something produced by human effort.   2. PRODUCT.
3. The amount or quantity produced.   3. YIELD *noun*.
4. *Geom.* The act of making something longer or the condition of being made longer.   4. EXTENSION.

productive *adjective*
1. Capable of reproducing.
2. Characterized by great productivity.
3. Acting effectively with minimal waste.
4. Producing or able to produce a desired effect.

1. FERTILE.
2. FERTILE.
3. EFFICIENT.
4. EFFECTIVE.

productivity *noun*
1. The quality or state of being fertile.
2. The quality of being efficient.

1. FERTILITY.
2. EFFICIENCY.

profanation *noun*
An act of disrespect or impiety toward something regarded as sacred.

SACRILEGE.

profane *adjective*
1. Not religious in subject matter, form, or use: *sacred and profane music.*
2. Offensive to accepted standards of decency.
3. Showing irreverence and contempt for something sacred.

1. *Syns:* lay², secular, temporal, worldly.
2. OBSCENE.
3. SACRILEGIOUS.

profane *verb*
To spoil or mar the sanctity of.

VIOLATE.

profanity *noun*
Something that is offensive to accepted standards of decency.

OBSCENITY.

proffer *verb*
To put before another for acceptance.

OFFER *verb.*

proffer *noun*
Something offered.

OFFER *noun.*

proficiency *noun*
Natural or acquired facility in a specific activity.

ABILITY.

proficient *adjective*
1. Having the ability to perform well.
2. Having or demonstrating a high degree of knowledge or skill.
3. Acting effectively with minimal waste.

1. ABLE.
2. EXPERT *adjective.*
3. EFFICIENT.

proficient *noun*
A person with a high degree of knowledge or skill in a particular field.

EXPERT *noun.*

profile *noun*
A line marking and shaping the outer form of an object.

OUTLINE *noun.*

profit *verb*
1. To be an advantage to: *It would profit you to learn to drive.*

1. *Syns:* avail, benefit, boot² (*Archaic*), serve. —*Idiom* stand someone in good stead.

2. To derive advantage.
3. To make a large profit.

2. BENEFIT *verb.*
3. CLEAN UP at **clean.**

profit *noun*
1. The quality of being suitable or adaptable to an end.
2. Something earned, won, or otherwise acquired.
3. Something beneficial.
4. Something that contributes to or increases one's well-being.

1. USE *noun.*
2. GAIN *noun.*
3. ADVANTAGE *noun.*
4. INTEREST *noun.*

profitable *adjective*
Affording profit: *a profitable business.*

Syns: advantageous, fat, lucrative, moneymaking, remunerative.
Near-syns: desirable, gainful, good, paying, pleasing, well-paying, worthwhile.
Ant: unprofitable.

profligacy *noun*
1. Excessive or imprudent expenditure.
2. Excessive freedom; lack of restraint.

1. EXTRAVAGANCE.
2. LICENSE *noun.*

profligate *adjective*
1. Lacking in moral restraint.
2. Characterized by excessive or imprudent spending.

profligate *noun*
1. An immoral or licentious man.
2. A person who spends money or resources wastefully.

profound *adjective*
1. Beyond the understanding of an average mind.
2. Resulting from or affecting one's innermost feelings.
3. Extending far downward or inward from a surface.

profoundness *noun*
Intellectual penetration or range.

profundity *noun*
1. Intellectual penetration or range.
2. Deep, thorough, or mature understanding.

profuse *adjective*
1. Given to or marked by unrestrained abundance: *profuse apologies.*

2. Growing profusely.

profusive *adjective*
Given to or marked by unrestrained abundance.

progenitive *adjective*
Biol. Employed in reproduction.

progenitor *noun*
A person from whom one is descended.

progeny *noun*
A group consisting of those descended directly from the same parents or ancestors: *Queen Victoria's progeny sat on many European thrones.*

prognosis *noun*
The act of predicting.

prognostic *adjective*
Of or relating to prediction.

prognostic *noun*
A phenomenon that serves as a sign or warning of some future good or evil.

prognosticate *verb*
To tell about or make known (future events) in advance, esp. by means of special knowledge or inference.

prognostication *noun*
1. A phenomenon that serves as a sign or warning of some future good or evil.
2. The act of predicting.

prognosticative *adjective*
Of or relating to prediction.

program *noun*
1. An organized list of procedures, activities, events, etc.: *On our program is a visit to Chinatown.*

2. A printed list of the order of events and other pertinent information for a public performance: *Why isn't her name on the program?*
3. An official or prescribed plan or course of action.

program *verb*
To enter on a schedule.

---

1. ABANDONED.
2. EXTRAVAGANT.

1. WANTON *noun.*
2. WASTREL.

1. DEEP *adjective.*
2. DEEP *adjective.*
3. DEEP *adjective.*

DEPTH.

1. DEPTH.
2. WISDOM.

1. **Syns:** extravagant, exuberant, lavish, lush, luxuriant, opulent, prodigal, profusive, riotous, superabundant. **Near-ants:** meager, measly, scant, scrimpy, skimpy, slight, small, sparse. **Ant:** exiguous.
2. THICK *adjective.*

PROFUSE.

REPRODUCTIVE.

ANCESTOR.

Syns: begats (*Slang*), brood, get, issue, offspring, posterity, seed.

PREDICTION.

PREDICTIVE.

OMEN.

PREDICT.

1. OMEN.

2. PREDICTION.

PREDICTIVE.

1. **Syns:** agenda, calendar, docket, line-up (*also* lineup), schedule, timetable. —*Idiom* order of the day.
2. **Syns:** bill[1], prospectus, syllabus.

3. LINE *noun.*

SCHEDULE *verb.*

progress *noun*
1. Steady improvement, as of an individual or a society: *progress in the economy of developing countries.*
2. Forward movement.
3. A progression from a simple form to a more complex one.

1. **Syns:** amelioration, betterment, development, improvement, melioration.
2. ADVANCE *noun.*
3. DEVELOPMENT.

progress *verb*
To go forward, esp. toward a conclusion.

COME.

progression *noun*
Forward movement.

ADVANCE *noun.*

progressive *adjective*
1. Favoring civil liberties and social progress.
2. Ahead of current trends or customs.
3. Not narrow or conservative in thought, expression, or conduct.

1. LIBERAL *adjective.*
2. ADVANCED.
3. BROAD.

progressive *noun*
A person with liberal political opinions.

LIBERAL *noun.*

prohibit *verb*
To refuse to allow.

FORBID.

prohibited *adjective*
Not allowed.

FORBIDDEN.

prohibition *noun*
A refusal to allow.

FORBIDDANCE.

project *noun*
1. Something undertaken, esp. something requiring extensive planning and work: *a five-year research project.*
2. A method for making, doing, or accomplishing something.

1. **Syns:** enterprise, undertaking, venture.

2. DESIGN *noun.*

project *verb*
1. To curve outward past the normal or usual limit.
2. To send out heat, light, or energy.
3. To launch with great force.
4. To form a strategy for.
5. To have in mind as a goal or purpose.

1. BULGE *verb.*
2. SHED.
3. SHOOT *verb.*
4. DESIGN *verb.*
5. INTEND.

projection *noun*
1. A part that protrudes or extends outward.
2. A natural land elevation.
3. The act of predicting.

1. BULGE *noun.*
2. HILL *noun.*
3. PREDICTION.

prolegomenon *noun*
A short section of preliminary remarks.

INTRODUCTION.

prolegomenous *adjective*
1. Serving to introduce a subject, person, etc.
2. Prior to or preparing for the main matter, action, or business.

1. INTRODUCTORY.
2. PRELIMINARY.

proliferate *verb*
To produce sexually or asexually others of one's kind.

REPRODUCE.

proliferation *noun*
1. The process by which an organism produces others of its kind.
2. The result or product of building up.

1. REPRODUCTION.

2. BUILD-UP at **build up.**

proliferous *adjective*
Biol. Capable of reproducing.

FERTILE.

prolific *adjective*
1. Capable of reproducing.
2. Characterized by great productivity.

1. FERTILE.
2. FERTILE.

prolix *adjective*
Using or containing an excessive number of words.

WORDY.

prolixity *noun*
Words or the use of words in excess of those needed for clarity or precision.   WORDINESS.

prolixness *noun*
Words or the use of words in excess of those needed for clarity or precision.   WORDINESS.

prologue *noun*
A short section of preliminary remarks.   INTRODUCTION.

prolong *verb*
To make or become longer.   LENGTHEN.

prolongate *verb*
To make or become longer.   LENGTHEN.

prolongation *noun*
The act of making something longer or the condition of being made longer.   EXTENSION.

prolonged *adjective*
1. Of long duration.   **1.** CHRONIC.
2. Extending tediously beyond a standard duration.   **2.** LONG¹ *adjective.*

promenade *verb*
To walk at a leisurely pace.   STROLL *verb.*

promenade *noun*
An act of walking, esp. for pleasure.   WALK *noun.*

prominence also **prominency** *noun*
1. A position of exalted, widely recognized importance.   **1.** EMINENCE.
2. A natural land elevation.   **2.** HILL *noun.*

prominency *noun*   SEE **prominence.**

prominent *adjective*
1. Standing out prominently.   **1.** BOLD.
2. Readily attracting notice.   **2.** NOTICEABLE.
3. Widely known and esteemed.   **3.** EMINENT.

promise *noun*
A declaration that one will or will not do a certain thing: *made a promise to repay the debt but defaulted; gave her his promise that he would return.*   *Syns:* covenant, guarantee, pledge, vow.

promise *verb*
1. To give reason for expecting: *dark clouds that promised a storm.*   **1.** *Syns:* betoken, foreshadow, foretoken, indicate, prefigure, presage.
2. To assume an obligation.   **2.** PLEDGE *verb.*
3. To guarantee by a solemn promise.   **3.** PLEDGE *verb.*

promising *adjective*
1. Showing great promise.   **1.** COMING.
2. Inspiring confidence or hope.   **2.** ENCOURAGING.

promote *verb*
1. To raise in rank: *promoted him from corporal to sergeant.*   **1.** *Syns:* advance, elevate, jump, raise, upgrade.
2. To cause to move forward or upward, as toward a goal.   **2.** ADVANCE *verb.*
3. To help bring about: *believed that TV violence promotes real violence.*   **3.** *Syns:* cultivate, encourage, feed, foster.
4. To make known vigorously the positive features of (a product).   **4.** ADVERTISE.
5. To increase or seek to increase the importance or reputation of by favorable publicity: *His press agent promoted the movie in feature stories.*   **5.** *Syns:* ballyhoo (*Informal*), boost, build up, enhance, hype (*Slang*), plug (*Informal*), publicize, puff, tout.
Near-ants: belittle, decry, deprecate, depreciate, discredit, impugn.
Ant: disparage.

promotion *noun*
1. A systematic effort to increase the importance or   **1.** *Syns:* ballyhoo (*Informal*), build-up

reputation of by favorable publicity: *spent $100,000 in promotion of the new product.*

2. A progression upward in rank.
3. The act or profession of promoting something, as a product.

prompt *adjective*
Occurring, acting, or performed exactly at the time appointed.

  prompt *verb*
  1. To cause to happen suddenly or unexpectedly.
  2. To elicit a strong emotional response from.
  3. To impel to action.

promulgate *verb*
1. To make (information) generally known.
2. To bring to public notice.
3. To put in force by legal authority.

promulgation *noun*
The act of announcing.

prone *adjective*
1. Lying down.
2. Having or showing a tendency or likelihood.
3. Tending to incur.

proneness *noun*
An inclination to something.

pronounce *verb*
To produce or make (speech sounds): *She pronounced her vowels with a southern drawl.*

pronounced *adjective*
1. Standing out prominently.
2. Without any doubt.

pronouncement *noun*
1. The act of announcing.
2. A public statement.
3. An authoritative or official decision, esp. one made by a court.

pronto *adverb*
Informal. In a rapid way.

proof *noun*
1. A fact or circumstance that gives logical support to an assertion, claim, or proposal.
2. A procedure that ascertains effectiveness, value, proper function, or other quality.
3. That which confirms.

  proof *adjective*
  Having the capacity to withstand.

prop *noun*
A means or device that keeps something erect, stable, or secure.

  prop *verb*
  To keep from yielding or failing during stress or difficulty.

propagandize *verb*
To teach to accept a system of thought uncritically.

propagate *verb*
1. To produce sexually or asexually others of one's kind.
2. To bring into existence and foster the development of.

(*also* buildup) (*Informal*), hype (*Slang*), pitch (*Slang*), publicity, puffery.
2. ADVANCEMENT.
3. ADVERTISING.

PUNCTUAL.

1. PRECIPITATE *verb*.
2. INSPIRE.
3. URGE *verb*.

1. ADVERTISE.
2. ANNOUNCE.
3. ESTABLISH.

ANNOUNCEMENT.

1. FLAT *adjective*.
2. INCLINED.
3. LIABLE.

BENT *noun*.

Syns: articulate, enunciate, say, utter[1], vocalize.

1. BOLD.
2. DECIDED.

1. ANNOUNCEMENT.
2. ANNOUNCEMENT.
3. RULING *noun*.

FAST *adverb*.

1. REASON *noun*.

2. TEST *noun*.

3. CONFIRMATION.

RESISTANT *adjective*.

SUPPORT *noun*.

SUSTAIN.

INDOCTRINATE.

1. REPRODUCE.

2. GROW.

propagation *noun*
The process by which an organism produces others of its kind. — REPRODUCTION.

propel *verb*
1. To set or keep going.
2. To force to move or advance with or as if with blows or pressure.
3. To launch with great force.
4. To impel to action.

1. DRIVE *verb.*
2. DRIVE *verb.*
3. SHOOT *verb.*
4. URGE *verb.*

propensity *noun*
An inclination to something. — BENT *noun.*

proper *adjective*
1. Conforming to accepted standards.
2. Suited to one's end or purpose.
3. In accordance with principles of right or good conduct.
4. Marked by excessive concern for propriety and good form.
5. Suitable for a particular person, condition, occasion, or place.
6. Conforming to fact.

1. CORRECT *adjective.*
2. CONVENIENT.
3. ETHICAL.
4. GENTEEL.
5. APPROPRIATE *adjective.*
6. ACCURATE.

properly *adverb*
In a fair, sporting manner. — FAIR *adverb.*

property *noun*
1. Something, as land and assets, legally possessed.
2. Usu. extensive real estate.
3. A distinctive element.

1. HOLDINGS.
2. LAND *noun.*
3. QUALITY.

prophecy *noun*
Something that is foretold by or as if by supernatural means: *The priest's prophecy was that the deposed king would regain his throne.* — **Syns:** cast, foretelling, oracle, vaticination, vision.

prophesier *noun*
A person who foretells future events by or as if by supernatural means. — PROPHET.

prophesy *verb*
To tell about or make known (future events) by or as if by supernatural means: *prophesied the coming end of civilization.* — **Syns:** augur, divine[2], foretell, soothsay, vaticinate.

prophet *noun*
A person who foretells future events by or as if by supernatural means: *When the flood came just as he predicted, the old man was revered as a prophet.* — **Syns:** augur, auspex, diviner, foreteller, haruspex (*also* aruspex), prophesier, seer[1], soothsayer, sibyl.

prophetic *also* **prophetical** *adjective*
Of or relating to the foretelling of events by or as if by supernatural means: *an old fortune teller believed to have prophetic powers.* — **Syns:** divinitory, fatidic (*also* fatidical), mantic, oracular, sibylline, vatic (*also* vatical), vaticinal.

prophylactic *adjective*
Defending against disease. — PREVENTIVE.

propitiate *verb*
To ease the anger or agitation of. — PACIFY.

propitious *adjective*
1. Affording benefit.
2. Occurring at a fitting or advantageous time.
3. Indicative of future success.

1. BENEFICIAL.
2. OPPORTUNE.
3. FAVORABLE.

proportion *noun*
1. Satisfying arrangement marked by even distribution of elements, as in a design: *sculpture of excellent proportion.*
2. Relative intensity or amount, as of a quality or attribute.

1. **Syns:** balance, harmony, symmetry.
2. DEGREE.

proportion *verb*

To bring into accord.

proportional *adjective*
1. Properly or correspondingly related in size, amount, or scale: *Happiness is not always proportional to virtue.*
2. Characterized by or displaying symmetry, esp. correspondence in scale or measure.

proportionate *adjective*
1. Properly or correspondingly related in size, amount, or scale.
2. Characterized by or displaying symmetry, esp. correspondence in scale or measure.

proportions *noun*
The amount of space occupied by something.

proposal *noun*
1. Something that is put forward for consideration: *a daring proposal to abolish the income tax.*
2. Something offered.

propose *verb*
1. To advance, as an idea, for consideration: *He proposed a trip to New York.*
2. To have in mind as a goal or purpose.

proposition *noun*
Something that is put forward for consideration.

propound *verb*
To advance, as an idea, for consideration.

proprieties *noun*
1. Courteous acts that contribute to smoothness and ease in dealings and social relationships.
2. Socially correct behavior.

proprietor *noun*
A person who has legal title to property.

proprietorship *noun*
1. Legal right to the possession of a thing.
2. The fact of possessing.

propriety *noun*
1. Conformity to recognized standards, as of conduct or appearance.
2. The moral quality of a course of action.

prosaic *adjective*
1. Of or suitable for ordinary days or routine occasions.
2. Lacking liveliness, charm, or surprise.

proscenium *noun*
The raised platform on which theatrical performances are given.

proscribe *verb*
To refuse to allow.

proscription *noun*
A refusal to allow.

prosecutable *adjective*
Subject to a lawsuit.

prosecute *verb*
1. To institute or subject to legal proceedings.
2. To begin and carry through to completion.
3. To engage in (a war or campaign).

prosecution *noun*
The act of beginning and carrying through to completion.

prosopopeia also **prosopopoeia** *noun*
Rhet. A physical entity typifying an abstraction.

prosopopoeia *noun*

HARMONIZE.

1. **Syns:** commensurable, commensurate, proportionate. —*Idiom* in proportion.

2. SYMMETRICAL.

1. PROPORTIONAL.

2. SYMMETRICAL.

SIZE.

1. **Syns:** proposition, submission, suggestion.
2. OFFER *noun*.

1. **Syns:** offer, pose, propound, put forth, submit, suggest.
2. INTEND.

PROPOSAL.

PROPOSE.

1. AMENITIES.

2. MANNERS.

OWNER.

1. OWNERSHIP.
2. POSSESSION.

1. DECENCY.

2. ETHICS.

1. EVERYDAY.
2. DULL *adjective*.

STAGE *noun*.

FORBID.

FORBIDDANCE.

LITIGABLE.

1. SUE.
2. PERFORM.
3. WAGE *verb*.

PERFORMANCE.

EMBODIMENT.

SEE **prosopopeia**.

prospect *noun*
1. The likelihood of a given event occurring.
2. Something expected.
3. Chance of success or advancement.
4. That which is or can be seen.

1. CHANCE *noun.*
2. EXPECTATION.
3. FUTURE *noun.*
4. VIEW *noun.*

prospectus *noun*
A printed list of the order of events and other pertinent information for a public performance.

PROGRAM.

prosper *verb*
To fare well: *The aerospace industry prospered during the 1960's.*

Syns: boom, flourish, go, make out (*Slang*), score (*Informal*), thrive. —*Idioms* do (*or* fare) well, get (*or* go) somewhere, go great guns, go strong.

prospering *adjective*
Improving, growing, or succeeding steadily.

FLOURISHING.

prosperity *noun*
1. Steady good fortune or financial security: *a struggling small businessman's dream of prosperity.*

1. *Syns:* comfort, ease, easy street (*also* Easy Street) (*Slang*), prosperousness. —*Idioms* comfortable (*or* easy) circumstances, the good life.

2. A state of health, happiness, and prospering.

2. WELFARE.

prosperous *adjective*
1. Enjoying steady good fortune or financial security: *fashionable new clothes that befit a prosperous young man-about-town.*

1. *Syns:* comfortable, easy, well-fixed (*Informal*), well-heeled (*Slang*), well-off, well-to-do. —*Idioms* comfortably off, in clover, on easy street.
Near-syns: affluent, opulent, rich, wealthy.
Ant: unprosperous.

2. Improving, growing, or succeeding steadily.
3. Occurring at a fitting or advantageous time.

2. FLOURISHING.
3. OPPORTUNE.

prosperousness *noun*
Steady good fortune or financial security.

PROSPERITY.

prostitute *noun*
A woman who engages in sexual intercourse for payment: *studied the psychological profiles of prostitutes.*

Syns: bawd, call girl, camp follower, courtesan, fille de joie (*French*), harlot, hooker (*Slang*), moll (*Slang*), streetwalker, whore. —*Idioms* lady of the night, lady of pleasure, scarlet woman, soiled dove.

prostrate *verb*
1. To cause to fall, as from a shot or blow.
2. To render powerless or motionless by inflicting severe injury.
3. To affect deeply or completely, as with emotion.

1. DROP *verb.*
2. DISABLE.

3. OVERWHELM.

prostrate *adjective*
Lying down.

FLAT *adjective.*

protagonist *noun*
The main performer in a theatrical production.

LEAD *noun.*

protean *adjective*
Having many aspects, uses, or abilities.

VERSATILE.

protect *verb*
To keep safe from danger, attack, or harm.

DEFEND.

protection *noun*
1. Something that physically protects, esp. from danger.
2. The act or a means of defending.

1. COVER *noun.*

2. DEFENSE.

protective *adjective*
1. Able to preserve.
2. Defending against disease.

1. PRESERVATIVE.
2. PREVENTIVE.

pro tem *adjective*
Temporarily assuming the duties of another.   TEMPORARY.

pro tempore *adjective*
Latin. Temporarily assuming the duties of another.   TEMPORARY.

protest *verb*
To express opposition by argument.   OBJECT².

protest *noun*
The act of expressing strong or reasoned opposition.   OBJECTION.

protestation *noun*
The act of expressing strong or reasoned opposition.   OBJECTION.

protocol *noun*
Strict observance of social conventions.   CEREMONY.

protoplast *noun*
Rare. A first form from which varieties arise or   ORIGINAL *noun.*
imitations are made.

prototypal *adjective*
Having the nature of, constituting, or serving as a   TYPICAL.
type.

prototype *noun*
1. A forerunner.   1. ANCESTOR.
2. A first form from which varieties arise or imitations   2. ORIGINAL *noun.*
   are made.

prototypic or **prototypical** *adjective*
Having the nature of, constituting, or serving as a   TYPICAL.
type.

protract *verb*
To make or become longer.   LENGTHEN.

protracted *adjective*
1. Of long duration.   1. CHRONIC.
2. Extending tediously beyond a standard duration.   2. LONG¹ *adjective.*

protraction *noun*
The act of making something longer or the condition of   EXTENSION.
being made longer.

protrude *verb*
To curve outward past the normal or usual limit.   BULGE *verb.*

protrusion *noun*
A part that protrudes or extends outward.   BULGE *noun.*

protuberance *noun*
1. A part that protrudes or extends outward.   1. BULGE *noun.*
2. An unevenness or elevation on a surface.   2. BUMP *noun.*

protuberate *verb*
To curve outward past the normal or usual limit.   BULGE *verb.*

proud *adjective*
1. Properly valuing oneself, one's honor, or one's   1. *Syns:* prideful, self-esteeming, self-
   dignity: *Poor but proud, he would not accept charity.*   respecting.
2. Overly convinced of one's own superiority and   2. ARROGANT.
   importance.
3. Marked by extraordinary elegance, beauty, and   3. GLORIOUS.
   splendor.
4. *Chiefly Regional.* Eagerly compliant.   4. GLAD.

prove *verb*
1. To establish as true or genuine: *He proved his*   1. *Syns:* authenticate, bear out, confirm,
   identity with a birth certificate.   corroborate, demonstrate, endorse,
                                                               establish, show, substantiate, validate,
                                                               verify.
2. To subject to a procedure that ascertains   2. TEST *verb.*
   effectiveness, value, proper function, or other
   quality.
3. *Archaic.* To participate in or partake of personally. 3. EXPERIENCE *verb.*

provenance *noun*
A point of origination.   ORIGIN.

provenience *noun*
A point of origination. ORIGIN.

prove out *verb*
To prove valid under scrutiny. WASH.

proverb *noun*
A usu. pithy and familiar statement expressing an observation or principle generally accepted as wise or true: *"A cat in gloves catches no mice" is a well-known proverb.* **Syns:** adage, aphorism, byword, maxim, saw, saying.

provide *verb*
1. To relinquish to the possession or control of another. 1. GIVE *verb.*
2. To make (something) readily available. 2. OFFER *verb.*

provide for *verb*
To supply with the necessities of life. SUPPORT *verb.*

provide for *verb* SEE **provide.**

providence *noun*
Careful use of material resources. ECONOMY.

provident *adjective*
Careful in the use of material resources. ECONOMICAL.

providential *adjective*
Characterized by luck or good fortune. HAPPY.

province *noun*
1. An area subject to rule by an outside power. 1. POSSESSION.
2. An area regularly covered, as by a policeman or reporter. 2. BEAT *noun.*
3. A sphere of activity, study, or interest. 3. AREA.

provincial *adjective*
1. Of or pertaining to the countryside. 1. COUNTRY *adjective.*
2. Having the restricted outlook often characteristic of geographic isolation. 2. LOCAL *adjective.*

provision *noun*
A restricting or modifying element: *a nuclear arms treaty with many provisions.* **Syns:** condition, proviso, qualification, reservation, specification, stipulation, string (*Informal*), term(s).

provisional *adjective*
1. Depending on or containing a condition or conditions. 1. CONDITIONAL.
2. Intended, used, or present for a limited time. 2. TEMPORARY.

provisionary *adjective*
Depending on or containing a condition or conditions. CONDITIONAL.

provisions *noun*
1. Plans made in preparation for some undertaking. 1. ARRANGEMENTS.
2. Something fit to be eaten. 2. FOOD.

proviso *noun*
A restricting or modifying element. PROVISION.

provisory *adjective*
Depending on or containing a condition or conditions. CONDITIONAL.

provocation *noun*
1. Something that incites esp. a violent response. 1. STIMULUS.
2. Behavior or an act that is intentionally provocative. 2. DEFIANCE.
3. The act of annoying. 3. ANNOYANCE.

provoke *verb*
1. To stir to action or feeling: *The insult provoked her to leave abruptly. His carelessness often provoked her to anger.* 1. **Syns:** arouse, egg on, excite, galvanize, goad, impel, incite, inflame, innerve, inspire, instigate, kindle, motivate, move, pique, rouse, spur, stimulate, work up.
Near-syns: awaken, bestir, rally, stir, wake; animate, exalt, fire.

2. To give rise to a particular development.
3. To trouble the nerves or peace of mind of, esp. by repeated vexations.
4. To solicit (danger) playfully and provocatively, often unwittingly.
5. To cause to feel or show anger.

2. GENERATE.
3. ANNOY.

4. COURT *verb*.

5. ANGER *verb*.

provoking *adjective*
Troubling the nerves or peace of mind, as by repeated vexations.

VEXATIOUS.

prowess *noun*
1. Skillfulness in the use of the hands or body.
2. The quality or state of being heroic.

1. DEXTERITY.
2. HEROISM.

prowl *verb*
To move silently and furtively.

SNEAK *verb*.

proximate *adjective*
1. Not far from another in space, time, or relation.
2. About to occur at any moment.

1. CLOSE[1] *adjective*.
2. MOMENTARY.

prude *noun*
A person who is too much concerned with being proper, modest, or righteous: *The prudes who once opposed coeducation now oppose sex education.*

Syns: bluenose, Mrs. Grundy, old maid, puritan, Victorian.
Near-syns: fuddy-duddy, old fogy, stuffed shirt; spoilsport, stick-in-the-mud, wet blanket.

prudence *noun*
1. The exercise of good judgment or common sense in practical matters: *showed a good deal of prudence when she chose the shop.*
2. Careful use of material resources.

1. *Syns:* caution, circumspection, foresight, forethought, precaution.

2. ECONOMY.

prudent *adjective*
1. Careful in the use of material resources.
2. Trying attentively to avoid danger, risk, or error.
3. Possessing, proceeding from, or exhibiting good judgment and prudence.

1. ECONOMICAL.
2. WARY.
3. SANE.

prudish *adjective*
Marked by excessive concern for propriety and good form.

GENTEEL.

prurience also **pruriency** *noun*
Sexual hunger.

DESIRE *noun*.

pruriency *noun*

SEE **prurience**.

prurient *adjective*
Feeling or devoted to sexual love or desire.

EROTIC.

pry *verb*
To look into or inquire about curiously, inquisitively, or in a meddlesome fashion.

SNOOP *verb*.

pryer *noun*

SEE **prier**.

prying *adjective*
Unduly interested in the affairs of others.

CURIOUS.

prying *noun*
Undue interest in the affairs of others.

CURIOSITY.

pseudo *adjective*
Fraudulently or deceptively imitative.

COUNTERFEIT *adjective*.

pseudonymic *adjective*
Being fictitious and not real.

ASSUMED.

pseudonymous *adjective*
Being fictitious and not real.

ASSUMED.

psyche *noun*
1. The thought processes characteristic of an individual or group.
2. The vital principle or animating force within living beings.

1. PSYCHOLOGY.

2. SPIRIT.

psychic also **psychical** *adjective*
Relating to or performed by the mind.   MENTAL.
psychological *adjective*
Relating to or performed by the mind.   MENTAL.
psychology *noun*
The thought processes characteristic of an individual or   **Syns:** ethos, mentality, mind, psyche.
group: *A good detective tries to understand the*   —*Idioms* mind set, what makes someone
psychology of the criminal.   tick.
psychopathy *noun*
Serious mental illness or disorder impairing a person's   INSANITY.
capacity to function normally and safely.
public *adjective*
1. Of, concerning, or affecting the community or the   1. **Syns:** civic, civil, national.
   people: *the public good.*
2. Not restricted or confined to few.   2. OPEN *adjective.*
3. Belonging to, shared by, or applicable to all alike.   3. COMMON *adjective.*
4. Of, representing, or carried on by people at large.   4. POPULAR.
public *noun*
1. Persons as an organized body: *rights and freedoms*   1. **Syns:** community, people, society.
   guaranteed to the public.
2. The common people.   2. COMMONALTY.
3. The body of persons who admire a public   3. **Syns:** audience, fans (*Informal*),
   personality, esp. an entertainer: *His public*   following.
   demanded an encore from the singer.
publication *noun*
1. The act or process of publishing printed matter: *The*   1. **Syns:** issue, printing, publishing.
   publication of a newly discovered piece by Mozart is
   a major event.
2. An issue of printed material offered for sale or   2. **Syns:** opus, title, volume, work.
   distribution: *a new publication on the breeding*
   habits of wild deer.
3. The act of announcing.   3. ANNOUNCEMENT.
publicity *noun*
1. The act or profession of promoting something, as a   1. ADVERTISING.
   product.
2. A systematic effort to increase the importance or   2. PROMOTION.
   reputation of by favorable publicity.
publicize *verb*
1. To make known vigorously the positive features of   1. ADVERTISE.
   (a product).
2. To increase or seek to increase the importance or   2. PROMOTE.
   reputation of by favorable publicity.
publish *verb*
1. To present for circulation, exhibit, or sale: *published* 1. **Syns:** bring out, issue, put out.
   a new one-volume edition.
2. To bring to public notice.   2. ANNOUNCE.
3. To be the author of (a published work or works): *She*   3. **Syns:** author, pen¹, write.
   published a biography of Marx.
publishing *noun*
The act or process of publishing printed matter.   PUBLICATION.
puddle *verb*
To waste time by engaging in aimless activity.   MESS AROUND at **mess.**
puddy *adjective*
Well-rounded and usu. short in physique.   PLUMP¹.
pudgy *adjective*
Well-rounded and usu. short in physique.   PLUMP¹.
puerile *adjective*
Of or characteristic of a child, esp. in immaturity.   CHILDISH.
puff *verb*
1. To be in a state of motion, as air.   1. BLOW¹ *verb.*
2. To breathe hard.   2. PANT.

3. To increase or seek to increase the importance or reputation of by favorable publicity.

3. PROMOTE.

puff *noun*
An inhalation, as of a cigar, pipe, or cigarette.

PULL *noun*.

puffed-up *adjective*
Characterized by an exaggerated show of dignity or self-importance.

POMPOUS.

puffery *noun*
A systematic effort to increase the importance or reputation of by favorable publicity.

PROMOTION.

puffy *adjective*
Characterized by an exaggerated show of dignity or self-importance.

POMPOUS.

pugnacious *adjective*
Having or showing an eagerness to fight.

BELLIGERENT.

pugnaciousness *noun*
The power or will to fight.

FIGHT *noun*.

pugnacity *noun*
1. Warlike or hostile attitude or nature.
2. The power or will to fight.

1. BELLIGERENCE.
2. FIGHT *noun*.

puissance *noun*
Capacity or power for work or vigorous activity.

ENERGY.

puissant *adjective*
1. Having or able to exert great power.
2. Having great physical strength.

1. POWERFUL.
2. STRONG.

pulchritudinous *adjective*
Having qualities that delight the eye.

BEAUTIFUL.

pule *verb*
To cry with soft, intermittent, often plaintive sounds.

WHINE.

pull *verb*
1. To exert force so as to move something toward the source of the force: *The boy pulled her hair. Everyone pulled on the rope.*
2. To remove from a fixed position: *pull a tooth.*
3. To direct or impel to oneself by some quality or action.

1. *Syns:* drag, draw, haul, tow, tug.

2. *Syns:* evulse, extract, pluck, tear[1].
3. ATTRACT.

pull down *verb*
1. To break up so that reconstruction is impossible.
2. To receive, as wages, for one's labor.

1. DESTROY.
2. EARN.

pull in *verb*
1. To come to a particular place.
2. To control, restrict, or arrest.

1. ARRIVE.
2. RESTRAIN.

pull off *verb*
1. *Informal.* To begin and carry through to completion.
2. *Informal.* To be responsible for or guilty of (an error or crime).

1. PERFORM.
2. COMMIT.

pull on *verb*
To put (an article of clothing) on one's person.

DON.

pull through *verb*
To exist in spite of adversity.

SURVIVE.

pull *noun*
1. The action or process of pulling: *gave the cord a pull.*
2. The act of drawing or pulling a load: *increased the pull of the tractor by shifting gears.*
3. An inhalation, as of a cigar, pipe, or cigarette: *took a pull on his meerschaum.*
4. An act of drinking or the amount swallowed.
5. *Slang.* The power to produce an effect by indirect means.
6. The power or quality of attracting.

1. *Syns:* jerk, tug.

2. *Syns:* draft, draw, haul, traction.

3. *Syns:* drag (*Informal*), draw, hit (*Slang*), puff.
4. DRINK *noun*.
5. INFLUENCE *noun*.

6. ATTRACTION.

pullback *noun*
The moving back of a military force in the face of enemy attack or after a defeat.   RETREAT *noun.*

pull down *verb*   SEE **pull.**

pull in *verb*   SEE **pull.**

pull off *verb*   SEE **pull.**

pull on *verb*   SEE **pull.**

pullout *noun*   SEE **pull out.**

pull out *verb*
To move or proceed away from a place.   GO *verb.*

   pullout *noun*
The moving back of a military force in the face of enemy attack or after a defeat.   RETREAT *noun.*

pull through *verb*   SEE **pull.**

pullulate *verb*
To overflow with.   TEEM[1].

pulp *verb*
To press forcefully so as to break up into a pulpy mass.   CRUSH *verb.*

pulpous *adjective*
Yielding easily to pressure or weight; not firm.   SOFT.

pulpy *adjective*
Yielding easily to pressure or weight; not firm.   SOFT.

pulsate *verb*
To make rhythmic contractions, sounds, or movements.   BEAT *verb.*

pulsating *adjective*
Marked by a regular rhythm.   RHYTHMICAL.

pulsation *noun*
A periodic contraction or sound of something coursing.   BEAT *noun.*

pulse *noun*
A periodic contraction or sound of something coursing.   BEAT *noun.*

   pulse *verb*
To make rhythmic contractions, sounds, or movements.   BEAT *verb.*

pulverize *verb*
1. To break up into tiny particles.   1. CRUSH *verb.*
2. To break up so that reconstruction is impossible.   2. DESTROY.

pulverous *adjective*
Consisting of small particles.   FINE[1].

pulverulent *adjective*
Consisting of small particles.   FINE[1].

pummel *verb*
To hit heavily and repeatedly.   BEAT *verb.*

pump *verb*
To remove (a liquid) by a steady, gradual process.   DRAIN.

punch *noun*
1. *Informal.* The capacity to create a powerful effect.   1. WALLOP *noun.*
2. *Informal.* A stimulating or intoxicating effect.   2. KICK *noun.*
3. An aggressive readiness to undertake taxing efforts.   3. DRIVE *noun.*

punctilio *noun*
A small, often specialized element of a whole.   DETAIL *noun.*

punctilious *adjective*
Fond of or given to ceremony.   CEREMONIOUS.

punctual *adjective*
Occurring, acting, or performed exactly at the time appointed: *a punctual arrival.*   ***Syns:*** prompt, timely. —*Idioms* on the dot, on time.

punctuate *verb*
To mark with punctuation.   POINT *verb.*

puncture *verb*
1. To make a hole or other opening in.   1. BREACH *verb.*
2. To pass into or through by overcoming resistance.   2. PENETRATE.
3. To cause to be no longer believed or valued.   3. DISCREDIT *verb.*

   puncture *noun*

A small mark or hole made by a sharp, pointed object.   PRICK *noun*.

pundit *noun*
A usu. elderly man noted for wisdom, knowledge, and   SAGE *noun*.
judgment.

pungent *adjective*
1. Affecting the organs of taste or smell with a strong   **1. Syns:** piquant, poignant (*Archaic*),
   and often harsh sensation: *a pungent smell; a*   sharp.
   pungent flavor.
2. So sharp as to cause mental pain.   **2.** BITING.

punish *verb*
1. To subject (one) to a penalty for a wrong: *punished*   **1. Syns:** correct, discipline.
   them for playing hooky.
2. *Informal.* To eat completely or entirely.   **2.** CONSUME.

punishing *adjective*
Inflicting or aiming to inflict punishment: *took*   **Syns:** disciplinary, punitive, punitory.
punishing action against the rebels.

punishment *noun*
A penalty imposed for wrongdoing: *The punishment for*   **Syns:** correction, discipline, punition.
armed robbery is a prison term.

punition *noun*
A penalty imposed for wrongdoing.   PUNISHMENT.

punitive *adjective*
Inflicting or aiming to inflict punishment.   PUNISHING.

punitory *adjective*
Inflicting or aiming to inflict punishment.   PUNISHING.

punk *noun*
Slang. A rough, violent person who engages in   TOUGH *noun*.
destructive actions.

puny *adjective*
1. Not physically strong.   **1.** INFIRM.
2. Conspicuously deficient in quantity, fullness, or   **2.** MEAGER.
   extent.

pup *noun*
An insignificant but arrogant and obnoxious young   SQUIRT *noun*.
person.

pupil *noun*
One who is being educated.   STUDENT.

puppet *noun*
A person used or controlled by others.   PAWN².

puppy *noun*
An insignificant but arrogant and obnoxious young   SQUIRT *noun*.
person.

purblind *adjective*
Unwilling or unable to perceive.   BLIND *adjective*.

purchasable *adjective*
Capable of being bribed.   CORRUPTIBLE.

purchase *verb*
1. To acquire in exchange for money or something of   **1.** BUY *verb*.
   equal value.
2. To subject (someone having the public's trust) to   **2.** CORRUPT *verb*.
   improper influence.

purchase *noun*
Something bought or capable of being bought.   BUY *noun*.

purchaser *noun*
One who buys goods or services.   PATRON.

pure *adjective*
1. Free from extraneous elements: *pure brilliance; pure*   **1. Syns:** absolute, perfect, plain, sheer²,
   necessity; pure gold.   unadulterated, undiluted, unmixed.
       Near-syns: authentic, genuine,
       unalloyed, unqualified, utter²;
       complete, out-and-out, total.

2. Not diluted or mixed with other substances.

3. Completely such, without qualification or exception.

4. Morally beyond reproach, esp. in sexual conduct.

5. Free from evil and corruption.

pure *verb*
Obs. To free from sin, guilt, or defilement.

pure *adverb*
Chiefly Regional. To a high degree.

pureblooded *adjective*
Of pure breeding stock.

purebred *adjective*
Of pure breeding stock.

purely *adverb*
Without exception; in its entirety: *Any such resemblance is purely coincidental.*

pureness *noun*
The condition of being clean and free of contaminants.

purgation *noun*
1. The act or process of discharging bodily wastes or foreign substances.

2. A freeing from sin, guilt, or defilement.

purgative *adjective*
1. Serving to purify of sin: *Confession is a purgative rite in the Russian Church.*

2. Of, relating to, or tending to eliminate.

purgatorial *adjective*
Serving to purify of sin.

purge *verb*
1. *Med.* To discharge (wastes or foreign substances) from the body.

2. To free from sin, guilt, or defilement.

3. *Law.* To free from a charge or imputation of guilt.

4. To get rid of, esp. by banishment or execution.

purge *noun*
The act or process of eliminating.

purificant *noun*
Something that purifies.

purification *noun*
1. The act or process of removing physical impurities: *water purification.*

2. A freeing from sin, guilt, or defilement: *purification of mind and soul through confession.*

purificator *noun*
Something that purifies.

purified *adjective*
Made pure, esp. by a commercial refining process.

purifier *noun*
Something that purifies: *Water purifiers are needed in some places.*

purify *verb*
1. To free from sin, guilt, or defilement: *prayed that her soul would be purified.*

2. To make or become clear by the removal of impurities.

purifying *adjective*
Serving to purify of sin.

puritan *noun*
A person who is too much concerned with being proper, modest, or righteous.

---

2. STRAIGHT.

3. UTTER[2].

4. CHASTE.

5. INNOCENT *adjective*.

PURIFY.

VERY *adverb*.

THOROUGHBRED *adjective*.

THOROUGHBRED *adjective*.

Syns: all, altogether, just, quite, utterly, wholly. —*Idioms* in all, in toto.

PURITY.

1. ELIMINATION.

2. PURIFICATION.

1. **Syns:** expiative, expiatory, expurgatory (*also* expurgatorial), lustral, lustrative, lustratory, purgatorial, purifying.

2. ELIMINATIVE.

PURGATIVE.

1. ELIMINATE.

2. PURIFY.

3. CLEAR *verb*.

4. ELIMINATE.

ELIMINATION.

PURIFIER.

1. **Syns:** clarification, cleaning, cleansing.

2. **Syns:** catharsis, cleansing, expurgation, lustration, purgation.

PURIFIER.

REFINED.

Syns: cleaner, cleanser, purificant, purificator.

1. **Syns:** cleanse, expurgate, lustrate, pure (*Obs.*), purge.

2. REFINE.

PURGATIVE.

PRUDE.

puritanical *adjective*
Marked by excessive concern for propriety and good form.

GENTEEL.

purity *noun*
1. The condition of being clean and free of contaminants: *tested the purity of the town's water supply.*
2. The condition of being chaste.

1. **Syns:** clarity, cleanliness, cleanness, pureness, taintlessness.

2. CHASTITY.

purloin *verb*
To take (another's property) without permission.

STEAL *verb.*

purloiner *noun*
A person who steals.

LARCENER.

purloining *noun*
The crime of taking someone else's property without consent.

LARCENY.

purport *noun*
1. The gist of a specific action or situation.
2. That which is signified by a word or expression.
3. The general sense or significance, as of an action, statement, etc.
4. The thread or current of thought uniting or occurring in all the elements of a text or discourse.

1. IDEA.
2. MEANING *noun.*
3. IMPORT *noun.*

4. THRUST *noun.*

purpose *noun*
1. What one intends to do or achieve.
2. The proper activity of a person or thing.

1. INTENTION.
2. FUNCTION *noun.*

purpose *verb*
To have in mind as a goal or purpose.

INTEND.

purposeless *adjective*
1. Without aim, purpose, or intent.
2. Lacking rational direction or purpose.
3. Having no particular pattern, purpose, organization, or structure.

1. AIMLESS.
2. MINDLESS.
3. RANDOM.

pursual *noun*
An attempting to accomplish or attain.

PURSUIT.

pursuance *noun*
An attempting to accomplish or attain.

PURSUIT.

pursue *verb*
1. To follow (another) with the intent of overtaking and capturing: *The police pursued the armed robbers across town.*
2. To move behind (another) in the same direction.
3. To strengthen the effect of (an action) by further action.
4. To go through (life) in a certain way.
5. To attempt to gain the affection of.
6. To work at, esp. as a profession.

1. **Syns:** chase, run after. —*Idioms* be (or go) in hot pursuit, give chase.
2. FOLLOW.
3. FOLLOW UP at **follow.**

4. LEAD *verb.*
5. COURT *verb.*
6. PRACTICE *verb.*

pursuing *noun*
An attempting to accomplish or attain.

PURSUIT.

pursuit *noun*
1. The following of another in an attempt to overtake and capture: *in pursuit of the hijackers.*
2. An attempting to accomplish or attain: *life, liberty, and the pursuit of happiness.*
3. Activity pursued as a livelihood.
4. A working at a profession or occupation.

1. **Syn:** chase. —*Idiom* hot pursuit.

2. **Syns:** pursual, pursuance, pursuing, quest, search.
3. BUSINESS.
4. PRACTICE *noun.*

purview *noun*
1. An area within which something or someone exists, acts, or has influence or power.
2. The extent of one's perception, understanding, knowledge, or vision.

1. RANGE *noun.*

2. KEN.

push *verb*
1. To do or achieve by forcing obstacles out of one's way: *pushed his way through the packed bar; pushed energy legislation through Congress.*
2. To exert pressure.
3. To act on with a steady pushing force.
4. To force to move or advance with or as if with blows or pressure.
5. To force one's way into a place or situation.
6. *Slang.* To make known vigorously the positive features of (a product).
7. *Slang.* To engage in the illicit sale of (narcotics): *pushing heroin on the street.*
8. To cause to stick out.

1. *Syns:* bulldoze (*Slang*), press, ram, shoulder, shove.
2. BEAR.
3. CROWD *verb.*
4. DRIVE *verb.*

5. MUSCLE *verb.*
6. ADVERTISE.

7. *Syns:* deal, peddle, shove.

8. POKE *verb.*

push off *verb*
Informal. To move or proceed away from a place.

GO *verb.*

push on *verb*
To move along a particular course.

GO *verb.*

push *noun*
1. An act or instance of using force so as to propel ahead: *gave him a quick push off the diving board.*
2. An organized effort to accomplish a purpose.
3. *Informal.* An aggressive readiness to undertake taxing efforts.
4. *Informal.* The wish, power, and ability to begin and follow through with a plan or task.
5. Something that causes and encourages a given response.

1. *Syns:* butt[1], prod, shove, thrust.

2. DRIVE *noun.*
3. DRIVE *noun.*

4. AMBITION.

5. STIMULUS.

pusher *noun*
Slang. A person who sells narcotics illegally: *heroin and cocaine pushers.*

Syns: candyman (*Slang*), dealer.

push off *verb*

SEE **push.**

push on *verb*

SEE **push.**

pushover *noun*
1. *Informal.* An easily accomplished task.
2. An easy victory.
3. *Informal.* A person who is easily deceived or victimized.

1. BREEZE *noun.*
2. RUNAWAY *noun* at **run away.**
3. DUPE *noun.*

pushy *adjective*
1. *Informal.* Having or exhibiting excessive and arrogant self-confidence.
2. *Informal.* Inclined to act in a hostile way.

1. PRESUMPTUOUS.

2. AGGRESSIVE.

pusillanimity *noun*
Ignoble lack of courage.

COWARDICE.

pusillanimous *adjective*
Ignobly lacking in courage.

COWARDLY.

puss *noun*
1. *Slang.* The front surface of the head.
2. *Slang.* The opening in the body through which food is ingested.

1. FACE *noun.*
2. MOUTH.

pussyfoot *verb*
1. *Slang.* To use evasive or deliberately vague language.
2. To move silently and furtively.

1. EQUIVOCATE.

2. SNEAK *verb.*

pussyfooting *adjective*
Slang. Deliberately ambiguous or vague.

EVASIVE.

put *verb*
1. To deposit in a specified position.
2. To place in proper position or location.
3. To convey in language or words of a particular form.

1. SET[1] *verb.*
2. POSITION *verb.*
3. PHRASE *verb.*

4. To express in another language, while systematically retaining the original sense.   **4.** TRANSLATE.

5. To utter publicly.   **5.** AIR *verb.*

6. To seek an answer to (a question).   **6.** ASK.

7. To establish and apply as compulsory.   **7.** IMPOSE.

8. To calculate approximately.   **8.** ESTIMATE *verb.*

9. To make a bet on.   **9.** BET *verb.*

put away *verb*

1. To eat completely or entirely.   **1.** CONSUME.

2. To take the life of (a person or persons) unlawfully.   **2.** MURDER *verb.*

put by *verb*

To reserve for the future.   SAVE.

put down *verb*

To bring to an end forcibly as if by imposing a heavy weight.   SUPPRESS.

put forth *verb*

1. To put forward a topic for discussion.   **1.** BROACH.

2. To advance, as an idea, for consideration.   **2.** PROPOSE.

put in *verb*

1. To use time in a particular way.   **1.** SPEND.

2. *Informal.* To spend or complete (time), as a prison term.   **2.** SERVE.

3. *Informal.* To ask for employment, acceptance, or admission.   **3.** APPLY.

4. *Naut.* To come or go into (a place).   **4.** ENTER.

put through *verb*

To carry to a successful conclusion.   EFFECT *verb.*

put to *verb*

To move an appropriate barrier into (an opening).   CLOSE[1] *verb.*

put together *verb*

To create by forming, combining, or altering materials.   MAKE.

put up *verb*

1. To make or form (a structure).   **1.** BUILD *verb.*

2. To raise upright.   **2.** ERECT.

3. To prepare (food) for storage and future use.   **3.** CONSERVE *verb.*

4. To provide with often temporary lodging.   **4.** HARBOR *verb.*

putative *adjective*

Assumed to be such.   REPUTED.

put away *verb*   SEE **put.**

put by *verb*   SEE **put.**

put down *verb*   SEE **put.**

put forth *verb*   SEE **put.**

put in *verb*   SEE **put.**

put-on *noun*   SEE **put on.**

put on *verb*

1. To produce on the stage.   **1.** STAGE *verb.*

2. To behave affectedly or insincerely.   **2.** ACT *verb.*

3. To take on or give a false appearance of.   **3.** ASSUME.

4. To put (an article of clothing) on one's person.   **4.** DON.

put-on *noun*

Slang. A deceptive outward appearance.   FAÇADE.

put-out *adjective*   SEE **put out.**

put out *verb*

1. To bring to bear steadily or forcefully.   **1.** EXERCISE *verb.*

2. To present for circulation, exhibit, or sale.   **2.** PUBLISH.

3. To cause inconvenience for.   **3.** INCONVENIENCE *verb.*

4. To cause to stop burning or giving light.   **4.** EXTINGUISH.

5. To cause (a person) to be self-consciously distressed.   **5.** EMBARRASS.

put-out *adjective*

Distressed and ill at ease.   EMBARRASSED.

putrefaction *noun*
The condition of being decayed.   DECAY *noun*.
putrefy *verb*
To become or cause to become rotten or unsound.   DECAY *verb*.
putresce *verb*
To become or cause to become rotten or unsound.   DECAY *verb*.
putrescence *noun*
The condition of being decayed.   DECAY *noun*.
putrid *adjective*
1. Impaired because of decay.   1. BAD.
2. Smelling of mildew or decay.   2. MOLDY.
putridness *noun*
The condition of being decayed.   DECAY *noun*.
putter *verb*
1. To move one's fingers or hands in a nervous or   1. FIDDLE.
   aimless fashion.
2. To waste time by engaging in aimless activity.   2. MESS AROUND at **mess**.
3. To be nervously or uselessly active.   3. FUSS *verb*.
put through *verb*   SEE **put**.
put to *verb*   SEE **put**.
put together *verb*   SEE **put**.
put up *verb*   SEE **put**.
puzzle *noun*
Anything that arouses curiosity or perplexes because it   MYSTERY.
is unexplained, inexplicable, or secret.
puzzle out *verb*
To find the key to.   BREAK *verb*.
puzzlement *noun*
Anything that arouses curiosity or perplexes because it   MYSTERY.
is unexplained, inexplicable, or secret.
puzzle out *verb*   SEE **puzzle**.
puzzler *noun*
Anything that arouses curiosity or perplexes because it   MYSTERY.
is unexplained, inexplicable, or secret.
pygmy also **pigmy** *adjective*
Extremely small.   TINY.
pyramid *noun*
A group of things gathered haphazardly.   HEAP *noun*.
pyretic *adjective*
Being at a higher temperature than is normal or   HOT *adjective*.
desirable.
pythonic *adjective*
Of extraordinary size and power.   GIANT *adjective*.

Q

quack *noun*
One who is not what he claims to be.   FAKE *noun*.
quad *noun*
An area partially or entirely enclosed by walls or   COURT *noun*.
buildings.

quadrangle *noun*
An area partially or entirely enclosed by walls or buildings.   COURT *noun*.

quadrate *adjective*
Having four equal sides and four right angles.   SQUARE *adjective*.

quadrate *verb*
To be compatible or in correspondence.   AGREE.

quaff *verb*
To take into the mouth and swallow (a liquid).   DRINK *verb*.

quaff *noun*
An act of drinking or the amount swallowed.   DRINK *noun*.

quag *noun*
A usu. low-lying area of soft, waterlogged ground and standing water.   SWAMP.

quaggy *adjective*
Yielding easily to pressure or weight; not firm.   SOFT.

quagmire *noun*
1. A difficult, embarrassing situation.   1. PREDICAMENT.
2. A usu. low-lying area of soft, waterlogged ground and standing water.   2. SWAMP.

quail *verb*
To draw away involuntarily, usu. due to fear or disgust.   FLINCH.

quaint¹ *adjective*
1. Agreeably curious, esp. in an old-fashioned or unusual way: *an old house with quaint, meandering stairways.*   1. **Syns:** funny, odd, oddball (*Informal*). **Near-syns:** antique, curious, peculiar, queer, singular, unusual.
2. Deviating from the customary.   2. ECCENTRIC *adjective*.

quaint² *verb*
Archaic. To make known socially.   ACQUAINT.

quake *verb*
1. To move to and fro in short, jerky movements.   1. SHAKE *verb*.
2. To move to and fro violently.   2. SHAKE *verb*.

quake *noun*
A shaking of the earth.   TREMOR *noun*.

quaking *adjective*
Marked by or affected with tremors.   TREMULOUS.

quaky *adjective*
Marked by or affected with tremors.   TREMULOUS.

qualification *noun*
1. The quality or state of being eligible: *His qualification for the senate is unquestioned.*   1. **Syns:** eligibility, eligibleness, fitness, suitableness.
2. A restricting or modifying element.   2. PROVISION.

qualified *adjective*
1. Not total, unlimited, or wholehearted: *a qualified plan for expansion.*   1. **Syns:** limited, modified, reserved, restricted. **Near-ants:** complete, entire, full, total, whole, wholehearted, unlimited, unrestricted. **Ants:** absolute, unqualified.
2. Having the ability to perform well.   2. ABLE.
3. Depending on or containing a condition or conditions.   3. CONDITIONAL.
4. Satisfying the requirements, as for selection.   4. ELIGIBLE.
5. Having the necessary strength or ability.   5. EQUAL *adjective*.

qualify *verb*
1. To make noticeable or different.   1. DISTINGUISH.
2. To give authority to.   2. AUTHORIZE.

quality *noun*
1. A distinctive element: *Honesty is her finest quality.*   1. **Syns:** affection², attribute, character, characteristic, feature, mark, peculiarity, property, savor, trait.

2. Degree of excellence: *yard goods of low quality.*
3. A level of superiority that is usu. high.
4. High style in quality, manner, or dress.
5. People of the highest social level.
quality *adjective*
Exceptionally good of its kind.
qualm *noun*
A feeling of uncertainty about the fitness or correctness of an action: *I had qualms about passing on the story.*

quantity *noun*
1. A measurable whole: *a large quantity of coal; a small quantity of evidence.*

2. An indefinite amount or extent.
quantum *noun*
1. A measurable whole.
2. That which is allotted.
quarrel *noun*
A discussion, often heated, in which a difference of opinion is expressed.
quarrel *verb*
To engage in a quarrel.
quarrelsome *adjective*
1. Given to arguing.
2. Having or showing an eagerness to fight.
quarter *noun*
1. One of four equal parts of something: *Each took a quarter of the profit.*
2. A part of the earth's surface.
3. A rather small part of a geographic unit considered in regard to its inhabitants or distinctive characteristics.
quarter *verb*
To provide with often temporary lodging.
quarterage *noun*
Dwellings in general.
quartern *noun*
One of four equal parts of something.
quash *verb*
To bring to an end forcibly as if by imposing a heavy weight.
quashing *noun*
The act of restraining forcefully.
quaver *verb*
To move to and fro in short, jerky movements.
quaver *noun*
A nervous shaking of the body.
queer *adjective*
1. Deviating from the customary.
2. Causing puzzlement; perplexing.
quell *verb*
To bring to an end forcibly as if by imposing a heavy weight.

Near-syns: affirmation, bent, element, factor, individuality, parameter, virtue.
2. **Syns:** caliber, class, grade.
3. MERIT *noun.*
4. CLASS *noun.*
5. SOCIETY.

EXCELLENT.

Syns: compunction, misgiving, reservation, scruple.
Near-syns: apprehension, conscience, demur, doubt, mistrust, objection, principle, reluctance, suspicion, unwillingness.

1. **Syns:** amount, body, budget, bulk, corpus, quantum.
Near-syns: aggregate, total; extent, limit, range; number, stock, sum, whole.
2. DEAL *noun.*

1. QUANTITY.
2. ALLOTMENT.

ARGUMENT.

ARGUE.

1. ARGUMENTATIVE.
2. BELLIGERENT.

1. **Syn:** quartern.

2. AREA.
3. NEIGHBORHOOD.

HARBOR *verb.*

SHELTER *noun.*

QUARTER *noun.*

SUPPRESS.

REPRESSION.

SHAKE *verb.*

TREMOR *noun.*

1. ECCENTRIC *adjective.*
2. FUNNY.

SUPPRESS.

quench *verb*
1. To cause to stop burning or giving light.
2. To bring to an end forcibly as if by imposing a heavy weight.
3. To hold (something requiring an outlet) in check.

1. EXTINGUISH.
2. SUPPRESS.
3. REPRESS.

quenching *noun*
The act of restraining forcefully.

REPRESSION.

querier *noun*
One who inquires.

INQUIRER.

querulent *adjective*
Easily annoyed.

IRRITABLE.

querulous *adjective*
1. Having or showing a bad temper.
2. Easily annoyed.

1. ILL-TEMPERED.
2. IRRITABLE.

query *noun*
A request for data.

INQUIRY.

query *verb*
To put a question to (someone).

ASK.

quest *noun*
1. A seeking of knowledge, data, or the truth about something.
2. An attempting to accomplish or attain.

1. INQUIRY.
2. PURSUIT.

quest *verb*
To try to find.

SEEK.

question *noun*
1. A request for data.
2. A lack of conviction or certainty.
3. A situation that presents difficulty, uncertainty, or perplexity.

1. INQUIRY.
2. DOUBT *noun*.
3. PROBLEM.

question *verb*
1. To put a question to (someone).
2. To be uncertain, disbelieving, or skeptical about.

1. ASK.
2. DOUBT *verb*.

questionable *adjective*
1. Of dubious character.
2. In doubt or dispute.
3. Not affording certainty.
4. Not likely.

1. SHADY.
2. DEBATABLE.
3. AMBIGUOUS.
4. DOUBTFUL.

questioner *noun*
1. One who inquires.
2. One who conducts an official inquiry, usu. with no regard for human rights.

1. INQUIRER.
2. INQUISITOR.

questioning *adjective*
1. Eager to acquire knowledge.
2. Refusing or reluctant to believe.

1. CURIOUS.
2. INCREDULOUS.

questioningly *adverb*
With skepticism.

SKEPTICALLY.

queue *noun*
A group of people or things arranged in a row.

LINE *noun*.

quibble *verb*
1. To raise unnecessary or trivial objections: *always quibbling about the silliest things.*

1. *Syns:* carp, cavil, niggle, nit-pick (*Informal*), pettifog. —*Idiom* pick to pieces.
Near-ants: applaud, commend, compliment, endorse, extol, recommend, sanction.

2. To engage in a quarrel.

2. ARGUE.

quick *adjective*
1. Accomplished in very little time: *a quick visit.*

1. *Syns:* brief, fast, flying, hasty, hurried, speedy.
Near-ants: dilatory, laggard, lagging,

leisurely, procrastinating, slow,
sluggish, unhasty, unhurried.

2. Characterized by great celerity.

2. FAST *adjective*.

3. Moving or performing quickly, lightly, and easily.

3. NIMBLE.

quick *noun*
A point of origin from which ideas, influences, etc.,
emanate.

CENTER *noun*.

quick *adverb*
In a rapid way.

FAST *adverb*.

quicken *verb*
1. To make alive: *Sun and showers quicken plants.*

1. *Syns:* animate, enliven, liven, vivify.
Near-syns: activate, awaken, energize,
vitalize; arouse, rouse, stir.
Ants: deactivate, deaden.

2. To increase the speed of.

2. SPEED UP at **speed.**

quickening *adjective*
Serving to enliven.

STIMULATING.

quickness *noun*
1. Rate of motion or performance.

1. SPEED *noun*.

2. The quality or state of being agile.

2. AGILITY.

quick-tempered *adjective*
Easily annoyed.

TESTY.

quick-witted *adjective*
Mentally quick and original.

CLEVER.

quidnunc *noun*
1. A person given to intruding in other people's affairs.

1. MEDDLER.

2. A person habitually engaged in idle talk about
others.

2. GOSSIP *noun*.

quiescence also **quiescency** *noun*
The condition of being temporarily inactive.

ABEYANCE.

quiescency *noun*

SEE **quiescence.**

quiescent *adjective*
Existing in a temporarily inactive and hidden form.

LATENT.

quiet *adjective*
1. Not showy or obtrusive: *a room decorated in a quiet,
pleasing style.*

1. *Syns:* inobtrusive, restrained, subdued,
tasteful, unobtrusive.
Near-ants: blatant, brash, brazen,
flashy, garish, gaudy, meretricious,
tinsel.
Ants: loud, tawdry.

2. Motionless and undisturbed.

2. STILL *adjective*.

3. Marked by, done with, or making no sound or noise.

3. SILENT.

4. Not irritating, strident, or loud.

4. SOFT.

quiet *noun*
1. An absence of motion or disturbance.

1. STILLNESS.

2. The absence of sound or noise.

2. SILENCE *noun*.

quiet *verb*
1. To cause to become silent.

1. SILENCE *verb*.

2. To make or become calm.

2. CALM *verb*.

quiet *adverb*
Without noise.

STILL *adverb*.

quieten *verb*
To cause to become silent.

SILENCE *verb*.

quietness *noun*
The absence of sound or noise.

SILENCE *noun*.

quietude *noun*
The absence of sound or noise.

SILENCE *noun*.

quietus *noun*
The act or fact of dying.

DEATH.

quintessence *noun*
1. A basic trait or set of traits that define and establish the character of something.
2. The most central and material part.

1. ESSENCE.

2. HEART.

quintessential *adjective*
Having the nature of, constituting, or serving as a type.

TYPICAL.

quintessential *noun*
A basic trait or set of traits that define and establish the character of something.

ESSENCE.

quip *noun*
1. Words or actions intended to excite laughter or amusement.
2. A flippant or sarcastic remark.

1. JOKE *noun.*

2. CRACK *noun.*

quirk *noun*
Peculiar behavior.

ECCENTRICITY.

quirky *adjective*
Deviating from the customary.

ECCENTRIC *adjective.*

quit *verb*
1. To relinquish one's engagement in or occupation with: *quit his job; quit drinking.*
2. To cease trying to accomplish or continue.
3. To give up without intending to return or claim again.
4. To move or proceed away from a place.
5. To conduct oneself in a specified way.
6. To come to a cessation.

1. ***Syns:*** leave[1], resign, terminate. ***Near-syns:*** drop, retire, withdraw.
2. ABANDON *verb.*
3. ABANDON *verb.*
4. GO *verb.*
5. ACT *verb.*
6. STOP *verb.*

quit *adjective*
Owing or being owed nothing.

EVEN[1] *adjective.*

quitclaim *noun*
A giving up of a possession, claim, or right.

ABDICATION.

quitclaim *verb*
To give up a possession, claim, or right.

ABDICATE.

quite *adverb*
1. To a considerable extent.
2. To the fullest extent.
3. Without exception; in its entirety.

1. CONSIDERABLY.
2. COMPLETELY.
3. PURELY.

quittance *noun*
Something to make up for loss or damage.

COMPENSATION.

quiver *verb*
To move to and fro in short, jerky movements.

SHAKE *verb.*

quiver *noun*
A nervous shaking of the body.

TREMOR *noun.*

quivering *adjective*
Marked by or affected with tremors.

TREMULOUS.

quivery *adjective*
Marked by or affected with tremors.

TREMULOUS.

quixotic *adjective*
Not compatible with reality.

IDEALISTIC.

quiz *verb*
1. To put a question to (someone).
2. *Brit.* To make fun of.

1. ASK.
2. RIDICULE *verb.*

quiz *noun*
1. A set of questions or exercises designed to determine knowledge or skill.
2. A person who is appealingly odd or curious.

1. TEST *noun.*

2. CHARACTER.

quodlibetic *adjective*
Characterized by a narrow concern for book learning and formal rules, without knowledge or experience of practical matters.

PEDANTIC.

quondam *adjective*
Having been such previously.

LATE *adjective*.

quota *noun*
That which is allotted.

ALLOTMENT.

quotidian *adjective*
Of or suitable for ordinary days or routine occasions.

EVERYDAY.

R

rabble *noun*
A group of persons regarded as the lowest class.

TRASH[1] *noun*.

rabid *adjective*
1. Marked by extreme excitement, confusion, or
   agitation.
2. Full of or marked by extreme anger.
3. Holding esp. political views that deviate drastically
   and fundamentally from conventional or traditional
   beliefs.

1. FRANTIC.

2. FURIOUS.
3. EXTREME *adjective*.

race *noun*
1. A struggle with others for victory or supremacy.
2. A swift advance or attack.

1. COMPETITION.
2. CHARGE *noun*.

race *verb*
To move swiftly.

RUSH *verb*.

rack *verb*
1. To bring great harm or suffering to.
2. To subject (another) to extreme physical cruelty, as
   in punishing.

1. AFFLICT.
2. TORTURE *verb*.

racket *noun*
1. Sounds or a sound, esp. when loud, confused, or
   disagreeable.
2. *Slang.* Activity pursued as a livelihood.

1. NOISE *noun*.

2. BUSINESS.

racy *adjective*
Bordering on indelicacy or impropriety: *shocked the
ladies by telling a racy story.*

Syns: blue, broad, dubious, off-color,
risqué, salty, scabrous, spicy, suggestive.
Near-syns: earthy, indecent, indecorous,
indelicate, naughty, raunchy, raw, ribald,
sexy, wicked.

radiance *noun*
1. Exceptional brightness and clarity, as of a cut and
   polished stone.
2. A feeling of pervasive emotional warmth.

1. FIRE *noun*.

2. GLOW *noun*.

radiant *adjective*
Giving off or reflecting light readily or in large
amounts.

BRIGHT.

radiate *verb*
1. To send out heat, light, or energy.
2. To emit a bright light.
3. To extend over a wide area.

1. SHED.
2. BEAM *verb*.
3. SPREAD *verb*.

radical *adjective*
1. Arising from or going to the root or source: *radical
   differences that can make activism and reason
   incompatible.*

1. *Syns:* basal, basic, bottom,
foundational, fundamental, original,
primary, underlying.

Near-syns: cardinal, elemental, essential, inherent, intrinsic, vital.
Ant: superficial.

2. Holding esp. political views that deviate drastically and fundamentally from conventional or traditional beliefs.

    2. EXTREME *adjective.*

radical *noun*
One who holds extreme views or advocates extreme measures.

    EXTREMIST *noun.*

rag *verb*
Slang. To tease or mock good-humoredly.

    JOKE *verb.*

ragamuffin *noun*
A person wearing ragged or tattered clothing.

    TATTERDEMALION.

rage *noun*
1. Violent or unrestrained anger.
2. The current custom.
3. A subject or activity that inspires lively interest.

    1. FURY.
    2. FASHION *noun.*
    3. ENTHUSIASM.

rage *verb*
To be or become angry.

    ANGER *verb.*

ragged *adjective*
1. Having a coarse, irregular surface.
2. Torn into or marked by shreds or tatters.

    1. ROUGH.
    2. TATTERED.

raggedy *adjective*
Torn into or marked by shreds or tatters.

    TATTERED.

raging *adjective*
1. Full of or marked by extreme anger.
2. Violently disturbed, as by storms.

    1. FURIOUS.
    2. ROUGH.

rags *noun*
Torn and ragged clothing.

    TATTERS.

ragtag also **ragtag and bobtail** *noun*
A group of persons regarded as the lowest class.

    TRASH[1] *noun.*

ragtag and bobtail *noun*

    SEE **ragtag.**

raid *noun*
An act of invading, esp. by military forces.

    INVASION.

raid *verb*
1. To enter in order to attack, plunder, destroy, or conquer.
2. To make a surprise attack on: *Apaches raided the outpost to discourage further expansion.*

    1. INVADE.
    2. *Syns:* harass, harry, maraud.

rail at (or **against**) *verb*
To attack with harsh, often insulting language.

    REVILE *verb.*

railing *noun*
Harsh, often insulting language.

    VITUPERATION.

raiment *noun*
Articles worn to cover the body.

    DRESS *noun.*

rain *verb*
To give in great abundance.

    SHOWER *verb.*

rainbow *noun*
A fantastic, impracticable plan or desire.

    ILLUSION.

rainless *adjective*
Having little or no precipitation.

    DRY *adjective.*

raise *verb*
1. To increase in amount: *raised prices; raised my rent.*
2. To make or form (a structure).
3. To move (something) to a higher position.
4. To raise upright.
5. To bring into existence and foster the development of.
6. To take care of and educate (a child).

    1. *Syns:* boost, hike, increase, jack (up), jump, up.
    2. BUILD *verb.*
    3. ELEVATE.
    4. ERECT *verb.*
    5. GROW.
    6. BRING UP at **bring.**

7. To increase markedly in level or intensity, esp. of sound.   **7.** ELEVATE.

8. To raise in rank.   **8.** PROMOTE.

9. To induce or elicit (a reaction or emotion).   **9.** AROUSE.

10. To put forward a topic for discussion.   **10.** BROACH.

11. To seek an answer to (a question).   **11.** ASK.

raise *noun*
The amount by which something is increased.   INCREASE *noun*.

raised *adjective*
1. Directed or pointed upward.   **1.** ERECT *adjective*.
2. Being positioned above a given level.   **2.** ELEVATED.
3. Abnormally increased, esp. in intensity.   **3.** ELEVATED.

rake¹ *noun*
An immoral or licentious man.   WANTON *noun*.

rake² *verb*
To depart or cause to depart from true vertical or horizontal.   INCLINE *verb*.

rakehell *adjective*
Given to heedless, unrestrained pursuit of pleasure.   FAST *adjective*.

rakish *adjective*
Given to heedless, unrestrained pursuit of pleasure.   FAST *adjective*.

rally *verb*
1. To assemble, prepare, or put into operation, as for war or a similar emergency.   **1.** MOBILIZE.
2. To regain one's health.   **2.** RECOVER.

rally *noun*
A return to normal health.   RECOVERY.

ram *verb*
1. To cause to penetrate with force: *rammed the bayonet into the target*.   **1.** *Syns:* dig, drive, plunge, run, sink, stab, stick, thrust.
2. To force to move or advance with or as if with blows or pressure.   **2.** DRIVE *verb*.
3. To do or achieve by forcing obstacles out of one's way.   **3.** PUSH *verb*.

ramble *verb*
1. To move about at random, esp. over a wide area.   **1.** ROVE.
2. To walk at a leisurely pace.   **2.** STROLL *verb*.

ramble *noun*
An act of walking, esp. for pleasure.   WALK *noun*.

ramify *verb*
To separate into branches or branchlike parts.   BRANCH *verb*.

rampage *noun*
A period of uncontrolled self-indulgence.   BINGE.

ramshackle *adjective*
Falling to ruin.   RUINOUS.

rancor *noun*
The quality or state of feeling bitter.   RESENTMENT.

rancorous *adjective*
Bitingly hostile.   RESENTFUL.

random *adjective*
1. Having no particular pattern, purpose, organization, or structure: *a random selection of his writings; random ideas; random acquaintanceships*.   **1.** *Syns:* desultory, haphazard, hit-or-miss, indiscriminate, objectless, purposeless, spot, stray, unconsidered, unplanned. *Near-syns:* accidental, aimless, designless, fortuitous, incidental, irregular.
2. Determined or marked by whim or caprice rather than reason.   **2.** ARBITRARY.

range *noun*
1. An area within which something or someone exists,   **1.** *Syns:* ambit, compass, extension,

acts, or has influence or power: *Extra fuel tanks greatly extend a bomber's range. The range of his mind was limited.*

extent, orbit, purview, reach, realm, scope, sphere, sweep.

Near-syns: area, circle, confines, domain, field, province, territory, width.

2. The extent of one's perception, understanding, knowledge, or vision.

2. KEN.

3. The ability or power to seize or attain.

3. GRASP *noun*.

4. Approximate size or amount.

4. NEIGHBORHOOD.

range *verb*

1. To place in or form a line or lines.

1. LINE *verb*.

2. To put into a deliberate order.

2. ARRANGE.

3. To change or fluctuate within limits.

3. GO.

4. To move about at random, esp. over a wide area.

4. ROVE.

rangy *adjective*

Tall, thin, and awkwardly built.

GANGLING.

rank¹ *noun*

1. A division of persons or things by quality, rank, or grade.

1. CLASS *noun*.

2. A group of people or things arranged in a row.

2. LINE *noun*.

3. Positioning of one individual vis-à-vis others.

3. PLACE *noun*.

rank *verb*

1. To put into a deliberate order.

1. ARRANGE.

2. To assign to a class or classes.

2. CLASS *verb*.

rank² *adjective*

1. Conspicuously bad or offensive.

1. FLAGRANT.

2. Growing profusely.

2. THICK *adjective*.

3. Smelling of mildew or decay.

3. MOLDY.

4. Offensive to accepted standards of decency.

4. OBSCENE.

rankness *noun*

The quality or state of being flagrant.

FLAGRANCY.

ransack *verb*

1. To make a thorough search of.

1. SCOUR.

2. To rob on a large scale.

2. LOOT *verb*.

rant *verb*

To speak in a loud, pompous, or prolonged manner: *ranted on and on about capital punishment.*

Syns: bloviate, harangue, mouth, perorate, rave.

ranting *adjective*

Full of or marked by extreme anger.

FURIOUS.

rap¹ *verb*

1. To make a noise by striking.

1. TAP¹ *verb*.

2. *Slang.* To find fault with.

2. BLAME *verb*.

3. *Informal.* To criticize for a fault or offense.

3. CALL DOWN at **call.**

rap out *verb*

To speak suddenly or sharply, as from surprise or emotion.

EXCLAIM.

rap *noun*

1. An audible blow.

1. TAP¹ *noun*.

2. *Slang.* A judicial decision, esp. one setting the punishment to be inflicted on a convicted person.

2. SENTENCE *noun*.

3. *Slang.* An exchanging of views.

3. CONFERENCE.

rap² *noun*

The least bit.

DAMN *noun*.

rapacious *adjective*

1. Having a strong urge to obtain or possess something, esp. material wealth, in quantity.

1. GREEDY.

2. Having an insatiable appetite for an activity or pursuit.

2. VORACIOUS.

rapacity *noun*

1. Excessive desire for more than one needs or deserves.

1. GREED.

2. The quality or condition of being voracious. — **2.** VORACITY.

rape *verb*
1. To compel (another) to participate in or submit to a sexual act: *Enemy soldiers pillaged the town and raped the women.* — **1.** *Syns:* assault, force, outrage, ravish, violate.
2. To rob of goods by force, esp. in time of war. — **2.** SACK² *verb.*

rapid *adjective*
Characterized by great celerity. — FAST *adjective.*

rapidity *noun*
1. Rate of motion or performance. — **1.** SPEED *noun.*
2. Rapidness of movement or activity. — **2.** HASTE *noun.*

rap out *verb* — SEE **rap¹.**

rapport *noun*
1. Harmonious mutual understanding. — **1.** AGREEMENT.
2. The state of individuals who are in utter agreement. — **2.** HARMONY.

rapprochement *noun*
A re-establishment of friendship or harmony. — RECONCILIATION.

rapt *adjective*
Having one's thoughts fully occupied. — ABSORBED.

rapture *noun*
A state of elated bliss. — HEAVEN.

rare *adjective*
1. Far beyond what is usual, normal, or customary: *a touch of rare wit.* — **1.** *Syns:* exceptional, extraordinary, remarkable, singular, uncommon, unusual.
Near-ants: common, commonplace, familiar, frequent, ordinary, unexceptional, usual.
2. Rarely occurring or appearing. — **2.** INFREQUENT.
3. Marked by great diffusion of component particles. — **3.** THIN *adjective.*

rarefied *adjective*
Marked by great diffusion of component particles. — THIN *adjective.*

rarefy *verb*
To become diffuse. — THIN *verb.*

rarely *adverb*
At rare intervals. — INFREQUENTLY.

raring *adjective*
Informal. Intensely desirous or interested. — EAGER.

rascal *noun*
One who causes minor trouble or damage. — MISCHIEF.

rash¹ *adjective*
1. Characterized by unthinking boldness and haste: *rash judgments.* — **1.** *Syns:* brash, foolhardy, harum-scarum, hasty, headlong, hotheaded, impetuous, impulsive, mad-brained, madcap, mad-headed, precipitant, precipitate, precipitous, reckless, slap-bang (*Informal*), slapdash, temerarious.
Near-ants: careful, cautious, circumspect, deliberate, premeditated; calm, collected, cool, level-headed; judicious, prudent, wise; calculating, considered, planned.
2. Lacking due thought or consideration. — **2.** PRECIPITATE *adjective.*

rash² *noun*
A sudden increase in something, as the occurrence of a disease. — OUTBREAK.

rashness *noun*
1. Careless, headlong action. — **1.** HASTE *noun.*
2. Foolhardy boldness or disregard of danger. — **2.** TEMERITY.

rasp *verb*
To bring or come into sliding, abrasive contact, often   SCRAPE *verb*.
with a harsh, grating sound.

raspberry *noun*
Slang. Any derisive sound of disapproval.   HISS *noun*.

rasping *adjective*
Disagreeable to the sense of hearing.   HARSH.

raspy *adjective*
Disagreeable to the sense of hearing.   HARSH.

rat *verb*
1. *Slang.* To be treacherous to.   1. BETRAY.
2. *Slang.* To abandon one's cause or party usu. to join   2. DEFECT *verb*.
   another.
3. *Slang.* To give incriminating information about   3. INFORM.
   others, esp. to the authorities.

  rat *noun*
1. *Slang.* One who betrays.   1. BETRAYER.
2. *Slang.* A person who has defected.   2. DEFECTOR.
3. *Slang.* One who gives incriminating information   3. INFORMER.
   about others.

rate¹ *verb*
1. To make a judgment as to the worth or value of.   1. ESTIMATE *verb*.
2. To assign to a class or classes.   2. CLASS *verb*.
3. *Informal.* To acquire as a result of one's behavior or 3. EARN.
   effort.

rate² *verb*
To reprimand loudly or harshly.   BAWL OUT at **bawl**.

rather *adverb*
To some extent.   FAIRLY.

ratification *noun*
An act of confirming officially.   CONFIRMATION.

ratify *verb*
To make valid and binding by a formal legal act.   CONFIRM.

ratiocinate *verb*
To use the powers of the mind, as in conceiving ideas,   THINK.
drawing inferences, and making judgments.

ratiocination *noun*
Exact, valid, and rational reasoning.   LOGIC.

ratiocinative *adjective*
Able to reason validly.   LOGICAL.

ration *noun*
That which is allotted.   ALLOTMENT.

rational *adjective*
1. Consistent with reason and intellect.   1. LOGICAL.
2. Of sound mind; mentally healthy.   2. SANE.
3. Possessing, proceeding from, or exhibiting good   3. SANE.
   judgment and prudence.

rationale *noun*
1. A statement of causes or motives.   1. ACCOUNT *noun*.
2. What is sound or reasonable.   2. SENSE *noun*.

rationality *noun*
1. Exact, valid, and rational reasoning.   1. LOGIC.
2. What is sound or reasonable.   2. SENSE *noun*.

rationalization *noun*
A statement of causes or motives.   ACCOUNT *noun*.

rationalize *verb*
1. To offer reasons for or a cause of.   1. ACCOUNT FOR at **account**.
2. To show to be just, right, or valid.   2. JUSTIFY.

rattle *verb*
1. To make or cause to make a succession of short, sharp sounds: *an old refrigerator that rattles; wind rattling the shutters.*
2. To talk volubly, persistently, and usu. inconsequentially.
3. *Informal.* To cause (a person) to be self-consciously distressed.

1. *Syns:* brattle (*Chiefly Scot.*), chatter, clack, clatter, clitter.
2. CHATTER *verb.*
3. EMBARRASS.

rattled *adjective*
Informal. Distressed and ill at ease.

EMBARRASSED.

ratty *adjective*
1. *Slang.* Showing signs of wear and tear or neglect.
2. *Chiefly Brit.* Easily annoyed.
3. *Chiefly Brit.* Having or showing a bad temper.

1. SHABBY.
2. TESTY.
3. ILL-TEMPERED.

raucous *adjective*
Disagreeable to the sense of hearing.

HARSH.

raunchiness *noun*
Slang. The quality or state of being obscene.

OBSCENITY.

raunchy *adjective*
Slang. Offensive to accepted standards of decency.

OBSCENE.

ravage *verb*
1. To destroy completely while conquering or occupying.
2. To rob of goods by force, esp. in time of war.

1. DEVASTATE.
2. SACK².

ravaging *adjective*
Tending to consume and destroy.

CONSUMPTIVE.

rave *verb*
1. To speak in a loud, pompous, or prolonged manner.
2. To show enthusiasm.

1. RANT.
2. ENTHUSE.

ravel *verb*
To make complex, intricate, or perplexing.

COMPLICATE.

ravenous *adjective*
1. Desiring or craving food: *The smells of cooking made us ravenous. Ravenous wild dogs ran down and ate the deer.*

2. Wanting to eat or drink more than one can reasonably consume.
3. Having an insatiable appetite for an activity or pursuit.

1. *Syns:* famished, hungry, starving. *Near-ants:* full, glutted, gorged, sated, satiated, satisfied. *Ant:* surfeited.
2. GREEDY.
3. VORACIOUS.

ravenousness *noun*
The quality or condition of being voracious.

VORACITY.

raving *adjective*
Full of or marked by extreme anger.

FURIOUS.

ravish *verb*
To compel (another) to participate in or submit to a sexual act.

RAPE.

ravishing *adjective*
Having qualities that delight the eye.

BEAUTIFUL.

raw *adjective*
1. Not cooked: *loves to munch on raw carrots.*
2. In a natural state and still not prepared for use.
3. Lacking experience and the knowledge gained from it.
4. Lacking expert, careful craftsmanship.
5. Lacking in delicacy or refinement.
6. Offensive to accepted standards of decency.

1. *Syn:* uncooked.
2. CRUDE.
3. INEXPERIENCED.
4. RUDE.
5. COARSE.
6. OBSCENE.

rawboned *adjective*
Having little flesh or fat on the body.

THIN *adjective.*

ray *noun*
A series of particles or waves traveling close together in parallel paths.

BEAM *noun.*

raze *verb*
To break up so that reconstruction is impossible.

DESTROY.

razz *noun*
Slang. Any derisive sound of disapproval.

HISS *noun.*

razz *verb*
1. *Slang.* To make fun of.
2. *Slang.* To tease or mock good-humoredly.

1. RIDICULE *verb.*
2. JOKE *verb.*

razzing *noun*
Slang. Words or actions intended to evoke contemptuous laughter.

RIDICULE *noun.*

reach *verb*
1. To extend, esp. an appendage: *reached out her hand to the child.*
2. To come to a particular place.
3. To succeed in communicating with: *Where can we reach you?*

4. To proceed on a certain course or for a certain distance.
5. To come to in number or quantity.
6. To succeed in doing.

1. *Syns:* outstretch, stretch (out).

2. ARRIVE.
3. *Syns:* contact (*Informal*), get. —*Idioms* get hold of, get in touch with, get through to, get to.
4. EXTEND.

5. AMOUNT *verb.*
6. ACCOMPLISH.

reach *noun*
1. An area within which something or someone exists, acts, or has influence or power.
2. The ability or power to seize or attain.
3. The measure of how far or long something goes in space, time, or degree.
4. A wide and open area, as of land, sky, or water.
5. The extent of one's perception, understanding, knowledge, or vision.

1. RANGE *noun.*

2. GRASP *noun.*
3. EXTENT.

4. EXPANSE.
5. KEN.

react *verb*
To act in return to something, as a stimulus.

RESPOND.

react to *verb*
To present with a specified reaction.

GREET.

reaction *noun*
1. The way in which a machine or other thing performs or functions.
2. An action elicited by a stimulus.

1. BEHAVIOR.

2. RESPONSE.

reactionary also **reactionist** *adjective*
1. Vehemently, often fanatically opposing progress or reform: *a reactionary backlash to progressive reforms.*
2. Clinging to obsolete ideas.

1. *Syns:* die-hard (*also* diehard), ultraconservative.

2. UNPROGRESSIVE.

reactionary also **reactionist** *noun*
A person who vehemently, often fanatically opposes progress and favors return to a previous condition: *a reactionary who clung to a belief in the monarchy.*

Syns: die-hard (*also* diehard), mossback, royalist, ultraconservative.

reactionist *adjective & noun*

SEE **reactionary.**

reactivate *verb*
To rouse from a state of inactivity or quiescence.

REVIVE.

react to *verb*

SEE **react.**

read *verb*
1. To perceive and recognize the meaning of.
2. To understand in a particular way.
3. To give a precise indication of, as on a register or scale.

1. UNDERSTAND.
2. INTERPRET.
3. SHOW *verb.*

readiness *noun*
1. Skillfulness in the use of the hands or body.

1. DEXTERITY.

2. The ability to perform without apparent effort.
3. The condition of being made ready beforehand.

reading *noun*
One's artistic conception as shown by the rendering of a dramatic role, musical composition, etc.

ready *adjective*
1. In a state of preparedness: *All systems are ready for liftoff.*

2. Marked by facility, esp. of expression.
3. Eagerly compliant.
4. Posing no difficulty.
5. Disposed to accept or agree.

ready *verb*
1. To cause to be ready, as for use, consumption, or a special purpose.
2. To prepare (oneself) for action.

real *adjective*
1. Having actual reality: *real evidence; real, not imaginary fears.*
2. Not counterfeit or copied.
3. In agreement or correspondence with fact.
4. Devoid of any hypocrisy or pretense.

realistic *adjective*
1. Accurately representing what is depicted or described: *a realistic novel.*
2. Having or indicating an awareness of things as they really are: *realistic about his chances of winning; a realistic evaluation of the company's financial posture.*

3. Described verbally in sharp and accurate detail.

reality *noun*
1. Something that exists.
2. The quality of being factual.

realization *noun*
1. The condition of being in full force or operation.
2. The condition of being fulfilled.
3. One's artistic conception as shown by the rendering of a dramatic role, musical composition, etc.

realize *verb*
1. To make real or actual: *By running the marathon she realized a lifelong dream.*

2. To succeed in doing.
3. To make as income or profit.
4. To achieve a certain price.

really *adverb*
1. In truth: *The walls really shook with his bellowing.*

2. In point of fact.

realm *noun*
1. A sphere of activity, study, or interest.
2. An area within which something or someone exists, acts, or has influence or power.

---

2. EASE *noun.*
3. PREPARATION.

INTERPRETATION.

1. **Syns:** go (*Informal*), prepared, primed, set[1], together (*Slang*). —*Idioms* all set, booted and spurred, in harness, in the saddle, in working order.
2. SMOOTH *adjective.*
3. GLAD.
4. EASY.
5. WILLING.

1. PREPARE.

2. GIRD.

1. **Syns:** concrete, substantial, substantive, tangible.
2. AUTHENTIC.
3. ACTUAL.
4. GENUINE.

1. **Syns:** lifelike, natural, naturalistic, true-to-life, truthful.
2. **Syns:** down-to-earth, hard, hard-boiled, hard-eyed, hardheaded, matter-of-fact, objective, practic, practical, pragmatic (*also* pragmatical), sober, tough-minded, unromantic.
   Near-ants: capricious, dreamy, idealistic, imaginative, impractical, irrational, romantic; fanciful, unrealistic, whimsical.
3. GRAPHIC.

1. ACTUALITY.
2. ACTUALITY.

1. EFFECT *noun.*
2. FULFILLMENT.
3. INTERPRETATION.

1. **Syns:** actualize, materialize. —*Idioms* bring to pass, carry into effect, carry out (*or* through).
2. ACCOMPLISH.
3. RETURN *verb.*
4. BRING.

1. **Syns:** absolutely, actually, fairly, indeed, positively, verily (*Archaic*). —*Idiom* for fair.
2. ACTUALLY.

1. AREA.
2. RANGE *noun.*

realness *noun*
The quality of being authentic.   AUTHENTICITY.

ream *noun*
An indeterminately great amount or number.   HEAP *noun*.

reanimation *noun*
The act of reviving or condition of being revived.   REVIVAL.

reap *verb*
1. To collect ripe crops.   1. GATHER.
2. To gather (grain) left by reapers.   2. GLEAN.

reaping *noun*
The act or process of bringing in a crop.   HARVEST *noun*.

reappear *verb*
To happen again or repeatedly.   RECUR.

reappearance *noun*
A repeated occurrence.   RECURRENCE.

rear¹ *noun*
1. The hindmost part of something.   1. TAIL *noun*.
2. The part or area farthest from the front.   2. BACK *noun*.
3. *Informal*. The part of one's back on which one rests   3. BOTTOM *noun*.
   in sitting.

rear *adjective*
Located in the rear.   BACK *adjective*.

rear² *verb*
1. To take care of and educate (a child).   1. BRING UP at **bring**.
2. To make or form (a structure).   2. BUILD *verb*.
3. To raise upright.   3. ERECT *verb*.

rearmost *adjective*
Bringing up the rear.   LAST¹ *adjective*.

rearward *adverb*
1. Toward the back.   1. BACKWARD *adverb*.
2. In or toward a former location or condition.   2. BACK *adverb*.

rearward *noun*
The part or area farthest from the front.   BACK *noun*.

reason *noun*
1. A fact or circumstance that gives logical support to   1. *Syns:* argument, ground, proof,
   an assertion, claim, or proposal: *What are your*   wherefore, why.
   reasons for voting as you did?
2. A basis for an action or decision.   2. CAUSE *noun*.
3. A statement of causes or motives.   3. ACCOUNT *noun*.
4. That which produces an effect.   4. CAUSE *noun*.
5. A justifying fact or consideration.   5. BASIS.
6. A course of reasoning.   6. ARGUMENT.
7. Exact, valid, and rational reasoning.   7. LOGIC.
8. What is sound or reasonable.   8. SENSE *noun*.
9. A healthy mental state.   9. SANITY.

reason *verb*
To use the faculty of reason: *Man's capacity to reason*   *Syns:* cogitate, deliberate, think.
sets him apart from other animals.

reasonable *adjective*
1. Possessing, proceeding from, or exhibiting good   1. SANE.
   judgment and prudence.
2. Consistent with reason and intellect.   2. LOGICAL.
3. Kept within sensible limits.   3. CONSERVATIVE *adjective*.
4. Not excessive or extreme in amount, degree, or   4. MODERATE *adjective*.
   force.
5. Suited to or within the means of ordinary people.   5. POPULAR.

reassume *verb*
To occupy or take again.   RESUME.

reawaken *verb*
To rouse from a state of inactivity or quiescence.   REVIVE.

rebate *noun*
An amount deducted.   DEDUCTION.

rebate *verb*
Rare. To grow or cause to grow gradually less.   DECREASE *verb*.

rebel *verb*
To refuse allegiance to and oppose by force a   **Syns:** insurrect, mutineer (*Archaic*),
government or ruling authority: *rebelled against the*   mutinize (*Archaic*), mutiny, revolt, rise
military government.   (up).

rebel *noun*
A person who rebels: *Dozens of rebels have been jailed*   **Syns:** insurgent, insurrectionist, mutineer.
by the regime.

rebellion *noun*
Organized opposition intended to change or overthrow   **Syns:** insurgence, insurgency,
existing authority: *a left-wing rebellion against the*   insurrection, mutiny, revolt, uprising.
dictator.

rebellious *adjective*
In open revolt against a government or ruling   **Syns:** insurgent, mutinous.
authority: *rebellious mobs barricading the streets.*

rebirth *noun*
1. The act of reviving or condition of being revived.   1. REVIVAL.
2. A fundamental change in one's beliefs.   2. CONVERSION.

rebound *verb*
1. To spring back after colliding with something.   1. BOUNCE *verb*.
2. To jerk backward, as a gun upon firing.   2. RECOIL.
3. To send back the sound of.   3. ECHO *verb*.
4. To produce an unexpected and undesired result.   4. BACKFIRE.

rebound *noun*
1. An act of bouncing or a bouncing movement.   1. BOUNCE *noun*.
2. Repetition of sound via reflection from a surface.   2. ECHO *noun*.

rebuff *noun*
A deliberate slight.   SNUB *noun*.

rebuff *verb*
To slight (someone) deliberately.   SNUB *verb*.

rebuild *verb*
To bring back to a previous normal condition.   RESTORE.

rebuke *noun*
Words expressive of strong disapproval: *The neighbor's*   **Syns:** admonishment, admonition, chiding,
rebuke took him by surprise.   reprimand, reproach, upbraiding.
                                                            Near-syns: lecture, lesson, scolding,
                                                            sermon, talking-to, tongue-lashing.

rebuke *verb*
1. To castigate for the purpose of improving.   1. CORRECT *verb*.
2. To criticize for a fault or offense.   2. CALL DOWN at **call**.

rebut *verb*
To prove or show to be false.   REFUTE.

recalcitrance or **recalcitrancy** *noun*
1. The disposition boldly to defy or resist authority or   1. DEFIANCE.
   an opposing force.
2. The quality or condition of being unruly.   2. UNRULINESS.

recalcitrancy *noun*   SEE **recalcitrance**.

recalcitrant *adjective*
1. Marked by defiance.   1. DEFIANT.
2. Not submitting to discipline or control.   2. UNRULY.

recalcitrate *verb*
To take a stand against.   CONTEST *verb*.

recall *verb*
1. To take back or remove.   1. LIFT *verb*.
2. To disavow (something previously written or said)   2. RETRACT.
   irrevocably and usu. formally.
3. To renew (an image or thought) in the mind.   3. REMEMBER.

recall *noun*

The power of retaining and recalling past experience.   MEMORY.

recant *verb*
To disavow (something previously written or said)   RETRACT.
irrevocably and usu. formally.

recantation *noun*
A formal statement of disavowal.   RETRACTION.

recanting *noun*
A formal statement of disavowal.   RETRACTION.

recap *noun*
A condensation of the essential or main points of   SUMMARY *noun.*
something.

recap *verb*
To recapitulate the salient facts of.   REVIEW *verb.*

recapitulation *noun*
A condensation of the essential or main points of   SUMMARY *noun.*
something.

recede *verb*
To move back or away from a point, limit, or mark: **Syns:** ebb, retract, retreat, retrocede,
tidal waters receding; a hairline that is receding.   retrograde, retrogress.
                                                          Near-syns: back, retire, withdraw.
                                                          Ants: advance, proceed.

receivable *adjective*
Owed as a debt.   DUE.

receive *verb*
1. To admit to one's possession, presence, or awareness: 1. **Syns:** accept, take.
   *received visitors graciously; received a present from
   an admirer; received instructions.*
2. To allow admittance, as to a group.   2. ACCEPT.

received *adjective*
1. Adhering to beliefs or practices approved by   1. ORTHODOX.
   authority or tradition.
2. Generally approved or agreed upon.   2. ACCEPTED.

recently *adverb*
1. Only a moment ago.   1. JUST *adverb.*
2. Not long ago.   2. LATE *adverb.*

receptive *adjective*
1. Ready and willing to receive favorably, as new   1. **Syns:** acceptant, acceptive, amenable,
   ideas: *The new symphony was played to a receptive*   open, open-minded, responsive.
   audience.   **Near-ants:** closed, closed-minded,
                                                           narrow, provincial, staid.
                                                           Ant: unreceptive.

2. *Physiol.* Transmitting impulses from sense organs to 2. SENSORY.
   nerve centers.

receptivity *noun*
Recognition of worth, quality, importance, etc.   APPRECIATION.

recess *noun*
A pause or interval, as from work or duty.   BREAK *noun.*

recess *verb*
To interrupt regular activity for a short period.   BREAK *verb.*

recession *noun*
A period of decreased business activity and high   DEPRESSION.
unemployment.

recidivate *verb*
To slip from a higher or better condition to a former,   RELAPSE *verb.*
usu. lower or poorer one.

recidivation *noun*
A slipping from a higher or better condition to a lower   LAPSE *noun.*
or poorer one.

recidivism *noun*
A slipping from a higher or better condition to a lower   LAPSE *noun.*
or poorer one.

reciprocal *adjective*
Having the same relationship each to the other.   MUTUAL.

reciprocate *verb*
1. To give or take mutually: *She reciprocated his*   **1. *Syns:*** requite, return.
   affection. He accepts invitations and never
   reciprocates.
2. To return like for like, esp. to return an unfriendly   **2.** RETALIATE.
   or hostile action with a similar one.

reciprocation *noun*
The act of retaliating.   RETALIATION.

reciprocative *adjective*
Having the same relationship each to the other.   MUTUAL.

recite *verb*
To give a verbal account of.   DESCRIBE.

reckless *adjective*
1. Characterized by unthinking boldness and haste.   **1.** RASH[1].
2. Lacking due thought or consideration.   **2.** PRECIPITATE *adjective*.
3. Lacking or showing a lack of a sense of   **3.** IRRESPONSIBLE.
   responsibility.

recklessness *noun*
Foolhardy boldness or disregard of danger.   TEMERITY.

reckon *verb*
1. To note (items) one by one so as to get a total.   **1.** COUNT *verb*.
2. To ascertain by mathematics.   **2.** CALCULATE.
3. To calculate approximately.   **3.** ESTIMATE *verb*.
4. To look upon in a particular way.   **4.** REGARD *verb*.
5. *Informal.* To take for granted without proof.   **5.** SUPPOSE.

  reckon on (or **upon**) *verb*
  To place trust or confidence in.   DEPEND ON at **depend**.

reckoning *noun*
1. The act, process, or result of calculating.   **1.** CALCULATION.
2. A noting of items one by one.   **2.** COUNT *noun*.
3. A precise list of fees or charges.   **3.** ACCOUNT *noun*.

reckon on (or **upon**) *verb*   SEE **reckon**.

reclaim *verb*
1. To extricate from an undesirable state.   **1.** RESCUE *verb*.
2. To bring back to a previous normal condition.   **2.** RESTORE.
3. To occupy or take again.   **3.** RESUME.

recline *verb*
1. To be or place oneself in a prostrate or recumbent   **1.** LIE[1].
   position.
2. To take repose by sleeping, lying quietly, or the like.   **2.** REST[1] *verb*.

recluse *adjective*
Solitary and shut off from society.   SECLUDED.

  recluse *verb*
  Obs. To put into solitude.   SECLUDE.

reclusion *noun*
The act of secluding or the state of being secluded.   SECLUSION.

recognition *noun*
Favorable notice, as of an achievement: *finally received*   ***Syns:*** acknowledgment (*also*
full recognition as a tenor.   acknowledgement), credit.

recognize *verb*
1. To perceive to be identical with something held in   **1. *Syn:*** know.
   the memory: *recognized his voice even over the*
   telephone.
2. To express recognition of.   **2.** ACKNOWLEDGE.
3. To establish the identification of.   **3.** PLACE *verb*.

recoil *verb*
1. To jerk backward, as a gun upon firing: *Stand back*   **1. *Syns:*** rebound, repercuss, ricochet.
   when the cannon recoils.

2. To draw away involuntarily, usu. due to fear or disgust.

2. FLINCH.

recollect *verb*
To renew (an image or thought) in the mind.

REMEMBER.

recollection *noun*
1. The power of retaining and recalling past experience.

1. MEMORY.

2. An act or instance of remembering.

2. MEMORY.

recommence *verb*
To go on after an interruption.

CONTINUE.

recommend *verb*
1. To give recommendations to (someone) about a decision or course of action.

1. ADVISE.

2. To pay a compliment to.

2. COMPLIMENT *verb.*

recommendable *adjective*
Worth doing, esp. for practical reasons.

ADVISABLE.

recommendation *noun*
1. An opinion as to a decision or course of action.

1. ADVICE.

2. A statement attesting to personal qualifications, character, and dependability.

2. REFERENCE.

recompense *verb*
1. To give compensation to.

1. COMPENSATE.

2. To give payment to in return for goods or services rendered.

2. PAY *verb.*

recompense *noun*
1. Something to make up for loss or damage.

1. COMPENSATION.

2. Something justly deserved.

2. DUE *noun.*

reconcile *verb*
1. To re-establish friendship between: *reconciling old enemies.*

1. *Syns:* conciliate, reunite. —*Idiom* heal the breach.

2. To bring (oneself) to accept: *reconciled herself to the loss of her friend.*

2. *Syn:* resign.

3. To bring into accord.

3. HARMONIZE.

4. To make or become suitable to a particular situation or use.

4. ADAPT.

5. To bring (something) into a state of agreement or accord.

5. SETTLE.

reconcilement *noun*
A re-establishment of friendship or harmony.

RECONCILIATION.

reconciliate *verb*
To bring into accord.

HARMONIZE.

reconciliation *noun*
A re-establishment of friendship or harmony: *effected a reconciliation between the warring countries.*

Syns: conciliation, rapprochement, reconcilement.

recondite *adjective*
Beyond the understanding of an average mind.

DEEP *adjective.*

recondition *verb*
1. To make new or as if new again.

1. RENEW.

2. To bring back to a previous normal condition.

2. RESTORE.

reconditioning *noun*
The act of making new or as if new again.

RENEWAL.

reconnaissance *noun*
The act or an instance of exploring or investigating.

EXPLORATION.

reconnoiter *verb*
To go into or through for the purpose of making discoveries or acquiring information.

EXPLORE.

reconsider *verb*
To consider again, esp. with the possibility of change: *Why not reconsider your foolish plan?*

Syns: re-evaluate, re-examine, rethink, review, think over.

reconstruct *verb*
To bring back to a previous normal condition.

RESTORE.

record *verb*
1. To place on a list or in a record.
2. To give a precise indication of, as on a register or scale.

recount *verb*
To give a verbal account of.

recoup *verb*
To get back.

  recoup *noun*
  The act of getting back or regaining.

recourse *noun*
That to which one turns for help when in desperation.

recover *verb*
1. To get back: *hopes to recover her stolen car.*

2. To regain one's health: *recovering after a long illness.*

3. To bring back to a previous normal condition.
4. To extricate from an undesirable state.

recovery *noun*
1. A return to normal health: *made a quick recovery.*
2. The act of getting back or regaining: *The Crusaders' objective was the recovery of the Holy Land.*
3. A return to former prosperity or status.

recreancy *noun*
An instance of defecting from or abandoning a cause.

recreant *adjective*
Not true to duty or obligation.

  recreant *noun*
  A person who has defected.

recreate *verb*
1. To occupy in an agreeable or pleasing way.
2. To occupy oneself with amusement or diversion.

recreation *noun*
1. Something, esp. a performance or show, designed to entertain.
2. Activity engaged in for relaxation and amusement.

recrudesce *verb*
To come back to a former condition.

rectify *verb*
1. To make right what is wrong.
2. To bring (something) into a state of agreement or accord.

rectitude *noun*
1. Moral or ethical strength.
2. The quality or state of being morally sound.
3. The quality of being honest.

recumbent *adjective*
Lying down.

recuperate *verb*
To regain one's health.

recuperation *noun*
A return to normal health.

recur *verb*
1. To happen again or repeatedly: *an area where typhoons recur.*
2. To come back to a former condition.

---

1. POST *verb*.
2. SHOW *verb*.

DESCRIBE.

RECOVER.

RECOVERY.

RESORT *noun*.

1. *Syns:* recoup, regain, repossess, retrieve.
   Near-syns: recapture, reclaim, redeem, retake; resume.
2. *Syns:* come around (*or* round), convalesce, gain, improve, mend, perk up, rally, recuperate.
3. RESTORE.
4. RESCUE *verb*.

1. *Syns:* rally, recuperation.
2. *Syns:* recoup, repossession, retrieval.

3. COMEBACK at **come back**.

DEFECTION.

FAITHLESS.

DEFECTOR.

1. AMUSE.
2. PLAY *verb*.

1. AMUSEMENT.

2. PLAY *noun*.

RETURN *verb*.

1. CORRECT *verb*.
2. SETTLE.

1. CHARACTER.
2. GOOD *noun*.
3. HONESTY.

FLAT *adjective*.

RECOVER.

RECOVERY.

1. *Syns:* reappear, reoccur, return.

2. RETURN *verb*.

recurrence *noun*
A repeated occurrence: *experienced a recurrence of her headaches.*

Syns: reappearance, reoccurrence, return.

recurrent *adjective*
Happening or appearing at regular intervals: *a recurrent problem.*

Syns: cyclic (*also* cyclical), isochronal (*also* isochronic, isochronous), periodic (*also* periodical), recurring. —*Idiom* as regular as (*or* like) clockwork.
Near-syn: seasonal.
Ants: continuous, incessant.

recurring *adjective*
Happening or appearing at regular intervals.

RECURRENT.

red-blooded *adjective*
Full of vigor.

LUSTY.

redden *verb*
To become red in the face.

BLUSH *verb.*

redeem *verb*
1. To make up for the defects of.
2. To extricate from an undesirable state.

1. COMPENSATE.
2. RESCUE *verb.*

red-hot *adjective*
1. Marked by much heat.
2. Fired with intense feeling.
3. Of great current interest.

1. HOT *adjective.*
2. PASSIONATE.
3. HOT *adjective.*

redolence *noun*
A sweet or pleasant odor.

FRAGRANCE.

redolent *adjective*
Having a pleasant odor.

FRAGRANT.

redouble *verb*
1. To make or become twice as great.
2. To increase in intensity or severity.

1. DOUBLE *verb.*
2. INTENSIFY.

redoubtable *adjective*
Widely known and esteemed.

EMINENT.

redress *verb*
1. To give compensation to.
2. To exact revenge for.

1. COMPENSATE.
2. AVENGE.

redress *noun*
Something to make up for loss or damage.

COMPENSATION.

reduce *verb*
1. To lose bodily weight, as by dieting: *Avoid sweets if you want to reduce.*
2. To grow or cause to grow gradually less.
3. To become or make less in price or value.
4. To decrease, as in length or amount, by or as if by severing or excising.
5. To lower in rank or grade.

1. *Syns:* slim (down), trim down.
2. DECREASE *verb.*
3. DEPRECIATE.
4. CUT BACK.
5. DEMOTE.

reduction *noun*
1. The act or process of decreasing.
2. An amount deducted.
3. The act or an instance of demoting.
4. A lowering in price or value.
5. The act or process of decreasing in length, amount, duration, etc.

1. DECREASE *noun.*
2. DEDUCTION.
3. DEMOTION.
4. DEPRECIATION.
5. CUTBACK at **cut back.**

redundant *adjective*
Characterized by excessive and obfuscatory wordiness.

TAUTOLOGICAL.

reduplicate *verb*
To make a copy of.

COPY *verb.*

reduplication *noun*
Something closely resembling another.

COPY *noun.*

re-echo *verb*
To send back the sound of.

ECHO *verb.*

reek *verb*
To have or give off a foul odor.

SMELL *verb*.

reeking *adjective*
Having an unpleasant odor.

SMELLY.

reel *verb*
1. To walk unsteadily.
2. To have the sensation of turning in circles.

1. LURCH *verb*.
2. SPIN *verb*.

reeling *adjective*
Having a sensation of whirling or falling.

DIZZY *adjective*.

re-evaluate *verb*
To consider again, esp. with the possibility of change.

RECONSIDER.

re-examine *verb*
To consider again, esp. with the possibility of change.

RECONSIDER.

ref *noun*
Slang. A person, usu. appointed, who decides the issues or results, or supervises the conduct, of a competition or conflict.

JUDGE *noun*.

refer *verb*
1. To direct (a person) elsewhere for help, information, etc.: *will refer the patient to a cardiologist*.
2. To call or direct attention to (an occurrence, situation, etc.): *I'll never refer to your indiscretion*.

3. To regard as belonging to or resulting from another.
4. To be pertinent.
5. To have recourse to when in need.

1. *Syns:* send, transfer, turn over.

2. *Syns:* advert, allude, bring up, mention, point out, touch on (*or* upon).
   Near-syns: cite, introduce, name, specify.

3. ATTRIBUTE *verb*.
4. APPLY.
5. RESORT TO at **resort**.

referee *noun*
A person, usu. appointed, who decides the issues or results, or supervises the conduct, of a competition or conflict.

JUDGE *noun*.

referee *verb*
To make a decision about (a controversy, dispute, etc.) after deliberation, as in a court of law.

JUDGE *verb*.

reference *noun*
A statement attesting to personal qualifications, character, and dependability: *Include three references with your application*.

Syns: character (*Archaic*), recommendation, testimonial.

refine *verb*
1. To make or become clear by the removal of impurities: *refining oil into gasoline; refining butter by heating it*.
2. To bring to perfection or completion.

1. *Syns:* clarify, clean, cleanse, purify.

2. PERFECT *verb*.

refined *adjective*
1. Made pure, esp. by a commercial refining process: *a lotion containing refined lanolin*.
2. Characterized by discriminating taste and broad knowledge as a result of development or education.
3. So slight as to be difficult to notice or appreciate.

1. *Syns:* clarified, purified.

2. CULTURED.

3. DELICATE.

refinement *noun*
1. Enlightenment and excellent taste resulting from intellectual development.
2. High style in quality, manner, or dress.
3. The ability to distinguish, esp. to recognize small differences or draw fine distinctions.

1. CULTURE.

2. CLASS *noun*.
3. DISCRIMINATION.

refining *adjective*
Promoting culture.

CULTURAL.

reflect *verb*
1. To send back or form an image of: *a pool that reflects nearby buildings*.
2. To send back the sound of.

1. *Syns:* image, mirror.

2. ECHO *verb*.

3. To copy (another) slavishly.

        3. ECHO *verb*.

4. To consider carefully and at length.

        4. PONDER.

5. To use the powers of the mind, as in conceiving ideas, drawing inferences, and making judgments.

        5. THINK.

reflection *noun*

1. Something that is reflected: *a reflection of clouds on the water.*

        1. *Syn:* image.

2. The act or process of thinking.

        2. THOUGHT.

3. An implied criticism: *His trouble cast no reflection on his parents.*

        3. *Syns:* reproach, slur.

4. Imitative reproduction, as of the style of another.

        4. ECHO *noun*.

reflective *adjective*

Of, characterized by, or disposed to thought.

        THOUGHTFUL.

reflex *adjective*

Acting or happening without apparent forethought, prompting, or planning.

        SPONTANEOUS.

reflex *noun*

Imitative reproduction, as of the style of another.

        ECHO *noun*.

reformatory *adjective*

Tending to correct.

        CORRECTIVE *adjective*.

refract *verb*

To cause to move, esp. at an angle.

        BEND *verb*.

refractoriness *noun*

1. The quality or state of being stubbornly unyielding.

        1. OBSTINACY.

2. The quality or condition of being unruly.

        2. UNRULINESS.

refractory *adjective*

1. Tenaciously unwilling to yield.

        1. OBSTINATE.

2. Not submitting to discipline or control.

        2. UNRULY.

refrain *verb*

To hold oneself back: *Please refrain from applauding.*

        Syns: abstain, forbear, hold off, keep, withhold.
        Near-syns: arrest, check, curb, inhibit, interrupt, restrain, stop.

refresh *verb*

1. To impart renewed energy and strength to (a person): *Sleep refreshed me.*

        1. *Syns:* freshen, reinvigorate, rejuvenate, renew, restore.
        Near-syns: animate, awake, awaken, energize, enliven, quicken, vivify.
        Ants: addle, jade.

2. To make new or as if new again.

        2. RENEW.

refreshing *adjective*

Producing or stimulating physical, mental, or emotional vigor.

        TONIC *adjective*.

refuge *noun*

1. The state of being protected or safeguarded, as from danger or hardship: *a political dissident seeking refuge in Sweden.*

        1. *Syns:* asylum, sanctuary, shelter.

2. Something that physically protects, esp. from danger.

        2. COVER *noun*.

3. An institution that provides care and shelter.

        3. HOME.

4. That to which one turns for help when in desperation.

        4. RESORT *noun*.

refugee *noun*

One who flees, as from home, confinement, captivity, justice, etc.

        FUGITIVE *noun*.

refulgent *adjective*

Giving off or reflecting light readily or in large amounts.

        BRIGHT.

refurbish *verb*

1. To make modern in appearance or style.

        1. MODERNIZE.

2. To make new or as if new again.

        2. RENEW.

refurbishing *noun*
The act of making new or as if new again.   RENEWAL.

refurbishment *noun*
The act of making new or as if new again.   RENEWAL.

refusal *noun*
1. A turning down of a request: *refusal of permission to*   1. **Syns:** denial, disallowance, rejection,
   leave early.   turn-down (*Informal*).
2. A negative response.   2. NO *noun.*

refuse *verb*
1. To be unwilling to grant: *refused him the right to*   1. **Syns:** deny, disallow, disapprove, turn
   visit the children.   down, withhold. —*Idiom* turn thumbs
                                                                 down on.
2. To be unwilling to accept, consider, or receive.   2. DECLINE *verb.*

refute *verb*
To prove or show to be false: *Evidence came to light*   **Syns:** belie, confute, discredit, disprove,
that refuted the theory.   rebut.
                                                             Near-syns: confound, contravene,
                                                             controver, disconfirm, evert, overturn,
                                                             traverse.
                                                             Ant: confirm.

regain *verb*
To get back.   RECOVER.

regal *adjective*
1. Marked by magnificently lavish ceremony and   1. GRAND.
   display.
2. Large and impressive in size, scope, or extent.   2. GRAND.

regard *verb*
1. To look upon in a particular way: *I regard him as a*   1. **Syns:** account, consider, esteem, reckon,
   fool.   view.
                                                                Near-syns: assess, estimate, rate,
                                                                value.
2. To have a high opinion of.   2. ADMIRE.
3. To direct the eyes on an object.   3. LOOK *verb.*

regard *noun*
1. Thoughtful attention.   1. CONSIDERATION.
2. The act of noting, observing, or taking into account.   2. NOTICE *noun.*
3. A feeling of deference, approval, and liking.   3. ESTEEM *noun.*
4. An act of directing the eyes on an object.   4. LOOK *noun.*
5. Cautious attentiveness.   5. CARE *noun.*
6. A being personally interested in.   6. CONCERN *noun.*

regards *noun*
Friendly greetings: *Give them our regards.*   **Syn:** respects.

regeneration *noun*
A fundamental change in one's beliefs.   CONVERSION.

regime *noun*
A system by which a political unit is controlled.   GOVERNMENT.

regimen *noun*
The systematic application of remedies to effect a cure.   TREATMENT.

region *noun*
A part of the earth's surface.   AREA.

register *verb*
1. To come as a realization: *His real meaning finally*   1. **Syns:** dawn on (*or* upon), sink in, soak
   registered with them.   in.
2. To place on a list or in a record.   2. POST *verb.*
3. To give a precise indication of, as on a register or   3. SHOW *verb.*
   scale.

register *noun*
A series of names, words, etc., printed or written down   LIST[1] *noun.*
item by item.

regnant *adjective*
1. Exercising controlling power or influence.   1. DOMINANT.

2. Most generally existing or encountered at a given
time.

    2. PREVAILING.

regress *verb*
To slip from a higher or better condition to a former,
usu. lower or poorer one.

    RELAPSE *verb*.

regress *noun*
A return to a former, usu. worse condition.

    REVERSION.

regression *noun*
A return to a former, usu. worse condition.

    REVERSION.

regret *verb*
To feel or express sorrow for: *He deeply regrets his
treatment of his wife.*

    Syns: deplore, repent, rue, wail (*Archaic*).
    Near-syns: bemoan, bewail, grieve,
    lament, mourn, sorrow.

regret *noun*
Unhappiness caused by the failure of one's hopes,
desires, or expectations.

    DISAPPOINTMENT.

regretful *adjective*
1. Expressing or inclined to express an apology.
2. Feeling or expressing regret for one's sins or
misdeeds.

    1. APOLOGETIC *adjective*.
    2. REMORSEFUL.

regrets *noun*
A statement of acknowledgment expressing regret or
asking pardon.

    APOLOGY.

regrettable *adjective*
Causing sorrow or regret.

    SORROWFUL.

regular *adjective*
1. Occurring quite often.
2. Commonly practiced or used.
3. Without imperfections or blemishes.
4. Having no variations.
5. Arranged or proceeding in a set, systematized
pattern.
6. Characterized by or displaying symmetry, esp.
correspondence in scale or measure.

    1. COMMON *adjective*.
    2. CUSTOMARY.
    3. CLEAN *adjective*.
    4. EVEN[1] *adjective*.
    5. METHODICAL.
    6. SYMMETRICAL.

regulate *verb*
1. To alter (parts of a device) for proper functioning.
2. To keep the mechanical operation of (a device)
within proper parameters.

    1. ADJUST.
    2. GOVERN.

regulation *noun*
1. A principle governing the affairs of man within or
among political units.
2. A code or set of codes governing action, procedure,
etc.

    1. LAW *noun*.
    2. RULE *noun*.

regulatory *adjective*
Of or relating to government.

    GOVERNMENTAL.

rehabilitate *verb*
To bring back to a previous normal condition.

    RESTORE.

rehearsal *noun*
Repetition of an action so as to develop or maintain
one's skill.

    PRACTICE *noun*.

rehearse *verb*
To give a verbal account of.

    DESCRIBE.

reign *verb*
1. To exercise the authority of a sovereign.
2. To occupy the pre-eminent position in.

    1. GOVERN.
    2. DOMINATE.

reimburse *verb*
To give compensation to.

    COMPENSATE.

rein *verb*
To control, restrict, or arrest.

    RESTRAIN.

reinforce *verb*
To make or become tight or tighter.

    TIGHTEN.

reinstate *verb*
1. To put (someone) in the possession of a prior position or office.
2. To bring back into existence or use.

1. RESTORE.

2. RESTORE.

reintroduce *verb*
To bring back into existence or use.

RESTORE.

reinvigorate *verb*
To impart renewed energy and strength to (a person).

REFRESH.

reinvigorating *adjective*
Producing or stimulating physical, mental, or emotional vigor.

TONIC *adjective*.

reiterate *verb*
To state again.

REPEAT.

reiterate *adjective*
Characterized by repetition.

REPETITIVE.

reiteration *noun*
The act or process of repeating.

REPETITION.

reiterative *adjective*
Characterized by repetition.

REPETITIVE.

reject *verb*
To be unwilling to accept, consider, or receive.

DECLINE *verb*.

rejection *noun*
1. A refusal to grant the truth of a statement or charge.
2. A turning down of a request.
3. A negative response.

1. DENIAL.

2. REFUSAL.

3. NO *noun*.

rejoice *verb*
1. To feel or take joy or pleasure: *The whole city rejoiced at the homecoming of its hero.*
2. To show happy satisfaction in an event, esp. by merrymaking.

1. **Syns:** delight, exult, joy.

2. CELEBRATE.

rejoicing *noun*
The act of showing happy satisfaction in an event.

CELEBRATION.

rejoin *verb*
To speak or act in response to.

ANSWER *verb*.

rejoinder *noun*
Something spoken or written as a return to a question, demand, etc.

ANSWER *noun*.

rejuvenate *verb*
1. To bring back to a previous normal condition.
2. To make new or as if new again.
3. To make modern in appearance or style.
4. To impart renewed energy and strength to (a person).

1. RESTORE.

2. RENEW.

3. MODERNIZE.

4. REFRESH.

rejuvenation *noun*
The act of making new or as if new again.

RENEWAL.

rekindle *verb*
To rouse from a state of inactivity or quiescence.

REVIVE.

rekindling *noun*
The act of reviving or condition of being revived.

REVIVAL.

relapse *verb*
To slip from a higher or better condition to a former, usu. lower or poorer one: *When untended, the garden relapsed into weeds.*

Syns: backslide, lapse, recidivate, regress, retrogress, revert.

relapse *noun*
A slipping from a higher or better condition to a lower or poorer one.

LAPSE *noun*.

relate *verb*
1. *Informal.* To interact with another or others in a meaningful fashion: *He doesn't relate with young people.*

1. **Syns:** click (*Informal*), communicate (*Informal*), connect (*Informal*). —Idiom be on the same wavelength.

2. To give a verbal account of.   2. DESCRIBE.
3. To unite or be united in a relationship.   3. ASSOCIATE *verb*.
4. To be pertinent.   4. APPLY.
5. To associate or affiliate oneself closely with a person   5. IDENTIFY.
   or group.

related *adjective*
Connected by or as if by kinship or common origin: *Syns:* agnate, akin, allied, cognate,
related to her through my father.   connate, connatural, consanguineous (*also*
                                                                        consanguine), kindred.
                                                                        Near-syns: affiliated, associated,
                                                                        connected, incident; alike, analogous,
                                                                        identical; germane, pertinent, relevant.
                                                                        Ant: unrelated.

relation *noun*
1. A logical or natural association between two or more   1. *Syns:* connection, correlation, hookup
   things: *the relation between hard work and success.*   (*Informal*), interconnection,
                                                                           interdependence, interrelation,
                                                                           interrelationship, link, relationship,
                                                                           tie-in.
2. A person connected to another person by blood.   2. RELATIVE *noun*.

relationship *noun*
A logical or natural association between two or more   RELATION.
things.

relative *adjective*
1. Being such by comparison with some standard.   1. COMPARATIVE.
2. Determined or to be determined by someone or   2. DEPENDENT *adjective*.
   something else.

relative *noun*
A person connected to another person by blood: *one of*   *Syns:* kin, kinsman, kinswoman, relation.
my relatives from the old country.

relax *verb*
1. To reduce in tension, pressure, or rigidity.   1. EASE *verb*.
2. To take repose by ceasing work or other effort for an   2. REST[1] *verb*.
   interval of time.

relaxation *noun*
Freedom from labor, responsibility, or strain.   REST[1] *noun*.

relaxed *adjective*
1. Unconstrained by rigid standards.   1. EASYGOING.
2. Not tautly bound to something else.   2. LOOSE *adjective*.

release *verb*
1. To free from something objectionable or undesirable.   1. RID.
2. To set at liberty.   2. FREE *verb*.
3. To discharge material, as vapor or fumes, usu.   3. EMIT.
   suddenly and violently.

released *adjective*
At liberty; not imprisoned or enslaved.   FREE *adjective*.

relegate *verb*
To give over to another for care, use, or performance.   ENTRUST.

relent *verb*
1. To become less active or intense.   1. SUBSIDE.
2. To moderate or change a position or course of action   2. WEAKEN.
   as a result of pressure.

relentless *adjective*
1. Existing or occurring without interruption or end.   1. CONTINUAL.
2. Firmly, often unreasonably immovable in purpose or   2. STUBBORN.
   will.

relevance also **relevancy** *noun*
1. The fact of being related to the matter at hand: 1. *Syns:* application, bearing,
   That idea has no relevance to our current situation.   germaneness, pertinence (*also*
                                                                           pertinency).
2. A connecting relation.   2. CONCERN *noun*.

relevancy *noun*

relevant *adjective*
Related to the matter at hand: *relevant questions; relevant issues.*

Syns: applicable, apposite, apropos, germane, material, pertinent. —*Idiom* to the point.
Near-ants: alien, extrinsic, foreign, inadmissible, inapplicable, inappropriate, unassociated, unconnected, unrelated.
Ants: extraneous, irrelevant.

reliable *adjective*
Capable of being depended upon.

DEPENDABLE.

reliance *noun*
Absolute certainty in the trustworthiness of another.

CONFIDENCE.

reliant *adjective*
Determined or to be determined by someone or something else.

DEPENDENT *adjective.*

relic *noun*
1. The remains of something destroyed, disintegrated, or decayed.
2. A mark or remnant that indicates the former presence of something.

1. RUIN *noun.*

2. TRACE *noun.*

relief *noun*
1. Assistance, esp. money, food, and other necessities, given to the needy or dispossessed: *received relief following the flood.*
2. Freedom, esp. from pain: *no relief from her suffering.*

3. The act or an instance of helping.
4. A person or persons taking over the duties of another: *His relief arrived early.*

1. *Syns:* dole, handout, welfare.

2. *Syns:* allayment, alleviation, assuagement, ease, mitigation.
3. HELP *noun.*
4. *Syn:* replacement.

relieve *verb*
1. To make less severe or more bearable: *takes medication to relieve the pain.*

1. *Syns:* allay, alleviate, assuage, comfort, ease, lessen, lighten, mitigate, palliate.
Near-syns: aid, appease, benefit, console, help, quiet, soften, soothe, subdue; moderate, temper.
Ant: intensify.

2. To free from an obligation or duty.
3. To free from a specific duty by acting as a substitute: *A new guard will relieve you at midnight.*
4. To free from something objectionable or undesirable.

2. EXCUSE *verb.*
3. *Syns:* spell[3], take over (for).

4. RID.

religion *noun*
A system of religious belief: *Many religions exist in the Orient.*

Syns: creed, denomination, faith, persuasion, sect.

religious *adjective*
1. Deeply concerned with God and the beliefs and practice of religion.
2. In the service or worship of God or a god.
3. Of or relating to a church or to an established religion.

1. HOLY.

2. DIVINE[1] *adjective.*
3. SPIRITUAL.

relinquish *verb*
1. To let (something) go: *relinquished his ambitions; relinquished my umbrella to the attendant.*

1. *Syns:* abandon, forgo (*also* forego), hand over, lay down, surrender, waive, yield.

2. To give up a possession, claim, or right.

2. ABDICATE.

relish *verb*
1. To regard with great pleasure or approval.
2. To receive pleasure from.
3. To be avidly interested in.
4. To recognize the worth, quality, importance, etc., of.

1. ADMIRE.
2. ENJOY.
3. EAT UP at **eat.**
4. APPRECIATE.

relish *noun*

1. A feeling of extreme gratification aroused by something good or desired.

2. A distinctive property of a substance affecting the gustatory sense.

3. A liking or personal preference for something.
4. Spirited enjoyment.

relocate *verb*
To change one's residence, place of business, etc.

relocation *noun*
The act or process of moving from one place to another.

reluctance *noun*
The state of not being disposed or inclined.

reluctant *adjective*
Not inclined or willing to do or undertake.

rely on (or **upon**) *verb*
To place trust or confidence in.

remain *verb*
To continue to be in a place: *She remained at home after he left for work.*

remainder *noun*
1. What remains after a part has been used or subtracted.
2. The remains of something destroyed, disintegrated, or decayed.

remainder *adjective*
That remains, esp. after a part has been removed.

remaining *adjective*
That remains, esp. after a part has been removed: *The remaining pie was quickly polished off.*

remains *noun*
1. What remains after a part has been used or subtracted.
2. A mark or remnant that indicates the former presence of something.
3. The physical frame of a dead person or animal.

remark *verb*
1. To make observations.
2. To perceive with a special effort of the senses or the mind.

remark *noun*
1. The act of noting, observing, or taking into account.
2. An expression of fact or opinion.
3. Something said.

remarkable *adjective*
1. Readily attracting notice.
2. Far beyond what is usual, normal, or customary.

remedial *adjective*
1. Tending to correct.
2. Serving to cure.

remedy *noun*
1. Something that corrects or counteracts: *There are no easy remedies for inflation.*

2. An agent used to restore health.

remedy *verb*
1. To rectify an undesirable or unhealthy condition.
2. To make right what is wrong.

---

1. DELIGHT *noun*.

2. FLAVOR *noun*.

3. TASTE *noun*.
4. ZEST.

MOVE *verb*.

REMOVAL.

INDISPOSITION.

INDISPOSED.

DEPEND ON at **depend.**

Syns: abide, bide, linger, stay[1], stick around (*Informal*), tarry, wait.
Near-syns: dally, delay, dillydally, lag, loiter, procrastinate.
Ant: depart.

1. BALANCE *noun*.

2. RUIN *noun*.

REMAINING.

Syns: leftover, remainder.

1. BALANCE *noun*.

2. TRACE *noun*.

3. BODY *noun*.

1. COMMENT *verb*.
2. NOTICE *verb*.

1. NOTICE *noun*.
2. COMMENT *noun*.
3. WORD *noun*.

1. NOTICEABLE.
2. RARE.

1. CORRECTIVE *adjective*.
2. CURATIVE *adjective*.

1. *Syns:* antidote, corrective, counteragent, countermeasure, curative, cure.

2. CURE *noun*.

1. CURE *verb*.
2. CORRECT *verb*.

remember *verb*
1. To renew (an image or thought) in the mind: *couldn't remember his name; couldn't remember what happened.*
2. To care enough to keep (someone) in mind: *How kind of you to remember me with flowers.*

1. **Syns:** bethink, mind (*Rare*), recall, recollect, retain, revive, think (of).
   —*Idiom* bring to mind.
2. **Syn:** think (of).

remembrance *noun*
1. Something that causes one to remember: *gave me an ashtray as a remembrance of my visit.*
2. The power of retaining and recalling past experience.
3. An act or instance of remembering.
4. Something, as a structure or custom, serving to honor or keep alive a memory.

1. **Syns:** keepsake, memento, reminder, souvenir, token, trophy.
2. MEMORY.
3. MEMORY.
4. MEMORIAL *noun*.

reminder *noun*
Something that causes one to remember.

REMEMBRANCE.

reminiscence *noun*
1. A narrative of experiences undergone by the writer.
2. An act or instance of remembering.
3. The power of retaining and recalling past experience.

1. COMMENTARY.
2. MEMORY.
3. MEMORY.

reminiscent *adjective*
Tending to bring something, as a memory, mood, or image, subtly or indirectly to mind.

SUGGESTIVE.

remiss *adjective*
Guilty of neglect; lacking due care or concern.

NEGLIGENT.

remission *noun*
1. The act or an instance of forgiving.
2. The condition of being temporarily inactive.

1. FORGIVENESS.
2. ABEYANCE.

remissive *adjective*
Existing in a temporarily inactive and hidden form.

LATENT.

remissness *noun*
The state or quality of being negligent.

NEGLIGENCE.

remit *verb*
1. To put off until a later time.
2. To grant forgiveness for a fault, offense, or injury.

1. DEFER[1].
2. FORGIVE.

remittent *adjective*
Existing in a temporarily inactive and hidden form.

LATENT.

remnant *noun*
1. Residual matter.
2. What remains after a part has been used or subtracted.
3. The remains of something destroyed, disintegrated, or decayed.

1. END *noun*.
2. BALANCE *noun*.
3. RUIN *noun*.

remonstrance *noun*
The act of expressing strong or reasoned opposition.

OBJECTION.

remonstrate *verb*
To express opposition by argument.

OBJECT[2].

remonstration *noun*
The act of expressing strong or reasoned opposition.

OBJECTION.

remorse *noun*
A feeling of regret for one's sins or misdeeds.

PENITENCE.

remorseful *adjective*
Feeling or expressing regret for one's sins or misdeeds: *made a remorseful admission that he had lied.*

Syns: compunctious, contrite, penitent, penitential, regretful, repentant, sorry.
Near-ants: hard, impenitent, unapologetic, unregretful, unrepentant, unsorrowful.
Ant: remorseless.

remorsefulness *noun*
A feeling of regret for one's sins or misdeeds.

PENITENCE.

remorseless *adjective*
1. Devoid of remorse: *a remorseless cad.*
2. Having or showing no mercy.
3. Having or showing uncompromising determination or resolution in purpose or action.

1. **Syns:** impenitent, unrepentant.
2. MERCILESS.
3. GRIM.

remote *adjective*
1. Small in degree, esp. of probability: *only a remote chance of survival.*
2. Far from others in space, time, or relationship.
3. Long past.
4. Far from centers of human population: *a remote outpost deep in the Andes.*

1. **Syns:** fat (*Slang*), negligible, off, outside, slender, slight, slim.
2. DISTANT.
3. HIGH.
4. **Syns:** isolated, insular, lonely, lonesome, obscure, out-of-the-way, removed, secluded, solitary. —*Idiom* off the beaten path (*or* track).

5. Not friendly, sociable, or warm in manner.

5. COOL *adjective.*

remoteness *noun*
1. Dissociation from one's surroundings or worldly affairs.
2. The fact or condition of being far removed or apart.

1. DETACHMENT.

2. DISTANCE.

remotion *noun*
The act or process of moving from one place to another.

REMOVAL.

removal *noun*
1. The act or process of moving from one place to another: *removal of the goods from the flooded warehouse to a new facility.*
2. The act or process of eliminating.

1. **Syns:** move, relocation, remotion.

2. ELIMINATION.

remove *verb*
1. To move (something) from a position occupied: *removed the dirty dishes from the table; removed the troops from the field.*
2. To go or cause to go from one place to another.
3. To change one's residence, place of business, etc.
4. To take from one's own person: *removed his coat and sat down.*
5. To destroy all traces of.
6. To get rid of, esp. by banishment or execution.
7. To take or leave out.
8. *Poetic.* To move or proceed away from a place.

1. **Syns:** take away, take off, take out, withdraw.

2. MOVE *verb.*
3. MOVE *verb.*
4. **Syns:** doff, douse, take off.

5. ANNIHILATE.
6. ELIMINATE.
7. DROP *verb.*
8. GO *verb.*

remove *noun*
Degree of separation, esp. in time: *It is difficult to judge the administration at this far remove.*

Syn: distance.

removed *adjective*
1. Far from others in space, time, or relationship.
2. Set away from all others.
3. Far from centers of human population.
4. Long past.

1. DISTANT.
2. SOLITARY.
3. REMOTE.
4. HIGH.

remunerate *verb*
1. To give compensation to.
2. To give payment to in return for goods or services rendered.

1. COMPENSATE.
2. PAY *verb.*

remuneration *noun*
1. Something to make up for loss or damage.
2. Something given in exchange for goods or services rendered.

1. COMPENSATION.
2. PAYMENT.

remunerative *adjective*
1. Affording compensation.
2. Affording profit.

1. COMPENSATORY.
2. PROFITABLE.

renaissance *noun*
The act of reviving or condition of being revived.

REVIVAL.

renascence *noun*
The act of reviving or condition of being revived.

REVIVAL.

rend *verb*
To separate or pull apart by force.   TEAR[1] *verb.*

render *verb*
1. To give up a possession, claim, or right.   1. ABDICATE.
2. To present a lifelike image of.   2. REPRESENT.
3. To perform according to one's artistic conception.   3. INTERPRET.
4. To deliver (an indictment or verdict).   4. RETURN *verb.*
5. To express in another language, while   5. TRANSLATE.
   systematically retaining the original sense.

rendering *noun*
A restating of something in other, esp. simpler, words.   PARAPHRASE *noun.*

rendezvous *noun*
1. A commitment to appear at a certain time and   1. ENGAGEMENT.
   place.
2. A frequently visited place.   2. HAUNT *noun.*

rendezvous *verb*
To come together face-to-face by arrangement.   MEET[1] *verb.*

rendition *noun*
One's artistic conception as shown by the rendering of a   INTERPRETATION.
dramatic role, musical composition, etc.

renegade *noun*
A person who has defected.   DEFECTOR.

renew *verb*
1. To make new or as if new again: *renewed the*   1. **Syns:** furbish, recondition, refresh,
   furniture by reupholstering it.   refurbish, rejuvenate, renovate, restore.
                                                                        —*Idiom* give a new look to.
                                                                        Near-ants: deplete, drain, exhaust,
                                                                        impoverish; bankrupt, consume.
2. To go on after an interruption.   2. CONTINUE.
3. To impart renewed energy and strength to (a   3. REFRESH.
   person).
4. To rouse from a state of inactivity or quiescence.   4. REVIVE.
5. To arrange for the extension of: *renew a contract.*   5. **Syn:** extend.
6. To bring back into existence or use.   6. RESTORE.

renewal *noun*
1. The act of making new or as if new again: *urban*   1. **Syns:** face lifting (*also* facelift),
   renewal.   reconditioning, refurbishing,
                                                                        refurbishment, rejuvenation,
                                                                        renovation, restoration.
2. A continuing after interruption: *renewal of United*   2. **Syns:** resumption, resurgence, revival.
   States-Soviet hostilities.
3. The act of reviving or condition of being revived.   3. REVIVAL.

renewing *adjective*
Producing or stimulating physical, mental, or emotional   TONIC *adjective.*
vigor.

renitence or **renitency** *noun*
The act of resisting.   RESISTANCE.

renitency *noun*   SEE **renitence.**

renitent *adjective*
Tending to resist, as an influence or idea.   RESISTANT *adjective.*

renounce *verb*
1. To give up a possession, claim, or right.   1. ABDICATE.
2. To cease trying to accomplish or continue.   2. ABANDON *verb.*

renovate *verb*
1. To make modern in appearance or style.   1. MODERNIZE.
2. To make new or as if new again.   2. RENEW.

renovation *noun*
The act of making new or as if new again.   RENEWAL.

renown *noun*
1. A position of exalted, widely recognized importance.   1. EMINENCE.
2. Wide recognition for one's deeds.   2. FAME.

renowned *adjective*
Widely known and esteemed. — EMINENT.

rent¹ *verb*
To engage the temporary use of (something) for a fee. — HIRE *verb*.

rent² *noun*
1. An opening, esp. in a solid structure.
2. An interruption in friendly relations.
3. A hole made by tearing.

1. BREACH *noun*.
2. BREACH *noun*.
3. TEAR¹ *noun*.

renunciation *noun*
A giving up of a possession, claim, or right. — ABDICATION.

reoccupy *verb*
To occupy or take again. — RESUME.

reoccur *verb*
1. To come back to a former condition.
2. To happen again or repeatedly.

1. RETURN *verb*.
2. RECUR.

reoccurrence *noun*
A repeated occurrence. — RECURRENCE.

reopen *verb*
To go on after an interruption. — CONTINUE.

repair *verb*
1. To restore to proper condition or functioning.
2. To have recourse to when in need.
3. To move along a particular course.

1. FIX *verb*.
2. RESORT TO at **resort**.
3. GO *verb*.

reparation *noun*
Something to make up for loss or damage. — COMPENSATION.

repartee *noun*
A spirited, incisive reply. — RETORT *noun*.

repay *verb*
1. To give compensation to.
2. To make as income or profit.
3. To exact revenge for.

1. COMPENSATE.
2. RETURN *verb*.
3. AVENGE.

repeal *verb*
1. To put an end to formally and with authority.
2. To annul (a decision or decree).
3. To take back or remove.

1. ABOLISH.
2. REVERSE *verb*.
3. LIFT *verb*.

repeal *noun*
1. An often formal act of putting an end to.
2. The act of reversing or annulling.

1. ABOLITION.
2. REVERSAL.

repeat *verb*
1. To state again: *repeated the oath of office after the Chief Justice.*
2. To send back the sound of.
3. To copy (another) slavishly.

1. *Syns:* iterate, reiterate, restate.
2. ECHO *verb*.
3. ECHO *verb*.

repel *verb*
1. To turn or drive away.
2. To offend the senses or feelings of.

1. PARRY.
2. DISGUST *verb*.

repellence also **repellency** *noun*
A state of mind brought on by something that is antipathetic. — ANTIPATHY.

repellency *noun* — SEE **repellence**.

repellent *adjective*
1. Arousing deep-seated dislike.
2. Extremely unpleasant to the senses or feelings.

1. ANTIPATHETIC.
2. OFFENSIVE.

repent *verb*
To feel or express sorrow for. — REGRET *verb*.

repentance *noun*
A feeling of regret for one's sins or misdeeds. — PENITENCE.

repentant *adjective*
1. Expressing or inclined to express an apology.
2. Feeling or expressing regret for one's sins or misdeeds.

1. APOLOGETIC *adjective*.
2. REMORSEFUL.

repercuss *verb*
To jerk backward, as a gun upon firing.   RECOIL.

repercussion *noun*
1. Repetition of sound via reflection from a surface.   **1.** ECHO *noun*.
2. The strong effect exerted by one person or thing on another.   **2.** IMPACT *noun*.

repetition *noun*
1. The act or process of repeating: *Children often learn by repetition. The repetition of your complaints is annoying.*   **1.** **Syns:** iteration, reiteration, restatement.
2. Imitative reproduction, as of the style of another.   **2.** ECHO *noun*.

repetitious *adjective*
Characterized by repetition.   REPETITIVE.

repetitive *adjective*
Characterized by repetition: *repetitive statements characteristic of some journalists.*   **Syns:** iterative, reiterate, reiterative, repetitious.

rephrase *verb*
To express the meaning of in other, esp. simpler, words.   PARAPHRASE *verb*.

replace *verb*
1. To remove (something) and substitute (another) for it: *replaced the broken pane with new glass.*   **1.** **Syns:** supplant, supersede.
2. To put (someone) in the possession of a prior position or office.   **2.** RESTORE.

replacement *noun*
1. One that takes the place of another.   **1.** SUBSTITUTE *noun*.
2. A person or persons taking over the duties of another.   **2.** RELIEF.

replete *adjective*
1. Completely filled.   **1.** FULL.
2. Full of animation and activity.   **2.** ALIVE.
3. Filled to satisfaction or excess.   **3.** SATIATED.

repletion *noun*
The condition of being full to or beyond satisfaction.   SATIATION.

replica *noun*
1. Something closely resembling another.   **1.** COPY *noun*.
2. A representation of a person or thing.   **2.** LIKENESS.

replicate *verb*
To make a copy of.   COPY *verb*.

replication *noun*
Something closely resembling another.   COPY *noun*.

reply *verb*
To speak or act in response to.   ANSWER *verb*.

reply *noun*
Something spoken or written as a return to a question, demand, etc.   ANSWER *noun*.

report *noun*
1. A sudden sharp, explosive noise: *From the reports of rifles we knew that hunters must be nearby.*   **1.** **Syns:** bang, bark, crack, explosion, pop, snap.
2. A recounting of past events.   **2.** STORY.
3. Idle, often sensational and groundless talk about others.   **3.** GOSSIP *noun*.
4. Public estimation of someone.   **4.** REPUTATION.

report *verb*
1. To give a verbal account of.   **1.** DESCRIBE.
2. To observe, analyze, and relate the details of (an event).   **2.** COVER *verb*.
3. To make known.   **3.** COMMUNICATE.
4. To spread as news.   **4.** NOISE *verb*.

reportage *noun*
The extent to which an event is reported.   COVERAGE.

repose *verb*
1. To be or place oneself in a prostrate or recumbent position.
2. To take repose by sleeping, lying quietly, or the like.
3. To have as an inherent basis.

repose *noun*
Freedom from labor, responsibility, or strain.

repository *noun*
1. A place where something is deposited for safekeeping.
2. One in whom secrets are confided.

repossess *verb*
1. To occupy or take again.
2. To get back.

repossession *noun*
The act of getting back or regaining.

reprehend *verb*
1. To find fault with.
2. To feel or express strong disapproval of.

reprehensible *adjective*
1. So objectionable as to elicit despisal.
2. Deserving strong condemnation.

reprehension *noun*
A finding fault.

represent *verb*
1. To serve as the image of: *The sword represents valor.*

2. To present a lifelike image of: *The painting represents the agony and crucifixion of Christ.*
3. To serve as an official delegate of: *My lawyer will represent me at the hearing.*
4. To play the part of.

representation *noun*
The act or process of describing in lifelike imagery: *a sculpture that is the representation of the heroism of the defenders of Leningrad.*

representative *noun*
1. One who stands for another: *representatives at a political convention.*
2. One that is representative of a group or class.

representative *adjective*
1. Serving to describe.
2. Having the nature of, constituting, or serving as a type.
3. Serving as a symbol.

repress *verb*
To hold (something requiring an outlet) in check: *repressed my laughter with difficulty; congressional whips repressing dissenting legislators.*

repression *noun*
1. The act of restraining forcefully: *repression of giggles; repression of the Young Turks' arguments.*

1. LIE[1].

2. REST[1] *verb.*
3. CONSIST.

REST[1] *noun.*

1. DEPOSITORY.

2. CONFIDANT.

1. RESUME.
2. RECOVER.

RECOVERY.

1. BLAME *verb.*
2. DEPLORE.

1. FILTHY.
2. INFAMOUS.

BLAME *noun.*

1. **Syns:** body (forth), embody, epitomize, exemplify, illustrate, personify, stand for, symbol, symbolize, typify.
   Near-syns: copy, denote, emblematize, imitate, impersonate, signify, substitute; mirror, personalize, reproduce.
   Ant: misrepresent.
2. **Syns:** delineate, depict, describe, image, limn, picture, portray, render, show.
3. **Syns:** speak for, stand for.

4. ACT *verb.*

Syns: delineation, depiction, description, picture, portraiture, portrayal.

1. **Syns:** delegate, deputy.

2. EXAMPLE *noun.*

1. DESCRIPTIVE.
2. TYPICAL.

3. SYMBOLIC.

Syns: choke, gag, hold back, hold down, hush (up), muffle, quench, shush, sit on (or upon) (*Informal*), smother, squelch, stifle, strangle, suppress, throttle.

1. **Syns:** choking, quashing, quenching, smothering, squelching, stifling, suppression, throttling.

2. Sudden punitive action.

repressive *adjective*
Serving to restrain forcefully: *took repressive measures against the rebels.*

reprieve *noun*
Temporary immunity from penalties.

reprimand *verb*
To criticize for a fault or offense.

reprimand *noun*
Words expressive of strong disapproval.

reprisal *noun*
The act of retaliating.

reproach *verb*
To criticize for a fault or offense.

reproach *noun*
1. Words expressive of strong disapproval.
2. An implied criticism.

reprobate *adjective*
Morally objectionable.

reprobate *verb*
1. To find fault with.
2. To feel or express strong disapproval of.

reprobation *noun*
A finding fault.

reproduce *verb*
1. *Biol.* To produce sexually or asexually others of one's kind: *Flies reproduce in astronomical numbers.*
2. To make a copy of.

reproduction *noun*
1. *Biol.* The process by which an organism produces others of its kind: *studied the reproduction of the monarch butterfly; a right-to-life group advocating unrestricted reproduction of the human race.*
2. Something closely resembling another.

reproductive *adjective*
1. *Biol.* Of or pertaining to reproduction: *reproductive cycles.*
2. *Biol.* Employed in reproduction: *reproductive organs.*

reprove *verb*
1. To castigate for the purpose of improving.
2. To criticize for a fault or offense.

repudiate *verb*
To refuse to recognize or acknowledge: *repudiating the black sheep of the family; repudiated his previous testimony.*

repugnance also **repugnancy** *noun*
Extreme hostility and dislike.

repugnancy *noun*

repugnant *adjective*
1. So objectionable as to elicit despisal.
2. *Logic.* Characterized by a natural or innate opposition.

repulse *verb*
1. To turn or drive away.
2. To offend the senses or feelings of.

repulsion *noun*
1. Extreme repugnance excited by something offensive.

Near-syns: check, control, curb, strangling.
2. SUPPRESSION.

Syn: suppressive.

GRACE *noun.*

CALL DOWN at **call.**

REBUKE *noun.*

RETALIATION.

CALL DOWN at **call.**

1. REBUKE *noun.*
2. REFLECTION.

EVIL *adjective.*

1. BLAME *verb.*
2. DEPLORE.

BLAME *noun.*

1. *Syns:* breed, multiply, procreate, proliferate, propagate, spawn.
2. COPY *verb.*

1. *Syns:* breeding, multiplication, procreation, proliferation, propagation, spawning.

2. COPY *noun.*

1. *Syns:* procreant (*Biol.*), procreative.

2. *Syns:* progenitive (*Biol.*), sexual.

1. CORRECT *verb.*
2. CALL DOWN at **call.**

Syns: deny, disacknowledge, disavow, disclaim, disown. —*Idiom* turn one's back on.
Near-syns: abandon, desert, forsake, reverse.

HATE *noun.*
SEE **repugnance.**

1. FILTHY.
2. CONTRARY *adjective.*

1. PARRY.
2. DISGUST *verb.*

1. DISGUST *noun.*

2. Extreme hostility and dislike.

3. A feeling of fear and repugnance.

repulsive *adjective*

Extremely unpleasant to the senses or feelings.

reputable *adjective*

Deserving honor or respect.

reputation *noun*

1. Public estimation of someone: *has a bad reputation.*

2. Wide recognition for one's deeds.

3. A person's high standing among others.

repute *verb*

To regard or be regarded in an appraising way: *Rasputin was reputed to be the power behind the Romanov throne.*

repute *noun*

1. Wide recognition for one's deeds.

2. A person's high standing among others.

3. Public estimation of someone.

reputed *adjective*

Assumed to be such: *the reputed father of the child.*

request *verb*

To endeavor to obtain (something) by expressing one's needs or desires: *requested a revised schedule to facilitate production of the book.*

requiescence *noun*

Freedom from labor, responsibility, or strain.

require *verb*

1. To oblige to do or not do by force of authority, propriety, or custom: *Men are required to wear ties in this restaurant.*

2. To have as a need or prerequisite.

3. To be without what is needed, required, or essential.

4. To ask for urgently or insistently.

5. To give orders to.

required *adjective*

1. Imposed on one by authority, command, or convention: *English composition is a required course at most colleges. He had to make the required apologies.*

2. Incapable of being dispensed with.

requirement *noun*

1. Something asked for or needed.

2. Something indispensable.

requisite *adjective*

1. Incapable of being dispensed with.

2. Imposed on one by authority, command, or convention.

requisite *noun*

Something indispensable.

requisition *verb*

To ask for urgently or insistently.

requisition *noun*

The act of demanding.

requital *noun*

1. Something to make up for loss or damage.

2. The act of retaliating.

requite *verb*

1. To give compensation to.

2. To give or take mutually.

3. To exact revenge for.

---

2. HATE *noun.*

3. HORROR.

OFFENSIVE *adjective.*

HONORABLE.

1. *Syns:* character, name, report, repute.

2. FAME.

3. HONOR *noun.*

Syns: suppose, think.

1. FAME *noun.*

2. HONOR *noun.*

3. REPUTATION.

Syns: putative, supposed.

Syns: ask (for), solicit.

REST[1] *noun.*

1. *Syns:* expect, suppose.

2. DEMAND *verb.*

3. LACK *verb.*

4. DEMAND *verb.*

5. COMMAND *verb.*

1. *Syns:* called-for, compulsory, imperative, mandatory, necessary, obligatory, requisite.

2. ESSENTIAL *adjective.*

1. DEMAND *noun.*

2. CONDITION *noun.*

1. ESSENTIAL *adjective.*

2. REQUIRED.

CONDITION *noun.*

DEMAND *verb.*

DEMAND *noun.*

1. COMPENSATION.

2. RETALIATION.

1. COMPENSATE.

2. RECIPROCATE.

3. AVENGE.

rescind *verb*
1. To put an end to formally and with authority.
2. To take back or remove.
3. To annul (a decision or decree).

1. ABOLISH.
2. LIFT *verb*.
3. REVERSE *verb*.

rescindment *noun*
An often formal act of putting an end to.

ABOLITION.

rescission *noun*
1. An often formal act of putting an end to.
2. The act of reversing or annulling.

1. ABOLITION.
2. REVERSAL.

rescue *verb*
1. To extricate, as from danger or confinement: *The Coast Guard rescued the shipwrecked sailors. Commandos rescued the hostages.*
2. To extricate from an undesirable state: *Federal funds are needed to rescue the city from bankruptcy.*

1. *Syns:* deliver, save. —*Idioms* come to the rescue of, snatch from the jaws of death.
2. *Syns:* reclaim, recover, redeem, salvage.

rescue *noun*
Extrication from danger or confinement: *a meticulously executed rescue of the shipwrecked sailors.*

Syns: deliverance, delivery, salvage, salvation.

resemblance *noun*
The quality or state of being alike.

LIKENESS.

resemble *verb*
To be similar to, as in appearance.

FAVOR *verb*.

resentful *adjective*
Bitingly hostile: *a resentful, unforgiving person; wrote a resentful letter.*

Syns: acrimonious, bitter, embittered, hard, rancorous, virulent.

resentfulness *noun*
The quality or state of feeling bitter.

RESENTMENT.

resentment *noun*
1. The quality or state of feeling bitter: *Let there be no resentment between us.*
2. Extreme displeasure caused by an insult or slight.

1. *Syns:* acridity, acrimony, bitterness, gall[1], rancor, resentfulness.
2. OFFENSE.

reservation *noun*
1. Public land kept for a special purpose: *an Indian reservation; a reservation for wildlife.*
2. A restricting or modifying element.
3. A feeling of uncertainty about the fitness or correctness of an action.

1. *Syns:* preserve, reserve.
2. PROVISION.
3. QUALM.

reserve *noun*
1. The keeping of one's thoughts and emotions to oneself: *a man of iron reserve.*

2. A supply stored or hidden for future use.
3. Public land kept for a special purpose.

1. *Syns:* control, restraint, reticence, self-control, self-restraint, taciturnity, uncommunicativeness.
2. HOARD *noun*.
3. RESERVATION.

reserve *verb*
1. To claim in advance.
2. To have and maintain in one's possession.

1. BOOK *verb*.
2. HOLD *verb*.

reserve *adjective*
Used or held in reserve.

AUXILIARY *adjective*.

reserved *adjective*
1. Tending to keep one's thoughts and emotions to oneself: *a reserved banker type.*

1. *Syns:* constrained, controlled, incommunicable, noncommittal, restrained, self-controlled, self-restrained.
   Near-ants: boisterous, bold, brazen, extroverted, open, outgoing, unrestrained; demonstrative, expansive, ostentatious.
   Ant: unreserved.

2. Not total, unlimited, or wholehearted.
3. Not speaking freely or openly.
4. Not friendly, sociable, or warm in manner.

2. QUALIFIED.
3. TACITURN.
4. COOL *adjective*.

reserves *noun*
The ability and the means to meet situations   RESOURCES.
effectively.
reservoir *noun*
A supply stored or hidden for future use.   HOARD *noun*.
reside *verb*
1. To have as one's domicile, usu. for an extended   1. LIVE[1].
   period.
2. To have as an inherent basis.   2. CONSIST.
residue *noun*
What remains after a part has been used or subtracted. BALANCE *noun*.
resign *verb*
1. To give up a possession, claim, or right.   1. ABDICATE.
2. To relinquish one's engagement in or occupation   2. QUIT.
   with.
resignation *noun*
1. A giving up of a possession, claim, or right.   1. ABDICATION.
2. The capacity of enduring hardship or inconvenience 2. PATIENCE.
   without complaint.
resigned *adjective*
Enduring or capable of enduring hardship or   PATIENT.
inconvenience without complaint.
resilience also **resiliency** *noun*
1. The ability to recover quickly from depression or   1. *Syns:* bounce, buoyancy, elasticity.
   discouragement: *His innate resilience helped him
   through the mid-life crisis.*
2. The quality or state of being flexible.   2. FLEXIBILITY.
resiliency *noun*   SEE **resilience**.
resilient *adjective*
Capable of withstanding stress without injury.   FLEXIBLE.
resist *verb*
1. To oppose actively and with force: *The Afghan rebels*   1. *Syns:* combat, duel, fight, withstand.
   resisted the Soviet invasion.   —*Idioms* mount (*or* offer) resistance,
                                                       put up a fight, stand up to (*or*
                                                       against).
2. To take a stand against.   2. CONTEST *verb*.
resistance *noun*
1. The capacity to withstand: *an unusually high*   1. *Syns:* immunity, imperviousness,
   resistance to viruses.   unsusceptibility.
2. The act of resisting: *overcame their resistance to*   2. *Syns:* opposition, renitence *or*
   school busing.   renitency.
3. A clandestine organization of freedom fighters in an   3. *Syn:* underground.
   oppressed land: *The French Resistance helped the
   Allies.*
resistant *adjective*
1. Having the capacity to withstand: *was totally*   1. *Syns:* immune, impervious, proof,
   resistant to our imprecations; a body very resistant to   resistive.
   viruses; a paint resistant to weathering.
2. Tending to resist, as an influence or idea: *a die-hard*   2. *Syns:* renitent, resisting, resistive.
   conservative resistant to change.
  resistant *noun*
  One who resists.   RESISTER.
resister *noun*
One who resists: *draft resisters.*   *Syns:* opponent, resistant.
resisting *adjective*
Tending to resist, as an influence or idea.   RESISTANT *adjective*.
resistive *adjective*
1. Tending to resist, as an influence or idea.   1. RESISTANT *adjective*.
2. Having the capacity to withstand.   2. RESISTANT *adjective*.
resolute *adjective*
1. On an unwavering course of action.   1. SET[1] *adjective*.

2. Not hesitating or wavering.

2. DECISIVE.

3. Indicating or possessing determination, resolution, or persistence.

3. FIRM[1].

4. Adhering firmly and devotedly, as to a person, a cause, or a duty.

4. FAITHFUL.

resoluteness *noun*

Unwavering firmness of character or action.

DECISION.

resolution *noun*

1. The quality of mind enabling one to face danger or hardship resolutely.

1. COURAGE.

2. A position reached after consideration.

2. DECISION.

3. Unwavering firmness of character or action.

3. DECISION.

4. The separation of a whole into its parts for study.

4. ANALYSIS.

5. The power to make choices and set goals and to act upon them firmly in spite of opposition or difficulty.

5. WILL[1] *noun*.

resolve *verb*

1. To find a solution for: *resolved the mystery; resolved the problem.*

1. *Syns:* clear up, decipher, dope out (*Informal*), explain, figure out, solve, unravel. —*Idiom* get to the bottom of.

2. To make up or cause to make up one's mind.

2. DECIDE.

3. To separate into parts for study.

3. ANALYZE.

4. To bring (something) into a state of agreement or accord.

4. SETTLE.

resolve *noun*

1. Unwavering firmness of character or action.

1. DECISION.

2. The power to make choices and set goals and to act upon them firmly in spite of opposition or difficulty.

2. WILL[1] *noun*.

resonant *adjective*

Having or producing a full, deep, or rich sound: *a resonant baritone.*

Syns: mellow, orotund, plangent, resounding, ringing, rotund, round, sonorous, vibrant.
Near-ants: faint, low, murmurous, muted, soft, weak; discordant, flat, off-key.

resort *noun*

1. That to which one turns for help when in desperation: *As a last resort I asked the bank for a loan.*

1. *Syns:* expediency (*also* expedience), expedient, recourse, refuge, resource, stopgap.

2. A frequently visited place.

2. HAUNT *noun*.

resort to *verb*

1. To have recourse to when in need: *The government has resorted to censorship. We were unwilling to resort to a loan shark for financial aid.*

1. *Syns:* apply, go, refer, repair, run, turn. —*Idiom* fall back on.

2. To visit regularly.

2. FREQUENT *verb*.

resort to *verb*

SEE **resort**.

resounding *adjective*

1. Expressed or performed with emphasis.

1. EMPHATIC.

2. Having or producing a full, deep, or rich sound.

2. RESONANT.

resounding *noun*

Repetition of sound via reflection from a surface.

ECHO *noun*.

resource *noun*

That to which one turns for help when in desperation.

RESORT.

resourceful *adjective*

Able to use the means at one's disposal to meet situations effectively: *a resourceful mind.*

Syns: fertile, ingenious, inventive.

resourcefulness *noun*

The ability and the means to meet situations effectively.

RESOURCES.

resources *noun*

1. The ability and the means to meet situations effectively: *Her inner resources sustained her during the illness.*

1. *Syns:* reserves, resourcefulness, wherewithal.

2. All property or goods having economic value: *It was hard to pinpoint the true extent of the deposed ruler's resources.*

respect *verb*
1. To have a high opinion of.
2. To recognize the worth, quality, importance, etc., of.

respect *noun*
1. A feeling of deference, approval, and liking.
2. The particular angle from which something is considered.

respectable *adjective*
1. Deserving honor or respect.
2. Conforming to accepted standards.
3. Proper in appearance.
4. Of moderately good quality but less than excellent.
5. Somewhat big.

respectful *adjective*
Marked by courteous submission or respect.

respects *noun*
Friendly greetings.

respiration *noun*
The act or process of breathing.

respire *verb*
To breathe in and out.

respite *noun*
1. A pause or interval, as from work or duty.
2. Temporary immunity from penalties.

resplendence or **resplendency** *noun*
Brilliant, showy splendor.

resplendency *noun*

resplendent *adjective*
Marked by extraordinary elegance, beauty, and splendor.

respond *verb*
1. To act in return to something, as a stimulus: *The patient is responding to treatment.*
2. To speak or act in response to.

respond to *verb*
To present with a specified reaction.

respondent *noun*
Law. A person against whom an action is brought.

respond to *verb*

response *noun*
1. An action elicited by a stimulus: *adverse patient responses to chemotherapy; a military response to the embargo.*
2. Something spoken or written as a return to a question, demand, etc.

responsibility *noun*
An act or course of action that is demanded of one, as by position, custom, law, or religion.

responsible *adjective*
1. Legally obligated.
2. Capable of being depended upon.

responsive *adjective*
1. Easily approached.
2. Ready and willing to receive favorably, as new ideas.
3. Able to receive and respond to external stimuli.

responsiveness *noun*
Recognition of worth, quality, importance, etc.

---

2. *Syns:* assets, capital, fortune, means, wealth, wherewithal.

1. ADMIRE.
2. APPRECIATE.

1. ESTEEM *noun.*
2. PHASE.

1. HONORABLE.
2. CORRECT *adjective.*
3. DECENT.
4. ACCEPTABLE.
5. SIZABLE.

DEFERENTIAL.

REGARDS.

BREATH.

BREATHE.

1. BREAK *noun.*
2. GRACE *noun.*

GLITTER *noun.*
SEE **resplendence.**

GLORIOUS.

1. *Syn:* react.

2. ANSWER *verb.*

GREET.

ACCUSED.
SEE **respond.**

1. *Syns:* reaction, retroaction.

2. ANSWER *noun.*

DUTY.

1. LIABLE.
2. DEPENDABLE.

1. APPROACHABLE.
2. RECEPTIVE.

3. SENSITIVE.

APPRECIATION.

rest¹ *noun*
   1. Freedom from labor, responsibility, or strain: *sat down and took his rest.*
   2. A pause or interval, as from work or duty.

   rest *verb*
   1. To take repose by sleeping, lying quietly, or the like: *rested for an hour before dinner.*
   2. To take repose by ceasing work or other effort for an interval of time: *We just want to rest during the vacation.*
   3. To take or serve as the basis for.
   4. To have as an inherent basis.

   rest on (or **upon**) *verb*
   To be determined by or contingent on something unknown, uncertain, or changeable.

rest² *noun*
   What remains after a part has been used or subtracted.

restart *verb*
   To go on after an interruption.

restate *verb*
   1. To state again.
   2. To express the meaning of in other, esp. simpler, words.

restatement *noun*
   1. A restating of something in other, esp. simpler, words.
   2. The act or process of repeating.

restitute *verb*
   To bring back to a previous normal condition.

restitution *noun*
   Something to make up for loss or damage.

restive *adjective*
   Feeling or exhibiting nervous tension.

restiveness *noun*
   An uneasy or nervous state.

restless *adjective*
   1. Affording no quiet, repose, or rest: *spent a restless night before the interview.*

   2. Feeling or exhibiting nervous tension.

restlessness *noun*
   An uneasy or nervous state: *We noticed the restlessness of the cattle.*

rest on (or **upon**) *verb*

restoration *noun*
   The act of making new or as if new again.

restorative *adjective*
   1. Serving to cure.
   2. Producing or stimulating physical, mental, or emotional vigor.

restorative *noun*
   A medicine that restores or increases vigor.

restore *verb*
   1. To bring back into existence or use: *restore law and order.*
   2. To cause to come back to life or consciousness.
   3. To bring back to a previous normal condition: *restored the Revolutionary house.*

---

   1. **Syns:** ease, leisure, relaxation, repose, requiescence.
   2. BREAK *noun.*

   1. **Syns:** lie, lie down, recline, repose, stretch out.
   2. **Syns:** relax, unbend, unwind. —*Idioms* live the life of Riley, take it easy.

   3. BASE¹ *verb.*
   4. CONSIST.

   DEPEND ON at **depend.**

   BALANCE *noun.*

   CONTINUE.

   1. REPEAT.
   2. PARAPHRASE *verb.*

   1. PARAPHRASE *noun.*

   2. REPETITION.

   RESTORE.

   COMPENSATION.

   EDGY.

   RESTLESSNESS.

   1. **Syns:** uneasy, unsettled.
      Near-ants: peaceful, quiet, serene, tranquil.
      Ant: restful.
   2. EDGY.

   Syns: disquiet, disquietude, inquietude, restiveness, uneasiness, unrest.
   SEE **rest¹.**

   RENEWAL.

   1. CURATIVE *adjective.*
   2. TONIC *adjective.*

   TONIC *noun.*

   1. **Syns:** reinstate, reintroduce, renew, return, revive.
   2. REVIVE.
   3. **Syns:** rebuild, reclaim, recondition, reconstruct, recover, rehabilitate, rejuvenate, restitute. —*Idiom* restore the first flower (or bloom) of.

4. To put (someone) in the possession of a prior position or office: *an emperor restored to the throne.*
5. To make modern in appearance or style.
6. To make new or as if new again.
7. To impart renewed energy and strength to (a person).
8. To send, put, or carry back to a former location.

restrain   *verb*
To control, restrict, or arrest: *restrained him from starting a fight; restrained my curiosity.*

4. **Syns:** give back, reinstate, replace, return.
5. MODERNIZE.
6. RENEW.
7. REFRESH.

8. RETURN *verb.*

Syns: bit², brake, bridle, check, constrain, curb, hold back, hold down, hold in, inhibit, keep, keep back, pull in, rein.
Near-syns: arrest, block, hinder, impede, interrupt, obstruct, prevent, withhold.
Ants: impel, incite.

restrained   *adjective*
1. Kept within sensible limits.
2. Not showy or obtrusive.
3. Tending to keep one's thoughts and emotions to oneself.

restraint   *noun*
1. Something that limits or restricts.
2. The keeping of one's thoughts and emotions to oneself.

restraints   *noun*
Something that physically confines the legs or arms.

restrict   *verb*
To place a limit on.

restricted   *adjective*
1. Kept within certain limits: *a restricted number of students.*
2. Of or being information available only to authorized persons.
3. Excluding or unavailable to certain minorities: *a restricted neighborhood.*
4. Confined to a particular location or site.
5. Not total, unlimited, or wholehearted.

restriction   *noun*
1. The act of limiting or condition of being limited: *Absolute rulers have power without restriction.*
2. Something that limits or restricts: *wanted restrictions on presidential power.*

1. CONSERVATIVE *adjective.*
2. QUIET.
3. RESERVED.

1. RESTRICTION.
2. RESERVE *noun.*

BONDS.

LIMIT *verb.*

1. **Syns:** circumscribed, determinate, fixed, limited.
2. CONFIDENTIAL.

3. **Syn:** segregated.

4. LOCAL *adjective.*
5. QUALIFIED.

1. **Syns:** circumscription, confinement, constrainment, constraint, limitation.
2. **Syns:** circumscription, constraint, cramp, limitation, restraint, stricture, trammel.

result   *noun*
1. Something brought about by a cause.
2. Something worked out to explain, resolve, or provide a method for dealing with and settling a problem.

result   *verb*
To occur as a consequence.

result in   *verb*
To be the cause of.

resultant   *noun*
Something brought about by a cause.

result in   *verb*

resume   *verb*
1. To occupy or take again: *The former prime minister resumed power.*

2. To go on after an interruption.

resumption   *noun*
A continuing after interruption.

1. EFFECT *noun.*
2. ANSWER *noun.*

FOLLOW.

CAUSE *verb.*

EFFECT *noun.*

SEE **result.**

1. **Syns:** reassume, reclaim, reoccupy, repossess, retake, take back.
   Near-syns: recoup, recover, regain, retrieve.
2. CONTINUE.

RENEWAL.

resurgence *noun*
  1. A continuing after interruption.   1. RENEWAL.
  2. The act of reviving or condition of being revived.   2. REVIVAL.
resurrect *verb*
  To rouse from a state of inactivity or quiescence.   REVIVE.
resurrection *noun*
  The act of reviving or condition of being revived.   REVIVAL.
resuscitate *verb*
  To cause to come back to life or consciousness.   REVIVE.
resuscitation *noun*
  The act of reviving or condition of being revived.   REVIVAL.
retail *verb*
  To offer for sale.   SELL *verb*.
retain *verb*
  1. To obtain the use or services of.   1. EMPLOY *verb*.
  2. To keep at one's disposal.   2. HAVE.
  3. To have and maintain in one's possession.   3. HOLD *verb*.
  4. To persevere in some condition, action, or belief.   4. KEEP *verb*.
  5. To renew (an image or thought) in the mind.   5. REMEMBER.
retake *verb*
  To occupy or take again.   RESUME.
retaliate *verb*
  To return like for like, esp. to return an unfriendly or   **Syns:** counter, hit back, reciprocate, retort,
  hostile action with a similar one: *retaliate against an*   strike back.
  enemy attack.
retaliation *noun*
  The act of retaliating: *an insult that provoked*   **Syns:** avengement, avenging,
  retaliation; attacked in retaliation for the attack on the   counteraction, counterattack, counterblow,
  ship.   counterstroke, reciprocation, reprisal,
                                                              requital, retribution, revanche, revenge,
                                                              vengeance. —*Idioms* an eye for an eye, a
                                                              tooth for a tooth, blow for blow, like for
                                                              like, measure for measure, tit for tat.
                                                              Near-ants: clemency, forgiveness, grace,
                                                              leniency, mercy, pardon, remission.

retard *verb*
  1. To cause to be later or slower than expected or   1. DELAY *verb*.
     desired.
  2. To interfere with the progress of.   2. HINDER.
retardation *noun*
  The condition or fact of being made late or slow.   DELAY *noun*.
retarded *adjective*
  Having only a limited ability to learn and understand.   BACKWARD *adjective*.
rethink *verb*
  To consider again, esp. with the possibility of change.   RECONSIDER.
reticence *noun*
  1. Reserve in speech, behavior, or dress.   1. MODESTY.
  2. The keeping of one's thoughts and emotions to   2. RESERVE *noun*.
     oneself.
reticent *adjective*
  1. Not speaking freely or openly.   1. TACITURN.
  2. Not friendly, sociable, or warm in manner.   2. COOL *adjective*.
retinue *noun*
  A group of attendants or followers: *Several translators*   **Syns:** entourage, following, suite, train.
  joined the President's retinue for the summit conference.
retire *verb*
  1. To go to bed: *retired at 11:00.*   1. **Syns:** bed (down), crash (*Slang*), flop
                                                                 (*Slang*), pile in (*Informal*), roll in
                                                                 (*Informal*), turn in (*Informal*).
                                                                 —*Idioms* call it a night, hit the hay (*or*
                                                                 sack), meet the sandman.

2. To move or proceed away from a place.

2. GO *verb.*

3. To withdraw from business or active life: *retired after 50 years on the job.*

3. **Syns:** demit, step down. —*Idioms* call it quits, hang up one's spurs, turn in one's badge.

4. To remove from active service: *retire a career officer.*

4. **Syns:** pension (off), superannuate. —*Idioms* put on the retired list, put out to pasture.

5. To move back in the face of enemy attack or after a defeat.

5. RETREAT *verb.*

retirement *noun*
1. The moving back of a military force in the face of enemy attack or after a defeat.

1. RETREAT *noun.*

2. The act of secluding or the state of being secluded.

2. SECLUSION.

retiring *adjective*
Reticent or reserved in manner.

MODEST.

retort *noun*
1. A spirited, incisive reply: *a master of the quick retort.*

1. **Syns:** comeback (*Slang*), counter, repartee, riposte (*also* ripost). —*Idiom* back answer.

2. Something spoken or written as a return to a question, demand, etc.

2. ANSWER *noun.*

retort *verb*
1. To speak or act in response to.
2. To return like for like, esp. to return an unfriendly or hostile action with a similar one.

1. ANSWER *verb.*
2. RETALIATE.

retouch *verb*
To improve by making minor changes or additions.

TOUCH UP at **touch.**

retract *verb*
1. To disavow (something previously written or said) irrevocably and usu. formally: *The senator retracted his previous denial.*

1. **Syns:** abjure, palinode, recall, recant, take back, withdraw.
Near-syns: disavow, eliminate, exclude, forswear, renounce, repudiate, suspend.

2. To move back or away from a point, limit, or mark.
3. To pull back in.

2. RECEDE.
3. WITHDRAW.

retraction *noun*
A formal statement of disavowal: *issued a retraction of the ethnic slur and made an apology.*

Syns: abjuration, palinode, recantation, recanting.

retreat *noun*
1. The moving back of a military force in the face of enemy attack or after a defeat: *In their hasty retreat the soldiers abandoned their arms.*

1. **Syns:** fallback, pullback, pullout, retirement, withdrawal (*also* withdrawment).

2. Something that physically protects, esp. from danger.

2. COVER *noun.*

3. An institution that provides care and shelter.

3. HOME.

retreat *verb*
1. To move back in the face of enemy attack or after a defeat: *Napoleon's forces retreating from Moscow.*

1. **Syns:** draw back, fall back, retire, withdraw. —*Idioms* beat (*or* sound) a retreat, give ground (*or* place *or* way).
Near-syns: decamp, depart, escape, evacuate, flee, fly, pull out, vacate.
Ant: attack.

2. To move in a reverse direction.
3. To abandon a former position or commitment.
4. To move back or away from a point, limit, or mark.

2. BACK *verb.*
3. BACK DOWN at **back.**
4. RECEDE.

retribution *noun*
The act of retaliating.

RETALIATION.

retrieval *noun*
The act of getting back or regaining.

RECOVERY.

retrieve *verb*
To get back.

RECOVER.

retroaction *noun*
An action elicited by a stimulus.   RESPONSE.

retrocede *verb*
1. To move in a reverse direction.   1. BACK *verb.*
2. To move back or away from a point, limit, or mark.   2. RECEDE.

retrograde *adjective*
Directed or facing toward the back or rear.   BACKWARD *adjective.*

    retrograde *verb*
1. To become lower in quality, character, or condition. 1. DETERIORATE.
2. To move back or away from a point, limit, or mark.   2. RECEDE.
3. To move in a reverse direction.   3. BACK *verb.*

retrogress *verb*
1. To move in a reverse direction.   1. BACK *verb.*
2. To move back or away from a point, limit, or mark.   2. RECEDE.
3. To slip from a higher or better condition to a former, usu. lower or poorer one.   3. RELAPSE *verb.*

retrogression *noun*
A return to a former, usu. worse condition.   REVERSION.

retrogressive *adjective*
Directed or facing toward the back or rear.   BACKWARD *adjective.*

return *verb*
1. To go again to a former place: *returned to my birthplace.*   1. **Syns:** come back, revert, revisit.
2. To come back to a former condition: *a disease that returned.*   2. **Syns:** recrudesce, recur, reoccur, revert.
3. To send, put, or carry back to a former location: *returning empty bottles to the store.*   3. **Syns:** give back, restore, take back.
4. To give or take mutually.   4. RECIPROCATE.
5. To speak or act in response to.   5. ANSWER *verb.*
6. To make as income or profit: *My investment returned 15 per cent.*   6. **Syns:** bring in, clear, draw, earn, gain, gross, net^2, pay, produce, realize, repay, yield.
7. To deliver (an indictment or verdict): *returned a verdict of guilty.*   7. **Syns:** hand down, render.
8. To put (someone) in the possession of a prior position or office.   8. RESTORE.
9. To bring back into existence or use.   9. RESTORE.
10. To happen again or repeatedly.   10. RECUR.

    return *noun*
1. A repeated occurrence.   1. RECURRENCE.
2. Something earned, won, or otherwise acquired.   2. GAIN *noun.*

reunite *verb*
To re-establish friendship between.   RECONCILE.

revamp *verb*
1. To restore to proper condition or functioning.   1. FIX *verb.*
2. To make modern in appearance or style.   2. MODERNIZE.
3. To prepare a new version of.   3. REVISE.

revamping *noun*
The act or process of revising.   REVISION.

revanche *noun*
The act of retaliating.   RETALIATION.

reveal *verb*
1. To make visible; bring to view: *A cleaning revealed the grain of the wood.*   1. **Syns:** bare, disclose, discover (*Archaic*). display, expose, lay open, show, unclothe, uncover, unmask, unveil. —*Idioms* bring to light (*or* view), lay bare, make plain.
2. To disclose in a breach of confidence.   2. BETRAY.

revel *verb*
1. To behave riotously: *drunken students reveling until dawn.*   1. **Syns:** carouse, frolic, hell (around) (*Informal*), riot, roister, spree. —*Idioms*

blow off steam, cut loose, kick over the traces, kick up one's heels, let go, let loose, make whoopee, paint the town red, raise Cain, raise hell, raise ned, whoop it up.

2. To show happy satisfaction in an event, esp. by merrymaking.

2. CELEBRATE.

3. To take extravagant pleasure.

3. LUXURIATE.

revel *noun*
Joyful, exuberant activity.

GAIETY.

revelation *noun*
Something disclosed, esp. something not previously known or realized: *a revelation about drug use among teen-agers.*

Syns: apocalypse, disclosure, exposé, exposure, eye opener, unveiling.

reveling *noun*
Joyful, exuberant activity.

GAIETY.

revelry *noun*
1. Joyful, exuberant activity.

1. GAIETY.

2. The act of showing happy satisfaction in an event.

2. CELEBRATION.

revels *noun*
The act of showing happy satisfaction in an event.

CELEBRATION.

revenant *noun*
A supernatural being.

GHOST *noun.*

revenge *noun*
1. The act of retaliating.

1. RETALIATION.

2. The quality or condition of being vindictive.

2. VINDICTIVENESS.

revengeful *adjective*
Disposed to seek revenge.

VINDICTIVE.

reverberate *verb*
To send back the sound of.

ECHO *verb.*

reverberation *noun*
Repetition of sound via reflection from a surface.

ECHO *noun.*

revere *verb*
To regard with great awe and devotion.

ADORE.

reverence *noun*
The act of adoring, esp. reverently.

ADORATION.

reverence *verb*
To regard with great awe and devotion.

ADORE.

reverend *noun*
Informal. A person ordained for service in a Christian church.

PREACHER.

reverent *adjective*
Feeling or showing reverence: *looked at the pope with reverent affection.*

Syns: adorant, adoring, reverential, worshipful.

reverential *adjective*
Feeling or showing reverence.

REVERENT.

reverie *noun*
1. The condition of being so lost in solitary thought as to be unaware of one's surroundings.

1. TRANCE.

2. An illusory mental image.

2. DREAM *noun.*

reversal *noun*
1. *Law.* The act of reversing or annulling: *a reversal of the decision in the appeals court.*

1. *Syns:* repeal, rescission, revocation.

2. A change from better to worse.

2. REVERSE *noun.*

3. The act of changing or being changed from one position, direction, or course to the opposite: *a reversal of figures resulting in a printer's error.*

3. *Syns:* inversion, transposition (*also* transposal).

reverse *noun*
1. A change from better to worse: *persevering in the face of sharp reverses.*

1. *Syns:* backset, reversal, setback.
—*Idiom* reverse of fortune.

2. That which is diametrically opposed to another.

2. OPPOSITE *noun.*

reverse *adjective*
Diametrically opposed.

OPPOSITE *adjective*.

reverse *verb*
1. To change to the opposite position, direction, or course: *reversed the empty glasses to fill them; will reverse the photographs in the album.*

1. **Syns:** inverse, invert, transpose, turn (around).
   Near-syns: change, exchange, interchange, overrule, overturn, shift, transfer, transplace.

2. *Law.* To annul (a decision or decree): *a judge reversing a decision.*
3. To turn sharply around.
4. To take back or remove.

2. **Syns:** repeal, rescind, revoke.
3. DOUBLE *verb*.
4. LIFT *verb*.

reversion *noun*
A return to a former, usu. worse condition: *reversion to old eating habits after the diet.*

Syns: regress, regression, retrogression.

revert *verb*
1. To slip from a higher or better condition to a former, usu. lower or poorer one.
2. To come back to a former condition.
3. To go again to a former place.

1. RELAPSE *verb*.
2. RETURN *verb*.
3. RETURN *verb*.

review *verb*
1. To write a critical report on: *His function is to review new plays.*
2. To consider again, esp. with the possibility of change.
3. To recapitulate the salient facts of: *The commentator reviewed the President's address after it was over.*

1. **Syns:** criticize, critique. —*Idiom* pass (or pronounce) judgment on.
2. RECONSIDER.
3. **Syns:** abstract, epitomize, go over, recap, run down, run through, summarize, sum up, synopsize.

review *noun*
1. A close or systematic study.
2. A formal military inspection: *The top brass turned out for the review.*
3. Evaluative and critical discourse: *The new book received rave reviews.*

1. ANALYSIS.
2. **Syn:** parade.
3. **Syns:** comment, commentary, criticism, critique, notice.

reviewer *noun*
A person who evaluates and reports on the worth of something.

CRITIC.

revile *verb*
To attack with harsh, often insulting language: *reviled his opponent in a stormy political debate.*

Syns: abuse, assail, rail at (or against), vituperate.
Near-syns: berate, defame, excoriate, impugn, jaw, libel, malign, slander, vilify.
Ants: applaud, laud.

revile *noun*
Obs. Harsh, often insulting language.

VITUPERATION.

revilement *noun*
Harsh, often insulting language.

VITUPERATION.

reviling *noun*
Harsh, often insulting language.

VITUPERATION.

reviling *adjective*
Of, relating to, or characterized by verbal abuse.

ABUSIVE.

revise *verb*
To prepare a new version of: *an almanac that is revised each year.*

Syns: amend, emend, emendate, revamp.
Near-syns: overhaul, redraw, restyle, rework, rewrite.

revision *noun*
The act or process of revising: *a complete revision of the dictionary.*

Syns: amendment, emendation, revamping, rewrite, rewriting.

revisit *verb*
To go again to a former place.

RETURN *verb*.

revitalization *noun*
The act of reviving or condition of being revived.   REVIVAL.
revitalize *verb*
To rouse from a state of inactivity or quiescence.   REVIVE.
revival *noun*
1. The act of reviving or condition of being revived: *a*   **1. *Syns:*** reanimation, rebirth, rekindling,
   revival of interest in crafts.   renaissance, renascence, renewal,
                                                                  resurgence, resurrection, resuscitation,
                                                                  revitalization, revivification.
2. A continuing after interruption.   **2.** RENEWAL.
revive *verb*
1. To cause to come back to life or consciousness: *They*   **1. *Syns:*** bring around, restore,
   revived her with artificial respiration.   resuscitate, revivify.
2. To bring back into existence or use.   **2.** RESTORE.
3. To rouse from a state of inactivity or quiescence: **3. *Syns:*** reactivate, reawaken, rekindle,
   revived my interest in Chaucer.   renew, resurrect, revitalize, revivify.
                                                                  Near-syns: reanimate, regenerate,
                                                                  reinvigorate, rejuvenate; activate,
                                                                  arouse, energize, quicken, start,
                                                                  stimulate, vitalize.
4. To renew (an image or thought) in the mind.   **4.** REMEMBER.
revivification *noun*
The act of reviving or condition of being revived.   REVIVAL.
revivify *verb*
1. To rouse from a state of inactivity or quiescence.   **1.** REVIVE.
2. To cause to come back to life or consciousness.   **2.** REVIVE.
revocation *noun*
The act of reversing or annulling.   REVERSAL.
revoke *verb*
1. To take back or remove.   **1.** LIFT *verb.*
2. To annul (a decision or decree).   **2.** REVERSE *verb.*
revolt *verb*
1. To refuse allegiance to and oppose by force a   **1.** REBEL *verb.*
   government or ruling authority.
2. To offend the senses or feelings of.   **2.** DISGUST *verb.*
revolt *noun*
Organized opposition intended to change or overthrow   REBELLION.
existing authority.
revolting *adjective*
1. Extremely unpleasant to the senses or feelings.   **1.** OFFENSIVE *adjective.*
2. Too awful to be described.   **2.** UNSPEAKABLE.
revolution *noun*
1. A momentous or sweeping change: *an invention that*   **1. *Syns:*** cataclysm, convulsion, upheaval.
   caused a revolution in the industry.
2. Circular movement around a point or about an axis: **2. *Syns:*** circuit, circulation,
   the earth's revolution around the sun; a phonograph   circumvolution, gyration, rotation,
   record rotating at 33 1/3 revolutions a minute.   turn, wheel, whirl.
revolutionary also **revolutionist** *noun*
One who holds extreme views or advocates extreme   EXTREMIST *noun.*
measures.
revolutionist *noun*   SEE **revolutionary.**
revolutionize *verb*
To bring about a radical change in: *an electronic*   ***Syns:*** metamorphose, transform.
advance that revolutionized broadcasting.
revolve *verb*
1. To move or cause to move in circles or around an   **1.** TURN *verb.*
   axis or center.
2. To consider carefully and at length.   **2.** PONDER.
revulsion *noun*
1. Extreme hostility and dislike.   **1.** HATE *noun.*
2. A feeling of fear and repugnance.   **2.** HORROR.

reward *noun*

1. Something given in return for a service or accomplishment: *received a reward for the brave rescue.*

2. A sum of money offered for a special service, as the apprehension of a criminal: *a reward for the return of the lost jewelry.*
3. Something justly deserved.

reward *verb*

To bestow a reward on: *rewarded her assistant with a day off.*

reword *verb*

To express the meaning of in other, esp. simpler, words.

rewording *noun*

A restating of something in other, esp. simpler, words.

rhapsodize *verb*

To show enthusiasm.

rhetoric *noun*

The art of public speaking.

rhetorical *adjective*

1. Of or relating to the art of public speaking.
2. Characterized by language that is elevated and sometimes pompous in style.

rhetorician *noun*

A public speaker.

rhodomontade *noun, adjective, & verb*

rhubarb *noun*

Slang. A discussion, often heated, in which a difference of opinion is expressed.

rhyme *noun*

A metrical composition.

rhyme *verb*

To be compatible or in correspondence.

rhythm *noun*

The regular recurrence of strong and weak elements, such as stressed and unstressed notes in music: *the rhythm of the tides; a lively waltz rhythm.*

rhythmical also **rhythmic** *adjective*

Marked by a regular rhythm: *rhythmical clapping at the end of the concert.*

rib *verb*

Slang. To tease or mock good-humoredly.

ribbing *noun*

Slang. Words or actions intended to evoke contemptuous laughter.

rich *adjective*

1. Possessing a large amount of money, land, or other material possessions: *His investments had made him rich.*

2. Characterized by extravagant, ostentatious magnificence.
3. Not readily digested because of richness.
4. Characterized by great productivity.
5. *Informal.* Extremely funny.

---

1. *Syns:* award, dividend, guerdon (*Poetic*), honorarium, plum, prize. —*Idiom* token of appreciation (*or* esteem).

2. *Syns:* bonus, bounty.

3. DUE *noun.*

Syn: guerdon (*Poetic*).

PARAPHRASE *verb.*

PARAPHRASE *noun.*

ENTHUSE.

ORATORY.

1. ORATORICAL.
2. SONOROUS.

ORATOR.

SEE **rodomontade.**

ARGUMENT.

POEM.

AGREE.

Syns: beat, cadence (*also* cadency), measure, meter, swing.

Syns: cadenced, measured, metrical (*also* metric), pulsating.

JOKE *verb.*

RIDICULE *noun.*

1. *Syns:* affluent, flush, loaded (*Slang*), moneyed, wealthy. —*Idioms* having money to burn, in the money, made of money, rolling in money. *Near-ants:* destitute, impoverished, indigent, penniless, penurious, poverty-stricken. *Ant:* poor.

2. LUXURIOUS.
3. HEAVY *adjective.*
4. FERTILE.
5. PRICELESS.

riches *noun*
A great amount of accumulated money and precious possessions: *the deposed monarch's riches.*

Syns: fortune, treasure, wealth, worth.

richness *noun*
The quality or state of being fertile.

FERTILITY.

rickety *adjective*
Not physically steady or firm.

UNSTABLE.

ricochet *verb*
1. To strike a surface at such an angle as to be deflected.
2. To jerk backward, as a gun upon firing.

1. GLANCE¹ *verb*.

2. RECOIL.

rid *verb*
To free from something objectionable or undesirable: *plans to rid himself of the unwanted responsibility.*

Syns: clear, disburden, disembarrass, disencumber, release, relieve, shake (off), throw off, unburden.
Near-ants: burden, charge, clog, encumber, load, saddle, task, tax, weigh.

riddance *noun*
1. The act of getting rid of something useless or used up.
2. The act or process of eliminating.

1. DISPOSAL.

2. ELIMINATION.

riddle *noun*
Anything that arouses curiosity or perplexes because it is unexplained, inexplicable, or secret.

MYSTERY.

ride *verb*
1. *Informal.* To torment with persistent insult or ridicule.
2. *Informal.* To tease or mock good-humoredly.

1. BAIT *verb*.

2. JOKE *verb*.

ride out *verb*
To exist in spite of adversity.

SURVIVE.

ride *noun*
A trip in a motor vehicle.

DRIVE *noun*.

ride out *verb*

SEE **ride**.

ridicule *verb*
To make fun of: *The angry fans ridiculed the losing quarterback.*

Syns: deride, fleer at, gibe at, jeer at, laugh at, mock, quiz (*Brit.*), razz (*Slang*), scoff (at), scout² , sneer at, taunt, twit.
—*Idioms* laugh out of court, poke fun at.
Near-syns: banter, burlesque, caricature, flout, jape, mimic; haze, ride, roast.

ridicule *noun*
Words or actions intended to evoke contemptuous laughter: *had to tolerate a storm of ridicule from his colleagues.*

Syns: derision, mockery, razzing (*Slang*), ribbing (*Slang*), taunt, twitting.

ridiculous *adjective*
1. Deserving laughter.
2. Beyond all reason.

1. LAUGHABLE.

2. OUTRAGEOUS.

rife *adjective*
1. Full of animation and activity.
2. Most generally existing or encountered at a given time.

1. ALIVE.

2. PREVAILING.

riffle *verb*
1. To look through reading matter casually.
2. To mix together so as to change the order of arrangement.

1. BROWSE.

2. SHUFFLE.

riffraff *noun*
A group of persons regarded as the lowest class.

TRASH¹ *noun*.

rift *noun*
1. An interruption in friendly relations.
2. A usu. narrow partial opening caused by splitting and rupture.

1. BREACH *noun*.

2. CRACK *noun*.

rig *noun*
1. A set or style of clothing.
2. Things needed for a task, journey, or other purpose.

rig *verb*
To supply what is needed for some activity or purpose.

1. DRESS *noun.*
2. OUTFIT *noun.*

FURNISH.

rigamarole *noun*

SEE **rigmarole.**

right *adjective*
1. Conforming to fact.
2. In accordance with principles of right or good conduct.
3. Conforming to accepted standards.
4. Suitable for a particular person, condition, occasion, or place.
5. Strongly favoring retention of the existing order.
6. Having good health.

1. ACCURATE.
2. ETHICAL.

3. CORRECT *adjective.*
4. APPROPRIATE *adjective.*

5. CONSERVATIVE *adjective.*
6. HEALTHY.

right *noun*
1. A privilege granted a person by virtue of birth.
2. Conferred power.
3. That which is morally proper, fitting, or good: *learning the difference between right and wrong.*

1. BIRTHRIGHT.
2. FACULTY.
3. *Syns:* rightfulness, rightness.

right *adverb*
1. With precision or absolute conformity.
2. Without the slightest deviation in any respect.

1. DIRECTLY.
2. PRECISELY.

right *verb*
1. To restore to an upright or proper position: *tipped the boat and then righted it.*
2. To make right what is wrong.
3. To restore to proper condition or functioning.

1. *Syns:* stand up, upright.

2. CORRECT *verb.*
3. FIX *verb.*

righteous *adjective*
1. In accordance with principles of right or good conduct.
2. Having or marked by uprightness in principle and action.

1. ETHICAL.

2. HONEST.

righteousness *noun*
1. The moral quality of a course of action.
2. The quality or state of being morally sound.

1. ETHICS.
2. GOOD *noun.*

rightful *adjective*
Being so legitimately.

TRUE.

rightfulness *noun*
That which is morally proper, fitting, or good.

RIGHT *noun.*

rightist *noun*
One who strongly favors retention of the existing order.

CONSERVATIVE *noun.*

rightist *adjective*
Strongly favoring retention of the existing order.

CONSERVATIVE *adjective.*

right-minded *adjective*
In accordance with principles of right or good conduct.

ETHICAL.

rightness *noun*
1. Freedom from error.
2. The moral quality of a course of action.
3. The quality or state of being morally sound.
4. That which is morally proper, fitting, or good.

1. ACCURACY.
2. ETHICS.
3. GOOD *noun.*
4. RIGHT *noun.*

right on *adverb*
Informal. It is so; as you say or ask.

YES *adverb.*

right-wing *adjective*
Strongly favoring retention of the existing order.

CONSERVATIVE *adjective.*

right-winger *noun*
One who strongly favors retention of the existing order.

CONSERVATIVE *noun.*

rigid *adjective*
1. Not changing shape or bending: *a rigid iron bar.*

1. *Syns:* inelastic, inflexible, stiff, unbending, unflexible, unyielding.

2. Firmly, often unreasonably immovable in purpose or will.   **2.** STUBBORN.

3. Incapable of changing or being modified.   **3.** INFLEXIBLE.

4. Rigorous and unsparing in treating others.   **4.** SEVERE.

rigmarole also **rigamarole** *noun*
Something that does not have or make sense.   NONSENSE.

rigor *noun*
1. Something that obstructs progress and requires great effort to overcome.   **1.** DIFFICULTY.

2. The fact or condition of being rigorous and unsparing.   **2.** SEVERITY.

rigorous *adjective*
1. Conforming to fact.   **1.** ACCURATE.

2. Imposing a severe test of bodily or spiritual strength.   **2.** BURDENSOME.

3. Not deviating from correctness, accuracy, or completeness.   **3.** CLOSE[1] *adjective*.

4. Conforming completely to established rule.   **4.** STRICT.

rim *noun*
A fairly narrow line or space forming a boundary.   BORDER *noun*.

rim *verb*
To put or form a border on.   BORDER *verb*.

rimple *noun*
A line made by the doubling of one part over another.   FOLD *noun*.

rimple *verb*
To make irregular folds in, esp. by pressing or twisting.   WRINKLE[1] *verb*.

rind *noun*
The outer covering of a fruit.   SKIN *noun*.

ring[1] *noun*
1. A closed plane curve everywhere equidistant from a fixed point or something shaped like this.   **1.** CIRCLE *noun*.

2. An organized group of criminals, hoodlums, or wrongdoers.   **2.** GANG.

3. A group of individuals united in a common cause.   **3.** COMBINE *noun*.

4. A length of line folded over and joined at the ends so as to form a curve or circle.   **4.** LOOP *noun*.

ring *verb*
To shut in on all sides.   SURROUND.

ring[2] *verb*
1. To give forth or cause to give forth a clear, resonant sound: *church bells ringing on Sunday morning.*   **1.** *Syns:* bong, chime, knell, peal, strike, toll[2], tintinnabulate (*Rare*).

2. *Informal.* To communicate with (someone) by telephone.   **2.** TELEPHONE.

ring *noun*
Informal. A telephone communication.   CALL *noun*.

ringer *noun*
Slang. One exactly resembling another.   DOUBLE *noun*.

ringing *adjective*
Having or producing a full, deep, or rich sound.   RESONANT.

ringleader *noun*
A professional politician who controls a party or political machine.   BOSS *noun*.

riot *noun*
1. A quarrel or fight marked by very noisy, disorderly, and often violent behavior.   **1.** BRAWL *noun*.

2. *Slang.* Something or someone uproariously funny or absurd.   **2.** SCREAM *noun*.

riot *verb*
1. To quarrel noisily.   **1.** BRAWL *verb*.

2. To behave riotously.   **2.** REVEL *verb*.

riot away *verb*

To spend (money) excessively and usu. foolishly.   WASTE *verb*.

riot away *verb*   SEE **riot**.

riotous *adjective*
1. Upsetting civil order or peace.   1. DISORDERLY.
2. Given to or marked by unrestrained abundance.   2. PROFUSE.

rip *verb*
1. To separate or pull apart by force.   1. TEAR¹ *verb*.
2. *Informal.* To criticize harshly and devastatingly.   2. SLAM *verb*.

rip *noun*
A hole made by tearing.   TEAR¹ *noun*.

ripe *adjective*
1. Having reached full growth and development.   1. MATURE *adjective*.
2. Brought to full flavor and richness by aging.   2. AGED.

ripe *verb*
Chiefly Regional. To bring or come to full development.   MATURE *verb*.

ripen *verb*
To bring or come to full development.   MATURE *verb*.

ripened *adjective*
Brought to full flavor and richness by aging.   AGED.

rip-off *noun*   SEE **rip off**.

rip off *verb*
1. *Slang.* To take property or possessions from (a   1. ROB.
   person, company, etc.) unlawfully and usu. forcibly.
2. *Slang.* To take (another's property) without   2. STEAL *verb*.
   permission.
3. *Slang.* To exploit (another) by charging too much for   3. SKIN *verb*.
   something.

rip-off *noun*
Slang. The act or crime of taking another's property   ROBBERY.
unlawfully and by force.

ripost *noun*   SEE **riposte**.

riposte also **ripost** *noun*
A spirited, incisive reply.   RETORT *noun*.

ripping *adjective*
Particularly excellent.   MARVELOUS.

rippling *adjective*
Emitting a murmuring sound felt to resemble a laugh.   LAUGHING.

rise *verb*
1. To move from a lower to a higher position: *Hot air*   1. *Syns:* arise, ascend, lift, mount, soar.
   rises.
2. To become greater in number, amount, or intensity: 2. *Syns:* build, burgeon, escalate, grow,
   Living costs continue to rise. Nationalistic feeling   heighten, increase, magnify, mount,
   rose higher every day.   multiply, soar.
3. To adopt a standing posture.   3. GET UP at **get**.
4. To leave one's bed.   4. GET UP at **get**.
5. To have as a source.   5. STEM *verb*.
6. To attain a higher status, rank, or condition: *rose*   6. *Syns:* advance, ascend, climb (up),
   through the ranks to become a general.   mount. —*Idiom* go up the ladder.
7. To gain wealth or fame.   7. SUCCEED.
8. To refuse allegiance to and oppose by force a   8. REBEL *verb*.
   government or ruling authority.

rise *noun*
1. The act of rising or moving upward: *watched the rise*   1. *Syns:* ascension, ascent, mounting,
   of the floodwaters.   rising.
2. The act of increasing or rising.   2. INCREASE *noun*.
3. The amount by which something is increased.   3. INCREASE *noun*.
4. A natural land elevation.   4. HILL *noun*.
5. An upward slope.   5. ASCENT.

risible *adjective*
1. Arousing laughter.   1. AMUSING.
2. Deserving laughter.   2. LAUGHABLE.

rising *noun*
The act of rising or moving upward.

RISE *noun*.

risk *verb*
1. To expose to possible loss or damage: *risked his money in commodity futures; risked the cause of peace by loose talk.*
2. To subject to danger or destruction.
3. To run the risk of.
4. To put up as a stake in a game or speculation.

1. *Syns:* adventure, compromise, hazard, luck (it), venture.

2. ENDANGER.
3. HAZARD *verb*.
4. GAMBLE *verb*.

risk *noun*
1. Exposure to possible harm, loss, or injury.
2. A possibility of danger or harm: *took the risk of walking against the traffic light.*

1. DANGER.
2. *Syns:* chance, gamble, hazard.

risky *adjective*
Involving possible risk, loss, or injury.

DANGEROUS.

risqué *adjective*
Bordering on indelicacy or impropriety.

RACY.

rite *noun*
A formal act or set of acts prescribed by ritual.

CEREMONY.

ritual *noun*
1. A conventional social gesture or act without intrinsic purpose: *Small talk at cocktail parties is mere ritual.*
2. A formal act or set of acts prescribed by ritual.

1. *Syns:* ceremony, form, formality.

2. CEREMONY.

ritual *adjective*
Of or characterized by ceremony: *the ritual incantations of priests.*

Syns: ceremonial, formal, liturgical.

ritzy *adjective*
Slang. Catering to, used by, or admitting only the wealthy or socially superior.

EXCLUSIVE.

rival *verb*
1. To come near in quality, amount, etc.: *a gourmet dinner that rivaled the cuisine of a top restaurant.*
2. To strive against (others) for victory.

1. *Syns:* approach, approximate, border (on *or* upon), challenge, verge on.

2. COMPETE.

rival *noun*
One that competes.

COMPETITOR.

rivalry *noun*
A struggle with others for victory or supremacy.

COMPETITION.

rive *verb*
1. To crack or split into two or more fragments by means of or as a result of force, a blow, or strain.
2. To separate or pull apart by force.

1. BREAK *verb*.

2. TEAR[1] *verb*.

rivet *verb*
To compel the attention, interest, imagination, etc., of.

GRIP *verb*.

road *noun*
A course affording passage from one place to another.

WAY.

roadway *noun*
A course affording passage from one place to another.

WAY *noun*.

roam *verb*
1. To go through a place, viewing or inspecting in a leisurely way.
2. To move about at random, esp. over a wide area.

1. BROWSE.

2. ROVE.

roaming *adjective*
1. Traveling about, esp. in search of adventure.
2. Leading the life of a person without a fixed domicile; moving from place to place.

1. ERRANT.

2. NOMADIC.

roar *verb*
1. To speak or say very loudly: *"Who goes there?" roared the sentry. The mob roared in rage.*

1. *Syns:* bawl, bellow, bluster, call, clamor, cry, halloo (*also* halloa), holler, shout, yawp (*also* yaup), yell.

2. To make an earsplitting, explosive noise.

2. BLAST *verb*.

3. To express great amusement or mirth.

roar *noun*

1. A loud, deep, prolonged sound: *heard a roar of excitement in the stadium.*
2. An earsplitting, explosive noise.

roaring *adjective*

1. Improving, growing, or succeeding steadily.
2. Marked by extremely high volume and intensity of sound.

roast *verb*

1. To feel or look hot.
2. *Informal.* To criticize harshly and devastatingly.

rob *verb*

1. To take property or possessions from (a person, company, etc.) unlawfully and usu. forcibly: *robbing pedestrians in the park; robbed a bank.*

2. To take or keep something away from.

robbery *noun*

The act or crime of taking another's property unlawfully and by force: *a bank robbery committed in broad daylight.*

robe *verb*

To cover as if with clothes.

robes *noun*

Clothing worn by members of a religious order.

roborant *adjective*

Producing or stimulating physical, mental, or emotional vigor.

roborant *noun*

A medicine that restores or increases vigor.

robust *adjective*

1. Improving, growing, or succeeding steadily.
2. Full of vigor.
3. Characterized by marked muscular development; powerfully built.

rock¹ *noun*

A stupid, clumsy mistake.

rock² *verb*

1. To cause to move to and fro violently.
2. To move to and fro violently.
3. To move vigorously from side to side or up and down.
4. To impair or destroy the composure of.

rocket *verb*

1. To move swiftly.
2. To rise abruptly and precipitously.

rockiness *noun*

A minor illness, esp. one of a temporary nature.

rocky *adjective*

1. Affected or tending to be affected with minor health problems.
2. Offensive to accepted standards of decency.

rococo *adjective*

Elaborately and heavily ornamented.

rod *noun*

A relatively long, straight, rigid piece of metal or other solid material.

---

3. BREAK UP at **break**.

1. *Syns:* bawl, bellow, clamor.

2. BLAST *noun*.

1. FLOURISHING.
2. LOUD *adjective*.

1. BURN *verb*.
2. SLAM *verb*.

1. *Syns:* bail³ (*Austral.*), heist (*Slang*), hit (*Slang*), hold up, knock off (*Slang*), knock over (*Slang*), rip off (*Slang*), stick up (*Informal*).
   Near-syns: cheat, hustle, swindle, thieve; burglarize, loot, plunder, ransack, rifle, roll; pilfer, purloin, steal.
2. DEPRIVE.

Syns: heist (*Slang*), holdup, rip-off (*Slang*), stickup (*Informal*).

CLOTHE.

HABIT.

TONIC *adjective*.

TONIC *noun*.

1. FLOURISHING.
2. LUSTY.
3. MUSCULAR.

BLUNDER *noun*.

1. AGITATE.
2. SHAKE *verb*.
3. TOSS *verb*.

4. AGITATE.

1. RUSH.
2. SOAR.

INDISPOSITION.

1. SICKLY.

2. OBSCENE.

ORNATE.

STICK *noun*.

rodomontade also **rhodomontade**   *noun*
  An act of boasting.   BOAST *noun*.
rodomontade also **rhodomontade**   *adjective*
  Characterized by or given to boasting.   BOASTFUL.
rodomontade also **rhodomontade**   *verb*
  To talk with excessive pride.   BOAST *verb*.
rogation   *noun*
  A formula of words used in praying.   PRAYER.
Roger   *adverb*
  Informal. It is so; as you say or ask.   YES *adverb*.
rogue   *noun*
  One who causes minor trouble or damage.   MISCHIEF.
roguery   *noun*
  Annoying yet harmless, usu. playful acts.   MISCHIEF.
roguishness   *noun*
  Annoying yet harmless, usu. playful acts.   MISCHIEF.
roiled   *adjective*
  1. Violently disturbed, as by storms.   1. ROUGH.
  2. Having sediment or foreign particles stirred up or   2. TURBID.
    suspended.
roily   *adjective*
  1. Violently disturbed, as by storms.   1. ROUGH.
  2. Having sediment or foreign particles stirred up or   2. TURBID.
    suspended.
roister   *verb*
  To behave riotously.   REVEL *verb*.
role also **rôle**   *noun*
  1. One's proper or expected function in a common   1. PART *noun*.
    effort.
  2. The proper activity of a person or thing.   2. FUNCTION *noun*.
roll   *verb*
  1. To lean suddenly, unsteadily, and erratically from   1. LURCH *verb*.
    the vertical axis.
  2. To move vigorously from side to side or up and   2. TOSS *verb*.
    down.
  3. To proceed with ease, esp. of expression.   3. FLOW *verb*.
  4. To make a continuous deep, reverberating sound.   4. RUMBLE.
  5. To cover completely and closely, as with clothing or   5. WRAP UP.
    bandages.
  6. To take extravagant pleasure.   6. LUXURIATE.
roll in   *verb*
  Informal. To go to bed.   RETIRE.
roll out   *verb*
  To leave one's bed.   GET UP at **get**.
roll up   *verb*
  To bring together so as to increase in mass or number.   ACCUMULATE.
roll   *noun*
  A series of names, words, etc., printed or written down   LIST[1] *noun*.
  item by item.
rollick   *verb*
  1. To leap and skip about playfully.   1. GAMBOL.
  2. To take extravagant pleasure.   2. LUXURIATE.
roll in   *verb*   SEE **roll**.
roll out   *verb*   SEE **roll**.
roll up   *verb*   SEE **roll**.
roly-poly   *adjective*
  Well-rounded and usu. short in physique.   PLUMP[1].
romance   *verb*
  Informal. To attempt to gain the affection of.   COURT *verb*.
romantic   *adjective*
  1. Not compatible with reality.   1. IDEALISTIC.

2. Affectedly or extravagantly emotional.

2. SENTIMENTAL.

romanticize *verb*
To regard or imbue with affected or exaggerated emotion.

SENTIMENTALIZE.

Romeo *noun*
A man amorously attentive to women.

GALLANT *noun.*

romp *verb*
To leap and skip about playfully.

GAMBOL.

romp *noun*
Slang. An easy victory.

RUNAWAY *noun* at **run away.**

roof *noun*
The highest point.

HEIGHT.

rook *verb*
Slang. To get money or something else from by deceitful trickery.

CHEAT *verb.*

rookie *noun*
Slang. One who is just starting to learn or do something.

BEGINNER.

room *noun*
1. Suitable opportunity to accept or allow something: *no room for error.*
2. *Archaic.* The function or position customarily occupied by another.

1. *Syns:* latitude, leeway, margin, play, scope.
2. PLACE *noun.*

room *verb*
To provide with often temporary lodging.

HARBOR *verb.*

roomy *adjective*
Having plenty of room: *a roomy house.*

Syns: ample, capacious, commodious, spacious.
Near-ants: circumscribed, confined, limited, narrow, restricted.

root¹ *noun*
1. A point of origination.
2. A fundamental principle or underlying concept.
3. The most central and material part.
4. A point of origin from which ideas, influences, etc., emanate.
5. *Ling.* The main part of a word to which affixes are attached.

1. ORIGIN.
2. BASIS.
3. HEART.
4. CENTER *noun.*
5. THEME.

root *verb*
To implant so deeply as to make change nearly impossible.

FIX *verb.*

root in *verb*
To take or serve as the basis for.

BASE¹ *verb.*

root out *verb*
To destroy all traces of.

ANNIHILATE.

root² *verb*
To express approval, esp. by clapping.

APPLAUD.

root in *verb*

SEE **root¹.**

root out *verb*

SEE **root¹.**

rootstock *noun*
A point of origination.

ORIGIN.

roseate *adjective*
1. Inspiring confidence or hope.
2. Expecting a favorable outcome or dwelling on hopeful aspects.

1. ENCOURAGING.
2. OPTIMISTIC.

rose-colored *adjective*
Inspiring confidence or hope.

ENCOURAGING.

roster *noun*
A series of names, words, etc., printed or written down item by item.

LIST¹ *noun.*

rosy *adjective*
1. Inspiring confidence or hope.
2. Expecting a favorable outcome or dwelling on hopeful aspects.
3. Of a healthy, reddish color.

1. ENCOURAGING.
2. OPTIMISTIC.

3. RUDDY.

rot *verb*
To become or cause to become rotten or unsound.

DECAY *verb*.

rot *noun*
The condition of being decayed.

DECAY *noun*.

rotate *verb*
1. To do, use, or occur in successive turns: *rotated their days off.*
2. To move or cause to move in circles or around an axis or center.

1. *Syns:* alternate, interchange (*Archaic*).

2. TURN *verb*.

rotation *noun*
1. Occurrence in successive turns: *worked weekends in rotation with other nurses.*
2. Circular movement around a point or about an axis.

1. *Syns:* alternation, interchange (*Archaic*).

2. REVOLUTION.

rotten *adjective*
1. Impaired because of decay.
2. *Informal.* Of decidedly inferior quality.
3. Utterly reprehensible in nature or behavior.
4. So objectionable as to elicit despisal.

1. BAD.
2. SHODDY.
3. CORRUPT *adjective*.
4. FILTHY.

rotund *adjective*
1. Well-rounded and usu. short in physique.
2. Having or producing a full, deep, or rich sound.

1. PLUMP[1].
2. RESONANT.

roué *noun*
An immoral or licentious man.

WANTON *noun*.

rough *adjective*
1. Having a coarse, irregular surface: *rough granite cliffs.*

1. *Syns:* asperous, coarse, cragged, craggy, harsh, ironbound, jagged, ragged, rugged, scabrous, uneven. *Near-syns:* abrasive, bumpy, choppy, scraggy, unsmooth. *Ant:* smooth.

2. Disagreeable to the sense of hearing.
3. Marked by vigorous physical exertion: *rugby and other rough games.*
4. Violently disturbed, as by storms: *rough seas.*

2. HARSH.
3. *Syns:* knockabout, rough-and-tumble, rugged, strenuous, tough.
4. *Syns:* agitated, dirty, heavy, raging, roiled, roily, stormy, tempestuous, tumultuous, turbid, turbulent, ugly, violent, wild.

5. Imposing a severe test of bodily or spiritual strength.
6. Lacking in delicacy or refinement.
7. Not perfected, elaborated, or completed: *the rough draft of a treaty.*
8. In a primitive state; not domesticated or cultivated.
9. Lacking expert, careful craftsmanship.
10. Consisting of or covered with large particles.

5. BURDENSOME.

6. COARSE.
7. *Syns:* preliminary, sketchy, tentative, unfinished, unperfected, unpolished.
8. WILD *adjective*.
9. RUDE.
10. COARSE.

rough *verb*
To be rough or brutal with.

SLAP AROUND at **slap**.

rough in *verb*
To draw up a preliminary plan or version of.

DRAFT *verb*.

rough out *verb*
To draw up a preliminary plan or version of.

DRAFT *verb*.

rough up *verb*
To injure or damage, as by abuse or heavy wear.

BATTER.

rough *noun*
A preliminary plan or version, as of a written work.

DRAFT *noun*.

rough-and-tumble *adjective*
Marked by vigorous physical exertion.   ROUGH.

rough in *verb*   SEE **rough.**

roughly *adverb*
Near to in quantity or amount.   APPROXIMATELY.

roughneck *noun*
A rough, violent person who engages in destructive   TOUGH *noun.*
actions.

roughness *noun*
Lack of smoothness or regularity.   IRREGULARITY.

rough out *verb*   SEE **rough.**

rough up *verb*   SEE **rough.**

round *adjective*
1. Having the shape of a curve everywhere equidistant   1. *Syns:* annular, circular, globoid,
   from a fixed point: *The world is round.*   globular, spherical (*also* spheric),
                                                                            spheroidal (*also* spheroidic,
                                                                            spheroidical).
2. Not more or less: *a round dozen.*   2. *Syns:* complete, entire, full, good,
                                                                            perfect, whole.
3. Well-rounded and usu. short in physique.   3. PLUMP[1].
4. Having or producing a full, deep, or rich sound.   4. RESONANT.

round *noun*
1. Something bent.   1. BEND *noun.*
2. An area regularly covered, as by a policeman or   2. BEAT *noun.*
   reporter.
3. An unbroken sequence of events.   3. RUN *noun.*
4. A course of action to be followed regularly.   4. ROUTINE *noun.*
5. A course, process, or journey that ends where it   5. CIRCLE *noun.*
   began or repeats itself.

round *adverb*
1. From one end to the other.   1. THROUGH *adverb.*
2. In or toward a former location or condition.   2. BACK *adverb.*
3. Toward the back.   3. BACKWARD *adverb.*

round *verb*
To swerve from a straight line.   BEND *verb.*

round off *verb*
To fill in what is lacking and make perfect.   COMPLEMENT *verb.*

round out *verb*
To fill in what is lacking and make perfect.   COMPLEMENT *verb.*

round up *verb*
To bring together.   ASSEMBLE.

roundabout *adjective*
Not taking a direct or straight line or course.   INDIRECT.

rounded *adjective*
Deviating from a straight line.   BENT *adjective.*

round off *verb*   SEE **round.**

round out *verb*   SEE **round.**

round-the-clock also **around-the-clock** *adjective*
Existing or occurring without interruption or end.   CONTINUAL.

round up *verb*   SEE **round.**

rouse *verb*
1. To induce or elicit (a reaction or emotion).   1. AROUSE.
2. To stir to action or feeling.   2. PROVOKE.
3. To cease sleeping.   3. WAKE *verb.*

rousing *adjective*
1. Serving to enliven.   1. STIMULATING.
2. Providing inspiration.   2. INSPIRING.

roustabout *noun*
One who labors.   LABORER.

rout¹ *noun*
Archaic. A very large number of things grouped
together.   CROWD *noun.*

rout² *verb*
To win a victory over, as in battle or a competition.   DEFEAT *verb.*

rout *noun*
The act of defeating or the condition of being defeated.   DEFEAT *noun.*

route *verb*
1. To show the way to.   **1.** GUIDE *verb.*
2. To cause (something) to be conveyed to a   **2.** SEND.
   destination.

route *noun*
1. An area regularly covered, as by a policeman or   **1.** BEAT *noun.*
   reporter.
2. A means or method of entering into or achieving   **2.** TICKET *noun.*
   something desirable.

routine *noun*
1. A course of action to be followed regularly: *a daily*   **1.** *Syns:* round, track.
   routine that includes exercise.
2. A habitual, laborious, often tiresome course of   **2.** GRIND *noun.*
   action.
3. A particular kind of activity.   **3.** BIT¹.

routine *adjective*
1. Familiar through repetition.   **1.** ACCUSTOMED.
2. Lacking in interest or originality: *a routine comedy.*   **2.** *Syns:* cut-and-dried, formulaic,
                                                                                 standard, stock.
3. Occurring quite often.   **3.** COMMON *adjective.*

rove *verb*
To move about at random, esp. over a wide area: *Syns:* drift, gad about (*or* around),
tourists roving around in the city.   gallivant, meander, peregrinate, ramble,
                                                                            range, roam, stray (over), traipse, wander.

roving *adjective*
1. Leading the life of a person without a fixed domicile;   **1.** NOMADIC.
   moving from place to place.
2. Traveling about, esp. in search of adventure.   **2.** ERRANT.

row¹ *noun*
A group of people or things arranged in a row.   LINE *noun.*

row² *noun*
1. A quarrel or fight marked by very noisy, disorderly,   **1.** BRAWL *noun.*
   and often violent behavior.
2. A discussion, often heated, in which a difference of   **2.** ARGUMENT.
   opinion is expressed.

rowdy *adjective*
Upsetting civil order or peace.   DISORDERLY.

rowdy *noun*
A rough, violent person who engages in destructive   TOUGH *noun.*
actions.

royal *adjective*
1. Large and impressive in size, scope, or extent.   **1.** GRAND.
2. Posing no difficulty.   **2.** EASY.

royalist *noun*
A person who vehemently, often fanatically opposes   REACTIONARY *noun.*
progress and favors return to a previous condition.

rozzer *noun*
Brit. Slang. A member of a law-enforcement agency.   POLICEMAN.

rub *noun*
A tricky or unsuspected condition.   CATCH *noun.*

rub out *verb*
1. To remove or invalidate by or as if by running a   **1.** CANCEL.
   line through or wiping clean.
2. To destroy all traces of.   **2.** ANNIHILATE.

3. *Slang.* To take the life of (a person or persons) unlawfully.   **3.** MURDER *verb.*

rubberneck also **rubbernecker** *noun*
One who travels for pleasure.   TOURIST.

rubbernecker *noun*   SEE **rubberneck.**

rubble *verb*
To break up so that reconstruction is impossible.   DESTROY.

rubicund *adjective*
Of a healthy, reddish color.   RUDDY.

rub out *verb*   SEE **rub.**

rubric *noun*
A code or set of codes governing action, procedure, etc.   RULE *noun.*

ruck[1] *noun*
1. A group of things gathered haphazardly.   1. HEAP *noun.*
2. The common people.   2. COMMONALTY.

ruck[2] *verb*
To bend together or crease so that one part lies over another.   FOLD *verb.*

ruck *noun*
A line made by the doubling of one part over another.   FOLD *noun.*

ruckle *verb*
Brit. To make irregular folds in, esp. by pressing or twisting.   WRINKLE[1] *verb.*

ruckus *noun*
Informal. A quarrel or fight marked by very noisy, disorderly, and often violent behavior.   BRAWL *noun.*

ruction *noun*
A quarrel or fight marked by very noisy, disorderly, and often violent behavior.   BRAWL *noun.*

ruddy *adjective*
1. Of a healthy, reddish color: *ruddy cheeks.*   1. ***Syns:*** blooming, florid, flush, flushed, full-blooded, glowing, rosy, rubicund, sanguine.
Near-ants: anemic, ashen, ashy, livid, pale, pallid, wan.
Ant: bloodless.

2. *Slang.* So annoying or detestable as to deserve condemnation.   2. DAMNED.

rude *adjective*
1. Lacking good manners: *rude, offensive behavior.*   1. ***Syns:*** bad-mannered, discourteous, ill-bred, ill-mannered, impolite, ungracious, unmannerly, unpolished.
Near-ants: affable, amiable, courteous, genteel, gracious, mannerly, smooth, suave, urbane, well-mannered.
Ants: civil, polite.

2. Lacking expert, careful craftsmanship: *a rude hut; a rude sculpture.*   2. ***Syns:*** crude, primitive, raw, rough, unpolished.
3. Not civilized.   3. UNCIVILIZED.
4. Lacking in delicacy or refinement.   4. COARSE.
5. Characterized by unpleasant discordance of sound.   5. INHARMONIOUS.

rudeness *noun*
The state or quality of being impudent.   IMPUDENCE.

rudiment *noun*
1. A fundamental principle or underlying concept.   1. BASIS.
2. A fundamental, irreducible constituent of a whole.   2. ELEMENT.

rudimental *adjective*
Of or treating the simplest aspects.   ELEMENTARY.

rudimentary *adjective*
Of or treating the simplest aspects.   ELEMENTARY.

rue *noun*
A feeling of regret for one's sins or misdeeds.   PENITENCE.

rue *verb*
To feel or express sorrow for.   REGRET *verb*.

rueful *adjective*
1. Arousing or deserving pity.   **1.** PITIFUL.
2. Causing sorrow or regret.   **2.** SORROWFUL.
3. Full of or expressive of sorrow.   **3.** SORROWFUL.

ruffian *noun*
A person who treats others violently and roughly, esp. for hire.   THUG.

ruffle *verb*
1. To trouble the nerves or peace of mind of, esp. by repeated vexations.   **1.** ANNOY.
2. To impair or destroy the composure of.   **2.** AGITATE.

rugged *adjective*
1. Having a coarse, irregular surface.   **1.** ROUGH.
2. Causing sharp, often prolonged discomfort.   **2.** BITTER *adjective*.
3. Disagreeable to the sense of hearing.   **3.** HARSH.
4. Physically toughened so as to have great endurance.   **4.** HARD *adjective*.
5. Marked by vigorous physical exertion.   **5.** ROUGH.

ruin *noun*
1. Severe damage or decay rendering something useless or worthless: *Moral turpitude hastened the ruin of the Roman Empire.*   **1.** *Syns:* decimation, degeneration, destruction, deterioration, devastation, disintegration, undoing.
2. The state of being destroyed.   **2.** DESTRUCTION.
3. Something that causes total loss or severe impairment of one's health, fortune, honor, hopes, etc.: *Adolf Hitler was the ruin of Germany. Gambling was his ruin.*   **3.** *Syns:* bane, destroyer, destruction, downfall, ruination, undoing.
4. The remains of something destroyed, disintegrated, or decayed: *the barnacled ruin of a pirate's brigantine; a land dotted with the ruins of past civilizations.*   **4.** *Syns:* relic, remainder, remnant, vestige, wrack, wreckage.

ruin *verb*
1. To cause the complete ruin or wreckage of.   **1.** DESTROY.
2. To reduce to financial insolvency: *Bad investments ruined him.*   **2.** *Syns:* bankrupt, break, bust (*Slang*), clean out (*Informal*), impoverish, pauper, sink. —*Idioms* drive to the wall, put (*or* shove) onto the rocks.
3. To make or become unusable or inoperative.   **3.** BREAK *verb*.
4. To impair severely the spirit, health, effectiveness, etc., of.   **4.** BREAK *verb*.

ruinate *verb*
Regional. To cause the complete ruin or wreckage of.   DESTROY.

ruination *noun*
1. The state of being destroyed.   **1.** DESTRUCTION.
2. Something that causes total loss or severe impairment of one's health, fortune, honor, hopes, etc.   **2.** RUIN *noun*.

ruinous *adjective*
1. Falling to ruin: *A ruinous old fortress was the island's only tourist attraction.*   **1.** *Syns:* dilapidated, ramshackle, tumbledown. —*Idiom* gone to seed.
2. Having the capability or effect of damaging irreparably.   **2.** DESTRUCTIVE.
3. Causing ruin or destruction.   **3.** FATAL.

rule *noun*
1. A code or set of codes governing action, procedure, etc.: *the rules of chess; a rule of grammar.*   **1.** *Syns:* dictate, prescript, regulation, rubric.
2. A system by which a political unit is controlled.   **2.** GOVERNMENT.

3. A principle governing the affairs of man within or among political units.

3. LAW *noun*.

4. The continuous exercise of authority over a political unit.

4. GOVERNMENT.

5. The act of exercising controlling power or the condition of being so controlled.

5. DOMINATION.

6. A regular or customary matter, condition, or course of events.

6. USUAL *noun*.

rule *verb*

1. To exercise authority or influence over.

1. CONTROL *verb*.

2. To exercise the authority of a sovereign.

2. GOVERN.

3. To make a decision about (a controversy, dispute, etc.) after deliberation, as in a court of law.

3. JUDGE *verb*.

4. To command in an arrogant manner.

4. BOSS *verb*.

5. To occupy the pre-eminent position in.

5. DOMINATE.

rule out *verb*

1. To keep from being admitted, included, or considered.

1. EXCLUDE.

2. To prohibit from occurring by advance planning or action.

2. PREVENT.

rule out *verb*

SEE **rule.**

ruling *noun*

An authoritative or official decision, esp. one made by a court: *an appellate court ruling; the Supreme Court's ruling on school integration.*

Syns: decree, determination, edict, judgment, pronouncement.

ruling *adjective*

1. Exercising controlling power or influence.

1. DOMINANT.

2. Having pre-eminent significance: *the ruling passion of his life.*

2. ***Syns:*** ascendant, dominant, predominant, prepotent, prevailing, supreme.

rum also **rummy** *adjective*

Brit. Slang. Deviating from the customary.

ECCENTRIC *adjective*.

rumble *verb*

1. To make a continuous deep, reverberating sound: *heard the convoy rumbling in the distance.*

1. ***Syns:*** boom, growl, grumble, roll. ***Near-syns:*** clap, crack, crash, roar, thunder.

2. To complain in low, indistinct tones.

2. MUTTER *verb*.

rumble *noun*

A low, indistinct utterance of complaint.

MUTTER *noun*.

ruminate *verb*

To consider carefully and at length.

PONDER.

rumination *noun*

The act or process of thinking.

THOUGHT.

ruminative *adjective*

Of, characterized by, or disposed to thought.

THOUGHTFUL.

rummage *verb*

To make a thorough search of.

SCOUR.

rummy[1] *noun*

Slang. A person who is habitually drunk.

DRUNKARD.

rummy[2] *adjective*

SEE **rum.**

rumor *noun*

Idle, often sensational and groundless talk about others.

GOSSIP *noun*.

rumor *verb*

To engage in or spread gossip.

GOSSIP *verb*.

rumorer *noun*

A person habitually engaged in idle talk about others.

GOSSIP *noun*.

rumormonger *noun*

A person habitually engaged in idle talk about others.

GOSSIP *noun*.

rump *noun*

The part of one's back on which one rests in sitting.

BOTTOM *noun*.

rumple *verb*
1. To put (the hair or clothes) into a state of disarray.
2. To make irregular folds in, esp. by pressing or twisting.

1. TOUSLE.
2. WRINKLE[1] *verb*.

rumpus *noun*
1. An interruption of regular procedure or of public peace.
2. Sounds or a sound, esp. when loud, confused, or disagreeable.
3. Offensively loud and insistent utterances, esp. of disapproval.

1. DISTURBANCE.

2. NOISE *noun*.

3. VOCIFERATION.

run *verb*
1. To move swiftly on foot so that both feet leave the ground during each stride: *The boy runs like a deer. We ran to the corner.*
2. To leave hastily: *hates people who eat and run; robbed the bank and ran.*

1. *Syns:* dash, fly (*Informal*), scamper, scoot, scurry, sprint, tear[1] (*Informal*). —*Idiom* run like the wind.
2. *Syns:* bolt, clear out (*Informal*), fly, get (*Regional & Informal*), get out, hightail (*Slang*), hotfoot (*Slang*), scram (*Slang*), skedaddle (*Informal*), skiddoo (*Informal*), split (*Slang*), take off (*Slang*), vamoose (*also* vamose) (*Slang*). —*Idioms* beat it, make tracks.

3. To move swiftly.
4. To have recourse to when in need.
5. To complete a race or competition in a specified position: *He ran third in a field of eight.*
6. To function effectively.
7. To have charge of (the affairs of others).
8. To control or direct the functioning of.
9. To set or keep going.
10. To urge to move along.
11. To change from a solid to a liquid.
12. To move freely as a liquid.
13. To proceed on a certain course or for a certain distance.
14. To change or fluctuate within limits.
15. To cause to penetrate with force.
16. To move or proceed away from a place.
17. To import or export secretly and illegally.
18. To look for and pursue (game) in order to capture or kill it.
19. To come to in number or quantity.

3. RUSH *verb*.
4. RESORT TO at **resort.**
5. *Syns:* come in, finish, place.

6. WORK *verb*.
7. ADMINISTER.
8. OPERATE.
9. DRIVE *verb*.
10. DRIVE *verb*.
11. MELT.
12. FLOW *verb*.
13. EXTEND.

14. GO *verb*.
15. RAM.
16. GO *verb*.
17. SMUGGLE.
18. HUNT.

19. AMOUNT *verb*.

run across *verb*
To find or meet by chance.

COME ACROSS at **come.**

run after *verb*
To follow (another) with the intent of overtaking and capturing.

PURSUE.

run along *verb*
To move or proceed away from a place.

GO *verb*.

run around *verb*
Informal. To keep company.

ASSOCIATE *verb*.

run dry *verb*
To make or become no longer active or productive.

DRY UP at **dry.**

run into *verb*
1. To find or meet by chance.
2. To come up against.

1. COME ACROSS at **come.**
2. ENCOUNTER *verb*.

run on *verb*
To talk volubly, persistently, and usu. inconsequentially.

CHATTER *verb*.

run out *verb*

1. To make or become no longer active or productive.
2. To prove deficient or insufficient.
3. *Slang.* To abandon one's cause or party usu. to join another.
4. To become void, esp. through passage of time or an omission.

run up *verb*
To make or become greater or larger.

run *noun*
1. An uninterrupted course.
2. An unbroken sequence of events: *a run of victories; a run of Broadway hits.*
3. A small stream.
4. A number of things placed or occurring one after the other.

run across *verb*
run after *verb*
runagate *noun*
Archaic. A person who has defected.
run along *verb*
run around *verb*
runaway *noun & adjective*
run away *verb*
To break loose and leave suddenly, as from confinement or from a difficult or threatening situation.

runaway *noun*
1. One who flees, as from home, confinement, captivity, justice, etc.
2. *Informal.* An easy victory: *The election was a runaway for our candidate.*

runaway *adjective*
1. Fleeing or having fled, as from home, confinement, captivity, justice, etc.
2. Out of control: *a runaway train; a runaway mob of angry protesters.*

run down *verb*
1. To lose so much strength and power as to become ineffective or motionless: *I seem to run down at about 4 o'clock in the afternoon.*
2. To pursue and locate: *The police were able to run down their missing witness.*

3. *Informal.* To think, represent, or speak of as small or unimportant.
4. To recapitulate the salient facts of.

run-down *noun*
A condensation of the essential or main points of something.

run-down *adjective*
1. Depleted of strength or robust health: *He's run-down from overwork.*
2. Showing signs of wear and tear or neglect.

run-down *noun & adjective*
run dry *verb*
rung *noun*
One of the units in a course, as on an ascending or descending scale.

run in *verb*
1. To go to or seek out the company of in order to socialize.
2. To take into custody as a prisoner.

---

1. DRY UP at **dry.**
2. FAIL.
3. DEFECT.

4. LAPSE *verb.*

INCREASE *verb.*

1. CONTINUANCE.
2. *Syns:* chain, round, series, string, succession, train.
3. BRANCH *noun.*
4. SERIES.

SEE **run.**
SEE **run.**

DEFECTOR.
SEE **run.**
SEE **run.**
SEE **run away.**

ESCAPE *verb.*

1. FUGITIVE *noun.*

2. *Syns:* pushover, romp (*Slang*), walkaway, walkover.

1. FUGITIVE *adjective.*

2. *Syns:* amuck (*also* amok), uncontrolled. —*Idioms* out of hand, running wild.

1. *Syns:* burn out, give out, play out, poop out (*Slang*).

2. *Syns:* hunt down, nose out (*Slang*), trace, track down. —*Idiom* run to earth.

3. BELITTLE.

4. REVIEW *verb.*

SUMMARY *noun.*

1. *Syns:* debilitated, drained, enervated, enfeebled, weakened.
2. SHABBY.

SEE **run down.**
SEE **run.**

DEGREE.

1. VISIT *verb.*

2. ARREST *verb.*

run-in *noun*
1. A brief, hostile exposure to or contact with something, as danger, opposition, etc.
2. A physical conflict involving two or more.
3. A discussion, often heated, in which a difference of opinion is expressed.

1. BRUSH *noun*.

2. FIGHT *noun*.
3. ARGUMENT.

run-in *noun*

SEE **run in.**

run into *verb*

SEE **run.**

runner *noun*
1. A person who carries messages or is sent on errands.
2. A person who engages in smuggling.
3. *Bot.* A young stemlike growth arising from a plant.

1. BEARER.

2. SMUGGLER.
3. SHOOT *noun*.

running *adjective*
1. In action or full operation.
2. Marked by facility, esp. of expression.

1. ACTIVE.
2. SMOOTH *adjective*.

run-of-the-mill *adjective*
Being of no special quality or type.

ORDINARY *adjective*.

run on *verb*

SEE **run.**

run out *verb*

SEE **run.**

run through *verb*
1. To use all of.
2. To be depleted.
3. To look through reading matter casually.
4. To recapitulate the salient facts of.

1. EXHAUST.
2. GO *verb*.
3. BROWSE.
4. REVIEW *verb*.

run-through *noun*
A condensation of the essential or main points of something.

SUMMARY *noun*.

run-through *noun*

SEE **run through.**

runty *adjective*
Regional. Having or showing a bad temper.

ILL-TEMPERED.

run up *verb*

SEE **run.**

rupture *noun*
1. An opening, esp. in a solid structure.
2. An interruption in friendly relations.

1. BREACH *noun*.
2. BREACH *noun*.

rupture *verb*
1. To make a hole or other opening in.
2. To undergo partial breaking.

1. BREACH *verb*.
2. CRACK *verb*.

rural *adjective*
Of or pertaining to the countryside.

COUNTRY *adjective*.

ruse *noun*
1. An action meant to deceive.
2. An indirect, usu. cunning means of gaining an end.

1. DECEPTION.
2. TRICK *noun*.

rush *verb*
1. To move swiftly: *rushed home from the airport.*

1. *Syns:* barrel (*Slang*), boil, bolt, bucket, bullet, bustle, dart, dash, dust (*Slang*), festinate, flash, fleet[1], flit, fly, haste (*Poetic*), hasten, hell (*Informal*), highball, hurry, hustle (*Informal*), nip[1] (*Brit. Slang*), pelt[2], race, rip (*Brit. Slang*), rocket, run, sail, scoot, scour, scurry, shoot, skin (out), speed, stave[2], tear[1], trot, whirl, whisk, whiz (*also* whizz), wing, zip, zoom. —*Idioms* beeline it, get a move on, get cracking, go like lightning, go like the wind, hotfoot it, make a beeline, make haste, make tracks, shake a leg, step (*or* jump) on it.

Near-ants: creep, dally, dawdle, drag, ease, glide, lag, linger, loiter, poke, saunter, stroll.

2. To come forth or emit in abundance.

   2. FLOW *verb.*

3. To attempt to gain the affection of.

   3. COURT *verb.*

rush *noun*

1. Careless, headlong action.

   1. HASTE *noun.*

2. Something suggestive of running water.

   2. FLOW *noun.*

3. A swift advance or attack.

   3. CHARGE *noun.*

rush *adjective*

Designed to meet emergency needs as quickly as possible.

CRASH *adjective.*

rustic *adjective*

1. Of a plain and unsophisticated nature: *the truth in his rustic philosophy; a rustic beauty.*

   1. **Syns:** artless, homely, homespun, natural, unadorned, unpolished.

2. Of or pertaining to the countryside.

   2. COUNTRY *adjective.*

rut *noun*

1. A habitual, laborious, often tiresome course of action.

   1. GRIND *noun.*

2. A regular period of sexual excitement in female mammals.

   2. HEAT *noun.*

ruthless *adjective*

Lacking scruples or principles.

UNSCRUPULOUS.

S

sable *adjective*

Of the darkest achromatic visual value.

BLACK *adjective.*

sabotage *noun*

A deliberate and underhanded effort to defeat or do harm to an endeavor: *Production was slowed down by industrial sabotage.*

Syns: subversion, undermining.

sabotage *verb*

To damage, destroy, or defeat by sabotage: *a campaign that was sabotaged by undercover agents.*

Syns: subvert, undermine.

saccharine *adjective*

1. Having or suggesting the taste of sugar.

   1. SWEET *adjective.*

2. Purposefully contrived to gain favor.

   2. INSINUATING.

sack[1] *noun*

Slang. The act of dismissing or the condition of being dismissed from employment.

DISMISSAL.

sack *verb*

Slang. To end the employment of.

DISMISS.

sack[2] *verb*

To rob of goods by force, esp. in time of war: *villages that were sacked by invaders.*

Syns: depredate, despoil, harrow, havoc (*Rare*), loot, pillage, plunder, rape, ravage, spoil (*Obs.*), spoliate.

sacrarium *noun*

Eccles. A sacred or holy place.

SANCTUARY.

sacred   *adjective*
1. Given over exclusively to a single use or purpose: *a place sacred to the memory of those who fell in battle.*
2. In the service or worship of God or a god.
3. Regarded with particular reverence or respect.
4. Protected from violation or abuse by custom, law, or feelings of reverence: *a sacred vow.*

1. **Syns:** consecrated, dedicated, devoted, hallowed.
2. DIVINE[1].
3. HOLY.
4. **Syns:** inviolable, sacrosanct.
   Near-syns: defended, guarded, immune, protected, shielded, untouchable.

sacredness   *noun*
1. The quality of being holy or sacred.
2. The quality or condition of being safe from assault, trespass, or violation.

1. HOLINESS.
2. SANCTITY.

sacrifice   *noun*
1. A living creature slain and offered to a deity as part of a religious rite: *The weapons of the sacrifice were shown to the priest.*
2. A loss sustained in the accomplishment of or as the result of something.

1. **Syns:** hecatomb, immolation, offering, victim.
2. COST *noun.*

sacrifice   *verb*
To offer as a sacrifice: *sacrificed two white doves on the altar of the temple.*

Syns: immolate, victimize.

sacrilege   *noun*
An act of disrespect or impiety toward something regarded as sacred: *The theft of the holy relics was a sacrilege.*

Syns: blasphemy, desecration, profanation, violation.

sacrilegious   *adjective*
Showing irreverence and contempt for something sacred: *sacrilegious mockery.*

Syns: blasphemous, profane.
Near-syns: evil, impious, irreverent, sinful, ungodly, wicked.
Ant: religious.

sacrosanct   *adjective*
1. Regarded with particular reverence or respect.
2. Protected from violation or abuse by custom, law, or feelings of reverence.

1. HOLY.
2. SACRED.

sacrosanctity   *noun*
The quality or condition of being safe from assault, trespass, or violation.

SANCTITY.

sad   *adjective*
1. Tending to cause sadness or low spirits: *a sad tale of family discord.*

1. **Syns:** depressing, dismal, gloomy, joyless, melancholy.
   Near-ants: bright, gay, lively, heartwarming, stimulating, stirring.
   Ant: happy.

2. In low spirits.
3. Causing sorrow or regret.

2. DEPRESSED.
3. SORROWFUL.

sadden   *verb*
To make sad or gloomy.

DEPRESS.

saddened   *adjective*
In low spirits.

DEPRESSED.

saddle   *verb*
1. To place a burden or heavy load on.
2. To ascribe (a misdeed, error, etc.) to.
3. To force (another) to accept a burden.

1. CHARGE *verb.*
2. FIX *verb.*
3. IMPOSE.

sadness   *noun*
A feeling or spell of dismally low spirits.

GLOOM.

safe   *adjective*
1. Free from danger, injury, or the threat of harm: *was perfectly safe at home.*

2. Affording protection: *a spot safe from enemy fire.*

1. **Syns:** unharmed, unhurt, uninjured, unscathed. —*Idioms* safe and sound, with a whole skin.
2. **Syn:** secure. —*Idiom* as safe as houses.

Near-syns: defended, guarded, protected, sheltered, shielded.
Ants: dangerous, insecure, unsafe.

safeguard *verb*
To keep safe from danger, attack, or harm.   DEFEND.

safeguard *noun*
The act or a means of defending.   DEFENSE.

safeness *noun*
The quality or state of being safe.   SAFETY.

safety *noun*
The quality or state of being safe: *guaranteed the safety of the children.*   *Syns:* assurance, safeness, security.

sag *verb*
1. To decline, as in value or quantity, very gradually.   1. SLIP *verb*.
2. To hang limply, loosely, and carelessly.   2. SLOUCH *verb*.
3. To become limp, as from loss of freshness.   3. WILT.

sag *noun*
An area sunk below its surroundings.   DEPRESSION.

sagacious *adjective*
1. Possessing or showing sound judgment and keen perception.   1. WISE[1].
2. Possessing, proceeding from, or exhibiting good judgment and prudence.   2. SANE.

sagacity *noun*
Skill in perceiving, discriminating, or judging.   DISCERNMENT.

sage *noun*
A usu. elderly man noted for wisdom, knowledge, and judgment: *Many considered Oliver Wendell Holmes a sage.*   *Syns:* Nestor, pundit, savant, scholar.

sage *adjective*
1. Possessing or showing sound judgment and keen perception.   1. WISE[1].
2. Possessing, proceeding from, or exhibiting good judgment and prudence.   2. SANE.

sageness *noun*
Skill in perceiving, discriminating, or judging.   DISCERNMENT.

sail *verb*
1. To move through the air with or as if with wings.   1. FLY.
2. To pass quickly and lightly through the air.   2. FLY.
3. To move swiftly.   3. RUSH *verb*.
4. To proceed with ease, esp. of expression.   4. FLOW *verb*.

sail in (or **into**) *verb*
1. To start work on vigorously.   1. ATTACK *verb*.
2. To set upon with violent force.   2. ATTACK *verb*.

sail in (or **into**) *verb*   SEE **sail**.

sailor *noun*
A person engaged in sailing or working on a ship: *A crew of 11 sailors manned the tanker.*   *Syns:* gob[1] (*Slang*), jack (*Informal*), jacktar (*Informal*), mariner, navigator, salt (*Informal*), sea dog (*Slang*), seafarer, seaman, tar (*Informal*).

salability *noun*
Market appeal.   SELL *noun*.

salableness *noun*
Market appeal.   SELL *noun*.

salary *noun*
Payment for work done.   WAGE(S) *noun*.

sales clerk *noun*
One who sells.   SELLER.

salesperson *noun*
One who sells.   SELLER.

salient *adjective*
Readily attracting notice.   NOTICEABLE.

salivate *verb*
To let saliva run from the mouth.   DROOL *verb*.

salivation *noun*
Saliva running from the mouth.   DROOL *noun*.

sallow *adjective*
Lacking color.   PALE *adjective*.

salmagundi *noun*
A collection of various things.   ASSORTMENT.

salt *noun*
1. The means needed to support life.   1. LIVING.
2. *Informal.* A person engaged in sailing or working on   2. SAILOR.
   a ship.

salt away *verb*
1. *Informal.* To place (money) in a bank.   1. BANK[1].
2. To reserve for the future.   2. SAVE.

salt away *verb*   SEE **salt.**

salty *adjective*
Bordering on indelicacy or impropriety.   RACY.

salubrious *adjective*
Promoting good health.   HEALTHFUL.

salutary *adjective*
1. Affording benefit.   1. BENEFICIAL.
2. Promoting good health.   2. HEALTHFUL.

salutation *noun*
An expression, in words or gestures, marking a meeting   GREETING.
of persons.

salute *verb*
To address in a friendly and respectful way.   GREET.

salute *noun*
1. An expression, in words or gestures, marking a   1. GREETING.
   meeting of persons.
2. A formal token of appreciation and admiration for a   2. TESTIMONIAL.
   person's high achievements.

salvage *verb*
To extricate from an undesirable state.   RESCUE *verb*.

salvage *noun*
Extrication from danger or confinement.   RESCUE *noun*.

salvation *noun*
Extrication from danger or confinement.   RESCUE *noun*.

salvo *noun*
1. A concentrated outpouring, as of missiles, words, or   1. BARRAGE *noun*.
   blows.
2. A formal token of appreciation and admiration for a   2. TESTIMONIAL.
   person's high achievements.

same *adjective*
1. Being one and not another or others; not different in 1. *Syns:* identic (*Archaic*), identical,
   nature or identity: *That is the same seat I had*   selfsame, very.
   yesterday.
2. Agreeing exactly in value, quantity, or effect.   2. EQUAL *adjective*.
3. Remaining continually unchanged.   3. CONSISTENT.

sameness *noun*
1. The quality or condition of being exactly the same   1. *Syns:* identicalness, identity, oneness,
   as something else: *the sameness of the fingerprints.*   selfsameness.
2. The state of being equivalent.   2. EQUIVALENCE.
3. A tiresome lack of variety.   3. MONOTONY.

sample *noun*
1. One that is representative of a group or class.   1. EXAMPLE.
2. A limited or anticipatory experience.   2. TASTE *noun*.

sanctified *adjective*
Regarded with particular reverence or respect.   HOLY.

sanctify *verb*
To make sacred by a religious rite: *sanctified the day*   *Syns:* bless, consecrate, hallow.
for the worship of God.

sanctimonious *adjective*
Of or practicing hypocrisy.   HYPOCRITICAL.

sanctimoniousness *noun*   SEE **sanctimony.**

sanctimony also **sanctimoniousness** *noun*
A show or expression of feelings or beliefs one does not   HYPOCRISY.
actually hold or possess.

sanction *verb*
To give one's consent to.   PERMIT *verb.*

  sanction *noun*
  1. A coercive measure intended to ensure compliance   1. *Syns:* interdict, interdiction, penalty.
    or conformity: *invoked sanctions against the*
    countries that flouted international law.
  2. Approval for an action, esp. as granted by one in   2. PERMISSION.
    authority.

sanctioned *adjective*
  1. Having or arising from authority.   1. AUTHORITATIVE.
  2. Generally approved or agreed upon.   2. ACCEPTED.
  3. Adhering to beliefs or practices approved by   3. ORTHODOX.
    authority or tradition.

sanctity *noun*
  1. The quality or condition of being safe from assault, 1. *Syns:* inviolability, sacredness,
    trespass, or violation: *the sanctity of the home.*   sacrosanctity.
  2. The quality of being holy or sacred.   2. HOLINESS.

sanctorium *noun*
A sacred or holy place.   SANCTUARY.

sanctuary *noun*
  1. A sacred or holy place: *the sanctuary of a church.* 1. *Syns:* sacrarium (*Eccles.*), sanctorium,
                                                                sanctum, shrine.
  2. Something that physically protects, esp. from   2. COVER *noun.*
    danger.
  3. The state of being protected or safeguarded, as from 3. REFUGE.
    danger or hardship.

sanctum *noun*
A sacred or holy place.   SANCTUARY.

sane *adjective*
  1. Of sound mind; mentally healthy: *a sane person.*   1. *Syns:* compos mentis (*Latin*), lucid,
                                                                rational. —*Idioms* all there, in one's
                                                                right mind, of sound mind.
  2. Possessing, proceeding from, or exhibiting good   2. *Syns:* balanced, commonsensible,
    judgment and prudence: *a sane decision.*   commonsensical, judicious, levelheaded,
                                                                prudent, rational, reasonable,
                                                                sagacious, sage, sapient, sensible,
                                                                sensical, sound^2, well-founded, well-
                                                                grounded, wise^1.
                                                                Near-syns: cogent, compelling,
                                                                convincing, logical.
                                                                Ants: imprudent, irrational.

saneness *noun*
A healthy mental state.   SANITY.

sang-froid *noun*
  1. Lack of emotional agitation.   1. CALM *noun.*
  2. The state or quality of being nonchalant.   2. NONCHALANCE.

sanguinary *adjective*
  1. Eager for bloodshed.   1. MURDEROUS.
  2. Attended by or causing bloodshed.   2. BLOODY *adjective.*

sanguine *adjective*
1. Expecting a favorable outcome or dwelling on hopeful aspects.
2. Of a healthy, reddish color.

1. OPTIMISTIC.

2. RUDDY.

sanguineness *noun*
A tendency to expect a favorable outcome or to dwell on hopeful aspects.

OPTIMISM.

sanguineous *adjective*
1. Attended by or causing bloodshed.
2. Eager for bloodshed.

1. BLOODY *adjective*.

2. MURDEROUS.

sanguinity *noun*
A tendency to expect a favorable outcome or to dwell on hopeful aspects.

OPTIMISM.

sanitize *verb*
To render free of microorganisms.

STERILIZE.

sanitized *adjective*
Free or freed from microorganisms.

STERILE.

sanity *noun*
A healthy mental state: *lost her sanity.*

Syns: lucidity, lucidness, marbles (*Slang*), mind, reason, saneness, sense, senses, soundness, wit, wits.

sap¹ *noun*
Slang. A person who is easily deceived or victimized.

DUPE *noun*.

sap² *verb*
To lessen or deplete the nerve, energy, or strength of.

ENERVATE.

sapience *noun*
Deep, thorough, or mature understanding.

WISDOM.

sapient *adjective*
1. Possessing, proceeding from, or exhibiting good judgment and prudence.
2. Possessing or showing sound judgment and keen perception.

1. SANE.

2. WISE¹.

sapor *noun*
A distinctive property of a substance affecting the gustatory sense.

FLAVOR *noun*.

sappy *adjective*
1. *Slang.* Affectedly or extravagantly emotional.
2. *Slang.* So senseless as to be laughable.

1. SENTIMENTAL.

2. FOOLISH.

sarcasm *noun*
Ironic, bitter humor designed to wound: *cruel and devastating sarcasm.*

Syns: acerbity, causticity, corrosiveness, mordacity, mordancy.

sarcastic *adjective*
Given to or expressing sarcasm: *a sarcastic, sneering critic; sarcastic remarks.*

Syns: acerb, acerbic, caustic, corrosive, mordant.
Near-syns: cynical, ironic, sardonic, satiric; biting, cutting, incisive, jeering, mocking, scornful.

sardonic *adjective*
Marked by or displaying contemptuous mockery of the motives or virtues of others.

CYNICAL.

sashay *verb*
Informal. To walk with exaggerated or unnatural motions expressive of self-importance or self-display.

STRUT.

sass *verb*
Informal. To utter an impertinent rejoinder.

TALK BACK at **talk.**

sassy *adjective*
Rude and disrespectful.

IMPUDENT:

satanic also **satanical** *adjective*
Perversely bad, cruel, or wicked.

FIENDISH.

sate *verb*
To satisfy to the full or to excess.

SATIATE.

sated *adjective*
Filled to satisfaction or excess.　　　　SATIATED.

satellite *noun*
One who supports and adheres to another.　　FOLLOWER.

satiate *verb*
To satisfy to the full or to excess: *The large meal* *satiated our hunger.*　**Syns:** cloy, glut, gorge, sate, surfeit.

　satiate *adjective*
　Filled to satisfaction or excess.　　SATIATED.

satiated *adjective*
Filled to satisfaction or excess: *Satiated with crime stories, readers turned to other amusements.*
　Syns: glutted, gorged, replete, sated, satiate, surfeited.
　Near-ants: ravenous.
　Ant: hungry.

satiation *noun*
The condition of being full to or beyond satisfaction: *Some dieticians advise stopping eating before the point of satiation.*
　Syns: engorgement, repletion, satiety, surfeit.

satiety *noun*
The condition of being full to or beyond satisfaction.　SATIATION.

satiny *adjective*
Smooth and lustrous as if polished.　SLEEK *adjective.*

satire *noun*
A work, as a novel or play, that exposes folly by the use of humor or irony: *wrote an amusing satire on pompous businessmen.*
　Syns: lampoon, lampoonery.

satisfaction *noun*
Something to make up for loss or damage.　COMPENSATION.

satisfactory *adjective*
1. Of moderately good quality but less than excellent.
2. Being what is needed without being in excess.
3. Serving to convince.
　1. ACCEPTABLE.
　2. SUFFICIENT.
　3. CONVINCING.

satisfied *adjective*
Having achieved satisfaction, as of one's goal.　FULFILLED.

satisfy *verb*
1. To grant or have what is demanded by (a need or desire): *satisfied his appetite for the time being; satisfying a lifelong desire to see Ireland.*
2. To be satisfactory to.
3. To supply fully or completely: *satisfied all requirements.*
4. To cause (another) to believe something.
5. To set right by giving what is due.
　1. **Syns:** appease, fulfill, gratify, indulge.
　　Near-syns: content, grant, placate, please.
　2. PLEASE.
　3. **Syns:** answer, fill, fulfill, meet[1].
　4. CONVINCE.
　5. SETTLE.

satisfying *adjective*
Affording pleasure or comfort.　GRATEFUL.

satisfyingly *adverb*
In the manner desired.　WELL[2] *adverb.*

saturate *verb*
1. To make thoroughly wet.
2. To cause to be filled with a particular mood or tone.
　1. WET *verb.*
　2. CHARGE *verb.*

saturnine *adjective*
Broodingly and sullenly unhappy.　GLUM.

satyr *noun*
An immoral or licentious man.　WANTON *noun.*

sauce *noun*
Informal. The state or quality of being impudent.　IMPUDENCE.

　sauce *verb*
　Informal. To utter an impertinent rejoinder.　TALK BACK at **talk.**

saucebox *noun*
One who is obnoxiously self-assertive and arrogant.　SMART ALECK.

sauciness *noun*
The state or quality of being impudent.   IMPUDENCE.

saucy *adjective*
Rude and disrespectful.   IMPUDENT.

saunter *verb*
To walk at a leisurely pace.   STROLL *verb*.

saunter *noun*
An act of walking, esp. for pleasure or exercise.   WALK *noun*.

savage *adjective*
1. Of or relating to beasts of prey: *a savage lion*.   1. **Syns:** feral, wild.
                                                             Near-ants: civilized, subdued, tamed.
                                                             Ants: domesticated, tame.
2. Showing or suggesting a disposition to be violently   2. FIERCE.
   destructive without scruple or restraint.
3. Not civilized.   3. UNCIVILIZED.
4. So intense as to cause extreme suffering.   4. CRUEL.

savant *noun*
A usu. elderly man noted for wisdom, knowledge, and   SAGE *noun*.
judgment.

save *verb*
1. To reserve for the future: *saved the old baby clothes* 1. **Syns:** keep, lay aside, lay away, lay by,
   for future grandchildren; save money each month in   lay in, put by, salt away, set by, spare.
   a Christmas club.   **Near-syns:** accumulate, collect,
                                                              conserve, heard, stockpile, store.
                                                              Ants: consume, spend.
2. To extricate, as from danger or confinement.   2. RESCUE *verb*.
3. To protect (an asset) from loss or destruction.   3. CONSERVE *verb*.
4. To accumulate and set aside for future use.   4. STOCKPILE *verb*.
5. To use without wasting.   5. ECONOMIZE.

saving *adjective*
Careful in the use of material resources.   ECONOMICAL.

savoir-faire *noun*
French. The ability to say and do the right thing at the TACT.
right time.

savor *noun*
1. A distinctive yet intangible quality deemed typical   1. FLAVOR *noun*.
   of a given thing.
2. A distinctive property of a substance affecting the   2. FLAVOR *noun*.
   gustatory sense.
3. A distinctive element.   3. QUALITY.

savor *verb*
1. To receive pleasure from.   1. ENJOY.
2. To undergo an emotional reaction.   2. FEEL *verb*.
3. To recognize the worth, quality, importance, etc., of. 3. APPRECIATE.
4. To have a particular flavor or suggestion of   4. SMACK[2] *verb*.
   something.

savory *adjective*
Highly pleasing, esp. to the sense of taste.   DELICIOUS.

savvy *noun*
Slang. Intellectual hold.   GRASP *noun*.

savvy *adjective*
Slang. Having or showing a clever awareness and   SHREWD.
resourcefulness in practical matters.

savvy *verb*
Slang. To perceive and recognize the meaning of.   UNDERSTAND.

saw *noun*
A usu. pithy and familiar statement expressing an   PROVERB.
observation or principle generally accepted as wise or
true.

saw off *verb*
 Slang. To stop suddenly, as a conversation, activity,   SUSPEND.
 relationship, etc.

say *verb*
 1. To put into words: *The speaker said what was on his*   1. **Syns:** articulate, communicate, convey,
    mind and then sat down.   declare, express, state, tell, utter[1],
                                                                     vent, vocalize, voice. —*Idiom* give vent
                                                                     (*or* voice *or* tongue) to.
                                                                     Near-syns: affirm, announce, assert,
                                                                     aver, avow, proclaim; comment, cite,
                                                                     quote, recite, remark.
 2. To produce or make (speech sounds).   2. PRONOUNCE.
 3. To state to be true.   3. CLAIM *verb*.

say *noun*
 The right or chance to express an opinion or participate   VOICE *noun*.
 in a decision.

saying *noun*
 A usu. pithy and familiar statement expressing an   PROVERB.
 observation or principle generally accepted as wise or
 true.

say-so *noun*
 1. *Informal.* The right and power to command, decide,   1. AUTHORITY.
    rule, or judge.
 2. *Informal.* The right or chance to express an opinion   2. VOICE *noun*.
    or participate in a decision.

scabrous *adjective*
 1. Bordering on indelicacy or impropriety.   1. RACY.
 2. Having a coarse, irregular surface.   2. ROUGH.

scad *noun*
 Informal. An indeterminately great amount or number.   HEAP *noun*.

scaffold *noun*
 A temporary framework with a floor, used by workmen.   STAGE *noun*.

scaffolding *noun*
 A temporary framework with a floor, used by workmen.   STAGE *noun*.

scalding *adjective*
 Marked by much heat.   HOT *adjective*.

scale¹ *verb*
 To remove the skin of.   SKIN *verb*.

scale² *verb*
 To move upward on or along.   ASCEND.

scaling *noun*
 The act of moving upward on or along.   ASCENT.

scalp *verb*
 Informal. To exploit (another) by charging too much for   SKIN *verb*.
 something.

scamp *noun*
 One who causes minor trouble or damage.   MISCHIEF.

scamper *verb*
 To move swiftly on foot so that both feet leave the   RUN *verb*.
 ground during each stride.

scan *verb*
 1. To look through reading matter casually.   1. BROWSE.
 2. To view broadly or from a height.   2. SURVEY *verb*.

scandal *noun*
 The expression of injurious, malicious statements about   LIBEL *noun*.
 someone.

scandal *verb*
 To make defamatory statements about.   LIBEL *verb*.

scandalize *verb*
 1. To make defamatory statements about.   1. LIBEL *verb*.
 2. To affect with a strong feeling of moral aversion.   2. SHOCK *verb*.

scandalmonger *noun*
A person habitually engaged in idle talk about others.   GOSSIP *noun.*

scandalous *adjective*
1. Damaging to the reputation.   1. LIBELOUS.
2. Disgracefully and grossly offensive.   2. OUTRAGEOUS.

scant *adjective*
1. Just sufficient.   1. BARE *adjective.*
2. Conspicuously deficient in quantity, fullness, or   2. MEAGER.
   extent.

scantiness *noun*
The condition or fact of being deficient.   SHORTAGE.

scanty *adjective*
1. Not enough to meet a demand or requirement.   1. INSUFFICIENT.
2. Conspicuously deficient in quantity, fullness, or   2. MEAGER.
   extent.

scapegoat *noun*
One who is made an object of blame: *The manager was*   **Syns:** fall guy (*Slang*), goat, patsy
a convenient scapegoat for the team's poor performance.   (*Slang*), whipping boy.

scarce *adjective*
1. Rarely occurring or appearing.   1. INFREQUENT.
2. Not enough to meet a demand or requirement.   2. INSUFFICIENT.
   scarce *adverb*
   By a very little.   BARELY.

scarceness *noun*
The condition or fact of being deficient.   SHORTAGE.

scarcity *noun*
The condition or fact of being deficient.   SHORTAGE.

scare *verb*
To fill with fear.   FRIGHTEN.

scarecrow *noun*
A person wearing ragged or tattered clothing.   TATTERDEMALION.

scared *adjective*
Filled with fear or terror.   AFRAID.

scaremonger *noun*
One who needlessly alarms others.   ALARMIST.

scarify *verb*
1. To criticize harshly and devastatingly.   1. SLAM *verb.*
2. *Regional.* To fill with fear.   2. FRIGHTEN.

scary *adjective*
Informal. Causing or able to cause fear.   FEARFUL.

scathe *verb*
To criticize harshly and devastatingly.   SLAM *verb.*

scathing *adjective*
So sharp as to cause mental pain.   BITING.

scatological also **scatologic** *adjective*
Offensive to accepted standards of decency.   OBSCENE.

scatter *verb*
1. To separate or cause to separate and go in various   1. **Syns:** dispel, disperse, dissipate.
   directions: *At a command the children scattered and*   **Near-ants:** amass, assemble,
   found hiding places.   concentrate, congregate, convene,
                                                                           crowd.
                                                                           Ant: gather.
2. To extend over a wide area.   2. SPREAD *verb.*
3. To disappear by or as if by rising.   3. LIFT *verb.*

scatterbrained *adjective*
Given to lighthearted silliness.   GIDDY.

scattergood *noun*
A person who spends money or resources wastefully.   WASTREL.

scene *noun*
1. The place where an action or event occurs: *Police*   1. **Syns:** locale, setting, site, stage.
   arrived on the scene shortly after the robbery.

2. That which is or can be seen.

3. The properties, backdrops, and other objects arranged for a dramatic presentation: *When the curtain rose, the audience applauded the beautifully designed scene.*

4. *Slang.* A sphere of activity, study, or interest.

scenery *noun*
The properties, backdrops, and other objects arranged for a dramatic presentation.

scent *noun*
1. The quality of something that may be perceived by the olfactory sense.
2. The sense by which odors are perceived.
3. A sweet or pleasant odor.
4. Evidence of passage left along a course followed by a hunted animal or fugitive.
5. A piece of information useful in a search.

scent *verb*
1. To perceive with the olfactory sense.
2. To fill with a pleasant odor: *Pine resin scented the air about the campsite.*

scented *adjective*
Having a pleasant odor.

schedule *noun*
1. A series of names, words, etc., printed or written down.
2. An organized list of procedures, activities, events, etc.

schedule *verb*
1. To enter on a schedule: *scheduled a dental appointment for next Thursday.*
2. To plan the details or arrangements of.
3. To set the time for (an event or occasion).

scheduled *adjective*
Known to be about to arrive.

schema *noun*
A method for making, doing, or accomplishing something.

scheme *noun*
1. A method for making, doing, or accomplishing something.
2. A secret plan to achieve an evil or illegal end.

scheme *verb*
To work out a secret plan to achieve an evil or illegal end.

scheming *adjective*
1. Coldly planning to achieve selfish aims.
2. Deceitfully clever.

schism *noun*
An interruption in friendly relations.

schismatic *noun*
A person who dissents from the doctrine of an established church.

schismatist *noun*
A person who dissents from the doctrine of an established church.

schlep *verb*
Slang. To move while supporting.

schlocky *adjective*
Slang. Of decidedly inferior quality.

---

2. VIEW *noun.*

3. *Syns:* mise en scène, scenery, set², setting.

4. AREA.

SCENE.

1. SMELL *noun.*

2. SMELL *noun.*

3. FRAGRANCE.

4. TRAIL *noun.*

5. LEAD *noun.*

1. SMELL *verb.*

2. *Syns:* aromatize, perfume.

FRAGRANT.

1. LIST¹ *noun.*

2. PROGRAM.

1. *Syns:* program, slate.

2. ARRANGE.

3. TIME *verb.*

DUE *adjective.*

DESIGN *noun.*

1. DESIGN *noun.*

2. PLOT *noun.*

PLOT *verb.*

1. CALCULATING.

2. ARTFUL.

BREACH *noun.*

SEPARATIST.

SEPARATIST.

CARRY *verb.*

SHODDY.

schmaltz *noun*
Slang. The quality or condition of being affectedly or overly emotional. SENTIMENTALITY.

schmaltzy *adjective*
Slang. Affectedly or extravagantly emotional. SENTIMENTAL.

schmo also **schmoe** *noun*
Slang. One deficient in judgment and good sense. FOOL *noun.*

schmoe *noun* SEE **schmo.**

schmuck *noun*
Slang. One deficient in judgment and good sense. FOOL *noun.*

schnozzle *noun*
Slang. The structure on the human face that contains the nostrils and organs of smell and forms the beginning of the respiratory tract. NOSE *noun.*

scholar *noun*
1. A usu. elderly man noted for wisdom, knowledge, and judgment. **1.** SAGE *noun.*
2. One who is being educated. **2.** STUDENT.

scholarly *adjective*
1. Having or showing profound knowledge and scholarship. **1.** LEARNED.
2. Devoted to study or reading. **2.** STUDIOUS.

scholarship *noun*
Known facts, ideas, and skill that have been imparted. EDUCATION.

scholastic *adjective*
1. Characterized by a narrow concern for book learning and formal rules, without knowledge or experience of practical matters. **1.** PEDANTIC.
2. Having or showing profound knowledge and scholarship. **2.** LEARNED.

scholastic *noun*
Obs. One who is being educated. STUDENT.

schooling *noun*
The act, process, or art of imparting knowledge and skill. EDUCATION.

science *noun*
Known facts, ideas, and skill that have been imparted. EDUCATION.

scilicet *adverb*
That is to say. NAMELY.

scintillate *verb*
To emit light suddenly in rays or sparks. FLASH *verb.*

scintillating *adjective*
Amusing or pleasing because of wit or originality. CLEVER.

scintillation *noun*
Sparkling, brilliant light. GLITTER *noun.*

scion *noun*
One descended directly from the same parents or ancestors. DESCENDANT.

scoff *verb*
To make fun of. RIDICULE *verb.*

scold *verb*
To criticize for a fault or offense. CALL DOWN at **call.**

scold *noun*
A person, esp. a woman, who habitually uses loud, abusive language: *If he came home late, his scold of a wife berated him unmercifully.* ***Syns:*** battle-ax *or* battle-axe, fishwife, fury, harpy, shrew, termagant, virago, vixen, Xanthippe.

scoop *verb*
To make by digging. DIG *verb.*

scoop up *verb*
To take a substance, as liquid, from a container by plunging the hand or a utensil into it. DIP *verb.*

scoop up *verb*   SEE **scoop.**

scoot *verb*
1. To move swiftly.   1. RUSH *verb.*
2. To move swiftly on foot so that both feet leave the   2. RUN *verb.*
   ground during each stride.

scope *noun*
1. Suitable opportunity to accept or allow something.   1. ROOM.
2. An area within which something or someone exists,   2. RANGE *noun.*
   acts, or has influence or power.
3. The ability or power to seize or attain.   3. GRASP *noun.*
4. The extent of one's perception, understanding,   4. KEN.
   knowledge, or vision.

scorch *verb*
1. To undergo or cause to undergo damage by or as if   1. BURN *verb.*
   by fire.
2. To feel or look hot.   2. BURN *verb.*
3. To criticize harshly and devastatingly.   3. SLAM *verb.*

scorch *noun*
Damage that results from burning.   BURN *noun.*

scorching *adjective*
Marked by much heat.   HOT *adjective.*

score *noun*
1. An incision, notch, or slight cut made with or as if 1. *Syns:* scotch, scratch, slash.
   with a knife: *made a score in the maple trunk to let
   the sap run.*
2. The total number of points made by a contestant,   2. *Syn:* tally. —*Idiom* the final count (*or*
   side, or team in a game or contest: *a final score of   result*).
   3–2.*
3. A harbored grievance demanding satisfaction: *We   3. *Syn:* account.
   have an old score to settle.*

score *verb*
1. To gain (a point or points) in a game or contest: 1. *Syns:* notch, post, tally. —*Idioms* bring
   scored three aces in the last set.   home, hang up another, put in one's
                                                            column.
2. *Informal.* To fare well.   2. PROSPER.
3. To succeed in doing.   3. ACCOMPLISH.
4. To evaluate and assign a grade to: *scored the test.* 4. *Syns:* grade, mark.
5. To criticize harshly and devastatingly.   5. SLAM *verb.*

scores *noun*
A very large number of things grouped together.   CROWD *noun.*

scorn *noun*
The feeling of despising.   DESPISAL.

scorn *verb*
To regard with utter contempt and disdain.   DESPISE.

scotch *noun*
An incision, notch, or slight cut made with or as if with SCORE *noun.*
a knife.

Scotch *adjective*
Careful in the use of material resources.   ECONOMICAL.

scoundrel *noun*
A mean, worthless character in a story or play.   HEAVY *noun.*

scour *verb*
1. To make a thorough search of: *I scoured the   1. *Syns:* comb, forage, ransack, rummage,
   bookstores for that novel.*   shake down (*Informal*). —*Idioms* beat
                                                            the bushes, leave no avenue
                                                            unexplored, leave no stone unturned,
                                                            look high and low, look up and down,
                                                            search the high heavens, turn inside
                                                            out, turn upside-down.
                                                            Near-syns: ferret, finecomb, rake, rout,
                                                            search, seek.

2. To move swiftly.   **2.** RUSH *verb.*
3. To rub hard in order to clean.   **3.** SCRUB.
4. To remove (an outer layer or adherent matter) by   **4.** SCRAPE *verb.*
rubbing a surface with considerable pressure.

scourge *noun*
A cause of suffering or harm.   CURSE *noun.*

  scourge *verb*
  1. To bring great harm or suffering to.   **1.** AFFLICT.
  2. To criticize harshly and devastatingly.   **2.** SLAM *verb.*

scout[1] *verb*
To go into or through for the purpose of making   EXPLORE.
discoveries or acquiring information.

scout[2] *verb*
  1. To regard with utter contempt and disdain. **1.** DESPISE.
  2. To make fun of.   **2.** RIDICULE *verb.*

scowl *noun*
  1. The act of wrinkling the brow, as in thought,   **1.** FROWN *noun.*
  puzzlement, or displeasure.
  2. A fixed, angry stare.   **2.** GLARE *noun.*

  scowl *verb*
  1. To wrinkle one's brow, as in thought, puzzlement, or   **1.** FROWN *verb.*
  displeasure.
  2. To stare fixedly and angrily.   **2.** GLARE *verb.*

scram *verb*
Slang. To leave hastily.   RUN *verb.*

scramble *verb*
  1. To move or climb hurriedly, esp. on all fours: **1.** *Syn:* clamber.
  scrambled over the hills to safety.
  2. To put into total disorder.   **2.** CONFUSE.
  3. To mix together so as to change the order of   **3.** SHUFFLE.
  arrangement.

  scramble *noun*
  A lack of order or regular arrangement.   DISORDER *noun.*

scrap[1] *noun*
  1. A tiny amount.   **1.** BIT[1].
  2. Residual matter.   **2.** END *noun.*

  scrap *verb*
  To let go or get rid of as being no longer of use, value,   DISCARD.
  etc.

scrap[2] *noun*
  1. A physical conflict involving two or more. **1.** FIGHT *noun.*
  2. The power or will to fight.   **2.** FIGHT *noun.*

scrape *verb*
  1. To remove (an outer layer or adherent matter) by   **1.** *Syns:* scour, scrub.
  rubbing a surface with considerable pressure: *scrape*
  the old paint off the bench.
  2. To bring or come into sliding, abrasive contact, often   **2.** *Syns:* grate, rasp, scratch.
  with a harsh, grating sound: *a chair scraping along*
  the floor.
  3. To be severely sparing in order to economize.   **3.** SCRIMP.
  4. To manage with difficulty or so as to barely escape   **4.** *Syn:* shave. —*Idiom* get through on a
  failure: *scraped through college.*   wing and a prayer.

  scrape *noun*
  Slang. A difficult, embarrassing situation.   PREDICAMENT.

scrappy *adjective*
  1. *Informal.* Having or showing an eagerness to fight.   **1.** BELLIGERENT.
  2. Given to arguing.   **2.** ARGUMENTATIVE.

scratch *noun*
  1. An incision, notch, or slight cut made with or as if   **1.** SCORE *noun.*
  with a knife.

2. *Slang.* Something, as coins, printed bills, etc., used as a medium of exchange.

2. MONEY.

scratch *verb*

1. To bring or come into sliding, abrasive contact, often with a harsh, grating sound.

1. SCRAPE *verb*.

2. *Informal.* To decide not to go ahead with (something previously arranged).

2. CANCEL.

scratch out *verb*

To remove or invalidate by or as if by running a line through or wiping clean.

CANCEL.

scratch out *verb*

SEE **scratch**.

scrawny *adjective*

Having little flesh or fat on the body.

THIN *adjective*.

screak also **screek** *noun*

A long, loud, piercing cry or sound.

SCREAM *noun*.

screak also **screek** *verb*

To utter a long, loud, piercing cry, as of pain or fright.

SCREAM *verb*.

scream *verb*

1. To utter a long, loud, piercing cry, as of pain or fright: *screamed when the bus hit the light pole.*

1. *Syns:* screak (*also* screek), screech, shriek, shrill.
Near-syns: caterwaul, cry, bellow, howl, wail.

2. To have or produce a blatantly startling effect: *His long hair and loud clothes screamed his nonconformity.*

2. *Syns:* blare, blaze[1], shout, shriek.

scream *noun*

1. A long, loud, piercing cry or sound: *gave a scream of terror.*

1. *Syns:* screak (*also* screek), screech, shriek, shrill.

2. *Slang.* Something or someone uproariously funny or absurd: *a comedy that was a real scream.*

2. *Syns:* absurdity, gas (*Slang*), hoot (*Slang*), howl (*Slang*), joke, laugh (*Informal*), panic (*Slang*), riot (*Slang*), screech (*Slang*). —*Idiom* a laugh a minute.

screaming *adjective*

Slang. Extremely funny.

PRICELESS.

screech *noun*

1. A long, loud, piercing cry or sound.

1. SCREAM *noun*.

2. *Slang.* Something or someone uproariously funny or absurd.

2. SCREAM *noun*.

screech *verb*

To utter a long, loud, piercing cry, as of pain or fright.

SCREAM *verb*.

screek *noun & verb*

SEE **screak**.

screen *verb*

1. To cut off from sight.

1. BLOCK OUT at **block**.

2. To shelter, esp. from light.

2. SHADE *verb*.

3. To examine (material) and remove parts considered harmful or improper for publication or transmission.

3. CENSOR.

screened *adjective*

Concealed from view.

SECLUDED.

screwball *noun*

An insanely foolish or strange person.

CRACKPOT.

screw-up *noun*

SEE **screw up**.

screw up *verb*

Slang. To harm irreparably through inept handling; make a mess of.

BOTCH.

screw-up *noun*

Slang. A stupid, clumsy mistake.

BLUNDER *noun*.

screwy *adjective*

Slang. Afflicted with or exhibiting irrationality and mental unsoundness.

INSANE.

scribe *verb*
To form letters, characters, or words on a surface with an instrument.   WRITE.

scrimp *verb*
To be severely sparing in order to economize: *scrimped for years to buy the house.*   **Syns:** pinch, scrape, skimp, stint. —*Idioms* pinch pennies, tighten one's belt, tighten the screws.

scriptural *adjective*
Of or pertaining to representation by means of writing.   GRAPHIC.

Scrooge *noun*
A stingy person.   MISER.

scrub *verb*
1. To rub hard in order to clean: *scrubbing the bathtub.*   1. **Syn:** scour.
2. To remove (an outer layer or adherent matter) by rubbing a surface with considerable pressure.   2. SCRAPE *verb*.
3. *Informal.* To decide not to go ahead with (something previously arranged).   3. CANCEL.

scrubby *adjective*
Showing signs of wear and tear or neglect.   SHABBY.

scruffy *adjective*
Showing signs of wear and tear or neglect.   SHABBY.

scrumptious *adjective*
Slang. Highly pleasing, esp. to the sense of taste.   DELICIOUS.

scrunch *verb*
To incline the body.   STOOP.

scruple *noun*
1. A tiny amount.   1. BIT[1].
2. A feeling of uncertainty about the fitness or correctness of an action.   2. QUALM.

scrupulous *adjective*
Showing or marked by attentiveness to all aspects or details.   CAREFUL.

scrupulousness *noun*
Attentiveness to detail.   THOROUGHNESS.

scrutinize *verb*
1. To look at carefully or critically.   1. EXAMINE.
2. To look at or on attentively or carefully.   2. WATCH *verb*.

scrutiny *noun*
1. The act of examining carefully.   1. EXAMINATION.
2. The act of observing, often for an extended time.   2. WATCH *noun*.

scuff *verb*
To drag (the feet) along the floor or ground while walking.   SHUFFLE.

scuffle *noun*
A physical conflict involving two or more.   FIGHT *noun*.
  scuffle *verb*
  1. To drag (the feet) along the floor or ground while walking.   1. SHUFFLE.
  2. To contend with an opponent, esp. by attempting to throw him.   2. WRESTLE.

scum *noun*
A group of persons regarded as the lowest class.   TRASH[1] *noun*.

scurrility *noun*
Harsh, often insulting language.   VITUPERATION.

scurrilous *adjective*
1. Of, relating to, or characterized by verbal abuse.   1. ABUSIVE.
2. Offensive to accepted standards of decency.   2. OBSCENE.

scurry *verb*
1. To move swiftly on foot so that both feet leave the ground during each stride.   1. RUN *verb*.
2. To move swiftly.   2. RUSH *verb*.

scuttlebutt *noun*
Slang. Idle, often sensational and groundless talk about others.

GOSSIP *noun.*

sea dog *noun*
Slang. A person engaged in sailing or working on a ship.

SAILOR.

seafarer *noun*
A person engaged in sailing or working on a ship.

SAILOR.

seam *noun*
A point or position at which two or more things are joined.

JOINT *noun.*

seaman *noun*
A person engaged in sailing or working on a ship.

SAILOR.

sear *verb*
1. To undergo or cause to undergo damage by or as if by fire.
2. To make or become no longer fresh or shapely because of loss of moisture.

1. BURN *verb.*

2. DRY UP at **dry.**

sear *noun*
Damage that results from burning.

BURN *noun.*

search *verb*
1. To examine the person or personal effects of in order to find something lost or concealed: *Customs inspectors searched him for narcotics.*
2. To try to find.

1. *Syns:* fan[1] (*Slang*), frisk, inspect, shake down (*Informal*). —*Idiom* give the once-over to.
2. SEEK.

search *noun*
A thorough search of a place or person.

SHAKEDOWN at **shake down.**

season *verb*
1. To impart flavor to.
2. To make resistant to hardship, esp. through continued exposure.

1. FLAVOR *verb.*
2. HARDEN.

season *noun*
1. A specific length of time characterized by the occurrence of certain conditions or events.
2. A span designated for a given activity.
3. A regular period of sexual excitement in female mammals.

1. PERIOD.

2. TIME *noun.*
3. HEAT *noun.*

seasonable *adjective*
Occurring at a fitting or advantageous time.

OPPORTUNE.

seasoned *adjective*
Skilled or knowledgeable through long practice.

EXPERIENCED.

seasoning *noun*
A substance that imparts taste.

FLAVORING.

seat *noun*
1. The part of one's back on which one rests in sitting.
2. The lowest or supporting part or structure.
3. A place of concentrated activity, influence, or importance.

1. BOTTOM *noun.*
2. BASE[1] *noun.*
3. CENTER *noun.*

seat *verb*
1. To cause to take a sitting position: *Seat yourself over there.*
2. To place securely in a position or condition.
3. To take or serve as the basis for.

1. *Syns:* sit, sit down.

2. ESTABLISH.
3. BASE[1] *verb.*

secede *verb*
To break away or withdraw from membership in an association or federation: *seceded from the party because of differences over fundamental issues.*

Syns: splinter (off), split.

seclude *verb*
1. To put into solitude: *a monk who secluded himself from all worldly influences.*
2. To set apart from a group.

1. *Syns:* cloister, recluse (*Obs.*), sequester, sequestrate.
2. ISOLATE *verb.*

secluded *adjective*
1. Solitary and shut off from society: *led a secluded life in a convent.*

2. Concealed from view: *a secluded garden surrounded by high walls.*
3. Far from centers of human population.

secluse *adjective*
Solitary and shut off from society.

seclusion *noun*
The act of secluding or the state of being secluded: *lived a life of seclusion after her husband's death.*

second¹ *noun*
A very brief time.

second² *noun*
A person who holds a position auxiliary to another and assumes some of his responsibilities.

secondary *adjective*
1. Of subordinate standing or importance.
2. In a position of subordination.
3. Stemming from an original source.

secondary *noun*
One belonging to a lower class or rank.

second-class *adjective*
Of mediocre quality.

second-rate *adjective*
Of mediocre quality.

secrecy *noun*
The habit, practice, or policy of keeping secrets: *believed that secrecy is a key ingredient to foreign-policy successes.*

secret *adjective*
1. Existing or operating in a way so as to ensure complete concealment and confidentiality: *secret counterintelligence operations; secret agents.*

2. Concealed from view.

secrete *verb*
To put or keep out of sight.

secretive *adjective*
Trickily secret.

secretiveness *noun*
The habit, practice, or policy of keeping secrets.

secretly *adverb*
In a secret way: *secretly planned to attack the smaller country.*

secretness *noun*
The habit, practice, or policy of keeping secrets.

sect *noun*
1. A system of religious belief.

---

1. **Syns:** cloistered, hermetic, recluse, secluse, sequestered, sequestrate (*Archaic*).
   Near-syns: alone, isolated, hidden, private, retired, withdrawn.
2. **Syns:** hidden, screened, secret, sequestered.
3. REMOTE.

SECLUDED.

Syns: reclusion, retirement, sequestration.
Near-syns: isolation, reclusiveness, separation, withdrawal.

FLASH *noun.*

ASSISTANT.

1. MINOR *adjective.*
2. SUBORDINATE *adjective.*
3. DERIVATIVE *adjective.*

SUBORDINATE *noun.*

INFERIOR.

INFERIOR.

Syns: concealment, huggermugger *or* hugger-mugger, hugger-muggery, secretiveness, secretness, wraps.

1. **Syns.** clandestine, cloak-and-dagger, covert, huggermugger *or* hugger-mugger, hush-hush (*Informal*), sub-rosa, undercover.
   Near-syns: concealed, hidden; classified, confidential, restricted, top-secret; surreptitious, underhanded.
   Ants: open, public.
2. SECLUDED.

HIDE¹ *verb.*

SLY *adjective.*

SECRECY.

Syns: clandestinely, huggermugger *or* hugger-mugger. —*Idioms* by stealth, on the sly, under cover.
Near-ants: forthrightly, plainly, publicly, straightforwardly; manifestly, overtly.
Ant: openly.

SECRECY.

1. RELIGION.

2. Those who accept and practice a particular religious belief.

sectary *noun*
1. One zealously devoted to a religion.
2. A person who dissents from the doctrine of an established church.

section *noun*
1. A particular subdivision of a written work: *The book contained a long section on controlled narcotics.*
2. One of the parts into which something is divided.
3. A part severed from a whole.
4. A thin piece, esp. of tissue, suitable for microscopic examination: *frozen sections of cancerous liver.*

section *verb*
To make a division into parts, sections, or branches.

sectional *adjective*
Pertaining to or restricted to a particular territory.

secular *adjective*
1. Pertaining to or characteristic of the earth or of human life on earth.
2. Not religious in subject matter, form, or use.

secure *verb*
1. To give a promise of payment to (a creditor): *secure a loan.*
2. To keep safe from danger, attack, or harm.
3. To make secure.
4. To join one thing to another.
5. To make fast or firmly fixed by means of a cord, rope, etc.
6. To render certain.
7. To come into possession of.
8. To gain possession of, esp. after a struggle or chase.
9. To be the cause of.

secure *adjective*
1. Affording protection.
2. Having a firm belief in one's own powers.
3. Firmly settled or positioned.
4. Persistently holding to something.
5. Not easily moved or shaken.

security *noun*
1. The quality or state of being safe.
2. Reliability in withstanding pressure, force, or stress.
3. The act or a means of defending.
4. Something given to guarantee the repayment of a loan or the fulfillment of an obligation.

sedate *adjective*
Full of or marked by dignity and seriousness.

sediment *noun*
Matter that settles on a bottom or collects on a surface by a natural process.

sedition *noun*
Willful violation of allegiance to one's country.

seditious *adjective*
Involving or constituting treason.

seditiousness *noun*
Willful violation of allegiance to one's country.

seduce *verb*
1. To lure or persuade into a sexual relationship: *a young girl seduced by a notorious roué.*

---

2. FAITH.

1. DEVOTEE.
2. SEPARATIST.

1. *Syns:* part, passage, segment.

2. DIVISION.
3. CUT *noun.*
4. *Syn:* slice.

DIVIDE.

TERRITORIAL.

1. EARTHLY.

2. PROFANE.

1. *Syns:* guarantee, pledge.

2. DEFEND.
3. FASTEN.
4. ATTACH.
5. TIE *verb.*

6. GUARANTEE *verb.*
7. GET *verb.*
8. TAKE *verb.*
9. CAUSE *verb.*

1. SAFE.
2. CONFIDENT.
3. SURE.
4. TIGHT *adjective.*
5. SOUND².

1. SAFETY.
2. STABILITY.
3. DEFENSE.
4. PAWN¹ *noun.*

GRAVE².

DEPOSIT *noun.*

TREASON.

TREASONOUS.

TREASON.

1. *Syns:* debauch, undo.

2. To beguile or draw into a wrong or foolish course of action: *was seduced into gambling by the vision of easy money.*

2. *Syns:* allure, entice, inveigle, lure, tempt.
Near-syns: coax, deceive, delude, mislead, tease; bait, decoy.

seducer *noun*
1. One that seduces: *Money is a well-known seducer.*

1. *Syns:* charmer, enticer, inveigler, tempter.

2. A man who seduces women: *a seducer without a conscience.*

2. *Syns:* debaucher, Don Juan.

seduction *noun*
1. The act or an instance of seducing sexually: *shot the man for the seduction of his sister.*

1. *Syns:* debauching, debauchment (*Obs.*).

2. Something that attracts, esp. with the promise of pleasure or reward.

2. LURE *noun.*

seductive *adjective*
Tending to seduce: *the seductive powers of some women; the seductive pull of money.*

Syns: alluring, bewitching, enticing, inviting, siren, sirenic or sirenical, tempting, witching.

seductress *noun*
A usu. unscrupulous woman who seduces or exploits men: *Mata Hari was a famous seductress.*

Syns: enchantress, femme fatale (*French*), siren, temptress, vamp, witch (*Informal*).

sedulous *adjective*
Characterized by steady attention and effort.

DILIGENT.

sedulousness *noun*
Steady attention and effort, as to one's occupation.

DILIGENCE.

see *verb*
1. To apprehend (images) by use of the eyes: *I could see the sailboat clearly. She sees very well even at ninety.*

1. *Syns:* behold, ken (*Archaic*), perceive.

2. To form mental images of.

2. IMAGINE.

3. To perceive with a special effort of the senses or the mind.

3. NOTICE *verb.*

4. To perceive and recognize the meaning of.

4. UNDERSTAND.

5. To know in advance.

5. FORESEE.

6. To participate in or partake of personally.

6. EXPERIENCE *verb.*

7. To be sure that.

7. LOOK *verb.*

8. To be together socially on a regular basis: *He has been seeing her for a year now.*

8. *Syns:* date, take out (*Informal*).

9. To go to or seek out the company of in order to socialize.

9. VISIT *verb.*

see to *verb*
To have the care and supervision of.

TEND[2].

seeable *adjective*
Capable of being seen.

VISIBLE.

seed *noun*
1. A fertilized plant ovule capable of germinating: *wheat and barley seeds.*

1. *Syns:* kernel, pip, pit, stone.

2. A propagative part of a plant: *looked at the tiny seeds on the backs of the fronds.*

2. *Syn:* spore.

3. A source of further growth and development.

3. GERM.

4. A group consisting of those descended directly from the same parents or ancestors.

4. PROGENY.

5. One's ancestors or their character.

5. ANCESTRY.

6. The male fluid of fertilization: *The seed of a prize bull can be sold for a high price.*

6. *Syns:* semen, sperm.

seed *verb*
To put (seeds) into the ground for growth: *seed a lawn.*

Syns: pitch, plant, sow.

seedtime *noun*
The season of the year during which the weather becomes warmer and plants revive.

SPRING *noun.*

seedy *adjective*
Showing signs of wear and tear or neglect.   SHABBY.

seeing *noun*
The faculty of seeing.   VISION.

seek *verb*
  1. To try to find: *sought the lost shoe; seeking just the*   **1.** *Syns:* cast about (for), hunt up, look
      right person for the job.   for, quest, search (for). —*Idiom* be in
                                                                              search of.
                                                                            Near-syns: delve, dig, fish, nose, root,
                                                                              smell out, sniff.
  2. To make an attempt to do or make.   **2.** ATTEMPT *verb*.
  3. To strive toward a goal.   **3.** AIM *verb*.

seeker *noun*
A person who applies for or seeks a job or position.   APPLICANT.

seem *verb*
To have the appearance of.   APPEAR.

seeming *adjective*
Appearing as such but not necessarily so.   APPARENT.

seemingly *adverb*
On the surface.   APPARENTLY.

seemliness *noun*
Conformity to recognized standards, as of conduct or   DECENCY.
appearance.

seemly *adjective*
Conforming to accepted standards.   CORRECT *adjective*.

seep *verb*
To flow or leak out slowly.   OOZE.

seer[1] *noun*
A person who foretells future events by or as if by   PROPHET.
supernatural means.

seer[2] *noun*
Someone who sees something occur.   WITNESS *noun*.

seesaw *verb*
To lean suddenly, unsteadily, and erratically from the   LURCH *verb*.
vertical axis.

seethe *verb*
  1. To be in a state of emotional or mental turmoil.   **1.** BOIL *verb*.
  2. *Archaic.* To cook (food) in liquid heated to the point   **2.** BOIL *verb*.
      of steaming.
  3. To be or become angry.   **3.** ANGER *verb*.
  4. To saturate (something) with a liquid.   **4.** STEEP[2].

seething *adjective*
Feeling or showing anger.   ANGRY.

see-through *adjective*
Admitting light so that objects beyond can be seen.   TRANSPARENT.

see to *verb*   SEE **see**.

segment *noun*
  1. One of the parts into which something is divided.   **1.** DIVISION.
  2. A part severed from a whole.   **2.** CUT *noun*.
  3. A particular subdivision of a written work.   **3.** SECTION *noun*.

  segment *verb*
To make a division into parts, sections, or branches.   DIVIDE.

segregate *verb*
To set apart from a group.   ISOLATE *verb*.

segregated *adjective*
Excluding or unavailable to certain minorities.   RESTRICTED.

segregation *noun*
  1. The policy or practice of excluding a minority group   **1.** *Syns:* apartheid, separatism.
      from full freedom or participation in a society: *the*
      evils of segregation.
  2. The act or process of isolating.   **2.** ISOLATION.

seize *verb*
1. To take quick and forcible possession of: *seized and nationalized all foreign industry; seized the smugglers' boat and impounded it.*
2. To get hold of (something moving).
3. To take firmly with the hand and maintain a hold on.
4. To have a sudden, overwhelming effect on: *was seized with a sneezing fit.*
5. To take into custody as a prisoner.
6. To lay claim to for oneself or as one's right.

1. *Syns:* commandeer, confiscate, expropriate, grab, snatch. —*Idiom* help oneself to.
2. CATCH *verb.*
3. GRASP *verb.*
4. *Syns:* catch, strike, take.
5. ARREST *verb.*
6. ASSUME.

seizure *noun*
1. The act of taking quick and forcible possession of: *seizure by customs agents of the illicit drug shipment; seizure of all personal property in a communist state.*
2. The act of catching, esp. a sudden taking and holding.
3. A seizing and holding by law.
4. The act of taking something for oneself.
5. A sudden and often acute manifestation of a disease: *has frequent seizures of gout.*

1. *Syns:* commandeering, confiscation, expropriation.
2. CATCH *noun.*
3. ARREST *noun.*
4. USURPATION.
5. *Syns:* access, attack, fit, spell.

seldom *adverb*
At rare intervals.

INFREQUENTLY.

select *verb*
To make a choice from a number of alternatives.

CHOOSE.

select *noun*
One that is selected.

ELECT *noun.*

select *adjective*
1. Singled out in preference: *Only a select group of Washington insiders knew the secret.*

1. *Syns:* choice, chosen, elect, exclusive. *Near-syns:* best, elite, favored, favorite, pick, selected. *Ant:* run-of-the-mill.

2. Of fine quality.
3. Able to recognize small differences or draw fine distinctions.

2. CHOICE *adjective.*
3. DISCRIMINATING.

selection *noun*
The act of choosing.

CHOICE *noun.*

selective *adjective*
Able to recognize small differences or draw fine distinctions.

DISCRIMINATING.

selectiveness *noun*
The ability to distinguish, esp. to recognize small differences or draw fine distinctions.

DISCRIMINATION.

selectivity *noun*
The ability to distinguish, esp. to recognize small differences or draw fine distinctions.

DISCRIMINATION.

self *noun*
An individual's awareness of what constitutes his or her essential nature and distinguishes him or her from all others: *a strong sense of self.*

Syn: ego.

self-absorbed *adjective*
Concerned only with oneself.

EGOTISTICAL.

self-absorption *noun*
Concern only for oneself.

EGOISM.

self-assurance *noun*
A firm belief in one's own powers.

CONFIDENCE.

self-assured *adjective*
Having a firm belief in one's own powers.

CONFIDENT.

self-centered *adjective*
Concerned only with oneself.

EGOTISTICAL.

self-centeredness *noun*
Concern only for oneself.   EGOISM.
self-confidence *noun*
A firm belief in one's own powers.   CONFIDENCE.
self-confident *adjective*
Having a firm belief in one's own powers.   CONFIDENT.
self-contained *adjective*
Free from the influence, guidance, or control of others.   INDEPENDENT.
self-control *noun*
The keeping of one's thoughts and emotions to oneself.   RESERVE *noun.*
self-controlled *adjective*
Tending to keep one's thoughts and emotions to oneself.   RESERVED.
self-denying *adjective*
Without concern for oneself.   SELFLESS.
self-determination *noun*
The capacity to manage one's own affairs, make one's   INDEPENDENCE.
own judgments, and provide for oneself.
self-effacing *adjective*
Reticent or reserved in manner.   MODEST.
self-esteem *noun*
A sense of one's own dignity or worth.   PRIDE *noun.*
self-esteeming *adjective*
Properly valuing oneself, one's honor, or one's dignity.   PROUD.
self-forgetful *adjective*
Without concern for oneself.   SELFLESS.
self-forgetting *adjective*
Without concern for oneself.   SELFLESS.
selfhood *noun*
The set of behavioral or personal characteristics by   IDENTITY.
which an individual is recognizable.
self-importance *noun*
An exaggerated belief in one's own importance.   EGOTISM.
self-important *adjective*
Characterized by an exaggerated show of dignity or   POMPOUS.
self-importance.
selfish *adjective*
Concerned only with oneself.   EGOTISTICAL.
selfishness *noun*
Concern only for oneself.   EGOISM.
selfless *adjective*
Without concern for oneself: *selfless devotion to duty.*   ***Syns:*** self-denying, self-forgetful, self-
                                                                     forgetting, unselfish.
                                                                     Near-syns: altruistic, elevated, generous,
                                                                     kind, high-minded, self-sacrificing.
                                                                     Ant: selfish.

self-possessed *adjective*
Having a firm belief in one's own powers.   CONFIDENT.
self-possession *noun*
1. A stable, calm state of the emotions.   **1.** BALANCE *noun.*
2. A firm belief in one's own powers.   **2.** CONFIDENCE.
self-regard *noun*
A sense of one's own dignity or worth.   PRIDE *noun.*
self-reliance *noun*
The capacity to manage one's own affairs, make one's   INDEPENDENCE.
own judgments, and provide for oneself.
self-reliant *adjective*
Free from the influence, guidance, or control of others.   INDEPENDENT.
self-respect *noun*
A sense of one's own dignity or worth.   PRIDE *noun.*
self-respecting *adjective*
Properly valuing oneself, one's honor, or one's dignity.   PROUD.

self-restrained *adjective*
Tending to keep one's thoughts and emotions to oneself. RESERVED.

self-restraint *noun*
The keeping of one's thoughts and emotions to oneself. RESERVE *noun*.

selfsame *adjective*
Being one and not another or others; not different in SAME.
nature or identity.

selfsameness *noun*
The quality or condition of being exactly the same as SAMENESS.
something else.

self-seeking *adjective*
Concerned only with oneself. EGOTISTICAL.

self-serving *adjective*
Concerned only with oneself. EGOTISTICAL.

self-sufficiency *noun*
The capacity to manage one's own affairs, make one's INDEPENDENCE.
own judgments, and provide for oneself.

self-sufficient *adjective*
1. Free from the influence, guidance, or control of 1. INDEPENDENT.
   others.
2. Able to support oneself financially. 2. INDEPENDENT.

self-supporting *adjective*
Able to support oneself financially. INDEPENDENT.

sell *noun*
1. Market appeal: *a product with a lot of sell to it*. 1. *Syns:* marketability, marketableness,
                                                           salability, salableness.
2. *Slang*. An action meant to deceive. 2. DECEPTION.

sell *verb*
1. To offer for sale: *We don't sell lawn mowers*. 1. *Syns:* deal in, handle, market,
                                                      merchandise, merchant, peddle, retail,
                                                      trade in, vend.
2. To achieve a certain price. 2. BRING.
3. To succeed in causing (a person) to act in a certain 3. PERSUADE.
   way.

sell for *verb*
1. To achieve a certain price. 1. BRING.
2. To require a specified price. 2. COST *verb*.

sell off *verb*
To get rid of completely by selling, esp. in quantity or *Syns:* close out, dump, sell out, sell up
at discount: *sold off all the water-damaged stock*. (*Brit.*), unload.

sell up *verb*
Brit. To get rid of completely by selling, esp. in SELL OFF.
quantity or at discount.

seller *noun*
One who sells: *sellers of books*. *Syns:* sales clerk, salesperson.

sell for *verb* SEE **sell.**
sell off *verb* SEE **sell.**
sellout *noun* SEE **sell out.**

sell out *verb*
1. To get rid of completely by selling, esp. in quantity 1. SELL OFF at **sell.**
   or at discount.
2. *Slang*. To be treacherous. 2. BETRAY.

sellout *noun*
Slang. An act of betraying. BETRAYAL.

sell up *verb* SEE **sell.**

semaphore *verb*
To communicate by means of such devices as lights or SIGNAL *verb*.
signs.

semblance *noun*
1. A deceptive outward appearance. 1. FAÇADE.
2. A slight amount. 2. SHADE *noun*.

semblant *adjective*
Appearing as such but not necessarily so.   APPARENT.

semen *noun*
The male fluid of fertilization.   SEED *noun.*

seminar *noun*
A meeting for the exchange of views.   CONFERENCE.

sempiternal *adjective*
Without beginning or end.   ETERNAL.

sempiternity *noun*
The totality of time without beginning or end.   ETERNITY.

send *verb*
1. To cause (something) to be conveyed to a   1. *Syns:* address, consign, dispatch,
   destination: *sent the package by air to Europe.*   forward, route, ship, transmit.
2. To direct (a person) elsewhere for help, information, 2. REFER.
   etc.
3. *Slang.* To move or excite greatly.   3. CARRY AWAY at **carry.**

send away *verb*
To direct or allow to leave.   DISMISS.

send for *verb*
To demand to appear, come, or assemble.   CALL *verb.*

send forth *verb*
To discharge material, as vapor or fumes, usu. suddenly   EMIT.
and violently.

send up *verb*
Informal. To place officially in confinement.   COMMIT.

send away *verb*   SEE **send.**
send for *verb*   SEE **send.**
send forth *verb*   SEE **send.**
send up *verb*   SEE **send.**

senectitude *noun*
Old age.   AGE *noun.*

senesce *verb*
To grow old.   AGE *verb.*

senescence *noun*
Old age.   AGE *noun.*

senile *adjective*
Exhibiting the mental and physical deterioration often   *Syns:* doddering, doddery, doting.
accompanying old age: *senile patients unable to care for* *Near-syns:* aged, aging, enfeebled, feeble,
themselves.   weak.

senility *noun*
The condition of being senile: *Old age does not*   *Syn:* dotage.
necessarily mean senility.

senior *adjective*
1. Of greater age than another: *The senior Mr. Walker* 1. *Syns:* elder, older.
   objected to his son's plans.
2. Far along in life or time.   2. OLD.
3. Being at a rank above another.   3. HIGHER.

senior *noun*
1. A person who is older than another: *She is my*   1. *Syn:* elder.
   senior by six years.
2. An elderly person: *seniors still able to make*   2. *Syns:* ancient, elder, golden ager,
   substantial contributions to society.   oldster (*Informal*), old-timer
                                                          (*Informal*), senior citizen.

3. One who stands above another in rank.   3. SUPERIOR *noun.*

senior citizen *noun*
An elderly person.   SENIOR *noun.*

sensation *noun*
1. The capacity for or an act of responding to a   1. *Syns:* feeling, sense, sensibility,
   stimulus: *lost all sensation in the arm; a sensation of*   sensitivity, sentiment (*Rare*).
   vague uneasiness.   *Near-syns:* consciousness, perception,
                                                          response, sensitiveness.

2. A condition of intense public interest or excitement: *The Watergate revelations created an international sensation.*

3. One that evokes great surprise and admiration.

sensational *adjective*
1. Of or pertaining to sensation or the senses: *sensational response to a stimulus.*
2. Particularly excellent.
3. Suggesting drama or a stage performance, as in emotionality or suspense.

sensatory *adjective*
1. Of or pertaining to sensation or the senses.
2. Transmitting impulses from sense organs to nerve centers.

sense *noun*
1. What is sound or reasonable: *There's no sense in waiting any longer.*
2. The capacity for or an act of responding to a stimulus.
3. The faculty of thinking, reasoning, and acquiring and applying knowledge.
4. The ability to make sensible decisions.
5. A healthy mental state.
6. That which is signified by a word or expression.

sense *verb*
1. To be intuitively aware of.
2. *Informal.* To perceive and recognize the meaning of.
3. To view in a certain way.

senseless *adjective*
1. Displaying a complete lack of forethought and good sense.
2. Lacking rational direction or purpose.
3. Lacking consciousness.

senselessness *noun*
Foolish behavior.

senses *noun*
A healthy mental state.

sensibility *noun*
1. The capacity for or an act of responding to a stimulus.
2. The quality or condition of being emotionally and intuitively sensitive.

sensible *adjective*
1. Composed of or relating to things that occupy space and can be perceived by the senses.
2. Able to receive and respond to external stimuli.
3. Marked by comprehension, cognizance, and perception.
4. Consistent with reason and intellect.
5. Possessing, proceeding from, or exhibiting good judgment and prudence.

sensical *adjective*
Possessing, proceeding from, or exhibiting good judgment and prudence.

sensile *adjective*
Able to receive and respond to external stimuli.

sensitive *adjective*
1. Able to receive and respond to external stimuli: *Frostbitten tissue always remains especially sensitive to the cold. She is a sensitive person, attuned to the moods of others.*

---

2. **Syns:** brouhaha, hoo-hah (*Slang*), stir[1], to-do (*Informal*), uproar.

3. MARVEL *noun.*

1. **Syns:** sensatory, sensitive, sensory (*also* sensorial), sensual.
2. MARVELOUS.
3. DRAMATIC.

1. SENSATIONAL.

2. SENSORY.

1. **Syns:** logic, rationale, rationality, reason. —*Idiom* rhyme or reason.
2. SENSATION.

3. INTELLIGENCE.

4. COMMON SENSE.
5. SANITY.
6. MEANING.

1. PERCEIVE.
2. UNDERSTAND.
3. FEEL *verb.*

1. MINDLESS.

2. MINDLESS.
3. UNCONSCIOUS.

FOOLISHNESS.

SANITY.

1. SENSATION.

2. SENSITIVENESS.

1. PHYSICAL.

2. SENSITIVE.
3. AWARE.

4. LOGICAL.
5. SANE.

SANE.

SENSITIVE.

1. **Syns:** impressible, impressionable, responsive, sensible, sensile, sentient, susceptible, susceptive.

2. Of or pertaining to sensation or the senses.
3. Readily stirred by emotion.
4. Showing sensitivity and skill in dealing with others.
5. Requiring great tact or skill.
6. Possessing or displaying perceptions of great
   accuracy and sensitivity.

2. SENSATIONAL.
3. EMOTIONAL.
4. DELICATE.
5. DELICATE.
6. ACUTE.

sensitiveness *noun*
The quality or condition of being emotionally and
intuitively sensitive: *fine-tuned sensitiveness to the
unspoken needs of others.*

Syns: feeling, sensibility, sensitivity.

sensitivity *noun*
1. The quality or condition of being emotionally and
   intuitively sensitive.
2. The capacity for or an act of responding to a
   stimulus.

1. SENSITIVENESS.

2. SENSATION.

sensorial *adjective*

SEE **sensory.**

sensory also **sensorial** *adjective*
1. Transmitting impulses from sense organs to nerve
   centers: *sensory nerve bundles.*
2. Of or pertaining to sensation or the senses.

1. *Syns:* afferent, receptive (*Physiol.*),
   sensatory.
2. SENSATIONAL.

sensual *adjective*
1. Suggesting sexuality: *a sensual belly dance.*

2. Relating to the desires and appetites of the body.
3. Of or preoccupied with material rather than
   spiritual or intellectual things.
4. Pertaining to, suggestive of, or appealing to sense
   gratification.
5. Of or pertaining to sensation or the senses.

1. *Syns:* sexual, sexy (*Slang*), suggestive,
   voluptuous.
2. PHYSICAL.
3. MATERIALISTIC.

4. SENSUOUS.

5. SENSATIONAL.

sensualism *noun*
The quality or condition of being sensuous.

SENSUOUSNESS.

sensualistic *adjective*
Pertaining to, suggestive of, or appealing to sense
gratification.

SENSUOUS.

sensuality *noun*
1. The quality or condition of being sensual: *the
   blatant sensuality of the stripper's movements.*
2. A preoccupation with the body and satisfaction of its
   desires.
3. The quality or condition of being sensuous.

1. *Syns:* sexiness (*Slang*), sexuality,
   suggestiveness, voluptuousness.
2. PHYSICALITY.

3. SENSUOUSNESS.

sensuous *adjective*
Pertaining to, suggestive of, or appealing to sense
gratification: *took sensuous pleasure in the gourmet
dinner; rich, sensuous velvet.*

Syns: epicurean, sensual, sensualistic,
voluptuary, voluptuous.

sensuousness *noun*
The quality or condition of being sensuous: *the
sensuousness of the music.*

Syns: sensualism, sensuality,
voluptuousness.

sentence *noun*
A judicial decision, esp. one setting the punishment to
be inflicted on a convicted person: *a ten-year sentence
for assault.*

Syns: judgment, rap[1] (*Slang*).

sentence *verb*
To pronounce judgment against.

CONDEMN.

sentient *adjective*
1. Marked by comprehension, cognizance, and
   perception.
2. Able to receive and respond to external stimuli.
3. Readily stirred by emotion.

1. AWARE.

2. SENSITIVE.
3. EMOTIONAL.

sentiment *noun*
1. A general cast of mind with regard to something:

1. *Syns:* attitude, disposition, feeling.

Anti-American sentiment was running high in the Islamic world.

2. Something believed or accepted as true by a person.

2. BELIEF.

3. A complex and usu. strong subjective response, as love, hate, etc.

3. EMOTION.

4. *Rare.* The capacity for or an act of responding to a stimulus.

4. SENSATION.

sentimental *adjective*
Affectedly or extravagantly emotional: *sentimental soap operas.*

Syns: bathetic, drippy (*Slang*), gooey (*Informal*), gushy, maudlin, mawkish, mushy (*Informal*), romantic, sappy (*Slang*), schmaltzy (*Slang*), sloppy (*Informal*), slushy (*Informal*), sobby, soft, soppy (*Slang*), soupy (*Informal*), tear-jerking (*Slang*).
Near-ants: dispassionate, unaffectionate, undemonstrative, unemotional, unresponsive, unromantic.
Ant: unsentimental.

sentimentalism *noun*
The quality or condition of being affectedly or overly emotional.

SENTIMENTALITY.

sentimentality *noun*
The quality or condition of being affectedly or overly emotional: *the cloying sentimentality of the novel.*

Syns: bathos, maudlinism, mawkishness, mush (*Informal*), mushiness (*Informal*), schmaltz (*Slang*), sentimentalism, sloppiness (*Informal*). —*Idiom* sob stuff.

sentimentalize *verb*
To regard or imbue with affected or exaggerated emotion: *vices sentimentalized into virtues.*

Syn: romanticize.

sentry *noun*
A person or special body of persons assigned to provide protection, keep watch over, etc.

GUARD *noun.*

separate *verb*
1. To terminate a relationship or association by or as if by leaving one another: *They have separated but have not yet filed for divorce. The two partners separated after a very serious and prolonged disagreement about finances.*

1. *Syns:* break off, break up, part, split (up). —*Idioms* call it quits, come to a parting of ways, part company.

2. To become or cause to become apart one from another.

2. DIVIDE.

3. To make a division into parts, sections, or branches.

3. DIVIDE.

4. To set apart from a group.

4. ISOLATE.

5. To set apart (one kind or type) from others.

5. SORT *verb.*

6. To recognize as being different.

6. DISTINGUISH.

7. To release from military duty.

7. DISCHARGE *verb.*

separate *adjective*
1. Being or related to a distinct entity.

1. INDIVIDUAL *adjective.*

2. Alone in a given category.

2. LONE.

3. Distinguished from others by nature or qualities.

3. DISTINCT.

separately *adverb*
As a separate unit: *Let's consider each problem separately.*

Syns: apart, discretely. —*Idioms* one at a time, one by one.

separateness *noun*
The quality of being individual.

INDIVIDUALITY.

separation *noun*
1. The act or an instance of separating one thing from another.

1. DIVISION.

2. The act or process of isolating.

2. ISOLATION.

3. The act or an instance of distinguishing.   3. DISTINCTION.
4. The act or process of detaching.   4. DETACHMENT.

separatism *noun*
The policy or practice of excluding a minority group   SEGREGATION.
from full freedom or participation in a society.

separatist *noun*
A person who dissents from the doctrine of an   ***Syns:*** dissenter, dissident, heretic,
established church: *The Puritans were separatists from*   nonconformist, schismatic, schismatist,
the Church of England.   sectary.

sepulcher *noun*
A burial place or receptacle for human remains.   GRAVE¹.

sepulture *noun*
Archaic. A burial place or receptacle for human   GRAVE¹.
remains.

sequel *noun*
Something brought about by a cause.   EFFECT *noun.*

sequence *noun*
  1. Something brought about by a cause.   1. EFFECT *noun.*
  2. A way or condition of being arranged.   2. ARRANGEMENT.
  3. A way in which things follow each other in space or   3. ORDER *noun.*
     time.
  4. A number of things placed or occurring one after the   4. SERIES.
     other.

sequent *adjective*
Following one after another in an orderly pattern.   CONSECUTIVE.

sequent *noun*
Something brought about by a cause.   EFFECT *noun.*

sequential *adjective*
Following one after another in an orderly pattern.   CONSECUTIVE.

sequester *verb*
  1. To set apart from a group.   1. ISOLATE *verb.*
  2. To put into solitude.   2. SECLUDE.

sequestered *adjective*
  1. Solitary and shut off from society.   1. SECLUDED.
  2. Concealed from view.   2. SECLUDED.

sequestrate *verb*
To put into solitude.   SECLUDE.

sequestrate *adjective*
Archaic. Solitary and shut off from society.   SECLUDED.

sequestration *noun*
  1. The act or process of isolating.   1. ISOLATION.
  2. The act of secluding or the state of being secluded.   2. SECLUSION.

sequin *noun*
A small, sparkling decoration.   GLITTER *noun.*

serene *adjective*
Not excited or emotionally agitated.   CALM *adjective.*

serenity *noun*
Lack of emotional agitation.   CALM *noun.*

serfdom *noun*
A state of subjugation to an owner or master.   SLAVERY.

serial *adjective*
Following one after another in an orderly pattern.   CONSECUTIVE.

series *noun*
  1. A number of things placed or occurring one after the   1. ***Syns:*** chain, consecution, course, order,
     other: *A series of hard winters decimated the deer*   run, sequence, streak (*Informal*),
     population.   string, succession, suite, train.
  2. An unbroken sequence of events.   2. RUN *noun.*

serious *adjective*
  1. Marked by sober sincerity: *Be serious and tell me*   1. ***Syns:*** businesslike, earnest, no-
     how you really feel. We had a serious talk about   nonsense, serious-minded, sobersided.
     business matters.   —*Idiom* serious as a judge.

2. Full of or marked by dignity and seriousness.

3. Having great consequence or weight.

4. Causing or marked by danger, pain, etc.

serious-minded *adjective*
Marked by sober sincerity.

serious-mindedness *noun*
Sober sincerity.

seriousness *noun*
1. Sober sincerity: *He told me that in complete seriousness.*
2. The condition of being grave and of involving serious consequences.

sermonize *verb*
To deliver (a sermon or sermons), esp. as a vocation.

serpentine *adjective*
Repeatedly curving in alternate directions.

serve *verb*
1. To work and care for: *a nurse who served her patients well.*
2. To place food before (someone): *The waitress still has not served us.*
3. To be an advantage to.
4. To spend or complete (time), as a prison term: *served 25 years for armed robbery.*
5. To meet a need or requirement: *a dictionary that will serve you well; a tool that serves my purpose efficiently.*
6. To perform the duties of another.

service *noun*
1. A formal act or set of acts prescribed by ritual.
2. The condition of being put to use.
3. A kindly act.

serviceable *adjective*
1. Affording support or assistance.
2. Serving or capable of serving a useful purpose.
3. In a condition to be used.

servile *adjective*
Excessively eager to serve or obey: *The hostess scurried about waiting on us in an unpleasantly servile way.*

servility *noun*
A state of subjugation to an owner or master.

serving *noun*
An individual quantity of food: *one serving of peas.*

servitude *noun*
A state of subjugation to an owner or master.

sesquipedalian *adjective*
Having many syllables.

set¹ *verb*
1. To deposit in a specified position: *Just set your bag on the floor.*

2. To alter (parts of a device) for proper functioning.
3. To move (a weapon, blow, etc.) in the direction of someone or something.

Near-syns: contemplative, intent, meditative, pensive, reflective, thoughtful.

2. GRAVE².

3. GRAVE².

4. GRIEVOUS.

SERIOUS.

SERIOUSNESS.

1. *Syns:* earnest, earnestness, serious-mindedness, sobriety.

2. GRAVITY.

PREACH.

WINDING.

1. *Syns:* attend, do for, minister (to), wait on (*or* upon).

2. *Syn:* wait on (*or* upon).

3. PROFIT *verb*.

4. *Syns:* do (*Informal*), put in (*Informal*).

5. *Syns:* answer, do, suffice, suit.

6. ACT FOR at **act**.

1. CEREMONY.

2. DUTY.

3. FAVOR *noun*.

1. HELPFUL.

2. PRACTICAL.

3. USABLE.

Syns: menial, obsequious, slavish, subservient.
Near-syns: bootlicking, groveling, submissive, toadish; obedient, passive.
Ant: authoritative.

SLAVERY.

Syns: helping, mess, portion.

SLAVERY.

LONG¹ *adjective*.

1. *Syns:* fix, lay¹, place, put, stick.
Near-syns: deposit, emplace, establish, install; ensconce.

2. ADJUST.

3. AIM *verb*.

4. To arrange tableware upon (a table) in preparation for a meal: *set the table for four.*

    4. **Syns:** lay¹, spread.

5. To change or be changed from a liquid into a soft, semisolid, or solid mass.

    5. COAGULATE.

6. To make or become physically hard.

    6. HARDEN.

7. To put up as a stake in a game or speculation.

    7. GAMBLE *verb.*

8. To calculate approximately.

    8. ESTIMATE *verb.*

9. To place in a designated setting.

    9. LAY¹.

10. To place in proper position or location.

    10. POSITION *verb.*

11. To appoint and send to a particular place.

    11. STATION *verb.*

12. To come to an agreement about.

    12. ARRANGE.

set apart *verb*
To make noticeable or different.

    DISTINGUISH.

set aside *verb*
To put an end to formally and with authority.

    ABOLISH.

set by *verb*
To reserve for the future.

    SAVE.

set down *verb*
To come to rest on the ground.

    LAND *verb.*

set out *verb*
1. To go about the initial step in doing (something).
2. To proceed in a specified direction.
3. To work out and arrange the parts or details of.

    1. START *verb.*
    2. BEAR.
    3. DESIGN *verb.*

set to *verb*
To go about the initial step in doing (something).

    START *verb.*

set up *verb*
1. To raise upright.
2. To bring into existence formally.
3. *Informal.* To pay for the food, drink, or entertainment of (another).

    1. ERECT *verb.*
    2. FOUND.
    3. TREAT *verb.*

set *adjective*
1. In a definite and final form; not likely to change.
2. On an unwavering course of action: *is set on going to Europe.*
3. Firmly established by long standing.
4. In a state of preparedness.
5. Fixed and distinct from others.

    1. FIRM¹ *adjective.*
    2. **Syns:** bent, decided, determined, fixed, intent, resolute.
    3. CONFIRMED.
    4. READY *adjective.*
    5. SPECIFIC.

set² *noun*
1. A number of individuals making up or considered a unit.
2. A subdivision of a larger group.
3. A group of people sharing an interest, activity, or achievement.
4. A particular social group.
5. The properties, backdrops, and other objects arranged for a dramatic presentation.

    1. GROUP *noun.*
    2. CLASS *noun.*
    3. CIRCLE *noun.*
    4. CROWD *noun.*
    5. SCENE.

set apart *verb*

    SEE **set¹.**

set aside *verb*

    SEE **set¹.**

setback *noun*

    SEE **set back.**

set back *verb*
To cause to be later or slower than expected or desired.

    DELAY *verb.*

  setback *noun*
A change from better to worse.

    REVERSE *noun.*

set by *verb*

    SEE **set¹.**

set down *verb*

    SEE **set¹.**

setoff *noun*

    SEE **set off.**

set off *verb*
1. To act as an equalizing weight or force to.
2. To compare so as to reveal differences.
3. To make up for the defects of.

    1. BALANCE *verb.*
    2. CONTRAST *verb.*
    3. COMPENSATE.

4. To endow with beauty and elegance by way of a notable addition.

4. GRACE *verb.*

setoff *noun*
Something to make up for loss or damage.

COMPENSATION.

set out *verb*

SEE **set**[1].

setting *noun*
1. The properties, backdrops, and other objects arranged for a dramatic presentation.
2. The place where an action or event occurs.

1. SCENE.
2. SCENE.

settle *verb*
1. To fall or drift down to the bottom: *The dust settled. Silt settles on the riverbed.*
2. To place securely in a position or condition.
3. To come to an agreement about.
4. To come to rest on the ground.
5. To make or become calm.
6. To put into correct or conclusive form: *The official settled the matter with a few quick calls.*
7. To bring (something) into a state of agreement or accord: *settle an argument.*
8. To set right by giving what is due: *finally had enough money to settle his debts.*
9. To make up or cause to make up one's mind.

1. *Syns:* gravitate, sink.
2. ESTABLISH.
3. ARRANGE.
4. LAND *verb.*
5. CALM *verb.*
6. *Syns:* arrange, attend to, conclude, dispose of, fix.
7. *Syns:* reconcile, rectify, resolve, smooth over, straighten out.
8. *Syns:* clear, discharge, liquidate, pay (up *or* off), satisfy, square.
9. DECIDE.

settled *adjective*
1. In a definite and final form; not likely to change.
2. Firmly established by long standing.

1. FIRM[1] *adjective.*
2. CONFIRMED.

set to *verb*

SEE **set**[1].

set up *verb*

SEE **set**[1].

sever *verb*
To separate into parts with or as if with a sharp-edged instrument.

CUT *verb.*

several *adjective*
1. Consisting of an indefinitely small number that is more than two or three but less than many: *Several friends stopped by to visit.*
2. Distinguished from others by nature or qualities.

1. *Syns:* divers (*Archaic*), some, sundry, various.
2. DISTINCT.

severe *adjective*
1. Rigorous and unsparing in treating others: *an excellent but severe teacher.*
2. Cold and forbidding.
3. Causing sharp, often prolonged discomfort.
4. Causing or marked by danger, pain, etc.
5. Having great consequence or weight.
6. Imposing a severe test of bodily or spiritual strength.
7. Conveying great physical force: *gave him a severe blow to the head.*

1. *Syns:* demanding, exacting, rigid, stern, strict, tough, unyielding.
2. BLEAK.
3. BITTER *adjective.*
4. GRIEVOUS.
5. GRAVE[2].
6. BURDENSOME.
7. *Syns:* hard, heavy, hefty, powerful.

severity *noun*
1. The fact or condition of being rigorous and unsparing: *an ordeal of extraordinary severity.*
2. Exceptionally great concentration, power, or force, esp. in activity.

1. *Syns:* austerity, harshness, rigor, stringency.
2. INTENSITY.

sexiness *noun*
Slang. The quality or condition of being sensual.

SENSUALITY.

sexual *adjective*
1. Of, concerning, or promoting sexual love or desire.
2. Employed in reproduction.
3. Suggesting sexuality.

1. EROTIC.
2. REPRODUCTIVE.
3. SENSUAL.

sexuality *noun*
The quality or condition of being sensual.

SENSUALITY.

sexy *adjective*
1. *Slang.* Arousing erotic desire.
2. *Slang.* Feeling or devoted to sexual love or desire.
3. *Slang.* Of, concerning, or promoting sexual love or desire.
4. *Slang.* Suggesting sexuality.

1. DESIRABLE.
2. EROTIC.
3. EROTIC.

4. SENSUAL.

shabby *adjective*
1. Showing signs of wear and tear or neglect: *a shabby couch; a shabby old building.*

1. **Syns:** bedraggled, broken-down, decaying, decrepit, dilapidated, dingy, down-at-heel *or* down-at-the-heel, faded, mangy, ratty (*Slang*), run-down, scrubby, scruffy, seedy, shoddy, sleazy, tacky[3] (*Informal*), tagrag, tattered, threadbare. —*Idioms* all the worse for wear, gone to seed (*or* pot), past cure (*or* hope).
Near-ants: fresh, neat, new, spruce, tidy, trim, well-kept.

2. So objectionable as to elicit despisal.
3. Meriting or causing shame or dishonor.

2. FILTHY.
3. DISGRACEFUL.

shackle *verb*
To restrict the activity or free movement of.

HAMPER.

shackles *noun*
Something that physically confines the legs or arms.

BONDS.

shade *noun*
1. Comparative darkness that results from the blocking of light rays: *sat in the shade of an oak tree.*
2. The degree of vividness of a color, as when modified by the addition of black or white pigment: *a delicate shade of pink; shades of gray and black.*
3. The property by which the sense of vision can distinguish between objects, as a red apple and a green apple, that are very similar or identical in form and size.
4. A slight variation between nearly identical entities: *not a shade of difference between the two politicians; shades of meaning.*
5. A barely perceivable indication of something.
6. A slight amount: *a shade of sadness in the music.*

1. **Syns:** adumbration, penumbra, shadow, umbra, umbrage (*Archaic*).
2. **Syns:** gradation, hue, tinge, tint.

3. COLOR *noun.*

4. **Syns:** gradation, nuance.

5. TRACE *noun.*
6. **Syns:** ghost, hair, hint, intimation, semblance, shadow, soupçon (*French*), strain[2], streak, suggestion, suspicion, tinge, touch, trace, whisker, whisper.

7. A supernatural being.

7. GHOST *noun.*

shade *verb*
1. To shelter, esp. from light: *A big hat shaded her face.*
2. To make dark or darker: *shaded in the background with pencil.*
3. *Informal.* To make a slight reduction in (a price): *The manager of the bookstore shaded the cost of the books for students.*

1. **Syns:** inumbrate, screen, shadow.

2. **Syns:** adumbrate, darken, shadow.

3. **Syns:** shave, trim.

shaded *adjective*
Full of shade.

SHADY.

shadiness *noun*
Lack of straightforwardness and honesty in action.

INDIRECTION.

shadow *noun*
1. Comparative darkness that results from the blocking of light rays.
2. A slight amount.
3. An agent assigned to observe and report on another.
4. A supernatural being.

1. SHADE *noun.*
2. SHADE *noun.*
3. TAIL *noun.*
4. GHOST *noun.*

shadow *verb*
1. To shelter, esp. from light.
2. To make dark or darker.
3. To make dim or indistinct.
4. To keep (another) under surveillance by moving along behind.

shadowy *adjective*
1. Full of shade.
2. Not clearly perceived or perceptible.

shady *adjective*
1. Full of shade: *shady lawns.*

2. Casting shade: *shady trees.*
3. Of dubious character: *a shady operator; a shady business deal.*

shaft *noun*
1. A relatively long, straight, rigid piece of metal or other solid material.
2. A series of particles or waves traveling close together in parallel paths.

shake *verb*
1. To cause to move to and fro with short, jerky movements: *shake the piggy bank to get out the last few coins.*
2. To move to and fro in short, jerky movements: *The dog was shaking like a leaf at the vet's.*
3. To cause to move to and fro violently.
4. To alter the settled state or position of.
5. To move to and fro violently: *The house shook as the jets flew overhead.*
6. To impair or destroy the composure of.
7. To deprive of courage or the power to act as a result of fear, anxiety, or disgust.
8. To get away from (a pursuer).
9. To free from something objectionable or undesirable.

shake *noun*
A shaking of the earth.

shakedown *noun*

shake down *verb*
1. *Informal.* To make a thorough search of.
2. *Informal.* To examine the person or personal effects of in order to find something lost or concealed.
3. *Informal.* To obtain by coercion or intimidation.

shakedown *noun*
Informal. A thorough search of a place or person: *gave the suspect a shakedown.*

shakes *noun*
A state of nervous restlessness or agitation.

shakeup *noun*

shake up *verb*
Informal. To fill with fear.

shakeup *noun*
A thorough or drastic reorganization: *The top three people in the office were fired in the company shakeup.*

shakiness *noun*
1. The quality or condition of being physically unsteady.

---

1. SHADE *verb*.
2. SHADE *verb*.
3. OBSCURE *verb*.
4. FOLLOW.

1. SHADY.
2. UNCLEAR.

1. ***Syns:*** bosky, shaded, shadowy, umbrous.
   Near-syns: dark, dusky, shadowed, sheltered.
   Ant: sunny.
2. ***Syn:*** umbrageous.
3. ***Syns:*** doubtful, equivocal, fishy, questionable, suspect, suspicious, uncertain.

1. STICK *noun*.

2. BEAM *noun*.

1. ***Syns:*** jiggle, joggle.

2. ***Syns:*** quake, quaver, quiver, shiver, shudder, tremble, tremor, twitter.
3. AGITATE.
4. DISTURB.
5. ***Syns:*** quake, rock[2], tremble, vibrate.

6. AGITATE.
7. DISMAY *verb*.

8. LOSE.
9. RID.

TREMOR *noun*.
SEE **shake down.**

1. SCOUR.
2. SEARCH *verb*.

3. EXTORT.

Syns: frisk, once-over (*Informal*), search.

JITTERS.
SEE **shake up.**

FRIGHTEN.

Syns: house-cleaning, overhaul.

1. UNSTABLENESS.

2. The quality or condition of being erratic and undependable.

shaking *adjective*
Marked by or affected with tremors.

shaky *adjective*
1. Marked by or affected with tremors.
2. Not physically steady or firm.
3. Lacking stability.

shallow *adjective*
1. Measuring little from bottom to top or surface: *a shallow river; a shallow bowl.*
2. Lacking in intellectual depth or thoroughness.

shallow *noun*
A shallow part of a body of water.

sham *noun*
1. A display of insincere behavior.
2. A fraudulent imitation.
3. A false, derisive, or impudent imitation of something.

sham *verb*
To behave affectedly or insincerely.

sham *adjective*
1. Fraudulently or deceptively imitative.
2. Made to imitate something else.

shamble *verb*
To drag (the feet) along the floor or ground while walking.

shambles *noun*
A ruinous state of disorder.

shame *noun*
1. A great disappointment or regrettable fact: *It's a shame she didn't get the job.*

2. Loss of or damage to one's reputation.

shame *verb*
To damage in reputation.

shameful *adjective*
1. Worthy of severe disapproval.
2. Meriting or causing shame or dishonor.

shamefulness *noun*
The condition of being infamous.

shameless *adjective*
Characterized by or done without shame: *a shameless display of greed and corruption.*

shanty *noun*
An ugly, squalid dwelling.

shape *noun*
1. The external outline of a thing.
2. *Informal.* A state of sound readiness.

shape *verb*
1. To give form to by or as if by pressing and kneading.
2. To create by forming, combining, or altering materials.

---

2. INSTABILITY.

TREMULOUS.

1. TREMULOUS.
2. UNSTABLE.
3. INSECURE.

1. *Syns:* ebb (*Brit. Regional*), fleet² (*Chiefly Regional*), shoal.
2. SUPERFICIAL.

SHOAL *noun.*

1. ACT *noun.*
2. COUNTERFEIT *noun.*
3. MOCKERY.

ACT *verb.*

1. COUNTERFEIT *adjective.*
2. ARTIFICIAL.

SHUFFLE.

BOTCH *noun.*

1. *Syns:* bummer (*Slang*), crime (*Informal*), pity. —*Idiom* a crying shame.
2. DISGRACE *noun.*

DISGRACE *verb.*

1. DEPLORABLE.
2. DISGRACEFUL.

INFAMY.

Syns: arrant, bald-faced, barefaced, blatant, brassy (*Informal*), brazen, brazenfaced, unabashed, unblushing. —*Idiom* dead (*or* lost) to shame. *Near-syns:* audacious, bold, brash, cheeky, presumptuous; immodest, lewd, profligate. *Ant:* modest.

HOLE *noun.*

1. FORM *noun.*
2. TRIM *noun.*

1. FORM *verb.*

2. MAKE.

shapeless *adjective*
Having no distinct shape: *a shapeless mass of goo.*

Syns: amorphous, formless, inchoate, unformed, unshaped.

shapely *adjective*
Having a full, voluptuous figure: *a shapely young gymnast.*

Syns: built (*Informal*), curvaceous, curvesome, curvy, rounded, stacked (*Informal*), well-developed.
Near-ants: dumpy, squat, stumpy.
Ants: shapeless, unshapely.

shard *noun*
Residual matter.

END *noun.*

share *noun*
1. That which is allotted.
2. One's proper or expected function in a common effort.

1. ALLOTMENT.
2. PART *noun.*

share *verb*
1. To give out in portions or shares.
2. To have a share in (an act, result, etc.); have a hand in.

1. DISTRIBUTE.
2. CONTRIBUTE.

sharing *noun*
The act or fact of participating.

PARTICIPATION.

sharp *adjective*
1. Having a fine edge, as for cutting: *a sharp knife.*
2. Clearly defined; not ambiguous: *a sharp distinction.*
3. Mentally quick and original.
4. Possessing or displaying perceptions of great accuracy and sensitivity.
5. Astute but lacking in ethics or principles: *sharp business practices.*
6. *Slang.* Being or in accordance with the current fashion.
7. Marked by severity or intensity: *a sharp pain in his abdomen.*
8. Having or suggesting keen, discerning intellect.
9. Having an end tapering to a point.
10. Affecting the organs of taste or smell with a strong and often harsh sensation.

1. **Syns:** honed, keen, whetted.
2. **Syns:** clear, distinct, unambiguous, unequivocal, unmistakable.
3. CLEVER.
4. ACUTE.
5. **Syns:** canny, clever, cunning, sharp, shifty, slick, sly, wily.
6. FASHIONABLE.
7. **Syns:** acute, gnawing, knifelike, lancinating, piercing, shooting, stabbing.
8. INCISIVE.
9. POINTED.
10. PUNGENT.

sharp *verb*
Regional. To give a sharp edge to.

SHARPEN.

sharpen *verb*
To give a sharp edge to: *sharpened the knife.*

Syns: acuminate, edge, hone[1], sharp (*Regional*), whet.

sharper *noun*
A person who cheats.

CHEAT *noun.*

sharpness *noun*
A cutting quality.

EDGE *noun.*

sharp-witted *adjective*
Mentally quick and original.

CLEVER.

shatter *verb*
1. To crack or split into two or more fragments by means of or as a result of force, a blow, or strain.
2. To cause the complete ruin or wreckage of.

1. BREAK *verb.*
2. DESTROY.

shattering *adjective*
Having the capability or effect of damaging irreparably.

DESTRUCTIVE.

shave *verb*
1. To make light and momentary contact with, as in passing.
2. To manage with difficulty or so as to barely escape failure.

1. BRUSH *verb.*
2. SCRAPE *verb.*

3. To make a slight reduction in (a price).   **3.** SHADE *verb*.

shear *verb*
To decrease, as in length or amount, by or as if by CUT BACK.
severing or excising.

sheath *noun*
A thin outer covering of an object.   SKIN *noun*.

sheathe *verb*
To furnish with a covering of a different material. FACE *verb*.

sheathing *noun*
A thin outer covering of an object.   SKIN *noun*.

shed *verb*
 1. To send out heat, light, or energy: *The moon shed a* **1.** *Syns:* cast, emit, irradiate, project,
  ghostly light over the yard.   radiate, throw.
 2. To cast off by natural process: *snakes that shed their* **2.** *Syns:* exuviate (*Zool.*), molt, slip,
  skins.   slough² , throw off.

sheen *noun*
A radiant brightness or glow, usu. due to light reflected GLOSS *noun*.
from a smooth surface.

sheer¹ *verb*
 1. To change the direction or course of.   **1.** TURN *verb*.
 2. To turn aside sharply from a straight course. **2.** SWERVE.

sheer² *adjective*
 1. Free from extraneous elements.   **1.** PURE *adjective*.
 2. Completely such, without qualification or exception. **2.** UTTER².
 3. So sharply inclined as to be almost perpendicular. **3.** STEEP¹.
 4. So light and insubstantial as to resemble air or a **4.** FILMY.
  thin film.

shellac *verb*
 1. *Slang.* To win a victory over, as in battle or a **1.** DEFEAT *verb*.
  competition.
 2. *Slang.* To render totally ineffective by decisive **2.** OVERWHELM.
  defeat.

shellacking *noun*
 1. *Slang.* The act of defeating or the condition of being **1.** DEFEAT *noun*.
  defeated.
 2. *Slang.* A severe defeat.   **2.** TROUNCING.

shell out *verb*
Informal. To distribute (money) as payment. SPEND.

shelter *noun*
 1. Dwellings in general: *How much of your salary goes* **1.** *Syns:* housing, lodging, quarterage.
  for shelter?   —*Idiom* a roof over one's head.
 2. Something that physically protects, esp. from **2.** COVER *noun*.
  danger.
 3. The state of being protected or safeguarded, as from **3.** REFUGE.
  danger or hardship.

 shelter *verb*
 To give refuge to.   HARBOR *verb*.

shelve *verb*
To put off until a later time.   DEFER¹.

shenanigan *noun*
 1. A mischievous act.   **1.** PRANK.
 2. *Informal.* An indirect, usu. cunning means of **2.** TRICK *noun*.
  gaining an end.

shepherd *verb*
To show the way to.   GUIDE *verb*.

shield *noun*
The act or a means of defending.   DEFENSE.

 shield *verb*
To keep safe from danger, attack, or harm. DEFEND.

shift *verb*
 1. To go or cause to go from one place to another. **1.** MOVE *verb*.

2. To leave or discard for another.   2. CHANGE verb.

3. To alter the settled state or position of.   3. DISTURB.

4. To change the direction or course of.   4. TURN verb.

5. To progress or perform adequately, esp. in difficult circumstances.   5. MANAGE.

6. To eat completely or entirely.   6. CONSUME.

shift *noun*

1. The act of exchanging or substituting.   1. CHANGE noun.

2. A usu. physical change of one thing into another.   2. CONVERSION.

3. An often sudden change or departure, as in a trend.   3. TURN noun.

4. The process or an instance of passing from one form, state, or stage to another.   4. TRANSITION.

5. A limited, often assigned period of activity, duty, or opportunity.   5. TURN noun.

6. Something used temporarily or reluctantly when other means are not available.   6. MAKESHIFT.

shiftless *adjective*

Resistant to exertion and activity.   LAZY.

shiftlessness *noun*

The quality or state of being lazy.   LAZINESS.

shifty *adjective*

1. Given to or marked by deliberate concealment or misrepresentation of the truth.   1. DISHONEST.

2. Deliberately ambiguous or vague.   2. EVASIVE.

3. Astute but lacking in ethics or principles.   3. SHARP adjective.

4. Marked by treachery or deceit.   4. UNDERHAND.

shilly-shally *verb*

To be irresolute in acting or doing.   HESITATE.

shilly-shally *noun*

The act or an instance of hesitating.   HESITATION.

shimmer *verb*

To emit light suddenly in rays or sparks.   FLASH verb.

shimmer *noun*

Sparkling, brilliant light.   GLITTER noun.

shindig *noun*

Slang. A big, exuberant party.   BLAST noun.

shine *verb*

1. To emit a bright light.   1. BEAM.

2. To give a gleaming luster to, usu. through friction.   2. GLOSS verb.

3. To be in one's prime.   3. FLOURISH.

shine *noun*

A radiant brightness or glow, usu. due to light reflected from a smooth surface.   GLOSS noun.

shiner *noun*

Slang. A bruise surrounding the eye.   BLACK EYE.

shining *adjective*

1. Giving off or reflecting light readily or in large amounts.   1. BRIGHT.

2. Having a high, radiant sheen.   2. GLOSSY.

shiny *adjective*

Having a high, radiant sheen.   GLOSSY.

ship *verb*

To cause (something) to be conveyed to a destination.   SEND.

shipshape *adjective*

In good order or clean condition.   NEAT.

shipwreck *verb*

To damage, disable, or destroy (a seacraft).   WRECK verb.

shirk *verb*

1. To pass time without working or in avoiding work.   1. IDLE verb.

2. To avoid the fulfillment of.   2. NEGLECT verb.

3. To move silently and furtively.   3. SNEAK verb.

shiver *verb*
1. To crack or split into two or more fragments by means of or as a result of force, a blow, or strain.
2. To move to and fro in short, jerky movements.

1. BREAK *verb*.

2. SHAKE *verb*.

shiver *noun*
A nervous shaking of the body.

TREMOR *noun*.

shivering *adjective*
Marked by or affected with tremors.

TREMULOUS.

shivers *noun*
A state of nervous restlessness or agitation.

JITTERS.

shivery *adjective*
1. Marked by a low temperature.
2. Marked by or affected with tremors.

1. COLD *adjective*.
2. TREMULOUS.

shoal *noun*
A shallow part of a body of water: *ran aground in the shoal.*

Syn: shallow.

shoal *adjective*
Measuring little from bottom to top or surface.

SHALLOW.

shock *verb*
1. To affect with a strong feeling of moral aversion: *Such shameless behavior shocked him.*
2. To cause to experience a sudden, momentary shock.
3. To inflict physical or mental injury or distress on.

1. *Syn:* scandalize. —*Idiom* stink in one's nostrils.
2. STARTLE *verb*.
3. TRAUMATIZE.

shock *noun*
1. Violent, forcible contact between two or more things.
2. Something that jars the mind or emotions: *Her death was a terrible shock to her family.*

1. COLLISION.
2. *Syns:* blow[2], jolt, trauma.

shocked *adjective*
Overcome with intense feeling, as of amazement, horror, or dismay: *was shocked by the bloodshed and violence of war.*

Syns: aghast, appalled, confounded, dismayed, dumfounded (*also* dumbfounded), horrified, horrorstruck, thunderstruck.
Near-syns: jarred, overwhelmed, shaken up; agape, bemused; offended, outraged.

shocking *adjective*
1. Very bad.
2. Deserving strong condemnation.
3. Too awful to be described.
4. Disgracefully and grossly offensive.
5. Beyond all reason.

1. TERRIBLE.
2. INFAMOUS.
3. UNSPEAKABLE.
4. OUTRAGEOUS.
5. OUTRAGEOUS.

shoddy *adjective*
1. Of decidedly inferior quality: *shoddy workmanship.*

1. *Syns:* base[2], cheap, cheesy (*Slang*), common, crappy (*Slang*), crummy (*also* crumby) (*Slang*), lousy (*Slang*), paltry, poor, rotten (*Informal*), schlocky (*Slang*), sleazy, tacky[2] (*Informal*), tatty, trashy.

2. Showing signs of wear and tear or neglect.

2. SHABBY.

shoo-in *noun*
Informal. A competitor regarded as the most likely winner.

FAVORITE *noun*.

shoot *noun*
A young stemlike growth arising from a plant: *new shoots at the base of the trunk.*

Syns: bine, offshoot, runner (*Bot.*), sprig, sprout, tendril.

shoot *verb*
1. To discharge a gun or firearm: *shot at a moving target.*
2. To wound or kill with a firearm: *Do you know who shot him?*
3. To launch with great force: *shoot rockets toward the moon; shoot arrows with a crossbow.*

1. *Syn:* fire. —*Idiom* take a shot at.
2. *Syns:* gun (down), pick off, plug (*Slang*). —*Idiom* stop in one's tracks.
3. *Syns:* discharge, fire, hurtle, loose, project, propel. —*Idiom* let fly.

4. To move swiftly.

5. To pass quickly and lightly through the air.

shoot down *verb*

To cause to be no longer believed or valued.

shoot up *verb*

To rise abruptly and precipitously.

shoot down *verb*

shooting *adjective*

Marked by severity or intensity.

shoot up *verb*

shop *noun*

A retail establishment where merchandise is sold.

shopworn *adjective*

Without freshness or appeal due to overuse.

shore *noun*

A means or device that keeps something erect, stable, or secure.

short *adjective*

1. Not long in time or duration.

2. Marked by or consisting of few words.

3. Rudely unceremonious.

4. Not enough to meet a demand or requirement.

short *adverb*

1. Without adequate preparation.

2. Without any warning: *stopped the car short.*

shortage *noun*

The condition or fact of being deficient: *a shortage of fuel.*

shortcoming *noun*

1. Something that mars the appearance or causes inadequacy or failure.

2. A liking or personal preference for something.

3. An unfavorable condition, circumstance, or characteristic.

shorten *verb*

1. To make short or shorter: *had to shorten their stay in Paris; wants to shorten the dress.*

2. To make short or shorter by or as if by cutting.

shorthanded *adjective*

Lacking the requisite workers or players.

short-lived *adjective*

Lasting or existing only for a short time.

short-range *adjective*

1. Intended, used, or present for a limited time.

2. Designed or implemented so as to gain a limited, temporary advantage.

short-spoken *adjective*

Rudely unceremonious.

short-term *adjective*

Intended, used, or present for a limited time.

shot *noun*

1. A brief trial.

2. *Informal.* A favorable or advantageous combination of circumstances.

3. A small amount of liquor.

---

4. RUSH *verb.*

5. FLY.

DISCREDIT *verb.*

SOAR.

SEE **shoot.**

SHARP *adjective.*

SEE **shoot.**

STORE *noun.*

TRITE.

SUPPORT *noun.*

1. BRIEF.

2. BRIEF.

3. ABRUPT.

4. INSUFFICIENT.

1. UNAWARES.

2. *Syns:* sudden, suddenly.

Syns: defect, deficit, deficiency (*also* deficience), failure, insufficiency (*also* insufficience), lack, paucity, poverty, scantiness, scarceness, scarcity, underage[1].

1. DEFECT *noun.*

2. WEAKNESS.

3. DISADVANTAGE.

1. *Syns:* abbreviate, curtail, cut back, cut down.
Near-syns: abridge, edit, decrease, diminish, lessen, reduce; condense, contract, shrink.
Ants: lengthen, prolong.

2. TRUNCATE.

UNDERHANDED.

TRANSITORY.

1. TEMPORARY.

2. TACTICAL.

ABRUPT *adjective.*

TEMPORARY.

1. TRY *noun.*

2. OPPORTUNITY.

3. DROP *noun.*

shotgun *verb*
Informal. To compel by pressure or threats.   COERCE.

shoulder *verb*
1. To take upon oneself.   1. ASSUME.
2. To do or achieve by forcing obstacles out of one's   2. PUSH *verb.*
   way.

shout *noun*
A loud cry: *a shout for help.*   *Syns:* call, halloo (*also* halloa), holler,
                                                             yell.

shout *verb*
1. To say (something) with a shout: *Fans shouted their*   1. *Syns:* bawl, bellow, cry, holler,
   approval.   vociferate, whoop, yell.
                                                               Near-syns: exclaim; howl, scream,
                                                               shriek; clamor, roar, thunder.
2. To speak or say very loudly.   2. ROAR *verb.*
3. To have or produce a blatantly startling effect.   3. SCREAM *verb.*
4. *Austral.* To pay for the food, drink, or entertainment 4. TREAT *verb.*
   of (another).

shove *verb*
1. To force to move or advance with or as if with blows   1. DRIVE *verb.*
   or pressure.
2. To do or achieve by forcing obstacles out of one's   2. PUSH *verb.*
   way.
3. To force one's way into a place or situation.   3. MUSCLE *verb.*
4. To cause to stick out.   4. POKE *verb.*
5. To engage in the illicit sale of (narcotics).   5. PUSH *verb.*

shove off *verb*
Slang. To move or proceed away from a place.   GO *verb.*

shove *noun*
An act or instance of using force so as to propel ahead.   PUSH *noun.*

shovel *verb*
1. To break, turn over, or remove (earth, sand, etc.)   1. DIG *verb.*
   with or as if with a tool.
2. To make by digging.   2. DIG *verb.*

shove off *verb*   SEE **shove.**

show *verb*
1. To make manifest or apparent: *showed prudence by*   1. *Syns:* demonstrate, display, evidence,
   driving carefully.   evince, exhibit, manifest, proclaim.
                                                               Near-syns: disclose, discover, divulge,
                                                               reveal, unveil.
2. To make visible; bring to view.   2. REVEAL.
3. To come into view.   3. APPEAR.
4. To make known or identify, as by signs.   4. DESIGNATE.
5. To present a lifelike image of.   5. REPRESENT.
6. To make a public and usu. ostentatious show of.   6. DISPLAY *verb.*
7. To give a precise indication of, as on a register or   7. *Syns:* indicate, mark, read, record,
   scale: *The thermometer shows 18°F.*   register.
8. To establish as true or genuine.   8. PROVE.

show off *verb*
To make a public and usu. ostentatious show of.   DISPLAY *verb.*

show up *verb*
1. *Informal.* To come into view.   1. APPEAR.
2. To come to a particular place.   2. ARRIVE.

show *noun*
1. An act of showing or displaying.   1. DISPLAY *noun.*
2. A large public display, as of goods, works of art, etc. 2. EXHIBITION.
3. A display of insincere behavior.   3. ACT *noun.*
4. A deceptive outward appearance.   4. FAÇADE.
5. Performance, as in a competition or test of skill.   5. SHOWING.

shower *noun*
A concentrated outpouring, as of missiles, words, or blows.

BARRAGE *noun.*

shower *verb*
1. To give in great abundance: *showered praise on her.*
2. To direct a barrage at.

1. **Syns:** heap, lavish, rain.
2. BARRAGE *verb.*

showing *noun*
Performance, as in a competition or test of skill: *made a brilliant showing in the finals.*

Syn: show.

show off *verb*

SEE **show.**

show up *verb*

SEE **show.**

showy *adjective*
1. Marked by outward, often extravagant display: *a showy diamond-encrusted watch.*

1. **Syns:** flamboyant, ostentatious, pretentious, splashy, splurgy.
   Near-syns: garish, gaudy, opulent, ornate.
   Ant: unshowy.

2. Full of color.

2. COLORFUL.

shred *noun*
1. A tiny amount.
2. The least bit.

1. BIT[1].
2. DAMN *noun.*

shrew *noun*
A person, esp. a woman, who habitually uses loud, abusive language.

SCOLD *noun.*

shrewd *adjective*
1. Having or showing a clever awareness and resourcefulness in practical matters: *a shrewd bargainer; a shrewd business deal.*

1. **Syns:** astute, cagey (*also* cagy), knowing, perspicacious, savvy (*Slang*), slick, sly (*Chiefly Regional*), smart, wise[1].
   Near-ants: foolable, foolhardy, green, gullible, naive.

2. Having or suggesting keen, discerning intellect.

2. INCISIVE.

shrewdness *noun*
Skill in perceiving, discriminating, or judging.

DISCERNMENT.

shriek *noun*
A long, loud, piercing cry or sound.

SCREAM *noun.*

shriek *verb*
1. To utter a long, loud, piercing cry, as of pain or fright.
2. To have or produce a blatantly startling effect.

1. SCREAM *verb.*
2. SCREAM *verb.*

shrieky *adjective*
Elevated in pitch.

HIGH.

shrill *adjective*
Elevated in pitch.

HIGH.

shrill *noun*
A long, loud, piercing cry or sound.

SCREAM *noun.*

shrill *verb*
To utter a long, loud, piercing cry, as of pain or fright.

SCREAM *verb.*

shrilly *adjective*
Elevated in pitch.

HIGH.

shrimp *noun*
Slang. A totally insignificant person.

NONENTITY.

shrine *noun*
A sacred or holy place.

SANCTUARY.

shrink *verb*
1. To reduce in size by or as if by drawing together.
2. To draw away involuntarily, usu. due to fear or disgust.

1. CONTRACT *verb.*
2. FLINCH.

shrivel *verb*
To make or become no longer fresh or shapely because
of loss of moisture.

DRY UP at **dry.**

shroud *verb*
1. To cut off from sight.
2. To prevent (something) from being known.
3. To surround and cover completely so as to obscure.

1. BLOCK OUT at **block.**
2. COVER *verb.*
3. WRAP *verb.*

shrouded *adjective*
Lying beyond what is obvious or avowed.

ULTERIOR.

shrunken *adjective*
Physically haggard.

WASTED.

shuck *verb*
To let go or get rid of as being no longer of use, value,
etc.

DISCARD.

shudder *verb*
To move to and fro in short, jerky movements.

SHAKE *verb.*

shudder *noun*
A nervous shaking of the body.

TREMOR *noun.*

shuffle *verb*
1. To drag (the feet) along the floor or ground while
walking: *Stop shuffling your feet.*

1. *Syns:* scuff, scuffle, shamble.
Near-syns: drag, draggle, scrape,
straggle.

2. To use evasive or deliberately vague language.
3. To mix together so as to change the order of
arrangement: *shuffled the cards, then dealt.*
4. To proceed or perform in an unsteady, faltering
manner.

2. EQUIVOCATE.
3. *Syns:* jumble, riffle, scramble.
4. MUDDLE.

shun *verb*
1. To keep away from.
2. To slight (someone) deliberately.

1. AVOID.
2. SNUB *verb.*

shush *verb*
1. To cause to become silent.
2. To hold (something requiring an outlet) in check.

1. SILENCE *verb.*
2. REPRESS.

shut *verb*
To move an appropriate barrier into (an opening).

CLOSE¹ *verb.*

shut in *verb*
To confine within a limited area.

ENCLOSE.

shut out *verb*
1. To exclude from normal social or professional
activities.
2. To rid one's mind of.
3. To cut off from sight.

1. BLACKBALL.
2. DISMISS.
3. BLOCK OUT at **block.**

shut up *verb*
1. To enclose so as to hinder or prohibit escape.
2. To cause to become silent.

1. IMPRISON.
2. SILENCE *verb.*

shut-eye *noun*
Slang. The natural recurring condition of suspended
consciousness by which the body rests.

SLEEP *noun.*

shut in *verb*
shut out *verb*
shut up *verb*

SEE **shut.**
SEE **shut.**
SEE **shut.**

shy¹ *adjective*
1. Reticent or reserved in manner.
2. Not enough to meet a demand or requirement.

1. MODEST.
2. INSUFFICIENT.

shy *verb*
To draw away involuntarily, usu. due to fear or disgust.

FLINCH.

shy² *verb*
To send through the air with a motion of the hand or
arm.

THROW *verb.*

shy *noun*
An act of throwing.

THROW *noun.*

sibilate *verb*
To make a sharp sibilant sound.   HISS *verb*.

sibyl *noun*
A person who foretells future events by or as if by   PROPHET.
supernatural means.

sibylline *adjective*
1. Liable to more than one interpretation.   1. AMBIGUOUS.
2. Of or relating to the foretelling of events by or as if   2. PROPHETIC.
   by supernatural means.

sick *adjective*
1. Suffering from or affected with an illness: *She's out*   1. *Syns:* down, ill, laid up (*Informal*).
   sick with the flu.
2. Of or associated with sickness.   2. SICKLY.
3. Susceptible to or marked by preoccupation with   3. MORBID.
   unwholesome matters.
4. Out of patience with: *sick of the whole situation.*   4. *Syns:* disgusted, fed up, tired, weary.
                                                                  —*Idiom* sick and tired.

sicken *verb*
1. To become affected with a disease.   1. CONTRACT *verb*.
2. To offend the senses or feelings of.   2. DISGUST *verb*.

sickening *adjective*
1. Extremely unpleasant to the senses or feelings.   1. OFFENSIVE *adjective*.
2. Too awful to be described.   2. UNSPEAKABLE.

sickly *adjective*
1. Affected or tending to be affected with minor health   1. *Syns:* ailing, indisposed, low, mean[2]
   problems: *He's been sickly all winter.*   (*Informal*), off-color, offish, poorly,
                                                                  rocky, unwell. —*Idiom* under the
                                                                  weather.
2. Of or associated with sickness: *You're looking a bit*   2. *Syns:* anemic, peaked, peaky, sick.
   sickly these days.
3. Susceptible to or marked by preoccupation with   3. MORBID.
   unwholesome matters.

sickness *noun*
1. The condition of being sick: *suffers from a lingering*   1. *Syns:* affliction, disorder, illness,
   sickness.   indisposition, infirmity.
2. A pathological condition of mind or body.   2. DISEASE.

side *noun*
1. One of two or more contrasted parts or places   1. *Syns:* flank, hand.
   identified by its location with respect to a center: *the*
   north side of the park; seated on both sides of the
   table.
2. One of two or more opposing opinions, actions, or   2. *Syn:* part.
   attitudes, as in a disagreement: *There's another side*
   to the story.
3. The particular angle from which something is   3. PHASE.
   considered.

side *verb*
To furnish with a covering of a different material.   FACE *verb*.

side with *verb*
To aid the cause of by approving or favoring.   SUPPORT *verb*.

sidekick *noun*
Slang. A person whom one knows well, likes, and   FRIEND.
trusts.

sidesplitting *adjective*
Extremely funny.   PRICELESS.

sidestep *verb*
1. To avoid fulfilling or answering completely.   1. EVADE.
2. To evade, as a topic, esp. by circumlocution.   2. SKIRT *verb*.

side with *verb*   SEE **side**.

sidle *verb*
To advance carefully and gradually.   EDGE *verb*.

siege *noun*
1. A prolonged surrounding of an objective by hostile troops: *the siege of Leningrad.*
2. An often prolonged period, as of illness: *a month-long siege of hepatitis.*

1. *Syn:* besiegement.

2. *Syns:* bout, go.

siege *verb*
To surround with hostile troops.

BESIEGE.

siesta *noun*
A brief sleep.

NAP *noun.*

siesta *verb*
To sleep for a brief period.

NAP *verb.*

sift *verb*
To set apart (one kind or type) from others.

SORT *verb.*

sigh *verb*
1. To exhale audibly in a long, deep breath, as in sorrow, weariness, or relief: *He sighed when he heard the news.*
2. To make a low, continuous, and indistinct sound.

1. *Syn:* sough.

2. MURMUR *verb.*

sigh *noun*
1. The act or sound of sighing: *heaved a sigh of relief when the plane landed safely.*
2. A low, indistinct, and often continuous sound.

1. *Syn:* sough.

2. MURMUR *noun.*

sight *noun*
1. The faculty of seeing.
2. An act of directing the eyes on an object.
3. That which is or can be seen.
4. An unsightly object.
5. *Chiefly Regional.* A great deal.

1. VISION.
2. LOOK *noun.*
3. VIEW *noun.*
4. MESS *noun.*
5. HEAP *noun.*

sightless *adjective*
Without the sense of sight.

BLIND *adjective.*

sightlessness *noun*
The condition of not being able to see.

BLINDNESS.

sightly *adjective*
Having qualities that delight the eye.

BEAUTIFUL.

sightseer *noun*
One who travels for pleasure.

TOURIST.

sign *noun*
1. Something visible or evident that gives grounds for believing in the existence or presence of something else: *A high forehead is thought to be a sign of intelligence.*
2. An expressive, meaningful bodily movement.
3. An action, motion, or gesture that conveys an idea, an order, or a desire.
4. A conventional mark used in a writing system.
5. Something that takes the place of words in communicating a thought or feeling.

1. *Syns:* evidence, index, indication, indicator, mark, manifestation, signification, stamp, symptom, token, witness.
2. GESTURE *noun.*
3. SIGNAL *noun.*
4. CHARACTER.
5. EXPRESSION.

sign *verb*
1. To affix one's signature to: *We signed the lease this morning.*

1. *Syns:* autograph, endorse, inscribe, subscribe, undersign. —*Idioms* put one's John Hancock on, set one's hand to.

2. To make bodily motions so as to convey an idea or complement speech.

2. GESTURE *verb.*

sign over *verb*
To change the ownership of (property) by means of a legal document.

TRANSFER.

sign up *verb*
1. To become a member of.
2. To ask for employment, acceptance, or admission.

1. JOIN.
2. APPLY.

signal *noun*
An action, motion, or gesture that conveys an idea, an order, or a desire: *gave us the signal to proceed.*

Syn: sign. —*Idiom* high sign.

signal *verb*
1. To communicate by means of such devices as lights or signs: *signaled the train to move ahead.*
2. To make bodily motions so as to convey an idea or complement speech.

1. *Syns:* flag[1], semaphore.

2. GESTURE *verb.*

signal *adjective*
Readily attracting notice.

NOTICEABLE.

signalize *verb*
1. To make noticeable or different.
2. To cause to be eminent or recognized.
3. To make bodily motions so as to convey an idea or complement speech.

1. DISTINGUISH.
2. DISTINGUISH.
3. GESTURE *verb.*

significance also **significancy** *noun*
1. That which is signified by a word or expression.
2. The quality or state of being important.
3. The gist of a specific action or situation.

1. MEANING *noun.*
2. IMPORTANCE.
3. IDEA.

significancy *noun*

SEE **significance.**

significant *adjective*
1. Having great significance.
2. Conveying hidden or unexpressed meaning.
3. Effectively conveying meaning, feeling, or mood.

1. IMPORTANT.
2. PREGNANT.
3. EXPRESSIVE.

signification *noun*
1. That which is signified by a word or expression.
2. Something visible or evident that gives grounds for believing in the existence or presence of something else.

1. MEANING *noun.*
2. SIGN *noun.*

signify *verb*
1. To have or convey a particular idea.
2. To be of significance or importance.

1. MEAN[1].
2. COUNT *verb.*

sign over *verb*

SEE **sign.**

sign up *verb*

SEE **sign.**

silence *noun*
1. The absence of sound or noise: *the silence of a starry night.*
2. The avoidance of speech: *maintained a silence on controversial issues.*

1. *Syns:* hush, quiet, quietness, quietude, soundlessness, still, stillness.
2. *Syns:* dumbness, muteness, speechlessness.

silence *verb*
To cause to become silent: *silenced the child with a menacing look.*

Syns: hush, quiet, quieten, shush, shut up, still.

silent *adjective*
1. Marked by, done with, or making no sound or noise: *a silent mountain valley; wept silent tears; silent guns.*

1. *Syns:* hush, hushed, noiseless, quiet, soundless, still, stilly.
Near-syns: calm, peaceful, placid, serene, tranquil.
Ant: noisy.

2. Not speaking freely or openly.
3. Temporarily unable or unwilling to speak, as from shock or fear.
4. Not voiced or expressed: *a silent admission of guilt.*

2. TACITURN.
3. SPEECHLESS.

4. *Syns:* tacit, undeclared, unexpressed, unsaid, unspoken, unuttered, unvoiced, wordless.

silhouette *noun*
A line marking and shaping the outer form of an object.

OUTLINE *noun.*

silliness *noun*
Foolish behavior.

FOOLISHNESS.

silly *adjective*
1. So senseless as to be laughable.

1. FOOLISH.

    2. Given to lighthearted silliness.

    3. Displaying a complete lack of forethought and good
       sense.

silver-tongued *adjective*

    1. Fluently persuasive and forceful.

    2. Characterized by ready but often insincere or
       superficial discourse.

similar *adjective*

  Possessing the same or almost the same characteristics.

similarity *noun*

  The quality or state of being alike.

similitude *noun*

  The quality or state of being alike.

simmer *verb*

    1. To cook (food) in liquid heated to the point of
       steaming.

    2. To be in a state of emotional or mental turmoil.

  simmer down *verb*

  To bring one's emotions under control.

simmer down *verb*

simper *verb*

  To smile in an insincere, knowing way.

  simper *noun*

  An affected, knowing smile.

simple *adjective*

    1. Posing no difficulty.

    2. Without addition, decoration, or qualification.

    3. Not formal or ceremonious.

    4. Not elaborate or showy, as in appearance or style.

    5. Free from guile, cunning, or deceit.

    6. Lacking in intelligence.

    7. Having only a limited ability to learn and
       understand.

    8. Displaying a complete lack of forethought and good
       sense.

    9. Of little distinction.

  simple *noun*

  One deficient in judgment and good sense.

simple-minded *adjective*

    1. Having only a limited ability to learn and
       understand.

    2. Lacking in intelligence.

simpleton *noun*

    1. One deficient in judgment and good sense

    2. A mentally deficient person.

simplicity *noun*

    1. Lack or avoidance of formality.

    2. Lack of ostentation or pretension.

simplify *verb*

  To reduce in complexity or scope.

simulacre *noun*

simulacrum also **simulacre** *noun*

  An inferior substitute imitating an original.

simulate *verb*

    1. To take on or give a false appearance of.

    2. To behave affectedly or insincerely.

    3. To contrive and present as genuine.

simulation *noun*

    1. A display of insincere behavior.

    2. An inferior substitute imitating an original.

---

2. GIDDY.

3. MINDLESS.

1. ELOQUENT.

2. GLIB.

LIKE². ANALOGOUS

LIKENESS.

LIKENESS.

1. BOIL *verb*.

2. BOIL *verb*.

COMPOSE.

SEE **simmer**.

SMIRK *verb*.

SMIRK *noun*.

1. EASY.

2. BARE *adjective*.

3. INFORMAL.

4. MODEST.

5. ARTLESS.

6. STUPID.

7. BACKWARD.

8. MINDLESS.

9. HUMBLE *adjective*.

FOOL *noun*.

1. BACKWARD *adjective*.

2. STUPID.

1. FOOL *noun*.

2. FOOL *noun*.

1. INFORMALITY.

2. MODESTY.

BOIL DOWN at **boil**.

SEE **simulacrum**.

COPY *noun*.

1. ASSUME.

2. ACT *verb*.

3. FAKE *verb*.

1. ACT *noun*.

2. COPY *noun*.

simultaneous *adjective*
Existing or occurring at the same moment:
simultaneous translations.

Syns: coincident, coinstantaneous,
contemporary.
Near-syns: coexistent, coexisting,
concurrent, contemporaneous.

sin *noun*
1. A wicked act.
2. That which is morally bad or objectionable.
3. Something that offends one's sense of propriety,
   fairness, or justice.

1. CRIME.
2. EVIL *noun.*
3. CRIME.

sin *verb*
To violate a moral or divine law.

OFFEND.

sincere *adjective*
Devoid of any hypocrisy or pretense.

GENUINE.

sine qua non *noun*
Something indispensable.

CONDITION *noun.*

sinew(s) *noun*
The state or quality of being physically strong.

STRENGTH.

sinewy *adjective*
Characterized by marked muscular development;
powerfully built.

MUSCULAR.

sinful *adjective*
Morally objectionable.

EVIL *adjective.*

sing *verb*
1. To utter words or sounds in musical tones: *learned
   to sing in a school chorus.*

1. *Syns:* carol, chant, tune (*Archaic*),
   vocalize.
   Near-syns: croon, hum, lull, lullaby,
   serenade.

2. *Slang.* To give incriminating information about
   others, esp. to the authorities.

2. INFORM.

singe *verb*
To undergo or cause to undergo damage by or as if by
fire.

BURN *verb.*

singe *noun*
Damage that results from burning.

BURN *noun.*

singer *noun*
A person who sings.

VOCALIST.

single *adjective*
1. Without a spouse: *a bar for single people.*

1. *Syns:* lone, sole, spouseless,
   unattached, unmarried, unwed.
   —*Idiom* footloose and fancy-free.
   Near-syns: celibate, free, maiden,
   unfettered, virgin.
   Ants: married, wed.

2. Alone in a given category.
3. Being or related to a distinct entity.
4. Not divided among or shared with others.

2. LONE.
3. INDIVIDUAL *adjective.*
4. EXCLUSIVE.

single out *verb*
To make a choice from a number of alternatives.

CHOOSE.

single-handedly *adverb*
Without the presence or aid of another.

ALONE *adverb.*

singleness *noun*
1. The quality or condition of being unique.
2. The condition of being one.

1. UNIQUENESS.
2. UNITY.

single out *verb*

SEE **single.**

singular *adjective*
1. Being or related to a distinct entity.
2. Far beyond what is usual, normal, or customary.
3. Deviating from the customary.

1. INDIVIDUAL *adjective.*
2. RARE.
3. ECCENTRIC *adjective.*

singularity *noun*
1. The quality of being individual.

1. INDIVIDUALITY.

2. The condition of being one.   2. UNITY.
3. Peculiar behavior.   3. ECCENTRICITY.

singularize *verb*
To make noticeable or different.   DISTINGUISH.

sinister *adjective*
Strongly suggestive of great harm, menace, or evil.   MALIGN *adjective.*

sink *noun*
1. An area sunk below its surroundings.   1. DEPRESSION.
2. A place known for its great filth or corruption.   2. PIT *noun.*

   sink *verb*
   1. To go beneath the surface or to the bottom of a   1. *Syns:* founder^2, submerge, submerse.
     liquid: *The* Titanic *sank in 1912.*   —*Idiom* go to Davy Jones's locker.
   2. To go from a more erect posture to a less erect   2. DROP *verb.*
     posture.
   3. To slope downward.   3. DESCEND.
   4. To undergo a sharp, rapid descent in value or   4. FALL *verb.*
     price.
   5. To become lower in quality, character, or condition.   5. DETERIORATE.
   6. To cause the complete ruin or wreckage of.   6. DESTROY.
   7. To undergo moral deterioration.   7. FALL *verb.*
   8. To bring oneself down to a lower level of behavior.   8. DESCEND.
   9. To cause to penetrate with force.   9. RAM *verb.*
   10. To fall or drift down to the bottom.   10. SETTLE.

   sink in *verb*
   To come as a realization.   REGISTER *verb.*

sink in *verb*   SEE **sink.**

sinuous *adjective*
Repeatedly curving in alternate directions.   WINDING.

sip *verb*
To take into the mouth and swallow (a liquid).   DRINK *verb.*

   sip *noun*
   1. An act of drinking or the amount swallowed.   1. DRINK *noun.*
   2. A small amount of liquor.   2. DROP *noun.*

sire *noun*
A male parent.   FATHER *noun.*

   sire *verb*
   1. To be the biological father of.   1. FATHER *verb.*
   2. To cause to come into existence.   2. PRODUCE.

siren *noun*
A usu. unscrupulous woman who seduces or exploits   SEDUCTRESS.
men.

   siren *adjective*
   Tending to seduce.   SEDUCTIVE.

sirenic or **sirenical** *adjective*
Tending to seduce.   SEDUCTIVE.

sissified *adjective*
Having qualities more appropriate to women than to   EFFEMINATE *adjective.*
men.

sit *verb*
1. To cause to take a sitting position.   1. SEAT *verb.*
2. To assume a particular position, as for a portrait.   2. POSE *verb.*

   sit in *verb*
   To act as a substitute.   SUBSTITUTE *verb.*

   sit on (or **upon**) *verb*
   Informal. To hold (something requiring an outlet) in   REPRESS.
   check.

site *noun*
1. The place where a person or thing is located.   1. POSITION *noun.*
2. The place where an action or event occurs.   2. SCENE.

   site *verb*
   To place in a proper position or location.   POSITION *verb.*

sit in *verb*   SEE **sit.**

sit on (or **upon**) *verb*   SEE **sit.**

situate *verb*
1. To put in or assign to a certain permanent place: *decided to situate the nuclear reactors far from major cities.*   1. **Syns:** install, locate, place, position, set[1], site.
2. To place in proper position or location.   2. POSITION *verb.*

situation *noun*
1. The place where a person or thing is located.   1. POSITION *noun.*
2. One's place and direction relative to one's surroundings. 2. BEARING.
3. Positioning of one individual vis-à-vis others.   3. PLACE *noun.*
4. Manner of being or form of existence.   4. CONDITION.
5. A post of employment.   5. POSITION *noun.*

sizable also **sizeable** *adjective*
1. Somewhat big: *a sizable inheritance; a sizable piece of land.*   1. **Syns:** biggish, goodly, largish (*also* largeish), respectable.
2. Notably above average in amount, size, or scope.   2. BIG *adjective.*

sizableness also **sizeableness** *noun*
The quality or state of being large in amount, extent, or importance.   SIZE.

size *noun*
1. The amount of space occupied by something: *measured the size of the room with a yardstick.*   1. **Syns:** amplitude, dimensions, extent, magnitude, measure, proportions.
2. The quality or state of being large in amount, extent, or importance: *a city that impressed me with its size.*   2. **Syns:** amplitude, bigness, extent, greatness, largeness, magnitude, sizableness (*also* sizeableness).
3. Great extent, amount, or dimension.   3. BULK.

size up *verb*
Informal. To make a judgment as to the worth or value of.   ESTIMATE *verb.*

sizeable *adjective*   SEE **sizable.**

sizeableness *noun*   SEE **sizableness.**

size up *verb*   SEE **size.**

sizzle *verb*
To make a sharp sibilant sound.   HISS *verb.*

sizzling *adjective*
Marked by much heat.   HOT *adjective.*

skedaddle *verb*
Informal. To leave hastily.   RUN *verb.*

skein *noun*
1. Something drawn or spun out like a fine, continuous filament.   1. THREAD *noun.*
2. Something that is intricately and often bewilderingly complex.   2. TANGLE *noun.*

skeletal *adjective*
Physically haggard.   WASTED.

skeleton *noun*
A preliminary plan or version, as of a written work.   DRAFT *noun.*

skeptic *noun*
One who habitually or instinctively doubts or questions: *Political skeptics called into question the administration's policy.*   **Syns:** doubter, doubting Thomas, headshaker, Humist, unbeliever.
Near-syns: agnostic, cynic, misanthrope, pessimist, questioner, scoffer.
Ant: believer.

skeptical *adjective*
1. Refusing or reluctant to believe.   1. INCREDULOUS.
2. Experiencing doubt.   2. DOUBTFUL.

skeptically *adverb*

With skepticism: *regarded that plan more than a little skeptically.*

Syns: askance, dubiously, questioningly.
—*Idioms* with a grain of salt, with a note of skepticism, with a skeptical eye.

skepticism *noun*

A lack of conviction or certainty.

DOUBT *noun.*

sketch *noun*

1. A short theatrical piece within a larger production: *a comic sketch in a variety show.*
2. A preliminary plan or version, as of a written work.

1. **Syns:** act, skit.

2. DRAFT *noun.*

sketch *verb*

To draw up a preliminary plan or version of.

DRAFT *verb.*

sketchy *adjective*

1. Not perfected, elaborated, or completed.
2. Lacking in intellectual depth or thoroughness.

1. ROUGH.

2. SUPERFICIAL.

skew *verb*

1. To turn aside sharply from a straight course.
2. To direct (material) to the interests of a particular group.

1. SWERVE.

2. BIAS *verb.*

skid *verb*

1. To lose one's balance and fall or almost fall.
2. To undergo a sharp, rapid descent in value or price.

1. SLIDE *verb.*

2. FALL *verb.*

skid *noun*

A usu. swift downward trend, as in prices.

FALL *noun.*

skiddoo *verb*

Informal. To leave hastily.

RUN *verb.*

skill *noun*

1. Skillfulness in the use of the hands or body.
2. Natural or acquired facility in a specific activity.

1. DEXTERITY.

2. ABILITY.

skilled *adjective*

1. Having the ability to perform well.
2. Very proficient as a result of practice and study.

1. ABLE.

2. ACCOMPLISHED.

skillful *adjective*

1. Having the ability to perform well.
2. Well done or executed.

1. ABLE.

2. NEAT.

skim *verb*

1. To make light and momentary contact with, as in passing.
2. To pass quickly and lightly through the air.
3. To strike a surface at such an angle as to be deflected.
4. To look through reading matter casually.

1. BRUSH *verb.*

2. FLY.

3. GLANCE[1] *verb.*

4. BROWSE.

skim *noun*

Light and momentary contact with another person or thing.

BRUSH *noun.*

skimp *verb*

To be severely sparing in order to economize.

SCRIMP.

skimpy *adjective*

1. Not enough to meet a demand or requirement.
2. Conspicuously deficient in quantity, fullness, or extent.

1. INSUFFICIENT.

2. MEAGER.

skin *noun*

1. The tissue forming the external covering of the body: *burned her skin in the sun.*
2. The outer covering of a fruit: *the skin of a tangerine.*
3. A thin outer covering of an object: *the skin of an aircraft.*

1. **Syns:** epidermis, integument.

2. **Syns:** peel, rind.

3. **Syns:** lamina, sheath, sheathing.

skin *verb*

1. To remove the skin of: *skinned an onion.*

2. To furnish with a covering of a different material.

1. **Syns:** decorticate, excorticate, peel, scale[1], strip[1].

2. FACE *verb.*

3. *Slang.* To exploit (another) by charging too much for something: *We really got skinned by that restaurant.*

3. **Syns:** clip[1] (*Slang*), gouge (*Informal*), hold up, nick (*Slang*), overcharge, rip off (*Slang*), scalp (*Informal*), soak (*Slang*), stick (*Slang*). —*Idioms* make someone pay through the nose, see someone coming, take someone for a ride, take someone to the cleaners.

4. To move swiftly.

4. RUSH *verb.*

skin-deep *adjective*
Lacking in intellectual depth or thoroughness.

SUPERFICIAL.

skinflint *noun*
Slang. A stingy person.

MISER.

skinny *adjective*
Having little flesh or fat on the body.

THIN *adjective.*

skip *verb*
1. To bound lightly: *children skipping around a Maypole.*
2. To strike a surface at such an angle as to be deflected.
3. To cease consideration or treatment of.
4. To fail to attend on purpose.
5. To break loose and leave suddenly, as from confinement or from a difficult or threatening situation.

1. **Syns:** hop, lope, skitter, spring, trip.

2. GLANCE[1] *verb.*

3. DROP *verb.*
4. CUT *verb.*
5. ESCAPE *verb.*

skip *noun*
1. A light bounding movement: *ran with skips and jumps across the playground.*
2. An unexcused absence.

1. **Syns:** hop, spring.

2. CUT *noun.*

skirmish *noun*
A brief, hostile exposure to or contact with something, as danger, opposition, etc.

BRUSH *noun.*

skirt *verb*
1. To pass around but not through: *skirted the many potholes in the road.*
2. To put or form a border on.
3. To evade, as a topic, esp. by circumlocution: *skirted all the touchy issues to avoid confrontations.*

1. **Syns:** bypass, circumnavigate, circumvent, detour, go around.
2. BORDER *verb.*
3. **Syns:** burke, bypass, circumvent, get around, hedge, sidestep.

skirts *noun*
The periphery of a city or town: *lived on the skirts of a huge metropolis.*

Syns: environs, fringe, outskirts, suburbs.

skit *noun*
A short theatrical piece within a larger production.

SKETCH *noun.*

skitter *verb*
To bound lightly.

SKIP *verb.*

skittish *adjective*
1. Feeling or exhibiting nervous tension.
2. Given to lighthearted silliness.

1. EDGY.
2. GIDDY.

skulk *verb*
To move silently and furtively.

SNEAK *verb.*

skulking *adjective*
So slow, deliberate, and secret as to escape observation.

STEALTHY.

sky *noun*
The celestial regions as seen from the earth.

AIR *noun.*

sky *verb*
To rise abruptly and precipitously.

SOAR.

sky-high *adjective*
1. Imposingly high.
2. Vastly exceeding a normal limit, as in cost.

1. LOFTY.
2. STEEP[1].

skyrocket *verb*
To rise abruptly and precipitously.

SOAR.

slab *noun*
A relatively long, straight, rigid piece of metal or other solid material.

STICK *noun*.

slack *adjective*
1. Not tautly bound to something else.
2. Guilty of neglect; lacking due care or concern.
3. Characterized by reduced economic activity.

1. LOOSE *adjective*.
2. NEGLIGENT.
3. SLOW *adjective*.

slack *verb*
1. To reduce in tension, pressure, or rigidity.
2. To avoid the fulfillment of.

1. EASE *verb*.
2. NEGLECT *verb*.

slacken *verb*
1. To reduce in tension, pressure, or rigidity.
2. To become less active or intense.
3. To moderate or change a position or course of action as a result of pressure.

1. EASE *verb*.
2. SUBSIDE.
3. WEAKEN.

slackening *noun*
The act or process of becoming less active or intense.

WANE *noun*.

slackness *noun*
The state or quality of being negligent.

NEGLIGENCE.

slam *noun*
A forceful movement causing a loud noise: *shut the door with a slam; hit his fist on the table with a slam.*

Syns: bang, crash, smash, wham.

slam *verb*
1. To strike, set down, or close in such a way as to make a loud noise.
2. To deliver (a powerful blow) suddenly and sharply.
3. *Slang.* To criticize harshly and devastatingly: *The candidate slammed his opponent for declining to debate.*

1. BANG *verb*.

2. HIT *verb*.
3. *Syns:* blister, drub, excoriate, flay, lash (into), rip (into) (*Informal*), roast (*Informal*), scarify, scathe, scorch, score, scourge, slap, slash. —*Idioms* burn someone's ears, crawl all over, give someone a roasting, pin someone's ears back, put someone on the griddle, put someone on the hot seat, rake over the coals, read the riot act to.

slammer *noun*
Slang. A place for the confinement of persons in lawful detention.

JAIL *noun*.

slander *noun*
The expression of injurious, malicious statements about someone.

LIBEL *noun*.

slander *verb*
To make defamatory statements about.

LIBEL *verb*.

slanderous *adjective*
Damaging to the reputation.

LIBELOUS.

slant *verb*
1. To depart or cause to depart from true vertical or horizontal.
2. To have a tendency or inclination.
3. To direct (material) to the interests of a particular group.

1. INCLINE *verb*.

2. TEND[1].
3. BIAS *verb*.

slant *noun*
1. Deviation from a particular direction.
2. A way of considering a matter.
3. The position from which something is observed or considered.

1. INCLINATION.
2. LIGHT[1] *noun*.
3. POINT OF VIEW.

slanted *adjective*
Angled at a slant.

BIAS *adjective*.

slanting *adjective*
Angled at a slant.

BIAS *adjective*.

slap *noun*
A quick, sharp blow, esp. with the hand: *gave the naughty child a slap on the bottom.*

Syns: box[2], buffet, bust (*Slang*), chop[1], clip[1] (*Informal*), cuff, smack[1], smacker, spank, spat (*Informal*).

slap *verb*
1. To hit with a quick, sharp blow of the hand: *slapped the child for having tantrums.*
2. To criticize harshly and devastatingly.

1. *Syns:* blip, box[2], buffet, bust, cuff, smack[1], spank.
2. SLAM *verb.*

slap around *verb*
To be rough or brutal with: *The police slapped the suspect around during questioning.*

Syns: knock about (*or* around) (*Informal*), manhandle, mess (up) (*Slang*), rough (up).
SEE **slap.**

slap around *verb*

slap-bang *adjective*
Informal. Characterized by unthinking boldness and haste.

RASH[1].

slapdash *adjective*
1. Indifferent to correctness, accuracy, or neatness.
2. Characterized by unthinking boldness and haste.

1. CARELESS.
2. RASH[1].

slash *verb*
1. To penetrate with a sharp edge.
2. To decrease, as in length or amount, by or as if by severing or excising.
3. To criticize harshly and devastatingly.

1. CUT *verb.*
2. CUT BACK.
3. SLAM *verb.*

slash *noun*
1. The result of cutting.
2. An incision, notch, or slight cut made with or as if with a knife.
3. The act or process of decreasing in length, amount, duration, etc.

1. CUT *noun.*
2. SCORE *noun.*
3. CUTBACK at **cut back.**

slashing *adjective*
So sharp as to cause mental pain.

BITING.

slate *noun*
1. A list of events to take place or of things to be done, often with their assigned times.
2. A list of candidates proposed or endorsed by a political party.

1. SCHEDULE *noun.*
2. TICKET *noun.*

slate *verb*
To enter on a schedule.

SCHEDULE *verb.*

slattern *noun*
A vulgar, promiscuous woman who flouts propriety.

SLUT.

slaughter *verb*
To kill savagely and indiscriminately.

ANNIHILATE.

slaughter *noun*
The savage killing of many victims.

MASSACRE *noun.*

slaughterer *noun*
One who murders another.

MURDERER.

slaughterous *adjective*
Eager for bloodshed.

MURDEROUS.

slave *verb*
To do tedious, laborious, and sometimes menial work.

GRIND *verb.*

slaver *verb*
1. To let saliva run from the mouth.
2. To compliment excessively and ingratiatingly.
3. To support slavishly every opinion or suggestion of a superior.

1. DROOL *verb.*
2. FLATTER.
3. FAWN.

slaver *noun*
1. Saliva running from the mouth.
2. *Archaic.* Excessive, ingratiating praise.

1. DROOL *noun.*
2. FLATTERY.

slavery *noun*
A state of subjugation to an owner or master: *sold into slavery.*

Syns: enslavement, helotry, serfdom, servility, servitude, thrall, thralldom *or*

thraldom, villeinage (*also* villainage),
yoke. —*Idioms* involuntary servitude, the
chains (*or* yoke) of slavery.

slavish   *adjective*
1. Excessively eager to serve or obey.
2. Copying another in an inferior or obsequious way.
3. Not easy to do, achieve, or master.

1. SERVILE.
2. IMITATIVE.
3. DIFFICULT.

slay   *verb*
1. To cause the death of.
2. To take the life of (a person or persons) unlawfully.

1. KILL.
2. MURDER *verb*.

slayer   *noun*
One who murders another.

MURDERER.

slaying   *noun*
The crime of murdering someone.

MURDER *noun*.

slaying   *adjective*
Slang. Extremely funny.

PRICELESS.

sleazy   *adjective*
1. Showing signs of wear and tear or neglect.
2. Of decidedly inferior quality.

1. SHABBY.
2. SHODDY.

sled   *verb*
To ride on a sled in the snow.

SLIDE *verb*.

sledge   *verb*
Brit. To ride on a sled in the snow.

SLIDE *verb*.

sleek   *adjective*
1. Smooth and lustrous as if polished: *the cat's sleek black fur.*

1. *Syns:* satiny, sleeky.
Near-syns: glassy, glossy, polished, smooth, sparkling.

2. Having slender and graceful lines: *a sleek new convertible.*
3. Affectedly and self-servingly earnest.

2. *Syns:* streamlined, trim.

3. UNCTUOUS.

sleek   *verb*
1. To give a gleaming luster to, usu. through friction.
2. To change or modify so as to prevent recognition of the true identity or character of.

1. GLOSS *verb*.
2. DISGUISE *verb*.

sleeky   *adjective*
Smooth and lustrous as if polished.

SLEEK *adjective*.

sleep   *noun*
The natural recurring condition of suspended consciousness by which the body rests: *needed a full eight hours of sleep.*

Syns: shut-eye (*Slang*), slumber, snooze (*Informal*). —*Idioms* land of Nod, the arms of Morpheus.

sleep   *verb*
To be asleep: *slept for twelve hours.*

Syns: slumber, snooze (*Informal*). —*Idioms* be in the land of Nod, be sunk in sleep, catch some shut-eye, rest in the arms of Morpheus, sleep like a log (*or* rock *or* top), sleep tight.

sleep in   *verb*
To sleep longer than intended: *slept in and was late to work.*

Syn: oversleep.

sleep with   *verb*
To engage in sexual relations with.

TAKE *verb*.

sleeper   *noun*
Informal. A dazzling, often sudden instance of success.

HIT *noun*.

sleep in   *verb*

SEE **sleep**.

sleeping   *adjective*
1. In a state of sleep: *Sleeping children are beautiful.*

1. *Syns:* asleep, out (*Informal*), slumbering, snoozing (*Informal*), unawake. —*Idioms* dead to the world, fast (*or* sound) asleep, in a sound (*or* wakeless) sleep, out like a light.

2. In a state of temporary inactivity: *a sleeping giant among the unaligned nations.*

2. *Syns:* dormant, inactive.

sleepless *adjective*
Marked by an absence of sleep.

WAKEFUL.
SEE **sleep.**

sleep with *verb*

sleepy *adjective*
1. Ready for or needing sleep: *tired, sleepy children.*

1. *Syns:* dozy, drowsy, nodding, slumberous (*also* slumbery, slumbrous), snoozy (*Informal*), somnolent, soporific.
Near-ants: awake, aroused, conscious, restless, sleepless, wide-awake.
Ant: wakeful.

2. Inducing sleep: *a hot, sleepy day.*

2. *Syns:* hypnotic, narcotic, slumberous (*also* slumbery, slumbrous), somnifacient, somniferous (*also* somnific), somnolent, somnorific, soporific.

sleer *verb*
Brit. Regional. To smile or laugh scornfully or derisively.

SNEER *verb.*

sleight *noun*
1. Skillfulness in the use of the hands or body.
2. An action meant to deceive.
3. An indirect, usu. cunning means of gaining an end.

1. DEXTERITY.
2. DECEPTION.
3. TRICK *noun.*

slender *adjective*
1. Having little flesh or fat on the body.
2. Small in degree, esp. of probability.

1. THIN *adjective.*
2. REMOTE.

sleuth *noun*
Informal. A person whose work is investigating crimes or obtaining hidden evidence or information.

DETECTIVE.

slew also **slue** *noun*
Informal. An indeterminately great amount or number.

HEAP *noun.*

slice *verb*
To separate into parts with or as if with a sharp-edged instrument.

CUT *verb.*

slice *noun*
1. The result of cutting.
2. A part severed from a whole.
3. A thin piece, esp. of tissue, suitable for microscopic examination.

1. CUT *noun.*
2. CUT *noun.*
3. SECTION *noun.*

slick *adjective*
1. So smooth and glassy as to offer insecure hold or footing: *steps slick with ice.*

1. *Syns:* lubricious, sliddery, slippery, slippy, slithery. —*Idioms* slick as a greased pig, slick as greased glass, slippery as an eel.
Near-ants: coarse, gritty, pitted, rough, uneven, unsmooth.

2. Exhibiting or possessing skill and ease in performance.
3. Having or showing a clever awareness and resourcefulness in practical matters.
4. Characterized by ready but often insincere or superficial discourse.
5. Astute but lacking in ethics or principles.

2. DEXTEROUS.

3. SHREWD.

4. GLIB.

5. SHARP *adjective.*

slick *verb*
1. To move smoothly, continuously, and effortlessly.
2. *Informal.* To dress in formal or special clothing.

1. GLIDE.
2. DRESS UP at **dress.**

sliddery *adjective*
So smooth and glassy as to offer insecure hold or footing.

SLICK.

slide *verb*

1. To pass smoothly, quietly, and undisturbed on or as if on a slippery surface: *skaters sliding across a frozen pond; decided to let the matter slide for the moment.*
2. To move smoothly, continuously, and effortlessly.
3. To move silently and furtively.
4. To move along in a crouching or prone position.
5. To lose one's balance and fall or almost fall: *slid on the freshly waxed floor.*
6. To maneuver gently and slowly into place.
7. To shift or be shifted out of place.
8. To ride on a sled in the snow: *The children went sliding on our hill.*

slide *noun*

A usu. swift downward trend, as in prices.

slight *adjective*

1. Of small intensity.
2. Small in degree, esp. of probability.

slight *verb*

1. To fail to care for or give proper attention to.
2. To refuse to pay attention to (a person); treat with contempt.

slight *noun*

An act or instance of neglecting.

slighting *adjective*

Tending or intending to belittle.

slim *adjective*

Small in degree, esp. of probability.

slim *verb*

To lose bodily weight, as by dieting.

slime *noun*

A viscous, usu. offensively dirty substance: *a swimming pool coated with green slime.*

slimy *adjective*

Of, pertaining to, or covered with slime: *slimy mud; a slimy, brackish pool.*

sling *verb*

1. To send through the air with a motion of the hand or arm.
2. To fasten or be fastened at one point with no support from below.

sling *noun*

An act of throwing.

slink *verb*

To move silently and furtively.

slink *noun*

1. One who behaves in a stealthy, furtive way.
2. The act of proceeding slowly, deliberately, and secretly to escape observation.

slinkiness *noun*

The act of proceeding slowly, deliberately, and secretly to escape observation.

slinking *adjective*

So slow, deliberate, and secret as to escape observation.

slinky *adjective*

So slow, deliberate, and secret as to escape observation.

slip *noun*

1. An act or thought that unintentionally deviates from what is correct, right, or true.
2. *Informal.* A minor mistake.

---

1. **Syns:** coast, drift.

2. GLIDE.
3. SNEAK *verb.*
4. CRAWL *verb.*
5. **Syns:** skid, slip, slither. —*Idiom* take a slide (*or* skid).
6. EASE *verb.*
7. SLIP *verb.*
8. **Syns:** sled, sledge (*Brit.*).

FALL *noun.*

1. LIGHT².
2. REMOTE.

1. NEGLECT *verb.*
2. IGNORE.

NEGLECT *noun.*

DISPARAGING.

REMOTE.

REDUCE.

Syns: muck, ooze.

Syns: mucky, oozy.

1. THROW *verb.*

2. HANG *verb.*

THROW *noun.*

SNEAK *verb.*

1. SNEAK *noun.*
2. STEALTH.

STEALTH.

STEALTHY.

STEALTHY.

1. ERROR.

2. LAPSE *noun.*

slip *verb*
1. To shift or be shifted out of place: *The boxes slipped from my grasp and crashed to the floor.*
2. To move smoothly, continuously, and effortlessly.
3. To move silently and furtively.
4. To lose one's balance and fall or almost fall.
5. To undergo moral deterioration.
6. *Informal.* To decline, as in value or quantity, very gradually: *Stock prices slipped an eighth of a point.*
7. To make an error or mistake.
8. To maneuver gently and slowly into place.
9. *Vet.Med.* To bring forth a nonviable fetus prematurely.
10. To cast off by natural process.
11. To displace (a bone) from a socket or joint: *slipped his shoulder in the soccer game.*

1. *Syn:* slide.
2. GLIDE.
3. SNEAK *verb.*
4. SLIDE *verb.*
5. FALL *verb.*
6. *Syns:* drop off, fall off, sag.

7. ERR.
8. EASE *verb.*
9. MISCARRY.

10. SHED.
11. *Syns:* dislocate, throw out. —*Idiom* throw out of joint.

slip away *verb*
To fail to be fixed by the mind, memory, or senses.

ESCAPE *verb.*

slip into *verb*
To put (an article of clothing) on one's person.

DON.

slip on *verb*
To put (an article of clothing) on one's person.

DON.

slip away *verb*

SEE **slip.**

slip into *verb*

SEE **slip.**

slip on *verb*

SEE **slip.**

slippery *adjective*
1. So smooth and glassy as to offer insecure hold or footing.
2. Characterized by or exhibiting evasion.
3. Astute but lacking in ethics or principles.

1. SLICK *adjective.*

2. EVASIVE.
3. SHARP *adjective.*

slippy *adjective*
So smooth and glassy as to offer insecure hold or footing.

SLICK *adjective.*

slipshod *adjective*
1. Indifferent to correctness, accuracy, or neatness.
2. Marked by an absence of cleanliness and order.

1. CARELESS.
2. MESSY.

slip-up *noun*

SEE **slip up.**

slip up *verb*
Informal. To make an error or mistake.

ERR.

slip-up *noun*
1. *Informal.* An act or thought that unintentionally deviates from what is correct, right, or true.
2. *Informal.* A minor mistake.

1. ERROR.

2. LAPSE *noun.*

slit *verb*
To penetrate with a sharp edge.

CUT *verb.*

slit *noun*
The result of cutting.

CUT *noun.*

slither *verb*
1. To move sinuously: *A large earthworm slithered in the garden.*
2. To lose one's balance and fall or almost fall.
3. To move smoothly, continuously, and effortlessly.

1. *Syns:* snake, undulate.

2. SLIDE *verb.*
3. GLIDE.

slithery *adjective*
So smooth and glassy as to offer insecure hold or footing.

SLICK *adjective.*

slobber *verb*
To let saliva run from the mouth.

DROOL *verb.*

slobber *noun*
Saliva running from the mouth.

DROOL *noun.*

slobbery *adjective*
Marked by an absence of cleanliness and order.

MESSY.

slog *verb*
1. To do tedious, laborious, and sometimes menial work.   1. GRIND *verb*.
2. To walk heavily, slowly, and with difficulty.   2. PLOD.
3. To deliver (a powerful blow) suddenly and sharply.   3. HIT *verb*.

slop *verb*
1. To walk heavily, slowly, and with difficulty.   1. PLOD.
2. To take on or move with an awkward, slovenly posture.   2. SLOUCH *verb*.
3. To hurl or scatter liquid upon.   3. SPLASH.

slope *verb*
To depart or cause to depart from true vertical or horizontal.   INCLINE *verb*.

slope *noun*
1. Deviation from a particular direction.   1. INCLINATION.
2. An upward slope.   2. ASCENT.

sloped *adjective*
Departing from true vertical or horizontal.   INCLINED.

sloping *adjective*
Departing from true vertical or horizontal.   INCLINED.

sloppiness *noun*
Informal. The quality or condition of being affectedly or overly emotional.   SENTIMENTALITY.

sloppy *adjective*
1. Indifferent to correctness, accuracy, or neatness.   1. CARELESS.
2. Marked by an absence of cleanliness and order.   2. MESSY.
3. *Informal.* Affectedly or extravagantly emotional.   3. SENTIMENTAL.

slosh *verb*
1. To hurl or scatter liquid upon.   1. SPLASH.
2. To flow or move with a low, slapping sound.   2. WASH.

sloshed *adjective*
Slang. Intoxicated with alcoholic liquor.   DRUNK *adjective*.

slot *noun*
1. A post of employment.   1. POSITION *noun*.
2. A particular position in a designated order of importance.   2. PLACE *noun*.

sloth *noun*
The quality or state of being lazy.   LAZINESS.

slothful *adjective*
Resistant to exertion and activity.   LAZY.

slothfulness *noun*
The quality or state of being lazy.   LAZINESS.

slouch *verb*
1. To take on or move with an awkward, slovenly posture: *He slouched into the room and fell into a big chair.*   1. *Syns:* loll, lop^2, slop, slump.
   Near-syns: lounge, saunter, shamble, shuffle, stoop.
2. To hang limply, loosely, and carelessly: *a hat with a wide, slouching brim.*   2. *Syns:* droop, flop, loll, lop^2, sag, wilt.

slouch *noun*
A self-indulgent person who spends time avoiding work or other useful activity.   WASTREL.

slough^1 *noun*
A usu. low-lying area of soft, waterlogged ground and standing water.   SWAMP *noun*.

slough^2 *verb*
To cast off by natural process.   SHED.

slovenly *adjective*
1. Indifferent to correctness, accuracy, or neatness.   1. CARELESS.
2. Marked by an absence of cleanliness and order.   2. MESSY.

slow   *adjective*
1. Proceeding at a rate less than usual or desired: *slow progress toward peace; slow traffic during rush hour.*

2. Characterized by reduced economic activity: *Car sales have been slow this year.*
3. Having only a limited ability to learn and understand.
4. Lacking in intelligence.

slow   *verb*
To cause to be later or slower than expected or desired.

slow   *adverb*
So as to fall behind schedule: *This clock runs slow. The train is an hour slow.*

slow-footed   *adjective*
Proceeding at a rate less than usual or desired.

slow-going   *adjective*
Proceeding at a rate less than usual or desired.

slow-paced   *adjective*
Proceeding at a rate less than usual or desired.

slowpoke   *noun*
Informal. One that lags.

slow-witted   *adjective*
1. Having only a limited ability to learn and understand.
2. Lacking in intelligence.

slue¹   *verb*
To turn aside sharply from a straight course.

slue²   *noun*

slug¹   *noun*
Informal. A small amount of liquor.

slug²   *verb*
Slang. To deliver (a powerful blow) suddenly and sharply.

slug³   *noun*
Informal. A self-indulgent person who spends time avoiding work or other useful activity.

slugabed   *noun*
A self-indulgent person who spends time avoiding work or other useful activity.

sluggard   *noun*
A self-indulgent person who spends time avoiding work or other useful activity.

sluggish   *adjective*
1. Lacking mental and physical alertness and activity.
2. Characterized by reduced economic activity.

sluggishness   *noun*
1. A deficiency in mental and physical alertness and activity.
2. The quality or state of being lazy.

slumber   *verb*
To be asleep.

slumber   *noun*
The natural recurring condition of suspended consciousness by which the body rests.

---

1. **Syns:** dilatory, dragging, flagging, laggard, lagging, poky (*also* pokey) (*Informal*), slow-footed, slow-going, slow-paced, tardy. —*Idioms* slow as a swamp turtle, slow as molasses in January.
   Near-ants: lightning, quick, rapid, swift.
   Ant: fast.
2. **Syns:** down, dull, off, slack, sluggish, soft.
3. BACKWARD *adjective.*
4. STUPID.

DELAY *verb.*

Syns: behind, behindhand, late. —*Idiom* behind time.

SLOW *adjective.*

SLOW *adjective.*

SLOW *adjective.*

LAGGARD *noun.*

1. BACKWARD *adjective.*
2. STUPID.

SWERVE.
SEE **slew.**

DROP *noun.*

HIT *verb.*

WASTREL.

WASTREL.

WASTREL.

1. LETHARGIC.
2. SLOW *adjective.*

1. LETHARGY.
2. LAZINESS.

SLEEP *verb.*

SLEEP *noun.*

slumbering *adjective*
In a state of sleep.   SLEEPING.

slumberless *adjective*
Marked by an absence of sleep.   WAKEFUL.

slumberous also **slumbery, slumbrous** *adjective*
1. Inducing sleep.   1. SLEEPY.
2. Ready for or needing sleep.   2. SLEEPY.

slumbery *adjective*   SEE **slumberous.**
slumbrous *adjective*   SEE **slumberous.**

slump *noun*
1. A usu. swift downward trend, as in prices.   1. FALL *noun.*
2. A period of decreased business activity and high   2. DEPRESSION.
   unemployment.

slump *verb*
1. To go from a more erect posture to a less erect   1. DROP *verb.*
   posture.
2. To take on or move with an awkward, slovenly   2. SLOUCH *verb.*
   posture.
3. To undergo a sharp, rapid descent in value or price.   3. FALL *verb.*

slur *verb*
To make defamatory statements about.   LIBEL *verb.*

slur *noun*
An implied criticism.   REFLECTION.

slushy *adjective*
Informal. Affectedly or extravagantly emotional.   SENTIMENTAL.

slut *noun*
A vulgar, promiscuous woman who flouts propriety: *a*   **Syns:** baggage, floozy (*also* floozey)
forward slut in tawdry finery.   (*Slang*), hussy, jade, slattern, strumpet,
                                                                            tart[2], tramp, wench, wanton.

sly *adjective*
1. Trickily secret: *a sly maneuver.*   1. **Syns:** furtive, secretive, surreptitious.
2. Deceitfully clever.   2. ARTFUL.
3. Astute but lacking in ethics or principles.   3. SHARP *adjective.*
4. *Chiefly Regional.* Having or showing a clever   4. SHREWD.
   awareness and resourcefulness in practical matters.

sly *verb*
To move silently and furtively.   SNEAK *verb.*

slyness *noun*
Lack of straightforwardness and honesty in action.   INDIRECTION.

smack[1] *verb*
1. To touch or caress with the lips, esp. as a sign of   1. KISS *verb.*
   passion or affection.
2. To deliver (a powerful blow) suddenly and sharply.   2. HIT *verb.*
3. To hit with a quick, sharp blow of the hand.   3. SLAP *verb.*

smack *noun*
1. The act or an instance of kissing.   1. KISS *noun.*
2. A sudden sharp, powerful stroke.   2. BLOW[2].
3. A quick, sharp blow, esp. with the hand.   3. SLAP *noun.*

smack *adverb*
Without the slightest deviation in any respect.   PRECISELY.

smack[2] *verb*
To have a particular flavor or suggestion of something: **Syns:** flavor, savor, smell, suggest, taste.
Those statements smack of treason.

smack *noun*
1. A distinctive property of a substance affecting the   1. FLAVOR *noun.*
   gustatory sense.
2. A distinctive yet intangible quality deemed typical   2. FLAVOR *noun.*
   of a given thing.

smacker *noun*
1. The act or an instance of kissing.   1. KISS *noun.*
2. A sudden sharp, powerful stroke.   2. BLOW[2].

3. A quick, sharp blow, esp. with the hand.   3. SLAP *noun*.

small *adjective*
1. Not yet large in size due to incomplete growth: 1. *Syn:* little.
   mothers with small children.
2. Notably below average in amount, size, or scope.   2. LITTLE.
3. *Brit. Regional.* Consisting of small particles.   3. FINE[1] *adjective*.
4. Of subordinate standing or importance.   4. MINOR *adjective*.
5. Not broad or elevated in scope or understanding.   5. NARROW.
6. Contemptibly unimportant.   6. PETTY.
7. Not irritating, strident, or loud.   7. SOFT.

smallest *adjective*
Comprising the least possible.   MINIMAL.

small-fry *adjective*
Informal. Of subordinate standing or importance.   MINOR *adjective*.

smallish *adjective*
Notably below average in amount, size, or scope.   LITTLE.

small-minded *adjective*
1. Not tolerant of the beliefs, opinions, etc., of others.   1. INTOLERANT.
2. Not broad or elevated in scope or understanding.   2. NARROW.
3. Contemptibly unimportant.   3. PETTY.

smallness *noun*
Contemptible unimportance.   PETTINESS.

small-time *adjective*
Informal. Of subordinate standing or importance.   MINOR *adjective*.

small-town *adjective*
Having the restricted outlook often characteristic of   LOCAL *adjective*.
geographic isolation.

smarm *verb*
Regional. To spread with a greasy, sticky, or dirty   SMEAR *verb*.
substance.

smarmy *adjective*
Affectedly and self-servingly earnest.   UNCTUOUS.

smart *verb*
To feel or cause to feel a sensation of heat or   STING *verb*.
discomfort.

smart *noun*
A sensation of physical discomfort occurring as the   PAIN *noun*.
result of disease or injury.

smart *adjective*
1. Mentally quick and original.   1. CLEVER.
2. Being or in accordance with the current fashion.   2. FASHIONABLE.
3. Amusing or pleasing because of wit or originality.   3. CLEVER.
4. Rude and disrespectful.   4. IMPUDENT.

smart aleck *noun*
Informal. One who is obnoxiously self-assertive and   *Syns:* know-it-all (*Informal*), malapert,
arrogant: *smart alecks who heckled the speaker; smart*   saucebox, smarty (*Informal*), smarty-pants
alecks cracking jokes during the love scene.   (*Slang*), wiseacre (*Informal*), wisecracker
                                                                    (*Slang*), wise guy (*Slang*), wisehead
                                                                    (*Informal*), wiseling (*Archaic*),
                                                                    wisenheimer (*also* weisenheimer)
                                                                    (*Informal*), witling (*Archaic*).
                                                                    Near-syns: blowhard, boaster, braggart,
                                                                    gasbag, windbag; exhibitionist, show-off.

smarten *verb*
To improve in appearance, esp. by refurbishing.   FIX UP at **fix**.

smarting *adjective*
Marked by, causing, or experiencing physical pain.   PAINFUL.

smarts *noun*
Slang. The faculty of thinking, reasoning, and   INTELLIGENCE.
acquiring and applying knowledge.

smarty *noun*
Informal. One who is obnoxiously self-assertive and arrogant.

SMART ALECK.

smarty-pants *noun*
Slang. One who is obnoxiously self-assertive and arrogant.

SMART ALECK.

smash *verb*
1. To crack or split into two or more fragments by means of or as a result of force, a blow, or strain.
2. To collapse or shatter by or as if by breaking.
3. To undergo wrecking.
4. To strike together with a loud, harsh noise.
5. To cause the complete ruin or wreckage of.
6. To deliver (a powerful blow) suddenly and sharply.

1. BREAK *verb.*
2. BREAK DOWN.
3. CRASH *verb.*
4. CLASH *verb.*
5. DESTROY.
6. HIT *verb.*

smash *noun*
1. An abrupt, disastrous failure.
2. Violent, forcible contact between two or more things.
3. A loud striking together.
4. A wrecking of a vehicle.
5. A forceful movement causing a loud noise.

1. COLLAPSE *noun.*
2. COLLISION.
3. CLASH *noun.*
4. CRASH *noun.*
5. SLAM *noun.*

smashed *adjective*
Slang. Intoxicated with alcoholic liquor.

DRUNK *adjective.*

smashup *noun*

SEE **smash up.**

smash up *verb*
To undergo wrecking.

CRASH *verb.*

smashup *noun*
1. A wrecking of a vehicle.
2. An abrupt, disastrous failure.

1. CRASH *noun.*
2. COLLAPSE *noun.*

smatterer *noun*
One lacking professional skill and ease in a particular pursuit.

AMATEUR.

smaze *noun*
A thick, heavy atmospheric condition offering reduced visibility due to the presence of suspended particles.

HAZE *noun.*

smear *verb*
1. To spread with a greasy, sticky, or dirty substance: *smeared the bricks with mortar.*

1. *Syns:* bedaub, besmear, butter, clart (*Brit. Regional*), dab[1], daub, plaster, smarm (*Regional*), smudge. —*Idiom* lay it on thick.
   Near-syns: coat, cover, encrust, lop, smirch, soil.

2. To cast aspersions on.
3. *Slang.* To win a victory over, as in battle or a competition.
4. *Slang.* To render totally ineffective by decisive defeat.

2. BLACKEN.
3. DEFEAT *verb.*

4. OVERWHELM.

smear *noun*
1. A discolored mark made by smearing: *had a huge smear of axle grease on his jeans.*
2. An attempt to destroy someone's reputation: *a carefully engineered smear by use of rumors.*

1. *Syns:* blot, blotch, dab[1], daub, smirch, smudge, smutch, splotch.
2. *Syns:* mudslinging, vilification. —*Idiom* smear campaign.

smell *noun*
1. The sense by which odors are perceived: *Rodents often identify their offspring by means of smell.*
2. The quality of something that may be perceived by the olfactory sense: *the mingled smells of food and seawater at the beach.*
3. A general impression produced by a predominant quality or characteristic.

1. *Syns:* nose, olfaction, scent.

2. *Syns:* aroma, odor, scent, snuff[1].

3. AIR *noun.*

smell *verb*

1. To perceive with the olfactory sense: *One could smell the smoke for miles.*

1. **Syns:** nose, scent, sniff, snuff¹, whiff.
   —*Idiom* catch (*or* get) a whiff of.
   Near-syns: detect, perceive, sense, snuffle.

2. To have or give off a foul odor: *This shrimp smells.*

2. **Syns:** funk¹, reek, stench, stink.
   —*Idiom* smell to high heaven.

3. To have a particular flavor or suggestion of something.

3. SMACK² *verb.*

smeller *noun*
Informal. The structure on the human face that contains the nostrils and organs of smell and forms the beginning of the respiratory tract.

NOSE *noun.*

smelly *adjective*
Informal. Having an unpleasant odor: *smelly fumes from a soap factory.*

Syns: fetid, foul, foul-smelling, malodorous, mephitic, noisome, reeking, stinking.

smidgen *noun*
Informal. A tiny amount.

BIT¹.

smile *noun*
A facial expression marked by an upward curving of the lips: *gave me a cheery smile.*

Syn: grin. —*Idiom* broad grin.

smile *verb*
To curve the lips upward in expressing amusement, pleasure, or happiness: *smiled and waved good-bye.*

Syns: beam, grin. —*Idioms* break into a smile, crack a smile, wreathe one's face in smiles.

smile on (or **upon**) *verb*
To lend supportive approval to.

ENCOURAGE.

smile on (or **upon**) *verb*

SEE **smile.**

smirch *noun*
A discolored mark made by smearing.

SMEAR *noun.*

smirk *verb*
To smile in an insincere, knowing way: *men smirking at peepshows.*

Syn: simper. —*Idiom* grin like a Cheshire cat.

smirk *noun*
An affected, knowing smile: *smirks and giggles in the back of the theater.*

Syn: simper. —*Idiom* sardonic grin.

smitch *noun*
Informal. A tiny amount.

BIT¹.

smite *verb*
1. To deliver (a powerful blow) suddenly and sharply.
2. To bring great harm or suffering to.

1. HIT *verb.*
2. AFFLICT.

smitten *adjective*
Affected with intense romantic attraction.

INFATUATED.

smolder *verb*
To be in a state of emotional or mental turmoil.

BOIL *verb.*

smooch *noun*
The act or an instance of kissing.

KISS *noun.*

smooch *verb*
To touch or caress with the lips, esp. as a sign of passion or affection.

KISS *verb.*

smooth *adjective*
1. Marked by facility, esp. of expression: *a smooth prose style.*
2. Having no irregularities, roughness, or indentations.
3. Posing no difficulty.
4. Free from severity or violence, as in movement.
5. Effortlessly gracious and tactful in social manner.

1. **Syns:** cursive, easy, effortless, flowing, fluent, fluid, graceful, ready, running.
2. EVEN¹ *adjective.*
3. EASY.
4. GENTLE *adjective.*
5. SUAVE.

smooth *verb*
1. To make even, smooth, or level.
2. To bring to perfection or completion.
3. To bring to perfection or completion.

1. EVEN¹ *verb.*
2. PERFECT *verb.*
3. PERFECT *verb.*

smooth over *verb*
To bring (something) into a state of agreement or accord.   SETTLE.

smooth over *verb*   SEE **smooth.**

smooth-spoken *adjective*
Fluently persuasive and forceful.   ELOQUENT.

smother *verb*
1. To stop the breathing of.   1. CHOKE.
2. To hold (something requiring an outlet) in check.   2. REPRESS.
3. To render totally ineffective by decisive defeat.   3. OVERWHELM.

smothering *noun*
The act of restraining forcefully.   REPRESSION.

smudge *verb*
1. To make dirty.   1. DIRTY *verb.*
2. To spread with a greasy, sticky, or dirty substance.   2. SMEAR *verb.*
3. To cast aspersions on.   3. BLACKEN.

smudge *noun*
A discolored mark made by smearing.   SMEAR *noun.*

smuggle *verb*
1. To import or export secretly and illegally: *smuggled in cocaine from South America.*   1. *Syns:* bootleg, contraband, run. —*Idiom* run contraband.
2. To bring in or take out secretly: *Friendly diplomats smuggled the hostages out of the country.*   2. *Syns:* sneak, spirit.

smuggler *noun*
A person who engages in smuggling: *arms smugglers operating out of Northern Ireland.*   *Syns:* bootlegger, contrabandist, runner.

smut *noun*
Something that is offensive to accepted standards of decency.   OBSCENITY.

smut *verb*
1. To soil with foreign matter.   1. STAIN *verb.*
2. To cast aspersions on.   2. BLACKEN.

smutch *verb*
To make dirty.   DIRTY *verb.*

smutch *noun*
A discolored mark made by smearing.   SMEAR *noun.*

smutty *adjective*
1. Covered or stained with or as if with dirt or other impurities.   1. DIRTY *adjective.*
2. Offensive to accepted standards of decency.   2. OBSCENE.

snack *noun*
A light meal.   BITE *noun.*

snafu *verb*
1. *Slang.* To harm irreparably through inept handling; make a mess of.   1. BOTCH *verb.*
2. *Slang.* To put into total disorder.   2. CONFUSE.

snafu *noun*
1. *Slang.* A lack of order or regular arrangement.   1. DISORDER *noun.*
2. *Slang.* A ruinous state of disorder.   2. BOTCH *noun.*

snag *noun*
1. Anything that impedes or prevents entry or passage.   1. BAR *noun.*
2. A tricky or unsuspected condition.   2. CATCH *noun.*

snake *verb*
1. To move along in a crouching or prone position.   1. CRAWL *verb.*
2. To move silently and furtively.   2. SNEAK *verb.*
3. To move sinuously.   3. SLITHER.
4. To move or proceed on a repeatedly curving course.   4. WIND^2.

snaky *adjective*
Repeatedly curving in alternate directions.   WINDING.

snap *verb*
1. To make a light, sharp noise: *The lock snapped shut.*
2. To make a sudden sharp, explosive noise.
3. To undergo partial breaking.
4. To give way mentally and emotionally.
5. To grasp at (something) eagerly, forcibly, and abruptly with the jaws: *sharks snapping at the bloody bait.*
6. To speak abruptly and sharply: *He snapped at me for no reason at all.*

1. **Syns:** clack, clacket (*Regional*), click.
2. CRACK *verb.*
3. CRACK *verb.*
4. BREAK DOWN.
5. **Syns:** catch, nip¹, snatch, strike.

6. **Syns:** bark, snarl². —*Idioms* bite someone's head off, snap someone's head (*or* nose) off.

snap *noun*
1. A light, sharp noise: *the snap of a light switch.*
2. A sudden sharp, explosive noise.
3. A sudden pull.
4. *Informal.* An aggressive readiness to undertake taxing efforts.
5. *Chiefly Brit. Regional.* A light meal.
6. A tiny amount.
7. *Informal.* An easily accomplished task.

1. **Syns:** clack, click.
2. REPORT *noun.*
3. JERK *noun.*
4. DRIVE *noun.*

5. BITE *noun.*
6. BIT¹ *noun.*
7. BREEZE *noun.*

snap *adjective*
1. Spoken, performed, or composed with little or no preparation or forethought.
2. *Informal.* Posing no difficulty.

1. EXTEMPORANEOUS.

2. EASY.

snappish *adjective*
1. Easily annoyed.
2. Having or showing a bad temper.

1. IRRITABLE.
2. ILL-TEMPERED.

snappy *adjective*
1. *Informal.* Disposed to action.
2. *Informal.* Full of or characterized by a lively, emphatic, eager quality.
3. *Informal.* Being or in accordance with the current fashion.
4. Easily annoyed.

1. VIGOROUS.
2. SPIRITED.

3. FASHIONABLE.

4. IRRITABLE.

snare *verb*
To gain control of or an advantage over by or as if by trapping.

CATCH *verb.*

snare *noun*
Something that leads one into a place or situation from which escape is difficult.

LURE *noun.*

snarl¹ *noun*
1. A lack of order or regular arrangement.
2. Something that is intricately and often bewilderingly complex.

1. DISORDER *noun.*
2. TANGLE *noun.*

snarl *verb*
1. To twist together so that separation is difficult.
2. To make complex, intricate, or perplexing.
3. To put into total disorder.

1. ENTANGLE.
2. COMPLICATE.
3. CONFUSE.

snarl² *verb*
To speak abruptly and sharply.

SNAP *verb.*

snatch *verb*
1. To get hold of (something moving).
2. To take quick and forcible possession of.
3. To take (another's property) without permission.
4. *Slang.* To seize and detain (a person) unlawfully.
5. To grasp at (something) eagerly, forcibly, and abruptly with the jaws.

1. CATCH *verb.*
2. SEIZE.
3. STEAL *verb.*
4. KIDNAP.
5. SNAP *verb.*

snatch *noun*
The act of catching, esp. a sudden taking and holding.

CATCH *noun.*

sneak *verb*

1. To move silently and furtively: *tried to sneak out of the room when my back was turned; a cat burglar sneaking onto the roof.*

1. **Syns:** creep, glide, gumshoe (*Slang*), lurk, mouse, prowl, pussyfoot, shirk, skulk, slide, slink, slip, sly, snake, steal.
   Near-ants: barge, clump, stamp, stride, strut, stump, swagger; march, parade, storm.

2. To bring in or take out secretly.

2. SMUGGLE.

sneak *noun*

One who behaves in a stealthy, furtive way: *Her sneak of a husband was deceiving her.*

Syns: slink, sneaker, weasel.

sneaker *noun*

One who behaves in a stealthy, furtive way.

SNEAK *noun*.

sneakiness *noun*

1. Lack of straightforwardness and honesty in action.
2. The act of proceeding slowly, deliberately, and secretly to escape observation.

1. INDIRECTION.
2. STEALTH.

sneaking *adjective*

1. So slow, deliberate, and secret as to escape observation.
2. Marked by treachery or deceit.

1. STEALTHY.

2. UNDERHAND.

sneakish *adjective*

So slow, deliberate, and secret as to escape observation.

STEALTHY.

sneaky *adjective*

1. So slow, deliberate, and secret as to escape observation.
2. Marked by treachery or deceit.

1. STEALTHY.

2. UNDERHAND.

sneer *noun*

A facial expression conveying scorn or derision: *He responded to my idea with a sneer.*

Syns: fleer, snicker (*also* snigger).

sneer *verb*

1. To smile or laugh scornfully or derisively: *The audience sneered at the politician's promises.*

1. **Syns:** fleer, sleer (*Brit. Regional*), snicker (*also* snigger). —*Idiom* curl one's lip.

2. To regard with utter contempt and disdain.

2. DESPISE.

sneer at *verb*

To make fun of.

RIDICULE *verb*.

sneer at *verb*

SEE **sneer.**

snicker *also* **snigger** *verb*

1. To laugh in a stifled way.
2. To smile or laugh scornfully or derisively.

1. GIGGLE *verb*.
2. SNEER *verb*.

snicker *also* **snigger** *noun*

1. A stifled laugh.
2. A facial expression conveying scorn or derision.

1. GIGGLE *noun*.
2. SNEER *noun*.

sniff *verb*

To perceive with the olfactory sense.

SMELL *verb*.

snigger *verb & noun*

SEE **snicker.**

snippety *adjective*

Rudely unceremonious.

ABRUPT.

snippy *adjective*

Rudely unceremonious.

ABRUPT.

snit *noun*

Slang. A condition of excited distress.

STATE *noun*.

snitch *verb*

1. *Slang.* To give incriminating information about others, esp. to the authorities.
2. *Slang.* To take (another's property) without permission.

1. INFORM.

2. STEAL *verb*.

snitch *also* **snitcher** *noun*

Slang. One who gives incriminating information about others.

snitcher *noun*

snob *noun*
One who despises people or things he regards as inferior, esp. because of social or intellectual pretension: *That snob feels all American movies are trash.*

snobbish *adjective*
Characteristic of or resembling a snob: *a snobbish attitude.*

snobby *adjective*
Characteristic of or resembling a snob.

snoop *verb*
Informal. To look into or inquire about curiously, inquisitively, or in a meddlesome fashion: *snooping into their private business, looking for gossip.*

snoop *noun*
Informal. A person who snoops: *an office snoop who repeated all the latest gossip.*

snooper *noun*
Informal. A person who snoops.

snoopiness *noun*
Informal. Undue interest in the affairs of others.

snoopy *adjective*
Informal. Unduly interested in the affairs of others.

snoot *noun*
1. *Slang.* The structure on the human face that contains the nostrils and organs of smell and forms the beginning of the respiratory tract.
2. *Informal.* One who despises people or things he regards as inferior, esp. because of social or intellectual pretension.

snooty *adjective*
Informal. Characteristic of or resembling a snob.

snooze *verb*
Informal. To be asleep.

snooze *noun*
Informal. The natural recurring condition of suspended consciousness by which the body rests.

snoozing *adjective*
Informal. In a state of sleep.

snoozy *adjective*
Informal. Ready for or needing sleep.

snort *noun*
Slang. A small amount of liquor.

snout *noun*
Slang. The structure on the human face that contains the nostrils and organs of smell and forms the beginning of the respiratory tract.

snowball *verb*
1. To make or become greater or larger.
2. To increase or expand suddenly, rapidly, or without control.

snub *verb*
1. To slight (someone) deliberately: *dared to address him familiarly and was roundly snubbed.*

INFORMER.

SEE **snitch.**

Syns: elitist (*also* élitist), high-hat (*Slang*), snoot (*Informal*).
Near-syns: bootlicker, sycophant, toady.

Syns: elitist (*also* élitist), high-hat (*Slang*), snobby, snooty (*Informal*), uppity (*also* uppish) (*Informal*).

SNOBBISH.

Syns: nose (around), poke, pry. —*Idiom* stick one's nose into.
Near-syns: peek, peep, peer; interfere, intrude, meddle.

Syns: busybody, meddler, prier (*also* pryer), snooper (*Informal*).

SNOOP *noun.*

CURIOSITY.

CURIOUS.

1. NOSE *noun.*

2. SNOB.

SNOBBISH.

SLEEP *verb.*

SLEEP *noun.*

SLEEPING.

SLEEPY.

DROP *noun.*

NOSE *noun.*

1. INCREASE *verb.*
2. EXPLODE.

1. **Syns:** cold-shoulder (*Informal*), cut, rebuff, shun, spurn. —*Idioms* give someone the cold shoulder, turn a cold shoulder on, turn one's back on, slam the door on.

2. To refuse to pay attention to (a person); treat with contempt.

2. IGNORE.

snub *noun*

A deliberate slight: *gave me a snub right in front of the boss.*

Syns: cold shoulder (*Informal*), cut, rebuff, spurn.

snuff¹ *verb*

To perceive with the olfactory sense.

SMELL *verb.*

snuff *noun*

The quality of something that may be perceived by the olfactory sense.

SMELL *noun.*

snuff² *verb*

To cause to stop burning or giving light.

EXTINGUISH.

snuff out *verb*

To destroy all traces of.

ANNIHILATE.

snuff out *verb*

SEE **snuff².**

snug *adjective*

1. Affording pleasurable ease.

1. COMFORTABLE.

2. Stretched tightly.

2. TAUT.

3. In good order or clean condition.

3. NEAT.

snuggle *verb*

To lie or press close together, usu. with another person or thing: *The cat snuggled on the blanket.*

Syns: cuddle, nestle, nuzzle.
Near-syns: burrow, curl up, huddle, snug.

soak *noun*

Slang. A person who is habitually drunk.

DRUNKARD.

soak *verb*

1. To saturate (something) with a liquid.

1. STEEP².

2. *Slang.* To take alcoholic liquor, esp. excessively or habitually.

2. DRINK *verb.*

3. *Slang.* To exploit (another) by charging too much for something.

3. SKIN *verb.*

soak in *verb*

To come as a realization.

REGISTER *verb.*

soak up *verb*

1. To take in (moisture or liquid).

1. DRINK *verb.*

2. To take in and incorporate, esp. mentally.

2. ABSORB.

soaked *adjective*

Covered with or full of liquid.

WET *adjective.*

soak in *verb*

SEE **soak.**

soak up *verb*

SEE **soak.**

soar *verb*

1. To rise abruptly and precipitously: *The price of gold has soared.*

1. **Syns:** rocket, shoot up, sky, skyrocket, upsoar.

2. To move from a lower to a higher position.

2. RISE *verb.*

3. To become greater in number, amount, or intensity.

3. RISE *verb.*

soaring *adjective*

Extending to a great height.

TALL.

sob *verb*

To make inarticulate sounds of grief or pain, usu. accompanied by tears.

CRY *verb.*

sobby *adjective*

Affected or extravagantly emotional.

SENTIMENTAL.

sober *adjective*

1. Exercising moderation and self-restraint in appetites and behavior.

1. TEMPERATE.

2. Full of or marked by dignity and seriousness.

2. GRAVE².

3. Having or indicating an awareness of things as they really are.

3. REALISTIC.

soberness *noun*

The practice of refraining from use of alcoholic liquors.

TEMPERANCE.

sobersided *adjective*

Marked by sober sincerity.

SERIOUS.

sobriety *noun*
1. High seriousness of manner or bearing.
2. Sober sincerity.
3. The practice of refraining from use of alcoholic liquors.

1. GRAVITY.
2. SERIOUSNESS.
3. TEMPERANCE.

sociable *adjective*
1. Of, characterized by, or inclined to living together in communities.
2. Liking company.
3. Characterized by kindness and warm, unaffected courtesy.
4. Spent, marked by, or enjoyed in the company of others.

1. SOCIAL.
2. COMPANIONABLE.
3. GRACIOUS.
4. SOCIAL.

social *adjective*
1. Of, characterized by, or inclined to living together in communities: *a social being.*

2. Spent, marked by, or enjoyed in the company of others: *a pleasant social afternoon.*
3. Liking company.
4. Of or pertaining to the structure, organization, or functioning of society.

1. *Syns:* gregarious, sociable.
   Near-ants: detached, insular, isolated, remote, withdrawn.
   Ant: antisocial.
2. *Syns:* companionable, convivial, sociable.
3. COMPANIONABLE.
4. SOCIETAL.

socialize *verb*
1. To place under government or group ownership or control: *socialize the steel industry.*
2. To fit for companionship with others, esp. in attitude or manners: *socializing small children.*
3. To take part in social activities: *The team members socialize together off the field.*

1. *Syns:* communalize, nationalize.
2. *Syns:* acculturate, civilize.
3. *Syn:* mingle.

societal *adjective*
Of or pertaining to the structure, organization, or functioning of society: *pressures for societal change.*

Syns: social, societary.

societary *adjective*
Of or pertaining to the structure, organization, or functioning of society.

SOCIETAL.

society *noun*
1. People of the highest social level: *was formally presented to New York society at a ball.*

2. Persons as an organized body.
3. A group of people united in a relationship and having some interest, activity, or purpose in common.
4. A pleasant association among people.

1. *Syns:* aristocracy, aristoi, blue blood, crème de la crème (*French*), elite (*also* élite), flower, gentility, gentry, haut monde (*French*), patriciate, quality, upper class, upper crust (*Informal*), who's who.
2. PUBLIC *noun.*
3. UNION.

4. COMPANY *noun.*

sock *noun*
1. *Slang.* A sudden sharp, powerful stroke.
2. *Slang.* The capacity to create a powerful effect.

1. BLOW[2].
2. WALLOP *noun.*

sock *verb*
Slang. To deliver (a powerful blow) suddenly and sharply.

HIT *verb.*

sock away *verb*
Informal. To place (money) in a bank.

BANK[1].

sock away *verb*

SEE **sock.**

sodden *verb*
To make thoroughly wet.

WET *verb.*

sodden *adjective*
1. Covered with or full of liquid.

1. WET *adjective.*

2. *Slang*. Intoxicated with alcoholic liquor.

soft *adjective*
1. Yielding easily to pressure or weight; not firm: *soft butter; a soft pillow.*

2. DRUNK *adjective*.

1. *Syns:* mushy, pappy, pulpous, pulpy, quaggy, spongy, squashy, squelchy, squishy, yielding.
   Near-syns: compressible, doughy, malleable, pliable, pliant, workable.

2. Free from severity or violence.
3. Of a kindly, considerate character.
4. Not irritating, strident, or loud: *a soft voice.*

2. GENTLE *adjective*.
3. GENTLE *adjective*.
4. *Syns:* hushed, low, low-key (*also* low-keyed), quiet, small, subdued.

5. Not strict or severe.
6. *Informal.* Lacking in intelligence.
7. *Informal.* Affording pleasurable ease.
8. Of small intensity.
9. Affectedly or extravagantly emotional.
10. Characterized by reduced economic activity.

5. TOLERANT.
6. STUPID.
7. COMFORTABLE.
8. LIGHT².
9. SENTIMENTAL.
10. SLOW *adjective*.

soften *verb*
1. To make or become less severe or extreme.
2. To moderate or change a position or course of action as a result of pressure.
3. To ease the anger or agitation of.

1. MODERATE *verb*.
2. WEAKEN.

3. PACIFY.

softheaded *adjective*
So senseless as to be laughable.

FOOLISH.

softhearted *adjective*
Of a kindly, considerate character.

GENTLE *adjective*.

soft-pedal *verb*
Informal. To make less emphatic or obvious: *soft-pedaled our contributions in an attempt to take most of the credit for herself.*

Syns: de-emphasize, play down, tone down.
Near-syns: cushion, dampen, muffle, subdue, suppress; conceal, disguise, silence.

soft-soap *verb*
1. *Informal.* To persuade or try to persuade by gentle, persistent urging or flattery.
2. *Informal.* To compliment excessively and ingratiatingly.

1. COAX.

2. FLATTER.

soggy *adjective*
1. Covered with or full of liquid.
2. Damp and warm.

1. WET *adjective*.
2. STICKY.

soil *verb*
1. To make dirty.
2. To cast aspersions on.
3. To make morally impure.

1. DIRTY *verb*.
2. BLACKEN.
3. TAINT *verb*.

soiled *adjective*
Covered or stained with or as if with dirt or other impurities.

DIRTY *adjective*.

soily *adjective*
Covered or stained with or as if with dirt or other impurities.

DIRTY *adjective*.

soiree also **soirée** *noun*
A large or important social gathering.

PARTY *noun*.

sojourn *verb*
To remain as a guest or lodger.

STAY¹ *verb*.

sojourn *noun*
A remaining in a place as a guest or lodger.

STAY¹ *noun*.

solace *verb*
To give hope to in time of grief or pain.

COMFORT *verb*.

solace *noun*
A consoling in time of grief or pain.

COMFORT *noun*.

soldier *noun*
One who engages in a combat or struggle.

FIGHTER.

soldierly *adjective*
Pertaining to, characteristic of, or performed by troops.   MILITARY.

sole *adjective*
1. Alone in a given category.   1. LONE.
2. Not divided among or shared with others.   2. EXCLUSIVE.
3. Without a spouse.   3. SINGLE *adjective*.

solecism *noun*
A term whose form offends against established usage   CORRUPTION.
standards.

solely *adverb*
1. To the exclusion of anyone or anything else: *I work*   1. *Syns:* alone, but, entirely, only.
   solely at night.
2. Without the presence or aid of another.   2. ALONE *adverb*.

solemn *adjective*
Full of or marked by dignity and seriousness.   GRAVE².

solemnity *noun*
High seriousness of manner or bearing.   GRAVITY.

solemnize *verb*
To mark (a day or event) with ceremonies of respect,   CELEBRATE.
festivity, or rejoicing.

solemnness *noun*
High seriousness of manner or bearing.   GRAVITY.

solicit *verb*
To endeavor to obtain (something) by expressing one's   REQUEST *verb*.
needs or desires.

solicitous *adjective*
1. Full of polite concern for the well-being of others.   1. ATTENTIVE.
2. Intensely desirous or interested.   2. EAGER.

solicitously *adverb*
In a considerate manner.   CONSIDERATELY.

solid *adjective*
1. Not easily moved or shaken.   1. SOUND².
2. Firmly settled or positioned.   2. SURE.
3. Unyielding to pressure or force.   3. FIRM¹.
4. Capable of being depended upon.   4. DEPENDABLE.
5. Serving to convince.   5. CONVINCING.
6. Being in or characterized by complete agreement.   6. UNANIMOUS.
7. Based on good judgment, reasoning, or evidence.   7. SOUND².

solidarity *noun*
An identity or coincidence of interests, purposes, or   UNITY.
sympathies among the members of a group.

solidify *verb*
To make or become physically hard.   HARDEN.

solidity *noun*
1. The condition of being free from defects or flaws.   1. SOUNDNESS.
2. The quality, condition, or degree of being thick.   2. THICKNESS.

solitary *adjective*
1. Set away from all others: *a solitary Norman*   1. *Syns:* alone, apart, detached, isolate,
   watchtower on the English coast.   isolated, lone, removed.
2. Lacking the company of others.   2. ALONE *adjective*.
3. Not friendly, sociable, or warm in manner.   3. COOL *adjective*.
4. Alone in a given category.   4. LONE.
5. Far from centers of human population.   5. REMOTE.

solitude *noun*
The quality or state of being alone.   ALONENESS.

solo *adverb*
Without the presence or aid of another.   ALONE *adverb*.

solution *noun*
Something worked out to explain, resolve, or provide a   ANSWER *noun*.
method for dealing with and settling a problem.

solve *verb*
1. To find a solution for.
2. To arrive at an answer to (a mathematical problem).

1. RESOLVE *verb*.
2. WORK *verb*.

somatic *adjective*
Of or pertaining to the human body.

BODILY.

somber also **sombre** *adjective*
1. Dark and depressing.
2. Full of or marked by dignity and seriousness.

1. GLOOMY.
2. GRAVE².

somberness *noun*
High seriousness of manner or bearing.

GRAVITY.

sombre *adjective*

SEE **somber.**

some *adjective*
Consisting of an indefinitely small number that is more than two or three but less than many.

SEVERAL.

somebody *noun*
Informal. An important, influential person.

DIGNITARY.

someone *noun*
Informal. An important, influential person.

DIGNITARY.

something *noun*
One that exists independently.

THING.

sometime *adjective*
Having been such previously.

LATE *adjective*.

somnifacient *adjective*
Inducing sleep.

SLEEPY.

somnifacient *noun*
Something that induces sleep.

SOPORIFIC *noun*.

somniferous also **somnific** *adjective*
Inducing sleep.

SLEEPY.

somnific *adjective*

SEE **somniferous.**

somnolent *adjective*
1. Ready for or needing sleep.
2. Inducing sleep.

1. SLEEPY.
2. SLEEPY.

somnorific *adjective*
Inducing sleep.

SLEEPY.

sonance *noun*
The sensation caused by vibrating wave motion that is perceived by the organs of hearing.

SOUND¹.

sonant *adjective*
Produced by the voice.

VOCAL.

songster *noun*
A person who sings.

VOCALIST.

songstress *noun*
A person who sings.

VOCALIST.

sonorous *adjective*
1. Characterized by language that is elevated and sometimes pompous in style: *sonorous phrases that stirred the crowd.*

1. *Syns:* aureate, bombastic, declamatory, fustian, grandiloquent, highfalutin *or* hifalutin (*also* highfaluting) (*Informal*), high-flown, high-sounding, magniloquent, orotund, rhetorical. *Near-ants:* plain, simple, unpretentious.

2. Having or producing a full, deep, or rich sound.

2. RESONANT.

soothe *verb*
1. To make or become calm.
2. To give hope to in time of grief or pain.
3. To ease the anger or agitation of.

1. CALM *verb*.
2. COMFORT *verb*.
3. PACIFY.

soothsay *verb*
To tell about or make known (future events) by or as if by supernatural means.

PROPHESY.

soothsayer *noun*
A person who foretells future events by or as if by supernatural means.

PROPHET.

sooty *adjective*
Of the darkest achromatic visual value.

BLACK *adjective*.

sop *verb*
1. To make thoroughly wet.
2. To take in (moisture or liquid).

1. WET *verb*.
2. DRINK *verb*.

sophism *noun*
Plausible but invalid reasoning.

FALLACY.

sophistic *adjective*
Containing fundamental errors in reasoning.

FALLACIOUS.

sophisticate *verb*
To make impure or inferior by deceptively adding foreign substances.

ADULTERATE.

sophisticated *adjective*
1. Experienced in the ways of the world; lacking natural simplicity: *tried to appear sophisticated but was really very naive.*

1. *Syns:* cosmopolitan, worldly, worldly-wise.
   Near-ants: artless, green, inexperienced, unseasoned, unworldly.
   Ants: naive, unsophisticated.

2. Appealing to or engaging the intellect.

2. INTELLECTUAL *adjective*.

sophistry *noun*
Plausible but invalid reasoning.

FALLACY.

soporific *noun*
Something that induces sleep: *a soporific prescribed by the doctor.*

Syns: hypnotic, narcotic, opiate, somnifacient.

soporific *adjective*
1. Inducing sleep.
2. Ready for or needing sleep.

1. SLEEPY.
2. SLEEPY.

sopping *adjective*
Covered with or full of liquid.

WET *adjective*.

soppy *adjective*
1. Covered with or full of liquid.
2. *Slang.* Affectedly or extravagantly emotional.

1. WET *adjective*.
2. SENTIMENTAL.

sorceress *noun*
A woman who practices magic.

WITCH *noun*.

sorcery *noun*
The use of supernatural powers to influence or predict events.

MAGIC *noun*.

sordid *adjective*
Having or proceeding from low moral standards: *His life was a sordid affair.*

Syns: base[2], contemptible, despicable, ignoble, low, low-down, mean[2], squalid, vile.
Near-ants: honest, honorable, moral, righteous, virtuous.

sore *adjective*
1. Marked by, causing, or experiencing physical pain.
2. *Informal.* Feeling or showing anger.

1. PAINFUL.
2. ANGRY.

sorehead *noun*
Slang. A person who habitually complains or grumbles.

GROUCH *noun*.

soreness *noun*
1. An instance of irritating, as of a part of the body.
2. A sensation of physical discomfort occurring as the result of disease or injury.

1. IRRITATION.
2. PAIN *noun*.

sorrow *noun*
Mental anguish or pain caused by loss or despair.

GRIEF.

sorrow *verb*
To feel, show, or express grief.

GRIEVE.

sorrowful *adjective*
1. Causing sorrow or regret: *a sorrowful and shameful death.*

2. Full of or expressive of sorrow: *a sorrowful smile.*

sorry *adjective*
1. Expressing or inclined to express an apology.
2. Feeling or expressing regret for one's sins or misdeeds.
3. Disturbing because of failure to measure up to a standard or produce the desired results.
4. So objectionable as to elicit despisal.

sort *noun*
A class that is defined by the common attribute or attributes possessed by all its members.

sort *verb*
1. To distribute into groups according to kinds.
2. To set apart (one kind or type) from others: *sort the wheat from the chaff; sorting out good ideas from bad.*
3. To put into a deliberate order.

sort out *verb*
To distribute into groups according to kinds.

sortilege *noun*
The use of supernatural powers to influence or predict events.

sort out *verb*

sot *noun*
A person who is habitually drunk.

sough *verb*
1. To exhale audibly in a long, deep breath, as in sorrow, weariness, or relief.
2. To make a low, continuous, and indistinct sound.

sough *noun*
1. The act or sound of sighing.
2. A low, indistinct, and often continuous sound.

soul *noun*
1. *Theol.* The essential being of a person, regarded as immaterial and immortal: *consigned his soul to God.*
2. The vital principle or animating force within living beings.
3. The seat of a person's innermost emotions and feelings.
4. A member of the human race.
5. The most central and material part.

sound¹ *noun*
1. The sensation caused by vibrating wave motion that is perceived by the organs of hearing: *What was that sound?*
2. Range of audibility.

sound *verb*
1. To have the appearance of.
2. To test the attitude of.
3. To make overtures to, esp. for the purpose of achieving a desired result.

sound² *adjective*
1. Not easily moved or shaken: *a house with a sound foundation.*

---

1. **Syns:** doleful, dolorous, grievous, lamentable, lugubrious, mournful, regrettable, rueful, sad, woeful (*also* woful).
2. **Syns:** doleful, dolorous, lugubrious, mournful, plaintive, rueful, woebegone (*also* wobegone), woeful (*also* woful).

1. APOLOGETIC *adjective.*
2. REMORSEFUL.

3. DISAPPOINTING.

4. FILTHY.

KIND².

1. ASSORT.
2. **Syns:** separate, sift, winnow.

3. ARRANGE.

ASSORT.

MAGIC *noun.*

SEE **sort.**

DRUNKARD.

1. SIGH *verb.*

2. MURMUR *verb.*

1. SIGH *noun.*
2. MURMUR *noun.*

1. **Syn:** spirit.

2. SPIRIT.

3. HEART.

4. HUMAN BEING.
5. HEART.

1. **Syns:** noise, sonance.

2. HEARING.

1. APPEAR.
2. FEEL OUT at **feel.**
3. APPROACH *verb.*

1. **Syns:** firm¹, secure, solid, stable, sturdy, sure.

2. In excellent condition.
3. Having good health.
4. Based on good judgment, reasoning, or evidence: *sound logic.*

5. Serving to convince.
6. Possessing, proceeding from, or exhibiting good judgment and prudence.

soundless *adjective*
Marked by, done with, or making no sound or noise.

soundlessness *noun*
The absence of sound or noise.

soundness *noun*
1. The condition of being free from defects or flaws: *tested the machine for soundness.*
2. The condition of being physically and mentally sound.
3. A healthy mental state.
4. Reliability in withstanding pressure, force, or stress.

soup *noun*
Slang. A difficult, embarrassing situation.

soupçon *noun*
1. *French.* A barely perceivable indication of something.
2. *French.* A slight amount.

soupy *adjective*
Informal. Affectedly or extravagantly emotional.

sour *adjective*
1. Having a taste characteristic of that produced by acids: *a very sour lemon.*

2. Having a noticeably sharp, pungent taste or smell.
3. Broodingly and sullenly unhappy.

sour *verb*
To make or become bitter.

sour *adverb*
1. *Informal.* In such a way as to inflict hardship or difficulty.
2. *Informal.* Not in the right way or on the proper course.

source *noun*
1. A point of origination.
2. An acquaintance who is in a position to help.

sourpuss *noun*
Slang. A person who habitually complains or grumbles.

souse *noun*
Slang. A person who is habitually drunk.

souse *verb*
1. To plunge briefly in or into a liquid.
2. To make thoroughly wet.

soused *adjective*
1. Covered with or full of liquid.
2. *Slang.* Intoxicated with alcoholic liquor.

souvenir *noun*
Something that causes one to remember.

sovereign *adjective*
1. Exceptionally good of its kind.

---

2. GOOD *adjective.*
3. HEALTHY.
4. **Syns:** cogent, just, solid, tight (*Slang*), valid.
Near-syns: convincing, flawless, impeccable, rational, well-founded.
Ant: unsound.

5. CONVINCING.
6. SANE.

SILENT.

SILENCE *noun.*

1. **Syns:** firmness, integrity, solidity, stability, strength, wholeness.
2. HEALTH.
3. SANITY.
4. STABILITY.

PREDICAMENT.

1. TRACE *noun.*

2. SHADE *noun.*

SENTIMENTAL.

1. **Syns:** acerb, acerbic, acetous (*also* acetose), acid, acidulous, dry, tart[1].
Near-syns: acrid, bitter, vinegary; sharp, tangy.
Ant: sweet.

2. BITTER *adjective.*
3. GLUM.

EMBITTER.

1. HARD *adverb.*

2. WRONG *adverb.*

1. ORIGIN.
2. CONTACT *noun.*

GROUCH *noun.*

DRUNKARD.

1. DIP *verb.*
2. WET *verb.*

1. WET *adjective.*
2. DRUNK *adjective.*

REMEMBRANCE.

1. EXCELLENT.

2. Having political independence.

sovereignty *noun*
The condition of being politically free.

sow *verb*
To put (seeds) into the ground for growth.

space *noun*
1. A wide and open area, as of land, sky, or water.
2. An extent, measured or unmeasured, of linear space.
3. A rather short period.

spaced-out *adjective*
Slang. Stupefied, intoxicated, or otherwise influenced by
the taking of drugs.

spacious *adjective*
1. Large in expanse.
2. Having plenty of room.

spade *verb*
1. To break, turn over, or remove (earth, sand, etc.)
with or as if with a tool.
2. To make by digging.

span *noun*
1. The measure of how far or long something goes in
space, time, or degree.
2. A specific length of time characterized by the
occurrence of certain conditions or events.
3. A limited or specific period of time during which
something happens, lasts, or extends.

spangle *verb*
To emit light suddenly in rays or sparks.

spangle *noun*
A small, sparkling decoration.

spank *verb*
To hit with a quick, sharp blow of the hand.

spank *noun*
A quick, sharp blow, esp. with the hand.

spanner *noun*
Chiefly Brit. A tool with jaws for gripping and twisting.

spare *verb*
1. To free from an obligation or duty.
2. To treat with inordinate gentleness and care.
3. To use without wasting.
4. To reserve for the future.

spare *adjective*
1. Being more than is needed, desired, or appropriate.
2. Conspicuously deficient in quantity, fullness, or
extent.
3. Having little flesh or fat on the body.
4. Characterized by an economy of artistic expression.

sparing *adjective*
Careful in the use of material resources.

spark *noun*
1. A sudden quick light.
2. A source of further growth and development.

spark *verb*
To attempt to gain the affection of.

sparkle *verb*
To emit light suddenly in rays or sparks.

sparkle *noun*
1. Sparkling, brilliant light.
2. Brilliant, showy splendor.

sparkling *adjective*
1. Amusing or pleasing because of wit or originality.

---

2. FREE *adjective*.

FREEDOM.

SEED *verb*.

1. EXPANSE.
2. DISTANCE.
3. BIT[1].

DRUGGED.

1. BROAD.
2. ROOMY.

1. DIG *verb*.

2. DIG *verb*.

1. EXTENT.

2. PERIOD.

3. TERM *noun*.

FLASH *verb*.

GLITTER *noun*.

SLAP *verb*.

SLAP *noun*.

WRENCH *noun*.

1. EXCUSE *verb*.
2. FAVOR *verb*.
3. ECONOMIZE.
4. SAVE.

1. SUPERFLUOUS.
2. MEAGER.

3. THIN *adjective*.
4. TIGHT *adjective*.

ECONOMICAL.

1. BLINK *noun*.
2. GERM.

COURT *verb*.

FLASH *verb*.

1. GLITTER *noun*.
2. GLITTER *noun*.

1. CLEVER.

2. Full of joyful, unrestrained high spirits.   **2.** EXUBERANT.

sparse *adjective*
Conspicuously deficient in quantity, fullness, or extent.   MEAGER.

spasm *noun*
A violent, excruciating seizure of pain.   THROE.

spat *noun*
1. A discussion, often heated, in which a difference of opinion is expressed.   **1.** ARGUMENT.
2. *Informal.* A quick, sharp blow, esp. with the hand.   **2.** SLAP *noun.*

spate *noun*
1. Something suggestive of running water.   **1.** FLOW *noun.*
2. An abundant, usu. overwhelming flow.   **2.** FLOOD *noun.*

spatter *verb*
1. To hurl or scatter liquid upon.   **1.** SPLASH.
2. To mark or soil with spots.   **2.** SPOT *verb.*
3. To make defamatory statements about.   **3.** LIBEL *verb.*

spawn *verb*
1. To produce sexually or asexually others of one's kind.   **1.** REPRODUCE.
2. To cause to come into existence.   **2.** PRODUCE.
3. To give rise to a particular development.   **3.** GENERATE.

spawning *adjective*
Capable of reproducing.   FERTILE.

spawning *noun*
The process by which an organism produces others of its kind.   REPRODUCTION.

speak *verb*
1. To express oneself in speech: *couldn't speak because of laryngitis; spoke to each parent who attended the play.*   **1.** *Syns:* talk, utter[1], verbalize, vocalize.
—*Idioms* break silence, open one's mouth (*or* lips), put in (*or* into) words, wag one's tongue.
Near-ants: gabble, gibber, jabber, mispronounce, misspeak, mumble, mutter.
2. To direct speech to.   **2.** ADDRESS *verb.*
3. To articulate (something) in words.   **3.** TALK *verb.*
4. To talk to (an audience) formally.   **4.** ADDRESS *verb.*
5. To engage in spoken exchange.   **5.** CONVERSE[1] *verb.*

speak for *verb*
To serve as an official delegate of.   REPRESENT.

speaker *noun*
1. One who delivers a public speech: *a moving and effective speaker.*   **1.** *Syns:* speechifier, speechmaker, talker.
2. A person who speaks on behalf of another or others: *The speaker for the governor made the announcement.*   **2.** *Syns:* mouth (*Informal*), mouthpiece (*Informal*), spokesman, spokesperson, spokeswoman.

speak for *verb*   SEE **speak.**

special *adjective*
1. Of, relating to, or intended for a distinctive thing or group: *a special medication for arthritis; a special entrance for the physically handicapped.*   **1.** *Syns:* especial, individual, particular, specific.
2. Fixed and distinct from others.   **2.** SPECIFIC.

specialty *noun*
1. An area of academic study that is part of a larger body of learning.   **1.** BRANCH *noun.*
2. Something at which a person excels.   **2.** FORTE.

species *noun*
A class that is defined by the common attribute or attributes possessed by all its members.   KIND[2].

specific *adjective*
1. Fixed and distinct from others: *had no specific purpose in mind.*
2. Of, relating to, or intended for a distinctive thing or group.
3. Clearly, fully, and sometimes emphatically expressed.

1. *Syns:* express, set[1], special.

2. SPECIAL.

3. DEFINITE.

specificate *verb*
To make specific.

STIPULATE.

specification *noun*
A restricting or modifying element.

PROVISION.

specify *verb*
1. To make known or identify, as by signs.
2. To refer to by name.
3. To make specific.

1. DESIGNATE.
2. NAME *verb*.
3. STIPULATE.

specimen *noun*
One that is representative of a group or class.

EXAMPLE.

specious *adjective*
1. Containing fundamental errors in reasoning.
2. Devoid of truth.

1. FALLACIOUS.
2. FALSE.

speciousness *noun*
Plausible but invalid reasoning.

FALLACY.

speck *noun*
A tiny amount.

BIT[1].

speck *verb*
To mark with many small spots.

SPECKLE.

speckle *verb*
To mark with many small spots: *a white horse speckled with brown spots.*

Syns: bespeckle, dapple, dot, fleck, freckle, mottle, pepper, speck, sprinkle, stipple.

spectacle *noun*
An impressive or ostentatious exhibition.

DISPLAY *noun*.

spectacular *adjective*
1. Suggesting drama or a stage performance, as in emotionality or suspense.
2. Of such a character as to overwhelm.

1. DRAMATIC.

2. STAGGERING.

spectator *noun*
Someone who observes.

WATCHER.

specter *noun*
A supernatural being.

GHOST *noun*.

spectral *adjective*
Gruesomely suggestive of ghosts or death.

GHASTLY.

spectrum *noun*
A supernatural being.

GHOST *noun*.

speculate *verb*
1. To use the powers of the mind, as in conceiving ideas, drawing inferences, and making judgments.
2. To take a risk in the hope of gaining advantage.

1. THINK.

2. GAMBLE *verb*.

speculation *noun*
1. The act or process of thinking.
2. A venture depending on chance.
3. Abstract reasoning.

1. THOUGHT.
2. GAMBLE *noun*.
3. THEORY.

speculative *adjective*
1. Of, characterized by, or disposed to thought.
2. Concerned with or restricted to a theory or theories.

1. THOUGHTFUL.
2. THEORETICAL.

speculator *noun*
1. One who speculates for quick profits: *stock-market speculators.*
2. One who bets.

1. *Syns:* adventurer, gambler, operator.

2. BETTOR.

speech *noun*
1. The faculty, act, or product of speaking: *a sore throat that made speech difficult; terms that occur in speech more than writing.*
2. A usu. formal oral communication to an audience: *a valedictory speech at graduation.*
3. A system of terms used by a people sharing a history and culture.

1. *Syns:* discourse, talk, utterance, verbalization, voice. —*Idiom* oral communication.
2. *Syns:* address, allocution, declamation, lecture, oration, prelection, talk.
3. LANGUAGE.

speechifier *noun*
One who delivers a public speech.

SPEAKER.

speechless *adjective*
1. Temporarily unable or unwilling to speak, as from shock or fear: *was speechless in her confusion and surprise.*
2. Lacking the power or faculty of speech.

1. *Syns:* dumb, mum, mute, silent, tight-lipped, wordless.
2. DUMB.

speechlessness *noun*
The avoidance of speech.

SILENCE *noun.*

speechmaker *noun*
One who delivers a public speech.

SPEAKER.

speed *noun*
1. Rate of motion or performance: *drove at a moderate speed; working at breakneck speed.*

2. Rapidness of movement or activity.
speed *verb*
1. To move swiftly.
2. To increase the speed of.

1. *Syns:* celerity, clip[1] (*Informal*), pace, quickness, rapidity, swiftness, tempo, velocity.
2. HASTE *noun.*

1. RUSH *verb.*
2. SPEED UP.

speed up *verb*
To increase the speed of: *We speeded up the loading so as to be done by quitting time.*

Syns: accelerate, expedite, hasten, hurry, quicken, speed, step up.

speediness *noun*
Rapidness of movement or activity.

HASTE *noun.*

speed up *verb*

SEE **speed.**

speedy *adjective*
1. Accomplished in very little time.
2. Characterized by great celerity.

1. QUICK *adjective.*
2. FAST *adjective.*

spell[1] *verb*
To have or convey a particular idea.

MEAN[1].

spell out *verb*
To make understandable.

EXPLAIN.

spell[2] *verb*
To act upon with or as if with magic.

CHARM *verb.*

spell[3] *noun*
1. A rather short period.
2. A limited, often assigned period of activity, duty, or opportunity.

1. BIT[1].
2. TURN *noun.*

spell *verb*
To free from a specific duty by acting as a substitute.

RELIEVE.

spellbind *verb*
1. To act upon with or as if with magic.
2. To compel the attention, interest, imagination, etc., of.

1. CHARM *verb.*
2. GRIP *verb.*

spell out *verb*

SEE **spell**[1].

spend *verb*
1. To distribute (money) as payment: *The studio spent a million dollars to promote the film.*

1. *Syns:* disburse, expend, fork out (*Informal*), give, lay out (*Informal*), outlay, pay, shell out (*Informal*).
Near-syns: blow, contribute, drop, lavish, squander, waste.
Ant: save.

2. To use all of.

3. To use time in a particular way: *spent summers at the beach; spent the day calculating her taxes.*

4. To be depleted.

spendthrift *adjective*
Characterized by excessive or imprudent spending.

spendthrift *noun*
A person who spends money or resources wastefully.

sperm *noun*
The male fluid of fertilization.

spew *verb*
To send forth (confined matter) violently.

sphere *noun*
An area within which something or someone exists, acts, or has influence or power.

spherical also **spheric** *adjective*
Having the shape of a curve everywhere equidistant from a fixed point.

spheroid also **spheroidic, spheroidical** *adjective*
Having the shape of a curve everywhere equidistant from a fixed point.

spheroidic also **spheroidical** *adjective*

spic-and-span *adjective*
In good order or clean condition.

spicy *adjective*
Bordering on indelicacy or impropriety.

spiel *verb*
Slang. To talk volubly, persistently, and usu. inconsequentially.

spill *verb*
1. To come to the ground suddenly and involuntarily.

2. *Informal.* To disclose in a breach of confidence.

3. To grow or spread in a disorderly or planless fashion.

spill *noun*
A sudden involuntary drop to the ground.

spin *noun*
Informal. A trip in a motor vehicle.

spin *verb*
1. To rotate rapidly: *spun the top; car wheels spinning on the ice.*

2. To have the sensation of turning in circles: *left the tavern with his head spinning.*

spin out *verb*
To make or become longer.

spindling *adjective*
Tall, thin, and awkwardly built.

spindly *adjective*
Tall, thin, and awkwardly built.

spin-off *noun*
Something derived from another.

spin out *verb*

spiny *adjective*
1. Full of sharp, needlelike protuberances.

2. So replete with interlocking points and complications as to be painfully irritating.

spiral *verb*
To move or proceed on a repeatedly curving course.

---

2. EXHAUST.

3. *Syns:* pass, put in.

4. GO *verb.*

EXTRAVAGANT.

WASTREL.

SEED *noun.*

ERUPT.

RANGE *noun.*

ROUND.

ROUND.

SEE **spheroid.**

NEAT.

RACY.

CHATTER *verb.*

1. FALL *verb.*

2. BETRAY.

3. SPRAWL.

FALL *noun.*

DRIVE *noun.*

1. *Syns:* gyrate, pirouette, swirl, twirl, whirl.
Near-syns: gyre, oscillate, revolve, rotate, wheel.

2. *Syns:* reel, swim, swirl, whirl.

LENGTHEN.

GANGLING.

GANGLING.

DERIVATIVE *noun.*

SEE **spin.**

1. THORNY.

2. THORNY.

WIND².

spirit *noun*

1. The vital principle or animating force within living beings: *understood life as matter infused with spirit.*

2. The essential being of a person, regarded as immaterial and immortal.
3. A supernatural being.
4. A prevailing quality, as of thought, behavior, or attitude.
5. A lively, emphatic, eager quality or manner: *She played the piece with spirit. The children had been drained of spirit by their oppressive guardian.*

6. The quality of mind enabling one to face danger or hardship resolutely.
7. The most central and material part.

spirit *verb*
To bring in or take out secretly.

spirit away *verb*
To seize and detain (a person) unlawfully.

spirit away *verb*

spirited *adjective*

1. Full of or characterized by a lively, emphatic, eager quality: *The mild disagreement grew into a spirited debate.*

2. Very brisk, alert, and high-spirited.

spiritless *adjective*
1. Lacking liveliness, charm, or surprise.
2. Lacking energy and vitality.
3. In low spirits.

spirits *noun*
A temporary state of mind or feeling.

spiritual *adjective*
1. Of or concerned with the spirit rather than the body or material things: *looked to music and literature for spiritual nourishment.*
2. Having no body, form, or substance.
3. Of or relating to a church or to an established religion: *the medieval popes' temporal and spiritual power.*

spirituous *adjective*
Containing alcohol.

spirt *noun & verb*

spite *noun*
1. A desire to harm others or to see others suffer.
2. The quality or condition of being vindictive.

spiteful *adjective*
1. Characterized by intense ill will or spite.
2. Disposed to seek revenge.

spitefulness *noun*
1. A desire to harm others or to see others suffer.
2. The quality or condition of being vindictive.

---

1. *Syns:* anima, animus, atman (*Hinduism*), pneuma, psyche, soul, vitality. —*Idioms* breath (*or* essence) of life, divine spark, élan vital, life force, vital force.

2. SOUL.

3. GHOST *noun.*
4. TEMPER *noun.*

5. *Syns:* animation, bounce, brio, dash, élan, esprit, ginger (*Informal*), life, liveliness, oomph (*Slang*), pep (*Informal*), verve, vigor, vim, vivacity, zip (*Informal*).
Near-syns: ardor, drive, enthusiasm, starch, vitality.

6. COURAGE.

7. HEART.

SMUGGLE.

KIDNAP.

SEE **spirit.**

1. *Syns:* fiery, high-spirited, mettlesome, peppery, snappy (*Informal*), vibrant.
Near-ants: boring, dull, languid, limp, unenthusiastic.
Ant: spiritless.

2. LIVELY.

1. DULL *adjective.*
2. LANGUID.
3. DEPRESSED.

MOOD.

1. *Syns:* numinous, otherworldly, unworldly.

2. IMMATERIAL.
3. *Syns:* church, churchly, ecclesiastical, religious.

HARD *adjective.*

SEE **spurt.**

1. MALEVOLENCE.
2. VINDICTIVENESS.

1. MALEVOLENT.
2. VINDICTIVE.

1. MALEVOLENCE.
2. VINDICTIVENESS.

splash *verb*
1. To hurl or scatter liquid upon: *splashed the counter with soup as he ladled it out; dove into the pool without splashing.*

           1. ***Syns:*** bespatter, dash, slop, slosh, spatter, splatter, swash.
           Near-syns: douse, drench, soak, spray, sprinkle, squirt, wet.

2. To flow or move with a low, slapping sound.

    2. WASH.

splashy *adjective*
Marked by outward, often extravagant display.

    SHOWY.

splatter *verb*
1. To hurl or scatter liquid upon.
2. To mark or soil with spots.

    1. SPLASH.
    2. SPOT *verb.*

spleen *noun*
A tendency to become angry or irritable.

    TEMPER *noun.*

splendid *adjective*
1. Marked by magnificently lavish ceremony and display.
2. Exceptionally good of its kind.
3. Particularly excellent.

    1. GRAND.

    2. EXCELLENT.
    3. MARVELOUS.

splendor *noun*
Something meriting the highest praise or regard.

    GLORY *noun.*

splendorous or **splendrous** *adjective*
Marked by extraordinary elegance, beauty, and splendor.

    GLORIOUS.

splendrous *adjective*

    SEE **splendorous.**

splinter *verb*
1. To crack or split into two or more fragments by means of or as a result of force, a blow, or strain.
2. To break away or withdraw from membership in an association or federation.

    1. BREAK *verb.*

    2. SECEDE.

split *noun*
1. A usu. narrow partial opening caused by splitting and rupture.
2. The result of cutting.
3. The condition of being divided, as in opinion.

    1. CRACK *noun.*

    2. CUT *noun.*
    3. DIVISION.

split *verb*
1. To undergo partial breaking.
2. To separate into parts with or as if with a sharp-edged instrument.
3. To become or cause to become apart one from another.
4. *Slang.* To move or proceed away from a place.
5. To terminate a relationship or association by or as if by leaving one another.
6. *Slang.* To leave hastily.
7. To break away or withdraw from membership in an association or federation.
8. To separate or pull apart by force.

    1. CRACK *verb.*
    2. CUT *verb.*

    3. DIVIDE.

    4. GO *verb.*
    5. SEPARATE *verb.*

    6. RUN *verb.*
    7. SECEDE.

    8. TEAR[1].

split-up *noun*
The act or an instance of separating one thing from another.

    DIVISION.

splotch *noun*
A discolored mark made by smearing.

    SMEAR *noun.*

splotch *verb*
To mark or soil with spots.

    SPOT *verb.*

splurgy *adjective*
Marked by outward, often extravagant display.

    SHOWY.

splutter *verb*
To make a series of short, sharp noises.

    CRACKLE.

spoil *verb*
1. To harm irreparably through inept handling; make a mess of.

    1. BOTCH *verb.*

2. To become or cause to become rotten or unsound.   **2.** DECAY *verb.*

3. *Obs.* To rob of goods by force, esp. in time of war.   **3.** SACK².

4. *Obs.* To destroy completely while conquering or occupying.   **4.** DEVASTATE.

5. To treat with indulgence and often overtender care.   **5.** BABY *verb.*

spoilage *noun*
The condition of being decayed.   DECAY *noun.*

spoiled *adjective*
Impaired because of decay.   BAD.

spoils *noun*
1. Goods or property seized unlawfully, esp. by a victor in wartime.   **1.** PLUNDER *noun.*

2. The political appointments or jobs that are at the disposal of those in power.   **2.** PATRONAGE.

spoken *adjective*
1. Produced by the voice.   **1.** VOCAL.

2. Expressed or transmitted in speech.   **2.** ORAL.

spokesman *noun*
A person who speaks on behalf of another or others.   SPEAKER.

spokesperson *noun*
A person who speaks on behalf of another or others.   SPEAKER.

spokeswoman *noun*
A person who speaks on behalf of another or others.   SPEAKER.

spoliate *verb*
1. To destroy completely while conquering or occupying.   **1.** DEVASTATE.

2. To rob of goods by force, esp. in time of war.   **2.** SACK².

sponge *noun*
1. One who depends on another for support without reciprocating.   **1.** PARASITE.

2. *Slang.* A person who is habitually drunk.   **2.** DRUNKARD.

spongy *adjective*
Yielding easily to pressure or weight; not firm.   SOFT.

sponsor *noun*
1. One who assumes financial responsibility for another: *became a generous sponsor of fledgling businessmen.*   **1. *Syns:*** angel, backer, guarantor, guaranty, surety, underwriter.

2. A person who supports or champions an activity, institution, etc.   **2.** PATRON.

sponsor *verb*
To act as a patron to.   PATRONIZE.

sponsorship *noun*
Aid or support given by a patron.   PATRONAGE.

spontaneity *noun*
Freedom from constraint, embarrassment, or awkwardness.   EASE *noun.*

spontaneous *adjective*
1. Acting or happening without apparent forethought, prompting, or planning: *The two suddenly embraced in a spontaneous gesture of affection.*   **1. *Syns:*** automatic, impulsive, instinctive, reflex, unpremeditated.
Near-ants: deliberate, intentional, planned, studied, thought-out, voluntary, willful.
Ant: premeditated.

2. Done by one's own choice.   **2.** VOLUNTARY *adjective.*

spook *noun*
1. A supernatural being.   **1.** GHOST *noun.*

2. *Informal.* A person who secretly observes others to obtain information.   **2.** SPY *noun.*

spook *verb*
Slang. To write for and credit authorship to another.   GHOST *verb.*

spoor *noun*
Evidence of passage left along a course followed by a hunted animal or fugitive.

TRAIL *noun*.

sporadic *adjective*
1. Happening or appearing now and then.
2. Rarely occurring or appearing.

1. INTERMITTENT.
2. INFREQUENT.

spore *noun*
A propagative part of a plant.

SEED *noun*.

sport *noun*
1. Activity engaged in for relaxation and amusement.
2. Actions taken as a joke.

1. PLAY *noun*.
2. PLAY *noun*.

sport *verb*
1. To occupy oneself with amusement or diversion.
2. To make a public and usu. ostentatious show of.

1. PLAY *verb*.
2. DISPLAY *verb*.

sporting *adjective*
1. According to the rules.
2. *Informal.* Neither favorable nor unfavorable.

1. SPORTSMANLIKE.
2. FAIR *adjective*.

sportiveness *noun*
Annoying yet harmless, usu. playful acts.

MISCHIEF.

sportsmanlike *adjective*
According to the rules: *a sportsmanlike fight; sportsmanlike play.*

Syns: clean, fair, sporting.

spot *noun*
1. A particular position in a designated order of importance.
2. A particular portion of space chosen for something.
3. A mark of discredit or disgrace.
4. *Chiefly Brit.* A tiny amount.
5. *Informal.* A difficult, embarrassing situation.
6. A very small mark.
7. A post of employment.

1. PLACE *noun*.
2. POINT *noun*.
3. STAIN *noun*.
4. BIT[1].
5. PREDICAMENT.
6. POINT *noun*.
7. POSITION *noun*.

spot *verb*
1. To mark or soil with spots: *The blood dripped from her finger and spotted her dress.*
2. To perceive, esp. barely or fleetingly.
3. To perceive and fix the identity of.
4. To look for and discover.

1. *Syns:* bespatter, blotch, spatter, splatter, splotch.
2. CATCH *verb*.
3. DISCERN.
4. FIND *verb*.

spot *adjective*
Having no particular pattern, purpose, organization, or structure.

RANDOM.

spotless *adjective*
Free from dirt, stain, or impurities.

CLEAN *adjective*.

spotty *adjective*
Lacking consistency or regularity in quality or performance.

UNEVEN.

spousal *adjective*
Of, relating to, or typical of marriage.

MARITAL.

spousal *noun*
The act or ceremony by which two people become husband and wife.

WEDDING.

spouse *noun*
A husband or wife: *Employees may bring their spouses to the company Christmas party.*

Syns: consort, mate, partner. —*Idiom* better half.

spouseless *adjective*
Without a spouse.

SINGLE *adjective*.

sprain *verb*
To injure (a bodily part) by twisting.

TURN *verb*.

sprat *noun*
An insignificant but arrogant and obnoxious young person.

SQUIRT *noun*.

sprawl *verb*

1. To sit or lie with the limbs spread out awkwardly: *staggered home exhausted and sprawled on the couch.*
2. To grow or spread in a disorderly or planless fashion: *handwriting that sprawled across the page; a crowd sprawling out of the stadium.*
3. To come to the ground suddenly and involuntarily.

sprawl *noun*

A sudden involuntary drop to the ground.

spread *verb*

1. To extend over a wide area: *a poisonous gas that spreads quickly.*

2. To move or arrange so as to cover a larger area: *spread the blanket on the grass; a bird spreading its wings for flight.*
3. To cause to become widely known: *spread the news.*

4. To become known far and wide.
5. To arrange tableware upon (a table) in preparation for a meal.
6. To cause (a disease) to pass to another or others.

spread over *verb*

To extend over the surface of.

spread *noun*

1. The act of increasing in dimensions, scope, or inclusiveness.
2. A wide and open area, as of land, sky, or water.
3. A large meal elaborately prepared or served.

spread-eagle *verb*

To sit or lie with the limbs spread out awkwardly.

spread over *verb*

spree *noun*

A period of uncontrolled self-indulgence.

spree *verb*

To behave riotously.

sprig *noun*

A young stemlike growth arising from a plant.

sprightliness *noun*

Capacity or power for work or vigorous activity.

sprightly *adjective*

1. Disposed to action.
2. Amusing or pleasing because of wit or originality.
3. Possessing, exerting, or displaying energy.
4. Free from care or worry.

spring *verb*

1. To move off the ground by a muscular effort of the legs and feet.
2. To bound lightly.
3. To move in a lively way.
4. To have as a source.
5. To have hereditary derivation.
6. *Slang.* To set at liberty.

spring *noun*

1. The act of jumping.
2. A light bounding movement.
3. A sudden lively movement.

---

1. *Syns:* drape, loll, spread-eagle, straddle.

2. *Syns:* spill, straggle.

3. FALL *verb.*

FALL *noun.*

1. *Syns:* diffuse, disperse, distribute, radiate, scatter, strew.
   Near-syns: broadcast, circulate, disseminate, dissipate, sow.
2. *Syns:* expand, extend, fan out, open (out *or* up), outstretch, unfold.

3. *Syns:* advertise (*also* advertize), blaze (around), blazon, broadcast, bruit (about), circulate, diffuse, disseminate, noise about (*or* abroad), propagate.

4. GET ABOUT at **get.**
5. SET[1] *verb.*

6. COMMUNICATE.

COVER *verb.*

1. EXPANSION.

2. EXPANSE.
3. FEAST.

SPRAWL.

SEE **spread.**

BINGE.

REVEL *verb.*

SHOOT *noun.*

ENERGY.

1. VIGOROUS.
2. CLEVER.
3. ENERGETIC.
4. LIGHT[2].

1. JUMP *verb.*

2. SKIP *verb.*
3. BOUNCE *verb.*
4. STEM *verb.*
5. DESCEND.
6. FREE *verb.*

1. JUMP *noun.*
2. SKIP *noun.*
3. BOUNCE *noun.*

4. Capacity to bounce.
5. A point of origination.
6. The initial stage of a developmental process.
7. The season of the year during which the weather becomes warmer and plants revive: *We're going to Paris this spring.*
8. The time of life between childhood and maturity.
9. A basis for an action or decision.

4. BOUNCE *noun.*
5. ORIGIN.
6. BIRTH *noun.*
7. *Syns:* seedtime, springtide, springtime.

8. YOUTH.
9. CAUSE *noun.*

spring *adjective*
Of, occurring in, or characteristic of the season of spring: *a spring thaw; spring cleaning.*

Syn: vernal.

springiness *noun*
1. Capacity to bounce.
2. The quality or state of being flexible.

1. BOUNCE *noun.*
2. FLEXIBILITY.

springtide *noun*
1. The season of the year during which the weather becomes warmer and plants revive.
2. The time of life between childhood and maturity.

1. SPRING *noun.*

2. YOUTH.

springtime *noun*
1. The season of the year during which the weather becomes warmer and plants revive.
2. The time of life between childhood and maturity.

1. SPRING *noun.*

2. YOUTH.

springy *adjective*
Capable of withstanding stress without injury.

FLEXIBLE.

sprinkle *verb*
1. To scatter or release in drops or small particles: *sprinkled shredded coconut over the pudding.*
2. To mark with many small spots.

1. *Syns:* besprinkle, dust, powder.

2. SPECKLE.

sprint *verb*
To move swiftly on foot so that both feet leave the ground during each stride.

RUN *verb.*

sprout *noun*
A young stemlike growth arising from a plant.

SHOOT *noun.*

spruce *verb*
1. To improve in appearance, esp. by refurbishing.
2. To make or keep (an area) clean and orderly.
3. To make neat and trim; make presentable.

1. FIX UP at **fix.**
2. TIDY *verb.*
3. TIDY *verb.*

spruce *adjective*
In good order or clean condition.

NEAT.

spry *adjective*
1. Disposed to action.
2. Moving or performing quickly, lightly, and easily.

1. VIGOROUS.
2. NIMBLE.

spume *noun*
A mass of bubbles in or on the surface of a liquid.

FOAM *noun.*

spume *verb*
To form or cause to form foam.

FOAM *verb.*

spumy *adjective*
Consisting of or resembling foam.

FOAMY.

spunk *noun*
Informal. The quality of mind enabling one to face danger or hardship resolutely.

COURAGE.

spur *verb*
1. To cause to happen suddenly or unexpectedly.
2. To stir to action or feeling.

1. PRECIPITATE *verb.*
2. PROVOKE.

spur *noun*
Something that causes and encourages a given response.

STIMULUS.

spurious *adjective*
1. Fraudulently or deceptively imitative.
2. Not genuine or sincere.
3. Containing fundamental errors in reasoning.

1. COUNTERFEIT *adjective.*
2. ARTIFICIAL.
3. FALLACIOUS.

4. Born out of wedlock.

4. ILLEGITIMATE.

spuriousness *noun*
Plausible but invalid reasoning.

FALLACY.

spurn *verb*
1. To slight (someone) deliberately.
2. To be unwilling to accept, consider, or receive.

1. SNUB *verb*.
2. DECLINE *verb*.

spurn *noun*
A deliberate slight.

SNUB *noun*.

spur-of-the-moment *adjective*
Spoken, performed, or composed with little or no preparation or forethought.

EXTEMPORANEOUS.

spurt also **spirt** *noun*
A sudden, swift stream of ejected liquid: *a spurt of blood.*

Syns: jet², squirt.

spurt also **spirt** *verb*
To eject or be ejected in a thin, swift stream: *Blood spurted from the ruptured artery.*

Syns: jet², squirt.

sputter *verb*
To make a series of short, sharp noises.

CRACKLE.

spy *noun*
A person who secretly observes others to obtain information: *A spy planted in the enemy high command smuggled out regular reports.*

Syns: operative, spook (*Informal*). —*Idiom* secret (*or* undercover) agent.
Near-syns: agent provocateur; detective, investigator, sleuth.

spy *verb*
1. To perceive, esp. barely or fleetingly.
2. To observe or listen in secret to obtain information: *spied on the thieves by hiding in a closet.*

1. CATCH *verb*.
2. *Syn:* eavesdrop.

squabble *noun*
A discussion, often heated, in which a difference of opinion is expressed.

ARGUMENT.

squabble *verb*
1. To engage in a quarrel.
2. To quarrel noisily.

1. ARGUE.
2. BRAWL *verb*.

squab *adjective*
Short, heavy, and solidly built.

STOCKY.

squabby *adjective*
Short, heavy, and solidly built.

STOCKY.

squalid *adjective*
1. Heavily soiled; very dirty or unclean.
2. Having or proceeding from low moral standards.

1. FILTHY.
2. SORDID.

squander *verb*
To spend (money) excessively and usu. foolishly.

WASTE *verb*.

squander *noun*
Excessive or imprudent expenditure.

EXTRAVAGANCE.

square *noun*
Slang. An old-fashioned person who is reluctant to change or innovate: *Some kids think that ballroom dancing is for squares.*

Syns: antediluvian, fogy, fossil, fuddy-duddy, mossback, stick-in-the-mud (*Informal*). —*Idiom* back number.

square *adjective*
1. Having four equal sides and four right angles: *a square plot of land.*
2. Free from bias in judgment.
3. Owing or being owed nothing.
4. Being an exact amount or number.
5. *Slang.* Conforming to established practice or standards.

1. *Syn:* quadrate.
2. FAIR *adjective*.
3. EVEN¹ *adjective*.
4. EVEN¹ *adjective*.
5. CONVENTIONAL.

square *verb*
1. To make equal.
2. To be compatible or in correspondence.

1. EQUALIZE.
2. AGREE.

3. To make or become suitable to a particular situation   3. ADAPT.
or use.
4. To set right by giving what is due.   4. SETTLE.
square *adverb*
1. Without the slightest deviation in any respect.   1. PRECISELY.
2. With precision or absolute conformity.   2. DIRECTLY.
squash *verb*
1. To press forcefully so as to break up into a pulpy   1. CRUSH *verb*.
mass.
2. To act on with a steady pushing force.   2. CROWD *verb*.
3. To congregate closely around or against.   3. CROWD *verb*.
4. To bring to an end forcibly as if by imposing a   4. SUPPRESS.
heavy weight.
squashy *adjective*
Yielding easily to pressure or weight; not firm.   SOFT.
squat *verb*
To sit on one's heels: *The boy squatted as he prepared to* *Syn:* hunker (down).
shoot his marble.
squat *adjective*
Short, heavy, and solidly built.   STOCKY.
squawk *verb*
Informal. To express opposition by argument.   OBJECT[2].
squawk *noun*
Informal. The act of expressing strong or reasoned   OBJECTION.
opposition.
squawky *adjective*
Disagreeable to the sense of hearing.   HARSH.
squeal *verb*
1. To utter a shrill, short cry.   1. YELP *verb*.
2. *Slang.* To give incriminating information about   2. INFORM.
others, esp. to the authorities.
squeal *noun*
A shrill, short cry.   YELP *noun*.
squealer *noun*
Slang. One who gives incriminating information about   INFORMER.
others.
squeeze *verb*
1. To subject to compression: *The tight collar squeezed*   1. *Syns:* compress, constrain, constrict,
my throat.   constringe.
2. To act on with a steady pushing force.   2. CROWD *verb*.
3. To extract from by applying pressure: *squeeze the*   3. *Syns:* crush, express, press.
juice from oranges.
4. To congregate closely around or against.   4. CROWD *verb*.
5. To put one's arms around affectionately.   5. EMBRACE *verb*.
6. To obtain by coercion or intimidation.   6. EXTORT.
squeeze *noun*
1. A compressing of something.   1. CONSTRICTION.
2. The act of embracing.   2. EMBRACE *noun*.
squeezing *noun*
A compressing of something.   CONSTRICTION.
squelch *verb*
1. To hold (something requiring an outlet) in check.   1. REPRESS.
2. To bring to an end forcibly as if by imposing a   2. SUPPRESS.
heavy weight.
squelching *noun*
The act of restraining forcefully.   REPRESSION.
squelchy *adjective*
Yielding easily to pressure or weight; not firm.   SOFT.
squiggle *verb*
To move or proceed with short, irregular motions up   WIGGLE.
and down or from side to side.

squinch *verb*
1. To draw away involuntarily, usu. due to fear or disgust.
2. To peer with the eyes partly closed.

squinch *adjective*
Marked by or affected with a squint.

squint *verb*
To peer with the eyes partly closed: *squinted at the fine print.*

squint toward (or **at**) *verb*
To have a tendency or inclination.

squint *noun*
1. The condition of not having the visual axes parallel: *The ophthalmologist recommended special eye exercises to rectify the child's squint.*
2. An inclination to something.

squint-eyed *adjective*
Marked by or affected with a squint.

squint toward (or **at**) *verb*

squinty *adjective*
Marked by or affected with a squint: *eyes squinty from sun and snow.*

squirm *verb*
1. To move or proceed with short, irregular motions up and down or from side to side.
2. To twist and turn, as in pain, struggle, or embarrassment.

squirrel *verb*
To store up (supplies or money), usu. well beyond one's needs.

squirt *verb*
To eject or be ejected in a sudden, swift stream.

squirt *noun*
1. A sudden, swift stream of ejected liquid.
2. *Informal.* An insignificant but arrogant and obnoxious young person: *had to tell the little squirt to get lost.*

squishy *adjective*
Yielding easily to pressure or weight; not firm.

squiz *noun*
Austral. & New Zeal. A quick look.

stab *verb*
To cause to penetrate with force.

stab *noun*
1. An act of thrusting into or against, as to attract attention.
2. A sudden, sharp, painful feeling.
3. A small mark or hole made by a sharp, pointed object.
4. A brief trial.

stabbing *adjective*
Marked by severity or intensity.

stability *noun*
1. Reliability in withstanding pressure, force, or stress: *tested the stability of the fuselage in the wind tunnel; a man lacking stability of character.*
2. The condition of being free from defects or flaws.

stabilize *verb*
1. To make stable: *tried in vain to stabilize the country on the verge of anarchy.*
2. To put in balance.

---

1. FLINCH.

2. SQUINT *verb.*

SQUINTY.

Syn: squinch. —*Idioms* look asquint, screw up one's eyes.

TEND[1].

1. *Syns:* cross-eye, strabismus.

2. BENT *noun.*

SQUINTY.
SEE **squint.**

Syns: cross-eyed, squinch, squinny, squint-eyed, strabismal *or* strabismic.

1. WIGGLE.

2. WRITHE.

HOARD *verb.*

SPURT *verb.*

1. SPURT *noun.*
2. *Syns:* pup, puppy, sprat, twerp (*also* twirp) (*Slang*).

SOFT.

GLANCE[1] *noun.*

RAM *verb.*

1. DIG *noun.*
2. PRICK *noun.*
3. PRICK *noun.*

4. TRY *noun.*

SHARP *adjective.*

1. *Syns:* firmness, security, soundness, stableness, steadiness, strength.

2. SOUNDNESS.

1. *Syn:* steady.

2. BALANCE *verb.*

stable *adjective*
1. Firmly settled or positioned.
2. Consistently reliable, esp. due to resistance to outside pressures.
3. Not easily moved or shaken.

1. SURE.
2. STEADY *adjective*.
3. SOUND².

stableness *noun*
Reliability in withstanding pressure, force, or stress.

STABILITY.

stack *noun*
A group of things gathered haphazardly.

HEAP *noun*.

stack *verb*
To put into a disordered pile.

HEAP *verb*.

stack up *verb*
Informal. To be equal or alike.

COMPARE.

stacked *adjective*
Informal. Having a full, voluptuous figure.

SHAPELY.

stack up *verb*

SEE **stack.**

staff *noun*
A fairly long, straight piece of solid material used esp. as a support in walking.

STICK *noun*.

stage *noun*
1. A temporary framework with a floor, used by workmen: *a window-washing stage.*
2. The raised platform on which theatrical performances are given: *the stage in Lincoln Center.*
3. The art and occupation of an actor.
4. One of the units in a course, as on an ascending or descending scale.
5. An interval regarded as a distinct evolutionary or developmental unit.
6. The place where an action or event occurs.

1. *Syns:* platform, scaffold, scaffolding.
2. *Syns:* the boards, proscenium.
3. ACTING *noun*.
4. DEGREE.
5. PERIOD.
6. SCENE.

stage *verb*
1. To produce on the stage: *staged a new performance every month.*
2. To organize and carry out (an activity).

1. *Syns:* act (out), do, dramatize, enact, give, perform, present², put on.
2. HAVE.

stagger *verb*
1. To overwhelm with surprise, wonder, or bewilderment: *The murder just staggered us.*
2. To walk unsteadily.
3. To be irresolute in acting or doing.
4. To proceed or perform in an unsteady, faltering manner.
5. To progress or perform adequately, esp. in difficult circumstances.

1. *Syns:* boggle, bowl over, dumfound (*also* dumbfound), flabbergast, floor.
2. LURCH *verb*.
3. HESITATE.
4. MUDDLE.
5. MANAGE.

staggering *adjective*
1. Of such a character as to overwhelm: *staggering acrobatic feats; staggering corruption.*

2. Awesomely or forbiddingly intense.

1. *Syns:* mind-blowing (*Slang*), mind-boggling (*Slang*), overwhelming, spectacular, stunning.
2. TOWERING.

staginess *noun*
Showy mannerisms and behavior.

THEATRICALISM.

stagnation *noun*
A lack of action or activity.

INACTION.

staid *adjective*
Full of or marked by dignity and seriousness.

GRAVE².

stain *verb*
1. To soil with foreign matter: *trousers stained with engine oil.*

2. To impart color to.
3. To ruin utterly in character or quality.
4. To cast aspersions on.

1. *Syns:* bestain, discolor, smut.
   Near-syns: blot, daub, smear, smudge, soil.
2. COLOR *verb*.
3. CORRUPT *verb*.
4. BLACKEN.

stain *noun*
1. Something that imparts color.
2. A mark of discredit or disgrace: *Watergate is a stain on American politics.*

1. COLOR *noun*.
2. *Syns:* attaint (*Archaic*), bar sinister, black eye, blemish, blot, onus, spot, stigma, taint, tarnish. —*Idioms* black mark, blot on the escutcheon.

stainless *adjective*
Free from dirt, stain, or impurities.

CLEAN *adjective*.

stake *noun*
1. Something valuable risked on an uncertain outcome.
2. A right or legal share in something.

1. BET *noun*.
2. INTEREST *noun*.

stake *verb*
1. To make a bet on.
2. *Informal.* To supply capital to or for.

1. BET *verb*.
2. FINANCE.

stale *adjective*
1. Having lost tang or effervescence.
2. Of a style or method formerly in vogue.
3. Without freshness or appeal due to overuse.

1. FLAT *adjective*.
2. OLD-FASHIONED.
3. TRITE.

stalemate *noun*
An equality of scores, votes, or performances in a contest.

TIE *noun*.

stalk *verb*
1. To walk with long steps, esp. in a vigorous manner.
2. To look for and pursue (game) in order to capture or kill it.

1. STRIDE.
2. HUNT *verb*.

stalwart *adjective*
Capable of exerting considerable effort or of withstanding considerable stress or hardship.

STRONG.

stamina *noun*
The quality or power of withstanding hardship or stress.

ENDURANCE.

stammer *verb*
1. To intrude involuntary repetitions and pauses into one's speech: *a nervous child who stammered and then fell silent.*
2. To walk unsteadily.

1. *Syns:* hammer (*Brit. Regional*), stutter. *Near-syns:* gibber, jabber, splutter, stumble; falter, hesitate.
2. LURCH *verb*.

stammer *noun*
A speech impediment marked by involuntary repetitions and pauses: *has suffered from a pronounced stammer since childhood.*

Syns: stutter, stuttering.

stamp *noun*
1. The visible effect made on a surface by pressure.
2. A class that is defined by the common attribute or attributes possessed by all its members.
3. Something visible or evident that gives grounds for believing in the existence or presence of something else.

1. IMPRESSION.
2. KIND².

3. SIGN *noun*.

stamp *verb*
1. To walk with loud, heavy steps.
2. To step on heavily and repeatedly so as to crush, injure, or destroy.
3. To produce a deep impression on.

1. TRAMP *verb*.
2. TRAMPLE.

3. ENGRAVE.

stamp out *verb*
To destroy all traces of.

ANNIHILATE.

stamp out *verb*

SEE **stamp**.

stance *noun*
1. The way in which a person holds or carries his body.
2. A frame of mind affecting one's thoughts or behavior.

1. POSTURE *noun*.
2. POSTURE *noun*.

stand *noun*
A shelter for concealing hunters.

BLIND *noun*.

stand *verb*
1. To put up with.
2. *Informal.* To pay for the food, drink, or entertainment of (another).

1. ENDURE.
2. TREAT *verb*.

stand behind *verb*
To aid the cause of by approving or favoring.

SUPPORT *verb*.

stand for *verb*
1. To serve as the image of.
2. To serve as an official delegate of.

1. REPRESENT.
2. REPRESENT.

stand up *verb*
1. To withstand stress or difficulty.
2. To adopt a standing posture.
3. To restore to an upright or proper position.
4. To prove valid under scrutiny.

1. BEAR UP at **bear**.
2. GET UP at **get**.
3. RIGHT *verb*.
4. WASH.

stand up for *verb*
To aid the cause of by approving or favoring.

SUPPORT *verb*.

standard *noun*
1. A means by which individuals are compared and judged: *Standards of public morality have clearly changed. The early American Presidents set a high standard.*

1. *Syns:* benchmark, criterion, gauge (*also* gage), mark, measure, test, touchstone, yardstick.
   Near-syns: average, mean, norm, par; belief, principle, rule; model, pattern.

2. Fabric used esp. as a symbol.
3. One that is worthy of imitation or duplication.

2. FLAG[1] *noun*.
3. MODEL *noun*.

standard *adjective*
1. Having or arising from authority.
2. Lacking in interest or originality.

1. AUTHORITATIVE.
2. ROUTINE *adjective*.

stand behind *verb*

SEE **stand**.

standby *adjective*
Used or held in reserve.

AUXILIARY *adjective*.

stand for *verb*

SEE **stand**.

stand-in *noun*

SEE **stand in**.

stand in *verb*
To act as a substitute.

SUBSTITUTE *verb*.

stand-in *noun*
One that takes the place of another.

SUBSTITUTE *noun*.

standing *noun*
1. The level of credit or respect at which one is regarded by others.
2. Positioning of one individual vis-à-vis others.

1. FACE *noun*.
2. PLACE *noun*.

stand-off *noun*
An equality of scores, votes, or performances in a contest.

TIE *noun*.

standoffish *adjective*
Not friendly, sociable, or warm in manner.

COOL *adjective*.

standout *adjective*

SEE **stand out**.

stand out *verb*
1. To curve outward past the normal or usual limit.
2. To be obtrusively conspicuous.

1. BULGE *verb*.
2. GLARE *verb*.

standout *adjective*
Far above others in quality or excellence.

OUTSTANDING.

standpoint *noun*
1. A way of considering a matter.
2. The position from which something is observed or considered.

1. LIGHT[1] *noun*.
2. POINT OF VIEW.

standstill *noun*
The condition of being stopped.

STOP *noun*.

stand up *verb*

SEE **stand**.

stand up for *verb*

SEE **stand**.

star *noun*
The main performer in a theatrical production.

LEAD *noun*.

starch *noun*
A quality of active mental and physical forcefulness.   VIGOR.

starchy *adjective*
So rigidly constrained, formal, or awkward as to lack all grace and spontaneity.   STIFF *adjective*.

star-crossed *adjective*
Involving or undergoing chance misfortune.   UNFORTUNATE *adjective*.

stare *verb*
To look intently and fixedly.   GAZE *verb*.

stare *noun*
An intent, fixed look.   GAZE *noun*.

stark *adjective*
Containing nothing.   EMPTY *adjective*.

starry-eyed *adjective*
Not compatible with reality.   IDEALISTIC.

start *verb*
1. To go about the initial step in doing (something): *starts every concert with a Bach fugue; is starting a new curriculum-development program.*

   1. *Syns:* approach, begin, commence, embark, enter, get off (*Informal*), inaugurate, initiate, kick off (*Informal*), launch, lead off (*Informal*), open, set out, set to, take on, take up, undertake. —*Idioms* get going, get the show on the road.

2. To come into being.   2. BEGIN.
3. To move suddenly and involuntarily.   3. JUMP *verb*.
4. To draw away involuntarily, usu. due to fear or disgust.   4. FLINCH.
5. To bring into existence formally.   5. FOUND.

start *noun*
1. The act or process of bringing or being brought into existence.   1. BEGINNING *noun*.
2. A sudden and involuntary movement.   2. JUMP *noun*.
3. The initial stage of a developmental process.   3. BIRTH *noun*.
4. A factor conducive to superiority and success.   4. ADVANTAGE *noun*.

startle *verb*
1. To cause to experience a sudden, momentary shock: *The cold shower startled him awake.*   1. *Syns:* jolt, shock.
2. To fill with fear.   2. FRIGHTEN.
3. To move suddenly and involuntarily.   3. JUMP *verb*.
4. To impress strongly by what is unexpected or unusual.   4. SURPRISE.

startle *noun*
A sudden and involuntary movement.   JUMP *noun*.

startling *adjective*
Causing momentary shock: *a startling sight.*   *Syns:* astonishing, astounding, electrifying, jolting, surprising.

starving *adjective*
Desiring or craving food.   RAVENOUS.

stash *verb*
1. To store up (supplies or money), usu. well beyond one's needs.   1. HOARD *verb*.
2. To put or keep out of sight.   2. HIDE[1] *verb*.
3. To have or put in a customary place.   3. KEEP *verb*.

stasis *noun*
A stable state characterized by the cancellation of all forces by equal opposing forces.   BALANCE *noun*.

state *noun*
1. An organized geopolitical unit: *France is one of the Western European states.*   1. *Syns:* country, land, nation, polity. —*Idiom* body politic.
2. Manner of being or form of existence.   2. CONDITION *noun*.

3. *Informal.* A condition of excited distress: *Don't get into a state because of this delay.*

3. **Syns:** fume, snit (*Slang*), sweat (*Informal*), swivet (*also* swivvet), tizzy (*Slang*).

state *verb*
1. To put into words.
2. To utter publicly.
3. To put into words positively and with conviction.
4. To declare by way of a systematic statement: *Einstein stated his theory of relativity in a rather short paper.*

1. SAY *verb.*
2. AIR *verb.*
3. ASSERT.
4. **Syns:** enounce, enunciate.

stately *adjective*
1. Marked by magnificently lavish ceremony and display.
2. Large and impressive in size, scope, or extent.

1. GRAND.
2. GRAND.

statement *noun*
1. The act or an instance of expressing in words.
2. A recounting of past events.
3. The act of asserting positively.
4. A precise list of fees or charges.
5. Something said.

1. EXPRESSION.
2. STORY.
3. ASSERTION.
4. ACCOUNT *noun.*
5. WORD *noun.*

station *noun*
1. An assigned position: *a sentry station; a duty station.*
2. Positioning of one individual vis-à-vis others.
3. A center of organization, supply, or activity.

1. **Syns:** post, posting.
2. PLACE *noun.*
3. BASE[1] *noun.*

station *verb*
To appoint and send to a particular place: *guards stationed on the border; airmen stationed on the DEW Line.*

Syns: assign, post, set[1].

stationary *adjective*
1. Firmly in position.
2. Not moving.

1. FIXED.
2. MOTIONLESS.

stature *noun*
A level of superiority that is usu. high.

MERIT *noun.*

status *noun*
1. Manner of being or form of existence.
2. Positioning of one individual vis-à-vis others.
3. A person's high standing among others.
4. The level of credit or respect at which one is regarded by others.
5. An established position from which to operate or deal with others.

1. CONDITION *noun.*
2. PLACE *noun.*
3. HONOR *noun.*
4. FACE *noun.*

5. BASIS.

statute *noun*
The formal product of a legislative or judicial body.

LAW *noun.*

staunch *adjective*
1. Firmly settled or positioned.
2. Adhering firmly and devotedly, as to a person, a cause, or a duty.

1. SURE.
2. FAITHFUL.

stave[1] *noun*
A fairly long, straight piece of solid material used esp. as a support in walking.

STICK *noun.*

stave off *verb*
To prohibit from occurring by advance planning or action.

PREVENT.

stave[2] *verb*
To move swiftly.

RUSH *verb.*

stave off *verb*

SEE **stave[1].**

stay[1] *verb*
1. To remain as a guest or lodger: *stayed with relatives instead of going to a hotel.*
2. To continue to be in a place.

1. **Syns:** sojourn, visit.

2. REMAIN.

3. To prevent the occurrence or continuation of a
movement, action, or operation.

4. To put off until a later time.

5. To remain fresh and unspoiled.

stay with *verb*

To persevere in some condition, action, or belief.

stay *noun*

1. A remaining in a place as a guest or lodger: *a six-
week stay with relatives.*

2. The act of stopping.

3. The act of putting off or the condition of being put
off.

4. An act or the time of waiting.

stay² *noun*

A means or device that keeps something erect, stable,
or secure.

stay with *verb*

stead *noun*

The function or position customarily occupied by
another.

steadfast *adjective*

1. Firmly in position.

2. Adhering firmly and devotedly, as to a person, a
cause, or a duty.

steadfastness *noun*

Faithfulness or devotion to a person, a cause,
obligations, or duties.

steadiness *noun*

Reliability in withstanding pressure, force, or stress.

steady *adjective*

1. Consistently reliable, esp. due to resistance to
outside pressures: *a steady hand on the wheel; a
steady job held for 20 years.*

2. Having no variations.

3. Adhering firmly and devotedly, as to a person, a
cause, or a duty.

steady *verb*

1. To make stable.

2. To put in balance.

steady-going *adjective*

Consistently reliable, esp. due to resistance to outside
pressures.

steal *verb*

1. To take (another's property) without permission:
accused him of stealing her bicycle.

2. To move silently and furtively.

steal *noun*

1. The crime of taking someone else's property without
consent.

2. *Slang.* Something offered or bought at a low price.

stealer *noun*

A person who steals.

stealing *noun*

The crime of taking someone else's property without
consent.

---

3. STOP *verb.*

4. DEFER¹.

5. KEEP *verb.*

KEEP *verb.*

1. *Syns:* sojourn, visit.

2. STOP *noun.*

3. DELAY *noun.*

4. WAIT *noun.*

SUPPORT *noun.*

SEE **stay¹.**

PLACE *noun.*

1. FIXED.

2. FAITHFUL *adjective.*

FIDELITY.

STABILITY.

1. *Syns:* stable, steady-going.

2. EVEN¹ *adjective.*

3. FAITHFUL.

1. STABILIZE.

2. BALANCE *verb.*

STEADY *adjective.*

1. *Syns:* cop (*Slang*), filch, hook (*Slang*),
lift (*Informal*), nip¹ (*Slang*), pilfer,
pinch (*Slang*), purloin, rip off (*Slang*),
snaffle (*Chiefly Brit. Regional*), snatch,
snitch (*Slang*), swipe (*Slang*), thieve.
—*Idioms* make off with, walk off with.
Near-syns: burglarize, loot, plunder,
rifle, rob; fleece, frisk.

2. SNEAK *verb.*

1. LARCENY.

2. BARGAIN *noun.*

LARCENER.

LARCENY.

stealth *noun*
The act of proceeding slowly, deliberately, and secretly to escape observation: *the stealth of a cat burglar.*

Syns: furtiveness, slink, slinkiness, sneakiness, stealthiness.

stealthiness *noun*
The act of proceeding slowly, deliberately, and secretly to escape observation.

STEALTH.

stealthy *adjective*
So slow, deliberate, and secret as to escape observation: *The mugger cast stealthy glances to the right and left and then attacked.*

Syns: catlike, feline, furtive, skulking, slinking, slinky, sneaking, sneakish, sneaky.
Near-syns: noiseless, quiet, silent, sly.

steam *noun*
1. Capacity or power for work or vigorous activity.
2. An aggressive readiness to undertake taxing efforts.

1. ENERGY.
2. DRIVE *noun.*

steam up *verb*
Informal. To cause to feel or show anger.

ANGER *verb.*

steamroller *verb*
To render totally ineffective by decisive defeat.

OVERWHELM.

steam up *verb*

SEE **steam.**

steel *verb*
To prepare (oneself) for action.

GIRD.

steep[1] *adjective*
1. So sharply inclined as to be almost perpendicular: *a steep cliff.*
2. Vastly exceeding a normal limit, as in cost: *steep gold prices this year.*

1. *Syns:* abrupt, arduous, bold, breakneck, precipitate, precipitous, sheer[2].
2. *Syns:* dizzy, dizzying, sky-high, stiff, stratospheric, towering, unconscionable.

steep[2] *verb*
To saturate (something) with a liquid: *steeped the tea bags in hot water.*

Syns: seethe, soak.

steer *verb*
1. To control the course of (an activity).
2. To show the way to.
3. To direct the course of carefully.

1. CONDUCT *verb.*
2. GUIDE *verb.*
3. MANEUVER *verb.*

steer *noun*
An item of advance or inside information given as a guide to action.

TIP[3] *noun.*

stem *verb*
To have as a source: *customs stemming from the past.*

Syns: arise, come, derive, emanate, flow, issue, originate, proceed, rise, spring, upspring.

stem *noun*
Ling. The main part of a word to which affixes are attached.

THEME.

stench *verb*
To have or give off a foul odor.

SMELL *verb.*

stentorian *adjective*
Marked by extremely high volume and intensity of sound.

LOUD *adjective.*

stentorious *adjective*
Marked by extremely high volume and intensity of sound.

LOUD *adjective.*

step *verb*
1. To go on foot.
2. To move rhythmically to music, using patterns of steps or gestures.

1. WALK *verb.*
2. DANCE *verb.*

step down *verb*
To withdraw from business or active life.

RETIRE.

step up *verb*
To increase the speed of.

SPEED UP at **speed.**

step *noun*
1. The act or manner of going on foot.

1. TREAD *noun.*

2. One of the units in a course, as on an ascending or descending scale.

2. DEGREE.

step-by-step *adjective*
Proceeding very slowly by degrees.

GRADUAL.

step down *verb*

SEE **step.**

step up *verb*

SEE **step.**

stereotype *noun*
A trite expression or idea.

CLICHÉ *noun.*

stereotyped *adjective*
Without freshness or appeal due to overuse.

TRITE.

stereotypic also **stereotypical** *adjective*
Without freshness or appeal due to overuse.

TRITE.

sterile *adjective*
1. Free or freed from microorganisms: *keeping the operating room sterile.*
2. Lacking originality: *a sterile play devoid of action and new ideas.*

1. *Syns:* sanitized, sterilized.

2. *Syns:* uncreative, unimaginative, uninspired, uninventive, unoriginative.
Near-ants: fertile, fruitful, potent, productive, prolific.
Ant: fecund.

3. Unable to produce offspring.
4. Arousing no interest or curiosity.

3. BARREN *adjective.*
4. BORING.

sterility *noun*
1. The state or condition of being unable to reproduce sexually: *Excess exposure to radiation can cause sterility.*
2. The state or condition of being free from microorganisms: *Sterility must be maintained in operating rooms.*

1. *Syns:* barrenness, infecundity, infertility, sterilization.

2. *Syn:* sterilization.

sterilization *noun*
1. The act or an instance of making one incapable of reproducing sexually: *enforced sterilization of prisoners; sterilization of farm animals.*
2. The state or condition of being unable to reproduce sexually.
3. The state or condition of being free from microorganisms.

1. *Syns:* castration, gelding, mutilation, unsexing.

2. STERILITY.

3. STERILITY.

sterilize *verb*
1. To render incapable of reproducing sexually: *had the cat sterilized.*
2. To render free of microorganisms: *sterilized the instruments in an autoclave.*

1. *Syns:* alter, castrate, change, fix, geld, neuter, unsex.
2. *Syns:* decontaminate, disinfect, sanitize.

sterilized *adjective*
Free or freed from microorganisms.

STERILE.

stern *adjective*
Rigorous and unsparing in treating others.

SEVERE.

stew *verb*
1. To cook (food) in liquid heated to the point of steaming.
2. To worry over trifles.
3. *Informal.* To turn over in the mind, moodily and at length.
4. To be troubled.

1. BOIL *verb.*

2. FUSS *verb.*
3. BROOD.

4. WORRY *verb.*

stew *noun*
Informal. A state of discomposure.

AGITATION.

stewardly *adjective*
Careful in the use of material resources.

ECONOMICAL.

stewed *adjective*
Slang. Intoxicated with alcoholic liquor.

DRUNK *adjective.*

stick *noun*

1. A fairly long, straight piece of solid material used esp. as a support in walking: *The old man was bent over his stick.*
2. A relatively long, straight, rigid piece of metal or other solid material: *a stick of pig iron; a stick of candy; a stick of wood.*

1. *Syns:* cane, staff, stave[1]. —*Idiom* walking stick.
2. *Syns:* bar, rod, shaft, slab.

stick *verb*

1. To cause to penetrate with force.
2. To become or cause to become stuck or lodged.
3. To deposit in a specified position.
4. *Informal.* To make incapable of finding something to think, do, or say.
5. *Slang.* To get money or something else from by deceitful trickery.
6. *Slang.* To exploit (another) by charging too much for something.
7. *Slang.* To force (another) to accept a burden.
8. To hold fast to.

1. RAM.
2. CATCH *verb.*
3. SET[1] *verb.*
4. NONPLUS.
5. CHEAT *verb.*
6. SKIN *verb.*
7. IMPOSE.
8. BOND *verb.*

stick around *verb*
Informal. To continue to be in a place.

REMAIN.

stick out *verb*

1. To curve outward past the normal or usual limit.
2. To be obtrusively conspicuous.

1. BULGE *verb.*
2. GLARE *verb.*

stick around *verb*

SEE **stick.**

stick-at-nothing *adjective*
Lacking scruples or principles.

UNSCRUPULOUS.

stick-in-the-mud *noun*
Informal. An old-fashioned person who is reluctant to change or innovate.

SQUARE *noun.*

stick out *verb*

SEE **stick.**

stick up *verb*
Informal. To take property or possessions from (a person, company, etc.) unlawfully and usu. forcibly.

ROB.

stickup *noun*
Informal. The act or crime of taking another's property unlawfully and by force.

ROBBERY.

stickup *noun*

SEE **stick up.**

sticky *adjective*

1. Having the property of adhering: *sticky icing.*

1. *Syns:* adhesive, claggy (*Regional*), cloggy, gluey, gooey (*Informal*), gummy, tacky[1].

2. Damp and warm: *a sticky day in the delta country.*

2. *Syns:* humid, mucky, muggy, soggy, sultry.
   Near-syns: close, oppressive, stifling, stuffy, sweltering.

3. *Informal.* Not easy to do, achieve, or master.
4. Hard to deal with or get out of.

3. DIFFICULT.
4. TIGHT *adjective.*

sticky-fingered *adjective*
Tending to larceny.

LARCENOUS.

stiff *adjective*

1. So rigidly constrained, formal, or awkward as to lack all grace and spontaneity: *a stiff, uncomfortable interview; a person who was stiff and ill at ease with others.*

1. *Syns:* buckram, cardboard, starchy, stilted, wooden.

2. Not changing shape or bending.
3. Incapable of changing or being modified.
4. Vastly exceeding a normal limit, as in cost.

2. RIGID.
3. INFLEXIBLE.
4. STEEP[1].

stiff *noun*

1. *Slang.* The physical frame of a dead person or animal.

1. BODY *noun.*

2. *Slang.* A person who is habitually drunk.   **2.** DRUNKARD.

3. *Slang.* A stingy person.   **3.** MISER.

stiff   *verb*

To make stiff or stiffer.   STIFFEN.

stiffen   *verb*

1. To make stiff or stiffer: *stiffen a collar with starch.*   **1.** *Syn:* stiff.

2. To make resistant to hardship, esp. through continued exposure.   **2.** HARDEN.

3. To make or become tense.   **3.** TENSE *verb.*

stiff-necked   *adjective*

Tenaciously unwilling to yield.   OBSTINATE.

stifle   *verb*

1. To stop the breathing of.   **1.** CHOKE.

2. To keep from being published or transmitted.   **2.** CENSOR.

3. To decrease or dull the sound of.   **3.** MUFFLE.

4. To hold (something requiring an outlet) in check.   **4.** REPRESS.

stifling   *adjective*

Oppressive due to a lack of fresh air.   AIRLESS.

stifling   *noun*

The act of restraining forcefully.   REPRESSION.

stigma   *noun*

1. *Med.* A mark on the skin indicative of a disease, as typhus: *a hemorrhaging stigma.*   **1.** *Syn:* petechia.

2. A mark of discredit or disgrace.   **2.** STAIN *noun.*

stigmatize   *verb*

To mark with disgrace or infamy: *a family stigmatized by congenital insanity; an administration stigmatized by scandal.*   *Syn:* brand. —*Idiom* give a bad name to.

still   *adverb*

1. Without noise: *He lay still and watched the attack.*   **1.** *Syn:* quiet. —*Idiom* still (*or* quiet) as a mouse.

2. In addition.   **2.** ADDITIONALLY.

3. To a more extreme degree.   **3.** EVEN[1] *adverb.*

4. In spite of a preceding event or consideration: *values that are age-old but still valid.*   **4.** *Syn:* yet. —*Idioms* be that as it may, still and all, still and on (*Scot.*).

still   *adjective*

1. Marked by, done with, or making no sound or noise.   **1.** SILENT.

2. Not moving.   **2.** MOTIONLESS.

3. Motionless and undisturbed: *the still waters of a secluded lagoon.*   **3.** *Syns:* calm, halcyon, placid, quiet, stilly (*Poetic*), untroubled.

4. Marked by an absence of circulating air.   **4.** AIRLESS.

still   *verb*

1. To cause to become silent.   **1.** SILENCE *verb.*

2. To make or become calm.   **2.** CALM *verb.*

still   *noun*

The absence of sound or noise.   SILENCE *noun.*

stillness   *noun*

1. An absence of motion or disturbance: *an ominous stillness before the storm.*   **1.** *Syns:* calm, hush, lull, placidity, quiet.

2. The absence of sound or noise.   **2.** SILENCE *noun.*

stilly   *adjective*

1. Marked by, done with, or making no sound or noise.   **1.** SILENT.

2. *Poetic.* Motionless and undisturbed.   **2.** STILL *adjective.*

stilted   *adjective*

So rigidly constrained, formal, or awkward as to lack all grace and spontaneity.   STIFF *adjective.*

stimulant   *noun*

Something that causes and encourages a given response.   STIMULUS.

stimulate   *verb*

1. To arouse to action.   **1.** ACTIVATE.

2. To impart courage, inspiration, and resolution to.
2. ENCOURAGE.

3. To elicit a strong emotional response from.
3. INSPIRE.

4. To stir to action or feeling.
4. PROVOKE.

stimulating *adjective*

1. Serving to enliven: *a stimulating debate on foreign policy; a stimulating night of good theater.*
1. *Syns:* animating, enlivening, quickening, rousing, stimulative, vitalizing, vivifying.

2. Producing or stimulating physical, mental, or emotional vigor.
2. TONIC *adjective.*

stimulation *noun*

1. Something that encourages.
1. ENCOURAGEMENT.

2. Something that causes and encourages a given response.
2. STIMULUS.

stimulative *adjective*

Serving to enliven.
STIMULATING.

stimulator *noun*

Something that causes and encourages a given response.
STIMULUS.

stimulus *noun*

1. Something that causes and encourages a given response: *laissez-faire economic policies serving as a stimulus to free enterprise.*
1. *Syns:* catalyst, fillip, impetus, impulse, incentive, motivation, prod, push, spur, stimulant, stimulation, stimulator.

2. Something that incites esp. a violent response: *Rumors of police brutality constituted the main stimulus for the riot.*
2. *Syns:* goad, incitation, incitement, instigation, provocation, trigger.

sting *noun*

1. A cutting quality.
1. EDGE *noun.*

2. A sudden, sharp, painful feeling.
2. PRICK *noun.*

3. *Informal.* A stimulating or intoxicating effect.
3. KICK *noun.*

sting *verb*

1. To feel or cause to feel a sensation of heat or discomfort: *Smoke made my eyes sting. Alcohol stings an open wound.*
1. *Syns:* bite, burn, smart.

2. To cause to become sore or inflamed.
2. IRRITATE.

3. *Slang.* To get money or something else from by deceitful trickery.
3. CHEAT *verb.*

stinging *adjective*

So sharp as to cause mental pain.
BITING.

stingy *adjective*

1. Ungenerously or pettily reluctant to spend money: *too stingy to pay his employees a living wage.*
1. *Syns:* cheap, close[1], close-fisted, costive, hardfisted, mean[2], miserly, narrow (*Regional*), niggard, niggardly, parsimonious, penny-pinching, penurious, pinching, tight, tightfisted. *Near-ants:* bountiful, generous, giving, liberal, philanthropic. *Ant:* sharing.

2. Conspicuously deficient in quantity, fullness, or extent.
2. MEAGER.

stink *verb*

To have or give off a foul odor.
SMELL *verb.*

stinking *adjective*

1. Having an unpleasant odor.
1. SMELLY.

2. *Slang.* Intoxicated with alcoholic liquor.
2. DRUNK *adjective.*

stint *verb*

To be severely sparing in order to economize.
SCRIMP.

stint *noun*

1. A limited, often assigned period of activity, duty, or opportunity.
1. TURN *noun.*

2. A piece of work that has been assigned.
2. TASK *noun.*

stipend *noun*
Payment for work done.   WAGE(S) *noun.*

stipple *verb*
To mark with many small spots.   SPECKLE.

stipulate *verb*
To make specific: *The contract stipulates the obligations*   **Syns:** detail, particularize, specificate,
of all parties.   specify.

stipulation *noun*
A restricting or modifying element.   PROVISION.

stir¹ *verb*
1. To impart movement to: *A slight smile stirred her*   1. **Syn:** move.
   lips. The breeze stirred my hair.
2. To put together into one mass so that the   2. MIX *verb.*
   constituent parts are more or less homogeneous.
3. To arouse the emotions of; make ardent.   3. FIRE *verb.*
4. To induce or elicit (a reaction or emotion).   4. AROUSE.
5. To elicit a strong emotional response from.   5. INSPIRE.
6. To give rise to a particular development.   6. GENERATE.
7. To make a slight movement: *The child stirred in his*   7. **Syns:** budge, move.
   sleep. He wouldn't stir from the TV set.
8. To cease sleeping.   8. WAKE.

stir *noun*
1. The act or process of moving.   1. MOTION *noun.*
2. Agitated, excited movement and activity: *an angry*   2. **Syns:** bustle, flurry, whirl, whirlpool.
   stir in the crowd.
3. An interruption of regular procedure or of public   3. DISTURBANCE.
   peace.
4. A condition of intense public interest or excitement.   4. SENSATION.

stir² *noun*
Slang. A place for the confinement of persons in lawful   JAIL *noun.*
detention.

stirred *adjective*
Emotionally aroused.   AFFECTED¹.

stirring *adjective*
1. Exciting a deep, usu. somber response.   1. AFFECTING.
2. Providing inspiration.   2. INSPIRING.

stitch *noun*
A sensation of physical discomfort occurring as the   PAIN *noun.*
result of disease or injury.

stock *adjective*
1. Being of no special quality or type.   1. ORDINARY *adjective.*
2. Lacking in interest or originality.   2. ROUTINE *adjective.*

stock *verb*
To have for sale.   CARRY.

stock *noun*
1. A group of people sharing common ancestry.   1. FAMILY.
2. A supply stored or hidden for future use.   2. HOARD *noun.*

stockpile *verb*
1. To accumulate and set aside for future use: *The air*   1. **Syns:** lay up, save (up), store (up).
   force stockpiled nuclear weapons for use in case of
   war.
2. To store up (supplies or money), usu. well beyond   2. HOARD *verb.*
   one's needs.

stockpile *noun*
A supply stored or hidden for future use.   HOARD *noun.*

stock-still *adjective*
Not moving.   MOTIONLESS.

stocky *adjective*
Short, heavy, and solidly built: *The coach made him a*   **Syns:** blocky, chunky, dumpy, squab,
shot-putter, since he was too stocky to run races.   squabby, squat, stodgy, stubby, stumpy.

Near-ants: lanky, lean, skinny, slim, thin, wiry.

stodgy *adjective*
1. Short, heavy, and solidly built.
2. Having so many constituent particles in suspension as to be condensed, often viscous.

1. STOCKY.
2. THICK *adjective*.

stole *noun*
A garment wrapped about a person.

WRAP *noun*.

stolid *adjective*
Without emotion or interest.

APATHETIC.

stolidity *noun*
Lack of emotion or interest.

APATHY.

stomach *noun*
A desire for food or drink.

APPETITE.

stomach *verb*
To put up with.

ENDURE.

stomp *verb*
1. To walk with loud, heavy steps.
2. To step on heavily and repeatedly so as to crush, injure, or destroy.

1. TRAMP *verb*.
2. TRAMPLE.

stone *noun*
A fertilized plant ovule capable of germinating.

SEED *noun*.

stoned *adjective*
1. *Slang.* Stupefied, intoxicated, or otherwise influenced by the taking of drugs.
2. *Slang.* Intoxicated with alcoholic liquor.

1. DRUGGED.

2. DRUNK *adjective*.

stonyhearted *adjective*
Totally lacking in compassion.

COLD-BLOODED.

stooge *noun*
A person used or controlled by others.

PAWN².

stool *verb*
Slang. To give incriminating information about others, esp. to the authorities.

INFORM.

stoolie *noun*
Slang. One who gives incriminating information about others.

INFORMER.

stool pigeon *noun*
Slang. One who gives incriminating information about others.

INFORMER.

stoop *verb*
1. To incline the body: *an old man stooped over his cane.*
2. To bring oneself down to a lower level of behavior.
3. To descend to a level considered inappropriate to one's dignity.

1. *Syns:* bend, bow, hump, hunch, scrunch.
2. DESCEND.
3. CONDESCEND.

stop *verb*
1. To prevent the occurrence or continuation of a movement, action, or operation: *The governor stopped the execution. Stop that noise!*

2. To plug up something, as a hole, space, or container.
3. To come to a cessation: *The snow has finally stopped. Work on the project stopped last week. The guard yelled for us to stop, and we froze in our tracks.*

4. To cut short; discontinue.
5. To bring or come to a forced end.
6. To cease trying to accomplish or continue.
7. To go to or seek out the company of in order to socialize.
8. To cause to cease regular activity.

1. *Syns:* arrest, belay (*Naut.*), cease, check, discontinue, halt¹, stay¹, surcease (*Archaic*). —*Idioms* bring to a standstill, call a halt to, put a stop to.

2. FILL.
3. *Syns:* belay (*Rare*), cease, desist, discontinue, halt¹, lay off (*Slang*), leave off, quit, surcease (*Archaic*). —*Idiom* come to a standstill (*or* stop).

4. BREAK *verb*.
5. BREAK UP at **break**.
6. ABANDON *verb*.
7. VISIT *verb*.

8. TIE UP.

stop *noun*
1. The act of stopping: *The skier made a fast stop at the bottom of the hill.*

2. The condition of being stopped: *Work on the dam has been at a total stop for a year.*
3. A concluding or terminating.
4. Anything that impedes or prevents entry or passage.

stopgap *noun*
1. Something used temporarily or reluctantly when other means are not available.
2. That to which one turns for help when in desperation.

stoppage *noun*
1. The act of stopping.
2. The condition of being stopped.
3. A cessation of normal activity caused by an accident, strike, etc.

store *noun*
1. A retail establishment where merchandise is sold: *a clothing store.*
2. A supply stored or hidden for future use.
3. A place where something is deposited for safekeeping.

store *verb*
1. To have or put in a customary place.
2. To accumulate and set aside for future use.

storehouse *noun*
A place where something is deposited for safekeeping.

storm *verb*
To set upon with violent force.

storm *noun*
A concentrated outpouring, as of missiles, words, or blows.

storm and stress *noun*
A state of uneasiness and usu. resentment brewing to an eventual explosion.

stormy *adjective*
1. Violently disturbed, as by storms.
2. Marked by unrest or disturbance.

story *noun*
1. A recounting of past events: *war stories.*

2. A usu. brief detail of news or information.
3. A narrative not based on fact.
4. An entertaining and often oral account of a real or fictitious occurrence.
5. The series of events and relationships forming the basis of a composition.
6. An untrue declaration.

storyteller *noun*
One who tells lies.

stout *adjective*
1. Having or showing courage.
2. Having a large body, esp. in girth.
3. Having too much flesh.
4. Capable of exerting considerable effort or of withstanding considerable stress or hardship.

stouthearted *adjective*
Having or showing courage.

---

1. **Syns:** arrest, cessation, check, cut-off, halt[1], stay[1], stoppage. —*Idiom* screeching halt.
2. **Syns:** cessation, halt[1], stoppage, standstill. —*Idiom* dead (*or* full) stop.
3. END *noun*.
4. BAR *noun*.

1. MAKESHIFT.

2. RESORT *noun*.

1. STOP *noun*.
2. STOP *noun*.
3. TIE-UP at **tie up.**

1. **Syns:** emporium, outlet, shop.

2. HOARD *noun*.
3. DEPOSITORY.

1. KEEP *verb*.
2. STOCKPILE *verb*.

DEPOSITORY.

ATTACK *verb*.

BARRAGE *noun*.

UNREST.

1. ROUGH.
2. TURBULENT.

1. **Syns:** account, chronicle, description, history, narrative, report, statement, version.
2. ITEM.
3. FICTION.
4. YARN.

5. PLOT *noun*.

6. LIE[2] *noun*.

LIAR.

1. BRAVE *adjective*.
2. BULKY.
3. FAT *adjective*.
4. STRONG.

BRAVE *adjective*.

strabismal or **strabismic** *adjective*
Marked by or affected with a squint.   SQUINTY.

strabismic *adjective*   SEE **strabismal.**

strabismus *noun*
The condition of not having the visual axes parallel.   SQUINT *noun.*

straddle *verb*
1. To sit or lie with the limbs spread out awkwardly.   1. SPRAWL.
2. To sit with a leg on each side of.   2. STRIDE.

straggle *verb*
To grow or spread in a disorderly or planless fashion.   SPRAWL.

straggler *noun*
One that lags.   LAGGARD *noun.*

straight *adjective*
1. Not diluted or mixed with other substances: *Straight* 1. *Syns:* full-strength, neat, plain, pure,
   vodka, bartender.   unblended *or* unblent, undiluted,
                                                              unmixed. —*Idiom* right off the top.
2. Proceeding or lying in an uninterrupted line or   2. DIRECT *adjective.*
   course.
3. Having no irregularities, roughness, or indentations. 3. EVEN[1] *adjective.*
4. In a definite and final form; not likely to change.   4. FIRM[1].
5. Speaking or spoken freely and sincerely.   5. FRANK.
6. *Slang.* Conforming to established practice or   6. CONVENTIONAL.
   standards.

straight *adverb*
1. Without the slightest deviation in any respect.   1. PRECISELY.
2. With precision or absolute conformity.   2. DIRECTLY.

straighten *verb*
To make or keep (an area) clean and orderly.   TIDY *verb.*

straighten out *verb*
To bring (something) into a state of agreement or   SETTLE.
accord.

straighten out *verb*   SEE **straighten.**

straightforward *adjective*
1. Proceeding or lying in an uninterrupted line or   1. DIRECT *adjective.*
   course.
2. Speaking or spoken freely and sincerely.   2. FRANK.
3. Executed without pretense or obfuscation.   3. PLAIN *adjective.*

straight-from-the-shoulder *adjective*
Informal. Speaking or spoken freely and sincerely.   FRANK.

straight-shooting *adjective*
1. Executed without pretense or obfuscation.   1. PLAIN *adjective.*
2. *Informal.* Having or marked by uprightness in   2. HONEST.
   principle and action.

strain¹ *verb*
To exert one's mental or physical powers, usu. under   LABOR *verb.*
difficulty and to the point of exhaustion.

strain *noun*
1. The act, condition, or effect of exerting force on   1. PRESSURE *noun.*
   someone or something.
2. The use of energy to do something.   2. EFFORT.

strain² *noun*
1. A pleasing succession of musical tones forming a   1. MELODY.
   usu. brief aesthetic unit.
2. An intermixture of a contrasting or unexpected   2. STREAK *noun.*
   quality, esp. in a person's character.
3. A slight amount.   3. SHADE *noun.*

strained *adjective*
Not natural or spontaneous.   FORCED.

strait-laced *adjective*
Marked by excessive concern for propriety and good   GENTEEL.
form.

strake *verb*
To mark with a line or band of different color or texture.   STREAK *verb*.

strand *noun*
Something drawn or spun out like a fine, continuous filament.   THREAD *noun*.

strange *adjective*
1. Deviating from the customary.   1. ECCENTRIC *adjective*.
2. Causing puzzlement; perplexing.   2. FUNNY.
3. Of, from, or characteristic of another place or part of   3. FOREIGN.
   the world.

stranger *noun*
A person coming from another country.   FOREIGNER.

strangle *verb*
1. To interfere with or stop the normal breathing of,   1. CHOKE *verb*.
   esp. by constricting the windpipe.
2. To hold (something requiring an outlet) in check.   2. REPRESS.

strapped *adjective*
Informal. Having little or no money or wealth.   POOR.

strapping *adjective*
Physically strong and healthy.   ABLE-BODIED.

stratagem *noun*
1. An indirect, usu. cunning means of gaining an end.   1. TRICK *noun*.
2. An action meant to deceive.   2. DECEPTION.

strategy *noun*
A method for making, doing, or accomplishing something.   DESIGN *noun*.

stratospheric *adjective*
1. Pre-eminent in rank or position.   1. HIGHEST.
2. Vastly exceeding a normal limit, as in cost.   2. STEEP[1].

straw *noun*
The least bit.   DAMN *noun*.

stray *verb*
1. To turn away from a prescribed course of action or   1. DEVIATE *verb*.
   conduct.
2. To turn aside from the main subject in writing or   2. DIGRESS.
   speaking.
3. To move about at random, esp. over a wide area.   3. ROVE.

stray *adjective*
1. Without a fixed or regular course.   1. ERRATIC.
2. Having no particular pattern, purpose, organization,   2. RANDOM.
   or structure.

streak *noun*
1. An intermixture of a contrasting or unexpected   1. *Syns:* strain[2], stripe, vein.
   quality, esp. in a person's character: *He's got a real
   mean streak.*
2. A slight amount.   2. SHADE *noun*.
3. *Informal.* A number of things placed or occurring   3. SERIES.
   one after the other.

streak *verb*
To mark with a line or band of different color or   *Syns:* strake, striate, stripe, variegate.
texture: *Lightning streaked the sky.*

stream *noun*
Something suggestive of running water.   FLOW *noun*.

stream *verb*
1. To move freely as a liquid.   1. FLOW *verb*.
2. To come forth or emit in abundance.   2. FLOW *verb*.

streamer *noun*
Fabric used esp. as a symbol.   FLAG[1] *noun*.

streamlined *adjective*
Having slender and graceful lines.   SLEEK *adjective*.

street *noun*
A course affording passage from one place to another.   WAY.

streetwalker *noun*
A woman who engages in sexual intercourse for   PROSTITUTE.
payment.

strength *noun*
1. The state or quality of being physically strong: *You*   1. ***Syns:*** brawn, might, muscle, potency
   could sense the strength in his legs and arms.   (*also* potence), power, powerfulness,
                                                                  puissance, sinew(s), thew(s), vigor,
                                                                  vigorousness.
                                                                  Near-syns: energy, force, health,
                                                                  toughness.
                                                                  Ant: weakness.
2. Capacity or power for work or vigorous activity.   2. ENERGY.
3. Power used to overcome resistance.   3. FORCE *noun*.
4. The condition of being free from defects or flaws.   4. SOUNDNESS.
5. Reliability in withstanding pressure, force, or stress.   5. STABILITY.

strengthen *verb*
1. To prepare (oneself) for action.   1. GIRD.
2. To make firmer in a particular conviction or habit.   2. CONFIRM.
3. To become or cause to become tough or strong.   3. TOUGHEN.
4. To make or become tight or tighter.   4. TIGHTEN.

strenuous *adjective*
1. Possessing, exerting, or displaying energy.   1. ENERGETIC.
2. Marked by vigorous physical exertion.   2. ROUGH.

stress *noun*
1. Special weight placed upon something considered   1. EMPHASIS.
   important.
2. The act, condition, or effect of exerting force on   2. PRESSURE *noun*.
   someone or something.

stress *verb*
To accord emphasis to.   EMPHASIZE.

stretch *verb*
1. To make or become longer.   1. LENGTHEN.
2. To proceed on a certain course or for a certain   2. EXTEND.
   distance.
3. To make (something) seem greater than is actually   3. EXAGGERATE.
   the case.
4. *Archaic.* To execute by suspending by the neck.   4. HANG.
5. To extend, esp. an appendage.   5. REACH.

stretch out *verb*
1. To be or place oneself in a prostrate or recumbent   1. LIE[1].
   position.
2. To take repose by sleeping, lying quietly, or the like. 2. REST[1] *verb*.

stretch *noun*
1. The measure of how far or long something goes in   1. EXTENT.
   space, time, or degree.
2. An extent, measured or unmeasured, of linear space.   2. DISTANCE.
3. A wide and open area, as of land, sky, or water.   3. EXPANSE.
4. A rather short period.   4. BIT[1].
5. A term of service, as in the military or in prison.   5. TIME *noun*.
6. A limited or specific period of time during which   6. TERM *noun*.
   something happens, lasts, or extends.

stretch *adjective*
Capable of being extended or expanded.   EXTENSIBLE.

stretchable *adjective*
Capable of being extended or expanded.   EXTENSIBLE.

stretch out *verb*   SEE **stretch**.

strew *verb*
To extend over a wide area.   SPREAD *verb*.

striate *verb*
To mark with a line or band of different color or texture.

STREAK *verb*.

strict *adjective*
1. Conforming completely to established rule: *a strict construction of the Constitution.*
2. Rigorous and unsparing in treating others.
3. Not deviating from correctness, accuracy, or completeness.

1. **Syns:** exact, rigorous, uncompromising.
2. SEVERE.
3. CLOSE[1] *adjective*.

stricture *noun*
1. Something that limits or restricts.
2. *Path.* A becoming narrow or narrower.

1. RESTRICTION.
2. CONSTRICTION.

stride *verb*
1. To walk with long steps, esp. in a vigorous manner: *strode into the office and demanded to see the manager.*
2. To sit with a leg on each side of: *stride the fence.*

1. **Syns:** march[1], stalk.
   Near-syns: clump, stamp, stomp, tramp, tromp.
2. **Syns:** bestride, straddle.

strident *adjective*
1. Disagreeable to the sense of hearing.
2. Offensively loud and insistent.

1. HARSH.
2. VOCIFEROUS.

strife *noun*
1. A state of disagreement and disharmony.
2. A state of open, prolonged fighting.
3. A struggle with others for victory or supremacy.

1. CONFLICT *noun*.
2. CONFLICT *noun*.
3. COMPETITION.

strike *verb*
1. To deliver (a powerful blow) suddenly and sharply.
2. To grasp at (something) eagerly, forcibly, and abruptly with the jaws.
3. To give forth or cause to give forth a clear, resonant sound.
4. To have a sudden, overwhelming effect on.
5. To set upon with violent force.
6. To bring great harm or suffering to.
7. To evoke a usu. strong mental or emotional response from.
8. To enter a person's mind.
9. To cease working in support of demands made upon an employer: *The miners decided to strike for higher pay.*

1. HIT *verb*.
2. SNAP *verb*.
3. RING[2].
4. SEIZE.
5. ATTACK *verb*.
6. AFFLICT.
7. AFFECT[1].
8. OCCUR.
9. **Syn:** walk out. —*Idiom* go on strike.

strike back *verb*
To return like for like, esp. to return an unfriendly or hostile action with a similar one.

RETALIATE.

strike out *verb*
1. To proceed in a specified direction.
2. To remove or invalidate by or as if by running a line through or wiping clean.

1. BEAR.
2. CANCEL.

strike *noun*
1. Something that has been discovered.
2. The act of attacking.

1. DISCOVERY.
2. ATTACK *noun*.

strike back *verb*
SEE **strike**.

strike out *verb*
SEE **strike**.

striking *adjective*
Readily attracting notice.

NOTICEABLE.

string *noun*
1. A number of things placed or occurring one after the other.
2. An unbroken sequence of events.
3. A group of people or things arranged in a row.
4. *Informal.* A restricting or modifying element.

1. SERIES.
2. RUN *noun*.
3. LINE *noun*.
4. PROVISION.

string *verb*
To put (objects) onto a fine, continuous filament.

THREAD *verb*.

string up *verb*
Informal. To execute by suspending by the neck.   HANG *verb.*

stringency *noun*
The fact or condition of being rigorous and unsparing.   SEVERITY.

string up *verb*   SEE **string.**

strip¹ *verb*
1. To remove all the clothing from: *stripped and*   1. ***Syns:*** denude, disrobe, unclothe,
   searched each suspect; quickly stripped and jumped   undress.
   into the pool.   ***Near-syns:*** bare, doff, expose, peel,
                                                                uncover.
2. To make bare.   2. BARE *verb.*
3. To remove the skin of.   3. SKIN *verb.*
4. To destroy completely while conquering or   4. DEVASTATE.
   occupying.
5. To take or keep something away from.   5. DEPRIVE.

strip² *noun*
A thin strip of material or color.   BAND¹ *noun.*

stripe *noun*
1. A thin strip of material or color.   1. BAND¹ *noun.*
2. A class that is defined by the common attribute or   2. KIND².
   attributes possessed by all its members.
3. An intermixture of a contrasting or unexpected   3. STREAK *noun.*
   quality, esp. in a person's character.

stripe *verb*
To mark with a line or band of different color or   STREAK *verb.*
texture.

stripped *adjective*
Not wearing any clothes.   NUDE.

strive *verb*
1. To make an attempt to do or make.   1. ATTEMPT *verb.*
2. To exert one's mental or physical powers, usu. under   2. LABOR *verb.*
   difficulty and to the point of exhaustion.

striving *noun*
1. A struggle with others for victory or supremacy.   1. COMPETITION.
2. The use of energy to do something.   2. EFFORT.

stroll *verb*
1. To walk at a leisurely pace: *We strolled about the*   1. ***Syns:*** amble, meander, mosey
   gardens as we talked.   (*Informal*), perambulate, promenade,
                                                                ramble, saunter, wander.
2. To go through a place, viewing or inspecting in a   2. BROWSE.
   leisurely way.

stroll *noun*
An act of walking, esp. for pleasure.   WALK *noun.*

strong *adjective*
1. Having great physical strength: *It takes two strong*   1. ***Syns:*** brawny, lusty, mighty, potent,
   men to move a piano.   powerful, puissant.
                                                                Near-syns: able, able-bodied, firm,
                                                                muscular, robust, sinewy, stout, tough.
                                                                Ant: weak.
2. Capable of exerting considerable effort or of   2. ***Syns:*** hardy, stalwart, stout, sturdy,
   withstanding considerable stress or hardship: *a*   tough.
   strong national economy; strong woolen fabric.
3. Full of or displaying force.   3. FORCEFUL.
4. Intensely violent in sustained velocity.   4. HIGH *adjective.*
5. Resulting from or affecting one's innermost feelings. 5. DEEP *adjective.*
6. Having a high concentration of the distinguishing   6. ***Syns:*** concentrated, potent, stiff.
   ingredient: *a strong drink.*
7. Containing alcohol.   7. HARD *adjective.*
8. Firmly settled or positioned.   8. SURE.

strong-arm *verb*
1. *Informal.* To domineer or drive into compliance by the use of threats, force, etc.
2. To force one's way into a place or situation.

1. INTIMIDATE.

2. MUSCLE *verb.*

strong-arm *adjective*
Informal. Accomplished by force.

FORCIBLE.

struck *adjective*
Emotionally aroused.

AFFECTED[1].

structure *noun*
A usu. permanent construction, as a house, store, etc.

BUILDING.

struggle *verb*
To strive in opposition to.

CONTEND.

struggle *noun*
1. An intense competition.
2. The use of energy to do something.

1. BATTLE *noun.*
2. EFFORT.

strumpet *noun*
A vulgar, promiscuous woman who flouts propriety.

SLUT.

strut *verb*
To walk with exaggerated or unnatural motions expressive of self-importance or self-display: *Modeling her new outfit, she strutted about like a peacock.*

Syns: flounce, peacock, sashay (*Informal*), swagger, swank, swash.

stubborn *adjective*
1. Firmly, often unreasonably immovable in purpose or will: *stubborn adherence to an unworkable plan.*

1. *Syns:* adamant, adamantine, brassbound, die-hard (*also* diehard), inexorable, inflexible, iron, obdurate, relentless, rigid, unbendable, unbending, uncompliant, uncompromising, unswayable, unyielding. —*Idiom* stubborn as a mule (*or* ox).
Near-ants: agreeable, amenable, compliant, docile, flexible, open-minded, pliant, responsive, yielding.

2. Tenaciously unwilling to yield.
3. Difficult to alleviate or cure: *a stubborn cold.*

2. OBSTINATE.
3. *Syns:* obstinate, persistent, pertinacious.

stubbornness *noun*
The quality or state of being stubbornly unyielding.

OBSTINACY.

stubby *adjective*
Short, heavy, and solidly built.

STOCKY.

stuck-up *adjective*
Informal. Thinking too highly of oneself.

EGOTISTICAL.

student *noun*
One who is being educated: *college students.*

Syns: educand, learner, pupil, scholar, scholastic (*Obs.*).

studied *adjective*
Resulting from deliberation and careful thought.

ADVISED.

studious *adjective*
1. Devoted to study or reading: *a studious young man who preferred books to sports.*
2. Characterized by steady attention and effort.
3. *Rare.* Resulting from deliberation and careful thought.

1. *Syns:* bookish, scholarly.
2. DILIGENT.
3. ADVISED.

study *noun*
1. The act of examining carefully.
2. A careful considering of a matter.
3. Repetition of an action so as to develop or maintain one's skill.
4. The condition of being so lost in solitary thought as to be unaware of one's surroundings.

1. EXAMINATION.
2. ADVISEMENT.
3. PRACTICE *noun.*
4. TRANCE.

study *verb*
1. To look at carefully or critically.
2. To think about seriously.
3. To apply one's mind to the acquisition of knowledge: *studying for an exam.*

1. EXAMINE.
2. CONSIDER.
3. *Syns:* con, lucubrate.

stuff *noun*
1. That from which things are or can be made.
2. The basic substance or essential elements of character that qualify a person for a specified role.
3. The most central and material part.
4. *Informal.* Those articles that belong to someone.
5. Something that does not have or make sense.

1. MATERIAL.
2. TIMBER.
3. HEART.
4. BELONGINGS.
5. NONSENSE.

stuff *verb*
To fill to excess by compressing or squeezing tightly.

CROWD *verb.*

stuffed *adjective*
Completely filled.

FULL.

stuffy *adjective*
1. Arousing no interest or curiosity.
2. Characterized by an exaggerated show of dignity or self-importance.
3. *Informal.* Marked by excessive concern for propriety and good form.
4. Oppressive due to a lack of fresh air.

1. BORING.
2. POMPOUS.
3. GENTEEL.
4. AIRLESS.

stumble *verb*
1. To catch the foot against something and lose one's balance: *stumbled on an electric cord and nearly fell.*
2. To move awkwardly or clumsily.
3. To walk unsteadily.
4. To proceed or perform in an unsteady, faltering manner.
5. To make an error or mistake.

1. *Syn:* trip. —*Idioms* lose one's footing, make a false step.
2. BLUNDER *verb.*
3. LURCH.
4. MUDDLE.
5. ERR.

stumble on (or **upon**) *verb*
To find or meet by chance.

COME ACROSS at **come.**

stumble *noun*
A stupid, clumsy mistake.

BLUNDER *noun.*

stumble on (or **upon**) *verb*

SEE **stumble.**

stump *verb*
1. To move heavily.
2. *Informal.* To make incapable of finding something to think, do, or say.

1. LUMP[1] *verb.*
2. NONPLUS.

stump *noun*
Informal. An act of taunting another to do something bold or rash.

DARE *noun.*

stumpy *adjective*
Short, heavy, and solidly built.

STOCKY.

stun *verb*
To render helpless, as by emotion.

PARALYZE.

stunner *noun*
1. A woman regarded as beautiful.
2. One that evokes great surprise and admiration.

1. BEAUTY.
2. MARVEL.

stunning *adjective*
Of such a character as to overwhelm.

STAGGERING.

stunt *noun*
1. A great or heroic deed.
2. A clever, dexterous act.

1. FEAT.
2. TRICK *noun.*

stupefy *verb*
1. To make or become less keen or responsive.
2. To stun the senses, as with a heavy blow, a shock, or fatigue.
3. To render helpless, as by emotion.

1. DULL *verb.*
2. DAZE *verb.*
3. PARALYZE.

stupendous *adjective*
1. Of extraordinary size and power.
2. So remarkable as to elicit disbelief.

1. GIANT *adjective*.
2. FABULOUS.

stupid *adjective*
1. Lacking in intelligence: *too stupid to grasp her meaning.*

1. **Syns:** blockheaded, dense, dimwitted, doltish, dumb (*Informal*), feeble-minded, half-witted, hebetudinous, obtuse, simple, simple-minded, slow, slow-witted, soft (*Informal*), thick, thickheaded, thick-witted.
Near-ants: alert, bright, clever, knowing, sharp.
Ants: intelligent, smart.

2. Lacking mental and physical alertness and activity.

2. LETHARGIC.

stupor *noun*
1. A deficiency in mental and physical alertness and activity.
2. A stunned or bewildered condition.

1. LETHARGY.
2. DAZE *noun*.

sturdy *adjective*
1. Physically strong and healthy.
2. Not easily moved or shaken.
3. Characterized by marked muscular development; powerfully built.
4. Capable of exerting considerable effort or of withstanding considerable stress or hardship.

1. ABLE-BODIED.
2. SOUND².
3. MUSCULAR.
4. STRONG.

Sturm und Drang *noun*
A state of uneasiness and usu. resentment brewing to an eventual explosion.

UNREST.

stutter *verb*
To intrude involuntary repetitions and pauses into one's speech.

STAMMER *verb*.

stutter *noun*
A speech impediment marked by involuntary repetitions and pauses.

STAMMER *noun*.

stuttering *noun*
A speech impediment marked by involuntary repetitions and pauses.

STAMMER *noun*.

style *noun*
1. A distinctive way of expressing oneself: *He wrote the script in a disjointed style.*
2. The current custom.
3. The manner in which something is done.
4. Behavior through which one reveals one's personality.
5. The word or words by which one is called and identified.

1. **Syns:** fashion, manner, mode, tone, vein.
2. FASHION *noun*.
3. WAY.
4. BEARING.
5. NAME *noun*.

style *verb*
1. To give a name or title to.
2. To describe with a word or term.

1. NAME *verb*.
2. CALL *verb*.

stylish *adjective*
Being or in accordance with the current fashion.

FASHIONABLE.

stylize *verb*
To make conventional.

CONVENTIONALIZE.

stymie *verb*
To prevent from accomplishing a purpose.

FRUSTRATE.

suave *adjective*
Effortlessly gracious and tactful in social manner: *a suave reply calculated to display his wit without arousing envy.*

Syns: bland, smooth, urbane.
Near-syns: affable, cordial, debonair, diplomatic, polished, refined, well-bred.

sub *noun*
Informal. One that takes the place of another.

SUBSTITUTE *noun*.

subaltern *noun*
One belonging to a lower class or rank.   SUBORDINATE *noun*.

subdivide *verb*
To separate into branches or branchlike parts.   BRANCH *verb*.

subdivision *noun*
1. One of the parts into which something is divided.   1. DIVISION.
2. A part of a family, tribe, or other group, or of such a   2. BRANCH *noun*.
   group's language, that is believed to stem from a
   common ancestor.

subdue *verb*
1. To win a victory over, as in battle or a competition.   1. DEFEAT *verb*.
2. To impair severely the spirit, health, effectiveness,   2. BREAK *verb*.
   etc., of.
3. To make or become less severe or extreme.   3. MODERATE *verb*.

subdued *adjective*
1. Not showy or obtrusive.   1. QUIET.
2. Not irritating, strident, or loud.   2. SOFT.

subject *adjective*
1. In a position of subordination.   1. SUBORDINATE *adjective*.
2. Determined or to be determined by someone or   2. DEPENDENT *adjective*.
   something else.
3. Tending to incur.   3. LIABLE.

subject *noun*
1. A person owing loyalty to and entitled to the   1. CITIZEN.
   protection of a given state.
2. What a speech, piece of writing, or artistic work is   2. *Syns:* argument, matter, point, text,
   about: *She chose the colonial prison system as the*   theme, topic. —*Idiom* subject matter.
   subject of her paper.
3. A sphere of activity, study, or interest.   3. AREA.

subject *verb*
1. To make a slave of.   1. ENSLAVE.
2. To lay open, as to something undesirable or   2. EXPOSE.
   injurious.

subjective *adjective*
Based on individual judgment or discretion.   ARBITRARY.

subjugate *verb*
To make a slave of.   ENSLAVE.

sublimation *noun*
The act of raising to a high position or status or the   EXALTATION.
condition of being so raised.

sublime *adjective*
1. Raised to or occupying a high position or rank.   1. EXALTED.
2. Marked by extraordinary elegance, beauty, and   2. GLORIOUS.
   splendor.
3. Large and impressive in size, scope, or extent.   3. GRAND.

submerge *verb*
1. To plunge briefly in or into a liquid.   1. DIP *verb*.
2. To go beneath the surface or to the bottom of a   2. SINK *verb*.
   liquid.
3. To flow over completely.   3. FLOOD *verb*.
4. To conceal in obscurity.   4. OBSCURE *verb*.

submerse *verb*
1. To go beneath the surface or to the bottom of a   1. SINK *verb*.
   liquid.
2. To plunge briefly in or into a liquid.   2. DIP *verb*.

submission *noun*
1. The quality or state of willingly carrying out the   1. OBEDIENCE.
   wishes of others.
2. The act of submitting or surrendering to the power   2. SURRENDER *noun*.
   of another.
3. Something that is put forward for consideration.   3. PROPOSAL.

submissive *adjective*
1. Willing to carry out the wishes of others.
2. Submitting without objection or resistance.

1. OBEDIENT.
2. PASSIVE.

submit *verb*
1. To commit to the consideration or judgment of another: *submitted his report to the authorities.*
2. To undergo capture, defeat, or ruin.
3. To give in from or as if from a gradual loss of strength.
4. To conform to the will or judgment of another, esp. out of respect or courtesy.
5. To advance, as an idea, for consideration.

1. *Syn:* turn in.
2. SURRENDER *verb.*
3. SUCCUMB.
4. DEFER^2.
5. PROPOSE.

subordinate *noun*
One belonging to a lower class or rank: *The supervisors kept a tight rein on their subordinates.*

Syns: inferior, junior, secondary, subaltern, underling.

subordinate *adjective*
In a position of subordination: *a subordinate territory of a major power.*

Syns: collateral, dependent (*also* dependant), secondary, subject, subservient.

sub-rosa *adjective*
Existing or operating in a way so as to ensure complete concealment and confidentiality.

SECRET *adjective.*

subscribe *verb*
1. To give in common with others.
2. To affix one's signature to.

1. CONTRIBUTE.
2. SIGN *verb.*

subscribe to *verb*
To be favorably disposed toward.

APPROVE.

subscriber *noun*
A person who gives to a charity or cause.

DONOR.

subscribe to *verb*

SEE **subscribe.**

subsequent *adjective*
1. Following something else in time.
2. Being or occurring in the time ahead.
3. Following one after another in an orderly pattern.
4. Going beyond what currently exists.

1. LATER *adjective.*
2. FUTURE *adjective.*
3. CONSECUTIVE.
4. FURTHER *adjective.*

subsequential *adjective*
1. Following one after another in an orderly pattern.
2. Following something else in time.

1. CONSECUTIVE.
2. LATER *adjective.*

subservient *adjective*
1. In a position of subordination.
2. Excessively eager to serve or obey.

1. SUBORDINATE *adjective.*
2. SERVILE.

subside *verb*
To become less active or intense: *The storm gradually subsided.*

Syns: abate, bate, die (down), ease off, ebb, fall, fall off, lapse, let up, moderate, relent, slacken, wane.

subsidiary *noun*
A local unit of a business or an auxiliary controlled by such a business: *A small subsidiary of the multinational corporation is located here.*

Syns: affiliate, branch, division.

subsidiary *adjective*
Giving or able to give help or support.

AUXILIARY *adjective.*

subsidize *verb*
To supply capital to or for.

FINANCE.

subsidy *noun*
Something, as a gift, granted for a definite purpose.

GRANT *noun.*

subsist *verb*
1. To have reality or life.
2. To have being or actuality.
3. To maintain existence in a certain way.

1. BE.
2. EXIST.
3. LIVE^1.

subsistence *noun*
The means needed to support life.

LIVING.

substance *noun*
1. That which occupies space and can be perceived by the senses.
2. That from which things are or can be made.
3. The most central and material part.
4. The general sense or significance, as of an action, statement, etc.
5. The main part.
6. The thread or current of thought uniting or occurring in all the elements of a text or discourse.

1. MATTER *noun.*
2. MATERIAL *noun.*
3. HEART.
4. IMPORT *noun.*

5. BODY *noun.*
6. THRUST *noun.*

substandard *adjective*
Of mediocre quality.

INFERIOR.

substantial *adjective*
1. Composed of or relating to things that occupy space and can be perceived by the senses.
2. Large in number or yield.
3. Having great significance.
4. Having actual reality.

1. PHYSICAL.

2. HEAVY *adjective.*
3. IMPORTANT.
4. REAL.

substantiate *verb*
1. To present evidence in support of.
2. To assure the certainty or validity of.
3. To represent (an abstraction) in or as if in bodily form.
4. To establish as true or genuine.

1. BACK *verb.*
2. CONFIRM.
3. EMBODY.

4. PROVE.

substantiation *noun*
1. That which confirms.
2. A physical entity typifying an abstraction.

1. CONFIRMATION.
2. EMBODIMENT.

substantive *adjective*
Having actual reality.

REAL.

substitute *noun*
One that takes the place of another: *a guest lecturer who is a substitute for a professor on sabbatical.*

Syns: alternate, fill-in, pinch hitter (*Informal*), replacement, stand-in, sub (*Informal*), surrogate.

substitute *verb*
1. To act as a substitute: *When the minister was sick, a church elder would substitute for him.*
2. To give up in return for something else.

1. **Syns:** fill in, pinch-hit (*Informal*), sit in, spell, stand in, supply.
2. CHANGE *verb.*

substitution *noun*
The act of exchanging or substituting.

CHANGE *noun.*

substratum *noun*
The lowest or supporting part or structure.

BASE[1] *noun.*

subsume *verb*
To have as an integral part.

CONTAIN *verb.*

subterfuge *noun*
An action meant to deceive.

DECEPTION.

subterrane *adjective*
Located or operating beneath the earth's surface.

UNDERGROUND *adjective.*

subterranean *adjective*
Located or operating beneath the earth's surface.

UNDERGROUND *adjective.*

subterrene *adjective*
Located or operating beneath the earth's surface.

UNDERGROUND *adjective.*

subterrestrial *adjective*
Located or operating beneath the earth's surface.

UNDERGROUND *adjective.*

subtle *adjective*
1. So slight as to be difficult to notice or appreciate.
2. Able to make or detect effects of great subtlety or precision.

1. DELICATE.
2. FINE[1].

subtract *verb*
To take away (a quantity) from another quantity.

DEDUCT.

suburbs *noun*
The periphery of a city or town.

SKIRTS.

subvention *noun*
Something, as a gift, granted for a definite purpose.

GRANT *noun.*

subversion *noun*
A deliberate and underhanded effort to defeat or do harm to an endeavor.

SABOTAGE *noun.*

subvert *verb*
1. To bring about the downfall of.
2. To damage, destroy, or defeat by sabotage.

1. OVERTHROW.
2. SABOTAGE *verb.*

succedent *adjective*
Following one after another in an orderly pattern.

CONSECUTIVE.

succeed *verb*
1. To turn out well: *The lower crime rate indicates that the campaign to make the streets safer has succeeded.*

1. ***Syns:*** click (*Slang*), come off, come through, go, go over, pan out (*Informal*), work out.

2. To gain wealth or fame: *sure to succeed as an architect.*

2. ***Syns:*** arrive, get ahead, get on, rise. —*Idioms* go far, go places, make good, make it.

3. To occur after (another) in time.

3. FOLLOW.

succeeding *adjective*
Following one after another in an orderly pattern.

CONSECUTIVE.

success *noun*
The achievement of something desired, planned, or attempted: *His efforts to enter high society ended in success.*

Syns: arrival, successfulness. —*Idiom* flying colors.

successfulness *noun*
The achievement of something desired, planned, or attempted.

SUCCESS.

succession *noun*
1. A way in which things follow each other in space or time.
2. A number of things placed or occurring one after the other.
3. An unbroken sequence of events.

1. ORDER *noun.*
2. SERIES.
3. RUN *noun.*

successional *adjective*
Following one after another in an orderly pattern.

CONSECUTIVE.

successive *adjective*
Following one after another in an orderly pattern.

CONSECUTIVE.

succinct *adjective*
Marked by or consisting of few words.

BRIEF.

succor *verb*
To give support or assistance.

HELP *verb.*

succor *noun*
The act or an instance of helping.

HELP *noun.*

succumb *verb*
1. To give in from or as if from a gradual loss of strength: *succumbed to the disease after a valiant struggle.*

1. ***Syns:*** bow, capitulate, fold (*Informal*), submit, surrender, yield.

2. To suddenly lose all health or strength.
3. To cease living.
4. To undergo capture, defeat, or ruin.

2. COLLAPSE *verb.*
3. DIE.
4. SURRENDER *verb.*

sucker *noun*
Slang. A person who is easily deceived or victimized.

DUPE *noun.*

suck in *verb*
Informal. To draw in in such a way that extrication is difficult.

INVOLVE.

sudden *adjective*
Happening quickly and without warning.

ABRUPT.

sudden *adverb*
Without any warning.

SHORT *adverb.*

sudoriferous *adjective*
Producing or covered with sweat.

SWEATY.

suds *noun*
1. A mass of bubbles in or on the surface of a liquid.
2. *Informal.* A feeling or spell of dismally low spirits.

1. FOAM *noun.*
2. GLOOM.

sudsy *adjective*
Consisting of or resembling foam.

FOAMY.

sue *verb*
1. To institute or subject to legal proceedings: *sued to regain custody of the child; suing the newspaper for libel.*
2. To bring an appeal or request to the attention of.
3. To make application to a higher authority.
4. *Archaic.* To attempt to gain the affection of.

1. **Syns:** action (*Law*), law (*Chiefly Regional*), litigate, prosecute. —*Idiom* bring suit (against).
2. ADDRESS *verb.*
3. APPEAL *verb.*
4. COURT *verb.*

suet *noun*
Adipose tissue.

FAT *noun.*

suffer *verb*
1. To participate in or partake of personally.
2. To put up with.
3. To feel, show, or express grief.
4. To neither forbid nor prevent.

1. EXPERIENCE *verb.*
2. ENDURE.
3. GRIEVE.
4. PERMIT *verb.*

sufferable *adjective*
Capable of being tolerated.

BEARABLE.

suffering *noun*
A state of prolonged anguish and privation.

MISERY.

suffering *adjective*
Having a painful ailment.

MISERABLE.

suffice *verb*
To meet a need or requirement.

SERVE.

sufficiency *noun*
An adequate quantity.

ENOUGH *noun.*

sufficient *adjective*
1. Being what is needed without being in excess: *We had just sufficient fuel to get us across the desert.*

1. **Syns:** adequate, comfortable (*Informal*), competent, decent, enough, satisfactory, sufficing.
Near-ants: deficient, inadequate; failing, lacking, wanting.
Ant: insufficient.

2. Of moderately good quality but less than excellent.

2. ACCEPTABLE.

sufficient *noun*
An adequate quantity.

ENOUGH *noun.*

sufficing *adjective*
Being what is needed without being in excess.

SUFFICIENT.

suffocate *verb*
To stop the breathing of.

CHOKE.

suffuse *verb*
1. To cause to be filled with a particular mood or tone.
2. To occupy the whole of; be found throughout.

1. CHARGE *verb.*
2. FILL.

sugar *verb*
To make superficially more acceptable or appealing.

SWEETEN.

sugarcoat *verb*
1. To give a deceptively attractive appearance to.
2. To make superficially more acceptable or appealing.

1. COLOR *verb.*
2. SWEETEN.

sugary *adjective*
1. Having or suggesting the taste of sugar.
2. Purposefully contrived to gain favor.

1. SWEET *adjective.*
2. INSINUATING.

suggest *verb*
1. To convey an idea by indirect, subtle means.
2. To lead to by logical inference.
3. To advance, as an idea, for consideration.
4. To have a particular flavor or suggestion of something.

1. HINT *verb.*
2. IMPLY.
3. PROPOSE.
4. SMACK[2] *verb.*

suggestion *noun*
1. A feeling, thought, idea, etc., associated in one's mind or imagination with someone or something specific: *What suggestion does the word "home" bring to mind?*
2. A subtle pointing out.
3. A barely perceivable indication of something.
4. A slight amount.
5. Something that is put forward for consideration.

1. **Syns:** association, connection, connotation.

2. HINT *noun.*
3. TRACE *noun.*
4. SHADE *noun.*
5. PROPOSAL.

suggestive *adjective*
1. Tending to bring something, as a memory, mood, or image, subtly or indirectly to mind: *music suggestive of an autumn woodland scene.*
2. Provoking a change of outlook and esp. gradual doubt and suspicion.
3. Bordering on indelicacy or impropriety.
4. Conveying hidden or unexpressed meaning.
5. Suggesting sexuality.

1. **Syns:** allusive, evocative, impressionistic, reminiscent.

2. INSINUATING.

3. RACY.
4. PREGNANT.
5. SENSUAL.

suggestiveness *noun*
The quality or condition of being sensual.

SENSUALITY.

suit *noun*
1. An earnest or urgent request.
2. An application to a higher authority, as for sanction or a decision.
3. *Law.* A legal proceeding to demand justice or enforce a right.
4. Romantic attentions.

1. APPEAL *noun.*
2. APPEAL *noun.*

3. LAWSUIT.

4. COURTSHIP.

suit *verb*
1. To be in keeping with.
2. To be appropriate or suitable to: *A less strident tone would suit you better.*
3. To make or become suitable to a particular situation or use.
4. To meet a need or requirement.
5. To be satisfactory to.
6. To look good on or with.

1. FIT *verb.*
2. **Syns:** become, befit, behoove, beseem (*Archaic*).
3. ADAPT.

4. SERVE.
5. PLEASE.
6. FLATTER.

suitable *adjective*
1. Suited to one's end or purpose.
2. Satisfying the requirements, as for selection.
3. Called for by right, convention, or justice.
4. Consistent with prevailing or accepted standards or circumstances.

1. CONVENIENT.
2. ELIGIBLE.
3. JUST *adjective.*
4. JUST *adjective.*

suitableness *noun*
The quality or state of being eligible.

QUALIFICATION.

suite *noun*
1. A group of attendants or followers.
2. A number of things placed or occurring one after the other.

1. RETINUE.
2. SERIES.

suited *adjective*
Suitable for a particular person, condition, occasion, or place.

APPROPRIATE *adjective.*

suitor *noun*
1. One who humbly entreats.
2. A man who courts a woman.
3. One that asks a higher authority for something, as a favor or redress.

1. SUPPLICANT.
2. BEAU.
3. APPEALER.

sulk *verb*
To be sullenly aloof or withdrawn, as in silent resentment or protest: *Angry at the slight, he sulked for the rest of the day.*

Syns: mope, pet[2], pout.
Near-syns: brood, frown, gloom, glower, scowl.

sulky *adjective*
Broodingly and sullenly unhappy. GLUM.

sullen *adjective*
1. Broodingly and sullenly unhappy. 1. GLUM.
2. Characterized by or expressive of a foreboding 2. DARK *adjective*.
somberness.

sully *verb*
To cast aspersions on. BLACKEN.

sultry *adjective*
1. Marked by much heat. 1. HOT *adjective*.
2. Damp and warm. 2. STICKY.

sum *verb*
To combine (figures) to form a sum. ADD.

sum up *verb*
To recapitulate the salient facts of. REVIEW *verb*.

sum *noun*
1. An organized array of individual elements and parts 1. SYSTEM.
forming and working as a unit.
2. A number or quantity obtained as a result of 2. TOTAL *noun*.
addition.
3. An amount or quantity from which nothing is left 3. WHOLE *noun*.
out or held back.
4. A condensation of the essential or main points of 4. SUMMARY *noun*.
something.

summarize *verb*
To recapitulate the salient facts of. REVIEW *verb*.

summary *noun*
A condensation of the essential or main points of
something: *a summary of the day's news*.

Syns: recap, recapitulation, run-down,
run-through, sum, summation, summing-
up, wrap-up.

summary *adjective*
Marked by or consisting of few words. BRIEF.

summate *verb*
To combine (figures) to form a sum. ADD.

summation *noun*
1. The act or process of adding. 1. ADDITION.
2. A number or quantity obtained as a result of 2. TOTAL *noun*.
addition.
3. A condensation of the essential or main points of 3. SUMMARY *noun*.
something.

summer *noun*
The season occurring between spring and autumn: *Syn:* summertime.
going to camp in the summer.

summertime *noun*
The season occurring between spring and autumn. SUMMER *noun*.

summing-up *noun*
A condensation of the essential or main points of SUMMARY *noun*.
something.

summit *noun*
1. The highest point or state. 1. CLIMAX *noun*.
2. The highest point. 2. HEIGHT.

summon *verb*
1. To demand to appear, come, or assemble. 1. CALL *verb*.
2. To bring together. 2. ASSEMBLE.

sumptuousness *noun*
Brilliant, showy splendor. GLITTER *noun*.

sum up *verb* SEE **sum**.

sunder *verb*
To crack or split into two or more fragments by means BREAK *verb*.
of or as a result of force, a blow, or strain.

sundries *noun*
Articles too small or numerous to be specified.   ODDS AND ENDS.

sundry *adjective*
1. Consisting of a number of different kinds.   1. VARIOUS.
2. Not limited to a single class.   2. GENERAL.
3. Consisting of an indefinitely small number that is   3. SEVERAL.
   more than two or three but less than many.

sunny *adjective*
1. Free from clouds, mist, etc.   1. CLEAR *adjective*.
2. Being in or showing good spirits.   2. CHEERFUL.

sunrise *noun*
The first appearance of daylight in the morning.   DAWN *noun*.

sunup *noun*
The first appearance of daylight in the morning.   DAWN *noun*.

sup *verb*
To take into the mouth and swallow (a liquid).   DRINK *verb*.

sup *noun*
An act of drinking or the amount swallowed.   DRINK *noun*.

super *adjective*
1. *Slang.* Exceptionally good of its kind.   1. EXCELLENT.
2. *Informal.* Particularly excellent.   2. MARVELOUS.

super *adverb*
Informal. Too much.   UNDULY.

superabundance *noun*
A condition of going or being beyond what is needed,   EXCESS *noun*.
desired, or appropriate.

superabundant *adjective*
Given to or marked by unrestrained abundance.   PROFUSE.

superannuate *verb*
1. To make or become obsolete.   1. OBSOLESCE.
2. To remove from active service.   2. RETIRE.

superb *adjective*
1. Exceptionally good of its kind.   1. EXCELLENT.
2. Particularly excellent.   2. MARVELOUS.
3. Marked by extraordinary elegance, beauty, and   3. GLORIOUS.
   splendor.
4. Large and impressive in size, scope, or extent.   4. GRAND.
5. Surpassing all others in quality.   5. BEST *adjective*.

superbness *noun*
The quality of being exceptionally good of its kind.   EXCELLENCE.

supercilious *adjective*
Overly convinced of one's own superiority and   ARROGANT.
importance.

superciliousness *noun*
The quality of being arrogant.   ARROGANCE.

supererogative *adjective*
Not required, necessary, or warranted by the   WANTON.
circumstances of the case.

supererogatory *adjective*
1. Being more than is needed, desired, or appropriate.   1. SUPERFLUOUS.
2. Not required, necessary, or warranted by the   2. WANTON.
   circumstances of the case.

superficial *adjective*
1. Lacking in intellectual depth or thoroughness: *the*   1. *Syns:* cursory, one-dimensional,
   superficial job television does in covering the news.   shallow, sketchy, skin-deep, uncritical.
                                                                Near-ants: critical, detailed, full,
                                                                inclusive, thorough.
                                                                Ant: exhaustive.

2. Appearing as such but not necessarily so.

2. APPARENT.

superfluity *noun*
1. A condition of going or being beyond what is needed, desired, or appropriate.
2. An amount or quantity beyond what is needed, desired, or appropriate.

1. EXCESS *noun.*

2. SURPLUS *noun.*

superfluous *adjective*
Being more than is needed, desired, or appropriate: *carried a raincoat that proved superfluous.*

Syns: de trop (*French*), excess, extra, spare, supererogatory, surplus.
Near-syns: needless, useless; dispensible, gratuitous, nonessential; unnecessary, unneeded, unwanted.

superhuman *adjective*
Of, coming from, or relating to forces or beings that exist outside the natural world.

SUPERNATURAL.

superintend *verb*
1. To direct and watch over the work and performance of others.
2. To have charge of (the affairs of others).

1. SUPERVISE.

2. ADMINISTER.

superintendence *noun*
1. Authoritative control over the affairs of others.
2. The function of watching, guarding, or overseeing.

1. ADMINISTRATION.

2. CARE *noun.*

superintendent *noun*
Someone who directs and supervises workers.

BOSS *noun.*

superior *adjective*
1. Being at a height or level above another.
2. Being at a rank above another.
3. Of greater excellence than another.
4. Exceptionally good of its kind.
5. Of fine quality.
6. Overly convinced of one's own superiority and importance.

1. HIGHER.
2. HIGHER.
3. BETTER[1] *adjective.*
4. EXCELLENT.
5. CHOICE *adjective.*
6. ARROGANT.

superior *noun*
One who stands above another in rank: *Servicemen must salute their superiors.*

Syns: better[1], elder, higher-up, senior.

superiority *noun*
1. The quality of being exceptionally good of its kind.
2. A dominating position, as in a conflict.
3. The quality of being arrogant.

1. EXCELLENCE.
2. ADVANTAGE *noun.*
3. ARROGANCE.

superlative *adjective*
Surpassing all others in quality.

BEST *adjective.*

supernatural *adjective*
1. Of, coming from, or relating to forces or beings that exist outside the natural world: *invoked the supernatural aid of the goddess.*

1. ***Syns:*** extramundane, extrasensory, metaphysical (*also* metaphysic), miraculous, preternatural, superhuman, superphysical, supersensible, transcendental, unearthly.
Near-syns: celestial, divine, heavenly, paranormal, unusual.

2. Greatly exceeding or departing from the normal course of nature.

2. PRETERNATURAL.

superphysical *adjective*
Of, coming from, or relating to forces or beings that exist outside the natural world.

SUPERNATURAL.

superscribe *verb*
To mark (a written communication) with its destination.

ADDRESS *verb.*

superscription *noun*
A written inscription on a deliverable item giving its destination.

ADDRESS *noun.*

supersede *verb*
To remove (something) and substitute (another) for it.

REPLACE.

superseded *adjective*
No longer in use.

OBSOLETE *adjective*.

supersensible *adjective*
Of, coming from, or relating to forces or beings that exist outside the natural world.

SUPERNATURAL.

supervene *verb*
To occur after (another) in time.

FOLLOW.

supervenient *adjective*
Not part of the real or essential nature of a thing.

ACCIDENTAL *adjective*.

supervise *verb*
1. To direct and watch over the work and performance of others: *supervised a team of investigators.*

1. ***Syns:*** boss, overlook, oversee, superintend.
   Near-syns: guide, steer; administer, conduct, manage, run; monitor, proctor.

2. To control the course of (an activity).

2. CONDUCT *verb*.

supervision *noun*
The function of watching, guarding, or overseeing.

CARE *noun*.

supervisor *noun*
Someone who directs and supervises workers.

BOSS *noun*.

supplant *verb*
1. To take the place of (another) against the other's will: *In the party caucus several committee chairmen were supplanted by young challengers.*

1. ***Syns:*** cut out, displace, usurp.

2. To remove (something) and substitute (another) for it.

2. REPLACE.

supple *adjective*
1. Capable of withstanding stress without injury.
2. Capable of being shaped, bent, or drawn out, as by hammering or pressure.

1. FLEXIBLE.
2. MALLEABLE.

supplement *noun*
1. Something that completes another.
2. Something that attaches as a supplementary part.

1. COMPLEMENT *noun*.
2. ATTACHMENT.

supplement *verb*
To fill in what is lacking and make perfect.

COMPLEMENT *verb*.

supplemental *adjective*
1. Forming or serving as a complement.
2. Used or held in reserve.

1. COMPLEMENTARY.
2. AUXILIARY *adjective*.

suppleness *noun*
The quality or state of being flexible.

FLEXIBILITY.

supplicant *noun*
One who humbly entreats: *The supplicants fell on their knees and begged for mercy.*

Syns: beggar, prayer, suitor, supplicator.

supplicate *verb*
1. To make an earnest or urgent request.
2. To offer a reverent petition to God or a god.

1. APPEAL *verb*.
2. PRAY.

supplication *noun*
1. An earnest or urgent request.
2. The act of praying.

1. APPEAL *noun*.
2. PRAYER.

supplicator *noun*
One who humbly entreats.

SUPPLICANT.

supply *verb*
1. To relinquish to the possession or control of another.
2. To act as a substitute.

1. GIVE *verb*.
2. SUBSTITUTE *verb*.

support *verb*
1. To aid the cause of by approving or favoring: *A majority of the voters supported his candidacy.*

1. ***Syns:*** advocate, back, champion, get behind, plump for, side with, stand behind, stand up for, uphold. —*Idioms* align oneself with, go to bat for, stick up for, take the part of.

2. To sustain the weight of: *columns designed to support the roof.*
3. To hold up.
4. To keep from yielding or failing during stress or difficulty.
5. To supply with the necessities of life: *Besides her own family, she supported her husband's elderly mother.*
6. To put up with.
7. To act as a patron to.

support *noun*
1. The act or an instance of helping.
2. A means or device that keeps something erect, stable, or secure: *used the railing as a support as he lifted himself up.*
3. The means needed to support life.

supporter *noun*
1. One who supports and adheres to another.
2. A person who supports or champions an activity, institution, etc.

supportive *adjective*
Affording support or assistance.

suppose *verb*
1. To take for granted without proof: *I suppose that he is feeling guilty.*

2. To draw an inference on the basis of inconclusive evidence or insufficient information.
3. To oblige to do or not do by force of authority, propriety, or custom.
4. To regard or be regarded in an appraising way.

supposed *adjective*
1. Presumed to be true, real, or genuine, esp. on inconclusive grounds: *He argued that deficit spending, the supposed cause of inflation, was in fact not the culprit.*

2. Based on inference, not fact.
3. Assumed to be such.

supposition *noun*
1. A judgment, estimate, or opinion arrived at by guessing.
2. Something taken to be true without proof.
3. A belief used as the basis for action.

suppositional *adjective*
Presumed to be true, real, or genuine, esp. on inconclusive grounds.

suppositious *adjective*
Presumed to be true, real, or genuine, esp. on inconclusive grounds.

suppress *verb*
1. To bring to an end forcibly as if by imposing a heavy weight: *The czar's forces easily suppressed the rebellion.*

2. To hold (something requiring an outlet) in check.
3. To keep from being published or transmitted.

suppression *noun*
1. Sudden punitive action: *suppression of narcotics trafficking.*

Near-ants: combat, counter, fight, oppose.
2. **Syns:** carry, hold, maintain, uphold.

3. BEAR.
4. SUSTAIN.

5. **Syns:** keep, maintain, provide for. —*Idiom* take care of.

6. ENDURE.
7. PATRONIZE.

1. HELP *noun.*
2. **Syns:** brace², buttress, crutch, prop, shore, stay², underpinning.

3. LIVING.

1. FOLLOWER.
2. PATRON.

HELPFUL.

1. **Syns:** assume, posit, postulate, premise, presume, presuppose, reckon (*Informal*).
2. GUESS *verb.*

3. REQUIRE.

4. REPUTE *verb.*

1. **Syns:** conjectural, hypothetical (*also* hypothetic), suppositional, suppositious.
   Near-ants: demonstrated, observed, recognized; known, proven.
2. PRESUMPTIVE.
3. REPUTED.

1. GUESS *noun.*

2. ASSUMPTION.
3. THEORY.

SUPPOSED.

SUPPOSED.

1. **Syns:** crush, extinguish, put down, quash, quell, quench, squash, squelch. —*Idiom* put the lid on.
2. REPRESS.
3. CENSOR.

1. **Syns:** clampdown (*Informal*), crackdown, repression.

2. The act of restraining forcefully.

2. REPRESSION.

suppressive *adjective*
Serving to restrain forcefully.

REPRESSIVE.

supremacy *noun*
The condition or fact of being dominant.

DOMINANCE.

supreme *adjective*
1. Having pre-eminent significance.
2. Of the greatest possible degree, quality, or intensity.
3. Conforming to an ultimate form of perfection or excellence.

1. RULING *adjective*.
2. ULTIMATE *adjective*.
3. IDEAL *adjective*.

surcease *verb*
1. *Archaic.* To come to a cessation.
2. *Archaic.* To prevent the occurrence or continuation of a movement, action, or operation.

1. STOP *verb*.
2. STOP *verb*.

sure *adjective*
1. Having no doubt: *I'm sure that you will succeed.*

2. Established beyond a doubt.
3. Known positively.
4. Such as could not possibly fail or disappoint: *a sure winner; a sure sign of illness.*
5. Firmly settled or positioned: *a sure footing on the slope; a sure friendship.*

6. Not easily moved or shaken.

1. *Syns:* assured, certain, confident, positive, undoubting.
2. CERTAIN.
3. DEFINITE.
4. *Syns:* certain, infallible, surefire, unerring, unfailing.
5. *Syns:* fast, firm¹, secure, solid, stable, staunch, strong. —*Idioms* firm as Gibraltar, solid as a rock.
6. SOUND².

sure-enough *adjective*
Based on fact.

ACTUAL.

surefire *adjective*
Such as could not possibly fail or disappoint.

SURE.

sureness *noun*
The fact or condition of being without doubt: *denying the rumor with absolute sureness.*

Syns: certainty, certitude, confidence, conviction, surety.

surety *noun*
1. The fact or condition of being without doubt.
2. An assumption of responsibility, as one given by a manufacturer, for the quality, worth, or durability of a product.
3. One who assumes financial responsibility for another.
4. An assurance that a condition will be met.

1. SURENESS.
2. GUARANTEE *noun*.

3. SPONSOR.

4. SECURITY.

surface *noun*
1. An outward appearance.
2. The outer layer covering something.

1. FACE *noun*.
2. FACE *noun*.

surfeit *noun*
1. A condition of going or being beyond what is needed, desired, or appropriate.
2. The condition of being full to or beyond satisfaction.

1. EXCESS *noun*.

2. SATIATION.

surfeit *verb*
To satisfy to the full or to excess.

SATIATE.

surfeited *adjective*
Filled to satisfaction or excess.

SATIATED.

surge *verb*
To come forth or emit in abundance.

FLOW *verb*.

surly *adjective*
1. Broodingly and sullenly unhappy.
2. Having or showing a bad temper.

1. GLUM.
2. ILL-TEMPERED.

surmise *verb*
To draw an inference on the basis of inconclusive evidence or insufficient information.

GUESS *verb*.

surmise *noun*
1. A judgment, estimate, or opinion arrived at by guessing.
2. Something taken to be true without proof.

1. GUESS *noun.*
2. ASSUMPTION.

surmount *verb*
To get the better of.

TRIUMPH *verb.*

surpass *verb*
1. To be greater or better than: *This year's wheat crop surpassed last year's by two million bushels.*

1. **Syns:** beat (*Informal*), best, better[1], exceed, excel, outdo, outmatch, outshine, outstrip, pass, top, transcend. —*Idioms* go beyond, go one better. **Near-syns:** distance, eclipse, outpace, overshadow.

2. To go beyond the limits of.

2. EXCEED.

surpassing *adjective*
1. Far above others in quality or excellence.
2. Of the greatest possible degree, quality, or intensity.

1. OUTSTANDING.
2. ULTIMATE *adjective.*

surplus *noun*
1. An amount or quantity beyond what is needed, desired, or appropriate: *With their earnings they paid their bills and split the surplus as profit.*

1. **Syns:** excess, fat, glut, overage, overflow, overmuch, overrun, overstock, oversupply, superfluity. **Near-syns:** overabundance, plethora, profusion, surfeit.

2. A condition of going or being beyond what is needed, desired, or appropriate.

2. EXCESS *noun.*

surplus *adjective*
Being more than is needed, desired, or appropriate.

SUPERFLUOUS.

surprise *verb*
1. To impress strongly by what is unexpected or unusual: *Truman's electoral victory in 1948 surprised most political observers.*

1. **Syns:** amaze, astonish, astound, startle. —*Idioms* catch (*or* take) unawares, take aback. **Near-syns:** bewilder, confound, disconcert, dismay, faze, rattle, stun.

2. To come upon, esp. suddenly or unexpectedly.
3. To attack suddenly and without warning.

2. TAKE *verb.*
3. AMBUSH.

surprising *adjective*
Causing momentary shock.

STARTLING.

surrender *verb*
1. To undergo capture, defeat, or ruin: *Paris surrendered in 1940 to the Nazis.*
2. To give up a possession, claim, or right.
3. To yield (oneself) unrestrainedly, as to a particular impulse.
4. To give in from or as if from a gradual loss of strength.
5. To let (something) go.

1. **Syns:** collapse, fall, go down, go under, submit, succumb, topple.
2. ABDICATE.
3. GIVE OVER at **give.**
4. SUCCUMB.
5. RELINQUISH.

surrender *noun*
1. The act of submitting or surrendering to the power of another: *The defeat forced the surrender of the entire army.*
2. A giving up of a possession, claim, or right.
3. The act of delivering or the condition of being delivered.

1. **Syns:** capitulation, submission.
2. ABDICATION.
3. DELIVERY.

surreptitious *adjective*
Trickily secret.

SLY *adjective.*

surrogate *noun*
One that takes the place of another.

SUBSTITUTE *noun.*

surround *verb*
To shut in on all sides: *A crowd surrounded the star. The city is surrounded by suburbs.*

Syns: begird, beset, besiege, circle, compass, encircle, enclose, encompass,

envelop, environ, gird, girdle, hedge (in), hem (in, about, *or* around), ring[1].
Near-syns: circumscribe, confine, enclave.

surroundings   *noun*
1. A surrounding area.
2. The totality of surrounding conditions and circumstances affecting growth or development.

1. ENVIRONMENT.
2. ENVIRONMENT.

surveillance   *noun*
The act of carefully watching.

LOOKOUT.

survey   *verb*
1. To view broadly or from a height: *surveyed the city from the top of a skyscraper.*
2. To look at carefully or critically.
3. To look at or on attentively or carefully.

1. ***Syns:*** look over, overlook, oversee, scan.
2. EXAMINE.
3. WATCH *verb*.

survey   *noun*
1. A close or systematic study.
2. A general or comprehensive view or treatment: *a course that offers a survey of world literature.*

1. ANALYSIS.
2. ***Syn:*** overview.

survive   *verb*
1. To exist in spite of adversity: *None of his family survived the Holocaust. A passing ship rescued the few crewmen who survived.*
2. To live, exist, or remain longer than.

1. ***Syns:*** come through, last[2], persist, pull through, ride out, weather.
2. OUTLAST.

susceptibility   *noun*
The condition of being laid open to something undesirable or injurious.

EXPOSURE.

susceptible   *adjective*
1. Easily imposed on or tricked.
2. Having or showing a tendency or likelihood.
3. Tending to incur.
4. Able to receive and respond to external stimuli.

1. EASY.
2. INCLINED.
3. LIABLE.
4. SENSITIVE.

susceptive   *adjective*
Able to receive and respond to external stimuli.

SENSITIVE.

suspect   *verb*
To lack trust or confidence in.

DISTRUST *verb*.

suspect   *adjective*
Of dubious character.

SHADY.

suspend   *verb*
1. To stop suddenly, as a conversation, activity, relationship, etc.: *The two sides suspended negotiations after a deadlock occurred.*
2. To fasten or be fastened at one point with no support from below.
3. To put off until a later time.

1. ***Syns:*** break off, cease, discontinue, interrupt, saw off (*Slang*), terminate.
2. HANG *verb*.
3. DEFER[1].

suspended   *adjective*
Hung or appearing to be hung from a support.

HANGING.

suspension   *noun*
1. A cessation of continuity or regularity.
2. The act of putting off or the condition of being put off.
3. The condition of being temporarily inactive.

1. BREAK *noun*.
2. DELAY *noun*.
3. ABEYANCE.

suspicion   *noun*
1. Lack of trust.
2. A lack of conviction or certainty.
3. Intuitive cognition.
4. A subtle quality underlying or felt to underlie a situation, action, or person.
5. A slight amount.

1. DISTRUST *noun*.
2. DOUBT *noun*.
3. FEELING.
4. HINT *noun*.
5. SHADE *noun*.

suspicious   *adjective*
1. Lacking trust or confidence.
2. Of dubious character.

1. DISTRUSTFUL.
2. SHADY.

sustain *verb*
1. To keep from yielding or failing during stress or difficulty: *At such desperate times her faith sustained her.*
2. To hold up.
3. To keep in a condition of good repair, efficiency, or use.
4. To put up with.

sustenance *noun*
1. The means needed to support life.
2. Something fit to be eaten.
3. That which sustains the mind or spirit.

susurration *noun*
A low, indistinct, and often continuous sound.

swaddle *verb*
To cover completely and closely, as with clothing or bandages.

swagger *verb*
To walk with exaggerated or unnatural motions expressive of self-importance or self-display.

swain *noun*
A man who courts a woman.

swallow *verb*
1. To cause to pass from the mouth into the stomach: *chewed and swallowed his food calmly.*
2. To do away with completely and destructively.
3. *Slang.* To regard (something) as true or real.
4. To put up with.

swallow *noun*
An act of swallowing: *took a swallow of coffee.*

swamp *noun*
A usu. low-lying area of soft, waterlogged ground and standing water: *birds that breed in the seclusion of tropical swamps.*

swampland *noun*
A usu. low-lying area of soft, waterlogged ground and standing water.

swank *verb*
To walk with exaggerated or unnatural motions expressive of self-importance or self-display.

swank also **swanky** *adjective*
1. Catering to, used by, or admitting only the wealthy or socially superior.
2. Being or in accordance with the current fashion.

swanky *adjective*

swap also **swop** *verb*
Informal. To give up in return for something else.

swap also **swop** *noun*
Informal. The act of exchanging or substituting.

swarm *verb*
1. To come or go in large numbers.
2. To overflow with.

swarm over *verb*
To enter in order to attack, plunder, destroy, or conquer.

swarm *noun*
An enormous number of persons gathered together.

swarm over *verb*

swarthy *adjective*
Of a complexion tending toward brown or black.

---

1. **Syns:** bolster, buoy up, prop, support, uphold.
2. BEAR.
3. MAINTAIN.
4. BEAR.

1. LIVING.
2. FOOD.
3. FOOD.

MURMUR *noun*.

WRAP UP.

STRUT.

BEAU.

1. **Syns:** down, ingest, take.
2. CONSUME.
3. BELIEVE.
4. ENDURE.

Syns: gobble, gulp, ingestion.

Syns: fen, marsh, marshland, mire, morass, muskeg, quag, quagmire, slough[1], swampland, wetland.

SWAMP.

STRUT.

1. EXCLUSIVE.
2. FASHIONABLE.

SEE **swank.**

CHANGE *verb*.

CHANGE *noun*.

1. POUR.
2. TEEM[1].

INVADE.

CROWD *noun*.

SEE **swarm.**

DARK *adjective*.

swash *verb*
1. To walk with exaggerated or unnatural motions expressive of self-importance or self-display.
2. To hurl or scatter liquid upon.
3. To flow or move with a low, slapping sound.

1. STRUT.
2. SPLASH.
3. WASH.

swat *noun*
A sudden sharp, powerful stroke.

BLOW².

swat *verb*
To deliver (a powerful blow) suddenly and sharply.

HIT *verb*.

swathe *verb*
To cover completely and closely, as with clothing or bandages.

WRAP UP.

sway *verb*
1. To move back and forth or from side to side, as if about to fall: *swayed dizzily at the top of the stairs.*
2. To evoke a usu. strong mental or emotional response from.
3. To influence or be influenced in a certain direction.
4. To exercise the authority of a sovereign.
5. To have an effect or impact upon.
6. To move rhythmically back and forth suspended or as if suspended from above.

1. *Syns:* teeter, totter, waver, weave, wobble.
2. AFFECT¹.
3. DISPOSE.
4. GOVERN.
5. INFLUENCE *verb*.
6. SWING *verb*.

sway *noun*
1. The act of exercising controlling power or the condition of being so controlled.
2. The right and power to command, decide, rule, or judge.
3. The power to produce an effect by indirect means.

1. DOMINATION.
2. AUTHORITY.
3. INFLUENCE *noun*.

swayed *adjective*
Emotionally aroused.

AFFECTED¹.

swear *verb*
1. To use profane or obscene language: *swore like a trooper; swore at the other motorist.*

2. To give evidence or testimony under oath.
3. To guarantee by a solemn promise.

1. *Syns:* bedamn, blaspheme, curse, cuss (*Informal*), damn, execrate, imprecate. —*Idioms* call names, use language.
2. TESTIFY.
3. PLEDGE *verb*.

swear off *verb*
Informal. To cease trying to accomplish or continue.

ABANDON *verb*.

swear *noun*
A profane or obscene term: *uttered a stream of swears.*

Syns: blasphemy, curse, cuss (*Informal*), cussword (*Informal*), epithet, expletive, invective, oath, swearword.

swear off *verb*

SEE **swear.**

swearword *noun*
A profane or obscene term.

SWEAR *noun*.

sweat *verb*
1. To excrete moisture through the pores of the skin: *sweating as he jogged.*
2. To exert one's mental or physical powers, usu. under difficulty and to the point of exhaustion.

1. *Syns:* lather, perspire.
2. LABOR *verb*.

sweat out *verb*
To carry on through despite hardships.

ENDURE.

sweat *noun*
1. Moisture excreted through the pores of the skin: *wiping the sweat from her forehead.*
2. Physical exertion that is usu. difficult and exhausting.
3. *Informal.* A condition of excited distress.

1. *Syns:* lather, perspiration.
2. LABOR *noun*.
3. STATE *noun*.

sweating *adjective*
Producing or covered with sweat.

SWEATY.

sweat out *verb*

SEE **sweat.**

sweaty *adjective*
Producing or covered with sweat: *left the gym all hot and sweaty.*

Syns: perspiring, sudoriferous, sweating.

sweep *noun*
1. A wide and open area, as of land, sky, or water.
2. An area within which something or someone exists, acts, or has influence or power.

1. EXPANSE.
2. RANGE *noun.*

sweep *verb*
To wield boldly and dramatically.

FLOURISH.

sweeping *adjective*
Covering a wide scope.

GENERAL.

sweet *adjective*
1. Having or suggesting the taste of sugar: *a sweet icing.*
2. Pleasing to the eye or mind.
3. Easy to love.

1. **Syns:** saccharine, sugary.
2. ATTRACTIVE.
3. ADORABLE.

sweet *noun*
A person who is much loved.

DARLING *noun.*

sweeten *verb*
1. To make superficially more acceptable or appealing: *sweetened his demands with the promise of a reward for obedience.*
2. To ease the anger or agitation of.

1. **Syns:** candy, gild, honey, sugar, sugarcoat.
2. PACIFY.

sweetheart *noun*
A person who is much loved.

DARLING *noun.*

sweet-talk *verb*
1. *Informal.* To persuade or try to persuade by gentle, persistent urging or flattery.
2. *Informal.* To compliment excessively and ingratiatingly.

1. COAX.
2. FLATTER.

swell *verb*
To make or become greater or larger.

INCREASE *verb.*

swell *adjective*
1. *Informal.* Exceptionally good of its kind.
2. *Informal.* Particularly excellent.

1. EXCELLENT.
2. MARVELOUS.

swelled head *noun*
Informal. An exaggerated belief in one's own importance.

EGOTISM.

swellheaded *adjective*
Informal. Thinking too highly of oneself.

EGOTISTICAL.

swelling *noun*
A small raised area of skin resulting from a light blow, an insect sting, etc.

BUMP *noun.*

swelter *verb*
To feel or look hot.

BURN *verb.*

sweltering *adjective*
Marked by much heat.

HOT *adjective.*

swerve *verb*
1. To turn aside sharply from a straight course: *swerved to avoid hitting a pedestrian.*
2. To turn away from a prescribed course of action or conduct.

1. **Syns:** chop² (*Naut.*), cut, sheer¹, skew, slue¹, veer, yaw.
2. DEVIATE *verb.*

swift *adjective*
Characterized by great celerity.

FAST *adjective.*

swiftness *noun*
1. Rate of motion or performance.
2. Rapidity of movement or activity.

1. SPEED *noun.*
2. HASTE *noun.*

swig *verb*
Informal. To take into the mouth and swallow (a liquid).

DRINK *verb.*

swig *noun*

Informal. An act of drinking or the amount swallowed.   DRINK *noun.*

swill *verb*
To swallow (food or drink) greedily or rapidly in large amounts.   GULP *verb.*

swill *noun*
An act of drinking or the amount swallowed.   DRINK *noun.*

swim *noun*
The act of swimming.   PLUNGE *noun.*

swim *verb*
To have the sensation of turning in circles.   SPIN *verb.*

swindle *verb*
To get money or something else from by deceitful trickery.   CHEAT *verb.*

swindle *noun*
An act of cheating.   CHEAT *noun.*

swindler *noun*
A person who cheats.   CHEAT *noun.*

swing *verb*
1. To move rhythmically back and forth suspended or as if suspended from above: *ship's lanterns swinging like pendulums.*   1. **Syns:** oscillate, sway.
2. To turn or cause to turn in place, as on a hinge or fixed point, tracing an arclike path: *a door swinging open; swung the tone arm carelessly across the record surface.*   2. **Syns:** pivot, wheel.
3. To change one's attitudes, policies, or the like: *swung from one position to another in the debate on abortion.*   3. **Syns:** vacillate, waver.
4. *Informal.* To execute by suspending by the neck.   4. HANG *verb.*
5. To change the direction or course of.   5. TURN *verb.*
6. *Slang.* To carry to a successful conclusion.   6. EFFECT *verb.*

swing *noun*
1. Ease of movement.   1. FREEDOM.
2. *Informal.* The proper method of doing, using, or handling something.   2. HANG *noun.*
3. The regular recurrence of strong and weak elements, such as stressed and unstressed notes in music.   3. RHYTHM.

swipe *verb*
Slang. To take (another's property) without permission.   STEAL *verb.*

swirl *verb*
1. To move or cause to move like a rapid rotary current of liquid: *water swirling over the dam; difficulties that swirled about her.*   1. **Syns:** eddy, gurge, whirl, whorl.
2. To have the sensation of turning in circles.   2. SPIN *verb.*
3. To rotate rapidly.   3. SPIN *verb.*

swish *verb*
1. To make a sharp sibilant sound.   1. HISS *verb.*
2. To flow or move with a low, slapping sound.   2. WASH.

swish *adjective*
1. *Slang.* Having qualities more appropriate to women than to men.   1. EFFEMINATE *adjective.*
2. *Chiefly Brit.* Being or in accordance with the current fashion.   2. FASHIONABLE.

switch *verb*
1. To give up in return for something else.   1. CHANGE *verb.*
2. To leave or discard for another.   2. CHANGE *verb.*
3. To move to and fro vigorously and usu. repeatedly.   3. WAG[1].

switch *noun*
The act of exchanging or substituting.   CHANGE *noun.*

swivel *verb*
To move, as a gun, laterally.   TRAVERSE *verb.*

swivet also **swivvet** *noun*
A condition of excited distress.   STATE.

swivvet *noun*   SEE **swivet.**

swoon *verb*
To suffer temporary loss of consciousness.   BLACK OUT.

swoon *noun*
A temporary loss of consciousness.   BLACKOUT at **black out.**

swoop *noun*
The act of plunging suddenly downward into or as if   PLUNGE *noun.*
into water.

swop *verb & noun*   SEE **swap.**

sybarite *noun*
A person devoted to pleasure and luxury: *an unlikely*   **Syns:** epicure (*Archaic*), hedonist,
breed of sybarites spawned by the 1849 Gold Rush.   voluptuary.

sybaritic or **sybaritical** *adjective*
Characterized by or devoted to pleasure and luxury as   **Syns:** epicurean, hedonic, hedonistic.
a lifestyle: *sybaritic tastes; a sybaritic young woman.*

sycophant *noun*
One who flatters another excessively: *Beware of*   **Syns:** adulator, apple-polisher (*Informal*),
sycophants and yes-men.   courtier, flatterer, truckler.

syllabus *noun*
A printed list of the order of events and other pertinent   PROGRAM.
information for a public performance.

symbol *noun*
  1. An object associated with and serving to identify   1. **Syns:** attribute, emblem.
     something else: *scales as the symbol of justice.*
  2. A conventional mark used in a writing system.   2. CHARACTER.

symbol *verb*
To serve as the image of.   REPRESENT.

symbolic also **symbolical** *adjective*
Serving as a symbol: *a gift symbolic of our appreciation;* **Syns:** emblematic (*also* emblematical),
the mark symbolic of division in arithmetic.   indicative, representative.

symbolize *verb*
To serve as the image of.   REPRESENT.

symmetrical also **symmetric** *adjective*
  1. Characterized by or displaying symmetry, esp.   1. **Syns:** balanced, commensurable,
     correspondence in scale or measure: *a symmetrical*   commensurate, proportional,
     floor plan; adjoining buildings that are symmetrical.   proportionate, regular.
  2. Having components pleasingly combined: *statuary*   2. **Syns:** accordant (to *or* with), balanced,
     symmetrical with the layout of the gardens.   concordant, congruous, harmonious.

symmetry *noun*
Satisfying arrangement marked by even distribution of   PROPORTION.
elements, as in a design.

sympathetic *adjective*
  1. Feeling or expressing sorrow: *a sympathetic note.*   1. **Syns:** commiserative, compassionate.
  2. Of or befitting a friend or friends.   2. FRIENDLY.
  3. Feeling or expressing pity.   3. PITYING.
  4. Cognizant of and comprehending the needs, feelings,   4. UNDERSTANDING.
     problems, and views of others.

sympathize *verb*
  1. To understand or be sensitive to another's feelings   1. **Syn:** empathize.
     or ideas: *We sympathized with his difficult position.*
  2. To experience or express compassion.   2. FEEL *verb.*
  3. To associate or affiliate oneself closely with a person 3. IDENTIFY.
     or group.

sympathy *noun*
  1. A very close relationship between persons, esp. one   1. **Syn:** empathy.
     resulting in mutual understanding or affection: *the*
     sympathy that often strengthens marriages in later
     and quieter years.
  2. Sympathetic, sad concern for someone in misfortune.   2. PITY *noun.*

symphonic *adjective*
Characterized by harmony of sound.   HARMONIOUS.

symptom *noun*
Something visible or evident that gives grounds for   SIGN *noun*.
believing in the existence or presence of something else.

synchronic also **synchronical** *adjective*
Belonging to the same period of time as another.   CONTEMPORARY *adjective*.

synchronous *adjective*
Belonging to the same period of time as another.   CONTEMPORARY *adjective*.

syncope *noun*
Path. A temporary loss of consciousness.   BLACKOUT at **black out.**

syndicate *noun*
A combination of businesses closely interconnected for   COMBINE *noun*.
common profit.

synergetic *adjective*
Working together toward a common end.   COOPERATIVE.

synergy *noun*
Joint work toward a common end.   COOPERATION.

synopsis *noun*
A short summary prepared by cutting down a larger   ***Syns:*** abridgment, abstract, brief,
work: *gave her a synopsis of the novel.*   condensation, epitome.

synopsize *verb*
To recapitulate the salient facts of.   REVIEW *verb*.

synthesize *verb*
To combine and adapt in order to attain a particular   HARMONIZE.
effect.

synthetic *adjective*
1. Made by human beings, not nature.   1. ARTIFICIAL.
2. Made to imitate something else.   2. ARTIFICIAL.
3. Marked by unnaturalness, pretension, and often a   3. PLASTIC.
   slavish love of fads.

system *noun*
1. An organized array of individual elements and parts   1. ***Syns:*** entity, integral, integrate, sum,
   forming and working as a unit: *The universe is a*   totality, whole.
   cosmic system.
2. Systematic arrangement and design.   2. METHOD.
3. The manner in which something is done.   3. WAY *noun*.
4. A usu. large entity composed of interconnected   4. COMPLEX *noun*.
   parts.

systematic also **systematical** *adjective*
1. Arranged or proceeding in a set, systematized   1. METHODICAL.
   pattern.
2. Showing characteristics advantageous to or of use in   2. BUSINESSLIKE.
   business.

systematize *verb*
1. To put into a deliberate order.   1. ARRANGE.
2. To arrange in an orderly manner.   2. METHODIZE.

T

tab *noun*
1. A precise list of fees or charges.
2. An amount paid or to be paid for a purchase.
3. A noting of items one by one.

1. ACCOUNT *noun*.
2. COST *noun*.
3. COUNT *noun*.

tab(s) *noun*
The act of observing, often for an extended time.

WATCH *noun*.

tabby *noun*
A person habitually engaged in idle talk about others.

GOSSIP *noun*.

table *noun*
An orderly, columnar display of data: *a table of census figures*.

Syns: chart, tabulation.

table *verb*
To put off until a later time.

DEFER[1].

taboo also **tabu** *noun*
A refusal to allow.

FORBIDDANCE.

taboo also **tabu** *adjective*
Not allowed.

FORBIDDEN.

tabu *noun, adjective*

SEE **taboo.**

tabulation *noun*
An orderly, columnar display of data.

TABLE *noun*.

tacit *adjective*
1. Conveyed indirectly without words or speech.
2. Not voiced or expressed.

1. IMPLICIT.
2. SILENT.

taciturn *adjective*
Not speaking freely or openly: *a taciturn Yankee farmer*.

Syns: close[1], close-mouthed, reserved, reticent, silent, tight-lipped, uncommunicative.
Near-ants: chatty, communicative, convivial, gabby, loquacious, talkative, uninhibited.
Ant: garrulous.

taciturnity *noun*
The keeping of one's thoughts and emotions to oneself.

RESERVE *noun*.

tack *noun*
1. A method used in dealing with something.
2. An often sudden change or departure, as in a trend.

1. APPROACH *noun*.
2. TURN *noun*.

tackle *noun*
Things needed for a task, journey, or other purpose.

OUTFIT.

tackle *verb*
1. To take upon oneself.
2. To start work on vigorously.

1. ASSUME.
2. ATTACK *verb*.

tacky[1] *adjective*
Having the property of adhering.

STICKY.

tacky[2] *adjective*
1. Lacking style and good taste: *tacky behavior*.

1. **Syns:** inelegant, tasteless, unbecoming.
Near-syns: cheap, crude, frumpy, gaudy, showy, tawdry.

2. *Informal.* Showing signs of wear and tear or neglect.
3. Quite outmoded: *tacky old clothes from the 1950's*.
4. Tastelessly showy.
5. *Informal.* Of decidedly inferior quality.

2. SHABBY.
3. **Syns:** dowdy, frumpish, out-of-date.
4. GAUDY.
5. SHODDY.

tact *noun*
The ability to say and do the right thing at the right time: *Tact is needed in dealing with high-strung people*.

Syns: address, diplomacy, savoir-faire (*French*), tactfulness.
Near-ants: abruptness, bluntness,

brashness, coarseness, discourtesy, rudeness.
Ant: tactlessness.

tactful *adjective*
Showing sensitivity and skill in dealing with others. DELICATE.

tactfulness *noun*
The ability to say and do the right thing at the right time. TACT.

tactic¹ *noun*
1. A method of deploying troops and equipment in combat: *used the tactic of encirclement to cut off the enemy.*
2. An action calculated to achieve an end.

1. *Syn:* maneuver.

2. MOVE *noun.*

tactic² *adjective*
Of, pertaining to, or arising from the sense of touch. TACTILE.

tactical *adjective*
Designed or implemented so as to gain a limited, temporary advantage: *took tactical rather than strategic measures to settle the crisis.*

Syn: short-range.

tactile *adjective*
1. Of, pertaining to, or arising from the sense of touch: *a tactile reflex.*
2. Discernible by touch.

1. *Syns:* tactic², tactual.

2. TANGIBLE.

tactility *noun*
1. The faculty or ability to perceive tactile stimulation.
2. The quality or condition of being discernible by touch.

1. TOUCH *noun.*
2. TANGIBILITY.

tactless *adjective*
Lacking sensitivity and skill in dealing with others: *took a tactless approach in the interview; tactless remarks made by a heavy-handed critic.*

Syns: brash, clumsy, impolitic, indelicate, maladroit, undiplomatic, unpolitic, untactful.
Near-syns: bungling, inept; brash, crude, impolite, inconsiderate, indelicate.
Ant: tactful.

tactual *adjective*
Of, pertaining to, or arising from the sense of touch. TACTILE.

tag *verb*
1. To describe with a word or term.
2. To follow closely or persistently.
3. To set off by or as if by a mark indicating ownership or manufacture.
4. To attach a ticket to.

1. CALL *verb.*
2. DOG *verb.*
3. MARK *verb.*

4. TICKET *verb.*

tag *noun*
1. *Slang.* The word or words by which one is called and identified.
2. An identifying or descriptive slip.

1. NAME *noun.*

2. TICKET *noun.*

tag end *noun*
The hindmost part of something. TAIL *noun.*

tagrag *adjective*
Showing signs of wear and tear or neglect. SHABBY.

tail *noun*
1. The hindmost part of something: *marched at the tail of the platoon.*
2. *Informal.* An agent assigned to observe and report on another: *Counterintelligence assigned a tail to the suspected spy.*
3. Something that follows or is drawn along behind.

1. *Syns:* end, rear¹, tag end, tail end.

2. *Syns:* shadow, watcher.

3. TRAIN *noun.*

tail *verb*
Informal. To keep (another) under surveillance by moving along behind. FOLLOW.

tail off *verb*

To grow or cause to grow gradually less.   DECREASE *verb*.

tailor *verb*

To make or become suitable to a particular situation or   ADAPT.
use.

tailor-made *adjective*

1. Suited to one's end or purpose.   1. CONVENIENT.
2. Made according to the specifications of the buyer.   2. CUSTOM *adjective*.

tailor-make *verb*

To make or become suitable to a particular situation or   ADAPT.
use.

taint *verb*

1. To make morally impure: *a young child's morals*   1. **Syns:** contaminate, corrupt, defile,
   tainted by delinquents.   infect, pollute, soil.
                                                                 Near-syns: besmirch, cloud, dirty,
                                                                 discolor, smear, stain, sully, tarnish.

2. To cast aspersions on.   2. BLACKEN.

taint *noun*

A mark of discredit or disgrace.   STAIN *noun*.

taintlessness *noun*

The condition of being clean and free of contaminants.   PURITY.

take *verb*

1. To go aboard (a means of transport): *took the six*   1. **Syns:** board, catch.
   o'clock train.
2. To obtain possession or control of.   2. CAPTURE.
3. To gain possession of, esp. after a struggle or   3. **Syns:** bag (*Slang*), capture, catch, get,
   chase: *took the thief after a high-speed pursuit.*   nail (*Slang*), net[1], secure.
4. To lay claim to for oneself or as one's right.   4. ASSUME.
5. To become affected with a disease.   5. CONTRACT.
6. To come upon, esp. suddenly or unexpectedly: *The*   6. **Syns:** catch, hit on (*or* upon),
   attackers took the enemy by surprise.   surprise.
7. To have a sudden, overwhelming effect on.   7. SEIZE *verb*.
8. To direct or impel to oneself by some quality or   8. ATTRACT.
   action.
9. To cause to pass from the mouth into the stomach.   9. SWALLOW *verb*.
10. To allow admittance, as to a group.   10. ACCEPT.
11. To engage in sexual relations with: *Abraham took*   11. **Syns:** bed, copulate (with), couple
    his slave girl.   with, have, mate (with), sleep with.
                                                                 —*Idioms* go to bed with, make love to
                                                                 (*or* with), take to bed.

12. To admit to one's possession, presence, or   12. RECEIVE.
    awareness.
13. To have as a need or prerequisite.   13. DEMAND *verb*.
14. To obtain from another source.   14. DERIVE.
15. To put up with.   15. ENDURE.
16. To perceive and recognize the meaning of.   16. UNDERSTAND.
17. To understand in a particular way.   17. INTERPRET.
18. To cause to come along with oneself.   18. BRING.
19. To take away (a quantity) from another quantity.   19. DEDUCT.
20. To get money or something else from by deceitful   20. CHEAT *verb*.
    trickery.
21. To react in a specified way.   21. FUNCTION.

take after *verb*

To be similar to, as in appearance.   FAVOR *verb*.

take away *verb*

To move (something) from a position occupied.   REMOVE *verb*.

take back *verb*

1. To send, put, or carry back to a former location.   1. RETURN *verb*.
2. To disavow (something previously written or said)   2. RETRACT.
   irrevocably and usu. formally.
3. To occupy or take again.   3. RESUME.

take down *verb*

1. To cause to descend.
2. To take (something) apart: *take down a Christmas tree; take down a rifle and clean it.*

take on *verb*
1. To obtain the use or services of.
2. To go about the initial step in doing (something).
3. *Informal.* To enter into conflict with.
4. To take, as another's idea, and make one's own.
5. To worry over trifles.
6. To take upon oneself.

take out *verb*
1. To move (something) from a position occupied.
2. *Informal.* To be together socially on a regular basis.

take over *verb*
1. To seize and move into by force.
2. To free from a specific duty by acting as a substitute.
3. To take upon oneself.

take to *verb*
To find agreeable.

take up *verb*
1. To move (something) to a higher position.
2. To go about the initial step in doing (something).
3. To go on after an interruption.
4. To be occupied or concerned.
5. To receive (something given or offered) willingly and gladly.
6. To take upon oneself.

take *noun*
1. *Slang.* The amount of money collected as admission, esp. to a sporting event: *Today's take amounts to $10,000.*
2. *Slang.* An effort to do or make something.

take after *verb*
take away *verb*
take back *verb*
take down *verb*
take-in *noun*
take in *verb*
1. To allow admittance, as to a group.
2. To have as an integral part.
3. To perceive and recognize the meaning of.
4. To cause to accept what is false, esp. by trickery or misrepresentation.

take-in *noun*
An action meant to deceive.

takeoff *noun*
take off *verb*
1. To rise up in flight: *The jet took off with a roar.*
2. To take from one's own person.
3. To move (something) from a position occupied.
4. To take away (a quantity) from another quantity.
5. *Informal.* To copy (the manner or expression of another), esp. in an exaggerated or mocking way.
6. *Slang.* To move or proceed away from a place.
7. *Slang.* To leave hastily.

takeoff *noun*
1. The act of rising in flight: *The plane crashed during takeoff.*
2. A usu. amusing caricature of another: *did a takeoff on the President.*

1. LOWER².
2. **Syns:** disassemble, dismantle, dismember, dismount.

1. EMPLOY *verb.*
2. START *verb.*
3. ENGAGE.
4. ADOPT.
5. FUSS *verb.*
6. ASSUME.

1. REMOVE *verb.*
2. SEE.

1. OCCUPY.
2. RELIEVE.

3. ASSUME.

LIKE¹.

1. ELEVATE.
2. START *verb.*
3. CONTINUE.
4. DEAL *verb.*
5. ACCEPT.

6. ASSUME.

1. **Syns:** gate, gate money. —*Idioms* box-office receipts, gate receipts.

2. ATTEMPT *noun.*

SEE **take.**
SEE **take.**
SEE **take.**
SEE **take.**
SEE **take in.**

1. ACCEPT.
2. CONTAIN.
3. UNDERSTAND.
4. DECEIVE.

DECEPTION.

SEE **take off.**

1. **Syn:** lift (off).
2. REMOVE *verb.*
3. REMOVE *verb.*
4. DEDUCT.
5. IMITATE.

6. GO *verb.*
7. RUN *verb.*

1. **Syn:** liftoff.

2. **Syns:** imitation, parody.

take on *verb*	SEE **take.**
take out *verb*	SEE **take.**
take over *verb*	SEE **take.**
take to *verb*	SEE **take.**
take up *verb*	SEE **take.**

taking *adjective*
1. Pleasing to the eye or mind.
2. Capable of transmission by infection.

1. ATTRACTIVE.
2. COMMUNICABLE.

tale *noun*
1. An entertaining and often oral account of a real or fictitious occurrence.
2. An untrue declaration.

1. YARN.
2. LIE² *noun*.

tale *verb*
To note (items) one by one so as to get a total.

COUNT *verb*.

talebearer *noun*
A person habitually engaged in idle talk about others.

GOSSIP *noun*.

talebearing *adjective*
Inclined to gossip.

GOSSIPY.

talent *noun*
An innate capability: *a talent for music; a talent for mathematics.*

Syns: aptitude, aptness, bent, faculty, flair, genius, gift, head, inclination, instinct, knack, turn.
Near-syns: ability, art, craft, expertise, forte, leaning, propensity, skill.

talented *adjective*
Having talent.

GIFTED.

taletelling *adjective*
Inclined to gossip.

GOSSIPY.

talisman *noun*
A small object worn or kept for its supposed magical power.

CHARM *noun*.

talk *verb*
1. To articulate (something) in words: *talk treason.*

1. **Syns:** speak, utter¹, verbalize. —*Idiom* put into words.

2. To express oneself in speech.
3. To direct speech to.
4. To engage in spoken exchange.
5. To meet and exchange views to reach a decision.
6. To engage in or spread gossip.
7. To give incriminating information about others, esp. to the authorities.

2. SPEAK.
3. ADDRESS *verb*.
4. CONVERSE¹ *verb*.
5. CONFER.
6. GOSSIP *verb*.
7. INFORM.

talk back *verb*
To utter an impertinent rejoinder: *talked back when his parents refused him the car.*

Syns: sass (*Informal*), sauce (*Informal*), talk up. —*Idiom* give someone some lip.

talk down *verb*
1. To think, represent, or speak of as small or unimportant.
2. To treat in a superciliously indulgent manner.

1. BELITTLE.
2. CONDESCEND.

talk into *verb*
To succeed in causing (a person) to act in a certain way.

PERSUADE.

talk over *verb*
To speak together and exchange ideas and opinions about.

DISCUSS.

talk up *verb*
1. To make known vigorously the positive features of (a product).
2. To utter an impertinent rejoinder.

1. ADVERTISE.
2. TALK BACK.

talk *noun*
1. Spoken exchange.
2. The faculty, act, or product of speaking.
3. A usu. formal oral communication to an audience.

1. CONVERSATION.
2. SPEECH.
3. SPEECH.

4. The act or process of dealing with another to reach an agreement: *the American-North Vietnamese peace talks*.

4. *Syns:* negotiation, parley.

talkative *adjective*
Given to conversation: *a very talkative person*.

Syns: chatty, conversational, free-spoken, gabby, garrulous, loquacious, multiloquent, talky.
Near-ants: laconic, reserved, reticent, speechless, uncommunicative.
Ant: silent.

talk back *verb*   SEE **talk.**
talk down *verb*   SEE **talk.**
talker *noun*
1. One given to conversation.   1. CONVERSATIONALIST.
2. One who delivers a public speech.   2. SPEAKER.
talk into *verb*   SEE **talk.**
talk over *verb*   SEE **talk.**
talk up *verb*   SEE **talk.**
talky *adjective*
Given to conversation.   TALKATIVE.
tall *adjective*
1. Extending to a great height: *tall mountains*.   1. ***Syns:*** elevated, high, lofty, soaring, towering.
2. Having a rather great upward projection.   2. HIGH *adjective*.
3. Not easy to do, achieve, or master.   3. DIFFICULT.
tally *verb*
1. To be compatible or in correspondence.   1. AGREE.
2. To combine (figures) to form a sum.   2. ADD.
3. To note (items) one by one so as to get a total.   3. COUNT *verb*.
4. To gain (a point or points) in a game or contest.   4. SCORE *verb*.
tally *noun*
1. A noting of items one by one.   1. COUNT *noun*.
2. The total number of points made by a contestant,   2. SCORE *noun*.
side, or team in a game or contest.
tallying *noun*
The act or state of agreeing or conforming.   AGREEMENT.
tame *adjective*
1. Trained or bred to live with and be of use to man.   1. DOMESTIC.
2. Easily managed or handled.   2. GENTLE *adjective*.
tame *verb*
1. To train to live with and be of use to man.   1. DOMESTICATE.
2. To make (an animal) docile.   2. GENTLE *verb*.
3. To make or become less severe or extreme.   3. MODERATE *verb*.
tamper *verb*
1. To handle something idly, ignorantly, or   1. ***Syns:*** fiddle, fool, meddle, mess,
destructively: *Someone tampered with the TV set*   monkey (*Informal*), tinker.
and spoiled the reception.
2. To prearrange the outcome of (a contest) unlawfully.   2. FIX *verb*.
tangent *noun*
An instance of digressing.   DIGRESSION.
tangential *adjective*
Marked by or given to digression.   DIGRESSIVE.
tangibility *noun*
The quality or condition of being discernible by touch: ***Syns:*** palpability, tactility, tangibleness,
The tangibility of the reward excited them.   touchability, touchableness.
tangible *adjective*
1. Discernible by touch: *tangible objects*.   1. ***Syns:*** palpable, tactile, touchable.
                                                          Near-ants: ethereal, spiritual, unreal.
                                                          Ant: intangible.

2. Having actual reality.

2. REAL.

3. Composed of or relating to things that occupy space and can be perceived by the senses.

3. PHYSICAL.

tangibleness *noun*

The quality or condition of being discernible by touch.

TANGIBILITY.

tangle *noun*

1. Something that is intricately and often bewilderingly complex: *a tangle of interlocking corporations; a tangle of freeways; a marital tangle.*

1. *Syns:* entanglement, jungle, knot, labyrinth, maze, mesh, morass, skein, snarl[1], web. —*Idiom* cat's cradle.

2. *Informal.* A discussion, often heated, in which a difference of opinion is expressed.

2. ARGUMENT.

tangle *verb*

1. To twist together so that separation is difficult.

1. ENTANGLE.

2. To make complex, intricate, or perplexing.

2. COMPLICATE.

3. To gain control of or an advantage over by or as if by trapping.

3. CATCH *verb.*

tangled *adjective*

Difficult to understand due to intricacy.

COMPLEX *adjective.*

tank up *verb*

Slang. To take alcoholic liquor, esp. excessively or habitually.

DRINK *verb.*

tantalize *verb*

To excite (another) by exposing something desirable while keeping it out of reach: *tantalized the dog with raw meat.*

Syns: bait, tease, torment. —*Idiom* make one's mouth water.

tantalizing *adjective*

Enticingly in sight, yet often out of reach: *had a tantalizing vision of an oasis.*

Syns: mouthwatering, teasing.

tantamount *adjective*

Agreeing exactly in value, quantity, or effect.

EQUAL *adjective.*

tantrum *noun*

An angry outburst.

TEMPER *noun.*

tap[1] *verb*

1. To make a noise by striking: *tapped at the door and called her name.*

1. *Syns:* bob (*Obs.*), knock, rap[1].

2. *Slang.* To select for an office or position.

2. APPOINT.

tap *noun*

An audible blow: *heard the tap of a pencil on the desk; a tap at the door.*

Syns: bob (*Obs.*), knock, rap[1].

tap[2] *verb*

1. To remove (a liquid) by a steady, gradual process.

1. DRAIN.

2. To monitor (telephone calls) with a concealed listening device connected to the circuit: *got a court order to tap the suspect's phone.*

2. *Syns:* bug, wiretap.

taper off *verb*

To grow or cause to grow gradually less.

DECREASE *verb.*

tar *noun*

Informal. A person engaged in sailing or working on a ship.

SAILOR.

tardiness *noun*

The quality or condition of not being on time.

LATENESS.

tardy *adjective*

1. Not being on time.

1. LATE *adjective.*

2. Proceeding at a rate less than usual or desired.

2. SLOW *adjective.*

target *noun*

1. One that is fired at, attacked, or abused: *The arrow fell short of its target. His pomposity made him a target of satirists.*

1. *Syns:* butt, mark.

2. What one intends to do or achieve.

2. INTENTION.

target *verb*

To make a target of: *The terrorists targeted the war hero as their prime victim.*

tariff *noun*
A compulsory contribution, usu. of money, that is required of persons or groups of persons for the support of a government.

TAX *noun.*

tarnish *verb*
1. To spoil the soundness or perfection of.
2. To cast aspersions on.

1. INJURE.
2. BLACKEN.

tarnish *noun*
A mark of discredit or disgrace.

STAIN *noun.*

tarry *verb*
1. To go or move slowly so that progress is hindered.
2. To continue to be in a place.
3. To stop temporarily and remain, as if reluctant to leave.

1. DELAY *verb.*
2. REMAIN.
3. PAUSE *verb.*

tart[1] *adjective*
Having a taste characteristic of that produced by acids.

SOUR *adjective.*

tart[2] *noun*
A vulgar, promiscuous woman who flouts propriety.

SLUT.

tartufe *noun*

SEE **tartuffe.**

tartuffe also **tartufe** *noun*
A person who practices hypocrisy.

HYPOCRITE.

tartuffery *noun*
A show or expression of feelings or beliefs one does not actually hold or possess.

HYPOCRISY.

tartuffian *adjective*
Of or practicing hypocrisy.

HYPOCRITICAL.

task *noun*
1. A piece of work that has been assigned: *His task is to prepare the publicity campaign.*
2. A difficult or tedious undertaking: *Writing letters is a real task for me.*

3. An assignment one is sent to carry out.

1. *Syns:* chore, duty, job, stint.
2. *Syns:* chore, effort, job, onus, taskwork.
   Near-syns: bother, burden, headache, nuisance, pain, strain, trouble.
3. MISSION.

task *verb*
To force to work.

WORK *verb.*

taskmaster *noun*
Someone who directs and supervises workers.

BOSS *noun.*

taskwork *noun*
A difficult or tedious undertaking.

TASK *noun.*

taste *verb*
1. To participate in or partake of personally.
2. To have a particular flavor or suggestion of something.
3. To undergo an emotional reaction.

1. EXPERIENCE *verb.*
2. SMACK[2] *verb.*
3. FEEL *verb.*

taste *noun*
1. A distinctive property of a substance affecting the gustatory sense.
2. A limited or anticipatory experience: *had a taste of success.*
3. A barely perceivable indication of something.
4. A liking or personal preference for something: *a taste for luxury.*

1. FLAVOR *noun.*
2. *Syns:* foretaste, sample.
3. TRACE *noun.*
4. *Syns:* appetite, fondness, inclination, partiality, predisposition, relish, weakness.
   Near-syns: bend, bias, leaning, penchant, proclivity, propensity.
   Ant: distaste.

5. Recognition of worth, quality, importance, etc.
6. A desire for food or drink.

5. APPRECIATION.
6. APPETITE.

7. The faculty or sense of discerning what is aesthetically pleasing or appropriate: *a house designed with taste and imagination.*

7. *Syn:* tastefulness.

tasteful *adjective*
 1. Showing good taste: *a tasteful and pleasing combination of colors.*
 2. *Rare.* Highly pleasing, esp. to the sense of taste.
 3. Not showy or obtrusive.

1. *Syns:* aesthetic *or* esthetic, artistic, tasty (*Rare*).
2. DELICIOUS.
3. QUIET.

tastefulness *noun*
The faculty or sense of discerning what is aesthetically pleasing or appropriate.

TASTE *noun.*

tasteless *adjective*
 1. Lacking an appetizing flavor.
 2. Lacking in delicacy or refinement.
 3. Lacking style and good taste.

1. FLAT *adjective.*
2. COARSE.
3. TACKY².

tasty *adjective*
 1. Highly pleasing, esp. to the sense of taste.
 2. *Rare.* Showing good taste.

1. DELICIOUS.
2. TASTEFUL.

tatterdemalion *noun*
A person wearing ragged or tattered clothing: *a shabby tatterdemalion begging for food.*

Syns: ragamuffin, scarecrow.
Near-syns: bum, hobo, loafer, tramp, vagabond, vagrant; orphan, waif; bag person.

tatterdemalion *adjective*
Torn into or marked by shreds or tatters.

TATTERED.

tattered *adjective*
 1. Torn into or marked by shreds or tatters: *tattered clothing.*
 2. Showing signs of wear and tear or neglect.

1. *Syns:* ragged, raggedy, tatterdemalion.
2. SHABBY.

tatters *noun*
Torn and ragged clothing: *dressed in tatters.*

Syn: rags.

tattle *verb*
 1. To engage in or spread gossip.
 2. To give incriminating information about others, esp. to the authorities.

1. GOSSIP *verb.*
2. INFORM.

tattle *noun*
 1. Idle, often sensational and groundless talk about others.
 2. A person habitually engaged in idle talk about others.

1. GOSSIP *noun.*
2. GOSSIP *noun.*

tattler *noun*
 1. A person habitually engaged in idle talk about others.
 2. One who gives incriminating information about others.

1. GOSSIP *noun.*
2. INFORMER.

tattletale *noun*
 1. A person habitually engaged in idle talk about others.
 2. One who gives incriminating information about others.

1. GOSSIP *noun.*
2. INFORMER.

tatty *adjective*
Of decidedly inferior quality.

SHODDY.

taunt *verb*
 1. To torment with persistent insult or ridicule.
 2. To make fun of.

1. BAIT *verb.*
2. RIDICULE *verb.*

taunt *noun*
Words or actions intended to evoke contemptuous laughter.

RIDICULE *noun.*

taut *adjective*
 1. Stretched tightly: *gloves with a taut fit; a taut anchor line.*

1. *Syns:* close¹, snug, tense, tight.

2. In good order or clean condition.

2. NEAT.

tauten *verb*
To make or become tense.

TENSE *verb*.

tautological *adjective*
Characterized by excessive and obfuscatory wordiness: *long-winded and tautological arguments*.

Syns: circumlocutional, circumlocutionary, circumlocutious, circumlocutory, pleonastic, redundant, roundabout.

tawdry *adjective*
Tastelessly showy.

GAUDY.

tax *noun*
1. A compulsory contribution, usu. of money, that is required of persons or groups of persons for the support of a government: *a tax on gasoline*.
2. A duty or responsibility that is a source of anxiety, worry, or hardship.

1. *Syns:* assessment, duty, impost, levy, tariff.

2. BURDEN *noun*.

tax *verb*
1. To place a burden or heavy load on.
2. To force to work.
3. To make an accusation against.
4. To criticize for a fault or offense.

1. CHARGE *verb*.
2. WORK *verb*.
3. ACCUSE.
4. CALL DOWN at **call**.

taxing *adjective*
1. Imposing a severe test of bodily or spiritual strength.
2. Requiring great effort.
3. Causing fatigue.

1. BURDENSOME.
2. DEMANDING.
3. TIRING.

TB also **T.B.** *noun*
A contagious disease producing lesions esp. of the lungs.

TUBERCULOSIS.

teach *verb*
To impart knowledge and skill to.

EDUCATE.

teachable *adjective*
Capable of being educated.

EDUCABLE.

teacher *noun*
One who educates.

EDUCATOR.

teaching *noun*
1. The act, process, or art of imparting knowledge and skill.
2. A principle taught or advanced for belief, as by a religious or philosophical group.

1. EDUCATION.

2. DOCTRINE.

team *noun*
A group of people organized for a particular purpose.

FORCE *noun*.

teamwork *noun*
Joint work toward a common end.

COOPERATION.

tear¹ *verb*
1. To separate or pull apart by force: *tore my stocking on a nail*.

1. *Syns:* cleave, rend, rip, rive, split.
   Near-syns: gash, sever, slash, sunder; break, crack, rupture.

2. To remove from a fixed position.
3. To move swiftly.
4. *Informal.* To move swiftly on foot so that both feet leave the ground during each stride.

2. PULL *verb*.
3. RUSH *verb*.
4. RUN *verb*.

tear down *verb*
1. To collapse or shatter by or as if by breaking.
2. To break up so that reconstruction is impossible.
3. To make defamatory statements about.

1. BREAK DOWN.
2. DESTROY.
3. LIBEL *verb*.

tear *noun*
1. A hole made by tearing: *mended the tears in the fabric*.
2. *Slang.* A drinking bout.

1. *Syns:* rent², rip.

2. BENDER.

tear² *noun*
A drop of the clear liquid secreted by the glands of the eyes: *A tear trickled down her cheek.*
Syn: teardrop.

tear *verb*
To fill with tears: *eyes that were tearing and smarting from the smoke.*
Syn: water.

tear down *verb*
SEE **tear¹**.

teardrop *noun*
A drop of the clear liquid secreted by the glands of the eye.
TEAR² *noun.*

tearful *adjective*
Filled with or shedding tears: *a sad and tearful child.*
Syns: lachrymose, teary, weeping, weepy.
—*Idiom* in (*or* to) tears.
Near-syns: bawling, crying, lamenting, mournful, sniveling, sobbing.
Ant: tearless.

tear-jerking *adjective*
Slang. Affectedly or extravagantly emotional.
SENTIMENTAL.

tears *noun*
A fit of crying.
CRY *noun.*

teary *adjective*
Filled with or shedding tears.
TEARFUL.

tease *verb*
1. To disturb by repeated attacks.
2. To excite (another) by exposing something desirable while keeping it out of reach.
1. ANNOY.
2. TANTALIZE.

teasing *adjective*
Enticingly in sight, yet often out of reach.
TANTALIZING.

technic *noun*
The degree of skill exhibited in any performance.
TECHNIQUE.

technicality *noun*
A small, often specialized element of a whole.
DETAIL *noun.*

technique *noun*
1. The degree of skill exhibited in any performance: *a faultless technique on the piano.*
2. The manner in which something is done.
3. A method used in dealing with something.
4. A skill in doing or performing that is attained by study, practice, or observation.
1. **Syns:** command, technic.
2. WAY *noun.*
3. APPROACH *noun.*
4. ART.

techy *adjective*
SEE **tetchy**.

tedious *adjective*
Arousing no interest or curiosity.
BORING.

tediousness *noun*
A tiresome lack of variety.
MONOTONY.

tedium *noun*
1. A tiresome lack of variety.
2. The condition of being bored.
1. MONOTONY.
2. BOREDOM.

tee-hee *verb & noun*
SEE **tehee**.

teem¹ *verb*
1. To overflow with: *a street teeming with pedestrians.*
1. **Syns:** abound, bristle, crawl, flow, formicate, pullulate, swarm.
Near-syns: bustle, busy, cram, crowd, jam, pack, overflow.

2. To come or go in large numbers.
2. POUR.

teem² *verb*
To rain heavily.
POUR.

teeming *adjective*
Full of animation and activity.
ALIVE.

teensy *adjective*
SEE **teeny**.

teeny also **teensy** *adjective*
Extremely small.
TINY.

teeter *verb*
1. To walk unsteadily.
2. To move back and forth or from side to side, as if about to fall.

1. LURCH *verb*.
2. SWAY *verb*.

teetotalism *noun*
The practice of refraining from use of alcoholic liquors.

TEMPERANCE.

tehee or **tee-hee** *verb*
To laugh in a stifled way.

GIGGLE *verb*.

tehee or **tee-hee** *noun*
A stifled laugh.

GIGGLE *noun*.

telephone *verb*
To communicate with (someone) by telephone: *She's telephoned me twice today.*

Syns: buzz (*Informal*), call, dial (*Informal*), phone, ring² (*Informal*). —*Idioms* get someone on the horn, give someone a buzz (*or* call *or* ring).

tell *verb*
1. To put into words.
2. To cause to know about or be aware of.
3. To make known.
4. To disclose in a breach of confidence.
5. To give orders to.
6. To recognize as being different.

1. SAY *verb*.
2. INFORM.
3. COMMUNICATE.
4. BETRAY.
5. COMMAND *verb*.
6. DISTINGUISH.

tell off *verb*
1. *Informal.* To reprimand loudly or harshly.
2. To note (items) one by one so as to get a total.

1. BAWL OUT at **bawl**.
2. COUNT *verb*.

telling *adjective*
Serving to convince.

CONVINCING.

tell off *verb*

SEE **tell**.

telltale *noun*
A person habitually engaged in idle talk about others.

GOSSIP *noun*.

tellurian *adjective*
Pertaining to or characteristic of the earth or of human life on earth.

EARTHLY.

telluric *adjective*
Pertaining to or characteristic of the earth or of human life on earth.

EARTHLY.

temerarious *adjective*
Characterized by unthinking boldness and haste.

RASH¹.

temblor *noun*
Regional. A shaking of the earth.

TREMOR *noun*.

temerity *noun*
1. Foolhardy boldness or disregard of danger: *had the temerity to challenge the dictator's authority.*

1. *Syns:* brashness, chutzpah (*Slang*), rashness, recklessness. *Near-syns:* daring, heedlessness, nerve; impatience, impetuosity. *Ant:* caution.

2. Excessive and arrogant self-confidence.

2. PRESUMPTION.

temper *noun*
1. A tendency to become angry or irritable: *was widely known for his temper.*

1. *Syns:* choler, irascibility, irascibleness, spleen, temperament. —*Idioms* low boiling point, short fuse.

2. A person's customary manner of emotional response.
3. A temporary state of mind or feeling.
4. An angry outburst: *flew into a temper.*

2. DISPOSITION.
3. MOOD.
4. *Syns:* conniption (*Informal*), fit, huff, passion, tantrum. *Near-syns:* anger, fury, outburst, rage.

5. A prevailing quality, as of thought, behavior, or attitude: *The temper of the early 1920's was one of optimism.*

5. *Syns:* climate, mood, spirit, tone.

temper *verb*
To make or become less severe or extreme.

MODERATE *verb*.

temperament *noun*
1. A person's customary manner of emotional response.
2. A tendency to become angry or irritable.

1. DISPOSITION.
2. TEMPER *noun.*

temperamental *adjective*
1. Given to changeable emotional states, esp. of anger or gloom.
2. Following no predictable pattern.

1. MOODY.
2. CAPRICIOUS.

temperance *noun*
1. The practice of refraining from use of alcoholic liquors: *believed that temperance was next to godliness.*
2. Avoidance of extremes of opinion, feeling, or personal conduct.

1. *Syns:* abstinence, dryness, nephalism, soberness, sobriety, teetotalism.

2. MODERATION.

temperate *adjective*
1. Exercising moderation and self-restraint in appetites and behavior: *is temperate in his tastes, unlike his high-living brother.*
2. Not excessive or extreme in amount, degree, or force.
3. Kept within sensible limits.
4. Free from extremes in temperature.

1. *Syns:* abstemious, abstentious, abstinent, continent, sober.

2. MODERATE *adjective.*
3. CONSERVATIVE *adjective.*
4. MILD.

tempestuous *adjective*
1. Marked by unrest or disturbance.
2. Violently disturbed, as by storms.

1. TURBULENT.
2. ROUGH.

tempo *noun*
Rate of motion or performance.

SPEED *noun.*

temporal *adjective*
1. Pertaining to or characteristic of the earth or of human life on earth.
2. Of or preoccupied with material rather than spiritual or intellectual things.
3. Not religious in subject matter, form, or use.
4. Lasting or existing only for a short time.

1. EARTHLY.

2. MATERIALISTIC.

3. PROFANE.
4. TRANSITORY.

temporary *adjective*
1. Intended, used, or present for a limited time: *temporary repairs; temporary employees.*
2. Lasting or existing only for a short time.
3. Temporarily assuming the duties of another: *temporary chairman.*

1. *Syns:* impermanent, interim, provisional, short-range, short-term.
2. TRANSITORY.
3. *Syns:* acting, ad interim (*Latin*), interim, pro tem, pro tempore (*Latin*).

tempt *verb*
1. To beguile or draw into a wrong or foolish course of action: *was tempted to destroy the records.*
2. To solicit (danger) playfully and provocatively, often unwittingly.

1. *Syns:* allure, entice, inveigle, lure, seduce. —*Idiom* lead astray.
2. COURT *verb.*

temptation *noun*
Something that attracts, esp. with the promise of pleasure or reward.

LURE *noun.*

tempter *noun*
One that seduces.

SEDUCER.

tempting *adjective*
1. Pleasing to the eye or mind.
2. Tending to seduce.

1. ATTRACTIVE.
2. SEDUCTIVE.

temptress *noun*
A usu. unscrupulous woman who seduces or exploits men.

SEDUCTRESS.

tenable *adjective*
1. Capable of being defended against armed attack: *an outpost that is no longer tenable.*

1. *Syns:* defendable, defensible.
   Near-ants: dangerous, precarious, risky, vulnerable; defenseless, helpless, unprotected.
   Ant: untenable.

2. Capable of being justified.	2. JUSTIFIABLE.
tenacious *adjective*	
1. Persistently holding to something.	1. TIGHT *adjective*.
2. Tenaciously unwilling to yield.	2. OBSTINATE.
tend[1] *verb*	
To have a tendency or inclination: *tends to stammer when excited*.	**Syns:** incline, lean[1] (to *or* toward), slant, squint toward (*or* at), trend.
tend[2] *verb*	
1. To have the care and supervision of: *tending the forgetful old man*.	1. **Syns:** attend, care for, look after, mind, minister to, see to, watch. —*Idioms* keep an eye on, look out for, take care (*or* charge) of, take under one's wing.
2. To prepare (soil) for the planting and raising of crops.	2. TILL.
tendency *noun*	
1. An inclination to something.	1. BENT *noun*.
2. The thread or current of thought uniting or occurring in all the elements of a text or discourse.	2. THRUST *noun*.
tendentious *adjective*	
Exhibiting bias.	BIASED.
tendentiousness *noun*	
An inclination for or against that inhibits impartial judgment.	BIAS *noun*.
tender[1] *adjective*	
Of a kindly, considerate character.	GENTLE *adjective*.
tender[2] *noun*	
Something offered.	OFFER *noun*.
tender *verb*	
To put before another for acceptance.	OFFER *verb*.
tenderfoot *noun*	
One who is just starting to learn or do something.	BEGINNER.
tenderhearted *adjective*	
Of a kindly, considerate character.	GENTLE *adjective*.
tendril *noun*	
A young stemlike growth arising from a plant.	SHOOT *noun*.
tenebrific *adjective*	
Dark and depressing.	GLOOMY.
tenebrosity *noun*	
Absence or deficiency of light.	DARK *noun*.
tenebrous *adjective*	
Deficient in brightness.	DARK *adjective*.
tenet *noun*	
A principle taught or advanced for belief, as by a religious or philosophical group.	DOCTRINE.
tenor *noun*	
The thread or current of thought uniting or occurring in all the elements of a text or discourse.	THRUST *noun*.
tense *verb*	
To make or become tense: *My muscles tensed when I heard the knock at the door*.	**Syns:** stiffen, tauten, tighten.
tense *adjective*	
1. Stretched tightly.	1. TAUT.
2. Feeling or exhibiting nervous tension.	2. EDGY.
tension *noun*	
The act, condition, or effect of exerting force on someone or something.	PRESSURE *noun*.
ten-strike *noun*	
Informal. A dazzling, often sudden instance of success.	HIT *noun*.
tentative *adjective*	
1. Depending on or containing a condition or conditions.	1. CONDITIONAL.

2. Given to or exhibiting hesitation.
3. Not perfected, elaborated, or completed.

tenuous *adjective*
Having little substance or significance; not solidly based: *tenuous reasoning.*

2. HESITANT.
3. ROUGH.

Syns: feeble, flimsy, insubstantial, unsubstantial.
Near-syns: implausible, insignificant, unsound, weak.
Ant: substantial.

tenure *noun*
The holding of something, such as a position: *a three-year tenure in office.*

Syns: incumbency, occupancy, occupation.

tepid *adjective*
Lacking warmth, interest, enthusiasm, or involvement: *her tepid approval of the plans.*

Syns: halfhearted, lukewarm, unenthusiastic.
Near-syns: colorless, dull, flat, lifeless, spiritless, unlively, weak.

tergiversate *verb*
1. To abandon one's cause or party usu. to join another.
2. To use evasive or deliberately vague language.

1. DEFECT *verb*.
2. EQUIVOCATE.

tergiversation *noun*
1. An instance of defecting from or abandoning a cause.
2. The use or an instance of equivocal language.
3. An expression or term liable to more than one interpretation.

1. DEFECTION.

2. EQUIVOCATION.
3. AMBIGUITY.

tergiversator *noun*
A person who has defected.

DEFECTOR.

term *noun*
1. A limited or specific period of time during which something happens, lasts, or extends: *a term of two years as chairman.*
2. The period during which someone or something exists.
3. A specific length of time characterized by the occurrence of certain conditions or events.
4. A sound or combination of sounds that symbolizes and communicates a meaning: *used the term in its most common sense.*
5. A restricting or modifying element.

1. *Syns:* duration, span, stretch, time.
Near-syns: hitch, tenure, tour, turn; period, phase.
2. LIFE.

3. PERIOD.

4. *Syns:* expression, word.

5. PROVISION.

term *verb*
1. To give a name or title to.
2. To describe with a word or term.

1. NAME *verb*.
2. CALL *verb*.

termagant *noun*
A person, esp. a woman, who habitually uses loud, abusive language.

SCOLD *noun*.

terminal *adjective*
1. Coming after all others.
2. Of or relating to a terminative condition, stage, or point.

1. LAST[1] *adjective*.
2. LAST[1] *adjective*.

terminate *verb*
1. To bring or come to a natural or proper end.
2. To stop suddenly, as a conversation, activity, relationship, etc.
3. To end the employment of.
4. To relinquish one's engagement in or occupation with.

1. CLOSE[1] *verb*.
2. SUSPEND.

3. DISMISS.
4. QUIT.

termination *noun*
1. A concluding or terminating.
2. The last part.
3. The act of dismissing or the condition of being dismissed from employment.

1. END *noun*.
2. END *noun*.
3. DISMISSAL.

terminology *noun*
Specialized expressions indigenous to a particular field, subject, trade, or subculture.   LANGUAGE.

terminus *noun*
1. A concluding or terminating.   1. END *noun.*
2. *Rare.* A fairly narrow line or space forming a boundary.   2. BORDER *noun.*

terms *noun*
An established position from which to operate or deal with others.   BASIS.

terpsichorean *noun*
A person who dances, esp. professionally.   DANCER.

terrain *noun*
1. The character, natural features, and configuration of land: *rocky, hilly terrain.*   1. **Syn:** topography. —*Idiom* the lay of the land.
2. A particular area used for or associated with a specific individual or activity.   2. TERRITORY.
3. A sphere of activity, study, or interest.   3. AREA.

terrene *adjective*
1. Pertaining to or characteristic of the earth or of human life on earth.   1. EARTHLY.
2. Consisting of or resembling soil.   2. EARTHY.

terrestrial *adjective*
1. Pertaining to or characteristic of the earth or of human life on earth.   1. EARTHLY.
2. Consisting of or resembling soil.   2. EARTHY.

terrible *adjective*
1. Very bad: *a terrible blunder.*   1. **Syns:** appalling, awful, dreadful, fearful, frightful, ghastly, horrendous, horrible, shocking.
2. Causing or able to cause fear.   2. FEARFUL.
3. Extreme in degree, strength, or effect.   3. INTENSE.

terrific *adjective*
1. Causing great horror.   1. HORRIBLE.
2. Particularly excellent.   2. MARVELOUS.
3. *Informal.* Exceptionally good of its kind.   3. EXCELLENT.

terrify *verb*
To fill with fear.   FRIGHTEN.

terrifying *adjective*
Causing great horror.   HORRIBLE.

territorial *adjective*
Pertaining to or restricted to a particular territory: *a territorial problem concerning land development.*   **Syn:** sectional.

territory *noun*
1. A particular area used for or associated with a specific individual or activity: *a salesman's territory; cattle territory.*   1. **Syns:** country (*Informal*), terrain, turf (*Slang*).
2. A sphere of activity, study, or interest.   2. AREA.

terror *noun*
Great agitation and anxiety caused by the expectation or the realization of danger.   FEAR.

terrorist *noun*
One who needlessly alarms others.   ALARMIST.

terrorize *verb*
To fill with fear.   FRIGHTEN.

test *noun*
1. A set of questions or exercises designed to determine knowledge or skill: *Tests were given at intervals during the course.*   1. **Syns:** catechism, catechization, exam (*Informal*), examination, quiz.

2. An operation employed to resolve an uncertainty: *ran tests to determine the effects of weightlessness on the human body.*
3. A procedure that ascertains effectiveness, value, proper function, or other quality: *The long hike was a test of our endurance.*
4. A means by which individuals are compared and judged.

test *verb*
1. To subject to a test of knowledge or skill: *tested the children's literacy levels.*
2. To subject to a procedure that ascertains effectiveness, value, proper function, or other quality: *He tested his headlights to be sure they were working.*
3. To engage in experiments: *scientists involved in testing; tested out the new theory.*

test *adjective*
Constituting a tentative model for future experiment or development.

testament *noun*
That which confirms.

testifier *noun*
One who testifies, esp. in court.

testify *verb*
1. To give evidence or testimony under oath: *A witness testified that he saw the defendant at the scene of the crime.*
2. To assure the certainty or validity of.
3. To confirm formally as true, accurate, or genuine.
4. To give grounds for believing in the existence or presence of.

testimonial *noun*
1. A formal token of appreciation and admiration for a person's high achievements: *a banquet as a testimonial to the hero.*

2. That which confirms.
3. A statement attesting to personal qualifications, character, and dependability.

testimony *noun*
1. A formal declaration of truth or fact given under oath: *A court reporter recorded the testimony.*
2. That which confirms.

testy *adjective*
1. Easily annoyed: *a frustrated, testy man.*

2. Having or showing a bad temper.

tetchy also **techy** *adjective*
Easily annoyed.

text *noun*
What a speech, piece of writing, or artistic work is about.

texture *noun*
1. A distinctive, complex underlying pattern or structure: *the texture of city life.*
2. A basic trait or set of traits that define and establish the character of something.

2. *Syns:* experiment, experimentation, trial.

3. *Syns:* assay, essay, proof, trial, try-out (*Informal*).

4. STANDARD *noun.*

1. *Syns:* check, examine.

2. *Syns:* assay, check, essay, examine, prove, try, try out. —*Idioms* bring to test, make trial of, put to the test (*or* proof).

3. *Syns:* experiment, try out.

PILOT *adjective.*

CONFIRMATION.

WITNESS *noun.*

1. *Syns:* attest, depone (*Archaic*), depose (*Law*), swear, witness (*Obs.*). —*Idioms* bear witness, take the stand.
2. CONFIRM.
3. CERTIFY.
4. INDICATE.

1. *Syns:* salute, salvo, tribute. *Near-syns:* appreciation, commemoration, jubilee, roast, triumph.
2. CONFIRMATION.
3. REFERENCE.

1. *Syns:* deposition (*Law*), witness (*Obs.*).

2. CONFIRMATION.

1. *Syns:* choleric, hot-tempered, irascible, peppery, quick-tempered, ratty (*Chiefly Brit.*), tetchy (*also* techy), touchy. *Near-syns:* cranky, cross, huffy, irritable, peevish, petulant.
2. ILL-TEMPERED.

TESTY.

SUBJECT *noun.*

1. *Syns:* contexture, fabric, fiber, web. —*Idiom* woof and warp.
2. ESSENCE.

thalassic *adjective*
Of or relating to the seas or oceans.   MARINE.

thank *verb*
To feel and express gratitude to: *I thank you for helping*   **Syn:** bless.
out.

thankful *adjective*
Showing or feeling gratitude.   GRATEFUL.

thankfulness *noun*
A being grateful.   APPRECIATION.

thankless *adjective*
1. Not showing or feeling gratitude: *a thankless*   1. **Syns:** unappreciative, ungrateful,
   sponger.   unthankful, unthanking.
                                                         Near-ants: appreciative, grateful,
                                                         heedful, thoughtful.
                                                         Ant: thankful.
2. Not apt to be appreciated: *a thankless task.*   2. **Syns:** unappreciated, ungrateful,
                                                         unthankful.

thanks *noun*
1. A being grateful.   1. APPRECIATION.
2. A short prayer said at meals.   2. GRACE *noun.*

thanksgiving *noun*
A short prayer said at meals.   GRACE *noun.*

thaumaturgic *adjective*
Having or brought about by supernatural powers.   MAGIC *adjective.*

thaumaturgy *noun*
The use of supernatural powers to influence or predict   MAGIC *noun.*
events.

thaw *verb*
To change from a solid to a liquid.   MELT.

theatrical also **theatric** *adjective*
1. Of or pertaining to drama or the theater.   1. DRAMATIC.
2. Suggesting drama or a stage performance, as in   2. DRAMATIC.
   emotionality or suspense.

theatricalism *noun*
Showy mannerisms and behavior: *a grand gesture*   **Syns:** dramaticism, staginess,
symptomatic of his theatricalism.   theatricality, theatricalness.

theatricality *noun*
Showy mannerisms and behavior.   THEATRICALISM.

theatricalness *noun*
Showy mannerisms and behavior.   THEATRICALISM.

theatricals *noun*
Overemotional, exaggerated behavior calculated for   THEATRICS.
effect.

theatrics *noun*
Overemotional, exaggerated behavior calculated for   **Syns:** dramatics, histrionics,
effect: *a child who used hysteria and theatrics to get*   melodramatics, theatricals.
what he wanted.

theft *noun*
The crime of taking someone else's property without   LARCENY.
consent.

thematic *adjective*
Of, constituting, or relating to a theme or themes: **Syn:** topical.
found a thematic tie-in between the two poems.

theme *noun*
1. *Ling.* The main part of a word to which affixes are   1. **Syns:** base[1], root[1], stem.
   attached: *The word "eat" is the theme on which the*
   derivative "eater" is based.
2. What a speech, piece of writing, or artistic work is   2. SUBJECT *noun.*
   about.
3. A relatively brief discourse written esp. as an   3. COMPOSITION.
   exercise.

theorem *noun*
A broad and basic rule or truth.
    LAW *noun.*

theoretical also **theoretic** *adjective*
1. Concerned with or restricted to a theory or theories: *theoretical mathematics.*
    1. **Syns:** abstract, academic, speculative.
2. Devoted to certain doctrines without regard to practicability.
    2. DOCTRINAIRE.
3. Existing only in concept and not in reality: *constructed a theoretical model of a society devoid of class conflict.*
    3. **Syns:** abstract, hypothetical (*also* hypothetic), ideal, transcendent, transcendental.

theory *noun*
1. A belief used as the basis for action: *Unstructured classroom activities resulted from the theory that children require free expression to learn.*
    1. **Syns:** hypothesis, supposition. **Near-syns:** base, basis, grounds, premise, understanding.
2. Something taken to be true without proof.
    2. ASSUMPTION.
3. Abstract reasoning: *the theory that the Romanovs survived execution.*
    3. **Syns:** conjecture, perhaps, speculation.

therapeutic *adjective*
Serving to cure.
    CURATIVE *adjective.*

therapy *noun*
The systematic application of remedies to effect a cure.
    TREATMENT.

thesis *noun*
1. A systematic, thorough written presentation of an original point of view: *a doctoral thesis.*
    1. **Syn:** dissertation.
2. A hypothetical, controversial proposition: *His thesis is that big government is the root of inflation.*
    2. **Syns:** contention, contestation. **Near-syns:** belief, opinion, view; point, position.
3. Something taken to be true without proof.
    3. ASSUMPTION.

thespian *noun*
A theatrical performer.
    ACTOR.

thespian *adjective*
Of or pertaining to drama or the theater.
    DRAMATIC.

theurgy *noun*
The use of supernatural powers to influence or predict events.
    MAGIC *noun.*

thew(s) *noun*
The state or quality of being physically strong.
    STRENGTH.

thick *adjective*
1. Relatively great in extent from one surface to the opposite: *cut himself a thick slice of bread.*
    1. **Syn:** fat.
2. Having a solid, compact build.
    2. HEAVY *adjective.*
3. Having all parts near to each other: *The pile in the carpet is thick.*
    3. **Syns:** close[1], compact[1], crowded, packed, tight.
4. Having so many constituent particles in suspension as to be condensed, often viscous: *a thick white sauce.*
    4. **Syns:** gelatinous, heavy, stodgy.
5. Lacking in intelligence.
    5. STUPID.
6. *Informal.* Very closely associated.
    6. FAMILIAR *adjective.*
7. Not plausible or believable.
    7. IMPLAUSIBLE.
8. Growing profusely: *thick jungle vegetation.*
    8. **Syns:** dense, heavy, lush, luxuriant, profuse, rank[2].

thick *noun*
The most intensely active central part: *the thick of the fighting; caught in the thick of the controversy.*
    Syns: eye, midst.

thickbodied *adjective*
Having a solid, compact build.
    HEAVY *adjective.*

thicken *verb*
To make thick or thicker, esp. through evaporation or condensation: *thickened the gravy by adding flour and heating it.*
    Syns: condense, inspissate.

thickhead   *noun*
A mentally dull person.   DULLARD.

thickheaded   *adjective*
Lacking in intelligence.   STUPID.

thickness   *noun*
The quality, condition, or degree of being thick: *measured the thickness of the wall.*   **Syns:** compactness, density, solidity.

thickset   *adjective*
Having a solid, compact build.   HEAVY *adjective.*

thick-witted   *adjective*
Lacking in intelligence.   STUPID.

thief   *noun*
A person who steals.   LARCENER.

thieve   *verb*
To take (another's property) without permission.   STEAL *verb.*

thievery   *noun*
The crime of taking someone else's property without consent.   LARCENY.

thieving   *noun*
The crime of taking someone else's property without consent.   LARCENY.

thieving   *adjective*
Tending to larceny.   LARCENOUS.

thievish   *adjective*
Tending to larceny.   LARCENOUS.

thin   *adjective*
1. Having little flesh or fat on the body: *became weak and thin during her illness.*

    1. **Syns:** angular, attenuate, bony, fleshless, gaunt, lank, lanky, lean[2], meager, rawboned, scrawny, skinny, spare, slender, twiggy, weedy. —*Idioms* all skin and bones, lean as a rake, thin as a rail.
    Near-ants: corpulent, fat, obese; heavy, massive, solid; piggish, plump.
    Ant: thick.

2. Marked by great diffusion of component particles: *the thin air in the high Sierras.*   2. **Syns:** rare, rarefied.
3. Lower than normal in strength or concentration due to admixture.   3. DILUTE *adjective.*
4. Not plausible or believable.   4. IMPLAUSIBLE.

thin   *verb*
1. To make physically thin or thinner: *a body thinned from malnutrition and malaria.*   1. **Syns:** extenuate (*Archaic*), gaunt, lean (down).
2. To lessen the strength of by or as if by admixture.   2. DILUTE *verb.*
3. To become diffuse: *At 50,000 feet the air thins markedly.*   3. **Syns:** attenuate, rarefy.

thing   *noun*
1. One that exists independently: *discerned three things on the horizon, one of which moved.*   1. **Syns:** being, entity, existence, existent, individual, object[1], something.
2. Something having material existence.   2. OBJECT[1].
3. A small, specialized mechanical device.   3. GADGET.
4. Something done.   4. ACT *noun.*
5. Something to be done, considered, or dealt with.   5. MATTER *noun.*
6. Something significant that happens.   6. EVENT.
7. An irrational preoccupation: *He has a thing about cleanliness.*   7. **Syns:** fetish, fixation (*Psychol.*), mania, obsession.
8. The current custom.   8. FASHION.
9. *Slang.* Something at which a person excels.   9. FORTE.
10. *Slang.* A temporary concentration of interest.   10. KICK *noun.*

thingamabob also **thingumabob**   *noun*
  Informal. A small, specialized mechanical device.   GADGET.
thingamajig also **thingumajig**   *noun*
  Informal. A small, specialized mechanical device.   GADGET.
things   *noun*
  1. Those articles that belong to someone.   **1.** BELONGINGS.
  2. One's portable property.   **2.** EFFECTS.
thingumabob   *noun*   SEE **thingamabob.**
thingumajig   *noun*   SEE **thingamajig.**
think   *verb*
  1. To use the powers of the mind, as in conceiving   **1.** *Syns:* cerebrate, cogitate, ratiocinate,
     ideas, drawing inferences, and making judgments: reflect, speculate. —*Idioms* put on one's
     took time and thought carefully before answering.   thinking cap, use one's head.
                                                                    Near-syns: consider, contemplate,
                                                                    deliberate, meditate, muse, ponder.
  2. To use the faculty of reason.   **2.** REASON *verb.*
  3. To have an opinion.   **3.** BELIEVE.
  4. To form mental images of.   **4.** IMAGINE.
  5. To view in a certain way.   **5.** FEEL *verb.*
  6. To regard or be regarded in an appraising way.   **6.** REPUTE *verb.*
  7. To renew (an image or thought) in the mind.   **7.** REMEMBER.
think of   *verb*
  1. To receive (an idea) and take it into consideration.   **1.** HEAR OF at **hear.**
  2. To renew (an image or thought) in the mind.   **2.** REMEMBER.
  3. To care enough to keep someone in mind.   **3.** REMEMBER.
think over   *verb*
  1. To consider carefully and at length.   **1.** PONDER.
  2. To consider again, esp. with the possibility of   **2.** RECONSIDER.
     change.
  3. To think about seriously.   **3.** CONSIDER.
think through   *verb*
  To consider carefully and at length.   PONDER.
think up   *verb*
  To use ingenuity in making, developing, or achieving.   INVENT.
thinkable   *adjective*
  Capable of being anticipated, considered, or imagined.   EARTHLY.
thinker   *noun*
  1. A person who seeks reason and truth by thinking   **1.** *Syn:* philosopher.
     and meditation: *Aristotle was a great thinker.*
  2. A person of great mental ability.   **2.** MIND *noun.*
thinking   *adjective*
  Of, characterized by, or disposed to thought.   THOUGHTFUL.
think of   *verb*   SEE **think.**
think over   *verb*   SEE **think.**
think through   *verb*   SEE **think.**
think up   *verb*   SEE **think.**
third-degree   *verb*
  To question thoroughly and relentlessly to verify facts.   INTERROGATE.
thirst   *noun*
  A desire for food or drink.   APPETITE.
thirst   *verb*
  To have a greedy, obsessive desire.   LUST *verb.*
thirsting   *adjective*
  Intensely desirous or interested.   EAGER.
thirsty   *adjective*
  1. Needing or desiring drink: *The hike left us hungry*   **1.** *Syns:* athirst, dry, parched.
     and thirsty.
  2. Intensely desirous or interested.   **2.** EAGER.
  3. Having little or no precipitation.   **3.** DRY *adjective.*
thistly   *adjective*
  Full of sharp, needlelike protuberances.   THORNY.

thorn *noun*
1. One that makes another totally miserable by causing sharp pain and irritation: *His wife had been a thorn in his life for many years.*
2. A sharp, pointed object.

1. **Syns:** pain, trial. —*Idioms* pain in the neck, pea in the shoe, thorn in the flesh (*or* side).
2. PRICK *noun*.

thorn *verb*
To trouble the nerves or peace of mind of, esp. by repeated vexations.

ANNOY.

thorny *adjective*
1. Full of sharp, needlelike protuberances: *a thorny shrub; a thorny marine animal.*
2. So replete with interlocking points and complications as to be painfully irritating: *the thorny problems of energy and inflation.*

1. **Syns:** briery (*also* briary), echinate, prickly, spiny, thistly.
2. **Syns:** nettlesome, prickly, spiny, vexatious. —*Idiom* set with thorns.
Near-syns: complicated, difficult, intricate, perplexing, troublesome, trying.

thorough *adjective*
1. Covering all aspects with painstaking accuracy: *a thorough physical examination; a thorough search.*

2. Characterized by attention to detail.
3. Completely such, without qualification or exception.

1. **Syns:** all-out, complete, exhaustive, full-dress, intensive, thoroughgoing, thoroughpaced, whole-hog (*Slang*).
2. DETAILED.
3. UTTER[2].

thoroughbred *adjective*
1. Of pure breeding stock: *thoroughbred horses.*

2. Of high birth or social position.

1. **Syns:** full-blooded, highbred, pureblooded, purebred.
2. NOBLE.

thoroughfare *noun*
A course affording passage from one place to another.

WAY.

thoroughgoing *adjective*
1. Covering all aspects with painstaking accuracy.
2. Completely such, without qualification or exception.

1. THOROUGH.
2. UTTER[2].

thoroughness *noun*
Attentiveness to detail: *edited the manuscript with great thoroughness.*

Syns: care, meticulousness, pains, painstaking, scrupulousness.

thoroughpaced *adjective*
Covering all aspects with painstaking accuracy.

THOROUGH.

thought *noun*
1. The act or process of thinking: *gave the matter much thought before reaching a decision.*

2. That which exists in the mind as the product of careful mental activity.

1. **Syns:** brainwork, cerebration, cogitation, deliberation, meditation, reflection, rumination, speculation.
2. IDEA.

thoughtful *adjective*
1. Of, characterized by, or disposed to thought: *a quiet, thoughtful child; a thoughtful pause before she began to play the music.*

1. **Syns:** cogitative, contemplative, deliberative, meditative, museful, pensive, reflective, ruminative, speculative, thinking. —*Idiom* in a brown study.
Near-ants: dull, empty-headed, inane, irrational, stupid, unthinking, vacuous.
Ant: thoughtless.

2. Appealing to or engaging the intellect.
3. Tending toward awareness and appreciation.
4. Full of polite concern for the well-being of others.

2. INTELLECTUAL *adjective*.
3. MINDFUL.
4. ATTENTIVE.

thoughtfulness *noun*
Thoughtful attention.

CONSIDERATION.

thoughtless *adjective*
1. Devoid of consideration for others' feelings: *a thoughtless person; a thoughtless remark.*

1. **Syns:** inconsiderate, ungracious, unthinking, unthoughtful.
Near-syns: careless, foolish, imprudent, impulsive, injudicious.
Ant: considerate.

2. Lacking or marked by a lack of care.

2. CARELESS.

thoughtlessness *noun*
1. A lack of consideration for others' feelings: *The thoughtlessness of his behavior is appalling.*
2. A careless, often reckless disregard for consequences.

1. *Syns:* disregard, inconsiderateness, inconsideration, unthoughtfulness.
2. ABANDON *noun*.

thought-out *adjective*
Resulting from deliberation and careful thought.

ADVISED.

thraldom *noun*

SEE **thralldom.**

thrall *noun*
A state of subjugation to an owner or master.

SLAVERY.

thralldom or **thraldom** *noun*
A state of subjugation to an owner or master.

SLAVERY.

thrash *verb*
1. To swing about or strike at wildly: *The wounded shark thrashed in the water. The delirious child thrashed about in his sleep.*
2. To hit heavily and repeatedly.
3. To punish with blows or lashes.
4. To win a victory over, as in battle or a competition.
5. To render totally ineffective by decisive defeat.
6. To beat (plants) with a machine or by hand to separate the grain from the straw: *thrashed the wheat.*

1. *Syns:* flail, thresh, toss. —*Idiom* toss and turn.
2. BEAT *verb*.
3. BEAT *verb*.
4. DEFEAT *verb*.
5. OVERWHELM.
6. *Syn:* thresh.

thrash out *verb*
To speak together and exchange ideas and opinions about.

DISCUSS.

thrashing *noun*
1. A punishment dealt with blows or lashes.
2. The act of defeating or the condition of being defeated.
3. A severe defeat.

1. BEATING.
2. DEFEAT *noun*.
3. TROUNCING.

thrash out *verb*

SEE **thrash.**

thread *noun*
1. A very fine, continuous strand: *polyester thread; threads trailing behind the tropical fish.*
2. Something drawn or spun out like a fine, continuous filament: *tried to follow the thread of the plot; lost the thread of the conversation.*

1. *Syns:* fiber, fibril (*also* fibrilla), filament.
2. *Syns:* skein, strand.

thread *verb*
To put (objects) onto a fine, continuous filament: *beads threaded into a necklace.*

Syn: string.

threadbare *adjective*
1. Showing signs of wear and tear or neglect.
2. Without freshness or appeal due to overuse.

1. SHABBY.
2. TRITE.

threads *noun*
Slang. Articles worn to cover the body.

DRESS *noun*.

threat *noun*
1. An expression of the intent to hurt or punish another: *The loan shark used threats of hideous beatings to collect his due.*
2. An indication of impending danger or harm: *the threat of a recession.*
3. One regarded as an imminent danger: *considered the other woman a threat to the marriage; felt that Soviet military presence in the Middle East was a threat to the oil fields.*

1. *Syns:* intimidation, menace.
2. *Syns:* forewarning, thundercloud. —*Idioms* gathering clouds, storm clouds.
3. *Syn:* menace. —*Idioms* clear and present danger, sword of Damocles.

threaten *verb*
1. To give warning signs of (impending peril): *economic indicators threatening recession. The company threatens to go under.*
2. To domineer or drive into compliance by the use of threats, force, etc.
3. To be imminent: *Civil Defense has announced that a typhoon threatens.*

threatening *adjective*
Expressing, indicating, or warning of an impending danger or misfortune: *gave me a threatening look; a threatening letter; threatening clouds.*

threesome *noun*
A group of three individuals.

thresh *verb*
1. To beat (plants) with a machine or by hand to separate the grain from the straw.
2. To swing about or strike at wildly.

threshold *noun*
A transitional interval beyond which some new action or different state of affairs is likely to begin or occur.

thrift *noun*
Careful use of material resources.

thriftiness *noun*
Careful use of material resources.

thriftless *adjective*
Reckless esp. in the use of material resources.

thrifty *adjective*
Careful in the use of material resources.

thrill *noun*
1. A strong, pleasant feeling of excitement or stimulation: *got a thrill out of bobsledding.*

2. A nervous shaking of the body.
thrill *verb*
To move or excite greatly.

thrilled *adjective*
Feeling a very strong emotion: *too thrilled by the day's events to sleep.*

thrive *verb*
1. To fare well.
2. To grow rapidly and luxuriantly.

thriving *adjective*
Improving, growing, or succeeding steadily.

throb *verb*
To make rhythmic contractions, sounds, or movements.
throb *noun*
A periodic contraction or sound of something coursing.

throe *noun*
1. A violent, excruciating seizure of pain: *the throes of a heart attack.*
2. A sensation of physical discomfort occurring as the result of disease or injury.
3. A condition of anguished struggle and disorder: *Lebanon is in the throes of a devastating civil war.*

throng *noun*
An enormous number of persons gathered together.
throng *verb*
To come or go in large numbers.

---

1. *Syns:* forebode, forewarn.

2. INTIMIDATE.

3. *Syns:* hang (over), impend, loom, lower[1] (*also* lour), menace, overhang.

Syns: menacing, minatory, overhanging.
Near-syns: approaching, brewing, imminent, impending, ominous.

TRIO.

1. THRASH.

2. THRASH.

VERGE *noun.*

ECONOMY.

ECONOMY.

IMPROVIDENT.

ECONOMICAL.

1. *Syns:* bang (*Slang*), boot[1], high (*Slang*), kick (*Slang*), lift, wallop (*Informal*).

2. TREMOR *noun.*

CARRY AWAY at **carry.**

Syns: atingle, excited, fired up, turned-on (*Slang*), worked up.

1. PROSPER.
2. FLOURISH.

FLOURISHING.

BEAT *verb.*

BEAT *noun.*

1. *Syns:* grip, paroxysm, spasm.

2. PAIN *noun.*

3. *Syns:* convulsion, paroxysm.

CROWD *noun.*

POUR.

throttle *verb*
1. To interfere with or stop the normal breathing of, esp. by constricting the windpipe.
2. To hold (something requiring an outlet) in check.

1. CHOKE *verb*.
2. REPRESS.

throttling *noun*
The act of restraining forcefully.

REPRESSION.

through *adverb*
1. From one end to the other: *worked furiously the whole day through.*
2. To an end or conclusion: *Let's see this thing through.*

1. *Syns:* around, over, round, throughout.
2. *Syn:* over.

through *adjective*
1. Proceeding or lying in an uninterrupted line or course.
2. Having reached completion.
3. No longer effective, capable, or valuable: *He's through as a ballplayer.*

4. Having no further relationship: *You and I are through.*

1. DIRECT *adjective*.
2. COMPLETE *adjective*.
3. *Syns:* done, done for, finished, kaput (*Slang*), washed-up. —*Idioms* at the end of the road (*or* line), over the hill, past one's prime.
4. *Syns:* done, finished, washed-up.

throughout *adverb*
From one end to the other.

THROUGH *adverb*.

throw *verb*
1. To send through the air with a motion of the hand or arm: *threw the ball to the catcher.*

1. *Syns:* cast, fire, fling, heave, hurl, pitch, shy^2, sling, toss.
Near-syns: drive, flick, flip, impel, propel, shoot, thrust.
Ant: catch.

2. To send out heat, light, or energy.
3. To cause to fall, as from a shot or blow.
4. To cause to be unclear in mind or intent.
5. To put (a mechanical device or process) in motion by releasing an activating mechanism.

2. SHED.
3. DROP *verb*.
4. CONFUSE.
5. TRIP *verb*.

throw away *verb*
1. To let go or get rid of as being no longer of use, value, etc.
2. To spend (money) excessively and usu. foolishly.

1. DISCARD.
2. WASTE *verb*.

throw off *verb*
1. To discharge material, as vapor or fumes, usu. suddenly and violently.
2. To free from something objectionable or undesirable.
3. To get away from (a pursuer).
4. To cast off by natural process.

1. EMIT.
2. RID.
3. LOSE.
4. SHED.

throw out *verb*
1. To let go or get rid of as being no longer of use, value, etc.
2. To put out by force.
3. To displace (a bone) from a socket or joint.

1. DISCARD.
2. EJECT.
3. SLIP *verb*.

throw over *verb*
To give up without intending to return or claim again.

ABANDON *verb*.

throw *noun*
An act of throwing: *a throw of 60 feet.*

Syns: cast, fling, heave (*Informal*), hurl, pitch, shy^2, sling, toss.

throw away *verb*
throw off *verb*
throw out *verb*
throw over *verb*

SEE **throw.**
SEE **throw.**
SEE **throw.**
SEE **throw.**

thrust *noun*
1. The thread or current of thought uniting or

1. *Syns:* aim, drift, intent, purport,

occurring in all the elements of a text or discourse: *the socialistic thrust of the new policy statement.*

substance, tendency, tenor.
Near-syns: core, crux, essence, gist, meat, pith, sense.

2. An act or instance of using force so as to propel ahead.

2. PUSH *noun.*

thrust *verb*
1. To force to move or advance with or as if with blows or pressure.
2. To cause to penetrate with force.
3. To cause to stick out.

1. DRIVE *verb.*

2. RAM.

3. POKE *verb.*

thud *verb*
To make a dull sound by or as if by striking a surface with a heavy object: *horses' hoofs thudding down the cobblestone street.*

Syns: clomp, clump, clunk.

thug *noun*
A person who treats others violently and roughly, esp. for hire: *The mobster sent his thugs to teach the welsher a lesson.*

Syns: ape (*Slang*), goon (*Slang*), gorilla (*Slang*), hood (*Slang*), hoodlum, hooligan, ruffian.
Near-syns: bully, gangster, gunman, mobster, punk, rowdy, tough.

thumb *verb*
To look through reading matter casually.

BROWSE.

thump *noun*
A repeated stroke or blow, esp. one that produces a sound.

BEAT *noun.*

thunder *noun*
An earsplitting, explosive noise.

BLAST *noun.*

thunder *verb*
To make an earsplitting, explosive noise.

BLAST *verb.*

thundercloud *noun*
An indication of impending danger or harm.

THREAT.

thunderstruck *adjective*
Overcome with intense feeling, as of amazement, horror, or dismay.

SHOCKED.

thwack *noun*
A sudden sharp, powerful stroke.

BLOW[2].

thwart *verb*
To prevent from accomplishing a purpose.

FRUSTRATE.

thwart *adjective*
Situated or lying across.

TRANSVERSE.

tic *noun*
A nervous shaking of the body.

TREMOR *noun.*

tick *noun*
Brit. Informal. A very brief time.

FLASH *noun.*

tick off *verb*
To name or specify one by one.

ENUMERATE.

ticker *noun*
Slang. The circulatory organ of the body.

HEART.

ticket *noun*
1. An identifying or descriptive slip: *a price ticket.*
2. A list of candidates proposed or endorsed by a political party: *the Republican state ticket.*
3. A means or method of entering into or achieving something desirable: *Hard work is the ticket to success.*

1. ***Syns:*** label, marker, tag.
2. ***Syns:*** line-up (*also* lineup), slate.

3. ***Syns:*** key, route, secret.

ticket *verb*
To attach a ticket to: *She's ticketing the new merchandise.*

Syns: label, tag.

tickle *verb*
To give great or keen pleasure to.

DELIGHT *verb.*

tickled   *adjective*
Eagerly compliant.   GLAD.

ticklish   *adjective*
1. Following no predictable pattern.   1. CAPRICIOUS.
2. Requiring great tact or skill.   2. DELICATE.

tick off   *verb*   SEE **tick.**

tidbit   *noun*
Something fine and delicious, esp. a food.   DELICACY.

tide   *noun*
Something suggestive of running water.   FLOW *noun.*

tidings   *noun*
New information, esp. about recent events and   NEWS.
happenings.

tidy   *verb*
1. To make or keep (an area) clean and orderly: *tidied*   1. **Syns:** clean (up), clear (up), neaten,
   the room for weekend houseguests.   police, spruce (up), straighten (up).
2. To make neat and trim; make presentable: *used*   2. **Syns:** freshen (up), groom, neaten,
   their bathroom in order to tidy up.   spruce (up), trig (up *or* out), trim.

tidy   *adjective*
1. In good order or clean condition.   1. NEAT.
2. *Informal.* Of moderately good quality but less than   2. ACCEPTABLE.
   excellent.
3. *Informal.* Notably above average in amount, size, or   3. BIG.
   scope.

tie   *verb*
1. To make fast or firmly fixed by means of a cord,   1. **Syns:** bind, fasten, knot, secure, tie up.
   rope, etc.: *tied the package with twine; tied her shoes.*   **Near-syns:** attach, join, link; anchor,
                                                                           moor.
                                                                           Ant: untie.
2. To do or make something equal to.   2. EQUAL *verb.*

tie down   *verb*
To restrict the activity or free movement of.   HAMPER.

tie   *noun*
1. That which unites or binds.   1. BOND *noun.*
2. The condition of being closely tied to another by   2. ATTACHMENT.
   affection or faith.
3. An equality of scores, votes, or performances in a   3. **Syns:** deadlock, draw, stalemate, stand-
   contest: *The teams played to a tie. The first game*   off. —*Idiom* dead heat.
   was a tie.

tie down   *verb*   SEE **tie.**

tie-in   *noun*
A logical or natural association between two or more   RELATION.
things.

tier   *noun*
1. A group of people or things arranged in a row.   1. LINE *noun.*
2. A division of persons or things by quality, rank, or   2. CLASS *noun.*
   grade.

tie-up   *noun*   SEE **tie up.**

tie up   *verb*
1. To cause to cease regular activity: *a wreck that tied*   1. **Syns:** idle, immobilize, stop. —*Idiom*
   up traffic.   bring to a screeching halt.
2. To make fast or firmly fixed by means of a cord,   2. TIE *verb.*
   rope, etc.
3. To cause to be busy or in use: *He's tied up until*   3. **Syns:** engage, monopolize, occupy, pre-
   noon. All the office telephones were tied up.   empt (*also* preempt).

tie-up   *noun*
A cessation of normal activity caused by an accident,   **Syn:** stoppage.
strike, etc.: *a traffic tie-up.*

tiff   *noun*
A discussion, often heated, in which a difference of   ARGUMENT.
opinion is expressed.

tiff *verb*
To engage in a quarrel.   ARGUE.

tiger *noun*
A perversely bad, cruel, or wicked person.   FIEND.

tight *adjective*
1. Hard to deal with or get out of: *in a tight spot.*
                                      1. **Syns:** rough, sticky, tricky.
                                        Near-syns: arduous, critical, difficult,
                                        distressing, tense, trying.
2. Having all parts near to each other.   2. THICK.
3. Nearly equivalent or even.   3. CLOSE[1] *adjective.*
4. Stretched tightly.   4. TAUT.
5. Affording little room for movement: *tight quarters.*   5. **Syns:** close[1], confining, cramped,
                                        crowded, narrow.
6. Persistently holding to something: *a tight embrace.*   6. **Syns:** fast, firm[1], secure, tenacious.
7. *Slang.* Very closely associated.   7. FAMILIAR *adjective.*
8. Ungenerously or pettily reluctant to spend money.   8. STINGY.
9. *Slang.* Intoxicated with alcoholic liquor.   9. DRUNK *adjective.*
10. Characterized by an economy of artistic expression: 10. **Syns:** compact[1], lean[2], spare.
    a tight writing style.
11. *Regional.* In good order or clean condition.   11. NEAT.
12. *Slang.* Based on good judgment, reasoning, or   12. SOUND[2].
    evidence.

tighten *verb*
1. To make or become tight or tighter: *tightened wage*   1. **Syns:** reinforce, strengthen.
    and price controls.
2. To make or become tense.   2. TENSE *verb.*

tightfisted *adjective*
Ungenerously or pettily reluctant to spend money.   STINGY.

tight-laced *adjective*
Marked by excessive concern for propriety and good   GENTEEL.
form.

tight-lipped *adjective*
1. Not speaking freely or openly.   1. TACITURN.
2. Temporarily unable or unwilling to speak, as from   2. SPEECHLESS.
    shock or fear.

tightwad *noun*
Slang. A stingy person.   MISER.

till *verb*
To prepare (soil) for the planting and raising of crops: **Syns:** cultivate, culture, dress, labor
farmers tilling their fields.   (*Archaic*), tend[2], work.
                                          Near-syns: harrow, hoe, mulch, plant,
                                          plow, sow, turn.

tilt *noun*
1. Any competition or test of opposing wills likened to   1. **Syns:** joust, tournament, tourney.
    the sport in which knights fought with lances: *her*
    frequent legal tilts with corporate management.
2. Deviation from a particular direction.   2. INCLINATION.

tilt *verb*
1. To depart or cause to depart from true vertical or   1. INCLINE.
    horizontal.
2. To lean suddenly, unsteadily, and erratically from   2. LURCH *verb.*
    the vertical axis.
3. To strive in opposition to.   3. CONTEND.

tilted *adjective*
Departing from true vertical or horizontal.   INCLINED.

tilting *adjective*
Departing from true vertical or horizontal.   INCLINED.

timber *noun*
1. A large, oblong piece of wood or other material, used   1. BEAM *noun.*
    esp. for construction.

2. The basic substance or essential elements of character that qualify a person for a specified role: *Without doubt she's presidential timber.*   **2. *Syns:*** material, stuff.

timbre *noun*
A sound of distinct pitch and quality.   TONE.

time *noun*
1. A term of service, as in the military or in prison: *put in his time in the army; did time for armed robbery.*   **1. *Syns:*** hitch, stretch.
2. The general point at which an event occurs.   **2.** OCCASION *noun.*
3. A particular time notable for its distinctive characteristics.   **3.** AGE *noun.*
4. A rather short period.   **4.** BIT[1] *noun.*
5. A limited, often assigned period of activity, duty, or opportunity.   **5.** TURN *noun.*
6. A limited or specific period of time during which something happens, lasts, or extends.   **6.** TERM *noun.*
7. A span designated for a given activity: *harvest time.*   **7. *Syns:*** period, season.

time *verb*
1. To set the time for (an event or occasion): *timed her absence so as not to interrupt our progress.*   **1. *Syn:*** schedule.
2. To record the speed or duration of: *timed the horse's workouts; timed the television show.*   **2. *Syn:*** clock.

time(s) *noun*
A particular time notable for its distinctive characteristics.   AGE *noun.*

time-honored *adjective*
Adhering to beliefs or practices approved by authority or tradition.   ORTHODOX.

timeless *adjective*
1. Existing unchanged forever.   **1.** AGELESS.
2. Existing or occurring without interruption or end.   **2.** CONTINUAL.

timely *adjective*
1. Occurring at a fitting or advantageous time.   **1.** OPPORTUNE.
2. Occurring, acting, or performed exactly at the time appointed.   **2.** PUNCTUAL.

time-out *noun*
A pause or interval, as from work or duty.   BREAK *noun.*

timetable *noun*
An organized list of procedures, activities, events, etc.   PROGRAM.

timeworn *adjective*
1. Belonging to, existing, or occurring in times long past.   **1.** OLD.
2. Without freshness or appeal due to overuse.   **2.** TRITE.

timid *adjective*
1. Reticent or reserved in manner.   **1.** MODEST.
2. Given to or exhibiting hesitation.   **2.** HESITANT.

tincture *noun*
Something that imparts color.   COLOR *noun.*

tinge *noun*
1. The degree of vividness of a color, as when modified by the addition of black or white pigment.   **1.** SHADE *noun.*
2. A shade of a color, esp. a pale or delicate variation.   **2.** TINT *noun.*
3. A slight amount.   **3.** SHADE *noun.*

tinker *verb*
1. To move one's fingers or hands in a nervous or aimless fashion.   **1.** FIDDLE.
2. To handle something idly, ignorantly, or destructively.   **2.** TAMPER.

tinsel *adjective*
Tastelessly showy.   GAUDY.

tint *noun*
1. A shade of a color, esp. a pale or delicate variation: *a tint of red in her hair.*
2. The degree of vividness of a color, as when modified by the addition of black or white pigment.

tint *verb*
To impart color to.

tintinnabulate *verb*
Rare. To give forth or cause to give forth a clear, resonant sound.

tiny *adjective*
Extremely small: *a tiny speck of soot in her eye.*

1. *Syns:* cast, hue, tinge, tone.
2. SHADE *noun.*

COLOR *verb.*

RING[2].

Syns: diminutive, dwarf, lilliputian, midget, miniature, minute, peewee, pint-size (*also* pint-sized), pygmy (*also* pigmy), teeny (*also* teensy), wee, weeny (*Informal*).
Near-ants: colossal, enormous, gargantuan, gigantic, immense, mammoth, vast.
Ant: huge.

tip[1] *noun*
A sharp or tapered end.

tip[2] *verb*
To depart or cause to depart from true vertical or horizontal.

tip[3] *noun*
1. An item of advance or inside information given as a guide to action: *a tip on the stock market; gave her a tip that she should buy gold ingots.*
2. A material favor or gift, usu. money, given in return for service.

tip-off *noun*
Informal. An item of advance or inside information given as a guide to action.

tipped *adjective*
Departing from true vertical or horizontal.

tipple *verb*
To take alcoholic liquor, esp. excessively or habitually.

tippler *noun*
A person who is habitually drunk.

tipster *noun*
One who gives incriminating information about others.

tipsy *adjective*
Slang. Intoxicated with alcoholic liquor.

tiptop *adjective*
Exceptionally good of its kind.

tirade *noun*
A long, violent, or blustering speech, usu. of censure or denunciation: *had to listen to her father's frequent tirades.*

POINT *noun.*

INCLINE *verb.*

1. *Syns:* pointer, steer, tip-off (*Informal*).
   Near-syns: clue, cue, forecast, hint, prediction.
2. GRATUITY.

TIP[3] *noun.*

INCLINED.

DRINK *verb.*

DRUNKARD.

INFORMER.

DRUNK *adjective.*

EXCELLENT.

Syns: diatribe, fulmination, harangue, jeremiad, obloquy, philippic.
Near-syns: abuse, censure, condemnation, denunciation, invective, vituperation; lecture, sermon.

tire *verb*
1. To diminish the strength and energy of.
2. To fatigue with dullness or tedium.

tired *adjective*
1. Without freshness or appeal due to overuse.
2. Out of patience with.

tiredness *noun*
The condition of being extremely tired.

1. FATIGUE *verb.*
2. BORE *verb.*

1. TRITE.
2. SICK.

EXHAUSTION.

tired out   *adjective*
Extremely tired.   EXHAUSTED.

tireless   *adjective*
Having or showing a capacity for protracted effort,   ***Syns:*** indefatigable, inexhaustible,
regardless of difficulty or frustration: *tireless efforts to*   unflagging, untiring, weariless.
resolve the labor dispute.   ***Near-ants:*** inactive, languid, listless, tired,
                                                        unenthusiastic.

tire out   *verb*
To make extremely tired.   EXHAUST.

tiresome   *adjective*
Arousing no interest or curiosity.   BORING.

tiring   *adjective*
   1. Causing fatigue: *a long, tiring walk; an*   1. ***Syns:*** exhausting, fatiguing, taxing,
      extraordinarily lengthy and tiring lecture on   wearying.
      entomology.
   2. Arousing no interest or curiosity.   2. BORING.

tissue   *noun*
A group of things that are linked or interconnected as WEB *noun.*
if by weaving.

titan   *noun*
One that is extraordinarily large and powerful.   GIANT *noun.*
   titan   *adjective*
Of extraordinary size and power.   GIANT *adjective.*

titanic   *adjective*
Of extraordinary size and power.   GIANT *adjective.*

title   *noun*
   1. A right or legal share in something.   1. INTEREST *noun.*
   2. Legal right to the possession of a thing.   2. OWNERSHIP.
   3. A legitimate or supposed right to demand something   3. CLAIM *noun.*
      as one's rightful due.
   4. The fact of possessing.   4. POSSESSION.
   5. An issue of printed material offered for sale or 5. PUBLICATION.
      distribution.
   title   *verb*
To give a name or title to.   NAME *verb.*

titter   *verb*
To laugh in a stifled way.   GIGGLE *verb.*
   titter   *noun*
A stifled laugh.   GIGGLE *noun.*

tittle   *noun*
A tiny amount.   BIT[1].

tittle-tattle   *noun*
Idle, often sensational and groundless talk about   GOSSIP *noun.*
others.
   tittle-tattle   *verb*
To engage in or spread gossip.   GOSSIP *verb.*

tizzy   *noun*
Slang. A condition of excited distress.   STATE *noun.*

to-and-fro   *noun*
The act or an instance of hesitating.   HESITATION.

toast   *noun*
The act of drinking to someone: *He proposed a toast to*   ***Syn:*** pledge.
the queen's health.
   toast   *verb*
To salute by raising and drinking from a glass.   DRINK *verb.*

tocsin   *noun*
A signal that warns of imminent danger.   ALARM *noun.*

today   *adverb*
At the present; these days.   NOW *adverb.*
   today   *noun*
The current time.   NOW *noun.*

to-do *noun*
1. *Informal.* An interruption of regular procedure or of public peace.
2. *Informal.* Busy and useless activity.
3. *Informal.* A condition of intense public interest or excitement.

1. DISTURBANCE.
2. FUSS *noun.*
3. SENSATION.

tog *verb*
Informal. To put clothes on.

DRESS *verb.*

tog out *verb*
Informal. To dress in formal or special clothing.

DRESS UP at **dress.**

tog up *verb*
Informal. To dress in formal or special clothing.

DRESS UP at **dress.**

together *adverb*
1. In, into, or as a single body: *six people singing together in perfect harmony.*

2. At the same time: *The bells rang out together.*

1. *Syns:* ensemble (*French*), jointly.
   —*Idioms* as one, in one breath, in the same breath, in unison, with one accord, with one voice.
2. *Syns:* concurrently, simultaneously, synchronously. —*Idioms* all at once, all together.

together *adjective*
Slang. In a state of preparedness.

READY *adjective.*

tog out *verb*

SEE **tog.**

togs *noun*
Informal. Articles worn to cover the body.

DRESS *noun.*

tog up *verb*

SEE **tog.**

toil *verb*
1. To exert one's mental or physical powers, usu. under difficulty and to the point of exhaustion.
2. To do tedious, laborious, and sometimes menial work.
3. To walk heavily, slowly, and with difficulty.

1. LABOR *verb.*
2. GRIND *verb.*
3. PLOD.

toil *noun*
Physical exertion that is usu. difficult and exhausting.

LABOR *noun.*

toilworn *adjective*
Pale and exhausted because of worry, sleeplessness, etc.

HAGGARD.

token *noun*
1. Something that takes the place of words in communicating a thought or feeling.
2. Something given to guarantee the repayment of a loan or the fulfillment of an obligation.
3. Something that causes one to remember.
4. Something visible or evident that gives grounds for believing in the existence or presence of something else.

1. EXPRESSION.
2. PAWN[1] *noun.*
3. REMEMBRANCE.
4. SIGN *noun.*

tolerable *adjective*
1. Of moderately good quality but less than excellent.
2. Capable of being tolerated.

1. ACCEPTABLE.
2. BEARABLE.

tolerance *noun*
Forbearing or lenient treatment: *an unintentional mistake that deserved tolerance.*

Syns: charitableness, charity, forbearance, indulgence, leniency (*also* lenience), toleration.
Near-ants: bigotry, dogmatism, narrow-mindedness, prejudice, provincialism.
Ant: intolerance.

tolerant *adjective*
1. Not strict or severe: *tolerant and understanding parents.*

2. Not narrow or conservative in thought, expression, or conduct.

1. *Syns:* charitable, clement, easy, forbearant (*Archaic*), forbearing, indulgent, lax, lenient, merciful, soft.
2. BROAD.

tolerate *verb*
1. To put up with.
2. To neither forbid nor prevent.

1. ENDURE.
2. PERMIT *verb*.

toleration *noun*
Forbearing or lenient treatment.

TOLERANCE.

toll[1] *noun*
1. A fixed amount of money charged for a privilege or service: *a toll of 50¢ to use the new bridge.*
2. A loss sustained in the accomplishment of or as the result of something.

1. *Syns:* charge, exaction, fee.

2. COST *noun*.

toll[2] *verb*
To give forth or cause to give forth a clear, resonant sound.

RING[2].

tomb *noun*
A burial place or receptacle for human remains.

GRAVE[1].

tome *noun*
A printed and bound work.

BOOK *noun*.

tomfool *noun*
One deficient in judgment and good sense.

FOOL *noun*.

tomfool *adjective*
So senseless as to be laughable.

FOOLISH.

tomfoolery *noun*
1. Foolish behavior.
2. Something that does not have or make sense.
3. A mischievous act.

1. FOOLISHNESS.
2. NONSENSE.
3. PRANK.

tommyrot *noun*
Informal. Something that does not have or make sense.

NONSENSE.

ton *noun*
The current custom.

FASHION *noun*.

tonality *noun*
A sound of distinct pitch and quality.

TONE.

tone *noun*
1. A sound of distinct pitch and quality: *the unmistakable tone of a violin.*
2. A particular vocal quality that indicates some emotion or feeling: *asked in an angry tone why I had gone.*
3. The property by which the sense of vision can distinguish between objects, as a red apple and a green apple, that are very similar or identical in form and size.
4. A shade of a color, esp. a pale or delicate variation.
5. A prevailing quality, as of thought, behavior, or attitude.
6. A general impression produced by a predominant quality or characteristic.

1. *Syns:* timbre, tonality. —*Idiom* tone color.
2. *Syns:* accent, inflection, intonation. —*Idiom* tone of voice.

3. COLOR *noun*.

4. TINT *noun*.
5. TEMPER *noun*.

6. AIR *noun*.

tone down *verb*
1. To make or become less severe or extreme.
2. To make less emphatic or obvious.

1. MODERATE *verb*.
2. SOFT-PEDAL.

tone down *verb*

SEE **tone.**

toney *adjective*

SEE **tony.**

tongue *noun*
A system of terms used by a people sharing a history and culture.

LANGUAGE.

tongue-lash *verb*
To reprimand loudly or harshly.

BAWL OUT at **bawl.**

tonic *noun*
A medicine that restores or increases vigor: *a spring tonic of sulfur and molasses.*

Syns: bracer, pick-me-up (*Informal*), restorative, roborant.

tonic *adjective*

Producing or stimulating physical, mental, or emotional vigor: *The mountain air proved very tonic.*

Syns: bracing, energizing, invigorating, refreshing, reinvigorating, renewing, restorative, roborant, stimulating. *Near-ants:* debilitating, enervating, enfeebling, exhausting, sapping.

tonish *adjective*
Being or in accordance with the current fashion.   FASHIONABLE.

tony also **toney** *adjective*
Being or in accordance with the current fashion.   FASHIONABLE.

tool *noun*
1. A device used to do work or perform a task: *the tools needed to repair a car.*
2. A person who is easily deceived or victimized.
3. A person used or controlled by others.

1. *Syns:* implement, instrument, utensil.
2. DUPE *noun.*
3. PAWN[2].

tool *verb*
Informal. To run and control (a motor vehicle).   DRIVE *verb.*

toothsome *adjective*
Highly pleasing, esp. to the sense of taste.   DELICIOUS.

top *noun*
1. The highest point.
2. The outer layer covering something.
3. That which is superlative.

1. HEIGHT.
2. FACE *noun.*
3. BEST *noun.*

top *adjective*
1. Of, being, located at, or forming the top: *the top shelf; typing at top speed.*
2. Exceptionally good of its kind.
3. Most important, influential, or significant.
4. Greatest in quantity or highest in degree that has been or can be attained.

1. *Syns:* highest, loftiest, topmost, uppermost.
2. EXCELLENT.
3. PRIMARY.
4. MAXIMUM *adjective.*

top *verb*
1. To put a topping on: *Top the sundae with a cherry.*
2. To be greater or better than.

1. *Syns:* cap, crown, top off.
2. SURPASS.

top off *verb*
1. To reach or bring to a climax.
2. To put a topping on.

1. CLIMAX *verb.*
2. TOP *verb.*

top-drawer *adjective*
Informal. Pre-eminent in rank or position.   HIGHEST.

topflight *adjective*
Exceptionally good of its kind.   EXCELLENT.

topic *noun*
What a speech, piece of writing, or artistic work is about.   SUBJECT *noun.*

topical *adjective*
Of, constituting, or relating to a theme or themes.   THEMATIC.

topmost *adjective*
1. Of, being, located at, or forming the top.
2. Greatest in quantity or highest in degree that has been or can be attained.

1. TOP *adjective.*
2. MAXIMUM *adjective.*

topnotch *adjective*
Informal. Exceptionally good of its kind.   EXCELLENT.

top off *verb*   SEE **top.**

topography *noun*
The character, natural features, and configuration of land.   TERRAIN.

topple *verb*
1. To turn or cause to turn from a vertical or horizontal position.
2. To come to the ground suddenly and involuntarily.
3. To undergo capture, defeat, or ruin.
4. To bring about the downfall of.

1. OVERTURN.
2. FALL *verb.*
3. SURRENDER.
4. OVERTHROW.

toppling *noun*
A disastrous, overwhelming defeat or ruin.   FALL *noun.*

top-quality *adjective*
Of fine quality.   CHOICE *adjective.*

top-ranking *adjective*
Pre-eminent in rank or position.   HIGHEST.

topsy-turviness *noun*
A lack of order or regular arrangement.   DISORDER *noun.*

topsy-turvy *adjective*
Characterized by physical confusion.   CONFUSED.

torch *verb*
Slang. To cause to burn or undergo combustion.   LIGHT[1] *verb.*

torment *verb*
1. To bring great harm or suffering to.   1. AFFLICT.
2. To subject (another) to extreme physical cruelty, as   2. TORTURE *verb.*
   in punishing.
3. To recur to continually.   3. HAUNT *verb.*
4. To excite (another) by exposing something desirable   4. TANTALIZE.
   while keeping it out of reach.

torment *noun*
Excruciating punishment.   HELL *noun.*

tormenting *adjective*
Extraordinarily painful or distressing: *a tormenting*   **Syns:** agonizing, excruciating, harrowing,
wait outside the operating room.   torturous.
                                                             Near-syns: racking, tearing; piercing,
                                                             sharp, shooting, stabbing.

torpedo *verb*
To cause the complete ruin or wreckage of.   DESTROY.

torpid *adjective*
Lacking mental and physical alertness and activity.   LETHARGIC.

torpidity *noun*
A deficiency in mental and physical alertness and   LETHARGY.
activity.

torpidness *noun*
A deficiency in mental and physical alertness and   LETHARGY.
activity.

torpor *noun*
1. A lack of action or activity.   1. INACTION.
2. A deficiency in mental and physical alertness and   2. LETHARGY.
   activity.

torrent *noun*
An abundant, usu. overwhelming flow.   FLOOD *noun.*

torrid *adjective*
1. Marked by much heat.   1. HOT *adjective.*
2. Fired with intense feeling.   2. PASSIONATE.

torridness *noun*
Intense warmth.   HEAT *noun.*

tort *noun*
A wicked act.   CRIME.

tortuous *adjective*
1. Not taking a direct or straight line or course.   1. INDIRECT.
2. Repeatedly curving in alternate directions.   2. WINDING.

torture *verb*
1. To subject (another) to extreme physical cruelty, as   1. **Syns:** crucify, rack, torment. —*Idiom*
   in punishing: *prisoners tortured by their captors.*   put on the rack (*or* wheel).
                                                                 Near-syns: agonize, hurt, maim,
                                                                 mutilate; oppress, persecute, vilify,
                                                                 wrong.

2. To bring great harm or suffering to.   2. AFFLICT.

torture *noun*
Excruciating punishment.   HELL *noun.*

torturous   *adjective*
Extraordinarily painful or distressing.   TORMENTING.

Tory   *noun*
One who strongly favors retention of the existing order.   CONSERVATIVE *noun.*
Tory   *adjective*
Strongly favoring retention of the existing order.   CONSERVATIVE *adjective.*

toss   *verb*
1. To move vigorously from side to side or up and   1. **Syns:** heave, pitch, rock², roll.
   down: *a small boat tossed by the waves; toss in one's
   sleep.*
2. To send through the air with a motion of the hand   2. THROW *verb.*
   or arm.
3. To impair or destroy the composure of.   3. AGITATE.
4. To throw (a coin) in order to decide something: *Let's 4. **Syns:** flip, toss up. —*Idioms* call heads
   toss to see which team will kick off.*   or tails, call the coin.
5. To swing about or strike at wildly.   5. THRASH.
6. To twist and turn, as in pain, struggle, or   6. WRITHE.
   embarrassment.

toss about   *verb*
Informal. To speak together and exchange ideas and   DISCUSS.
opinions about.

toss around   *verb*
Informal. To speak together and exchange ideas and   DISCUSS.
opinions about.

toss down   *verb*
To take into the mouth and swallow (a liquid).   DRINK *verb.*

toss off   *verb*
To take into the mouth and swallow (a liquid).   DRINK *verb.*

toss up   *verb*
To throw (a coin) in order to decide something.   TOSS *verb.*

toss   *noun*
An act of throwing.   THROW *noun.*

toss about   *verb*   SEE **toss.**
toss around   *verb*   SEE **toss.**
toss down   *verb*   SEE **toss.**
toss off   *verb*   SEE **toss.**
toss up   *verb*   SEE **toss.**

tot¹   *noun*
1. A young person between birth and puberty.   1. CHILD.
2. A small amount of liquor.   2. DROP *noun.*

tot²   *verb*
To combine (figures) to form a sum.   ADD.

total   *noun*
1. A number or quantity obtained as a result of   1. **Syns:** aggregate, amount, sum,
   addition: *Losses reached a new total.*   summation, totality, tote². —*Idiom* sum
                                                              total.
2. An amount or quantity from which nothing is left   2. WHOLE *noun.*
   out or held back.

total   *adjective*
1. Including every constituent or individual.   1. WHOLE *adjective.*
2. Completely such, without qualification or exception.   2. UTTER².

total   *verb*
1. To combine (figures) to form a sum.   1. ADD.
2. To come to in number or quantity.   2. AMOUNT *verb.*
3. To cause the complete ruin or wreckage of.   3. DESTROY.

totalitarian   *noun*
An absolute ruler, esp. one who is harsh and   DICTATOR.
oppressive.

totalitarian   *adjective*
1. Characterized by or favoring absolute obedience to   1. AUTHORITARIAN *adjective.*
   authority.

2. Having and exercising complete political power and control.

2. ABSOLUTE.

totalitarianism *noun*

1. A political doctrine advocating the principle of absolute rule.

1. ABSOLUTISM.

2. Absolute power, esp. when exercised unjustly or cruelly.

2. TYRANNY.

totality *noun*

1. The state of being entirely whole.

1. COMPLETENESS.

2. A number or quantity obtained as a result of addition.

2. TOTAL *noun*.

3. An organized array of individual elements and parts forming and working as a unit.

3. SYSTEM.

4. An amount or quantity from which nothing is left out or held back.

4. WHOLE *noun*.

totalization *noun*

The act or process of adding.

ADDITION.

totalize *verb*

To combine (figures) to form a sum.

ADD.

tote¹ *verb*

Informal. To move while supporting.

CARRY.

tote² *noun*

A number or quantity obtained as a result of addition.

TOTAL *noun*.

tote *verb*

To combine (figures) to form a sum.

ADD.

tottery *adjective*

Lacking stability.

INSECURE.

touch *verb*

1. To bring into contact with, esp. by means of the hands or fingers, so as to give or receive a physical sensation: *The doctor gently touched the wound.*

1. *Syns:* feel, finger, handle, palp, palpate. *Near-syns:* caress, fondle, rub, stroke; brush, graze.

2. To bring into or make contact with.

2. CONTACT *verb*.

3. To be contiguous or next to.

3. ADJOIN.

4. To be equal or alike.

4. COMPARE.

5. To evoke a usu. strong mental or emotional response from.

5. AFFECT¹.

touch down *verb*

To come to rest on the ground.

LAND *verb*.

touch off *verb*

1. To release or cause to release energy suddenly and violently, esp. with a loud noise.

1. EXPLODE.

2. To give rise to a particular development.

2. GENERATE.

touch on (or **upon**) *verb*

To call or direct attention to (an occurrence, situation, etc.).

REFER.

touch up *verb*

To improve by making minor changes or additions: *touched up his speech to make it more lively.*

Syns: polish, retouch. *Near-syns:* improve, perfect.

touch *noun*

1. An act of touching: *felt a gentle touch on her shoulder.*

1. *Syns:* feeling, palpation.

2. The faculty or ability to perceive tactile stimulation: *the sense of touch.*

2. *Syns:* feel, feeling, tactility.

3. A particular sensation conveyed by means of physical contact: *the soft touch of velvet.*

3. *Syns:* feel, feeling.

4. A coming together so as to be touching.

4. CONTACT *noun*.

5. A situation allowing exchange of ideas or messages: *tried in vain to get in touch with her.*

5. *Syns:* communication, contact, intercommunication.

6. A barely perceivable indication of something.

6. TRACE *noun*.

7. A slight amount.

7. SHADE *noun*.

touchability *noun*
The quality or condition of being discerned by touch.   TANGIBILITY.

touchable *adjective*
Discernible by touch.   TANGIBLE.

touchableness *noun*
The quality or condition of being discerned by touch.   TANGIBILITY.

touch-and-go *adjective*
Requiring great tact or skill.   DELICATE.

touch down *verb*   SEE **touch**.

touched *adjective*
1. Emotionally aroused.   1. AFFECTED[1].
2. Afflicted with or exhibiting irrationality and mental   2. INSANE.
   unsoundness.

touching *adjective*
1. Sharing a common boundary.   1. ADJOINING.
2. Exciting a deep, usu. somber response.   2. AFFECTING.

touch off *verb*   SEE **touch**.

touch on (or **upon**) *verb*   SEE **touch**.

touchstone *noun*
A means by which individuals are compared and   STANDARD *noun*.
judged.

touch up *verb*   SEE **touch**.

touchy *adjective*
1. Requiring great tact or skill.   1. DELICATE.
2. Easily annoyed.   2. TESTY.

tough *adjective*
1. Capable of exerting considerable effort or of   1. STRONG.
   withstanding considerable stress or hardship.
2. Not easy to do, achieve, or master.   2. DIFFICULT.
3. Requiring great effort.   3. DEMANDING.
4. Imposing a severe test of bodily or spiritual   4. BURDENSOME.
   strength.
5. Rigorous and unsparing in treating others.   5. SEVERE.
6. Tenaciously unwilling to yield.   6. OBSTINATE.
7. Physically toughened so as to have great endurance.   7. HARD *adjective*.
8. Indicating or possessing determination, resolution,   8. FIRM[1].
   or persistence.
9. Marked by vigorous physical exertion.   9. ROUGH.

tough *noun*
A rough, violent person who engages in destructive   *Syns:* mug, punk (*Slang*), roughneck,
actions: *neighborhood toughs breaking windows.*   rowdy, toughie (*also* toughy).
                                                              Near-syns: bully, goon, hood, ruffian,
                                                              thug.

tough out *verb*
To carry on through despite hardships.   ENDURE.

toughen *verb*
1. To become or cause to become tough or strong: *The*   1. *Syn:* strengthen.
   soles of her feet toughened from going barefoot.
2. To make resistant to hardship, esp. through   2. HARDEN.
   continued exposure.

toughie *also* **toughy** *noun*
A rough, violent person who engages in destructive   TOUGH *noun*.
actions.

tough-minded *adjective*
Having or indicating an awareness of things as they   REALISTIC.
really are.

tough out *verb*   SEE **tough**.

toughy *noun*   SEE **toughie**.

tour *noun*
1. A course, process, or journey that ends where it   1. CIRCLE *noun*.
   began or repeats itself.

2. A limited, often assigned period of activity, duty, or opportunity.

    2. TURN *noun.*

tour de force *noun*
1. *French.* A great or heroic deed.
2. *French.* An outstanding and ingenious work.

    1. FEAT.
    2. MASTERPIECE.

tourist *noun*
One who travels for pleasure: *saw a group of tourists snapping pictures.*

    Syns: excursionist, rubberneck (*also* rubbernecker) (*Slang*), sightseer, tripper (*Chiefly Brit.*).

tournament *noun*
Any competition or test of opposing wills likened to the sport in which knights fought with lances.

    TILT *noun.*

tourney *noun*
Any competition or test of opposing wills likened to the sport in which knights fought with lances.

    TILT *noun.*

tousle *also* **touzle** *verb*
To put (the hair or clothes) into a state of disarray: *The wind tousled the child's curls.*

    Syns: disarrange, dishevel, disorder, mess (up), muss (up), rumple.

tout *verb*
To increase or seek to increase the importance or reputation of by favorable publicity.

    PROMOTE.

touzle *verb*

    SEE **tousle.**

tow *verb*
To exert force so as to move something toward the source of the force.

    PULL *verb.*

toward *adjective*
Rare. Affording benefit.

    BENEFICIAL.

tower above *verb*
To rise above, esp. so as to afford a view of.

    DOMINATE.

towering *adjective*
1. Awesomely or forbiddingly intense: *in a towering fury.*
2. Extending to a great height.
3. Imposingly high.
4. Far above others in quality or excellence.
5. Vastly exceeding a normal limit, as in cost.

    1. *Syns:* overpowering, overwhelming, staggering.
    2. TALL.
    3. LOFTY.
    4. OUTSTANDING.
    5. STEEP[1].

towheaded *adjective*
Having light hair.

    FAIR *adjective.*

toxic *adjective*
Capable of injuring or killing by poison.

    POISONOUS.

toxicant *adjective*
Capable of injuring or killing by poison.

    POISONOUS.

toxin *noun*
Anything that is injurious, destructive, or fatal.

    POISON *noun.*

toy *noun*
1. An object for children to play with: *Toys and games are sold on the third floor.*
2. A small, showy article.

    1. *Syn:* plaything.
    2. NOVELTY.

toy *verb*
1. To make amorous advances without serious intentions.
2. To treat lightly or flippantly.
3. To solicit (danger) playfully and provocatively, often unwittingly.
4. To move one's fingers or hands in a nervous or aimless fashion.

    1. FLIRT *verb.*
    2. FLIRT *verb.*
    3. COURT *verb.*
    4. FIDDLE.

trace *noun*
1. A mark or remnant that indicates the former presence of something: *traces of an ancient civilization.*

    1. *Syns:* relic, remains, vestige.

2. A visible sign or mark of the passage of someone or something.
3. A barely perceivable indication of something: *not a trace of scandal*.

4. A slight amount.

trace *verb*
1. To follow the traces or scent of, as in hunting.
2. To pursue and locate.

track *noun*
1. A visible sign or mark of the passage of someone or something: *tire tracks in the mud*.
2. Evidence of passage left along a course followed by a hunted animal or fugitive.
3. A course of action to be followed regularly.

track *verb*
1. To follow the traces or scent of, as in hunting: *tracked the bear for miles before treeing it*.
2. To keep (another) under surveillance by moving along behind.
3. To journey over (a specified distance).

track down *verb*
To pursue and locate.

track down *verb*

tract *noun*
1. A part of the earth's surface.
2. A piece of land.

tractable *adjective*
Willing to carry out the wishes of others.

traction *noun*
The act of drawing or pulling a load.

trade *noun*
1. Activity pursued as a livelihood.
2. Commercial, industrial, or professional activity in general.
3. The commercial transactions of customers with a supplier.
4. The act of exchanging or substituting.

trade *verb*
To give up in return for something else.

trade in *verb*
To offer for sale.

trade in *verb*

trademark *noun*
A name or other device placed on merchandise to signify its ownership or manufacture.

trader *noun*
A person engaged in buying and selling.

tradesman *noun*
A person engaged in buying and selling.

trading *noun*
Commercial, industrial, or professional activity in general.

tradition *noun*
1. Something immaterial, as a style or philosophy, that is passed from one generation to another.
2. A body of traditional beliefs and notions accumulated about a particular subject.

---

2. TRACK *noun*.

3. *Syns:* breath, dash, hint, shade, soupçon (*French*), suggestion, taste, touch, whiff.
Near-syns: inkling, insinuation, innuendo, notion.

4. SHADE *noun*.

1. TRACK *verb*.
2. RUN DOWN.

1. *Syns:* print, trace, tread.

2. TRAIL *noun*.

3. ROUTINE *noun*.

1. *Syns:* trace, trail.

2. FOLLOW.

3. TRAVERSE *verb*.

RUN DOWN.
SEE **track**.

1. AREA.
2. LOT *noun*.

OBEDIENT.

PULL *noun*.

1. BUSINESS.
2. BUSINESS.

3. PATRONAGE.

4. CHANGE *noun*.

CHANGE *verb*.

SELL *verb*.
SEE **trade**.

MARK *noun*.

DEALER.

DEALER.

BUSINESS.

1. HERITAGE.

2. LORE.

traditional *adjective*
Conforming to established practice or standards. — CONVENTIONAL.

traditionalist also **traditionalistic** *adjective*
Strongly favoring retention of the existing order. — CONSERVATIVE *adjective*.

traditionalistic *adjective* — SEE **traditionalist**.

traffic *noun*
1. Commercial, industrial, or professional activity in general. — 1. BUSINESS.
2. The commercial transactions of customers with a supplier. — 2. PATRONAGE.

trafficker *noun*
A person engaged in buying and selling. — DEALER.

tragedy *noun*
An occurrence inflicting widespread destruction and distress. — DISASTER.

trail *verb*
1. To hang or cause to hang down and be pulled along behind: *The dog raced away, its leash trailing.* — 1. *Syns:* drag, draggle, train. *Near-syns:* droop, hang, sag.
2. To move behind (another) in the same direction. — 2. FOLLOW.
3. To follow closely or persistently. — 3. DOG *verb*.
4. To go or move slowly so that progress is hindered. — 4. DELAY *verb*.
5. To follow the traces or scent of, as in hunting. — 5. TRACK *verb*.
6. To keep (another) under surveillance by moving along behind. — 6. FOLLOW.

trail *noun*
1. Something that follows or is drawn along behind. — 1. TRAIN *noun*.
2. Evidence of passage left along a course followed by a hunted animal or fugitive: *He crossed a stream to throw the pursuers off his trail.* — 2. *Syns:* scent, spoor, track.

train *noun*
1. Something that follows or is drawn along behind: *a wedding gown with a long train.* — 1. *Syns:* tail, trail.
2. A number of things placed or occurring one after the other. — 2. SERIES.
3. A group of attendants or followers. — 3. RETINUE.
4. An unbroken sequence of events. — 4. RUN *noun*.

train *verb*
1. To impart knowledge and skill to. — 1. EDUCATE.
2. To move (a weapon, blow, etc.) in the direction of someone or something. — 2. AIM *verb*.
3. To hang or cause to hang down and be pulled along behind. — 3. TRAIL *verb*.

training *noun*
1. The act, process, or art of imparting knowledge and skill. — 1. EDUCATION.
2. Repetition of an action so as to develop or maintain one's skill. — 2. PRACTICE *noun*.

traipse *verb*
To move about at random, esp. over a wide area. — ROVE.

trait *noun*
A distinctive element. — QUALITY.

traitor *noun*
One who betrays. — BETRAYER.

traitorous *adjective*
1. Not true to duty or obligation. — 1. FAITHLESS.
2. Involving or constituting treason. — 2. TREASONOUS.

traitorousness *noun*
Willful violation of allegiance to one's country. — TREASON.

trammel *noun*
Something that limits or restricts. — RESTRICTION.

trammel *verb*

1. To restrict the activity or free movement of.
2. To gain control of or an advantage over by or as if by trapping.

tramp *verb*
1. To walk with loud, heavy steps: *I was awakened by a neighbor tramping up the stairs.*
2. To step on heavily and repeatedly so as to crush, injure, or destroy.

tramp *noun*
A vulgar, promiscuous woman who flouts propriety.

trample *verb*
1. To step on heavily and repeatedly so as to crush, injure, or destroy: *Occasionally a bull will trample and gore a matador.*
2. To walk with loud, heavy steps.

trample on *verb*
To exercise absolute power, esp. arbitrarily or cruelly.

trample on *verb*

trance *noun*
1. The condition of being so lost in solitary thought as to be unaware of one's surroundings: *sat gazing at the fire in a trance.*
2. A stunned or bewildered condition.

tranquil *adjective*
Not excited or emotionally agitated.

tranquility *noun*

tranquilize also **tranquillize** *verb*
To make or become calm.

tranquillity or **tranquility** *noun*
Lack of emotional agitation.

tranquillize *verb*

transaction *noun*
An agreement, esp. one involving a sale or exchange.

transcend *verb*
To be greater or better than.

transcendent *adjective*
1. Far above others in quality or excellence.
2. Of the greatest possible degree, quality, or intensity.
3. Existing only in concept and not in reality.

transcendental *adjective*
1. Of, coming from, or relating to forces or beings that exist outside the natural world.
2. Existing only in concept and not in reality.

transfer *verb*
1. To change the ownership of (property) by means of a legal document: *persuaded large landholders to transfer their unused acres to the national forest system.*
2. To go or cause to go from one place to another.
3. To change one's residence, place of business, etc.
4. To change into a different form, substance, or state.
5. To relinquish to the possession or control of another.
6. To direct (a person) elsewhere for help, information, etc.

transfer *noun*
1. The act of delivering or the condition of being delivered.
2. A making over of legal ownership or title.

transfiguration *noun*
The process or result of giving a different form or appearance.

---

1. HAMPER.
2. CATCH *verb.*

1. *Syns:* trample, tromp, stamp, stomp.
   Near-syns: march, plod, thud, trudge.
2. TRAMPLE.

SLUT.

1. *Syns:* stamp, stomp, tramp, tread, tromp.

2. TRAMP *verb.*

TYRANNIZE.
SEE **trample.**

1. *Syns:* abstraction, muse, reverie, study.

2. DAZE *noun.*

CALM *adjective.*
SEE **tranquillity.**

CALM *verb.*

CALM *noun.*
SEE **tranquilize.**

BARGAIN *noun.*

SURPASS.

1. OUTSTANDING.
2. ULTIMATE *adjective.*
3. THEORETICAL.

1. SUPERNATURAL.

2. THEORETICAL.

1. *Syns:* alien, alienate (*Law*), assign (*Law*), cede, convey (*Law*), deed, grant, make over, sign over.

2. MOVE *verb.*
3. MOVE *verb.*
4. CONVERT.
5. GIVE *verb.*
6. REFER.

1. DELIVERY.

2. GRANT *noun.*

CHANGE *noun.*

transfigure *verb*
To change into a different form, substance, or state.   CONVERT.

transfix *verb*
To compel the attention, interest, imagination, etc., of.   GRIP *verb*.

transform *verb*
1. To change into a different form, substance, or state.   1. CONVERT.
2. To bring about a radical change in.   2. REVOLUTIONIZE.

transformation *noun*
1. A usu. physical change of one thing into another.   1. CONVERSION.
2. The process or result of giving a different form or
appearance.   2. CHANGE *noun*.

transfuse *verb*
To cause to be filled with a particular mood or tone.   CHARGE *verb*.

transgress *verb*
1. To fail to fulfill (a promise) or conform to (a
regulation).   1. VIOLATE.
2. To violate a moral or divine law.   2. OFFEND.

transgression *noun*
1. An act or instance of breaking a law or regulation
or of nonfulfillment of an obligation, promise, etc.   1. BREACH *noun*.
2. A wicked act.   2. CRIME.

transient *adjective*
Lasting or existing only for a short time.   TRANSITORY.

transit *noun*
1. The process or an instance of passing from one form,
state, or stage to another.   1. TRANSITION.
2. The moving of persons or goods from one place to
another.   2. TRANSPORTATION.

transit *verb*
To go across.   CROSS *verb*.

transition *noun*
The process or an instance of passing from one form,   *Syns:* changeover, passage, shift, transit.
state, or stage to another: *transition from an*   *Near-syns:* alteration, change, conversion,
agricultural to an industrial economy.   development, evolution, transformation.

transitory *adjective*
Lasting or existing only for a short time: *the transitory*   *Syns:* ephemeral, evanescent, fleeing,
Arctic summer.   fleeting, fugacious, fugitive, momentary,
passing, short-lived, temporal, temporary,
transient.
Near-ants: durable, lasting, permanent,
substantial.
Ant: perpetual.

translate *verb*
1. To express in another language, while   1. *Syns:* construe, put, render.
systematically retaining the original sense:
translated the Italian into English with the help of a
dictionary.
2. To express the meaning of in other, esp. simpler,   2. PARAPHRASE *verb*.
words.
3. To change into a different form, substance, or state.   3. CONVERT.

translation *noun*
1. A restating of something in other, esp. simpler,   1. PARAPHRASE *noun*.
words.
2. The process or result of giving a different form or   2. CHANGE *noun*.
appearance.

translucent *adjective*
Admitting light so that objects beyond can be seen.   TRANSPARENT.

transmigrant *noun*
One who emigrates.   EMIGRANT.

transmigrate *verb*
1. To leave one's native land and to settle in another.   1. EMIGRATE.

2. To change habitat seasonally.

2. MIGRATE.

transmigration *noun*
Departure from one's native land to settle in another.

EMIGRATION.

transmigratory *adjective*
Moving from one habitat to another on a seasonal basis.

MIGRATORY.

transmit *verb*
1. To cause (something) to be conveyed to a destination.
2. To cause to be transferred from one to another.
3. To convey (something) from one generation to the next.
4. To cause (a disease) to pass to another or others.
5. To serve as a conduit.
6. To make known.

1. SEND.

2. PASS *verb*.
3. HAND DOWN at **hand**.

4. COMMUNICATE.
5. CONDUCT *verb*.
6. COMMUNICATE.

transmogrify *verb*
To change into a different form, substance, or state.

CONVERT.

transmutation *noun*
The process or result of giving a different form or appearance.

CHANGE *noun*.

transmute *verb*
To change into a different form, substance, or state.

CONVERT.

transparent *adjective*
1. Admitting light so that objects beyond can be seen: *transparent glass*.

1. *Syns:* clear, crystal-clear, crystalline, limpid, see-through, translucent.
Near-ants: cloudy, dark, foggy, hazy, misty, murky, smoky.
Ant: opaque.

2. Free from what obscures or dims.
3. So light and insubstantial as to resemble air or a thin film.

2. CLEAR *adjective*.
3. FILMY.

transpire *verb*
1. To take place.
2. To be made public.
3. To flow or leak out slowly.

1. COME.
2. COME OUT at **come**.
3. OOZE *verb*.

transport *verb*
1. To move while supporting.
2. To move or excite greatly.
3. To force to leave a country or place by official decree.

1. CARRY.
2. CARRY AWAY at **carry**.
3. BANISH.

transport *noun*
1. The moving of persons or goods from one place to another.
2. A state of elated bliss.

1. TRANSPORTATION.

2. HEAVEN.

transportable *adjective*
Capable of moving or being moved from place to place.

MOBILE.

transportation *noun*
The moving of persons or goods from one place to another: *A central mountain range hampers transportation between the east and west coasts.*

Syns: carriage, conveyance, transit, transport.

transposal *noun*

SEE **transposition**.

transpose *verb*
1. To change to the opposite position, direction, or course.
2. To change into a different form, substance, or state.

1. REVERSE *verb*.

2. CONVERT.

transposition also **transposal** *noun*
1. The act of changing or being changed from one position, direction, or course to the opposite.
2. The act of exchanging or substituting.

1. REVERSAL.

2. CHANGE *noun*.

transubstantiate *verb*
To change into a different form, substance, or state.

CONVERT.

transude *verb*
To flow or leak out slowly.

OOZE *verb.*

transversal *adjective*
Situated or lying across.

TRANSVERSE *adjective.*

transverse *adjective*
Situated or lying across: *transverse beams visible above the room.*

Syns: crossing, crosswise, thwart, transversal, traverse.
Near-syns: across, diagonal, oblique, sideways.
Ant: longitudinal.

transverse *verb*
To go across.

CROSS *verb.*

trap *noun*
1. Something that leads one into a place or situation from which escape is difficult.

1. LURE *noun.*

2. A source of danger or difficulty not easily foreseen and avoided.

2. PITFALL.

3. *Slang.* The opening in the body through which food is ingested.

3. MOUTH *noun.*

4. *Brit.* A member of a law-enforcement agency.

4. POLICEMAN.

trap *verb*
To gain control of or an advantage over by or as if by trapping.

CATCH *verb.*

trash¹ *noun*
1. A group of persons regarded as the lowest class: *racism promulgated by trash.*

1. **Syns:** dregs, hoi polloi, rabble, ragtag (*also* ragtag and bobtail), riffraff, scum. —*Idioms* dregs of society, lumpen proletariat, other half, scum of the earth, tag and rag, the great unwashed.
Near-ants: aristocracy, elite, gentility, nobility, upper class.

2. Something that does not have or make sense.

2. NONSENSE.

trash *verb*
Slang. To injure or destroy (property) maliciously: *A gang of youths trashed the store.*

Syns: vandalize, wreck.

trash² *verb*
Brit. Regional. To walk heavily, slowly, and with difficulty.

PLOD.

trashy *adjective*
Of decidedly inferior quality.

SHODDY.

trauma *noun*
1. *Pathol.* Marked tissue damage, esp. when produced by physical injury: *trauma in the lower lumbar region.*

1. **Syns:** traumatism, wound.

2. Something that jars the mind or emotions.

2. SHOCK *noun.*

traumatic *adjective*
Causing trauma: *a traumatic injury sustained in the collision.*

Syn: traumatizing.

traumatism *noun*
Marked tissue damage, esp. when produced by physical injury.

TRAUMA.

traumatize *verb*
To inflict physical or mental injury or distress on: *victims traumatized by the plane crash.*

Syns: shock, wound.

traumatizing *adjective*
Causing trauma.

TRAUMATIC.

travail *noun*
1. Physical exertion that is usu. difficult and exhausting.

1. LABOR *noun.*

2. The act or process of bringing forth young.

2. BIRTH *noun.*

travail *verb*
To exert one's mental or physical powers, usu. under difficulty and to the point of exhaustion.

LABOR *verb*.

travel *verb*
1. To make or go on a journey.
2. To move along a particular course.
3. To become known far and wide.

1. JOURNEY *verb*.
2. GO *verb*.
3. GET ABOUT at **get**.

traveling *adjective*
Capable of moving or being moved from place to place.

MOBILE.

traversal *noun*
Law. A refusal to grant the truth of a statement or charge.

DENIAL.

traverse *verb*
1. To descend, as a ski slope, by crossing and recrossing laterally: *traversed the hill and then began to parallel.*
2. To go across.
3. To journey over (a specified distance): *traversed 400 miles a day.*
4. To move, as a gun, laterally: *The gunner traversed the tank's cannon and raked the farmhouse with withering fire.*
5. To look at carefully or critically.
6. To take a stand against.
7. *Law.* To refuse to admit the truth, reality, value, or worth of.

1. **Syn:** zigzag.

2. CROSS *verb*.
3. **Syns:** cover, do, make, pass, track.
4. **Syns:** pivot, swivel.

5. EXAMINE.
6. CONTEST *verb*.
7. DENY.

traverse *adjective*
Situated or lying across.

TRANSVERSE *adjective*.

traverse *noun*
Anything that impedes or prevents entry or passage.

BAR *noun*.

travesty *noun*
A false, derisive, or impudent imitation of something.

MOCKERY.

travesty *verb*
To copy (the manner or expression of another), esp. in an exaggerated or mocking way.

IMITATE.

treacherous *adjective*
1. Characterized by duplicity.
2. Not true to duty or obligation.
3. Involving possible risk, loss, or injury.

1. DOUBLE *adjective*.
2. FAITHLESS.
3. DANGEROUS.

treacherousness *noun*
Willful betrayal of fidelity, confidence, or trust.

TREACHERY.

treachery *noun*
1. Willful betrayal of fidelity, confidence, or trust: *The treachery of a double agent compromised the lives of the resistance fighters.*

1. **Syns:** perfidiousness, perfidy, treacherousness, treason (*Rare*).
—*Idioms* dirty work at the crossroads, Judas kiss, knife in the back.
Near-ants: constancy, fidelity, loyalty, reliability.
Ants: dependability, trustworthiness.

2. An act of betraying.

2. BETRAYAL.

tread *noun*
1. The act or manner of going on foot: *heard his heavy tread on the stairs.*
2. A visible sign or mark of the passage of someone or something.

1. **Syns:** footfall, footstep, step.

2. TRACK *noun*.

tread *verb*
1. To step on heavily and repeatedly so as to crush, injure, or destroy.
2. To go on foot.

1. TRAMPLE.

2. WALK *verb*.

treadmill *noun*
A habitual, laborious, often tiresome course of action.

GRIND *noun*.

treason *noun*
1. Willful violation of allegiance to one's country: *was hanged for treason.*

   1. **Syns:** sedition, seditiousness, traitorousness.
   Near-syns: disloyalty, misprison, treachery.
   Ant: allegiance.

2. *Rare.* Willful betrayal of fidelity, confidence, or trust.

   2. TREACHERY.

treasonable *adjective*
Involving or constituting treason.

TREASONOUS.

treasonous *adjective*
Involving or constituting treason: *aiding and abetting the enemy and other treasonous activities.*

Syns: Iscariotic *or* Iscariotical, seditious, traitorous, treasonable.

treasure *noun*
1. Someone or something considered exceptionally precious: *That editor is a real treasure.*

   1. **Syns:** diamond, gem, pearl, prize.

2. A great amount of accumulated money and precious possessions.

   2. RICHES.

3. A supply stored or hidden for future use.

   3. HOARD *noun*.

treasure *verb*
1. To store up (supplies or money), usu. well beyond one's needs.

   1. HOARD *verb*.

2. To recognize the worth, quality, importance, etc., of.

   2. APPRECIATE.

3. To have the highest regard for.

   3. CHERISH.

treasure-house *noun*
A place where one keeps one's valuables.

TREASURY.

treasury *noun*
A place where one keeps one's valuables: *the king's treasury deep in the bowels of the fortress.*

Syn: treasure-house.
Near-syns: archive, depository, museum, repository, storehouse.

treat *verb*
1. To pay for the food, drink, or entertainment of (another): *He treated me to dinner and a concert.*

   1. **Syns:** blow[1] (*Slang*), set up (*Informal*), shout (*Austral.*), stand (*Informal*).
   —*Idioms* go (*or* stand) treat, pick up the tab for.

2. To behave in a specified way toward.
3. To be occupied or concerned.
4. To give medical aid to: *was treated by a cardiologist.*

   2. DEAL WITH at **deal**.
   3. DEAL *verb*.
   4. **Syn:** doctor.

treat *noun*
Something fine and delicious, esp. a food.

DELICACY.

treatise *noun*
A formal, lengthy exposition of a topic.

DISCOURSE *noun*.

treatment *noun*
The systematic application of remedies to effect a cure: *treatment prescribed by a physician; dietary treatment for obesity.*

Syns: care, regimen, therapy.

treaty *noun*
A formal, usu. written settlement between nations: *an arms-limitation treaty.*

Syns: accord, agreement, concord, convention, pact.
Near-syns: charter, compact, covenant, understanding; alliance.

treble *adjective*
Elevated in pitch.

HIGH.

trek *verb*
To make or go on a journey.

JOURNEY *verb*.

tremble *verb*
1. To move to and fro in short, jerky movements.
2. To move to and fro violently.

   1. SHAKE *verb*.
   2. SHAKE *verb*.

tremble(s) *noun*
A state of nervous restlessness or agitation.

JITTERS.

trembler *noun*

SEE **tremblor**.

trembling *adjective*
Marked by or affected with tremors.

TREMULOUS.

tremblor or **trembler** *noun*
A shaking of the earth.

TREMOR *noun.*

tremendous *adjective*
1. Causing or able to cause fear.
2. Of extraordinary size and power.
3. *Informal.* Particularly excellent.

1. FEARFUL.
2. GIANT *adjective.*
3. MARVELOUS.

tremendousness *noun*
The quality of being enormous.

ENORMOUSNESS.

tremor *noun*
1. A shaking of the earth: *a tremor measuring eight points on the Richter scale.*

2. A nervous shaking of the body: *A tremor ran through his body as he watched the massacre from a hiding place.*

1. *Syns:* earthquake, quake, shake, temblor (*Regional*), tremblor or trembler.
2. *Syns:* quaver, quiver, shiver, shudder, thrill, tic, twitch.

tremor *verb*
To move to and fro in short, jerky movements.

tremulant *adjective*

tremulent *adjective*

SHAKE *verb.*
SEE **tremulous.**
SEE **tremulous.**

tremulous also **tremulant, tremulent** *adjective*
Marked by or affected with tremors: *the tremulous hands of a patient with Parkinson's disease.*

Syns: aquake, aquiver, ashake, ashiver, quaking, quaky, quivering, quivery, shaking, shaky, shivering, shivery, trembling.
Near-ants: calm, firm, secure, settled, stable, steady, unmoving.

trenchant *adjective*
Having or suggesting keen, discerning intellect.

INCISIVE.

trend *noun*
The current custom.

FASHION *noun.*

trend *verb*
To have a tendency or inclination.

TEND[1].

trendy *adjective*
Informal. Being or in accordance with the current fashion.

FASHIONABLE.

trepidation *noun*
Great agitation and anxiety caused by the expectation or the realization of danger.

FEAR *noun.*

trespass *verb*
1. To enter forcibly and illegally.
2. To violate a moral or divine law.

1. BREAK IN at **break.**
2. OFFEND.

trespass *noun*
1. An act or instance of breaking a law or regulation or of nonfulfillment of an obligation, promise, etc.
2. A serious breaking of the public law.

1. BREACH *noun.*

2. CRIME.

triable *adjective*
Subject to a lawsuit.

LITIGABLE.

trial *noun*
1. *Law.* The examination and deciding upon evidence, charges, and claims in court: *testified at the trial.*
2. An operation employed to resolve an uncertainty.
3. A state of pain or anguish that tests one's resiliency and character: *The death of her parents was a great trial for her.*

1. *Syn:* hearing (*Law*).

2. TEST *noun.*
3. *Syns:* crucible, ordeal, tribulation, visitation. —*Idioms* crown of thorns, fiery ordeal, time of trial, trial by fire, trial and tribulation.
Near-syns: agony, difficulty, distress, hardship, rigor; anguish, grief.

4. Something hard to bear physically or emotionally.
5. An earnest try.

4. BURDEN *noun.*
5. EFFORT.

6. An effort to do or make something.   **6.** ATTEMPT *noun*.
7. One that makes another totally miserable by   **7.** THORN *noun*.
causing sharp pain and irritation.
8. A procedure that ascertains effectiveness, value,   **8.** TEST *noun*.
proper function, or other quality.

trial *adjective*
Constituting a tentative model for future experiment or   PILOT *adjective*.
development.

tribe *noun*
A group of people sharing common ancestry.   FAMILY.

tribulation *noun*
A state of pain or anguish that tests one's resiliency   TRIAL *noun*.
and character.

tribunal *noun*
A judicial assembly.   COURT *noun*.

tribute *noun*
1. An expression of admiration or congratulation.   **1.** COMPLIMENT *noun*.
2. A formal token of appreciation and admiration for a **2.** TESTIMONIAL.
person's high achievements.

trice *noun*
A very brief time.   FLASH *noun*.

trick *noun*
1. An indirect, usu. cunning means of gaining an end: **1.** *Syns:* artifice, device, feint, gimmick
used every trick in the bag to win the election.   (*Slang*), jig (*Slang*), maneuver, play,
                                                            ploy, ruse, shenanigan (*Informal*),
                                                            sleight, stratagem, wile.
                                                            Near-syns: bluff, curve, dodge, sham,
                                                            stall; fraud, red herring.
2. An action meant to deceive.   **2.** DECEPTION.
3. A mischievous act.   **3.** PRANK.
4. The proper method for doing, using, or handling   **4.** HANG *noun*.
something.
5. A clever, dexterous act: *magicians' tricks.*   **5.** *Syns:* feat, stunt.
6. A limited, often assigned period of activity, duty, or **6.** TURN *noun*.
opportunity.

trick *adjective*
So weak or defective as to be liable to fail: *a trick lock;* *Syns:* tricky, undependable, unreliable.
a trick knee.

trick *verb*
To cause to accept what is false, esp. by trickery or   DECEIVE.
misrepresentation.

trick out *verb*
To dress in formal or special clothing.   DRESS UP at **dress**.

trick up *verb*
To dress in formal or special clothing.   DRESS UP at **dress**.

trickery *noun*
Lack of straightforwardness and honesty in action.   INDIRECTION.

trickiness *noun*
Lack of straightforwardness and honesty in action.   INDIRECTION.

trickle *verb*
To fall or let fall in drops of liquid.   DRIP *verb*.

trickle *noun*
The process or sound of dripping.   DRIP *noun*.

trick out *verb*   SEE **trick**.

trickster *noun*
A person who cheats.   CHEAT *noun*.

trick up *verb*   SEE **trick**.

tricky *adjective*
1. Requiring great tact or skill.   **1.** DELICATE.
2. Hard to deal with or get out of.   **2.** TIGHT *adjective*.
3. Deceitfully clever.   **3.** ARTFUL.

4. So weak or defective as to be liable to fail.

trifle *noun*
A small, showy article.

trifle *verb*
1. To move one's fingers or hands in a nervous or aimless fashion.
2. To pass (time) without working or in avoiding work.
3. To make amorous advances without serious intentions.
4. To treat lightly or flippantly.

trifle away *verb*
To spend (money) excessively and usu. foolishly.

trifle away *verb*

trifles *noun*
Unimportant matters or concerns.

trifling *adjective*
1. Contemptibly unimportant.
2. *Chiefly Regional.* Resistant to exertion and activity.

trig *adjective*
1. Being or in accordance with the current fashion.
2. In good order or clean condition.
3. *Brit. Regional.* Completely filled.

trig *verb*
To make neat and trim; make presentable.

trigger *noun*
Something that incites esp. a violent response.

trigger *verb*
To put (a mechanical device or process) in motion by releasing an activating mechanism.

triggerman *noun*
Slang. One who murders another.

trillion *noun*
An indeterminately great amount or number.

trim *verb*
1. To decrease, as in length or amount, by or as if by severing or excising.
2. To make a slight reduction in (a price).
3. To furnish with decorations.
4. To make neat and trim; make presentable.
5. *Informal.* To punish with blows or lashes.
6. *Informal.* To win a victory over, as in battle or a competition.
7. *Informal.* To get money or something else from by deceitful trickery.

trim down *verb*
To lose bodily weight, as by dieting.

trim *adjective*
1. In good order or clean condition.
2. Having slender and graceful lines.

trim *noun*
1. A state of sound readiness: *got into trim for the race.*

2. Something that adorns.

trim down *verb*

trimming *noun*
1. Something that adorns.
2. *Informal.* The act of defeating or the condition of being defeated.

trine *noun*
A group of three individuals.

---

4. TRICK *adjective.*

NOVELTY.

1. FIDDLE.

2. IDLE *verb.*

3. FLIRT *verb.*

4. FLIRT *verb.*

WASTE *verb.*

SEE **trifle.**

TRIVIA.

1. PETTY.
2. LAZY.

1. FASHIONABLE.
2. NEAT.
3. FULL.

TIDY *verb.*

STIMULUS.

TRIP *verb.*

MURDERER.

HEAP *noun.*

1. CUT BACK.

2. SHADE *verb.*
3. ADORN.
4. TIDY *verb.*
5. BEAT *verb.*
6. DEFEAT *verb.*

7. CHEAT *verb.*

REDUCE.

1. NEAT.
2. SLEEK *adjective.*

1. *Syns:* condition, fettle, fitness, form, kilter, order, shape (*Informal*).
2. ADORNMENT.
SEE **trim.**

1. ADORNMENT.
2. DEFEAT *noun.*

TRIO.

trinity also **triunity**   *noun*
A group of three individuals.   TRIO.

trinket   *noun*
A small, showy article.   NOVELTY.

trio   *noun*
A group of three individuals: *a trio of generals*   **Syns:** threesome, trine, trinity (*also*
conspiring to overthrow the government; a trio of   triunity), triple, triumvirate, triune,
musicians.   troika.

trip   *verb*
1. To put (a mechanical device or process) in motion by   1. **Syns:** throw, trigger.
   releasing an activating mechanism: *trip a light*
   switch.
2. To catch the foot against something and lose one's   2. STUMBLE *verb.*
   balance.
3. To bound lightly.   3. SKIP *verb.*
4. To make an error or mistake.   4. ERR.
5. *Rare.* To make or go on a journey.   5. JOURNEY *verb.*

trip   *noun*
1. A setting out or venturing forth: *a trip to the French*   1. **Syns:** excursion, jaunt, junket, outing.
   Quarter.
2. *Slang.* An illusion of perceiving something that does   2. HALLUCINATION.
   not really exist.
3. An act or thought that unintentionally deviates   3. ERROR.
   from what is correct, right, or true.
4. A stupid, clumsy mistake.   4. BLUNDER *noun.*
5. *Slang.* A temporary concentration of interest.   5. KICK *noun.*

triple   *noun*
A group of three individuals.   TRIO.

tripper   *noun*
Chiefly Brit. One who travels for pleasure.   TOURIST.

tristful   *adjective*
1. *Archaic.* Suggestive of or expressing deep, often   1. PENSIVE.
   melancholy thoughtfulness.
2. *Archaic.* In low spirits.   2. DEPRESSED.

trite   *adjective*
Without freshness or appeal due to overuse: *Trite*   **Syns:** banal, bathetic, bromidic, cliché,
expressions spoiled the writing.   commonplace, corny (*Slang*), hackneyed,
                                                           musty, platitudinous, shopworn, stale,
                                                           stereotyped, stereotypic (*also*
                                                           stereotypical), threadbare, timeworn,
                                                           tired, warmed-over, well-worn,
                                                           worn-out.
                                                           Near-ants: creative, imaginative, novel,
                                                           unique; first, new.
                                                           Ants: fresh, original.

triturate   *verb*
To break up into tiny particles.   CRUSH *verb.*

triumph   *verb*
1. To get the better of: *triumphed over all obstacles.*   1. **Syns:** best, conquer, master, overcome,
                                                              prevail (over *or* against), surmount,
                                                              worst.
2. To win a victory over, as in battle or a competition.   2. DEFEAT *verb.*
3. To feel or express an uplifting joy over a success or   3. EXULT.
   victory.

triumph   *noun*
1. The act of conquering.   1. CONQUEST.
2. The act or condition of feeling an uplifting joy over   2. EXULTATION.
   a success or victory.

triumphal *adjective*
Pertaining to, having the nature of, or experiencing triumph.   VICTORIOUS.

triumphant *adjective*
1. Pertaining to, having the nature of, or experiencing triumph.   1. VICTORIOUS.
2. Feeling or expressing an uplifting joy over a success or victory.   2. EXULTANT.

triumvirate *noun*
A group of three individuals.   TRIO.

triune *noun*
A group of three individuals.   TRIO.

triunity *noun*   SEE **trinity.**

trivia *noun*
1. Unimportant matters or concerns: *the trivia of suburban living.*   1. *Syns:* minutiae, trifles, triviality.
   —*Idioms* small change, small potatoes.
2. Something lacking substance or depth.   2. FROTH *noun.*

trivial *adjective*
1. Not of great importance.   1. LITTLE.
2. Contemptibly unimportant.   2. PETTY.

triviality *noun*
1. Something lacking substance or depth.   1. FROTH *noun.*
2. Contemptible unimportance.   2. PETTINESS.
3. Unimportant matters or concerns.   3. TRIVIA.

trivialness *noun*
Contemptible unimportance.   PETTINESS.

troika *noun*
A group of three individuals.   TRIO.

tromp *verb*
1. To walk with loud, heavy steps.   1. TRAMP *verb.*
2. To step on heavily and repeatedly so as to crush, injure, or destroy.   2. TRAMPLE.

troop *verb*
1. To come or go in large numbers.   1. POUR.
2. To keep company.   2. ASSOCIATE *verb.*

troop *noun*
1. A number of persons who have come or been gathered together.   1. ASSEMBLY.
2. A group of performers.   2. BAND[2] *noun.*

trophy *noun*
1. A memento received as a symbol of excellence or victory: *The Oscar is a much-sought-after trophy.*   1. *Syns:* award, prize.
2. Something that causes one to remember.   2. REMEMBRANCE.

tropic *adjective*
Of or relating to the tropics.   TROPICAL.

tropical *adjective*
Of or relating to the tropics: *a tropical climate in South America.*   *Syn:* tropic.

trot *noun*
1. A person's steady, easy gait that is faster than a walk but slower than a run: *The child came across the yard at a trot.*   1. *Syns:* jog, lope.
2. *Archaic.* An ugly, frightening old woman.   2. WITCH.

trot *verb*
1. To move with a steady, easy gait faster than a walk but slower than a run: *The football players trotted around the field to warm up.*   1. *Syns:* jog, lope.
2. To move swiftly.   2. RUSH *verb.*

troth *noun*
The act or condition of being pledged to marry.

ENGAGEMENT.

trouble *noun*
1. A condition or situation characterized by danger, distress, or annoyance: *Walking alone at night in the city is just asking for trouble. He didn't watch what he said and got in trouble.*
2. A cause of worry.
3. The condition of being in need of immediate assistance.
4. The use of energy to do something.
5. The state or quality of being inconvenient.

1. **Syns:** difficulty, Dutch (*Informal*), hot water (*Slang*).
2. CARE *noun*.
3. DISTRESS *noun*.
4. EFFORT.
5. INCONVENIENCE *noun*.

trouble *verb*
1. To cause anxious uneasiness in.
2. To cause inconvenience for.
3. To recur to continually.

1. WORRY *verb*.
2. INCONVENIENCE *verb*.
3. HAUNT *verb*.

troubled *adjective*
In a state of uneasiness.

ANXIOUS.

troublesome *adjective*
1. Hard to treat, manage, or cope with: *a troublesome hitter who usually gets on base.*

1. **Syns:** mean[2] (*Slang*), pesky, vexatious, wicked (*Slang*).
   Near-syns: annoying, bothersome, disquieting, disturbing, upsetting, vexing.
   Ant: benign.

2. Troubling to the mind or emotions.
3. Troubling the nerves or peace of mind, as by repeated vexations.
4. Causing difficulty, trouble, or discomfort.

2. DISTURBING.
3. VEXATIOUS.

4. INCONVENIENT.

trounce *verb*
1. To render totally ineffective by decisive defeat.
2. To win a victory over, as in battle or a competition.

1. OVERWHELM.
2. DEFEAT *verb*.

trouncing *noun*
A severe defeat: *The voters gave the incumbent a trouncing.*

Syns: drubbing (*Slang*), dusting, lambasting (*Slang*), licking (*Slang*), shellacking (*Slang*), thrashing.

troupe *noun*
A group of performers.

BAND[2] *noun*.

truancy *noun*
An unexcused absence.

CUT *noun*.

truce *noun*
A temporary cessation of hostilities by mutual consent of the contending parties: *called for a truce so the wounded could be removed from the area.*

Syns: armistice, cease-fire. —*Idiom* cooling-off period.
Near-syns: accord, de-escalation, lull, pause, peace.

truckle *verb*
To support slavishly every opinion or suggestion of a superior.

FAWN.

truckler *noun*
One who flatters another excessively.

SYCOPHANT.

truculence also **truculency** *noun*
1. A cruel act or an instance of cruel behavior.
2. Warlike or hostile attitude or disposition.

1. CRUELTY.
2. BELLIGERENCE.

truculency *noun*

SEE **truculence.**

truculent *adjective*
1. Having or showing an eagerness to fight.
2. Showing or suggesting a disposition to be violently destructive without scruple or restraint.
3. So sharp as to cause mental pain.

1. BELLIGERENT.
2. FIERCE.

3. BITING.

trudge *verb*
To walk heavily, slowly, and with difficulty.

PLOD.

true *adjective*
1. Being so legitimately: *the true heir to the throne; the true victor of the contest.*

2. Conforming to fact.
3. In agreement or correspondence with fact.
4. Not counterfeit or copied.
5. Devoid of any hypocrisy or pretense.
6. Adhering firmly and devotedly, as to a person, a cause, or a duty.
7. Worthy of belief because of precision, faithfulness to an original, etc.
8. Having or marked by uprightness in principle and action.

1. **Syns:** legitimate, rightful.
   Near-ants: illegitimate, spurious.
   Ant: false.
2. ACCURATE.
3. ACTUAL.
4. AUTHENTIC.
5. GENUINE.
6. FAITHFUL.

7. AUTHENTIC.

8. HONEST.

truelove *noun*
A person who is much loved.

DARLING *noun*.

true-to-life *adjective*
Accurately representing what is depicted or described.

REALISTIC.

truism *noun*
A trite expression or idea.

CLICHÉ *noun*.

trump *noun*
Something, esp. something held in reserve, that gives one a decisive advantage: *The attorney decided to use his trump and call the witness' bluff.*

Syns: ace², clincher (*Informal*). —*Idioms* ace in the hole, trump card.

trump *verb*
To outmaneuver (an opponent), esp. with the aid of some extra resource: *The incumbent President trumped the other candidate by sending federal aid to the cities on election eve.*

Syns: finesse, one-up (*Slang*).

truncate *verb*
To make short or shorter by or as if by cutting: *a speech that was truncated to fit into the allotted time.*

Syns: abbreviate, abridge, brief, crop, lop¹, shorten.

trust *noun*
1. Absolute certainty in the trustworthiness of another.
2. The function of watching, guarding, or overseeing.
3. A combination of businesses closely interconnected for common profit.

1. CONFIDENCE.
2. CARE *noun*.
3. COMBINE *noun*.

trust *verb*
1. To have confidence in the truthfulness of.
2. To place trust or confidence in.
3. To place a trust upon.

1. BELIEVE.
2. DEPEND ON at **depend.**
3. ENTRUST.

trustless *adjective*
Not to be depended on.

UNDEPENDABLE.

trustworthy *adjective*
1. Capable of being depended upon.
2. Worthy of belief because of precision, faithfulness to an original, etc.

1. DEPENDABLE.
2. AUTHENTIC.

trusty *adjective*
Capable of being depended upon.

DEPENDABLE.

truth *noun*
1. Freedom from deceit or falseness: *a claim having the ring of truth.*

2. Correspondence with fact or truth.

1. **Syns:** truthfulness, veracity, verity.
   Near-ants: deception, equivocation, evasion, falseness.
   Ant: untruth.
2. VERACITY.

truthful *adjective*
1. Consistently telling the truth: *so truthful that she had our absolute confidence.*

1. **Syns:** veracious, veridical.
   Near-syns: candid, forthright, frank, honest, sincere, trustful.
   Ant: untruthful.

2. Accurately representing what is depicted or described.

2. REALISTIC.

truthfulness *noun*
1. Freedom from deceit or falseness.
2. The quality of being authentic.

1. TRUTH.
2. AUTHENTICITY.

truthless *adjective*
Devoid of truth.

FALSE.

truthlessness *noun*
The practice of lying.

MENDACITY.

try *noun*
1. A brief trial: *I'll give the task a try.*

1. *Syns:* crack (*Slang*), fling (*Informal*), go (*Informal*), shot, stab, whack (*Informal*), whirl (*Informal*).

2. An effort to do or make something.

2. ATTEMPT *noun.*

try *verb*
1. To make an attempt to do or make.
2. To subject to a procedure that ascertains effectiveness, value, proper function, or other quality.

1. ATTEMPT *verb.*
2. TEST *verb.*

trying *adjective*
Imposing a severe test of bodily or spiritual strength.

BURDENSOME.

try out *verb*
1. To subject to a procedure that ascertains effectiveness, value, proper function, or other quality.
2. To engage in experiments.

1. TEST *verb.*

2. TEST *verb.*

try-out *noun*
Informal. A procedure that ascertains effectiveness, value, proper function, or other quality.

TEST *noun.*

try-out *noun*

SEE **try out.**

tryst *noun*
A commitment to appear at a certain time and place.

ENGAGEMENT.

tubby *adjective*
Well-rounded and usu. short in physique.

PLUMP[1].

tubercular *adjective*
Pertaining to or afflicted with tuberculosis: *tubercular therapy; tubercular patients.*

Syns: consumptive (*Path.*), phthisic (*also* phthisical) (*Path.*), tuberculous.

tuberculosis *noun*
A contagious disease producing lesions esp. of the lungs: *pains and a cough that suggested tuberculosis.*

Syns: consumption, phthisis (*also* phthisic) (*Path.*), TB (*also* T.B.), white plague.

tuberculous *adjective*
Pertaining to or afflicted with tuberculosis.

TUBERCULAR.

tucker *verb*
Informal. To make extremely tired.

EXHAUST.

tuckered *adjective*
Informal. Extremely tired.

EXHAUSTED.

tug *verb*
1. To exert force so as to move something toward the source of the force.
2. To exert one's mental or physical powers, usu. under difficulty and to the point of exhaustion.
3. To move or cause to move with a sudden, abrupt motion.

1. PULL *verb.*

2. LABOR *verb.*

3. JERK *verb.*

tug *noun*
A sudden pull.

JERK *noun.*

tuition *noun*
The act, process, or art of imparting knowledge and skill.

EDUCATION.

tumble *verb*
1. To come to the ground suddenly and involuntarily.
2. To undergo a sharp, rapid descent in value or price.
3. To bring about the downfall of.
4. To put out of proper order.
5. To find or meet by chance.

1. FALL *verb*.
2. FALL *verb*.
3. OVERTHROW *verb*.
4. DISORDER *verb*.
5. COME ACROSS at **come**.

tumble *noun*
1. A usu. swift downward trend, as in prices.
2. A sudden involuntary drop to the ground.
3. A lack of order or regular arrangement.
4. A group of things gathered haphazardly.

1. FALL *noun*.
2. FALL *noun*.
3. DISORDER *noun*.
4. HEAP *noun*.

tumble-down *adjective*
Falling to ruin.

RUINOUS.

tumescent *adjective*
Filled up with or as if with something insubstantial.

INFLATED.

tumid *adjective*
Filled up with or as if with something insubstantial.

INFLATED.

tumult *noun*
1. An interruption of regular procedure or of public peace.
2. A quarrel or fight marked by very noisy, disorderly, and often violent behavior.
3. A state of discomposure.
4. Sounds or a sound, esp. when loud, confused, or disagreeable.

1. DISTURBANCE.
2. BRAWL *noun*.
3. AGITATION.
4. NOISE *noun*.

tumultuous *adjective*
1. Violently disturbed, as by storms.
2. Marked by unrest or disturbance.

1. ROUGH *adjective*.
2. TURBULENT.

tune *noun*
1. A pleasing succession of musical tones forming a usu. brief aesthetic unit.
2. Pleasing agreement, as of musical sounds.
3. Harmonious mutual understanding.

1. MELODY.
2. HARMONY.
3. AGREEMENT.

tune *verb*
1. To bring into accord.
2. To bring (oneself) into harmony with one's environment.
3. To alter (parts of a device) for proper functioning.
4. *Archaic*. To utter words or sounds in musical tones.

1. HARMONIZE.
2. ADJUST.
3. ADJUST.
4. SING.

tuneful *adjective*
1. Having or producing a pleasing melody.
2. Resembling or having the effect of music, esp. pleasing music.

1. MELODIOUS.
2. MELODIOUS.

turbid *adjective*
1. Having sediment or foreign particles stirred up or suspended: *turbid water*.

1. *Syns:* muddy, roiled, roily.
Near-syns: clouded, cloudy, dark, dense, mucky, murky, opaque, thick.
Ant: clear.

2. Heavy, dark, or dense, esp. with impurities: *atmosphere made turbid by smoke from factories*.
3. Violently disturbed, as by storms.

2. *Syns:* hazy, murky (*also* mirky).
3. ROUGH *adjective*.

turbulence *noun*
1. The condition of being physically agitated.
2. An interruption of regular procedure or of public peace.

1. AGITATION.
2. DISTURBANCE.

turbulent *adjective*
1. Marked by unrest or disturbance: *the turbulent times just before and after the revolution; a turbulent love affair*.

1. *Syns:* stormy, tempestuous, tumultuous.
Near-ants: calm, controlled, orderly, placid, quiet, serene, tranquil.

2. Violently disturbed, as by storms.　　　　　　　　　**2.** ROUGH *adjective*.

turf *noun*
Slang. A particular area used for or associated with a
specific individual or activity.　　　　　　　　　　　　TERRITORY.

turgid *adjective*
Filled up with or as if with something insubstantial.　　INFLATED.

turkey *noun*
Slang. One deficient in judgment and good sense.　　　FOOL *noun*.

turmoil *noun*
1. A state of uneasiness and usu. resentment brewing　**1.** UNREST.
　　to an eventual explosion.
2. A state of discomposure.　　　　　　　　　　　**2.** AGITATION.
3. A lack of order or regular arrangement.　　　　　**3.** DISORDER *noun*.

turn *verb*
1. To move or cause to move in circles or around an　**1.** *Syns:* circle, gyrate, revolve, rotate,
　　axis or center: *a weather vane turning in the breeze.*　　wheel.
　　　　　　　　　　　　　　　　　　　　　　　　　　Near-syns: eddy, orbit, spin, twirl,
　　　　　　　　　　　　　　　　　　　　　　　　　　whirl.
2. To cause to move, esp. at an angle.　　　　　　　**2.** BEND *verb*.
3. To change to the opposite position, direction, or　**3.** REVERSE *verb*.
　　course.
4. To spade or dig (soil) to bring the undersoil to the　**4.** *Syns:* break, plow, turn over.
　　surface: *turn the earth before planting.*
5. To injure (a bodily part) by twisting: *turn an ankle.*　**5.** *Syns:* sprain, wrench.
6. To change the direction or course of: *turn the*　**6.** *Syns:* avert, deflect, divert, pivot,
　　bicycle into the driveway.　　　　　　　　　　　sheer[1], shift, swing, veer.
　　　　　　　　　　　　　　　　　　　　　　　　　　Near-syns: depart, deviate, diverge,
　　　　　　　　　　　　　　　　　　　　　　　　　　move, switch, swivel, zigzag.
7. To make or become different.　　　　　　　　　**7.** CHANGE *verb*.
8. To devote (oneself or one's efforts).　　　　　　**8.** APPLY.
9. To move (a weapon, blow, etc.) in the direction of　**9.** AIM *verb*.
　　someone or something.
10. To become or cause to become rotten or unsound.　**10.** DECAY *verb*.
11. To abandon one's cause or party usu. to join　**11.** DEFECT *verb*.
　　another.
12. To have recourse to when in need.　　　　　　**12.** RESORT TO at **resort**.
13. To make or become less sharp-edged.　　　　　**13.** DULL *verb*.
14. To come to be.　　　　　　　　　　　　　　**14.** BECOME.
15. To disturb the health or physiological functioning　**15.** UPSET *verb*.
　　of.

turn aside *verb*
To prohibit from occurring by advance planning or　　PREVENT.
action.

turn in *verb*
1. To commit to the consideration or judgment of　**1.** SUBMIT.
　　another.
2. *Informal.* To go to bed.　　　　　　　　　　**2.** RETIRE.

turn off *verb*
1. *Slang.* To be very disagreeable to.　　　　　　**1.** OFFEND.
2. *Rare.* To execute by suspending by the neck.　　**2.** HANG *verb*.

turn on *verb*
Slang. To arouse the interest and attention of.　　　INTEREST *verb*.

turn on (or **upon**) *verb*
To be determined by or contingent on something　　DEPEND ON at **depend**.
unknown, uncertain, or changeable.

turn over *verb*
1. To relinquish to the possession or control of another.　**1.** GIVE *verb*.
2. To give over to another for care, use, or　　　　**2.** ENTRUST.
　　performance.
3. To consider carefully and at length.　　　　　　**3.** PONDER.

4. To spade or dig (soil) to bring the undersoil to the surface.

    4. TURN *verb*.

5. To turn or cause to turn from a vertical or horizontal position.

    5. OVERTURN.

turn up *verb*
1. To find by investigation.
2. To come to a particular place.

    1. UNCOVER.
    2. ARRIVE.

turn *noun*
1. Circular movement around a point or about an axis.
2. Something bent.
3. An often sudden change or departure, as in a trend: *a new turn of events since yesterday.*
4. A calculated change in position.
5. A limited, often assigned period of activity, duty, or opportunity: *I took a turn at the wheel while Frank rested. We took turns washing the dishes.*
6. An inclination to something.
7. An innate capability.
8. A usu. brief and regular journey on foot, esp. for exercise.
9. A course, process, or journey that ends where it began or repeats itself.

    1. REVOLUTION.
    2. BEND *noun*.
    3. *Syns:* shift, tack, twist.
    4. MOVEMENT.
    5. *Syns:* bout, go, hitch, innings, shift, spell[3], stint, time, tour, trick, watch.
    6. BENT *noun*.
    7. TALENT.
    8. CONSTITUTIONAL *noun*.
    9. CIRCLE *noun*.

turn aside *verb*

    SEE **turn.**

turncoat *noun*
A person who has defected.

    DEFECTOR.

turn-down *noun*

    SEE **turn down.**

turn down *verb*
1. To be unwilling to accept, consider, or receive.
2. To be unwilling to grant.
3. To prevent or forbid authoritatively.

    1. DECLINE *verb*.
    2. REFUSE.
    3. VETO.

    turn-down *noun*
    Informal. A turning down of a request.

    REFUSAL.

turned-on *adjective*
1. *Slang.* Feeling a very strong emotion.
2. *Slang.* Feeling great delight and joy.
3. *Slang.* Stupefied, intoxicated, or otherwise influenced by the taking of drugs.

    1. THRILLED.
    2. ELATED.
    3. DRUGGED.

turn in *verb*

    SEE **turn.**

turnkey *noun*
A guard or keeper of a prison.

    JAILER.

turn off *verb*

    SEE **turn.**

turn on *verb*

    SEE **turn.**

turn on (or **upon**) *verb*

    SEE **turn.**

turn out *verb*
1. To supply what is needed for some activity or purpose.
2. To leave one's bed.

    1. FURNISH.
    2. GET UP at **get.**

    turnout *noun*
    1. Things needed for a task, journey, or other purpose.
    2. A set or style of clothing.

    1. OUTFIT *noun*.
    2. DRESS *noun*.

turnout *noun*

    SEE **turn out.**

turn over *verb*

    SEE **turn.**

turn up *verb*

    SEE **turn.**

turpitude *noun*
Immoral, degrading acts or habits.

    CORRUPTION.

tussle *noun*
A physical conflict involving two or more.

    FIGHT *noun*.

    tussle *verb*
    To contend with an opponent, esp. by attempting to throw him.

    WRESTLE.

tutelage *noun*
The act, process, or art of imparting knowledge and skill. — EDUCATION.

tutor *verb*
To impart knowledge and skill to. — EDUCATE.

tutoring *noun*
The act, process, or art of imparting knowledge and skill. — EDUCATION.

twaddle *noun*
1. Something that does not have or make sense. — 1. NONSENSE.
2. Unintelligible or foolish talk. — 2. BABBLE *noun*.

twang *noun*
A distinctive property of a substance affecting the gustatory sense. — FLAVOR *noun*.

twelvemonth *noun*
A period of time of approx. 12 months, esp. that period during which the earth completes a single revolution around the sun. — YEAR.

twerp also **twirp** *noun*
Slang. An insignificant but arrogant and obnoxious young person. — SQUIRT *noun*.

twiddle *verb*
To move one's fingers or hands in a nervous or aimless fashion. — FIDDLE.

twiggy *adjective*
Having little flesh or fat on the body. — THIN *adjective*.

twilight *noun*
The period between afternoon and nighttime. — EVENING.

twin *adjective*
Consisting of two identical or similar related things, parts, or elements: *the twin evils of drink and lust.* — **Syns:** double, dual, paired. **Near-syns:** identical, like, matched, similar.

twin *noun*
One of a matched pair of things. — MATE *noun*.

twine *verb*
To move or proceed on a repeatedly curving course. — WIND².

twinge *noun*
A sensation of physical discomfort occurring as the result of disease or injury. — PAIN *noun*.

twinkle *verb*
1. To shine with intermittent gleams. — 1. BLINK *verb*.
2. To emit light suddenly in rays or sparks. — 2. FLASH *verb*.
3. *Archaic.* To open and close the eyes rapidly. — 3. BLINK *verb*.

twinkle *noun*
1. A sudden quick light. — 1. BLINK *noun*.
2. A very brief time. — 2. FLASH *noun*.

twinkling *noun*
A very brief time. — FLASH *noun*.

twirl *verb*
To rotate rapidly. — SPIN *verb*.

twirp *noun* — SEE **twerp.**

twist *verb*
1. To move or proceed on a repeatedly curving course. — 1. WIND².
2. To give an inaccurate view of by representing falsely or misleadingly. — 2. DISTORT.
3. To alter and spoil the natural form or appearance of. — 3. DEFORM.

twist *noun*
1. An often sudden change or departure, as in a trend. — 1. TURN *noun*.
2. A clever, unexpected new trick or method. — 2. WRINKLE².

twisting *adjective*
1. Having bends, curves, or angles. — 1. CROOKED.

2. Repeatedly curving in alternate directions.

2. WINDING.

twit   *verb*
To make fun of.

RIDICULE *verb.*

twitch   *verb*
To move or cause to move with a sudden, abrupt motion.

JERK *verb.*

    twitch   *noun*
    1. A sudden pull.
    2. A nervous shaking of the body.

    1. JERK *noun.*
    2. TREMOR *noun.*

twitchy   *adjective*
Feeling or exhibiting nervous tension.

EDGY.

twitter   *verb*
To move to and fro in short, jerky movements.

SHAKE *verb.*

twitting   *noun*
Words or actions intended to evoke contemptuous laughter.

RIDICULE *noun.*

two bits   *noun*
Informal. A small or trifling amount of money.

PEANUTS.

two-faced   *adjective*
    1. Characterized by duplicity.
    2. Of or practicing hypocrisy.

    1. DOUBLE *adjective.*
    2. HYPOCRITICAL.

two-facedness   *noun*
A show or expression of feelings or beliefs one does not actually hold or possess.

HYPOCRISY.

two-fisted   *adjective*
Informal. Indulging in drink to an excessive degree.

HEAVY *adjective.*

twofold   *adjective*
    1. Twice as much or as large.
    2. Composed of two parts or things.

    1. DOUBLE *adjective.*
    2. DOUBLE *adjective.*

twosome   *noun*
Two persons united, as by marriage.

PAIR *noun.*

type   *noun*
A class that is defined by the common attribute or attributes possessed by all its members.

KIND[2].

typical also **typic**   *adjective*
    1. Having the nature of, constituting, or serving as a type: *a piece of jewelry typical of Fabergé; typical weather for this part of the country.*

    1. *Syns:* archetypal, archetypic (*also* archetypical), classic, classical, model, paradigmatic, prototypal, prototypic *or* prototypical, quintessential, representative.
    Near-syns: characteristic, emblematic, symbolic; ideal.
    Ants: atypical, untypical.

    2. To be expected.
    3. Serving to identify or set apart an individual or group.

    2. COMMON *adjective.*
    3. DISTINCTIVE.

typically   *adverb*
In an expected or customary manner.

USUALLY.

typify   *verb*
To serve as the image of.

REPRESENT.

tyrannical also **tyrannic**   *adjective*
    1. Having and exercising complete political power and control.
    2. Characterized by or favoring absolute obedience to authority.

    1. ABSOLUTE.

    2. AUTHORITARIAN *adjective.*

tyrannize   *verb*
    1. To exercise absolute power, esp. arbitrarily or cruelly: *The occupying army tyrannized the vanquished.*
    2. To command in an arrogant manner.

    1. *Syn:* trample on. —*Idiom* grind someone's face in the dirt (*or* mud).

    2. BOSS *verb.*

tyrannous *adjective*
Having and exercising complete political power and control.

ABSOLUTE.

tyranny *noun*
Absolute power, esp. when exercised unjustly or cruelly: *fascist tyranny.*

Syns: autocracy, despotism, dictatorship, totalitarianism.
Near-syns: absolutism, authoritarianism, fascism, monocracy, oppression.

tyrant *noun*
1. An absolute ruler, esp. one who is harsh and oppressive.

1. DICTATOR.

2. One who imposes or favors absolute obedience to authority.

2. AUTHORITARIAN *noun.*

tyro *noun*
1. One lacking professional skill and ease in a particular pursuit.

1. AMATEUR.

2. One who is just starting to learn or do something.

2. BEGINNER.

U

ubiquitous *adjective*
Ever present in all places.

UNIVERSAL *adjective.*

ugliness *noun*
1. The quality or condition of being ugly: *the ugliness of ghetto squalor.*

1. **Syns:** frightfulness, hideousness, unsightliness.

2. An unsightly object.

2. MESS *noun.*

ugly *adjective*
1. Extremely displeasing to the eye: *An ugly scar disfigured his face.*

1. **Syns:** hideous, ill-favored, ill-looking, unsightly. —*Idioms* enough to stop a clock, ugly as sin.
Near-syns: homely, plain, unattractive.
Ant: beautiful.

2. Extremely unpleasant to the senses or feelings.

2. OFFENSIVE.

3. Violently disturbed, as by storms.

3. ROUGH *adjective.*

4. *Informal.* Having or showing a bad temper.

4. ILL-TEMPERED.

ugly *noun*
An unsightly object.

MESS *noun.*

uh-huh *adverb*
Informal. It is so; as you say or ask.

YES *adverb.*

ulterior *adjective*
1. Lying beyond what is obvious or avowed: *The President tried to discern the Soviets' ulterior motives.*

1. **Syns:** buried, concealed, covert, hidden, obscured, shrouded. —*Idiom* under cover (*or* wraps).
Near-syns: ambiguous, cryptic, dark, elusive, enigmatic, equivocal, evasive, inscrutable.

2. Going beyond what currently exists.

2. FURTHER *adjective.*

ultimate *adjective*
1. Of the greatest possible degree, quality, or intensity: *His death was the ultimate proof of his patriotism.*

1. **Syns:** supreme, surpassing, transcendent, unsurpassable.

2. Of or relating to a terminative condition, stage, or point.

2. LAST[1] *adjective.*

3. Most distant or remote from a center.
4. Of or being an irreducible element.
5. Greatest in quantity or highest in degree that has been or can be attained.

ultimate *noun*
The greatest quantity or highest degree attainable.

ultimate *verb*
To bring or come to a natural or proper end.

ultimately *adverb*
After a considerable length of time, usu. after a delay.

ultra *adjective*
Holding esp. political views that deviate drastically and fundamentally from conventional or traditional beliefs.

ultra *noun*
One who holds extreme views or advocates extreme measures.

ultraconservative *adjective*
Vehemently, often fanatically opposing progress or reform.

ultraconservative *noun*
A person who vehemently, often fanatically opposes progress and favors return to a previous condition.

ululate *verb*
To utter or emit a long, mournful, plaintive sound.

ululation *noun*
A long, mournful cry.

umbra *noun*
1. Comparative darkness that results from the blocking of light rays.
2. A supernatural being.

umbrage *noun*
1. Extreme displeasure caused by an insult or slight.
2. *Archaic.* Comparative darkness that results from the blocking of light rays.

umbrageous *adjective*
Casting shade.

umbrous *adjective*
Full of shade.

ump *noun*
Slang. A person, usu. appointed, who decides the issues or results, or supervises the conduct, of a competition or conflict.

umpire *verb*
To make a decision about (a controversy, dispute, etc.) after deliberation, as in a court of law.

unabashed *adjective*
Characterized by or done without shame.

unable *verb*
To make incapable, as of doing a job.

unabridged *adjective*
Not shortened by omissions.

unacceptable *adjective*
Arousing disapproval.

unaccompanied *adjective*
Lacking the company of others.

unaccountable *adjective*
1. Difficult to explain or understand.
2. That cannot be explained.

unacquainted *adjective*
Not aware or informed.

---

3. EXTREME *adjective*.
4. ELEMENTAL.
5. MAXIMUM *adjective*.

MAXIMUM *noun*.

CLOSE[1] *verb*.

AT LAST.

EXTREME *adjective*.

EXTREMIST *noun*.

REACTIONARY *adjective*.

REACTIONARY *noun*.

HOWL *verb*.

HOWL *noun*.

1. SHADE *noun*.

2. GHOST *noun*.

1. OFFENSE.
2. SHADE *noun*

SHADY.

SHADY.

JUDGE *noun*.

JUDGE *verb*.

SHAMELESS.

UNFIT *verb*.

COMPLETE *adjective*.

OBJECTIONABLE.

ALONE *adjective*.

1. MYSTERIOUS.
2. INEXPLICABLE.

IGNORANT.

unadorned *adjective*
1. Without addition, decoration, or qualification.
2. Of a plain and unsophisticated nature.

1. BARE *adjective.*
2. RUSTIC *adjective.*

unadulterated *adjective*
1. Produced by nature; not artificial or manmade.
2. Free from extraneous elements.

1. NATURAL *adjective.*
2. PURE *adjective.*

unadvantageous *adjective*
Tending to discourage, retard, to make more difficult.

UNFAVORABLE.

unaffected *adjective*
1. Devoid of any hypocrisy or pretense.
2. Free from guile, cunning, or deceit.
3. Not affected by or showing emotion.

1. GENUINE.
2. ARTLESS.
3. COLD *adjective.*

unafraid *adjective*
Having or showing courage.

BRAVE *adjective.*

unalterable *adjective*
1. That cannot be revoked or undone.
2. Incapable of changing or being modified.

1. IRREVOCABLE.
2. INFLEXIBLE.

unambiguous *adjective*
1. Clearly, fully, and sometimes emphatically expressed.
2. Clearly defined; not ambiguous.

1. DEFINITE.

2. SHARP *adjective.*

unanimity *noun*
The quality or condition of being in complete mutual agreement: *The unanimity of their disapproval was disconcerting.*

Syns: accord, consensus, unanimousness.

unanimous *adjective*
Being in or characterized by complete agreement: *unanimous in wanting to return home; a unanimous opinion of the court.*

Syns: concurrent, solid. —*Idioms* as one, of one mind, with one voice.
Near-ants: differing, discordant, inharmonious; divided.

unanimousness *noun*
The quality or condition of being in complete mutual agreement.

UNANIMITY.

unappeasable *adjective*
Having an insatiable appetite for an activity or pursuit.

VORACIOUS.

unappetizing *adjective*
So unpleasant in flavor as to be inedible.

UNPALATABLE.

unappreciable *adjective*
Incapable of being apprehended by the mind or the senses.

IMPERCEPTIBLE.

unappreciated *adjective*
Not apt to be appreciated.

THANKLESS.

unappreciative *adjective*
Not showing or feeling gratitude.

THANKLESS.

unapproachable *adjective*
1. Unable to be reached.
2. Not friendly, sociable, or warm in manner.

1. INACCESSIBLE.
2. COOL *adjective.*

unapt *adjective*
1. Not suited to circumstances.
2. Lacking the qualities, as efficiency or skill, required to produce desired results.

1. IMPROPER.
2. INEFFICIENT.

unassuming *adjective*
Having or expressing feelings of humility.

HUMBLE *adjective.*

unattached *adjective*
Without a spouse.

SINGLE *adjective.*

unattainable *adjective*
1. Unable to be reached.
2. Not capable of happening or being done.

1. INACCESSIBLE.
2. IMPOSSIBLE.

unattractive *adjective*
Not handsome or beautiful.

PLAIN *adjective.*

unavailing *adjective*
Having no useful result.   FUTILE.

unavoidable *adjective*
Sure to happen.   CERTAIN.

unawake *adjective*
In a state of sleep.   SLEEPING.

unaware *adjective*
Not aware or informed.   IGNORANT.

unaware *adverb*
Without adequate preparation.   UNAWARES.

unawares *adverb*
Without adequate preparation: *The sudden accusation*   ***Syns:*** aback, short, unaware. —*Idioms* by
caught her unawares.   surprise, off base.

unbalance *verb*
To make insane.   DERANGE.

unbalance *noun*
Serious mental illness or disorder impairing a person's   INSANITY.
capacity to function normally and safely.

unbalanced *adjective*
Afflicted with or exhibiting irrationality and mental   INSANE.
unsoundness.

unbearable *adjective*
Not capable of being endured or tolerated: *had to flee*   ***Syns:*** impossible, insufferable,
the unbearable heat.   insupportable, intolerable, unendurable,
                                                  unsufferable, unsupportable.
                                                  Near-syns: agonizing, distressing, painful,
                                                  trying.
                                                  Ants: bearable, sufferable, tolerable.

unbecoming *adjective*
1. Not in keeping with conventional mores.   1. IMPROPER.
2. Not suited to circumstances.   2. IMPROPER.
3. Lacking style and good taste.   3. TACKY[2].

unbefitting *adjective*
1. Not in keeping with conventional mores.   1. IMPROPER.
2. Not suited to circumstances.   2. IMPROPER.

unbelief *noun*
The refusal or reluctance to believe.   DISBELIEF.

unbelievable *adjective*
1. Not plausible or believable.   1. IMPLAUSIBLE.
2. Not to be believed.   2. INCREDIBLE.
3. So remarkable as to elicit disbelief.   3. FABULOUS.

unbelieve *verb*
To give no credence to.   DISBELIEVE.

unbeliever *noun*
One who habitually or instinctively doubts or   SKEPTIC.
questions.

unbelieving *adjective*
Refusing or reluctant to believe.   INCREDULOUS.

unbend *verb*
To take repose by ceasing work or other effort for an   REST[1] *verb.*
interval of time.

unbendable *adjective*
Firmly, often unreasonably immovable in purpose or   STUBBORN.
will.

unbending *adjective*
1. Not changing shape or bending.   1. RIGID.
2. Indicating or possessing determination, resolution,   2. FIRM[1].
   or persistence.
3. Having or showing uncompromising determination   3. GRIM.
   or resolution in purpose or action.

4. Firmly, often unreasonably immovable in purpose or will.   **4.** STUBBORN.

unbiased *adjective*
  1. Free from bias in judgment.   **1.** FAIR *adjective*.
  2. Not inclining toward or actively taking either side in a matter under dispute.   **2.** NEUTRAL.

unbind *verb*
To free from ties or fasteners.   UNDO.

unblamable *adjective*
Beyond reproach.   EXEMPLARY.

unblemished *adjective*
  1. Free from flaws or blemishes.   **1.** CLEAR *adjective*.
  2. In excellent condition.   **2.** GOOD *adjective*.
  3. Free from evil and corruption.   **3.** INNOCENT *adjective*.

unblended or **unblent** *adjective*
Not diluted or mixed with other substances.   STRAIGHT *adjective*.

unblent *adjective*   SEE **unblended.**

unblushing *adjective*
Characterized by or done without shame.   SHAMELESS.

unbodied *adjective*
Having no body, form, or substance.   IMMATERIAL.

unbounded *adjective*
  1. Having no ends or limits.   **1.** ENDLESS.
  2. Completely such, without qualification or exception.   **2.** UTTER^2.

unbridled *adjective*
Lacking in moral restraint.   ABANDONED.

unbroken *adjective*
  1. Free from flaws or blemishes.   **1.** CLEAR *adjective*.
  2. In excellent condition.   **2.** GOOD *adjective*.

unburden *verb*
To free from something objectionable or undesirable.   RID.

uncalled-for *adjective*
  1. Not necessary.   **1.** UNNECESSARY.
  2. Not required, necessary, or warranted by the circumstances of the case.   **2.** WANTON *adjective*.

uncandor *noun*
Lack of sincerity.   INSINCERITY.

uncanny *adjective*
Of a mysteriously strange and usu. frightening nature.   WEIRD.

uncaring *adjective*
Not sympathetic.   UNSYMPATHETIC.

unceasing *adjective*
Existing or occurring without interruption or end.   CONTINUAL.

unceremonious *adjective*
Not formal or ceremonious.   INFORMAL.

unceremoniousness *noun*
Lack or avoidance of formality.   INFORMALITY.

uncertain *adjective*
  1. Experiencing doubt.   **1.** DOUBTFUL.
  2. Not affording certainty.   **2.** AMBIGUOUS.
  3. Liable to more than one interpretation.   **3.** AMBIGUOUS.
  4. In doubt or dispute.   **4.** DEBATABLE.
  5. Marked by lack of firm decision or commitment; of questionable outcome.   **5.** INDEFINITE.
  6. Capable of or liable to change.   **6.** CHANGEABLE.
  7. Given to or exhibiting hesitation.   **7.** HESITANT.
  8. Following no predictable pattern.   **8.** CAPRICIOUS.
  9. Of dubious character.   **9.** SHADY.

uncertainty *noun*
  1. A lack of conviction or certainty.   **1.** DOUBT *noun*.
  2. The quality or state of being ambiguous.   **2.** VAGUENESS.

unchangeable *adjective*
Incapable of changing or being modified.   INFLEXIBLE.

unchanging *adjective*
1. Remaining continually unchanged.   1. CONSISTENT.
2. Having no variations.   2. EVEN[1] *adjective.*

uncharitable *adjective*
Not sympathetic.   UNSYMPATHETIC.

unchaste *adjective*
Not chaste or moral.   IMPURE.

uncivil *adjective*
1. Having or showing a lack of respect.   1. DISRESPECTFUL.
2. Not civilized.   2. UNCIVILIZED.

uncivilized *adjective*
1. Not civilized: *an uncivilized people.*   1. ***Syns:*** barbarian, barbaric, barbarous,
                                                               primitive, rude, savage, uncivil,
                                                               uncultivated, wild.
                                                               Near-ants: cultured, enlightened,
                                                               humane, sophisticated; refined, well-
                                                               bred, well-mannered; domestic, tame.
                                                               Ant: civilized.

2. Lacking in delicacy or refinement.   2. COARSE.

unclad *adjective*
Not wearing any clothes.   NUDE.

unclasp *verb*
To free from ties or fasteners.   UNDO.

unclean *adjective*
1. Covered or stained with or as if with dirt or other   1. DIRTY *adjective.*
   impurities.
2. Not chaste or moral.   2. IMPURE.
3. Ceremonially or religiously unfit.   3. IMPURE.

uncleanliness *noun*
The condition or state of being dirty.   DIRTINESS.

uncleanly *adjective*
1. Covered or stained with or as if with dirt or other   1. DIRTY *adjective.*
   impurities.
2. Not chaste or moral.   2. IMPURE.

uncleanness *noun*
1. The condition or state of being dirty.   1. DIRTINESS.
2. Impure condition.   2. IMPURITY.

unclear *adjective*
1. Not clearly perceived or perceptible: *an unclear view   1. ***Syns:*** blear, bleary, cloudy, dim, faint,
   through the smog; an unclear recollection.*   foggy, fuzzy, hazy, indefinite,
                                                               indistinct, misty, obscure, shadowy,
                                                               undistinct, vague, vaporous (*also*
                                                               vapory).

2. Not affording certainty.   2. AMBIGUOUS.
3. Liable to more than one interpretation.   3. AMBIGUOUS.

unclearness *noun*
The quality or state of being ambiguous.   VAGUENESS.

unclose *verb*
To become or cause to become open.   OPEN *verb.*

unclothe *verb*
1. To remove all the clothing from.   1. STRIP[1].
2. To make visible; bring to view.   2. REVEAL.

unclothed *adjective*
Not wearing any clothes.   NUDE.

unclouded *adjective*
Free from clouds, mist, etc.   CLEAR *adjective.*

uncomely *adjective*
Not handsome or beautiful.   PLAIN *adjective.*

uncomfortable *adjective*
1. Causing discomfort: *a lumpy, uncomfortable mattress.*

    1. **Syns:** comfortless, uncomforting, uncomfy (*Informal*).
    Near-syns: discomforting, distressing, harsh, uneasy.
    Ant: comfortable.

2. Characterized by embarrassment and discomfort.

    2. AWKWARD.

uncomforting *adjective*
Causing discomfort.

UNCOMFORTABLE.

uncomfy *adjective*
Informal. Causing discomfort.

UNCOMFORTABLE.

uncommitted *adjective*
Not inclining toward or actively taking either side in a matter under dispute.

NEUTRAL.

uncommon *adjective*
1. Rarely occurring or appearing.
2. Far beyond what is usual, normal, or customary.

1. INFREQUENT.
2. RARE.

uncommunicative *adjective*
1. Not friendly, sociable, or warm in manner.
2. Not speaking freely or openly.

1. COOL *adjective*.
2. TACITURN.

uncommunicativeness *noun*
The keeping of one's thoughts and emotions to oneself.

RESERVE *noun*.

uncompassionate *adjective*
Not sympathetic.

UNSYMPATHETIC.

uncompelled *adjective*
Done by one's own choice.

VOLUNTARY *adjective*.

uncompensated *adjective*
Contributing one's time without pay.

UNPAID.

uncompliant *adjective*
1. Firmly, often unreasonably immovable in purpose or will.
2. Refusing or failing to obey.

1. STUBBORN.
2. DISOBEDIENT.

uncomplimentary *adjective*
Tending or intending to belittle.

DISPARAGING.

uncomprehending *adjective*
Unwilling or unable to perceive.

BLIND *adjective*.

uncomprehensible *adjective*
Incapable of being grasped by the intellect or understanding.

INCOMPREHENSIBLE.

uncompromising *adjective*
1. Indicating or possessing determination, resolution, or persistence.
2. Conforming completely to established rule.
3. Firmly, often unreasonably immovable in purpose or will.

1. FIRM[1].
2. STRICT.
3. STUBBORN.

unconceivable *adjective*
Not plausible or believable.

IMPLAUSIBLE.

unconcern *noun*
Lack of emotion or interest.

APATHY.

unconcerned *adjective*
1. Lacking or marked by a lack of care.
2. Lacking interest in one's surroundings or worldly affairs.
3. Without emotion or interest.

1. CARELESS.
2. DETACHED.
3. APATHETIC.

unconditional *adjective*
1. Without limitations or mitigating conditions: *an unconditional surrender.*
2. Having no reservations.

1. **Syns:** absolute, unconditioned, unqualified, unreserved.
2. IMPLICIT.

unconditioned *adjective*
Without limitations or mitigating conditions.

UNCONDITIONAL.

unconfined *adjective*
Able to move about at will without bounds or restraint.

LOOSE *adjective*.

uncongenial *adjective*
1. Devoid of harmony and accord.
2. Arousing deep-seated dislike.

1. INHARMONIOUS.
2. ANTIPATHETIC.

unconquerable *adjective*
Incapable of being conquered, overrun, or subjugated.

INVINCIBLE.

unconscionable *adjective*
1. Beyond all reason.
2. Vastly exceeding a normal limit, as in cost.
3. Lacking scruples or principles.

1. OUTRAGEOUS.
2. STEEP[1].
3. UNSCRUPULOUS.

unconscious *adjective*
1. Lacking consciousness: *knocked unconscious by the punch.*

1. *Syns:* cold (*Informal*), inconscious, insensible, senseless. —*Idiom* out like a light.

2. Not aware or informed.

2. IGNORANT.

unconsequential *adjective*
Contemptibly unimportant.

PETTY.

unconsidered *adjective*
1. Having no particular pattern, purpose, organization, or structure.
2. Contemptibly unimportant.

1. RANDOM.
2. PETTY.

unconspicuous *adjective*
Not readily noticed or seen.

INCONSPICUOUS.

unconstrained *adjective*
Lacking in moral restraint.

ABANDONED.

uncontrollability *noun*
The quality or condition of being unruly.

UNRULINESS.

uncontrollable *adjective*
Not submitting to discipline or control.

UNRULY.

uncontrollableness *noun*
The quality or condition of being unruly.

UNRULINESS.

uncontrolled *adjective*
1. Out of control.
2. Lacking in moral restraint.

1. RUNAWAY *adjective* at **run away.**
2. ABANDONED.

unconventional *adjective*
Not usual or ordinary.

UNUSUAL.

unconvincing *adjective*
Not plausible or believable.

IMPLAUSIBLE.

uncooked *adjective*
Not cooked.

RAW.

uncorporal *adjective*
Having no body, form, or substance.

IMMATERIAL.

uncorrupted *adjective*
Free from evil and corruption.

INNOCENT *adjective*.

uncountable *adjective*
Too great to be calculated.

INCALCULABLE.

uncouple *verb*
To separate one thing from another thing.

DETACH.

uncoupling *noun*
The act or process of detaching.

DETACHMENT.

uncouth *adjective*
Lacking in delicacy or refinement.

COARSE.

uncover *verb*
1. To find by investigation: *a reporter who uncovered the true facts of the murder.*
2. To make bare.
3. To make visible; bring to view.
4. To disclose in a breach of confidence.
5. To lay open, as to something undesirable or injurious.

1. *Syns:* dig up (*or* out), turn up, unearth. —*Idiom* bring to light.
2. BARE *verb*.
3. REVEAL.
4. BETRAY.
5. EXPOSE.

uncovered *adjective*
Having no protecting or concealing cover.　OPEN *adjective*.

uncreative *adjective*
Lacking originality.　STERILE.

uncritical *adjective*
Lacking in intellectual depth or thoroughness.　SUPERFICIAL.

unctious *adjective*
Affectedly and self-servingly earnest.　UNCTUOUS.

unctuous *adjective*
1. Affectedly and self-servingly earnest: *The ambassador had an oozing, unctuous manner.*

1. **Syns:** fulsome, oily, oleaginous, sleek, smarmy, unctious.
Near-syns: bland, glib, hypocritical, ingratiating, sanctimonious; flattering, wheedling.

2. Having the qualities of fat.　2. FATTY *adjective*.

uncultivated *adjective*
1. Lacking in delicacy or refinement.　1. COARSE.
2. Not civilized.　2. UNCIVILIZED.
3. In a primitive state; not domesticated or cultivated.　3. WILD *adjective*.

uncut *adjective*
Not shortened by omissions.　COMPLETE *adjective*.

undamaged *adjective*
In excellent condition.　GOOD *adjective*.

undaunted *adjective*
Having or showing courage.　BRAVE *adjective*.

undecided *adjective*
1. Experiencing doubt.　1. DOUBTFUL.
2. Not affording certainty.　2. AMBIGUOUS.
3. Marked by lack of firm decision or commitment; of questionable outcome.　3. INDEFINITE.

undecisive *adjective*
Given to or exhibiting hesitation.　HESITANT.

undeclared *adjective*
1. Not voiced or expressed.　1. SILENT.
2. Conveyed indirectly without words or speech.　2. IMPLICIT.

undefiled *adjective*
Free from evil and corruption.　INNOCENT *adjective*.

undemonstrated *adjective*
Not tested or proved.　UNTRIED.

undemonstrative *adjective*
Not friendly, sociable, or warm in manner.　COOL *adjective*.

undeniable *adjective*
1. In agreement or correspondence with fact.　1. ACTUAL.
2. Established beyond a doubt.　2. CERTAIN.

undependable *adjective*
1. Not to be depended on: *an undependable bridge needing maintenance; undependable weather.*

1. **Syns:** trustless, unreliable, untrustworthy.

2. So weak or defective as to be liable to fail.　2. TRICK *adjective*.

under *adjective*
Of subordinate standing or importance.　MINOR *adjective*.

underage¹ *noun*
The condition or fact of being deficient.　SHORTAGE.

underage² *adjective*
Not yet a legal adult.　MINOR *adjective*.

undercover *adjective*
Existing or operating in a way so as to ensure complete concealment and confidentiality.　SECRET *adjective*.

underdeveloped *adjective*
Not progressing and developing as fast as others, as in economic and social aspects.　BACKWARD *adjective*.

underdog *noun*
A person living under very unhappy circumstances.   UNFORTUNATE *noun.*

undergo *verb*
To participate in or partake of personally.   EXPERIENCE *verb.*

underearth *adjective*
Located or operating beneath the earth's surface.   UNDERGROUND *adjective.*

underground *adjective*
Located or operating beneath the earth's surface: *wells*   **Syns:** hypogeal (*also* hypogean,
that tap underground pools of fresh water.   hypogeous), subterrane, subterranean,
                                                                          subterrene, subterrestrial, underearth.

underground *noun*
A clandestine organization of freedom fighters in an   RESISTANCE.
oppressed land.

underhand *adjective*
Marked by treachery or deceit: *such underhand*   **Syns:** devious, disingenuous, duplicitous,
business practices as profiteering and false advertising.   guileful, indirect, shifty, sneaking,
                                                                          sneaky, underhanded.
                                                                          Near-ants: candid, frank, honest, open,
                                                                          plain; straight-forward.
                                                                          Ant: aboveboard.

underhanded *adjective*
1. Lacking the requisite workers or players: *an*   1. **Syns:** shorthanded, undermanned.
   underhanded typing pool.   **Near-syns:** short, understaffed,
                                                                            wanting.
2. Marked by treachery or deceit.   2. UNDERHAND.

underhandedness *noun*
Lack of straightforwardness and honesty in action.   INDIRECTION.

underline *verb*
To accord emphasis to.   EMPHASIZE.

underlined *adjective*
Expressed or performed with emphasis.   EMPHATIC.

underling *noun*
One belonging to a lower class or rank.   SUBORDINATE *noun.*

underlying *adjective*
1. Of or being an irreducible element.   1. ELEMENTAL.
2. Arising from or going to the root or source.   2. RADICAL *adjective.*

undermanned *adjective*
Lacking the requisite workers or players.   UNDERHANDED.

undermine *verb*
1. To lessen or deplete the nerve, energy, or strength   1. ENERVATE.
   of.
2. To damage, destroy, or defeat by sabotage.   2. SABOTAGE *verb.*

undermining *noun*
A deliberate and underhanded effort to defeat or do   SABOTAGE *noun.*
harm to an endeavor.

undermost *adjective*
Opposite to or farthest from the top.   BOTTOM *adjective.*

underneath *noun*
A side or surface that is below or under.   BOTTOM *noun.*

underpinning *noun*
1. The lowest or supporting part or structure.   1. BASE[1] *noun.*
2. A means or device that keeps something erect,   2. SUPPORT *noun.*
   stable, or secure.

underprivileged *adjective*
Economically and socially below standard.   DEPRESSED.

underprivileged *noun*
A person living under very unhappy circumstances.   UNFORTUNATE *noun.*

underscore *verb*
To accord emphasis to.   EMPHASIZE.

underscored *adjective*
Expressed or performed with emphasis.   EMPHATIC.

underside *noun*
A side or surface that is below or under.

BOTTOM *noun*.

undersign *verb*
To affix one's signature to.

SIGN *verb*.

understand *verb*
1. To perceive and recognize the meaning of: *The teacher spoke slowly and simply so that all could understand him.*

1. **Syns:** accept, apprehend, catch, catch on (*Informal*), compass, comprehend, conceive, dig (*Slang*), fathom, follow, get (*Informal*), grasp, ken (*Scot.*), make out, read, savvy (*Slang*), see, sense (*Informal*), take, take in, twig. —*Idiom* get the picture.

2. To perceive directly with the intellect.

2. KNOW.

understandable *adjective*
Capable of being readily understood: *mumbled in a way that his audience found scarcely understandable.*

Syns: comprehensible, fathomable, intelligible, knowable.
Near-ants: abstruse, cryptic, esoteric, hidden, mysterious, obscure, strange, vague.

understanding *adjective*
Cognizant of and comprehending the needs, feelings, problems, and views of others: *an understanding counselor.*

Syns: empathic (*also* empathetic), sympathetic.

understanding *noun*
1. The faculty of thinking, reasoning, and acquiring and applying knowledge.
2. Intellectual hold.
3. An act or state of agreeing between parties regarding a course of action.

1. INTELLIGENCE.

2. GRASP *noun*.
3. AGREEMENT.

understood *adjective*
Conveyed indirectly without words or speech.

IMPLICIT.

undertake *verb*
1. To go about the initial step in doing (something).
2. To take upon oneself.
3. To make an attempt to do or make.
4. To assume an obligation.

1. START *verb*.
2. ASSUME.
3. ATTEMPT *verb*.
4. PLEDGE *verb*.

undertaking *noun*
1. An effort to do or make something.
2. Something undertaken, esp. something requiring extensive planning and work.

1. ATTEMPT *noun*.
2. PROJECT *noun*.

undertone *noun*
A subtle quality underlying or felt to underlie a situation, action, or person.

HINT *noun*.

underwriter *noun*
One who assumes financial responsibility for another.

SPONSOR.

undescribable *adjective*
That cannot be described.

UNSPEAKABLE.

undesigned *adjective*
Not intended.

UNINTENTIONAL.

undesirable *adjective*
1. Not welcome or wanted.
2. Arousing disapproval.

1. UNWELCOME *adjective*.
2. OBJECTIONABLE.

undesired *adjective*
Not welcome or wanted.

UNWELCOME *adjective*.

undetected *adjective*
Not found.

UNFOUND.

undetermined *adjective*
1. Lacking precise limits.
2. Marked by lack of firm decision or commitment; of questionable outcome.

1. INDEFINITE.
2. INDEFINITE.

undeveloped *adjective*
Not progressing and developing as fast as others, as in economic and social aspects.   BACKWARD *adjective*.

undevised *adjective*
Not intended.   UNINTENTIONAL.

undiluted *adjective*
1. Free from extraneous elements.   1. PURE *adjective*.
2. Not diluted or mixed with other substances.   2. STRAIGHT *adjective*.

undiplomatic *adjective*
Lacking sensitivity and skill in dealing with others.   TACTLESS.

undisciplined *adjective*
Not submitting to discipline or control.   UNRULY.

undiscovered *adjective*
Not found.   UNFOUND.

undisguised *adjective*
Speaking or spoken freely and sincerely.   FRANK.

undisputable *adjective*
Established beyond a doubt.   CERTAIN.

undissembling *adjective*
Executed without pretense or obfuscation.   PLAIN *adjective*.

undistinct *adjective*
Not clearly perceived or perceptible.   UNCLEAR.

undistinguishable *adjective*
Incapable of being apprehended by the mind or the senses.   IMPERCEPTIBLE.

undistinguished *adjective*
Of little distinction.   HUMBLE *adjective*.

undivided *adjective*
Not diffused or dispersed.   CONCENTRATED.

undo *verb*
1. To free from ties or fasteners: *She gently undid the bow and opened the package.*   1. **Syns:** disengage, loose, loosen, slip, unbind, unclasp, unfasten, unloose, unloosen, untie.
2. To remove or invalidate by or as if by running a line through or wiping clean.   2. CANCEL.
3. To become or cause to become open.   3. OPEN *verb*.
4. To cause the complete ruin or wreckage of.   4. DESTROY.
5. To lessen or deplete the nerve, energy, or strength of.   5. ENERVATE.
6. To lure or persuade into a sexual relationship.   6. SEDUCE.

undoing *noun*
1. Something that causes total loss or severe impairment of one's health, fortune, honor, hopes, etc.   1. RUIN *noun*.
2. Severe damage or decay rendering something useless or worthless.   2. RUIN *noun*.

undomesticated *adjective*
In a primitive state; not domesticated or cultivated.   WILD *adjective*.

undoubted *adjective*
Not counterfeit or copied.   AUTHENTIC.

undoubting *adjective*
1. Having no reservations.   1. IMPLICIT.
2. Having no doubt.   2. SURE.

undress *noun*
The state of being without clothes.   NUDITY.
 undress *verb*
To remove all the clothing from.   STRIP[1].

undressed *adjective*
Not wearing any clothes.   NUDE.

undue *adjective*
Exceeding a normal or reasonable limit.   EXCESSIVE.

undulate *verb*
1. To have or cause to have a curved or sinuous form or surface.
2. To move sinuously.

1. WAVE.
2. SLITHER.

unduly *adverb*
Too much: *unduly conceited.*

Syns: over, overmuch, super (*Informal*).

undying *adjective*
Not being subject to death.

IMMORTAL.

unearth *verb*
To find by investigation.

UNCOVER.

unearthly *adjective*
1. Of, coming from, or relating to forces or beings that exist outside the natural world.
2. Of a mysteriously strange and usu. frightening nature.
3. So senseless as to be laughable.

1. SUPERNATURAL.
2. WEIRD.
3. FOOLISH.

unease *noun*
Anxious concern.

ANXIETY.

uneasiness *noun*
1. Anxious concern.
2. An uneasy or nervous state.

1. ANXIETY.
2. RESTLESSNESS.

uneasy *adjective*
1. Affording no quiet, repose, or rest.
2. In a state of uneasiness.
3. Feeling or exhibiting nervous tension.
4. Characterized by embarrassment and discomfort.

1. RESTLESS.
2. ANXIOUS.
3. EDGY.
4. AWKWARD.

uneducated *adjective*
Without education or knowledge.

IGNORANT.

unemotional *adjective*
1. Not affected by or showing emotion.
2. With little or no emotion or expression.

1. COLD *adjective.*
2. DRY *adjective.*

unemployed *adjective*
1. Out of work.
2. Not occupied or put to use.

1. WORKLESS.
2. IDLE *adjective.*

unending *adjective*
1. Existing or occurring without interruption or end.
2. Enduring for all time.

1. CONTINUAL.
2. ENDLESS.

unendurable *adjective*
Not capable of being endured or tolerated.

UNBEARABLE.

unenlightened *adjective*
1. Not aware or informed.
2. Exhibiting lack of education or knowledge.

1. IGNORANT.
2. IGNORANT.

unenthusiastic *adjective*
Lacking warmth, interest, enthusiasm, or involvement.

TEPID.

unequal *adjective*
1. Not fair, right, or just.
2. Lacking capability.

1. UNFAIR.
2. INADEQUATE.

unequaled *adjective*
Without equal or rival.

UNIQUE.

unequivocal *adjective*
1. Clearly, fully, and sometimes emphatically expressed.
2. Clearly defined; not ambiguous.
3. Completely such, without qualification or exception.

1. DEFINITE.
2. SHARP *adjective.*
3. UTTER[2].

unerring *adjective*
Such as could not possibly fail or disappoint.

SURE.

unessential *adjective*
Not necessary.

UNNECESSARY.

unethical *adjective*
1. Ruthlessly seeking personal advantage.
2. Lacking scruples or principles.

1. CORRUPT *adjective.*
2. UNSCRUPULOUS.

uneven *adjective*
1. Lacking consistency or regularity in quality or performance: *an uneven novel, at times flat and at times moving.*
2. Not straight, uniform, or symmetrical.
3. Having a coarse, irregular surface.

1. *Syns:* on-again-off-again, patchy, spotty, unsteady, variable.
2. IRREGULAR.
3. ROUGH.

unevenness *noun*
Lack of smoothness or regularity.

IRREGULARITY.

unexampled *adjective*
Without equal or rival.

UNIQUE.

unexceptional *adjective*
Being of no special quality or type.

ORDINARY *adjective.*

unexplainable *adjective*
1. That cannot be explained.
2. Difficult to explain or understand.

1. INEXPLICABLE.
2. MYSTERIOUS.

unexposed *adjective*
Not found.

UNFOUND.

unexpressed *adjective*
1. Not voiced or expressed.
2. Conveyed indirectly without words or speech.

1. SILENT.
2. IMPLICIT.

unexpressible *adjective*
That cannot be described.

UNSPEAKABLE.

unexpurgated *adjective*
Not shortened by omissions.

COMPLETE *adjective.*

unfailing *adjective*
1. Remaining continually unchanged.
2. Such as could not possibly fail or disappoint.

1. CONSISTENT.
2. SURE.

unfair *adjective*
Not fair, right, or just: *unfair housing laws.*

Syns: inequitable, injust (*Obs.*), unequal, unjust.
Near-ants: equal, just, impartial, nondiscriminatory, objective; balanced, rational, reasonable.
Ant: fair.

unfairness *noun*
Lack of justice.

INJUSTICE.

unfaithful *adjective*
Not true to duty or obligation.

FAITHLESS.

unfaithfulness *noun*
Betrayal, esp. of a moral obligation.

FAITHLESSNESS.

unfamiliar *adjective*
1. Showing marked departure from previous practice.
2. Not aware or informed.

1. NEW.
2. IGNORANT.

unfamiliarity *noun*
The condition of being uninformed.

IGNORANCE.

unfasten *verb*
To free from ties or fasteners.

UNDO.

unfastened *adjective*
Freed from contact or connection.

CLEAR *adjective.*

unfathomable *adjective*
1. Difficult to explain or understand.
2. Incapable of being grasped by the intellect or understanding.

1. MYSTERIOUS.
2. INCOMPREHENSIBLE.

unfavorable *adjective*
1. Tending to discourage, retard, or make more difficult: *weather unfavorable for hang-gliding; an unfavorable economic climate.*
2. Bringing, predicting, or characterized by misfortune.

1. *Syns:* adverse, disadvantageous, negative, unadvantageous, unsatisfactory, untoward.
2. BAD.

unfeasible *adjective*
Not capable of happening or being done.

IMPOSSIBLE.

unfeeling *adjective*
1. Lacking physical feeling or sensitivity.
2. Totally lacking in compassion.

1. DEAD *adjective*.
2. COLD-BLOODED.

unfeigned *adjective*
Devoid of any hypocrisy or pretense.

GENUINE.

unfinished *adjective*
Not perfected, elaborated, or completed.

ROUGH.

unfit *adjective*
1. Not suited to a given purpose: *a house unfit for human habitation; an aircraft unfit for flight.*
2. Totally incapable of doing a job.
3. Lacking capability.

1. *Syns:* ill-suited, inappropriate, inapt, unsuitable, unsuited.
2. INCOMPETENT.
3. INADEQUATE.

unfit *verb*
To make incapable, as of doing a job: *a heart condition unfitting him to be a pilot.*

Syns: disable, disqualify, unable, unqualify.

unfitness *noun*
The condition of being improper.

IMPROPRIETY.

unfitting *adjective*
Not suited to circumstances.

IMPROPER.

unflagging *adjective*
Having or showing a capacity for protracted effort, regardless of difficulty or frustration.

TIRELESS.

unflappable *adjective*
Slang. Not easily excited, even under pressure.

COOL *adjective*.

unflawed *adjective*
Supremely excellent in quality or nature.

PERFECT *adjective*.

unflexible *adjective*
Not changing shape or bending.

RIGID.

unfold *verb*
1. To move or arrange so as to cover a larger area.
2. To be disclosed gradually.

1. SPREAD *verb*.
2. DEVELOP.

unfolding *noun*
A progression from a simple form to a more complex one.

DEVELOPMENT.

unforbearing *adjective*
Not able or willing to tolerate or endure with equanimity.

INTOLERANT.

unforced *adjective*
Done by one's own choice.

VOLUNTARY *adjective*.

unforgivable *adjective*
Impossible to excuse, pardon, or justify.

INEXCUSABLE.

unformed *adjective*
Having no distinct shape.

SHAPELESS.

unfortunate *adjective*
1. Involving or undergoing chance misfortune: *an unfortunate turn of events; an unfortunate marriage.*

2. Characterized by inappropriateness and gracelessness, esp. in expression: *an unfortunate, ill-timed remark.*
3. Worthy of severe disapproval.

1. *Syns:* hapless, ill-fated, ill-starred, luckless, misfortunate, star-crossed, unhappy, unlucky, untoward.
2. *Syns:* awkward, ill-chosen, inappropriate, inept, infelicitous, unhappy.
3. DEPLORABLE.

unfortunate *noun*
A person living under very unhappy circumstances: *social workers trying to help the world's unfortunates.*

Syns: loser, miserable, underdog, underprivileged, wretch. —*Idiom* poor devil.

unfound *adjective*
Not found: *hitherto unfound Egyptian tombs.*

Syns: undetected, undiscovered, unexposed.

unfounded *adjective*
Having no basis or foundation in fact.

BASELESS.

unfoundedly *adverb*
Without basis or foundation in fact; *was unfoundedly charged with theft.*   **Syns:** groundlessly, unwarrantedly.

unfrequented *adjective*
Empty of people.   LONELY.

unfriendly *adjective*
Feeling or showing unfriendliness.   HOSTILE.

ungainly *adjective*
Lacking dexterity and grace in physical movement.   AWKWARD.

ungovernable *adjective*
Not submitting to discipline or control.   UNRULY.

ungovernableness *noun*
The quality or condition of being unruly.   UNRULINESS.

ungoverned *adjective*
Lacking in moral restraint.   ABANDONED.

ungraceful *adjective*
Lacking dexterity and grace in physical movement.   AWKWARD.

ungracious *adjective*
1. Lacking good manners.   1. RUDE.
2. Devoid of consideration for others' feelings.   2. THOUGHTLESS.

ungraciousness *noun*
Lack of cordiality and hospitableness.   UNWELCOME *noun*.

ungrateful *adjective*
1. Not apt to be appreciated.   1. THANKLESS.
2. Not showing or feeling gratitude.   2. THANKLESS.

unguarded *adjective*
Inadequately protected.   INSECURE.

unhandy *adjective*
1. Difficult to handle or manage.   1. AWKWARD.
2. Not accessible or handy.   2. INCONVENIENT.

unhappiness *noun*
1. A state of prolonged anguish and privation.   1. MISERY.
2. A feeling or spell of dismally low spirits.   2. GLOOM.

unhappy *adjective*
1. In low spirits.   1. DEPRESSED.
2. Involving or undergoing chance misfortune.   2. UNFORTUNATE *adjective*.
3. Characterized by inappropriateness and   3. UNFORTUNATE *adjective*.
   gracelessness, esp. in expression.

unharmed *adjective*
Free from danger, injury, or the threat of harm.   SAFE.

unharmonious *adjective*
1. Devoid of harmony and accord.   1. INHARMONIOUS.
2. Characterized by unpleasant discordance of sound.   2. INHARMONIOUS.

unhealthy *adjective*
1. Not sustaining or promoting health.   1. UNWHOLESOME.
2. Utterly reprehensible in nature or behavior.   2. CORRUPT *adjective*.
3. Susceptible to or marked by preoccupation with   3. MORBID.
   unwholesome matters.
4. Morally detrimental.   4. UNWHOLESOME.

unheard-of *adjective*
Unknown by name.   OBSCURE *adjective*.

unheeding *adjective*
Showing no concern, attention, or regard.   MINDLESS.

unhesitating *adjective*
Having no reservations.   IMPLICIT.

unhinge *verb*
1. To disturb the health or physiological functioning of. 1. UPSET *verb*.
2. To make insane.   2. DERANGE.

unhorse *verb*
To bring about the downfall of.   OVERTHROW.

unhospitable *adjective*
So disagreeably austere as to discourage approach.   FORBIDDING.

unhurried *adjective*
Careful and slow in acting, moving, or deciding.   DELIBERATE *adjective*.

unhurt *adjective*
1. Free from danger, injury, or the threat of harm.   1. SAFE.
2. In excellent condition.   2. GOOD *adjective*.

unicity *noun*
The quality or condition of being unique.   UNIQUENESS.

unification *noun*
1. A bringing together into a whole: *The USSR is a*   1. *Syns:* coalition, consolidation, union,
   vast nation resulting from the unification of many   unity.
   autonomous republics.
2. The result of combining.   2. COMBINATION.

unified *adjective*
Closely connected by or as if by a treaty.   ALLIED.

uniform *adjective*
1. Having no variations.   1. EVEN[1] *adjective*.
2. Possessing the same or almost the same   2. LIKE[2].
   characteristics.

unify *verb*
1. To make into a whole by joining a system of parts.   1. INTEGRATE *verb*.
2. To combine and adapt in order to attain a particular   2. HARMONIZE.
   effect.

unimaginable *adjective*
Not to be believed.   INCREDIBLE.

unimaginative *adjective*
1. Lacking liveliness, charm, or surprise.   1. DULL *adjective*.
2. Lacking originality.   2. STERILE.

unimpaired *adjective*
In excellent condition.   GOOD *adjective*.

unimpeded *adjective*
Free from obstructions.   CLEAR *adjective*.

unimportance *noun*
Lack of importance.   INDIFFERENCE.

unimportant *adjective*
Not of great importance.   LITTLE.

unimpressionable *adjective*
Not capable of being affected or impressed.   INSENSITIVE.

uninformed *adjective*
Not aware or informed.   IGNORANT.

uninhibited *adjective*
Lacking in moral restraint.   ABANDONED.

uninitiate *noun*
One lacking professional skill and ease in a particular   AMATEUR.
pursuit.

uninjured *adjective*
1. Free from danger, injury, or the threat of harm.   1. SAFE.
2. In excellent condition.   2. GOOD *adjective*.

uninspired *adjective*
1. Lacking liveliness, charm, or surprise.   1. DULL *adjective*.
2. Lacking originality.   2. STERILE.

unintelligent *adjective*
Displaying a complete lack of forethought and good   MINDLESS.
sense.

unintelligible *adjective*
1. Liable to more than one interpretation.   1. AMBIGUOUS.
2. Incapable of being grasped by the intellect or   2. INCOMPREHENSIBLE.
   understanding.

unintended *adjective*
Not intended.

UNINTENTIONAL.

unintentional *adjective*
Not intended: *an unintentional delay; an unintentional gaffe.*

Syns: inadvertent, undesigned, undevised, unintended, unmeant, unplanned, unpremeditated, unthinking, unwitting.

uninterested *adjective*
1. Without emotion or interest.
2. Lacking interest in one's surroundings or worldly affairs.

1. APATHETIC.
2. DETACHED.

uninteresting *adjective*
Arousing no interest or curiosity.

BORING.

uninterrupted *adjective*
Existing or occurring without interruption or end.

CONTINUAL.

uninvited *adjective*
Not welcome or wanted.

UNWELCOME *adjective*.

uninviting *adjective*
So disagreeably austere as to discourage approach.

FORBIDDING.

uninvolved *adjective*
Not inclining toward or actively taking either side in a matter under dispute.

NEUTRAL.

union *noun*
1. A group of people united in a relationship and having some interest, activity, or purpose in common: *a trade union; a union of draft resisters.*

2. An association, esp. of nations for a common cause.
3. The result of combining.
4. A point or position at which two or more things are joined.
5. An identity or coincidence of interests, purposes, or sympathies among the members of a group.
6. A bringing together into a whole.

1. *Syns:* association, club, confederation, congress, federation, fellowship, fraternity, guild, league, order, organization, society.
2. ALLIANCE.
3. COMBINATION.
4. JOINT *noun*.

5. UNITY.

6. UNIFICATION.

unique *adjective*
1. Without equal or rival: *an artist unique in creativity.*

2. Alone in a given category.

1. *Syns:* alone, apart, incomparable, matchless, nonpareil, only, peerless, unequaled (*also* unequalled), unexampled, unmatched, unparalleled, unrivaled (*also* unrivalled).
2. LONE.

uniqueness *noun*
The quality or condition of being unique: *the uniqueness of the diamond.*

Syns: oneness, singleness, unicity, uniquity.
Near-syns: oddity, peculiarity, quaintness, singularity; memorability, notability.

uniquity *noun*
The quality or condition of being unique.

UNIQUENESS.

unit *noun*
A group of people organized for a particular purpose.

FORCE *noun*.

unite *verb*
1. To bring or come together into a united whole.
2. To assemble or join in a group.

1. COMBINE *verb*.
2. BAND^2 *verb*.

unity *noun*
1. The condition of being one: *argued the unity of God and nature.*
2. The state of individuals who are in utter agreement.
3. A bringing together into a whole.
4. An identity or coincidence of interests, purposes, or sympathies among the members of a group: *believed that there was strength in unity.*

1. *Syns:* oneness, singleness, singularity.

2. HARMONY.
3. UNIFICATION.
4. *Syns:* oneness, solidarity, union.

universal *adjective*
1. So pervasive and all-inclusive as to exist in or affect the whole world: *a universal fear of nuclear war; universal truths.*
2. Belonging or pertaining to the whole.
3. Ever present in all places: *believed in a universal divine spirit guiding men.*

universal *noun*
A broad and basic rule or truth.

universalize *verb*
To make universal: *rules governing the treatment of POW's universalized by the Geneva Convention.*

universe *noun*
1. The totality of all existing things: *studied the beginnings and the continuing development of the universe.*
2. The human race.

unjust *adjective*
Not fair, right, or just.

unjustifiable *adjective*
Impossible to excuse, pardon, or justify.

unjustness *noun*
Lack of justice.

unkempt *adjective*
Marked by an absence of cleanliness and order.

unknowing *adjective*
Not aware or informed.

unlade *verb*
To remove the cargo or load from.

unlawful *adjective*
1. Contrary to accepted, esp. moral conventions: *an unlawful love.*
2. Prohibited by law.
3. Of, involving, or being a crime.
4. Born out of wedlock.

unlawfulness *noun*
The state or quality of being illegal.

unlearned *adjective*
1. Without education or knowledge.
2. Lacking the requisite scholarship or instruction.

unlike *adjective*
Not like another in nature, quality, amount, or form.

unlikely *adjective*
Not likely.

unlikeness *noun*
The condition of being unlike or dissimilar.

unlimited *adjective*
1. Having no ends or limits.
2. Completely such, without qualification or exception.

unload *verb*
1. To remove the cargo or load from: *longshoremen unloading cars from a freighter.*
2. To unburden oneself of by pouring out (one's troubles): *He unloaded all of his marital problems on me.*
3. To get rid of completely by selling, esp. in quantity or at discount.

unloose *verb*
To free from ties or fasteners.

unloosen *verb*
To free from ties or fasteners.

---

1. **Syns:** catholic, cosmic, cosmopolitan, ecumenical, global, pandemic, planetary, worldwide.
2. GENERAL.
3. **Syns:** omnipresent, ubiquitous.

LAW *noun*.

Syn: generalize.

1. **Syns:** cosmos, creation, macrocosm, macrocosmos, megacosm, nature, world.
2. MANKIND.

UNFAIR.

INEXCUSABLE.

INJUSTICE.

MESSY.

IGNORANT.

UNLOAD.

1. **Syns:** illicit, lawless, wrongful.
2. ILLEGAL.
3. CRIMINAL *adjective*.
4. ILLEGITIMATE.

ILLEGALITY.

1. IGNORANT.
2. UNSCHOLARLY.

DIFFERENT.

DOUBTFUL.

DIFFERENCE.

1. ENDLESS.
2. UTTER[2].

1. **Syns:** disburden, discharge, unlade.
2. **Syn:** dump.

3. SELL OFF at **sell**.

UNDO.

UNDO.

unlovely *adjective*
Not handsome or beautiful.   PLAIN *adjective*.

unluck *noun*
Chiefly Regional. Bad fortune.   MISFORTUNE.

unluckiness *noun*
Bad fortune.   MISFORTUNE.

unlucky *adjective*
1. Involving or undergoing chance misfortune.   1. UNFORTUNATE *adjective*.
2. Portending future disaster.   2. FATEFUL.
3. Disturbing because of failure to measure up to a   3. DISAPPOINTING.
standard or produce the desired results.

unmanageability *noun*
The quality or condition of being unruly.   UNRULINESS.

unmanageable *adjective*
1. Not submitting to discipline or control.   1. UNRULY.
2. Difficult to handle or manage.   2. AWKWARD.

unmanliness *noun*
Ignoble lack of courage.   COWARDICE.

unmanly *adjective*
1. Ignobly lacking in courage.   1. COWARDLY.
2. Having qualities more appropriate to women than to   2. EFFEMINATE *adjective*.
men.

unmannered *adjective*
Executed without pretense or obfuscation.   PLAIN *adjective*.

unmannerly *adjective*
Lacking good manners.   RUDE.

unmarked *adjective*
Free from flaws or blemishes.   CLEAR *adjective*.

unmarred *adjective*
In excellent condition.   GOOD *adjective*.

unmarried *adjective*
Without a spouse.   SINGLE *adjective*.

unmask *verb*
To make visible; bring to view.   REVEAL.

unmatched *adjective*
Without equal or rival.   UNIQUE.

unmeant *adjective*
Not intended.   UNINTENTIONAL.

unmentionable *adjective*
That may not be spoken of or uttered.   UNSPEAKABLE.

unmerciful *adjective*
Having or showing no mercy.   MERCILESS.

unmindful *adjective*
Showing no concern, attention, or regard.   MINDLESS.

unmistakable *adjective*
1. Easily seen through due to a lack of subtlety.   1. UNSUBTLE.
2. Clearly defined; not ambiguous.   2. SHARP *adjective*.

unmitigated *adjective*
Completely such, without qualification or exception. UTTER^2.

unmixed *adjective*
1. Free from extraneous elements.   1. PURE *adjective*.
2. Not diluted or mixed with other substances.   2. STRAIGHT *adjective*.

unmovable *adjective*
Firmly in position.   FIXED.

unmoved *adjective*
Not sympathetic.   UNSYMPATHETIC.

unmoving *adjective*
Firmly in position.   FIXED.

unmusical *adjective*
Characterized by unpleasant discordance of sound.   INHARMONIOUS.

unnamed *adjective*
Having an unknown name or author. — ANONYMOUS.

unnatural *adjective*
1. Departing from the normal. — 1. ABNORMAL.
2. Greatly exceeding or departing from the normal course of nature. — 2. PRETERNATURAL.

unnecessary *adjective*
Not necessary: *unnecessary roughness in football; avoided making unnecessary trips in the car.* — *Syns:* inessential, needless, nonessential, uncalled-for, unessential, unneeded, unrequired.

unneeded *adjective*
Not necessary. — UNNECESSARY.

unnegotiable *adjective*
Incapable of being used or availed of to advantage. — IMPRACTICABLE.

unnerve *verb*
To lessen or deplete the nerve, energy, or strength of. — ENERVATE.

unnoticeable *adjective*
1. Not readily noticed or seen. — 1. INCONSPICUOUS.
2. Incapable of being apprehended by the mind or the senses. — 2. IMPERCEPTIBLE.

unobjectionable *adjective*
Capable of being accepted. — ACCEPTABLE.

unobservable *adjective*
Incapable of being apprehended by the mind or the senses. — IMPERCEPTIBLE.

unobstructed *adjective*
Free from obstructions. — CLEAR *adjective.*

unobtrusive *adjective*
1. Not readily noticed or seen. — 1. INCONSPICUOUS.
2. Not showy or obtrusive. — 2. QUIET.

unoccupied *adjective*
Not spoken for or occupied. — UNRESERVED.

unoffensive *adjective*
Devoid of hurtful qualities. — HARMLESS.

unordinary *adjective*
Not usual or ordinary. — UNUSUAL.

unoriginative *adjective*
Lacking originality. — STERILE.

unostentatious *adjective*
Not elaborate or showy, as in appearance or style. — MODEST.

unostentatiousness *noun*
Lack of ostentation or pretension. — MODESTY.

unpaid *adjective*
1. Contributing one's time without pay: *unpaid hospital volunteers.* — 1. *Syns:* uncompensated, unrecompensed, unremunerated, unsalaried.
2. Owed as a debt. — 2. DUE *adjective.*

unpalatable *adjective*
1. So unpleasant in flavor as to be inedible: *sent the unpalatable meal back to the kitchen.* — 1. *Syns:* distasteful, unappetizing, unsavory.
Near-syns: flat, flavorless, insipid, tasteless, watery, weak.
Ant: palatable.
2. Difficult to accept. — 2. BITTER *adjective.*

unparalleled *adjective*
Without equal or rival. — UNIQUE.

unpardonable *adjective*
Impossible to excuse, pardon, or justify. — INEXCUSABLE.

unperceptive *adjective*
Unwilling or unable to perceive. — BLIND *adjective.*

unperfected *adjective*
Not perfected, elaborated, or completed. — ROUGH.

unpitying *adjective*
Not sympathetic.

UNSYMPATHETIC.

unplanned *adjective*
1. Not intended.
2. Having no particular pattern, purpose, organization, or structure.

1. UNINTENTIONAL.
2. RANDOM.

unpleasant *adjective*
Not pleasant or agreeable: *an unpleasant odor; in an unpleasant mood.*

Syns: bad, disagreeable, displeasing, offensive.

unpleasantness *noun*
A discussion, often heated, in which a difference of opinion is expressed.

ARGUMENT.

unpolished *adjective*
1. Not perfected, elaborated, or completed.
2. Lacking expert, careful craftsmanship.
3. Of a plain and unsophisticated nature.
4. Lacking good manners.
5. Lacking in delicacy or refinement.

1. ROUGH.
2. RUDE.
3. RUSTIC *adjective.*
4. RUDE.
5. COARSE.

unpolitic *adjective*
Lacking sensitivity and skill in dealing with others.

TACTLESS.

unpracticed *adjective*
1. Lacking experience and the knowledge gained from it.
2. Not tested or proved.

1. INEXPERIENCED.
2. UNTRIED.

unprecedented *adjective*
Showing marked departure from previous practice.

NEW *adjective.*

unpredictable *adjective*
Following no predictable pattern.

CAPRICIOUS.

unprejudiced *adjective*
1. Not inclining toward or actively taking either side in a matter under dispute.
2. Free from bias in judgment.

1. NEUTRAL.
2. FAIR *adjective.*

unpremeditated *adjective*
1. Acting or happening without apparent forethought, prompting, or planning.
2. Not intended.

1. SPONTANEOUS.
2. UNINTENTIONAL.

unpresuming *adjective*
Having or expressing feelings of humility.

HUMBLE *adjective.*

unpretentious *adjective*
1. Of little distinction.
2. Not formal or ceremonious.
3. Not elaborate or showy, as in appearance or style.

1. HUMBLE *adjective.*
2. INFORMAL.
3. MODEST.

unpretentiousness *noun*
Lack of ostentation or pretension.

MODESTY.

unprincipled *adjective*
1. Lacking scruples or principles.
2. Ruthlessly seeking personal advantage.

1. UNSCRUPULOUS.
2. CORRUPT *adjective.*

unprocessed *adjective*
In a natural state and still not prepared for use.

CRUDE.

unproductive *adjective*
Lacking or unable to produce growing plants or crops.

BARREN *adjective.*

unprogressive *adjective*
Clinging to obsolete ideas: *unprogressive views about minority rights.*

Syns: backward, benighted, reactionary (*also* reactionist).

unprotected *adjective*
1. Having no protecting or concealing cover.
2. Devoid of help or protection.
3. Inadequately protected.

1. OPEN *adjective.*
2. HELPLESS.
3. INSECURE.

unproved *adjective*
Not tested or proved.

UNTRIED.

unqualified *adjective*
1. Totally incapable of doing a job.
2. Lacking capability.
3. Completely such, without qualification or exception.
4. Without limitations or mitigating conditions.

1. INCOMPETENT.
2. INADEQUATE.
3. UTTER[2].
4. UNCONDITIONAL.

unqualify *verb*
To make incapable, as of doing a job.

UNFIT *verb*.

unquestionable *adjective*
1. Established beyond a doubt.
2. Without any doubt.
3. Not counterfeit or copied.

1. CERTAIN.
2. DECIDED.
3. AUTHENTIC.

unquestioning *adjective*
Having no reservations.

IMPLICIT.

unravel *verb*
To find a solution for.

RESOLVE.

unreachable *adjective*
Unable to be reached.

INACCESSIBLE.

unreal *adjective*
Existing only in the imagination.

IMAGINARY.

unrealistic *adjective*
Not compatible with reality.

IDEALISTIC.

unrealizable *adjective*
Not capable of happening or being done.

IMPOSSIBLE.

unreason *noun*
The absence of reason: *demands based purely on unreason, not rationality.*

Syns: irrationality, unreasonableness.

unreasonable *adjective*
1. Not governed by or predicated on reason: *an unreasonable demand; an unreasonable expectation.*
2. Beyond all reason.

1. *Syns:* illogical, irrational, unreasoned.

2. OUTRAGEOUS.

unreasonableness *noun*
The absence of reason.

UNREASON.

unreasoned *adjective*
Not governed by or predicated on reason.

UNREASONABLE.

unreceptiveness *noun*
Lack of cordiality and hospitableness.

UNWELCOME *noun*.

unrecompensed *adjective*
Contributing one's time without pay.

UNPAID.

unrefined *adjective*
1. In a natural state and still not prepared for use.
2. Lacking in delicacy or refinement.

1. CRUDE.
2. COARSE.

unrehearsed *adjective*
Spoken, performed, or composed with little or no preparation or forethought.

EXTEMPORANEOUS.

unrelenting *adjective*
Having or showing uncompromising determination or resolution in purpose or action.

GRIM.

unreliable *adjective*
1. Not to be depended on.
2. So weak or defective as to be liable to fail.

1. UNDEPENDABLE.
2. TRICK *adjective*.

unrelieved *adjective*
Completely such, without qualification or exception.

UTTER[2].

unremitting *adjective*
1. Existing or occurring without interruption or end.
2. Obstinately maintaining a stand.

1. CONTINUAL.
2. INSISTENT.

unremunerated *adjective*
Contributing one's time without pay.

UNPAID.

unrepentant *adjective*
Devoid of remorse.

REMORSELESS.

unrequired *adjective*
Not necessary.

UNNECESSARY.

unreserved *adjective*
1. Not spoken for or occupied: *unreserved seats; unreserved computer time.*
2. Completely such, without qualification or exception.
3. Without limitations or mitigating conditions.
4. Having no reservations.
5. Disposed to be open, sociable, and talkative.
6. Executed without pretense or obfuscation.

1. **Syns:** free, open, unoccupied.
2. UTTER[2].
3. UNCONDITIONAL.
4. IMPLICIT.
5. OUTGOING.
6. PLAIN *adjective.*

unresolved *adjective*
Marked by lack of firm decision or commitment; of questionable outcome.

INDEFINITE.

unresponsive *adjective*
1. Without emotion or interest.
2. Lacking responsiveness or alertness.
3. Deficient in or lacking sexual desire.

1. APATHETIC.
2. DULL *adjective.*
3. FRIGID.

unresponsiveness *noun*
Lack of emotion or interest.

APATHY.

unrest *noun*
1. A state of uneasiness and usu. resentment brewing to an eventual explosion: *Stringent new laws fomented unrest throughout the country.*
2. An uneasy or nervous state.

1. **Syns:** ferment, storm and stress, Sturm und Drang, turmoil.
2. RESTLESSNESS.

unrestrained *adjective*
1. Able to move about at will without bounds or restraint.
2. Lacking in moral restraint.

1. LOOSE *adjective.*
2. ABANDONED.

unrestraint *noun*
1. Freedom from constraint, embarrassment, or awkwardness.
2. A complete surrender of inhibitions.

1. EASE *noun.*
2. ABANDON *noun.*

unrestricted *adjective*
Not restricted or confined to few.

OPEN *adjective.*

unrivaled *adjective*
Without equal or rival.

UNIQUE.

unroll *verb*
To cause (a line) to become longer and less taut.

PLAY OUT at **play.**

unromantic *adjective*
Having or indicating an awareness of things as they really are.

REALISTIC.

unruffled *adjective*
1. Not easily excited, even under pressure.
2. Not excited or emotionally agitated.

1. COOL *adjective.*
2. CALM *adjective.*

unruliness *noun*
1. The quality or condition of being unruly: *the unruliness of classroom troublemakers.*

1. **Syns:** fractiousness, obstreperousness, recalcitrance *or* recalcitrancy, refractoriness, uncontrollability, uncontrollableness, ungovernableness, unmanageability, wildness.

2. The condition or practice of not obeying.
3. The disposition boldly to defy or resist authority or an opposing force.

2. DISOBEDIENCE.
3. DEFIANCE.

unruly *adjective*
1. Not submitting to discipline or control: *an unruly student who was expelled; an unruly mob.*

1. **Syns:** fractious, indocile, indomitable, obstreperous, recalcitrant, refractory, uncontrollable, undisciplined, ungovernable, unmanageable, untoward, wild.

2. Upsetting civil order or peace.
3. Refusing or failing to obey.
4. Marked by defiance.

2. DISORDERLY.
3. DISOBEDIENT.
4. DEFIANT.

unsafe *adjective*
1. Involving possible risk, loss, or injury.
2. Inadequately protected.

1. DANGEROUS.
2. INSECURE.

unsaid *adjective*
1. Not voiced or expressed.
2. Conveyed indirectly without words or speech.

1. SILENT.
2. IMPLICIT.

unsalaried *adjective*
Contributing one's time without pay.

UNPAID.

unsalutary *adjective*
Not sustaining or promoting health.

UNWHOLESOME.

unsatisfactory *adjective*
1. Below a standard of quality.
2. Tending to discourage, retard, or make more difficult.

1. BAD.
2. UNFAVORABLE.

unsavory *adjective*
So unpleasant in flavor as to be inedible.

UNPALATABLE.

unscathed *adjective*
Free from danger, injury, or the threat of harm.

SAFE.

unscholarly *adjective*
Lacking the requisite scholarship or instruction: *an unscholarly approach to the writing of history.*

Syns: unlearned, unstudious.

unschooled *adjective*
Without education or knowledge.

IGNORANT.

unscrupulous *adjective*
1. Lacking scruples or principles: *an unscrupulous courtier who stopped at nothing to gain power.*

1. *Syns:* conscienceless, ruthless, stick-at-nothing, unconscionable, unethical, unprincipled.
Near-syns: crafty, deceitful, dishonest; contriving, cunning, manipulating.
Ant: scrupulous.

2. Ruthlessly seeking personal advantage.

2. CORRUPT *adjective*.

unseasonable *adjective*
Not suitable for or characteristic of the season: *unseasonable weather for January.*

Syn: untimely.

unseasoned *adjective*
Lacking experience and the knowledge gained from it.

INEXPERIENCED.

unseeing *adjective*
Without the sense of sight.

BLIND *adjective*.

unseemliness *noun*
The condition of being improper.

IMPROPRIETY.

unseemly *adjective*
1. Not in keeping with conventional mores.
2. Not suited to circumstances.

1. IMPROPER.
2. IMPROPER.

unselfish *adjective*
1. Without concern for oneself.
2. Willing to give of oneself and one's possessions.

1. SELFLESS.
2. GENEROUS.

unserviceable *adjective*
Incapable of being used or availed of to advantage.

IMPRACTICABLE.

unsettle *verb*
1. To impair or destroy the composure of.
2. To put out of proper order.
3. To disturb the health or physiological functioning of.

1. AGITATE.
2. DISORDER *verb*.
3. UPSET *verb*.

unsettled *adjective*
1. Capable of or liable to change.
2. Not affording certainty.
3. Marked by lack of firm decision or commitment; of questionable outcome.
4. Affording no quiet, repose, or rest.
5. In a state of uneasiness.
6. Owed as a debt.

1. CHANGEABLE.
2. AMBIGUOUS.
3. INDEFINITE.

4. RESTLESS.
5. ANXIOUS.
6. DUE *adjective*.

unsettling *adjective*
Troubling to the mind or emotions. — DISTURBING.

unsex *verb*
To render incapable of reproducing sexually. — STERILIZE.

unsexing *noun*
The act or an instance of making one incapable of reproducing sexually. — STERILIZATION.

unshaped *adjective*
Having no distinct shape. — SHAPELESS.

unsightliness *noun*
The quality or condition of being ugly. — UGLINESS.

unsightly *adjective*
Extremely displeasing to the eye. — UGLY *adjective*.

unsigned *adjective*
Having an unknown name or author. — ANONYMOUS.

unskilled *adjective*
1. Lacking the required professional skill. — 1. AMATEURISH.
2. Lacking the qualities, as efficiency or skill, required to produce desired results. — 2. INEFFICIENT.

unskillful *adjective*
1. Clumsily lacking in the ability to do or perform: *an unskillful attempt to explain*. — 1. *Syns:* awkward, bumbling, clumsy, gauche, heavy-handed, inept, maladroit.
2. Lacking the qualities, as efficiency or skill, required to produce desired results. — 2. INEFFICIENT.
3. Lacking the required professional skill. — 3. AMATEURISH.

unsleeping *adjective*
Not in a state of sleep. — WAKEFUL.

unsoiled *adjective*
Free from dirt, stain, or impurities. — CLEAN *adjective*.

unsophisticate *noun*
A guileless, unsophisticated person. — INNOCENT.

unsophisticated *adjective*
Free from guile, cunning, or deceit. — ARTLESS.

unsought *adjective*
Not welcome or wanted. — UNWELCOME *adjective*.

unsound *adjective*
1. Containing an error or errors. — 1. ERRONEOUS.
2. Devoid of truth. — 2. FALSE.
3. Not physically strong. — 3. INFIRM.
4. Afflicted with or exhibiting irrationality and mental unsoundness. — 4. INSANE.
5. Not wise. — 5. UNWISE.

unsoundness *noun*
The condition of being infirm or physically weak. — INFIRMITY.

unsparing *adjective*
Characterized by bounteous giving. — GENEROUS.

unspeakable *adjective*
1. That cannot be described: *unspeakable happiness*. — 1. *Syns:* incommunicable, indefinable, indescribable, ineffable, inenarrable, inexpressible, undescribable, unexpressible, unutterable. —*Idioms* beyond description (*or* words), defying description.
2. Too awful to be described: *unspeakable acts of genocide*. — 2. *Syns:* abominable, frightful, nauseating, revolting, shocking, sickening.
3. That may not be spoken of or uttered: *unspeakable words of abuse*. — 3. *Syn:* unmentionable.

unspoken *adjective*
1. Conveyed indirectly without words or speech. — 1. IMPLICIT.

2. Not voiced or expressed. — **2.** SILENT.

unstability *noun*
1. The quality or condition of being erratic and undependable. — **1.** INSTABILITY.
2. The quality or condition of being physically unsteady. — **2.** UNSTABLENESS.

unstable *adjective*
1. Not physically steady or firm: *an unstable ladder.* — **1.** *Syns:* rickety, shaky, tottering, unsteady, wobbly.
2. Capable of or liable to change. — **2.** CHANGEABLE.
3. Following no predictable pattern. — **3.** CAPRICIOUS.
4. Lacking stability. — **4.** INSECURE.

unstableness *noun*
1. The quality or condition of being physically unsteady: *The unstableness of the scaffolding frightened the painters.* — **1.** *Syns:* instability, precariousness, shakiness, unstability, unsteadiness.
2. The quality or condition of being erratic and undependable. — **2.** INSTABILITY.

unstained *adjective*
Free from evil and corruption. — INNOCENT *adjective.*

unsteadiness *noun*
The quality or condition of being physically unsteady. — UNSTABLENESS.

unsteady *adjective*
1. Lacking stability. — **1.** INSECURE.
2. Not physically steady or firm. — **2.** UNSTABLE.
3. Lacking consistency or regularity in quality or performance. — **3.** UNEVEN.
4. Capable of or liable to change. — **4.** CHANGEABLE.
5. Following no predictable pattern. — **5.** CAPRICIOUS.

unstinting *adjective*
Characterized by bounteous giving. — GENEROUS.

unstirred *adjective*
Not sympathetic. — UNSYMPATHETIC.

unstudied *adjective*
Free from guile, cunning, or deceit. — ARTLESS.

unstudious *adjective*
Lacking the requisite scholarship or instruction. — UNSCHOLARLY.

unsubstantial *adjective*
1. Not physically strong. — **1.** INFIRM.
2. Having no body, form, or substance. — **2.** IMMATERIAL.
3. Not plausible or believable. — **3.** IMPLAUSIBLE.
4. Having little substance or significance; not solidly based. — **4.** TENUOUS.

unsubtle *adjective*
Easily seen through due to a lack of subtlety: *The host gave the drunken guest a very unsubtle hint to leave.* — *Syns:* broad, clear, obvious, patent, plain, unmistakable.

unsuccess *noun*
The condition of not achieving the desired end. — FAILURE.

unsuccessful *adjective*
Having no useful result. — FUTILE.

unsuccessfulness *noun*
The condition of not achieving the desired end. — FAILURE.

unsufferable *adjective*
Not capable of being endured or tolerated. — UNBEARABLE.

unsuitability *noun*
The condition of being improper. — IMPROPRIETY.

unsuitable *adjective*
1. Not suited to circumstances. — **1.** IMPROPER.
2. Not suited to a given purpose. — **2.** UNFIT *adjective.*

unsuitableness *noun*
The condition of being improper. — IMPROPRIETY.

unsuited *adjective*
Not suited to a given purpose.   UNFIT *adjective*.

unsullied *adjective*
1. Free from dirt, stain, or impurities.   1. CLEAN *adjective*.
2. Free from evil and corruption.   2. INNOCENT *adjective*.

unsupportable *adjective*
Not capable of being endured or tolerated.   UNBEARABLE.

unsure *adjective*
1. Experiencing doubt.   1. DOUBTFUL.
2. Not affording certainty.   2. AMBIGUOUS.
3. Marked by lack of firm decision or commitment; of questionable outcome.   3. INDEFINITE.
4. Lacking stability.   4. INSECURE.

unsurmountable *adjective*
Incapable of being negotiated or overcome.   INSUPERABLE.

unsurpassable *adjective*
Of the greatest possible degree, quality, or intensity.   ULTIMATE *adjective*.

unsurpassed *adjective*
Surpassing all others in quality.   BEST *adjective*.

unsusceptibility *noun*
The capacity to withstand.   RESISTANCE.

unsusceptible *adjective*
Not capable of being affected or impressed.   INSENSITIVE.

unswayable *adjective*
Firmly, often reasonably immovable in purpose or will.   STUBBORN.

unswerving *adjective*
Not diffused or dispersed.   CONCENTRATED.

unsympathetic *adjective*
1. Not sympathetic: *The old miser was unsympathetic toward charitable causes.*   1. *Syns:* uncaring, uncharitable, uncompassionate, unmoved, unpitying, unstirred, untouched.
2. Arousing deep-seated dislike.   2. ANTIPATHETIC.

unsystematic *adjective*
Lacking regular or logical order.   DISORDERLY.

untactful *adjective*
Lacking sensitivity and skill in dealing with others.   TACTLESS.

untainted *adjective*
Free from evil and corruption.   INNOCENT *adjective*.

untamed *adjective*
In a primitive state; not domesticated or cultivated.   WILD *adjective*.

untangle *verb*
To free from an entanglement.   CLEAR *verb*.

untaught *adjective*
Without education or knowledge.   IGNORANT.

untested *adjective*
Not tested or proved.   UNTRIED.

unthankful *adjective*
1. Not showing or feeling gratitude.   1. THANKLESS.
2. Not apt to be appreciated.   2. THANKLESS.

unthanking *adjective*
Not showing or feeling gratitude.   THANKLESS.

unthinkable *adjective*
1. Not capable of happening or being done.   1. IMPOSSIBLE.
2. Not to be believed.   2. INCREDIBLE.

unthinking *adjective*
1. Devoid of consideration for others' feelings.   1. THOUGHTLESS.
2. Not intended.   2. UNINTENTIONAL.

unthoughtful *adjective*
Devoid of consideration for others' feelings.   THOUGHTLESS.

unthoughtfulness *noun*
A lack of consideration for others' feelings.   THOUGHTLESSNESS.

untidy *adjective*
1. Marked by an absence of cleanliness and order.
2. Indifferent to correctness, accuracy, or neatness.

1. MESSY.
2. CARELESS.

untie *verb*
To free from ties or fasteners.

UNDO.

untighten *verb*
To reduce in tension, pressure, or rigidity.

EASE *verb*.

untimely *adjective*
1. Developing, occurring, or appearing before the expected time.
2. Not occurring at a favorable time.
3. Not suitable for or characteristic of the season.

1. EARLY *adjective*.

2. INCONVENIENT.
3. UNSEASONABLE.

untiring *adjective*
Having or showing a capacity for protracted effort, regardless of difficulty or frustration.

TIRELESS.

untouched *adjective*
Not sympathetic.

UNSYMPATHETIC.

untoward *adjective*
1. Tending to discourage, retard, or make more difficult.
2. Not submitting to discipline or control.
3. Involving or undergoing chance misfortune.
4. Not in keeping with conventional mores.

1. UNFAVORABLE.

2. UNRULY.
3. UNFORTUNATE *adjective*.
4. IMPROPER.

untried *adjective*
1. Not tested or proved: *options as yet untried*.

2. Lacking experience and the knowledge gained from it.

1. **Syns:** undemonstrated, unpracticed, unproved, untested.
2. INEXPERIENCED.

untroubled *adjective*
Motionless and undisturbed.

STILL *adjective*.

untrue *adjective*
1. Containing an error or errors.
2. Not true to duty or obligation.

1. ERRONEOUS.
2. FAITHLESS.

untrusting *adjective*
Lacking trust or confidence.

DISTRUSTFUL.

untrustworthy *adjective*
Not to be depended on.

UNDEPENDABLE.

untruth *noun*
1. An erroneous or false idea.
2. An untrue declaration.

1. FALLACY.
2. LIE^2 *noun*.

untruthful *adjective*
1. Given to or marked by deliberate concealment or misrepresentation of the truth.
2. Devoid of truth.

1. DISHONEST.

2. FALSE.

untruthfulness *noun*
The practice of lying.

MENDACITY.

unusable *adjective*
1. Incapable of being used or availed of to advantage.
2. Having no useful purpose.

1. IMPRACTICABLE.
2. USELESS.

unused *adjective*
Not occupied or put to use.

IDLE *adjective*.

unusual *adjective*
1. Not usual or ordinary: *a ring of unusual design*.

2. Deviating from the customary.
3. Rarely occurring or appearing.
4. Far beyond what is usual, normal, or customary.

1. **Syns:** atypical (*also* atypic), novel, offbeat (*Informal*), unconventional, unordinary, unwonted.
2. ECCENTRIC *adjective*.
3. INFREQUENT.
4. RARE.

unusually *adverb*
In a manner or to a degree that is unusual: *The child is unusually gifted. It is an unusually oppressive day.*

Syns: exceptionally, extraordinarily.

unutterable *adjective*
That cannot be described.

UNSPEAKABLE.

unuttered *adjective*
1. Conveyed indirectly without words or speech.
2. Not voiced or expressed.

1. IMPLICIT.
2. SILENT.

unvarnished *adjective*
Without addition, decoration, or qualification.

BARE *adjective*.

unvarying *adjective*
Having no variations.

EVEN[1] *adjective*.

unveil *verb*
1. To make visible; bring to view.
2. To disclose in a breach of confidence.

1. REVEAL.
2. BETRAY.

unveiling *noun*
Something disclosed, esp. something not previously known or realized.

REVELATION.

unveracity *noun*
The practice of lying.

MENDACITY.

unveridical *adjective*
Given to or marked by deliberate concealment or misrepresentation of the truth.

DISHONEST.

unversed *adjective*
Lacking experience and the knowledge gained from it.

INEXPERIENCED.

unvoiced *adjective*
Not voiced or expressed.

SILENT.

unwanted *adjective*
1. Not welcome or wanted.
2. Arousing disapproval.

1. UNWELCOME *adjective*.
2. OBJECTIONABLE.

unwarranted *adjective*
Having no basis or foundation in fact.

BASELESS.

unwarrantedly *adverb*
Without basis or foundation in fact.

UNFOUNDEDLY.

unwashed *adjective*
Lacking high station or birth.

LOWLY.

unwed *adjective*
Without a spouse.

SINGLE *adjective*.

unwelcome *adjective*
1. Not welcome or wanted: *an unwelcome phone call late at night.*

1. *Syns:* undesirable, undesired, uninvited, unsought, unwanted, unwished-for.

2. Arousing disapproval.

2. OBJECTIONABLE.

unwelcome *noun*
Lack of cordiality and hospitableness: *Upon entering the room we felt a strong sense of unwelcome.*

Syns: inhospitableness, inhospitality, ungraciousness, unreceptiveness.

unwell *adjective*
Affected or tending to be affected with minor health problems.

SICKLY.

unwholesome *adjective*
1. Not sustaining or promoting health: *unwholesome foods.*
2. Morally detrimental: *fell into an unwholesome way of life.*
3. Susceptible to or marked by preoccupation with unwholesome matters.
4. Extremely unpleasant to the senses or feelings.

1. *Syns:* insalubrious, insalutary, unhealthy, unsalutary.
2. *Syns:* contaminating, contaminative, corrupting, demoralizing, unhealthy.
3. MORBID.
4. OFFENSIVE *adjective*.

unwholesomeness *noun*
Impure condition.

IMPURITY.

unwieldy *adjective*
Difficult to handle or manage.

AWKWARD.

unwilling *adjective*
Not inclined or willing to do or undertake.

INDISPOSED.

unwillingness *noun*
The state of not being disposed or inclined. INDISPOSITION.

unwind *verb*
1. To cause (a line) to become longer and less taut. 1. PLAY OUT at **play.**
2. To take repose by ceasing work or other effort for an 2. REST[1] *verb.*
interval of time.

unwise *adjective*
Not wise: *impoverished by some unwise investments;* **Syns:** ill-advised, ill-considered, ill-judged,
unwise decisions. impolitic, improvident, imprudent,
injudicious, unsound.

unwished-for *adjective*
Not welcome or wanted. UNWELCOME *adjective.*

unwitting *adjective*
1. Not intended. 1. UNINTENTIONAL.
2. Not aware or informed. 2. IGNORANT.

unwonted *adjective*
Not usual or ordinary. UNUSUAL.

unworkable *adjective*
1. Incapable of being used or availed of to advantage. 1. IMPRACTICABLE.
2. Not capable of happening or being done. 2. IMPOSSIBLE.

unworkmanlike *adjective*
Lacking the qualities, as efficiency or skill, required to INEFFICIENT.
produce desired results.

unworldly *adjective*
Of or concerned with the spirit rather than the body or SPIRITUAL.
material things.

unwritten *adjective*
Expressed or transmitted in speech. ORAL.

unyielding *adjective*
1. Not changing shape or bending. 1. RIGID.
2. Incapable of changing or being modified. 2. INFLEXIBLE.
3. Indicating or possessing determination, resolution, 3. FIRM[1].
or persistence.
4. Having or showing uncompromising determination 4. GRIM.
or resolution in purpose or action.
5. Firmly, often unreasonably immovable in purpose or 5. STUBBORN.
will.
6. Rigorous and unsparing in treating others. 6. SEVERE.

up *adjective*
Informal. Having the necessary strength or ability. EQUAL *adjective.*
up *verb*
To increase in amount. RAISE *verb.*

up-and-comer *noun*
One showing much promise. COMER.

up-and-coming *adjective*
Showing great promise. COMING.

upbeat *adjective*
1. *Informal.* Expecting a favorable outcome or dwelling 1. OPTIMISTIC.
on hopeful aspects.
2. *Informal.* Of a constructive nature. 2. POSITIVE.

upbraid *verb*
To criticize for a fault or offense. CALL DOWN at **call.**

upbraiding *noun*
Words expressive of strong disapproval. REBUKE *noun.*

upcoming *adjective*
In the relatively near future. COMING.

update *verb*
To make modern in appearance or style. MODERNIZE.

upgrade *verb*
1. To raise in rank. 1. PROMOTE.
2. To advance to a more desirable state. 2. IMPROVE.

upgrading *noun*
1. A progression upward in rank.
2. Something that improves.

1. ADVANCEMENT.
2. IMPROVEMENT.

upheaval *noun*
A momentous or sweeping change.

REVOLUTION.

uphill *adjective*
Not easy to do, achieve, or master.

DIFFICULT.

uphold *verb*
1. To sustain the weight of.
2. To move (something) to a higher position.
3. To aid the cause of by approving or favoring.
4. To keep from yielding or failing during stress or difficulty.

1. SUPPORT *verb.*
2. ELEVATE.
3. SUPPORT *verb.*
4. SUSTAIN.

upkeep *noun*
The means needed to support life.

LIVING.

uplift *verb*
1. To move (something) to a higher position.
2. To raise to a high position or status.
3. To raise the spirits of.

1. ELEVATE.
2. EXALT.
3. ELATE *verb.*

uplift *noun*
High spirits.

ELATION.

uplifted *adjective*
1. Feeling great delight and joy.
2. Being positioned above a given level.

1. ELATED.
2. ELEVATED.

up on *adjective*
Informal. Having good knowledge of.

FAMILIAR.

upper class *noun*
People of the highest social level.

SOCIETY.

upper crust *noun*
Informal. People of the highest social level.

SOCIETY.

uppermost *adjective*
Of, being, located at, or forming the top.

TOP *adjective.*

upper story *noun*
Informal. The seat of the faculty of intelligence and reason.

HEAD *noun.*

upperworks *noun*
Informal. The seat of the faculty of intelligence and reason.

HEAD *noun.*

uppish *adjective*

SEE **uppity.**

uppitiness *noun*
Informal. Excessive and arrogant self-confidence.

PRESUMPTION.

uppity also **uppish** *adjective*
1. *Informal.* Having or exhibiting excessive and arrogant self-confidence.
2. *Informal.* Characteristic of or resembling a snob.

1. PRESUMPTUOUS.
2. SNOBBISH.

upraise *verb*
1. To raise upright.
2. To move (something) to a higher position.

1. ERECT *verb.*
2. ELEVATE.

upraised *adjective*
1. Directed or pointed upward.
2. Being positioned above a given level.

1. ERECT *adjective.*
2. ELEVATED.

uprear *verb*
To raise upright.

ERECT *verb.*

upright *adjective*
1. Directed or pointed upward.
2. At right angles to the horizon or to level ground.
3. Having or marked by uprightness in principle and action.

1. ERECT *adjective.*
2. VERTICAL.
3. HONEST.

upright *verb*
To restore to an upright or proper position.

RIGHT *verb.*

uprightness *noun*
1. The quality or state of being morally sound.
2. The quality of being honest.

1. GOOD *noun.*
2. HONESTY.

uprise *verb*
1. To leave one's bed.
2. To adopt a standing posture.

1. GET UP at **get.**
2. GET UP at **get.**

uprisen *adjective*
Being positioned above a given level.

ELEVATED.

uprising *noun*
Organized opposition intended to change or overthrow existing authority.

REBELLION.

uproar *noun*
1. A quarrel or fight marked by very noisy, disorderly, and often violent behavior.
2. An interruption of regular procedure or of public peace.
3. Sounds or a sound, esp. when loud, confused, or disagreeable.
4. A condition of intense public interest or excitement.
5. Offensively loud and insistent utterances, esp. of disapproval.

1. BRAWL *noun.*
2. DISTURBANCE.
3. NOISE *noun.*
4. SENSATION.
5. VOCIFERATION.

uproot *verb*
To destroy all traces of.

ANNIHILATE.

upset *verb*
1. To disturb the health or physiological functioning of: *Heavy meals upset my stomach.*
2. To turn or cause to turn from a vertical or horizontal position.
3. To put out of proper order.
4. To break up the order or progress of.
5. To impair or destroy the composure of.

1. *Syns:* derange, disorder, turn, unhinge, unsettle.
2. OVERTURN.
3. DISORDER *verb.*
4. DISRUPT.
5. AGITATE.

upset *noun*
1. The act or an example of upsetting: *an upset in our plans.*
2. The condition of being physically agitated.
3. A state of discomposure.

1. *Syns:* disordering, disorganization, disruption.
2. AGITATION.
3. AGITATION.

upset *adjective*
Overturned completely.

UPSIDE-DOWN.

upsetting *adjective*
Troubling to the mind or emotions.

DISTURBING.

upshot *noun*
Something brought about by a cause.

EFFECT *noun.*

upside *adjective*
Informal. Greatest in quantity or highest in degree that has been or can be attained.

MAXIMUM *adjective.*

upside-down *adjective*
1. Overturned completely: *an upside-down car in the ditch.*
2. Characterized by physical confusion.

1. *Syns:* inverted, upset, upturned.
2. CONFUSED.

upsoar *verb*
To rise abruptly and precipitously.

SOAR.

upspring *verb*
1. To have as a source.
2. To adopt a standing posture.

1. STEM *verb.*
2. GET UP at **get.**

upstanding *adjective*
1. Directed or pointed upward.
2. Having or marked by uprightness in principle and action.

1. ERECT *adjective.*
2. HONEST.

upsurge *verb*
To make or become greater or larger.

INCREASE *verb.*

upswing *noun*
The act of increasing or rising.

INCREASE *noun*.

up tight also **uptight** *adjective*
Slang. Feeling or exhibiting nervous tension.

EDGY.

up-to-date *adjective*
Modern.

CONTEMPORARY *adjective*.

up-to-the-minute *adjective*
Modern.

CONTEMPORARY *adjective*.

upturn *noun*
The act of increasing or rising.

INCREASE *noun*.

upturned *adjective*
Overturned completely.

UPSIDE-DOWN.

urban *adjective*
Of, in, or belonging to a city.

CITY *adjective*.

urbane *adjective*
1. Characterized by discriminating taste and broad knowledge as a result of development or education.
2. Effortlessly gracious and tactful in social manner.

1. CULTURED.

2. SUAVE.

urbanity *noun*
Refined, effortless beauty of manner, form, and style.

ELEGANCE.

urbanize *verb*
To imbue with city ways, manners, and customs.

CITIFY.

urge *verb*
1. To impel to action: *We urged the President to be more decisive. My conscience urged me to tell the truth at last.*
2. To solicit insistently.

1. *Syns:* exhort, press, prick, prod, prompt, propel.

2. INSIST.

urgence *noun*
Urgent solicitation.

INSISTENCE.

urgency *noun*
Urgent solicitation.

INSISTENCE.

urgent *adjective*
Of immediate import.

BURNING.

urging *noun*
Urgent solicitation.

INSISTENCE.

usable *adjective*
1. In a condition to be used: *Does he really think this manuscript is usable?*
2. Available for use.

1. *Syns:* employable, serviceable, utilizable.

2. OPEN *adjective*.

usage *noun*
1. The act of putting into play.
2. A habitual way of behaving.
3. An accepted way of doing something.
4. A quantity consumed.

1. EXERCISE *noun*.
2. CUSTOM *noun*.
3. CONVENTION.
4. CONSUMPTION.

use *verb*
1. To put into action or use: *Use the utmost caution at intersections. He used the money to pay off debts. I used the brakes as quickly as possible. We want to use her talents to our advantage.*

2. To control or direct the functioning of.
3. *Informal.* To take advantage of unfairly.
4. To be depleted.

1. *Syns:* actuate, apply, employ, exercise, exploit, implement, practice, utilize.
—*Idioms* bring into play, bring to bear, make use of, put into practice, put to use.

2. OPERATE.
3. ABUSE *verb*.
4. GO *verb*.

use up *verb*
1. To use all of.
2. To lessen or weaken severely, as by removing something essential.

1. EXHAUST.
2. DEPLETE.

use *noun*
1. The act of putting into play.
2. The condition of being put to use.

1. EXERCISE *noun*.
2. DUTY.

3. The quality of being suitable or adaptable to an end: *found a use for the extra chair; a lazy person of no earthly use to us.*
4. A habitual way of behaving.
5. A quantity consumed.

used to *adjective*
In the habit of.

useful *adjective*
1. Suited to one's end or purpose.
2. Affording benefit.
3. Serving or capable of serving a useful purpose.

usefulness *noun*
The quality of being suitable or adaptable to an end.

useless *adjective*
1. Having no useful purpose: *A dead battery is useless in starting a car.*
2. Having no useful result.
3. Incapable of being used or availed of to advantage.

uselessness *noun*
The condition or quality of being useless or ineffective.

user *noun*
One who consumes goods and services.

use up *verb*

usher *verb*
To show the way to.

usher in *verb*
1. To make known the presence or arrival of: *Falling leaves usher in autumn. The doorkeeper ushered in the President as members of Congress applauded.*
2. To begin (something) with preliminary or prefatory material.
3. To bring into currency, use, fashion, or practice.

usher in *verb*

usual *noun*
A regular or customary matter, condition, or course of events: *Fair weather is the usual here.*

usual *adjective*
1. To be expected.
2. Commonly practiced or used.

usually *adverb*
1. In an expected or customary manner: *August is usually warm here.*

2. For the most part: *He is usually out of town once a week.*

usualness *noun*
The quality or condition of being usual: *the usualness of rain in the tropics.*

usurp *verb*
1. To lay claim to for oneself or as one's right.
2. To take the place of (another) against the other's will.

usurpation *noun*
The act of taking something for oneself: *usurpation of authority by mutinous sailors.*

utensil *noun*
A device used to do work or perform a task.

utilitarian *adjective*
Serving or capable of serving a useful purpose.

---

3. **Syns:** account, advantage, avail, benefit, profit, usefulness, utility.
4. CUSTOM *noun*.
5. CONSUMPTION.

ACCUSTOMED TO at **accustomed**.

1. CONVENIENT.
2. BENEFICIAL.
3. PRACTICAL.

USE *noun*.

1. **Syns:** ineffectual, inutile, unusable, worthless.
2. FUTILE.
3. IMPRACTICABLE.

FUTILITY.

CONSUMER.
SEE **use**.

GUIDE *verb*.

1. **Syns:** announce, herald, introduce, presage, proclaim.

2. INTRODUCE.

3. INTRODUCE.
SEE **usher**.

Syns: commonplace, ordinary, rule.

1. COMMON *adjective*.
2. CUSTOMARY.

1. **Syns:** consistently, customarily, naturally, normally, typically. —*Idioms* as usual, per usual.
2. **Syns:** commonly, frequently.

Syns: ordinariness, prevalence.

1. ASSUME.
2. SUPPLANT.

Syns: appropriation, arrogation, assumption, pre-emption (*also* preemption, preëmption), seizure.

TOOL.

PRACTICAL.

utility   *noun*
The quality of being suitable or adaptable to an end.   USE *noun.*

utilizable   *adjective*
In a condition to be used.   USABLE.

utilization   *noun*
1. The condition of being put to use.   1. DUTY.
2. A specific use.   2. APPLICATION.

utilize   *verb*
To put into action or use.   USE *verb.*

utmost   *adjective*
1. Of the greatest or highest degree.   1. EXTREME *adjective.*
2. Most distant or remote from a center.   2. EXTREME *adjective.*
3. Greatest in quantity or highest in degree that has   3. MAXIMUM *adjective.*
   been or can be attained.

utopian   *noun*
A person inclined to be imaginative or idealistic but   DREAMER.
impractical.

utopian   *adjective*
Showing a tendency to envision things in perfect but   IDEALISTIC.
unrealistic form.

utter[1]   *verb*
1. To produce or make (speech sounds).   1. PRONOUNCE.
2. To put into words.   2. SAY *verb.*
3. To articulate (something) in words.   3. TALK *verb.*
4. To express oneself in speech.   4. SPEAK.

utter[2]   *adjective*
Completely such, without qualification or exception: *an*   ***Syns:*** absolute, all-out, arrant, blooming
utter fool; a room in utter chaos; had utter confidence in (*Slang*), complete, consummate, crashing,
his ability.   damned, dead, downright, flat, flat-out,
                                                             out-and-out, outright, perfect, positive
                                                             (*Informal*), pure, sheer[2], thorough,
                                                             thoroughgoing, total, unbounded,
                                                             unequivocal, unlimited, unmitigated,
                                                             unqualified, unrelieved, unreserved.

utterance   *noun*
1. The act or an instance of expressing in words.   1. EXPRESSION.
2. The faculty, act, or product of speaking.   2. SPEECH.
3. The use of the speech organs to produce sounds.   3. VOICING.
4. Something said.   4. WORD *noun.*

uttered   *adjective*
Produced by the voice.   VOCAL.

utterly   *adverb*
Without exception; in its entirety.   PURELY.

uttermost   *adjective*
1. Of the greatest or highest degree.   1. EXTREME *adjective.*
2. Most distant or remote from a center.   2. EXTREME *adjective.*

V

vacancy *noun*
1. Total absence of matter.
2. Total lack of ideas, meaning, or substance.

1. EMPTINESS.
2. EMPTINESS.

vacant *adjective*
1. Lacking intelligent thought or content: *a vacant mind; vacant rhetoric.*
2. Containing nothing.
3. Not occupied or put to use.
4. Lacking value, use, or substance.

1. **Syns:** empty, empty-headed, vacuous.
2. EMPTY *adjective.*
3. IDLE *adjective.*
4. EMPTY *adjective.*

vacate *verb*
1. To remove the contents of.
2. *Law.* To remove or invalidate by or as if by running a line through or wiping clean.

1. EMPTY *verb.*
2. CANCEL.

vacation *noun*
A regularly scheduled period spent away from work or duty, often in recreation: *teachers enjoying their long summer vacation.*

Syns: furlough, holiday, leave[2].
Near-syns: break, intermission, recess, respite, rest.

vacillant *adjective*
Given to or exhibiting hesitation.

HESITANT.

vacillate *verb*
1. To be irresolute in acting or doing.
2. To change one's attitudes, policies, or the like.

1. HESITATE.
2. SWING *verb.*

vacillating also **vacillatory** *adjective*
Given to or exhibiting hesitation.

HESITANT.

vacillation *noun*
The act or an instance of hesitating.

HESITATION.
SEE **vacillating.**

vacillatory *adjective*

vacuity *noun*
1. Total absence of matter.
2. Total lack of ideas, meaning, or substance.
3. A space in an otherwise solid mass.
4. Absence of anything perceptible.

1. EMPTINESS.
2. EMPTINESS.
3. HOLE *noun.*
4. NOTHINGNESS.

vacuous *adjective*
1. Containing nothing.
2. Lacking intelligent thought or content.

1. EMPTY *adjective.*
2. VACANT.

vacuum *noun*
1. Total absence of matter.
2. A desolate sense of loss.

1. EMPTINESS.
2. EMPTINESS.

vagabond *adjective*
Leading the life of a person without a fixed domicile; moving from place to place.

NOMADIC.

vagary *noun*
An impulsive, often illogical turn of mind.

FANCY *noun.*

vagrant *adjective*
Leading the life of a person without a fixed domicile; moving from place to place.

NOMADIC.

vague *adjective*
1. Liable to more than one interpretation.
2. Marked by lack of firm decision or commitment; of questionable outcome.
3. Not clearly perceived or perceptible.

1. AMBIGUOUS.
2. INDEFINITE.

3. UNCLEAR.

vagueness *noun*
The quality or state of being ambiguous: *suggestions impractical due to their vagueness.*

Syns: ambiguity, ambiguousness, cloudiness, equivocalness, indefiniteness, obscurity, uncertainty, unclearness.

vain *adjective*
1. Unduly preoccupied with one's own appearance: *A vain man, he would pluck out his gray hairs as soon as he noticed them.*

2. Having no useful result.
3. Lacking value, use, or substance.

vainglorious *adjective*
Thinking too highly of oneself.

vainglory *noun*
A regarding of oneself with undue favor.

vainness *noun*
A regarding of oneself with undue favor.

valedictory *adjective*
Of, done, given, or said on departing.

valiance or **valiancy** *noun*
1. The quality or state of being heroic.
2. The quality of mind enabling one to face danger or hardship resolutely.

valiancy *noun*

valiant *adjective*
Having or showing courage.

valid *adjective*
1. Based on good judgment, reasoning, or evidence.
2. Worthy of belief because of precision, faithfulness to an original, etc.

validate *verb*
1. To establish as true or genuine.
2. To assure the certainty or validity of.

validation *noun*
That which confirms.

validity *noun*
The quality of being authentic.

valor *noun*
1. The quality of mind enabling one to face danger or hardship resolutely.
2. The quality or state of being heroic.

valorous *adjective*
Having or showing courage.

valorousness *noun*
The quality or state of being heroic.

valuable *adjective*
Of great value: *valuable Georgian silver.*

valuate *verb*
To make a judgment as to the worth or value of.

valuation *noun*
1. The act or result of judging the worth or value of something or someone.
2. A measure of those qualities that determine merit, desirability, usefulness, or importance.

value *noun*
1. A measure of those qualities that determine merit, desirability, usefulness, or importance.
2. A level of superiority that is usu. high.
3. That which is signified by a word or expression.

value *verb*

---

1. **Syns:** conceited, narcissistic.
   Near-syns: egotistic, haughty, proud, stuck-up (*Informal*), vainglorious.
   Ant: modest.
2. FUTILE.
3. EMPTY *adjective.*

EGOTISTICAL.

EGOTISM.

EGOTISM.

PARTING *adjective.*

1. HEROISM.
2. COURAGE.

SEE **valiance.**

BRAVE *adjective.*

1. SOUND[2].
2. AUTHENTIC.

1. PROVE.
2. CONFIRM.

CONFIRMATION.

AUTHENTICITY.

1. COURAGE.
2. HEROISM.

BRAVE *adjective.*

HEROISM.

Syns: costly, inestimable, invaluable, precious, priceless, worthy. —*Idioms* beyond price, of great price.
Near-syns: dear, expensive, pricey; prized, treasured, valued.
Ants: valueless, worthless.

ESTIMATE *verb.*

1. ESTIMATE *noun.*
2. WORTH *noun.*

1. WORTH *noun.*
2. MERIT *noun.*
3. MEANING.

1. To make a judgment as to the worth or value of.	1. ESTIMATE *verb*.
2. To recognize the worth, quality, importance, etc., of.	2. APPRECIATE.
3. To have a high opinion of.	3. ADMIRE.

valueless *adjective*
Lacking all worth and value. — WORTHLESS.

vamoose also **vamose** *verb*
Slang. To leave hastily. — RUN *verb*.

vamose *verb* — SEE **vamoose**.

vamp *noun*
A usu. unscrupulous woman who seduces or exploits men. — SEDUCTRESS.

vampire *noun*
A perversely bad, cruel, or wicked person. — FIEND.

vandalize *verb*
To injure or destroy (property) maliciously. — TRASH[1] *verb*.

vanish *verb*
To pass out of sight either gradually or suddenly. — DISAPPEAR.

vanished *adjective*
No longer in use, force, or operation: *the vanished languages of ancient peoples*. — *Syns:* dead, defunct, extinct, lost.

vanity *noun*
A regarding of oneself with undue favor. — EGOTISM.

vanquish *verb*
To win a victory over, as in battle or a competition. — DEFEAT *verb*.

vantage *noun*

1. A factor conducive to superiority and success.	1. ADVANTAGE *noun*.
2. A dominating position, as in a conflict.	2. ADVANTAGE *noun*.

vapid *adjective*
Lacking the qualities requisite for spiritedness and originality. — INSIPID.

vapidity *noun*
The state or quality of being insipid. — INSIPIDITY.

vaporize *verb*
To pass off as vapor, esp. due to being heated. — EVAPORATE.

vaporous also **vapory** *adjective*

1. So light and insubstantial as to resemble air or a thin film.	1. FILMY.
2. Not clearly perceived or perceptible.	2. UNCLEAR.

vapory *adjective* — SEE **vaporous**.

variable *adjective*

1. Capable of or liable to change.	1. CHANGEABLE.
2. Following no predictable pattern.	2. CAPRICIOUS.
3. Lacking consistency or regularity in quality or performance.	3. UNEVEN.

variance *noun*

1. The condition or fact of varying.	1. VARIATION.
2. A state of disagreement and disharmony.	2. CONFLICT *noun*.

variant *noun*
One that is slightly different from others of the same kind or designation. — VARIATION.

variant *adjective*

1. Not like another in nature, quality, amount, or form.	1. DIFFERENT.
2. Capable of or liable to change.	2. CHANGEABLE.

variation *noun*

1. The condition or fact of varying: *A wind shift can bring a sharp variation in temperature*.	1. *Syns:* difference, variance.
2. The process or result of making or becoming different.	2. CHANGE *noun*.

3. One that is slightly different from others of the same kind or designation: *Several variations of hopscotch are played in this neighborhood.*

varicolored *adjective*
Having many different colors.

varied *adjective*
Consisting of a number of different kinds.

variegate *verb*
To mark with a line or band of different color or texture.

variegated *adjective*
1. Having many different colors.
2. Consisting of a number of different kinds.

variety *noun*
1. The quality of being made of many different elements, forms, kinds, or individuals: *a monotonous life without variety; the variety of cultural expression in a great metropolis.*
2. A collection of various things.
3. One that is slightly different from others of the same kind or designation.
4. A class that is defined by the common attribute or attributes possessed by all its members.

various *adjective*
1. Consisting of a number of different kinds: *various books on the shelves; dresses of various colors.*

2. Not like another in nature, quality, amount, or form.
3. Distinguished from others by nature or qualities.
4. Consisting of an indefinitely small number that is more than two or three but less than many.
5. Having many aspects, uses, or abilities.
6. *Archaic.* Capable of or liable to change.

variousness *noun*
The quality of being made of many different elements, forms, kinds, or individuals.

varnish *verb*
To give a deceptively attractive appearance to.

vary *verb*
1. To make or become different.
2. To be unlike or dissimilar.
3. To be of different opinion.
4. To change or fluctuate within limits.

vast *adjective*
Of extraordinary size and power.

vastness *noun*
The quality of being enormous.

vatic also **vatical** *adjective*
Of or relating to the foretelling of events by or as if by supernatural means.

vaticinal *adjective*
Of or relating to the foretelling of events by or as if by supernatural means.

vaticinate *verb*
To tell about or make known (future events) by or as if by supernatural means.

---

3. *Syns:* variant, variety, version.

MULTICOLORED.

VARIOUS.

STREAK *verb.*

1. MULTICOLORED.
2. VARIOUS.

1. *Syns:* diverseness, diversity, heterogeneity, multifariousness, multiformity, multiplicity, polymorphism (*Biol.*), variousness.
2. ASSORTMENT.
3. VARIATION.

4. KIND².

1. *Syns:* assorted, divers, diverse, diversified, heterogeneous, miscellaneous, mixed, motley, multifarious, sundry, varied, variegated.
2. DIFFERENT.

3. DISTINCT.
4. SEVERAL.

5. VERSATILE.
6. CHANGEABLE.

VARIETY.

COLOR *verb.*

1. CHANGE *verb.*
2. DIFFER.
3. DIFFER.
4. GO *verb.*

GIANT *adjective.*

ENORMOUSNESS.

PROPHETIC.

PROPHETIC.

PROPHESY.

vaticination *noun*
Something that is foretold by or as if by supernatural   PROPHECY.
means.

vault[1] *noun*
A burial place or receptacle for human remains.   GRAVE[1].

vault[2] *verb*
To move off the ground by a muscular effort of the legs   JUMP *verb*.
and feet.

  vault *noun*
  The act of jumping.   JUMP *noun*.

vaunt *verb*
To talk with excessive pride.   BOAST *verb*.

vector *noun*
The compass direction in which a ship or aircraft   HEADING.
moves.

veer *verb*
  1. To turn aside sharply from a straight course.   1. SWERVE.
  2. To change the direction or course of.   2. TURN *verb*.

vehemence *noun*
Exceptionally great concentration, power, or force, esp.   INTENSITY.
in activity.

vehement *adjective*
Extreme in degree, strength, or effect.   INTENSE.

veil *noun*
A deceptive outward appearance.   FAÇADE.

  veil *verb*
  1. To surround and cover completely so as to obscure.   1. WRAP *verb*.
  2. To prevent (something) from being known.   2. COVER *verb*.

vein *noun*
  1. A distinctive way of expressing oneself.   1. STYLE *noun*.
  2. A temporary state of mind or feeling.   2. MOOD.
  3. An intermixture of a contrasting or unexpected   3. STREAK *noun*.
     quality, esp. in a person's character.

velocity *noun*
Rate of motion or performance.   SPEED *noun*.

venal *adjective*
  1. Marked by dishonesty, esp. in matters of public   1. CORRUPT *adjective*.
     trust.
  2. Ruthlessly seeking personal advantage.   2. CORRUPT *adjective*.
  3. Capable of being bribed.   3. CORRUPTIBLE.

vend *verb*
  1. To travel about selling goods.   1. PEDDLE.
  2. To offer for sale.   2. SELL *verb*.

veneer *noun*
A deceptive outward appearance.   FAÇADE.

  veneer *verb*
  To give a deceptively attractive appearance to.   COLOR *verb*.

venerable *adjective*
Belonging to, existing, or occurring in times long past.   OLD.

venerate *verb*
  1. To regard with great awe and devotion.   1. ADORE.
  2. To pay tribute or homage to.   2. HONOR *verb*.

veneration *noun*
The act of adoring, esp. reverently.   ADORATION.

vengeance *noun*
The act of retaliating.   RETALIATION.

vengeful *adjective*
Disposed to seek revenge.   VINDICTIVE.

vengefulness *noun*
The quality or condition of being vindictive.   VINDICTIVENESS.

venial *adjective*
Admitting of forgiveness or pardon.   PARDONABLE.

venom *noun*
Anything that is injurious, destructive, or fatal.   POISON *noun.*

venomous *adjective*
1. Capable of injuring or killing by poison.   1. POISONOUS.
2. Characterized by intense ill will or spite.   2. MALEVOLENT.

vent *verb*
1. To discharge material, as vapor or fumes, usu.   1. EMIT.
   suddenly and violently.
2. To pass or pour out into.   2. DISCHARGE *verb.*
3. To put into words.   3. SAY *verb.*
4. To utter publicly.   4. AIR *verb.*

vent *noun*
1. An open space allowing passage.   1. HOLE *noun.*
2. The act or an instance of expressing in words.   2. EXPRESSION.

ventilate *verb*
1. To expose to circulating air.   1. AIR *verb.*
2. To utter publicly.   2. AIR *verb.*

ventilation *noun*
An exchanging of views.   CONFERENCE.

venture *noun*
1. An exciting, often hazardous undertaking.   1. ADVENTURE *noun.*
2. Something undertaken, esp. something requiring   2. PROJECT *noun.*
   extensive planning and work.

venture *verb*
1. To expose to possible loss or damage.   1. RISK *verb.*
2. To run the risk of.   2. HAZARD *verb.*
3. To take a risk in the hope of gaining advantage.   3. GAMBLE *verb.*
4. To have the courage to put forward, as an idea, esp. 4. PRESUME.
   when rebuff or criticism is likely.
5. To put up as a stake in a game or speculation.   5. GAMBLE *verb.*

venturer *noun*
One who engages in exciting, risky pursuits.   ADVENTURER.

venturesome *adjective*
Taking or willing to take risks.   ADVENTUROUS.

venturous *adjective*
1. Taking or willing to take risks.   1. ADVENTUROUS.
2. Involving possible risk, loss, or injury.   2. DANGEROUS.

veracious *adjective*
1. Conforming to fact.   1. ACCURATE.
2. Consistently telling the truth.   2. TRUTHFUL.

veracity *noun*
1. Correspondence with fact or truth: *No one doubted* 1. ***Syns:*** accuracy, correctness, exactitude,
   the veracity of the prediction.   exactness, fidelity, truth.
2. Freedom from deceit or falseness.   2. TRUTH.

verbal *adjective*
1. Pertaining to, consisting of, or having the nature of 1. ***Syn:*** wordy.
   words: *a verbal war between the two candidates.*
2. Expressed or transmitted in speech.   2. ORAL.
3. Employing the very same words as another.   3. LITERAL.

verbalism *noun*
Choice of words and the way in which they are used.   WORDING.

verbalization *noun*
The faculty, act, or product of speaking.   SPEECH.

verbalize *verb*
1. To express oneself in speech.   1. SPEAK.
2. To articulate (something) in words.   2. TALK *verb.*

verbatim *adjective*
Employing the very same words as another.   LITERAL.

verbose *adjective*
Using or containing an excessive number of words.   WORDY.

verboseness *noun*
Words or the use of words in excess of those needed for   WORDINESS.
clarity or precision.

verbosity *noun*
Words or the use of words in excess of those needed for   WORDINESS.
clarity or precision.

verboten *adjective*
Not allowed.   FORBIDDEN.

verge *noun*
1. A transitional interval beyond which some new   **1. *Syns:*** borderline (*also* border line),
   action or different state of affairs is likely to begin   brink, edge, point, threshold.
   or occur: *The Middle East is on the verge of war.*
2. A fairly narrow line or space forming a boundary.   **2.** BORDER *noun.*

verge *verb*
1. To put or form a border on.   **1.** BORDER *verb.*
2. To be contiguous or next to.   **2.** ADJOIN.

verge on *verb*
To come near in quality, amount, etc.   RIVAL *verb.*

verge on *verb*   SEE **verge.**

veridical *adjective*
1. Conforming to fact.   **1.** ACCURATE.
2. Consistently telling the truth.   **2.** TRUTHFUL.

verification *noun*
That which confirms.   CONFIRMATION.

verify *verb*
1. To assure the certainty or validity of.   **1.** CONFIRM.
2. To establish as true or genuine.   **2.** PROVE.

verily *adverb*
1. Not just this but also.   **1.** EVEN[1] *adverb.*
2. *Archaic.* In truth.   **2.** REALLY.

verisimilitude *noun*
Appearance of truth or authenticity: *statistics that lend*   ***Syns:*** color, plausibility.
verisimilitude to the story.

verity *noun*
Freedom from deceit or falseness.   TRUTH.

vernacular *noun*
1. An often regional form of a language not considered   **1.** DIALECT.
   standard.
2. Specialized expressions indigenous to a particular   **2.** LANGUAGE.
   field, subject, trade, or subculture.
3. A system of terms used by a people sharing a   **3.** LANGUAGE.
   history and culture.

vernal *adjective*
Of, occurring in, or characteristic of the season of   SPRING *adjective.*
spring.

versant *adjective*
Having good knowledge of.   FAMILIAR *adjective.*

versatile *adjective*
Having many aspects, uses, or abilities: *a versatile*   ***Syns:*** all-round (*also* all-around),
athlete who excels in all track events; a versatile   ambidextrous, many-sided, multifaceted,
building material.   protean, various.
     Near-syns: adaptable, adroit, dexterous,
     facile, flexible, skillful.

verse *noun*
A metrical composition.   POEM.

versed *adjective*
1. Skilled or knowledgeable through long practice.   **1.** EXPERIENCED.
2. Having good knowledge of.   **2.** FAMILIAR *adjective.*

versicolor also **versicolored** *adjective*
Having many different colors. MULTICOLORED.

versicolored *adjective* SEE **versicolor.**

version *noun*
1. A recounting of past events. 1. STORY.
2. A restating of something in other, esp. simpler, words. 2. PARAPHRASE *noun.*
3. One that is slightly different from others of the same kind or designation. 3. VARIATION.

vertical *adjective*
At right angles to the horizon or to level ground: *careful to make the doorposts vertical.* *Syns:* perpendicular, plumb, upright.

vertiginous *adjective*
1. Having a sensation of whirling or falling. 1. DIZZY *adjective.*
2. Producing dizziness or vertigo. 2. GIDDY.

vertigo *noun*
A sensation of whirling or falling. DIZZINESS.

verve *noun*
1. A lively, emphatic, eager quality or manner. 1. SPIRIT.
2. A quality of active mental and physical forcefulness. 2. VIGOR.

very *adverb*
To a high degree: *very cold; very pleased to see her.* *Syns:* awfully (*Informal*), dreadfully (*Informal*), eminently, exceptionally, extra, mighty (*Informal*), most, muchly, notably, pure (*Chiefly Regional*).
Near-syns: exceedingly, extremely, greatly, highly, strikingly, thoroughly.

very *adjective*
1. Being one and not another or others. 1. SAME.
2. Strictly distinguished from others. 2. PRECISE.
3. Being what is specified and nothing more. 3. MERE.

vesper *noun*
Archaic. The period between afternoon and nighttime. EVENING.

vestige *noun*
1. A mark or remnant that indicates the former presence of something. 1. TRACE *noun.*
2. The remains of something destroyed, disintegrated, or decayed. 2. RUIN *noun.*

vestments *noun*
Clothing worn by members of a religious order. HABIT.

vet *noun*
One who has had long experience in a given activity or capacity. VETERAN *noun.*

veteran *noun*
One who has had long experience in a given activity or capacity: *a veteran of 20 years' service on the police force.* *Syns:* old-timer (*Informal*), vet. —*Idiom* old hand.

veteran *adjective*
1. Skilled or knowledgeable through long practice. 1. EXPERIENCED.
2. Resulting from experience or practice. 2. PRACTICAL.

veto *verb*
To prevent or forbid authoritatively: *The board vetoed the plan.* *Syns:* blackball, negative, nix (*Slang*), turn down. —*Idiom* turn thumbs down on.
Near-syns: decline, deny, disallow, forbid, negate, prohibit, refuse, reject.

vex *verb*
To trouble the nerves or peace of mind of, esp. by repeated vexations. ANNOY.

vexation *noun*
1. The act of annoying. 1. ANNOYANCE.
2. The feeling of being annoyed. 2. ANNOYANCE.

3. Needless trouble.

vexatious *adjective*
1. Troubling the nerves or peace of mind, as by repeated vexations: *had a vexatious habit of cracking his knuckles.*

2. Hard to treat, manage, or cope with.
3. So replete with interlocking points and complications as to be painfully irritating.

vexing *adjective*
Troubling the nerves or peace of mind, as by repeated vexations.

viable *adjective*
Capable of occurring or being done.

vibrant *adjective*
1. Having or producing a full, deep, or rich sound.
2. Full of or characterized by a lively, emphatic, eager quality.

vibrate *verb*
To move to and fro violently.

vice *noun*
Immoral, degrading acts or habits.

vicinity *noun*
1. A surrounding area.
2. A surrounding site.
3. Approximate size or amount.

vicious *adjective*
1. Morally objectionable.
2. Showing or suggesting a disposition to be violently destructive without scruple or restraint.
3. Characterized by intense ill will or spite.
4. So intense as to cause extreme suffering.

viciousness *noun*
A cruel act or an instance of cruel behavior.

vicissitude *noun*
Something that obstructs progress and requires great effort to overcome.

victim *noun*
1. One that is made to suffer injury, loss, or death: *The plague claimed millions of victims.*
2. A living creature slain and offered to a deity as part of a religious rite.
3. A person who is easily deceived or victimized.

victimize *verb*
1. To offer as a sacrifice.
2. To get money or something else from by deceitful trickery.

victor *noun*
1. One that conquers.
2. One that wins a contest or competition.

Victorian *adjective*
Marked by excessive concern for propriety and good form.

Victorian *noun*
A person who is too much concerned with being proper, modest, or righteous.

victorious *adjective*
Pertaining to, having the nature of, or experiencing triumph: *a victorious entry into the conquered city; victorious teams.*

---

3. BOTHER *noun.*

1. **Syns:** aggravating (*Informal*), annoying, bothersome, galling, irksome, irritating, nettlesome, plaguy (*also* plaguey) (*Informal*), provoking, troublesome, vexing.
2. TROUBLESOME.
3. THORNY.

VEXATIOUS.

POSSIBLE.

1. RESONANT.
2. SPIRITED.

SHAKE *verb.*

CORRUPTION.

1. ENVIRONMENT.
2. LOCALITY.
3. NEIGHBORHOOD.

1. EVIL *adjective.*
2. FIERCE.
3. MALEVOLENT.
4. CRUEL.

CRUELTY.

DIFFICULTY.

1. **Syns:** casualty, prey.
2. SACRIFICE *noun.*
3. DUPE *noun.*

1. SACRIFICE *verb.*
2. CHEAT *verb.*

1. CONQUEROR.
2. WINNER.

GENTEEL.

PRUDE.

Syns: conquering, triumphal, triumphant.

victory *noun*
  The act of conquering.

CONQUEST.

videlicet *adverb*
  That is to say.

NAMELY.

vie *verb*
  1. To strive against (others) for victory.
  2. To strive in opposition to.

1. COMPETE.
2. CONTEND.

view *noun*
  1. That which is or can be seen: *stepped out on the porch to enjoy the ocean view.*
  2. An act of directing the eyes on an object.
  3. An outward appearance.
  4. The position from which something is observed or considered.
  5. Something believed or accepted as true by a person.
  6. What one intends to do or achieve.

1. *Syns:* lookout, outlook, perspective, prospect, scene, sight, vista.
2. LOOK *noun.*
3. FACE *noun.*
4. POINT OF VIEW.
5. BELIEF.
6. INTENTION.

view *verb*
  1. To direct the eyes on an object.
  2. To look at carefully or critically.
  3. To look upon in a particular way.

1. LOOK *verb.*
2. EXAMINE.
3. REGARD *verb.*

viewable *adjective*
  Capable of being seen.

VISIBLE.

viewer *noun*
  Someone who sees something occur.

WITNESS *noun.*

viewpoint *noun*
  1. A way of considering a matter.
  2. The position from which something is observed or considered.

1. LIGHT[1] *noun.*
2. POINT OF VIEW.

vigil *noun*
  1. The act of carefully watching.
  2. A watch over the body of a dead person before burial.

1. LOOKOUT.
2. WAKE *noun.*

vigilance *noun*
  The act of carefully watching.

LOOKOUT.

vigilant *adjective*
  Vigilantly attentive.

ALERT *adjective.*

vigor *noun*
  1. A quality of active mental and physical forcefulness: *the vigor of early manhood; the vigor of a bright, inquisitive mind.*
  2. The state or quality of being physically strong.
  3. An aggressive readiness to undertake taxing efforts.
  4. The capacity to exert an influence.
  5. Capacity or power for work or vigorous activity.
  6. A lively, emphatic, eager quality or manner.

1. *Syns:* dash, starch, verve, vigorousness, vitality. —*Idiom* vim and vigor.
2. STRENGTH.
3. DRIVE *noun.*
4. FORCE *noun.*
5. ENERGY.
6. SPIRIT.

vigorous *adjective*
  1. Disposed to action: *a vigorous fellow who found retirement a bore.*

1. *Syns:* active, brisk, brisky, driving, dynamic (*also* dynamical), energetic, enterprising, lively, peppy, snappy (*Informal*), sprightly, spry, zippy.
  Near-syns: daring, dashing, exuberant, mettlesome, red-blooded, rough-and-ready, zealous.
  Ant: lethargic.

  2. Full of vigor.
  3. Possessing, exerting, or displaying energy.
  4. Full of or displaying force.

2. LUSTY.
3. ENERGETIC.
4. FORCEFUL.

vigorously *adverb*
  With intense energy and force.

HARD *adverb.*

vigorousness *noun*
  1. The state or quality of being physically strong.

1. STRENGTH.

2. A quality of active mental and physical forcefulness. | **2.** VIGOR.

vile *adjective*
1. So objectionable as to elicit despisal. | **1.** FILTHY.
2. Deserving strong condemnation. | **2.** INFAMOUS.
3. Extremely unpleasant to the senses or feelings. | **3.** OFFENSIVE *adjective*.
4. Having or proceeding from low moral standards. | **4.** SORDID.

vilification *noun*
An attempt to destroy someone's reputation. | SMEAR *noun*.

vilify *verb*
To make defamatory statements about. | LIBEL *verb*.

vilifying *adjective*
Damaging to the reputation. | LIBELOUS.

villain *noun*
A mean, worthless character in a story or play. | HEAVY *noun*.

villainage *noun* | SEE **villeinage.**

villainous *adjective*
Utterly reprehensible in nature or behavior. | CORRUPT *adjective*.

villainy *noun*
The condition of being infamous. | INFAMY.

villeinage also **villainage** *noun*
A state of subjugation to an owner or master. | SLAVERY.

vim *noun*
1. A lively, emphatic, eager quality or manner. | **1.** SPIRIT.
2. Capacity or power for work or vigorous activity. | **2.** ENERGY.

vincible *adjective*
Open to attack and capture because of a lack of protection. | VULNERABLE.

vinculum *noun*
That which unites or binds. | BOND *noun*.

vindicate *verb*
1. To free from a charge or imputation of guilt. | **1.** CLEAR *verb*.
2. To support against arguments, attack, or criticism. | **2.** DEFEND.
3. To exact revenge for. | **3.** AVENGE.
4. To defend, maintain, or insist on the recognition of (one's rights, for example). | **4.** ASSERT.
5. To show to be just, right, or valid. | **5.** JUSTIFY.

vindictive *adjective*
Disposed to seek revenge: *a bitter, vindictive man.* | *Syns:* revengeful, spiteful, vengeful, wreakful (*Archaic*).
Near-syns: implacable, malicious, malign, merciless, relentless, unrelenting.
Ant: unvindictive.

vindictiveness *noun*
The quality or condition of being vindictive: *actions motivated by pure vindictiveness.* | *Syns:* revenge, spite, spitefulness, vengefulness.

vintage *noun*
Informal. A period of origin: *a good vintage for that wine; a car of 1942 vintage.* | *Syn:* year.

vintage *adjective*
1. Characterized by enduring excellence, appeal, and importance: *vintage paintings of the Cubist period.* | **1.** *Syns:* classic, classical.
2. Of a style or method formerly in vogue. | **2.** OLD-FASHIONED.
3. Serving to identify or set apart an individual or group. | **3.** DISTINCTIVE.

violate *verb*
1. To spoil or mar the sanctity of: *an altar violated by vandals.* | **1.** *Syns:* defile, desecrate, profane.

2. To fail to fulfill (a promise) or conform to (a regulation): *violated his sacred oath; violated the traffic laws.*

2. *Syns:* breach, break, contravene, transgress.
Near-ants: abide by, carry out, fulfill, heed, keep, mind.
Ants: observe, obey.

3. To deprive of virginity: *a young girl violated by an older man.*

3. *Syns:* defile (*Obs.*), deflorate, deflower.

4. To compel (another) to participate in or submit to a sexual act.

4. RAPE.

violation *noun*
1. An act of disrespect or impiety toward something regarded as sacred.

1. SACRILEGE.

2. An act or instance of breaking a law or regulation or of nonfulfillment of an obligation, promise, etc.

2. BREACH *noun.*

3. A serious breaking of the public law.

3. CRIME.

violence *noun*
1. Power used to overcome resistance.

1. FORCE *noun.*

2. Exceptionally great concentration, power, or force, esp. in activity.

2. INTENSITY.

violent *adjective*
1. Accomplished by force.

1. FORCIBLE.

2. Extreme in degree, strength, or effect.

2. INTENSE.

3. Violently disturbed, as by storms.

3. ROUGH.

VIP *noun*
Informal. An important, influential person.

DIGNITARY.

virago *noun*
A person, esp. a woman, who habitually uses loud, abusive language.

SCOLD *noun.*

virgin *noun*
A pure, uncorrupted person.

INNOCENT *noun.*

virginal *adjective*
Free from evil and corruption.

INNOCENT *adjective.*

virile *adjective*
Of, characteristic of, or befitting the male sex.

MANLY.

virtual *adjective*
Involved in the essential nature of something but not shown or developed.

IMPLICIT.

virtue *noun*
1. A special feature or quality that confers superiority: *The virtue of the faculty lies in its diversity.*

1. *Syns:* beauty, distinction, excellence, merit, perfection.

2. The condition of being chaste.

2. CHASTITY.

3. The quality or state of being morally sound.

3. GOOD *noun.*

4. A level of superiority that is usu. high.

4. MERIT *noun.*

virtuous *adjective*
1. Morally beyond reproach, esp. in sexual conduct.

1. CHASTE.

2. *Rare.* Producing or able to produce a desired effect.

2. EFFECTIVE.

virtuousness *noun*
1. The condition of being chaste.

1. CHASTITY.

2. The quality or state of being morally sound.

2. GOOD *noun.*

virulent *adjective*
1. Extremely destructive or harmful: *virulent rumors.*

1. *Syns:* baneful, deadly, malignant, noxious, pernicious, pestilent, pestilential.

2. Capable of injuring or killing by poison.

2. POISONOUS.

3. Bitingly hostile.

3. RESENTFUL.

virus *noun*
Anything that is injurious, destructive, or fatal.

POISON *noun.*

visage *noun*
1. A disposition of the facial features that conveys meaning, feeling, or mood.

1. EXPRESSION.

2. The front surface of the head.

3. An outward appearance.

2. FACE *noun.*

3. FACE *noun.*

vis-à-vis *noun*

One holding a position corresponding to that of one in another organization or hierarchy.

COUNTERPART.

visceral *adjective*

1. Derived from or prompted by a natural tendency or impulse.

2. Of, pertaining to, or arising from one's mental or spiritual being.

1. INSTINCTIVE.

2. INNER.

viscerous *adjective*

Of, pertaining to, or arising from one's mental or spiritual being.

INNER.

viscid *adjective*

Having a heavy, gluey quality.

VISCOUS.

viscidity *noun*

The physical property of being viscous.

VISCOSITY.

viscose *adjective*

Having a heavy, gluey quality.

VISCOUS.

viscosity *noun*

The physical property of being viscous: *measured the viscosity of the oil.*

Syn: viscidity.

viscous *adjective*

Having a heavy, gluey quality: *Unrefined oil is viscous.*

Syns: glutinous, mucilaginous, viscid, viscose.

visibility *noun*

The quality, condition, or degree of being visible: *Visibility was zero because of fog.*

Syn: visuality.

visible *adjective*

1. Capable of being seen: *Yellow headlights are visible even in fog.*

2. Readily seen, perceived, or understood.

1. *Syns:* perceivable, perceptible, seeable, viewable, visual.

2. APPARENT.

vision *noun*

1. The faculty of seeing: *Her vision has deteriorated since the accident.*

2. An illusory mental image.

3. Unusual or creative discernment or perception: *We need a leader who is a man of vision.*

4. Something that is foretold by or as if by supernatural means.

1. *Syns:* eyes, eyesight, light[1] (*Poetic*), seeing, sight.

2. DREAM *noun.*

3. *Syns:* far-sightedness, foresight, prescience.

4. PROPHECY.

vision *verb*

To form mental images of.

IMAGINE.

visionary *adjective*

1. Characterized by foresight: *a visionary film about the aftereffects of nuclear war.*

2. Given to daydreams or reverie.

3. Showing a tendency to envision things in perfect but unrealistic form.

1. *Syns:* far-sighted, prescient.

2. DREAMY.

3. IDEALISTIC.

visionary *noun*

A person inclined to be imaginative or idealistic but impractical.

DREAMER.

visit *verb*

1. To go to or seek out the company of in order to socialize: *visited relatives.*

1. *Syns:* call, come by, come over (*Informal*), drop by, drop in, look in, look up, pop in, run in, see, stop (in *or* by). —*Idiom* pay a visit.

2. To remain as a guest or lodger.

3. *Informal.* To engage in spoken exchange.

4. To cause to undergo or bear, as something unwelcome or damaging.

2. STAY[1] *verb.*

3. CONVERSE[1] *verb.*

4. INFLICT.

visit *noun*

1. An act or an instance of going or coming to see another: *She paid a visit to her aunt.*
2. A remaining in a place as a guest or lodger.

1. **Syns:** call, visitation.

2. STAY[1] *noun.*

visitant *noun*
1. A person or persons visiting one.
2. A supernatural being.

1. COMPANY *noun.*
2. GHOST *noun.*

visitation *noun*
1. An act or an instance of going or coming to see another.
2. A state of pain or anguish that tests one's resiliency and character.

1. VISIT *noun.*

2. TRIAL.

visitor *noun*
1. One that arrives.
2. A person or persons visiting one.

1. ARRIVAL.
2. COMPANY *noun.*

vista *noun*
That which is or can be seen.

VIEW *noun.*

visual *adjective*
1. Serving, resulting from, or pertaining to the sense of sight: *visual cues; visual images; visual acuity.*
2. Capable of being seen.

1. **Syns:** optic, optical.

2. VISIBLE.

visuality *noun*
The quality, condition, or degree of being visible.

VISIBILITY.

visualize *verb*
To form mental images of.

IMAGINE.

vital *adjective*
1. Marked by or exhibiting life.
2. Full of vigor.
3. Constituting or forming part of the essence of something.
4. *Archaic.* Causing or tending to cause death.

1. ALIVE.
2. LUSTY.
3. ESSENTIAL *adjective.*

4. DEADLY.

vitality *noun*
1. The vital principle or animating force within living beings.
2. The capacity to exert an influence.
3. A quality of active mental and physical forcefulness.

1. SPIRIT.

2. FORCE *noun.*
3. VIGOR.

vitalizing *adjective*
Serving to enliven.

STIMULATING.

vitiate *verb*
1. To ruin utterly in character or quality.
2. To undergo moral deterioration.
3. To spoil the soundness or perfection of.
4. To put an end to formally and with authority.

1. CORRUPT *verb.*
2. FALL *verb.*
3. INJURE.
4. ABOLISH.

vitiated *adjective*
Lowered in character or quality.

CORRUPTED.

vitriolic *adjective*
So sharp as to cause mental pain.

BITING.

vituperate *verb*
To attack with harsh, often insulting language.

REVILE *verb.*

vituperation *noun*
Harsh, often insulting language: *a family row characterized by much vituperation.*

Syns: abuse, billingsgate, contumely, invective, obloquy, railing, revile (*Obs.*), revilement, reviling, scurrility.

vituperative *adjective*
1. Of, relating to, or characterized by verbal abuse.
2. So sharp as to cause mental pain.

1. ABUSIVE.
2. BITING.

vivacious *adjective*
1. Full of joyful, unrestrained high spirits.
2. Very brisk, alert, and high-spirited.

1. EXUBERANT.
2. LIVELY.

vivacity *noun*
A lively, emphatic, eager quality or manner.

SPIRIT.

vivid *adjective*
1. Full of color.
2. Evoking strong mental images through distinctiveness.
3. Described verbally in sharp and accurate detail.

1. COLORFUL.
2. COLORFUL.
3. GRAPHIC.

vivifying *adjective*
Serving to enliven.

STIMULATING.

vivify *verb*
To make alive.

QUICKEN.

vixen *noun*
A person, esp. a woman, who habitually uses loud, abusive language.

SCOLD *noun*.

vocabulary *noun*
1. An alphabetical list of words often defined or translated: *The vocabulary includes idioms and two-word verbs.*
2. All the words of a language: *The vocabulary of Russian is very expressive.*
3. Specialized expressions indigenous to a particular field, subject, trade, or subculture.

1. *Syns:* dictionary, lexicon, wordbook.

2. *Syns:* lexicon, word-hoard, word-stock.

3. LANGUAGE.

vocal *adjective*
1. Produced by the voice: *a vocal prayer.*

2. Speaking or spoken without reserve.
3. *Phon.* Characterized by, containing, or functioning as a vowel or vowels: *vocal as opposed to consonant sounds.*

1. *Syns:* articulate, oral, sonant, spoken, uttered, voiced.
2. OUTSPOKEN.
3. *Syns:* vocalic, vowel.

vocalic *adjective*
Characterized by, containing, or functioning as a vowel or vowels.

VOCAL.

vocalism *noun*
The use of the speech organs to produce sounds.

VOICING.

vocalist *noun*
A person who sings: *a vocalist who performs at weddings.*

Syns: singer, songster, songstress, voice.

vocalization *noun*
The use of the speech organs to produce sounds.

VOICING.

vocalize *verb*
1. To put into words.
2. To express oneself in speech.
3. To utter words or sounds in musical tones.

1. SAY *verb*.
2. SPEAK *verb*.
3. SING.

vocation *noun*
1. An inner urge to pursue an activity or perform a service: *the vocation of the priesthood.*
2. Activity pursued as a livelihood.

1. *Syns:* calling, mission.

2. BUSINESS.

vociferant *adjective*

SEE **vociferous.**

vociferate *verb*
To say (something) with a shout.

SHOUT *verb*.

vociferation *noun*
Offensively loud and insistent utterances, esp. of disapproval: *Gas rationing was greeted by widespread public vociferation.*

Syns: clamor, hullabaloo (*also* hullaballoo), outcry, rumpus, uproar.
—*Idiom* hue and cry.

vociferous also **vociferant** *adjective*
Offensively loud and insistent: *vociferous complaints from the demoralized staff.*

Syns: blatant, boisterous, clamorous, loudmouthed, multivocal, obstreperous, strident.
Near-ants: calm, close-mouthed, noiseless, quiet, silent, still.

vogue *noun*
The current custom.

FASHION *noun*.

voice *noun*
1. The right or chance to express an opinion or participate in a decision: *was allowed no voice in choosing his replacement.*
2. The act or an instance of expressing in words.
3. The faculty, act, or product of speaking.
4. A person who sings.

voice *verb*
To put into words.

voiced *adjective*
Produced by the voice.

voiceless *adjective*
Lacking the power or faculty of speech.

voicing *noun*
The use of the speech organs to produce sounds: *a loud voicing of hitherto unspoken resentment.*

void *adjective*
1. Containing nothing.
2. Lacking a desirable element.

void *noun*
1. Empty, unfilled space.
2. A space in an otherwise solid mass.
3. An interval during which continuity is suspended.
4. A desolate sense of loss.

void *verb*
1. To put an end to formally and with authority.
2. To pass or pour out into.
3. To remove the contents of.

volatile *adjective*
Following no predictable pattern.

volatilize *verb*
To pass off as vapor, esp. due to being heated.

volition *noun*
The mental faculty by which one deliberately chooses or decides.

volitional *adjective*
Of or relating to free exercise of the will.

volley *noun*
A concentrated outpouring, as of missiles, words, or blows.

volume *noun*
1. Great extent, amount, or dimension.
2. A printed and bound work.
3. An issue of printed material offered for sale or distribution.

voluminous *adjective*
1. Of full measure; not narrow or restricted.
2. Large in number or yield.
3. Amounting to or consisting of a large, indefinite number.

voluntarily *adverb*
Of one's own free will: *voluntarily gave up his seat to the old lady.*

voluntary *adjective*
1. Done by one's own choice: *voluntary enlistment into the army; voluntary labor.*

1. **Syns:** say, say-so (*Informal*), suffrage.

2. EXPRESSION.
3. SPEECH.
4. VOCALIST.

SAY *verb.*

VOCAL.

DUMB.

Syns: articulation, utterance, vocalism, vocalization.

1. EMPTY *adjective.*
2. EMPTY *adjective.*

1. NOTHINGNESS.
2. HOLE *noun.*
3. GAP.
4. EMPTINESS.

1. ABOLISH.
2. DISCHARGE *verb.*
3. EMPTY *verb.*

CAPRICIOUS.

EVAPORATE.

WILL[1] *noun.*

VOLUNTARY *adjective.*

BARRAGE *noun.*

1. BULK.
2. BOOK *noun.*
3. PUBLICATION.

1. FULL.
2. HEAVY *adjective.*
3. MANY.

Syns: voluntary, willingly. —*Idioms* of one's own accord, on one's own volition.

1. **Syns:** free, spontaneous, uncompelled, unforced, willful (*Obs.*).
   Near-ants: coerced, compelled, forced, prescribed, unintentional, unplanned, unwilling, unwitting.
   Ant: involuntary.

2. Of or relating to free exercise of the will: *voluntary sacrifices; voluntary acts.*

2. *Syns:* volitional, willing.

3. Done or said on purpose.

3. DELIBERATE *adjective*.

voluntary *adverb*
Of one's own free will.

VOLUNTARILY.

voluntary *noun*
Someone who offers his or her services freely.

VOLUNTEER *noun*.

volunteer *noun*
Someone who offers his or her services freely: *unpaid political volunteers.*

Syn: voluntary.

volunteer *verb*
To put before another for acceptance.

OFFER *verb*.

voluptuary *noun*
A person devoted to pleasure and luxury.

SYBARITE.

voluptuary *adjective*
Pertaining to, suggestive of, or appealing to sense gratification.

SENSUOUS.

voluptuous *adjective*
1. Suggesting sexuality.

1. SENSUAL.

2. Pertaining to, suggestive of, or appealing to sense gratification.

2. SENSUOUS.

voluptuousness *noun*
The quality or condition of being sensual.

SENSUALITY.

voracious *adjective*
1. Having an insatiable appetite for an activity or pursuit: *a voracious reader.*

1. *Syns:* avid, edacious, omnivorous, rapacious, ravenous, unappeasable.

2. Wanting to eat or drink more than one can reasonably consume.

2. GREEDY.

voracity *noun*
The quality or condition of being voracious: *The hungry wolf consumed its fallen prey with frightening voracity.*

Syns: avidness, edacity, gulosity, rapacity, ravenousness.

votary *noun*
One zealously devoted to a religion.

DEVOTEE.

vote *verb*
To select by vote for an office.

ELECT *verb*.

voter *noun*
One who votes.

ELECTOR.

vouch for *verb*
To confirm formally as true, accurate, or genuine.

CERTIFY.

vouchsafe *verb*
1. To descend to a level considered inappropriate to one's dignity.

1. CONDESCEND.

2. To let have as a favor or privilege.

2. GRANT *verb*.

vow *noun*
A declaration that one will or will not do a certain thing.

PROMISE *noun*.

vow *verb*
To guarantee by a solemn promise.

PLEDGE *verb*.

vowel *adjective*
Characterized by, containing, or functioning as a vowel or vowels.

VOCAL.

vulgar *adjective*
1. Lacking in delicacy or refinement.

1. COARSE.

2. Lacking high station or birth.

2. LOWLY.

vulgarian *noun*
An unrefined, rude person.

BOOR.

vulgarism *noun*
A term whose form offends against established usage standards.

CORRUPTION.

vulnerability *noun*
The condition of being laid open to something
undesirable or injurious.

EXPOSURE.

vulnerable *adjective*
1. Open to attack and capture because of a lack of
protection: *a strategic position vulnerable to
counterattack.*
2. Tending to incur.

1. **Syns:** assailable, attackable, pregnable,
vincible.

2. LIABLE.

vulnerableness *noun*
The condition of being laid open to something
undesirable or injurious.

EXPOSURE.

vying *noun*
An intense competition.

BATTLE *noun.*

vying *adjective*
Given to competition.

COMPETITIVE.

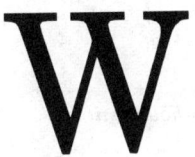

wacky also **whacky** *adjective*
1. *Slang.* Afflicted with or exhibiting irrationality and
mental unsoundness.
2. *Slang.* So senseless as to be laughable.

1. INSANE.

2. FOOLISH.

wad *noun*
1. An irregularly shaped mass of indefinite size.
2. *Informal.* An indeterminately great amount or
number.
3. *Informal.* A large sum of money.

1. LUMP[1] *noun.*

2. HEAP *noun.*

3. FORTUNE.

waffle *verb*
Informal. To use evasive or deliberately vague
language.

EQUIVOCATE.

wag[1] *verb*
To move to and fro vigorously and usu. repeatedly: *The
dog wagged its tail.*

Syns: lash, switch, waggle, wave.
Near-syns: beat, shake, toss, twitch,
wiggle.

wag[2] *noun*
A person whose words or actions provoke or are
intended to provoke amusement or laughter.

JOKER.

wage *verb*
To engage in (a war or campaign): *waged war on two
fronts; waging an antipoverty campaign.*

Syns: carry on, carry out, conduct,
prosecute.

wager *verb*
1. To make a bet on.
2. To put up as a stake in a game or speculation.

1. BET *verb.*
2. GAMBLE *verb.*

wager *noun*
1. A venture depending on chance.
2. Something valuable risked on an uncertain outcome.

1. GAMBLE *noun.*
2. BET *noun.*

wage(s) *noun*
1. Payment for work done: *an hourly wage of $8.50;
high union wages.*

2. Something justly deserved.

1. **Syns:** earnings, emolument, fee, hire,
pay, salary, stipend. —*Idioms* pay
envelope, pay packet (*Brit.*).
2. DUE *noun.*

waggle *verb*
1. To move (wings, arms, etc.) up and down.

1. FLAP *verb.*

2. To move to and fro vigorously and usu. repeatedly.

3. To move or proceed with short, irregular motions up and down or from side to side.

wail *verb*

1. To make inarticulate sounds of grief or pain, usu. accompanied by tears.

2. To cry loudly, as a healthy child does from pain or distress.

3. To utter or emit a long, mournful, plaintive sound.

4. *Archaic.* To feel or express sorrow for.

wail *noun*

A long, mournful cry.

wailing *noun*

A fit of crying.

wait *verb*

1. To continue to be in a place.

2. To stop temporarily and remain, as if reluctant to leave.

3. *Informal.* To put off until a later time.

wait on (or **upon**) *verb*

1. To work and care for.

2. To place food before (someone).

wait *noun*

An act or the time of waiting: *had a two-hour wait in the doctor's office.*

waiting *noun*

An act or the time of waiting.

wait on (or **upon**) *verb*

waive *verb*

1. To give up a possession, claim, or right.

2. To let (something) go.

3. To put off until a later time.

waiver *noun*

A giving up of a possession, claim, or right.

wake *verb*

To cease sleeping: *woke at six in the morning.*

wake *noun*

A watch over the body of a dead person before burial: *laid in a plentiful supply of food and drink for the wake.*

wake *adjective*

Not in a state of sleep.

wakeful *adjective*

1. Not in a state of sleep: *a wakeful, fretting baby.*

2. Marked by an absence of sleep: *had a wakeful, restless night.*

3. Vigilantly attentive.

waken *verb*

1. To cease sleeping.

2. To induce or elicit (a reaction or emotion).

wale *noun*

A ridge or bump raised on the flesh by a lash or blow.

walk *noun*

1. An act of walking, esp. for pleasure: *With time between trains, he checked his luggage and took a walk.*

2. A usu. brief and regular journey on foot, esp. for exercise.

walk *verb*

---

2. WAG[1].

3. WIGGLE.

1. CRY *verb*.

2. BAWL.

3. HOWL *verb*.

4. REGRET *verb*.

HOWL *noun*.

CRY *noun*.

1. REMAIN.

2. PAUSE *verb*.

3. DEFER[1].

1. SERVE.

2. SERVE.

Syns: stay[1], waiting.

WAIT *noun*.

SEE **wait**.

1. ABDICATE.

2. RELINQUISH.

3. DEFER[1].

ABDICATION.

Syns: arouse, awake, awaken, rouse, stir[1], waken.

Syn: vigil.

WAKEFUL.

1. *Syns:* awake, unsleeping, wake, wide-awake.

2. *Syns:* sleepless, slumberless.

3. ALERT *adjective*.

1. WAKE *verb*.

2. AROUSE.

WELT.

1. *Syns:* amble, perambulation, promenade, ramble, saunter, stroll.

2. CONSTITUTIONAL *noun*.

To go on foot: *walked to and fro in deep thought.*

walk out *verb*
To cease working in support of demands made upon an employer.

walk out on *verb*
To give up without intending to return or claim again.

walkaway *noun*
1. *Informal.* An easily accomplished task.
2. An easy victory.

walk out *verb*

walk out on *verb*

walkover *noun*
1. *Informal.* An easily accomplished task.
2. An easy victory.

wall *noun*
1. A solid structure that encloses an area or separates one area from another: *We knocked down a wall between two bedrooms to make a large studio for our son.*
2. Anything that impedes or prevents entry or passage.

wall *verb*
1. To separate with or as if with a wall: *We have walled off part of our yard for a patio.*
2. To confine within a limited area.
3. To shut in with or as if with bars.

wallop *verb*
1. *Informal.* To deliver (a powerful blow) suddenly and sharply.
2. *Informal.* To render totally ineffective by decisive defeat.

wallop *noun*
1. *Informal.* A sudden sharp, powerful stroke.
2. Violent, forcible contact between two or more things.
3. *Informal.* The capacity to create a powerful effect: *Today's editorial really packs a wallop.*
4. *Informal.* A strong, pleasant feeling of excitement or stimulation.

walloping *adjective*
Informal. Of extraordinary size and power.

wallow *verb*
1. To move about in an indolent or clumsy manner: *two drunks wallowing in the snow.*
2. To move awkwardly or clumsily.
3. To take extravagant pleasure.

waltz *verb*
To move swiftly and effortlessly.

wampum *noun*
Something, as coins, printed bills, etc., used as a medium of exchange.

wan *adjective*
1. Pale and exhausted because of worry, sleeplessness, etc.
2. Lacking color.

wan *verb*
To lose normal coloration; turn pale.

wander *verb*
1. To move about at random, esp. over a wide area.
2. To walk at a leisurely pace.
3. To go through a place, viewing or inspecting in a leisurely way.

Syns: ambulate, foot (it), hoof (*Informal*), pace, step, tread.

STRIKE *verb.*

ABANDON *verb.*

1. BREEZE *noun.*
2. RUNAWAY *noun* at **run away.**
SEE **walk.**
SEE **walk.**

1. BREEZE *noun.*
2. RUNAWAY *noun* at **run away.**

1. **Syns:** barrier, partition.

2. BAR *noun.*

1. **Syns:** fence (off), partition.

2. ENCLOSE.
3. BAR *verb.*

1. HIT *verb.*

2. OVERWHELM.

1. BLOW^2.
2. COLLISION.
3. **Syns:** impact, punch (*Informal*), sock (*Slang*).
4. THRILL *noun.*

GIANT *adjective.*

1. **Syns:** flounder, welter.

2. BLUNDER *verb.*
3. LUXURIATE.

BREEZE *verb.*

MONEY.

1. HAGGARD.

2. PALE *adjective.*

PALE *verb.*

1. ROVE.
2. STROLL *verb.*
3. BROWSE.

4. To turn aside from the main subject in writing or speaking.

4. DIGRESS.

wandering *adjective*
1. Leading the life of a person without a fixed domicile; moving from place to place.
2. Traveling about, esp. in search of adventure.
3. Without a fixed or regular course.

1. NOMADIC.

2. ERRANT.
3. ERRATIC.

wane *verb*
1. To become less active or intense.
2. To lose strength or power.

1. SUBSIDE.
2. FADE *verb*.

wane *noun*
The act or process of becoming less active or intense: *popularity that was on the wane.*

Syns: abatement, ebb, letup, slackening.

wangle *verb*
Informal. To make, achieve, or get through contrivance or guile: *How did you wangle an interview with such a reclusive man?*

Syns: engineer, finagle (*also* fenagle) (*Informal*), finesse, worm.

want *verb*
1. To be without what is needed, required, or essential.
2. To have the desire or inclination to.

1. LACK *verb*.
2. CHOOSE.

want *noun*
1. The condition of lacking a usual or needed amount.
2. The condition of being extremely poor.
3. Something asked for or needed.

1. ABSENCE.
2. POVERTY.
3. DEMAND *noun*.

wanting *adjective*
1. Not present.
2. Lacking an essential element.
3. Not enough to meet a demand or requirement.
4. Lacking a desirable element.

1. ABSENT.
2. DEFICIENT.
3. INSUFFICIENT.
4. EMPTY *adjective*.

wanton *adjective*
1. Sexually promiscuous: *a wanton woman.*

1. *Syns:* easy, fast, libertine, light[2], loose, whorish. —*Idiom* of easy virtue.

2. Not required, necessary, or warranted by the circumstances of the case: *wanton killing; the wanton destruction of Sheridan's army.*
3. Lacking in moral restraint.

2. *Syns:* gratuitous, supererogative, supererogatory, uncalled-for.

3. ABANDONED.

wanton *noun*
1. A vulgar, promiscuous woman who flouts propriety.
2. An immoral or licentious man: *a toothless old wanton still chasing young girls.*

1. SLUT.
2. *Syns:* lecher, libertine, profligate, rake[1], roué, satyr. —*Idiom* dirty old man.

wantonness *noun*
A complete surrender of inhibitions.

ABANDON *noun*.

war *noun*
1. A state of open, prolonged fighting.
2. A struggle with others for victory or supremacy.

1. CONFLICT *noun*.
2. COMPETITION.

ward *noun*
1. A person who relies on another for support.
2. The act or a means of defending.
3. A person or special body of persons assigned to provide protection, keep watch over, etc.

1. DEPENDENT *noun*.
2. DEFENSE.
3. GUARD *noun*.

ward *verb*
To prohibit from occurring by advance planning or action.

PREVENT.

ward off *verb*
To turn or drive away.

PARRY.

warden *noun*
1. A person who is legally responsible for the person or property of another considered by law to be incompetent to manage his affairs.
2. A guard or keeper of a prison.

1. GUARDIAN.

2. JAILER.

warder *noun*
   Brit. A guard or keeper of a prison.   JAILER.

ward off *verb*   SEE **ward.**

wares *noun*
   Products bought and sold in commerce.   GOODS.

warfare *noun*
   1. A state of open, prolonged fighting.   **1.** CONFLICT *noun.*
   2. A struggle with others for victory or supremacy.   **2.** COMPETITION.

wariness *noun*
   Careful forethought to avoid harm or risk.   CAUTION *noun.*

warlike *adjective*
   1. Having or showing an eagerness to fight.   **1.** BELLIGERENT.
   2. Of, pertaining to, or inclined toward war.   **2.** MILITARY.

warm *adjective*
   1. Easily approached.   **1.** APPROACHABLE.
   2. Showing or having enthusiasm.   **2.** ENTHUSIASTIC.

warmed-over *adjective*
   Informal. Without freshness or appeal due to overuse.   TRITE.

warmhearted *adjective*
   Of or befitting a friend or friends.   FRIENDLY.

warmth *noun*
   Intensity of feeling or reaction.   HEAT *noun.*

warn *verb*
   To notify (someone) of imminent danger or risk: *warned*   ***Syns:*** alarm, alert, caution, forewarn.
   them about the cyclone's approach.

warning *noun*
   1. Advice to beware, as of a person or thing: **1.** ***Syns:*** admonishment, admonition,
   disregarded her friend's warnings.   caution, caveat, forewarning, monition.
   2. A signal that warns of imminent danger.   **2.** ALARM *noun.*
   3. An instance that warns or discourages prospective   **3.** EXAMPLE.
      imitators.

   warning *adjective*
   Giving warning.   CAUTIONARY.

warp *verb*
   1. To cause to have a prejudiced view.   **1.** BIAS *verb.*
   2. To give an inaccurate view of by representing falsely   **2.** DISTORT.
      or misleadingly.
   3. To ruin utterly in character or quality.   **3.** CORRUPT *verb.*

warrant *noun*
   1. Legal permission to do something.   **1.** LICENSE *noun.*
   2. A justifying fact or consideration.   **2.** BASIS.
   3. An assumption of responsibility, as one given by a   **3.** GUARANTEE *noun.*
      manufacturer, for the quality, worth, or durability of
      a product.
   4. Something given to guarantee the repayment of a   **4.** PAWN[1] *noun.*
      loan or the fulfillment of an obligation.
   5. A statement that expresses a commitment on the   **5.** WORD *noun.*
      part of its maker as to its truthfulness or to the
      fulfillment of its conditions.

   warrant *verb*
   1. To be a proper or sufficient occasion for.   **1.** CALL FOR at **call.**
   2. To assure the certainty or validity of.   **2.** CONFIRM.
   3. To render certain.   **3.** GUARANTEE *verb.*
   4. To assume responsibility for the quality, worth, or   **4.** GUARANTEE *verb.*
      durability of.

warranty *noun*
   An assumption of responsibility, as one given by a   GUARANTEE *noun.*
   manufacturer, for the quality, worth, or durability of a
   product.

warring *adjective*
   Of or engaged in warfare.   BELLIGERENT.

wary *adjective*
1. Trying attentively to avoid danger, risk, or error: *a wary driver.*

2. Vigilantly attentive.
3. Careful in the use of material resources.

wash *verb*
1. To make moist: *flowers washed by dew; cheeks washed by tears.*
2. To flow against or along: *waves that washed the rocks.*
3. To move along with or be carried away by the action of water: *The skiff washed down the stream in the storm.*
4. To flow or move with a low, slapping sound: *could hear water washing about the floor of the ship's engine room.*
5. *Informal.* To prove valid under scrutiny: *Her alibi doesn't wash.*

wash up *verb*
To be depleted.

washed-up *adjective*
1. Having no further relationship.
2. No longer effective, capable, or valuable.

washout *noun*

wash out *verb*
To receive less than a passing grade.

washout *noun*
One that fails completely.

wash up *verb*

washy *adjective*
1. Lower than normal in strength or concentration due to admixture.
2. Lacking the qualities requisite for spiritedness and originality.

waspish *adjective*
1. Having or showing a bad temper.
2. Easily annoyed.

waste *verb*
1. To use up foolishly or needlessly: *wasted gas by joyriding; a poorly insulated house that wastes energy.*
2. To spend (money) excessively and usu. foolishly: *wasted their inheritance gambling.*

3. To pass (time) without working or in avoiding work.
4. To do away with completely and destructively.
5. To destroy completely while conquering or occupying.
6. To lose strength or power.
7. To fail to take advantage of.
8. *Slang.* To take the life of (a person or persons) unlawfully.

waste *noun*
1. Excessive or imprudent expenditure.
2. A tract of unproductive land.

---

1. **Syns:** careful, cautious, chary, circumspect, gingerly, prudent. **Near-ants:** careless, feckless, heedless, irresponsible, thoughtless, uncautious. **Ant:** foolhardy.
2. ALERT *adjective.*
3. ECONOMICAL.

1. **Syns:** bathe, dampen, moisten.

2. **Syns:** bathe, lap, lave, lip.

3. **Syns:** drift, float.

4. **Syns:** burble, gurgle, lap, slosh, splash, swash, swish.

5. **Syns:** hold up, prove out, stand up. —*Idioms* hold water, pass muster, ring true.

GO *verb.*

1. THROUGH *adjective.*
2. THROUGH *adjective.*
SEE **wash out.**

FAIL.

FAILURE.
SEE **wash.**

1. DILUTE *adjective.*

2. INSIPID.

1. ILL-TEMPERED.
2. IRRITABLE.

1. **Syns:** consume, devour, expend, squander.

2. **Syns:** blow[1] (*Slang*), blue (*Brit. Slang*), consume, dissipate, fool away, fritter away, riot away, squander, throw away, trifle away.
3. IDLE *verb.*
4. CONSUME.
5. DEVASTATE.

6. FADE.
7. LOSE.
8. MURDER *verb.*

1. EXTRAVAGANCE.
2. BARREN *noun.*

wasted *adjective*
Physically haggard: *the wasted remains of famine victims.*

Syns: cadaverous, emaciated, gaunt, shrunken, skeletal. —*Idiom* all skin and bones.

wasteful *adjective*
Characterized by excessive or imprudent spending.

EXTRAVAGANT.

wastefulness *noun*
Excessive or imprudent expenditure.

EXTRAVAGANCE.

wasteland *noun*
A tract of unproductive land.

BARREN *noun.*

waster *noun*
A person who spends money or resources wastefully.

WASTREL.

wasting *adjective*
Tending to consume and destroy.

CONSUMPTIVE.

wastrel *noun*
1. A person who spends money or resources wastefully: *a wastrel who squandered his fortune on clothes and cars.*
2. A self-indulgent person who spends time avoiding work or other useful activity: *joined his fellow wastrels for the daily visit to the poolroom.*

1. *Syns:* prodigal, profligate, scattergood, spendthrift, waster.

2. *Syns:* bum, dolittle, do-nothing, drone[1], fainéant, good-for-nothing, idler, lazybones (*Slang*), loafer, ne'er-do-well, no-good, slouch, slug[3] (*Informal*), slugabed, sluggard. —*Idiom* Weary Willie.

watch *verb*
1. To look at or on attentively or carefully: *The guard watched the prisoner closely. He demonstrated the wrestling hold while we watched.*
2. To use the power of vision.
3. To be sure that.
4. To have the care and supervision of.

1. *Syns:* eye, observe, scrutinize, survey. —*Idiom* keep an eye on.

2. LOOK *verb.*
3. LOOK *verb.*
4. TEND[2].

watch out *verb*
To be careful.

LOOK OUT.

watch *noun*
1. The act of observing, often for an extended time: *The guards kept a 24-hour watch on the prisoner.*
2. The act of carefully watching.
3. A person or special body of persons assigned to provide protection, keep watch over, etc.
4. A limited, often assigned period of activity, duty, or opportunity.

1. *Syns:* eye, observance, observation, scrutiny, tab(s).
2. LOOKOUT at **look out.**
3. GUARD *noun.*

4. TURN *noun.*

watcher *noun*
1. Someone who observes: *Kremlin watchers tried to predict new Soviet moves.*
2. An agent assigned to observe and report on another.

1. *Syns:* beholder, by-sitter, bystander, looker-on, observer, spectator.
2. TAIL *noun.*

watchful *adjective*
1. Vigilantly attentive.
2. Cautiously attentive.

1. ALERT *adjective.*
2. CAREFUL.
SEE **watch.**

watch out *verb*

water *verb*
1. To lessen the strength of by or as if by admixture.
2. To fill with tears.

1. DILUTE *verb.*
2. TEAR[2] *verb.*

watered *adjective*
Lower than normal in strength or concentration due to admixture.

DILUTE *adjective.*

watered-down *adjective*
Lower than normal in strength or concentration due to admixture.

DILUTE *adjective.*

waterish *adjective*
1. Lower than normal in strength or concentration due to admixture.

1. DILUTE *adjective.*

2. Lacking the qualities requisite for spiritedness and originality.

2. INSIPID.

3. Being weak in quality or substance.

3. PALE *adjective*.

waterless *adjective*

Having little or no liquid or moisture.

DRY *adjective*.

Waterloo *noun*

A disastrous, overwhelming defeat or ruin.

FALL *noun*.

watershed *noun*

The region drained by a river system.

BASIN.

watery *adjective*

1. Lower than normal in strength or concentration due to admixture.

1. DILUTE *adjective*.

2. Lacking the qualities requisite for spiritedness and originality.

2. INSIPID.

3. Being weak in quality or substance.

3. PALE *adjective*.

wave *verb*

1. To have or cause to have a curved or sinuous form or surface: *hair that waves naturally; waved her hair with a hot iron.*

1. *Syns:* curl, curve, undulate.

2. To move (wings, arms, etc.) up and down.

2. FLAP *verb*.

3. To move or cause to move about while being fixed at one edge.

3. FLAP *verb*.

4. To move to and fro vigorously and usu. repeatedly.

4. WAG[1].

5. To wield boldly and dramatically.

5. FLOURISH.

waver *verb*

1. To be irresolute in acting or doing.

1. HESITATE.

2. To change one's attitudes, policies, or the like.

2. SWING *verb*.

3. To move back and forth or from side to side, as if about to fall.

3. SWAY.

wavering *adjective*

Given to or exhibiting hesitation.

HESITANT.

wavering *noun*

The act or an instance of hesitating.

HESITATION.

wax *verb*

1. To come to be.

1. BECOME.

2. To make or become greater or larger.

2. INCREASE *verb*.

waxen *adjective*

Lacking color.

PALE *adjective*.

way *noun*

1. A course affording passage from one place to another: *historic houses on both sides of the way.*

1. *Syns:* avenue, boulevard, drive, freeway, highway, path, road, roadway, street, thoroughfare.
Near-syns: alley, byway, drag (*Slang*), lane, passage, route.

2. An extent, measured or unmeasured, of linear space.

2. DISTANCE.

3. The manner in which something is done: *demonstrated various ways of tackling in football; a circuitous way of expressing himself.*

3. *Syns:* fashion, method, mode, modus, modus operandi (*Latin*), style, system, technique, wise[2].

4. The manner in which one behaves.

4. BEHAVIOR.

5. A habitual way of behaving.

5. CUSTOM *noun*.

waylay *verb*

To attack suddenly and without warning.

AMBUSH.

wayward *adjective*

Given to acting in opposition to others.

CONTRARY *adjective*.

weak *adjective*

1. Not physically strong.

1. INFIRM.

2. So lacking in strength as to be barely audible.

2. FAINT *adjective*.

3. Lacking stability.

3. INSECURE.

4. Not capable of accomplishing anything.

4. INEFFECTUAL.

5. Not plausible or believable.

5. IMPLAUSIBLE.

6. Lower than normal in strength or concentration due to admixture.

weaken *verb*
1. To moderate or change a position or course of action as a result of pressure: *did not weaken in spite of public opinion.*
2. To lessen or deplete the nerve, energy, or strength of.
3. To lose strength or power.
4. To lessen the strength of by or as if by admixture.

weakened *adjective*
Depleted of strength or robust health.

weakening *noun*
A marked loss of strength or effectiveness.

weakling *noun*
A person who behaves in a childish, weak, or spoiled way.

weakly *adjective*
Not physically strong.

weakly *adverb*
In a barely audible way.

weak-minded *adjective*
1. Displaying a complete lack of forethought and good sense.
2. Having only a limited ability to learn and understand.

weakness *noun*
1. A liking or personal preference for something: *A love of rich food is my weakness.*

2. The condition of being infirm or physically weak.

weal¹ *noun*
A state of health, happiness, and prospering.

weal² *noun*
A ridge or bump raised on the flesh by a lash or blow.

wealth *noun*
1. A great amount of accumulated money and precious possessions.
2. All property or goods having economic value.
3. A great deal.

wealthy *adjective*
Possessing a large amount of money, land, or other material possessions.

wear *verb*
1. To diminish the strength and energy of.
2. To consume gradually, as by chemical reaction, friction, etc.

wear away *verb*
To consume gradually, as by chemical reaction, friction, etc.

wear down *verb*
To diminish the strength and energy of.

wear out *verb*
1. To diminish the strength and energy of.
2. To make extremely tired.

wear away *verb*

wear down *verb*

wearied *adjective*
Extremely tired.

weariful *adjective*
1. Extremely tired.

6. DILUTE *adjective.*

1. *Syns:* ease off, relent, slacken, soften, yield. —*Idiom* give way (*or* ground).

2. ENERVATE.

3. FADE *verb.*

4. DILUTE *verb.*

RUN-DOWN *adjective* at **run down.**

FAILURE.

BABY *noun.*

INFIRM.

FAINTLY.

1. MINDLESS.

2. BACKWARD *adjective.*

1. *Syns:* failing, fault, foible, frailty, infirmity, shortcoming. —*Idiom* weak point.
2. INFIRMITY.

WELFARE.

WELT.

1. RICHES.

2. RESOURCES.
3. HEAP *noun.*

RICH.

1. FATIGUE *verb.*
2. BITE *verb.*

BITE *verb.*

FATIGUE *verb.*

1. FATIGUE *verb.*
2. EXHAUST.
SEE **wear.**
SEE **wear.**

EXHAUSTED.

1. EXHAUSTED.

2. Arousing no interest or curiosity.
2. BORING.

weariless *adjective*
Having or showing a capacity for protracted effort, regardless of difficulty or frustration.
TIRELESS.

wearily *adverb*
In a weary way: *yawned and sat down wearily.*
Syn: heavily.

weariness *noun*
The condition of being extremely tired.
EXHAUSTION.

wearisome *adjective*
Arousing no interest or curiosity.
BORING.

wear out *verb*
SEE **wear.**

weary *adjective*
1. Extremely tired.
1. EXHAUSTED.
2. Arousing no interest or curiosity.
2. BORING.
3. Out of patience with.
3. SICK.

weary *verb*
1. To diminish the strength and energy of.
1. FATIGUE *verb.*
2. To fatigue with dullness or tedium.
2. BORE.

wearying *adjective*
Causing fatigue.
TIRING.

weasel *noun*
One who behaves in a stealthy, furtive way.
SNEAK *noun.*

weasel *verb*
To use evasive or deliberately vague language.
EQUIVOCATE.

weather *verb*
To exist in spite of adversity.
SURVIVE.

weave *verb*
1. To walk unsteadily.
1. LURCH *verb.*
2. To move back and forth or from side to side, as if about to fall.
2. SWAY *verb.*
3. To move or proceed on a repeatedly curving course.
3. WIND².

web *noun*
1. An open fabric woven of strands that are interlaced and knotted at usu. regular intervals: *a light, filmy web of lace.*
1. *Syns:* mesh, net¹, netting, network.
2. A distinctive, complex underlying pattern or structure.
2. TEXTURE.
3. A group of things that are linked or interconnected as if by weaving: *a web of lies.*
3. *Syns:* network, tissue.
4. Something that is intricately and often bewilderingly complex.
4. TANGLE *noun.*

web *verb*
To gain control of or an advantage over by or as if by trapping.
CATCH *verb.*

wed *verb*
1. To join or be joined in marriage.
1. MARRY.
2. To bring or come together into a united whole.
2. COMBINE *verb.*

wedded *adjective*
Of, relating to, or typical of marriage.
MARITAL.

wedding *noun*
The act or ceremony by which two people become husband and wife: *an outdoor wedding.*
Syns: bridal, espousal, marriage, nuptial, spousal.

wedlock *noun*
The state of being united as husband and wife.
MARRIAGE.

wee *adjective*
Extremely small.
TINY.

weeny *adjective*
Informal. Extremely small.
TINY.

weep *verb*
1. To make inarticulate sounds of grief or pain, usu. accompanied by tears.
1. CRY *verb.*

2. To flow or leak out slowly.
3. To fall or let fall in drops of liquid.

weeping *adjective*
Filled with or shedding tears.

weeping *noun*
A fit of crying.

weepy *adjective*
Filled with or shedding tears.

weigh *verb*
1. To place a burden or heavy load on.
2. To consider carefully and at length.
3. To be of significance or importance.

weigh down *verb*
To make sad or gloomy.

weigh on (or **upon**) *verb*
To recur to continually.

weigh down *verb*

weighed *adjective*
Resulting from deliberation and careful thought.

weigh on (or **upon**) *verb*

weight *noun*
1. The greatest part or portion: *the weight of the evidence.*
2. The state or quality of being physically heavy.
3. A duty or responsibility that is a source of anxiety, worry, or hardship.
4. Effective means of influencing, compelling, or punishing.
5. The power to produce an effect by indirect means.
6. The quality or state of being important.

weight *verb*
To place a burden or heavy load on.

weightiness *noun*
1. The state or quality of being physically heavy.
2. The quality or state of being important.
3. The condition of being grave and of involving serious consequences.

weightless *adjective*
Having little weight; not heavy.

weighty *adjective*
1. Having a relatively great weight.
2. Having too much flesh.
3. Imposing a severe test of bodily or spiritual strength.
4. Having great significance.
5. Having great consequence or weight.
6. Having or exercising influence.

weird *adjective*
1. Of a mysteriously strange and usu. frightening nature: *a weird premonition of disaster.*

2. Deviating from the customary.
3. Causing puzzlement; perplexing.

weirdie also **weirdy, weirdo** *noun*
Slang. An insanely foolish or strange person.

weirdo *noun*

weirdy *noun*

weisenheimer *noun*

welcome *adjective*
1. To one's liking.

---

2. OOZE.
3. DRIP *verb*.

TEARFUL.

CRY *noun*.

TEARFUL.

1. CHARGE *verb*.
2. PONDER.
3. COUNT *verb*.

DEPRESS.

HAUNT.
SEE **weigh**.

ADVISED.
SEE **weigh**.

1. *Syns:* bulk, mass, preponderance (*also* preponderancy).
2. HEAVINESS.
3. BURDEN *noun*.

4. MUSCLE *noun*.

5. INFLUENCE *noun*.
6. IMPORTANCE.

CHARGE *verb*.

1. HEAVINESS.
2. IMPORTANCE.
3. GRAVITY.

LIGHT^2.

1. HEAVY *adjective*.
2. FAT *adjective*.
3. BURDENSOME.

4. IMPORTANT.
5. GRAVE^2.
6. INFLUENTIAL.

1. *Syns:* eerie (*also* eery), uncanny, unearthly.
   Near-syns: awful, dreadful, fearful, horrible; creepy, haunting, spooky.
2. ECCENTRIC *adjective*.
3. FUNNY.

CRACKPOT.
SEE **weirdie**.
SEE **weirdie**.
SEE **wisenheimer**.

1. AGREEABLE.

2. Affording pleasure or comfort.

welcome *noun*

An expression, in words or gestures, marking a meeting of persons.

welcome *verb*

1. To receive (something given or offered) willingly and gladly.

2. To address in a friendly and respectful way.

welcoming *adjective*

Easily approached.

welfare *noun*

1. A state of health, happiness, and prospering: *A government ought to seek the welfare of all its citizens.*

2. Assistance, esp. money, food, and other necessities, given to the needy or dispossessed.

welkin *noun*

Archaic. The celestial regions as seen from the earth.

well¹ *noun*

A point of origination.

well *verb*

To come forth or emit in abundance.

well² *adverb*

1. In the manner desired: *The program is going well.*

2. In a considerate manner.

3. To a considerable extent.

4. To the fullest extent.

well *adjective*

1. Having good health.

2. Worth doing, esp. for practical reasons.

well-being *noun*

A state of health, happiness, and prospering.

well-born *adjective*

Of high birth or social position.

well-bred *adjective*

1. Characterized by good manners.

2. Characterized by discriminating taste and broad knowledge as a result of development or education.

well-developed *adjective*

Having a full, voluptuous figure.

well-fixed *adjective*

Informal. Enjoying steady good fortune or financial security.

well-founded *adjective*

Possessing, proceeding from, or exhibiting good judgment and prudence.

well-groomed *adjective*

In good order or clean condition.

well-grounded *adjective*

Possessing, proceeding from, or exhibiting good judgment and prudence.

well-heeled *adjective*

Slang. Enjoying steady good fortune or financial security.

well-known *adjective*

Widely known and discussed.

well-liked *adjective*

Being a favorite.

---

2. GRATEFUL.

GREETING.

1. ACCEPT.

2. GREET.

APPROACHABLE.

1. *Syns:* advantage, benefit, good, prosperity, weal¹, well-being.
Near-syns: contentment, fortune, happiness, luck, success.
Ants: destitution, illfare.

2. RELIEF.

AIR *noun.*

ORIGIN.

FLOW *verb.*

1. *Syn:* satisfyingly.

2. CONSIDERATELY.

3. CONSIDERABLY.

4. COMPLETELY.

1. HEALTHY.

2. ADVISABLE.

WELFARE.

NOBLE.

1. COURTEOUS.

2. CULTURED.

SHAPELY.

PROSPEROUS.

SANE.

NEAT.

SANE.

PROSPEROUS.

FAMOUS.

FAVORITE *adjective.*

well-mannered *adjective*
Characterized by good manners.   COURTEOUS.

well-off *adjective*
Enjoying steady good fortune or financial security.   PROSPEROUS.

well-timed *adjective*
Occurring at a fitting or advantageous time.   OPPORTUNE.

well-to-do *adjective*
Enjoying steady good fortune or financial security.   PROSPEROUS.

well-worn *adjective*
Without freshness or appeal due to overuse.   TRITE.

welt *noun*
1. A ridge or bump raised on the flesh by a lash or   1. *Syns:* wale, weal², wheal, whelk
   blow: *The beating left raw welts on the boy's back*   (*Path.*).
   and shoulders.
2. *Informal.* A sudden sharp, powerful stroke.   2. BLOW².

welter *verb*
To move about in an indolent or clumsy manner.   WALLOW.

wench *noun*
A vulgar, promiscuous woman who flouts propriety.   SLUT.

wend *verb*
Archaic. To move along a particular course.   GO *verb.*

wet *adjective*
Covered with or full of liquid: *removed her wet bathing*   *Syns:* drenched, soaked, sodden, soggy,
suit.   sopping, soppy, soused.
                                                           Near-syns: damp, dank, dripping,
                                                           saturated, soaking, water-logged.
                                                           Ant: dry.

wet *verb*
To make thoroughly wet: *wetted the sponge and watched*   *Syns:* douse, drench, saturate, soak,
it grow.   sodden, sop, souse.

wetland *noun*
A usu. low-lying area of soft, waterlogged ground and   SWAMP *noun.*
standing water.

whack *verb*
1. To deliver (a powerful blow) suddenly and sharply.   1. HIT *verb.*
2. To strike, set down, or close in such a way as to   2. BANG *verb.*
   make a loud noise.

  whack *noun*
  1. A sudden sharp, powerful stroke.   1. BLOW².
  2. *Informal.* A brief trial.   2. TRY *noun.*

whacky *adjective*   SEE **wacky.**

wham *noun*
A forceful movement causing a loud noise.   SLAM *noun.*

  wham *verb*
  To deliver (a powerful blow) suddenly and sharply.   HIT *verb.*

whatnot *noun*
A small, showy article.   NOVELTY.

wheal *noun*
A ridge or bump raised on the flesh by a lash or blow.   WELT.

wheedle *verb*
To persuade or try to persuade by gentle, persistent   COAX.
urging or flattery.

wheel *noun*
1. A closed plane curve everywhere equidistant from a   1. CIRCLE *noun.*
   fixed point or something shaped like this.
2. Circular movement around a point or about an axis.   2. REVOLUTION.

  wheel *verb*
  1. To run and control (a motor vehicle).   1. DRIVE *verb.*
  2. To turn or cause to turn in place, as on a hinge or 2. SWING *verb.*
     fixed point, tracing an arclike path.

3. To move or cause to move in circles or around an axis or center.

3. TURN *verb*.

whelk *noun*
Path. A ridge or bump raised on the flesh by a lash or blow.

WELT.

whelm *verb*
1. To affect as if by an outpouring of water.
2. To flow over completely.

1. FLOOD *verb*.
2. FLOOD *verb*.

wherefore *noun*
A fact or circumstance that gives logical support to an assertion, claim, or proposal.

REASON *noun*.

wherewithal *noun*
1. All property or goods having economic value.
2. The ability and the means to meet situations effectively.

1. RESOURCES.
2. RESOURCES.

whet *verb*
To give a sharp edge to.

SHARPEN.

whiff *noun*
A barely perceivable indication of something.

TRACE *noun*.

whiff *verb*
To perceive with the olfactory sense.

SMELL *verb*.

while *noun*
1. A rather short period.
2. The use of energy to do something.

1. BIT[1].
2. EFFORT.

while *verb*
To pass (time) without working or in avoiding work.

IDLE *verb*.

whilom *adjective*
Having been such previously.

LATE *adjective*.

whim *noun*
An impulsive, often illogical turn of mind.

FANCY *noun*.

whimper *verb*
To cry with soft, intermittent, often plaintive sounds.

WHINE.

whimsey *noun*

SEE **whimsy**.

whimsical *adjective*
1. Appealing to fancy.
2. Following no predictable pattern.
3. Determined or marked by whim or caprice rather than reason.

1. FANCIFUL.
2. CAPRICIOUS.
3. ARBITRARY.

whimsy also **whimsey** *noun*
An impulsive, often illogical turn of mind.

FANCY *noun*.

whim-whams also **wim-wams** *noun*
A state of nervous restlessness or agitation.

JITTERS.

whine *verb*
1. To cry with soft, intermittent, often plaintive sounds: *The frightened kitten began to whine pitifully.*
2. To express negative feelings, esp. of dissatisfaction or resentment.

1. *Syns:* pule, whimper.

2. COMPLAIN.

whip *verb*
1. To punish with blows or lashes.
2. To mix rapidly to a frothy consistency.
3. *Informal.* To win a victory over, as in battle or a competition.

1. BEAT *verb*.
2. BEAT *verb*.
3. DEFEAT *verb*.

whipping *noun*
1. A punishment dealt with blows or lashes.
2. *Informal.* The act of defeating or the condition of being defeated.

1. BEATING.
2. DEFEAT *noun*.

whipping boy *noun*
One who is made an object of blame.

SCAPEGOAT.

whir *verb*
To make a continuous low-pitched droning sound.

HUM *verb*.

whir *noun*
A continuous low-pitched droning sound.

HUM *noun*.

whirl *verb*
1. To rotate rapidly.
2. To have the sensation of turning in circles.
3. To move or cause to move like a rapid rotary current of liquid.
4. To move swiftly.

1. SPIN.
2. SPIN.
3. SWIRL.

4. RUSH *verb*.

whirl *noun*
1. Circular movement around a point or about an axis.
2. Agitated, excited movement and activity.
3. *Informal.* A trip in a motor vehicle.
4. *Informal.* A brief trial.

1. REVOLUTION.
2. STIR[1] *noun*.
3. DRIVE *noun*.
4. TRY *noun*.

whirlpool *noun*
Agitated, excited movement and activity.

STIR[1] *noun*.

whisk *verb*
1. To mix rapidly to a frothy consistency.
2. To move swiftly.
3. To make a sharp sibilant sound.

1. BEAT *verb*.
2. RUSH *verb*.
3. HISS *verb*.

whisker *noun*
A slight amount.

SHADE *noun*.

whisper *verb*
1. To speak or utter indistinctly, as by lowering the voice or partially closing the mouth.
2. To tell in confidence.
3. To make a low, continuous, and indistinct sound.

1. MUTTER *verb*.

2. CONFIDE.
3. MURMUR *verb*.

whisper *noun*
1. A low, indistinct, and often continuous sound.
2. A slight amount.

1. MURMUR *noun*.
2. SHADE *noun*.

whispering *noun*
Idle, often sensational and groundless talk about others.

GOSSIP *noun*.

whit *noun*
1. A tiny amount.
2. The least bit.

1. BIT[1].
2. DAMN *noun*.

white plague *noun*
A contagious disease producing lesions esp. of the lungs.

TUBERCULOSIS.

whitewash *verb*
1. To give a deceptively attractive appearance to.
2. To conceal or make light of a fault or offense.

1. COLOR *verb*.
2. EXTENUATE.

whiz also **whizz** *verb*
1. To move swiftly.
2. To make a sharp sibilant sound.
3. To make a continuous low-pitched droning sound.

1. RUSH *verb*.
2. HISS *verb*.
3. HUM *verb*.

whiz also **whizz** *noun*
1. *Slang.* A person with a high degree of knowledge or skill in a particular field.
2. A continuous low-pitched droning sound.

1. EXPERT *noun*.

2. HUM *noun*.

whizz *verb & noun*

SEE **whiz**.

whole *adjective*
1. Including every constituent or individual: *The whole town backed the mayor.*
2. Lacking nothing essential or normal.
3. In excellent condition.
4. Having good health.
5. Not diffused or dispersed.
6. Not more or less.

1. *Syns:* all, complete, entire, gross, total.

2. COMPLETE *adjective*.
3. GOOD *adjective*.
4. HEALTHY.
5. CONCENTRATED.
6. ROUND *adjective*.

whole *noun*

1. An amount or quantity from which nothing is left out or held back: *spent the whole of our cash reserve.*

    1. *Syns:* aggregate, all, entirety, gross, sum, total, totality. —*Idioms* kit and caboodle; lock, stock, and barrel; the works.

2. An organized array of individual elements and parts forming and working as a unit.

    2. SYSTEM.

wholehearted *adjective*
Having no reservations.

    IMPLICIT.

whole-hog *adjective*
Slang. Covering all aspects with painstaking accuracy.

    THOROUGH.

wholeness *noun*
1. The state of being entirely whole.
2. The condition of being physically and mentally sound.
3. The condition of being free from defects or flaws.

    1. COMPLETENESS.
    2. HEALTH.
    3. SOUNDNESS.

wholesome *adjective*
1. Not lewd or obscene.
2. Having good health.
3. Promoting good health.

    1. CLEAN *adjective.*
    2. HEALTHY.
    3. HEALTHFUL.

wholly *adverb*
1. To the fullest extent.
2. Without exception; in its entirety.

    1. COMPLETELY.
    2. PURELY.

whoop *verb*
To say (something) with a shout.

    SHOUT *verb.*

whoopee *noun*
Slang. Joyful, exuberant activity.

    GAIETY.

whoosh *verb*
To make a sharp sibilant sound.

    HISS *verb.*

whop *noun*
A sudden sharp, powerful stroke.

    BLOW[2].

whopper *noun*
1. One that is extraordinarily large and powerful.
2. An untrue declaration.

    1. GIANT *noun.*
    2. LIE[2] *noun.*

whopping *adjective*
Of extraordinary size and power.

    GIANT *adjective.*

whore *noun*
A woman who engages in sexual intercourse for payment.

    PROSTITUTE.

whorish *adjective*
Sexually promiscuous.

    WANTON *adjective.*

whorl *verb*
To move or cause to move like a rapid rotary current of liquid.

    SWIRL.

who's who *noun*
People of the highest social level.

    SOCIETY.

why *noun*
A fact or circumstance that gives logical support to an assertion, claim, or proposal.

    REASON *noun.*

wicked *adjective*
1. Morally objectionable.
2. Characterized by intense ill will or spite.
3. *Slang.* Hard to treat, manage, or cope with.

    1. EVIL *adjective.*
    2. MALEVOLENT.
    3. TROUBLESOME.

wickedness *noun*
1. That which is morally bad or objectionable.
2. Immoral, degrading acts or habits.
3. The condition of being infamous.

    1. EVIL *noun.*
    2. CORRUPTION.
    3. INFAMY.

wide *adjective*
1. Extending over a large area from side to side.
2. Of full measure; not narrow or restricted.

    1. BROAD.
    2. FULL.

wide-awake *adjective*
1. Not in a state of sleep.

    1. WAKEFUL.

2. Vigilantly attentive.

widen *verb*
1. To make or become broad or broader.
2. To make or become more comprehensive or inclusive.

wideness *noun*
The extent of something from side to side.

wide-ranging *adjective*
Covering a wide scope.

wide-reaching *adjective*
Covering a wide scope.

widespread *adjective*
1. Covering a wide scope.
2. Occurring quite often.
3. Most generally existing or encountered at a given time.

width *noun*
The extent of something from side to side: *measured the width of the windowpane.*

wield *verb*
1. To bring to bear steadily or forcefully.
2. To use with or as if with the hands.

wig *verb*
Brit. To reprimand loudly or harshly.

wiggle *verb*
To move or proceed with short, irregular motions up and down or from side to side: *He wiggled his toes to be sure the new shoes were roomy.*

wild *adjective*
1. In a primitive state; not domesticated or cultivated: *wild countryside; wild animals.*

2. Not civilized.
3. Of or relating to beasts of prey.
4. Lacking in moral restraint.
5. Given to heedless, unrestrained pursuit of pleasure.
6. Violently disturbed, as by storms.
7. Marked by extreme excitement, confusion, or agitation.
8. Not submitting to discipline or control.

wild *noun*
An uninhabited region left in its natural state: *a resourceful backpacker, at home in the wild.*

wilderness *noun*
1. A tract of unproductive land.
2. An uninhabited region left in its natural state.

wildness *noun*
1. A complete surrender of inhibitions.
2. An uninhabited region left in its natural state.
3. The quality or condition of being unruly.

wile *noun*
An indirect, usu. cunning means of gaining an end.

wile *verb*
To pass (time) without working or in avoiding work.

wiliness *noun*
Deceitful cleverness.

will[1] *noun*
1. The mental faculty by which one deliberately chooses or decides: *He stood hesitant in a paralysis of will.*

---

2. ALERT *adjective.*

1. BROADEN.
2. EXTEND.

WIDTH.

GENERAL.

GENERAL.

1. GENERAL.
2. COMMON *adjective.*
3. PREVAILING.

Syns: breadth, broadness, wideness.

1. EXERCISE *verb.*
2. HANDLE.

BAWL OUT at **bawl.**

Syns: squiggle, squirm, waggle, worm, wriggle, writhe.

1. *Syns:* agrestal (*also* agrestial), native, natural, rough, uncultivated, undomesticated, untamed.
2. UNCIVILIZED.
3. SAVAGE.
4. ABANDONED.
5. FAST *adjective.*
6. ROUGH.
7. FRANTIC.

8. UNRULY.

Syns: backland, bush, wilderness, wildness.

1. BARREN *noun.*
2. WILD *noun.*

1. ABANDON *noun.*
2. WILD *noun.*
3. UNRULINESS.

TRICK *noun.*

IDLE *verb.*

ART.

1. *Syn:* volition.

2. The power to make choices and set goals and to act upon them firmly in spite of opposition or difficulty: *lacked the will to carry his theories into practical social action.*

3. Unrestricted freedom to choose: *wandered about at will.*

4. A desire for a particular thing or activity.

will *verb*
To have the desire or inclination to.

will² *verb*
To give (property) to another person after one's death.

willful *adjective*
1. Done or said on purpose.
2. Tenaciously unwilling to yield.
3. Determined or marked by whim or caprice rather than reason.
4. *Obs.* Done by one's own choice.

willfulness *noun*
The quality or state of being stubbornly unyielding.

willies *noun*
Slang. A state of nervous restlessness or agitation.

willing *adjective*
1. Disposed to accept or agree: *asked her for one last dance, and she was willing.*

2. Of or relating to free exercise of the will.

willingly *adverb*
Of one's own free will.

will-o'-the-wisp *noun*
An erroneous perception of reality.

willy-nilly *adverb*
Without regard to desire or inclination.

wilt *verb*
1. To become limp, as from loss of freshness: *Cut wildflowers wilt quickly.*
2. To hang limply, loosely, and carelessly.

wily *adjective*
Deceitfully clever.

wim-wams *noun*

win *verb*
1. To obtain possession or control of.
2. To come into possession of.
3. To acquire as a result of one's behavior or effort.
4. To receive, as wages, for one's labor.

win over *verb*
To cause (another) to believe something.

win *noun*
The act of conquering.

wince *verb*
To draw away involuntarily, usu. due to fear or disgust.

wind¹ *noun*
A natural movement or current of air: *plant seeds that are scattered and blown by the wind.*

wind *verb*
To expose to circulating air.

---

2. *Syns:* decision, determination, resolution, resolve. —*Idiom* will power.

3. *Syns:* choice, discretion, pleasure.

4. LIKING.

CHOOSE.

LEAVE¹.

1. DELIBERATE *adjective*.
2. OBSTINATE.
3. ARBITRARY.

4. VOLUNTARY *adjective*.

OBSTINACY.

JITTERS.

1. *Syns:* acquiescent, agreeable, fain (*Archaic*), game (*Informal*), inclined, minded, ready.
Near-ants: averse, disinclined, indisposed, loath, reluctant, reticent.
Ant: unwilling.
2. VOLUNTARY *adjective*.

VOLUNTARILY.

ILLUSION.

HELPLESSLY.

1. *Syns:* droop, flag², sag.

2. SLOUCH *verb*.

ARTFUL.

SEE **whim-whams**.

1. CAPTURE.
2. GET.
3. EARN.
4. EARN.

CONVINCE.

CONQUEST.

FLINCH.

Syns: air, blow, breeze, gale (*Archaic*), gust, zephyr.

AIR *verb*.

wind² *verb*
1. To move or proceed on a repeatedly curving course: *A staircase wound its way up the tower. The river wound slowly through the plain.*
2. To introduce gradually and slyly.

1. ***Syns:*** coil, corkscrew, curl, entwine, meander, snake, spiral, twine, twist, weave, wreathe.
2. INSINUATE.

windiness *noun*
Words or the use of words in excess of those needed for clarity or precision.

WORDINESS.

winding *adjective*
Repeatedly curving in alternate directions: *a winding footpath down a mountain.*

Syns: anfractuous, flexuous (*also* flexuose), meandering, meandrous, serpentine, sinuous, snaky, tortuous, twisting.
Near-syns: bending, convoluted, curving; circuitous, indirect, roundabout.
Ant: straight.

windless *adjective*
Marked by an absence of circulating air.

AIRLESS.

window-dressing *also* **window dressing** *noun*
A deceptive outward appearance.

FAÇADE.

wind-up *noun*

SEE **wind up.**

wind up *verb*
Informal. To bring or come to a natural or proper end.

CLOSE¹ *verb.*

wind-up *noun*
1. *Informal.* A concluding or terminating.
2. *Informal.* The last part.

1. END *noun.*
2. END *noun.*

windy *adjective*
1. Exposed to or characterized by the presence of freely circulating air or wind.
2. *Chiefly Scot.* Filled up with or as if with something insubstantial.

1. AIRY.

2. INFLATED.

wing *noun*
A component of government that performs a given function.

BRANCH *noun.*

wing *verb*
1. To move through the air with or as if with wings.
2. To move swiftly.

1. FLY.
2. RUSH *verb.*

wink *verb*
1. To open and close the eyes rapidly.
2. To shine with intermittent gleams.

1. BLINK *verb.*
2. BLINK *verb.*

wink at *verb*
To pretend not to see.

BLINK AT at **blink.**

wink *noun*
1. A brief closing of the eyes.
2. A sudden quick light.
3. A very brief time.

1. BLINK *noun.*
2. BLINK *noun.*
3. FLASH *noun.*

wink at *verb*

SEE **wink.**

winner *noun*
1. One that wins a contest or competition: *the winner of the tennis match.*
2. One that conquers.

1. ***Syn:*** victor.

2. CONQUEROR.

winning *adjective*
Pleasing to the eye or mind.

ATTRACTIVE.

winnow *verb*
1. To be in a state of motion, as air.
2. To set apart (one kind or type) from others.

1. BLOW¹ *verb.*
2. SORT *verb.*

win over *verb*

SEE **win.**

winsome *adjective*
Pleasing to the eye or mind.

ATTRACTIVE.

wintry *adjective*
Very cold.

FRIGID.

wiped-out *adjective*
Slang. Stupefied, intoxicated, or otherwise influenced by   DRUGGED.
the taking of drugs.

wipe out *verb*
1. To remove or invalidate by or as if by running a   **1.** CANCEL.
   line through or wiping clean.
2. To get rid of, esp. by banishment or execution.   **2.** ELIMINATE.
3. To destroy all traces of.   **3.** ANNIHILATE.
4. *Informal.* To take the life of (a person or persons)   **4.** MURDER *verb.*
   unlawfully.

wiretap *verb*
To monitor (telephone calls) with a concealed listening   TAP² *verb.*
device connected to the circuit.

wisdom *noun*
1. Deep, thorough, or mature understanding: *an old*   **1.** *Syns:* insight, profundity,
   judge famous for his wisdom.   sagaciousness, sagacity, sageness,
      sapience.
2. The ability to make sensible decisions.   **2.** COMMON SENSE.
3. That which is known; the sum of what has been   **3.** KNOWLEDGE.
   perceived, discovered, or inferred.

wise¹ *adjective*
1. Possessing or showing sound judgment and keen   **1.** *Syns:* discerning, knowing, sagacious,
   perception: *a wise elder statesman.*   sage, sapient.
      Near-ants: obtuse, slow, unintelligent,
      unknowing.
      Ant: unwise.
2. Possessing, proceeding from, or exhibiting good   **2.** SANE.
   judgment and prudence.
3. Having or showing profound knowledge and   **3.** LEARNED.
   scholarship.
4. Having or showing a clever awareness and   **4.** SHREWD.
   resourcefulness in practical matters.
5. Marked by comprehension, cognizance, and   **5.** AWARE.
   perception.
6. Rude and disrespectful.   **6.** IMPUDENT.

wise² *noun*
The manner in which something is done.   WAY.

wiseacre *noun*
Informal. One who is obnoxiously self-assertive and   SMART ALECK.
arrogant.

wisecrack *noun*
A flippant or sarcastic remark.   CRACK *noun.*

wisecracker *noun*
Slang. One who is obnoxiously self-assertive and   SMART ALECK.
arrogant.

wise guy *noun*
Slang. One who is obnoxiously self-assertive and   SMART ALECK.
arrogant.

wisehead *noun*
Informal. One who is obnoxiously self-assertive and   SMART ALECK.
arrogant.

wiseling *noun*
Archaic. One who is obnoxiously self-assertive and   SMART ALECK.
arrogant.

wisenheimer also **weisenheimer** *noun*
Informal. One who is obnoxiously self-assertive and   SMART ALECK.
arrogant.

wish *verb*
1. To have a strong longing for.   **1.** DESIRE *verb.*
2. To have the desire or inclination to.   **2.** CHOOSE.

wishy-washy *adjective*
Informal. Lacking the qualities requisite for spiritedness and originality.

INSIPID.

wistful *adjective*
Suggestive of or expressing deep, often melancholy thoughtfulness.

PENSIVE.

wit *noun*
1. The faculty of thinking, reasoning, and acquiring and applying knowledge.
2. A healthy mental state.
3. Skill in perceiving, discriminating, or judging.
4. The quality of being laughable or comical.
5. A person whose words or actions provoke or are intended to provoke amusement or laughter.

1. INTELLIGENCE.
2. SANITY.
3. DISCERNMENT.
4. HUMOR *noun.*
5. JOKER.

witch *noun*
1. A woman who practices magic: *The witch turned the handsome prince into a frog.*
2. An ugly, frightening old woman: *children scared by the evil-looking old witch.*

1. *Syns:* enchantress, hag, hex, lamia, sorceress.
2. *Syns:* bag (*Slang*), bat[2] (*Slang*), beldam (*also* beldame), biddy (*also* biddie) (*Slang*), crone, drab[2], drone, hag, trot (*Archaic*).

3. *Informal.* A usu. unscrupulous woman who seduces or exploits men.

3. SEDUCTRESS.

witch *verb*
To act upon with or as if with magic.

CHARM *verb.*

witchcraft *noun*
The use of supernatural powers to influence or predict events.

MAGIC *noun.*

witchery *noun*
1. The use of supernatural powers to influence or predict events.
2. The power or quality of attracting.

1. MAGIC *noun.*
2. ATTRACTION.

witching *noun*
The use of supernatural powers to influence or predict events.

MAGIC *noun.*

witching *adjective*
1. Pertaining to magic: *the witching hour.*

2. Tending to seduce.

1. *Syns:* bewitching, magic (*also* magical).
2. SEDUCTIVE.

withdraw *verb*
1. To pull back in: *The cat withdrew its claws.*
2. To move (something) from a position occupied.
3. To disavow (something previously written or said) irrevocably and usu. formally.
4. To remove from association with.
5. To move or proceed away from a place.
6. To move back in the face of enemy attack or after a defeat.

1. *Syns:* draw in, retract.
2. REMOVE *verb.*
3. RETRACT.
4. DETACH.
5. GO *verb.*
6. RETREAT *verb.*

withdrawal *also* **withdrawment** *noun*
1. The act of leaving.
2. The moving back of a military force in the face of enemy attack or after a defeat.

1. DEPARTURE.
2. RETREAT *noun.*

withdrawment *noun*

SEE **withdrawal.**

withdrawn *adjective*
Not friendly, sociable, or warm in manner.

COOL *adjective.*

wither *verb*
1. To render (another) speechless or incapable of action: *He withered me with that ugly look.*
2. To make or become no longer fresh or shapely because of loss of moisture.
3. To waste away from longing or grief.

1. *Syn:* petrify.

2. DRY UP at **dry.**

3. LANGUISH.

withhold *verb*
1. To be unwilling to grant.
2. To have and maintain in one's possession.
3. To hold oneself back.

1. REFUSE.
2. HOLD *verb*.
3. REFRAIN.

with-it *adjective*
Slang. Being or in accordance with the current fashion.

FASHIONABLE.

withstand *verb*
To oppose actively and with force.

RESIST.

witless *adjective*
1. Afflicted with or exhibiting irrationality and mental unsoundness.
2. Displaying a complete lack of forethought and good sense.

1. INSANE.
2. MINDLESS.

witling *noun*
Archaic. One who is obnoxiously self-assertive and arrogant.

SMART ALECK.

witness *noun*
1. Someone who sees something occur: *a witness to murder.*
2. One who testifies, esp. in court: *a witness for the defense.*
3. Something visible or evident that gives grounds for believing in the existence or presence of something else.
4. *Obs.* A formal declaration of truth or fact given under oath.

1. *Syns:* eyewitness, seer[2], viewer.
2. *Syns:* attestant, deponent (*Law*), testifier.
3. SIGN *noun*.
4. TESTIMONY.

witness *verb*
1. To confirm formally as true, accurate, or genuine.
2. To give grounds for believing in the existence or presence of.
3. *Obs.* To give evidence or testimony under oath.

1. CERTIFY.
2. INDICATE.
3. TESTIFY.

wits *noun*
A healthy mental state.

SANITY.

witticism *noun*
Words or actions intended to excite laughter or amusement.

JOKE *noun*.

wittiness *noun*
The quality of being laughable or comical.

HUMOR *noun*.

witting *adjective*
Done or said on purpose.

DELIBERATE *adjective*.

witty *adjective*
1. Intended to excite laughter or amusement.
2. Amusing or pleasing because of wit or originality.

1. HUMOROUS.
2. CLEVER.

wizard *noun*
A person with a high degree of knowledge or skill in a particular field.

EXPERT *noun*.

wizardly *adjective*
Having or brought about by supernatural powers.

MAGIC *adjective*.

wizardry *noun*
The use of supernatural powers to influence or predict events.

MAGIC *noun*.

wizen *verb*
To make or become no longer fresh or shapely because of loss of moisture.

DRY UP at **dry**.

wobble *verb*
1. To walk unsteadily.
2. To move back and forth or from side to side, as if about to fall.

1. LURCH *verb*.
2. SWAY *verb*.

wobbly *adjective*
1. Given to or exhibiting hesitation.
2. Lacking stability.

1. HESITANT.
2. INSECURE.

3. Not physically steady or firm.   3. UNSTABLE.

wobegone *adjective*   SEE **woebegone.**

woe *noun*

1. Mental anguish or pain caused by loss or despair.   1. GRIEF.
2. A state of physical or mental suffering.   2. DISTRESS.
3. A state of prolonged anguish and privation.   3. MISERY.
4. A cause of suffering or harm.   4. CURSE *noun*.

woebegone also **wobegone** *adjective*

1. *Archaic*. Suffering from usu. prolonged anguish.   1. MISERABLE.
2. Full of or expressive of sorrow.   2. SORROWFUL.

woeful also **woful** *adjective*

1. Full of or expressive of sorrow.   1. SORROWFUL.
2. Causing sorrow or regret.   2. SORROWFUL.
3. Suffering from usu. prolonged anguish.   3. MISERABLE.

woful *adjective*   SEE **woeful.**

wolf *noun*

   Slang. A man who philanders.   PHILANDERER.

   wolf *verb*

   To swallow (food or drink) greedily or rapidly in large   GULP *verb*.
   amounts.

womanish *adjective*

   Having qualities more appropriate to women than to   EFFEMINATE *adjective*.
   men.

womanishness *noun*

   The quality of being effeminate.   EFFEMINACY.

womanity *noun*

   The quality or condition of being feminine.   FEMININITY.

womanize *verb*

   To be sexually unfaithful to another.   PHILANDER *verb*.

womanizer *noun*

   A man who philanders.   PHILANDERER.

womankind *noun*

   Women in general.   FEMININITY.

womanliness *noun*

   The quality or condition of being feminine.   FEMININITY.

womanly *adjective*

   Of, relating to, or characteristic of women.   FEMININE.

womanness *noun*

   The quality or condition of being feminine.   FEMININITY.

womenfolk *noun*

   Women in general.   FEMININITY.

wonder *noun*

1. The emotion aroused by something awe-inspiring or   1. *Syns:* admiration (*Archaic*), amaze
   astounding: *viewed the northern lights with wonder.*   (*Archaic*), amazement, awe, dread,
                                                              marveling, wonderment.
2. One that evokes great surprise and admiration.   2. MARVEL *noun*.
3. An event inexplicable by the laws of nature.   3. MIRACLE.
4. A lack of conviction or certainty.   4. DOUBT *noun*.

   wonder *verb*

   To have a feeling of great awe and rapt admiration: *Syn:* marvel.
   wondered at the beauty and engineering excellence of the
   Great Pyramid.

wonderful *adjective*

1. So remarkable as to elicit disbelief.   1. FABULOUS.
2. Particularly excellent.   2. MARVELOUS.

wonderment *noun*

1. One that evokes great surprise and admiration.   1. MARVEL.
2. The emotion aroused by something awe-inspiring or   2. WONDER *noun*.
   astounding.

wondrous *adjective*

   So remarkable as to elicit disbelief.   FABULOUS.

wont *adjective*
In the habit of.   ACCUSTOMED TO at **accustomed**.
wont *verb*
To make familiar through constant practice or use.   ACCUSTOM.
wont *noun*
A habitual way of behaving.   CUSTOM *noun*.
woo *verb*
To attempt to gain the affection of.   COURT *verb*.
wooden *adjective*
1. Lacking responsiveness or alertness.   1. DULL *adjective*.
2. So rigidly constrained, formal, or awkward as to   2. STIFF *adjective*.
lack all grace and spontaneity.
woolgathering *adjective*
Given to daydreams or reverie.   DREAMY.
woolly *adjective*
Covered with hair.   HAIRY.
wooziness *noun*
A sensation of whirling or falling.   DIZZINESS.
woozy *adjective*
Having a sensation of whirling or falling.   DIZZY *adjective*.
word *noun*
1. Something said: *May I say a word about that?*   1. *Syns:* comment, remark, statement,
Remember: not a word about this to anyone!   utterance.
2. A sound or combination of sounds that symbolizes   2. TERM *noun*.
and communicates a meaning.
3. Something communicated, as information.   3. COMMUNICATION.
4. A statement that expresses a commitment on the   4. *Syns:* assurance, guarantee, warrant.
part of its maker as to its truthfulness or to the   —*Idioms* solemn word, word of honor.
fulfillment of its conditions: *gave my word that I had*
not revealed his identity.
5. An authoritative indication to be obeyed.   5. COMMAND *noun*.
6. New information, esp. about recent events and   6. NEWS.
happenings.
7. Idle, often sensational and groundless talk about   7. GOSSIP *noun*.
others.
word *verb*
To convey in language or words of a particular form.   PHRASE *verb*.
wordage *noun*
Choice of words and the way in which they are used.   WORDING.
wordbook *noun*
An alphabetical list of words often defined or   VOCABULARY.
translated.
word-for-word *adjective*
Employing the very same words as another.   LITERAL.
word-hoard *noun*
All the words of a language.   VOCABULARY.
wordiness *noun*
Words or the use of words in excess of those needed for   *Syns:* prolixity, prolixness, verboseness,
clarity or precision: *Instead of getting to the point, he* verbosity, windiness.
obscured his meaning with wordiness.
wording *noun*
Choice of words and the way in which they are used: *Syns:* diction, parlance, phrase,
complex wording in a contract.   phraseology, phrasing, verbalism,
                                                            wordage.
wordless *adjective*
1. Conveyed indirectly without words or speech.   1. IMPLICIT.
2. Temporarily unable or unwilling to speak, as from   2. SPEECHLESS.
shock or fear.
3. Not voiced or expressed.   3. SILENT.
word-of-mouth *adjective*
Expressed or transmitted in speech.   ORAL.

words *noun*
A discussion, often heated, in which a difference of opinion is expressed. — ARGUMENT.

word-stock *noun*
All the words of a language. — VOCABULARY.

wordy *adjective*
1. Using or containing an excessive number of words: *a halting, wordy apology that made everyone impatient.*
   1. **Syns:** diffuse, longwinded, periphrastic, pleonastic, prolix, verbose.
      Near-syns: glib, loquacious, talkative, vocal, voluble; flatulent, inflated, windy.
      Ant: laconic.
2. Pertaining to, consisting of, or having the nature of words.
   2. VERBAL.

work *noun*
1. The technique, style, and quality of working: *did excellent work on the watch; the exquisite work of Fabergé.*
   1. **Syns:** craftsmanship, workmanship.
2. Physical exertion that is usu. difficult and exhausting.
   2. LABOR *noun.*
3. Activity pursued as a livelihood.
   3. BUSINESS.
4. Something that is the result of creative effort.
   4. COMPOSITION.
5. An issue of printed material offered for sale or distribution.
   5. PUBLICATION.

work *verb*
1. To force to work: *The overseer worked the slaves unmercifully.*
   1. **Syns:** drive, labor, task, tax. —*Idiom* crack the whip.
2. To exert one's mental or physical powers, usu. under difficulty and to the point of exhaustion.
   2. LABOR *verb.*
3. To function effectively: *The car doesn't work half the time.*
   3. **Syns:** function, go, operate, run.
4. To react in a specified way.
   4. FUNCTION.
5. To introduce gradually and slyly.
   5. INSINUATE.
6. To control or direct the functioning of.
   6. OPERATE.
7. To handle in a way so as to mix, form, and shape: *worked the dough into a ball.*
   7. **Syns:** knead, manipulate.
8. To arrive at an answer to (a mathematical problem): *worked two problems.*
   8. **Syns:** figure out (*Informal*), solve, work out.
9. To prepare (soil) for the planting and raising of crops.
   9. TILL *verb.*

work out *verb*
1. To arrive at an answer to (a mathematical problem).
   1. WORK *verb.*
2. To plan the details or arrangements of.
   2. ARRANGE *verb.*
3. To turn out well.
   3. SUCCEED.
4. To subject to forms of exertion in order to train, strengthen, or condition.
   4. EXERCISE *verb.*

work up *verb*
To stir to action or feeling. — PROVOKE.

workable *adjective*
1. Capable of being shaped, bent, or drawn out, as by hammering or pressure.
   1. MALLEABLE.
2. Capable of occurring or being done.
   2. POSSIBLE.

workaday *adjective*
Of or suitable for ordinary days or routine occasions. — EVERYDAY.

workday *adjective*
Of or suitable for ordinary days or routine occasions. — EVERYDAY.

worked up *adjective*
Feeling a very strong emotion. — THRILLED.

worker *noun*
1. One who labors.
   1. LABORER.
2. One who is employed by another.
   2. EMPLOYEE.

workhand *noun*
One who labors.   LABORER.

working *noun*
The way in which a machine or other thing performs or   BEHAVIOR.
functions.

working *adjective*
1. In action or full operation.   1. ACTIVE.
2. Having a job.   2. EMPLOYED.

workingman *noun*
One who labors.   LABORER.

workless *adjective*
Out of work: *workless coal miners.*   *Syns:* jobless, unemployed.

workman *noun*
One who labors.   LABORER.

workmanship *noun*
The technique, style, and quality of working.   WORK *noun.*

work out *verb*   SEE **work.**

works *noun*
A building or complex in which an industry is located: *Syns:* mill, plant.
the Krupp works.

work up *verb*   SEE **work.**

world *noun*
1. The celestial body where humans live.   1. EARTH.
2. The totality of all existing things.   2. UNIVERSE.
3. The human race.   3. MANKIND.
4. A sphere of activity, study, or interest.   4. AREA.
5. The totality of surrounding conditions and   5. ENVIRONMENT.
   circumstances affecting growth or development.
6. A great deal.   6. HEAP *noun.*

worldly *adjective*
1. Pertaining to or characteristic of the earth or of   1. EARTHLY.
   human life on earth.
2. Of or preoccupied with material rather than   2. MATERIALISTIC.
   spiritual or intellectual things.
3. Not religious in subject matter, form, or use.   3. PROFANE.
4. Experienced in the ways of the world; lacking   4. SOPHISTICATED.
   natural simplicity.

worldly-wise *adjective*
Experienced in the ways of the world; lacking natural   SOPHISTICATED.
simplicity.

worldwide *adjective*
So pervasive and all-inclusive as to exist in or affect UNIVERSAL *adjective.*
the whole world.

world-without-end *adjective*
Enduring for all time.   ENDLESS.

world-without-end *noun*
1. Endless life after death.   1. IMMORTALITY.
2. The quality or state of having no end.   2. ENDLESSNESS.

worm *verb*
1. To move along in a crouching or prone position.   1. CRAWL *verb.*
2. To introduce gradually and slyly.   2. INSINUATE.
3. To move or proceed with short, irregular motions up   3. WIGGLE.
   and down or from side to side.
4. To make, achieve, or get through contrivance or   4. WANGLE.
   guile.

worn *adjective*
1. Extremely tired.   1. EXHAUSTED.
2. Pale and exhausted because of worry, sleeplessness,   2. HAGGARD.
   etc.

worn-down *adjective*
Extremely tired.   EXHAUSTED.

worn-out *adjective*
1. Extremely tired.
2. Without freshness or appeal due to overuse.

worried *adjective*
In a state of uneasiness.

worry *verb*
1. To be troubled: *I worry about his sanity.*

2. To turn over in the mind, moodily and at length.
3. To cause anxious uneasiness in: *The patient's high fever worried the doctors.*
4. To disturb by repeated attacks.

worry *noun*
Anxious concern.

worrywart *noun*
Informal. A prophet of misfortune or disaster.

worsen *verb*
To become lower in quality, character, or condition.

worsening *noun*
Descent to a lower level or condition.

worship *verb*
1. To regard with great awe and devotion.
2. To feel deep, devoted love for.

worship *noun*
The act of adoring, esp. reverently.

worshipful *adjective*
Feeling or showing reverence.

worst *verb*
1. To win a victory over, as in battle or a competition.
2. To get the better of.

worth *noun*
1. A measure of those qualities that determine merit, desirability, usefulness, or importance: *the innate worth of the individual; a book of little worth or interest; a Caucasian rug of great worth.*
2. A great amount of accumulated money and precious possessions.
3. A level of superiority that is usu. high.

worthless *adjective*
1. Lacking all worth and value: *worthless junk jewelry; a worthless occupation.*

2. Having no useful purpose.

worthy *adjective*
1. Satisfying the requirements, as for selection.
2. Deserving admiration.
3. Deserving honor or respect.
4. Of great value.

wound *noun*
Marked tissue damage, esp. when produced by physical injury.

wound *verb*
1. To cause physical damage to.
2. To inflict physical or mental injury or distress on.

wow *noun*
Informal. A dazzling, often sudden instance of success.

---

1. EXHAUSTED.
2. TRITE.

ANXIOUS.

1. **Syns:** cark, pother, stew. —*Idioms* bite one's nails, play with the worry beads, worry one's head over.
2. BROOD.
3. **Syns:** ail, cark, concern, distress, trouble.
4. ANNOY.

ANXIETY.

PESSIMIST.

DETERIORATE.

DETERIORATION.

1. ADORE.
2. ADORE.

ADORATION.

REVERENT.

1. DEFEAT *verb.*
2. TRIUMPH *verb.*

1. **Syns:** account, valuation, value.

2. RICHES.

3. MERIT *noun.*

1. **Syns:** drossy, good-for-nothing, inutile, no-good, nothing (*Slang*), valueless.
   Near-syns: inferior, mediocre, poor, second-rate, useless; defective, flawed, imperfect.
   Ant: priceless.
2. USELESS.

1. ELIGIBLE.
2. ADMIRABLE.
3. HONORABLE.
4. VALUABLE.

TRAUMA.

1. HURT *verb*
2. TRAUMATIZE.

HIT *noun.*

wrack *noun*
  1. The state of being destroyed.
  2. The remains of something destroyed, disintegrated, or decayed.

  1. DESTRUCTION.
  2. RUIN *noun*.

wrack *verb*
To cause the complete ruin or wreckage of.

DESTROY.

wraith *noun*
A supernatural being.

GHOST *noun*.

wrangle *verb*
  1. To quarrel noisily.
  2. To engage in a quarrel.

  1. BRAWL *verb*.
  2. ARGUE.

wrangle *noun*
A discussion, often heated, in which a difference of opinion is expressed.

ARGUMENT.

wrap *verb*
  1. To cover and tie (something), as with paper and string: *wrap a box for mailing.*
  2. To surround and cover completely so as to obscure: *Fog wrapped the lonely moors.*

  1. *Syns:* do up, package.
  2. *Syns:* cloak, clothe, enfold (*also* infold), enshroud, envelop, enwrap, invest, shroud, veil.

wrap *noun*
  1. A garment wrapped about a person: *a mink wrap.*
  2. The material in which something is wrapped.

  1. *Syns:* cloak, hap^2 (*Regional*), stole.
  2. WRAPPER.

wrapped up *adjective*
Having one's thoughts fully occupied.

ABSORBED.

wrapper *noun*
The material in which something is wrapped: *foil candy wrappers.*

Syns: wrap, wrapping (*also* wrappings).

wrapping also **wrappings** *noun*
The material in which something is wrapped.

WRAPPER.

wrappings *noun*

SEE **wrapping**.

wraps *noun*
The habit, practice, or policy of keeping secrets.

SECRECY.

wrap-up *noun*

SEE **wrap up**.

wrap up *verb*
  1. To cover completely and closely, as with clothing or bandages: *Infants were formerly wrapped up in strips of linen called swaddling clothes.*
  2. To put on warm clothes: *They wrapped up in furs.*
  3. To bring or come to a natural or proper end.

  1. *Syns:* enfold (*also* infold), enswathe, envelop, enwrap, invest, roll, swaddle, swathe.
  2. *Syns:* bundle (up), hap^2 (*Regional*).
  3. CLOSE^1 *verb*.

wrap-up *noun*
  1. A concluding or terminating.
  2. The last part.
  3. A condensation of the essential or main points of something.

  1. END *noun*.
  2. END *noun*.
  3. SUMMARY *noun*.

wrath *noun*
Violent or unrestrained anger.

FURY.

wrathful *adjective*
Feeling or showing anger.

ANGRY.

wrathfulness *noun*
Violent or unrestrained anger.

FURY.

wreak *verb*
To cause to undergo or bear, as something unwelcome or damaging.

INFLICT.

wreathe *verb*
To move or proceed on a repeatedly curving course.

WIND^2.

wreck *verb*
  1. To damage, disable, or destroy (a seacraft): *The violent storm in the Irish Sea wrecked the racing yachts.*

  1. *Syns:* cast away, pile up, shipwreck.

2. To spoil or destroy.

3. To cause the complete ruin or wreckage of.

4. To injure or destroy (property) maliciously.

wreck *noun*

1. A wrecking of a vehicle.

2. The state of being destroyed.

3. An abrupt, disastrous failure.

wreckage *noun*

1. The remains of something destroyed, disintegrated, or decayed.

2. An act, instance, or consequence of breaking.

3. The state of being destroyed.

wrench *verb*

1. To alter the position of by a sharp, forcible twisting or turning movement: *wrenched the steering wheel to the right; wrenched the child from the deep water.*

2. To injure (a bodily part) by twisting.

3. To move or cause to move with a sudden, abrupt motion.

4. To obtain by coercion or intimidation.

5. To give an inaccurate view of by representing falsely or misleadingly.

wrench *noun*

1. A sudden pull.

2. A tool with jaws for gripping and twisting: *opened the pipe with a big wrench.*

wrest *verb*

1. To obtain by coercion or intimidation.

2. To alter the position of by a sharp, forcible twisting or turning movement.

wrestle *verb*

1. To contend with an opponent, esp. by attempting to throw him: *heavyweights wrestling in amateur competition; wrestled the skyjacker to the ground and disarmed him.*

2. To strive in opposition to.

wretch *noun*

A person living under very unhappy circumstances.

wretched *adjective*

1. Suffering from usu. prolonged anguish.

2. Having a painful ailment.

3. So objectionable as to elicit despisal.

wretchedness *noun*

A state of prolonged anguish and privation.

wriggle *verb*

To move or proceed with short, irregular motions up and down or from side to side.

wring *verb*

1. To obtain by coercion or intimidation.

2. To alter the position of by a sharp, forcible twisting or turning movement.

wrinkle[1] *verb*

To make irregular folds in, esp. by pressing or twisting: *The overloaded washer wrinkled all the clothes.*

wrinkle *noun*

1. A line made by the doubling of one part over another.

2. An indentation or seam on the skin, esp. on the face.

---

2. BLAST *verb.*

3. DESTROY.

4. TRASH[1] *verb.*

1. CRASH *noun.*

2. DESTRUCTION.

3. COLLAPSE *noun.*

1. RUIN *noun.*

2. BREAKAGE.

3. DESTRUCTION.

1. *Syns:* wrest, wring, wry.

2. TURN *verb.*

3. JERK *verb.*

4. EXTORT.

5. DISTORT.

1. JERK *noun.*

2. *Syn:* spanner (*Chiefly Brit.*).

1. EXTORT.

2. WRENCH *verb.*

1. *Syns:* grapple, scuffle, tussle. —*Idiom* go to the mat with.

2. CONTEND.

UNFORTUNATE *noun.*

1. MISERABLE.

2. MISERABLE.

3. FILTHY.

MISERY.

WIGGLE.

1. EXTORT.

2. WRENCH *verb.*

Syns: crimp, crimple, crinkle, crumple, rimple, ruckle (*Brit.*), rumple.

1. FOLD *noun.*

2. LINE *noun.*

wrinkle²   *noun*

Informal. A clever, unexpected new trick or method: *a strategy with some new wrinkles guaranteed to increase sales.*

Syns: angle (*Slang*), gimmick (*Slang*), kick, kicker, twist.

write   *verb*

1. To form letters, characters, or words on a surface with an instrument: *wrote the equation on the blackboard with chalk; wrote a message on the card.*

   1. *Syns:* engross, indite, inscribe, scribe. —*Idiom* put in writing.

2. To form by artistic effort.

   2. COMPOSE.

3. To be the author of (a published work or works).

   3. PUBLISH.

write down   *verb*

To become or make less in price or value.

DEPRECIATE.

write off   *verb*

To put out of one's mind as a loss or failure: *wrote off the incident as an exercise in futility.*

Syn: discount.

write down   *verb*

SEE **write**.

write off   *verb*

SEE **write**.

writhe   *verb*

1. To twist and turn, as in pain, struggle, or embarrassment: *The patient writhed in a convulsion.*

   1. *Syns:* agonize, squirm, toss.

2. To move or proceed with short, irregular motions up and down or from side to side.

   2. WIGGLE.

written   *adjective*

Of or pertaining to representation by means of writing.

GRAPHIC.

wrong   *adjective*

1. Containing an error or errors.

   1. ERRONEOUS.

2. Devoid of truth.

   2. FALSE.

3. Morally objectionable.

   3. EVIL *adjective*.

4. Not in accordance with what is usual or expected.

   4. AMISS *adjective*.

5. Afflicted with or exhibiting irrationality and mental unsoundness.

   5. INSANE.

wrong   *adverb*

Not in the right way or on the proper course: *Our plans went wrong at the last minute.*

Syns: afield, amiss, astray, badly, sour (*Informal*). —*Idiom* off the mark.

wrong   *noun*

1. That which is morally bad or objectionable.

   1. EVIL *noun*.

2. A wicked act.

   2. CRIME *noun*.

3. An act that is not just.

   3. INJUSTICE.

4. Lack of justice.

   4. INJUSTICE.

wrong   *verb*

To do a wrong to; treat unjustly: *wronged and injured those who had trusted him.*

Syns: aggrieve, oppress, outrage, persecute.

wrongdoing   *noun*

1. A wicked act.

   1. CRIME.

2. Improper, often rude behavior.

   2. MISBEHAVIOR.

wrongful   *adjective*

1. Contrary to accepted, esp. moral conventions.

   1. UNLAWFUL.

2. Prohibited by law.

   2. ILLEGAL.

3. Of, involving, or being a crime.

   3. CRIMINAL *adjective*.

wry   *adjective*

Marked by or displaying contemptuous mockery of the motives or virtues of others.

CYNICAL.

wry   *verb*

To alter the position of by a sharp, forcible twisting or turning movement.

WRENCH *verb*.

XYZ

Xanthippe *noun*
A person, esp. a woman, who habitually uses loud, abusive language.   SCOLD *noun.*

x out *verb*
To remove or invalidate by or as if by running a line through or wiping clean.   CANCEL.

---

yahoo *noun*
An unrefined, rude person.   BOOR.

yak *noun*
Slang. Incessant and usu. inconsequential talk.   CHATTER *noun.*

yak *verb*
Slang. To talk volubly, persistently, and usu. inconsequentially.   CHATTER *verb.*

yank *verb*
Informal. To move or cause to move with a sudden, abrupt motion.   JERK *verb.*

yank *noun*
Informal. A sudden pull.   JERK *noun.*

yap *verb*
To utter a shrill, short cry.   YELP *verb.*

yap *noun*
A shrill, short cry.   YELP *noun.*

yard *noun*
An area partially or entirely enclosed by walls or buildings.   COURT *noun.*

yardstick *noun*
A means by which individuals are compared and judged.   STANDARD *noun.*

yarn *noun*
Informal. An entertaining and often oral account of a real or fictitious occurrence: *told the children yarns about his adventures.*
    Syns: anecdote, fable, story, tale. —*Idiom* tall story (*or* tale).
    Near-syns: description, folktale, legend; account, narration, narrative.
    SEE **yawp.**

yaup *verb & noun*

yaw *verb*
1. To turn aside sharply from a straight course.
2. To lean suddenly, unsteadily, and erratically from the vertical axis.
3. *Regional.* To open the mouth wide with a deep inward breath, as when tired or bored.
    1. SWERVE *verb.*
    2. LURCH *verb.*
    3. YAWN *verb.*

yawn *verb*
1. To open the mouth wide with a deep inward breath, as when tired or bored: *yawning and nodding in front of the fire.*
2. To open wide: *The chasm yawned at our feet.*
    1. *Syns:* gape, yaw (*Regional*).
    Near-syns: catnap, doze, drowse, nap, snooze, wink.
    2. *Syns:* gap (*Regional*), gape.

yawn *noun*
Informal. The condition of being bored.   BOREDOM.

yawning *adjective*
Open wide: *a yawning gulf.*
    Syns: abysmal, abyssal, cavernous, gaping.

yawp also **yaup** *verb*
1. To speak or say very loudly.
2. To express negative feelings, esp. of dissatisfaction or resentment.
    1. ROAR *verb.*
    2. COMPLAIN.

3. To utter a shrill, short cry.

3. YELP *verb*.

4. *Regional.* To look intently and fixedly.

4. GAZE *verb*.

yawp also **yaup** *noun*
A shrill, short cry.

YELP *noun*.

yea *adverb*
Archaic. It is so; as you say or ask.

YES *adverb*.

yea *noun*
An affirmative vote or voter.

YES *noun*.

yeah also **yeh** *adverb*
Informal. It is so; as you say or ask.

YES *adverb*.

year *noun*
1. A period of time of approx. 12 months, esp. that period during which the earth completes a single revolution around the sun: *spent a year in London.*

1. *Syn:* twelvemonth.

2. A period of origin.

2. VINTAGE *noun*.

yearn *verb*
1. To have a strong longing for.

1. DESIRE *verb*.

2. To experience or express compassion.

2. FEEL *verb*.

yearner *noun*
One who aspires.

ASPIRANT.

yearning *noun*
A strong wish for what promises enjoyment or pleasure.

DESIRE *noun*.

years *noun*
Old age.

AGE *noun*.

yeast *noun*
1. A mass of bubbles in or on the surface of a liquid.

1. FOAM *noun*.

2. An agent that stimulates or precipitates a reaction, development, or change.

2. CATALYST.

yeh *adverb*

SEE **yeah.**

yell *verb*
1. To say (something) with a shout.

1. SHOUT *verb*.

2. To speak or say very loudly.

2. ROAR *verb*.

yell *noun*
A loud cry.

SHOUT *noun*.

yellow *adjective*
Slang. Ignobly lacking in courage.

COWARDLY.

yellow-bellied *adjective*
Slang. Ignobly lacking in courage.

COWARDLY.

yellow-belly *noun*
Slang. An ignoble, uncourageous person.

COWARD.

yellowness *noun*
Slang. Ignoble lack of courage.

COWARDICE.

yelp *verb*
To utter a shrill, short cry: *a dog that yelped at strangers; yelped with pain.*

Syns: squeal, yap, yawp (*also* yaup), yip.

yelp *noun*
A shrill, short cry: *gave a yelp of surprise.*

Syns: squeal, yap, yawp (*also* yaup), yip.

yen *noun*
Informal. A strong wish for what promises enjoyment or pleasure.

DESIRE *noun*.

yenta *noun*
Slang. A person habitually engaged in idle talk about others.

GOSSIP *noun*.

yep also **yup** *adverb*
Slang. It is so; as you say or ask.

YES *adverb*.

yes *adverb*
It is so; as you say or ask: *Yes, he was here yesterday.*

Syns: absolutely, agreed, all right, aye (*also* ay), certainly, O.K. *or* OK (*Informal*), okeydoke (*also* okeydokey) (*Slang*), right on (*Informal*), Roger (*Informal*), uh-huh (*Informal*), yea

(*Archaic*), yeah (*also* yeh) (*Informal*), yep (*also* yup) (*Slang*).
Near-syns: assuredly, gladly, indubitably, undoubtedly, unquestionably, willingly.

yes *noun*
1. The act or process of accepting.
2. An affirmative vote or voter: *The yeses were in the majority, and the bill became law.*

1. ACCEPTANCE.
2. **Syns:** aye (*also* ay), yea.

yesterday *noun*
A former period of time or of one's life.

PAST *noun*.

yesteryear *noun*
A former period of time or of one's life.

PAST *noun*.

yet *adverb*
1. Up to this time.
2. To a more extreme degree.
3. In spite of a preceding event or consideration.

1. EARLIER.
2. EVEN[1] *adverb*.
3. STILL *adverb*.

yield *verb*
1. To give up a possession, claim, or right.
2. To bring forth (a product).
3. To make as income or profit.
4. To let (something) go.
5. To conform to the will or judgment of another, esp. out of respect or courtesy.
6. To moderate or change a position or course of action as a result of pressure.
7. To give in from or as if from a gradual loss of strength.
8. To cease opposition.

1. ABDICATE.
2. BEAR.
3. RETURN *verb*.
4. RELINQUISH.
5. DEFER[2].
6. WEAKEN.
7. SUCCUMB.
8. GIVE IN at **give**.

yield *noun*
1. The amount or quantity produced: *a high yield of corn per acre.*

2. The produce gathered from the land.

1. **Syns:** output, product, production.
   Near-syns: gain, get, harvest, profit, take, turnout.
2. HARVEST *noun*.

yielding *adjective*
1. Submitting without objection or resistance.
2. Yielding easily to pressure or weight; not firm.

1. PASSIVE.
2. SOFT.

yip *noun*
A shrill, short cry.

YELP *noun*.

yip *verb*
To utter a shrill, short cry.

YELP *verb*.

yoke *noun*
1. That which unites or binds.
2. A state of subjugation to an owner or master.

1. BOND *noun*.
2. SLAVERY.

yoke *verb*
To bring or come together in a united whole.

COMBINE *verb*.

yore *noun*
A former period of time or of one's life.

PAST *noun*.

young *adjective*
Being in an early period of growth or development: *a young country full of the pioneer spirit.*

Syns: green, immature, infant, juvenile, youthful.
Near-syns: fresh, new, unfinished; crude, raw, unripe.
Ants: adult, mature, old.

young *noun*
1. Young people collectively: *had a great influence on the young.*
2. The offspring, as of an animal, bird, etc., that are the result of one breeding season: *a lioness with her young.*

1. **Syns:** juvenility, youth.
2. **Syns:** brood, litter.

youngster *noun*
A young person between birth and puberty.

CHILD.

youth *noun*

1. The time of life between childhood and maturity: *In her youth she lived in Europe.*

    1. **Syns:** greenness, juvenescence, juvenility, prime (*Rare*), spring, springtide, springtime, youthfulness. —*Idiom* salad days.
    Near-syns: adolescence, immaturity, inexperience, puberty, pubescence.
    Ant: age.

2. Young people collectively.

    2. YOUNG *noun*.

youthful *adjective*
Being in an early period of growth or development.

    YOUNG *adjective*.

youthfulness *noun*
The time of life between childhood and maturity.

    YOUTH.

yowl *verb*

1. To cry loudly, as a healthy child does from pain or distress.

    1. BAWL.

2. To make inarticulate sounds of grief or pain, usu. accompanied by tears.

    2. CRY *verb*.

3. To utter or emit a long, mournful, plaintive sound.

    3. HOWL *verb*.

yowl *noun*
A long, mournful cry.

    HOWL *noun*.

yummy *adjective*
Slang. Highly pleasing, esp. to the sense of taste.

    DELICIOUS.

yup *adverb*

    SEE **yep.**

---

zaftig or **zoftig** *adjective*
Well-rounded and usu. short in physique.

    PLUMP[1].

zany *adjective*

1. Arousing laughter.

    1. AMUSING.

2. So senseless as to be laughable.

    2. FOOLISH.

zany *noun*
A person whose words or actions provoke or are intended to provoke amusement or laughter.

    JOKER.

zap *verb*

1. *Slang.* To take the life of (a person or persons) unlawfully.

    1. MURDER *verb*.

2. *Slang.* To cause the death of.

    2. KILL.

zeal *noun*
Passionate devotion to or interest in a cause, subject, etc.

    ENTHUSIASM.

zealot *noun*
A person who is ardently devoted to a particular subject or activity.

    ENTHUSIAST.

zealous *adjective*
Showing or having enthusiasm.

    ENTHUSIASTIC.

zealousness *noun*
Passionate devotion to or interest in a cause, subject, etc.

    ENTHUSIASM.

zenith *noun*
The highest point or state.

    CLIMAX *noun*.

zephyr *noun*

1. A gentle wind.

    1. BREEZE *noun*.

2. A natural movement or current of air.

    2. WIND[1] *noun*.

zero *noun*
A totally insignificant person.

    NONENTITY.

zero in *verb*
To move (a weapon, blow, etc.) in the direction of someone or something.

    AIM *verb*.

zero in *verb*

    SEE **zero.**

zest *noun*
Spirited enjoyment: *ate and drank with zest.*

Syns: gusto, relish.
Near-syns: enthusiasm, flair, joi de vivre, verve, vigor.

zigzag *verb*
To descend, as a ski slope, by crossing and recrossing laterally.

TRAVERSE *verb.*

zilch *noun*
1. *Slang.* A totally insignificant person.
2. *Slang.* No thing; not anything.

1. NONENTITY.
2. NOTHING *noun.*

zillion *noun*
Informal. An indeterminately great amount or number.

HEAP *noun.*

zip *noun*
1. *Informal.* Capacity or power for work or vigorous activity.
2. *Informal.* A lively, emphatic, eager quality or manner.

1. ENERGY.
2. SPIRIT.

zip *verb*
1. To move swiftly.
2. To move swiftly and effortlessly.

1. RUSH *verb.*
2. BREEZE *verb.*

zippy *adjective*
Disposed to action.

VIGOROUS.

zoftig *adjective*

SEE **zaftig.**

zonked *adjective*
1. *Slang.* Stupefied, intoxicated, or otherwise influenced by the taking of drugs.
2. *Slang.* Intoxicated with alcoholic liquor.

1. DRUGGED.
2. DRUNK *adjective.*

zoom *verb*
To move swiftly.

RUSH *verb.*